GAULT

GAULT MILLAU

The Guide to German Wines

Armin Diel • Joel Payne

Profiles the top 842 Producers
Rates over 6,800 Wines

Table of Contents

The Authors

When publisher Johannes Heyne set out in search of competent editors in chief for the new German Gault Millau WeinGuide in the early Nineties, he was on the look-out for accomplished experts of the German wine scene – and found them speedily, in the form of Armin Diel and Joel Payne. This pair had

already worked well together and in tandem on many wine tasting projects. They are well placed to assess top-class German wines based on their extensive experience of great wines from around the world. The Diel/Payne duo had already made quite a name for itself based on wine tastings and reviews in the German business magazine "Capital," as well as in the wine publication "Alles über Wein" (All about wine), which they still write for today. **Armin Diel** was born in the Nahe region on October 1, 1953, and it was also here, exactly 34 years later, that he took over the Burg Layen wine estate from his father. Before that, he had studied business sciences in Mainz, and law in Münster. Since 1990, Diel has been heading up the German Barrique Forum (Deutsches Barrique Forum), and since 1993 he has also been in charge of the regional VDP chapter in the Nahe region. The culinary wine trips to the leading wine-growing regions in Europe, which he organizes and leads, have attained cult status. His gastronomic series on TV reach an audience of millions. In his rare moments of spare time, Diel likes to go out on his bicycle, he is also a passionate card player, focusing on the German game Skat, and also sings as a baritone in the local mens' choir. **Joel Brian Payne**, too, was born in 1953, the son of a lawyer in the US state of Kansas. His work for the United Nations took him to Africa and to South-East Asia. In the early Eighties, he ended up in Europe, and worked as a sommelier in the Gala Restaurant in Aachen, Germany. A competition showed him to be the best sommelier in Germany for French and German wines. In 1990 Payne moved into the wine trade, first to the Schlumberger group, then to Segnitz, and finally to Schlee & Popken. Payne is an artistically inclined person, and plays several instruments from the flute to the piano, and his reading interests are focused on classical literature. To balance things out, his sporting interests include running, e.g. the marathon run in the Médoc, north of Bordeaux.

Following on stations at the Traube Tonbach restaurant as well as at the Bülow Residenz of his home town Dresden, **Mathias Dathan** was head sommelier at the Brandenburger Hof Hotel in Berlin, until going into business on his own in Berlin in 2004. For this edition he has been responsible for the Sachsen and Saale-Unstrut regions. After completing an apprenticeship as a winemaker, **Christoph Dirksen** spent a few years working as a sommelier in top-class restaurants. For the past decade he has been working at the Meckenheim-based wine trading company Schlumberger. In terms of the WeinGuide he is once again responsible for the Mosel-Saar-Ruwer region.

Dr. Peter Henk is a qualified chemist, and works in the pharmaceutical industry. He has been tasting wines for the Gault Millau WeinGuide for the past five years, and for this edition he has once again been responsible for the Baden region. **Carsten Henn** has been writing about wine for many years, and is active as a journalist, contributing to various wine magazines as well as to the Deutschlandfunk state-run German radio broadcasting corporation. In the WeinGuide, Henn takes care of the chapter on the Nahe region. Carsten Henn combines journalism and literature in his wine-related crime thrillers such as "In Vino Veritas."

Frank Kämmer discovered the fascination of wine while undergoing his training at the Schlosshotel Friedrichsruhe. After spending many years at the "Délice" in Stuttgart, he now runs the restaurant at the Art Museum. Master-Sommelier Kämmer has written several books on wine. He looks after the chapter on Württemberg. **Rudolf Knoll**, who was born in Munich, has worked as a wine journalist for more than 20 years, and he has written more than 35 books on wine-related topics in this time. He is also the organizer of the "Deutschen Rotweinpreis" (German Red Wine Prize) as well as of the "Riesling-Erzeugerpreises" (Riesling Producer Prize) competitions. Rudolf Knoll brings his many years of experience to bear on the chapter on Rheinhessen.

Jürgen Mathäß was born in Landau, is a qualified economist, and spent many years as a business journalist before taking over as editor-in-chief of a major wine magazine. Mathäß has written a number of books, and few people know the wines of his home region, the Pfalz, better than he does. **Hans-Jürgen Podzun** is the chief executive of the IHK (Chamber of Commerce) in Koblenz, and has many connections with the world of wine. Among other projects, he initiated the founding of one of the leading sommelier schools in Germany. The wine region he is responsible for in the WeinGuide is the Mittelrhein, located at his front door.

Kai Schattner was born in Heidelberg, and as the long-standing sommelier at the Ente restaurant in Wiesbaden he is one of the grandees of his profession. He is an important source of support for the editorial board, not only for his intimate knowledge of the Rheingau region. Sommelière **Claudia Stern** decided to go into business on her own in 1992. She runs the "Vintage" in Cologne, which combines a restaurant, retail wine sales and lifestyle seminars. Claudia Stern has participated for the first time, contributing to the chapter on the Mosel, Saar and Ruwer region.

Preface

We have been following the evolution of the German wine industry for most of the past generation and have published the definitive annual guide on each German vintage since 1992. The book in your hands is a compendium of the last three editions of our German book, highlighting the vintages 2003, 2002 and 2001. It is only the second time it has been published in English. The first English version appeared six years ago and covered the vintages 1997, 1996 and 1995. Since that time the German wine industry has matured considerably. The new generation of young winemakers that had at that time only just risen to the fore has begun to change the international perception of German wines; and new talents emerge with each vintage. This guide is intended to give them a voice as well.

Because of the hot dry summer, 2003 was being treated as a phenomenal vintage long before the grapes were harvested. Today we are beginning to see a more nuanced picture. Sheer opulence is not always the hallmark of a great wine. The high alcoholic levels and relatively low acidities have left many of the wines a touch heavy. However, the finest Auslese can easily be compared to the excellent 1959s, phenomenally dense but unmarked by botrytis. The 2002s may have been less compact, but are as a whole better balanced and more pleasurable to drink. The vintage 2001 has, perhaps because it was less stunning elsewhere, been a bit forgotten. The foreign press picked it up as the finest German vintage since 1976, which was certainly an overstatement, but many of the wines are rather closed today. However, given the depth of fruit and tight acidic structure, 2001 will probably age more gracefully than the two more recent vintages.

At the end of the 19th century German Rieslings from the Mosel and the Rheingau were the most expensive wines in the world, commanding prices higher than those of the top Bordeaux growths. Although the quality of the finest wines remained high, the fall from zenith to nadir took less than 50 years. Only two decades ago, "German wine" was a synonym for cheap, sweet plonk. Since then dry wines have become immensely popular in Germany, heralding a rebirth in national pride for the quality of wines "Made in Germany." At the same time it created a schism for the producers. In the German market many estates sell only dry wines; on the export market, nothing but delicately sweet Spätlese and Auslese. We have included a selection of both in this guide. However, given the fact that the finest wines are often produced only in small volumes, they may be difficult to find in many markets.

The last few years have certainly been lean due to the difficult economic environment. But as beer and spirit consumption continue to wane, wine sales are growing in Germany, the largest import market for wine in the world; and today's generation is also willing, if only occasionally, to spend a bit more money on finer wines, creating new markets for quality oriented producers. But fierce competition has its advantages, especially for the wine lover. The finest estates have been obliged to focus even more intensely on quality to justify their prices – and even modest estates must produce better wines or perish. And as the wheat is separated from the chaff an interesting range of intermediate quality has emerged at extremely interesting prices. These wines have never been better.

Wine lovers have always sworn by the varietal Riesling. The wine consumer has tended to acknowledge its inherent quality, but not buy it. As the "Anything But Chardonnay" movement continues to grow, and overly oaked wines lambasted, that is changing. But fashions die hardly. On the other hand, various other local varietals are beginning to receive the same privileged treatment once reserved only for Riesling. They are being planted in the finest sites, yields held low and, in the case of the Pinot varietals, often given a touch of oak. Silvaner, Weißburgunder (Pinot Blanc) and Spätburgunder (Pinot Noir) have never been so good before. Which estates do each style best is documented in the tables on pages 60 to 61.

❦ ❦ ❦

Many in Germany realize, though politicians are loathe to discuss it in public, that this country's future cannot lie in exporting Liebfrauenmilch. Total volumes are down significantly in recent years, but a large part of Germany's wine production is still exported at prices that barely cover the costs of production. Farmers are going out of business and few shippers can seriously speak of a return on investment. Many of these companies though have risen to the challenge and are now producing wines that can hold their own in the international arena. We have included a selection of these shippers in a chapter on global players.

❦ ❦ ❦

The best vineyards in Germany are extremely steep. As most of the work must be done by hand, many sites have been abandoned. Labor costs are so high that the producers must increasingly concentrate on their unique sales proposition, which is the expression of pure Riesling fruit from the choicest sites. We have for that reason included a tentative selection of the finest vineyard sites in a table at the head of each chapter that is based on the classification done by the local "Verband der Prädikatsweigüter," an association of the best estates in that region. This is certainly not yet a definitive list. Great wines are always a marriage of vineyard potential, local weather conditions and the ability of the vintner.

❦ ❦ ❦

For the past twelve years we have endeavored to simplify your buying strategies with this guide. That so many readers feel that we have succeeded makes it easier for us to bear the occasional criticism from those estates who feel that they have not been sufficiently praised. But German wine is not a public relations' gimmick, it's the quality of the wine in the glass that counts! We hope this book will help you to find the wine you want to drink.

With best wishes and "Prost!"

Armin Diel

Joel B. Payne

About This Book...

We have tried to keep this book as simple as possible, so that every reader will be able to find the wines that he wants to drink from a producer that he admires. Obviously the easiest thing to do for any reader unfamiliar with German wine is to look at the lists on pages 32 to 38 and buy only from the best estates. Even easier would be to buy nothing other than the select group of top wines listed on pages 50 to 57. Unfortunately, few of the finest wines are produced in quantity. Lots of 360 bottles are not uncommon; lots of 12,000 the exception. Thus, many of these wines will be difficult to find.

The 13 wine-growing regions, which are presented in alphabetical order, are our point of departure. Although we refer to English names in the introductions, we have left the German names as the headlines, as these are the names that will appear on the labels.

Similarly, the individual producers are portrayed exactly as they are known in German – with ä, ö, ü and ß – in alphabetical order within their respective growing region. Because many of the obscure German names are difficult to decipher, we have highlighted the defining letter for each estate in order to make the search easier. This is clearly better than presenting the producers in the order of their ranking, as such a list is already provided both on pages 32 to 38 and, for each region, in the introduction to the corresponding chapter. Anyone who is not able to find a particular producer or wine should search for the name in the index of the estates, the vineyard sites or individuals listed at the end of the guide.

Any ranking of producers is always a subjective matter, and often one of contention. In our assessment we have endeavored to provide an accurate picture of how each individual estate has performed over the last 12 vintages. Thus, on the one hand, a given estate may appear highly rated in light of a poor performance in 2002 or 2003. On the other hand, another producer with excellent results in one of those vintages may appear

underrated, generally owing to the fact that the estate has at most but only few vintages of that quality under its belt. The criteria for the ranking of the individual estates are provided on page 30.

The telephone and fax numbers we have listed are valid for calls within Germany. Anyone phoning from abroad should use his own international access number, plus Germany's national code of 49 and delete the first 0 of the area code for the village. To date, not all of the German estates are online, but where applicable we have also included e-mail and homepage addresses.

In the presentation of the growing regions and individual estates, we have left the vineyard sizes in hectares. One hectare equals approximately 2.5 acres. Similarly, we have left the yields in hectoliters per hectare, which is the common standard in Europe. For those not familiar with this measure, we provide the following vague conversions as a guide:

35 hl/ha	2 tons/acre
50 hl/ha	3 tons/acre
68 hl/ha	4 tons/acre
85 hl/ha	5 tons/acre

Any given producer's yields are an average. Thus an estate may produce an average of 60 hectoliters per hectare, while having yields of 75 or 80 hectoliters for its simple liter bottling but only 30 hectoliters per hectare for the finest wines. More importantly, the average consumer has been misled by the French vaunting their low productions. Except for the top estates, their claims seldom bear close scrutiny.

In the line "Member" we have tried to include any reference to organizations that have international significance. The most prominent is the VDP, a club that unites the majority – albeit not all – of Germany's best estates. There is also the Barrique Forum, which, as the name implies, is a group of producers promoting the use of oak barrels for a richer style of wine. Many of the best producers of Pinot varietals are members of this forum. Most of the other names such as Naturland, Bioland and BÖW are organizations insuring the organic production of their members' wines. The remaining groups such as the Bernkastler Ring have, although their members are carefully chosen, primarily local significance.

The presentation of the individual wines from any given estate has been restricted, by and large, to the 2002 and 2003 whites. 2001 reds that are currently in the market are also included. Although we have tried to include most of every estate's finest wines, the selection is often no more than a fraction of the total number produced. Many of the botrytis dessert wines are bottled only in halves. All wines have been presented exactly as they are mentioned on the German label, using the German names for the grape varieties. The red wines have, additionally, been separated from the whites in order to make them more easily recognizable.

Although it may be frustrating, we have chosen not to print any cellar door prices as listed in each estate's current consumer list. Although those are the prices that you would pay, were you to purchase the wines directly at the estate, given limited availability, freight costs, customs and excise taxes, margins and value added taxes, the true prices vary so widely from what you will see on your local shelf that any mention that we might make here would hardly even provide a frame of reference. More likely it would create confusion.

German wines can be sublime at low alcoholic strengths. As this is rather unusual, we have included a mention of total alcohol for all wines. The German Wine Institute is right in promoting the theme "naturally light," for a Spätlese from the Mosel at 8.5% is a far different animal from the New World Chardonnay at 14%. Both have their merits, and both their clientele, but no other country in the world produces top-notch quality at such low levels of alcohol.

The description and scoring of each wine is our personal judgement. We do not pretend to be totally objective. We have been tasting most wines from almost all of the well-known producers in Germany from every vintage for more than two decades and hope to have provided the reader with an accurate picture of each wine's intrinsic quality. In order to save space, and thus present a wider range of wines, we have deleted all tasting notes. Our German guide began basing all wine scores on a 20-point scale, which is the scholastic rating system used in France that was long one of the two standards widely accepted in Germany (the other being that from 1 to 5, like the A to F used in America). In order to make the scoring in the English guide more understandable for an international public, we adopted America's 100-point scale for the first English translation and now use that system in our German edition.

The criteria for scoring are provided on page 30.

Given the fact that we are presenting only the finest wines from a select group of estates, this guide's apparently low scoring of many wines may appear disheartening. This is, however, a misunderstanding. European educators have traditionally been very strict. There is no political correctness that requires teachers to give every child a pass, much less an A or a B. Most children in Germany are tickled pink to take home Cs, marks above 90 are rare, 95 is almost unheard of and 100 essentially never given. More disheartening for the consumer, though, is the fact that there are seldom more than a few thousand bottles of the highly scored wines produced. You will have to search out a merchant who specializes in German wines to find any of them.

Lastly, the recommended drinking dates are only tentative. It is very difficult to predict how a given wine will develop, but the reader should not lay down wines that he could have been drinking. Further, today's consumer tends to prefer fresh, youthful fruit rather than the complexities of bottle aging. For this reason we have been very conservative in our estimations. Many wines will probably age better than stated in this guide.

9

Ever since 1994, the Gault Millau WineGuide Germany has honored outstanding personalities of the German wine world – in addition to the Producer of the Year. Exceptional performances in the categories of Rising Stars, Discovery of the Year and Winery Manager of the Year are also honored each year. Furthermore, the WineGuide selects the best sommeliers to be found in gourmet restaurants, as well as some restaurants that have, in their wine lists, done the most to promote German wine. All these stars are portrayed here for your information and guidance.

Helmut Dönnhoff
Weingut Hermann Dönnhoff
Oberhausen, Nahe
Producer of the year 1999

Gerhard Biffar, Weingut Josef Biffar
Deidesheim, Pfalz
Discovery of the year 1994

Stéphane Gass
Restaurant "Schwarzwaldstube"
Baiersbronn-Tonbach
Sommelier of the year 1997

Christina Fischer
"Fischers Weingenuss & Tafelfreuden"
Köln
Sommelier of the year 2001

Johannes Geil-Bierschenk
Weingut Ökonomierat Joh. Geil Erben
Bechtheim, Rheinhessen
Discovery of the year 2004

German Wine World

Gerhard and Werner Leve
Hotel "Im Engel," Warendorf
Wine list of the year 1999

Gert Aldinger, Weingut Aldinger
Fellbach, Württemberg
Rising star of the year 2004

Klaus Keller, Weingut Keller
Flörsheim-Dalsheim, Rheinhessen
Producer of the year 2000

Hendrick Thoma
Restaurant Louis C. Jacob
Hamburg-Nienstedten
Wine list of the year 2005

Horst Kolesch
Weingut Juliusspital
Würzburg, Franken
Estate manager of the year 1996

Kai Schattner
Restaurant "Ente," Wiesbaden
Sommelier of the year 2003

Marie-Helen Krebs
Restaurant "Marcobrunn"
Schloss Reinhartshausen
Eltville-Erbach, Rheingau
Sommelier of the year 1998

Roman Niewodniczanski
Weingut van Volxem, Wiltingen, Saar
Discovery of the year 2002

Johannes van Toorn
Restaurant "Die Ente vom Lehel"
Wiesbaden
Wine list of the year 1997

Matthias Müller
Weingut Heinrich Müller
Spay, Mittelrhein
Discovery of the year 1998

Fritz Waßmer
Weingut Fritz Waßmer
Bad Krozingen-Schlatt, Baden
Discovery of the year 2005

German Wine World

Werner Schönleber
Weingut Emrich-Schönleber
Monzingen, Nahe
Range of the year 2004

Robert Haller
Weingut Fürst Löwenstein
Franken and Rheingau
Estate manager of the year 2004

Gerhard Stodden,Weingut Jean Stodden
Rech, Ahr
Rising star of the year 2002

Christoph Tyrell
Weingut Karthäuserhof
Trier-Eitelsbach, Ruwer
Producer of the year 2005

Markus Otto Graf
Hotel Brandenburger Hof, Berlin
Wine list of the year 2003

Wilhelm Weil
Weingut Robert Weil
Kiedrich, Rheingau
Range of the year 2005

13

Dieter Müller, Silvio Nitzsche
Restaurant Dieter Müller, Schloss-
hotel Lerbach, Bergisch Gladbach
Wine list of the year 2004

Egon Müller
Weingut Egon Müller – Scharzhof
Wiltingen, Saar
Producer of the year 1998

Dr. Manfred Prüm
Weingut Joh. Jos. Prüm
Bernkastel-Wehlen, Mosel
Producer of the year 1996

Dr. Carl-Ferdinand von Schubert
and Alfons Heinrich
Gutsverwaltung von Schubert
Maximin Grünhaus, Ruwer
Producer of the year 1995

Daniel Vollenweider
Weingut Vollenweider
Traben-Trarbach, Mosel
Discovery of the year 2003

German Wine World

Heinfried and Gerold Pfannebecker
Weingut Michel-Pfannebecker
Flomborn, Rheinhessen
Discovery of the year 1999

Hans-Günther Schwarz
Weingut Müller-Catoir
Neustadt-Haardt, Pfalz
Estate manager of the year 1998

Christina Göbel
Restaurant Speisemeisterei, Stuttgart
Sommelier of the year 2005

Bernd and Andreas Spreitzer,
Weingut Josef Spreitzer
Oestrich, Rheingau
Discovery of the year 2001

Alexander Spinner
Weingut Schloss Neuweier
Baden-Baden, Baden
Discovery of the year 1995

Stefan Männle
Winzergenossenschaft Pfaffenweiler
Baden
Estate manager of the year 2002

H. B. Ullrich
Historischer Gasthof "Krone"
Rüdesheim-Assmannshausen
Wine list of the year 1998

Alfred Voigt
Restaurant "Residence"
Essen-Kettwig
Sommelier of the year 1996

Carl Geisel
Hotel "Königshof," München
Wine list of the year 2000

Rakhshan Zhouleh
Restaurant "Margaux," Berlin
Sommelier of the year 2002

Wilhelm Weil
Weingut Robert Weil, Kiedrich, Rheingau
Rising star of the year 1994 and
Producer of the year 1997

German Wine World

Dr. Rowald Hepp
Weingut Schloss Vollrads
Oestrich-Winkel, Rheingau
Estate manager of the year 2001

Willi Schaefer
Weingut Willi Schaefer, Graach, Mosel
Rising star of the year 1997

Markus Molitor, Weingut Molitor
Bernkastel-Wehlen, Mosel
Rising star of the year 1999

Tim Fröhlich
Weingut Schäfer-Fröhlich
Bockenau, Nahe
Rising star of the year 2005

Bernhard Breuer †
Weingut Georg Breuer
Rüdesheim, Rheingau
Rising star of the year 1996

Joachim Heger, Weingut Dr. Heger
Ihringen, Baden
Rising star of the year 1998

Paul Fürst, Weingut Rudolf Fürst
Bürgstadt, Franken
Producer of the year 2003

Helmut Mathern †
Weingut Oskar Mathern
Niederhausen, Nahe
Discovery of the year 1997

Hansjörg Rebholz
Weingut Ökonomierat Rebholz
Siebeldingen, Pfalz
Producer of the year 2002

Hans-Joachim Krautkrämer
Hotel Krautkrämer, Münster/Westfalen
Wine list of the year 2001

Thomas Seeger
Weingut Seeger, Leimen, Baden
Discovery of the year 1996

Jürgen Off, Günter Hübner
Weinmanufaktur Untertürkheim eG
Württemberg
Estate manager of the year 2005

German Wine World

Rudolf Mies and Rolf Münster
Winzergenossenschaft Mayschoss-Altenahr
Mayschoss, Ahr
Discovery of the year 2000

Werner Näkel
Weingut Meyer-Näkel, Dernau, Ahr
Producer of the year 2004

Peter Jost
Weingut Toni Jost – Hahnenhof
Bacharach, Mittelrhein
Rising star of the year 1995

Jürgen Fendt
Restaurant Bareiss, Baiersbronn-Mitteltal
Sommelier of the year 2000

Heinrich Hillenbrand
Staatsweingut Bergstraße
Bensheim, Hessische Bergstraße
Estate manager of the year 1999

Hendrik Thoma
Hotel "Louis C. Jacob," Hamburg
Sommelier of the year 1999

Karl-Heinz Wehrheim
Weingut Dr. Wehrheim
Birkweiler, Pfalz
Rising star of the year 2003

Dieter L. Kaufmann
Restaurant "Zur Traube," Grevenbroich
Wine list of the year 1996

Günter Wittmann, Weingut Wittmann
Westhofen, Rheinhessen
Rising star of the year 2001

Rudolf Frieß
Weingut Bürgerspital zum Heiligen Geist
Würzburg, Franken
Estate manager of the year 2000

Karl-Josef Krötz
Ratskeller, Bremen
Wine list of the year 2002

German Wine World

Wolfgang Schleicher
Schloss Johannisberg, Rheingau
Estate manager of the year 2003

Wilhelm Haag, Weingut Fritz Haag
Brauneberg, Mosel
Producer of the year 1994

Andreas Laible, Weingut Andreas Laible
Durbach, Baden
Rising star of the year 2000

Susanne Spies
Restaurant "La Table," Dortmund
Sommelier of the year 2004

Norbert Holderrieth
Geheimrat J. Wegeler Erben
Oestrich-Bernkastel-Deidesheim
Estate manager of the year 1997

Ernst F. Loosen, Weingut Dr. Loosen
Bernkastel, Mosel
Producer of the year 2001

The thirteen wine-growing regions of

Rheinhessen	**26,171 hectares**	**Baden**	**15,944 hectares**
18% Müller-Thurgau	71% white	35% Pinot Noir	59% white
13% Dornfelder	29% red	21% Müller-Thurgau	41% red
10% Silvaner		10% Pinot Gris	

Pfalz	**23,394 hectares**	**Württemberg**	**11,459 hectares**
20% Riesling	62% white	22% Trollinger	31% white
12% Dornfelder	38% red	19% Riesling	69% red
13% Müller-Thurgau		17% Pinot Meunier	

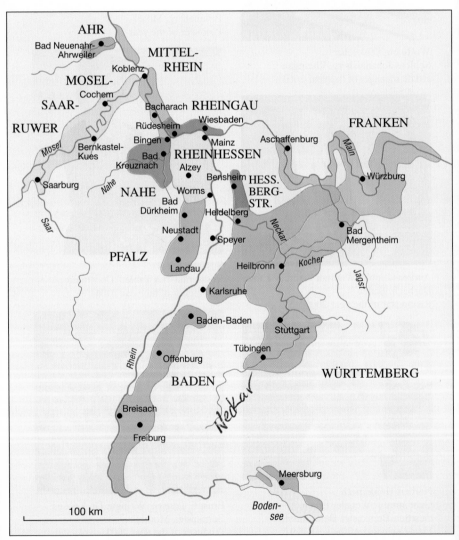

Regions

Germany and their key grape varieties

Mosel-Saar-Ruwer		**9,533 hectares**
57% Riesling		92% white
16% Müller-Thurgau		8% red
7% Elbling		

Nahe		**4**
25% Riesling		
16% Müller-Thurgau		23% red
10% Dornfelder		

Franken   **6,005 hectares**
36% Müller-Thurgau   86% white
21% Silvaner   14% red
12% Bacchus

Rheingau   **3,167 hectares**
78% Riesling   84% white
13% Pinot Noir   16% red
 2% Müller-Thurgau

Saale-Unstrut   **652 hectares**
22% Müller-Thurgau   76% white
12% Pinot Blanc   24% red
 9% Silvaner

Ahr   **529 hectares**
61% Pinot Noir   12% white
11% Portugieser   88% red
 7% Riesling

Mittelrhein   **495 hectares**
69% Riesling   87% white
 8% Pinot Noir   13% red
 7% Müller-Thurgau

Sachsen   **446 hectares**
21% Müller-Thurgau   85% white
16% Riesling   15% red
13% Pinot Blanc

Hessische Bergstraße   **444 hectares**
51% Riesling   84% white
 9% Müller-Thurgau   16% red
 8% Pinot Gris

Germany total   **102,489 hectares**

White varieties: 67,663 hectares (66%)

20.2% Riesling	**20,770 hectares**
15.6% Müller-Thurgau	**16,078 hectares**
5.7% Silvaner	**5,820 hectares**
4.9% Kerner	**5,053 hectares**

Red varieties: 34,826 hectares (34%)

10.7% Pinot Noir	**11,022 hectares**
7.5% Dornfelder	**7,686 hectares**
4.8% Portugieser	**4,931 hectares**
2.5% Trollinger	**2,597 hectares**

Source: German Federal Bureau of Statistics
(Statistisches Bundesamt)

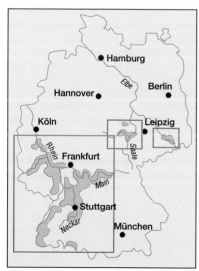

23

the beginning, there was the predicate designation: Based on the sugar content of the grapes, terms such as Spätlese and Auslese informed the consumer that these were wines of better quality, made from grapes whose natural sugar content made chaptalization by means of adding saccharose or concentration by reverse osmosis unnecessary. Right up to the Eighties of the last century, these wines almost always tasted sweet. There was hardly any market at the time for better quality dry white wines. Experts then estimated the market share at five percent – with not much hope for an increase. How wrong they could be!

Suddenly – the demand for dry wine

Together with the "miracle of German cuisine" there was suddenly, almost overnight, a great demand for good dry wines. A trend that was enhanced by the glycol scandal of 1985. All of a sudden, it was almost impossible to sell sweet wines, and wine producers who were able to offer a range of good dry wines were able to do brisk business. In order to document the high quality of these wines on the label, many winemakers now took these Spätlese and Auslese wines that had been fermented more or less dry, and added the designation *dry* (trocken) on the label. Of course, consumers who had hitherto associated the term Auslese were now confused, but that was considered acceptable. Even today, quite well-known producers expect their customers to distinguish between dry, off-dry and sweet Auslese wines.

Classic and strict Selection

Everything was going to be made much simpler when in 2001 the term *Selection* was introduced as a separate designation for top-quality dry wines. A level below this, the term *Classic* was created to cover all everyday wines that tasted (fairly) dry. In the wine-growing regions, the permitted grapes for *Classic* and *Selection* were determined. In addition, strict production rules apply to *Selection* wines: yield is limited to 60 hectoliters per hectare (approx. 3 tons/acre). Grapes must have

must weights equal to Auslese wines, must be exclusively from a single vineyard, and must be picked by hand. The wines may only be sold after September 1st of the year following the harvest. For the first time, the German legislature had managed to pass a new regulation that was based on real criteria of quality.

Divided we are weak!

The elite association of wine estates, *VDP – Verband Deutscher Prädikatsweingüter* decided to create its own term for designating top-quality dry wines, the *Großes Gewächs* (Great Growth, or *Grand Cru*). The reason behind this seemed superficially reasonable: The legislature had omitted to consider the quality of individual vineyard sites in the sense of a special terroir. With a view to the situation in the Rheingau, where all vineyards had been subjected to a classification procedure, and the top sites were named *Erstes Gewächs* (First Growth), and the federal state implemented a set of regulations to legalize this, in other growing regions one now uses the term *Großes Gewächs*. A significant disadvantage compared to the Rheingau solution was that initially this term could not be legally mentioned on the label.

Special bottle for *Grand Crus*

This has been partly rectified, beginning with the 2003 vintage, as many of these *Grands Crus* are now bottled in a special bottle that carries a special embossed logo – a bunch of grapes combined with the numeral "1." In addition, the VDP has patented the designation *Großes Gewächs-VDP* and is busy working on the legalization of this term on labels. What would really help is if all growing regions could agree on a single definition of the term, as in some areas a *Grand Cru* is still a dry Spätlese, while in other regions it is a quality wine, with or without *dry* in the designation. And in the Mosel region, they use the term *Erste Lage*, causing even more confusion for the poor consumer: In this region, the term is used for both dry and naturally sweet wines.

Looking back at the last century, one can say that there was a reasonably uniform style that was applied in the first half of the century: At that time, apart from a small number of naturally sweet exceptions, German wine was usually fermented dry. This can only very approximately be equated with the current definition of *dry*, as depending on the must weight and the temperature in the cellar, many of these wines had a very restrained residual sweetness. Even today, quality-conscious producers utilize temperature-controlled fermentation to produce wines with some natural residual sugar.

Only in the Sixties did the wine producers in the Rhein and Mosel regions start to systematically stop fermentation by the addition of sulfur, and using pressure tanks. Then in the early Seventies, the development of so-called sweet reserve revolutionized cellar practices. Part of the grape must was sterilized using sulfur, and then added back to the wine, which had been fermented dry, in whatever dosage was deemed desirable. Thanks to modern technology, gone were the days when naturally sweet wines could only be produced in particularly warm, sunny vintages. From then on, cellar technicians and beverage technologists determined the practices in German wine cellars – which could have been real progress, if only people had handled the new technology sensibly.

Even the new wine law of 1971, much praised before it was published, did little to help German wine regain its formerly excellent reputation in world markets.

New quality classifications were created, which were based exclusively on the must weight of the grapes at the time of picking. The so-called must weight, expressed in degrees *Oechsle*, even today still determines whether the resulting wine may later be sold as a *Quality Wine* or as a *Quality Wine with Predicate*. The production of table wine plays only a very minor role.

Unfortunately at the time the authorities omitted to link a particular quality classification with a specific taste or style, allegedly in order to give consumers a greater choice. It was basically left up to each wine producer what the taste or style of a wine should be.

Quality wines bear the name of the growing region, are usually chaptalized (the name originated in France) either before or during fermentation by the addition of saccharose. This procedure increases the level of alcohol, and initially has no influence on whether the resulting wine will taste tart or sweet.

From a certain degree of ripeness upward – and this is defined at a lower level in the North than in the South of Germany – one arrives at the classification Quality Wine with Predicate. Here, chaptalization is not permitted, the must has to be fermented as the grapes were picked. Theoretically, therefore, the wines of the entry level **Kabinett** have the lowest alcohol levels.

The next step up on the scale of ripeness is the **Spätlese**. The style and taste can vary significantly: from sweet and light to off-dry and medium-weight or up to dry and full-bodied. For the **Auslese** level, too, there is no clearly defined taste profile, it is made in a confusing multitude of styles from dry to botrytized dessert wines.

To make a **Beerenauslese** wine, overripe grapes showing signs of botrytis (noble rot) are selected and cut out of the bunches by hand. Because of their highly concentrated fruit they produce decidedly sweet wines with considerable maturation potential.

The **Trockenbeerenauslese** wines are even more rare, and are produced exclusively. From individually selected shriveled raisin-like berries with botrytis. These botrytized sweet dessert wines represent the pinnacle of German winemaking, can mature beautifully for decades.

Eiswein is a specialty produced from grapes that have a must weight of at least Beerenauslese level. They can only be produced at vineyard temperatures of minus 7° C (19° F) or below, and are vinified while the grapes are frozen. The cold temperature binds the water, and the wines produced show botrytis character as well as very high extract values.

The Wine Label

Obligatory information:

1. **The name of the producer or bottler.** The term *Erzeugerabfüllung* (bottled by producer) is based on the bottler also being the producer. Under certain conditions, wine estates may also use the term *Gutsabfüllung* (estate bottled), or more recently also *Schlossabfüllung* (château bottled).

2. **The official control number.** This must be stated for quality and predicate wines. It consists of several numeric designations: in this case the 7 stands for the control office of the growing region, 763 indicates the town or commune, 19 is the producer's number, and 20 indicates a running number, showing how many wines that producer has presented for approval in the current year, in this case 1993. Table wines must display a batch number, from which the bottler can be derived.

3. **The location of the producer or bottler.** This must be stated together with a reference to the country of origin, which in the case of Germany can be indicated by the letter *D*.

8. **The volume** (contents) of the bottle, e.g. 0.75 l or 750 ml.

9. **The growing region.** This must be stated for quality and predicate wines.

10. **Alcoholic strength** of each wine.

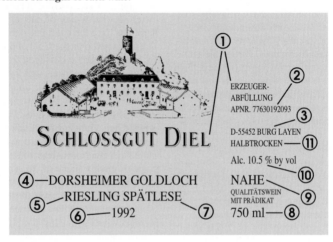

Optional information:

4. **Town/Commune and vineyard** in which the wine was grown may be stated.

5. **The grape variety** (or two) from which the wine was produced.

6. **The vintage** in which the wine was grown. For instance, an Eiswein picked on the 2nd of January 2002, nevertheless carries the 2001 vintage!

7. **The quality level** is determined by the sugar content of the grapes, the so-called must weight, at picking. Each growing area has its own specific regulations for this. The minimum levels in each class are lower in the North, higher in the (warmer) South. In the Rheingau there has for some years been the option of stating *Erstes Gewächs* (First Growth) on dry wines of particularly high quality, from specific vineyards.

11. **The taste or style.** A wine designated dry may contain a maximum of 9 g/l (0.9%) of residual sugar, depending on the level of acidity, while for an off-dry wine the maximum level is 18 g/l (1.8%).

As of August 2003 a number of additional items of information may be stated on the label. The basic premise remains that whatever is stated on the label must be true.

The Grape Varieties

Although the law does not require the variety to be stated on the label, and the number of blends produced is on the increase, it is usually mentioned prominently on the label.

Riesling is without a doubt Germany's most important contribution to the world of fine wines. In no other country is it cultivated so intensively, nor are the results as excellent elsewhere. This variety covers 20,770 hectares. The best examples are characterized by complex layers of aromas and considerable maturation potential. An elegantly fruity Riesling from the Mosel can be extremely delicate, an off-dry version from the Rhein or Nahe can be stately, and a dry wine from the Pfalz or the Ortenau in Baden can often express a certain baroque opulence.

Second position is held by the **Müller-Thurgau** grape. This is decreasing rapidly: The total area is now 16,080 hectares, a dramatic decline of almost 2,600 hectares in only two years. When handled correctly, it can produce wines with a nutty aroma and clear fruit. Unfortunately yields are often very high. In an effort to get away from the negative image that has resulted from this, many more quality-conscious winemakers today use the alternative name **Rivaner**.

In the 19th century, **Silvaner** was the most widely planted variety in Germany. Its total area is currently 5,820 hectares, showing a slower decrease of around 300 hectares compared to last year. In many cases it is handled with equally little regard as is the Müller-Thurgau. The resultant wines are basic wines for everyday quaffing. However, when planted on good soils and where yields are kept low, Silvaner can produce wines of remarkable character. The best examples are to be found in Franken and Rheinhessen.

Of the many newly-crossed and bred grape varieties that appeared in the vineyards in the Seventies, it is mainly **Kerner** (5,050 hectares, minus 500) and **Bacchus** (2,520 hectares, minus 250) that are still of any importance today. Given proper care and the right location, **Scheurebe** (2,200 hectares, minus 240) and **Rieslaner** (80 hectares) can provide the base material for truly outstanding wines. A mature Scheurebe Auslese, for instance, can be the perfect match for dessert. The Rieslaner, too, requires high must weights to put in its best performance. The classic varieties include **Gewürztraminer** (825 hectares) and **Muskateller** (101 hectares), both of which used to be much more widely grown. However, their popularity declined significantly for a while because of their inconsistent performance and their strong aromatic notes. In the meantime they are experiencing at least a slight Renaissance. The trend toward grape varieties that combine restrained aromatic components with relatively low acidity has also been on the increase in Germany.

The **Graue Burgunder** (Pinot Gris), for long better known in Baden as Ruländer, has developed a loyal following, and currently covers 3,430 hectares (plus 280). The **Weiße Burgunder** (Pinot Blanc) is one of the rising stars of the past ten years: it has doubled its area to 3,100 hectares. The southern Pfalz and the Kaiserstuhl area in Baden tend to produce the best Pinot Blanc. This trio includes **Chardonnay**, which continues to grow in popularity, and now covers 890 hectares. German **red wines** have gained tremendously in popularity. Its area of 11,020 hectares (plus around 400) makes the **Spätburgunder** (Pinot Noir) far and away the leading red wine variety in Germany. The best examples come from the Ahr, Rheingau, Pfalz and Kaiserstuhl regions. The best wines can hold their own in a comparison with the *Premier Crus* of Burgundy. Moving up quickly is the second-placed **Dornfelder**, which produces dark-colored wines in copious quantities, and now covers a remarkable 7,700 hectares (doubled since 1999). **Portugieser** remains in third place with just on 5,000 hectares. Varieties such as **Trollinger** (2,600 hectares) and **Schwarzriesling** (Pinot Meunier – 2,500 hectares) generally are only of regional importance. Specialties such as **Lemberger** (1,440 hectares) and **Sankt Laurent** (600 hectares) would certainly be worthy of more attention.

Wine and Food

One of the main duties of a host is to know something about the matching of food and wine. Long gone are the days when it was sufficient to serve white wine with fish and red wine with meat. It is true that there are few hard-and-fast rules, but there are some general guidelines based on experience that may serve the interested reader well.

1. The intensity of taste of the food and wine must be in balance, neither the food nor the wine should be strongly dominant. The wine should thus be chosen with a view to the most intensively tasting product on the plate.

2. Sweetness and acidity of the food and wine should be compatible. Generally it is not the meat that primarily determines the taste of a dish, but the sauce or gravy. The old rule of *white wine with fish and red wine with meat* is only of limited application these days.

3. Sugar as an ingredient of a dish, no matter in what form it is added, makes an acidic wine taste even more aggressive.

4. Acetic or lactic acid in a dish have an unpleasant additive effect with the acidity in wine.

5. On the other hand, sweetness in a sauce and sweetness in a wine tend to cancel each other out.

6. Lots of salt in a dish is not compatible with lots of acidity in a wine. Instead, salt in the sauce and sweetness in the wine tend to have a positive balancing effect.

7. Bitter components in food do not often match well with tannins and acidity in a wine. It is more likely that they will go well with some sweetness in the wine.

To be able to make an optimum wine recommendation, it is particularly important that the sommelier should understand the interactions of the components of food and wine.

In most cases it can be assumed that the **sauce** will be the component of a dish that determines the overall taste.

First let us look at sauces based on butter and cream. It does not matter whether the sauce was made with crème fraîche, double or single cream or butter, the lactose content of all these ingredients will add some sweetness to the reduced sauce. Frequent variations of this are dark or glazed sauces, possibly thickened with cold butter. These are given a bit of acidity by the addition of wine, vinegar or fruit juice.

A wine served to accompany a sauce must match this in sweetness and acidity. Since there, concerning sweet glazed sauces and acid-dominated butter sauces, it is particularly important to know how a particular sauce was prepared if you are to find the ideal wine accompaniment based on the principles mentioned above. While **vegetables** are usually just a complement to most dishes, there are enormous differences in their taste interactions with wine. For instance, peas, carrots, Brussels sprouts, cabbage, fennel and onions all have some innate sweetness. You would want to match this with a white wine that is not overly dry, and certainly not acid-dominated.

In a certain sense, zucchini, aubergines and beans are neutral. By contrast, steamed chicory or radicchio can develop some bitter notes, which are of great importance in choosing a suitable wine. Chicory served as an accompaniment to a beef fillet, could well unbalance a red wine, since the tannins of the vegetable will have an additive effect on the tannins of the wine, particularly if the wine has been matured in barriques.

Soups are beverages in a sense, and it is unusual for a wine to be served with the soup. If a wine is selected, the same principles apply as for sauces. For instance, an off-dry Riesling matched with a creamy soup may be more successful than an overly acidic dry white wine.

Herbs and spices used in a dish also play an important part. Parsley, dill, chervil, oregano, marjoram, thyme, rosemary, sweet basil, curry, sage, juniper, pimento, bay leaves, muscat and pepper all go very well with wine. On the other hand, caution is indicated when using herbs that have a high level of ethereal oils, such as garlic, tarragon, chives, horse-radish or mint. These flavorants should be boiled several times to take away the edge, and give the wine the chance it deserves to stand up to their flavors.

There was a time when it was unthinkable to match **salads** with wine. We now know that a balanced dressing, consisting of not more than one part vinegar to three parts oil, can harmonize quite well with a white wine that is not overly acidic.

As **cheese** always contains lactic acid to a greater or lesser degree, one should always take care to match cheese with wine that is not too acidic. Which wine best goes with which cheese is dependent on many factors: the pressing, the maturation, the level of salt and the type of fungus used in the production of a specific type of cheese. It still appears to be a rule of thumb that red wine is usually served with cheese. This is just as wrong as saying that red wine should be served at room temperature – a habit that predates the advent of central heating.

In fact, some cheeses are simply difficult to match with wine. Lots of salt and a high level of lactic acid are generally not promising signs for a good match with wine, since the lactic acid and the acidity of the wine have an additive effect. If the cheese has also been washed in a saline solution, such as the red-crusted soft cheeses, this doubles the intensity of the wine's acidity. You should definitely avoid serving red wine with such a cheese. A Vintage Port would be much more suitable. The sweetness of the wine would balance the salt and acidity of the cheese, and the overall taste combination would be much more harmonious.

When selecting cheeses, the host should thus try to put together a range of cheeses with similar intensity of taste. To serve fresh cottage cheeses on the same plate as a Stilton or a red-crusted cheese would be just as nonsensical as pouring together a Riesling Kabinett and a Traminer Beerenauslese. In the long run, you will only enjoy well-balanced, harmonious tastes.

There is no such thing as the ideal wine for cheese, just types of wine that may go better with certain types of cheeses. Speaking very broadly, an aromatic white wine with some residual sweetness is more likely to work than a tannic red wine. For interest's sake, try an off-dry Scheurebe or Muskateller Auslese.

For obvious reasons, only wines with some residual sweetness will harmonize with **desserts**, and the same goes, in most cases, for sparkling wines. Dessert dishes often consist of chocolate, coffee, or many different kinds of fruit. Citrus fruit will only very rarely go well with wine. That does not mean you must do completely without this ingredient. For instance blanched lemon rind can be used without hesitation.

On the other hand, all **fruits** based on malice (apple) acid go particularly well with sweet botrytized Auslese wines. The following harmonize well with wine: apple, apricot, peach, mango, papaya, passion fruit, plum, quince, pear, black currant, elderberry, fig and melon.

Mocca and chocolate often contain too many bitter components to really make an interesting match with wine. We would also recommend that you steer away from sauces rich in egg-yolk, including zabaione, as these bind the flavorants, and cause them to stick to the tongue. Just generally it is interesting to observe and experience the interaction of sweet wines and sweet dishes: Where a Beerenauslese with a strong botrytis character might appear too sweet on its own, it could actually taste bitter when paired with an even sweeter caramel sauce. Just remember the basic principle: sweetness and sweetness cancel each other out!

The ideal case is that the acidity of the fruit will combine and harmonize with the acidity of the wine, leading to an interesting and refreshing combination. Good appetite!

Our Rating System

Classification of the producers

In classifying a producer, the editors base their verdict on the quality of wines produced over the past five to ten years. Extra weight is given to current developments and trends.

Highest rating,
for world-class wine producers

Excellent producers
counted as among
the best in Germany

Very good producers
who have been making
consistently high quality wines
for many years

Good producers who do better
than make just everyday wines

Reliable producers making
decent standard quality wines

Classification of the wines

The authors use the internationally accepted 100 points system.

100

A perfect wine that
justifies virtually any price

95 to 99

Outstanding wines from
exceptional vintages with long
maturation potential. Such rare
wines can command a high price

90 to 94

Excellent quality wines with a
considerable maturation potential.
They are rarely inexpensive

85 to 89

Very good, harmonious wines
that generally also mature well.
This category often provides
the best value for money

80 to 84

Good quality, well above average.
There are some bargains to
be had in this category

75 to 79

Average quality
for everyday consumption

For each wine, the alcoholic strength is stated, e. g. 11.5%.

The ratings refer exclusively to the quality of the wine, and not reflect value for money.

↗ indicates an auction wine

♀ the suggested best time of drinking is indicated for each wine. However, these ar not *Best by* of *Sell by* dates.

Producer of the Year

Every year since 1994, the Gault Millau WineGuide Germany has selected a Producer of the Year. The editorial board sees this as a means of honoring outstanding wineries that have in many cases produced top-class wines for many years or even decades. These are the top quality wine producers in Germany, and indeed some of them are among the best in the world. To date, 12 producers have been awarded this highest accolade presented by the WineGuide, of which no fewer than six were from the Mosel-Saar-Ruwer growing region.

2005

Christoph Tyrell
Weingut Karthäuserhof
Trier-Eitelsbach, Ruwer

2004

Werner Näkel
Weingut Meyer–Näkel
Dernau, Ahr

2003

Paul Fürst
Weingut Rudolf Fürst
Bürgstadt, Franken

2002

Hansjörg Rebholz
Weingut Ökonomierat Rebholz
Siebeldingen, Pfalz

2001

Ernst F. Loosen
Weingut Dr. Loosen
Bernkastel, Mosel

2000

Klaus Keller
Weingut Keller
Flörsheim-Dalsheim, Rheinhessen

1999

Helmut Dönnhoff
Weingut Hermann Dönnhoff
Oberhausen, Nahe

1998

Egon Müller
Weingut Egon Müller – Scharzhof
Wiltingen Saar

1997

Wilhelm Weil
Weingut Robert Weil
Kiedrich, Rheingau

1996

Dr. Manfred Prüm
Weingut Joh. Jos. Prüm
Bernkastel-Wehlen, Mosel

1995

Dr. Carl-Ferdinand von Schubert
Gutsverwaltung von Schubert
Maximin Grünhaus, Ruwer

1994

Wilhelm Haag
Weingut Fritz Haag
Brauneberg, Mosel

Germany's Best Estates

Highest rating,
for world-class wine producers

Mosel-Saar-Ruwer

FRITZ HAAG
LOOSEN
EGON MÜLLER
JOH. JOS. PRÜM

Nahe

DÖNNHOFF
EMRICH-SCHÖNLEBER

Pfalz

REBHOLZ

Rheingau

ROBERT WEIL

Rheinhessen

KELLER

Excellent producers counted
as among the best in Germany

Ahr

DEUTZERHOF
MEYER-NÄKEL
STODDEN

Baden

HEGER
BERNHARD HUBER
ANDREAS LAIBLE
SALWEY
R. U. C. SCHNEIDER

Franken

FÜRST CASTELL
RUDOLF FÜRST
HORST SAUER

Mittelrhein

WEINGART

Mosel-Saar-Ruwer

J. J. CHRISTOFFEL
GRANS-FASSIAN
REINHOLD HAART
HEYMANN-LÖWENSTEIN
KARTHÄUSERHOF
R. U. B. KNEBEL
SCHLOSS LIESER
MARKUS MOLITOR
SANKT URBANS-HOF
SELBACH-OSTER

Nahe

SCHÄFER-FRÖHLICH

Pfalz

BASSERMANN-JORDAN
BÜRKLIN-WOLF
A. CHRISTMANN
KNIPSER
KOEHLER-RUPRECHT
MOSBACHER
MÜLLER-CATOIR
WEHRHEIM

Rheingau

BREUER
KESSELER
P. J. KÜHN
JOSEF LEITZ

Rheinhessen

GUNDERLOCH
WITTMANN

Württemberg

ALDINGER
DAUTEL

Note: The Schlossgut Diel estate, Burg Layen, is not rated, as Armin Diel, the owner, is editor in chief of the Gault Millau WineGuide.

Germany's Best Estates

Very good producers
who have been making consistently
high quality wines for many years

Ahr

ADENEUER
KREUZBERG
WG MAYSCHOSS-ALTENAHR
NELLES

Baden

AUFRICHT
BERCHER
DUIJN
FISCHER
FRANKENSTEIN
GLEICHENSTEIN
ERNST HEINEMANN
KARL H. JOHNER
FRANZ KELLER
KNAB
MICHEL
SCHLOSS NEUWEIER
SCHLOSS ORTENBERG
WG PFAFFENWEILER
SCHLUMBERGER
SEEGER
STIGLER
WOLFF METTERNICH

Franken

GLASER-HIMMELSTOSS
JULIUSSPITAL
LÖWENSTEIN
JOHANN RUCK
SCHMITT'S KINDER
SCHLOSS SOMMERHAUSEN
AM STEIN
STÖRRLEIN
WIRSCHING
ZEHNTHOF

Hessische Bergstraße

STAATSWEINGUT BERGSTRASSE

Mittelrhein

DIDINGER
TONI JOST
MATTHIAS MÜLLER
A. U. TH. PERLL
RATZENBERGER

Mosel-Saar-Ruwer

BEULWITZ
CLÜSSERATH-EIFEL
CLÜSSERATH-WEILER
F.-J. EIFEL
JOH. HAART
HAIN
HERRENBERG
HÖVEL
IMMICH
KARLSMÜHLE
KEES-KIEREN
KESSELSTATT
KIRSTEN
LOEWEN
MÖNCHHOF
OTHEGRAVEN
PAULINSHOF
PAULY-BERGWEILER
S. A. PRÜM
REINERT
MAX FERD. RICHTER
ROSCH
SCHLOSS SAARSTEIN
WILLI SCHAEFER
HEINZ SCHMITT
SCHUBERT – GRÜNHAUS
THANISCH, MÜLLER-BURGGRAEF
THANISCH, ERBEN THANISCH
VOLLENWEIDER
WEGELER – BERNKASTEL
WEINS-PRÜM
ZILLIKEN

Nahe

CRUSIUS
GÖTTELMANN
HEXAMER
KORRELL
KRUGER-RUMPF
SALM-DALBERG
SCHWEINHARDT
TESCH

Germany's Best Estates

Pfalz
F. BECKER
BERGDOLT
BERNHART
BIFFAR
BUHL
DEINHARD
KLEINMANN
MÜNZBERG
PFEFFINGEN
KARL SCHAEFER
SIEGRIST
ULLRICHSHOF
WEEGMÜLLER
WILHELMSHOF
J. L. WOLF

Rheingau
J. B. BECKER
DOMDECHANT WERNER
FLICK
PRINZ VON HESSEN
SCHLOSS JOHANNISBERG
JOHANNISHOF
JAKOB JUNG
KRONE
KÜNSTLER
HANS LANG
LÖWENSTEIN
PRINZ
SCHLOSS SCHÖNBORN
SPREITZER
SCHLOSS VOLLRADS
WEGELER – OESTRICH

Rheinhessen
GUTZLER
HEYL ZU HERRNSHEIM
MANZ
SANKT ANTONY
G. A. SCHNEIDER
WAGNER-STEMPEL

Württemberg
ADELMANN
DRAUTZ-ABLE
ELLWANGER
KARL HAIDLE

NEIPPERG
SCHNAITMANN
SCHWEGLER
WÖHRWAG

Good producers who do better
than make just everyday wines

Ahr
BROGSITTER
BURGGARTEN
SONNENBERG
DOMÄNE MARIENTHAL

Baden
ABRIL
BERCHER-SCHMIDT
BLANKENHORN
WG BRITZINGEN
DÖRFLINGER
WG DURBACH
JOACHIM HEGER
HOENSBROECH
HUMMEL
SCHLOSSGUT ISTEIN
JÄHNISCH
KOCH
KONSTANZER
LÄMMLIN-SCHINDLER
MÄNNLE
MARKGRAF BADEN –
SCHLOSS STAUFENBERG
NÄGELSFÖRST
BURG RAVENSBURG
SCHÄTZLE
SCHLÖR
STAATSWEINGUT FREIBURG
STADT LAHR
FRITZ WASSMER
MARTIN WASSMER

Franken
BICKEL-STUMPF
BRAUN
BRENNFLECK
BÜRGERSPITAL

Germany's Best Estates

Good producers who do better
than make just everyday wines

Franken
CHRIST
FRÖHLICH
HEIGEL
HOFMANN
WG NORDHEIM
ROTH
RAINER SAUER
SCHÄFFER
STAATLICHER HOFKELLER
STICH
WELTNER

Hessische Bergstraße
SIMON-BÜRKLE
STADT BENSHEIM

Mittelrhein
FRITZ BASTIAN
DR. KAUER
GOSWIN LAMBRICH
LANIUS-KNAB
LORENZ

Mosel-Saar-Ruwer
BISCHÖFLICHE WEINGÜTER
BRAUNEBERGER HOF
BUSCH
CHRISTOFFEL JUN.
ANSGAR CLÜSSERATH
ERNST CLÜSSERATH
EHLEN
FRANZEN
FRIEDRICH-KERN
FUCHS
WILLI HAAG
HEDDESDORFF
KERPEN
KUNTZ
LAUER
LUBENTIUSHOF
MERKELBACH
MEULENHOF
MILZ

MOLITOR – ROSENKREUZ
MÜLLEN
WALTER RAUEN
REGNERY
SCHMITGES
STUDERT-PRÜM
VEREINIGTE HOSPITIEN
VAN VOLXEM
HEINZ WAGNER
WELLER-LEHNERT

Nahe
BAMBERGER
HAHNMÜHLE
LINDENHOF
MATHERN
MONTIGNY
GUTSVERWALUNG
NIEDERHAUSEN
JOH. BAPT. SCHÄFER
JAKOB SCHNEIDER
STAATSWEINGUT
BAD KREUZNACH

Pfalz
ACHAM-MAGIN
BENDERHOF
BRENNEIS-KOCH
DARTING
EYMANN
FREY
GAUL
GIES-DÜPPEL
HENSEL
HEUSSLER
IMMENGARTEN HOF
JÜLG
KAUB
KRANZ
KUHN
LEININGERHOF
LERGENMÜLLER
LUCASHOF
MESSMER
FRANK MEYER
MINGES
EUGEN MÜLLER
PETRI

Germany's Best Estates

Good producers who do better
than make just everyday wines

KARL PFAFFMANN
SCHEU
EGON SCHMITT
SCHUMACHER
SIENER
SPINDLER

Rheingau
ALTENKIRCH
BARTH
CORVERS-KAUTER
JOST
GRAF KANITZ
BARON KNYPHAUSEN
ROBERT KÖNIG
KÖNIGIN-VICTORIABERG
LANGWERTH VON SIMMERN
NIKOLAI
QUERBACH
SCHLOSS REINHARTSHAUSEN
RESS
SCHÖNLEBER
SPEICHER-SCHUTH
STAATSWEINGUT
ASSMANNSHAUSEN
STAATSWEINGUT
KLOSTER EBERBACH

Rheinhessen
BATTENFELD-SPANIER
DR. BECKER
BUSCHER
FLEISCHER
GEHRING
JOH. GEIL ERBEN
GROEBE
KISSINGER
KÜHLING-GILLOT
MICHEL-PFANNEBECKER
MILCH
POSTHOF
SANDER
SCHALES
SCHERNER-KLEINHANSS

SEEBRICH
SEEHOF
STRUB
VILLA SACHSEN

Saale-Unstrut
LÜTZKENDORF
PAWIS

Sachsen
SCHLOSS PROSCHWITZ
ZIMMERLING

Württemberg
BEURER
G. A. HEINRICH
SCHLOSSGUT HOHENBEILSTEIN
HOHENLOHE-OEHRINGEN
KISTENMACHER-HENGERER
KUSTERER
STAATSWEINGUT WEINSBERG
WG UNTERTÜRKHEIM
WACHTSTETTER
HERZOG VON WÜRTTEMBERG

Reliable producers making
decent standard qualitiy wines

Ahr
DAGERNOVA
LINGEN
MAIBACHFARM
RISKE
SERMANN-KREUZBERG

Baden
WG ACHKARREN
AFFENTALER WG
WG ALDE GOTT
WG AUGGEN
L. BASTIAN
CONSEQUENCE
EHRENSTETTER WINZERKELLER
ENGIST
HAGENBUCHER
WINZERVEREIN HAGNAU
WG HALTINGEN
HEX VOM DASENSTEIN

Germany's Best Estates

HOLUB
HUCK-WAGNER
KALKBÖDELE
KLUMPP
WG KÖNIGSCHAFFHAUSEN
KOPP
KRESS
LEO MAIER
MARKGRAF BADEN –
SCHLOSS SALEM
GEBRÜDER MÜLLER
WG OBERBERGEN
PIX
PROBST
WG SASBACH
C. u. S. SCHNEIDER
STAATSWEINGUT MEERSBURG
TAUBERFR. WG BECKSTEIN
TRAUTWEIN
ZÄHRINGER

Franken
BARDORF
BLENDEL
BRÜGEL
ERHARD
HÖFLER
AM LUMP
MAY
MEINTZINGER
MAX MÜLLER
RUDLOFF
TROCKENE SCHMITTS
SCHWAB
SCHWANE
WINZERKELLER SOMMERACH
STEINMANN
WG THÜNGERSHEIM

Hessische Bergstraße
BERGSTRÄSSER WINZER EG
ROTHWEILER

Mittelrhein
EMMERICH
HOHN
ALBERT LAMBRICH
MADES
WALTER PERLL
SCHEIDGEN
SELT
SONNENHANG

Mosel-Saar-Ruwer
BASTGEN
BLEES-FERBER
BOCH
BERNHARD EIFEL
EIFEL-PFEIFFER
ERBES
FRIES
HERRENBERG – B. SIMON
KRÖBER
LEHNERT-VEIT
MELSHEIMER
PHILIPPS-ECKSTEIN
PIEDMONT
FAMILIE RAUEN
REH
RESCH
REUSCHER-HAART
RICHARD RICHTER
RÖMERHOF
SCHÖMANN
SPÄTER-VEIT
TERGES

Nahe
ADELSECK
EDELBERG
EMRICH-MONTIGNY
ANTON FINKENAUER
KAUER
KLOSTERMÜHLE
LÖTZBEYER
RAPP
ROHR

Germany's Best Estates

SCHAUSS
SCHMIDT
SCHÖMEHL
SITZIUS

Pfalz

ACKERMANN
BECK
BORELL-DIEHL
CASTEL PETER
DENGLER-SEYLER
FADER
FITZ-RITTER
GRASSMÜCK
KARST
KASSNER-SIMON
KLEIN
BERNHARD KOCH
LEINER
LIDY
LUDI NEISS
PFIRMANN
PFLEGER
STOLLEIS
VIER JAHRESZEITEN WG
WAGECK-PFAFFMANN
WEGNER
WEIK
WILKER
ZIEGLER
ZIMMERMANN

Rheingau

BISCHÖFL. WEINGUT RÜDESHEIM
DIEFENHARDT
FENDEL
FREIMUTH
HAMM
LAMM-JUNG
MOHR
DETLEV RITTER VON OETINGER
OHLIG
W. J. SCHÄFER
SCHAMARI-MÜHLE

Rheinhessen

BERNHARD
FOGT
GALLÉ
GEILS SEKT- UND WEINGUT
GÖHRING
HEDESHEIMER HOF
HUFF
HUFF-DOLL
JOHANNINGER
KREICHGAUER
AXEL MÜLLER
NEUS
PETH-WETZ
RIFFEL
SCHAETZEL
SCHEMBS
SCHICK
SPIESS
DOMÄNE OPPENHEIM
STEITZ
STROHM
WERNER
WINTER
WÜRTZ

Saale-Unstrut

BÖHME
GUSSEK
THÜRINGER WEINGUT

Sachsen

SCHWARZ
SCHLOSS WACKERBARTH

Württemberg

AMALIENHOF
BADER
WG GRANTSCHEN
HIRTH
KLOPFER
KUHNLE
LEISS
MEDINGER
WG ROTENBERG
SANKT ANNAGARTEN
SONNENHOF

Vintage Chart

The Vintages in the Growing Regions

Vintages are important in a country that is as far north as Germany, but it is impossible to give a single value to the quality of any given year for all of the 13 growing regions. On the whole, however, the last years have brought a string of above average vintages unparalleled in German history. We have tried to provide a frame of reference using the grape symbols of this book, but this will not describe the quality of the wines from any given producer. Some make excellent wines even in poor vintages, others poor wines in great vintages.

Legend:

- 🍇🍇🍇🍇🍇 Excellent
- 🍇🍇🍇🍇 Very good
- 🍇🍇🍇 Good
- 🍇🍇 Average
- 🍇 Poor

	1994	1995	1996	1997	1998	1999	2000	2001	2002	2003
Ahr										
Baden										
Franken										
Hessische Bergstraße										
Mittelrhein										
Mosel-Saar-Ruwer										
Nahe										
Pfalz										
Rheingau										
Rheinhessen										
Saale-Unstrut										
Sachsen										
Württemberg										
	1994	1995	1996	1997	1998	1999	2000	2001	2002	2003

Beyond sweet and cheap

After France, Italy and Spain, Germany is the fourth-largest wine exporter in Europe. Each year, 2 million hectoliters of German wine are exported to more than 140 countries around the world. This represents a fourth of the annual production. A large part of this volume is bottled by shippers. They are all based in the wine-growing regions and most can thus be found either in Rheinhessen or along the Mosel River. Up to the Eighties, life was pleasant for these global players. They were extremely successful with sweet wines, especially Liebfraumilch, of which no less than 175 million bottles were sold in 1984. This volume has been almost reduced, to less than 95 million bottles.

This loss can largely be ascribed to a change in consumer taste and demand. The German wine export trade was slow to respond to new modern trends, to the growing demand for red wines as well as dry white wines in a modern style. When a working group of the German Wine Institute assessed the industry status in the mid-Nineties, the findings did not make pleasant reading. German wine was stigmatized with an image that can be summarized as cheap, sweet and for elderly people. With regard to style, presentation and descriptive labeling, most producers – although successfully establishing a new generation of wines on the German market – were clearly neglecting the changing demands of the foreign markets. Further, they had simply ignored the shift in the mid-price segment of the market and left this to the foreign competition, while the prices for Liebfraumilch and similar products fell to record lows.

New and drier profile wines with an attractive modern presentation were developed in a bid to put a stop to this decline and have been rigorously put into practice by the major shippers. Label descriptions have been simplified, and clear indications of taste have been added in order to build a higher recognition factor for these wines – important if you want to compete on retailers' shelves. Today, the focus is on grape varieties combined with large-scale definitions of origin, such as Riesling from the Mosel region. In this context, the Classic range concept, introduced in 2000, has proven successful and is being implemented in many export markets.

The new wave of success of German wine abroad can primarily be attributed to the astonishing renaissance of Riesling, which had its origins in the USA and which is gaining momentum worldwide. The opinion leaders, such as sommeliers and journalists, have long since come out in favor of Riesling, and after many years of decline, German Riesling is winning back market share on the expanding American wine-market. Similar trends can be observed in other markets. There is a lot of catching up to be done, though, particularly in Japan, where many consumers have developed a taste for red wine. However, Steffen Schindler, responsible for export marketing at the German Wine Institute, is optimistic that the nigh-perfect matching of Asian cuisine with German Riesling will lead to a wave of demand, not only from Japan.

Initially, German wines became famous abroad mainly through the appeal of Riesling from the Rhine and Mosel, and more specifically for the top-class sweet botrytized dessert wines. Although Liebfraumilch, formerly the most important export article, is on the wane, other major brands such as Black Tower or Blue Nun have maintained their share of the market. However, bottles bearing these brand names are no longer filled with sweet and insipid wines. Increasingly they contain the Riesling, Silvaner as well as Pinot varieties in a modern drier style.

Among other positive developments the global players have brought to the German wine scene is the use of international winemakers from the New World. This has led to the production of large volumes of good-quality, usually cold-fermented, wines. On the other hand, these players have also created regional wines with distinctive style and character, proving that Germany is capable of producing much more than just basic sweet wines.

BINDERER ST. URSULA WEINKELLEREI

General Manager: Peter Binderer
Export Sales Manager: Ariane Binderer
Lerchenstraße 66, D-80995 München
Tel. ++49 (0)89-3 14 00 30,
Fax 31 40 03 55
e-mail: info@binderer.de
Internet: www.devils-rock.co.uk

Annual sales value: 60 mill. Euros
Annual sales volume: 50 mill. bottles
Export share: 30 percent
Exports: Since the early Seventies
Most important export markets:
United Kingdom, Scandinavia,
Canada, Benelux
Key brands: Devil's Rock Riesling and
Devil's Rock Pinot Grigio

This winery was formerly based in Bingen on the Rhine, and the Devil's Rock, which is depicted on the labels, actually does exist in the South of the Pfalz region. The Riesling grapes, which Binderer St. Ursula processes to must and wine are sourced from this area. The wines are made in a modern style, presenting clear fruit and freshness with quite pronounced lemon and grapefruit notes. The Pinot Grigio, too, shows good balance and medium body, the grapes for this are obtained from the neighboring Rheinhessen region. The realization that the erstwhile exports mainstay Liebfraumilch and Piesporter are in continual decline, has led the Binderer family to promote the Devils's Rock product line. St. Binderer sees good opportunities primarily for Riesling as well as for the Pinot varieties, made in a modern style.

HENKEL & SÖHNLEIN SEKTKELLEREIEN KG

Export Manager:
Dr. Hans-Henning Wiegmann
Export Director: Dieter Ballo
Biebricher Allee 142
D-65187 Wiesbaden
Tel. ++49 (0)6 11-6 30, Fax 6 37 12 22
e-mail: balldi@hs-kg.de
Internet: www.deinhard.com

Annual sales value: 480 mill. Euros
Annual sales volume: 200 mill. liters
Export share: 65 percent (Deinhard)
Exports: Deinhard has been exporting
since 1794
Important export markets: Canada,
Norway, Sweden, USA, Netherlands
Key brands: Classic wines from Ries-
ling, Pinot Blanc, Pinot Gris, Deinhard
Green Label Riesling

For some time now, the largest sparkling wine producer in Germany has been generating a significant share of its turnover in the new markets of Eastern Europe. Also for some time, the Deinhard KG company, a further sparkling wine producer with a long tradition, has been part of the Henkell & Söhnlein group. Deinhard has always also had a program of branded wines, of which two-thirds are still exported even today. In addition to the Green Label Riesling and the Piesporter Riesling, the range of Classic wines has in recent years also gained a foothold in export markets. Fresh, medium-bodied Pinot Blanc and Pinot Gris wines as well as a fruity, invigorating Riesling, have all found their friends around the world.

F. W. LANGGUTH ERBEN

Manager: Thomas Langguth, Rainer Trumm
Dr.-Ernst-Spies-Allee 2
D-56841 Traben-Trarbach
Tel. ++49 (0)65 41-1 70, Fax 64 74
e-mail: carmen.beyer@langguth.de
Internet: www.langguth.de

Annual sales value: 97 mill. Euros
Annual sales volume: 48 mill. bottles
Export share: 40 percent
Exports: Since 1921
Most important export markets: United Kingdom, USA, Scandinavia
Key brands: Blue Nun, Langguth's Erben wines

At one stage, Blue Nun was practically synonymous with Liebfraumilch in Great Britain. Although the fortunes of this former export star of the German wine industry have been on the wane since the Nineties, recent market research has revealed that Blue Nun is still today the best-known wine brand in England. Langguth intends to build on this solid foundation, and soon after acquiring the brand from H. Sichel in 1996 embarked on a complete repositioning of the brand. The Liebfraumilch is now a quality wine with a much-reduced sugar content. Also, the Blue Nun range now encompasses wines from a number of different countries: Merlot from France, Shiraz from Australia, Rosé from Spain. This concept appears to be working out: By the year 2002 Blue Nun had again attained the high sales figures of the Seventies – and the brand continues to grow.

PETER MERTES WEINKELLER

Manager: Michael Willkomm
In der Bornwiese 4
D-54470 Bernkastel-Kues
Tel. ++49 (0)65 31-5 51 45, Fax 5 51 29
e-mail: H.Wiele@mertes.de
Internet: www.mertes.de

Annual sales value: 130 mill. Euros
Annual production: 120 mill. bottles
Export share: 30 percent
Exports: Since the early Seventies
Most important export markets: United Kingdom and Ireland, Scandinavia, USA, Japan, Benelux
Own vineyard area: 44 hectares

After Racke, Peter Mertes is the second-largest winery in Germany. The company concentrates on domestic business, with own brands accounting for only a small share of sales. The main focus is on bottling wines on a large scale for all the leading food and supermarket chains – mainly vineyard- and varietal-designated wines grown in Germany. Red wines play an increasingly important role in the product mix. In addition, Mertes has transformed its traditional cellar in Bernkastel-Kues into the largest barrique cellar facility in Germany. A spacious visitor center is being developed above this, due to be opened in mid-2005. Traditional export wines such as Hock, Zeller Schwarze Katz or Niersteiner Gutes Domtal still play quite an important part here. In addition, one has seen the signs of the times here as well, and the focus in future will be increasingly on varietal wines, primarily Riesling.

MOSELLAND EG

General Manager: Werner Kirchhoff
Export Sales Manager:
Martin Henrichs
Bornwiese 6
D-54470 Bernkastel-Kues
Tel. ++49 (0)65 31-5 70, Fax 5 71 37
e-mail: info@moselland.de
Internet: www.moselland.de

Annual sales value: 40 mill. Euros
Annual sales volume: 25 mill. liters
Export share: 50 percent
Exports: Since foundation of the
company in 1968
Most important export markets:
Great Britain, North America, Scandinavia, Benelux, Japan
Key brands: Divinum, Insignum
Vineyard area: 2,400 hectares

This is the co-operative winery that probably has the highest export share of all German co-operatives. 3,200 members cultivate some 2,400 hectares of vineyard in the Mosel-Saar-Ruwer and Nahe regions – much of this on labor-intensive steep slopes. More than 50 percent of the vineyard area is planted with Riesling. This makes Moselland the largest Riesling producer in the world. This position is further strengthened by means of strategic agreements with additional co-operatives in the Pfalz and Rheinhessen regions. The wines of the four growing regions are marketed under different brands. The main demand in export markets is for Riesling from the Mosel, Saar and Ruwer. The top-level wines are to be found in the Divinum series. The Insignum brand includes vineyard-specific Riesling wines, such as those from the Lieserer Schlossberg or the Ürziger Würzgarten sites.

A. RACKE

Chairman of the board:
Marcus Moller-Racke
Gaustraße 20, D-55411 Bingen
Tel. ++49 (0)67 21-18 80, Fax 18 82 20
e-mail: r.zoeller@racke.de
Internet: www.racke.de

Annual sales value: 200 mill. Euros
Annual sales volume: 75 mill. bottles
Export share: 10 percent
Exports: Since 1960
Most important export markets:
Poland, Netherlands, Switzerland,
Japan, Canada
Key brand: Rebian's

Under the stewardship of Marcus Moller-Racke, this largest winery/cellar in Germany is increasing its focus on wine. Racke first made a name for itself in the Sixties when they launched the first German Whisky, the logo of which, a fox, has become the corporate logo. In the wine sector, co-operation agreements have been established, including some with South African producers. In fact, the head of Racke International, Marian Kopp, is of the opinion that many mid-priced German wines still lack marketing/brand orientation. Racke has been marketing a German branded wine for many years, Rebian's Riesling, a quality wine produced primarily for the export markets.

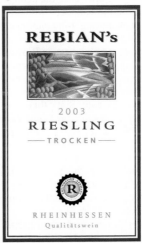

REH-KENDERMANN WEINKELLEREI

Owners: Carl and Andrea Reh
Export Sales Director:
Alison Flemming MW
Am Ockenheimer Graben 35
D-55411 Bingen/Rhein
Tel. ++49 (0)67 21-90 10, Fax 90 12 40
e-mail:
alison.flemming@reh-kendermann.de
Internet: www.reh-kendermann.de

Annual sales value: 85 mill. Euros
Annual sales volume: 70 mill. bottles,
of this 85% from Rhine and Mosel
Export share: 65 percent
Exports: Since the 1920's
Most important export markets:
United Kingdom, Scandinavia,
North America, Netherlands
Key brands: Black Tower, The Bend
in the River, Carl Reh, Kendermann's

In 1920, Carl Reh established a trading company for grapes, must and wine in the small cellar at his parents' house on the Mosel. Only a few years later, the first larger winery and cellar was built in Leiwen on the Mosel. The business was so successful that in the next few years additional cellar facilities had to be rented in surrounding villages. After the Second World War, the founder was still able to experience the dedication of one of the most modern wine cellars in Europe, featuring fully automatic bottling lines. In 1992, the merger with the H. Kendermann winery in Bingen led to the creation of the leading German wine exporting company, featuring the Black Tower brand, the international number one market leader. Since then, Carl Reh, who represents the third generation, has implemented a strong drive for improved quality. By now, a total of five winemakers is constantly on the road, in order to ensure the high standards of quality at all facilities. They take in only healthy grapes at the optimum moment of ripeness from long-term contract growers. A new container transport system was introduced in 1999, designed to ensure the grapes are transported from vineyard to the nearest cellar as quickly as possible. Efforts are mainly focused on key quality varietals: Riesling, Rivaner, Pinot Gris and Pinot Blanc as well as Silvaner. Reh-Kendermann operates extremely modern cellar facilities at various locations (Bingen on the Rhine, Leiwen on the Mosel, Gau-Bickelheim in Rheinhessen). Up to 12 million liters of wine can be fermented under temperature-controlled conditions. A comprehensive tasting of the wines confirmed that this attention to detail is starting to bear fruit, and in particular the dry wines have benefited from the efforts. For instance, the 2002 Kendermann's Dry Riesling "Kalkstein" from the Palatinate shows spicy fruit and elegant acid balance. The Rheinhessen Riesling "Roter Hang" is dense and powerful and the Riesling "Schiefer" from Moselle shows interesting minerals. Even the basic wines of the Black Tower range are always clean and very attractive, showing fruit and sometimes a little delicate sweetness. The volume sold has been doubled in only five years, to 10.7 million bottles annually. The flagship of a large and ambitious range is the stylish Riesling Auslese from the Leiwener Laurentiuslay vineyard (Carl Reh, Mosel). In recent years, Carl Reh has purchased additional vineyard parcels in top-class Mosel sites, including a parcel of the famous Trittenheimer Apotheke site.

RUPPERTSBERGER WINZERVEREIN HOHEBURG EG

General Manager: Gerhard Brauer
Hauptstraße 74, D-67152 Ruppertsberg
Tel. ++49 (0)63 26-96 29 70, Fax 96 29 79
e-mail: info@ruppertsberger.de
Internet: www.ruppertsberger.de

Annual sales value: 5.5 mill. Euros
Annual production: 2 mill. liters
Export share: 25 percent
Exports: Since the late Eighties
Most important export markets:
Sweden, United Kingdom, Belgium,
Netherlands, Japan, Switzerland,
Norway, Denmark
Vineyard area: 245 hectares
Key brand: Riesling Classic

Gerhard Brauer of the Ruppertsberg wine co-operative is not really comfortable being placed in a list of global players. The general manager of the co-operative right in the heart of the Pfalz region is very happy about the level of exports, which make up a quarter of total sales, and are thus much higher than the average co-operative, many of which have no foreign sales at all. The Classic wines, launched only a few years ago, dominate export sales, and account for almost two-thirds of exports, with Riesling playing the key role. Gerhard Brauer looks to the future with confidence, particularly if the German wine industry continues to work on improving quality, especially for the export markets, with a focus on fruity and harmonious Riesling wines instead of basic sweet wines.

SCHMITT SÖHNE WEINKELLEREI

President: Thomas Schmitt
Weinstraße 8, D-54340 Longuich
Tel. ++49 (0)65 02-40 90, Fax 4 09 36
e-mail: info@schmitt-soehne.com
Internet: www.schmitt-soehne.com

Annual sales value: 35 mill. Euros
Annual production: 24 mill. bottles
Export share: 90 percent
Exports: Since the mid-Seventies
Most important export markets:
United Kingdom, USA, Netherlands,
Scandinavia
Key brands: Blue Riesling,
Relax Riesling

Whereas most German wholesale producers also process at least some imported wines, Schmitt Söhne maintains a tradition of bottling only German wines. A further distinguishing characteristic of this winery, which is located in Longuich in the Mosel region: practically 100 percent of wines sold are exported. In fact, in terms of the US market, Schmitt Söhne is by far the largest German exporter. The range still features the old classics: from Liebfraumilch right through to Niersteiner Gutes Domtal. However, these are increasingly giving way to varietal wines, with Riesling at the forefront. A wine has been created specifically for the American market: Relax Riesling – easy in name, easy to understand and enjoy. One of the most successful brands is Blue Riesling, derived from grapes grown in the Mosel region.

P. J. VALCKENBERG

President: Wilhelm G. Steifensand
Postfach 23 45
D-67513 Worms am Rhein
Tel. ++49 (0)62 41-9 11 10,
Fax 9 11 11 60
e-mail: info@valckenberg.com
Internet: www.valckenberg.com
Sales: "Der Weinladen," Worms
Weckerlingplatz 1
Tel. ++49 (0)62 41-91 11 80

Annual sales value: 12 mill. Euros
Annual sales volume: 5.5 mill. bottles
Export share: 75 percent
Exports: Since more than 200 years
Key export markets: USA, Scandinavia, Baltic states, Japan

Dutchman Peter Joseph Valckenberg founded the wine house, which today is the oldest family-owned wine merchant house in Germany, in Worms on the Rhine, a few years before the French Revolution. In April 1808 he purchased the major part of the Liebfrauenstift-Kirchenstück vineyard site on an auction, this being the documented origin of the "Liebfraumilch" designation. Exports today are split evenly between bottlings of own wines and those of major German VDP estates. The United States remain the most important export market, with a first delivery of Liebfraumilch to Ohio being documented in 1865. General manager Wilhelm Steifensand represents the seventh generation of the founder family.

WIV WEIN INTERNATIONAL AG

Executive board: Dr. Herbert Rasenberger, Dr. Johannes Pieroth, Andreas Pieroth
Hauptstraße 1, D-55452 Burg Layen
Tel. ++49 (0)67 21-96 50, Fax 96 54 99
e-mail: info@ wiv-ag.com
Internet: www.wiv-ag.com

Annual sales value: approx. 490 mill.
Euros (includes other divisions)
Annual sales volume: 53 mill. bottles
Export share: 25 percent
Exports: Since 1958
Most important export markets:
United Kingdom, Japan, USA,
Australia and 20 additional countries

Ever since company founder Elmar Pieroth made his first foreign trip to London in the late Fifties, carrying his case of samples, exports have become an important part of the business. This is the largest direct-marketing wine company in the world, with a range of products on offer that could not be more diverse. WIV has the complete spectrum available, from consumer friendly basic wines right up to First Growths from top producers. In the export markets, wines bearing the name of the owner's family, Pieroth have always been important players. The latest innovation is a range of varietal wines in the premium segment, in modern presentation. The company is particularly successful in Great Britain and Japan. For example, in Japan Pieroth is one of the most important distributors of top Bordeaux wines as well as of a number of the most highly regarded German VDP estates. New challenges that the management has decided to tackle entail is the development of further markets in Asia and Russia.

ZIMMERMANN-GRAEFF & MÜLLER

Executive shareholders: Johannes Hübinger and Erik Rundquist
Marientaler Au 23
D-56856 Zell/Mosel
Tel. ++49 (0)65 42-41 90, Fax 41 91 50
e-mail: info@zgm.de
Internet: www.zgm.de

Annual sales value: 105 mill. Euros
Annual sales volume: 100 mill. bottles
Export share: 60 percent
Export: Since 1976
Most important export markets: United Kingdom, Benelux, Scandinavian, USA, Russia, Poland, Canada, Japan
Key brands: Königsmosel, Bishop of Riesling, Fire Mountain

This dynamic company is probably the biggest export producer in Germany. It has grown out of a merger of two family-owned companies in 1998. Zimmermann-Graeff was founded in Zell on the Mosel in 1886, and since the Seventies, under the direction of Johannes Hübinger, has developed to be one of the leading wine producers in the Mosel region. Rudolf Müller founded his company in Reil in 1919. The attached winery in Kinheim is specialized on sparkling and carbonated wines. Erik Rundquist of Rudolf Müller is the second executive shareholder in the merged company that bears the abbreviated name ZGM. The efforts at improving quality are exceptional for a company of this size. Last year, five cellar facilities took in a total of 23 million liters of fresh must. Six "flying winemakers" from South Africa, Australia and New Zealand ensured the musts were handled with care and stored under optimum conditions. Temperature-controlled fermentation and extended lees contact are by now standard procedures. Each year, 53 million liters of German wine are bottled on state-of-the-art bottling lines that can handle 420,000 bottles per day. Ever since Johannes Hübinger joined the business in the mid-Seventies, the company engaged in export business, which now makes up a formidable 60 percent of total sales. The program on offer covers just about every possible facet, and is exported to more than 30 countries. The merchant house of Rudolf Müller has a long tradition of export sales. In fact, a separate concept of a range of wines from steep slopes has been developed under this roof. Other distribution companies that today are also part of the ZGM group likewise play an important part in exports. For example, the merchant company of Ewald Theod. Drathen is well-known in Japan and Scandinavia. In addition, the name of Michel Schneider has a good reputation in world markets, and is also a division of ZGM. The key varietal, Riesling, is available both in traditional presentation (Königsmosel brand), and as a cold-fermented varietal wine in modern style and presentation (Fire Mountain). Apart from the trade in bottled wines, another form of packaging is currently very much in demand: the three liter bag-in-box, which is particularly popular in the Anglo-Saxon and Scandinavian markets. In addition, the range includes wines very much in the premium segment. The wine estate of Wwe Dr. Thanisch – Erben Müller-Burggraef (see page 382) provides access to a parcel of the world-famous Bernkasteler Doctor site, appealing to even the most discerning Mosel enthusiasts.

RUDOLF MÜLLER

2004
RIESLING
CLASSIC
Qualitätswein
MOSEL

Rudolf Müller

© Armin Faber & Partner

Finest estate-bottled sparkling wine
2000 Blanc de Noir Brut "Prestige"
Raumland (Rheinhessen)

Finest dry red wine
2002 Blauer Spätburgunder Tafelwein "Res."
Friedrich Becker (Pfalz)

Finest dry white Pinot
2003 Siebeldinger im Sonnenschein Weißer Burgunder Spätlese "Großes Gewächs"
Ökonomierat Rebholz (Pfalz)

Finest dry Riesling
2003 "G-Max"
Keller (Rheinhessen)

Finest off-dry Riesling
2003 Winninger Röttgen "Erste Lage"
Heymann-Löwenstein (Mosel-Saar-Ruwer)

Favorites

Finest Riesling Classic
2003 Riesling Classic
Wilfried Querbach (Rheingau)

Finest naturally sweet Riesling
2003 Ockfener Bockstein Spälese
Sankt Urbans-Hof (Mosel-Saar-Ruwer)

Finest Riesling Spätlese
2003 Wehlener Sonnenuhr – 22 –
Joh. Jos. Prüm (Mosel-Saar-Ruwer)

Finest Riesling Auslese
2003 Scharzhofberger – 26 – Goldkapsel
Egon Müller – Scharzhof (Mosel-Saar-Ruwer)

Finest botrytis dessert wine
2003 Kiedricher Gräfenberg Riesling Trockenbeerenauslese Goldkapsel
Robert Weil (Rheingau)

Wines of the Year

Dry red wine

For many years, German red wines were not in the same league as the top products of other wine-producing countries, and, based on their limited availability, were often excessively expensive and overpriced. However, the progress made in wine quality the past few years bears some comment, particularly in those wineries that have the right feel for the use of oak, and specifically small oak or barriques. Generally speaking, the best red wines are from Baden, from the Pfalz and from the Ahr region. In addition, Franken, Württemberg as well as the Rheingau have some remarkable wines on offer.

2002	Blauer Spätburgunder Tafelwein "Res." Friedrich Becker (Pfalz)	**94**
2001	Blauer Spätburgunder Tafelwein "Res." Friedrich Becker (Pfalz)	**93**
2000	Spätburgunder "R" Bernhard Huber (Baden)	**93**
1999	Walporzheimer Kräuterberg Spätburgunder Auslese Meyer-Näkel (Ahr)	**93**
1998	Dalsheimer Bürgel Spätburgunder "Felix" Keller (Rheinhessen)	**91**
1997	Spätburgunder Rotwein "B 52" Nelles (Ahr)	**93**
1996	Assmannshäuser Höllenberg Spätburgunder Spätlese ** Kesseler (Rheingau)	**92**
1995	Spätburgunder Rotwein "Reserve" Bernhard Huber (Baden)	**91**
1994	Spätburgunder "S" Meyer-Näkel (Ahr)	**91**
1993	Spätburgunder Tafelwein "S" Dautel (Württemberg)	**91**
1992	Burkheimer Feuerberg Spätburgunder Rotwein Spätlese "SE" Bercher (Baden)	**92**

Wines of the Year

Dry white Pinot varieties

The success of the dry white Pinot varieties can be explained in terms of what most consumers expect from a dry wine: It should be full-bodied and smooth, but not too acidic. The best examples are found primarily in Baden and in the Pfalz region, as well as in Rheinhessen. Based on their full flavor they are ideal partners for food, while their full body as well as the usually higher alcohol levels means they are not really quaffing wines.

2003	Siebeldinger im Sonnenschein Weißer Burgunder Spätlese "Großes Gewächs" Ökonomierat Rebholz (Pfalz)	**93**
2002	Birkweiler Mandelberg Weißer Burgunder Spätlese "Großes Gewächs" Dr. Wehrheim (Pfalz)	**93**
2001	Siebeldinger im Sonnenschein Weißer Burgunder Spätlese "Großes Gewächs" Ökonomierat Rebholz (Pfalz)	**93**
2000	Grauer Burgunder "SJ" Karl H. Johner (Baden)	**92**
1999	Chardonnay Spätlese "R" Ökonomierat Rebholz (Pfalz)	**92**
1998	Weißer Burgunder Spätlese *** R. u. C. Schneider (Baden)	**92**
1997	Burkheimer Feuerberg Grauer Burgunder Auslese "SE" Bercher (Baden)	**92**
1996	Burkheimer Feuerberg Grauer Burgunder Spätlese "SE" Bercher (Baden)	**92**
1995	Chardonnay "SJ" Tafelwein Karl H. Johner (Baden)	**92**
1994	Burkheimer Feuerberg Weißburgunder Auslese "SE" Bercher (Baden)	**92**
1993	Grauburgunder Tafelwein "SJ" Karl H. Johner (Baden)	**93**
1992	Chardonnay Tafelwein Karl H. Johner (Baden)	**90**

Wines of the Year
Dry Riesling

The quality of top-class dry Riesling has improved significantly in the past decade. Good dry wines must have a full body as well as extract and substance, while the fruit acid should not be too dominant on the palate. The ideal natural conditions for the production of this type of Riesling wine can be found primarily in the Pfalz as well as in the Ortenau region in Baden, as well as in the Rheingau, Rheinhessen and in the Nahe region. We really do wish German producers would finally decide on a mutually agreed name or designation for dry premium-quality Riesling.

2003	G-Max Keller (Rheinhessen)	**94**
2002	Forster Kirchenstück Riesling "Großes Gewächs" Dr. Bürklin-Wolf (Pfalz)	**94**
2001	Westhofener Morstein Riesling "Großes Gewächs" Wittmann (Rheinhessen)	**94**
2000	Königsbacher Idig Riesling Spätlese "Großes Gewächs" Christmann (Pfalz)	**92**
1999	Forster Jesuitengarten Riesling Spätlese J. L. Wolf (Pfalz)	**92**
1998	Durbacher Plauelrain Riesling Auslese Andreas Laible (Baden)	**93**
1997	Dalsheimer Hubacker Riesling Auslese Keller (Rheinhessen)	**92**
1996	Forster Kirchenstück Riesling Spätlese Dr. Bürklin-Wolf (Pfalz)	**92**
1995	Ruppertsberger Gaisböhl Riesling Spätlese Dr. Bürklin-Wolf (Pfalz)	**92**
1994	Durbacher Plauelrain Riesling Spätlese "SL" Andreas Laible (Baden)	**92**
1993	Rauenthaler Nonnenberg Riesling Georg Breuer (Rheingau)	**94**
1992	Wachenheimer Gerümpel Riesling Auslese Josef Biffar (Pfalz)	**94**

Wines of the Year

Riesling Classic

This category was created in 2000, with the objective of creating a new middle-class category of dry to off-dry ("classically" dry) wines along the lines of a basic estate wine. Classic wines may not carry a village or single vineyard designation on the label. However, to date only a fairly small portion of producers has opted to use this category. In the 2003 vintage, the best examples come primarily from the Rheingau, as well as from the Pfalz, Mittelrhein and the Nahe regions.

2002	2003
87	**87**
Joh. Bapt. Schäfer (Nahe)	Wilfried Querbach (Rheingau)
86	**86**
Peter Jakob Kühn (Rheingau)	Joh. Bapt. Schäfer (Nahe)
Korrell – Johanneshof (Nahe)	Peter Jakob Kühn (Rheingau)
Joachim Flick (Rheingau)	Schloss Reinhartshausen (Rheingau)
85	Heinz Nikolai (Rheingau)
Klosterweingut Abtei St. Hildegard (Rheingau)	**85**
Johannes Ohlig (Rheingau)	Jakob Jung (Rheingau)
Posthof Doll & Göth (Rheinhessen)	Domdechant Werner (Rheingau)
Weinmanufaktur Dagernova (Ahr)	Karl-Heinz Gaul (Pfalz)
Immengarten Hof (Pfalz)	**84**
Domdechant Werner (Rheingau)	Lamm-Jung (Rheingau)
	Peter Hohn (Mittelrhein)

Wines of the Year

Off-dry Riesling

The best examples in this category provide, in terms of taste, a combination of the full-bodied dry Riesling type characteristic of the warmer growing regions in the South and the elegantly fruity Riesling style of the cooler Northern regions. They are frequently a better accompaniment for food than some of the extremely dry and tart wines. Nevertheless, the range of wines available in this category has been decreasing consistently in recent years. The best off-dry Rieslings can be found in the Rheingau, along the Mittelrhein and in the Nahe region, as well as in sections of the Mosel, Rheinhessen and Pfalz regions.

2003	Winninger Röttgen "Erste Lage" Heymann-Löwenstein (Mosel-Saar-Ruwer)	**91**
2002	Wehlener Klosterberg Riesling Spätlese feinherb Markus Molitor (Mosel-Saar-Ruwer)	**90**
2001	Winninger Brückstück Riesling Spätlese R. u. B. Knebel (Mosel-Saar-Ruwer)	**89**
2000	Rüdesheimer Berg Schlossberg Riesling Spätlese Josef Leitz (Rheingau)	**89**
1999	Wehlener Klosterberg Riesling Spätlese Markus Molitor (Mosel-Saar-Ruwer)	**89**
1998	Brauneberger Kammer Riesling Auslese Paulinshof (Mosel-Saar-Ruwer)	**91**
1997	Hochheimer Hölle Riesling Spätlese Franz Künstler (Rheingau)	**91**
1996	Bopparder Hamm Feuerlay Riesling Spätlese Weingart (Mittelrhein)	**91**
1995	Rüdesheimer Kirchenpfad Riesling Kabinett Josef Leitz (Rheingau)	**91**
1994	Ruppertsberger Linsenbusch Riesling Spätlese Christmann (Pfalz)	**91**
1993	Riesling Spätlese Robert Weil (Rheingau)	**92**
1992	Nackenheimer Rothenberg Riesling Auslese *** Gunderloch (Rheinhessen)	**94**

Riesling Spätlese

The renaissance of fruity Riesling has been encouraged by the new trend to lighter styles of enjoyment. There are few grape varieties that can produce attractive wines even at low alcohol levels. Riesling can achieve just that with ease and style. The Riesling Spätlese wines most noted for their filigree structure and elegant style are those from the Mosel, Saar and Ruwer, from the Mittelrhein, from the Nahe and from the Rheingau region. The wines from Rheinhessen, the Ortenau and the Pfalz tend to have more extract and body.

2003	Wehlener Sonnenuhr – 22 – Joh. Jos. Prüm (Mosel-Saar-Ruwer)	**95**
2002	Nackenheimer Rothenberg Gunderloch (Rheinhessen)	**93**
2001	Wehlener Sonnenuhr Riesling Spätlese – 16 – Joh. Jos. Prüm (Mosel-Saar-Ruwer)	**94**
2000	Wehlener Sonnenuhr Riesling Spätlese – 18 – Joh. Jos. Prüm (Mosel-Saar-Ruwer)	**92**
1999	Wehlener Sonnenuhr Riesling Spätlese Joh. Jos. Prüm (Mosel-Saar-Ruwer)	**92**
1998	Wintricher Ohligsberg Riesling Spätlese Reinhold Haart (Mosel-Saar-Ruwer)	**93**
1997	Wehlener Sonnenuhr Riesling Spätlese – 34 – Joh. Jos. Prüm (Mosel-Saar-Ruwer)	**94**
1996	Kiedricher Gräfenberg Riesling Spätlese Robert Weil (Rheingau)	**94**
1995	Winkeler Jesuitengarten Riesling Spätlese Johannishof (Rheingau)	**94**
1994	Hochheimer Kirchenstück Riesling Spätlese Domdechant Werner (Rheingau)	**94**
1993	Brauneberger Juffer-Sonnenuhr Riesling Spätlese – 9 – Fritz Haag (Mosel-Saar-Ruwer)	**95**
1992	Kiedricher Gräfenberg Riesling Spätlese Robert Weil (Rheingau)	**95**

Wines of the Year

Riesling Auslese

The best wines in this category were most often from the Mosel, Saar and Ruwer regions. While the primary taste is fully sweet, their real elegance and harmony are achieved as a result of their finely balanced acidity. The Rheingau too, as well as the Nahe, parts of Rheinhessen and of the Pfalz are predestined for the production of full-bodied Riesling Auslese wines with a piquant fruity acidity. These wines reveal their full complexity and finesse only after extended maturation in bottle.

2003 Scharzhofberger – 26 – Goldkapsel
Egon Müller – Scharzhof (Mosel-Saar-Ruwer)   **99**

2002 Graacher Himmelreich lange Goldkapsel
Joh. Jos. Prüm (Mosel-Saar-Ruwer)   **95**

2001 Dalsheimer Hubacker Riesling Auslese *** Goldkapsel
Keller (Rheinhessen)   **97**

2000 Dalsheimer Hubacker Riesling Auslese *** – 29 –
Keller (Rheinhessen)   **95**

1999 Scharzhofberger Riesling Auslese Goldkapsel – 33 –
Egon Müller – Scharzhof (Mosel-Saar-Ruwer)   **95**

1998 Dalsheimer Hubacker Riesling Auslese *** – 29 –
Keller (Rheinhessen)   **96**

1997 Kiedricher Gräfenberg Riesling Auslese Goldkapsel
Robert Weil (Rheingau)   **97**

1996 Kiedricher Gräfenberg Riesling Auslese Goldkapsel
Robert Weil (Rheingau)   **98**

1995 Scharzhofberger Riesling Auslese Goldkapsel
Egon Müller – Scharzhof (Mosel-Saar-Ruwer)   **98**

1994 Dalsheimer Hubacker Riesling Auslese ***
Keller (Rheinhessen)   **97**

1993 Erdener Prälat Riesling Auslese lange Goldkapsel
Dr. Loosen (Mosel-Saar-Ruwer)   **98**

on same level

Brauneberger Juffer-Sonnenuhr Riesling Auslese lange Goldkapsel
Fritz Haag (Mosel-Saar-Ruwer)

1992 Brauneberger Juffer-Sonnenuhr
Riesling Auslese lange Goldkapsel
Fritz Haag (Mosel-Saar-Ruwer)   **97**

Wines of the Year

Botrytis dessert wines

These top-class wines are produced from overripe berries that are wrinkled and raisiny, in which both sweetness and acidity have been concentrated. The ice wines (Eiswein) produced only when there is severe frost, represent a special category of rare and exceptional wines. The more pronounced the balancing fruit acid is, the more piquant the taste sensation. The finest botrytis Riesling wines are obtained from the Mosel, Saar and Ruwer, from the Nahe, from Rheinhessen and from the Rheingau. Other grape varieties, such as Rieslaner and Scheurebe, can sometimes compete in this category. These treasures of German wine culture are among the most long-lived wines in the world.

2003	Kiedricher Gräfenberg Riesling Trockenbeerenauslese Goldkapsel Robert Weil (Rheingau)	**100**
2002	Monzinger Halenberg Riesling Eiswein Goldkapsel Emrich-Schönleber (Nahe)	**100**
2001	Mülheimer Helenenkloster Riesling Eiswein ** Max Ferd. Richter (Mosel-Saar-Ruwer)	**100**
2000	Monzinger Frühlingsplätzchen Riesling Eiswein *** Emrich-Schönleber (Nahe)	**98**
1999	Dalsheimer Hubacker Riesling Trockenbeerenauslese Goldkapsel Keller (Rheinhessen)	**100**
1998	Oberhäuser Brücke Riesling Eiswein "Montag" – 24 – Hermann Dönnhoff (Nahe)	**99**
1997	Erdener Treppchen Riesling Beerenauslese Dr. Loosen (Mosel-Saar-Ruwer)	**98**
1996	Oberhäuser Brücke Riesling Eiswein – 28 – Hermann Dönnhoff (Nahe)	**99**
1995	Kiedricher Gräfenberg Riesling Trockenbeerenauslese Goldkapsel Robert Weil (Rheingau)	**100**
1994	Brauneberger Juffer-Sonnenuhr Riesling Trockenbeerenauslese – 17 – Fritz Haag (Mosel-Saar-Ruwer)	**100**
1993	Piesporter Goldtröpfchen Riesling Eiswein Reinhold Haart (Mosel-Saar-Ruwer)	**99**
1992	Kiedricher Gräfenberg Riesling Trockenbeerenauslese Robert Weil (Rheingau)	**99**

The Best – From the Beginning

On the following pages, we have compiled our list of best performers in all twelve issues of the guide that have appeared so far in Germany. This is a unique documentation of the elite of German winemaking in the past twelve years: A total of 1024 wines from 164 wineries have so far made it into the hit list of top performers in their respective vintages. This does not include wines in liter bottles, sparkling wines and distilled products, which have only been included in our reviews in the past few years.

With eight nominations in the current edition, Klaus Keller from Rheinhessen continues on his irresistible path to success, further underlining his commanding position at the top of the list of best producers, followed by the Robert Weil estate in the Rheingau. This duo at the top is followed by two Riesling stars from the Saar and Mosel, Egon Müller and Fritz Haag. All these exceptional producers were also honored as "Producers of the year" in recent years, as were Dr. Carl von Schubert, Dr. Manfred Prüm, Helmut Dönnhoff and Ernst Loosen, as well as this year Christoph Tyrell. Hansjörg Rebholz, Paul Fürst and Werner Näkel are living proof that the highest accolades are not reserved exclusively for the producers of botrytis dessert Riesling.

The statistics also reveal interesting information regarding the various wine categories: The red wine category is strongly dominated by Meyer-Näkel, while Dr. Heger is similarly dominant in the field of white Pinot varieties.

In the dry Riesling class, the Pfalz has long since taken on the leading role: To date Bürklin-Wolf and Christmann have collected the highest number of accolades, followed by Keller (Rheinhessen) and Breuer (Rheingau). Speaking of the Rheingau: This area also does very well in the off-dry Riesling category, as do the Nahe, the Mosel and particularly the Mittelrhein. This can probably mainly be attributed to the good balance of alcohol, sweetness and acidity found in these centrally located growing regions. The more the residual sugar in Riesling is a part of the equation, the more do the producers of Mosel, Saar and Ruwer dominate the scene; most of the wines in these regions are grown on slate, and show a characteristic delicacy. Looking at the classic Spätlese wines, two Mosel wineries are right at the top, Joh. Jos. Prüm and Fritz Haag, and the same applies to the Auslese category, here Haag (again) and Egon Müller are the most successful producers. In the most difficult and prestigious category of botrytis dessert wines – Beerenauslese and Trockenbeerenauslese wines as well as Eiswein – Wilhelm Weil came in first, a short head in front of Klaus Keller, our "Producer of the Decade."

Certain trends are also interesting to note: Several wineries that started off with a bang twelve years ago, are today showing some weakness. Others were hardly ever seen in the top rankings in the early years, only to forge ahead, such as our serial winner Keller.

Following on a phase of slightly weaker quality in recent years, Robert Weil has now returned to the five-bunch category with his world-class botrytis dessert wines. Truly rock-solid are the two Mosel producers Fritz Haag and Joh. Jos. Prüm. Only these two estates achieved placings in the top-rated lists in all 12 issues of the guide, without a single interruption!

Number of top-ranked wines by edition from 1994 to 2005

		Total	'94	'95	'96	'97	'98	'99	'00	'01	'02	'03	'04	'05
								Edition Gault Millau WeinGuide						
1. Keller	Rheinhessen	63	–	–	2	–	3	5	8	10	9	10	8	8
2. Weil	Rheingau	45	8	3	5	8	7	3	3	2	–	1	–	5
3. Egon Müller	Saar	40	3	3	4	5	4	5	3	5	2	–	2	4
4. Fritz Haag	Mosel	38	4	5	6	4	3	4	1	2	1	2	4	2
5. Dr. Heger	Baden	25	–	3	5	3	4	4	5	–	1	–	–	–
Dönnhoff	Nahe	25	4	2	1	4	2	4	4	–	–	1	–	3
7. Joh. Jos. Prüm	Mosel	23	2	1	3	2	1	2	1	2	2	2	2	3
Rebholz	Pfalz	23	–	1	–	–	1	–	1	3	4	4	5	4
9. Dr. Loosen	Mosel	21	1	3	3	2	3	4	1	2	2	–	–	–
Christmann	Pfalz	21	–	–	2	1	3	1	3	–	5	3	2	1
11. Johner	Baden	20	2	3	3	4	1	2	–	1	3	–	1	–
12. Karthäuserhof	Ruwer	18	3	4	1	2	–	2	–	2	–	1	2	1
13. Meyer-Näkel	Ahr	17	–	1	1	3	3	1	5	–	2	1	–	–
Bürklin-Wolf	Pfalz	17	–	–	2	2	5	3	2	1	–	–	1	1
15. Bercher	Baden	16	2	3	3	–	3	3	–	2	–	–	–	–
Künstler	Rheingau	16	2	2	2	1	1	3	3	2	–	–	–	–
Huber	Baden	16	–	–	1	–	2	1	4	2	2	1	1	2
18. Müller-Catoir	Pfalz	15	4	2	–	–	1	–	2	1	–	5	–	–
19. Molitor	Mosel	14	–	–	–	–	–	2	2	2	1	2	3	2
Leitz	Rheingau	14	–	1	1	2	–	–	1	–	3	1	2	3
21. Breuer	Rheingau	13	–	2	4	2	1	2	–	–	1	–	1	–
Kühn	Rheingau	13	–	2	–	3	3	2	–	1	–	–	1	1
Dr. Wehrheim	Pfalz	13	1	–	–	–	3	1	1	–	1	4	1	1
St. Urbans-Hof	Mosel-Saar	13	2	–	1	–	1	1	2	–	3	1	–	2
25. Jost	Mittelrhein	12	1	5	2	2	–	1	–	–	1	–	–	–
von Schubert	Ruwer	12	3	5	1	1	1	1	–	–	–	–	–	–
Em.-Schönleber	Nahe	12	–	–	–	1	–	–	–	–	5	1	5	–
28. Gunderloch	Rheinhessen	11	3	2	2	1	–	2	–	–	–	–	1	–
Fürst	Franken	11	1	–	1	1	–	1	2	–	–	2	2	1
Wittmann	Rheinhessen	11	–	–	–	1	–	–	1	2	1	4	–	2

Note: In the WineGuide 2005 the white wines of the 2003 vintage are included in the lists of leading wines and producers, and these are therefore also taken into consideration in this list; in the WineGuide 2004 we considered those of the 2002 vintage, etc. In the case of red wines, this edition looks at the 2002 vintage, i.e. in each case one year older than the white wines.

The Best in Their Categories

Top producers from 1994 to 2005 Sorted by category of wine		Total	Red wine	White Pinot varieties	Riesling dry	Riesling Classic	Riesling off-dry	Riesling Spätlese	Riesling Auslese	Botrytis dessert
1. Keller	Rheinhessen	63	2	6	10	–	1	9	14	21
2. Weil	Rheingau	45	–	–	3	–	2	7	11	22
3. Egon Müller	Saar	40	–	–	–	–	–	9	17	14
4. Fritz Haag	Mosel	38	–	–	–	–	–	13	20	5
5. Dr. Heger	Baden	25	3	22	–	–	–	–	–	–
Dönnhoff	Nahe	25	–	2	2	–	1	5	5	10
7. Joh. Jos. Prüm	Mosel	23	–	–	–	–	–	15	6	2
Rebholz	Pfalz	23	3	15	5	–	–	–	–	–
9. Dr. Loosen	Mosel	21	–	–	–	–	–	5	12	4
Christmann	Pfalz	21	–	–	14	–	3	–	2	2
11. Johner	Baden	20	7	13	–	–	–	–	–	–
12. Karthäuserhof	Ruwer	18	–	–	4	–	3	1	8	2
13. Meyer-Näkel	Ahr	17	17	–	–	–	–	–	–	–
Bürklin-Wolf	Pfalz	17	–	–	16	–	1	–	–	–
15. Bercher	Baden	16	3	13	–	–	–	–	–	–
Künstler	Rheingau	16	–	–	5	–	4	6	1	–
Huber	Baden	16	11	5	–	–	–	–	–	–
18. Müller-Catoir	Pfalz	15	–	1	3	–	3	–	1	7
19. Molitor	Mosel	14	–	–	–	–	8	4	1	1
Leitz	Rheingau	14	–	–	6	–	6	2	–	–
21. Breuer	Rheingau	13	–	–	10	–	2	–	–	1
Kühn	Rheingau	13	–	–	2	2	1	1	3	4
Dr. Wehrheim	Pfalz	13	2	10	1	–	–	–	–	–
St. Urbans-Hof	Mosel-Saar	13	–	–	–	–	2	5	2	4
25. Jost	Mittelrhein	12	–	–	5	–	4	1	1	1
von Schubert	Ruwer	12	–	–	–	–	–	6	4	2
Em.-Schönleber	Nahe	12	–	–	1	–	4	2	2	3
28. Gunderloch	Rheinhessen	11	–	–	2	–	1	5	1	2
Fürst	Franken	11	6	5	–	–	–	–	–	–
Wittmann	Rheinhessen	11	–	6	4	–	–	–	1	–

The Specialists

The top producers and the number of their wines achieving top placings in their respective categories from 1994 to 2005

Dry Riesling

1. Bürklin-Wolf	Pfalz	16
2. Christmann	Pfalz	14
3. Breuer	Rheingau	10
Keller	Rheinhessen	10
5. Mosbacher	Pfalz	7
6. Laible	Baden	6
Biffar	Pfalz	6
Leitz	Rheingau	6
9. Künstler	Rheingau	5
Jost	Mittelrhein	5
11. Wittmann	Rheinhessen	4
Karthäuserhof	Ruwer	4
Heyl zu H'heim	Rheinhessen	4

Riesling off-dry

1. Molitor	Mosel	8
2. Kruger-Rumpf	Nahe	6
3. Leitz	Rheingau	5
Weingart	Mittelrhein	5
Paulinshof	Mosel	5
Matthias Müller	Mittelrhein	5
7. Em.-Schönl.	Nahe	4
August Perll	Mittelrhein	4
Lorenz	Mittelrhein	4
Künstler	Rheingau	4
Jost	Mittelrhein	4
A. Eser	Rheingau	4

Riesling Spätlese

1. Joh. Jos. Prüm	Mosel	15
2. Fritz Haag	Mosel	13
3. Keller	Rheinhessen	9
Egon Müller	Saar	9
5. Weil	Rheingau	7
6. Künstler	Rheingau	6
von Schubert	Ruwer	6
8. Dr. Loosen	Mosel	5
Reinh. Haart	Mosel	5
Gunderloch	Rheinhessen	5
St. Urbans-Hof	Mosel-Saar	5
Dönnhoff	Nahe	5

Red wine

1. Meyer-Näkel	Ahr	17
2. Huber	Baden	11
3. Deutzerhof	Ahr	10
4. Johner	Baden	7
Knipser	Pfalz	7
6. Dautel	Württemberg	6
Friedr. Becker	Pfalz	6
Fürst	Franken	6
9. Stodden	Ahr	5
Kesseler	Rheingau	5
Nelles	Ahr	5
12. Seeger	Baden	4
R./C. Schneider	Baden	4

White Pinot varieties

1. Dr. Heger	Baden	22
2. Rebholz	Pfalz	15
3. Johner	Baden	13
Bercher	Baden	13
5. Bergdolt	Pfalz	10
Dr. Wehrheim	Pfalz	10
7. Keller	Rheinhessen	6
Wittmann	Rheinhessen	6
9. Fürst	Franken	5
Huber	Baden	5

Riesling Auslese

1. Fritz Haag	Mosel	20
2. Egon Müller	Saar	17
3. Keller	Rheinhessen	14
4. Dr. Loosen	Mosel	12
5. Weil	Rheingau	11
6. Karthäuserhof	Ruwer	8
7. Joh. Jos. Prüm	Mosel	6
8. Dönnhoff	Nahe	5
9. Schloss Lieser	Mosel	4
Willi Schaefer	Mosel	4
von Schubert	Ruwer	4

Botrytis dessert white wine

1. Weil	Rheingau	22
2. Keller	Rheinhessen	21
3. Egon Müller	Saar	14
4. Dönnhoff	Nahe	10
5. Müller-Catoir	Pfalz	7
6. Fritz Haag	Mosel	5
7. St. Urbans-Hof	Mosel-Saar	4
Dr. Loosen	Mosel	4
Kühn	Rheingau	4

Top Producers by Region

Each year, the Gault Millau WineGuide documents the best wines of the vintage in its "Best of" lists. The leading producers are almost always represented on this lists with one or more wines. The following table shows clearly who are the leading producers of top-rated wines in each region.

Ahr (4)

1. Meyer-Näkel	17
2. Deutzerhof	10
3. Stodden	5
Nelles	5

Mosel-Saar-Ruwer (24)

1. Egon Müller *	40
2. Fritz Haag	38
3. Joh. Jos. Prüm	23
4. Dr. Loosen	21
5. Karthäuserhof	18
6. Molitor	14
7. St. Urbans-Hof	13
8. von Schubert	12
9. Reinhold Haart	9
10. Willi Schaefer	8
11. Heymann-Löwenstein	6
12. Schloss Lieser	5
Grans-Fassian	5
Paulinshof	5
von Kesselstatt	5
16. Knebel	4
Karlsmühle	4
Joh. Jos. Christoffel	4
Selbach-Oster	4
20. Clüsserath-Weiler	3
Schloss Saarstein	3
Dr. Wagner	3
Erben Wwe. Thanisch	3
von Hövel	3

* includes Le Gallais

Mittelrhein (5)

1. Jost	12
2. Weingart	7
3. M. Müller	6
4. A. Perll	5
5. Lorenz	4

Nahe (8)

1. Dönnhoff	25
2. Emrich-Schönleber	12
3. Niederhausen	6
Kruger-Rumpf	6
5. Göttelmann	4
Prinz Salm	4
Mathern	4
Crusius	4

Rheingau (16)

1. Weil	45
2. Künstler	16
3. Leitz	14
4. Breuer	13
5. Kühn	12
6. Kesseler	7
7. Johannishof	6
A. Eser	6
Domdechant Werner	6
10. Wegeler	5
11. Hans Lang	4
Johannisberg	4
Jakob Jung	4
Reinhartshausen	4
15. Prinz von Hessen	3
Spreitzer	3

Rheinhessen (4)

1. Keller	63
2. Gunderloch	11
Wittmann	11
4. Heyl zu Herrnsheim	9

Hessische Bergstraße (1)

1. Staatsweingut	5

Pfalz (16)

1. Rebholz	23
2. Christmann	21
3. Bürklin-Wolf	17
4. Müller-Catoir	15
5. Dr. Wehrheim	13
6. Bergdolt	10
von Buhl	10
8. Knipser	9
9. Mosbacher	8
10. Biffar	7
Friedr. Becker	7
12. Koehler-Ruprecht	6
13. Bassermann-Jordan	5
14. Bernhart	4
15. Pfeffingen-Fuhrmann	3
Münzberg	3

Franken (1)

1. Fürst	11

Württemberg (1)

1. Dautel	9

Baden (9)

1. Dr. Heger	25
2. Johner	20
3. Bercher	16
Huber	16
5. R. u. C. Schneider	8
6. Laible	6
Salwey	6
8. Seeger	5
9. Duijn	3

The Guide to German Wines

The Regions, the Producers, the Wines

The battle for Marienthal

For quite some time it looked as though there were no buyers for the state domain at Marienthal. Carrying a price tag of "at least five million Euros," all potential buyers decided to give this opportunity of acquiring the former jewel of the Ahr region a miss. Then in early July rumours started that cult-winemaker Werner Näkel, together with the Mayschoß-Altenahr co-operative, had mutually managed to bag the whole operation for a bargain price of less than two million Euros. That spelled the need of the peaceful atmosphere in the sleepy Ahr valley. Suddenly there was an uproar of protest. So the bidding period was extended, and suddenly there was lively interest. Now, the largest co-operative on the Ahr was willing to pay more than the Näkel/Mayschoß partnership, and Hans-Joachim Brogsitter too, owner of the largest wine estate in the Ahr valley, decided to join the battle for ownership of Marienthal. In no time the bids exceeded the previous offer by half a million. To put an end to the bidding frenzy a meeting of the four Ahr grandees was called, who found themselves asking "Why should we try to outbid each other?" The quartet decided to withdraw all previous offers, and put in a mutual purchase offer, which is reputed to have been very close to the original offer. It remains to be seen what will become of the remnants of the erstwhile proud state domain in the hands of the new owners, who have decided to continue operations – albeit at a much reduced scale – under the name of Kloster Marienthal (abbey).

It remains a mystery why there appears to be a system that ensures the Ahr, especially, will produce excellent red wines in odd-numbered vintages, producing only average wines in the even years. This belief dates back to the 1993 vintage, which first attracted attention to the area. The 1995 vintage produced full-bodied, hearty wines, 1997 saw perhaps the most sun-drenched Pinot Noirs of the Nineties, and 1999, too, produced an amazing range of high-quality Pinot Noir (both Spätburgunder and Frühburgunder). The 2001 vintage was in some places even an improvement on 1999, producing many top-quality wines. This was followed by 2002, which like so often in even years simply could not rise to the same standard. After the grapes had ripened with great promise, rain during the harvest led to an excess of water in the grapes. Only in rare exceptions were the winemakers of the Ahr able to bottle wines with any sort of promise of long maturation potential. These exceptions include the Deutzerhof in Mayschoß, Nelles in Heimersheim and Jean Stodden in Rech – their wines show both, firmness and structure as well as the velvety smooth-

ness of good Pinot Noir. In any case, Gerhard Stodden is always remarkably consistent and true to style, and his efforts now take him into the top category of producers in the region. Other than that, there have been virtually no changes in the hierarchy of this region. Two wineries have been awarded bunches of grapes for the first time: The Peter Lingen winery as well as the Maibach Farm, which was renovated at a cost of millions at the end of the Nineties. Taking a brief look to the 2003 vintage, wine producers on the Ahr are unanimous in praising this vintage in the highest notes, promising a wide availability of rich, opulent wines.

The Ahr region covers a vineyard area of just more than 500 hectares, and stretches along the Ahr valley over a distance of 25 kilometers from Altenahr to Heimersheim. The lower Ahr valley, with its basalt cones and garden landscapes differs significantly in geological terms from the middle Ahr valley, with its towering rock formations along the winding river. Soils, rock formations and vineyard walls of dark slate and grey wacke absorb and store the sun's heat during daytime, reflecting it back to the vines at night. The result of this greenhouse effect is a Mediterranean climate with surprisingly high average temperatures.

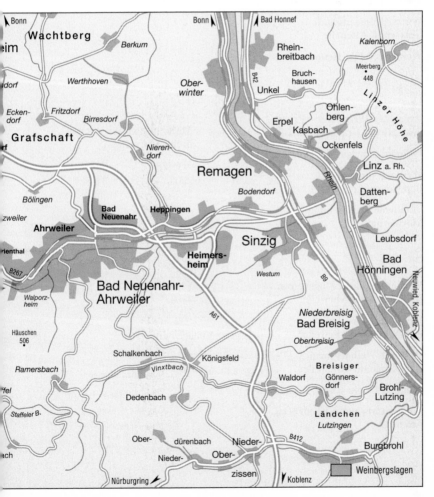

Ahr

The leading producers on the Ahr

**Weingut Deutzerhof –
Cossmann-Hehle, Mayschoß**

Weingut Meyer-Näkel, Dernau

Weingut Jean Stodden, Rech

Weingut J. J. Adeneuer, Ahrweiler

Weingut Kreuzberg, Dernau

**Winzergenossenschaft
Mayschoß-Altenahr**

Weingut Nelles, Heimersheim

**Brogsitter Weingüter – Privat-
Sektkellerei, Grafschaft-Gelsdorf**

Weingut Burggarten, Heppingen

**Weingut Sonnenberg,
Bad Neuenahr**

**Staatliche Weinbaudomäne
Marienthal**

**Weinmanufaktur Dagernova,
Bad Neuenahr-Ahrweiler**

**Weingut Peter Lingen,
Bad Neuenahr-Ahrweiler**

**Weingut Maibachfarm,
Bad Neuenahr-Ahrweiler**

Weingut Erwin Riske, Dernau

**Weingut Sermann-Kreuzberg,
Altenahr**

The best vineyard sites on the Ahr*

Ahrweiler: Rosenthal, Silberberg

Altenahr: Eck

Dernau: Pfarrwingert, Hardtberg

Heimersheim: Landskrone, Burggarten

Marienthal: Klostergarten, Trotzenberg

Mayschoß: Mönchberg

Neuenahr: Sonnenberg, Schieferlay

Walporzheim: Gärkammer,
Kräuterberg, Domlay

---

* Source: VDP Nahe-Ahr

Major and minor vintages in the Ahr valley

Vintage	Rating
2003	❦❦❦❦❦
2002	❦❦
2001	❦❦❦❦
2000	❦❦
1999	❦❦❦❦
1998	❦❦❦
1997	❦❦❦❦
1996	❦❦❦
1995	❦❦❦❦
1994	❦❦❦

Vintage rating:

❦❦❦❦❦ : Excellent vintage

❦❦❦❦ : Very good vintage

❦❦❦ : Good vintage

❦❦ : Average vintage

❦ : Poor vintage

WEINGUT J. J. ADENEUER

Owner: Frank and Marc Adeneuer
Winemaker: Frank Adeneuer
53474 Ahrweiler, Max-Planck-Straße 8
Tel. (0 26 41) 3 44 73, Fax 3 73 79
e-mail: JJAdeneuer@t-online.de
Internet: www.adeneuer.de
Directions: A 61 Köln–Koblenz,
Ahrweiler exit
Sales: Marc Adeneuer
Opening hours: Mon.–Fri. 09:00 to
12:00 and 14:00 to 18:00, Sat. 10:00 to
15:00 hours, Sun. by appointment
History: Winemaking in the family for
500 years

Vineyard area: 8.5 hectares
Annual production: 80,000 bottles
Top sites: Walporzheimer
Gärkammer and Ahrweiler Rosenthal
Soil types: Decomposed slate
Grape varieties: 83% Spätburgunder,
10% Frühburgunder, 5% Portugieser,
2% Dornfelder
Average yield: 74 hl/ha
Best vintages: 1999, 2001, 2003
Member: VDP

A lot has happened here since brothers Frank and Marc Adeneuer took over this traditional operation in the Eighties. The cellar has been brought up to modern standards, and the vineyard area has been increased by five hectares. Usually the highlight of the range is made up of the red wines from the monopole Walporzheimer Gärkammer site. This vineyard has a nearly Mediterranean climate, so that Auslese level wines can be made even in an average year. The Adeneuers presented a very respectable range even in the difficult 2000 vintage, while the 2001 vintage was better than practically anything we have ever tasted from this estate. The 2002 wines did not quite reach this standard. The 2003 vintage shows the winery back on its usual good form. We were pleasantly surprised by the Frühburgunder from the Sonnenberg site, which was able to stand up to the No. 1.

———— Red wines ————

2003 Ahrweiler
Spätburgunder trocken
13%, ♀ till 2008 **86**

2003 Walporzheimer Gärkammer
Spätburgunder Auslese trocken
14%, ♀ till 2007 **86**

2002 Walporzheimer Gärkammer
Spätburgunder Auslese trocken
13.5%, ♀ till 2008 **87**

2003 Spätburgunder trocken No. 2
14%, ♀ till 2009 **87**

2002 Spätburgunder trocken No. 2
13%, ♀ till 2008 **87**

2001 Spätburgunder trocken No. 2
14%, ♀ till 2006 **87**

2003 Neuenahrer Sonnenberg
Frühburgunder trocken
14%, ♀ till 2010 **88**

2001 Walporzheimer Gärkammer
Spätburgunder Spätlese trocken
13.5%, ♀ till 2007 **88**

2001 Ahrweiler Rosenthal
Spätburgunder Auslese trocken
14%, ♀ till 2008 **88**

2003 Spätburgunder
Auslese trocken No. 1
14.5%, ♀ till 2010 **88**

2001 Walporzheimer Gärkammer
Spätburgunder Auslese trocken
14%, ♀ till 2009 **89**

2001 Spätburgunder
Auslese trocken No. 1
14%, ♀ till 2009 **90**

The wines: **100** Perfect · **95–99** Outstanding · **90–94** Excellent · **85–89** Very good · **80–84** Good · **75–79** Average

67

BROGSITTER WEINGÜTER – PRIVAT-SEKTKELLEREI

Owner: Hans-Joachim Brogsitter
Manager: Elmar Sermann
Winemaker: Elmar Sermann,
Markus Hallerbach
53501 Grafschaft-Gelsdorf,
Max-Planck-Straße 1
Tel. (0 22 25) 91 81 11, Fax 91 81 12
e-mail: verkauf@brogsitter.de
Internet: www.brogsitter.de
Directions: A 61, Altenahr exit, A 565/ B 257, Gelsdorf industrial area exit
Sales: Harald Gerhard
Opening hours: Mon.–Fri. 08:00 to 20:00, Sat. 09:00 to 15:00 hours
Restaurant: Historical restaurant and inn "Sanct Peter" with vinotheque and garden terrace, 09:00 to 24:00 hours
Closed Thu. except on public holidays
Tel. (0 26 41) 9 77 50, Fax 97 75 25
Specialties: Duo of Eifel lamb, Fillet of pike-perch on lentils, Gratinated Eifel goats' cheese
History: Previously wine estate attached to Cologne cathedral, from 1246 to 1805

Vineyard area: 33 hectares
Annual production: 180,000 bottles
Top sites: Walporzheimer Alte Lay, Domlay and Kräuterberg, Ahrweiler Silberberg, Neuenahrer Sonnenberg
Soil types: Decomposed slate, loess-clay
Grape varieties: 65% Spätburgunder, 15% Frühburgunder, 12% Portugieser, 6% Dornfelder, 2% Riesling
Average yield: 55 hl/ha
Best vintages: 1999, 2001, 2003

This historical estate owns parcels of the best vineyard sites, and is at the core of the Brogsitter group, which includes a sparkling wine operation as well as the renowned and traditional restaurant and inn "Sanct Peter." In recent times, the owners have invested considerably in the cellar. Following on from a number of excellent 2001 wines, the opulent 2003 vintage Auslese wines of the "Hommage Sanct Peter" Selection showed themselves in outstanding form.

——— Red wines ———

2002 Frühburgunder
trocken AD ARAM
13.5%, ♀ till 2007 — **86**

2001 Ahrweiler Silberberg
Spätburgunder Auslese trocken
13.5%, ♀ till 2008 — **87**

2002 Spätburgunder
trocken AD ARAM
13.5%, ♀ till 2008 — **87**

2003 Ahrweiler Forstberg
Spätburgunder Auslese trocken
"Hommage Sanct Peter"
15%, ♀ till 2009 — **87**

2003 Walporzheimer Alte Lay
Spätburgunder Auslese trocken
"Hommage Sanct Peter"
15%, ♀ till 2010 — **87**

2001 Walporzheimer Kräuterberg
Spätburgunder Auslese trocken
13.5%, ♀ till 2008 — **88**

2003 Walporzheimer Pfaffenberg
Frühburgunder Auslese trocken
"Hommage Sanct Peter"
14.5%, ♀ till 2010 — **88**

2003 Ahrweiler Rosenthal
Spätburgunder Auslese trocken
"Hommage Sanct Peter"
15.5%, ♀ till 2010 — **88**

2003 Walporzheimer Kräuterberg
Spätburgunder Auslese trocken
"Hommage Sanct Peter"
15%, ♀ till 2012 — **89**

UNFILTERED
Brogsitter
Der Botschafter guten Weines

HOMMAGE SANCT PETER

2003
WALPORZHEIMER ALTE LAY
SPÄTBURGUNDER
AUSLESE TROCKEN

The estates: ✦✦✦✦✦ World's finest · ✦✦✦✦ Germany's best · ✦✦✦ Very good · ✦✦ Good · ✦ Reliable

WEINGUT BURGGARTEN

Owner: Paul-Josef Schäfer
Manager: Paul-Josef Schäfer
Winemaker: Paul-Michael Schäfer
53474 Heppingen, Landskronerstr. 61
Tel. (0 26 41) 2 12 80, Fax 7 92 20
e-mail: burggarten@t-online.de
*Directions: A 61 Köln–Koblenz,
Bad Neuenahr-Ahrweiler exit,
in Heppingen suburb*
Sales: Paul-Josef and Gitta Schäfer
Opening hours: Mon.–Fri. 10:00 to
12:00 and 13:00 to 18:00 hours
Sat. and Sun. 10:00 to 13:00 hours
Accommodation: 14 double rooms as
well as a holiday apartment
Worth seeing: Historical vaulted wine
cellar of quarry stone

Vineyard area: 15 hectares
Annual production: 120,000 bottles
Top sites: Neuenahrer Sonnen-
berg, Ahrweiler Ursulingarten,
Heimersheimer Burggarten
Soil types: Loess-clay,
gravel und volcanic formation
Grape varieties: 58% Spätburgunder,
12% Domina, 10% each of Portugie-
ser and Dornfelder, 5% Frühburgun-
der, 3% Riesling, 2% Grauburgunder
Average yield: 60 hl/ha
Best vintages: 2000, 2001, 2002

It has been quite obvious in recent years that Paul Schäfer is determined to keep his winery on the path of the best quality possible. It was interesting to note that here the wines of the 2000 vintage by and large were better than those of the much-vaunted 1999 vintage. While it is true that Schäfers top wines have gained in concentration and depth, the thing that really stands out here in comparison to the competition are the very commendable everyday wines, which are available at very reasonable prices. This applies to the 2003 vintage as well. However, most of the so-called "better" are only marginally better than the basic wines, many of them clumsy and even boring.

——— Red wines ———

2003 Heimersheimer Burggarten
Spätburgunder trocken
13.5%, ♀ till 2007   **83**

2003 Neuenahrer Sonnenberg
Dornfelder trocken
13.5%, ♀ till 2007   **84**

2003 Neuenahrer Sonnenberg
Frühburgunder trocken
14%, ♀ till 2008   **84**

2003 Neuenahrer Sonnenberg
Spätburgunder Auslese trocken
14.5%, ♀ till 2008   **85**

2003 Neuenahrer Sonnenberg
Spätburgunder trocken
13.5%, ♀ till 2007   **85**

2003 Ahrweiler Ursulingarten
Spätburgunder Auslese trocken
14%, ♀ till 2007   **86**

2003 "Filius"
Spätburgunder trocken
14%, ♀ till 2008   **86**

2002 Spätburgunder
trocken "P. J. Signatur"
13.5%, ♀ till 2007   **86**

2002 Neuenahrer Sonnenberg
Frühburgunder trocken
13%, ♀ till 2008   **87**

2001 Ahrweiler Ursulingarten
Spätburgunder Auslese trocken
14%, ♀ till 2007   **87**

2003 Spätburgunder
trocken "P.J. Signatur"
14%, ♀ till 2009   **87**

2002 Ahrweiler Ursulingarten
Spätburgunder trocken
14%, ♀ till 2008   **88**

The wines: **100** Perfect · **95–99** Outstanding · **90–94** Excellent · **85–89** Very good · **80–84** Good · **75–79** Average

69

WEINMANUFAKTUR DAGERNOVA

General manager: Friedhelm Nelles
Winemaker: Günter Schüller
53474 Bad Neuenahr-Ahrweiler,
Heerstraße 91–93
Tel. (0 26 41) 9 47 20, Fax 94 72 94
e-mail: info@dagernova.de
Internet: www.dagernova.de
Directions: A 61, Bad Neuenahr-Ahrweiler exit
Sales: In Dernau: Mon.–Fri. 08:00 to 12:00 hours and 13:00 to 18:00 hours Sat., Sun. and public holidays 10:00 to 12:00 hours and 13:00 to 17:30 hours In Neuenahr: Mon.–Fri. 08:00 to 18:00 hours, Sat. 08:00 to 12:00 hours
Wine tasting: Wolfgang Hennemann by appointment
Restaurant: In Dernau, Ahrweg 7, 11:00 to 21:00 hours
History: Established 1873
Worth seeing: Cellar hewn from rock at headquarters in Dernau

---

Vineyard area: 146 hectares
Number of members: 582
Annual production: 1.5 mill. bottles
Top sites: Dernauer Pfarrwingert and Goldkaul, Neuenahrer Sonnenberg, Ahrweiler Rosenthal
Soil types: Decomposed slate, clay with gravel, loess-clay
Grape varieties: 76% Spätburgunder, 7% Portugieser, 5% Frühburgunder, 4% Riesling, 8% other varieties
Average yield: 79 hl/ha
Best vintages: 1997, 1999, 2001

This is the largest co-operative in the Ahr valley, covering around 30 percent of the vineyard area in this region, and it was only a matter of time until somebody found a full-sounding name for the business. Apparently, "Dagernova" was the name of a Frankish settlement here in the 8th century. The managers also point out that they deserve the description of "Manufaktur," since all grapes are picked by hand. The wines have been of a reliable

good quality in recent years, among them the 2002 vintage Selection wines from the Kräuterberg and Daubhaus. The first 2003 tasted were also attractive.

2003 Riesling Classic
13%, ♀ till 2006   **83**

———— Red wines ————

2003 Dernauer
Spätburgunder trocken
13.5%, ♀ till 2008   **83**

2003 Spätburgunder trocken
13.5%, ♀ till 2008   **83**

2002 Ahrweiler Daubhaus
Spätburgunder trocken Selection
14%, ♀ till 2007   **84**

2002 Walporzheimer Kräuterberg
Spätburgunder trocken Selection
14%, ♀ till 2008   **85**

2001 Bachemer Sonnenschein
Spätburgunder trocken Selection Barrique
13%, ♀ till 2006   **85**

2002 Spätburgunder
Auslese trocken
13%, ♀ till 2008   **86**

2001 Walporzheimer Kräuterberg
Spätburgunder trocken Selection Barrique
14%, ♀ till 2007   **86**

Only a few vines can be grown on these small terraces, close to Bad Neuenahr.
Photo: DWI/Dieth

WEINGUT DEUTZERHOF – COSSMANN-HEHLE

Owner: Hella and Wolfgang Hehle
Winemaker: Wolfgang Hehle
53508 Mayschoß, Deutzerwiese 2
Tel. (0 26 43) 72 64, Fax 32 32
e-mail: info@weingut-deutzerhof.de
Internet: www.weingut-deutzerhof.de
Directions: A 61 Köln–Koblenz,
Altenahr exit
Sales: Hella and Wolfgang Hehle
Hans-Jörg Lüchau, by appointment
History: Wines made here since 1574,
family-owned for more than 400 years

Vineyard area: 9 hectares
Annual production: 60,000 bottles
Top sites: Altenahrer Eck,
Mayschosser Mönchberg,
Heimersheimer Landskrone
Soil types: Decomposed slate with
loess
Grape varieties: 75% Spätburgunder,
10% Dornfelder, 7% Riesling,
5% Frühburgunder , 2% Chardonnay,
1% Portugieser
Average yield: 51 hl/ha
Best vintages: 1999, 2001, 2002
Member: VDP,
Deutsches Barrique Forum

The Deutzerhof has been one of the leading red wine producers in Germany for many years. This success story is inextricably linked to the name of Wolfgang Hehle, an ex-tax consultant who, together with his wife Hella has really made something of his father-in-law's winery. Today, single vineyard designation are used virtually only for the excellent wines from the Altenahrer Eck and Mayschosser Mönchberg sites. Instead, Hehle markets most of his Pinot Noir wines as varietal wines, or uses brand names that tend to use family names. In this respect, his creativity knows virtually no bounds. A further excellent example of the Hehle creations is the "Melchior C.," which now makes up a trio together with Caspar and Balthasar – the three sages of the East

were involved somewhere. However, no Melchior wine was made in 2002, the grapes were just not of the standard demanded. On the other hand, Hehle has once again presented a Dornfelder wine that is destined to shine up the image of this variety, which is often decried as a mass-producing variety. The grapes for this are grown on the steep slopes of the narrow Ahr valley. The forest growing above the vineyards protects the vines from cold air. Soils, rock formations and vineyard terrace walls of dark slate and grey wacke store the heat of the day, and release it to the vines again at night. The result of this natural underfloor heating with its nightly storage effect is virtually a Mediterranean climate. The vineyards of the Deutzerhof consist of small, steeply terraced parcels of land. In recent years, considerable effort has been invested in repairing and restoring the terrace walls, some of which had already collapsed, and the small terraces have been fully restored. After a series of good to excellent vintages, Hehle's perhaps best wines of his as yet brief career were those of the 1997 vintage. We initially underrated the red wines of the equally excellent 1999 vintage simply because of their power and voluptousness, but these have developed beautifully. The 2001 vintage range is characterized by Hehle's overriding ambition to outdo everything he has achieved in the past. Now the star winemaker of Mayschoß has produced a 2002 range that stands out, together with that of his colleague Jean Stodden in Rech, as simply the best in the Ahr valley. The highlight is the powerful Pinot Noir from the Mayschosser Mönchberg site, followed by the incredibly complex "Große Gewächs" (First Growth) from the Altenahrer Eck site. Most of the red wines of the 2003 vintage have so far only been tasted as barrel samples, but even at this early stage their exceptional structure and concentrated fruit has raised our expectations, and we very much look forward to tasting these wines in finished form.

The estates: ♦♦♦♦♦ World's finest · ♦♦♦♦ Germany's best · ♦♦♦ Very good · ♦♦ Good · ♦ Reliable

2003 Riesling trocken
12%, ♀ till 2006   **82**

2003 "Catharina C."
Riesling trocken
12.5%, ♀ till 2006   **83**

2002 Chardonnay trocken
13.5%, ♀ till 2006   **85**

2003 Chardonnay trocken
13.5%, ♀ till 2008   **87**

2003 Riesling halbtrocken
12%, ♀ till 2006   **80**

2003 Altenahrer Eck
Riesling Eiswein
8%, ♀ till 2010   **88**

2003 Altenahrer Eck
Riesling Auslese
9%, ♀ till 2008   **89**

2002 Altenahrer Eck
Riesling Auslese
9%, ♀ till 2015   **89**

2003 Altenahrer Eck
Riesling Trockenbeerenauslese
7.5%, ♀ till 2015   **92**

——— Red wines ———

2003 "Saumon de l'Ahr"
Spätburgunder Rosé trocken
13%, ♀ till 2006   **83**

2002 "Cuvée Rot Légère" trocken
12%, ♀ till 2006   **83**

2002 "Cuvée Rot Légère" trocken
13%, ♀ till 2006   **84**

2002 Spätburgunder trocken
13.5%, ♀ till 2006   **84**

2001 Spätburgunder trocken
13%, ♀ till 2008   **85**

2002 "Balthasar C."
Spätburgunder trocken
13.5%, ♀ till 2007   **86**

2001 "Balthasar C."
Spätburgunder trocken
13%, ♀ till 2009   **86**

2002 "Grand Duc"
Spätburgunder trocken
13.5%, ♀ till 2010   **88**

2002 "Caspar C."
Spätburgunder trocken
13.5%, ♀ till 2008   **88**

2002 Dornfelder trocken
13.5%, ♀ till 2007   **88**

2001 Dornfelder trocken
13.5%, ♀ till 2007   **88**

2002 Mayschosser Mönchberg
Spätburgunder trocken
↗ auction wine, 14%, ♀ till 2010   **89**

2001 "Caspar C."
Spätburgunder trocken
13.5%, ♀ till 2009   **89**

2002 Altenahrer Eck
Spätburgunder trocken
"Großes Gewächs"
14%, ♀ till 2010   **89**

2001 "Grand Duc"
Spätburgunder trocken
14%, ♀ till 2010   **90**

2001 Altenahrer Eck
Spätburgunder trocken
14%, ♀ till 2010   **91**

2001 Mayschosser Mönchberg
Spätburgunder trocken
14%, ♀ till 2013   **92**

2001 "Melchior C."
Spätburgunder trocken
14%, ♀ till 2013   **92**

2001 "Apollo"
Spätburgunder trocken
14%, ♀ till 2015   **92**

CASPAR C.
SPÄTBURGUNDER
TROCKEN
Deutzerhof
COSSMANN-HEHLE

The wines: **100** Perfect · **95–99** Outstanding · **90–94** Excellent · **85–89** Very good · **80–84** Good · **75–79** Average

WEINGUT KREUZBERG

Owner: Ludwig Kreuzberg
Winemaker:
Hermann-Josef Kreuzberg
53507 Dernau,
Benedikt-Schmittmann-Straße 30
Tel. (0 26 43) 16 91, Fax 32 06
e-mail: info@weingut-kreuzberg.de
Internet: www.weingut-kreuzberg.de
Directions: A 61, Altenahr exit,
5 km downriver in direction of
Bad Neuenahr-Ahrweiler
Sales: Ludwig Kreuzberg and Paul
Schneider
Opening hours: Mon.–Fri. 08:00 to
18:00, Sat. and Sun. 10:00 to 15:00 hours
Restaurant: May to October
Fri. from 15:00, Sat. and Sun. from
12:00 hours

Vineyard area: 8,5 hectares
Annual production: 70,000 bottles
Top sites: Neuenahrer Schieferlay
and Sonnenberg, Dernauer Pfarr-
wingert and Ahrweiler Silberberg
Soil types: Slate, partly with loess
Grape varieties: 70% Spätburgunder,
10% Frühburgunder, 7% Portugieser,
6% Dornfelder, 7% other varieties
Average yield: 68 hl/ha
Best vintages: 2000, 2001, 2002
Member: VDP

The wine restaurant at the Kreuzberg
estate is one of the oldest and most popular restaurants in the Ahr valley, and an
enjoyable evening can be expected when-
ever father Kreuzberg gets out his guitar.
In addition, the winery has in recent produced wines that are among the best in
the region. The Kreuzbergs love to experiment: there are some interesting results
with Cabernet Sauvignon, Cabernet
Franc and Regent. However, we regularly
prefer the "Devonschiefer" blends, which
are named after the soil (slate) on which
they are grown. The good Frühburgunder
wines add to the overall impression that
the 2002 vintage here is more than just
fairly good.

——— Red wines ———

2002 Neuenahrer Sonnenberg
Frühburgunder trocken
13.5%, ♀ till 2008   86

2002 "Devonschiefer"
Spätburgunder trocken
13.5%, ♀ till 2009   87

2001 Ahrweiler Silberberg
Spätburgunder Auslese trocken
14.5%, ♀ till 2007   87

2003 Frühburgunder
Auslese trocken
14%, ♀ till 2010   88

2003 "Devonschiefer"
Spätburgunder trocken
14%, ♀ till 2010   88

2003 Dernauer Pfarrwingert
Spätburgunder Auslese trocken
14%, ♀ till 2010   88

2001 Dernauer Pfarrwingert
Spätburgunder Auslese trocken
14%, ♀ till 2008   88

2001 Neuenahrer Sonnenberg
Frühburgunder trocken
13.5%, ♀ till 2007   88

2002 "Devonschiefer"
Spätburgunder trocken Goldkapsel
14%, ♀ till 2009   88

2003 Neuenahrer Schieferlay
Spätburgunder Auslese trocken
⟶ auction wine, 14%, ♀ till 2010   89

WEINGUT PETER LINGEN

Owner: Peter Lingen
53474 Bad Neuenahr-Ahrweiler,
Teichstraße 3
Tel. (0 26 41) 2 95 45, Fax 20 11 36
e-mail: Weingut-Lingen@t-online.de
*Directions: A 61, Bad Neuenahr exit,
1. right (Weinbergstraße), across inter-
section in Teichstraße*
Sales: Lingen family
Opening hours: Mon.–Sat. 08:00 to
19:00, Sun. 10:00 to 13:00 hours
by appointment
History: Winemaking in family since
1599
Worth a visit: Wine tasting with hearty
vintner's platter, Burgundian (Pinot)
festival (4th weekend in July)

Vineyard area: 4 hectares
Annual production: 40,000 bottles
Top sites: Neuenahrer
Sonnenberg and Schieferlay
Soil types: Decomposed grey wacke,
loess with clay
Grape varieties: 45% Spätburgunder,
30% Portugieser, 10% each of Früh-
burgunder and Dornfelder, 5% Ries-
ling and Rivaner
Average yield: 85 hl/ha
Best vintages: 2002, 2003

The Peter Lingen winery has for many
years been one of the reliable producers of
the Ahr valley, working mainly in the
classic style. Peter Lingen only started experimenting with the use of barriques in
2002. Winemaking has run in the family
for ten generations, but for a long time the
grapes were delivered to the co-operative.
It was grandfather Peter-Josef who started
making his own wines, and Peter's father
was quite successful at selling these wines
via the wine bar, which used to be located
on the estate. Peter Lingen has been working in the family business since 1982. The
2002 Spätburgunder from the Sonnenberg
site, matured in barrique, sets new standards. Not to mention the ratings accorded
the wines of the 2003 vintage.

———— Red wines ————

2003 Neuenahrer Schieferlay
Portugieser trocken
13%, ♀ till 2006 — **82**

2003 Neuenahrer Schieferlay
Spätburgunder trocken
13.5%, ♀ till 2007 — **83**

2003 Neuenahrer Sonnenberg
Spätburgunder trocken
13.5%, ♀ till 2007 — **83**

2003 "J*A*C"
Spätburgunder trocken Barrique
14.5%, ♀ till 2007 — **84**

2002 Neuenahrer Sonnenberg
Spätburgunder trocken Barrique
14%, ♀ till 2008 — **86**

2003 Ahrweiler Ursulinengarten
Frühburgunder Auslese trocken
14%, ♀ till 2008 — **87**

2003 Neuenahrer Sonnenberg
Spätburgunder Auslese trocken
14%, ♀ till 2008 — **88**

2003 Neuenahrer Sonnenberg
Spätburgunder Auslese trocken Barrique
14.5%, ♀ till 2010 — **88**

2003 Ahrweiler Sonnenberg
Spätburgunder halbtrocken
12%, ♀ till 2006 — **83**

WEINGUT
PETER
LINGEN

AHR
2003er
Ahrweiler Ursulinengarten
**Frühburgunder
Auslese**
Trocken
ERZEUGERABFÜLLUNG
A. P. Nr. 1 791 506 09 04
Peter Lingen · Teichstraße 3
D-53474 Bad Neuenahr
Telefon 0 26 41/2 95 45
13,5% vol   0,75 l

The wines: **100** Perfect · **95–99** Outstanding · **90–94** Excellent · **85–89** Very good · **80–84** Good · **75–79** Average

75

WEINGUT MAIBACHFARM

Owner: Gatzmaga family
Manager: Günter Gatzmaga
Winemaker: Andreas Gatzmaga
53474 Bad Neuenahr-Ahrweiler,
Im Maibachtal 100
Tel. (0 26 41) 3 66 79, Fax 3 66 43
e-mail: info@weingut-maibachfarm.de
Internet: www.weingut-maibachfarm.de
Directions: A 61, Ahrweiler exit, winery is on the south-westerly border of Ahrweiler, above the Kalvarienberg abbey
Sales: Gatzmaga family
Opening hours: Tue.–Fri. 11:00 to 20:00, Sat. and Sun. 11:00 to 22:00 hours by appointment
Restaurant: Jun., Aug., Sep. and Oct. from 11:00 to 21:00 hours, closed Mon.
Specialties: Roast lamb with Spätzle noodles
Worth seeing: Own sheep farm, cheese production

Vineyard area: 15 hectares
Annual production: 120,000 bottles
Top sites: Walporzheimer Domlay, Neuenahrer Sonnenberg
Soil types: Slate, grey wacke, clay
Grape varieties: 35% Spätburgunder, 15% Portugieser, 13% each of Riesling and Dornfelder, 10% Frühburgunder, 5% Regent, 4% Rivaner, 5% other varieties
Average yield: 55 hl/ha
Best vintages: 2002, 2003
Member: Bioland

This interesting operation was only established as a winery in 1998. By now Günter Gatzmaga and his son Andreas are working 15 hectares of vineyard according to organic practices, and provide quite a multi-faceted programme: Spätburgunder and Frühburgunder grown on some of the best terraced sites of the Ahr valley, but also attractive Rivaner wines for quaffing as well as some hearty Regent wines. The wines of the 2002 vintage were already quite good, those of the succeeding vintage are even better. Our favorites are the Frühburgunder Auslese as well as the Spätburgunder, both from the Klosterberg site. Most of the red wines are matured in barriques. Their investment in a brand-new cellar is another step on the way to building one of the leading wineries in the region.

———— Red wines ————

2003 Walporzheimer Himmelchen
Spätburgunder trocken
12.5%, ♀ till 2006   82

2003 Dernauer Goldkaul
Regent trocken
12.5%, ♀ till 2007   82

2003 Ahrweiler Silberberg
Acolon trocken
13%, ♀ till 2007   83

2003 Walporzheimer Domlay
Spätburgunder trocken
13.5%, ♀ till 2007   84

2003 Dernauer Goldkaul
Spätburgunder trocken
14%, ♀ till 2007   84

2003 Ahrweiler Klosterberg
Spätburgunder trocken
14%, ♀ till 2008   85

2003 Frühburgunder
Auslese trocken
14%, ♀ till 2008   85

WINZERGENOSSENSCHAFT MAYSCHOSS-ALTENAHR

General manager: Rudolf Mies
Winemaker: Rolf Münster
53508 Mayschoß, Ahrrotweinstr. 42
Tel. (0 26 43) 9 36 00, Fax 93 60 93
e-mail: wmayschoss@t-online.de
Internet: www.winzergenossenschaft-mayschoss.de
Directions: A 61 Köln–Koblenz, Bad Neuenahr exit, in direction of Altenahr
Sales: Rudolf Stodden
Opening hours: Mon.–Fri. 08:00 to 18:30 hours, Sat., Sun. and public holidays 9:00 to 18:30 hours
History: Oldest wine co-operative in Germany
Worth seeing: Old barrel cellar, small wine museum

Vineyard area: 112 hectares
Number of members: 305
Annual production: 1 mill. bottles
Top sites: Mayschosser Mönchberg, Burgberg and Laacherberg, Altenahrer Eck, Ahrweiler Daubhaus, Neuenahrer Sonnenberg
Soil types: Decomposed slate, partly with loess-clay
Grape varieties: 60% Spätburgunder, 20% Riesling, 5% Portugieser, 15% other varieties
Average yield: 70 hl/ha
Best vintages: 1999, 2001, 2003

One really has to show respect for what the enterprising members of the Mayschoß co-operative are doing: By now there are 305 members producing wine on 112 hectares of vineyard. They have a wide-ranging list of wines, but there is never a really disappointing wine in this line-up. Following on the excellent ranges of the 1999 and 2001 vintages, the 2002 vintage red wines are again of reliable good quality. Looking to the white wines of the 2003 vintage, the Auslese wines as well as the Eiswein from the Laacherberg site are again among the very best botrytis dessert Rieslings of the whole Ahr valley.

2003 Mayschosser Mönchberg
Riesling Spätlese halbtrocken
12%, ♀ till 2008 — **85**

2003 Mayschosser Laacherberg
Riesling Auslese – 21 –
8.5%, ♀ till 2012 — **89**

2003 Mayschosser Laacherberg
Riesling Auslese – 22 –
7.5%, ♀ till 2014 — **90**

2003 Mayschosser Laacherberg
Riesling Eiswein
7%, ♀ till 2014 — **90**

———— Red wines ————

2002 Spätburgunder
trocken Selection "12 Trauben"
14.5%, ♀ till 2007 — **84**

2003 Dornfelder trocken
13.5%, ♀ till 2008 — **86**

2002 Spätburgunder
trocken "Edition Ponsart"
13.5%, ♀ till 2008 — **86**

2002 Spätburgunder
trocken "Edition Ponsart" Goldkapsel
14%, ♀ till 2014 — **86**

2003 Ahrweiler Daubhaus
Spätburgunder Auslese trocken
15.5%, ♀ till 2008 — **87**

2001 Neuenahrer Sonnenberg
Spätburgunder Auslese trocken
14%, ♀ till 2007 — **87**

2003 Frühburgunder trocken
14.5%, ♀ till 2009 — **88**

2001 Spätburgunder
trocken "Ponsart" Goldkapsel
13.5%, ♀ till 2008 — **88**

The wines: **100** Perfect · **95–99** Outstanding · **90–94** Excellent · **85–89** Very good · **80–84** Good · **75–79** Average

77

WEINGUT MEYER-NÄKEL

Owner: Werner Näkel
53507 Dernau, Friedensstraße 15
Tel. (0 26 43) 16 28, Fax 33 63
e-mail: weingut@meyer-naekel.de
Internet: www.meyer-naekel.de
Directions: A 61 Köln–Koblenz, Bad
Neuenahr exit, in direction of Altenahr
Sales: Entrance Friedensstraße 15,
by appointment only
Closed Sun.
Restaurant/Wine bar: "Im Hofgarten,"
Bachstraße 26, next to the church, open
daily from 11:00 to 23:00 hours
Hartwig Näkel, Tel. (0 26 43) 15 40
Historical wine and beer restaurant:
Family-owned for 200 years

Vineyard area: 13.2 hectares
Annual production: 100,000 bottles
Top sites: Dernauer Pfarrwingert,
Neuenahrer Sonnenberg,
Walporzheimer Kräuterberg
Soil types: Decomposed slate,
partly with loess-clay
Grape varieties: 75% Spätburgunder,
15% Frühburgunder, 5% each of
Dornfelder and Riesling
Average yield: 51 hl/ha
Best vintages: 1997, 2001, 2003
Member: VDP,
Deutsches Barrique Forum

Last year we honoured Werner Näkel as our "Producer of the year," out of respect for his life's work (so far). Hardly any other winemaker in Germany has had a greater impact on the production of high-quality red wines than he. Particularly since the mid-Nineties, he has presented exceptional ranges of wines in a biennial rhythm, always coinciding with the uneven years. Starting with the 1997 vintage, the head of the regional VDP association presented a picture-perfect collection that was without equal in his 15-year career. The way in which Näkel also coaxed the optimum out of his grapes in 1999, using careful vinification in small oak barrels to maximize the natural potential of the ma-

terial, was nothing short of masterly. Later tastings of these wines have shown that their development is progressing much better than that of wines from the early Nineties. If there was any slight criticism of Näkel's wines in the past, then it was that wines that were highly rated in their youth did not mature as elegantly as one had originally anticipated. The 2001 range set new standards. All five wines were rated 90 points or higher, with the Frühburgunder Auslese as well as the spicy Spätburgunder Auslese, both from the Pfarrwingert site, among our very favorite wines. The 2000 vintage was a difficult one, and there were not quite as many top wines, and a similar picture applies with regard to the 2002 vintage. However, to Werner Näkels strong credit, he never tried to talk up these two vintages in any way. And the very well-ballanced 2002 Spätburgunder "S" is clear evidence that this was not an altogether poor year. The red wines of the 2003 vintage, tasted shortly after bottling, herald a paradigm change: Here a range of red wines is maturing that boasts density of fruit and fullness of body such as has not been seen from this winery in the past 20 years – just as things should be in an uneven-year vintage at the Näkel estate! The latest entrepreneurial exercise of this indefatigable man from Dernau, who keeps on commuting to his joint ventures in South Africa and Portugal, is his part in taking over the state domain at Marienthal. This is however a cake he is sharing with Hajo Brogsitter as well as with the Mayschoß and Dagernova co-operatives. It would seem that Näkel's portfolio of vineyard sites is due to grow again by quite a few hectares.

2003 Riesling trocken
12.5%, ♀ till 2006   **84**

2003 Weißer Burgunder trocken
13.5%, ♀ till 2006   **85**

——— Red wines ———

2003 Spätburgunder Weißherbst
trocken
13%, ♀ till 2006   **82**

2002 Spätburgunder Weißherbst
trocken
12%, ♀ till 2005   **83**

2003 Spätburgunder trocken
13%, ♀ till 2008   **84**

2002 "Blauschiefer"
Spätburgunder trocken
13%, ♀ till 2006   **84**

2002 Spätburgunder trocken
12.5%, ♀ till 2006   **84**

2003 "Illusion"
Spätburgunder trocken
13%, ♀ till 2006   **85**

2002 Frühburgunder trocken
13.5%, ♀ till 2006   **85**

2003 Frühburgunder trocken
14%, ♀ till 2008   **86**

2002 Spätburgunder
trocken "Illusion"
11.5%, ♀ till 2006   **86**

2003 "Blauschiefer"
Spätburgunder trocken
14%, ♀ till 2009   **87**

2001 "Blauschiefer"
Spätburgunder trocken
14%, ♀ till 2006   **87**

2001 Spätburgunder trocken "G"
14%, ♀ till 2006   **87**

2002 Spätburgunder trocken "S"
13.5%, ♀ till 2008   **88**

2003 Spätburgunder trocken "S"
14%, ♀ till 2010   **89**

2001 Spätburgunder trocken "S"
14%, ♀ till 2008   **89**

2003 Neuenahrer Sonnenberg
Frühburgunder trocken
14.5%, ♀ till 2012   **90**

2001 Bad Neuenahrer Sonnenberg
Frühburgunder trocken
14%, ♀ till 2008   **90**

2001 Spätburgunder
trocken "S" Goldkapsel
14%, ♀ till 2008   **90**

2001 Dernauer Pfarrwingert
Frühburgunder Auslese trocken
14.5%, ♀ till 2010   **91**

2001 Dernauer Pfarrwingert
Spätburgunder Auslese trocken
➶ auction wine, 14.5%, ♀ till 2010   **91**

2003 Dernauer Pfarrwingert
Frühburgunder Auslese trocken
Goldkapsel
14.5%, ♀ till 2014   **91**

2003 Neuenahrer Sonnenberg
Spätburgunder Auslese trocken
Goldkapsel
➶ auction wine, 14%, ♀ till 2012   **91**

2001 Walporzheimer Kräuterberg
Spätburgunder Auslese trocken
14.5%, ♀ till 2010   **92**

2003 Dernauer Pfarrwingert
Spätburgunder Auslese trocken
Goldkapsel
14.5%, ♀ till 2012   **92**

2003 Walporzheimer Kräuterberg
Spätburgunder Auslese trocken
14.5%, ♀ till 2012   **93**

The wines: **100** Perfect · **95–99** Outstanding · **90–94** Excellent · **85–89** Very good · **80–84** Good · **75–79** Average

WEINGUT NELLES

Owner: Thomas Nelles
Winemaker: Alfred Emmerich
53474 Bad Neuenahr-Heimersheim,
Göppinger Straße 13a
Tel. (0 26 41) 2 43 49, Fax 7 95 86
e-mail: info@weingut-nelles.de
Internet: www.weingut-nelles.de
Directions: A 61, triangle Sinzig exit –
A 571, in direction of Bad Neuenahr,
Heimersheim exit
Sales: Thomas Nelles
Opening hours: Mon.–Fri. 09:00 to
12:00 and 14:00 to 18:00 hours
Sat. 10:00 to 12:00 hours
Restaurant: Weinhaus Nelles
Tel. (0 26 41) 68 68, Wed.–Sat. from
17:30 to 23:00 hours, Sun. and public
holidays from 11:30 hours
Specialties: Regional wine-related dishes
History: Wine has been made here for
more than 500 years

Vineyard area: 6,5 hectares
Annual production: 35,000 bottles
Top site: Heimersheimer Landskrone
Soil types: Decomposed slate,
grey wacke and loess-clay
Grape varieties: 65% Spätburgunder,
10% each of Frühburgunder, Riesling
and Grauburgunder, 5% Portugieser
Average yield: 63 hl/ha
Best vintages: 1999, 2001, 2002
Member: VDP

The year of 1479 dominates the label, re-
fering to the first mention of the Nelles
vineyards in the 15th century. Of particular interest here is a trio of refreshing summer wines sporting the names "Albus,"
"Clarus" and "Ruber," indicating the respective colors of the wines. However, the
reputation of the winery is based primarily on the delicate red wines, often reminiscent of an elegant Volnay. Following
on excellent ranges in the 1999 and 2001
vintages, Nelles has presented a remarkably good range of 2002 wines. The Pinot
Noirs labeled "B 52" are among the best
red wines in the Ahr region.

——— Red wines ———

2002 Spätburgunder
trocken Classic
13.5%, ♀ till 2007   84

2003 "Pinot Madeleine"
Frühburgunder trocken
13%, ♀ till 2007   85

2002 "Ruber"
Spätburgunder trocken
13%, ♀ till 2008   85

2002 Spätburgunder trocken "B"
13.5%, ♀ till 2008   86

2001 Spätburgunder
trocken "B 48"
13.5%, ♀ till 2008   88

2002 Spätburgunder
trocken "B 48"
14%, ♀ till 2010   89

2002 Spätburgunder
trocken "B 52"
14.5%, ♀ till 2010   89

2001 Spätburgunder
trocken "B 52"
14%, ♀ till 2009   89

2002 Spätburgunder
trocken "B 52" Goldkapsel
➤ auction wine, 14.5%, ♀ till 2012   89

2001 Spätburgunder
trocken "B 59"
13.5%, ♀ till 2008   90

2001 Spätburgunder
trocken "B 52" Goldkapsel
➤ auction wine, 14.5%, ♀ till 2010   91

WEINGUT ERWIN RISKE

Owner: Volker Riske
Manager and winemaker: Volker Riske
53507 Dernau, Wingertstraße 26–28
Tel. (0 26 43) 84 06, Fax 35 31
e-mail: Weingut-Riske@t-online.de
Internet: www.weingut-riske.de
*Directions: A 61, Bad Neuenahr-Ahr-
weiler exit, in direction of Altenahr*
Sales: Mechthild Riske
Opening hours: Mon.–Fri. by appoint-
ment, Sat. 10:00 to 18:00 hours, Sun.
and public holidays 15:00 to 18:00 hours
and as for the restaurant opening times
Restaurant: May and June, Sept.–Nov.
Fri. open from 15:00 to 22:00 hours
Sat. u. public holidays 12:00 to 22:00
hours, Sun. from 12:00 to 20:00 hours
Specialties: Home-made cream of pota-
to and leek soup, oven-baked potatoes
with sour cream and herbs

Vineyard area: 5 hectares
Annual production: 45,000 bottles
Top sites: Dernauer Pfarrwingert, Neuenahrer Sonnenberg
Soil types: Decomposed slate, loess
Grape varieties: 75% Spätburgunder, 8% Portugieser, 5% Frühburgunder, 12% other varieties
Average yield: 75 hl/ha
Best vintages: 1999, 2002, 2003

Volker Riske is yet another enterprising
man from Dernau who has come to wine
later in life. After finishing school, he began studying to teach sport and Fine Arts.
However, when his father fell ill in the
early Eighties, he switched his studies,
completed his degree as an enologist,
and now heads up the winery in the
fourth generation. A new sense of quality has
been evident here since the 1999 vintage.
Following on the good range of 2002 vintage wines, the wines of the 2003 vintage
are again of respectable quality, and the
Frühburgunder Auslese from the Hardtberg site is truly excellent. The wines
taste even better when enjoyed in the restaurant "Turmgarten."

———— Red wines ————

2003 Neuenahrer Sonnenberg
Spätburgunder trocken
13.5%, ♀ till 2008   **84**

2002 Dernauer Schieferlay
Spätburgunder trocken
13%, ♀ till 2007   **84**

2003 Ahrweiler Ursulinengarten
Spätburgunder trocken
13%, ♀ till 2008   **85**

2003 Dernauer Pfarrwingert
Spätburgunder Auslese trocken
14%, ♀ till 2008   **85**

2001 Dernauer Pfarrwingert
Spätburgunder Auslese trocken
14%, ♀ till 2007   **85**

2002 Spätburgunder
trocken "Schieferturm"
12.5%, ♀ till 2008   **85**

2003 Dernauer Hardtberg
Frühburgunder Auslese trocken
13%, ♀ till 2010   **87**

2002 Dernauer Pfarrwingert
Spätburgunder trocken
13%, ♀ till 2008   **87**

2001 Dernauer Schieferlay
Spätburgunder trocken Barrique
14%, ♀ till 2005   **87**

2001 Dernauer Pfarrwingert
Spätburgunder Auslese trocken Barrique
14%, ♀ till 2006   **88**

The wines: **100** Perfect · **95–99** Outstanding · **90–94** Excellent · **85–89** Very good · **80–84** Good · **75–79** Average

81

WEINGUT
SERMANN-KREUZBERG

Owner and manager: Klaus Sermann
53505 Altenahr, Seilbahnstraße 22
Tel. (0 26 43) 71 05, Fax 90 16 46
e-mail: weingut-sermann@t-online.de
Internet: www.sermann.de
Directions: A 61, Altenahr exit, at center
of town in direction of Nürburgring,
after the bridge right into Seilbahnstraße
Sales: Luzia and Rasema Sermann
Opening hours: Thur.–Tue. 10:00 to
18:00 hours or by appointment
Restaurant: Easter to All Saints
Thur.–Tue. 10:00 to 18:00 hours,
Wed. by arrangement
Specialties: Fried white bread marinated
in Riesling, goat's cheese provencale style
History: Winemaking since 1775

Vineyard area: 6 hectares
Annual production: 60,000 bottles
Top sites: Altenahrer Eck,
Mayschosser Burgberg
Soil types: Slate, clay, loess
Grape varieties: 68% Spätburgunder,
12% Frühburgunder, 10% Riesling,
4% Müller-Thurgau, 3% each of Dorn-
felder and Regent
Average yield: 83 hl/ha
Best vintages: 2001, 2002

The small Sermann winery in Altenahr
has begun to build a reputation in recent
years. Following on its merger with the
Kreuzberg winery in Reimerzhofen there
are now six hectares under vine, and
the investment in the cellar is beginning
to bear fruit. The range of 2001 vintage
wines presented last year earned K. Sermann his first bunch of grapes. The wine
we liked best was the Spätburgunder
from the Altenahrer Eck site, which has
fragrant hazelnut and black currant
aromas. It deserves special mention that
the two 2002 vintage Frühburgunder wines
from the Burgberg site now present themselves in even better form than last year,
and the two 2003 vintage Rieslings tasted
were also of satisfactory quality.

2002 "Bellabianca"
Spätburgunder trocken "Blanc de Noir"
12.5%, ♀ till 2005   **83**

2003 Mayschosser Laacherberg
Riesling trocken
12.5%, ♀ till 2006   **84**

2001 Altenahrer Eck
Riesling Auslese
10%, ♀ till 2008   **84**

2003 Altenahrer Eck
Riesling Spätlese
9.5%, ♀ till 2007   **85**

———————— Red wines ————————

2003 Altenahrer Eck
Spätburgunder trocken
13%, ♀ till 2006   **82**

2003 Ahrweiler Forstberg
Spätburgunder trocken
13.5%, ♀ till 2006   **82**

2001 Ahrweiler Forstberg
Spätburgunder trocken
13.5%, ♀ till 2006   **83**

2002 Mayschosser Burgberg
Frühburgunder trocken
13.5%, ♀ till 2007   **85**

2001 Mayschosser Burgberg
Frühburgunder trocken Barrique
13.5%, ♀ till 2006   **85**

2001 Ahrweiler Rosenthal
Spätburgunder Auslese trocken Barrique
13.5%, ♀ till 2006   **85**

2002 Mayschosser Burgberg
Frühburgunder trocken Barrique
13.5%, ♀ till 2009   **87**

2001 Altenahrer Eck
Spätburgunder trocken Barrique
13.5%, ♀ till 2007   **87**

WEINGUT SONNENBERG

Owner: Görres and Linden families
Manager and winemaker:
Manfred Linden
53474 Bad Neuenahr, Heerstraße 98
Tel. (0 26 41) 67 13, Fax 20 10 37
e-mail: info@weingut-sonnenberg.de
Internet: www.weingut-sonnenberg.de
Directions: A 61 Köln–Koblenz,
Bad Neuenahr exit
Sales: Manfred and Birgit Linden
Opening hours: Mon.–Fri. 09:00 to
18:00 hours, Sat. 10:00 to 14:00 hours,
Sun. 10:00 to 12:00 hours
Restaurant: On six weekends in May
and October
Specialties: Home-made vintner's platter

Vineyard area: 5.5 hectares
Annual production: 50,000 bottles
Top sites: Neuenahrer
Sonnenberg and Schieferlay,
Ahrweiler Silberberg
Soil types: Grey wacke with loess-clay
Grape varieties: 72% Spätburgunder,
6% Frühburgunder,
22% other varieties
Average yield: 60 hl/ha
Best vintages: 1997, 1999, 2001

In 1981, Manfred Linden turned his back
on a secure job and ventured into the ris-
ky life of the winemaker. He has expanded the small operation to five and a half
hectares of vineyard, including one and a
half hectares of terraced land that is a registered heritage site. The vineyard designations are used only for the predicate-
level wines as well as for respectively the
best Frühburgunder and Spätburgunder
quality wines. Manfred Linden's wines
took a step forward in 1999, while those
of the 2001 vintage were better than ever
before. The wines of the 2002 vintage did
not achieve this standard. The overly rich
wines of the 2003 vintage are, we regret,
disappointing. The dry Auslese from the
Sonnenberg site is alcoholic, and the Beerenauslese, fermented dry, is no pleasure
to drink.

--------- Red wines ---------

2003 Neuenahrer Schieferlay
Spätburgunder trocken
13.5%, ♀ till 2006 **84**

2003 Ahrweiler Ursulinengarten
Frühburgunder trocken
14%, ♀ till 2006 **84**

2003 Neuenahrer Sonnenberg
Spätburgunder Beerenauslese trocken
15.5%, ♀ till 2006 **84**

2003 Neuenahrer Sonnenberg
Spätburgunder Auslese trocken
15%, ♀ till 2007 **85**

2002 Ahrweiler Ursulinengarten
Frühburgunder trocken
13%, ♀ till 2007 **86**

2001 Ahrweiler Ursulinengarten
Frühburgunder Auslese trocken
12.5%, ♀ till 2005 **87**

2001 Spätburgunder
trocken "Feanor"
13%, ♀ till 2009 **87**

2001 Spätburgunder
trocken "Tradition"
13.5%, ♀ till 2005 **87**

2001 Neuenahrer Sonnenberg
Spätburgunder Auslese trocken
14%, ♀ till 2006 **88**

The wines: **100** Perfect · **95–99** Outstanding · **90–94** Excellent · **85–89** Very good · **80–84** Good · **75–79** Average

83

STAATLICHE WEINBAU-DOMÄNE MARIENTHAL

Owner: State of Rheinland-Pfalz
Manager: Sigmund Lawnik
Winemaker: Heinz-Peter Bier
53507 Marienthal, Klosterstraße 3
Tel. (0 26 41) 9 80 60, Fax 98 06 20
e-mail: domaene.slva-
aw@agrarinfo.rlp.de
Internet: www.staatsweingueter.rlp.de
Directions: A 61, Bad Neuenahr-Ahr-weiler exit, in the direction of Altenahr
Sales: Mon.–Fri. 08:00 to 12:00 hours and 13:00 to 16:00 hours
Worth seeing: Abbey garden with ruins and cloisters and wine cellar. The Augustine abbey was founded in 12th century.

Vineyard area: 18.5 hectares
Annual production: 100,000 bottles
Top sites: Ahrweiler Rosenthal and Silberberg, Walporzheimer Kräuterberg, Marienthaler Klostergarten (monopole)
Soil types: Decomposed slate, grey wacke, loess on a rubble base
Grape varieties: 66% Spätburgunder, 14% Portugieser, 6% Domina, 5% Dornfelder, 3% each of Frühburgunder, Weißburgunder and Riesling
Average yield: 59 hl/ha
Best vintages: 1999, 2001, 2002
Member: VDP

For many years, the state wine domain housed in the historic Augustine abbey of Marienthal was the pride of vineyards owned by the federal state of Rheinland-Pfalz. The estate, which comprises 18.5 hectares of vineyards, was sold to an energetic quartet of investors just prior to the 2004 harvest. It still remains to be seen, who will take over which vineyard site, and how the old domain facilities will be used. So far it has been announced that a small winery under the name of Kloster Marienthal is to continue there. As the stocks of wines have also been acquired by the new owners, the 2003 vintage will be the last to bear the Prussian eagle on wine bottled in the Ahr region.

——— Red wines ———

2003 Ahrweiler Silberberg
Spätburgunder Auslese trocken
13.5%, ♀ till 2007 — **84**

2002 Spätburgunder trocken
13%, ♀ till 2007 — **85**

2002 Ahrweiler Klostergarten
Spätburgunder Spätlese trocken
12.5%, ♀ till 2007 — **85**

2002 Frühburgunder trocken
13.5%, ♀ till 2007 — **85**

2001 Frühburgunder trocken
13.5%, ♀ till 2005 — **85**

2001 Ahrweiler Rosenthal
Frühburgunder Spätlese trocken
12%, ♀ till 2007 — **86**

2001 Frühburgunder trocken – 30 –
13.5%, ♀ till 2007 — **86**

2001 Spätburgunder
Auslese trocken
13%, ♀ till 2008 — **87**

2001 Ahrweiler Silberberg
Spätburgunder Auslese trocken
14.5%, ♀ till 2007 — **87**

2001 Spätburgunder trocken
12.5%, ♀ till 2008 — **87**

2001 Frühburgunder trocken – 22 –
13.5%, ♀ till 2008 — **88**

Staatliche
Weinbaudomäne
Marienthal
Domäne
2001
SPÄTBURGUNDER
TROCKEN

AHR

The estates: ♛♛♛♛♛ World's finest · ♛♛♛♛ Germany's best · ♛♛♛ Very good · ♛♛ Good · ♛ Reliable

WEINGUT JEAN STODDEN

Owner: Gerhard Stodden
Manager and winemaker: Alexander and Gerhard Stodden
53506 Rech, Rotweinstraße 7–9
Tel. (0 26 43) 30 01, Fax 30 03
e-mail: info@stodden.de
Internet: www.stodden.de
Directions: A 61 Köln–Koblenz, Bad Neuenahr exit, in direction of Altenahr
Sales: Dr. Brigitta Stodden
Opening hours: Mon.–Fri. 09:00 to 18:00 hours, Sat. 10:00 to 14:00 hours
History: Winemaking in the family since 1578
Worth seeing: Art gallery in the vinotheque

Vineyard area: 6,5 hectares
Annual production: 45,000 bottles
Top sites: Recher Herrenberg, Dernauer Hardtberg, Ahrweiler Rosenthal
Soil types: Decomposed slate, partly with loess-clay
Grape varieties: 83% Spätburgunder, 7% Frühburgunder, 5% Riesling, 5% other varieties
Average yield: 48 hl/ha
Best vintages: 1999, 2001, 2002

Gerhard Stodden has never been a proponent of the light and gentle style of Pinot Noir so typical of the Ahr region. Quite the contrary, his idols are at home in the Côte de Nuits of Burgundy, and carry names as Dujac, Ponsot and Roumier. Stodden has tasted their products extensively, and has learnt a lot, by now he is on regular friendly terms with some of them. Until a few years ago he sent the grapes to fermentation with their stems – just as is common among his colleagues – until he realized that this practice was a source of unwanted green tannins. Now, Stodden de-stems his grapes, and extends the time of maceration on skins to 14 and sometimes even 21 days, to ensure he extracts sufficient substance from the skins. Immediately after racking the wine into barriques, Stodden induces malolactic fermentation. The wines matured in barrique are bottled 16 months after the vintage, and are recognizable by the designation "JS" on the label. These wines generally need some time to develop their fruit. The best wines are matured in exclusively new, heavily toasted pièce barrels. The oak is sourced from the French Central Massif. Following on his excellent 1997 vintage, Stodden served up breathtakingly good wines of the 1999 vintage, which were among the best red wines in Germany. We found cause to comment his efforts even in the difficult 2000 vintage, but these were followed by a 2001 vintage that produced inaccessible wines, to avoid the terms hard and tannic. Now, Gerhard Stodden has set himself a monument in the form of his 2002 vintage wines: No other winemaker on the Ahr has produced such a uniformly good range from the rather average vintage. Stodden had noted as early as November that the wines were taking on a brickish hue, although they had been dark red at pressing. This may be attributable to the increased water uptake in the autumn. However, Stodden is not concerned about the maturation potential of these wines: "The wines are not quite as robust as those of 1999, but a lifespan of ten years will be no problem!" Son Alexander is now also involved, since 2001, following on his winemaking studies and practical stints in South Africa and Oregon, a fact that is also hinted at in the form of a new wine bearing the apt name "Next Generation." Just a few words on the wines of the 2003 vintage, which we tasted from barrel samples, and which uniformly impressed us with their density and complexity. A highlight is the dry Auslese wine from the Herrenberg site, which is to be bottled as a gold capsule wine. Gerhard Stodden knows he has never had better wines in his cellar than these: "They will easily beat the big wines we made in 1999!"

The wines: **100** Perfect · **95–99** Outstanding · **90–94** Excellent · **85–89** Very good · **80–84** Good · **75–79** Average

2002 "Cuvée Blanc" trocken "JS"
13%, ♀ till 2006   **83**

2001 "Cuvée Blanc" trocken "JS"
13.5%, ♀ till 2006   **86**

2003 Recher Herrenberg
Riesling halbtrocken
12.5%, ♀ till 2006   **81**

2002 Recher Herrenberg
Riesling Spätlese
7.5%, ♀ till 2007   **87**

——— Red wines ———

2002 Recher Herrenberg
Spätburgunder Auslese trocken
"JS" Alte Reben
14%, ♀ till 2012   **91**

2002 Recher Herrenberg
Spätburgunder trocken
13.5%, ♀ till 2006   **83**

2001 "Cuvée Jeanne" trocken "JS"
13.5%, ♀ till 2005   **83**

2001 Spätburgunder trocken "JS"
13.5%, ♀ till 2007   **84**

2002 Spätburgunder trocken "JS"
13.5%, ♀ till 2006   **85**

2002 "Cuvée Jeanne" trocken "JS"
13.5%, ♀ till 2010   **87**

2002 Recher Herrenberg
Frühburgunder trocken "JS"
13.5%, ♀ till 2008   **87**

2001 Recher Herrenberg
Spätburgunder trocken "JS"
13.5%, ♀ till 2007   **87**

2001 Ahrweiler Rosenthal
Spätburgunder trocken "JS"
13.5%, ♀ till 2007   **87**

2002 Recher Herrenberg
Spätburgunder trocken "JS"
13.5%, ♀ till 2008   **88**

2002 Ahrweiler Rosenthal
Spätburgunder trocken "JS"
13.5%, ♀ till 2008   **88**

2001 Recher Herrenberg
Frühburgunder trocken "JS"
13.5%, ♀ till 2007   **88**

2001 "Next Generation"
Spätburgunder Auslese trocken "JS"
14%, ♀ till 2010   **88**

2002 "Next Generation"
Spätburgunder trocken "JS"
14.5%, ♀ till 2010   **89**

2002 Recher Herrenberg
Spätburgunder Auslese*** trocken "JS"
13%, ♀ till 2012   **89**

2001 Recher Herrenberg
Spätburgunder Auslese*** trocken "JS"
Alte Reben
13.5%, ♀ till 2008   **89**

2001 Recher Herrenberg
Spätburgunder Auslese*** trocken "JS"
13%, ♀ till 2010   **90**

2002 Spätburgunder
trocken "JS Reserve"
14%, ♀ till 2012   **90**

Jean Stodden

2002
Recher Herrenberg
Spätburgunder JS
Alte Reben
Auslese
Qualitätswein mit Prädikat · Trocken
Unfiltriert – Dekantieren empfohlen
Ahr · A.P.Nr. 1 795 090 2 04
14,0%vol   0,75 l
Erzeuger-Abfüllung
Weingut Jean Stodden D-53506 Rech/Ahr

Other recommended producers

Weingut Alois Grimmiger – Im Kräutergarten
53474 Walporzheim
Walporzheimer Str. 143
Tel. (0 26 41) 3 44 14

In the Eighties, when many winemakers in the Ahr region were still producing light-bodied sweetish wines for the tourist trade, Alois Grimmiger was one of the pioneers of uncompromisingly dry wines. It is true that, compared to the current stars of the region, he has lost touch somewhat, but his alcoholic Auslese wines of the 2003 vintage, which are reminiscent in style of an Amarone from the Veneto, should not be ignored.

Weingut Klosterhof – Familie Gilles
53507 Marienthal, Rotweinstraße 7
Tel. (0 26 41) 3 62 80, Fax 3 58 54

In the past few years, this producer has become a reliable supplier. Although the quality still does not quite match that of the established wineries in the Ahr valley, the wines are of acceptably good quality right across the board, the 2002 Spätburgunder (Pinot Noir, 82 points) is a typical example. However, in some cases the wines are quite rustic, such as the 2003 Spätburgunder Classic (79 points).

Weingut Reinhold Riske
53507 Dernau, Wingertstraße 32
Tel. (0 26 43) 70 20, Fax 90 05 66

If Bernd Riske were to submit wines regularly that are as good as those of the 2001 vintage, he would have been awarded a bunch of grapes long ago. Last year we were impressed by a Spätburgunder Weißherbst (Pinot Noir rosé) Eiswein (90 points), that reminded us of biscuits dipped in raspberry distillate. More recently, we found the red wines of the 2002 vintage to be a touch too rustic, and the Spätburgunder Auslese 2003 from the Karlskopf site was even slightly faulty.

Winzergenossenschaft Walporzhe
53474 Bad Neuenahr-Ahrweiler
Walporzheimer Straße 173
Tel. (0 26 41) 3 47 63, Fax 3 14 10

The quality of wines presented here in the past few years has been a rollercoaster ride. The 2001 wines were all of commendable quality, those of the 2002 vintage less so. The wines produced in 2003 are back to the high level of 2001: Now as then we particularly liked the dry Spätburgunder Auslese "Bunte Kuh" as well as the Frühburgunder from the Pfaffenberg site (both rated 84 points).

Recommended by our wine producers

Hotels and inns
Adenbach: Burghotel
Ahrweiler: Hohenzollern, Rodder Hof
Dernau: Kreuzberg
Gimmingen: Haus am Berg
Heppingen: Steinheuers Landhaus
Mayschoß: Saffenburg
Bad Neuenahr: Aurora, Goldener Anker, Krupp, Steigenberger
Rech: Appel
Walporzheim: Romantikhotel St. Peter

Gourmet restaurants
Heppingen: Steinheuers Alte Post
Walporzheim: Brogsitters St. Peter

Restaurants, wine bars and winery facilities
Ahrweiler: Eifelstube, Prümer Hof
Altenahr: Schäferkarre
Bad Neuenahr: Idille
Dernau: Kreuzberg
Heimersheim: Weinhaus Nelles
Heppingen: Burggarten
Lorsdorf: Köhlerhof
Marienthal: Gilles
Mayschoß: Bahnsteig I, Saffenburg

Baden

A year of extremes

'ere complaining about a
y contrast the 2003 vin-
rised by extreme drought
itures such as are usually
only experienced in southern Europe. Vineyard irrigation is now permitted in this
region, and many producers made use of
this option. Faced by an extremely early
vintage, producers had to distinguish
carefully between high must weights and
physiological ripeness. Producers who
were able to pick their red grapes at just
the right time were rewarded with excellent quality. The white wines are clean,
full-bodied and have medium concentration, with white grapes suffering more in
the extreme heat than did red grapes.

The top red wines of the 2002 vintage
have proven to be very good indeed.
Among the best – and this includes comparison with wines across Germany – are
the Pinot Noir wines produced by Franz
Keller, Duijn, Bernhard Huber, Reinhold
and Cornelia Schneider, Salwey and Fritz
Waßmer.

This year, the absolute top positions in
Baden have been taken by Reinhold and
Cornelia Schneider and by Bernhard
Huber. Both, the white and red wines presented by these producers, are of a uniformly high standard. Salwey impresses
mainly with his red wines. Considering
how difficult the vintage was in the Durbach area, Andreas Laible has presented a
remarkably good range. On the other
hand, we were by and large disappointed
by the wines presented by Bercher, Heger
und Johner.

The rising star of the year in Baden is the
Knab estate. Here, classical Pinot Noirs
stand side by side with elegant fruity
white wines. We were also very pleased to
note the positive development at the Freiherr Franckenstein estate. Here, Hubert
Doll, assisted by his daughter, has produced a homogeneous range of elegant,
strongly typical varietal white wines. In
addition to these wineries that have risen
up to three-bunch status, there are two
new wineries rated with two bunches. The
first we would like to mention here is our

discovery of the year, Fritz Waßmer. We
were throughly thrilled by his red wines:
dense, classically Burgundian in style,
with no attempt to deny their French idols.
In recognition of its good red wines, the
Bernd Hummel estate in Malsch receives
its second bunch of grapes. Two wineries
that presented particularly impressive ranges were Herrmann Dörflinger as well as
the Staatsweingut (state winery) Freiburg.
Seven estates were awarded their first
bunch of grapes. The Winzerverein Hagnau, the Leo Maier estate, and Schloss
Salem, the Markgraf zu Baden estate, all
confirmed the positive trend to be seen in
the Bodensee (Lake Constance) area.

This area has in recent years seen increased experimentation with international grape varieties. Chardonnay has been
quite well established, and more recently
Sauvignon Blanc is increasingly been
planted here. However, whether Merlot
and Cabernet Sauvignon really represent a
move forward remains to be seen. In addition, Nebbiolo (Bercher-Schmidt estate,
Oberrotweil) as well as Syrah (Ziereisen
estate, Efringen) are also planted here.

Spätburgunder (Pinot Noir) remains the
red wine variety par excellence for this region, combining as it does full-bodied
fruit with elegance and depth. Riesling
produces excellent results, too, and not
just in the Ortenau area. The Kaiserstuhl,
on the other hand, particularly brings out
the best in the white Pinot varieties. And if
you like heady aromatic wines, you will
find Gewürztraminer and Muskateller to
satisfy your fancy. Last but not least, one
should give a thought to Gutedel (Chasselas), the specialty of the Markgräfler area.
The history of this variety can be traced
back some 5,000 years, though it has been
planted in the area south of Freiburg only
in the past 200 years, often producing excellent table wines.

Baden is the third-largest wine-producing
region in Germany, encompassing 16,000
hectares of vineyard, and producing 1 million hectoliters of wine each year. It is the
most southerly region, and is the only area
in Germany classified as climatic zone B

in the European Union classification – on a par with Alsace, Champagne and the Loire valley. The minimum must weight requirements for quality and predicate wines are thus higher here than elsewhere in Germany. The winegrowing region of Baden stretches over a length of some 400 kilometers, and encompasses nine sub-regions: Tauberfranken, Badische Bergstraße, Kraichgau, Ortenau, Breisgau, Kaiserstuhl, Tuniberg, Markgräflerland and Bodensee (Lake Constance).

The idyllic Tauber river flows through a small part of northern Baden, which was known as Badisches Frankenland until 1992. Here, wine grows exclusively on south-facing slopes. The key grape variety here is Müller-Thurgau, which is capable of producing some quite attractive everyday wines.

Picturesque villages characterise the Badische Bergstraße, spread betweeen Weinheim and Heidelberg. The Bergstraße attracts an annual pilgrimage of tourists in early spring, when cherry, almond and peach trees are in full bloom.

The Kraichgau consists of gently rolling hills, rich farm land stretching from the Black Forest to the Odenwald forest. This is a happy region, characteristics reflected in both its inhabitants and its wines.

The Ortenau is to be found betweeen Baden-Baden and Lahr. Flowers and vines are everywhere to be seen, fruit is produced in copious quantities. The landscape is characterised by narrow valleys and steep slopes. The vineyards enjoy the protection of the Black Forest, and are interrupted only by the villages.

The Kaiserstuhl, or Emperor's Seat, lies between Freiburg and the Rhine valley. In times gone by, dust from the lower Alpine area was deposited here, creating a fertile layer of loess, with the result that wide areas of terraced vineyards could be established here. Every little speck of soil here is planted with vines. Encouraged by the warmest climate in Germany, one-third of the wine produced in Baden grows here.

To the south of the Kaiserstuhl lies the smallest sub-region in Baden, the Tuniberg area: a limestone ridge dating back to Jurassic times, covered in later times by a thick layer of loess. These are fertile soils, and mainly Pinot varieties are grown here. The Breisgau stretches from Lahr to Freiburg. The Glottertal valley enjoys a particularly warm climate. Nature lovers assure us this small area is among the most beautiful to be found anywhere.

Between Freiburg and Basel, in the foothills of the southern Black Forest, lies the Markgräflerland region, the home of Gutedel (Chasselas) for more than 200 years. The Black Forest mountains rise up steeply, to fall of gently as hills towards the Rhine. Dark pine forest, rich fruit orchards and vineyards characterize the landscape.

The German side of the Bodensee (Lake Constance) region is primarily part of Baden. The wines produced within sight of the lake are known as Seewein (lake wine), and the steep slopes here are among the most southerly in Baden, and thus in Germany as a whole. Not only does the sun shine here a great deal, its energy is reflected by the water, and the lake itself stores some of the sun's energy, warming the whole area.

Major and minor vintages in Baden

Vintage	white	red
2003	♦♦♦	♦♦♦♦♦
2002	♦♦♦	♦♦♦
2001	♦♦♦♦	♦♦♦♦
2000	♦♦♦	♦♦
1999	♦♦♦♦	♦♦♦♦
1998	♦♦♦	♦♦
1997	♦♦♦	♦♦♦♦♦
1996	♦♦♦♦	♦♦♦
1995	♦♦♦	♦♦♦♦
1994	♦♦♦	♦♦♦

Vintage rating:

♦♦♦♦♦ : Excellent vintage

♦♦♦♦ : Very good vintage

♦♦♦ : Good vintage

♦♦ : Average vintage

♦ : Poor vintage

Baden

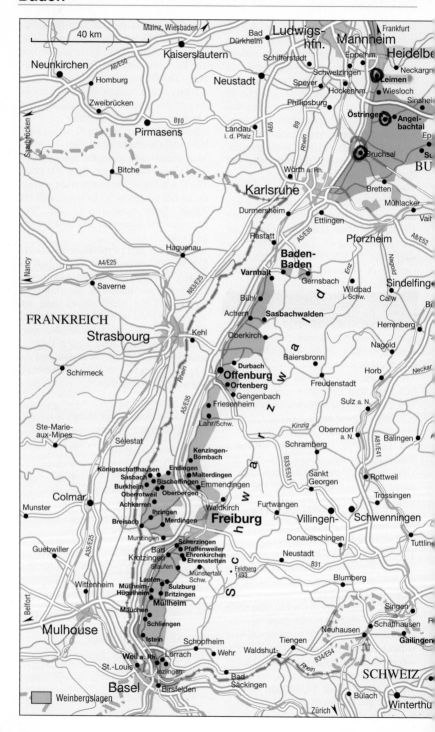

The best vineyard sites i

Breisgau

Hecklingen: Schlossberg

Malterdingen: Bienenberg

Kaiserstuhl

Achkarren: Schlossberg

Burkheim: Schlossgarten, Feuerberg

Freiburg: Schlossberg

Glottertal: Eichberg

Ihringen: Winklerberg, Fohrenberg

Jechtingen: Eichert

Oberrotweil: Kirchberg, Eichberg, Henkenberg, Käsleberg

Sasbach: Limburg

Kraichgau

Michelfeld: Himmelberg

Sulzfeld: Burg Ravensburger Löchle, Husarenkappe, Dicker Franz

Tiefenbach: Schellenbrunnen, Spiegelberg

Markgräflerland

Auggen: Schäf

Istein: Kirchberg

Mauchen: Sonnenstück

Schliengen: Sonnenstück

Ortenau

Berghaupten: Schützenberg

Durbach: Plauelrain

Neuweier: Schlossberg, Mauerberg, Heiligenstein

Zell-Weierbach: Abtsberg, Neugesetz

---

* Source: VDP Baden

91

he leading producers in Baden

Weingut Dr. Heger, Ihringen

Weingut Bernhard Huber, Malterdingen

Weingut Andreas Laible, Durbach

Weingut Salwey, Oberrotweil

Weingut Reinhold und Cornelia Schneider, Endingen

Weingut Aufricht, Meersburg am Bodensee

Weingut Bercher, Vogtsburg-Burkheim

Weingut Duijn, Bühl-Kappelwindeck

Weingut Fischer, Nimburg-Bottingen

Weingut Freiherr von und zu Franckenstein, Offenburg

Weingut Freiherr von Gleichenstein, Oberrotweil

Weingut Ernst Heinemann, Ehrenkirchen-Scherzingen

Weingut Karl H. Johner, Bischoffingen

Franz Keller Schwarzer Adler, Oberbergen

Weingut Knab, Endingen

Weingut Michel, Achkarren

Weingut Schloss Neuweier, Baden-Baden

Weingut Schloss Ortenberg

Winzergenossenschaft Pfaffenweiler EG

Weingut Hartmut Schlumberger, Laufen

Weingut Seeger, Leimen

Weingut Stigler, Ihringen

Weingut Graf Wolff Metternich, Durbach

Weingut Abril, Bischoffingen

Weingut Bercher-Schmidt, Oberrotweil

Weingut Blankenhorn, Schliengen

Winzergenossenschaft Britzingen

Weingut Hermann Dörflinger, Müllheim

Durbacher Winzergenossenschaft

Weinhaus Joachim Heger, Ihringen

Weingut Reichsgraf und Marquis zu Hoensbroech, Angelbachtal-Michelfeld

Weingut Bernd Hummel, Malsch

Schlossgut Istein

Weingut Achim Jähnisch, Ehrenkirchen/Kirchhofen

Weingut Holger Koch, Bickensohl

Weingut Konstanzer, Ihringen

Weingut Lämmlin-Schindler, Mauchen

Weingut Heinrich Männle, Durbach

Weingut Markgraf von Baden – Schloss Staufenberg, Durbach

Gut Nägelsförst, Baden-Baden (Varnhalt)

Weingut Burg Ravensburg, Sulzfeld

Weingut Gregor und Thomas Schätzle, Vogtsburg-Schelingen

Weingut Konrad Schlör, Wertheim-Reicholzheim

Staatsweingut Freiburg und Blankenhornsberg

Weingut **S**tadt Lahr – Familie Wöhrle, Lahr

Weingut Fritz **W**aßmer, Bad Krozingen-Schlatt

Weingut Martin **W**aßmer, Bad Krozingen-Schlatt

Winzergenossenschaft **A**chkarren, Vogtsburg-Achkarren

Affentaler Winzergenossenschaft, Bühl-Eisental

Alde Gott Winzer EG, Sasbachwalden

Winzergenossenschaft **A**uggen

Weingut L. **B**astian, Endingen

Hofgut **C**onsequence, Bischoffingen

Ehrenstetter Winzerkeller EG, Ehrenstetten

Weingut Herbert Daniel **E**ngist, Vogtsburg-Achkarren

Weingut Thomas **H**agenbucher, Sulzfeld

Winzerverein **H**agnau, Hagnau

Winzergenossenschaft **H**altingen, Weil am Rhein

Winzerkeller **H**ex vom Dasenstein EG, Kappelrodeck

Weingut **H**olub, Herbolzheim-Tutschfelden

Weingut **H**uck-Wagner, Efringen-Kirchen

Weingut **K**alkbödele, Merdingen

Weingut **K**lumpp, Bruchsal

Winzergenossenschaft **K**önigschaffhausen

Weingut **K**opp, Sinzheim-Ebenung

Seegut **K**ress, Hagnau

Weingut Leo **M**aier, Stetten bei Meersburg

Weingut **M**arkgraf von Baden – Schloss Salem

Weingut Gebrüder **M**üller, Breisach

Winzergenossenschaft **O**berbergen, Vogtsburg-Oberbergen

Weingut **P**ix, Ihringen

Weingut Reiner **P**robst, Achkarren

Winzergenossenschaft **S**asbach am Kaiserstuhl

Weingut Claus und Susanne **S**chneider, Weil am Rhein

Staatsweingut Meersburg

Tauberfränkische Winzergenossenschaft Beckstein, Lauda-Königshofen

Weingut **T**rautwein, Bahlingen

Weingut Wilhelm **Z**ähringer, Heitersheim

Classification of producers

Highest rating,
for world-class wine producers

Excellent producers counted
as among the best in Germany

Very good producers
who have been making consistently
high quality wines for many years

Good producers who do better
than make just everyday wines

Reliable producers making
decent standard qualitiy wines

WEINGUT ABRIL

Owner: Hans-Friedrich Abril
Manager and winemaker:
Hans-Friedrich Abril
79235 Bischoffingen, Talstraße 9
Tel. (0 76 62) 2 55, Fax 60 76
e-mail: weingut@abril.de
Internet: www.abril.de
Directions: A 5 Frankfurt–Basel,
Riegel exit, in direction of Breisach
Opening hours: Mon.–Fri. 08:00 to
12:00 hours and 14:00 to 18:00 hours
Sat. by appointment
History: Winemaking since 1740, in the
eighth generation
Worth seeing: Half-timbered house
dating to 1803, collection of corkscrews

Vineyard area: 6.6 hectares
Annual production: 40,000 bottles
Top sites: Bischoffinger Enselberg
and Steinbuck
Soil types: Stony decomposed volcanic formation and loess-clay
Grape varieties: 30% each of Spätburgunder and Grauburgunder,
15% Müller-Thurgau, 9% Silvaner,
6% Riesling, 5% Weißburgunder,
5% other varieties
Average yield: 61 hl/ha
Best vintages: 1998, 1999, 2001

His ownership of part of the Bischoffinger Enselberg gives Hans-Friedrich Abril
the opportunity to produce classic white
and red Pinot wines. This potential was
demonstrated by the elegant dry 2001
Spätburgunder (Pinot Noir) Auslese with
its cherry nose. From the 2003 vintage,
the Weißburgunder (Pinot Blanc) Spätlese, for instance, achieves a similarly high
standard. While the fruity Spätlese wines
have plenty of fruit, they are lacking a
little in elegance and finesse. Abril wants
to concentrate even more on the classic
varieties in the years to come, with the
Pinot varieties, in particular, destined to
gain in importance. While this is commendable, he would do well to also pay a
little more attention to his basic wines.

2003 Bischoffinger Enselberg
Riesling Spätlese trocken
13.5%, ♀ till 2006   **82**

2003 Bischoffinger Enselberg
Weißer Burgunder Spätlese trocken
14%, ♀ till 2006   **86**

2001 Schelinger Kirchberg
Riesling Kabinett trocken
11.5%, ♀ till 2005   **87**

2003 Bischoffinger Enselberg
Riesling Spätlese
11%, ♀ till 2006   **83**

2003 Schelinger Kirchberg
Scheurebe Spätlese
11.5%, ♀ till 2006   **84**

2002 Bischoffinger Enselberg
Ruländer Spätlese
11%, ♀ till 2006   **85**

——————— Red wines ———————

2003 Bischoffinger Steinbuck
Spätburgunder Weißherbst Spätlese
trocken
14.5%, ♀ till 2006   **83**

2003 Bischoffinger Enselberg
Spätburgunder trocken
14%, ♀ till 2006   **83**

2000 Bischoffinger Steinbuck
Spätburgunder Spätlese trocken
14.5%, ♀ till 2006   **86**

2001 Bischoffinger Enselberg
Spätburgunder Auslese trocken
15%, ♀ till 2007   **87**

WINZERGENOSSENSCHAFT ACHKARREN EG

General manager: Waldemar Isele
Winemaker: Anton Kiefer,
Christoph Rombach
79235 Vogtsburg-Achkarren,
Schlossbergstraße 2
Tel. (0 76 62) 9 30 40, Fax 93 04 93
e-mail: info@winzergenossenschaft-achkarren.de
Internet: www.achkarrer-wein.com
Directions: A 5, Bad Krozingen
or Riegel exit, in direction of Breisach
Sales: Florian Graner, Tobias Mattmüller and Marlene Schächtele
Opening hours: Mon.–Fri. 08:00 to 12:30 hours and 13:30 to 17:30 hours
From March to December also
Sat. 09:00 to 13:00 hours
History: Founded 1929
Worth seeing: Kaiserstühler viticultural museum, vinotheque with old wines going back to 1942 vintage, guided vineyard trail

---

Vineyard area: 155 hectares
Number of members: 320
Annual production: 1.7 mill. bottles
Top sites: Achkarrer Schlossberg and Castellberg
Soil types: Decomposed volcanic formation, loess-clay
Grape varieties: 35% Grauburgunder, 33% Spätburgunder, 16% Müller-Thurgau, 9% Weißburgunder, 3% Silvaner, 4% other varieties
Average yield: 73 hl/ha
Best vintages: 2000, 2001, 2002

The co-operative at Achkarren is one of the solid co-operative wineries in Baden. Members are very disciplined in keeping their yields low. Last year we tasted both good 2001 vintage red wines and solid 2002 whites. Unfortunately the current range is not an improvement. We can thus only hope that the investments made to improve careful grape handling – such as the new presses – will bear fruit in the near future.

2003 Achkarrer Castellberg
Grauer Burgunder Kabinett trocken
14.5%, ♀ till 2006   **83**

2003 Achkarrer Schlossberg
Gewürztraminer Spätlese trocken
"Bestes Fass"
14.5%, ♀ till 2006   **83**

2001 Achkarrer Schlossberg
Grauer Burgunder Spätlese
"Bestes Fass" trocken
13.5%, ♀ till 2006   **84**

2002 Achkarrer Schlossberg
Chardonnay trocken "Bestes Fass"
13%, ♀ till 2006   **84**

2000 Achkarrer Schlossberg
Gewürztraminer Auslese "Bestes Fass"
12%, ♀ till 2006   **84**

2003 Achkarrer Schlossberg
Muskateller Beerenauslese
13%, ♀ till 2007   **85**

2000 Achkarrer Schlossberg
Muskateller Eiswein
10.5%, ♀ till 2020   **90**

——— Red wines ———

2002 Achkarrer Schlossberg
"Diavolo" trocken
13%, ♀ till 2006   **84**

2001 Achkarrer Schlossberg
Spätburgunder trocken Barrique
14%, ♀ till 2006   **85**

2001 Achkarrer Schlossberg
Cuvée "Diavolo" trocken
14%, ♀ till 2006   **86**

2000 Achkarrer Schlossberg
Spätburgunder "Bestes Fass" trocken
14.5%, ♀ till 2006   **86**

The wines: **100** Perfect · **95–99** Outstanding · **90–94** Excellent · **85–89** Very good · **80–84** Good · **75–79** Average

AFFENTALER WINZERGENOSSENSCHAFT

General manager: Dr. Ralf Schäfer
Manager: Leo Klär
Winemaker: Leo Klär, Medard Jung
77815 Bühl-Eisental, Betschgräblerplatz
Tel. (0 72 23) 9 89 80, Fax 98 98 30
e-mail: info@affentaler.de
Internet: www.affentaler.de
*Directions: A 5 Frankfurt–Basel, Bühl
exit, direction of Schwarzwaldhochstraße,
B 3 exit, direction of Baden-Baden*
Sales: Dr. Ralf Schäfer, Günther Weber
Opening hours: Mon.–Fri. 08:00 to
18:00 hours, Sat. 09:00 to 13:00 hours
March to Dec. Sun. 10:00 to 14:00 hours

Vineyard area: 228 hectares
Number of members: 950
Annual production: 2.5 mill. bottles
Top sites: Affentaler, Eisentaler
Betschgräbler
Soil types: Soils of decomposed
granite, gneiss and sandstone
Grape varieties: 50% Riesling,
35% Spätburgunder, 12% Müller-
Thurgau, 3% Pinot Blanc, Pinot Gris
and Traminer
Average yield: 75 hl/ha
Best vintages: 1998, 1999, 2001
Member: Deutsches Barrique Forum

Pinot Noir was first vinified in the Cistercian abbey at Affental in the 13th century. In 1908, 24 wine producers amalgamated to form the "Naturweinbauverein Affental" association. The co-operative, which uses its own bottle shape (Buddel) to compete with the Bocksbeutel shape used by other communes in the Ortenau area, has been successful in recent years in marketing its Spätburgunder (Pinot Noir) wines. Following on years of stability, 2001 saw the implementation of a new concept involving significantly reduced yields. The white wines in 2003 were not a success, while the 2003 red wines provide a continuation from the good wines of 2001.

2003 Eisentaler Betschgräbler
Riesling Kabinett trocken
12%, ♀ till 2006 — **82**

2003 Affentaler
Riesling trocken "SLK"
12.5%, ♀ till 2006 — **82**

2002 Weißer Burgunder
trocken "Primus"
12.5%, ♀ till 2006 — **84**

2001 Riesling trocken
12%, ♀ till 2006 — **86**

2001 Grauer Burgunder
Auslese trocken
14%, ♀ till 2006 — **86**

2003 Affentaler
Riesling Auslese "SLK"
10.5%, ♀ till 2006 — **82**

———— Red wines ————

2003 Affentaler
Spätburgunder trocken
15%, ♀ till 2006 — **83**

2003 Affentaler
Spätburgunder Auslese trocken
14.5%, ♀ till 2006 — **84**

2003 Affentaler
Spätburgunder trocken "Primus"
15%, ♀ till 2006 — **84**

2003 Affentaler
Spätburgunder trocken "SLK"
15%, ♀ till 2007 — **85**

2001 Spätburgunder
Auslese trocken "SLK"
14%, ♀ till 2006 — **86**

2001 Spätburgunder
Auslese trocken "SLK B"
14%, ♀ till 2006 — **87**

BADEN
2002

Affentaler
WINZERGENOSSENSCHAFT

SLK

RIESLING
TROCKEN

ALDE GOTT WINZER EG

General manager: Günter Lehmann
Winemaker: Hermann Bähr
77887 Sasbachwalden, Talstraße 2
Tel. (0 78 41) 2 02 90, Fax 20 29 18
e-mail: info@aldegott.de
Internet: www.aldegott.de
Directions: A 5 Frankfurt–Basel, Achern exit, in direction of Sasbachwalden, right at town entrance
Sales: Friedrich Wäldele
Opening hours: Mon.–Fri. 08:00 to 12:00 hours and 13:30 to 18:00 hours
Sat. 08:30 to 12:00 hours
May to Oct.: Sat. to 17:00 hours
and Sun. 13:00 to 17:00 hours
History: Founded 1948
Worth seeing: Barrique and sparkling wine cellar

Vineyard area: 246 hectares
Number of members: 418
Annual production: 2.2 mill. bottles
Top site: Sasbachwaldener
Alde Gott
Soil types: Decomposed granite
Grape varieties: 62% Spätburgunder, 14% Riesling, 12% Müller-Thurgau, 8% Grauburgunder, 4% other varieties
Average yield: 78 hl/ha
Best vintages: 2000, 2001, 2003

According to legend, the name of the vineyard came about through the exclamation of a man at the end of the Thirty Years War, on seeing another survivor: "The old god (alde Gott) is still alive!". The co-operative was founded under this name only 300 years later, in 1948. It enjoys considerable success in competitions, particularly for its red wines, and has in recent years again been producing wines of an attractive quality. Good red wines from three vintages, as well as a juicy Grauburgunder Spätlese (Pinot Gris) characterized by melon fruit underline this development. However, only a small part of the range was presented to us for tasting.

2001 Sasbachwaldener Alde Gott
Grauer Burgunder Kabinett trocken
12.5%, ♀ till 2005   **82**

2003 Weißer Burgunder
Kabinett trocken
14.5%, ♀ till 2006   **83**

2002 Grauer Burgunder
Spätlese trocken
13%, ♀ till 2006   **83**

2001 Sasbachwaldener Alde Gott
Chardonnay trocken
14%, ♀ till 2006   **83**

2003 Grauer Burgunder
Spätlese trocken
14.5%, ♀ till 2006   **85**

2001 Sasbachwaldener Alde Gott
Riesling Kabinett trocken
11.5%, ♀ till 2005   **85**

——— Red wines ———

2003 Spätburgunder trocken
15%, ♀ till 2006   **84**

2002 Spätburgunder
Auslese trocken
14%, ♀ till 2008   **85**

2001 Spätburgunder
Auslese trocken Barrique
14%, ♀ till 2006   **85**

2001 Spätburgunder
Auslese trocken
14.5%, ♀ till 2008   **86**

2003 Spätburgunder
Spätlese trocken
15.5%, ♀ till 2008   **86**

The wines: **100** Perfect · **95–99** Outstanding · **90–94** Excellent · **85–89** Very good · **80–84** Good · **75–79** Average

97

WEINGUT AUFRICHT

Owner: Robert and Manfred Aufricht
Winemaker: Robert Markheiser
88709 Meersburg am Bodensee,
Weinkundeweg 8/Höhenweg 8
Tel. (0 75 32) 24 27 und 61 23, Fax 24 21
e-mail: weingut-aufricht@t-online.de
Internet: www.aufricht.de
Directions: B 31 between Meersburg
and Hagnau
Sales: Aufricht family
Opening hours: Mon.–Sat. 08:00 to
11:30 and 13:30 to 18:30 hours, Sun.
10:00 to 11:30 hours, by appointment
Worth seeing: Idyllic location close to na-
ture reserve on shores of Lake Constance

Vineyard area: 19 hectares
Annual production: 125,000 bottles
Top sites: Meersburger Sänger-
halde and Fohrenberg
Soil types: Sandy clay with limestone
Grape varieties: 39% Spätburgunder
15% Grauburgunder, 10% Weißbur-
gunder, 8% each of Chardonnay and
Auxerrois, 7% each of Riesling and
Müller-Thurgau, 6% other varieties
Average yield: 75 hl/ha
Best vintages: 2000, 2001, 2002

The Aufricht brothers have extended their
vineyard area on the southerly slopes
of Lake Constance almost five-fold in
recent years. This development has gone
hand in hand with a significant improvement in quality. Since the autumn of 2002
the Aufrichts have also had a newly-built
"wine house," which also includes a cellar, in the midst of their vineyards, and
which is appropiate for the size of the
operation, and the quality to which they
aspire. The range presented last year was
very good indeed, the 2001 Spätburgunder (Pinot Noir) "Isabel" was one of the
very best red wines in Germany. The successor from the 2002 vintage is also good,
but currently dominated by oak. Of the
2003 vintage white wines we particularly
liked the fresh Rieslings as well as the
two Grauburgunder-Chardonnay blends.

2003 Meersburger Sängerhalde
Riesling trocken
13.5%, ♀ till 2006   **85**

2003 Meersburger Sängerhalde
"Inspiration Blanc" trocken
13.5%, ♀ till 2007   **86**

2002 Meersburger Sängerhalde
"Inspiration Blanc" trocken
12.5%, ♀ till 2006   **87**

2003 Meersburger Sängerhalde
Grauer Burgunder & Chardonnay trocken
14%, ♀ till 2008   **89**

2003 Meersburger Sängerhalde
Chardonnay & Grauer Burgunder trocken
13.5%, ♀ till 2008   **89**

2003 Meersburger Sängerhalde
Riesling
12%, ♀ till 2007   **86**

———— Red wines ————

2002 Meersburger Sängerhalde
Spätburgunder trocken
13%, ♀ till 2007   **86**

2002 Meersburger Sängerhalde
Spätburgunder trocken "Isabel"
13%, ♀ till 2010   **89**

2001 Meersburger Sängerhalde
Spätburgunder trocken "Isabel"
13%, ♀ till 2010   **92**

BODENSEE

Aufricht

2 0 0 3
MEERSBURGER SÄNGERHALDE
Chardonnay
QUALITÄTSWEIN · A.P. NR. 117/06/04
T R O C K E N

BADEN

GUTSABFÜLLUNG
ROBERT UND MANFRED AUFRICHT
WEINKUNDEWEG · D-88709 MEERSBURG
TELEFON 0 75 32/24 27 · FAX 0 75 32/24 21
www.aufricht.de

0,75 l · 14 % vol

WINZERGENOSSENSCHAFT AUGGEN

Chairman: Martin Schmidt
Manager: Thomas Basler
Winemaker: Andreas Philipp
79424 Auggen, An der B 3
Tel. (0 76 31) 3 68 00, Fax 36 80 80
e-mail: info@auggener-wein.de
Internet: www.auggener-wein.de
Directions: A 5 Frankfurt–Basel,
Neuenburg exit, B 3 in direction of
Lörrach/Basel
Sales: Thomas Basler
Opening hours: Mon.–Fri. 08:00 to
18:30 hours, Sat. 09:00 to 13:00 hours
Sun. 10:00 to 13:00 hours
History: Founded 1922

Vineyard area: 290 hectares
Number of members: 400
Annual production: 2.2 mill. bottles
Top sites: Auggener Letten and Schäf
Soil types: Kaolin, limestone-slate
with clay
Grape varieties: 45% Gutedel,
18% Spätburgunder, 10% each of
Weißburgunder, Müller-Thurgau and
Regent, 7% other varieties
Average yield: 80 hl/ha
Best vintages: 2000, 2002, 2003

The co-operative, which has 400 members cultivating 290 hectares of vineyard, could look to a solid base when it celebrated its 80th anniversary in 2002. The co-operative collected the largest number of gold medals of any producer in Baden – though it must be said these are awarded generously. They also took two high places in the Gutedel Cup awards, and were able to improve on this in 2003 when the 2002 Gutedel Qualitätswein came first in its category. The 2003 Gutedel wines are once again juicy quaffing wines. As in the previous year, the Regent, which sees judicious oak treatment, is an attractive wine, while the highlight of the range is a Gutedel Trockenbeerenauslese from the Auggener Letten site.

2003 Auggener Schäf
Gutedel Kabinett trocken
12%, ♀ till 2006 — **81**

2003 Auggener Schäf
Gutedel Spätlese trocken
12%, ♀ till 2006 — **82**

2003 Auggener Schäf
Weißer Burgunder Spätlese trocken
14.5%, ♀ till 2006 — **83**

2002 Auggener Schäf
Chardonnay Auslese trocken
14.5%, ♀ till 2006 — **83**

2003 Auggener Schäf
Chardonnay Auslese trocken
15.5%, ♀ till 2006 — **83**

2003 Auggener Schäf
Grauer Burgunder Auslese trocken
16%, ♀ till 2006 — **84**

2003 Auggener Letten
Gutedel Trockenbeerenauslese
9%, ♀ till 2008 — **87**

2001 Auggener Schäf
Gutedel Eiswein
10%, ♀ till 2007 — **87**

——— Red wines ———

2002 Auggener Schäf
Regent trocken
14%, ♀ till 2007 — **85**

2001 Auggener Schäf
Regent trocken
13.5%, ♀ till 2006 — **86**

The wines: **100** Perfect · **95–99** Outstanding · **90–94** Excellent · **85–89** Very good · **80–84** Good · **75–79** Average

WEINGUT L. BASTIAN

Owner and manager:
Andreas Neymeyer
Winemaker: Bernd Hildwein and
Andreas Neymeyer
79346 Endingen am Kaiserstuhl,
Königschaffhauser Straße 8
Tel. (0 76 42) 60 09, Fax 38 62
e-mail: service@weingut-bastian.de
Internet: www.weingut-bastian.de
Directions: A 5 Karlsruhe–Basel, Riegel
exit, in Endingen on the main road just
behind the city gate
Sales: Bruno Müller
Opening hours: Mon.–Fri. 08:00 to
12:00 and 14:00 to 17:00, Sat. 08:00 to
12:00 hours, and by appointment
Worth seeing: Burkheim castle ruins
with smallest single vineyard site at the
Kaiserstuhl, historic vaulted barrel cellar
Worth a visit: "Lyrical Summer" in
palace ballroom July/August

Vineyard area: 10 hectares
Contracted growers: 32 hectares
Annual production: 420,000 bottles
Top sites: Burkheimer Schlossberg
(monopole), Endinger Engelsberg
Soil types: Loess, decomposed vol-
canic formation
Grape varieties: 40% Spätburgunder,
15% each of Müller-Thurgau and
Grauburgunder, 10% Riesling,
5% each of Chardonnay and Weiß-
burgunder, 10% other varieties
Average yield: 65 hl/ha
Best vintages: 1999, 2000, 2001

Leopold Bastian was a pioneer in viticulture. In the 19th century he founded a
winery, and by 1900 was maturing a million liters. The Neymeyer family came into
the business by marriage. Apart from ten
hectares of own vineyards, the production
of 180 contract growers is vinified into
some quite attractive wines. The wines produced in their own vineyards, presented
here, are marketed under the "SL" label.
Of the current range, the wines we liked
best were the 2003 Gewürztraminer,
which is attractively fruity, and the 2002
Spätburgunder matured in barrique.

2003 Endinger Engelsberg
Weißer Burgunder trocken
14%, ♀ till 2006 — 82

2003 Endinger Engelsberg
Chardonnay trocken
13.5%, ♀ till 2006 — 83

2003 Burkheimer Schlossberg
Grauer Burgunder trocken
13.5%, ♀ till 2006 — 83

2003 Endinger Tannacker
Gewürztraminer
13.5%, ♀ till 2006 — 85

2001 Endinger Tannacker
Gewürztraminer Eiswein
11%, ♀ till 2007 — 87

——— Red wines ———

2001 Endinger Engelsberg
Spätburgunder trocken Barrique
13%, ♀ till 2006 — 84

2002 Endinger Engelsberg
Spätburgunder trocken Barrique
13.5%, ♀ till 2007 — 86

The estates: ✟✟✟✟✟ World's finest · ✟✟✟✟ Germany's best · ✟✟✟ Very good · ✟✟ Good · ✟ Reliable

WEINGUT BERCHER

Owner: Eckhardt and Rainer Bercher
Winemaker: Werner Rehbein
79235 Vogtsburg-Burkheim,
Mittelstadt 13
Tel. (0 76 62) 9 07 60, **Fax** 82 79
e-mail: info@weingutbercher.de
Internet: www.weingutbercher.de
Directions: A 5 Karlsruhe–Basel,
Riegel or Bad Krozingen exit, in direc-
tion of Breisach
Sales: Bercher families
Opening hours: Mon.–Sat. 09:00 to
11:30 hours and 13:30 to 17:00 hours
History: Winemaking in 9th generation
Worth seeing: Old vaulted barrel cellar

Vineyard area: 24 hectares
Annual production: 170,000 bottles
Top sites: Burkheimer Feuerberg
and Schlossgarten, Sasbacher
Limburg, Jechtinger Eichert
Soil types: Decomposed volcanic
formation and loess
Grape varieties: 42% Spätburgunder,
20% Grauburgunder, 14% Weißbur-
gunder, 10% Riesling, 7% Chardonnay,
2% Müller-Thurgau, 5% other varieties
Average yield: 54 hl/ha
Best vintages: 1998, 1999, 2000
Member: VDP,
Deutsches Barrique Forum

This beautifully located winery in the center of the town of Burkheim on the western escarpment of the Kaiserstuhl mountain can trace its history back to the 15th century. For the past forty years the focus has been on growing grapes and fruit (for the distillery). Throughout the Nineties, the winery maintained its place among the best producers in Baden, based on its reliability and homogeneous good quality from basic wine in liter bottles right up to the most noble products. However, since 2001 we have observed a marked decline in quality. The wines are correctly made, but there are no exciting highlights, even among the top wines. This is a good three-bunch standard.

2003 Sasbacher Limburg
Weißer Burgunder Spätlese trocken
14.5%, ♀ till 2007 — **86**

2003 Burkheimer Feuerberg
Grauer Burgunder Spätlese trocken
14%, ♀ till 2007 — **86**

2003 Burkheimer Feuerberg
Weißer Burgunder Spätlese trocken
"Großes Gewächs"
15%, ♀ till 2006 — **86**

2003 Burkheimer Feuerberg
Grauer Burgunder Spätlese trocken
"Großes Gewächs"
15%, ♀ till 2007 — **87**

2002 Burkheimer Feuerberg
Weißer Burgunder Spätlese trocken
"Großes Gewächs"
13%, ♀ till 2008 — **89**

2003 Burkheimer Schlossgarten
Muskateller Spätlese
13%, ♀ till 2007 — **88**

——— Red wines ———

2002 Jechtinger Eichert
Spätburgunder Spätlese trocken
13%, ♀ till 2006 — **83**

2002 Burkheimer Feuerberg
Spätburgunder Spätlese trocken
"Großes Gewächs"
13%, ♀ till 2008 — **87**

2001 Burkheimer Feuerberg
Spätburgunder Spätlese trocken
"Großes Gewächs"
13%, ♀ till 2010 — **90**

The wines: **100** Perfect · **95–99** Outstanding · **90–94** Excellent · **85–89** Very good · **80–84** Good · **75–79** Average

101

WEINGUT
BERCHER-SCHMIDT

**Owner: Beate Wiedemann-Schmidt
and Franz Wilhelm Schmidt
Winemaker: Franz Wilhelm Schmidt
79235 Oberrotweil, Herrenstraße 28
Tel. (0 76 62) 3 72, Fax 63 33
e-mail: weingut@bercher-schmidt.de
Internet:
www.weingut-bercher-schmidt.de**
*Directions: A 5 Karlsruhe–Basel,
Riegel exit, in direction of Vogtsburg*
Sales: Beate Wiedemann-Schmidt
and Annemarie Wiedemann
Opening hours: Mon.–Fri. 09:00 to 18:00
hours, Sat. and Sun. by appointment
Worth seeing: Open studio in old court-
yard on last weekend in June

Vineyard area: 10 hectares
Annual production: 60,000 bottles
Top sites: Oberrotweiler Henken-
berg and Käsleberg, Bischoffinger
Enselberg, Steinbuck and Rosen-
kranz, Burkheimer Feuerberg
Soil types: Decomposed volcanic
formation, loess and clay
Grape varieties: 35% Grauburgunder,
33% Spätburgunder, 9% Weißbur-
gunder, 8% Müller-Thurgau, 5% Ries-
ling, 4% Silvaner, 6% other varieties
Average yield: 50 hl/ha
Best vintages: 2000, 2001, 2003

This family-owned winery in Oberrotweil is a strong defender of the terroir
concept. Parcels of the old core sections
of the best vineyard sites of the Kaiserstuhl provide the base for producing
wines full of character. Whereas the white
wines are vinified in stainless steel tanks,
the red wines are vinified in oak, including new barriques, resulting in wines
with considerable potential. The 2001
Spätburgunder (Pinot Noir), which was
still very closed a year ago, impressed us
now with its deep fruit, complexity and
long finish. The 2003 white wines are all
very well made, with some juicy Spätlese
wines at the top of the range.

2003 Oberrotweiler Käsleberg
Weißer Burgunder Kabinett trocken
13%, ♀ till 2006 — **83**

2003 Bischoffinger Steinbuck
Silvaner Spätlese trocken
13%, ♀ till 2006 — **85**

2003 Oberrotweiler Käsleberg
Weißer Burgunder Spätlese trocken ***
13%, ♀ till 2007 — **86**

2003 Bischoffinger Steinbuck
Grauer Burgunder Spätlese trocken ***
14.5%, ♀ till 2008 — **86**

2003 Bischoffinger Rosenkranz
Weißer Burgunder Spätlese trocken ***
13.5%, ♀ till 2008 — **87**

—— Red wines ——

2003 Oberrotweiler Käsleberg
Spätburgunder Spätlese trocken ***
13.5%, ♀ till 2007 — **83**

2002 Oberrotweiler Henkenberg
Spätburgunder Spätlese trocken ***
13%, ♀ till 2008 — **85**

2003 Bischoffinger Enselberg
Spätburgunder Auslese trocken ***
14%, ♀ till 2008 — **87**

2001 Oberrotweiler Henkenberg
Spätburgunder Spätlese trocken ***
13%, ♀ till 2011 — **90**

WEINGUT
Bercher - Schmidt
D-79235 Oberrotweil a.K.
☆☆☆
BADEN
2000er
*Bischoffinger Steinbuck
Grauburgunder*
Spätlese · trocken
Qualitätswein mit Prädikat

13%vol   A.P.Nr. 304-07-01 · Gutsabfüllung   0,75 L

WEINGUT BLANKENHORN

Owner: Rosemarie Blankenhorn
Manager: Fritz Deutschmann
79418 Schliengen, Baslerstraße 2
Tel. (0 76 35) 8 20 00, Fax 82 00 20
e-mail:
weingut-blankenhorn@t-online.de
Internet: www.gutedel.de
Directions: A 5 Frankfurt–Basel, Müll-
heim exit, 8 kilometers to Schliengen
Sales: Rosemarie Blankenhorn
Opening hours: Mon.–Fri. 08:00 to
12:00 and 14:00 to 18:00, Sat. 09:00 to
13:00 hours, and by appointment
Restaurant/Wine bar: 11:00 to 15:00
and 17:00 to 24:00 hours, closed Mon.
Managers Thomas and Renate Vierk
Tel. (0 76 35) 82 25 90
History: Founded by Johann Blanken-
horn in 1847
Worth seeing: Former Thurn &
Taxis postal station

Vineyard area: 20 hectares
Annual production: 170,000 bottles
Top sites: Schliengener
Sonnenstück, Auggener Schäf
Soil types: Loess-clay and loam
with limestone and marl
Grape varieties: 30% Gutedel,
25% Spätburgunder, 10% each of
Grau- and Weißburgunder,
25% other varieties
Average yield: 65 hl/ha
Best vintages: 1999, 2001, 2003
Member: VDP

The Blankenhorn family has been one of
the best known producers in the Markgräfler Land area for the past 150 years.
The enthusiastic owner Rosemarie Blankenhorn and manager Fritz Deutschmann
keep the operation in good shape. Last
year, we tasted acceptable white wines
here, and some very good 2001 vintage
red wines. The current range is very solid,
with a very good Spätburgunder from old
vines at the top of the range. On the other
hand, the Merlot and Cabernet are only
powerful, and lack elegance.

2003 Schliengener Sonnenstück
Weißer Burgunder Kabinett trocken
14%, ♀ till 2006 — **84**

2002 Schliengener Sonnenstück
Chardonnay Spätlese trocken
13%, ♀ till 2006 — **84**

2003 Schliengener Sonnenstück
Grauer Burgunder Auslese trocken
15%, ♀ till 2006 — **84**

2002 Schliengener Sonnenstück
Grauer Burgunder Kabinett trocken
12%, ♀ till 2006 — **85**

——— Red wines ———

2002 Schliengener Sonnenstück
Merlot trocken
13%, ♀ till 2006 — **83**

2002 Schliengener Sonnenstück
Cabernet Sauvignon trocken
13.5%, ♀ till 2007 — **85**

2001 Schliengener Sonnenstück
Spätburgunder trocken
13.5%, ♀ till 2006 — **86**

2002 Schliengener Sonnenstück
Spätburgunder "Alte Reben" trocken
13.5%, ♀ till 2008 — **87**

The wines: **100** Perfect · **95–99** Outstanding · **90–94** Excellent · **85–89** Very good · **80–84** Good · **75–79** Average

WINZERGENOSSENSCHAFT BRITZINGEN

General manager: Achim Frey
Winemaker: Hermann Zenzen, Bruno Kiefer
79379 Müllheim-Britzingen, Markgräfler Straße 25–29
Tel. (0 76 31) 1 77 10, **Fax** 40 13
e-mail: info@britzinger-wein.de
Internet: www.britzinger-wein.de
Directions: A 5, Bad Krozingen exit, Müllheim or Heitersheim
Sales: Florian Mayer
Opening hours: Mon.–Fri. 09:00 to 12:30 hours and 14:00 to 18:00 hours
Sat. 09:00 to 12:30 hours
History: Founded 1950
Worth seeing: Terrace at "Muggardter Berg"
Worth a visit: May–Oct., Thu. 15:00 hours, tour in vineyards, with lovely view to Alsace, culinary wine tastings

---

Vineyard area: 190 hectares
Number of members: 209
Annual production: 1.7 mill. bottles
Top sites: Britzinger Sonnhole and Rosenberg, Badenweiler Römerberg
Soil types: Loess and clay on a limestone-rich sub-soil
Grape varieties: 32% Gutedel, 29% Spätburgunder, 12% Weißburgunder, 8% Ruländer, 6% Müller-Thurgau, 5% Nobling, 8% other varieties
Average yield: 80 hl/ha
Best vintages: 1998, 1999, 2001

The Britzingen co-operative first attracted attention in the Eighties with their dry Selection wines. After some variable vintages, the potential was again fulfilled with the 2001 vintage. However, this level could not quite be maintained in 2002. The basic dry wines were poor, although the dry and botrytized Auslese wines were much better. The 2003 Gutedel as well as some of the botrytized Auslese wines are very good indeed. However, the red as well as the rosé and sparkling wines are decidedly not up to standard.

2003 Britzinger Rosenberg
Gutedel Kabinett trocken
11.5%, ♀ till 2006 — **82**

2003 Britzinger Sonnhole
Gutedel Spätlese trocken
12.5%, ♀ till 2006 — **83**

2003 Britzinger Sonnhole
Grauer Burgunder Auslese trocken
15.5%, ♀ till 2006 — **85**

2002 Britzinger Sonnhole
Grauer Burgunder Auslese trocken
14.5%, ♀ till 2006 — **85**

2001 Britzinger Rosenberg
Gutedel Auslese trocken
14%, ♀ till 2006 — **86**

2003 Britzinger Sonnhole
Weißer Burgunder Auslese
11.5%, ♀ till 2007 — **86**

2003 Badenweiler Römerberg
Gewürztraminer Auslese
10.5%, ♀ till 2007 — **86**

2003 Britzinger Rosenberg
Weißer Burgunder Trockenbeerenauslese
8.5%, ♀ till 2009 — **88**

2003 Britzinger Sonnhole
Ruländer Trockenbeerenauslese
9.5%, ♀ till 2009 — **89**

2002 Badenweiler Römerberg
Chardonnay Trockenbeerenauslese
10%, ♀ till 2010 — **91**

——————— Red wines ———————

2003 Britzinger Rosenberg
Spätburgunder Kabinett trocken
13%, ♀ till 2006 — **81**

2002 Britzinger Sonnhole
Spätburgunder trocken
13%, ♀ till 2006 — **82**

Baden

HOFGUT CONSEQUENCE

**Owner: Manfred and
Eva Maria Schmidt
79235 Bischoffingen, Talstraße 15
Tel. (0 76 62) 9 40 87, Fax 9 40 86
e-mail: info@hofgut-consequence.de
Internet: www.hofgut-consequence.de**
*Directions: A 5 Frankfurt–Basel,
Riegel exit, in direction of Breisach*
Sales: Mon.–Sat. 14:00 to 18:00 hours
Sat. 09:00 to 11:00 hours
and by appointment
June to August Fri. and Sat. only

Vineyard area: 7.5 hectares
Annual production: 20,000 bottles
Top sites: No vineyard sites stated on labels
Soil types: Decomposed volcanic formation and loess terraces
Grape varieties: 30% Spätburgunder, 21% Grauburgunder, 12% each of Weißburgunder and Müller-Thurgau, 7% Cabernet and Merlot, 18% fungus-resistant varieties
Average yield: 40 hl/ha
Best vintages: 1999, 2000, 2002
Member: EcoVin

Manfred and Eva Maria Schmidt were members of the co-operative in Bischoffingen until 1994. Then they dared to venture into an independent operation, at the same time changing over to organic viticultural practices. Since then they have not stated vineyard names on their labels, nor do they state predicate quality levels for their dry wines. The extremely low yields must certainly be beneficial for the quality of the wines. Quite contrary to the general trend, the 2002 vintage here was rather good. Only a small range of 2003 wines was presented: a somewhat weak sparkling wine, plus four wines of quite a good standard. It appears that no red wines of either the 2001 or 2002 vintages were bottled. We certainly expect to see a little more next year.

2002 Grauer Burgunder trocken
12.5%, ♀ till 2005 — 81

2003 Weißer Burgunder trocken
13%, ♀ till 2006 — 83

2003 Grauer Burgunder trocken
14%, ♀ till 2006 — 83

2002 Weißer Burgunder trocken
12.5%, ♀ till 2006 — 83

2000 Grauer Burgunder trocken
14%, ♀ till 2005 — 84

2000 Weißer Burgunder trocken
12.5%, ♀ till 2005 — 84

2001 Grauer Burgunder
trocken Barrique
14%, ♀ till 2006 — 84

2003 Weißer Burgunder
trocken ***
13.5%, ♀ till 2007 — 85

2000 Gewürztraminer trocken
12.5%, ♀ till 2005 — 85

2003 Müller-Thurgau & Kerner
12%, ♀ till 2006 — 82

2001 Grauer Burgunder Auslese
13%, ♀ till 2006 — 86

———— Red wines ————

2002 "Création Consequence"
Rosé trocken
12%, ♀ till 2005 — 81

2002 Spätburgunder Weißherbst
trocken
11.5%, ♀ till 2005 — 84

2000 Spätburgunder Weißherbst
trocken
12%, ♀ till 2005 — 85

2002 Spätburgunder Weißherbst
Auslese
12%, ♀ till 2006 — 85

WEISSER BURGUNDER
2003
***

The wines: **100** Perfect · **95–99** Outstanding · **90–94** Excellent · **85–89** Very good · **80–84** Good · **75–79** Average

WEINGUT
HERMANN DÖRFLINGER

Owner: Hermann Dörflinger
Manager and winemaker:
Hermann Dörflinger
79379 Müllheim, Mühlenstraße 7
Tel. (0 76 31) 22 07, Fax 41 95
e-mail: mail@weingut-doerflinger.de
Directions: A 5 Frankfurt–Basel,
Müllheim exit
Sales: Hermann and Doris Dörflinger
Opening hours: Mon.–Fri. 08:00 to
12:00 and 13:30 to 18:00 hours
Sat. 09:00 to 16:00 hours
Worth seeing: Attractive barrel cellar,
courtyard with Mediterranean flair

Vineyard area: 20 hectares
Annual production: 140,000 bottles
Top sites: Müllheimer Reggenhag,
Pfaffenstück and Sonnhalde,
Badenweiler Römerberg
Soil types: Limestone-rich loess,
Brown Jurassic and sandy clay
Grape varieties: 48% Gutedel, 15% Spät-
burgunder, 11% Weißburgunder, 10%
Grauburgunder, 16% other varieties
Average yield: 65 hl/ha
Best vintages: 2001, 2002, 2003

This family winery was founded in 1900.
Hermann Dörflinger has always been un-
compromising in allowing his wines to
ferment completely dry. This philosophy
means that one accepts vintage variances,
and does not try to hide them. Nevertheless – or perhaps because of this attitude –
he mastered the problems of the difficult
2002 vintage rather well. The best wine
was an elegant Grauburgunder (Pinot
Gris) Spätlese characterized by melon
fruit. The 2003 vintage has produced an
attractive Gutedel Kabinett as well as
good Silvaner, Weißburgunder (Pinot
Blanc), Grauburgunder Spätlese wines.
We also liked the red wines, the barrel
sample of Spätburgunder (Pinot Noir)
Auslese holds great promise. The winery
is a reliable supplier of juicy, no-frills
wines typical of their variety.

2003 Müllheimer Reggenhag
Gutedel Kabinett trocken
12%, ♀ till 2006   **83**

2003 Badenweiler Römerberg
Weißer Burgunder Kabinett trocken
13%, ♀ till 2006   **83**

2003 Müllheimer Pfaffenstück
Silvaner Spätlese trocken
13%, ♀ till 2006   **86**

2002 Badenweiler Römerberg
Weißer Burgunder Spätlese trocken
13%, ♀ till 2006   **86**

2003 Badenweiler Römerberg
Weißer Burgunder Spätlese trocken
13.5%, ♀ till 2007   **88**

2003 Müllheimer Sonnhalde
Grauer Burgunder Spätlese trocken
Barrique
14.5%, ♀ till 2007   **88**

2002 Müllheimer Sonnhalde
Grauer Burgunder Spätlese trocken
13.5%, ♀ till 2006   **89**

———— Red wines ————

2001 Badenweiler Römerberg
Merlot trocken
12.5%, ♀ till 2006   **85**

2003 Müllheimer Pfaffenstück
Spätburgunder Spätlese trocken
14.5%, ♀ till 2007   **85**

2001 Badenweiler Römerberg
Spätburgunder Spätlese trocken
13%, ♀ till 2006   **86**

2003 Müllheimer Sonnhalde
Spätburgunder Spätlese trocken
14.5%, ♀ till 2009   **87**

BADEN   Markgräflerland

DÖRFLINGER
2oo1er
CHARDONNAY
MÜLLHEIMER REGGENHAG
KABINETT TROCKEN
Gutsabfüllung · Qualitätswein mit Prädikat · 13,0 % vol. · RZ LO g/l · 0,75 ltr
Weingut Hermann Dörflinger D-79379 Müllheim/Baden/Markgräflerland

APNr 674 08 04

The estates: ✚✚✚✚✚ World's finest · ✚✚✚✚ Germany's best · ✚✚✚ Very good · ✚✚ Good · ✚ Reliable

WEINGUT DUIJN

Owner: Jacob Duijn
77815 Bühl-Kappelwindeck,
Klotzbergstraße 1a
Tel. (0 72 23) 2 14 97, Fax 8 37 73
e-mail: info@weingut-duijn.com
Internet: www.weingut-duijn.com
Directions: A 5 Frankfurt–Basel,
Bühl exit
Sales: Martina Duijn
by appointment
Worth seeing: Vaulted cellar dating
to 1638

Vineyard area: 8 hectares
Annual production: 30,000 bottles
Top sites: Bühlertaler
Engelsfelsen and Sternenberg,
Laufer Gut Alsenhof
Soil types: Decomposed granite
Grape varieties: 100% Spätburgunder
Average yield: 35 hl/ha
Best vintages: 2000, 2001, 2002

Jacob Duijn has realized his dream in the Bühlertal near Baden-Baden. He was sommelier at Eckart Witzigmann's restaurant in Munich, and then moved to the noble Bühler Höhe restaurant. After this, the Dutch-born wine-lover moved into wine sales and distribution. He bought his first vineyard in 1994, an extremely steep site with a grade of up to 75 percent. When he bought a vaulted cellar dating back to 1638, the foundation was laid by this ambitious self-taught man to produce high-quality Pinot Noir wines. He admits readily that his determination alone would not have been enough. It is fortunate that his best friend is also one of the best red wine producers in Germany. Bernhard Huber from Malterdingen has given him many useful hints, and in the initial phases helped to iron out some weak points. In the meantime, the vineyard area has been increased to eight hectares. A new cellar was completed in August 2001, giving Duijn adequate capacity for the maturation of his wines. The use of 100 percent new barriques is standard here, and wines are kept in barrel for more than eighteen months. The 2001 vintage wines presented last year were very good, though it must be said that the difference between the top selection "SD" and the regular Spätburgunder (Pinot Noir) is not all that great. The massive use of oak tended to hide some of the finesse of the wine. Considering the problems of the vintage, the 2002 wines presented now are more than just good, showing a clarity of fruit and elegantly firm structure rarely found in German Pinot Noir. In addition, a new basic Spätburgunder wine of excellent quality, called "Gut Alsenhof," was introduced this year. Our compliments!

———— Red wines ————

2002 Spätburgunder
trocken "Gut Alsenhof"
13%, ♀ till 2007   **86**

2000 Spätburgunder trocken
13.5%, ♀ till 2008   **87**

2001 Spätburgunder trocken
13%, ♀ till 2007   **89**

2002 Spätburgunder
trocken "Jannin"
13.5%, ♀ till 2009   **89**

2001 Spätburgunder trocken "SD"
13.5%, ♀ till 2009   **90**

2000 Spätburgunder trocken "SD"
13.5%, ♀ till 2012   **91**

2002 Spätburgunder trocken "SD"
13.5%, ♀ till 2012   **92**

DUIJN

0,75 L ALC. 13% VOL.
QUALITÄTSWEIN

2001
SPÄTBURGUNDER
TROCKEN
BADEN

GUTSABFÜLLUNG
WEINGUT: DUIJN · D-77815 BÜHL BADEN · A.P.NR. 3273 01 03

DURBACHER WINZERGENOSSENSCHAFT

Director: Konrad Geppert
Winemaker: Arndt Köbelin
77770 Durbach, Nachtweide 2
Tel. (07 81) 9 36 60, Fax 3 65 47
e-mail: WG@durbacher.de
Internet: www.durbacher.de
Directions: A 5 Frankfurt–Basel, Appenweier or Offenburg-Süd exit
Sales: Frank Huber, Ulrich Litterst
Opening hours: Mon.–Fri. 08:00 to 12:00 and 13:30 to 18:00 hours Sat. and Sun. 09:00 to 12:30 hours Cellar tours and wine tastings by appointment with Ms. Benz, Tel. 93 66 43
History: Founded 1928
Worth seeing: Barrel cellar, vintner's hall for 200 persons, rustic sales room

---

Vineyard area: 340 hectares
Number of members: 300
Annual production: 3 mill. bottles
Top sites: Durbacher Ölberg, Plauelrain, Kochberg and Steinberg (monopole)
Soil types: Decomposed granite, gneiss
Grape varieties: 42% Spätburgunder, 27% Riesling, 15% Müller-Thurgau, 6% each of Clevner (Traminer) and Grauburgunder, 4% other varieties
Average yield: 80 hl/ha
Best vintages: 2001, 2002, 2003

Of the 450 hectares of steep and rocky vineyards around Durbach, 340 hectares are operated by the co-operative. The benefits of the Durbach sites are particularly noticeable in the Riesling wines. After some variable vintages, the co-operative has again produced very attractive ranges in the past two years. The higher rating implemented last year has been confirmed by a good range of Rieslings, dry white Pinots and some elegant botrytis wines. Only the 2003 Spätburgunder Auslese is disappointing. It is particularly pleasing to note that both basic and top wines are of commendable quality.

2003 Durbacher Steinberg
Riesling Spätlese trocken
13%, ♀ till 2006   83

2003 Durbacher Plauelrain
Riesling Spätlese trocken
13%, ♀ till 2006   84

2003 Durbacher Steinberg
Weißer Burgunder Spätlese trocken
14%, ♀ till 2007   85

2001 Durbacher Plauelrain
Riesling Spätlese trocken
12%, ♀ till 2006   86

2003 Durbacher Steinberg
Scheurebe Auslese
10.5%, ♀ till 2009   88

2003 Durbacher Kochberg
Müller-Thurgau Auslese
11.5%, ♀ till 2009   88

2002 Durbacher Steinberg
Muskateller Auslese
10.5%, ♀ till 2007   89

2003 Durbacher Steinberg
Riesling Eiswein
7.5%, ♀ till 2013   91

2002 Durbacher Plauelrain
Riesling Eiswein
8%, ♀ till 2015   91

2002 Durbacher Plauelrain
Scheurebe Trockenbeerenauslese
8%, ♀ till 2017   94

The estates: ♦♦♦♦♦ World's finest · ♦♦♦♦ Germany's best · ♦♦♦ Very good · ♦♦ Good · ♦ Reliable

EHRENSTETTER WINZERKELLER EG

General manager: Dr. Dominik Müller
Winemaker: Norbert Faller
79238 Ehrenstetten, Kirchbergstraße 9
Tel. (0 76 33) 9 50 90, Fax 5 08 53
e-mail:
info@ehrenstetter-winzerkeller.de
Internet:
www.ehrenstetter-winzerkeller.de
Directions: A 5 Frankfurt–Basel, Bad Krozingen exit, in direction of Staufen, then in direction of Ehrenkirchen, in suburb of Ehrenstetten
Sales: Mon.–Fri. 08:00 to 18:00 hours
Sat. 09:00 to 12:00 hours
History: Founded 1952
Worth seeing: Large barrel cellar, Oelberg chapel with view to Markgräflerland, Oelberg is a nature reserve

---

Vineyard area: 143 hectares
Number of members: 300
Annual production: 1.2 mill. bottles
Top sites: Ehrenstetter Oelberg and Bollschweiler Steinberg
Soil types: Loess, clay and limestone-rich primordial rock
Grape varieties: 30% Gutedel, 28% Spätburgunder, 18% Müller-Thurgau, 14% Weiß- and Grauburgunder, 10% other varieties
Average yield: 82 hl/ha
Best vintages: 1999, 2000, 2003

Ehrenstetten is an old wine-producing community in the Markgräflerland area. The vineyards form a cauldron-shaped valley, with a specific micro-climate. The co-operative, which celebrated its 50th anniversary in 2002, covers 97 percent of the vineyard area. The ambitious managers of the Ehrenstetten co-operative have decided to focus more on red wines in the coming years – a wise decision, as evidenced by last year's range. In the current range, we liked both the white and the red wines. The juicy 2003 Auxerrois Spätlese as well as the "Camenot" red blend are both worthy of special mention.

2003 Ehrenstetter Oelberg
Gutedel trocken "Chasslie"
12.5%, ♀ till 2006   **83**

2001 Ehrenstetter Oelberg
Chardonnay "SL" trocken
13.5%, ♀ till 2005   **83**

2001 Ehrenstetter Oelberg
Gutedel Kabinett "SL" trocken
12%, ♀ till 2005   **84**

2003 Ehrenstetter Oelberg
Auxerrois Spätlese trocken
13%, ♀ till 2006   **85**

2001 Ehrenstetter Oelberg
Grauer Burgunder Spätlese "SL" trocken
14%, ♀ till 2006   **85**

2003 Ehrenstetter
Muskateller Spätlese halbtrocken
12.5%, ♀ till 2006   **84**

——— Red wines ———

2002 Ehrenstetter Oelberg
Pinot Noir trocken
13.5%, ♀ till 2006   **83**

2002 Ehrenstetter Oelberg
Spätburgunder Spätlese trocken
13.5%, ♀ till 2006   **84**

2002 Ehrenstetter Oelberg
trocken "Camenot"
13.5%, ♀ till 2008   **86**

2001 Ehrenstetter Oelberg
trocken "Camenot"
13.5%, ♀ till 2006   **86**

The wines: **100** Perfect · **95–99** Outstanding · **90–94** Excellent · **85–89** Very good · **80–84** Good · **75–79** Average

109

WEINGUT HERBERT DANIEL ENGIST

Owner: Herbert Daniel Engist
79235 Vogtsburg-Achkarren,
Winzerweg 6
Tel. (0 76 62) 3 73, Fax 91 22 03
e-mail:
weingut-herbert-engist@t-online.de
*Directions: A 5 Frankfurt–Basel,
Bad Krozingen or Riegel exit, in direction of Breisach*
Sales: Herbert and Simone Engist
by appointment
Worth a visit: Vineyard tours, distillery, winery festival in May

---

Vineyard area: 3 hectares
Annual production: 15,000 bottles
Top site: Achkarrer Schlossberg
Soil types: Decomposed volcanic formation, loess
Grape varieties: 25% Spätburgunder, 20% Grauburgunder, 10% each of Gutedel and Weißburgunder, 35% other varieties
Average yield: 40 hl/ha
Best vintage: 2003

We were very pleasantly surprised by this small estate in Achkarren. The success is hard-earned – Herbert Engist has planted his vines on extremely narrow terraces, and keeps the yields very low. This ensures that the sun reaches the bunches of grapes easily, and good ventilation is also guaranteed. In the cellar, the accent is on quick processing and minimum intervention, fermentation is temperature-controlled. All wines have good body, clear fruit and are fresh. A few wines deserve a special mention: the powerful Grauburgunder (Pinot Gris) Auslese, and particularly the classy, elegant and typical Muskateller Spätlese. The wines can be tasted in the "Probierstüble" tasting room, and if you make reservations you can also order food, which is of the hearty regional variety, such as "Gschwellti mit Bibbeleskäs." Don't worry about a translation, order it and enjoy.

2003 Achkarrer Schlossberg
Weißer Burgunder Spätlese trocken
14%, ♀ till 2006 **83**

2003 Achkarrer Schlossberg
Chardonnay Spätlese trocken
15%, ♀ till 2006 **84**

2003 Achkarrer Schlossberg
Grauer Burgunder Auslese trocken
15.5%, ♀ till 2007 **86**

2003 Achkarrer Schlossberg
Muskateller Spätlese trocken
13.5%, ♀ till 2007 **88**

2003 Achkarrer Schlossberg
Müller-Thurgau Spätlese
13%, ♀ till 2006 **84**

——— Red wine ———

2003 Achkarrer Schlossberg
Spätburgunder Spätlese trocken
13.5%, ♀ till 2006 **83**

WEINGUT HERBERT DANIEL ENGIST

0,75 l 13,5% vol

2003
Baden
Achkarrer
Schlossberg
Muskateller
Spätlese trocken

QUALITÄTSWEIN MIT PRÄDIKAT · A.P.NR. 941/05/04 · ERZEUGERABFÜLLUNG
WEINGUT HERBERT DANIEL ENGIST · WINZERWEG 6 · D-79235 VOGTSBURG-ACHKARREN
TELEFON 07662/373

The estates: ♦♦♦♦♦ World's finest · ♦♦♦♦ Germany's best · ♦♦♦ Very good · ♦♦ Good · ♦ Reliable

Baden

WEINGUT FISCHER

Owner and manager:
Silvia and Joachim Heger
Manager and sales: Franz Herbster
Administrator and winemaker:
Manfred Zimmermann
79331 Nimburg-Bottingen,
Auf der Ziegelbreite 8
Tel. (0 76 63) 17 47, Fax 5 01 75
e-mail: info@weingut-fischer-baden.de
Internet: www.weingut-fischer-baden.de
Directions: A 5 Frankfurt–Basel, Teningen/Nimburg exit
Opening hours: Mon.–Fri. 13:00 to 17:00 hours or by appointment

> Vineyard area: 17.5 hectares
> Annual production: 100,000 bottles
> Top site: Nimburg-Bottinger Steingrube
> Soil types: Brown Jurassic limestone, shell limestone, loess top layer
> Grape varieties: 38% Spätburgunder, 22% Grauburgunder, 16% Weißburgunder, 5% Chardonnay, 4% Riesling, 2% Müller-Thurgau, 13% other varieties
> Average yield: 55 hl/ha
> Best vintages: 2000, 2001, 2003

This old and renowned winery was acquired by Silvia and Joachim Heger in the mid-Nineties. The quality of wines is based mainly on the Steingrube site on the south-western rim of the Nimberg, a small volcanic hill about one kilometer east of Kaiserstuhl mountains. This vineyard is characterized by its own microclimate, as well as a specific soil structure (brown Jurassic and shell limestone). The new management team consists of Manfred Zimmermann, responsible for the cellar and vineyards, as well as general manager Franz Herbster. Together they presented a good range of 2003 wines, which fitted in seamlessly with the 2001 vintage. The top wine is a well-structured Spätburgunder (Pinot Noir) Auslese, which has clear fruit, but was perhaps released a little too early – this is a big wine that needs time.

2002 Nimburg-Bottinger Steingrube
Chardonnay trocken
12.5%, ♀ till 2006   **84**

2003 Nimburg-Bottinger Steingrube
Auxerrois Spätlese trocken
12.5%, ♀ till 2006   **84**

2003 Nimburg-Bottinger Steingrube
Chardonnay Spätlese trocken
13.5%, ♀ till 2007   **85**

2003 Nimburg-Bottinger Steingrube
Weißer Burgunder Auslese trocken
14.5%, ♀ till 2007   **86**

2001 Nimburg-Bottinger Steingrube
Chardonnay trocken
13%, ♀ till 2006   **88**

2001 Nimburg-Bottinger Steingrube
Weißer Burgunder trocken
12.5%, ♀ till 2006   **88**

2003 Nimburg-Bottinger Steingrube
Chardonnay Auslese trocken
14.5%, ♀ till 2008   **88**

———— Red wines ————

2002 Nimburg-Bottinger Steingrube
Pinot Noir trocken
13%, ♀ till 2006   **85**

2002 Nimburg-Bottinger Steingrube
Frühburgunder trocken
13%, ♀ till 2008   **87**

2003 Nimburg-Bottinger Steingrube
Spätburgunder Auslese trocken
14.5%, ♀ till 2010   **88**

NIMBURG-BOTTINGER STEINGRUBE
QUALITÄTSWEIN B.A. · A.P.Nr. 356-06-03
IN BARRIQUE GEREIFT · GUTSABFÜLLUNG
WEINGUT FISCHER · INH. SILVIA & JOACHIM HEGER
D-79331 NIMBURG-BOTTINGEN AM KAISERSTUHL
750 ml Alc.13.0% by Vol.

FISCHER

2001 **SPÄTBURGUNDER*****
TROCKEN
BARRIQUE
BADEN

The wines: **100** Perfect · **95–99** Outstanding · **90–94** Excellent · **85–89** Very good · **80–84** Good · **75–79** Average

WEINGUT FREIHERR VON UND ZU FRANCKENSTEIN

Owner: Hubert Doll
77654 Offenburg, Weingartenstraße 66
Tel. (07 81) 3 49 73, Fax 3 60 46
e-mail:
weingut-franckenstein@t-online.de
Internet: www.germanwine.de/
weingut/franckenstein
*Directions: A 5 Frankfurt–Basel, Offen-
burg exit, in direction of Zell-Weierbach*
Sales: Hubert and Lioba Doll
Opening hours: Mon.–Fri. 09:00 to
12:00 hours and 14:00 to 18:00 hours
Sat. 09:00 to 13:00 hours
and by appointment
History: Oldest document dates winemaking here to 1517; owned by
Franckenstein family since 1710

Vineyard area: 14 hectares
Annual production: 80,000 bottles
Top sites: Zell-Weierbacher
Neugesetz and Abtsberg,
Berghauptener Schützenberg
Soil types: Decomposed granite,
decomposed gneiss and loess-clay
Grape varieties: 31% Riesling, 20%
Grauburgunder, 24% Spätburgunder,
23% Müller-Thurgau, 8% Weißbur-
gunder, 5% other varieties
Average yield: 62 hl/ha
Best vintages: 2000, 2001, 2003
Member: VDP

The property of the barons of Franckenstein, whose winemaking tradition dates
back to 1517, is located on the outskirts
of the city of Offenburg. Hubert Doll took
over as lessee in 1985. While vinifying
the current vintage he was assisted for the
first time by his daughter, who has a degree in viticulture and enology. The
2003 vintage fully confirms the good reputation of the vineyard sites in Zell-Weierbach and Berghaupten. Juicy, typical
Riesling wines with good body and an
elegant finish as well as similarly good
Pinot Gris and Pinot Blanc wines justify
the higher rating. Congratulations!

2003 Zell-Weierbacher Neugesetz
Riesling Kabinett trocken
12.5%, ♀ till 2006   86

2003 Berghauptener Schützenberg
Weißer Burgunder Kabinett trocken
14%, ♀ till 2006   86

2003 Berghauptener Schützenberg
Weißer Burgunder Spätlese trocken
14.5%, ♀ till 2006   86

2002 Zell-Weierbacher Neugesetz
Riesling Spätlese trocken
12%, ♀ till 2006   86

2003 Zell-Weierbacher Neugesetz
Riesling Spätlese trocken
13%, ♀ till 2007   87

2003 Zell-Weierbacher Abtsberg
Grauer Burgunder Kabinett trocken
14%, ♀ till 2007   87

2001 Zell-Weierbacher Neugesetz
Riesling Spätlese trocken
12%, ♀ till 2006   87

2003 Zell-Weierbacher Abtsberg
Grauer Burgunder Spätlese trocken
15.5%, ♀ till 2007   88

2003 Zell-Weierbacher Neugesetz
Riesling Spätlese
12.5%, ♀ till 2008   87

2003 Zell-Weierbacher Neugesetz
Traminer
13%, ♀ till 2009   88

———— Red wine ————

2001 Zell-Weierbacher Neugesetz
Spätburgunder Spätlese trocken Barrique
13%, ♀ till 2007   87

WEINGUT FREIHERR VON GLEICHENSTEIN

Owner: Johannes Freiherr von Gleichenstein
Vineyard manager: Franz Orth
Winemaker: Odin Bauer
79235 Oberrotweil, Bahnhofstraße 12
Tel. (0 76 62) 2 88, Fax 18 56
e-mail: weingut@gleichenstein.de
Internet: www.gleichenstein.de
Directions: A 5 Frankfurt–Basel, Riegel exit via Endingen or Bad Krozingen
Sales: Freiherr von Gleichenstein
Opening hours: Mon.–Sun. 09:00 to 18:00 hours and by appointment
History: Family-owned since 1634
Worth seeing: Old barrel cellar from 1580, former tithe barn of Saint Blasien abbey

---

Vineyard area: 24 hectares
Annual production: 150,000 bottles
Top sites: Oberrotweiler Eichberg, Henkenberg and Käsleberg, Achkarrer Schlossberg, Oberbergener Bassgeige
Soil types: Decomposed volcanic formation und loess
Grape varieties: 30% each of Spätburgunder and Weißburgunder, 20% Grauburgunder, 10% Müller-Thurgau, 3% Riesling, 7% other varieties
Average yield: 65 hl/ha
Best vintages: 2000, 2001, 2002

This winery in Oberrotweil has one of the longest traditions in Baden. Winemaker Odin Bauer came here armed with experience gained in Bordeaux, Burgundy and Australia. Following on a very good 2001 vintage and a good 2002 vintage, he has now presented rather a mixed bag for the 2003 vintage. Some of the basic wines are disappointing. However, this does not apply to the refreshing Müller-Thurgau from the Käsleberg site. We had high expectations of the concentrated juicy Chardonnay Spätlese and the powerful Grauburgunder Auslese, which were not quite fulfilled. On the other hand, the 2002 Spätburgunder from the Eichberg site is most enjoyable.

2003 Oberrotweiler Käsleberg
Müller-Thurgau trocken
12.5%, ♀ till 2006   83

2003 Oberrotweiler Eichberg
Weißer Burgunder Spätlese trocken
14%, ♀ till 2006   84

2003 Oberrotweiler Eichberg
Grauer Burgunder Spätlese trocken
14.5%, ♀ till 2006   85

2003 Oberrotweiler Eichberg
Chardonnay Spätlese trocken
13.5%, ♀ till 2007   86

2003 Oberrotweiler Eichberg
Muskateller Auslese trocken
15%, ♀ till 2006   86

2003 Grauer Burgunder
Auslese trocken
15%, ♀ till 2008   87

2002 Weißer Burgunder
Spätlese trocken
13.5%, ♀ till 2006   89

——————— Red wines ———————

2002 Oberbergener Bassgeige
Spätburgunder trocken
13%, ♀ till 2006   84

2002 Oberrotweiler Eichberg
Spätburgunder trocken
13%, ♀ till 2007   86

2001 Spätburgunder trocken
12%, ♀ till 2006   86

The wines: **100** Perfect · **95–99** Outstanding · **90–94** Excellent · **85–89** Very good · **80–84** Good · **75–79** Average

113

WEINGUT
THOMAS HAGENBUCHER

Owner: Thomas Hagenbucher
75056 Sulzfeld, Friedrichstraße 36
Tel. (0 72 69) 91 11 20, Fax 91 11 22
e-mail: info@weingut-hagenbucher.de
Internet: www.weingut-hagenbucher.de
Directions: A 5 Frankfurt–Basel,
Karlsruhe-Durlach exit,
B 293 in direction of Heilbronn
Opening hours: Mon.–Fri. 14:00 to
18:00 hours, Sat. 10:30 to 15:00 hours
and by appointment

Vineyard area: 8.5 hectares
Annual production: 60,000 bottles
Top sites: No vineyard sites stated on labels
Soil types: Red marl with high kaolin content, loess, gravel
Grape varieties: 25% Riesling, 21% Schwarzriesling, 13% Müller-Thurgau, 10% each of Weißburgunder and Spätburgunder, 5% each of Grauburgunder and Chardonnay, 6% Lemberger, 5% other varieties
Average yield: 60 hl/ha
Best vintages: 1999, 2001, 2003

Following on his training as a cellar technician, Thomas Hagenbucher started his own winery in 1992 in Sulzfeld, which is midway between the upper Rhine and the Neckar valley. Since there are very few designated vineyard sites here – just those attached to Burg Ravensburg, as well as the Lerchenberg site – he has decided to do without vineyard site mentions on his labels. After a bit of a roller coaster ride in recent years, he presented six wines in 2003, of which four were quite attractive. We can particularly recommend the Riesling in the liter bottle, which has fresh, clear fruit, as well as the Riesling Kabinett and the crisp Lemberger. Hagenbucher used synthetic closures in stead of natural cork on most of his bottles. However, the clearest fruit was shown by the wine in the liter bottle, which has a screw-cap closure.

2003 Sulzfelder
Grauer Burgunder trocken
14%, ♀ till 2006 — **81**

2001 Weißer Burgunder
Spätlese trocken
13%, ♀ till 2005 — **83**

2003 Sulzfelder
Weißer Burgunder trocken
15%, ♀ till 2006 — **84**

2003 Sulzfelder Riesling trocken
13%, ♀ till 2006 — **84**

2001 Riesling Kabinett trocken
11.5%, ♀ till 2005 — **85**

2001 Grauer Burgunder
Spätlese trocken
13%, ♀ till 2006 — **85**

2001 Chardonnay trocken
13.5%, ♀ till 2006 — **85**

2003 Sulzfelder
Riesling Kabinett trocken
13%, ♀ till 2007 — **85**

2001 Ruländer Beerenauslese
9%, ♀ till 2006 — **84**

——— Red wines ———

2003 Sulzfelder
Schwarzriesling trocken
14%, ♀ till 2006 — **81**

2003 Sulzfelder
Lemberger trocken
14%, ♀ till 2007 — **84**

2000 Schwarzriesling trocken
13.5%, ♀ till 2006 — **85**

WINZERVEREIN HAGNAU

General manager: Franz Gutemann
Winemaker: Herbert Senft
88709 Hagnau, Strandbadstraße 7
Tel. (0 75 32) 10 30, Fax 13 41
e-mail: info@hagnauer.de
Internet: www.hagnauer.de
Directions: B 31 on Lake Constance,
follow signs in Hagnau
Sales: Tobias Keck
Opening hours: Mon.–Fri. 08:00 to
18:00 hours, Sat. 09:00 to 13:00 hours
History: Oldest wine co-operative in
Baden, founded 1881

Vineyard area: 140 hectares
Number of members: 112
Annual production: 1 mill. bottles
Top site: Hagnauer Burgstall
Soil types: Clay, loess
Grape varieties: 41% each of Müller-
Thurgau and Spätburgunder, 11%
Grauburgunder, 7% other varieties
Average yield: 83 hl/ha
Best vintage: 2003

The co-operative was founded in 1881 by
the Rev. Heinrich Hansjakob, in an effort
to protect the wine producers of Hagnau
from a further decline in wine prices. It is
the oldest co-operative in Baden. Today
its 112 members produce around 1.2 million liters of wine each year from 140
hectares of vineyard. Sustainable viticultural practices as well as exclusively
hand-picked grapes provide the foundation for the quality of the wines, and also
support the maintenance of the unique
Lake Constance environment. In the current range, both the fresh, juicy Müller-
Thurgau and the velvety smooth Spätburgunder (Pinot Noir) wines can be recommended. As the botrytis dessert wines are
also very good – headed up by an impressive Müller-Thurgau Beerenauslese and
an interesting Ruländer Eiswein – it is our
pleasure to reward the new team's good
work by awarding the winery its first
bunch of grapes.

2003 Hagnauer
Müller-Thurgau trocken
12.5%, ♀ till 2006 — 82

2003 Hagnauer Sonnenufer
Müller-Thurgau trocken
12.5%, ♀ till 2006 — 84

2003 Hagnauer Burgstall
Grauer Burgunder Spätlese trocken
14%, ♀ till 2006 — 85

2003 Hagnauer Sonnenufer
Müller-Thurgau
11.5%, ♀ till 2006 — 84

2003 Hagnauer Burgstall
Müller-Thurgau Beerenauslese
8.5%, ♀ till 2008 — 89

2003 Hagnauer Burgstall
Ruländer Eiswein
10%, ♀ till 2010 — 90

———— Red wines ————

2003 Hagnauer Burgstall
Spätburgunder Weißherbst Kabinett
12.5%, ♀ till 2006 — 83

2003 Hagnauer Burgstall
Spätburgunder trocken
14.5%, ♀ till 2006 — 84

2003 Hagnauer Burgstall
Spätburgunder halbtrocken
13.5%, ♀ till 2006 — 83

The wines: **100** Perfect · **95–99** Outstanding · **90–94** Excellent · **85–89** Very good · **80–84** Good · **75–79** Average

115

WINZERGENOSSENSCHAFT HALTINGEN

General manager: Gerd Martini
Winemaker: Christoph Schell
79576 Weil am Rhein, Winzerweg 8
Tel. (0 76 21) 6 24 49, Fax 6 57 25
e-mail: wgh@wg-haltingen.de
Internet: www.wg-haltingen.de
Directions: A 5 Karlsruhe–Basel, Lörrach exit, via A 98, Weil am Rhein-Haltingen turn-off, in center of town
Sales: Gerd Martini
Opening hours: Mon.–Fri. 08:00 to 12:00 hours and 14:00 to 18:00 hours
Sat. 09:00 to 12:00 hours
History: Founded 1936

Vineyard area: 43 hectares
Number of members: 110
Annual production: 400,000 bottles
Top sites: Haltinger Stiege,
Weiler Schlipf
Soil types: Clay and loess, partly with limestone
Grape varieties: 51% Gutedel, 26% Spätburgunder, 10% Müller-Thurgau, 5% Graubunder, 3% Weißburgunder, 5% other varieties
Average yield: 77 hl/ha
Best vintage: 2001
Member: EcoVin

Haltingen is in the most southerly corner of Germany, in the Rhine bend opposite Basle, and viticulture has been practised here for the past 1200 years. The main variety planted by this small co-operative is the Gutedel (Chasselas), which is always of respectable quality. Sustainable viticultural practices are implemented, in parts of the Haltinger Stiege site organic practices have been introduced. While the 2001 vintage was successful across the board, the difficult 2002 vintage also left its mark here. The 2003 range is very solid, but lacks highlights. The only exception is the concentrated Gewürztraminer Spätlese with its rose-petal bouquet.

2003 Ötlinger Sonnhole
Gutedel trocken
11.5%, ♀ till 2006   **81**

2003 Haltinger Stiege
Grauer Burgunder Spätlese trocken
14.5%, ♀ till 2006   **82**

2003 Haltinger Stiege
Weißer Burgunder Spätlese trocken
14%, ♀ till 2006   **83**

2003 Haltinger Stiege
Chardonnay Spätlese trocken
13.5%, ♀ till 2006   **83**

2001 Haltinger Stiege
Weißer Burgunder Spätlese trocken
13%, ♀ till 2006   **85**

2001 Haltinger Stiege
Gutedel Spätlese trocken
13%, ♀ till 2006   **86**

2003 Haltinger Stiege
Gewürztraminer Spätlese
14%, ♀ till 2007   **85**

2001 Haltinger Stiege
Müller-Thurgau Eiswein
8.5%, ♀ till 2006   **86**

——— Red wines ———

2003 Haltinger Stiege
Regent Spätlese trocken
13%, ♀ till 2006   **83**

2001 Haltinger Stiege
Spätburgunder Spätlese trocken
13%, ♀ till 2006   **84**

2001
*Haltinger
Stiege*
Grauburgunder
Spätlese trocken
Qualitätswein mit Prädikat

WINZERGENOSSENSCHAFT
HALTINGEN EG
BADEN/MARKGRÄFLERLAND

WEINHAUS JOACHIM HEGER

Owner: Silvia and Joachim Heger
Vineyard manager: Jürgen Kühnle
Winemaker: Joachim Heger
79241 Ihringen, Bachenstraße 19
Tel. (0 76 68) 2 05 und 78 33, Fax 93 00
e-mail: info@heger-weine.de
Internet: www.heger-weine.de
Directions: A 5 Frankfurt–Basel, Frei-burg-Mitte exit, direction of Breisach
Sales: Silvia and Joachim Heger
Opening hours: Mon.–Fri. 09:00 to
12:00 hours and 13:30 to 17:30 hours
Sat. 10:00 to 14:00 hours
and by appointment
Closed Sun. and public holidays

Vineyard area: 20 hectares
Members: 16 contract growers
Annual production: 150,000 bottles
Top sites: Munzinger Kapellenberg,
Merdinger Bühl, Ihringer Fohrenberg
Soil types: Limestone-rich loess,
decomposed volcanic soil
Grape varieties: 55% Spätburgunder,
18% each of Weiß- and Grauburgun-
der, 9% other varieties
Average yield: 60 hl/ha
Best vintages: 2000, 2001, 2003

Apart from the top-class Dr. Heger win-ery, the wine house Joachim Heger has been in operation for a number of years, supplying attractive wines for everyday restaurant use. The project was launched in 1986, when Joachim Heger leased the vineyards of the former Graf von Kagen-eck winery on the slopes of the Tuniberg. A sort of producer group has developed out of these beginnings. All grapes are picked by hand, but the yields are higher than those of the Dr. Heger estate. A number of Kabinett wines of the 2003 vintage also bear the designation "Oktav" to indicate the higher quality of grapes used, and these are quite good, providing enjoyable drinking. The wines of the "Vi-tus" range have body, but are superficial-ly dominated by oak.

2003 Silvaner
Kabinett trocken "Oktav"
13%, ♀ till 2006 — **83**

2003 Grauer Burgunder
Kabinett trocken "Oktav"
14.5%, ♀ till 2006 — **84**

2003 Weißer Burgunder
Kabinett trocken "Oktav"
14%, ♀ till 2006 — **85**

2003 Weißer Burgunder
"Vitus" trocken
14%, ♀ till 2006 — **85**

2001 Muskat-Ottonel
Kabinett trocken
12%, ♀ till 2005 — **86**

2003 Grauer Burgunder
"Vitus" trocken
14%, ♀ till 2007 — **86**

2001 Weißer Burgunder
"Vitus" trocken
13%, ♀ till 2006 — **87**

2001 Grauer Burgunder
"Vitus" trocken
13%, ♀ till 2007 — **88**

———— Red wines ————

2003 Spätburgunder trocken
14%, ♀ till 2006 — **84**

2001 Merdinger Bühl
Spätburgunder trocken
13%, ♀ till 2006 — **84**

2002 Spätburgunder
trocken "Vitus"
13%, ♀ till 2008 — **85**

The wines: **100** Perfect · **95–99** Outstanding · **90–94** Excellent · **85–89** Very good · **80–84** Good · **75–79** Average

WEINGUT DR. HEGER

Owner and manager: Joachim Heger
Vineyard manager: Jürgen Kühnle
Winemaker: Joachim Heger
79241 Ihringen, Bachenstraße 19
Tel. (0 76 68) 2 05 und 78 33, Fax 93 00
e-mail: info@heger-weine.de
Internet: www.heger-weine.de
Directions: A 5 Frankfurt–Basel,
Freiburg-Mitte exit, in direction of
Breisach
Sales: Heger family
Opening hours: Mon.–Fri. 09:00 to
12:00 hours and 13:30 to 17:30 hours
Sat. 10:00 to 14:00 hours
and by appointment

Vineyard area: 17 hectares
Annual production: 100,000 bottles
Top sites: Ihringer Winklerberg,
Achkarrer Schlossberg, Freiburger
Schlossberg
Soil types: Decomposed volcanic
formation, loess
Grape varieties: 24% each of Spät-
burgunder and Riesling, 19% Grau-
burgunder, 13% Weißburgunder,
8% Silvaner, 5% Chardonnay,
7% other varieties
Average yield: 50 hl/ha
Best vintages: 1998, 2000, 2001
Member: VDP, Deutsches Barrique
Forum

This highly renowned estate was established in 1935 by medical doctor Dr. Max
Heger. As most of his patients were wine
producers, he could not help learning that
the volcanic Kaiserstuhl area provides
ideal conditions for viticulture. He changed jobs, and selectively purchased the
best sections of the vineyard sites Ihringer
Winklerberg and Achkarrer Schlossberg.
Son Wolfgang Heger took over the business in 1949. Today, the operation is in
the hands of Joachim Heger, the third generation, who has owned the estate since
1992. For many years now, this winery has
set the standard for white Pinot varieties.
The white wines of the 2001 vintage were

of nigh-perfect quality. The highlight was
a concentrated, fruity, well-bred Grauburgunder (Pinot Gris) Auslese from the Achkarrer Schlossberg site. Great wine! However, the 2002 vintage saw a step back-
wards in quality. We tasted clean, juicy
wines that lacked somewhat in concentration. To be honest, this year's range is a
disappointment. Neither the Silvaner nor
the Riesling Spätlese come up to standards this winery has itself set in the past.
The Pinot varieties, too, are only of average
quality, and are no longer among the best
Baden wines.

2003 Ihringer Winklerberg
Silvaner Spätlese trocken
13%, ♀ till 2006 **81**

2003 Ihringer Winklerberg
Riesling Spätlese trocken
12%, ♀ till 2006 **83**

2003 Ihringer Winklerberg
Weißer Burgunder Spätlese trocken
14%, ♀ till 2006 **84**

2002 Ihringer Winklerberg
Grauer Burgunder Spätlese trocken
12.5%, ♀ till 2006 **85**

2002 Ihringer Winklerberg
Riesling Spätlese trocken ✱✱✱
11%, ♀ till 2006 **86**

2003 Ihringer Winklerberg
Grauer Burgunder Spätlese trocken
14%, ♀ till 2007 **86**

2003 Ihringer Winklerberg
Weißer Burgunder Spätlese trocken ✱✱✱
14%, ♀ till 2006 **86**

2002 Ihringer Winklerberg
Weißer Burgunder Spätlese trocken
12.5%, ♀ till 2007 **87**

2003 Ihringer Winklerberg
Chardonnay Spätlese trocken
14%, ♀ till 2007 **87**

2001 Ihringer Winklerberg
Grauer Burgunder Auslese trocken ✱✱✱
13.5%, ♀ till 2007 **88**

2002 Achkarrer Schlossberg
Grauer Burgunder Spätlese trocken ✱✱✱
13.5%, ♀ till 2006 **88**

The estates: ✦✦✦✦✦ World's finest · ✦✦✦✦ Germany's best · ✦✦✦ Very good · ✦✦ Good · ✦ Reliable

2002 Ihringer Winklerberg
Weißer Burgunder Auslese trocken ***
13.5%, ♀ till 2007 **88**

2001 Ihringer Winklerberg
Silvaner Spätlese trocken
12%, ♀ till 2006 **88**

2001 Ihringer Winklerberg
Weißer Burgunder Spätlese trocken
13%, ♀ till 2006 **88**

2003 Achkarrer Schlossberg
Grauer Burgunder Spätlese trocken ***
14.5%, ♀ till 2008 **88**

2001 Ihringer Winklerberg
Weißer Burgunder Spätlese trocken
Holzfass
13%, ♀ till 2006 **88**

2001 Ihringer Winklerberg
Weißer Burgunder Spätlese trocken ***
13.5%, ♀ till 2006 **89**

2001 Ihringer Winklerberg
Chardonnay Spätlese trocken
13.5%, ♀ till 2006 **89**

2002 Ihringer Winklerberg
Weißer Burgunder Spätlese trocken ***
13%, ♀ till 2007 **89**

2002 Achkarrer Schlossberg
Weißer Burgunder Spätlese trocken ***
12.5%, ♀ till 2007 **89**

2001 Ihringer Winklerberg
Muskateller Spätlese trocken
12.5%, ♀ till 2006 **89**

2001 Ihringer Winklerberg
Riesling Spätlese trocken ***
12%, ♀ till 2006 **89**

2001 Achkarrer Schlossberg
Weißer Burgunder Spätlese trocken ***
12.5%, ♀ till 2007 **91**

2001 Achkarrer Schlossberg
Grauer Burgunder Auslese trocken ***
14%, ♀ till 2008 **93**

2002 Achkarrer Schlossberg
Riesling Spätlese
9.5%, ♀ till 2006 **86**

2001 Achkarrer Schlossberg
Silvaner Spätlese
10.5%, ♀ till 2006 **86**

2003 Ihringer Winklerberg
Gewürztraminer Auslese
11%, ♀ till 2008 **86**

2001 Achkarrer Schlossberg
Riesling Spätlese
11%, ♀ till 2008 **88**

2003 Ihringer Winklerberg
Muskateller Auslese
11.5%, ♀ till 2010 **88**

2001 Ihringer Winklerberg
Muskateller Spätlese
11.5%, ♀ till 2010 **89**

———— Red wines ————

2001 Ihringer Winklerberg
Spätburgunder "Mimus" trocken
13%, ♀ till 2006 **86**

2002 Ihringer Winklerberg
Spätburgunder "Mimus" trocken
13%, ♀ till 2008 **87**

2002 Ihringer Winklerberg
Spätburgunder trocken ***
13.5%, ♀ till 2009 **88**

2001 Ihringer Winklerberg
Spätburgunder trocken ***
13%, ♀ till 2008 **90**

2001 Achkarrer Schlossberg
Spätburgunder trocken ***
12.5%, ♀ till 2008 **90**

BADEN

DR. HEGER

2001
Silvaner ***

IHRINGER WINKLERBERG
SPÄTLESE · TROCKEN
QUALITÄTSWEIN MIT PRÄDIKAT
A.P.-NR. 311-03-02
ERZEUGERABFÜLLUNG
WEINGUT DR. HEGER
D-79241 IHRINGEN/KAISERSTUHL
PRODUCE OF GERMANY

750 ml · Alc. 12% by Vol.

The wines: **100** Perfect · **95–99** Outstanding · **90–94** Excellent · **85–89** Very good · **80–84** Good · **75–79** Average

WEINGUT
ERNST HEINEMANN

Owner: Lothar Heinemann
Winemaker: Lothar Heinemann
79238 Ehrenkirchen-Scherzingen,
Mengener Straße 4
Tel. (0 76 64) 63 51, Fax 60 04 65
e-mail:
weingut-heinemann@t-online.de
Internet: www.weingut-heinemann.de
*Directions: A 5 Frankfurt–Basel,
Freiburg-Süd exit, via Tiengen, Mengen
and Scherzingen*
Sales: Heinemann family
Opening hours: Mon.–Fri. from 09:00
to 12:00 hours and 13:30 to 18:00 hours
Sat. 09:00 to 12:00 hours and 13:00 to
16:00 hours and by appointment
Worth seeing: 200-year-old vaulted cellar

Vineyard area: 13 hectares
Contracted growers: 20 members
Annual production: 100,000 bottles
Top site: Scherzinger Batzenberg
Soil types: Clay with kaolin, very rich
in limestone, decomposed stone
Grape varieties: 35% Gutedel,
30% Spätburgunder, 12% Chardon-
nay, 8% Weißburgunder, 5% Rivaner,
4% Muskateller, 6% other varieties
Average yield: 65 hl/ha
Best vintages: 1999, 2000, 2001

The Heinemann family has been involved
in viticulture in Scherzingen for 450
years. Grapes are bought in from around
20 growers to satisfy the demand for Gutedel (Chasselas) Müller-Thurgau and
Spätburgunder. The winery first attracted
attention for its good quality in the Eighties, particularly for its Chardonnay, a variety that has been planted here for the
past 40 years. The 2002 range was solid,
but without real highlights. Looking to
the 2003 vintage, we again liked the
Chardonnays, which combine clarity of
fruit, smoothness and good breeding in
the most attractive manner. We wish the
same style could be achieved with the remainder of the wines produced here.

2003 Scherzinger Batzenberg
Weißer Burgunder Spätlese trocken
14.5%, ♀ till 2006   83

2003 Scherzinger Batzenberg
Gutedel Spätlese trocken
13%, ♀ till 2006   84

2003 Scherzinger Batzenberg
Muskateller Spätlese trocken
13.5%, ♀ till 2006   84

2002 Scherzinger Batzenberg
Muskateller Kabinett trocken
11%, ♀ till 2006   85

2003 Scherzinger Batzenberg
Grauer Burgunder Spätlese trocken
14.5%, ♀ till 2006   85

2002 Scherzinger Batzenberg
Chardonnay Spätlese trocken Barrique
13%, ♀ till 2006   86

2003 Scherzinger Batzenberg
Chardonnay Kabinett trocken
13.5%, ♀ till 2007   87

2003 Scherzinger Batzenberg
Chardonnay Spätlese trocken
14.5%, ♀ till 2008   87

2003 Scherzinger Batzenberg
Gewürztraminer Auslese
13%, ♀ till 2008   87

———— Red wines ————

2002 Scherzinger Batzenberg
Spätburgunder trocken Alte Reben
12.5%, ♀ till 2007   83

2003 Scherzinger Batzenberg
Spätburgunder Spätlese trocken
13.5%, ♀ till 2008   85

2001 Scherzinger Batzenberg
Spätburgunder Spätlese trocken Barrique
12.5%, ♀ till 2006   86

WINZERKELLER
HEX VOM DASENSTEIN EG

General manager: Jürgen Decker
Winemaker: Robert Schnurr
77876 Kappelrodeck, Burgunderplatz 1
Tel. **(0 78 42) 9 93 80, Fax 99 38 38**
e-mail: info@winzerkeller.net
Internet: **www.hex-vom-dasenstein.de**
Directions: A 5 Frankfurt–Basel, Achern
exit, in direction of Schwarzwaldhochstraße
Sales: Ingrid Oberle, Alex Schwank,
Anette Schneider, Irmgard Spinner
Opening hours: Mon.–Fri. 08:00 to
12:00 hours and 13:30 to 17:30 hours
Sat. 09:00 to 13:00 hours
Sun. 10:00 to 13:00 hours
History: Founded 1934

Vineyard area: 143 hectares
Number of members: 277
Annual production: 1.3 mill. bottles
Top site: Kappelrodecker
Hex vom Dasenstein
Soil types: Decomposed granitic rock
Grape varieties: 78% Spätburgunder,
7% Müller-Thurgau, 5% each of Ries-
ling and Grauburgunder, 3% Weißbur-
gunder, 2% other varieties
Average yield: 74 hl/ha
Best vintages: 1999, 2001, 2003

Where the pine trees of the Black Forest
give way to chestnut groves, you will find
the Pinot Noir vineyards of the Hex vom
Dasenstein. The locals love telling the
story of the noble young lady who was
turned into a red wine witch (Hexe). The
achievement of the co-operative members was first honored in the shape of a
Federal gold medal in 1994. The team is
proud of the fact that this award was repeated in the years from 1999 to 2002.
The red wines have their own specific
fruity character, which is augmented this
year by chewy tannins. One can sense the
ambition to take the range up a notch in
quality. If the wines could be a little more
balanced and elegant, this is a realistic
endeavor.

2001 Gewürztraminer
Beerenauslese
12.5%, ♀ till 2007 — **85**

2000 Gewürztraminer
Trockenbeerenauslese
11.5%, ♀ till 2010 — **89**

———— Red wines ————

2002 Spätburgunder
Spätlese trocken "Alte Reben"
13%, ♀ till 2006 — **84**

2002 Spätburgunder
Auslese trocken
14.5%, ♀ till 2007 — **85**

2003 Spätburgunder
Spätlese trocken
14.5%, ♀ till 2006 — **85**

2003 Spätburgunder
trocken "Avantgarde"
15%, ♀ till 2007 — **85**

2003 Spätburgunder
Auslese trocken
14.5%, ♀ till 2008 — **87**

2003 Spätburgunder Auslese
13%, ♀ till 2007 — **85**

2002 Spätburgunder Beerenauslese
12.5%, ♀ till 2010 — **88**

2001 Spätburgunder Weißherbst
Eiswein
12.5%, ♀ till 2011 — **91**

The wines: **100** Perfect · **95–99** Outstanding · **90–94** Excellent · **85–89** Very good · **80–84** Good · **75–79** Average

121

WEINGUT REICHSGRAF UND MARQUIS ZU HOENSBROECH

Owner: Rüdiger Graf Hoensbroech
Manager and winemaker:
Rüdiger Graf Hoensbroech
74918 Angelbachtal-Michelfeld,
Hermannstraße 12
Tel. (0 72 65) 91 10 34, Fax 91 10 35
e-mail:
mail@weingut-graf-hoensbroech.com
Internet:
www.weingut-graf-hoensbroech.com
Directions: A 6, Sinsheim exit, Angel-
bachtal, Michelfeld Schulstraße
Sales: Graf Hoensbroech
Opening hours: Mon.–Fri. 09:00 to
18:00 hours, Sat. 10:00 to 16:00 hours

Vineyard area: 17 hectares
Annual production: 120,000 bottles
Top site: Michelfelder Himmelberg
Soil types: Loess and coloured marl
Grape varieties: 35% Weißburgunder,
15% each of Riesling and Graubur-
gunder, 8% Spätburgunder,
27% other varieties
Average yield: 65 hl/ha
Best vintages: 2001, 2002, 2003
Member: VDP

Following on his training at Geisenheim and at Weinsberg, and a brief interlude involving an inherited winery in the Saar region, Rüdiger Graf Hoensbroech settled in Baden in 1968, and proceeded to build an operation that enjoys a respectable reputation. He has become known mainly for his white Pinot wines, his philosophy of not chaptalising and not fining the wines gives them a definite character of their own. The range of 2002 vintage wines was attractive, the vintage can be blamed for the absence of top wines. The 2003 vintage range is very homogeneous, and that at a very high overall level. In particular the Pinot Blanc wines, from the juicy basic wine in liter bottles up to a very good Auslese are in line with the best tradition of this winery.

2003 Michelfelder Himmelberg
Auxerrois Kabinett trocken
12.5%, ♀ till 2006   83

2003 Michelfelder Himmelberg
Weißer Burgunder trocken
12.5%, ♀ till 2006   84

2002 Michelfelder Himmelberg
Weißer Burgunder trocken
12%, ♀ till 2006   85

2002 Michelfelder Himmelberg
Weißer Burgunder Kabinett trocken
12%, ♀ till 2006   85

2002 Michelfelder Himmelberg
Auxerrois Kabinett trocken
12%, ♀ till 2006   85

2003 Michelfelder Himmelberg
Weißer Burgunder Kabinett trocken
12.5%, ♀ till 2007   85

2002 Michelfelder Himmelberg
Chardonnay trocken
13%, ♀ till 2006   86

2001 Michelfelder Himmelberg
Riesling Spätlese trocken
13%, ♀ till 2006   86

2003 Michelfelder Himmelberg
Riesling Spätlese trocken
13%, ♀ till 2007   86

2001 Michelfelder Himmelberg
Weißer Burgunder Spätlese trocken
13%, ♀ till 2006   87

2003 Michelfelder Himmelberg
Weißer Burgunder Spätlese trocken
13%, ♀ till 2008   87

2003 Michelfelder Himmelberg
Weißer Burgunder Auslese
14.5%, ♀ till 2010   89

WEINGUT HOLUB

Owner and manager: Horst Holub
Administrator: Dieter Schunk
**79336 Herbolzheim-Tutschfelden,
Weinstraße 4**
Tel. (0 76 43) 9 14 14 12, Fax 9 14 14 14
e-mail: info@weingut-holub.com
Internet: www.weingut-holub.com
Directions: A 5 Karlsruhe–Basel, Herbolzheim exit, the winery is at entrance to Tutschfelden suburb
Sales: Christian Gmoser
Opening hours: Mon.–Fri. 09:00 to 17:00 hours and by appointment

---

Vineyard area: 1.1 hectares
Annual production: 5,000 bottles
Top site: Herbolzheimer Kaiserberg
Soil types: Clay and loess
Grape varieties: 60% Spätburgunder, 30% Grauburgunder, 10% Weißburgunder
Average yield: 40 hl/ha
Best vintages: 2002, 2003

For his 50th birthday, Horst Holub was given 700 square meters of vineyard, planted with Pinot Noir vines. This was in 1999, and marked the beginning of the Holub winery. By now, the vineyard area has grown to a little more than one hectare, planted to Pinot Noir, Pinot Gris and Pinot Blanc. A policy of minimal intervention applies in the cellar, using gravity wherever possible. The Pinot Noir is fermented in temperature-controlled stainless steel tanks, while the white Pinot varieties are moved into barrique immediately after fermentation is completed. All wines undergo malo-lactic fermentation. The two wines of the 2002 vintage were very attractive, both the Pinot Noir, with cherry fruit, good concentration and a long finish as well as the Pinot Gris, which has clear fruit and shows elegant use of oak. The white wines of the 2003 vintage also show clear fruit and judicious use of oak, although they lack a little concentration, a vintage characteristic.

2003 Amolterer Steinhalde
Weißer Burgunder Spätlese trocken
13%, ♀ till 2006   84

2003 Amolterer Steinhalde
Grauer Burgunder Spätlese trocken
13.5%, ♀ till 2006   84

2003 Malterdinger Bienengarten
Grauer Burgunder Spätlese trocken
13%, ♀ till 2006   86

2002 Grauer Burgunder
Spätlese trocken
13.5%, ♀ till 2008   86

——————— Red wine ———————

2002 Spätburgunder trocken
13.5%, ♀ till 2008   87

Grauer Burgunder

The wines: **100** Perfect · **95–99** Outstanding · **90–94** Excellent · **85–89** Very good · **80–84** Good · **75–79** Average

123

WEINGUT
BERNHARD HUBER

Owner: Barbara and Bernhard Huber
Manager: Bernhard Huber
Chef de culture: Egon Meyer
Winemaker: Stefan Beck
79364 Malterdingen,
Heimbacher Weg 19
Tel. (0 76 44) 12 00, Fax 82 22
e-mail: info@weingut-huber.com
Internet: www.weingut-huber.com
*Directions: A 5 Frankfurt–Basel,
Riegel exit*
Sales: Barbara Huber
Opening hours: Mon.–Fri. 14:00 to
18:00 hours, Sat. 10:00 to 12:00 hours
Worth seeing: Gate house dating to the
16th century, stone wall of shell lime-
stone with fossils

Vineyard area: 26 hectares
Annual production: 170,000 bottles,
10,000 bottles sparkling wine
Top sites: Hecklinger Schlossberg,
Malterdinger Bienenberg
Soil types: Decomposed shell limestone
Grape varieties: 70% Spätburgunder,
10% Chardonnay, 9% Weißburgun-
der, 6% Grauburgunder,
5% other varieties
Average yield: 48 hl/ha
Best vintages: 2001, 2002, 2003
Member: VDP,
Deutsches Barrique Forum

When Bernhard Huber set out to help the "Malterer," a formerly well-known blend, regain its erstwhile popularity, he was perhaps already dreaming of one day becoming one of the leading red wine producers in Germany. The first step was to slowly withdraw from the co-opera-tive, initially using only parts of the fam-ily-owned vineyards; his development was evident from each year to the next. His first major success came in 1990, when he took first place in the Vinum Red Wine Awards. Since then he has also enjoyed many top placings in this guide. Hubers red wines are often inaccessible in their youth. However, they are among the small elite of red wines in Germany that can show really outstanding matura-tion. They need time to develop and show their best – a characteristic of all great red wines. In his first vintages as an indepen-dent winemaker, Huber produced mainly opulent, powerful wines. In the mean-time, Pinot Noirs have added a dimen-sion of elegance – and that applies even to the more basic categories. The basic red wines of the 2002 vintage are good, but not as outstanding as those of the pre-vious vintage. On the other hand, the Spätburgunder (Pinot Noir) from old vines, as well as the Reserve, referred to here as "R," which are bottled during a waxing moon, are again among the very best wines produced in Baden. Excellent white wines round off the range, most of these go through extended lees contact, are generally fermented in stainless steel, while some also see barriques. The "Mal-terer" blend of the 2003 vintage is just as good as are the excellent Chardonnays. A newcomer to the range is a Weißburgun-der Spätlese "Erstes Gewächs" (Pinot Blanc Spätlese First Growth). This wine has been slotted in below the top white wines of the estate in terms of price, a de-cision that accurately reflects the quality of the wine, but indicates a half-hearted approach to the First Growth concept. The sweet botrytis finale is provided by a racy, fresh Muskateller Auslese.

2002 Malterdinger Bienenberg
Grauer Burgunder trocken
13%, ♀ till 2006 **85**

2003 Weißer Burgunder trocken
13.5%, ♀ till 2006 **85**

2003 Grauer Burgunder trocken
14%, ♀ till 2006 **86**

2002 Malterdinger Bienenberg
Weißer Burgunder trocken
12.5%, ♀ till 2006 **87**

2001 Malterdinger Bienenberg
Grauer Burgunder Spätlese trocken
13%, ♀ till 2006 **87**

2003 Malterdinger Bienenberg
Auxerrois Kabinett trocken
12%, ♀ till 2006   **87**

2001 "Malterer" trocken
13.5%, ♀ till 2006   **88**

2002 Chardonnay trocken
13%, ♀ till 2006   **88**

2003 Malterer trocken
13.5%, ♀ till 2007   **88**

2003 Malterdinger Bienenberg
Weißer Burgunder Spätlese trocken
"Erstes Gewächs"
14%, ♀ till 2007   **89**

2002 Weißer Burgunder
trocken "S"
13%, ♀ till 2007   **89**

2000 "Malterer" trocken
13%, ♀ till 2008   **90**

2003 Chardonnay trocken
14%, ♀ till 2008   **90**

2000 Chardonnay trocken "R"
14%, ♀ till 2006   **90**

2001 Weißer Burgunder
trocken "S"
13%, ♀ till 2008   **90**

2001 Grauer Burgunder
trocken "S"
13%, ♀ till 2008   **91**

2003 Chardonnay trocken "R"
14%, ♀ till 2010   **92**

2002 Malterdinger Bienenberg
Muskateller Kabinett
11.5%, ♀ till 2006   **86**

2001 Malterdinger Bienenberg
Muskateller Kabinett
11.5%, ♀ till 2006   **87**

2001 Malterdinger Bienenberg
Riesling Auslese
10%, ♀ till 2010   **89**

2002 Chardonnay Auslese
14.5%, ♀ till 2008   **90**

2003 Malterdinger Bienenberg
Muskateller Auslese
10.5%, ♀ till 2010   **91**

——— Red wines ———

2002 Malterdinger Bienenberg
Spätburgunder trocken
13%, ♀ till 2007   **86**

2002 Spätburgunder
trocken "Junge Reben"
13%, ♀ till 2007   **86**

2000 Malterdinger Bienenberg
Spätburgunder trocken
13%, ♀ till 2006   **88**

2001 Spätburgunder
trocken "Junge Reben"
13%, ♀ till 2006   **88**

2001 Malterdinger Bienenberg
Spätburgunder trocken
13%, ♀ till 2007   **89**

2000 Spätburgunder
trocken "Alte Reben"
13%, ♀ till 2010   **90**

2002 Spätburgunder
trocken "Alte Reben"
13%, ♀ till 2009   **90**

2001 Spätburgunder
trocken "Alte Reben"
13%, ♀ till 2008   **91**

2001 Spätburgunder trocken "R"
13.5%, ♀ till 2010   **92**

2002 Spätburgunder trocken "R"
13%, ♀ till 2010   **92**

2000 Spätburgunder trocken "R"
13%, ♀ till 2012   **93**

The wines: **100** Perfect · **95–99** Outstanding · **90–94** Excellent · **85–89** Very good · **80–84** Good · **75–79** Average

WEINGUT HUCK-WAGNER

Owner: Huck-Wagner family
Winemaker:
Christiane Huck-Wagner
79588 Efringen-Kirchen,
Engetalstraße 31
Tel. (0 76 28) 14 62, Fax 80 03 19
e-mail: huck-wagner@gmx.de
*Directions: A 5 Frankfurt–Basel, Efrin-
gen-Kirchen exit, at entrance to Efringen
turn left, left after railway bridge*
Sales: Mon.–Sat. 08:00 to 19:00 hours
Worth seeing: 500-year-old barrel cel-
lar, lovely view from Efringer
Ölberg towards Drei-Länder-Eck

Vineyard area: 10 hectares
Annual production: 70,000 bottles
Top sites: Efringer Ölberg,
Binzener Sonnhole
Soil types: Sandy clay with loess,
Jurassic limestone
Grape varieties: 35% Gutedel,
30% Spätburgunder, 10% Graubur-
gunder, 5% each of Müller-Thurgau
and Silvaner, 15% other varieties
Average yield: 70 hl/ha
Best vintages: 2001, 2003

Roland Wagner was a wine producer supplying the co-operative when he married
Christiane Huck, a winemaker's daughter, in 1992. The joint winery that emerged from this union was large enough to
allow the young couple to go it alone as a
winery. Wagner's left the Markgräflerland regional co-operative, which he sup-
plied from his vineyards, and also termi-
nated his activities at the co-operative in
Schliengen. One of the focal points of the
range is certainly the Gutedel (Chasselas). While the Kabinett wine was this
year's winner of the Gutedel Cup, we
much preferred the racy and invigorating
Roter Gutedel. Both Grauburgunder (Pinot Gris) and Chardonnay show good
fruit and breeding, but unfortunately the
Ruländer Beerenauslese has been fermented for too long.

2003 Efringer Ölberg
Gutedel Kabinett trocken
11.5%, ♀ till 2006 — **80**

2003 Efringer Ölberg
Silvaner Kabinett trocken
12%, ♀ till 2006 — **81**

2003 Roter Gutedel trocken
12%, ♀ till 2006 — **83**

2003 Efringer Ölberg
Grauer Burgunder Spätlese trocken
13.5%, ♀ till 2006 — **84**

2001 Efringer Ölberg
Grauer Burgunder Spätlese trocken
13.5%, ♀ till 2006 — **84**

2003 Efringer Ölberg
Chardonnay Spätlese trocken
14%, ♀ till 2006 — **85**

2001 Efringer Ölberg
Gewürztraminer Spätlese trocken
14%, ♀ till 2006 — **86**

2003 Efringer Ölberg
Ruländer Beerenauslese
14.5%, ♀ till 2008 — **86**

2001 Efringer Ölberg
Ruländer Beerenauslese
12.5%, ♀ till 2010 — **87**

——— Red wines ———

2003 Efringer Ölberg
Spätburgunder Weißherbst Auslese
12.5%, ♀ till 2007 — **85**

2002 Efringer Ölberg
Spätburgunder trocken
12%, ♀ till 2006 — **82**

2000 Efringer Ölberg
Spätburgunder trocken
12.5%, ♀ till 2005 — **84**

WEINGUT
HUCK-WAGNER

2001er
EFRINGER ÖLBERG
Grauburgunder
SPÄTLESE TROCKEN

BADEN

The estates: ✿✿✿✿✿ World's finest · ✿✿✿✿ Germany's best · ✿✿✿ Very good · ✿✿ Good · ✿ Reliable

WEINGUT BERND HUMMEL

Owner: Bernd Hummel
Winemaker: Bernd Hummel
69254 Malsch, Oberer Mühlweg 5
Tel. (0 72 53) 2 71 48, Fax 2 57 99
e-mail: info@weingut-hummel.de
Internet: www.weingut-hummel.de
Directions: Via the B 3, south of
Heidelberg, or via the B 39
Sales: Bernd Hummel
Opening hours: Mon.–Fri. 17:00 to
19:00 hours, Sat. 09:00 to 13:00 hours
and by appointment

Vineyard area: 7.5 hectares
Annual production: 50,000 bottles
Top sites: Malscher Ölbaum
and Rotsteig
Soil types: Loess, clay, sandstone,
red marl and shell limestone
Grape varieties: 55% Spätburgunder,
10% white Pinot varieties, 8% each
of Riesling and Auxerrois, 19% other
varieties
Average yield: 54 hl/ha
Best vintages: 1999, 2001, 2002

Malsch is located on the western border
of the Kraichgau, and it is here that the
trained economist Bernd Hummel began
his career as a winemaker. Faced with the
decision in 1984, he did not want to sell
his father-in-law's vineyards, and decided
instead to take over the reins himself,
at the same time leaving the co-operative.
Strict pruning and green harvesting reduce the yield in the vineyard, the best
grapes are matured in barriques. Particular attention is regularly focussed on the
quality of the red wines. We particularly
liked the Pinot Noir wines. Both the basic
wine in liter bottles, which has clear
fruit, as well as the concentrated Auslese
wine contribute to the reputation of the
estate. While the white wines are not yet
quite up to the same standard, the overall
performance certainly warrants awarding Hummel the second bunch of grapes.
Congratulations!

2003 Malscher Öll
Weißer Burgunder Spätl
13.5%, ♀ till 2006

2003 Malscher Öll
Chardonnay Spätlese trocken
13.5%, ♀ till 2006   **84**

2002 Malscher Ölbaum
Chardonnay Spätlese trocken "S"
13%, ♀ till 2006   **84**

2003 Malscher Ölbaum
Riesling Spätlese
12%, ♀ till 2006   **83**

———— Red wines ————

2002 Malscher Ölbaum
Dornfelder trocken
12.5%, ♀ till 2006   **84**

2002 Malscher
Spätburgunder trocken
12.5%, ♀ till 2006   **85**

2002 Malscher Rotsteig
Cabernet Sauvignon trocken
14%, ♀ till 2007   **85**

2001 Malscher Rotsteig
Cabernet Sauvignon trocken
13.5%, ♀ till 2006   **85**

2001 Malscher Rotsteig
Spätburgunder trocken "R"
13.5%, ♀ till 2006   **85**

2002 Malscher Rotsteig
Schwarzriesling trocken
12.5%, ♀ till 2007   **86**

2002 Malscher Rotsteig
Spätburgunder Auslese trocken
14%, ♀ till 2009   **88**

The wines: **100** Perfect · **95–99** Outstanding · **90–94** Excellent · **85–89** Very good · **80–84** Good · **75–79** Average

127

SCHLOSSGUT ISTEIN

Owner: District of Lörrach administration
Manager and winemaker: Albert Soder
79588 Istein, Im Innerdorf 23
Tel. (0 76 28) 12 84, Fax 86 32
e-mail: soder.schlossgut@t-online.de
Internet: www.soder-schlossgut.de
Directions: A 5 Freiburg–Basel,
Efringen-Kirchen exit
Sales: Albert and Anita Soder
Opening hours: Mon.–Sat. 09:00 to
17:00 hours by appointment
Worth seeing: Saint Vitus' chapel,
Isteiner Klotz

Vineyard area: 10 hectares
Annual production: 65,000 bottles
Top site: Isteiner Kirchberg
Soil types: Decomposed Jurassic
limestone, loess-clay
Grape varieties: 30% Gutedel,
25% Spätburgunder, 25% Weiß- and
Grauburgunder, 10% Riesling,
10% Chardonnay and Gewürztraminer
Average yield: 53 hl/ha
Best vintages: 1999, 2000, 2001
Member: VDP

The Isteiner Klotz rock formation rises from the gently rolling pastures of the Markgräflerland, visible far and wide. Sun-drenched vineyard slopes reach down into the ancient wine-producing village. The village, which is close to Basle, was first mentioned in a document dated 1139, and signed by Pope Innocent II. in Rome. Later on, it belonged to the bishops of Baden, then the margrave, then the city of Karlsruhe, and now the district of Lörrach. The Schlossgut, implying a castle, was in a rather sorry state when Albert and Anita Soder arrived here as lessees in 1977. The 2001 range was good, followed by a rather variable 2002 vintage. The 2003 wines are clearly not homogeneous: The full-bodied Grauburgunder Auslese and the powerful Chardonnay Spätlese stand in juxtaposition to some really poor wines.

2003 Isteiner Gutedel trocken
11.5%, ♀ till 2006 — **80**

2003 Isteiner
Weißer Burgunder Spätlese trocken
13.5%, ♀ till 2006 — **82**

2003 Isteiner
Riesling Spätlese trocken
12.5%, ♀ till 2006 — **83**

2001 Isteiner Kirchberg
Grauer Burgunder Kabinett trocken
12.5%, ♀ till 2005 — **84**

2003 Isteiner
Chardonnay Spätlese trocken
13%, ♀ till 2006 — **85**

2003 Isteiner
Grauer Burgunder Auslese trocken
14.5%, ♀ till 2007 — **86**

2002 Isteiner Kirchberg
Chardonnay Spätlese trocken
13%, ♀ till 2006 — **86**

2001 Isteiner Kirchberg
Weißer Burgunder Spätlese trocken
13.5%, ♀ till 2006 — **86**

2001 Isteiner Kirchberg
Riesling Spätlese trocken
12.5%, ♀ till 2006 — **86**

2001 Isteiner Kirchberg
Gewürztraminer Spätlese trocken
13.5%, ♀ till 2006 — **87**

—— Red wines ——

2002 Isteiner
Spätburgunder Kabinett trocken
12%, ♀ till 2006 — **81**

2001 Isteiner Kirchberg
Spätburgunder Auslese trocken
14%, ♀ till 2006 — **86**

Baden/Markgräflerland

2001
Gutedel
Kabinett
Schloßgut Istein
A. Soder

11%vol
0,4 g/l R.Z.
750 ml

Qualitätswein mit Prädikat, Trocken
Gutsabfüllung A.P.Nr. 221 04 02
Weingut des Landkreises Lörrach
D-79588 Istein

The estates: ♦♦♦♦♦ World's finest · ♦♦♦♦ Germany's best · ♦♦♦ Very good · ♦♦ Good · ♦ Reliable

WEINGUT ACHIM JÄHNISCH

Owner: Achim Jähnisch and Sarah Oberle
Manager and winemaker: Achim Jähnisch
Viticulturists: Achim Jähnisch and Sarah Oberle
79238 Ehrenkirchen/Kirchhofen, Hofmattenweg 19
Tel. (0 76 33) 80 11 61, Fax 80 11 61
e-mail: a.jaehnisch@t-online.de
Internet: www.weingut-jaehnisch.de
Directions: Coming from the north: A 5 Frankfurt–Basel, Freiburg-Süd exit, in direction of Staufen; from the south: A 5, Bad Krozingen exit
Sales: Sarah Oberle
Opening hours: Mon.–Fri. 13:00 to 20:00 hours, Sat. 09:00 to 18:00 hours and by appointment
Worth seeing: Old vaulted cellar

Vineyard area: 2.8 hectares
Annual production: 15,000 bottles
Top site: Staufener Schlossberg
Soil types: Decomposed shell limestone, granite and porphyrite
Grape varieties: 40% Spätburgunder, 23% Riesling, 16% Grauburgunder, 12% Gutedel, 6% Chardonnay, 3% Weißburgunder
Average yield: 45 hl/ha
Best vintages: 2000, 2001, 2002

Achim Jähnisch discovered his love for wine while studying the history of art. He served an apprenticeship as winemaker with Bernhard Huber in Malterdingen, then studied viticulture and enology in Geisenheim. In 1999 he was able to lease a small winery in the Markgräflerland, and began to realize his dream. Low yields and minimal intervention in the handling of healthy grapes are the foundation for the production of good wines. We particularly liked the Riesling and Gutedel (Chasselas) wines in 2002. The current range maintains a good standard, but is not quite up to the level of the previous years. The Pinot Noir is basically very good, but suffers from a massive dose of oak. On the other hand, the sparkling wine deserves a special recommendation: a creamy 2001 Pinot Brut with an elegant long finish.

2003 Gutedel trocken
12%, ♀ till 2006 — **82**

2003 Spätburgunder "Blanc de Noir" trocken
14.5%, ♀ till 2006 — **82**

2002 Weißer Burgunder & Chardonnay trocken
13%, ♀ till 2006 — **85**

2003 Staufener Schlossberg Riesling trocken
12.5%, ♀ till 2006 — **86**

2002 Staufener Schlossberg Grauer Burgunder trocken
13.5%, ♀ till 2007 — **86**

2002 Staufener Schlossberg Riesling trocken
12.5%, ♀ till 2006 — **88**

2001 Staufener Schlossberg Riesling
12%, ♀ till 2006 — **87**

2002 Grauer Burgunder "XL"
9%, ♀ till 2007 — **88**

——— Red wines ———

2002 Spätburgunder trocken
13%, ♀ till 2006 — **83**

2002 Pinot Noir trocken
13%, ♀ till 2007 — **85**

2001 Pinot Noir trocken
13%, ♀ till 2006 — **86**

The wines: **100** Perfect · **95–99** Outstanding · **90–94** Excellent · **85–89** Very good · **80–84** Good · **75–79** Average

129

WEINGUT
KARL H. JOHNER

Owner: Karl Heinz and Patrick Johner
Winemaker: Karl Heinz and
Patrick Johner
79235 Bischoffingen, Gartenstraße 20
Tel. (0 76 62) 60 41, Fax 83 80
e-mail: info@johner.de
Internet: www.johner.de
Directions: A 5 Frankfurt–Basel, Riegel
exit, direction of Breisach and Vogtsburg
Sales: Irene Johner
Opening hours: Mon.–Fri. 14:00 to
17:00, Sat. 10:00 to 12:00 and 14:00 to
16:00 hours, and by appointment
Worth seeing: Unusual building in
Tuscan style, round barrel cellar

Vineyard area: 15.3 hectares
Annual production: 80,000 bottles
Top site: Bischoffinger Steinbuck,
but no sites mentioned on label
Soil types: Decomposed volcanic
formation
Grape varieties: 34% Blauer Spät-
burgunder, 17% Weißburgunder,
16% Grauburgunder, 9% Rivaner, 6%
Chardonnay, 3% Sauvignon Blanc,
15% other varieties
Average yield: 48 hl/ha
Best vintages: 1999, 2000, 2001
Member: Deutsches Barrique Forum

Karl Heinz Johner received his training at
the educational facility at Blankenhornsberg, then took his degree at Geisenheim.
This was followed by a stint of several
years as winemaker at the Lamberhurst
estate in England. After this, he proceeded to establish his winery back home
in Baden. He soon attracted attention
for the fact that his entire range was matured in barriques. And something else
was unusual ten years ago: Each of these
wines showed real class. Johner has
maintained his enthusiasm for innovative
practices. He was one of the first in Germany to experiment with concentration
techniques. Unfortunately, among all this
innovation, wine quality appears to have
taken a back seat. In 2003 only the Grauburgunder and Spätburgunder "SJ" are
reminiscent of better times.

2003 Grauer Burgunder trocken
14%, ♀ till 2006 — **84**

2003 Weißer Burgunder
trocken "SJ"
14.5%, ♀ till 2006 — **84**

2002 Sauvignon Blanc trocken
13%, ♀ till 2006 — **86**

2003 Weißer Burgunder & Chardonnay
trocken
13.5%, ♀ till 2007 — **86**

2003 Chardonnay trocken "SJ"
14.5%, ♀ till 2007 — **87**

2002 Chardonnay trocken "SJ"
14%, ♀ till 2007 — **88**

2003 Grauer Burgunder
trocken "SJ"
14.5%, ♀ till 2008 — **89**

2002 Grauer Burgunder
trocken "SJ"
14%, ♀ till 2008 — **91**

2003 Grauer Burgunder Auslese
12%, ♀ till 2008 — **86**

———— Red wines ————

2002 Spätburgunder trocken
14%, ♀ till 2007 — **84**

2001 Spätburgunder trocken
13.5%, ♀ till 2007 — **88**

2002 Spätburgunder trocken "SJ"
14%, ♀ till 2009 — **89**

2001 Spätburgunder trocken "SJ"
14%, ♀ till 2009 — **91**

WEINGUT KALKBÖDELE

Owner: Bernhard Mathis family
Administrator and winemaker:
Martin Schärli
79291 Merdingen, Enggasse 21
Tel. (0 76 68) 90 26 72, Fax 9 45 05
e-mail: weingut@kalkboedele.de
Internet: www.kalkboedele.de
Directions: A 5 Karlsruhe–Basel,
Freiburg-Mitte exit, in direction of
Umkirch, via the Tuniberg
Sales: Andrea Koch
Opening hours: Mon.–Fri. 10:00 to
12:00 hours and 14:00 to 17:00 hours
Sat. 10:00 to 13:00 hours
Specialty: Spätburgunder (Pinot Noir)
matured in chestnut barriques
Worth seeing: Large barrel cellar

Vineyard area: 14.5 hectares
Annual production: 130,000 bottles
Top sites: Merdinger Bühl,
Munzinger Kapellenberg
Soil types: Limestone formation with
loess top layer
Grape varieties: 67% Spätburgunder,
13% Grauburgunder, 11% Weiß-
burgunder, 7% Müller-Thurgau,
2% Riesling, Cabernet Sauvignon
on experimental basis
Average yield: 65 hl/ha
Best vintages: 1998, 1999, 2000
Member: Deutsches Barrique Forum

This winery first attracted attention in the
Eighties for its Pinot Noir, matured in
small barriques of French oak. In later
years the white Pinot varieties showed increasing form. That this potential is still
there to be taped is shown by the juicy,
elegant Spätburgunder (Pinot Noir) "Edition" of the 2002 vintage, and the smooth
Weißburgunder (Pinot Blanc) Spätlese.
Unfortunately, the basic range as well as
the botrytis dessert wines are still significantly weaker. One can but hope that the
planned investments in sorting tables
and temperature-controlled fermentation
tanks for red wine will provide a much-
needed impetus.

2003 Merdinger Bühl
Weißer Burgunder Kabinett trocken
13.5%, ♀ till 2006   **82**

2003 Merdinger Bühl
Grauer Burgunder Kabinett trocken
13.5%, ♀ till 2006   **82**

2001 Merdinger Bühl
Weißer Burgunder Spätlese trocken
13%, ♀ till 2006   **84**

2001 Merdinger Bühl
Riesling Spätlese trocken
12.5%, ♀ till 2006   **84**

2003 Merdinger Bühl
Weißer Burgunder Spätlese trocken
14%, ♀ till 2006   **85**

2003 Merdinger Bühl
Weißer Burgunder Beerenauslese
10%, ♀ till 2008   **85**

———— Red wines ————

2000 Merdinger Bühl
Spätburgunder trocken
13.5%, ♀ till 2005   **84**

2002 Merdinger Bühl
Spätburgunder trocken "Edition"
13.5%, ♀ till 2008   **86**

2003 Merdinger Bühl
Spätburgunder Beerenauslese
16.5%, ♀ till 2006   **82**

Kalkbödele®

Weingut der Gebrüder Mathis · D-79291 Merdingen

2001
Merdinger Bühl
Spätburgunder Rotwein
trocken
Qualitätswein
A.P.Nr. 340 03 02
Gutsabfüllung

13,5 % vol   Baden   1 ℓ

The wines: **100** Perfect · **95–99** Outstanding · **90–94** Excellent · **85–89** Very good · **80–84** Good · **75–79** Average

131

FRANZ KELLER
SCHWARZER ADLER

Owner and manager: Fritz Keller
Winemaker: Uwe Barnickel,
Hubert Zöllin
79235 Vogtsburg-Oberbergen,
Badbergstraße 23
Tel. (0 76 62) 9 33 00, Fax 7 19
e-mail: keller@franz-keller.de
Internet: www.franz-keller.de
*Directions: A 5 Frankfurt–Basel,
Riegel exit, in direction of Breisach*
Sales: Werner Geiser
Opening hours: Mon.–Fri. 08:00 to
17:00, Sat. 08:00 to 13:00 hours
and by appointment
Hotel and restaurant: "Schwarzer
Adler," closed Wed. and Thu.
Specialty: Top-class Baden/French cuisine
Worth seeing: Cellars hewn out of the
mountainside, up to 100 meters deep

Vineyard area: 48 hectares
Annual production: 350,000 bottles
Top sites: Oberbergener Bassgeige
and Pulverbuck, Oberrotweiler Kirch-
berg, Jechtinger Eichert, Achkarrer
Schlossberg
Soil types: Loess, volcanic and
decomposed basalt
Grape varieties: 34% Grauburgunder,
30% Spätburgunder, 13% Weiß-
burgunder, 10% Müller-Thurgau,
13% other varieties
Average yield: 59 hl/ha
Best vintages: 2001, 2002, 2003

Fritz Keller, whose father Franz was one
of the early advocates of dry wines in the
Eighties, took over the winery in 1990.
He has built his own style, his wines
show elegant varietal characteristics, they
are concentrated and juicy, showing in-
dividuality and character, wines that are
excellent companions for food, and more.
The 2003 white wines are good examples
of the house style. Just as in 2001, the
best wine is the Spätburgunder "A,"
which has clean fruit and an elegant long
finish – a typically Burgundian wine.

2003 Silvaner Spätlese trocken
13.5%, ♀ till 2006 — **83**

2003 Oberbergener Bassgeige
Grauer Burgunder trocken
14%, ♀ till 2006 — **84**

2003 Grauer Burgunder
trocken "S"
14.5%, ♀ till 2007 — **86**

2003 Chardonnay trocken "S"
14.5%, ♀ till 2007 — **86**

2003 Grauer Burgunder
trocken "A"
14.5%, ♀ till 2007 — **87**

2003 Chardonnay trocken "A"
14.5%, ♀ till 2008 — **88**

2003 Weißer Burgunder
trocken "S"
14.5%, ♀ till 2007 — **88**

2003 Weißer Burgunder
trocken "A"
14.5%, ♀ till 2009 — **89**

2002 Grauer Burgunder
trocken "A"
13.5%, ♀ till 2007 — **89**

——————— Red wines ———————

2002 Spätburgunder trocken "S"
13%, ♀ till 2008 — **88**

2001 Spätburgunder
trocken "S"
13%, ♀ till 2006 — **88**

2001 Spätburgunder
trocken "A"
13.5%, ♀ till 2009 — **92**

2002 Spätburgunder trocken "A"
14%, ♀ till 2010 — **93**

WEINGUT KLUMPP

Owner and manager: Ulrich Klumpp
Winemaker: Ulrich and
Markus Klumpp
76646 Bruchsal, Heidelberger Str. 100
Tel. (0 72 51) 1 67 19, **Fax** 1 05 23
e-mail: info@weingutklumpp.de
Internet: www.weingutklumpp.de
*Directions: Head out of town on the B 3
in direction of Heidelberg, 300 meters
after town limits, above the parking loop*
Sales: Marietta and Ulrich Klumpp
Opening hours: Mon.–Fri. 16:00 to
19:00 hours, Sat. 09:00 to 13:00 hours
and by appointment
Wine bistro: Jan., Mar., May, July,
Sept., Nov. from 1st to 14th, open from
17:00 hours, Sun. from 16:00 hours
Specialties: Vegetarian, Mediterranean

Vineyard area: 14 hectares
Annual production: 80,000 bottles
Top sites: Bruchsaler Weinhecke
and Klosterberg
Soil types: Sandy clay, kaolin with
clay, red marl
Grape varieties: 23% Spätburgunder,
21% Riesling, 13% Weißburgunder,
10% Grauburgunder, 8% each of
Auxerrois and St. Laurent, 7% Lem-
berger, 10% other varieties
Average yield: 60 hl/ha
Best vintages: 2000, 2001, 2003
Member: EcoVin

Together with his wife Marietta, Ulrich
Klumpp set out in 1990 to lay the foundation for his current winery by starting a
new operation on the outskirts of Bruchsal. A modern wine bistro provides an opportunity to get acquainted with the estate's wines, which are produced using
organic practices. The winery produces
three ranges of differing quality: one star
(estate wine), two stars (Edition Klumpp)
and three stars (Premium). In addition,
predicate designations such as Kabinett
are used for some wines. The juicy 2003
Auxerrois Kabinett proves that Klumpp
certainly knows how to make good wine.

2003 Weißer Burg...
Kabinett trocke...
12%, ♀ till 2006

2003 Chardonnay tr...
12.5%, ♀ till 2006

64

2003 Weißer Burgunder
trocken ***
12.5%, ♀ till 2006

84

2003 Chardonnay trocken *
13%, ♀ till 2006

84

2002 Grauer Burgunder
trocken ***
12%, ♀ till 2006

84

2003 Auxerrois
Kabinett trocken **
12%, ♀ till 2007

85

2001 Weißer Burgunder
"Premium" trocken
12%, ♀ till 2005

85

2001 Chardonnay
"Premium" trocken
13%, ♀ till 2006

85

——— Red wines ———

2003 Cuvée Nr. 1 trocken
12%, ♀ till 2006

81

2001 Cuvée No. 1 trocken *
12%, ♀ till 2006

84

2001 Pinot Noir trocken *
12.5%, ♀ till 2006

84

2003 St. Laurent trocken *
13.5%, ♀ till 2007

84

2003 Cuvée "M" trocken *
13.5%, ♀ till 2008

85

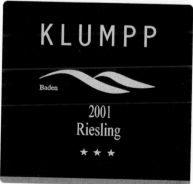

KLUMPP
Baden
2001
Riesling
★ ★ ★

The wines: **100** Perfect · **95–99** Outstanding · **90–94** Excellent · **85–89** Very good · **80–84** Good · **75–79** Average

133

EINGUT KNAB

Owner: Thomas and Regina Rinker
Winemaker: Thomas Rinker
79346 Endingen, Hennengärtle 1a
Tel. (0 76 42) 61 55, Fax 93 13 77
e-mail: regina-rinker@t-online.de
Directions: A 5 Frankfurt–Basel,
Riegel exit
Sales: Rinker family
Opening hours: Mon.–Fri. 17:00 to
18:30 hours, Sat. 10:00 to 14:00 hours
and by appointment
Worth a visit: "Vinological Unimog
Tour" through the loess paths to the
nature reserve Amolterer Heide

Vineyard area: 15 hectares
Annual production: 100,000 bottles
Top site: Endinger Engelsberg
Soil types: Loess-clay and decom-
posed volcanic soil
Grape varieties: 40% Spätburgunder,
30% Weißburgunder, 15% Grau-
burgunder, 5% each of Chardonnay,
Riesling and Müller-Thurgau
Average yield: 65 hl/ha
Best vintages: 2001, 2002, 2003

Thomas Rinker is a cellar technician. Together with his wife Regina, an artist, he
took over the Knab winery in the eastern
Kaiserstuhl area in the mid-Nineties. One
of the most attractive labels in Baden
adorns the bottles. In order to impart
more knowledge about nature and viticulture to his customers, Rinker organizes
drives through the vineyards to the Amolterer Heide nature conservation area.
The development in recent years has been
very positive, and the red wines of the
2001 vintage showed Rinker moving into
the elite of Baden producers. The range
tasted this year was thoroughly convincing. The elegantly fruity and clean 2002
Spätburgunder (Pinot Noir) wines as
well as the smooth and elegant white wines
are exemplary. The reward can be seen in
the third bunch of grapes now awarded.

2003 Endinger Engelsberg
Auxerrois Kabinett trocken
13.5%, ♀ till 2007   86

2003 Endinger Engelsberg
Weißer Burgunder Spätlese trocken
14%, ♀ till 2006   86

2003 Endinger Engelsberg
Grauer Burgunder Spätlese trocken
14.5%, ♀ till 2007   87

2002 Endinger Engelsberg
Chardonnay Spätlese trocken
13%, ♀ till 2007   87

2002 Endinger Engelsberg
Grauer Burgunder Spätlese trocken ***
13.5%, ♀ till 2007   87

2001 Endinger Engelsberg
Chardonnay Spätlese trocken
13.5%, ♀ till 2006   87

2003 Endinger Engelsberg
Weißer Burgunder Spätlese trocken ***
14.5%, ♀ till 2008   89

2003 Endinger Engelsberg
Grauer Burgunder Spätlese trocken ***
14.5%, ♀ till 2009   90

———— Red wines ————

2003 Endinger Engelsberg
Spätburgunder trocken
13%, ♀ till 2007   87

2001 Endinger Engelsberg
Spätburgunder trocken Barrique
13%, ♀ till 2006   88

2002 Endinger Engelsberg
Spätburgunder trocken ***
13.5%, ♀ till 2010   90

2001 Endinger Engelsberg
Spätburgunder trocken "Reserve" ***
13%, ♀ till 2010   90

WEINGUT KNAB

2001 ENDINGER ENGELSBERG
WEISSER BURGUNDER
TROCKEN

BADEN · SPÄTLESE · 12.5% vol. 0,75 l
QUALITÄTSWEIN MIT PRÄDIKAT · A.P.NR. 268/08/03

WEINGUT HOLGER KOCH

Owner: Holger Koch
Vineyard manager: Erna and Hubert Koch
79235 Bickensohl, Mannwerk 3
Tel. (0 76 62) 91 22 58, Fax 94 98 59
e-mail: hk@weingut-holger-koch.de
Internet: www.weingut-holger-koch.de
Directions: A 5 Frankfurt–Basel, Riegel exit, coming from the south Bad Krozingen exit, via Breisach and Achkarren
Sales: By appointment
Worth seeing: Natural monument "Lösshohlgasse" around Koch's vineyard in the "Katzenloch" site, also barrique cellar in former water tower

---

Vineyard area: 6 hectares
Annual production: 33,000 bottles
Top sites: Bickensohler Katzenloch, Halbuck and Eichbuck
Soil types: Loess
Grape varieties: 50% Spätburgunder, 34% Grauburgunder, 16% Weißburgunder
Average yield: 50 hl/ha
Best vintages: 2001, 2002, 2003

Holger Koch worked as winemaker for five years at the Franz Keller estate. In 1999, he started his own winery, based on vineyards owned by his parents, who had in the past delivered their grapes to the local co-operative. The vineyard area has since grown from half a hectare to six hectares. Beginning with the 2001 vintage, Koch has been involved full-time with the production in his own winery. The wines are left to mature in an old water cistern that is a 100 years old, and is located underground below the Katzenloch vineyard. His aim is to produce outstanding selected Spätburgunder (Pinot Noir) wines from Pinot Noir clones imported from Burgundy. The 2002 vintage has taken him another step closer to realizing this dream, the French style of the wines is most attractive. The good white wines of the 2003 vintage, too, underline the positive trend at this winery.

2003 Weißer Burgunder
trocken "S"
14.5%, ♀ till 2007   86

2001 Grauer Burgunder
trocken "S" *
13%, ♀ till 2006   86

2002 Grauer Burgunder
trocken "S"
13%, ♀ till 2006   86

2003 Grauer Burgunder
trocken "S" ***
15%, ♀ till 2007   87

2001 Weißer Burgunder
trocken "S"
13%, ♀ till 2006   87

2003 Grauer Burgunder
trocken "S"
14.5%, ♀ till 2008   88

———— Red wines ————

2001 Spätburgunder
trocken "S" ***
13.5%, ♀ till 2007   86

2000 Spätburgunder
trocken "S ***"
13%, ♀ till 2008   86

2002 Spätburgunder trocken "S"
13.5%, ♀ till 2008   87

2002 Spätburgunder
trocken "S" ***
13.5%, ♀ till 2010   88

HOLGER KOCH
kaiserstuhl

Grauburgunder 2003

Gutsabfüllung Holger Koch, D-79235 Bickensohl, A.P. Nr. 3416 12 03
Baden Qualitätswein 14% vol 750 ml

The wines: **100** Perfect · **95–99** Outstanding · **90–94** Excellent · **85–89** Very good · **80–84** Good · **75–79** Average

135

WINZERGENOSSENSCHAFT KÖNIGSCHAFFHAUSEN

General manager: Edmund Schillinger
Winemaker: Rainer Roßwog
79346 Königschaffhausen,
Kiechlinsberger Straße 2
Tel. (0 76 42) 9 08 46, Fax 25 35
e-mail:
wg-koenigschaffhausen@t-online.de
Internet:
www.koenigschaffhauser-wein.de
*Directions: A 5 Frankfurt–Basel,
Riegel exit, in direction of Rhine*
Sales: Harald Henninger, Elke Feser
Opening hours: Mon.–Fri. 08:00 to
12:00 hours and 13:30 to 17:00 hours
Sat. 09:00 to 12:00 hours
Worth seeing: Signposted wine hiking
path, old vaulted barrel cellar

Vineyard area: 199 hectares
Number of members: 380
Annual production: 1.55 mill. bottles
Top sites: Königschaffhauser
Hasenberg and Steingrüble
Soil types: Loess-clay, partly on
decomposed volcanic formation
Grape varieties: 42% Spätburgunder,
23% Müller-Thurgau, 22% Graubur-
gunder, 8% Weißburgunder, 5% other
varieties
Average yield: 69 hl/ha
Best vintages: 1999, 2001, 2002
Member: Deutsches Barrique Forum

The co-operative at Königschaffhausen started investing in modern cellar equipment in the early Seventies, which put it ahead of most of its competitors in Baden for many years. Following on a good range presented last year, we have to report a definite disappointment here. Many of the basic wines can hardly be recommended. But there are some good wines too: The Scheurebe Trockenbeerenauslese as well as the 2001 Spätburgunder (Pinot Noir) "Regnum" are attractive wines, and the dry Grauburgunder (Pinot Gris) Spätlese, matured in barriques, can also be recommended.

2003 Königschaffhauser Hasenberg
Weißer Burgunder trocken
14%, ♀ till 2006   **82**

2003 Königschaffhauser Hasenberg
Grauer Burgunder Spätlese trocken
Barrique
14.5%, ♀ till 2006   **84**

2002 Königschaffhauser Hasenberg
Chardonnay Spätlese trocken
13%, ♀ till 2006   **85**

2002 Königschaffhauser Vulkanfelsen
Scheurebe Trockenbeerenauslese
10%, ♀ till 2010   **88**

——— Red wines ———

2002 Königschaffhauser Steingrüble
Spätburgunder Weißherbst Eiswein
12%, ♀ till 2007   **85**

2003 Königschaffhauser Steingrüble
Spätburgunder Auslese trocken
14.5%, ♀ till 2006   **80**

2003 Königschaffhauser Steingrüble
Spätburgunder trocken Selection
14%, ♀ till 2006   **80**

2002 Königschaffhauser Vulkanfelsen
Spätburgunder Auslese trocken
13.5%, ♀ till 2006   **83**

2000 Königschaffhauser Steingrüble
Spätburgunder trocken "Regnum"
13.5%, ♀ till 2006   **85**

2001 Königschaffhauser Steingrüble
Spätburgunder Spätlese trocken Selection
12.5%, ♀ till 2006   **85**

2001 Königschaffhauser Steingrüble
Spätburgunder trocken "Regnum"
13.5%, ♀ till 2007   **86**

WEINGUT KONSTANZER

Owner: Horst and Petra Konstanzer
79241 Ihringen, Quellenstraße 22
Tel. (0 76 68) 55 37, Fax 50 97
e-mail: info@weingut-konstanzer.de
Internet: www.weingut-konstanzer.de
Directions: A 5 Frankfurt–Basel,
Freiburg-Mitte exit, in direction of
Breisach
Opening hours: Mon.–Fri. 17:00 to
19:00 hours, Sat. 09:00 to 16:30 hours
and by appointment

Vineyard area: 6.5 hectares
Annual production: 50,000 bottles
Top site: Ihringer Winklerberg
Soil types: Decomposed volcanic formation, loess
Grape varieties: 45% Spätburgunder, 30% Grauburgunder, 10% Weißburgunder, 6% Silvaner, 3% each of Riesling, Muskateller and Chardonnay
Average yield: 60 hl/ha
Best vintages: 1999, 2001, 2002

Horst and Petra Konstanzer started off this small winery at the southernmost tip of the Kaiserstuhl area in 1983, with less than a hectare of vineyard, as a side-line. 1989 they took over their parents operation, which until then had delivered its grapes to the co-operative. The vineyard area has been expanded, two hectares in recent years, and the Pinot Gris plantings increased to 30 percent of the total. Today, vines are planted on more than six hectares. Minimal intervention is used in handling the grapes, which are all fermented dry. In the previous year's range we particularly liked the 2001 Chardonnay and Spätburgunder (Pinot Noir) Spätlese wines, which had been matured in barriques. The 2002 vintage white wines were juicy and clean. Unfortunately, the 2003 vintage represents a step backward. The only slight exceptions are some solid Silvaner wines and an attractive Weißburgunder (Pinot Blanc) Spätlese.

2003 Ihringer Winklerberg
Gewürztraminer Spätlese trocken
13.5%, ♀ till 2006 · · · · · · · · · · · · · · 83

2003 Ihringer Winklerberg
Silvaner Kabinett trocken
13%, ♀ till 2006 · · · · · · · · · · · · · · · 83

2003 Ihringer Winklerberg
Grauer Burgunder Spätlese trocken
14%, ♀ till 2006 · · · · · · · · · · · · · · · 83

2003 Ihringer Winklerberg
Weißer Burgunder Kabinett trocken
14%, ♀ till 2006 · · · · · · · · · · · · · · · 83

2002 Ihringer Winklerberg
Chardonnay Spätlese trocken
13%, ♀ till 2006 · · · · · · · · · · · · · · · 84

2003 Ihringer Winklerberg
Silvaner Spätlese trocken
13%, ♀ till 2006 · · · · · · · · · · · · · · · 84

2002 Ihringer Winklerberg
Grauer Burgunder Spätlese trocken
13%, ♀ till 2006 · · · · · · · · · · · · · · · 85

2001 Ihringer Winklerberg
Chardonnay Spätlese trocken
13%, ♀ till 2006 · · · · · · · · · · · · · · · 86

2003 Ihringer Winklerberg
Weißer Burgunder Spätlese trocken
15%, ♀ till 2006 · · · · · · · · · · · · · · · 86

————— Red wine —————

2001 Ihringer Winklerberg
Spätburgunder Spätlese trocken Barrique
13.5%, ♀ till 2006 · · · · · · · · · · · · · · 86

konstanzer

Baden
2003
Ihringer Winklerberg
Silvaner
Spätlese · Trocken
Qualitätswein mit Prädikat

Gutsabfüllung
Weingut Horst + Petra Konstanzer
D-79241 Ihringen/Kaiserstuhl

75 cl · 13%vol · A.P.Nr. 377/10/03

The wines: **100** Perfect · **95–99** Outstanding · **90–94** Excellent · **85–89** Very good · **80–84** Good · **75–79** Average

WEINGUT KOPP

Owner and manager:
Ewald and Birgit Kopp
Winemaker: Ewald Kopp
76547 Sinzheim-Ebenung,
Ebenunger Straße 21
Tel. (0 72 21) 80 36 01, Fax 80 36 02
e-mail: info@weingut-kopp.com
Internet: www.weingut-kopp.com
Directions: A 5 Frankfurt–Basel, Baden-
Baden exit, at end of town in Sinzheim
turn left in direction of Ebenung
Sales: Birgit Kopp
Opening hours: Mon. 10:00 to 12:00
hours and 14:30 to 18:00 hours
Wed., Thur. and Fri. 14:30 to 18:00
hours, Sat. 10:00 to 14:30 hours

Vineyard area: 7 hectares
Annual production: 45,000 bottles
Top sites: No vineyard sites stated on
labels
Soil types: Red sandstone und
decomposed granite, clay und loess
Grape varieties: 41% Riesling,
32% Spätburgunder, 12% Weißbur-
gunder, 7% Grauburgunder, 5% Char-
donnay, 3% other varieties
Average yield: 57 hl/ha
Best vintages: 2001, 2002

When he took over the vineyards of the
last producer of bottled wine in town in
1996, this was a signal for Ewald Kopp to
seek independence for himself. Ewald
Kopp initially trained as a mechanic for
agricultural machinery, then followed
this with an apprenticeship in winemaking, part of which was spent under the
tutelage of Bernhard Huber in Malterdingen. He is totally focussed on quality in
his own winery, and his Chardonnay and
Spätburgunder (Pinot Noir) wines bear
testimony to this. Only the Riesling wines
are not yet quite up to standard. This summary of last year's reviews is confirmed by the current range. We particularly
liked the 2002 Spätburgunder (Pinot
Noir) "Alte Reben" (Old Vines). It has an
elegant fruity finish. Looking at the 2003

white wines, the Chardonnay is once
again the outstanding wine of the range.

2002 Riesling Kabinett trocken
11.5%, ♀ till 2005   **83**

2003 Riesling Kabinett trocken
13%, ♀ till 2006   **83**

2003 Riesling Spätlese trocken
13%, ♀ till 2006   **83**

2003 Grauer Burgunder trocken
14%, ♀ till 2006   **83**

2002 Grauer Burgunder trocken
11.5%, ♀ till 2006   **84**

2003 Chardonnay trocken
13.5%, ♀ till 2006   **84**

2002 Chardonnay trocken "S"
13.5%, ♀ till 2006   **85**

2002 Chardonnay trocken
12%, ♀ till 2006   **86**

2001 Chardonnay trocken
13%, ♀ till 2007   **88**

—————— Red wines ——————

2001 Spätburgunder
trocken "Alte Reben"
13.5%, ♀ till 2007   **86**

2000 Spätburgunder trocken "S"
13.5%, ♀ till 2006   **87**

2002 Spätburgunder trocken "S"
13.5%, ♀ till 2009   **87**

2002 Spätburgunder
trocken "Alte Reben"
13.5%, ♀ till 2009   **88**

2001 Spätburgunder trocken "R"
13.5%, ♀ till 2009   **89**

SEEGUT KRESS

Owner: Kristin and Thomas Kress
Winemaker: Thomas Kress
88709 Hagnau, Hauptstraße 2
Tel. (0 75 32) 62 05, Fax 29 09
e-mail: info@seegut-kress.de
Internet: www.seegut-kress.de
Directions: A 7 Stuttgart–Singen, in direction of Lindau at Kreuz Singen; on the B 31 at town exit of Hagnau, building with red wine glass on wall
Sales: Kristin and Thomas Kress
Opening hours: Anytime by appointment

Vineyard area: 7 hectares
Annual production: 55,000 bottles
Top sites: No vineyard sites stated on labels
Soil types: Sandy, limestone-rich clay, fresh water molasse
Grape varieties: 40% Spätburgunder, 25% Müller-Thurgau, 15% each of Grau- and Weißburgunder, 5% Auxerrois
Average yield: 70 hl/ha
Best vintages: 2001, 2002

A pleasant surprise on Lake Constance. The winery is located in the center of Hagnau – a five meter high banner showing a red wine glass ensures you cannot miss it. Thomas and Kristin Kress left the Hagnau co-operative a few years ago. 2001 was the second vintage in which they had not delivered grapes to the co-operative, and the first vintage mentioned in this guide. The successor vintage 2002 was so successful that it was an easy decision awarding the first bunch of grapes. All the wines showed clean and elegant varietal typicity, coupled with dense fruit and good structure in the case of the best varieties. Half of the production is sold to restaurants. The succession here is also secure: son Johannes served his apprenticeship in winemaking with Dr. Heger in Ihringen, and practical stints overseas (South Africa, New Zealand) are destined to widen his horizons. The current collection is solid, but lacks the charm of the previous vintage.

2003 Müller-Thurgau trocken
12%, ♀ till 2006 — 81

2002 Müller-Thurgau trocken
11.5%, ♀ till 2006 — 81

2002 Weißer Burgunder trocken
12.5%, ♀ till 2006 — 83

2003 Weißer Burgunder trocken
14%, ♀ till 2006 — 84

2003 Grauer Burgunder trocken
14%, ♀ till 2006 — 84

2002 Grauer Burgunder trocken
12.5%, ♀ till 2006 — 85

——— Red wines ———

2002 Kress Rosé trocken
12.5%, ♀ till 2006 — 85

2003 Rosé halbtrocken
14.5%, ♀ till 2006 — 84

2003 Spätburgunder trocken
14%, ♀ till 2006 — 82

2001 Spätburgunder trocken
13%, ♀ till 2006 — 85

2002 Spätburgunder
trocken Barrique
13%, ♀ till 2007 — 85

2001 Spätburgunder
trocken Barrique
13%, ♀ till 2007 — 87

The wines: **100** Perfect · **95–99** Outstanding · **90–94** Excellent · **85–89** Very good · **80–84** Good · **75–79** Average

139

WEINGUT LÄMMLIN-SCHINDLER

Owner and manager: Gerd Schindler
Winemaker: Friedhelm Maier
79418 Mauchen, Müllheimer Straße 4
Tel. (0 76 35) 4 40, Fax 4 36
e-mail: weingut@laemmlin-schindler.de
Internet: www.laemmlin-schindler.de
Directions: A 5 Freiburg–Basel, Neuen-burg exit, in direction of Schliengen
Sales: Mon.–Fri. 09:00 to 12:00 hours and 14:00 to 18:00 hours, Sat. 09:00 to 12:00 hours and 14:00 to 16:30 hours and by appointment
Restaurant: "Zur Krone" in Mauchen from 11:00 to 23:00 hours, closed Mon. and Tue.
Specialties: Veal sausage, roast beef with horse-radish
History: Winemaking in family since 12th century

Vineyard area: 19.2 hectares
Annual production: 150,000 bottles
Top sites: Mauchener Frauenberg and Sonnenstück
Soil types: Decomposed limestone, loess-clay
Grape varieties: 41% Spätburgunder, 15% Gutedel, 12% each of Weißburgunder and Chardonnay, 20% other varieties
Average yield: 67 hl/ha
Best vintages: 2000, 2001, 2003

Gerd Schindler has for some years been producing concentrated white wines, typical of their vintages. The red wines tend not quite to match up to this standard. The restaurant and inn "Zur Krone" has been run by the family since 1826, and provides convivial surroundings in which to get acquainted with the wines while enjoying hearty local food. Following on from the good 2001 vintage, the 2003 wines remain on the same solid level as those of the previous vintage. The Grauburgunder, Chardonnay and Gewürztraminer Spätlese wines all show clear fruit and good concentration.

2003 Mauchener Sonnenstück
Weißer Burgunder Kabinett trocken
13.5%, ♀ till 2006 **84**

2003 Mauchener Sonnenstück
Gewürztraminer Spätlese trocken
14%, ♀ till 2006 **85**

2003 Mauchener Frauenberg
Chardonnay Spätlese trocken
14.5%, ♀ till 2007 **85**

2003 Mauchener Sonnenstück
Grauer Burgunder Spätlese trocken
14.5%, ♀ till 2007 **86**

2001 Mauchener Sonnenstück
Gewürztraminer Spätlese trocken
13%, ♀ till 2006 **88**

2001 Mauchener Sonnenstück
Weißer Burgunder Trockenbeerenauslese
8.5%, ♀ till 2020 **91**

——— Red wines ———

2003 Mauchener Sonnenstück
Spätburgunder Weißherbst Kabinett trocken
14.5%, ♀ till 2006 **83**

2003 Mauchener Sonnenstück
Spätburgunder Weißherbst Spätlese trocken
13.5%, ♀ till 2006 **84**

2002 Mauchener Sonnenstück
Spätburgunder Auslese trocken
15%, ♀ till 2006 **84**

WEINGUT
ANDREAS LAIBLE

Owner: Andreas and Ingrid Laible
Winemaker: Andreas Laible
and Andreas Chr. Laible
77770 Durbach, Am Bühl 6
Tel. (07 81) 4 12 38, Fax 3 83 39
e-mail: info@weingut-laible.de
Internet: www.weingut-laible.de
Directions: A 5 Frankfurt–Basel, Appen-
weier or Offenburg exit, in direction of
Durbach
Sales: Ingrid and Andreas Laible
Opening hours: Mon.–Fri. 08:00 to
11:30 hours and 13:30 to 18:00 hours
Sat. 08:00 to 11:30 hours
and 13:30 to 16:00 hours
and by appointment
History: Family-owned since 1672

Vineyard area: 7 hectares
Annual production: 40,000 bottles
Top site: Durbacher Plauelrain
Soil types: Decomposed granite
Grape varieties: 58% Riesling (Klingel-
berger), 15% Spätburgunder,
6% each of Traminer, Gewürztraminer
and Scheurebe, 6% Weißburgunder
and Grauburgunder, 3% Chardonnay
and other varieties
Average yield: 53 hl/ha
Best vintages: 1996, 1998, 2002
Member: VDP

Andreas Laible heads up what is probably
the winery in all of Baden-Württemberg
that has collected the most medals and
awards. A total of more than 600 gold
medals at state and national competitions
speaks for itself. 22 special state awards,
11 special national awards (2 golds) also
bear testimony to the creativity, and continuity on a very high level. This effort was
rewarded with the title "Rising star of the
year" in 2000. Laible has to work hard to
achieve these successes, in contrast to
many other producers he has to work the
steep rocky slopes of the Durbacher Plauelrain site, the best sections of which can
only be worked by hand. Against this

background the restlessly active winemaker, who has been dubbed by regional
media the "Star of the steep slopes," is
naturally happy to see the next generation
growing up to take over duties successively
in the winery. Andreas junior has already
graduated as a viticultural technician, and
the same goes for son Alexander. There is
plenty of work to be found on the estate.
Apart from making wines, the Laibles also
distill some high-quality spirits. The ingredients for Kirschwasser and Williams pear
distillates come from the own orchards,
and Marc made from Gewürztraminer is
also one of the specialties. Even bread is
baked in the one stone baking oven. 200
meters from the winery, under the vines of
the Plauelrain site, Andreas Laible has had
an underground cellar hewn out of the
rocks. He wants to use this for barrique
maturation, but also for wine tastings with
a special ambience. His wines are as individual, but also full of character, as Laible
is himself. He is quick to point out that his
results run without the use of any modern concentration techniques. The Scheurebe wines were the outstanding feature of
the 2002 vintage: From the elegant and
racy dry Spätlese via the incredibly juicy
fruity Spätlese to the wonderful Beerenauslese, one wine was better than the
next. The wines of the hot 2003 vintage are
well made, but they cannot entirely deny
the stresses the vines had to endure during
the heat-wave. The "Achat," which is full
of character, is the best of the dry wines.
Our tasting "Ten Years After" proves that
these wines have excellent maturation potential. The top 1994 dry Riesling of the
estate was fresh and dominated by clear
fruit, though mature, when tasted recently.
Two botrytized Auslese wines confirm the
potential of the 2003 vintage, and round
off the range rather nicely.

2003 Durbacher Plauelrain
Riesling Kabinett trocken – 6 –
12.5%, ♀ till 2006 **85**

2002 Durbacher Plauelrain
Riesling Spätlese trocken – 31 –
12.5%, ♀ till 2006 **85**

The wines: **100** Perfect · **95–99** Outstanding · **90–94** Excellent · **85–89** Very good · **80–84** Good · **75–79** Average

2003 Durbacher Plauelrain
Chardonnay Spätlese trocken
13%, ♀ till 2006 — 85

2003 Durbacher Plauelrain
Riesling Spätlese trocken "SL"
13%, ♀ till 2006 — 86

2003 Durbacher Plauelrain
Weißer Burgunder Spätlese trocken
14%, ♀ till 2007 — 87

2003 Durbacher Plauelrain
Grauer Burgunder Spätlese trocken
14%, ♀ till 2007 — 87

2002 Durbacher Plauelrain
Riesling Spätlese trocken
12.5%, ♀ till 2006 — 87

2003 Durbacher Plauelrain
Gewürztraminer Spätlese trocken
14%, ♀ till 2007 — 88

2003 Durbacher Plauelrain
Riesling Spätlese trocken "Achat"
13.5%, ♀ till 2007 — 88

2002 Durbacher Plauelrain
Riesling Spätlese trocken "SL"
12.5%, ♀ till 2007 — 88

2002 Durbacher Plauelrain
Scheurebe Spätlese trocken
13.5%, ♀ till 2007 — 89

2002 Durbacher Plauelrain
Riesling Spätlese trocken "Achat"
13%, ♀ till 2008 — 89

2002 Durbacher Plauelrain
Chardonnay Spätlese trocken
12.5%, ♀ till 2007 — 90

2002 Durbacher Plauelrain
Riesling Auslese halbtrocken
13%, ♀ till 2006 — 87

2003 Durbacher Plauelrain
Riesling Spätlese
11.5%, ♀ till 2008 — 87

2003 Durbacher Plauelrain
Traminer Auslese
11.5%, ♀ till 2008 — 88

2002 Durbacher Plauelrain
Traminer Auslese
11%, ♀ till 2008 — 88

2002 Durbacher Plauelrain
Gewürztraminer Beerenauslese
9%, ♀ till 2008 — 88

2002 Durbacher Plauelrain
Scheurebe Auslese
12%, ♀ till 2010 — 89

2002 Durbacher Plauelrain
Gewürztraminer Auslese
11.5%, ♀ till 2008 — 89

2003 Durbacher Plauelrain
Scheurebe Auslese
11.5%, ♀ till 2010 — 90

2003 Durbacher Plauelrain
Gewürztraminer Auslese
12%, ♀ till 2010 — 90

2002 Durbacher Plauelrain
Riesling Auslese
12%, ♀ till 2010 — 90

2002 Durbacher Plauelrain
Scheurebe Spätlese
12.5%, ♀ till 2012 — 91

2002 Durbacher Plauelrain
Scheurebe Beerenauslese
10%, ♀ till 2020 — 94

——— Red wines ———

2002 Durbacher Plauelrain
Spätburgunder Spätlese trocken – 26 –
14%, ♀ till 2007 — 84

2003 Durbacher Plauelrain
Spätburgunder Auslese trocken – 37 –
14%, ♀ till 2009 — 86

2003 Durbacher Plauelrain
Spätburgunder Auslese trocken – 39 –
14.5%, ♀ till 2009 — 88

Baden   Ortenau

LAIBLE

Qualitätswein mit Prädikat · Weingut Andreas Laible · D-77770 Durbach · Gutsabfüllung

2000
Durbacher Plauelrain

Riesling
Spätlese trocken »Achat«

13% vol   A. P. Nr. 514/35/01   0,75 L

The estates: ✿✿✿✿✿ World's finest · ✿✿✿✿ Germany's best · ✿✿✿ Very good · ✿✿ Good · ✿ Reliable

WEINGUT
HEINRICH MÄNNLE

Owner: Heinrich and Wilma Männle
Manager and winemaker: Heinrich Männle
77770 Durbach, Sendelbach 16
Tel. (07 81) 4 11 01, Fax 44 01 05
e-mail: weingutmaennle@aol.com
Internet: www.weingutmaennle.de
Directions: A 5 Frankfurt–Basel, Appenweier or Offenburg exit, in direction of Durbach, to center of village, then to suburb of Sendelbach
Sales: Wilma Männle
Opening hours: Mon.–Sat. 08:00 to 18:00 hours and by appointment
History: Winery family-owned since 1737
Worth seeing: Granite vaulted cellar in half-timbered house

Vineyard area: 5.5 hectares
Annual production: 40,000 bottles
Top site: Durbacher Kochberg
Soil types: Decomposed granite
Grape varieties: 56% Spätburgunder, 10% Weißburgunder, 9% Scheurebe, 8% Riesling (Klingelberger), 6% Grauburgunder, 11% other varieties
Average yield: 73 hl/ha
Best vintages: 2000, 2001, 2002

The Männle family winery lies embedded in the vineyards in the heart of the town of Durbach. Heinrich Männle took over this 18th century property in 1956, and established soon a solid reputation for the good Riesling wines produced here. Last year the highlights were two dry 2002 Spätlese wines from the Durbacher Kochberg site. The 2003 counterparts cannot quite equal that standard. It thus comes as no surprise that the wines we liked best were two mature reds from the 2000 and 2001 vintages. The owner's plans for the future include the construction of a new vaulted cellar from quarry stone, and the maturation of all wines in oak barrels.

2003 Durbacher Kochberg
Grauer Burgunder Spätlese trocken
13.5%, ♀ till 2006 — **84**

2002 Durbacher Kochberg
Riesling Spätlese trocken – 2 –
11.5%, ♀ till 2006 — **86**

2001 Durbacher Kochberg
Riesling Spätlese trocken
11.5%, ♀ till 2006 — **86**

2003 Durbacher Kochberg
Weißer Burgunder Spätlese halbtrocken
13%, ♀ till 2006 — **84**

2003 Durbacher Kochberg
Scheurebe Spätlese
12%, ♀ till 2007 — **85**

2003 Durbacher Kochberg
Weißer Burgunder Beerenauslese
12.5%, ♀ till 2008 — **85**

2003 Durbacher Oelberg
Gewürztraminer Auslese
12.5%, ♀ till 2008 — **86**

2001 Durbacher Kochberg
Traminer (Clevner) Eiswein
9%, ♀ till 2015 — **89**

——— Red wines ———

2000 Durbacher Kochberg
Cabernet Sauvignon trocken
13.5%, ♀ till 2006 — **85**

2001 Durbacher Kochberg
Spätburgunder Spätlese trocken
13%, ♀ till 2008 — **86**

2003 Durbacher Kochberg
Spätburgunder Auslese
14%, ♀ till 2007 — **85**

The wines: **100** Perfect · **95–99** Outstanding · **90–94** Excellent · **85–89** Very good · **80–84** Good · **75–79** Average

143

WEINGUT LEO MAIER

Owner and manager: Leo Maier
88719 Stetten bei Meersburg,
Hauptstraße 15
Tel. (0 75 32) 92 31, Fax 21 81
e-mail: weingut.leo.maier@t-online.de
Directions: B 31, coming from Meersburg, go on to B 33 in direction of Ravensburg, at town exit Stetten
Sales: Leo Maier
Opening hours: Mon.–Fri. 09:00 to 18:00 hours, Sat. 09:00 to 16:00 hours and by appointment
Restaurant: May, June and Sept. from 18:00 to 24:00 hours, closed Mon.
Specialties: Vintner's bread, whitefish from Lake Constance
Worth seeing: View from the vineyards over Lake Constance, model vineyard

---

Vineyard area: 5.5 hectares
Annual production: 45,000 bottles
Top site: Meersburger Sängerhalde
Soil types: Sand, clay, terminal moraine
Grape varieties: 34% Müller-Thurgau, 30% Spätburgunder, 9% GraubFurgunder, 8% Sauvignon Blanc, 7% each of Weißburgunder and Regent, 5% other varieties
Average yield: 70 hl/ha
Best vintages: 2001, 2002, 2003

Leo Maier sought independence in 1988, at the age of 25. By now his operation includes 5.5 hectares of vineyards, plus 4.5 hectares of fruit orchards (cherries, plums, yellow plums, pears and apples) from the fruits of which Maier produces 25 different distilled spirits. We were impressed by last year's attractive range: Juicy Müller-Thurgau and good red wines showed the potential. The very homogeneous quality of the 2003 white wines and good 2002 red wines have convinced us the time has come to award a first bunch of grapes. The 2002 Spätburgunder deserves special mention for its clean fruit, elegant use of oak and good length. Maier has no problems selling his wine: "We are sold out every year!"

2003 Meersburger Sängerhalde
Sauvignon Blanc Spätlese trocken
13.5%, ♀ till 2006   81

2003 Stettener
Grauer Burgunder trocken
13%, ♀ till 2006   82

2003 Meersburger Sängerhalde
Müller-Thurgau trocken "18.04."
12%, ♀ till 2006   82

2003 Meersburger Sängerhalde
Weißer Burgunder Spätlese trocken
13%, ♀ till 2006   83

2003 Meersburger Sängerhalde
Müller-Thurgau trocken "06.04."
12%, ♀ till 2006   83

2003 Meersburger Sängerhalde
Müller-Thurgau Spätlese
12%, ♀ till 2006   82

——— Red wines ———

2003 Meersburger Sängerhalde
Spätburgunder Weißherbst Spätlese trocken
13.5%, ♀ till 2006   83

2003 Meersburger Fohrenberg
Spätburgunder Spätlese trocken
13%, ♀ till 2006   83

2002 Meersburger Sängerhalde
Regent trocken
13%, ♀ till 2006   84

2002 Meersburger Sängerhalde
Spätburgunder trocken
13%, ♀ till 2008   87

WEINGUT MARKGRAF VON BADEN – SCHLOSS SALEM

Owner: Max Markgraf von Baden
Manager: Steffen Brahner, Volker Faust
Winemaker: Martin Kölble
88682 Schloss Salem, Rentamt
Tel. (0 75 53) 8 14 02, Fax 8 15 69
e-mail: Weingut@Salem.de
Internet: www.markgraf-von-baden.de
Directions: A 81 to end of Autobahn at Stockach, B 31 as far as Überlingen, Salem
Sales: Mon.–Sat. 09:00 to 18:00 hours
Sun. and public holidays 12:00 to 18:00 hours (April to Oct.)
Restaurant: 11:00 to 21:00 hours, open daily, closed Jan. and Feb.
History: Founded as Cistercian abbey in 1197, owned by House of Baden since 1802, winemaking since 13th century
Worth seeing: 17 ha castle precincts, Gothic church, impressive interior

Vineyard area: 110 hectares
Annual production: 800,000 bottles
Top site: Gailinger Schloss Rheinburg
Soil types: Decomposed glacial moraine
Grape varieties: 40% Spätburgunder, 30% Müller-Thurgau, 10% Grauburgunder, 5% each of Weißburgunder and Bacchus, 10% other varieties
Average yield: 67 hl/ha
Best vintages: 2002, 2003

The large margrave's estate has always been a surprisingly inexpensive source for attractive clean quaffing white wines. As this quality has been further improved upon with the 2003 vintage, we were happy to award the first bunch of grapes to this producer. Wines such as the Grauburgunder (Pinot Gris) "Fidelitas" and the Sauvignon Blanc show real class. One should also not ignore the fresh, juicy Müller-Thurgau wines from Birnau and Meersburg – quaffing wines in the best sense of the word. The quality of the red wines does not yet come up to the standard of the white wines.

2003 Gailinger Schloss Rheinburg
Grauer Burgunder trocken
13.5%, ♀ till 2006   **81**

2003 Birnauer Kirchhalde
Müller-Thurgau trocken
12%, ♀ till 2006   **83**

2003 Gailinger Schloss Rheinburg
Chardonnay trocken
12.5%, ♀ till 2006   **84**

2003 Bernatinger Leopoldsberg
Grauer Burgunder trocken "Fidelitas"
13%, ♀ till 2007   **85**

2003 Gailinger Schloss Rheinburg
Sauvignon Blanc trocken
13.5%, ♀ till 2006   **86**

2003 Meersburger Sängerhalde
Müller-Thurgau
11.5%, ♀ till 2006   **84**

———— Red wines ————

2001 Bernatinger Leopoldsberg
Spätburgunder Weißherbst Eiswein
9.5%, ♀ till 2011   **89**

2002 Bernatinger Leopoldsberg
Spätburgunder trocken
13.5%, ♀ till 2006   **81**

2003 Bernatinger Leopoldsberg
Spätburgunder trocken
14%, ♀ till 2006   **83**

Baden Bodensee

Markgraf von Baden

2003

Bermatiner Leopoldsberg
Müller-Thurgau
trocken

The wines: **100** Perfect · **95–99** Outstanding · **90–94** Excellent · **85–89** Very good · **80–84** Good · **75–79** Average

Baden

WEINGUT MARKGRAF VON BADEN – SCHLOSS STAUFENBERG

Owner: Max Markgraf von Baden
General manager:
Bernhard Prinz von Baden
Winery manager: Achim Kirchner
Winemaker: Martin Kölble
77770 Durbach, Schloss Staufenberg 1
Tel. (07 81) 4 27 78, Fax 44 05 78
e-mail: info@schloss-staufenberg.de
Internet: www.markgraf-von-baden.de
Directions: A 5 Frankfurt–Basel, Appen-weier exit, in direction of Oberkirch, then in direction of Durbach
Sales: Achim Kirchner
Opening hours: Mon.–Fri. 09:00 to 17:00 hours, Sat. and Sun. 11:00 to 14:00 hours, by appointment
Restaurant: From 10:00 to 21:00 hours open daily
History: Winemaking since 1391
Worth seeing: Old castle buildings on Schlossberg with view onto Rhine plains and Strasbourg cathedral

---

Vineyard area: 23 hectares
Annual production: 140,000 bottles
Top site: Durbacher Schlossberg
Soil types: Decomposed granite, granite with clay
Grape varieties: 45% Riesling, 35% Spätburgunder, 5% each of Graubur-gunder and Weißburgunder, 3% Sauvignon Blanc, 7% other varieties
Average yield: 42 hl/ha
Best vintages: 2000, 2001, 2003

The distinctive palace behind Durbach has been owned by the margraves of Baden since the 14th century. Riesling (Klingelberger) and Traminer (Clevner) grapes have been cultivated here since the 18th century. Prince Bernhard of Baden is now in charge of operations, assisted by technical and sales managers. The current range is good, and fits in seamlessly with the good 2001 vintage. Special mention can be accorded to the elegant and racy top Riesling "Carl Friedrich," the

Spätburgunder from the Schlossberg site as well as the typical Gewürztraminer Beerenauslese.

2003 Chardonnay trocken
14%, ♀ till 2006 · **81**

2003 Riesling trocken
13%, ♀ till 2006 · **82**

2003 Grauer Burgunder trocken
13%, ♀ till 2006 · **82**

2003 Weißer Burgunder
Kabinett trocken
13%, ♀ till 2006 · **83**

2003 Riesling Kabinett trocken
12%, ♀ till 2006 · **84**

2002 Grauer Burgunder
Spätlese trocken
13%, ♀ till 2006 · **85**

2003 Riesling
trocken "Carl Friedrich"
12.5%, ♀ till 2007 · **86**

2001 Durbacher Schlossberg
Riesling trocken
14%, ♀ till 2007 · **88**

2001 Clevner (Traminer) Auslese
13.5%, ♀ till 2006 · **86**

2001 Riesling (Klingelberger)
Beerenauslese
11%, ♀ till 2012 · **88**

2002 Gewürztraminer
Beerenauslese
6%, ♀ till 2012 · **90**

——— Red wine ———

2002 Durbacher Schlossberg
Spätburgunder trocken
13.5%, ♀ till 2007 · **86**

The estates: ✦✦✦✦✦ World's finest · ✦✦✦✦ Germany's best · ✦✦✦ Very good · ✦✦ Good · ✦ Reliable

WEINGUT MICHEL

Owner: Josef Michel
Winemaker: Josef Michel
79235 Achkarren, Winzerweg 24
Tel. (0 76 62) 4 29, Fax 7 63
e-mail: weingutmichel@t-online.de
Directions: A 5 Frankfurt–Basel,
Bad Krozingen or Riegel exit, in direc-
tion of Breisach
Sales: Michel family
Opening hours: Mon.–Fri. 09:00 to
12:00 and 13:00 to 17:00, Sat. 09:00 to
12:00 hours, and by appointment
Worth seeing: Wine museum and
educational wine trail

Vineyard area: 12.5 hectares
Annual production: 90,000 bottles
Top sites: Achkarrer Schlossberg
and Castellberg
Soil types: Decomposed volcanic
formation, loess and clay
Grape varieties: 40% Spätburgunder,
30% Grauburgunder, 20% Weiß-
burgunder, 5% Müller-Thurgau,
4% Chardonnay, 1% Silvaner
Average yield: 65 hl/ha
Best vintages: 1999, 2000, 2002

Walter and Margarete Michel founded
their own winery in 1983 on a farm on the
outskirts of Achkarren. Son Josef took
over responsibility in the cellar. Their
ownership of part of the top Schlossberg
vineyard site is the key to the production
of exceptional wines. Extensive pruning,
selective hand-picking and careful handling during fermentation are keywords in
realizing this potential. The quality has
been continuously improved over the past
ten years. The wines are always clean,
fruit-driven and invigorating. The range
presented last year was very reliable, and
founded on the known strength of the
Grauburgunder (Pinot Gris). Unfortunately, the 2003 wines do not quite attain
this standard. Only the Grauburgunder
Spätlese *** shows some of the expected
class. The 2002 red wines are of good
quality.

2003 Achkarrer Schlossberg
Grauer Burgunder Spätlese trocken
13.5%, ♀ till 2006   **85**

2003 Achkarrer Schlossberg
Weißer Burgunder Spätlese trocken
14.5%, ♀ till 2006   **85**

2002 Achkarrer Schlossberg
Chardonnay trocken
13.5%, ♀ till 2006   **87**

2003 Achkarrer Schlossberg
Grauer Burgunder *** Spätlese trocken
14.5%, ♀ till 2008   **88**

2002 Achkarrer Schlossberg
Grauer Burgunder Spätlese trocken
13%, ♀ till 2006   **88**

———— Red wines ————

2002 Achkarrer Schlossberg
Spätburgunder trocken
13.5%, ♀ till 2007   **86**

2002 "Alte Reben"
Spätburgunder trocken
13.5%, ♀ till 2007   **86**

2002 Ihringer Winklerberg
Spätburgunder trocken
13.5%, ♀ till 2008   **87**

2002 Achkarrer Schlossberg
Spätburgunder trocken Barrique
13.5%, ♀ till 2008   **87**

2001 Achkarrer Schlossberg
Spätburgunder trocken Barrique
13.5%, ♀ till 2008   **89**

The wines: **100** Perfect · **95–99** Outstanding · **90–94** Excellent · **85–89** Very good · **80–84** Good · **75–79** Average

147

WEINGUT GEBRÜDER MÜLLER

Owner: Peter Bercher
Manager and winemaker:
Joachim Lang
79206 Breisach,
Richard-Müller-Straße 5
Tel. (0 76 67) 5 11, Fax 65 81
e-mail: info@weingut-gebr-mueller.de
Internet: www.weingut-gebr-mueller.de
Directions: A 5 Frankfurt–Basel,
Bad Krozingen exit, in direction of
Breisach-Stadtmitte
Sales: J. Lang and E. Bercher
Opening hours: Mon.–Fri. 08:30 to
12:00 hours and 14:30 to 17:00 hours
Sat. 09:00 to 12:00 hours
and by appointment
Worth seeing: Vaulted cellar with rare
wines dating back to 1943

Vineyard area: 10 hectares
Annual production: 70,000 bottles
Top sites: Ihringer Winklerberg,
Breisacher Eckartsberg
Soil types: Decomposed volcanic
formation, loess and rocky soils
Grape varieties: 50% Spätburgunder,
26% Weißburgunder, 10% Graubur-
gunder, 5% Riesling, 5% Silvaner,
4% other varieties
Average yield: 65 hl/ha
Best vintages: 1998, 1999, 2000
Member: Deutsches Barrique Forum

This winery was founded by Johann Bap-
tist Hau who was the first to promote the
wines of the Kaiserstuhl area outside Germany. Today the winery is owned by Peter Bercher. So far, winemaker Joachim
Lang has applied his strengths mainly to
the red wines. This was shown last year,
among others, by the 2001 Spätburgunder
(Pinot Noir) Spätlese from the Winklerberg site. The white wines of the 2002
vintage were rather poor. Unfortunately,
this trend has continued into the current
range. The wines are too basic and too
rustic to warrant a two-bunch rating.

2003 Breisacher Eckartsberg
Weißer Burgunder Kabinett trocken
13.5%, ♀ till 2006   **82**

2003 Breisacher Eckartsberg
Grauer Burgunder Kabinett trocken
13.5%, ♀ till 2006   **82**

2003 Ihringer Fohrenberg
Grauer Burgunder Spätlese trocken
15.5%, ♀ till 2006   **83**

2003 Ihringer Winklerberg
Riesling Spätlese trocken
13%, ♀ till 2006   **83**

2003 Breisacher Eckartsberg
Weißer Burgunder Spätlese trocken
14.5%, ♀ till 2006   **84**

2001 Breisacher Eckartsberg
Weißer Burgunder Spätlese trocken
13.5%, ♀ till 2006   **86**

2001 Ihringer Fohrenberg
Weißer Burgunder Eiswein
10%, ♀ till 2009   **89**

———— Red wines ————

2001 Ihringer Winklerberg
Cabernet Franc trocken
13%, ♀ till 2006   **83**

2001 Ihringer Winklerberg
Cabernet Sauvignon & Merlot trocken
13%, ♀ till 2007   **84**

2001 Ihringer Winklerberg
Spätburgunder Spätlese trocken
13.5%, ♀ till 2007   **86**

BADEN
2003
GRAUER BURGUNDER
IHRINGER FOHRENBERG
SPÄTLESE · TROCKEN
QUALITÄTSWEIN MIT PRÄDIKAT
A.P.Nr. 316/13/04

15,5 % vol

GUTSABFÜLLUNG
Weingut Gebrüder Müller
D-79206 BREISACH/KAISERSTUHL

0,75 l

GUT NÄGELSFÖRST

Owner: Reinhard J. Strickler
Manager: Robert Schätzle
76534 Baden-Baden (Varnhalt),
Nägelsförst 1
Tel. (0 72 21) 3 55 50, Fax 35 55 56
e-mail: info@naegelsfoerst.de
Internet: www.naegelsfoerst.de
Directions: A 5 Frankfurt–Basel,
Baden-Baden exit, follow signs from city
center to winery
Sales: Albert Mirbach
Opening hours: Mon.–Fri. 09:00 to
18:00 hours, Sat. 10:00 to 16:00 hours
and by appointment
History: Founded 1268 as estate of
Lichtenthal abbey, Pinot Noir planted
on Klosterberg site since 1344

Vineyard area: 30 hectares
Annual production: 170,000 bottles
Top sites: Varnhalter Klosterberg-
felsen, Neuweier Mauerberg,
Umweger Stich den Buben,
Waldulmer Pfarrberg
Soil types: Decomposed porphyry,
granite and gneiss
Grape varieties: 40% Riesling,
35% Spätburgunder, 20% white Pinot
varieties, 5% other varieties
Average yield: 50 hl/ha
Best vintages: 2001, 2002, 2003

Reinhard J. Strickler has made considerable investments in rebuilding the former winery of the Cistercian abbey at Lichtental. Robert Schätzle, who joined the business as general manager in 2002, presented a good maiden vintage. The dry Riesling wines showed mineral notes and clean fruit. The basic wines of the 2003 vintage have turned out rather simple, but the top wines, by contrast, are particularly good. The top dry Riesling of the vintage in the whole of Baden is the minerally smooth "RJS Prestige," with a nose that reminds one of good Wachau wines. The exquisite Trockenbeerenauslese provides strong evidence of what was possible in 2003 in the botrytis dessert style.

2003 Chardonnay trocken
13.5%, ♀ till 2006 — **82**

2003 Riesling trocken
13%, ♀ till 2006 — **83**

2003 Riesling Spätlese trocken
13%, ♀ till 2006 — **84**

2002 Neuweier Mauerberg
Riesling trocken Selection
12.5%, ♀ till 2006 — **86**

2003 Neuweier Mauerberg
Riesling trocken
13.5%, ♀ till 2007 — **87**

2001 Neuweier Mauerberg
Riesling Auslese trocken
8%, ♀ till 2010 — **88**

2003 Riesling
trocken "RJS Prestige"
13.5%, ♀ till 2008 — **89**

2001 Neuweier Mauerberg
Riesling Beerenauslese
8%, ♀ till 2020 — **91**

2001 Neuweier Mauerberg
Riesling Trockenbeerenauslese
8%, ♀ till 2030 — **92**

2003 Neuweier Mauerberg
Riesling Trockenbeerenauslese
8%, ♀ till 2023 — **95**

——— Red wines ———

2002 Spätburgunder trocken
13.5%, ♀ till 2006 — **84**

2002 Spätburgunder trocken "RJS"
13%, ♀ till 2008 — **86**

2001 Spätburgunder trocken "RJS"
13%, ♀ till 2007 — **87**

The wines: **100** Perfect · **95–99** Outstanding · **90–94** Excellent · **85–89** Very good · **80–84** Good · **75–79** Average

Discovery of the year 1995

Baden

WEINGUT
SCHLOSS NEUWEIER

Owner: Gisela Joos
Administrator: Jürgen Guntert
Winemaker: Alexander Spinner
76534 Baden-Baden, Mauerbergstr. 21
Tel. (0 72 23) 9 66 70, Fax 6 08 64
e-mail:
kontakt@weingut-schloss-neuweier.de
Internet:
www.weingut-schloss-neuweier.de
*Directions: A 5 Frankfurt–Basel, Bühl
or Baden-Baden exit, via Steinbach*
Sales: In château courtyard
Opening hours: Mon.–Fri. 09:00 to
12:00 hours and 13:00 to 17:00 hours
Sat. 09:00 to 13:00 hours
Restaurant: High-class cuisine in castle
Worth seeing: Terraces with dry-stone
walls, Schloss Neuweier (not open
to visitors)

Vineyard area: 10.5 hectares
Annual production: 65,000 bottles
Top sites: Neuweier Schlossberg
and Mauerberg
Soil types: Decomposed granite,
decomposed porphyry
Grape varieties: 85% Riesling, 12%
Spätburgunder, 3% other varieties
Average yield: 50 hl/ha
Best vintages: 2000, 2002, 2003
Member: VDP

The beginnings of Schlossgut Neuweier
go back to the 12th century. In 1992 Gisela Joos, a businesswoman from Frankfurt and her husband Helmut purchased
the run-down château, which has been restored to its former glory. There has been
investment in both vineyards and cellar,
and the focus is on producing top-quality
dry Riesling. This was demonstrated in
the 2002 vintage by wines with strong
mineral backbones, with depth and
length. In 2003 too, the Schlossberg "Alte Reben" and the Mauerberg "Goldenes
Loch" are the highlights of the range. The
off-dry and botrytis dessert wines did not
quite live up to our expectations.

2003 Neuweier Mauerberg
Weißer Burgunder Spätlese trocken
14.5%, ♀ till 2006 **84**

2003 Neuweier Mauerberg
Riesling Kabinett trocken
12.5%, ♀ till 2006 **85**

2003 Neuweier Schlossberg
Riesling Kabinett trocken
12.5%, ♀ till 2006 **86**

2003 Neuweier Mauerberg
Riesling Spätlese trocken
13%, ♀ till 2007 **87**

2003 Neuweier Schlossberg
Riesling Spätlese trocken "Alte Reben"
13.5%, ♀ till 2007 **88**

2002 Neuweier Schlossberg
Riesling Spätlese trocken "Alte Reben"
12.5%, ♀ till 2007 **89**

2003 Neuweier Mauerberg
Riesling Spätlese trocken
"Goldenes Loch"
13%, ♀ till 2008 **89**

2002 Neuweier Mauerberg
Riesling Spätlese trocken
"Goldenes Loch"
12.5%, ♀ till 2007 **89**

2003 Neuweier Mauerberg
Riesling Spätlese
12%, ♀ till 2007 **86**

2003 Neuweier Mauerberg
Riesling Auslese
10%, ♀ till 2008 **86**

2003 Neuweier Schlossberg
Gewürztraminer Spätlese
13.5%, ♀ till 2007 **87**

The estates: World's finest · Germany's best · Very good · Good · Reliable

150

WINZERGENOSSENSCHAFT OBERBERGEN

General manager: Rolf Hofschneider
Winemaker: Wolfgang Schupp
79235 Vogtsburg-Oberbergen,
Badbergstraße 2
Tel. (0 76 62) 9 46 00, Fax 94 60 24
e-mail: info@wg-oberbergen.com
Internet: www.wg-oberbergen.com
Directions: A 5 Karlsruhe–Basel, Riegel or Teningen exit, via Bahlingen, Schelingen to Oberbergen
Sales: Udo Beck, Ralf Kreutner
Opening hours: Mon.–Fri. 07:30 to 12:00 hours and 13:30 to 17:00 hours Sat. 08:30 to 12:30 hours (April–Dec.)
History: Founded 1924
Worth seeing: Barrel cellar built 1952, Badberg and Haselschacher Buck nature reserves

Vineyard area: 325 hectares
Number of members: 430
Annual production: 3 mill. bottles
Top site: Oberbergener Bassgeige
Soil types: Decomposed volcanic formation, loess
Grape varieties: 39% Müller-Thurgau, 28% Spätburgunder, 22% Grauburgunder, 11% other varieties
Average yield: 84 hl/ha
Best vintages: 2002, 2003

It is a fact: The Oberbergen co-operative, founded in 1924, has always been a good, reliable source for solid everyday wines. Last year, we first noticed a particularly good Muskateller Kabinett. Now this grape variety provides the foundation for a higher rating. The juicy, elegantly aromatic Kabinett as well as the very elegant Beerenauslese are top-class wines. The basic wines, too, can sincerely be recommended. The Grauburgunder and Weißburgunder (Pinot Gris and Pinot Blanc) Kabinett wines provide excellent value for money. An interesting product of the hot 2003 vintage is the Spätburgunder (Pinot Noir) Beerenauslese with its aromas of blackcurrants and blackberries.

2003 Oberbergener Baßgeige
Weißer Burgunder trocken
13.5%, ♀ till 2006 — **81**

2003 Oberbergener Baßgeige
Müller-Thurgau Kabinett trocken
13%, ♀ till 2006 — **81**

2003 Oberbergener Baßgeige
Weißer Burgunder Auslese trocken
15.5%, ♀ till 2006 — **81**

2003 Oberbergener Baßgeige
Weißer Burgunder Kabinett trocken
13.5%, ♀ till 2006 — **82**

2003 Oberbergener Baßgeige
Grauer Burgunder Kabinett trocken
13.5%, ♀ till 2006 — **83**

2003 Oberbergener Baßgeige
Gewürztraminer Spätlese
12.5%, ♀ till 2006 — **83**

2003 Oberbergener Baßgeige
Muskateller Kabinett
13%, ♀ till 2007 — **85**

2003 Oberbergener Baßgeige
Muskateller Beerenauslese
8%, ♀ till 2013 — **90**

———— Red wines ————

2002 Oberbergener Baßgeige
Spätburgunder trocken
13%, ♀ till 2006 — **81**

2003 Oberbergener Baßgeige
Spätburgunder Spätlese trocken
14%, ♀ till 2007 — **84**

2003 Oberbergener Baßgeige
Spätburgunder Beerenauslese
11.5%, ♀ till 2010 — **88**

The wines: **100** Perfect · **95–99** Outstanding · **90–94** Excellent · **85–89** Very good · **80–84** Good · **75–79** Average

151

WEINGUT SCHLOSS ORTENBERG

Owner: Ortenau district, city of Offenburg
General manager: Winfried Köninger
Administrator: Urban Jung
Winemaker: Hans-Peter Rieflin
77799 Ortenberg, Am Sankt Andreas 1
Tel. (07 81) 9 34 30, Fax 93 43 20
e-mail:
info@weingut-schloss-ortenberg.de
Internet:
www.weingut-schloss-ortenberg.de
Directions: A 5 Frankfurt–Basel, Offenburg exit, 3 kilometers on the B 33 in the direction of Donaueschingen
Sales: Mon.–Fri. 08:00 to 12:00 and 13:00 to 17:00, Sat. 09:00 to 12:30 hours
Worth seeing: Château Ortenberg wine gallery

Vineyard area: 46 hectares
Annual production: 300,000 bottles
Top sites: Ortenberger Schlossberg and Andreasberg, Zeller Abtsberg
Soil types: Decomposed primordial rock
Grape varieties: 31% Riesling, 24% Spätburgunder, 10% Müller-Thurgau, 7% each of Grauburgunder, Weißburgunder, Chardonnay, Scheurebe and Sauvignon Blanc
Average yield: 59 hl/ha
Best vintages: 1999, 2000, 2001

The third-largest winery in Baden came about through the merger of two communal wineries in 1997. The district of Ortenau and the city of Offenburg now command a respectable 46 hectares. Estate manager Winfried Köninger is proud not only of the quality of the wines, but also of the profits that are made here – not a given for a communal operation. The 2002 vintage range provided a number of elegantly fruity dry white wines. Their successors are robust, with good fruit. 2003 is not characterized by elegance or nuances. The best wine is the concentrated Weißburgunder Spätlese "SL."

2003 Chardonnay Spätlese trocken
13%, ♀ till 2006   83

2003 Sauvignon Blanc et Gris
trocken
13.5%, ♀ till 2006   84

2003 Riesling trocken "SL"
12.5%, ♀ till 2006   85

2003 Weißer Burgunder
Spätlese trocken "SL"
14.5%, ♀ till 2007   86

2002 Sauvignon Blanc et Gris
trocken
12.5%, ♀ till 2006   87

2003 Weißer Burgunder
Auslese halbtrocken
14.5%, ♀ till 2007   84

2002 Scheurebe
Trockenbeerenauslese
10%, ♀ till 2008   87

——— Red wines ———

2003 Spätburgunder
Spätlese trocken
14.5%, ♀ till 2008   85

2003 Spätburgunder trocken
13.5%, ♀ till 2006   86

2000 Spätburgunder
Auslese trocken
14%, ♀ till 2006   86

2003 Spätburgunder
Trockenbeerenauslese
11%, ♀ till 2013   88

WINZERGENOSSENSCHAFT PFAFFENWEILER EG

General manager:
Heinrich Stefan Männle
Winemaker: Roland Braun
79292 Pfaffenweiler, Weinstraße 40
Tel. (0 76 64) 9 79 60, Fax 97 96 44
e-mail: info@wg-pfaffenweiler.de
Internet: www.pfaffenweiler-wein.de
Directions: A 5 Frankfurt–Basel, Freiburg-Süd exit, B 3 direction of Bad Krozingen
Sales: Eric Schweigler
Opening hours: Mon.–Fri. 08:00 to 12:00 hours and 13:00 to 17:00 hours Sat. 09:00 to 12:00 hours
History: Co-operative founded 1950, but winemaking in the valley since 716
Worth a visit: "Schnecke-Fescht" (festival) on 1st weekend in September

---

Vineyard area: 99 hectares
Number of members: 170
Annual production: 800,000 bottles
Top sites: Pfaffenweiler Batzenberg and Oberdürrenberg
Soil types: Clay, loess with limestone
Grape varieties: 35% Gutedel, 20% Spätburgunder, 12% Müller-Thurgau, 9% Weißburgunder, 5% each of Grauburgunder and Sauvignon Blanc, 14% other varieties
Average yield: 70 hl/ha
Best vintages: 2000, 2001, 2002

General manager Heinrich Stefan Männle, whose father runs the eponymous winery in Durbach, has focussed on quality ever since taking over here. The highlights of the 2002 range included a very typical dry Sauvignon Blanc Spätlese as well as some very good red wines from the 2001 vintage. Unfortunately the top red wines of the 2002 vintage had not yet been bottled by the deadline for our tasting. It remains to assess the 2003 white wines, and these tended to be rather alcoholic. Exceptions are the fresh Gutedel (Chasselas) as well as the Sauvignon Blanc Spätlese. Of the sweet wines we liked the classic Ruländer Auslese.

2003 Pfaffenweiler Batzenberg
Gutedel trocken
12%, ♀ till 2006   **83**

2003 Pfaffenweiler Oberdürrenberg
Gewürztraminer Spätlese trocken "Primus"
14.5%, ♀ till 2006   **84**

2003 Pfaffenweiler Oberdürrenberg
Sauvignon Blanc Spätlese trocken
14.5%, ♀ till 2007   **86**

2002 Pfaffenweiler Oberdürrenberg
Sauvignon Blanc Spätlese trocken
13%, ♀ till 2006   **87**

2001 Pfaffenweiler Oberdürrenberg
Gutedel Auslese trocken "Primus"
14%, ♀ till 2006   **87**

2003 Pfaffenweiler Oberdürrenberg
Ruländer Auslese
12%, ♀ till 2008   **87**

——————— Red wines ———————

2001 Pfaffenweiler Oberdürrenberg
Merlot trocken
14%, ♀ till 2007   **87**

2002 Pfaffenweiler Oberdürrenberg
Spätburgunder Spätlese trocken – 31 –
13%, ♀ till 2008   **88**

2001 Pfaffenweiler Oberdürrenberg
Cabernet Sauvignon trocken – 32 –
14%, ♀ till 2008   **89**

The wines: **100** Perfect · **95–99** Outstanding · **90–94** Excellent · **85–89** Very good · **80–84** Good · **75–79** Average

WEINGUT PIX

Owner: Helga and Reinhold Pix
Manager and winemaker:
Reinhold Pix
79241 Ihringen, Eisenbahnstraße 19
Tel. (0 76 68) 8 79, Fax 90 26 78
e-mail: info@weingut-pix.de
Internet: www.weingut-pix.de
Directions: A 5 Karlsruhe–Basel, Umkirch exit, Gottenheim, Wasenweiler
Sales: Helga Pix
Opening hours: Mon.–Sat. 09:00 to 12:00 hours and 13:00 to 18:00 hours and by appointment
Worth seeing: Art exhibitions in the foyer of the estate

Vineyard area: 4 hectares
Annual production: 30,000 bottles
Top sites: Ihringer Winklerberg and Fohrenberg, Achkarrer Castellberg
Soil types: Loess, decomposed volcanic formation
Grape varieties: 25% Spätburgunder, 21% each of Silvaner and Grauburgunder, 7% each of Weißburgunder, Gewürztraminer and Lemberger, 6% each of Chardonnay and Müller-Thurgau
Average yield: 60 hl/ha
Best vintages: 2001, 2003
Member: Bioland

Reinhold and Helga Pix started their winery in 1984, working right from the word go according to the guidelines of the Bioland Organic Farming Association. At the same time, their Hinterwälder cattle herd was a source of manure. The winery is located in the town center of Ihringen, and has grown to four hectares. The current range has shown that our decision last year to downgrade the winery was taken in haste. We tasted typical, attractive and juicy white wines that cried out to be drunk. The wines we liked best were an elegantly aromatic Gewürztraminer Spätlese, a powerful Grauburgunder (Pinot Gris) Auslese and a Silvaner Spätlese that was both clean and juicy.

2003 Ihringer Winklerberg
Chardonnay Spätlese trocken
14%, ♀ till 2006 — 84

2002 Ihringer Fohrenberg
Pinoxx Cuvée trocken Barrique
13%, ♀ till 2006 — 84

2001 Ihringer Fohrenberg
Grauer Burgunder Spätlese trocken
13%, ♀ till 2006 — 85

2003 Ihringer Fohrenberg
Gewürztraminer Spätlese trocken
14.5%, ♀ till 2006 — 86

2003 Ihringer Winklerberg
Grauer Burgunder Auslese trocken
15%, ♀ till 2007 — 87

2003 Ihringer Fohrenberg
Silvaner feinherb
14%, ♀ till 2006 — 83

2003 Ihringer Winklerberg
Silvaner Spätlese feinherb
14%, ♀ till 2007 — 88

2003 Ihringer Winklerberg
Silvaner Auslese
13%, ♀ till 2006 — 84

2001 Ihringer Fohrenberg
Gewürztraminer Spätlese
14%, ♀ till 2006 — 85

2003 Ihringer Winklerberg
Grauer Burgunder Auslese
14.5%, ♀ till 2007 — 86

Baden
Ihringer Winklerberg

H·PIX·R

2001

SPÄTBURGUNDER
ROSÉ

Kabinett

0,75l trocken 12%vol

Qualitätswein mit Prädikat
Gutsabfüllung · A. P. Nr. 940 04 02
Weingut Pix · D-79241 Ihringen
Öko-Kontrollstelle DE-002
Bioland
Betrieb A-79388

The estates: ♦♦♦♦♦ World's finest · ♦♦♦♦ Germany's best · ♦♦♦ Very good · ♦♦ Good · ♦ Reliable

WEINGUT REINER PROBST

Owner: Reiner Probst
79235 Achkarren,
Castellbergstraße 21
Tel. (0 76 62) 3 29, Fax 2 29
e-mail: weingutprobst@t-online.de
Directions: A 5, Bad Krozingen
or Riegel exit, in direction of Breisach
Sales: Marion Probst
Opening hours: Mon.–Fri. 08:00 to
12:00 hours and 13:00 to 17:00 hours
Sat., Sun., public holidays from 09:00
hours, Tue. by appointment only
Restaurant: Mon.–Fri. 17:00 to 24:00
hours, Sat., Sun., public holidays 10:00
to 24:00 hours, Closed Tue.
Specialties: Dishes with "Brägele"
(sautéed potatoes)

Vineyard area: 9 hectares
Annual production: 40,000 bottles
Top sites: Achkarrer Schlossberg
and Castellberg
Soil types: Loess-clay and decom-
posed volcanic soils
Grape varieties: 60% Spätburgunder,
20% Grauburgunder, 15% Weiß-
burgunder, 5% Müller-Thurgau,
Muskateller and Gewürztraminer
Average yield: 60 hl/ha
Best vintages: 1999, 2000, 2002

Reiner Probst has been running his
parents winery, the oldest such operation
in Achkarren, since 1985. A wine bar
and restaurant, run by his wife Marion, is
attached to the winery. Probst has more
than four hectares of vineyards in the
Schlossberg site, planted almost exclusively to Pinot Gris and Pinot Noir. Both
the top Spätlese wines of these varieties
of the 2002 vintage ("Plus") as well as the
2003 red wines clearly show the potential of both the vineyard and the winery.
At the same time, we must put on record
our disappointment with some of the
more basic wines in the range, which need
a bit more clarity and polish to succeed.

2003 Achkarrer Schlossberg
Weißer Burgunder Kabinett trocken
13.5%, ♀ till 2006 **78**

2003 Achkarrer Castellberg
Grauer Burgunder Kabinett trocken
13.5%, ♀ till 2006 **81**

2002 Achkarrer Schlossberg
Grauer Burgunder Spätlese trocken
Barrique
13.5%, ♀ till 2007 **86**

2001 Achkarrer Schlossberg
Ruländer Spätlese
14%, ♀ till 2006 **84**

2001 Achkarrer Schlossberg
Muskateller Beerenauslese
14.5%, ♀ till 2010 **86**

——————— Red wines ———————

2002 Achkarrer Schlossberg
Spätburgunder Spätlese trocken
13%, ♀ till 2006 **82**

2003 Achkarrer Schlossberg
Spätburgunder trocken
14%, ♀ till 2007 **84**

2001 Achkarrer Schlossberg
Spätburgunder Auslese trocken
14%, ♀ till 2006 **84**

2002 Achkarrer Schlossberg
Spätburgunder Kabinett trocken "Pius"
12.5%, ♀ till 2006 **84**

2002 Achkarrer Schlossberg
Spätburgunder trocken "Pius"
13%, ♀ till 2008 **86**

2003 Achkarrer Schlossberg
Spätburgunder Auslese
13.5%, ♀ till 2008 **86**

The wines: **100** Perfect · **95–99** Outstanding · **90–94** Excellent · **85–89** Very good · **80–84** Good · **75–79** Average

WEINGUT
BURG RAVENSBURG

**Owner: Freiherren Göler
von Ravensburg
General manager: Claus Burmeister
Winemaker: Jürgen Kern
75056 Sulzfeld, Hauptstraße 44
Tel. (0 72 69) 9 14 10, Fax 91 41 40
e-mail: weingut@burg-ravensburg.de
Internet: www.burg-ravensburg.de**
Directions: A 5 Frankfurt–Basel, Bruchsal exit, B 293 in direction of Heilbronn
Sales: Claus Burmeister
Opening hours: Mon.–Fri. 09:00 to
12:00 hours and 14:00 to 17:00 hours
Sat. 10:00 to 13:00 hours
Restaurant: Burg Ravensburg
Closed Mon. and Tue., Tel. 91 41 91
Closed for winter break mid-Dec.–late Feb.
Specialties: Game, hunted in own
forests, Kraichgau regional cuisine
History: Winemaking since 1251
Worth seeing: Ravensburg castle, estate
building with vinotheque

Vineyard area: 28 hectares
Annual production: 200,000 bottles
Top sites: Burg Ravensburger Löchle,
Dicker Franz and Husarenkappe
Soil types: Red marl, coloured marl,
gypsum-red marl, loess, kaolin
Grape varieties: 30% Riesling, 24%
Lemberger, 22% Schwarzriesling, 10%
Spätburgunder, 8% Weißburgunder,
4% Grauburgunder, 2% other varieties
Average yield: 60 hl/ha
Best vintages: 2000, 2001, 2002
Member: VDP

The barons von Göler are the oldest wine-producing family in Baden. Documents show a vineyard being sold in 1251 by the knight Berthold Göler von Ravensburg. A combination of investments and the efforts of the general manager Claus Burmeister's team has brought about significant improvements in quality. The 2001 red wines provided ample evidence of this development. The 2003 vintage is not as homogeneous. The basic wines are partly weak, but there are also two good First Growths wines as well as a very elegant 2002 "Corvus" Spätburgunder.

2003 Burg Ravensburger Husarenkappe
Riesling Kabinett trocken
12%, ♀ till 2006   **82**

2002 Burg Ravensburger Husarenkappe
Riesling Kabinett trocken
11.5%, ♀ till 2006   **85**

2003 Burg Ravensburger Löchle
Grauer Burgunder trocken
"Großes Gewächs"
14%, ♀ till 2007   **86**

2003 Burg Ravensburger Husarenkappe
Riesling trocken "Großes Gewächs"
12.5%, ♀ till 2007   **87**

2002 Burg Ravensburger Husarenkappe
Riesling Spätlese trocken
"Großes Gewächs"
12%, ♀ till 2006   **87**

——————— Red wines ———————

2003 Burg Ravensburger Dicker Franz
Lemberger trocken
13%, ♀ till 2007   **85**

2002 "Corvus"
Spätburgunder trocken
13.5%, ♀ till 2008   **87**

2001 "Corvus" Lemberger trocken
13%, ♀ till 2007   **88**

2001 "Corvus"
Spätburgunder trocken
13%, ♀ till 2008   **89**

Baden

WEINGUT SALWEY

Owner: Wolf-Dietrich Salwey
79235 Oberrotweil, Hauptstraße 2
Tel. (0 76 62) 3 84, Fax 63 40
e-mail: weingut@salwey.de
Internet: www.salwey.de
Directions: A 5 Frankfurt–Basel, Riegel
exit, in direction of Rhine, or Bad Kro-
zingen exit, in direction of Breisach
Opening hours: Mon.–Fri. 08:00 to 12:00
and 14:00 to 17:00 hours
Sat. 08:00 to 12:00 hours
and 14:00 to 16:00 hours
History: Family-owned since 1763
Worth seeing: Newly built underground
cellar

Vineyard area: 23 hectares
Annual production: 150,000 bottles
Top sites: Oberrotweiler Kirchberg
and Eichberg, Glottertaler Eichberg
Soil types: Decomposed volcanic
formation, loess and decomposed
gneiss
Grape varieties: 40% Spätburgunder,
30% Grauburgunder, 10% Weiß-
burgunder, 6% each of Riesling and
Silvaner, 8% other varieties
Average yield: 53 hl/ha
Best vintages: 2000, 2001, 2002
Member: VDP,
Deutsches Barrique Forum

This renowned estate in Oberrotweil was
built up by Benno Salwey, the father of
the current owner Wolf-Dietrich, following an inheritance and subsequent parti-
tion of land in 1950. Konrad Salwey now
represents the next generation to enter the
business. While his father continues to
be responsible for the red wines, he has
taken over vinification of the whites. The
estate is known for its elegantly fruity
Weißherbst (Rosé) wines, its classical
Spätburgunder (Pinot Noir) and the elegant Weißburgunder (Pinot Blanc) wines.
The improvement in the Pinot Gris in recent years has been noticeable. The variety is popular in Oberrotweil. Salwey:
"With a Pinot Gris is passion involved,

emotions are raised, while a Riesling
only leads to sophisticated discussions."
Vinification in the new cellar (dug into the mountainside) appears to have
changed slightly. The wines appear more
modern in style, they have fewer rough
edges, and are more polished as well
as spicy. This can be said not only of the
wines sourced from the Kaiserstuhl, also
those from the Glottertal in the Breisgau
area, from which the Salweys produce a
very good Weißherbst (Rosé) and a surprisingly elegant Riesling. All of the 2001
Spätburgunder (Pinot Noir) wines were
good, right across the board. We preferred the Oberrotweiler Eichberg "RS,"
which has prominent cherry fruit, as well
as a smooth, elegant finish to the Spätlese
*** from the Kirchberg site, which was
almost overripe. The 2002 white wines
were variable, as befits the vintage. Even
their successors from the 2003 vintage
do not present a homogeneous picture.
There are some fresh Rieslings and some
solid red wines, but also some wines that
cannot deny the problems associated with
the extremely hot vintage. The 2002 red
wines were most enjoyable. These classic
Pinot Noir wines are characterized by
concentrated fruit and an aromatic depth.
There is no doubt that the Kirchberg
Spätlese *** was placed in the top ten red
wines of the vintage.

2003 Glottertaler Eichberg
Riesling Kabinett trocken
12%, ♀ till 2006 **84**

2003 Oberrotweiler Käsleberg
Weißer Burgunder Kabinett trocken
13.5%, ♀ till 2006 **84**

2003 Chardonnay trocken "RS"
14%, ♀ till 2006 **84**

2003 Oberrotweiler Henkenberg
Weißer Burgunder Spätlese trocken
14%, ♀ till 2006 **85**

2003 Oberrotweiler Henkenberg
Grauer Burgunder Spätlese trocken
14.5%, ♀ till 2006 **85**

2003 Weißer Burgunder trocken
15.5%, ♀ till 2007 **85**

The wines: **100** Perfect · **95–99** Outstanding · **90–94** Excellent · **85–89** Very good · **80–84** Good · **75–79** Average

2003 Gewürztraminer
Spätlese trocken
13.5%, ♀ till 2006 **85**

2002 Chardonnay Kabinett trocken
13%, ♀ till 2006 **85**

2002 Oberrotweiler Kirchberg
Muskateller Kabinett trocken
12.5%, ♀ till 2006 **85**

2002 Oberrotweiler Henkenberg
Grauer Burgunder Spätlese trocken
12.5%, ♀ till 2006 **87**

2002 Oberrotweiler Kirchberg
Weißer Burgunder Spätlese trocken ***
13%, ♀ till 2006 **87**

2000 Grauer Burgunder
Tafelwein trocken
12.5%, ♀ till 2006 **87**

2001 Oberrotweiler Henkenberg
Weißer Burgunder Spätlese trocken
13.5%, ♀ till 2006 **88**

2001 Oberrotweiler Henkenberg
Grauer Burgunder Spätlese trocken
13%, ♀ till 2006 **88**

2000 Chardonnay
Tafelwein trocken
12.5%, ♀ till 2007 **88**

2003 Oberrotweiler Kirchberg
Weißer Burgunder Spätlese trocken ***
14.5%, ♀ till 2008 **88**

2003 Oberrotweiler Eichberg
Grauer Burgunder Spätlese trocken ***
14.5%, ♀ till 2008 **88**

2002 Oberrotweiler Eichberg
Grauer Burgunder Spätlese trocken ***
14%, ♀ till 2008 **89**

2001 Oberrotweiler Kirchberg
Riesling Spätlese *** trocken
13%, ♀ till 2007 **89**

2001 Glottertaler Eichberg
Riesling Spätlese trocken
13%, ♀ till 2008 **90**

2003 Glottertaler Eichberg
Riesling Kabinett
11.5%, ♀ till 2007 **86**

2003 Grauer Burgunder
Auslese ***
13%, ♀ till 2008 **87**

—————— Red wines ——————

2003 Glottertaler Eichberg
Spätburgunder Weißherbst
Spätlese trocken
14%, ♀ till 2006 **85**

2001 Glottertaler Eichberg
Spätburgunder Weißherbst
Auslese trocken
15%, ♀ till 2010 **90**

2002 Spätburgunder trocken
13%, ♀ till 2006 **82**

2002 Oberrotweiler Henkenberg
Spätburgunder trocken
13.5%, ♀ till 2007 **86**

2000 Spätburgunder trocken "RS"
13%, ♀ till 2006 **86**

2001 Glottertaler Eichberg
Spätburgunder trocken "RS"
13%, ♀ till 2007 **87**

2001 Oberrotweiler Kirchberg
Spätburgunder Spätlese *** trocken
13.5%, ♀ till 2007 **88**

2001 Oberrotweiler Eichberg
Spätburgunder trocken
13%, ♀ till 2009 **90**

2000 Oberrotweiler Kirchberg
Spätburgunder Spätlese *** trocken
13%, ♀ till 2010 **90**

2002 Oberrotweiler Eichberg
Spätburgunder trocken "RS"
13.5%, ♀ till 2010 **90**

2002 Oberrotweiler Kirchberg
Spätburgunder Spätlese trocken
"Großes Gewächs" ***
13.5%, ♀ till 2010 **91**

BADEN · KAISERSTUHL
Oberrotweiler Eichberg
Ruländer Spätlese trocken
***
750 ml   Qualitätswein mit Prädikat
Alc. 14 % / Vol.   Erzeugerabfüllung AP Nr. 307 56 00
Weingut Salwey D-79235 Oberrotweil am Kaiserstuhl

The estates: ♦♦♦♦♦ World's finest · ♦♦♦♦ Germany's best · ♦♦♦ Very good · ♦♦ Good · ♦ Reliable

WINZERGENOSSENSCHAFT SASBACH AM KAISERSTUHL

General manager: Rolf Eberenz
Winemaker: Gerhard Staiblin
79361 Sasbach, Jechtinger Straße 26
Tel. (0 76 42) 9 03 10, Fax 90 31 50
e-mail: info@sasbacher.de
Internet: www.sasbacher.de
Directions: A 5 Frankfurt–Basel,
Riegel exit, in direction of France
Sales: Bertram Bohn
Opening hours: Mon.–Fri. 08:00 to
12:30 hours and 13:30 to 17:00 hours
Sat. 09:00 to 12:00 hours
and by appointment
Worth seeing: Scientific signposted educational trail "Limberg" at Kaiserstuhl

---

Vineyard area: 108 hectares
Number of members: 337
Annual production: 815,000 bottles
Top sites: Sasbacher Rote Halde
and Limburg
Soil types: Decomposed volcanic
formation, partly with top layer of
clay and loess
Grape varieties: 55% Spätburgunder,
21% Müller-Thurgau, 11% Grauburgunder, 10% Weißburgunder,
3% other varieties
Average yield: 76 hl/ha
Best vintages: 1999, 2000, 2001
Member: Deutsches Barrique Forum

The Sasbach co-operative operates 108 hectares, and is one of the smallest co-operatives in the Kaiserstuhl area. Conditions here are equally good for Pinot Noir as well as for the white Pinot varieties. The red wines here have enjoyed the better reputation for many years, a fact which was confirmed by the 2001 red wines. Regrettably, the current range represents a step backward. With the exception of the Muskateller all the white wines are poor, and the reds no better than solid. The presentation of some of the bottles is unusual, to say the least.

2003 Sasbacher Limburg
Rivaner Kabinett trocken
12%, ♀ till 2006 — 82

2003 Sasbacher Limburg
Grauer Burgunder Spätlese trocken
13.5%, ♀ till 2006 — 82

2002 Sasbacher Limburg
Grauer Burgunder Kabinett trocken
12.5%, ♀ till 2006 — 83

2001 Sasbacher Limburg
Muskateller Spätlese trocken
12.5%, ♀ till 2005 — 83

2003 Sasbacher Limburg
Muskateller Auslese
12%, ♀ till 2007 — 85

——— Red wines ———

2003 Sasbacher Rote Halde
Spätburgunder Spätlese trocken
14%, ♀ till 2205 — 82

2003 Sasbacher Rote Halde
Spätburgunder Auslese trocken
14.5%, ♀ till 2006 — 83

2003 Sasbacher Rote Halde
Cabernet Sauvignon trocken
13.5%, ♀ till 2006 — 84

2002 Sasbacher Rote Halde
Spätburgunder Spätlese trocken
12.5%, ♀ till 2006 — 84

2001 Sasbacher Rote Halde
Spätburgunder Spätlese trocken
12.5%, ♀ till 2006 — 85

2001 Sasbacher Rote Halde
Spätburgunder Auslese trocken
13.5%, ♀ till 2007 — 86

2001 Sasbacher Rote Halde
Cabernet Sauvignon trocken
13%, ♀ till 2007 — 87

The wines: **100** Perfect · **95–99** Outstanding · **90–94** Excellent · **85–89** Very good · **80–84** Good · **75–79** Average

159

Baden

WEINGUT GREGOR UND THOMAS SCHÄTZLE

Owner: Thomas Schätzle
79235 Vogtsburg-Schelingen,
Heinrich-Kling-Straße 38
Tel. (0 76 62) 9 46 10, Fax 94 61 20
e-mail: info@weingutschaetzle.de
Internet: www.weingutschaetzle.de
*Directions: A 5 Frankfurt–Basel,
Riegel exit, via Bahlingen*
Sales: Schätzle family
Opening hours: Mon.–Fri. 08:00 to
12:00 hours and 13:30 to 18:00 hours
Sat. 08:00 to 12:00 hours
and 13:30 to 17:00 hours
Sun. by appointment
Worth seeing: Nature reserve with
orchid section

Vineyard area: 11 hectares
Annual production: 80,000 bottles
Top sites: Schelinger Kirchberg,
Oberbergener Bassgeige, Amolterer
Steinhalde
Soil types: Loess, clay and decom-
posed volcanic soils
Grape varieties: 37% Spätburgunder ,
33% Grauburgunder, 9% Müller-
Thurgau, 8% Weißburgunder,
7% Chardonnay, 6% other varieties
Average yield: 75 hl/ha
Best vintages: 2000, 2001, 2003

An inheritance and division of land in the early Sixties interrupted the family wine-making tradition. Then in 1982 Thomas Schätzle and his father Gregor resumed marketing their own wines. He took over the winery in 1994, together with his wife Friederike. His first successes came with the 1998 range of wines produced. The 2003 vintage has produced a number of powerful, juicy wines. Both the concentrated dry Grauburgunder (Pinot Gris) Spätlese, with its honey melon aromas and the typical Muskateller Auslese are worthy of special mention. In future we would like to see a little more finesse and elegance being added to the power that is already abundantly evident.

2003 Schelinger Kirchberg
Weißer Burgunder Spätlese trocken
14%, ♀ till 2006 — 84

2002 Schelinger Kirchberg
Grauer Burgunder Spätlese trocken
13.5%, ♀ till 2006 — 85

2003 Schelinger Kirchberg
Grauer Burgunder Spätlese trocken
14.5%, ♀ till 2007 — 86

2001 Schelinger Kirchberg
Chardonnay Spätlese trocken
13.5%, ♀ till 2007 — 87

2001 Schelinger Kirchberg
Grauer Burgunder Spätlese trocken
13.5%, ♀ till 2005 — 87

2003 Schelinger Kirchberg
Grauer Burgunder Spätlese halbtrocken
15%, ♀ till 2006 — 84

2003 Schelinger Kirchberg
Weißer Burgunder Auslese
15%, ♀ till 2007 — 85

2003 Schelinger Kirchberg
Grauer Burgunder Auslese
15%, ♀ till 2007 — 86

2003 Muskateller Auslese
14%, ♀ till 2008 — 87

——— Red wines ———

2002 Schelinger Kirchberg
Spätburgunder trocken
12.5%, ♀ till 2007 — 85

2003 Schelinger Kirchberg
Spätburgunder Spätlese trocken
13%, ♀ till 2008 — 85

2001 Schelinger Kirchberg
Spätburgunder Spätlese trocken
13%, ♀ till 2007 — 86

WEINGUT KONRAD SCHLÖR

Owner: Konrad Schlör
Winemaker: Konrad Schlör
97877 Wertheim-Reicholzheim,
Martin-Schlör-Straße 22
Tel. (0 93 42) 49 76, Fax 69 59
e-mail: info@weingut-schloer.de
Internet: www.weingut-schloer.de
Directions: *A 81 Würzburg–Heilbronn,
Tauberbischofsheim exit; A 3 Frank-
furt–Würzburg, Wertheim exit*
Sales: Schlör family
by appointment

Vineyard area: 4.4 hectares
Annual production: 20,000 bottles
Top site: Reicholzheimer First
Soil types: Shell limestone
Grape varieties: 21% Spätburgunder,
18% each of Müller-Thurgau and
Schwarzriesling, 11% Riesling,
9% each of Silvaner and Weißburgun-
der, 8% Kerner, 6% Dornfelder
Average yield: 45 hl/ha
Best vintages: 1999, 2000, 2001

The Tauber valley borders on Franken, and is rapidly developing on both sides of the state border into a region from which one can expect outstanding wines. Konrad Schlör is busy trying to establish the Reicholzheimer First vineyard site in the public mind, basing on his motto: "It is the winemaker who makes a vineyard famous, not the other way round." He started off delivering grapes to the co-operative, then in 1982 he added a small wine bar, and years later he finally took the risk of marketing his own wines. He resisted the temptation of producing bigger quantities for the restaurant, and developed ambitions to produce good wines, which is reflected in the very low yields per hectare. The dry 2003 wines are solid, the Schwarzriesling (Pinot Meunier) Trockenbeerenauslese shows richness and length. Above all we liked the blackberry fruit of the 2002 dry Spät-burgunder (Pinot Noir) Spätlese.

2003 Reicholzheimer First
Silvaner Spätlese trocken
13%, ♀ till 2006   **83**

2002 Reicholzheimer First
Riesling Spätlese trocken
13%, ♀ till 2006   **83**

2003 Reicholzheimer First
Riesling Spätlese trocken
13.5%, ♀ till 2006   **84**

2002 Reicholzheimer First
Weißer Burgunder Spätlese trocken
13%, ♀ till 2006   **84**

2003 Reicholzheimer First
Kabinett "S"
12%, ♀ till 2006   **83**

———— Red wines ————

2002 Reicholzheimer First
Schwarzriesling Spätlese trocken
13%, ♀ till 2006   **82**

2003 "Tauber-Edition" trocken
12.5%, ♀ till 2006   **84**

2002 Reicholzheimer First
trocken "M"
12.5%, ♀ till 2007   **85**

2001 Reicholzheimer First
Schwarzriesling Spätlese trocken
12.5%, ♀ till 2006   **86**

2001 Reicholzheimer First
Spätburgunder Spätlese trocken
13.5%, ♀ till 2008   **88**

2002 Reicholzheimer First
Spätburgunder Spätlese trocken
13%, ♀ till 2009   **89**

2003 Reicholzheimer First
Schwarzriesling Trockenbeerenauslese
9%, ♀ till 2013   **89**

TAUBERFRANKEN · BADEN
Schlör
WEINGUT
2002
SCHWARZRIESLING
SPÄTLESE
» im Barrique gereift «

The wines: **100** Perfect · **95–99** Outstanding · **90–94** Excellent · **85–89** Very good · **80–84** Good · **75–79** Average

161

WEINGUT HARTMUT SCHLUMBERGER

Owner: Claudia Schlumberger-Bernhart, Ulrich Bernhart
Winemaker: Ulrich Bernhart
79295 Laufen, Weinstraße 19
Tel. (0 76 34) 89 92, Fax 82 55
e-mail: info@schlumbergerwein.de
Internet: www.schlumbergerwein.de
Directions: A 5 Frankfurt–Basel, Neuenburg exit, direction of Müllheim/Sulzburg
Sales: Hella Schlumberger, Claudia Schlumberger-Bernhart
Opening hours: Mon.–Fri. 09:00 to 12:00 hours and 14:00 to 18:00 hours Sat. 09:00 to 12:00 hours and 14:00 to 16:00 hours
History: Winemaking in the family since 16th century

Vineyard area: 7.5 hectares
Annual production: 55,000 bottles
Top sites: Vineyard sites not stated on labels
Soil types: Loess and clay
Grape varieties: 30% each of Spätburgunder and Weißburgunder, 20% Gutedel 8% Grauburgunder, 5% Chardonnay, 5% Riesling, 2% other varieties
Average yield: 60 hl/ha
Best vintages: 2000, 2001, 2002

The cellar of the Schlumberger family still houses oak barrels made by the grandfather. For many generations, winemakers and coopers have lived here under the same roof. Since Ulrich Bernhart from Schweigen and his wife Claudia (née Schlumberger) have leased the winery and are responsbile for the wine production, the already high standard has been further improved. The top wine, a Pinot Noir labelled "R" provides evidence of this. The 2002 vintage, just like its predecessor, shows classical fruit, substance and spice. The 2003 white wines are fresh, but appear rather made, and are not really well-balanced. The highlight is the juicy Grauburgunder (Pinot Gris) Spätlese with its clean, abundant fruit.

2003 Gutedel Kabinett trocken
11%, ♀ till 2006   83

2003 Weißer Burgunder
Kabinett trocken
13%, ♀ till 2006   83

2003 Riesling Spätlese trocken
12.5%, ♀ till 2006   83

2003 Grauer Burgunder
Kabinett trocken
13%, ♀ till 2006   84

2003 Scheurebe Spätlese trocken
13.5%, ♀ till 2006   85

2002 Grauer Burgunder
Spätlese trocken
13.5%, ♀ till 2006   85

2003 Weißer Burgunder
Spätlese trocken
14%, ♀ till 2006   86

2002 Riesling Spätlese trocken
12.5%, ♀ till 2007   86

2001 Chardonnay Spätlese trocken
13.5%, ♀ till 2007   87

2003 Grauer Burgunder
Spätlese trocken
14%, ♀ till 2007   88

————— Red wines —————

2002 Spätburgunder trocken "S"
13.5%, ♀ till 2006   84

2002 Pinot Noir trocken
13.5%, ♀ till 2007   85

2002 Cabernet Sauvignon & Merlot
trocken
13.5%, ♀ till 2007   85

2001 Pinot Noir trocken
13.5%, ♀ till 2006   86

2002 Pinot Noir trocken "R"
13.5%, ♀ till 2008   88

2001 Pinot Noir trocken "R"
13.5%, ♀ till 2009   88

GUTSABFÜLLUNG
H.SCHLUMBERGER
PRIVAT-WEINGUT
BADEN
2003
WEISSBURGUNDER
KABINETT TROCKEN
13%vol   75cl
QUALITÄTSWEIN m. PRÄD.   D-79295 LAUFEN/MARKGRÄFLERLAND   A.P.Nr. 300904

WEINGUT CLAUS UND SUSANNE SCHNEIDER

Owner: Claus and Susanne Schneider
Winemaker: Claus Schneider
79576 Weil am Rhein, Lörracher Str. 4
Tel. (0 76 21) 7 28 17, Fax 7 80 14
e-mail: info@schneiderweingut.de
Internet: www.schneiderweingut.de
Directions: A 5 Frankfurt–Basel, Weil am Rhein exit, in direction of Weil am Rhein-Ost, 3. traffic lights left., 3. street left
Sales: Susanne Hagin-Schneider
Opening hours: Tue.–Sat. 09:00 to 12:30 hours, Mon., Tue., Thur., Fri. 14:30 to 18:30 hours and by appointment
History: Winemaking in the family since 1425; "Weiler Schlipf" vineyard, classified 1825 as best site in southern Markgräflerland
Worth seeing: Vaulted cellar built 1780

Vineyard area: 8.8 hectares
Annual production: 60,000 bottles
Top site: Weiler Schlipf
Soil types: Deep clay, limestone-rich
Grape varieties: 40% Spätburgunder, 30% Gutedel, 12% Weißburgunder, 10% Grauburgunder, 5% Chardonnay, 3% other varieties
Average yield: 60 hl/ha
Best vintages: 2000, 2001, 2003

Claus Schneider is a viticultural technician trained in Weinsberg. He took over his parents winery in 1982. Together with his wife Susanne he grows vines in the most southwesterly region in Germany, benefitting from Mediterranean climates of the so-called Burgundian Pforte (gateway to Burgundy). The Pinot varieties fare particularly well here, and the Weiler Schlipf vineyard provides high-quality terroir potential. Unfortunately, we were able to taste only four wines of the 2003 vintage. Just as the 2002 Spätburgunder (Pinot Noir) these were of a solid quality, and came over as a homogeneous range. The aim in the next few years will be to bring out the vineyard character more strongly.

2003 Gutedel Kabinett trocken
11%, ♀ till 2006   **81**

2003 Weiler Schlipf
Chardonnay Spätlese trocken "CS"
14%, ♀ till 2006   **83**

2002 Weiler Schlipf
Grauer Burgunder Kabinett trocken "CS"
12.5%, ♀ till 2006   **83**

2001 Weiler Schlipf
Weißer Burgunder Kabinett trocken
13.5%, ♀ till 2005   **84**

2002 Weiler Schlipf
Chardonnay Kabinett trocken "CS"
12%, ♀ till 2006   **84**

2001 Weiler Schlipf
Weißer Burgunder Spätlese trocken
13.5%, ♀ till 2006   **85**

2003 Weiler Schlipf
Grauer Burgunder Spätlese trocken "CS"
14.5%, ♀ till 2007   **85**

2001 Weiler Schlipf
Grauer Burgunder Spätlese trocken
13.5%, ♀ till 2006   **86**

2001 Weiler Schlipf
Chardonnay Spätlese trocken
13.5%, ♀ till 2006   **87**

2003 Weiler Schlipf
Weißer Burgunder Spätlese "CS"
14.5%, ♀ till 2006   **83**

2001 Weiler Schlipf
Grauer Burgunder Eiswein
8.5%, ♀ till 2011   **90**

————— Red wine —————

2002 Weiler Schlipf
Spätburgunder trocken
13.5%, ♀ till 2006   **83**

Schneider
2003
CHARDONNAY
WEILER SCHLIPF
BADEN
SPÄTLESE

The wines: **100** Perfect · **95–99** Outstanding · **90–94** Excellent · **85–89** Very good · **80–84** Good · **75–79** Average

WEINGUT REINHOLD UND CORNELIA SCHNEIDER

Owner: Reinhold and Cornelia Schneider
Winemaker: Reinhold and Alexander Schneider
79346 Endingen,
Königschaffhauser Straße 2
Tel. (0 76 42) 52 78 and 92 41 30,
Fax 20 91
e-mail: weingutschneider@aol.com
Internet: www.weingutschneider.com
Directions: A 5 Frankfurt–Basel, Riegel exit, in Endingen after the old city gate, 2nd entrance on right
Sales: Cornelia Schneider
Opening hours: Fri. 14:30 to 18:00 hours, Sat. 09:00 to 14:00 hours and by appointment

---

Vineyard area: 6.7 hectares
Annual production: 40,000 bottles
Top sites: No vineyards stated on labels
Soil types: Loess, clay and decomposed volcanic formation
Grape varieties: 49% Spätburgunder, 21% Ruländer, 12% Weißburgunder, 5% Auxerrois, 4% each of Riesling and Muskateller, 3% Müller-Thurgau, 2% Silvaner
Average yield: 48 hl/ha
Best vintages: 2001, 2002, 2003

When Reinhold and Cornelia Schneider founded the winery in 1981, they committed themselves to sustainable viticultural practices as well as to the production of dry wines. At the time, according to Schneider, "this did not always suit the official tasting panels," so some of his wines had to be classified as lowly table wines. The customers did not mind, nor did they object to the vineyard sites not being stated on the label. Instead, the labels today bear designations that indicate the source of the wine. For instance, "A" indicates red wines that have grown on clay soils, "C" indicates wines grown of loess soils, and "R" is for wines grown on volcanic soils. The term "trio" logically indicates

a blend of wines from three different vineyard sites. The best wines of each vintage are marked with three stars. Wine lovers and fans of this winery have been enthusiastic for many years about the value-for-money provided here. Schneider's improvements in recent years can almost be described as breathtaking. From his point of view it is all terribly simple: No complicated technology is involved in fermentation, all that happens is that hand-picked grapes are handled with great care through temperature-controlled fermentation, which takes place on the skins in the case of the Pinot Noir. The white wines are given extended lees contact. Reinhold Schneider has always refused to go along with the "Grauburgunder fashion." For this reason he still calls his Pinot Gris wines Ruländer, the traditional name. In our opinion, his 1999 Ruländer Auslese "R" (sold out) was one of the best dry white wines ever made in Germany. As in other difficult vintages, Schneider succeeded in presenting a very respectable range in 2002. The highlight was the Ruländer Spätlese "C" with three stars, which was matured in barriques. The white wines of the 2003 vintage stand out in their homogeneously high quality, and are probably unequalled in Baden. The wines show great clarity of fruit, while being juicy and of elegant structure. The excellent 2002 vintage red wines follow on seamlessly from the 2001 "R," which was one of the three best red wines last year. In summary: the best range in Baden. Our compliments!

2002 Muskateller
Kabinett trocken
11%, ♀ till 2006 — **82**

2002 Auxerrois Kabinett trocken
11.5%, ♀ till 2006 — **83**

2002 Silvaner Kabinett trocken
11%, ♀ till 2006 — **84**

2003 Auxerrois Spätlese trocken
13%, ♀ till 2006 — **86**

2002 Weißer Burgunder
Spätlese trocken ***
13%, ♀ till 2006 — **86**

2001 Ruländer Kabinett trocken
13%, ♀ till 2006   **86**

2001 Weißer Burgunder
Spätlese trocken ***
13%, ♀ till 2006   **87**

2002 Ruländer
Spätlese trocken "C" ***
13%, ♀ till 2007   **87**

2001 Ruländer Spätlese trocken
14%, ♀ till 2006   **88**

2001 Riesling Spätlese trocken
13%, ♀ till 2006   **88**

2002 Weißer Burgunder
Spätlese trocken "trio" ***
13%, ♀ till 2006   **88**

2003 Weißer Burgunder
Spätlese trocken ***
14.5%, ♀ till 2008   **89**

2001 Muskateller
Spätlese trocken ***
12.5%, ♀ till 2006   **89**

2000 Ruländer Spätlese trocken
13%, ♀ till 2006   **89**

2001 Ruländer
Spätlese trocken "C"
13%, ♀ till 2008   **89**

2003 Ruländer
Spätlese trocken "R" ***
15%, ♀ till 2010   **89**

2002 Ruländer
Spätlese trocken "R" ***
13%, ♀ till 2008   **89**

2001 Weißer Burgunder
Spätlese trocken *** "trio"
13%, ♀ till 2008   **89**

2003 Ruländer
Spätlese trocken "C" ***
14.5%, ♀ till 2008   **90**

2002 Ruländer
Spätlese trocken "C" *** Barrique
13%, ♀ till 2008   **90**

2001 Ruländer
Spätlese trocken "R"
13%, ♀ till 2008   **90**

2003 Weißer Burgunder
Auslese trocken "R" ***
15%, ♀ till 2010   **91**

2003 Weißer Burgunder
Spätlese trocken "trio" ***
14.5%, ♀ till 2010   **91**

2001 Ruländer
Auslese trocken ***
14%, ♀ till 2009   **92**

2002 Riesling
Spätlese halbtrocken
11%, ♀ till 2006   **85**

2003 Muskateller Spätlese *
14%, ♀ till 2008   **88**

———— Red wines ————

2001 Spätburgunder trocken
13%, ♀ till 2006   **85**

2000 Spätburgunder trocken
13%, ♀ till 2007   **87**

2001 Spätburgunder
trocken "C" ***
13%, ♀ till 2007   **88**

2000 Spätburgunder
trocken "C" ***
13%, ♀ till 2010   **90**

2002 Spätburgunder
trocken "R" ***
13%, ♀ till 2010   **90**

2002 Spätburgunder
trocken "C" ***
13%, ♀ till 2010   **91**

2000 Spätburgunder
trocken "R" ***
13%, ♀ till 2012   **91**

2001 Spätburgunder
trocken "R" ***
13%, ♀ till 2010   **93**

WEINGUT
Reinhold & Cornelia
SCHNEIDER

BADEN   2002

Muskateller

QUALITÄTSWEIN MIT PRÄDIKAT · TROCKEN
A.P.NR. 354 12 03
KABINETT

Alc. 11%ol
750 ml

GUTSABFÜLLUNG
REINHOLD UND CORNELIA SCHNEIDER
D-79346 Endingen am Kaiserstuhl

PRODUCT OF GERMANY

The wines: **100** Perfect · **95–99** Outstanding · **90–94** Excellent · **85–89** Very good · **80–84** Good · **75–79** Average

WEINGUT SEEGER

Owner: Seeger family
Manager: Helmut Seeger
Winemaker: Thomas Seeger
69181 Leimen, Rohrbacher Straße 101
Tel. (0 62 24) 7 21 78, Fax 7 83 63
e-mail: info@seegerweingut.de
Internet: www.seegerweingut.de
Directions: A 5 Frankfurt–Basel, Heidelberg/Leimen/Schwetzingen exit
Sales: Thomas Seeger
by appointment
Sat. 10:00 to 14:00 hours
Restaurant: "Jägerlust,"
Tue.–Fri. 18:00 to 23:00 hours
Specialties: Regional cuisine
History: Restaurant/Wine bar since 1895
Worth seeing: Old Harley-Davidson

Vineyard area: 6.5 hectares
Annual production: 40,000 bottles
Top sites: Heidelberger Herren-
berg, Leimener Herrenberg
Soil types: Loess-clay on shell lime-
stone and sandstone
Grape varieties: 25% Spätburgunder,
20% Weißburgunder, 15% each of
Riesling and Grauburgunder, 10%
Lemberger, 5% each of Portugieser,
Schwarzriesling and Müller-Thurgau
Average yield: 50 hl/ha
Best vintages: 2000, 2001, 2002
Member: Deutsches Barrique Forum

This winery has a long tradition dating
back to 1665, and Thomas Seeger has
taken it right to the top of producers in
North Baden. The red wines have tremendous maturation potential, and often only
show their true potential after several
years. Over time the man from Leimen
has also developed a feeling for white
wines. This is confirmed by the 2003
Auxerrois and Grauburgunder Spätlese
wines. The Riesling wines are not quite
of the same standard. Looking to the red
wines, the 2002 Spätburgunder are good,
headed up by an outstanding "RR":
a thoroughly impressive combination
of fruit, substance and length.

2003 Heidelberger Herrenberg
Grauer Burgunder Kabinett trocken
13.5%, ♀ till 2006 **84**

2003 Heidelberger Herrenberg
Grauer Burgunder Spätlese trocken
14.5%, ♀ till 2007 **86**

2003 Heidelberger Herrenberg
Auxerrois Spätlese trocken
13.5%, ♀ till 2007 **87**

2002 Grauer Burgunder trocken
13.5%, ♀ till 2007 **87**

2002 Heidelberger Herrenberg
Grauer Burgunder Spätlese trocken
13%, ♀ till 2007 **87**

——— Red wines ———

2002 Spätburgunder trocken "S"
14%, ♀ till 2007 **87**

2002 Heidelberger Herrenberg
Spätburgunder trocken "R"
13.5%, ♀ till 2008 **88**

2001 Schwarzriesling trocken "S"
13.5%, ♀ till 2009 **89**

2002 Heidelberger Herrenberg
Spätburgunder trocken "RR"
14%, ♀ till 2012 **91**

2001 Heidelberger Herrenberg
Spätburgunder trocken "RR"
13.5%, ♀ till 2011 **91**

STAATSWEINGUT FREIBURG UND BLANKENHORNSBERG

Owner: Federal state of Baden-Württemberg
Manager: Peter Wohlfarth
Administrator: Tobias Burtsche
Winemaker: Hans Breisacher and Werner Scheffelt
79100 Freiburg im Breisgau, Merzhauser Straße 119
Tel. (07 61) 4 01 65 44, Fax 4 01 65 70
e-mail: staatsweingut@wbi.bwl.de
Internet: www.landwirtschaft-mlr.ba-den-wuerttemberg.de/la/wbi
Directions: A 5 Frankfurt–Basel, Freiburg-Mitte exit, via Merdingen and Ihringen to Blankenhornsberg
Sales: Peter Wohlfarth, Tobias Burtsche
Opening hours: Mon.–Fri. 08:00 to 12:00 hours and 13:00 to 17:00 hours
Worth seeing: Vaulted cellar dating back to founding years (1847)

Vineyard area: 36.2 hectares
Annual production: 280,000 bottles
Top sites: Blankenhornsberger Doktorgarten, Freiburger Schlossberg
Soil types: Decomposed volcanic formation, loess-clay, decomposed gneiss
Grape varieties: 30% Spätburgunder, 21% Weißburgunder, 18% Grauburgunder, 16% Riesling, 8% Müller-Thurgau, 7% other varieties
Average yield: 65 hl/ha
Best vintages: 2000, 2001, 2003
Member: VDP, EcoVin

The community-run wineries of Blankenhornsberg and Freiburg were combined into a single state domain in 1997. The Doktorgarten site, established 1842, remains the core of the operation. It's headed by Peter Wohlfarth and Tobias Burtsche, and it appears they are determined to lead the winery to new heights. The 2003 white wines are of good quality across the board, and the 2000 Spätburgunder wines show deep fruit, power and maturation potential.

2003 Blankenhornsl
Riesling Kabinett tr
11.7%, ♀ till 2006

2003 Blankenhornsl
Grauer Burgunder Kabinett trocken
13.9%, ♀ till 2006 **85**

2003 Freiburger Schlossberg
Riesling Spätlese trocken
12%, ♀ till 2006 **85**

2002 Blankenhornsberger
Weißer Burgunder Spätlese trocken
12.5%, ♀ till 2006 **85**

2003 Blankenhornsberger Doktorgarten
Grauer Burgunder Spätlese trocken
14.8%, ♀ till 2007 **86**

2003 Blankenhornsberger Doktorgarten
Weißer Burgunder Spätlese trocken
14.7%, ♀ till 2007 **87**

2002 Blankenhornsberger
Muskateller Spätlese
12%, ♀ till 2007 **86**

——— Red wines ———

2000 Blankenhornsberger
Spätburgunder Spätlese trocken
13.5%, ♀ till 2007 **86**

2000 Blankenhornsberger
Spätburgunder trocken
13.5%, ♀ till 2008 **87**

2001 Blankenhornsberger
Spätburgunder trocken
13%, ♀ till 2009 **88**

2002
Blankenhornsberger

MUSKATELLER
QUALITÄTSWEIN TROCKEN

BADEN

The wines: **100** Perfect · **95–99** Outstanding · **90–94** Excellent · **85–89** Very good · **80–84** Good · **75–79** Average

167

STAATSWEINGUT MEERSBURG

**Owner: Federal state of
Baden-Württemberg
Director: Dr. Jürgen Dietrich
Vineyard manager: Otto Kopp
Winemaker: Harald Gutemann
88709 Meersburg, Seminarstraße 6
Tel. (0 75 32) 3 57, Fax 3 58
e-mail:
info@staatsweingut-meersburg.de
Internet:
www.staatsweingut-meersburg.de**
*Directions: Via B 31/B 33 to Meersburg,
in direction of Schloss, Parking at winery*
Sales: Marion Schäfer
Opening hours: Mon.–Fri. 09:00 to
18:00 hours, Sat. 09:00 to 16:00 hours
Restaurant/Wine bar: With view over
the lake, daily from 11:00 to 24:00 hours,
closed Wed.
Specialties: Foamy cheese-wine soup
with bread crust
History: Winemaking since 1210, state-
owned winery since 1803

Vineyard area: 61 hectares
Annual production: 450,000 bottles
Top sites: Meersburger
Rieschen and Jungfernstieg
Soil types: Glacial moraine rubble
on fresh water molasse
Grape varieties: 50% Spätburgunder,
22% Müller-Thurgau, 9% Weißbur-
gunder, 4% Grauburgunder,
3% Riesling, 12% other varieties
Average yield: 52 hl/ha
Best vintages: 2002, 2003

This winery was once the leading producer on Lake Constance. This year it presented a enjoyable range of wines. The
new estate director is Dr. Jürgen Dietrich,
who came from the state-run Hofkellerei
in Würzburg, and it seems the measures
he has introduced show long-term promise. Across the board we tasted juicy
white wines that are a joy to drink. We
would like to give special mention to the
concentrated Weißburgunder from the

Olgaberg site as well as the elegant Chardonnay from the Chorherrenhalde.

2003 Weißer Burgunder trocken
12.5%, ♀ till 2006 — **83**

2003 Meersburger Chorherrenhalde
Weißer Burgunder trocken ***
13.5%, ♀ till 2006 — **84**

2003 Meersburger Chorherrenhalde
Chardonnay trocken ***
13%, ♀ till 2006 — **85**

2002 Meersburger Chorherrenhalde
Weißer Burgunder & Chardonnay
trocken
13%, ♀ till 2006 — **85**

2002 Meersburger Jungfernstieg
Weißer Burgunder trocken
6.4%, ♀ till 2006 — **85**

2003 Hohentwieler Olgaberg
Weißer Burgunder trocken ***
13.5%, ♀ till 2007 — **86**

———— Red wines ————

2003 Meersburger Jungfernstieg
Spätburgunder Weißherbst
12%, ♀ till 2006 — **83**

2002 Gailinger Ritterhalde
Spätburgunder trocken
14%, ♀ till 2006 — **83**

2003 Meersburger Bengel
Spätburgunder trocken ***
14%, ♀ till 2007 — **84**

WEINGUT STADT LAHR – FAMILIE WÖHRLE

Owner: Wöhrle family GbR
Manager: Hans and Markus Wöhrle
Winemaker: Markus Wöhrle
77933 Lahr, Weinbergstraße 3
Tel. (0 78 21) 2 53 32 und 95 71 90,
Fax 3 93 98
e-mail: info@weingut-stadt-lahr.de
Internet: www.weingut-stadt-lahr.de
Directions: A 5 Frankfurt–Basel,
Lahr exit, in direction of city center,
at city park in direction of Terrassenbad
Sales: Wöhrle family
Opening hours: Mon.–Fri. 17:00 to
19:00 hours, Sat. 09:00 to 13:00 hours
and by appointment
History: The city-owned estate was
privatized by merging with the Wöhrle
family business in 1979

Vineyard area: 11.5 hectares
Annual production: 75,000 bottles
Top site: Lahrer Schutterlindenberg
Soil types: Loess-clay with humus
Grape varieties: 23% Spätburgunder,
15% Auxerrois, 12% Weißburgunder,
10% Grauburgunder, 9% Müller-Thur-
gau, 6% Riesling, 25% other varieties
Average yield: 55 hl/ha
Best vintages: 2001, 2002, 2003
Member: EcoVin

Hans Wöhrle and his wife Monika leased
the winery of the city of Lahr, which was
completely run down, and have breathed
new life into it. In 1997 the Wöhrles
purchased the building from the city. The
changeover to organic viticultural practices was accompanied by some variable
quality, but by now the standard is again
reliable at a high level. Wöhrle is assisted
by his son Markus, who has learnt a lot
from Hans-Günther Schwarz in the Pfalz.
The 2002 white wines were clean and
showed unusual concentration and length
for this vintage. The 2003 range is well
made, the wines we liked best were the
juicy Auxerrois Kabinett as well as the
expressive Grauburgunder Spätlese.

2003 Weißer Burgunder
Kabinett trocken
13.5%, ♀ till 2006   83

2003 Grauer Burgunder
Kabinett trocken
13.5%, ♀ till 2006   84

2003 Weißer Burgunder
Spätlese trocken
14%, ♀ till 2006   85

2003 Auxerrois
Kabinett trocken
13%, ♀ till 2006   86

2003 Chardonnay
Spätlese trocken
15%, ♀ till 2007   86

2002 Chardonnay
Spätlese trocken
13.5%, ♀ till 2007   86

2002 Lahrer Schutterlindenberg
Grauer Burgunder Spätlese trocken
13%, ♀ till 2007   87

2002 Lahrer Schutterlindenberg
Chardonnay Spätlese trocken
13%, ♀ till 2007   87

2003 Grauer Burgunder
Spätlese trocken
14.5%, ♀ till 2008   88

2001 Lahrer Schutterlindenberg
Chardonnay Spätlese trocken
13.5%, ♀ till 2007   88

2003 Riesling
Beerenauslese
10.5%, ♀ till 2010   88

WEINGUT STADT LAHR
INH. FAMILIE WÖHRLE
2003
LAHRER SCHUTTERLINDENBERG
WEISSBURGUNDER
SPÄTLESE TROCKEN
14% 0,75 l
QUALITÄTSWEIN MIT PRÄDIKAT
GUTSABFÜLLUNG
A.P. NR. 810 09/04   D-77933 LAHR
BADEN
DE-005 Öko-Kontrollst.
ECO VIN

The wines: **100** Perfect · **95–99** Outstanding · **90–94** Excellent · **85–89** Very good · **80–84** Good · **75–79** Average

WEINGUT STIGLER

Owner: Andreas Stigler
79241 Ihringen, Bachenstraße 29
Tel. (0 76 68) 2 97, Fax 9 41 20
e-mail: info@weingut-stigler.de
Internet: www.weingut-stigler.de
Directions: A 5 Frankfurt–Basel,
Teningen exit, in direction of Eichstetten
Sales: Regina Stigler
Opening hours: Mon.–Fri. 10:00 to
12:00 hours and 15:00 to 18:00 hours
Sat. 10:00 to 12:00 hours
and 15:00 to 17:00 hours
and by appointment
History: Family-owned since 1881
Worth a visit: Series of culinary events
(Stigler's wine calendar)

Vineyard area: 10 hectares
Annual production: 70,000 bottles
Top sites: Ihringer Winklerberg,
Freiburger Schlossberg,
Oberrotweiler Eichberg
Soil types: Volcanic and decomposed
gneiss soils
Grape varieties: 36% Spätburgunder,
24% Riesling, 11% Weißburgunder,
10% Grauburgunder, 9% Silvaner,
5% Traminer, 5% other varieties
Average yield: 45 hl/ha
Best vintages: 2000, 2001, 2003
Member: VDP

This winery has a long tradition, and owns six hectares of the famous Ihringer Winklerberg site, as well as good parcels of the Freiburger Schlossberg site. Low yields ensure that virtually all grapes harvested are of predicate level, and the wines are given unusually long time in the cellar to develop. Owner Andreas Stigler is also responsible for the cellar. For his red wines, he likes to emphasize ripeness, and favors an almost oxidative style that can work very well in good vintages such as 1999. The 2001 Schlossberg is rather light in color, and does not quite achieve this standard. The 2003 white wines are of good quality, and the strong suits are Silvaner, Riesling and Chardonnay.

2003 Freiburger Schlossberg
Weißer Burgunder Kabinett trocken
13%, ♀ till 2006   **84**

2002 Ihringer Winklerberg
Grauer Burgunder Spätlese trocken
12.5%, ♀ till 2006   **85**

2003 Ihringer Winklerberg
Grauer Burgunder Spätlese trocken
14.5%, ♀ till 2006   **85**

2003 Ihringer Winklerberg
Weißer Burgunder Spätlese trocken
14.5%, ♀ till 2006   **86**

2003 Ihringer Winklerberg
Silvaner Spätlese trocken "F 66"
13%, ♀ till 2006   **86**

2003 Ihringer Winklerberg
Chardonnay Spätlese trocken
14.5%, ♀ till 2008   **87**

2003 Ihringer Winklerberg
Riesling Spätlese trocken "F 36"
14.5%, ♀ till 2008   **88**

2003 Ihringer Winklerberg
Traminer Spätlese
13%, ♀ till 2008   **87**

——————— Red wines ———————

2003 Freiburger Schlossberg
Spätburgunder Weißherbst Spätlese
trocken
14.5%, ♀ till 2006   **86**

2001 Freiburger Schlossberg
Spätburgunder Spätlese trocken
13.5%, ♀ till 2008   **85**

BADEN

STIGLER

Ihringer Winklerberg

Silvaner
Spätlese F66
trocken

2003

Qualitätswein mit Prädikat
A.P.Nr. 312-07-04
Gutsabfüllung Weingut Stigler
13,0% vol.   D-79241 Ihringen / Kaiserstuhl   0,75 L

TAUBERFRÄNKISCHE WINZERGENOSSENSCHAFT BECKSTEIN

General manager: Bernhard Stahl
Technical manager: Stefan Steffen
97922 Lauda-Königshofen,
Weinstraße 30
Tel. (0 93 43) 50 00, Fax 52 77
e-mail: info@beckstein.de
Internet: www.beckstein.de
Directions: A 81 Würzburg–Heilbronn,
Tauberbischofsheim exit
Sales: Manager Ms. Hönninger
Opening hours: Mon.–Fri. 08:00 to
18:00 hours, Sat. 09:00 to 18:00 hours
Sun. 09:00 to 17:00 hours
Mar.–Nov. only Sat. 09:00 to 13:00 hours
Restaurant: Weinstuben Beckstein
10:00 to 24:00 hours, closed Wed.
Specialties: Green rye dishes
History: Founded 1894

Vineyard area: 345 hectares
Number of members: 575
Annual production: 3.5 mill. bottles
Top sites: Becksteiner Kirchberg
and Nonnenberg
Soil types: Shell limestone
Grape varieties: 39% Müller-Thurgau,
29% Schwarzriesling, 8% Kerner, 5%
each of Spätburgunder and Bacchus,
4% Silvaner, 10% other varieties
Average yield: 70 hl/ha
Best vintages: 1998, 2001, 2003

The magic of Tauberfranken captivates the wine-lover travelling along the "Romantic Route," investigating medieval towns and modern wines. Here the Müller-Thurgau grape dominates, and Pinot Meunier is the most important red variety. The co-operative is responsible for 40 percent of the total vineyard area of 800 hectares. The 2003 range is of homogeneous good quality. The basic Schwarzriesling is just as convincing as is the Beerenauslese. There is also a remarkable Auslese made from the ancient variety Tauberschwarz, with aromas of cherries and blackcurrants.

2003 Becksteiner Kirchberg
Müller-Thurgau Kabinett trocken
13.5%, ♀ till 2006   **81**

2003 Gerlachsheimer Herrenberg
Silvaner Spätlese trocken
13.5%, ♀ till 2006   **83**

2002 Marbacher Frankenberg
Grauer Burgunder Auslese trocken
14%, ♀ till 2006   **84**

2001 Marbacher Frankenberg
Grauer Burgunder Auslese trocken
14%, ♀ till 2006   **85**

2003 Becksteiner Kirchberg
Riesling Spätlese
11.5%, ♀ till 2006   **83**

2003 Becksteiner Kirchberg
Riesling Auslese
11.5%, ♀ till 2007   **85**

2000 Marbacher Frankenberg
Müller-Thurgau Trockenbeerenauslese
12%, ♀ till 2015   **89**

———— Red wines ————

2003 Dittwarer Ölkuchen
Schwarzriesling trocken
13.5%, ♀ till 2006   **82**

2003 Becksteiner Kirchberg
Tauberschwarz Auslese
15%, ♀ till 2006   **85**

2003 Becksteiner Kirchberg
Schwarzriesling Beerenauslese
14.5%, ♀ till 2010   **88**

The wines: **100** Perfect · **95–99** Outstanding · **90–94** Excellent · **85–89** Very good · **80–84** Good · **75–79** Average

WEINGUT TRAUTWEIN

Owner: Hans-Peter and Elfriede Trautwein
Manager: Hans-Peter Trautwein
79353 Bahlingen, Riegeler Straße 2
Tel. (0 76 63) 26 50, Fax 5 00 27
e-mail: info@trautweingut.com
Internet: www.trautweingut.com
Directions: A 5, Riegel exit, left at town entrance to Bahlingen; A 5, Teningen exit, through Bahlingen in direction of Riegel, right at town exit
Sales: Trautwein family
Opening hours: Mon.–Fri. 08:30 to 12:30 hours and 14:00 to 18:00 hours Sat. 08:30 to 16:00 hours
History: Winemaking and coopering tradition in family since 1649
Worth seeing: Working on organic principles, sparkling wine cellar 400 years old

---

Vineyard area: 8 hectares
Annual production: 35,000 bottles
Top sites: Vineyard not stated on labels
Soil types: Loess, loess-clay, decomposed volcanic soil
Grape varieties: 45% Spätburgunder, 20% Grauburgunder, 10% each of Weißburgunder and Müller-Thurgau, 5% each of Gewürztraminer and Regent, 5% other varieties
Average yield: 50 hl/ha
Best vintages: 2001, 2002, 2003
Member: Bioland, Demeter

Hans-Peter and Elfriede Trautwein have been implementing organic viticultural practices since 1980. Their winery in Bahlingen has always produced very interesting wines, but the quality has often been variable. We upgraded their rating last year, based mainly on to excellent Gewürztraminer wines. The 2001 vintage Spätburgunder "Edition RS" rounded off the positive impression. Now, the current range is again well made. Good basic wines made from the white Pinot varieties are complemented by a good Chardonnay and a Gewürztraminer Auslese. The 2002 red wines show a solid quality.

2003 Bahlinger
Grauer Burgunder trocken
14.5%, ♀ till 2006 — **83**

2003 Bahlinger
Weißer Burgunder trocken
15%, ♀ till 2006 — **84**

2001 Bahlinger
Chardonnay Spätlese trocken
14%, ♀ till 2006 — **86**

2002 Bahlinger
Gewürztraminer Spätlese trocken
12.5%, ♀ till 2006 — **86**

2002 Bahlinger
Chardonnay trocken "Edition RS"
14%, ♀ till 2007 — **86**

2003 Bahlinger
Gewürztraminer Auslese
15%, ♀ till 2006 — **86**

2001 Bahlinger
Gewürztraminer Eiswein
11%, ♀ till 2011 — **89**

——— Red wines ———

2002 Bahlinger
Spätburgunder trocken
13.5%, ♀ till 2006 — **84**

2002 Bahlinger Regent trocken
13%, ♀ till 2006 — **84**

2001 Bahlinger
Spätburgunder trocken
13.5%, ♀ till 2006 — **85**

2001 Bahlinger
Spätburgunder trocken "Edition RS"
14%, ♀ till 2007 — **87**

The estates: ♯♯♯♯♯ World's finest · ♯♯♯♯ Germany's best · ♯♯♯ Very good · ♯♯ Good · ♯ Reliable

WEINGUT
FRITZ WASSMER

Owner and manager:
Fritz Waßmer
79189 Bad Krozingen-Schlatt,
Lazariterstraße 3
Tel. (0 76 33) 39 65, Fax 44 58
e-mail: Fwassmer@gmx.de
Internet:
www.weingut-wassmer-schlatt.de
Directions: A 5 Karlsruhe–Basel, Bad Krozingen exit
Sales: Fritz Waßmer
by appointment
Worth seeing: Lazariterquelle mineral water spring

Vineyard area: 15 hectares
Annual production: 74,000 bottles
Top site: Malterdinger Bienenberg
Soil types: Loess with decomposed limestone soil, red kaolin, shell limestone
Grape varieties: 67% Spätburgunder, 10% Weißburgunder, 5% each of Grauburgunder and Syrah, 13% other varieties
Average yield: 36 hl/ha
Best vintages: 2002, 2003

Fritz Waßmer received his training in winemaking at Blankenhornsberg. He decided in the late Nineties to implement what he had learnt in his own winery. He bought and leased vineyards in Malterdingen and Kenzingen, concentrating on the production of top-quality red wines. But his white wines, too, as shown by the 2003 range, should not be disregarded. When planting new vines, he uses French Pinot clones grafted onto low-vigour rootstocks, with a plant density of 8,000 to 12,000 vines per hectare. He ferments the must in open tanks, and adds no cultured yeasts. The red wines of the 2001 vintage were already very good. Now, the quality of the 2002 wines is so convincing that we have named Fritz Waßmer our "Discovery of the year 2005." Our sincere congratulations!

2003 Weißer Burgunder trocken
13%, ♀ till 2006 — 82

2003 Weißer Burgunder
trocken "Reserve"
15%, ♀ till 2006 — 84

2003 Grauer Burgunder
trocken "Reserve"
14.5%, ♀ till 2006 — 84

2003 Muskateller trocken
14%, ♀ till 2006 — 86

2003 Muskateller Spätlese
13%, ♀ till 2007 — 86

——— Red wines ———

2002 Spätburgunder trocken
13%, ♀ till 2006 — 83

2001 Spätburgunder trocken
13.5%, ♀ till 2006 — 85

2002 Spätburgunder
trocken "Alte Reben"
13.5%, ♀ till 2010 — 90

2002 Spätburgunder
trocken "Reserve"
13.5%, ♀ till 2010 — 91

The wines: **100** Perfect · **95–99** Outstanding · **90–94** Excellent · **85–89** Very good · **80–84** Good · **75–79** Average

173

WEINGUT
MARTIN WASSMER

Owner and manager:
Martin Waßmer
79189 Bad Krozingen-Schlatt,
Am Sportplatz 3
Tel. (0 76 33) 1 52 92, Fax 1 33 84
e-mail:
wassmer-krozingen@t-online.de
Internet: www.weingut-wassmer.de
*Directions: A 5 Frankfurt–Basel, exit
and in direction of Bad Krozingen, right
after two kilometers, next to sports field
at Schlatt town limits*
Sales: Martin and Sabine Waßmer
Opening hours: April, May, June 08:00
to 20:00 hours, Sat. 09:00 to 14:00
hours, otherwise by appointment

Vineyard area: 9 hectares
Annual production: 48,000 bottles
Top sites: Schlatter Malteser-
garten, Laufener Altenberg
Soil types: Loess with limestone,
loess and clay
Grape varieties: 70% Spätburgunder,
12% Weißburgunder, 7% Graubur-
gunder, 4% each of Müller-Thurgau
and Gutedel, 3% Muskateller
Average yield: 51 hl/ha
Best vintages: 2000, 2001, 2002

Martin Waßmer started off as a producer
of excellent asparagus, and running a
handicraft shop, turning to winemaking
only in 1999 – and getting off to an impressive start. He first attracted attention
when he garnered some top placings in
the Vinum Red Wine Competition. Since
then he has even further improved his almost intuitive feeling for Pinot Noir. This
development was crowned last year,
when he presented a range of outstanding
2001 red wines, as well as good white
wines. His current range is equally attractive. The highlight is the Spätburgunder
(Pinot Noir) "SW" with its elegant cherry
fruit. The white wines can still be improved, what they need is a little more
elegance and polish.

2003 Schlatter Maltesergarten
Weißer Burgunder Spätlese trocken
14.5%, ♀ till 2006   **84**

2003 Grauer Burgunder
Spätlese trocken
14.5%, ♀ till 2006   **85**

2001 Schlatter Maltesergarten
Weißer Burgunder
Spätlese trocken "SW"
14%, ♀ till 2006   **85**

2002 Schlatter Maltesergarten
Weißer Burgunder
Spätlese trocken "SW"
13.5%, ♀ till 2006   **85**

2002 Grauer Burgunder
trocken "R"
13.5%, ♀ till 2007   **87**

2001 Grauer Burgunder trocken
14%, ♀ till 2007   **89**

2003 Markgräfler Muskateller
12%, ♀ till 2007   **87**

——— Red wines ———

2002 Markgräfler
Spätburgunder trocken
13.5%, ♀ till 2006   **84**

2002 Schlatter Maltesergarten
Spätburgunder trocken
13.5%, ♀ till 2008   **86**

2002 Schlatter
Spätburgunder trocken "SW"
13.5%, ♀ till 2010   **89**

2001 Schlatter
Spätburgunder trocken "SW"
13.5%, ♀ till 2010   **90**

WEINGUT GRAF WOLFF METTERNICH

Owner: G. and R. Hurrle
Manager: Hans-Bert Espe
Winemaker: Franz Schwörer
77770 Durbach, Grol 4
Tel. (07 81) 4 27 79, Fax 4 25 53
e-mail: info@weingut-metternich.de
Internet: www.weingut-metternich.de
Directions: A 5 Frankfurt–Basel,
Offenburg or Appenweier exit, in direc-
tion of Durbach
Sales: Mon.–Fri. 08:00 to 12:00 and
13:00 to 17:00, Sat. 09:30 to 12:30
hours, and by appointment
History: Winemaking since 1180
Worth seeing: Former castle cellar, ren-
ovated Trott house, vinotheque, oldest
Sauvignon Blanc vineyard in Germany

Vineyard area: 34 hectares
Annual production: 140,000 bottles
Top sites: Durbacher Schloss
Grohl and Schlossberg, Lahrer
Herrentisch (all monopole)
Soil types: Decomposed granite
Grape varieties: 28% Riesling,
31% Spätburgunder, 10% each of
Weißburgunder and Grauburgunder,
6% Müller-Thurgau, 5% Chardonnay,
4% Traminer, 6% other varieties
Average yield: 42 hl/ha
Best vintages: 1999, 2001, 2002

This winery looks back on a long tradition, and has recently experienced a significant positive development, ever since
the new manager Hans-Bert Espe has
been at the helm. Looking to the 2002 vintage, we liked both: dry wines, and particularly the botrytis dessert wines. Riesling Auslese wines as well as a Traminer
Trockenbeerenauslese were the highlights of the range. Unfortunately the
2003 wines are not of the same standard.
Only the Riesling Trockenbeerenauslese
makes up slightly for the deficits. We
hope that this was a single poor range,
not to be repeated.

2003 Durbacher Schlossberg
Traminer Spätlese
10.5%, ♀ till 2007 — **84**

2003 Durbacher Schloss Grohl
Scheurebe Auslese
10%, ♀ till 2008 — **85**

2003 Durbacher Schlossberg
Traminer Auslese – 18 –
10%, ♀ till 2009 — **86**

2002 Durbacher Schlossberg
Riesling Spätlese
10%, ♀ till 2007 — **88**

2002 Durbacher Schlossberg
Riesling Auslese
9%, ♀ till 2009 — **89**

2001 Durbacher Schloss Grohl
Riesling Eiswein – 10 –
7.5%, ♀ till 2011 — **89**

2003 Durbacher Schloss Grohl
Riesling Trockenbeerenauslese
8.5%, ♀ till 2018 — **90**

2002 Durbacher Schlossberg
Traminer Trockenbeerenauslese
9%, ♀ till 2015 — **90**

———— Red wines ————

2002 Durbacher Schlossberg
Cabernet Sauvignon & Merlot trocken
13.5%, ♀ till 2006 — **82**

2002 Durbacher Schlossberg
Spätburgunder Spätlese trocken
13.5%, ♀ till 2007 — **84**

2001 Durbacher Schlossberg
Spätburgunder Auslese trocken
13.5%, ♀ till 2006 — **85**

The wines: **100** Perfect · **95–99** Outstanding · **90–94** Excellent · **85–89** Very good · **80–84** Good · **75–79** Average

WEINGUT
WILHELM ZÄHRINGER

Owner and manager:
Wolfgang Zähringer
Administrator: Paulin Köpfer
Winemaker: Uli Klee
79423 Heitersheim, Johanniterstr. 61
Tel. (0 76 34) 10 25, Fax 10 27
e-mail: weingut.zaehringer@t-online.de
Internet: www.weingut-zaehringer.de
*Directions: B 3, first or second round-
about, through the town, opposite
Catholic church*
Sales: Wolfgang Zähringer
Opening hours: Mon.–Fri. 09:00 to
12:00 hours and 14:00 to 18:00 hours
Sat. 10:00 to 12:00 hours
History: Founded 1844

Vineyard area: 9 hectares
Annual production: 50,000 bottles
Top sites: Heitersheimer
Sonnhole and Maltesergarten
Soil types: Clay, loess
Grape varieties: 42% Spätburgunder,
11% each of Gutedel and Graubur-
gunder, 10% each of Weißburgunder
and Chardonnay, 16% other varieties
Average yield: 64 hl/ha
Best vintages: 2001, 2002, 2003
Member: EcoVin

Wolfgang Zähringer took over the family
winery in Heitersheim in 1971. He converted to organic viticultural practices in
the mid-Eighties. The owner is supported
in this by his manager Paulin Köpfer.
Apart from running his own winery,
Zähringer also manages a small producer
group. The current range remains faithful
to the house's powerful style, and retains
a good one-bunch standard. Why the rather good Gewürztraminer, which has 15
percent (!) alcohol, should be declared as
a Kabinett is a mystery to us. As in the
previous vintage, the "Villa Urbana"
blend is the best red wine. We also liked
the Grauburgunder Sekt (Pinot Gris sparkling wine).

2003 Heitersheimer Maltesergarten
Muskateller trocken
13%, ♀ till 2006 **83**

2003 Heitersheimer Maltesergarten
Grauer Burgunder trocken
14%, ♀ till 2006 **83**

2001 Heitersheimer Maltesergarten
Gutedel trocken
11.5%, ♀ till 2005 **83**

2002 "Zähringer Löwe Nr. 28"
Weißer Burgunder Auslese trocken
14%, ♀ till 2006 **84**

2001 Heitersheimer Sonnhole
Grauer Burgunder Auslese trocken
14%, ♀ till 2006 **84**

2001 Weißer Burgunder
trocken "SZ"
13.5%, ♀ till 2006 **84**

2002 "Zähringer Löwe Nr. 29"
Grauer Burgunder Auslese trocken
14%, ♀ till 2006 **85**

2003 Gewürztraminer
Kabinett trocken
15%, ♀ till 2006 **87**

2001 Grauer Burgunder
trocken "SZ"
13.5%, ♀ till 2007 **87**

———— Red wines ————

2002 Spätburgunder trocken "SZ"
13%, ♀ till 2006 **84**

2001 Spätburgunder trocken "SZ"
13%, ♀ till 2006 **84**

2002 "Villa Urbana" trocken
13%, ♀ till 2007 **85**

2001 "Villa Urbana" trocken
12.5%, ♀ till 2006 **86**

Weinhaus S. Bastian

79346 Endingen, Königschaffhauser Str. 8
Tel. (0 76 42) 60 09, Fax 38 62

The S. Bastian wine house (see also estate of the same name) processes the grapes of 180 contract growers, and is a reliable supplier of fresh standard-quality wines. A good example is the Spätburgunder (Pinot Noir) Rosé "Stephanie" (82 points).

Weingut Michael Baumer

79235 Oberbergen, Kapellenstraße 16
Tel. (0 76 62) 94 91 91, Fax 94 91 92
weingut-michael-baumer@t-online.de

Michael Baumer and Melanie Sommer established their winery, which now covers 1.8 hectares of vineyard, in 1999. By far the best current wine is a 2001 Grauburgunder (Pinot Gris) Spätlese, bottled in 2004 (88 points). More of the same, please!

Weingut Dr. Benz – Kirchberghof

79341 Kenzingen-Bombach, Pfadweg 5
Tel. (0 76 44) 12 61, Fax 40 54

This winery has been owned by Marina and Eribert Benz since 2003, they are currently still being assisted by previous owners Herta and Gert Hügle. There are promising signs in the Grauburgunder, the Spätburgunder "Hummelberg" and a barrique-matured Chardonnay.

Winzergenossenschaft Bickensohl

79235 Bickensohl, Neulindenstraße 25
Tel. (0 76 62) 9 31 10, Fax 93 11 50
e-mail: info@bickensohler-wein.com

This co-operative, founded in 1924, was regarded in the early Eighties as one of the "inventors" of the Pinot Gris renaissance, and was a reliable producer of solid quality wines. It's currently in a phase of changing quality. The 2002 Spätburgunder Steinfelsen "SC" sets a positive sign.

View of the wine-growing village of Kappelrodeck in Baden, picturesquely located amidst the vineyards. Photo: DWI/Hartmann

Baden

Weingut Bimmerle

77871 Renchen, Kirchstraße 4
Tel. (0 78 43) 6 54, Fax 15 02

The wine estate and merchant Bimmerle has presented a solid range, with two Rieslings from the Oberkircher Schlossberg site standing out as highlights. We liked both the racy fresh Kabinett (84 points) as well as the juicy, clearly defined Spätlese (86).

Winzergenossenschaft Bischoffingen

79235 Bischoffingen, Bacchusstraße 14
Tel. (0 76 62) 9 30 10, Fax 93 01 93
e-mail: info@wg-bischoffingen.de
Internet: www.wg-bischoffingen.de

The Bischoffingen co-operative has built its reputation on classically produced Pinot Gris and Pinot Noir wines. In recent years, the wines have been solid, but have rarely shown any polish or character. This development has continued through the 2003 vintage. We liked the fresh Muskateller Spätlese (84 points).

Weingut Peter Briem

79241 Ihringen-Wasenweiler, Weinstr. 1
Tel. (0 76 68) 52 57, Fax 99 54 16
e-mail: info@weingut-briem.de
Internet: www.weingut-briem.de

This family winery was founded in 1977. In recent years, we have had our problems with the wines here, and this, unfortunately, continues through the 2003 vintage. The only exception is the 2002 Cabernet Sauvignon (86 points), which is really well made. Nevertheless, the exclusion from the ranks of wineries rated with bunches of grapes was inevitable.

Weingut Otto und Martin Frey

79211 Denzlingen, Im Brühl 1
Tel. (0 76 66) 52 53, Fax 23 14
e-mail: weingut-frey@t-online.de

The Frey winery presented a homogeneous 2003 vintage range. We liked both a Chardonnay that has been partly matured in barriques (84 points), and a clean, typical Gewürztraminer Spätlese (85). The wines need a little more extract and concentration to warrant a higher rating.

Weingut Heitlinger

76684 Östringen-Tiefenbach, Mühlberg
Tel. (0 72 59) 9 11 20, Fax 91 12 99
e-mail: info@heitlinger-wein.de
Internet: www.heitlinger-wein.de

Literally millions were invested here – and that includes expensive marketing. A wine forum was created, featuring a cultural stage and a bistro. The final culmination of this hectic development was a court proceeding for insolvency, at the end of which the business re-emerged as Weingut Heitlinger GmbH (private limited company). The quality of wines presented has not improved.

Weingut Hermann

79235 Vogtsburg, Alt-Vogtsburg 19
Tel. (0 76 62) 62 02, Fax 62 02

The wines of this winery reached us only just before the publishing deadline – and an interesting discovery they make. White wines typical of their varieties and two very well made Pinot Noirs from the 2001 and 2002 vintages make us look forward with great interest to the next vintage.

Winzergenossenschaft Jechtingen

79361 Sasbach-Jechtingen, Winzerstr. 1
Tel. (0 76 62) 9 32 30, Fax 82 41
e-mail: info@jechtinger-wein.de
Internet: www.jechtinger-wein.de

The emblem of the historic wine-producing commune is the Burg Sponeck castle, 700 years old, the coat-of-arms of which is reproduced on the label of the co-operative. Apart from the 2002 Hochberg Spätburgunder we found nothing to enthuse over in the latest range.

Weingut – Weinkellerei Karl Karle

79241 Ihringen, Am Krebsbach 3
Tel. (0 76 68) 50 50, Fax 92 50
e-mail: karlkarle@gmx.de
Internet: www.weingut-karl-karle.de

The 2003 vintage range is characterized by clean but extremely alcoholic wines. Both, the Sekt (sparkling wine) and the Ihringer Winklerberg Merlot are disappointing. We liked the delicately sweet Gewürztraminer Spätlese (84 points).

Weingut Friedrich Kiefer

79356 Eichstetten, Bötzinger Straße 13
Tel. (0 76 63) 10 63, Fax 39 27

The wines presented by the Friedrich Kiefer wine-growers group are rock-solid. A good example is the Graubur-gunder (Pinot Gris) Kabinett (83 points). The botrytis dessert Muskateller wines (Auslese 86, Beerenauslese 88) have been a little overfermented, but show the ambitions presents here.

Weingut Landmann

79112 Freiburg-Waltershofen
Umkircher Straße 29
Tel. (0 76 65) 67 56, Fax 5 19 45
e-mail: weingut-landmann@t-online.de
Internet: www.weingut-landmann.de

Peter and Jürgen Landmann took over the vineyards from their parents in 1995. An emerald lizard is displayed on the label. The volume of the press kit is a little in advance of the quality of the wines. The highlights of this year's range are the 2002 Kapellenberg Spätburgun-der (Pinot Noir) and the 2003 Gewürztra-miner from the same site (both 83 points).

Weingut Clemens Lang

79112 Freiburg-Munzingen
Reinachstraße 19
Tel. (0 76 64) 58 63, Fax 5 94 16

The Clemens Lang winery presented a ho-mogeneous range, the only disappointment being the Riesling in liter bottles. The best wine is the 2002 Munzinger Kapellenberg Spätburgunder (Pinot Noir) Kabinett (84 points), with a red fruit nose.

Weingut Andreas Männle

77770 Durbach, Heimbach 12
Tel. (07 81) 4 14 86, Fax 4 29 81
e-mail: alfred@weingut-maennle.de
Internet: www.weingut-maennle.de

The 2002 Spätburgunder (Pinot Noir) Auslese from the Bienengarten site (owned exclusively by Männle) is the best of this year's range. The white wines of the 2003 range are solid, but provide little drinking pleasure.

Weingut Klaus-Martin M

79423 Heitersheim, Johann
Tel. (0 76 34) 22 54, Fax 3
e-mail: Weingut.Marget@

Klaus-Martin Marget ha_ solid range, headed up by an elegant Chardonnay Kabinett and a clear, fruity Spätburgunder Blanc de Noir Spätlese (both 84 points). There is room for im-provement in the Gutedel, the Sekt as well as the Spätburgunder in liter bottles.

Bezirkskellerei Markgräflerland

79588 Efringen-Kirchen, Winzerstraße 2
Tel. (0 76 28) 9 11 40, Fax 29 76
e-mail: bezirkskellerei@t-online.de
Internet: www.badischer-wein.com

The co-operative was founded in 1953, with members producing from approx. 350 hectares of vineyard, and produces a solid basic range of wines. A good example is the Blansinger Wolfer Gutedel Kabinett (82 points). The 2002 Pinot Noirs from the Weiler Schlipf site are also pleasant.

Gutshof Edwin Menges

69231 Rauenberg, Suttenweg 1
Tel. (0 62 22) 95 10, Fax 95 11 00
e-mail: gutshof-menges@t-online.de
Internet: www.gutshof-menges.de

This sizeable winery includes a restau-rant as well as a hotel with 30 beds, and is located between Heidelberg and Heil-bronn. The white wines of the 2003 vin-tage could certainly be improved on. The reds of 2002 are better, headed up by a concentrated Lemberger (85 points).

Weingut Adam Müller

69181 Leimen, Adam-Müller-Straße 1
Tel. (0 62 24) 9 71 00, Fax 97 10 47
e-mail: verkauf@weingut-adam-mueller.de

The Adam Müller winery draws on 22 hectares of vineyard in the Leimen and Heidelberg communes. We tasted a solid basic range, as well as two wines that aspire to something better: the typical Muscat Ottonel Spätlese (84 points) as well as the Heidelberger Sonnenseite ob der Bruck Spätburgunder (Pinot Noir) Spätlese (86 points).

179

...erkircher Winzergenossenschaft

, 7704 Oberkirch, Renchener Straße 42
Tel. (0 78 02) 9 25 80, Fax 92 58 38
e-mail: info@oberkircher-winzer.de
Internet: www.oberkircher-winzer.de

This year, the co-operative in Oberkir-
chen presented a range that was split down
the middle: While one has to be generous
to describe the white wines as being solid,
we liked the 2003 Pinot Noirs quite a lot.
The dry Spätlese (85 points) has cherry
fruit, while the Auslese has aromas of
black currant and mulberries (86 points).

Weingut St. Remigius

79291 Merdingen, Rittgasse 17
Tel. (0 76 68) 57 18, Fax 72 52
e-mail: st.remigius@web.de

The small winery, run by Edgar Bärmann
and Conrad Isele, has produced a solid
range of wines, with no great exceptions
in either direction. The best wines are
two Kabinett wines of the 2003 vintage, a
Pinot Blanc and a Pinot Gris, both from
the Merdinger Bühl vineyard, and both
rated 82 points.

Weingut Freiherr Roeder
von Diersburg

77749 Diersburg, Kreisstraße 20
Tel. (0 78 08) 22 21, Fax 22 26
e-mail: weingut@von-roeder.de

This is a traditional winery, run by an
established blue-blooded family, and in-
cludes a small museum. They have man-
aged to handle the 2003 vintage quite well,
the best wine is a Diersburger Schloss-
berg Riesling Spätlese, a juicy wine rated
at 83 points.

Biologisches Weingut Schambachhof

79268 Bötzingen, Schambachhof
Tel. (0 76 63) 14 74, Fax 14 61
e-mail: info@schambachhof.de
Internet: www.schambachhof.de

Matthias and Sonja Höfflin run their
vineyard along organic lines. The wines
of the 2003 vintage are of very solid qual-
ity, headed up by an exciting Scheurebe
Trockenbeerenauslese (91 points), with
an aroma of pink grapefruit.

Weingut Dr. Schneider

79379 Müllheim-Zunzingen
Rosenbergstraße 10
Tel. (0 76 31) 29 15, Fax 1 53 99
e-mail: info@weingut-dr-schneider.de
Internet: www.weingut-dr-schneider.de

The white wines of the 2003 vintage have
turned out quite well here: For instance, a
juicy Chardonnay Spätlese with typical
varietal character (84 points). The "Edi-
tion Antoine," a blend of Cabernet Sau-
vignon, Cabernet Franc and Merlot, was
presented in two vintage editions, 2001
and 2002, of which we clearly preferred
the older vintage (rated 87 and 83 points
respectively). Overall, we discern a dis-
tinct positive trend here.

Weingut Schneider

79423 Heitersheim, Kolpingstraße 7
Tel. (0 76 34) 28 36, Fax 55 13 93
e-mail: weingut-schneider-heiters-
heim@t-online.de

This was our new discovery in the Mark-
gräflerland area last year. One's interest
is stimulated visually right away – attrac-
tive bottles and labels. The current range
is very heterogeneous, running from weak
Riesling and Gutedel to solid white Pinot
wines and a very well made Sauvignon
Blanc Auslese (85 points).

Weingut Schwörer

77770 Durbach, Grol 8
Tel. (07 81) 4 23 62, Fax 3 34 08
e-mail: info@weingut-schwoerer.de
Internet: www.weingut-schwoerer.de

The Schwörer winery and merchant
house was founded in 1812, and was
initially focused on making wooden
barrels, with the production of wine
becoming more important only at a later
stage. Hermann Schwörer made the 2002
vintage his last one. The business was
taken over by Josef Rohrer, who had pre-
viously worked as manager of the Gräf-
lich Wolff Metternich winery. The range
presented has left us mystified. Only the
dry Durbacher Riesling "HS" (84 points)
bore any resemblance to the quality pre-
sented in the previous vintage.

Weingut Lothar Schwörer

77971 Schmieheim, Waldstraße 6
Tel. (0 78 25) 74 11, Fax 23 81
e-mail: weingut.schwoerer@t-online.de

Lothar Schwörer, who took over his parents' winery in 1992, presented an uneven range. The wine we liked best was the dry Riesling Spätlese "Selektion Kalkofen." On the other hand, the sparkling wines as well as some of the basic wines are really poor this year.

Winzergenossenschaft Waldulm

77876 Kappelrodeck-Waldulm,
Weinstraße 37
Tel. (0 78 42) 9 48 90, Fax 94 89 20

The red wines presented here are solid across the board. The highlight is the 2002 Pfarrberg Spätburgunder (Pinot Noir, 83 points) matured in barrique. In fact, the good basic quality of the wine might be even more evident if less oak had been used.

Weingut Josef Walz

79423 Heitersheim, Hauptstraße 34
Tel. (0 76 34) 55 30 30, Fax 55 30 33
e-mail: weinwalz@t-online.de
Internet: www.weingut-walz.de

Thomas Walz took over this winery in 1996, when he was only 24 years old. He was a rising star last year, but this vintage collection shows up a number of really poor wines. Only the Gutedel Selektion Johannes (82 points), the 2001 "Cuvée Jakob" (83) and the Nobling Auslese (84) bear any resemblance to the good wines presented from the previous vintage.

Winzergenossenschaft Wasenweiler

79241 Wasenweiler, Raiffeisenstraße 6
Tel. (0 76 68) 50 76, Fax 50 08

Wasenweiler is a suburb of Ihringen. The small Kaiserstuhl co-operative (around 90 hectares) has occasionally attracted attention for its quite good red wines. The 2003 Pinot Noir is an attractive wine, with typical fruit and a juicy style (85 points). Some of the white wines are also quite pleasant this year. More of the same, please!

Weingut Rudolf Zimmerlin

79268 Bötzingen, Kirchweg 2
Tel. (0 76 63) 12 96, Fax 35 10

The Zimmerlin estate produces solid basic white wines, such as a fresh Riesling Kabinett (82 points) or a typical Chardonnay with clean fruit (83 points). The red wines are not yet quite of the same standard. The highlight is a rounded, mouth-filling 2002 Weißburgunder Eiswein (89 points).

Weingut Zimmermann

79418 Schliengen
Tel. (0 76 35) 6 65
e-mail: info@zimmermann-wein.de

This new discovery from the Markgräflerland area produces clean white wines, as well as some red wines headed up by a Roter Gutedel (83 points), which is full of character, and a 2002 Spätburgunder (85 points) that shows expert handling of oak.

Weingut Julius Zotz

79423 Heitersheim, Staufener Straße 3
Tel. (0 76 34) 10 59, Fax 47 58
e-mail: weingut.zotz@t-online.de

Unfortunately we have to confirm that this producer has shown a negative development compared to the previous year. Only the soft Chasslie (83 points) and the red blend of the 2000 vintage (84 points) as well as two botrytis dessert wines deserve the accolade "recommended."

Other wineries tasted

- Weingut Augit – Treffeisen & Würstlin, Bahlingen
- Susanne und Berthold Clauß, Lottstetten-Nack
- Weingut Engelhof, Hohentengen
- Weingut Felix und Kilian Hunn, Gottenheim
- Weingut Martin Mössner, Teningen-Köndringen
- Spitalkellerei Konstanz
- Winzergenossenschaft Varnhalt, Baden-Baden-Varnhalt
- Weingut Werner Weber, Ettenheim

Baden

Recommended by our wine producers

Hotels and inns

Baden-Baden: Brenners Parkhotel, Europäischer Hof, Kleiner Prinz
Badenweiler: Römerbad, Schwarzmatt
Beckstein: Adler
Blansingen: Traube
Bretten: Eulenspiegel
Durbach: Ritter, Rebstock, Linde
Eppingen: Wilde Rose
Freiburg: Bären, Colombi, Schiller
Friesenheim-Oberweier: Mühlenhof
Heitersheim: Krone, Löwen
Ihringen: Bräutigam
Kappelrodeck: Prinzen, Rebstock
Kirchhofen: Krone
Bad Krozingen: Adler
Lahr: Grüner Baum
Lahr-Reichenbach: Grüner Baum
Lindau: Villino
Malterdingen: Hotel de Charme
Neuweier: Heiligenstein
Oberdingen: Lindner
Oberkirch: Obere Linde
Pfinztal-Söllingen: Hammerschmiede
Rauenberg: Winzerhof
Reute: Hirschen
Sasbachwalden: Engel, Talmühle
Schliengen-Obereggenen: Rebstock
Staufen: Kreuzpost
Sulzburg: Hirschen
Vogtsburg-Achkarren: Krone
Vogtsburg-Bischoffingen: Steinbuck
Vogtsburg-Oberbergen: Schwarzer Adler
Weil am Rhein: Adler, Krone
Wiesloch: Palatin

Gourmet restaurants

Freiburg: Zirbelstube im Colombi
Kuppenheim: Raubs Restaurant
Pfinztal-Söllingen: Hammerschmiede
Sulzburg: Hirschen
Vogtsburg-Oberbergen: Schwarzer Adler

Restaurants, wine bars and winery facilities

Baden-Baden: Jardin de France
Badenweiler: Markgräfler Weinstube
Beckstein: Zur alten Kelter
Blansingen: Traube
Bombach: Sonne
Dielheim: Zur Pfalz
Durbach: Ritter
Ehrenstetten: Löwen
Eichstetten: Ochsen
Emmendingen-Wasser: Ochsen
Endingen: Rebstock
Endingen-Kiechlinsbergen: Dutters
Freiburg: Bären, Enoteca, Kreuzblume, Oberkirch, Traube
Freiburg-Herdern: Eichhalde
Freiburg-Lehen: Bierhäusle, Hirschen
Hagnau: Löwen
Ihringen: Bräutigam, Holzöfele, Sonne
Kenzingen: Scheidel's
Bad Krozingen-Biengen: Krone
Lahr-Reichenbach: Grüner Baum
Leimen: Jägerlust
Malsch: Zehntkeller
Malterdingen: Keller
Mauchen: Krone
Meersburg: Becher
Neuweier: Lamm, Schloss Neuweier, Alde Gott
Nimburg-Bottingen: Krone, Rebstock
Östringen-Tiefenbach: Heitlinger
Ortenberg: Glattfelder
Pfaffenweiler: Zehner
Rauenberg: Gutshof
Sasbachwalden: Fallert
Schliengen: Blankenhorn
Schmiedhofen: Storchen
Sulzfeld: Burg Ravensburg
Vogtsburg-Bischoffingen: Steinbuck
Vogtsburg-Niederrotweil: Kaiserstuhl
Vogtsburg-Oberbergen: Rebstock
Waldulm: Rebstock
Weil am Rhein: Adler, Kronen
Wertheim: Baunachshof

Franken

Escherndorf on the Main river in Franken produces some of the best wines in this region.
Photo: DWI/Dieth

Not a picture-perfect summer

2003 was not a picture-perfect summer for the wine producers of Franken. Usually, their biggest problem in this region is frost. Last year, they had to endure extreme weather conditions of different kind. The summer was hotter and drier than usual, quickly giving rise to the rumor that this would be the wine of the century. But winemakers in this area are not used to such extremes. The result is that, instead of producing exceptionally good wines, many have simply produced alcoholic wines lacking in elegance and in lively acidity. Just to have the highest must weights recorded in the past 80 years is not on its own a guarantee of quality.

No vintage in recent years has been more unforgiving in separating the men from the boys, winemakers were called upon to draw on their reserves and really show their ability. If you were not absolutely meticulous in handling the grapes, the result was inevitably dull wines with not enough fruit or acidity. This ripe vintage required mastery and restraint, and few winemakers rose to the challenge. One of the exceptions is the Silvaner wizard Horst Sauer, who attracted not only our attention, but has also been honoured by the judges of the London International Wine Challenge as the "White Wine Maker of the Year 2004," in recognition of his achievements and success over many years. The international Silvaner competition was held for the thrid time, attracting no less than 445 entries, and here, too, Franken stood out with positive results.

It is no surprise that Franken is such an important area for the Silvaner grape. It is documented that the first Silvaner vines were planted in the Castell vineyards on 5. April 1659. While its image suffered in fairly recent times because of mass production, and a resultant decline in quality, Silvaner has overcome this problem, and is now on an upward curve – not least because leading winemakers have planted the variety on their best vineyard sites. While Riesling is not the pre-eminent variety in Franken, lovers of this grape can find good examples in the area around Würzburg. The Riesling wines produced by the top wineries provide excellent quality, with regional typicity.

However, it is still the heavy-bearing Müller-Thurgau grape that covers more than a third (36 percent) of the vineyard area in Franken, 2,168 hectares in all, considerably more than Silvaner, which

manages to account for just more than 20 percent. Interestingly, the red wine boom has not really spread to Franken yet, and only 14.4 percent of the area is planted to red varieties.

The area of "Weinfranken" stretches from Aschaffenburg to Schweinfurt. The heartland of this region is the Maindreieck (Main triangle) in and around Würzburg. Here, the vines flourish on shell limestone soils, with admixtures of clay and loess. The famous single vineyard site "Stein," whose wines used to be known as "Stein wine" and which were considered to be the archetypal Franken wines, is to be found on the outskirts of Würzburg, directly on the Main river.

Because of the defined continental climate with hot, dry summers and cold winters, the vineyards, which are spread quite

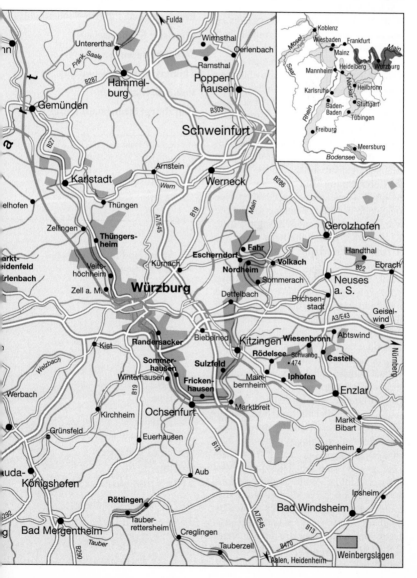

Franken

far apart, are located mainly on south-facing slopes above the Main river, and on the red marl soils on the westerly slopes of Steigerwald forest. The climate is a little more temperate in the Mainviereck (Main square), to the west of lower Franken.

Exceptionally good red wines are grown on the primordial decomposed soils and layered multi-coloured sandstone soils found primarily above the town of Bürgstadt. Of the roughly 6,000 hectares of vineyards found in Franken, roughly half the production is marketed through the seven co-operatives in the region. Some of these cellars are so filled to bursting that the wines are dumped on the market at ridiculously low prices.This of necessity has an effect on the image of the whole region, and also negatively affects the market opportunities of the leading renowned wineries, who find it difficult to establish realistic prices in the face of such competition. But there are fans of the good wines, and when Goethe wrote to his wife in 1816: "Send me some more Würzburg wine, I cannot develop a taste for any other wine," the wine-lover was certainly not referring to the mass-produced wines.

While their colleagues in other German wine-growing regions have experienced highs and lows from one vintage to the next, the wine producers in Franken have been able to enjoy relatively stable conditions since the late Nineties. This can probably be ascribed to the more stable continental climate of this only wine-growing region in Bavaria.

This difference was particularly evident in the 2000 millennium vintage: While other regions were virtually drowned by the rain, Franken enjoyed one of the best vintages in the past decade. 2001 was almost as good, and the 2002 vintage was also very similar. While in other regions the proportion of predicate wines that could be produced was strictly limited by weather conditions, in Franken wine producers were able to declare three quarters of their grapes as being of Kabinett quality or better.

The best vineyard sites in Franken *

Bürgstadt: Centgrafenberg

Castell: Schlossberg

Escherndorf: Lump

Frickenhausen: Kapellenberg

Homburg: Kallmuth

Iphofen: Julius-Echter-Berg

Randersacker: Pfülben, Sonnenstuhl

Rödelsee: Küchenmeister

Sommerhausen: Steinbach

Thüngersheim: Johannisberg

Volkach: Karthäuser

Würzburg: Stein, Innere Leiste

* Source: VDP Franken

Major and minor vintages in Franken

Vintage	Rating
2003	⚜⚜⚜
2002	⚜⚜⚜
2001	⚜⚜⚜
2000	⚜⚜⚜⚜
1999	⚜⚜⚜
1998	⚜⚜⚜
1997	⚜⚜⚜⚜
1996	⚜⚜⚜
1995	⚜⚜
1994	⚜⚜⚜⚜

Vintage rating:

⚜⚜⚜⚜⚜ : Excellent vintage

⚜⚜⚜⚜ : Very good vintage

⚜⚜⚜ : Good vintage

⚜⚜ : Average vintage

⚜ : Poor vintage

The leading producers in Franken

Fürstlich Castellsches
Domänenamt, Castell

Weingut Rudolf Fürst, Bürgstadt

Weingut Horst Sauer, Escherndorf

Weingut Glaser-Himmelstoß,
Nordheim

Weingut Juliusspital, Würzburg

Weingut Fürst Löwenstein,
Kreuzwertheim

Weingut Johann Ruck, Iphofen

Weingut Schmitt's Kinder,
Randersacker

Weingut Schloss Sommerhausen

Weingut am Stein, Würzburg

Weingut Störrlein, Randersacker

Weingut Hans Wirsching, Iphofen

Weingut Zehnthof, Sulzfeld

Weingut Bickel-Stumpf,
Frickenhausen

Weingut Waldemar Braun,
Nordheim

Weingut Brennfleck, Sulzfeld

Weingut Bürgerspital
zum Heiligen Geist, Würzburg

Weingut Helmut Christ, Nordheim

Weingut Michael Fröhlich,
Escherndorf

Weingut Dr. Heigel, Zeil am Main

Weingut Hofmann, Röttingen

Winzergenossenschaft Nordheim

Weingut Roth, Wiesenbronn

Weingut Rainer Sauer,
Escherndorf

Weinbau Egon Schäffer,
Escherndorf

Staatlicher Hofkeller Würzburg

Weingut Stich – "Im Löwen",
Bürgstadt

Weingut Wolfgang Weltner,
Rödelsee

Weingut Günther Bardorf,
Randersacker

Weingut Michael Blendel,
Volkach-Escherndorf

Weingut Brügel, Greuth

Weingut Walter Erhard,
Volkach

Weingut Höfler,
Alzenau-Michelbach

Weingut "Am Lump", Escherndorf

Weingut Rudolf May, Retzstadt

Weingut Meintzinger,
Frickenhausen

Weingut Max Müller I, Volkach

Weingut Rudloff, Nordheim

Weingut Trockene Schmitts,
Randersacker

Weingut Schwab, Thüngersheim

Weingut "Zur Schwane", Volkach

Winzerkeller Sommerach

Weingut Artur Steinmann –
Im Pastoriushaus, Sommerhausen

Winzergenossenschaft
Thüngersheim

WEINGUT
GÜNTHER BARDORF

Owner and manager:
Günther Bardorf
Winemaker: Stefan Bardorf
97236 Randersacker,
Ochsenfurter Straße 4
Tel. (09 31) 7 05 50, Fax 7 05 52 22
e-mail: info@loewen-randersacker.de
Internet: www.loewen-randersacker.de
Directions: A 3 Frankfurt–Nürnberg,
Würzburg-Randersacker exit
Sales: Günther and Stefan Bardorf
Opening hours: Mon.–Fri. 07:30 to 22:30
hours, Sat. and Sun. 08:00 to 22:30 hours
Restaurant: Hotel and restaurant
"Löwen," Mon.–Fri. 15:00 to 24:00
hours, Sat., Sun. and public holidays
11:00 to 24:00 hours
Specialties: Franconian seasonal cuisine

Vineyard area: 2.3 hectares
Annual production: 20,000 bottles
Top sites: Randersacker
Marsberg and Sonnenstuhl
Soil types: Deep shell limestone
Grape varieties: 23% Silvaner, 12%
Bacchus, 10% Müller-Thurgau,
8% each of Weißburgunder, Scheure-
be and Spätburgunder, 7% each of
Riesling and Schwarzriesling,
17% other varieties
Average yield: 80 hl/ha
Best vintage: 2003

When Günther Bardorf established this small winery in 1965, the vineyard area was only 0.18 hectares, which has grown to 2.3 hectares today. The restaurant "Löwen" is attached to the winery, here you can drink the wines to accompany Franconian regional dishes. Best wines produced by Günther Bardorf in the exceptional 2003 vintage: the sweet Spätlese and Auslese wines made from Riesling, Kerner and Silvaner grapes. It may be added that the dry Silvaner Auslese from the Dabug vineyard (86 points) also left a good impression, while the basic dry wines still need a bit of work.

2003 Randersacker Ewig Leben
Bacchus Kabinett trocken
11%, ♀ till 2006   80

2003 Randersacker Sonnenstuhl
Müller-Thurgau Kabinett trocken
12%, ♀ till 2011   80

2003 Randersacker Marsberg
Silvaner Spätlese trocken
14%, ♀ till 2009   81

2003 Randersacker Dabug
Silvaner Auslese trocken
15%, ♀ till 2011   86

2003 Randersacker Dabug
Silvaner Auslese
11%, ♀ till 2011   81

2003 Randersacker Marsberg
Scheurebe Eiswein
7%, ♀ till 2020   82

2003 Randersacker Sonnenstuhl
Riesling Auslese
9%, ♀ till 2011   83

2003 Randersacker Ewig Leben
Kerner Auslese
8.5%, ♀ till 2011   85

2003 Randersacker
Riesling Spätlese
12%, ♀ till 2009   86

2003 Randersacker Sonnenstuhl
Riesling Auslese "SL"
6%, ♀ till 2009   87

WEINGUT
BICKEL-STUMPF

Owner: Reimund and Carmen Stumpf
Winemaker: Reimund Stumpf
97252 Frickenhausen, Kirchgasse 5
Tel. (0 93 31) 28 47, Fax 71 76
e-mail: info@bickel-stumpf.de
Internet: www.bickel-stumpf.de
Directions: A 3 Würzburg–Nürnberg,
Randersacker exit, via the B 13,
17 kilometers along the Main river
A 7, Marktbreit exit
Sales: Carmen Stumpf
Opening hours: Mon.–Sat. 09:00 to
17:00 hours and by appointment
Worth seeing: Medieval winery with
modern vinotheque

Vineyard area: 8 hectares
Annual production: 70,000 bottles
Top sites: Frickenhäuser
Kapellenberg, Thüngersheimer
Johannisberg
Soil types: Shell limestone, sandstone
Grape varieties: 32% Silvaner,
20% Müller-Thurgau, 11% Riesling,
10% Spätburgunder, 9% Portugieser,
4% each of Rieslaner and Cabernet
Dorsa, 3% Domina, 7% other varieties
Average yield: 62 hl/ha
Best vintages: 2001, 2002, 2003
Member: VDP

When the two winemakers Carmen
Bickel and Reimund Stumpf got married
in 1976, one of the results was that their
parents' wineries, with a total of eight
hectares of vineyard area, were combined. The head office, including a newly-
opened vinotheque, is in the former Bickel
winery in Frickenhausen, tucked away behind the church. The shell limestone soils
of Frickenhausen are particularly suitable
for white wines, whereas red varieties prefer the vineyards of Thüngersheim. In the
past few years the ranges tasted from this
winery have always been reliably good.
The "Große Gewächse" (First Growths)
of the 2003 vintage are among the best of
the vintage in Franken.

2003 Frickenhäuser Kapellenberg
Riesling Kabinett trocken
12.5%, ♀ till 2006   **85**

2002 Frickenhäuser Kapellenberg
Silvaner Spätlese trocken
12%, ♀ till 2007   **86**

2002 Frickenhäuser Kapellenberg
Riesling Kabinett trocken
12%, ♀ till 2006   **87**

2002 Thüngersheimer Johannisberg
Riesling Spätlese trocken
12%, ♀ till 2007   **87**

2003 Frickenhäuser Kapellenberg
Silvaner trocken Barrique
14.5%, ♀ till 2008   **87**

2003 Thüngersheimer Johannisberg
Riesling trocken "Großes Gewächs"
13.5%, ♀ till 2007   **87**

2003 Frickenhäuser Kapellenberg
Silvaner trocken "Großes Gewächs"
14.5%, ♀ till 2007   **87**

2003 Frickenhäuser Kapellenberg
Riesling trocken "Großes Gewächs"
13.5%, ♀ till 2008   **88**

2003 Frickenhäuser Kapellenberg
Rieslaner Auslese
13%, ♀ till 2011   **85**

——————— Red wines ———————

2002 Thüngersheimer Johannisberg
Spätburgunder trocken
13%, ♀ till 2008   **84**

2002 Thüngersheimer Johannisberg
trocken "Cuvée C"
13%, ♀ till 2007   **85**

The wines: **100** Perfect · **95–99** Outstanding · **90–94** Excellent · **85–89** Very good · **80–84** Good · **75–79** Average

Franken

WEINGUT
MICHAEL BLENDEL

Owner and manager:
Michael Blendel
97332 Volkach-Escherndorf,
Bocksbeutelstraße 13
Tel. (0 93 81) 91 30, Fax 69 36
e-mail: infopost@weingut-blendel.de
Internet: www.weingut-blendel.de
Directions: A 3 Würzburg–Nürnberg,
Kitzingen exit, via Schwarzach
Sales: Edith Blendel
Opening hours: Mon.–Fri. 08:00 to
18:00 hours, Sat. 08:00 to 17:00 hours
Sun. 10:00 to 12:00 hours
or by appointment
History: Winemaking for ten generations
Worth seeing: Lovely inner courtyard,
garden pavilion

> Vineyard area: 5.6 hectares
> Annual production: 45,000 bottles
> Top sites: Escherndorfer Lump
> and Fürstenberg
> Soil types: Shell limestone, clay
> Grape varieties: 24% Müller-Thurgau,
> 20% Silvaner, 15% Riesling,
> 12% Spätburgunder, 10% Domina,
> 8% each of Bacchus and Kerner,
> 3% other varieties
> Average yield: 83 hl/ha
> Best vintages: 2002, 2003

Currently the tenth generation is working
this winery in the Main river loop. Blendel gives his vines intensive care, and
aims at retaining the typical varietal
characteristics of grapes by a policy of
minimum intervention in the cellar. The
quality of the 2002 vintage was already
very homogeneous: from fresh Müller-
Thurgau in liter bottles up to the flagship
dry Riesling Spätlese. The wines of the
2003 vintage provide a worthy continuation of this standard. In particular the
Riesling wines are again particularly
good, with only the 2002 Spätburgunder
(Pinot Noir) not quite living up to our expectations.

2003 Escherndorfer Lump
Riesling Kabinett trocken
14%, ♀ till 2006   83

2002 Escherndorfer Lump
Silvaner Spätlese trocken
13%, ♀ till 2007   85

2003 Escherndorfer Lump
Silvaner Kabinett trocken
14.5%, ♀ till 2006   85

2002 Escherndorfer Lump
Riesling Spätlese trocken
12.5%, ♀ till 2007   86

2003 Escherndorfer Lump
Riesling Spätlese trocken
14%, ♀ till 2009   86

2003 Escherndorfer Lump
Riesling Spätlese
13%, ♀ till 2009   84

2002 Escherndorfer Lump
Silvaner Kabinett
11.5%, ♀ till 2006   85

2002 Escherndorfer Lump
Silvaner Spätlese
13%, ♀ till 2007   85

2002 Escherndorfer Fürstenberg
Kerner Spätlese
12%, ♀ till 2007   86

————— Red wines —————

2002 Escherndorfer Fürstenberg
Spätburgunder Kabinett trocken
12.5%, ♀ till 2006   83

2001 Escherndorfer Fürstenberg
Spätburgunder trocken
13%, ♀ till 2006   86

The estates: ♛♛♛♛♛ World's finest · ♛♛♛♛ Germany's best · ♛♛♛ Very good · ♛♛ Good · ♛ Reliable

WEINGUT
WALDEMAR BRAUN

Owner: Waldemar Braun
Manager: Waldemar Braun
Winemaker: Patrick Braun
97334 Nordheim, Langgasse 10
Tel. (0 93 81) 90 61, Fax 7 11 79
e-mail:
info@weingut-waldemar-braun.de
Internet:
www.weingut-waldemar-braun.de
Directions: A 3 Würzburg–Nürnberg,
Kitzingen/Schwarzach exit, in direction
of Volkach; A 70, Gerolzhofen exit, in
direction of Volkach
Sales: Heidi Braun
Opening hours: Mon.–Sat. 09:00 to
18:00 hours, Sun. 10:00 to 16:00 hours
and by appointment
Worth seeing: Tasting room in old
vaulted cellar

Vineyard area: 10.5 hectares
Annual production: 70,000 bottles
Top sites: Nordheimer Vögelein
and Kreuzberg
Soil types: Shell limestone with loose
sandy top layer
Grape varieties: 35% Müller-Thurgau,
20% Silvaner, 10% Bacchus, 8% Ries-
ling, 6% Domina, 5% Rieslaner, 4%
Spätburgunder, 12% other varieties
Average yield: 76 hl/ha
Best vintages: 2001, 2002, 2003

Waldemar Braun has for some years been
bottling his wines with screw-cap closures – his logical reaction to bad experiences with cork that spoiled part of his
1998 vintage. This is a typical successful family winery in which two generations work together harmoniously. The
vineyards are worked in accordance with
the guidelines for sustainable viticulture.
The 2003 wines are again recommended
across the board, and are characterized by
an invigorating freshness. We particularly liked the dry Weißburgunder (Pinot
Blanc) from the premium range "Wie-
Waldi."

2003 Nordheimer Vögelein
Riesling Kabinett trocken
13%, ♀ till 2006 — **83**

2003 "WieWaldi"
Chardonnay trocken
14.5%, ♀ till 2007 — **83**

2003 "WieWaldi" Silvaner trocken
14.5%, ♀ till 2007 — **84**

2002 Nordheimer Vögelein
Weißer Burgunder Kabinett trocken
13.5%, ♀ till 2006 — **85**

2003 "WieWaldi" Riesling trocken
14.5%, ♀ till 2008 — **85**

2002 Nordheimer Vögelein
Silvaner Kabinett trocken
13%, ♀ till 2006 — **86**

2002 Nordheimer Vögelein
Riesling Kabinett trocken
12.5%, ♀ till 2006 — **86**

2003 "WieWaldi"
Weißer Burgunder trocken
15%, ♀ till 2008 — **86**

2003 Sommeracher Rosenberg
Scheurebe Kabinett
15%, ♀ till 2006 — **84**

2002 Sommeracher Rosenberg
Scheurebe Kabinett
11.5%, ♀ till 2006 — **85**

2002 Nordheimer Vögelein
Silvaner Auslese
10%, ♀ till 2013 — **89**

2002 Nordheimer Vögelein
Rieslaner Eiswein
6%, ♀ till 2018 — **89**

The wines: **100** Perfect · **95–99** Outstanding · **90–94** Excellent · **85–89** Very good · **80–84** Good · **75–79** Average

WEINGUT BRENNFLECK

Owner and manager:
Hugo Brennfleck
97320 Sulzfeld, Papiusgasse 7
Tel. (0 93 21) 43 47, Fax 43 45
e-mail: info@weingut-brennfleck.de
Internet: www.weingut-brennfleck.de
*Directions: A 3 Würzburg–Nürnberg,
Kitzingen/Schwarzach exit; A 7 Kassel–
Ulm, Kitzingen/Repperndorf exit*
Sales: Susanne Brennfleck, Sandra Holler
Opening hours: Mon.–Fri. 07:30 to
17:30 hours, weekends by appointment
History: Wine made here since 1591
Worth seeing: Medieval winery,
ensemble of vaulted cellars
Worth a visit: Winery festival on
3rd weekend in July

Vineyard area: 18 hectares
Annual production: 180,000 bottles
Top sites: Iphöfer Kalb and Krons-
berg, Escherndorfer Lump, Sulzfelder
Maustal and Cyriakusberg
Soil types: Red marl, shell limestone
Grape varieties: 40% Silvaner,
20% Pinot varieties, 10% each of
Müller-Thurgau and Riesling,
20% other varieties
Average yield: 75 hl/ha
Best vintages: 2001, 2002, 2003
Member: Frank & Frei

In the old winery, originally built in 1479,
in the medieval village of Sulzfeld, Hugo and Susanne Brennfleck represent the
13th generation of winemakers. The
young couple with their two daughters
took over the 18 hectares operation from
the parents in 1998. The main focus remains on Silvaner, which achieves remarkable results here based on low yields. Just
as last year, Hugo Brennfleck convinced
us by presenting a range of straightforward and exceptionally hearty wines. The
highlights of the 2003 vintage range are
two Auslese wines made from Riesling
and Silvaner respectively.

2003 "Frank & Frei"
Müller-Thurgau trocken
12.5%, ♀ till 2006 — 83

2003 Iphöfer Kalb
Silvaner Kabinett trocken
13%, ♀ till 2006 — 85

2003 "Anna-Lena"
Silvaner Kabinett trocken
13%, ♀ till 2006 — 86

2003 Sulzfelder Cyriakusberg
Grauer Burgunder Spätlese trocken
14%, ♀ till 2009 — 86

2003 Iphöfer Kronsberg
Scheurebe Spätlese trocken
14%, ♀ till 2009 — 87

2003 Iphöfer Kalb
Silvaner Spätlese trocken
14%, ♀ till 2009 — 87

2003 Sulzfelder Maustal
Silvaner Spätlese trocken
14.5%, ♀ till 2009 — 87

2003 Sulzfelder Maustal
Riesling Kabinett trocken
13.5%, ♀ till 2006 — 87

2003 Escherndorfer Lump
Riesling Spätlese trocken
13.5%, ♀ till 2009 — 88

2003 Sulzfelder Cyriakusberg
Huxelrebe Auslese
10.5%, ♀ till 2011 — 86

2003 Escherndorfer Lump
Riesling Auslese
8%, ♀ till 2015 — 90

2003 Sulzfelder Cyriakusberg
Silvaner Auslese
7%, ♀ till 2011 — 91

WEINGUT BRÜGEL

Owner: Heinrich Brügel
Manager and winemaker:
Harald Brügel
97355 Greuth, Hauptstraße 49
Tel. (0 93 83) 76 19, Fax 67 33
e-mail: info@weingut-bruegel.de
Internet: www.weingut-bruegel.de
Directions: A 3 Würzburg–Nürnberg,
Wiesentheid exit, through Rüdenhausen
to Greuth
Sales: Harald Brügel
Opening hours: Mon.–Fri. 08:00 to
18:00 hours, Sat. 09:00 to 18:00 hours
and by appointment

Vineyard area: 3.5 hectares
Annual production: 30,000 bottles
Top sites: Greuther Bastel
and Abtswinder Altenberg
Soil types: Red decomposed marl
with kaolin
Grape varieties: 33% Silvaner,
30% Müller-Thurgau, 8% Spätburgunder, 7% Bacchus, 6% Domina,
5% Portugieser, 4% Riesling,
7% other varieties
Average yield: 80 hl/ha
Best vintages: 2001, 2002, 2003

This winery at the foot of the Steigerwald mountains has only recently been created from a mixed farming operation. Father Heinrich Brügel still delivered his grapes to a co-operative. Son Harald Brügel completed an apprenticeship as a cooper and followed this with studies at the viticultural school in Veitshöchheim. He has been working full-time in the winery since 1998. The grapes processed here come either from the 3.5 hectares of own vineyards, or from a further 1.7 hectares as bought-in grapes. Following on an all-round attractive range of 2002 wines, we tasted a very good range of mainly dry wines from the 2003 vintage, headed up by a Silvaner Eiswein. This time around the Silvaner Spätlese matured in barriques is particularly good. The Pinot Noir red wines also provide very solid quality.

2003 Greuther Bastel
Silvaner Kabinett trocken
12.5%, ♀ till 2006 — **84**

2003 Abtswinder Altenberg
Silvaner Spätlese trocken
13.5%, ♀ till 2007 — **85**

2003 Casteller Kirchberg
Weißer Burgunder Spätlese trocken
15.5%, ♀ till 2008 — **85**

2003 Silvaner
Spätlese trocken Barrique
13.5%, ♀ till 2008 — **85**

2002 Abtswinder Altenberg
Silvaner Spätlese trocken
13%, ♀ till 2007 — **86**

2002 Casteller Kirchberg
Weißer Burgunder Spätlese trocken
13%, ♀ till 2007 — **86**

2002 Greuther Bastel
Silvaner Spätlese trocken "B"
13.5%, ♀ till 2007 — **86**

2001 Weißer Burgunder
Spätlese trocken Barrique
13%, ♀ till 2007 — **87**

2003 Greuther Bastel
Scheurebe Spätlese
12.5%, ♀ till 2009 — **86**

2003 Greuther Bastel
Silvaner Eiswein
7.5%, ♀ till 2020 — **90**

——— Red wines ———

2002 Casteller Kirchberg
Spätburgunder trocken
13%, ♀ till 2006 — **83**

2001 Spätburgunder
trocken Barrique
13.5%, ♀ till 2007 — **85**

WEINGUT BÜRGERSPITAL ZUM HEILIGEN GEIST

Owner: Public Foundation
Winery directors: Helmut Plunien and Sonja Höferlin
Winemaker: Helmut Plunien, Elmar Nun
97070 Würzburg, Theaterstraße 19
Tel. (09 31) 3 50 34 41, Fax 3 50 34 44
e-mail: weinverkauf@buergerspital.de
Internet: www.buergerspital.de
Directions: In the center of Würzburg, near Mainfranken-Theater
Sales: Reinhard Sauer
Mon.–Fri. 08:00 to 17:00 hours
Shop sales: Heinrich Bauer
Opening hours: Mon.–Fri. 09:00 to 18:00 hours, Sat. 09:00 to 15:00 hours
Restaurant: Bürgerspital Weinstuben, from 09:00 to 24:00 hours
History: Founded 1316 as hospital for the sick, and for travelers
Worth seeing: Spitalkirche church, baroque courtyard, vaulted cellar

---

Vineyard area: 110 hectares
Annual production: 820,000 bottles
Top sites: Würzburger Stein, Stein-Harfe, Abtsleite and Innere Leiste, Randersacker Pfülben, Teufelskeller
Soil types: Shell limestone, gypsum with red marl
Grape varieties: 28% Riesling, 24% Silvaner, 14% Müller-Thurgau, 6% Bacchus, 4% each of Weißburgunder and Spätburgunder, 20% other varieties
Average yield: 67 hl/ha
Best vintages: 2001, 2002, 2003
Member: VDP

This formerly renowned traditional winery is returning to its previous good form under the guidance of Helmut Plunien and Sonja Höferlin. The vineyard area has been reduced from 120 to 110 hectares. Following on quite good ranges in the 2001 and 2002 vintages, we were again pleased to see a wide range of harmonious wines from the rather difficult 2003 vintage. The highlights are the "First Growths" from the Würzburger Stein site.

2003 Randersacker Teufelskeller
Riesling Spätlese trocken
13.5%, ♀ till 2007 — **84**

2003 Würzburger Stein
Silvaner Spätlese trocken
14%, ♀ till 2007 — **85**

2003 Würzburger Stein
Riesling Spätlese trocken
14.5%, ♀ till 2007 — **85**

2003 Würzburger Stein
Riesling Hagemann "Großes Gewächs"
14%, ♀ till 2008 — **85**

2003 Würzburger Stein
Silvaner "Großes Gewächs"
14%, ♀ till 2008 — **86**

2003 Würzburger Stein
Weißer Burgunder "Großes Gewächs"
14.5%, ♀ till 2008 — **86**

2002 Würzburger Stein
Riesling Spätlese trocken "Großes Gewächs"
13%, ♀ till 2009 — **88**

2003 Würzburger Stein-Harfe
Riesling Spätlese feinherb
12.5%, ♀ till 2008 — **86**

2002 Würzburger Stein
Silvaner Eiswein
7.5%, ♀ till 2018 — **88**

2002 Würzburger Stein
Silvaner Trockenbeerenauslese
7%, ♀ till 2023 — **89**

2001
Würzburger Stein
Silvaner
Spätlese
trocken

FÜRSTLICH CASTELLSCHES DOMÄNENAMT

Owner: Ferdinand Graf zu Castell-Castell
Manager: Karl-Heinz Rebitzer
Vineyard manager: Peter Hemberger
Winemaker: Christian Frieß and Reinhard Firnbach
97335 Castell, Schlossplatz 5
Tel. (0 93 25) 6 01 60, Fax 6 01 88
e-mail: weingut@castell.de
Internet: www.castell.de
Directions: A 3 Würzburg–Nürnberg, Wiesentheid exit 75, via the B 286 in the direction of Neustadt/Aisch
Opening hours: Mon.–Fri. 08:00 to 18:00 hours, Sat. 10:00 to 16:00 hours and by appointment
Restaurant: "Weinstall"
Tel. (0 93 25) 90 25 61, from 11:00 to 23:00 hours, closed Mon. and Tue.
Specialties: Typical regional cuisine
History: Wine made here since the 13th century
Worth seeing: Vaulted cellar, attractive walking paths in château garden

---

Vineyard area: 65 hectares
Annual production: 400,000 bottles
Top sites: Casteller Schlossberg, Hohnart, Kugelspiel, Trautberg, Bausch
Soil types: Gypsum with red marl
Grape varieties: 34% Silvaner, 21% Müller-Thurgau, 6% each of Riesling, Rieslaner and Bacchus, 18% red varieties, 9% other varieties
Average yield: 60 hl/ha
Best vintages: 1999, 2000, 2001
Member: VDP

At Schloss Castell they are used working in very long time-frames. The wine estate has been owned by the family since the 11th century, making it one of the oldest in the whole of Germany. The top sites such as the Schlossberg and Hohnart have been documented since 1258. Silvaner, which had been imported from Austria, was planted in Franken for the first time – and in Germany – on 5th April 1659, this was meant to show a sign of hope for the future after the chaos of the Thirty Years' War (1618/1648). Since 1996 Count Ferdinand Graf zu Castell-Castell has been running the estate in the 26th generation, supported by a hard-working team headed by general manager Karl-Heinz Rebitzer. The estate's own internal classification starts off with the varietal wines in modern style, labelled "Castell-Castell." The next level are the wines blended from several vineyards, labelled "Schloss Castell," above this are the vineyard-specific wines, including the new "Edition Graf Ferdinand." Right at the top is the fourth level, the "Große Gewächse" (First Growths), all from the Casteller Schlossberg site. This is an extremely steep slope, and low-yielding Riesling and Silvaner produce top quality here. In the cellar, these wines are kept on the lees for an extremely long time. A few years ago, the wines from this estate were overly commercial, and sometimes a little on the sour side, but today they are juicy, crisp, spicy, concentrated as well as elegant, sometimes even downright sophisticated. Red wine side: The 2002 vintage "Cuvée C" is once again an impressive wine, and a great Pinot Noir with considerable potential was also produced. The dry white wines of the 2003 vintage range fit in seamlessly with the ranges of previous vintages, although the basic dry wines are not quite up to standard. The highlights are the "Große Gewächse" from the top Schlossberg site: a dry Silvaner Spätlese as well as an equally delicious Riesling Spätlese from the same vineyard.

2003 Casteller Hohnart
Silvaner Kabinett trocken
14%, ♀ till 2006 **84**

2003 Casteller Kugelspiel
Silvaner Spätlese trocken
14%, ♀ till 2008 **85**

2003 Casteller Trautberg
Silvaner & Traminer trocken
"Edition Graf Ferdinand"
13%, ♀ till 2008 **85**

The wines: **100** Perfect · **95–99** Outstanding · **90–94** Excellent · **85–89** Very good · **80–84** Good · **75–79** Average

2002 Casteller Hohnart
Silvaner Spätlese trocken
12.5%, ♀ till 2006 — 86

2001 Casteller Trautberg
Silvaner Spätlese trocken
12.5%, ♀ till 2007 — 87

2001 Casteller Hohnart
Riesling Spätlese trocken
13%, ♀ till 2007 — 87

2002 Casteller Hohnart
Riesling Kabinett trocken
12.5%, ♀ till 2006 — 87

2001 Casteller Hohnart
Silvaner Spätlese trocken
13%, ♀ till 2007 — 88

2003 Casteller Schlossberg
Riesling Spätlese "Großes Gewächs"
13.5%, ♀ till 2010 — 88

2001 Casteller Schlossberg
Silvaner Spätlese trocken
13%, ♀ till 2007 — 89

2002 Casteller Schlossberg
Silvaner Spätlese trocken
12.5%, ♀ till 2007 — 89

2002 Casteller Schlossberg
Riesling Spätlese trocken
12.5%, ♀ till 2007 — 89

2003 Casteller Schlossberg
Silvaner Spätlese "Großes Gewächs"
14%, ♀ till 2009 — 89

2001 Casteller Schlossberg
Riesling Spätlese trocken
12.5%, ♀ till 2007 — 90

2003 Casteller Kugelspiel
Rieslaner Spätlese
14%, ♀ till 2009 — 86

2002 Casteller Kugelspiel
Rieslaner Spätlese
12%, ♀ till 2007 — 88

2001 Casteller Kugelspiel
Silvaner Eiswein
11%, ♀ till 2017 — 89

2002 Casteller Schlossberg
Rieslaner Auslese
11.5%, ♀ till 2013 — 89

2001 Casteller Schlossberg
Rieslaner Trockenbeerenauslese
11.5%, ♀ till 2023 — 90

2002 Casteller Kugelspiel
Rieslaner Beerenauslese
11.5%, ♀ till 2018 — 90

2002 Casteller Schlossberg
Rieslaner Beerenauslese
10.5%, ♀ till 2018 — 91

2002 Casteller Kugelspiel
Silvaner Eiswein
11%, ♀ till 2018 — 91

2003 Casteller Kugelspiel
Rieslaner Trockenbeerenauslese
9.5%, ♀ till 2020 — 91

2003 Casteller Kugelspiel
Silvaner Trockenbeerenauslese
10%, ♀ till 2022 — 92

2002 Casteller Schlossberg
Silvaner Trockenbeerenauslese
9%, ♀ till 2025 — 93

——— Red wines ———

2002 Schloss Castell
"Cuvée C" trocken
13%, ♀ till 2007 — 86

2001 Castell Cuvée trocken
13%, ♀ till 2006 — 87

2002 Casteller Reitsteig
Spätburgunder trocken
13%, ♀ till 2009 — 87

2001 Casteller Reitsteig
Spätburgunder trocken
13%, ♀ till 2006 — 88

CASTELL·CASTELL

12
24

Rotwein trocken

2003

F · R · A · N · K · E · N

The estates: ⚜⚜⚜⚜⚜ World's finest · ⚜⚜⚜⚜ Germany's best · ⚜⚜⚜ Very good · ⚜⚜ Good · ⚜ Reliable

WEINGUT
HELMUT CHRIST

Owner: Helmut Christ
97334 Nordheim, Volkacher Straße 6
Tel. (0 93 81) 28 06, Fax 66 40
e-mail: Christ-Nordheim@t-online.de
Internet: www.weingut-helmut-christ.de
*Directions: A 3 Würzburg–Nürnberg,
Volkach exit, via Schwarzach and Som-
merach*
Sales: Angelika Christ
Opening hours: Mon.–Sat. 10:00 to
12:00 hours and 13:00 to 18:00 hours
and by appointment
Restaurant: In the courtyard, May to
October on weekends only
Specialties: Only organic ingredients
used in kitchen
Worth seeing: Baroque buildings

Vineyard area: 9.5 hectares
Annual production: 65,000 bottles
Top sites: Volkacher Ratsherr,
Nordheimer Vögelein, Dettelbacher
Berg Rondell
Soil types: Shell limestone, sandy clay,
clay with sand
Grape varieties: 29% Müller-Thurgau,
27% Silvaner, 8% Dornfelder,
5% Spätburgunder, 4% each of Ker-
ner, Riesling, Domina and Bacchus,
15% other varieties
Average yield: 65 hl/ha
Best vintages: 2001, 2002, 2003
Member: Bioland

Helmut Christ was one of the first organic
wine-growers in Germany. He began
converting his vineyards in earnest in the
mid-Seventies. In 1975 he decided to
market his own wines, and was soon attracting attention for his above-average
quality. We have tasted only first-class
wines here since the 2000 vintage. It must
be admitted that Christ, who produces
some 20 different wines each year, bottles them very late, and has always been
able to present only a small selection for
tasting. From the 2003 vintage we liked
particularly two Riesling Spätlese wines.

2002 Volkacher Kirchberg
Silvaner Kabinett trocken
11.5%, ♀ till 2006 — 84

2002 Volkacher Kirchberg
Kerner Kabinett trocken
12.5%, ♀ till 2006 — 84

2002 Stammheimer Eselsberg
Silvaner Kabinett trocken
12.5%, ♀ till 2006 — 85

2003 Volkacher Ratsherr
Riesling Spätlese trocken
13.5%, ♀ till 2009 — 85

2002 Nordheimer Kreuzberg
Müller-Thurgau Spätlese trocken
12.5%, ♀ till 2007 — 87

2002 Volkacher Ratsherr
Riesling Spätlese trocken
13%, ♀ till 2007 — 88

2003 Nordheimer Vögelein
Riesling Spätlese halbtrocken
14%, ♀ till 2009 — 84

———— Red wines ————

2002 Spätburgunder
Spätlese trocken
13%, ♀ till 2009 — 85

2002 Blaufränkisch
trocken Barrique
13%, ♀ till 2006 — 85

The wines: **100** Perfect · **95–99** Outstanding · **90–94** Excellent · **85–89** Very good · **80–84** Good · **75–79** Average

WEINGUT
WALTER ERHARD

Owner and manager: Walter Erhard
97332 Volkach, Weinstraße 21
Tel. (0 93 81) 26 23, Fax 7 11 16
e-mail: info@weingut-erhard.de
Internet: www.weingut-erhard.de
*Directions: A 3, Hörblach exit, A 7
Estenfeld exit, in direction of Volkach
town center*
Sales: Sabine Erhard
Opening hours: Tue.–Sat. 09:00 to
18:00 hours, Sun. 10:00 to 12:00 hours
and by appointment
Restaurant: "Schoppenhäusle"
April/May and Oct./Nov. Fri. to Sun.
from 17:00 hours
Specialties: Kitchen uses exclusively
Franconian farm produce

Vineyard area: 6 hectares
Annual production: 50,000 bottles
Top site: Volkacher Ratsherr,
Escherndorfer Lump
Soil types: Shell limestone with clay,
kaolin or sand
Grape varieties: 23% each of Müller-
Thurgau and Silvaner, 8% Bacchus,
7% Weißburgunder 6% each of Ries-
ling, Kerner, Spätburgunder and
Domina, 15% other varieties
Average yield: 79 hl/ha
Best vintages: 2002, 2003
Member: Frank & Frei

When Walter and Sabine Erhard took
over the mixed agricultural operation
from their parents in 1989, they set plans
in motion to handle their own wine marketing. By now more than 80 percent of
their clients are private customers, and a
lot is done to make sure they remain loyal to the winery. This includes guided
vineyard tours as well as a cosy small
restaurant and wine bar, in which never
more than three tables are occupied by
design, where hearty regional dishes
are served to accompany the wines. And
these are most enjoyable to drink, including those of the 2003 vintage.

2003 Volkacher Ratsherr
Silvaner Spätlese trocken
14%, ♀ till 2007   83

2003 Obervolkacher Landsknecht
Riesling Kabinett trocken
12.5%, ♀ till 2006   83

2003 Escherndorfer Lump
Riesling Spätlese trocken
13.5%, ♀ till 2007   84

2002 Obervolkacher Landsknecht
Riesling Kabinett trocken
12%, ♀ till 2006   86

2002 Volkacher Ratsherr
Silvaner Kabinett trocken
12.5%, ♀ till 2006   87

2002 Volkacher Ratsherr
Scheurebe Spätlese trocken
12.5%, ♀ till 2007   87

2002 Volkacher Ratsherr
Silvaner Spätlese trocken
13%, ♀ till 2007   88

2003 Escherndorfer Lump
Silvaner Spätlese halbtrocken
13.5%, ♀ till 2009   84

2003 Volkacher Ratsherr
Kerner Spätlese halbtrocken
13.5%, ♀ till 2009   85

2002 Obervolkacher Landsknecht
Riesling Auslese
9.5%, ♀ till 2011   86

2002 Obervolkacher Landsknecht
Riesling Eiswein
10%, ♀ till 2020   87

WEINGUT
MICHAEL FRÖHLICH

Owner: Michael Fröhlich
97332 Escherndorf,
Bocksbeutelstraße 41
Tel. (0 93 81) 28 47, Fax 7 13 60
e-mail:
info@weingut-michael-froehlich.de
Internet: weingut-michael-froehlich.de
Directions: A 7 Würzburg–Kassel, Würz-
burg-Estenfeld exit, in direction of
Volkach; A 3 Würzburg–Nürnberg, Kit-
zingen exit, in direction of Volkach
Opening hours: Mon.–Sat. 09:00 to
18:00 hours, Sun. by appointment
Worth a visit: Hofschoppen wine festival on two last weekends in August

---

Vineyard area: 10 hectares
Annual production: 85,000 bottles
Top sites: Escherndorfer Lump and
Fürstenberg
Soil types: Shell limestone
Grape varieties: 25% Müller-Thurgau,
20% Silvaner, 10% Riesling,
20% red varieties, 25% other varieties
Average yield: 80 hl/ha
Best vintages: 1999, 2000, 2001
Member: VDP

Michael and Eva Fröhlich see their work
in the vineyard as a "cautious accompaniment of the annual process of growing
and ripening," and they practice minimal
intervention as a philosophy in making
wine. The quality throughout is good, and
the wines are enjoyable to drink. This includes the elegantly fruity Muskateller
from the Untereisenheim site. The sweet
Scheurebe wine from the same vineyard
can also be very good. Fröhlich knows
how to make the best of the advantages
provided by the steep Escherndorfer
Lump vineyards, his Riesling and Silvaner wines from that site show off their
good quality. We particularly applaud the
typical straightforward Franken style,
which has become the exception in recent
times. A newly-built facility now provides more space for wine sales.

2003 Escherndorfer Lump
Silvaner Spätlese trocken
14.5%, ♀ till 2007 — 83

2003 Escherndorfer Lump
Riesling Kabinett trocken
13%, ♀ till 2006 — 83

2003 Escherndorfer Lump
Riesling Spätlese trocken
14%, ♀ till 2007 — 84

2002 Frank & Frei
Müller-Thurgau trocken
11.5%, ♀ till 2006 — 85

2002 Untereisenheimer Sonnenberg
Muskateller Kabinett trocken
10%, ♀ till 2006 — 85

2002 Escherndorfer Lump
Riesling Kabinett trocken
11.5%, ♀ till 2006 — 86

2001 Escherndorfer Lump
Riesling Spätlese trocken
13%, ♀ till 2007 — 87

2002 Escherndorfer Lump
Riesling Spätlese trocken
12.5%, ♀ till 2007 — 87

2003 Escherndorfer Lump
Silvaner Spätlese
12%, ♀ till 2009 — 84

2003 Escherndorfer Lump
Rieslaner Spätlese
13.5%, ♀ till 2009 — 85

2003 Untereisenheimer Sonnenberg
Muskateller Spätlese
11.5%, ♀ till 2009 — 86

2003 Untereisenheimer Sonnenberg
Scheurebe Spätlese
11%, ♀ till 2009 — 86

The wines: **100** Perfect · **95–99** Outstanding · **90–94** Excellent · **85–89** Very good · **80–84** Good · **75–79** Average

WEINGUT RUDOLF FÜRST

Owner: Paul and Monika Fürst
Manager viticulture and distillery:
Franz Dumbsky
63927 Bürgstadt, Hohenlindenweg 46
Tel. (0 93 71) 86 42, Fax 6 92 30
e-mail:
weingut-rudolf-fuerst@t-online.de
Internet: www.weingut-rudolf-fuerst.de
Directions: A 3 Frankfurt–Würzburg,
Stockstadt or Wertheim exit, in direction
of Miltenberg
Sales: Monika Fürst
Opening hours: Mon.–Fri. 09:00 to
12:00 hours and 14:00 to 18:00 hours
Sat. 10:00 to 15:00 hours, by appointment
History: Winemaking in family since 1638

Vineyard area: 17 hectares
Annual production: 100,000 bottles
Top sites: Bürgstadter Centgrafen-
berg, Volkacher Karthäuser,
Großheubacher Bischofsberg,
Klingenberger Schlossberg
Soil types: Sandstone with clay
and kaolin layers, shell limestone
Grape varieties: 40% Spätburgunder,
18% Riesling, 14% Weißburgunder,
10% each of Silvaner and Früh-
burgunder, 8% other varieties
Average yield: 53 hl/ha
Best vintages: 1998, 2000, 2001
Member: VDP, Trias,
Deutsches Barrique Forum

Paul Fürst has had a cellar drilled into the layered sandstone right in the middle of the Bürgstadter Centgrafenberg vineyard, providing the ideal natural climate as well as a view of the valley and of Miltenberg. All this has grown from a small mixed farming operation that was located in the center of Bürgstadt, and which rapidly became too small for the grand plans developed by Fürst. Fürst likes to point out that the area around Klingenberg has traditionally been a red wine region, and that the soils are particularly suitable for the Pinot varieties. When you can build on traditions such as these, you can remain calm when observing the sometimes hectic pace at which red varieties are being planted in other regions, sometimes on completely unsuitable soils. Although Fürst, who took over the winery at the tender age of 21, is considered a pioneer of red wine in Franken, 50 percent of his vineyard area is planted to white varieties. That is not to say that he is ignoring the red wines. Fürst has by now increased the share of Frühburgunder to ten percent of the area. Nor does our "Producer of the year 2003" want to rest on his laurels in other respects. Oak fermenting vats have been acquired for the red Pinot varieties, and in Feb. 2004 Paul and son Sebastian Fürst acquired 1.3 hectares of the best parcels of the Klingenberg site, with the aim of producing a big Pinot Noir from this renowned vineyard. The reds of the 2002 vintage here are at once both expressive and very balanced within themselves. As usual, the Spätburgunder wines (Pinot Noir) are a little more accessible at this stage than the Frühburgunder, which are still a little closed. The "Reserves" of both varieties as well as the "Parzival" are among the very best red wines in Germany this year. We expressed admiration for the white wines here last year, and with very small reservations this also applies to the wines of the 2003 vintage.

2003 "Buntsandsteinterrassen"
Riesling & Silvaner trocken "Alter Satz"
13%, ♀ till 2006   **86**

2003 Bürgstadter Centgrafenberg
Silvaner Spätlese trocken
13%, ♀ till 2007   **87**

2003 Bürgstadter Centgrafenberg
Riesling Spätlese trocken
13%, ♀ till 2007   **87**

2003 Riesling trocken
13%, ♀ till 2007   **87**

2002 Bürgstadter Centgrafenberg
Riesling Spätlese trocken
12.5%, ♀ till 2007   **88**

2002 "Buntsandsteinterrassen"
Riesling & Silvaner trocken
12.5%, ♀ till 2006   **88**

The estates: 🍷🍷🍷🍷🍷 World's finest · 🍷🍷🍷🍷 Germany's best · 🍷🍷🍷 Very good · 🍷🍷 Good · 🍷 Reliable

2003 Bürgstadter Centgrafenberg
Weißer Burgunder trocken
14%, ♀ till 2008 **88**

2002 Bürgstadter Centgrafenberg
Weißer Burgunder trocken
13.5%, ♀ till 2007 **89**

2003 Bürgstadter Centgrafenberg
Riesling Spätlese trocken "R"
13.5%, ♀ till 2008 **89**

2001 Bürgstadter Centgrafenberg
Riesling Spätlese trocken "R"
12.5%, ♀ till 2007 **90**

2001 Bürgstadter Centgrafenberg
Weißer Burgunder trocken "R"
13.5%, ♀ till 2007 **90**

2003 Bürgstadter Centgrafenberg
Weißer Burgunder trocken "R"
14%, ♀ till 2009 **90**

2002 Bürgstadter Centgrafenberg
Weißer Burgunder trocken "R"
13.5%, ♀ till 2008 **91**

2003 Bürgstadter Centgrafenberg
Riesling Spätlese Goldkapsel
12%, ♀ till 2009 **86**

2003 Bürgstadter Centgrafenberg
Riesling Auslese
8.5%, ♀ till 2011 **89**

2001 Bürgstadter Centgrafenberg
Riesling Eiswein
6%, ♀ till 2017 **91**

2001 Bürgstadter Centgrafenberg
Rieslaner Trockenbeerenauslese
7.5%, ♀ till 2023 **92**

2002 Bürgstadter Centgrafenberg
Riesling Auslese
7%, ♀ till 2009 **92**

——— Red wines ———

2002 "Parzival" Cuvée trocken
13%, ♀ till 2008 **85**

2002 Spätburgunder
trocken "Tradition"
13%, ♀ till 2008 **85**

2001 "Parzival" trocken
13%, ♀ till 2009 **87**

2002 Bürgstadter Centgrafenberg
Frühburgunder trocken
13.5%, ♀ till 2008 **88**

2001 Spätburgunder
trocken "Tradition"
13%, ♀ till 2009 **88**

2000 Bürgstadter Centgrafenberg
Spätburgunder trocken
13.5%, ♀ till 2007 **89**

2000 Bürgstadter Centgrafenberg
Frühburgunder trocken
13.5%, ♀ till 2007 **89**

2001 Bürgstadter Centgrafenberg
Spätburgunder trocken
13.5%, ♀ till 2009 **89**

2001 Bürgstadter Centgrafenberg
Frühburgunder trocken
13.5%, ♀ till 2009 **89**

2002 Bürgstadter Centgrafenberg
Spätburgunder trocken "R"
13.5%, ♀ till 2010 **89**

2001 "Parzival" trocken "R"
13%, ♀ till 2011 **90**

2002 "Parzival"
Cuvée trocken "R" von alten Reben
13.5%, ♀ till 2008 **90**

2000 Bürgstadter Centgrafenberg
Spätburgunder trocken "R"
13.5%, ♀ till 2010 **91**

2000 Bürgstadter Centgrafenberg
Frühburgunder trocken "R"
13.5%, ♀ till 2013 **91**

2001 Bürgstadter Centgrafenberg
Spätburgunder trocken "R"
13.5%, ♀ till 2011 **91**

2002 Bürgstadter Centgrafenberg
Frühburgunder trocken "R"
13.5%, ♀ till 2012 **91**

2001 Bürgstadter Centgrafenberg
Frühburgunder trocken "R"
13.5%, ♀ till 2011 **93**

The wines: **100** Perfect · **95–99** Outstanding · **90–94** Excellent · **85–89** Very good · **80–84** Good · **75–79** Average

WEINGUT
GLASER-HIMMELSTOSS

Owner: Wolfgang and Monika Glaser
Winemaker: Wolfgang Glaser
97334 Nordheim, Langgasse 7
Tel. (0 93 81) 46 02, Fax 64 02
e-mail:
info@weingut-glaser-himmelstoss.de
Internet:
www.weingut-glaser-himmelstoss.de
Directions: A 3 Würzburg–Nürnberg,
Kitzingen exit, via Schwarzach
Sales: Mon.–Fri. 09:00 to 18:00 hours,
except Tue.; Sat. and Sun. 10:00 to
16:00 hours. Sales also in Dettelbach,
Bamberger Straße 3, Tel. (0 93 24) 23 05
Restaurant: Restaurant "Himmelstoß,"
Bamberger Straße 3, Dettelbach
Tel. (0 93 24) 47 76, Wed.–Sun. 12:00 to
14:00 hours and 18:00 to 24:00 hours
Specialties: Creative regional cuisine

Vineyard area: 12 hectares
Annual production: 100,000 bottles
Top sites: Dettelbacher Berg-
Rondell, Sommeracher Katzenkopf,
Nordheimer Vögelein
Soil types: Shell limestone, sand, clay
Grape varieties: 28% Müller-Thurgau,
22% Silvaner, 9% Riesling, 8% Spät-
burgunder, 5% each of Weißburgunder
and Scheurebe, 23% other varieties
Average yield: 65 hl/ha
Best vintages: 1998, 2000, 2003
Member: VDP

Wolfgang and Monika Glaser continue to
run their parents wineries in Dettelbach
and Nordheim, which have been combined under the name of Glaser-Himmelstoß with a total area of 12 hectares. The
winery in Dettelbach is a half-timbered
building dating back to the 17th century,
with a pretty restaurant and wine sales
facility. We tasted the extensive range of
some two dozen 2003 vintage wines,
which were significantly better across
the board than the wines of the previous
vintage. We particularly liked the full-
bodied Spätburgunder "Rebell."

2003 Dettelbacher Berg-Rondell
Riesling Kabinett trocken
13.5%, ♀ till 2006   **85**

2003 Nordheimer Vögelein
Silvaner Spätlese trocken
14%, ♀ till 2007   **85**

2003 "Denker"
Grauer Burgunder Spätlese trocken
15%, ♀ till 2007   **85**

2003 Nordheimer Vögelein
Weißer Burgunder Spätlese trocken
14%, ♀ till 2008   **86**

2003 Nordheimer Vögelein
Scheurebe Spätlese
13.5%, ♀ till 2009   **86**

2003 Nordheimer Vögelein
Traminer Spätlese
13.5%, ♀ till 2009   **86**

2003 Nordheimer Vögelein
Riesling Spätlese
13%, ♀ till 2009   **86**

2003 Dettelbacher Berg-Rondell
Riesling Trockenbeerenauslese
7%, ♀ till 2025   **90**

2003 Nordheimer Vögelein
Silvaner Trockenbeerenauslese
8%, ♀ till 2025   **91**

——— Red wine ———
2002 "Rebell"
Spätburgunder trocken Barrique
13%, ♀ till 2008   **86**

WEINGUT DR. HEIGEL

Owner and winemaker:
Dr. Klaus-Peter Heigel
97475 Zeil am Main, Haßfurter Str. 30
Tel. (0 95 24) 31 10, Fax 31 09
e-mail: Weingut-Dr-Heigel@t-online.de
Directions: A 70 Bamberg–Schweinfurt,
Knetzgau exit
Sales: Birgit Heigel, by appointment
Worth seeing: Oldest vineyard in Ober-
main area – monopole vineyard site
"Zeiler Mönchshang"

Vineyard area: 13.8 hectares
Annual production: 100,000 bottles
Top sites: Randersackerer Pfülben,
Zeiler Mönchshang, Würzburger
Abtsleite
Soil types: Shell limestone, sandstone
with red marl
Grape varieties: 26% red varieties,
23% Silvaner, 18% Müller-Thurgau,
8% Rieslaner, 5% each of Riesling and
Weißburgunder, 15% other varieties
Average yield: 69 hl/ha
Best vintages: 1998, 2002, 2003
Member: Frank & Frei

Klaus-Peter Heigel is an agronomist with
a degree, who studied in Gießen, far from
any wineries. Since 1994 he has turned
his father's small part-time business into
a respectable operation, which was expanded yet again last year, by almost 50
percent, with a vineyard area now of
almost 14 hectares. Heigel has enough
space around his existing buildings to
cope with the demands of his enlarged
business. The 2000 and 2001 vintages
from here will not go down in the history
books. In 2002 Heigel presented a range
of almost 25 wines. Even the most basic
Müller-Thurgau in liter bottles was very
good. It is possible that the new cellar,
with temperature-controlled fermentation
facilities, contributed to the improved
quality. The highlights of the 2003 range
are some very good botrytis dessert wines
made from Rieslaner grapes. Our personal favorite is the Eiswein.

2003 Zeiler Mönchshang
Silvaner "S" Spätlese trocken
14%, ♀ till 2007   **84**

2003 Randersackerer Pfülben
Riesling "S" Spätlese trocken
13.5%, ♀ till 2007   **85**

2002 Kitzinger Hofrat
Silvaner Spätlese trocken
12.5%, ♀ till 2007   **86**

2002 Kitzinger Hofrat
Weißer Burgunder Kabinett trocken
12%, ♀ till 2006   **87**

2002 Randersackerer Pfülben
Riesling Spätlese trocken
12.5%, ♀ till 2007   **87**

2003 Würzburger Abtsleite
Riesling Auslese
10.5%, ♀ till 2010   **86**

2003 Zeiler Mönchshang
Rieslaner Auslese
9.5%, ♀ till 2012   **88**

2003 Zeiler Mönchshang
Rieslaner Beerenauslese
7.5%, ♀ till 2020   **89**

2003 Zeiler Mönchshang
Rieslaner Trockenbeerenauslese
6.5%, ♀ till 2025   **89**

2003 Zeiler Mönchshang
Rieslaner Eiswein
7.5%, ♀ till 2020   **90**

The wines: **100** Perfect · **95–99** Outstanding · **90–94** Excellent · **85–89** Very good · **80–84** Good · **75–79** Average

WEINGUT HÖFLER

Owner and manager:
Bernhard Höfler
Winemaker: Stefan Kunkel
63755 Alzenau-Michelbach,
Albstädter Straße 1
Tel. (0 60 23) 54 95, Fax 3 14 17
e-mail: info@weingut-hoefler.de
Internet: www.weingut-hoefler.de
*Directions: A 45, Alzenau-Nord exit, in
direction of Michelbach, left at first traf-
fic light, in direction of Gelnhausen*
Sales: Edeltraud Höfler
Opening hours: Mon.–Fri. 09:00 to
12:00 hours and 14:00 to 19:00 hours
Sat. 09:00 to 16:00 hours
Worth seeing: Michelbacher Apostel-
garten vineyard in original state, a pro-
tected monument since 1985
Worth a visit: Winery festival in July

Vineyard area: 7.2 hectares
Annual production: 50,000 bottles
Top sites: Michelbacher
Apostelgarten and Steinberg
Soil types: Crystalline primordial rock,
slate, light loess-clay
Grape varieties: 30% Riesling,
25% Müller-Thurgau, 8% each of Sil-
vaner and Weißburgunder, 5% each
of Spätburgunder, Schwarzriesling
and Domina, 14% other varieties
Average yield: 70 hl/ha
Best vintages: 2001, 2002
Member: VDP

Michelbach makes up the north-west tip
of the growing region, is located close
to Frankfurt, although it belongs terri-
torially to the Bavarian region of Franken. At the tip of the western foothills of
the Spessart mountains, not far from the
lower Main river, the Höfler family has
been involved in winemaking since 1924,
working steep vineyard slopes. Last year,
we liked the fresh style of two of the 2002
Rieslings. The current 2003 range does
not quite measure up to this. The wine we
liked best is the fruity Riesling Spätlese
from the Apostelgarten site.

2001 Michelbacher Apostelgarten
Weißer Burgunder Spätlese trocken
12%, ♀ till 2007 **86**

2001 Michelbacher Apostelgarten
Silvaner Kabinett halbtrocken
11%, ♀ till 2006 **87**

2003 Michelbacher Steinberg
Müller-Thurgau
12.5%, ♀ till 2006 **83**

2003 Michelbacher Apostelgarten
Riesling Kabinett
12.5%, ♀ till 2006 **83**

2003 Michelbacher Apostelgarten
Rieslaner Auslese
14%, ♀ till 2008 **83**

2003 Michelbacher Apostelgarten
Riesling Auslese
10%, ♀ till 2009 **84**

2003 Michelbacher Apostelgarten
Riesling "S"
14%, ♀ till 2007 **84**

2002 Michelbacher Riesling
11.5%, ♀ till 2006 **85**

2003 Michelbacher Apostelgarten
Riesling Spätlese
13%, ♀ till 2009 **85**

2002 Michelbacher Apostelgarten
Riesling "Urgestein Sommer"
12%, ♀ till 2006 **86**

———— Red wines ————

2001 Michelbacher Steinberg
Spätburgunder trocken
13%, ♀ till 2006 **85**

2001 Michelbacher Steinberg
Schwarzriesling trocken
13%, ♀ till 2006 **85**

HÖFLER
2003 er
Michelbacher Steinberg
Müller-Thurgau „S"
Qualitätswein
12,5%vol   A.P.Nr. 1027-011-04   750ml
Gutsabfüllung
Weingut Höfler Albstädter Straße1·D-63755 Alzenau-Michelbach
Tel 10 60 23) 54 95·Fax 10 60 23) 3 14 17
FRANKEN

The estates: ✦✦✦✦✦ World's finest · ✦✦✦✦ Germany's best · ✦✦✦ Very good · ✦✦ Good · ✦ Reliable

WEINGUT HOFMANN

Owner: Jürgen and Alois Hofmann
Winemaker: Jürgen Hofmann
97285 Röttingen, Strüther Straße 7
Tel. (0 93 38) 15 77, Fax 99 33 75
e-mail: weingut.a.hofmann@t-online.de
Directions: A 3 Frankfurt–Würzburg, Hei-
dingsfeld exit, to Röttingen on the B 19
Sales: Gertrud, Alois, Jürgen Hofmann
Opening hours: Mon.–Sat. 08:00 to
18:00 hours and by appointment
Restaurant: Spring and fall
Fri. and Sat. from 18:00 hours,
Sun. from 15:00 hours

Vineyard area: 6.5 hectares
Annual production: 35,000 bottles
Top sites: Röttinger Feuerstein,
Tauberrettersheimer Königin
Soil types: Shell limestone with quartz
and high proportion of rocks
Grape varieties: 20% Müller-Thurgau,
17% Silvaner, 15% Spätburgunder,
11% Riesling, 10% each of Bacchus
and Schwarzriesling, 9% Tauber-
schwarz, 8% other varieties
Average yield: 70 hl/ha
Best vintages: 2001, 2002, 2003

Röttingen lies in the triangle created by
Würzburg, Bad Mergentheim and Ro-
thenburg. Here you find the most southerly vineyards in Franken. Until 1990,
Alois Hofmann delivered his grapes to
another winery, and has been making his
wines independently since then. Son Jürgen, born 1977, took over work in the cellar when not yet 20, and while he was still
being trained by top winemaker Paul
Fürst. Now that he has completed his
studies he can turn his full attention to the
winery. The 2003 vintage range probably represents the highest natural levels
of acidity seen anywhere in Franken.
We particularly liked his modern-style
"Flint," a blend of classical varieties from
the Feuerstein vineyard. Even the
Bacchus is a good quaffing wine here,
representative of a standard we believe
is worthy of the second bunch of grapes.

2003 Röttinger Feuerstein
Bacchus trocken
11.5%, ♀ till 2006   83

2003 Röttinger Feuerstein
Riesling Kabinett trocken
12%, ♀ till 2006   85

2002 "Flint" Cuvée Blanc trocken
11.5%, ♀ till 2006   87

2003 Röttinger Feuerstein
Riesling trocken ***
12.5%, ♀ till 2008   87

2002 Röttinger Feuerstein
Riesling trocken ***
11.5%, ♀ till 2006   88

2002 Röttinger Feuerstein
Silvaner Spätlese trocken
12%, ♀ till 2007   88

2002 Röttinger Feuerstein
trocken "Tauber-Edition"
12%, ♀ till 2006   88

2003 Röttinger Feuerstein
Silvaner Spätlese trocken
12.5%, ♀ till 2008   89

2003 "Tauberedition"
12.5%, ♀ till 2008   87

——————— Red wines ———————

2003 Röttinger Feuerstein
Tauberschwarz trocken "R"
13%, ♀ till 2008   85

2002 Röttinger Feuerstein
Spätburgunder trocken "R"
13%, ♀ till 2008   85

The wines: **100** Perfect · **95–99** Outstanding · **90–94** Excellent · **85–89** Very good · **80–84** Good · **75–79** Average

205

WEINGUT JULIUSSPITAL

Owner: Juliusspital Foundation
Manager: Horst Kolesch
Winemaker: Benedikt Then
97070 Würzburg, Klinikstraße 1
Tel. (09 31) 3 93 14 00, Fax 3 93 14 14
e-mail: weingut@juliusspital.de
Internet: www.juliusspital.de
Directions: Center of Würzburg, between congress center and railroad terminal
Sales: Wolfgang Apel, Kordula Geier
Opening hours: Mon.–Thur. 07:30 to 16:30, Fri. 07:30 to 12:00 hours and at the Weineck Julius Echter, Koelliker-straße 1/2, Mon.–Fri. 09:00 to 18:00, Sat. 09:00 to 16:00 hours
Restaurant: Wine bar/restaurant "Juliusspital," 10:00 to 24:00 hours
Specialties: Franconian fish dishes
History: Founded 1576 by prince bishop Julius Echter von Mespelbrunn
Worth seeing: Baroque buildings, pavilion, oak barrel cellar, historic barn

---

Vineyard area: 168 hectares
Annual production: 1 mill. bottles
Top sites: Würzburger Stein, Iphöfer Julius-Echter-Berg, Randersacker Pfülben, Escherndorfer Lump
Soil types: Shell limestone, clay, gypsum with red marl and sandstone
Grape varieties: 40% Silvaner, 20% Riesling, 16% Müller-Thurgau, 8% Spätburgunder, 16% other varieties
Average yield: 63 hl/ha
Best vintages: 2001, 2002, 2003
Member: VDP

This traditional winery is among the most imposing representatives of wine culture in the country, and we suggest you go and see this for yourself. We have noted an improvement in quality since 2001, which has been continued in 2002 and 2003. From a basic Silvaner through to an excellent dry Weißburgunder (Pinot Blanc) Spätlese from the Volkacher Karthäuser vineyard and a great dry white wine blend "BT," every single wine here is very good part of a faultless range.

2003 Thüngersheimer Johannisberg
Grauer Burgunder Spätlese trocken
15%, ♀ till 2008   86

2003 Würzburger Innere Leiste
Silvaner Spätlese trocken
"Großes Gewächs"
14%, ♀ till 2008   86

2003 Würzburger Stein
Riesling Spätlese trocken
"Großes Gewächs"
14%, ♀ till 2009   86

2003 Würzburger Stein
Silvaner Spätlese trocken
14%, ♀ till 2009   87

2003 Würzburger Abtsleite
Traminer Spätlese trocken
14%, ♀ till 2009   87

2002 Würzburger Innere Leiste
Riesling Spätlese trocken
12.5%, ♀ till 2007   88

2003 Volkacher Karthäuser
Weißer Burgunder Spätlese trocken
"Großes Gewächs"
15%, ♀ till 2009   88

2002 Iphöfer Julius-Echter-Berg
Riesling Spätlese trocken
13%, ♀ till 2007   89

2003 "Cuvée BT" trocken
14.5%, ♀ till 2008   89

2002 Volkacher Karthäuser
Weißer Burgunder Spätlese trocken
13.5%, ♀ till 2007   90

WEINGUT FÜRST LÖWENSTEIN

Owner: Carl-Friedrich Erbprinz zu Löwenstein-Wertheim-Rosenberg
Manager and winemaker:
Robert Haller
97892 Kreuzwertheim, Rathausgasse 5
Tel. (0 93 42) 9 23 50, Fax 92 35 50
e-mail:
kreuzwertheim@loewenstein.de
Internet: www.loewenstein.de
Directions: A 3 Würzburg–Frankfurt,
Wertheim or Marktheidenfeld exit
Sales: Robert Macgregor
Opening hours: Mon.–Fri. 09:00 to
12:00 hours and 13:00 to 17:00 hours
Sat. 10:00 to 14:00 hours
and by appointment
Worth seeing: Renovated Renaissance
building, stepped gable from 1594
Worth a visit: Walking through steep
slopes of Homburger Kallmuth vineyard

Vineyard area: 25 hectares
Annual production: 150,000 bottles
Top sites: Homburger Kallmuth,
Bürgstadter Centgrafenberg, Reicholz-
heimer Satzenberg, Lengfurter Oberrot
Soil types: Shell limestone, sandstone
Grape varieties: 37% Silvaner,
19% Spätburgunder, 18% Müller-
Thurgau, 11% Riesling, 9% Bacchus,
6% other varieties
Average yield: 55 hl/ha
Best vintages: 2001, 2002, 2003
Member: VDP, Trias

Our "Estate administrator of the year
2004," Robert Haller, and a massive investment are helping this traditional winery to maintain its positive momentum.
There have been no poor wines produced
here in recent years. The 2003 range is remarkably good, the highlights are the top
dry Spätlese wines, the Silvaner "Asphodill" and the Riesling "Coronilla," both
from the Homburger Kallmuth site,
which has been cultivated for 900 years.
The red wines, too, are good, with elegant
spice and showing judicious use of oak.

2003 Homburger Kallmuth
Riesling Spätlese trocken
13%, ♀ till 2007 — **84**

2003 Homburger Kallmuth
Silvaner Spätlese trocken
13.5%, ♀ till 2008 — **87**

2003 "Kallmuth Tradition"
Spätlese trocken
13%, ♀ till 2009 — **89**

2002 Homburger Kallmuth
Silvaner Spätlese trocken
12.5%, ♀ till 2007 — **90**

2003 Homburger Kallmuth
Silvaner Spätlese trocken "Asphodill"
13.5%, ♀ till 2010 — **90**

2002 Homburger Kallmuth
Riesling Spätlese trocken "Coronilla"
13.5%, ♀ till 2009 — **90**

2003 Homburger Kallmuth
Riesling Spätlese trocken "Coronilla"
13.5%, ♀ till 2010 — **90**

2002 Homburger Kallmuth
Silvaner Spätlese trocken "Asphodill"
13%, ♀ till 2009 — **91**

2001 Homburger Kallmuth
Silvaner Beerenauslese
8.5%, ♀ till 2017 — **90**

2001 Homburger Kallmuth
Rieslaner Beerenauslese
6%, ♀ till 2017 — **91**

——— Red wines ———

2001 Lengfurter Alter Berg
Spätburgunder trocken
12.5%, ♀ till 2006 — **87**

2002 Lengfurter Oberrot
Spätburgunder trocken
12.5%, ♀ till 2008 — **87**

The wines: **100** Perfect · **95–99** Outstanding · **90–94** Excellent · **85–89** Very good · **80–84** Good · **75–79** Average

207

WEINGUT "AM LUMP"

Owner: Albrecht Sauer
Manager and winemaker:
Albrecht Sauer
97332 Escherndorf,
Bocksbeutelstraße 60
Tel. (0 93 81) 90 35, Fax 61 35
e-mail: Weingut-Am-Lump@t-online.de
Directions: A 3 Würzburg–Nürnberg,
Kitzingen-Schwarzach exit, in direction
of Dettelbach; A 7 Kassel–Würzburg,
Estenfeld exit, in direction of Volkach
Sales: Margarete and Paul,
Anne and Albrecht Sauer
Opening hours: Mon.–Sat. 09:00 to
12:00 and 13:00 to 18:00, Sun. 10:00 to
12:00 and 13:00 to 14:00 hours
Worth seeing: Historical wine press from
19th century, renovated Lourdes chapel
Worth a visit: Rafting on the Main river

Vineyard area: 10.7 hectares
Annual production: 85,000 bottles
Top sites: Escherndorfer Lump
and Fürstenberg
Soil types: Shell limestone, red marl,
loess-clay
Grape varieties: 26% Silvaner,
21% Riesling, 20% Müller-Thurgau,
7% each of Spätburgunder and
Schwarzriesling, 5% Portugieser,
4% each of Weißburgunder and
Bacchus, 3% each of Scheurebe
and Rieslaner
Average yield: 75 hl/ha
Best vintages: 1998, 2001, 2002

The winery building of the Sauer family
is located in idyllic scenery at the foot of
the steep Escherndorfer Lump vineyard,
with a view of the Main loop at Volkach.
From May to October that is where you
will find son Michael and daughter Monika offering raft rides on the river – providing music and wine to the guests. The
two previous vintages were very good
here, and the 2003 range fits in seamlessly. We particularly liked the fruity Riesling and Silvaner Spätlese wines from the
top-class Escherndorfer Lump vineyard.

2003 Escherndorfer Lump
Silvaner Kabinett trocken
12.5%, ♀ till 2006 — **82**

2003 Escherndorfer Lump
Weißer Burgunder Spätlese trocken
12.9%, ♀ till 2007 — **85**

2002 Escherndorfer Lump
Riesling Kabinett trocken
12.5%, ♀ till 2006 — **86**

2002 Escherndorfer Lump
Weißer Burgunder Spätlese trocken
12.5%, ♀ till 2007 — **88**

2003 Escherndorfer Lump
Silvaner Kabinett halbtrocken
12.3%, ♀ till 2006 — **83**

2003 Escherndorfer Fürstenberg
Kerner Spätlese
13.5%, ♀ till 2009 — **82**

2003 Escherndorfer Lump
Silvaner Spätlese
12.7%, ♀ till 2009 — **85**

2003 Escherndorfer Lump
Riesling Spätlese
12%, ♀ till 2009 — **85**

2002 Escherndorfer Lump
Rieslaner Spätlese
9.5%, ♀ till 2007 — **87**

2003 Escherndorfer Fürstenberg
Riesling Beerenauslese
10.4%, ♀ till 2020 — **88**

2002 Escherndorfer Lump
Riesling Spätlese
10%, ♀ till 2007 — **89**

2002 Escherndorfer Lump
Weißer Burgunder Eiswein
9.5%, ♀ till 2018 — **90**

0,75 L   12,5 % vol
2001er
Escherndorfer Lump
Silvaner trocken
Spätlese
Gutsabfüllung
Qualitätswein mit Prädikat
A. P. Nr. 4173-024-02
Paul Sauer · D-97332 FRANKEN Volkach-Escherndorf

The estates: ♦♦♦♦♦ World's finest · ♦♦♦♦ Germany's best · ♦♦♦ Very good · ♦♦ Good · ♦ Reliable

WEINGUT RUDOLF MAY

Owner: Petra and Rudolf May
Manager and winemaker:
Rudolf May
97282 Retzstadt, Im Eberstal
Tel. (0 93 64) 57 60, Fax 89 64 34
e-mail: info@weingut-may.de
Internet: www.weingut-may.de
*Directions: A 7, Gramschatzer Wald
exit, via Gramschatz to Retzstadt*
Sales: Petra May
Opening hours: Mon.–Fri. 09:00 to
18:00 hours, Sat. 09:00 to 15:00 hours
and by appointment
Restaurant: May, Nov. and Dec.,
Thur.–Sat. 16:00, Sun. 11:30 hours
History: Winemaking tradition for over
300 years
Worth seeing: New winery in attractive
natural surroundings

Vineyard area: 8.4 hectares
Annual production: 56,000 bottles
Top sites: Retzstadter Langenberg
and Benediktusberg, Stettener Stein
Soil types: Shell limestone
Grape varieties: 34% Silvaner, 14%
Müller-Thurgau, 10% each of Weiß-
and Spätburgunder, 8% each of Ries-
ling and Grauburgunder,
16% other varieties
Average yield: 65 hl/ha
Best vintages: 2001, 2002
Member: Frank & Frei

Rudolf May established a new winery on
the outskirts of Retzstadt in 1999, and has
gone into business with great enthusiasm.
Sustainable practices are maintained in
the vineyard, involving intensive work on
the vines. Yields are kept low, and all
grapes are picked by hand. In the cellar, a
policy of minimal intervention is practised. All this effort has again produced a
good range, the highlights being a dry Silvaner Kabinett and an elegant Grauburgunder (Pinot Gris). It is particularly
pleasant to enjoy the wines in the wine
bar and restaurant, which is open for a
few weeks in spring and fall.

2003 Silvaner trocken
12.5%, ♀ till 2006 — **82**

2003 Retzstadter Langenberg
Silvaner Spätlese trocken
14%, ♀ till 2009 — **83**

2003 Retzstadter Langenberg
Weißer Burgunder Spätlese trocken
13.5%, ♀ till 2009 — **83**

2003 Stettener Stein
Grauer Burgunder Spätlese trocken
14.5%, ♀ till 2009 — **85**

2003 Retzstadter Langenberg
Silvaner Kabinett trocken
12.5%, ♀ till 2006 — **86**

2003 Retzstadter Langenberg
Silvaner Spätlese
13.5%, ♀ till 2009 — **84**

2002 Retzstadter Langenberg
Rieslaner Auslese
11%, ♀ till 2013 — **87**

——————— Red wines ———————

2003 Retzstadter Langenberg
Regent Spätlese trocken
13.5%, ♀ till 2009 — **83**

2001 Retzstadter Benediktusberg
Spätburgunder trocken
14%, ♀ till 2007 — **87**

The wines: **100** Perfect · **95–99** Outstanding · **90–94** Excellent · **85–89** Very good · **80–84** Good · **75–79** Average

209

WEINGUT MEINTZINGER

Owner: Götz, Peter and Jochen Meintzinger
Manager: Götz Meintzinger
Winemaker: Jochen Meintzinger and Volker Pfaff
97252 Frickenhausen, Babenbergplatz 2
Tel. (0 93 31) 8 71 10, Fax 75 78
e-mail: weingut.meintzinger@t-online.de
Internet: www.meintzinger.de
Directions: A 3, Randersacker exit, B 13 in direction of Ochsenfurt, in Ochsenfurt continue straight to Frickenhausen
Sales: Peter Meintzinger
Opening hours: Mon.–Fri. 08:00 to 12:00 and 13:00 to 18:00, Sat. 09:00 to 17:00, Sun. 10:00 to 12:00 hours
History: Previously winery of bishops of Würzburg, vaulted cellar dating to 1475
Worth seeing: Extensive operation with integrated hotel

Vineyard area: 25 hectares
Annual production: 200,000 bottles
Top sites: Frickenhäuser Kapellenberg and Fischer
Soil types: Shell limestone
Grape varieties: 20% Silvaner, 15% Müller-Thurgau, 14% Bacchus, 12% Domina, 8% Riesling, 7% Spätburgunder, 5% Weißburgunder, 19% other varieties
Average yield: 78 hl/ha
Best vintages: 2000, 2001, 2002
Member: Frank & Frei

The winery is housed in a historical building complex that has been owned by the Meintzinger family since 1790. Götz Meintzinger took over the business in 1966 at the age of only 23, following the early death of his father. Starting with only 1.5 hectares of vineyards, he went through several stages of restructuring, and today has a respectable 25 hectares of vineyard. The complex includes an attractive hotel. By now, the seventh and eighth generations of the family have joined the business, and continue to produce a reliable high level of quality.

2003 Frickenhäuser Kapellenberg
Riesling Kabinett trocken
13%, ♀ till 2006 — **84**

2002 Frickenhäuser Kapellenberg
Silvaner Spätlese trocken
12%, ♀ till 2007 — **86**

2003 Frickenhäuser Kapellenberg
Weißer Burgunder Kabinett trocken
13.5%, ♀ till 2006 — **86**

2002 Frickenhäuser Kapellenberg
Riesling Kabinett trocken
11.5%, ♀ till 2006 — **87**

2003 Frickenhäuser Fischer
Rieslaner Kabinett
14%, ♀ till 2006 — **82**

2003 Frickenhäuser Kapellenberg
Traminer Spätlese
14%, ♀ till 2009 — **83**

2003 Frickenhäuser Kapellenberg
Riesling Spätlese
13.5%, ♀ till 2009 — **84**

2003 Frickenhäuser Kapellenberg
Weißer Burgunder Spätlese
14%, ♀ till 2009 — **85**

2003 Frickenhäuser Fischer
Silvaner Spätlese
13.5%, ♀ till 2009 — **85**

2003 Frickenhäuser Fischer
Rieslaner Auslese
13%, ♀ till 2011 — **86**

2002 Frickenhäuser Kapellenberg
Traminer Spätlese
12.5%, ♀ till 2007 — **87**

The estates: ⬥⬥⬥⬥⬥ World's finest · ⬥⬥⬥⬥ Germany's best · ⬥⬥⬥ Very good · ⬥⬥ Good · ⬥ Reliable

WEINGUT MAX MÜLLER I

Owner: Rainer and Monika Müller family
Winemaker: Rainer Müller
97332 Volkach, Hauptstraße 46
Tel. (0 93 81) 12 18, Fax 16 90
e-mail: info@max-mueller.de
Internet: www.max-mueller.de
Directions: A 3 Würzburg–Nürnberg, Schwarzach exit, in direction of Volkach
Sales: Monika and Rainer Müller
Opening hours: Mon.–Fri. 09:00 to 18:00 hours, Sat. 09:00 to 15:00 hours Sun. 10:00 to 12:00 hours
History: Winery building built by prince bishops of Würzburg 1692
Worth seeing: Baroque tasting room, treasure trove in old vaulted cellar, Franconian courtyard
Worth a visit: Culinary events in wine kitchen with guest chefs

---

Vineyard area: 10 hectares
Annual production: 87,000 bottles
Top sites: Volkacher Ratsherr, Sommeracher Katzenkopf
Soil types: Shell limestone
Grape varieties: 32% Silvaner, 25% Müller-Thurgau, 12% Riesling, 15% red varieties, 7% Bacchus, 9% other varieties
Average yield: 76 hl/ha
Best vintages: 2001, 2002, 2003

The Müllers have been making wine in the deep vaulted cellar in the center of Volkach for many centuries. Rainer Müller builds on the long tradition, but is not against modern technology. All white musts are fermented exclusively in stainless steel tanks, while the red wines mature by traditional style in large oak vats. The wines are kept on the lees for an extended period to maintain the freshness of young wines. Following on a solid succession of ranges in 2000, 2001 and 2002, Müller has presented a very good 2003 range, the highlights of which are a dry Riesling Spätlese as well as a fruity sweet Scheurebe Spätlese.

2003 Volkacher Ratsherr
Silvaner Spätlese trocken
13.5%, ♀ till 2007 — 83

2003 Sommeracher Katzenkopf
Riesling Kabinett trocken
12%, ♀ till 2006 — 84

2002 Sommeracher Katzenkopf
Riesling Kabinett trocken
11.5%, ♀ till 2006 — 86

2002 Volkacher Ratsherr
Silvaner Spätlese trocken
13%, ♀ till 2007 — 86

2003 Sommeracher Katzenkopf
Riesling Spätlese trocken
13.5%, ♀ till 2008 — 86

2002 Sommeracher Katzenkopf
Riesling Spätlese trocken
13%, ♀ till 2007 — 87

2003 Volkacher Ratsherr
Rieslaner Auslese
10.5%, ♀ till 2009 — 84

2003 Sommeracher Katzenkopf
Riesling Spätlese
12%, ♀ till 2009 — 85

2003 Volkacher Ratsherr
Scheurebe Spätlese
11%, ♀ till 2009 — 86

2003 Sommeracher Katzenkopf
Riesling Beerenauslese
10%, ♀ till 2020 — 86

2002 Sommeracher Katzenkopf
Riesling Beerenauslese
10%, ♀ till 2018 — 88

2002 Volkacher Ratsherr
Scheurebe Beerenauslese
10%, ♀ till 2018 — 88

MAX MÜLLER I
2001   RIESLING   0,75 l
        KABINETT   12,0% vol
        TROCKEN
        Sommeracher Katzenkopf
        Qualitätswein mit Prädikat
        Gutsabfüllung · A.P.Nr. 4016-007-02
        D-97332 Volkach
FRANKEN

The wines: **100** Perfect · **95–99** Outstanding · **90–94** Excellent · **85–89** Very good · **80–84** Good · **75–79** Average

Franken

WINZERGENOSSENSCHAFT NORDHEIM

General manager: Oskar Georg Noppenberger
Quality control: Paul Glaser
Winemaker: Ernst Braun
97334 Nordheim, Langgasse 33
Tel. (0 93 81) 8 09 90, Fax 80 99 32
e-mail: info@wgn.de
Internet: www.wgn.de
Directions: A 3, Kitzingen-Schwarzach exit, in direction of Volkach, before Volkach turn left in direction of Nordheim
Sales: Rita Wendel
Opening hours: Mon.–Fri. 08:00 to 18:00 hours, Sat. 09:00 to 17:00 hours Sun. 13:00 to 17:00 hours
History: Founded 1951 by village priest
Worth seeing: Vinotheque "Divino"
Worth a visit: Concerts in courtyard

Vineyard area: 293 hectares
Number of members: 240
Annual production: 2.2 mill. bottles
Top sites: Nordheimer Vögelein and Kreuzberg, Escherndorfer Lump and Fürstenberg
Soil types: Shell limestone
Grape varieties: 40% Müller-Thurgau, 20% Silvaner, 15% red varieties, 10% Bacchus, 5% each of Riesling, Grau- and Weißburgunder
Average yield: 83 hl/ha
Best vintages: 2000, 2001, 2002

When the co-operative was founded in Nordheim in the early Fifties, the main objective was to overcome the poverty of the post-War years. Today the second-largest co-operative in Franken is uncompromisingly focussed on high quality. The 240 members have again shown their strengths in the current range, the highlights include a dry Weißburgunder and a Grauburgunder "Divino" as well as a fruity-sweet Rieslaner Auslese on the white side, and also the outstanding red wines matured in barrique, which are among the best in the region, and are offered at an affordable price.

2003 Grauer Burgunder
trocken "Divino"
14%, ♀ till 2007 — 84

2003 Riesling trocken "Juventa"
12.5%, ♀ till 2006 — 85

2002 Grauer Burgunder
trocken "Divino"
12.5%, ♀ till 2006 — 87

2003 Nordheimer Vögelein
Traminer Auslese "Franconia"
12%, ♀ till 2009 — 86

2002 Nordheimer Vögelein
Silvaner Auslese "Franconia"
11.5%, ♀ till 2013 — 88

2003 Nordheimer Vögelein
Rieslaner Auslese "Franconia"
11.5%, ♀ till 2010 — 88

2002 Nordheimer Vögelein
Silvaner Eiswein "Franconia"
8%, ♀ till 2016 — 88

——— Red wines ———

2002 Cabernet Dorsa
trocken "Divino" Barrique
13.5%, ♀ till 2008 — 85

2002 Frühburgunder
trocken "Divino" Barrique
13.5%, ♀ till 2008 — 85

2001 Cabernet Dorsa
trocken "Divino" Barrique
13%, ♀ till 2009 — 87

2002 Spätburgunder
trocken "Divino" Barrique
13%, ♀ till 2009 — 87

2001 Spätburgunder
trocken "Divino" Barrique
14%, ♀ till 2009 — 88

2001 Frühburgunder
trocken "Divino" Barrique
13.5%, ♀ till 2009 — 89

WEINGUT ROTH

Owner: Gerhard Roth
Manager and winemaker:
Gerhard Roth
97355 Wiesenbronn, Büttnergasse 11
Tel. (0 93 25) 90 20 04, Fax 90 25 20
e-mail: info@weingut-roth.de
Internet: www.weingut-roth.de
Directions: A 3 Würzburg–Nürnberg,
Schweinfurt Süd/Wiesentheid exit
Opening hours: Mon.–Sat. 09:00 to
11:00 hours and 13:00 to 17:00 hours
History: Pioneer of organic wine
production in Franken – since 1974
Worth seeing: Winery building with
closed energy circulation, barrel cellar as
"living room for wine"

Vineyard area: 13 hectares
Annual production: 85,000 bottles
Top sites: Wiesenbronner
Wachhügel and Geißberg,
Abtswinder Altenberg
Soil types: Red marl
Grape varieties: 20% Silvaner,
15% each of Riesling and Spätbur-
gunder, 10% each of Portugieser and
Blaufränkisch, 5% each of Weißbur-
gunder and Müller-Thurgau,
20% other varieties
Average yield: 56 hl/ha
Best vintages: 2000, 2001, 2003
Member: VDP, Naturland

Gerhard Roth decided to follow the strict
route of organic viticulture as early as
1974. In recent years, the whole operation
has been rebuilt, using exclusively natural materials. Roth has further reduced
the yields since 2000, and is also setting
himself higher standards than the ones legally required for predicate quality wines.
Grapes and must are processed using
gravity feed, without any pumps. We particularly liked the dry 2003 Kerner and
Riesling Spätlese wines, and of the red
wines we liked the elegant 2002 barrique-
matured Pinot Noir. Good spirits (fruit-
based and grappa) from the own distillery
round off an attractive range.

2003 Wiesenbronner Geißberg
Silvaner Kabinett trocken
12%, ♀ till 2006 — **85**

2002 Wiesenbronner Geißberg
Silvaner Spätlese trocken
13%, ♀ till 2007 — **86**

2002 Müller-Thurgau
Spätlese trocken
12.5%, ♀ till 2007 — **86**

2003 Wiesenbronner Geißberg
Silvaner Spätlese trocken
13%, ♀ till 2007 — **86**

2003 Wiesenbronner Geißberg
Riesling Spätlese trocken
12%, ♀ till 2008 — **86**

2003 Wiesenbronner Geißberg
Kerner Spätlese trocken
14.5%, ♀ till 2007 — **86**

2002 Wiesenbronner Geißberg
Weißer Burgunder Spätlese trocken
13%, ♀ till 2007 — **87**

——— Red wines ———

2003 Domina
trocken "Holzfassausbau"
13%, ♀ till 2008 — **84**

2001 Regent trocken
13%, ♀ till 2006 — **85**

2002 Pinot Noir trocken Barrique
13%, ♀ till 2009 — **86**

2001 Wiesenbronner Geißberg
Spätburgunder Spätlese trocken
13%, ♀ till 2009 — **87**

The wines: **100** Perfect · **95–99** Outstanding · **90–94** Excellent · **85–89** Very good · **80–84** Good · **75–79** Average

213

WEINGUT JOHANN RUCK

Owner: Johann Ruck
Manager: Johannes Ruck
97346 Iphofen, Marktplatz 19
Tel. (0 93 23) 80 08 80, Fax 80 08 88
e-mail: info@ruckwein.de
Internet: www.ruckwein.de
Directions: A 3 Würzburg–Nürnberg,
Kitzingen or Schweinfurt-
Wiesentheid exit
Sales: Birgit Ruck
Opening hours: Mon.–Sat. 09:00 to
12:00 hours and 13:00 to 18:00 hours
Sun. 10:00 to 12:00 hours

Vineyard area: 12 hectares
Annual production: 80,000 bottles
Top site: Iphöfer Julius-Echter-Berg
Soil types: Gypsum with red marl, with
reed sandstone in Julius-Echter-Berg
Grape varieties: 28% Silvaner,
17% Müller-Thurgau, 16% Pinot varie-
ties, 11% Riesling, 28% other varieties
Average yield: 60 hl/ha
Best vintages: 2000, 2002, 2003
Member: VDP, Trias

Father Hans Ruck is one of best-known personalities in wine-making circles in Franken. However, for the past three years he has been working mainly in the background, as the young generation took over the business at the turn of the century. Son Johannes "Hansi" Ruck completed his university studies in Geisenheim as well as a practical term at a top winery in South Tyrol, and has now taken over. Looking to the 2003 vintage range, we particularly liked the wines from the top-class Julius-Echter-Berg vineyard, which are famous for their exotic notes – Hans Ruck simply calls it a "God-given terroir." The Silvaner "Myophorium," matured in Iphofen oak, as well as the "Grauer Burgunder Alte Reben" (Pinot Gris from old vines), both of the 2002 vintage, were also very good; the absolute star that had us breathless with excitement is the 2003 Scheurebe "Estheria." Bravo!

2003 Iphöfer Kalb
Silvaner trocken
13.5%, ♀ till 2007 — 84

2002 Rödelseer Schwanleite
Grauer Burgunder Spätlese trocken
13%, ♀ till 2008 — 86

2002 Iphöfer Julius-Echter-Berg
Silvaner Spätlese trocken "Trias"
12.5%, ♀ till 2008 — 86

2003 Iphöfer Julius-Echter-Berg
Silvaner Spätlese trocken
14%, ♀ till 2008 — 87

2003 Iphöfer Julius-Echter-Berg
Riesling Spätlese trocken
"Großes Gewächs" Trias
14%, ♀ till 2009 — 87

2003 Rödelseer Küchenmeister
Rieslaner Spätlese
13.5%, ♀ till 2010 — 87

2002 "Myophorium"
13%, ♀ till 2009 — 88

2003 Iphöfer Julius-Echter-Berg
Traminer Spätlese
14%, ♀ till 2010 — 88

2003 Iphöfer Julius-Echter-Berg
Rieslaner Auslese
11%, ♀ till 2011 — 89

2002 Rödelseer Schwanleite
Grauer Burgunder Alte Reben
13.5%, ♀ till 2009 — 89

2003 "Estheria" Scheurebe
14.5%, ♀ till 2011 — 90

WEINGUT RUDLOFF

Owner and manager:
Dorothea Rudloff
Winemaker: Peter Rudloff
97334 Nordheim, Mainstraße 19
Tel. (0 93 81) 21 30, Fax 21 36
e-mail: info@weingut-rudloff.de
*Directions: A 3 Würzburg–Nürnberg,
Kitzingen/Schwarzach exit, in direction
of Volkach; A 70, Gerolzhofen exit, in
direction of Volkach*
Sales: Rudloff family
Opening hours: Mon.–Sat. 09:00 to
19:00 hours and by appointment

Vineyard area: 4.5 hectares
Annual production: 30,000 bottles
Top sites: Nordheimer Vögelein
and Sommeracher Katzenkopf
Soil types: Shell limestone with
sandsoil
Grape varieties: 29% Müller-Thurgau,
22% Silvaner, 11% Domina, 9% Weiß-
burgunder, 8% Bacchus, 5% each of
Blauer Zweigelt and Cabernet Dorio,
11% other varieties
Average yield: 72 hl/ha
Best vintage: 2002

The Rudloff winery in Nordheim has decided to present its wines using a new internal classification system. The term
"Gute Traube" (Good Grape) is used for
the basic wines, "Junge Triebe" (Young
Sprout) refers to particularly inexpensive
wines in a colorful, rather avantgarde
packaging design. The "Klassische Beere" (Classical Berry) is filled in Bocksbeutel bottles, and is meant to express all
the traditional values of Franken wines.
At the top of the pyramid is the "Edle Rebe" (Noble Vine), "legendary wines of
the vintage characterized by absolutely
outstanding quality." However that may
be, the 2003 wines fit in fairly seamlessly
as a follow-on to the 2002 vintages, but
without quite reaching the same quality
level. You can best get into the mood for
tasting the wines if you visit the tasting
room with its Mediterranean decor.

2003 Silvaner
Kabinett trocken "Junge Triebe"
13.5%, ♀ till 2006   **84**

2003 Gewürztraminer
Kabinett trocken "Junge Triebe"
13.5%, ♀ till 2006   **84**

2003 Sommeracher Katzenkopf
Silvaner Kabinett trocken
"Klassische Beere"
13.5%, ♀ till 2006   **84**

2002 Sommeracher Katzenkopf
Silvaner Kabinett trocken
12.5%, ♀ till 2006   **85**

2003 Weißer Burgunder
Kabinett trocken "Junge Triebe"
13%, ♀ till 2006   **85**

2003 Nordheimer Vögelein
Weißer Burgunder Kabinett trocken
"Klassische Beere"
13.5%, ♀ till 2007   **85**

2002 Nordheimer Vögelein
Weißer Burgunder Kabinett trocken
13%, ♀ till 2006   **86**

2002 Silvaner Spätlese trocken
13%, ♀ till 2007   **86**

2003 Silvaner
Spätlese trocken "Edle Rebe"
14%, ♀ till 2007   **86**

2002 Weißer Burgunder
Spätlese trocken
13.5%, ♀ till 2007   **87**

2002 Gewürztraminer Spätlese
13%, ♀ till 2007   **88**

Klassische Beere*
2002
Weißer Burgunder
Kabinett trocken
Weingut Rudloff
Franken

The wines: **100** Perfect · **95–99** Outstanding · **90–94** Excellent · **85–89** Very good · **80–84** Good · **75–79** Average

215

WEINGUT HORST SAUER

Owner: Magdalena and Horst Sauer
Manager and winemaker: Horst Sauer
97332 Escherndorf,
Bocksbeutelstraße 14
Tel. (0 93 81) 43 64, Fax 68 43
e-mail: Mail@Weingut-Horst-Sauer.de
Internet: www.Weingut-Horst-Sauer.de
Directions: A 3 Würzburg–Nürnberg,
Wiesentheid exit, via Volkach;
From A 7 Kassel–Würzburg, Estenfeld
exit, in direction of Volkach
Sales: Magdalena Sauer
Opening hours: Mon.–Fri. 10:00 to
12:00 hours and 13:00 to 18:00 hours
Sat. 10:30 to 17:00 hours
Sun. 10:00 to 12:00 hours
by appointment
Guest rooms: At winery

Vineyard area: 12 hectares
Annual production: 110,000 bottles
Top sites: Escherndorfer Lump
and Fürstenberg
Soil types: Shell limestone, loam with
red marl and loess-clay
Grape varieties: 34% Silvaner,
29% Müller-Thurgau, 13% Riesling,
6% Kerner, 6% red varieties,
5% Bacchus, 4% Weißburgunder,
3% Scheurebe
Average yield: 76 hl/ha
Best vintages: 2001, 2002, 2003
Member: VDP

We do not want to get involved in discussions as to whether the Escherndorfer Lump is the best vineyard site in Franken, but we do agree that the best white wines in Bavaria have been grown here in recent years, and most probably the best Silvaner wines in the world! This is thanks exclusively to the efforts of the diffident Horst Sauer, in spite of the fact that he is no extreme proponent of low yields in the vineyard. But then a lot here also depends on how the vines are tended. "The secret is not to copy others, but to use your experience and your ability to combine the familiar with new scientific findings, and then to find your own way," that is how this shy winemaker describes his work. One of the important elements in the new cellar is that the grapes, must and wine are moved over a four-storey system by means of gravity feed. The absence of pumps means even greater care in handling the raw material. Following on the institution of a section of the cellar with old rarities and the opening of a new sales facility, Sauer now wants to tackle the redesign of the marketing rooms as well as of the outside facilities. The botrytis dessert wines are always exceptionally good, and in 2003 these wines are again the very best in Franken. The Riesling and Silvaner Auslese wines and the Beerenauslese are simply unequalled in the region, and the delightful Trockenbeerenauslese crowns the range. At the same time, Horst Sauer produces wines in the basic categories that are a joy to drink and represent real bargains. Even new crossings such as Bacchus – particularly the Spätlese in 2003 – and Kerner are excellent in the current vintage. Just as a representative of all the other fine Riesling and Silvaner wines produced here, we should this time around like to give a special mention to a 2003 Silvaner with the promising name of "Sehnsucht" (Yearning).

2003 "Frank & Frei"
Müller-Thurgau trocken
12%, ♀ till 2006 **84**

2003 Escherndorfer Fürstenberg
Müller-Thurgau Kabinett trocken
12.5%, ♀ till 2006 **84**

2003 Escherndorfer Fürstenberg
Silvaner Kabinett trocken
12.5%, ♀ till 2006 **84**

2003 Escherndorfer Fürstenberg
Müller-Thurgau Spätlese trocken
13.5%, ♀ till 2009 **85**

2003 Escherndorfer Lump
Silvaner Kabinett trocken
13%, ♀ till 2006 **86**

The estates: ♛♛♛♛♛ World's finest · ♛♛♛♛ Germany's best · ♛♛♛ Very good · ♛♛ Good · ♛ Reliable

2003 Escherndorfer Lump
Riesling Kabinett trocken
13%, ♀ till 2006 — 86

2003 Escherndorfer Lump
Silvaner Spätlese trocken
13.5%, ♀ till 2009 — 87

2003 Escherndorfer Lump
Riesling Spätlese trocken
14%, ♀ till 2009 — 87

2003 "Sehnsucht"
Silvaner trocken
14.5%, ♀ till 2006 — 88

2002 Escherndorfer Lump
Silvaner Spätlese trocken
13%, ♀ till 2007 — 90

2002 Escherndorfer Lump
Riesling Spätlese trocken
12.5%, ♀ till 2007 — 90

2003 Escherndorfer Lump
Silvaner trocken "Großes Gewächs"
14%, ♀ till 2006 — 90

2003 Escherndorfer Lump
Riesling trocken "Großes Gewächs"
14.5%, ♀ till 2006 — 90

2002 Escherndorfer Lump
Silvaner Auslese trocken
"Großes Gewächs"
14%, ♀ till 2008 — 91

2002 Escherndorfer Lump
Riesling Auslese trocken
"Großes Gewächs"
14%, ♀ till 2008 — 91

2003 Escherndorfer Fürstenberg
Kerner Spätlese
13.5%, ♀ till 2009 — 85

2003 Escherndorfer Fürstenberg
Blauer Silvaner
13.5%, ♀ till 2008 — 86

2003 Escherndorfer Fürstenberg
Bacchus Spätlese
12%, ♀ till 2009 — 87

2003 Escherndorfer Lump
Scheurebe Spätlese
12%, ♀ till 2009 — 88

2003 Escherndorfer Lump
Scheurebe Auslese
9%, ♀ till 2011 — 88

2003 Escherndorfer Lump
Silvaner Auslese
9%, ♀ till 2011 — 89

2003 Escherndorfer Lump
Riesling Auslese
8.5%, ♀ till 2012 — 89

2003 Escherndorfer Lump
Silvaner Beerenauslese
8.5%, ♀ till 2016 — 90

2002 Escherndorfer Lump
Riesling Auslese
8%, ♀ till 2013 — 91

2002 Escherndorfer Lump
Silvaner Beerenauslese
7%, ♀ till 2018 — 91

2002 Escherndorfer Lump
Silvaner Trockenbeerenauslese
7%, ♀ till 2023 — 92

2002 Escherndorfer Lump
Silvaner Eiswein
7.5%, ♀ till 2018 — 92

2003 Escherndorfer Lump
Riesling Beerenauslese
8.5%, ♀ till 2018 — 92

2002 Escherndorfer Lump
Riesling Beerenauslese
9%, ♀ till 2018 — 93

2002 Escherndorfer Lump
Riesling Eiswein
8.5%, ♀ till 2018 — 93

2003 Escherndorfer Lump
Silvaner Trockenbeerenauslese
8%, ♀ till 2026 — 93

2002 Escherndorfer Lump
Riesling Trockenbeerenauslese
6.5%, ♀ till 2023 — 94

The wines: **100** Perfect · **95–99** Outstanding · **90–94** Excellent · **85–89** Very good · **80–84** Good · **75–79** Average

217

WEINGUT RAINER SAUER

Owner: Helga and Rainer Sauer
Manager and winemaker:
Rainer Sauer
97332 Escherndorf,
Bocksbeutelstr. 15
Tel. (0 93 81) 25 27, Fax 7 13 40
e-mail: info@weingut-rainer-sauer.de
Internet: www.weingut-rainer-sauer.de
*Directions: A 3, Wiesentheid exit,
via Volkach; A 7, Estenfeld exit, in direc-
tion of Volkach*
Sales: Helga Sauer
Opening hours: Mon.–Sat. 09:00 to
18:00 hours, Sun. 10:00 to 12:00 hours
and by appointment
Wine bar/Restaurant: On weekends in
March and April
Worth a visit: Summer wine festival on
third weekend in July

Vineyard area: 8 hectares
Annual production: 68,000 bottles
Top sites: Escherndorfer Lump
and Fürstenberg
Soil types: Shell limestone, loam with
red marl and loess-clay
Grape varieties: 50% Silvaner,
26% Müller-Thurgau, 9% Riesling,
5% red varieties, 4% Kerner,
6% other varieties
Average yield: 72 hl/ha
Best vintages: 2000, 2001, 2002
Member: Frank & Frei

The wines produced here clearly reflect
Rainer Sauer's striving for quality. They
are all characterized by a straightforward
clarity, even a certain austerity – a welcome alternative to the many featureless
wines "designed" in the cellar. The classic
dry Riesling Spätlese from the top Lump
vineyard site, but especially the Weißburgunder (Pinot Blanc) Spätlese "L" have
real staying power, and should by no
means be drunk too soon. Overall, the
wines of the 2003 vintage do not quite
achieve the extremely high standard of the
previous vintage's wines.

2003 Escherndorfer Fürstenberg
Silvaner Spätlese trocken
14.5%, ♀ till 2009 — **84**

2003 Escherndorfer Lump
Riesling Spätlese trocken
14%, ♀ till 2009 — **85**

2003 Weißer Burgunder
Spätlese trocken "L"
14.5%, ♀ till 2009 — **86**

2002 Escherndorfer Lump
Riesling Spätlese trocken
13.5%, ♀ till 2007 — **87**

2002 Escherndorfer Lump
Weißer Burgunder Spätlese trocken
13%, ♀ till 2007 — **87**

2002 Escherndorfer Lump
Silvaner Spätlese trocken
13.5%, ♀ till 2007 — **88**

2002 Escherndorfer Lump
Traminer Spätlese trocken
14%, ♀ till 2007 — **88**

2003 Silvaner
Spätlese trocken "L"
15%, ♀ till 2009 — **88**

2002 Escherndorfer Lump
Silvaner Spätlese trocken "L"
14.5%, ♀ till 2007 — **89**

2001 Escherndorfer Lump
Riesling Eiswein
9%, ♀ till 2018 — **91**

WEINBAU
EGON SCHÄFFER

Owner: Egon Schäffer
97332 Volkach-Escherndorf,
Astheimer Straße 17
Tel. (0 93 81) 93 50, Fax 48 34
e-mail: info@weingut-schaeffer.de
Internet: www.weingut-schaeffer.de
Directions: A 3 Würzburg–Nürnberg,
Wiesentheid exit, via Volkach;
A 7 Fulda–Würzburg, Estenfeld exit, in
direction of Volkach
Opening hours: Mon.–Sat. 09:00 to
19:00 hours by appointment
Vacation apartment: In winery for two
to four persons

Vineyard area: 3.4 hectares
Annual production: 25,000 bottles
Top sites: Escherndorfer Lump
and Fürstenberg
Soil types: Shell limestone
Grape varieties: 41% Silvaner,
33% Müller-Thurgau, 14% Riesling,
5% Schwarzriesling, 4% Weiß-
burgunder, 3% Bacchus
Average yield: 80 hl/ha
Best vintages: 2001, 2002, 2003
Member: VDP

Shortly after taking over the small operation from his father in the late Eighties,
Egon Schäffer produced a real explosion
of quality. This winery was one of the
very best in the region till the mid-Nineties. The wines were always straightforward and clear. However, in 1999 and
2000 we were less happy with the wines.
Then in 2001 there appeared to be an improvement, and this trend was continued
in 2002. These again were Schäffer's u-
nique products, fermented dry and traditionally matured in oak. The highlights of
the range were an excellent dry Riesling
Spätlese as well as a well-balanced Weißburgunder. The 2003 vintage provides a
seamless continuation of this. Special
mention deserve two outstanding dry
Riesling and Silvaner Spätlese wines as
well as an intense dry Silvaner Auslese.

2002 Escherndorfer Fürstenberg
Müller-Thurgau Kabinett trocken
12%, ♀ till 2006   **85**

2002 Escherndorfer Lump
Silvaner Kabinett trocken
12.5%, ♀ till 2006   **85**

2002 Escherndorfer Lump
Silvaner Spätlese trocken
13%, ♀ till 2007   **85**

2003 Escherndorfer Fürstenberg
Weißer Burgunder Spätlese trocken
11.1%, ♀ till 2009   **85**

2003 Untereisenheimer Sonnenberg
Silvaner Spätlese trocken
11.4%, ♀ till 2009   **85**

2002 Escherndorfer Lump
Riesling Kabinett trocken
13%, ♀ till 2006   **86**

2003 Escherndorfer Fürstenberg
Silvaner Spätlese trocken
11%, ♀ till 2009   **86**

2003 Escherndorfer Lump
Riesling Spätlese trocken
10.8%, ♀ till 2009   **86**

2003 Escherndorfer Lump
Silvaner Auslese trocken
12%, ♀ till 2011   **87**

2002 Escherndorfer Lump
Riesling Spätlese trocken
12.5%, ♀ till 2007   **88**

2002 Escherndorfer Fürstenberg
Weißer Burgunder Spätlese trocken
13.5%, ♀ till 2007   **88**

2003 Escherndorfer Fürstenberg
Müller-Thurgau Kabinett
10%, ♀ till 2006   **84**

The wines: **100** Perfect · **95–99** Outstanding · **90–94** Excellent · **85–89** Very good · **80–84** Good · **75–79** Average

219

WEINGUT
SCHMITT'S KINDER

Owner: Karl Martin Schmitt
Manager: Karl Martin Schmitt,
Renate Marie Schmitt
Winemaker: Martin Joh. Schmitt
97236 Randersacker, Am Sonnenstuhl
Tel. (09 31) 7 05 91 97, **Fax** 7 05 91 98
e-mail:
schmitts-kinder@randersacker.de
Internet: www.schmitts-kinder.de
Directions: A 3 Würzburg–Nürnberg,
Randersacker exit near Würzburg
Sales: Renate Marie Schmitt
Opening hours: Mon.–Fri. 08:00 to
18:00 hours, Sat. 09:00 to 17:00 hours
and by appointment
History: Winemaking in family since 1710
Worth seeing: Various exhibitions by
landscape artist Andi Schmitt

> Vineyard area: 16.8 hectares
> Annual production: 110,000 bottles
> Top sites: Randersacker
> Pfülben, Sonnenstuhl, Marsberg
> and Teufelskeller
> Soil types: Decomposed shell limestone
> Grape varieties: 29% Silvaner,
> 18% Müller-Thurgau, 14% Bacchus,
> 13% Riesling, 11% red varieties,
> 5% each of Scheurebe,
> Weißburgunder and Rieslaner
> Average yield: 62 hl/ha
> Best vintages: 1998, 2000, 2003
> Member: VDP, Trias

This is one of the thoroughly solid producers in Franken. With hard work and careful planning, Karl Schmitt has succeeded in maneuvering this family operation
with its 14 hectares of vineyard to the top.
The last few vintages have confirmed his
rank, and he has found like-minded colleagues in the "Trias" group, together
with four other winemakers in the area.
Following on from quite a good range last
year, it is particularly the sweet Spätlese
and Auslese wines of the 2003 vintage
that we liked. The highlight is the Rieslaner Auslese gold capsule.

2003 Randersackerer Teufelskeller
Riesling Spätlese trocken
13%, ♀ till 2009   **85**

2003 Randersackerer Marsberg
Silvaner Spätlese trocken
14%, ♀ till 2007   **85**

2003 Randersackerer Pfülben
Riesling Spätlese trocken
14%, ♀ till 2009   **86**

2003 Randersackerer Sonnenstuhl
Silvaner Spätlese trocken
14%, ♀ till 2008   **86**

2003 Randersackerer Pfülben
Silvaner Spätlese trocken "Großes Gewächs"
14%, ♀ till 2008   **86**

2002 Randersackerer Pfülben
Riesling Spätlese trocken
12.5%, ♀ till 2007   **87**

2003 Randersackerer Sonnenstuhl
Scheurebe Spätlese
13.5%, ♀ till 2009   **88**

2003 Randersackerer Sonnenstuhl
Riesling Spätlese
12.5%, ♀ till 2009   **88**

2003 Randersackerer Sonnenstuhl
Scheurebe Auslese
11.5%, ♀ till 2009   **88**

2003 Randersackerer Sonnenstuhl
Rieslaner Auslese
10%, ♀ till 2010   **88**

2002 Randersackerer Marsberg
Riesling Eiswein
8.5%, ♀ till 2018   **89**

2003 Randersackerer Sonnenstuhl
Rieslaner Auslese Goldkapsel "S"
9.5%, ♀ till 2011   **89**

WEINGUT
TROCKENE SCHMITTS

Owner and manager:
Paul and Bruno Schmitt
97236 Randersacker,
Flecken 1/Maingasse 14a
Tel. (09 31) 70 82 06 und 70 04 90,
Fax 70 82 22
e-mail: info@durchgegorene-weine.de
Internet: www.durchgegorene-weine.de
Directions: A 3 Frankfurt–Nürnberg,
Randersacker exit
Sales: Angela and Bruno Schmitt
Opening hours: Mon.–Fri. 08:00 to
18:00 hours, Sat. 09:00 to 16:00 hours
and by appointment
History: Family-owned since 1680

Vineyard area: 12.5 hectares
Annual production: 100,000 bottles
Top sites: Randersacker Pfülben,
Sonnenstuhl and Marsberg
Soil types: Shell limestone
Grape varieties: 30% Müller-Thurgau,
28% Silvaner, 12% Riesling, 7% red
varieties, 5% Weißburgunder, 4% Ge-
würztraminer, 14% other varieties
Average yield: 68 hl/ha
Best vintage: 2002
Member: VDP

Beginning with the 2002 vintage, the two winemaking brothers Paul and Bruno Schmitt have combined their formerly independent operations (Paul Schmitt and Robert Schmitt wineries) into an operation now known as the Trockene Schmitts winery. The philosophy is clear and simple: All the wines are fermented dry, with no chaptalisation – the pure Franken style! This involved no changes for the brothers, since both wineries had in recent years worked "strictly according to the principles of the former association of natural wine auctioneers," as Bruno Schmitt explains. The 2003 wine we liked best is the dry Rieslaner Spätlese. 95 percent of the production goes to private customers, the remainder is poured in the attached wine bar.

2003 Randersacker Marsberg
Riesling Kabinett trocken
12%, ♀ till 2006   **82**

2003 Randersacker Sonnenstuhl
Silvaner Spätlese trocken
13%, ♀ till 2007   **82**

2003 Randersacker Marsberg
Weißer Burgunder Kabinett trocken
13%, ♀ till 2006   **83**

2003 Randersacker Pfülben
Riesling Spätlese trocken
13%, ♀ till 2008   **84**

2003 Randersacker Pfülben
Weißer Burgunder Spätlese trocken
13.5%, ♀ till 2007   **84**

2002 Randersackerer Marsberg
Weißer Burgunder Kabinett trocken
12%, ♀ till 2006   **86**

2002 Randersackerer Sonnenstuhl
Rieslaner Spätlese trocken
13.5%, ♀ till 2006   **86**

2003 Randersacker Sonnenstuhl
Rieslaner Spätlese trocken
14%, ♀ till 2008   **86**

2002 Randersackerer Pfülben
Riesling Spätlese trocken
13%, ♀ till 2006   **87**

2002 Randersackerer Lämmerberg
Traminer Spätlese trocken
13%, ♀ till 2006   **88**

The wines: **100** Perfect · **95–99** Outstanding · **90–94** Excellent · **85–89** Very good · **80–84** Good · **75–79** Average

221

WEINGUT SCHWAB

Owner: Thomas Schwab
97291 Thüngersheim, Bühlstraße 17
Tel. (0 93 64) 8 91 83, Fax 8 91 84
e-mail:
info@weingut-schwab-franken.de
Internet:
www.weingut-schwab-franken.de
*Directions: B 27 Würzburg–Fulda, last
Thüngersheim exit in direction of Karlstadt*
Sales: Andrea Schwab
Opening hours: Mon.–Fri. 08:00 to 18:00
hours, Sat. and Sun. by appointment
Worth a visit: Music and cabaret in
courtyard, cheese seminars

Vineyard area: 10.5 hectares
Annual production: 80,000 bottles
Top sites: Thüngersheimer
Johannisberg and Scharlachberg
Soil types: Decomposed shell limestone
Grape varieties: 29% Müller-Thurgau,
18% Silvaner, 15% Riesling, 14%
Bacchus, 8% Dornfelder, 6% Kerner,
5% Spätburgunder, 5% other varieties
Average yield: 78 hl/ha
Best vintages: 1998, 1999, 2000
Member: VDP

Considerable investments were made following the take-over of the family business in Thüngersheim by Thomas Schwab.
In the vineyards, quality varietals have
been planted, and in the cellar stainless
steel tanks have taken the place of plastic.
The share of red wines is to be increased
in the coming years. At the same time,
Silvaner, which has a long tradition in the
region, is to be a focus, and more Pinot
Blanc is also to be planted. In the cellar,
Schwab intends to use whole-bunch pressing increasingly, and also to experiment
with barrique maturation for white wines.
In addition, Thomas Schwab's "Klein-
kunstauslese" provides a remarkable artis-
tic program to go along with the wines.
The wine we liked best of the 2003 range
is a dry Riesling Kabinett from the Scharlachberg site.

2003 Thüngersheimer Johannisberg
Müller-Thurgau Kabinett trocken
12.5%, ♀ till 2006 **83**

2003 Thüngersheimer Johannisberg
Silvaner Kabinett trocken
13%, ♀ till 2006 **83**

2002 "Blanc de Barrique"
Spätlese trocken
13.5%, ♀ till 2009 **84**

2002 Thüngersheimer
Riesling trocken
12%, ♀ till 2006 **85**

2002 Thüngersheimer Johannisberg
Riesling Kabinett trocken
12%, ♀ till 2006 **85**

2003 Thüngersheimer Scharlachberg
Riesling Kabinett trocken
12.5%, ♀ till 2006 **85**

2002 Thüngersheimer Johannisberg
Silvaner Spätlese trocken
12.5%, ♀ till 2007 **86**

2002 Thüngersheimer Johannisberg
Riesling trocken Selection
12.5%, ♀ till 2006 **86**

2001 Thüngersheimer Scharlachberg
Kerner Auslese
11%, ♀ till 2013 **87**

———— Red wines ————

2001 Thüngersheimer Johannisberg
Spätburgunder trocken
12%, ♀ till 2006 **84**

2002 Thüngersheimer Johannisberg
Spätburgunder trocken
13%, ♀ till 2008 **84**

WEINGUT "ZUR SCHWANE"

Owner: Eva Pfaff-Düker and
Ralph Düker
Winemaker: Stefan Ott and
Eva Pfaff-Düker
97332 Volkach,
Hauptstraße 12, Erlachhof 7
Tel. (0 93 81) 7 17 60, Fax 71 76 20
e-mail: weingut@schwane.de
Internet: www.schwane.de
*Directions: A 3 Würzburg–Nürnberg,
Kitzingen/Schwarzach/Volkach exit*
Sales winery: Eva Pfaff-Düker
and Ralph Düker
Opening hours: Mon.–Sat. 08:00 to
18:00 hours, Sun. by appointment
Winery restaurant: "Zur Schwane"
12:00 to 14:00 and 18:00 to 21:30 hours
Specialties: Hearty fare at lunch-time, in
the evenings high-level Franken cuisine
History: Oldest restaurant in Franken
preserved in original state
Worth seeing: Newly built winery

Vineyard area: 20 hectares
Annual production: 180,000 bottles
Top sites: Volkacher Ratsherr,
Escherndorfer Lump
Soil types: Shell limestone
Grape varieties: 34% Silvaner, 28%
Riesling, 17% Müller-Thurgau, 15%
Spätburgunder, 6% other varieties
Average yield: 64 hl/ha
Best vintages: 2001, 2002, 2003
Member: VDP

The trade-mark of this estate goes back to
the Schwan (swan) family, which built
the Schwan inn at this site on the Main
loop near Volkach. Josef Pfaff II bought
the inn in 1935, today it is part of the
chain of Romantikhotels. Eva Pfaff-
Düker and Ralph-Düker, the young owners, have in recent years decorated the
luxurious rooms in country manor-style.
There have also been some new developments in the winery, which is demonstrated in the 2003 range particularly with
the dry Spätburgunder Auslese.

2003 "Fervor Oloris"
Silvaner trocken
13%, ♀ till 2006 — **82**

2002 Volkacher Ratsherr
Silvaner Spätlese trocken
13%, ♀ till 2007 — **84**

2002 Riesling trocken
11.5%, ♀ till 2006 — **84**

2002 Volkacher Ratsherr
Riesling Spätlese trocken
13%, ♀ till 2007 — **85**

2003 "Fervor Oloris"
Riesling trocken
13%, ♀ till 2007 — **85**

2001 "Ex Vineto Oloris"
Riesling Spätlese trocken
13%, ♀ till 2007 — **86**

2002 Volkacher Ratsherr
Silvaner trocken "Großes Gewächs"
13%, ♀ till 2009 — **87**

2003 Scheurebe Spätlese
13%, ♀ till 2009 — **83**

2002 Volkacher Ratsherr
Rieslaner Auslese
11%, ♀ till 2011 — **84**

2001 Escherndorfer Lump
Rieslaner Spätlese
12%, ♀ till 2008 — **87**

——— Red wines ———

2000 "Fervor Oloris"
Spätburgunder trocken
12.5%, ♀ till 2007 — **85**

2003 Spätburgunder
Auslese trocken
15%, ♀ till 2011 — **85**

2001 "Fervor Oloris"
Spätburgunder trocken
14%, ♀ till 2006 — **87**

The wines: **100** Perfect · **95–99** Outstanding · **90–94** Excellent · **85–89** Very good · **80–84** Good · **75–79** Average

223

WINZERKELLER SOMMERACH

General manager: Eugen Preißinger and Frank Dietrich
Winemaker: Helmut Glaser, Anton Troll
97334 Sommerach, Zum Katzenkopf 1
Tel. (0 93 81) 8 06 10, Fax 45 51
e-mail:
info@winzerkeller-sommerach.de
Internet:
www.winzerkeller-sommerach.de
Directions: A 3 Würzburg–Nürnberg, Kitzingen-Schwarzach exit, in direction of Volkach, turn off after Sommerach
Sales: Frank Dietrich
Opening hours: Mon.–Fri. 08:00 to 17:30 hours
Wine bar: Sat. 09:30 to 16:00 hours and Sun. 13:00 to 18:00 hours
History: Founded 1901
Worth seeing: Old barrel cellar

Vineyard area: 170 hectares
Number of members: 225
Annual production: 1.4 mill. bottles
Top sites: Sommeracher Katzenkopf, Volkacher Ratsherr
Soil types: Shell limestone, sand, clay
Grape varieties: 29% Müller-Thurgau, 20% Silvaner, 18% Bacchus, 9% Domina, 5% Schwarzriesling, 19% other varieties
Average yield: 88 hl/ha
Best vintages: 2002, 2003

There is no lack of self-confidence at this co-operative. According to general manager Preißinger, the goal "for the near future" is no less than "to be the leaders," which he then qualifies "at least among co-operatives in Franken." This is to be achieved by demanding specified quality from the members, with checks carried out in the vineyards. The management team has already been augmented by the addition of the motivated Frank Dietrich. We tasted a homogeneous 2003 range, with no weak links, and highlighted by two dry Weißburgunder Spätlese wines.

2003 Sommeracher Katzenkopf
Silvaner Kabinett trocken
13%, ♀ till 2006 **84**

2003 Sommeracher Katzenkopf
Riesling Kabinett trocken
13.5%, ♀ till 2006 **84**

2003 Sommeracher Katzenkopf
Grauer Burgunder trocken "Conventus"
14%, ♀ till 2007 **84**

2003 Sommeracher Katzenkopf
Riesling Spätlese trocken
14%, ♀ till 2007 **85**

2003 Sommeracher Katzenkopf
Silvaner trocken "Conventus"
14%, ♀ till 2007 **85**

2003 Sommeracher Katzenkopf
Silvaner Spätlese trocken "Supremus"
14%, ♀ till 2008 **85**

2003 Sommeracher Katzenkopf
Weißer Burgunder Spätlese trocken "Supremus"
14.5%, ♀ till 2008 **85**

2003 Sommeracher Katzenkopf
Weißer Burgunder Spätlese trocken
14.5%, ♀ till 2008 **86**

2003 Sommeracher Katzenkopf
Rieslaner Auslese
11.5%, ♀ till 2011 **85**

2002 Sommeracher Gold
Gewürztraminer Spätlese
12.5%, ♀ till 2007 **86**

2002 Sommeracher Katzenkopf
Rieslaner Spätlese
12.5%, ♀ till 2007 **88**

WEINGUT SCHLOSS SOMMERHAUSEN

Owner: Martin Steinmann family
Manager and winemaker:
Martin Steinmann
Vineyard manager: Walter Blomeyer
97286 Sommerhausen,
Ochsenfurter Straße 17–19
Tel. (0 93 33) 2 60, **Fax** 14 88
e-mail: info@sommerhausen.com
Internet: www.sommerhausen.com
Directions: A 3 Würzburg–Nürnberg, Randersacker exit near Würzburg
Sales: Martin Steinmann, Günter Höhn
Opening hours: Mon.–Sat. 08:00 to 17:00 hours and by appointment
Guest house: At the château
History: Steinmann family has been making wine in Sommerhausen for 350 years
Worth seeing: Château buildings, sparkling wine cellar, built 1435

Vineyard area: 28 hectares
Annual production: 170,000 bottles
Top sites: Sommerhäuser
Steinbach and Reifenstein,
Randersacker Sonnenstuhl
Soil types: Shell limestone
Grape varieties: 25% Silvaner,
20% Riesling, 30% Pinot varieties,
25% other varieties
Average yield: 60 hl/ha
Best vintages: 2001, 2002, 2003
Member: VDP

Now that the vine grafting operation has been hived off, the management at the Schloss Sommerhausen wine estate can concentrate fully on the production of wine. Martin Steinmann, who represents the 11th generation of the family, continues to restore the old buildings, and celebrated the 350th anniversary by purchasing four hectares of the Sommerhäuser Steinbach vineyard. The last vintages brought about a noticeable improvement in the wines. We again tasted a homogeneously good range of 2003 wines, headed up by a many good dry Weißburgunder. The "First Growths" are also convincing.

2003 Eibelstadter Kapellenberg
Weißer Burgunder Spätlese trocken
14%, ♀ till 2009 — **86**

2003 Sommerhäuser Steinbach
Riesling Spätlese "Großes Gewächs"
13.5%, ♀ till 2009 — **86**

2003 Sommerhäuser Steinbach
Silvaner Spätlese "Großes Gewächs"
14.5%, ♀ till 2009 — **87**

2002 Eibelstadter Kapellenberg
Weißer Burgunder Kabinett trocken
12.5%, ♀ till 2006 — **88**

2002 Sommerhäuser Steinbach
Riesling Kabinett trocken
12%, ♀ till 2006 — **88**

2002 Sommerhäuser Steinbach
Riesling Spätlese trocken
12%, ♀ till 2007 — **88**

2002 Eibelstadter Kapellenberg
Weißer Burgunder Spätlese trocken
13.5%, ♀ till 2007 — **89**

2002 Sommerhäuser Steinbach
Riesling Spätlese trocken "Großes Gewächs"
12.5%, ♀ till 2009 — **89**

2003 Sommerhäuser Steinbach
Riesling Spätlese
13%, ♀ till 2009 — **87**

2003 Sommerhäuser Steinbach
Silvaner Trockenbeerenauslese
8.5%, ♀ till 2025 — **88**

2002 Randersackerer Sonnenstuhl
Silvaner Beerenauslese
8.5%, ♀ till 2018 — **91**

2002 Sommerhäuser Steinbach
Riesling Eiswein
7.5%, ♀ till 2020 — **92**

The wines: **100** Perfect · **95–99** Outstanding · **90–94** Excellent · **85–89** Very good · **80–84** Good · **75–79** Average

225

STAATLICHER HOFKELLER WÜRZBURG

Director: Dr. Andreas Becker
Vineyard manager: Edgar Sauer
Winemaker: Klaus Kuhn, Alexander Ley, Mathias Krönert
97070 Würzburg, Residenzplatz 3
Tel. (09 31) 3 05 09 21, Fax 3 05 09 33
e-mail: hofkeller-wuerzburg@t-online.de
Internet: www.hofkeller.de
Directions: Würzburg-Stadtmitte, in Rosenbach palace of Fürstbischöfliche Residenz
Sales: Siegbert Henkelmann
Opening hours: Mon.–Fri. 09:00 to 18:00 hours, Sat. 09:00 to 14:00 hours
Events: Bernd van Elten
Restaurant: Residenz restaurant in Würzburg, daily except Monday
Specialties: Franken regional cuisine
History: Royal court cellars since 1128
Worth seeing: Würzburg royal residence, historic barrel cellar

Vineyard area: 150 hectares
Annual production: 850,000 bottles
Top sites: Würzburger Stein and Innere Leiste, Randersacker Pfülben
Soil types: Primordial rock, striated sandstone, shell limestone, red marl, Main terrace sands, loess
Grape varieties: 22% Riesling, 19% Silvaner, 17% Müller Thurgau, 8% Spätburgunder, 6% Rieslaner, 5% each of Kerner and Bacchus, 18% other varieties
Average yield: 65 hl/ha
Best vintages: 2001, 2002, 2003
Member: VDP

Dr. Andreas Becker has constructed a new outfit for this giant operation with its long tradition (875 years), aiming at a "Mediterranean feel for Franken wine." The master of 150 hectares of vineyard wants to "make wine culture an experience with every sip, through the harmonious combination of tradition and innovation." He has achieved this particularly well in 2003 in the form of two dry Riesling Spätlese wines.

2003 Würzburger Innere Leiste
Riesling Spätlese trocken
13.5%, ♀ till 2009 — 86

2003 Randersacker Pfülben
Riesling Spätlese trocken
13%, ♀ till 2009 — 86

2002 Thüngersheimer Scharlachberg
Weißer Burgunder Spätlese trocken
13%, ♀ till 2007 — 87

2002 Würzburger Stein
Riesling Spätlese trocken
12.5%, ♀ till 2007 — 88

2002 Würzburger Innere Leiste
Riesling Spätlese trocken
12.5%, ♀ till 2007 — 88

2003 Thüngersheimer Scharlachberg
Traminer Spätlese
13%, ♀ till 2009 — 86

2003 Würzburger Stein
Rieslaner Auslese
12%, ♀ till 2011 — 86

2003 Hörsteiner Abtsberg
Riesling Auslese
12.5%, ♀ till 2011 — 86

2003 Hörsteiner Abtsberg
Riesling Trockenbeerenauslese
7%, ♀ till 2026 — 88

2001 Hörsteiner Abtsberg
Riesling Beerenauslese
10.5%, ♀ till 2018 — 89

WEINGUT AM STEIN

Owner: Ludwig Knoll
Winemaker: Ludwig Knoll and
Dr. Manfred Stoll
97080 Würzburg,
Mittlerer Steinbergweg 5
Tel. (09 31) 2 58 08, Fax 2 58 80
e-mail: mail@weingut-am-stein.de
Internet: www.weingut-am-stein.de
Directions: In Würzburg right next to the Stein vineyard, at starting point of guided vineyard trail
Sales: Sandra Knoll and Christian Lau
Opening hours: Mon.–Fri. 09:00 to 13:00 hours and 14:00 to 18:00 hours Sat. 10:00 to 14:00 hours
Restaurant and wine bar: "Weinstein" Mon.–Sat. 17:00 to 24:00 hours, closed Sun.
Worth seeing: View of the city, "New Architecture at the Stein site"
Worth a visit: Cooking courses in "Kitchen House"

Vineyard area: 20 hectares
Annual production: 150,000 bottles
Top sites: Würzburger Innere Leiste and Stein, Stettener Stein, Randersacker Sonnenstuhl
Soil types: Shell limestone
Grape varieties: 25% Silvaner, 22% Müller-Thurgau, 16% Riesling, 12% Spätburgunder, 9% Grauburgunder, 6% Weißburgunder, 10% other varieties
Average yield: 65 hl/ha
Best vintages: 2000, 2001, 2002
Member: VDP, Frank & Frei

The winery of Sandra and Ludwig Knoll is located amidst the vineyards of the famous Würzburger Stein site. It is always worth a visit to come here, whether you wish to taste the wines or to enjoy the food at the "Weinstein" restaurant and wine bar later. Ludwig Knoll follows a clear, straightforward style that has taken him into the upper echelons of wine producers in the region in recent years. The "Montonia" barrique-matured wines are very good, the range is crowned by a superb sweet 2003 Rieslaner Auslese.

2003 Würzburger Stein
Silvaner Spätlese trocken
14.5%, ♀ till 2007 **85**

2003 Escherndorfer Lump
Silvaner Spätlese trocken
13.5%, ♀ till 2008 **86**

2003 Stettener Stein
Weißer Burgunder Spätlese trocken
14%, ♀ till 2008 **86**

2002 "Montonia"
Weißer Burgunder trocken Barrique
13.5%, ♀ till 2008 **86**

2002 Würzburger Stein
Silvaner Kabinett trocken
12%, ♀ till 2006 **88**

2002 Würzburger Innere Leiste
Riesling Spätlese trocken
13.5%, ♀ till 2007 **88**

2003 Escherndorfer Lump
Riesling Spätlese
12%, ♀ till 2008 **86**

2003 Würzburger Stein
Silvaner Auslese
9%, ♀ till 2010 **87**

2003 Stettener Stein
Riesling Eiswein
7%, ♀ till 2016 **87**

2003 Stettener Stein
Rieslaner Auslese
8.5%, ♀ till 2012 **90**

——— Red wine ———

2001 "Montonia"
Spätburgunder trocken Barrique
13.5%, ♀ till 2009 **89**

Escherndorfer Lump
Riesling
2003

The wines: **100** Perfect · **95–99** Outstanding · **90–94** Excellent · **85–89** Very good · **80–84** Good · **75–79** Average

WEINGUT ARTUR STEINMANN – IM PASTORIUSHAUS

Owner: Artur Steinmann
Manager and winemaker:
Artur Steinmann
Administrator: Frank Schönig
97286 Sommerhausen, Plan 4
Tel. (0 93 33) 9 04 60, Fax 90 46 27
e-mail: artur.steinmann@t-online.de
Internet: www.pastoriushaus.de
Directions: A 7, Randersacker exit,
4 km in direction of Ochsenfurt/Ansbach
Opening hours: Mon.–Sat. 07:30 to
18:30 hours, Sun. 09:00 to 12:00 hours
History: Winery located in the house, in
which Franz Daniel Pastorius was born,
first German emigrant to North America
Worth seeing: Beautiful courtyard,
vaulted cellar, rarities in cellar

Vineyard area: 11 hectares Annual production: 100,000 bottles Top sites: Sommerhäuser Steinbach, Frickenhäuser Kapellenberg Soil types: Shell limestone, loess Grape varieties: 20% Müller-Thurgau, 17% Silvaner, 10% each of Bacchus, Scheurebe and Dornfelder, 9% Ries- ling, 5% each of Zweigelt and Schwarzriesling, 4% Spätburgunder, 10% other varieties Average yield: 80 hl/ha Best vintages: 2000, 2002 Member: Frank & Frei

Franz Daniel Pastorius, who gave the
winery and residential building its nick-
name, was the first German to emigrate
to North America in 1683, and was born
here. The winery itself was founded in
1916 by grandfather Karl. His son concentrated exclusively on wine production
from 1960 onward, and was also the local
mayor. His son Artur, born 1955, who also trained as a brewer (!), took over in
1982. He is the man with the basic idea
behind the successful "Frank & Frei" in-
itiative. His 2003 range is good, the best
wine is a dry Riesling Spätlese.

2003 Frickenhäuser Kapellenberg
Silvaner Spätlese trocken
13%, ♀ till 2009 — **84**

2003 Sommerhäuser Steinbach
Silvaner Spätlese trocken
13%, ♀ till 2009 — **84**

2003 Sommerhäuser Steinbach
Riesling Spätlese trocken
13.5%, ♀ till 2009 — **85**

2003 Sommerhäuser Ölspiel
Traminer Auslese
12%, ♀ till 2011 — **85**

2003 Sommerhäuser Steinbach
Silvaner Auslese
10.5%, ♀ till 2011 — **85**

2003 Sommerhäuser Steinbach
Riesling Eiswein
10%, ♀ till 2020 — **85**

2002 Sommerhäuser Steinbach
Riesling Spätlese
12%, ♀ till 2007 — **88**

2002 Sommerhäuser Ölspiel
Traminer Eiswein
9%, ♀ till 2018 — **88**

2002 Sommerhäuser Ölspiel
Silvaner Eiswein
10.5%, ♀ till 2018 — **88**

2002 Sommerhäuser Ölspiel
Traminer Spätlese
12.5%, ♀ till 2007 — **89**

WEINGUT STICH – "IM LÖWEN"

Owner: Gerhard Stich
Manager and winemaker:
Gerhard and Helga Stich
63927 Bürgstadt,
Freudenberger Straße 73
Tel. (0 93 71) 57 05, Fax 8 09 73
e-mail: info@weingut-stich.de
Internet: www.weingut-stich.de
Directions: A 3 Frankfurt–Würzburg, Stockstadt or Wertheim exit, in direction of Miltenberg
Sales: Gerhard and Helga Stich
Opening hours: Mon.–Fri. 08:30 to 18:30 hours, Sat. to 16:00 hours
Restaurant: For three weeks from Easter Monday, daily 12:00 to 24:00 hours
Specialties: Franken Must Soup, blood sausages, marinated goat's cheese, beef salad with pumpkin seed oil

---

Vineyard area: 7 hectares
Annual production: 50,000 bottles
Top sites: Bürgstadter Centgrafenberg, Prichsenstadter Krone
Soil types: Decomposed sandstone, shell limestone
Grape varieties: 35% Spätburgunder 20% Müller-Thurgau, 15% Silvaner, 10% Bacchus, 20% other varieties
Average yield: 65 hl/ha
Best vintages: 1999, 2001, 2002
Member: Frank & Frei

The Belle-Epoque ambience in the former "Zum Löwen" inn provides the ideal backdrop for wine tastings presented by Gerhard and Helga Stich. During the Easter period the facility is open to the public as a restaurant and wine bar. The 2002 range, which included elegant Pinot Blanc wines as well as the red wines of the 2001 vintage was fully convincing. Looking to the 2003 range, a juicy Gewürztraminer Spätlese is particularly outstanding. The Spätburgunder-Tresterbrand (Pinot Noir grappa) here can also be recommended.

2003 "Frank & Frei"
Müller-Thurgau trocken
12%, ♀ till 2006 **83**

2003 Bürgstadter Centgrafenberg
Silvaner Spätlese trocken
14.5%, ♀ till 2007 **83**

2002 Bürgstadter Centgrafenberg
Riesling Kabinett trocken
11.5%, ♀ till 2006 **86**

2002 Prichsenstadter Krone
Weißer Burgunder Spätlese trocken
12.5%, ♀ till 2007 **87**

2001 Prichsenstadter Krone
Weißer Burgunder Spätlese trocken
Barrique
12.5%, ♀ till 2007 **87**

2003 Bürgstadter Centgrafenberg
Gewürztraminer Spätlese
13%, ♀ till 2009 **86**

——— Red wines ———

2002 Bürgstadter Centgrafenberg
Spätburgunder Spätlese trocken Barrique
12.5%, ♀ till 2009 **83**

2003 "Frank & Frei"
Cuvée trocken
13%, ♀ till 2008 **84**

2001 Bürgstadter Centgrafenberg
Schwarzriesling trocken
12.5%, ♀ till 2006 **86**

2001 Bürgstadter Centgrafenberg
Spätburgunder trocken
12.5%, ♀ till 2006 **86**

2001 Bürgstadter Centgrafenberg
Spätburgunder Spätlese trocken Barrique
12.5%, ♀ till 2009 **87**

WEINGUT STÖRRLEIN

Owner: Armin Störrlein
97236 Randersacker, Schulstraße 14
Tel. (09 31) 70 82 81, Fax 70 11 55
e-mail: info@stoerrlein.de
Internet: www.stoerrlein.de
Directions: A 3 Würzburg–Nürnberg,
Randersacker exit near Würzburg
Sales: Ruth Störrlein
Opening hours: Mon.–Sat. 08:00 to
19:00 hours, Sun. by appointment
Worth a visit: Cultural-culinary events
several times a year

Vineyard area: 8.5 hectares
Annual production: 65,000 bottles
Top sites: Randersacker
Marsberg, Sonnenstuhl and Dabug
Soil types: Shell limestone
Grape varieties: 30% Silvaner,
20% Müller-Thurgau, 10% each of
Riesling and Spätburgunder,
6% Schwarzriesling, 5% Weißbur-
gunder, 19% other varieties
Average yield: 69 hl/ha
Best vintages: 1998, 2001, 2002
Member: VDP, Trias

Armin Störrlein appears convincing
when he declaims his motto: Quality is
born in the vineyard. And the vineyard,
according to him, is "not a high-perform-
ance plantation." In order to achieve a
classical varietal style, he generally ferments his white wines in stainless steel
tanks, then matures them in oak barrels,
and bottles them relatively late. This results in a slight loss of freshness, but also
produces very harmonious wines. The
wines we found most impressive in this
year's range are the two "Trias" wines, a
2003 dry Riesling Spätlese as well as an
elegant 2002 Spätburgunder (Pinot Noir).
By the way, customers ordering wines
bottled in Bocksbeutel bottles have a
choice of either traditional natural cork or
crown-cork closures. Störrlein has plans
to plant more white and red Pinot varieties, and to expand his barrel maturation
cellar in his Randersacker winery.

2003 Randersacker Sonnenstuhl
Silvaner Kabinett trocken
13%, ♀ till 2006 **84**

2003 Randersacker Sonnenstuhl
Silvaner Spätlese trocken
13.5%, ♀ till 2008 **85**

2003 Randersacker Sonnenstuhl
Weißer Burgunder Spätlese trocken
13%, ♀ till 2008 **85**

2003 Randersacker Sonnenstuhl
Weißer Burgunder Spätlese trocken
"Großes Gewächs" Trias
13%, ♀ till 2009 **87**

2002 Randersacker Sonnenstuhl
Riesling Kabinett trocken
12%, ♀ till 2006 **88**

2002 Randersacker Sonnenstuhl
Riesling Spätlese trocken
13%, ♀ till 2007 **88**

2003 Randersacker Sonnenstuhl
Riesling Spätlese trocken
"Großes Gewächs" Trias
13.5%, ♀ till 2009 **88**

2002 Randersacker Sonnenstuhl
Riesling Spätlese
12.5%, ♀ till 2007 **87**

——— Red wines ———

2002 Randersacker Domina trocken
13%, ♀ till 2008 **84**

2000 Randersacker Ewig Leben
Schwarzriesling Spätlese trocken
12.5%, ♀ till 2009 **87**

2002 Randersacker Sonnenstuhl
Spätburgunder trocken "Trias"
13%, ♀ till 2009 **87**

Weingut Störrlein
D-97236 Randersacker

FRANKEN

2001er
Randersackerer Sonnenstuhl
Silvaner · Kabinett · Trocken

Qualitätswein mit Prädikat
Gutsabfüllung
A. P. Nr. 3143 - 114 - 02
0,75 l   12 % vol

WINZERGENOSSENSCHAFT THÜNGERSHEIM

Chairman of the board: Georg Lutz
Technical manager: Norbert Gerhard
Winemaker: Reinhold Full
97291 Thüngersheim,
Untere Hauptstraße 1
Tel. (0 93 64) 5 00 90, Fax 50 09 10
e-mail: info@wg-thuengersheim.de
Internet: www.wg-thuengersheim.de
Directions: A 7/A 9, B 27
Würzburg–Karlstadt exit
Sales: Manager Christian Heßdörfer
Opening hours: Mon.–Fri. 08:00 to
18:00 hours, Sat. 09:00 to 14:00 hours
Restaurant: Altes Wasserhaus (old
water house)
History: Founded 1930
Worth seeing: Extensive barrel cellar,
beautiful view of Main valley

Vineyard area: 240 hectares
Number of members: 348
Annual production: 2.5 mill. bottles
Top sites: Thüngersheimer
Johannisberg and Scharlachberg,
Retzbacher Benediktusberg
Soil types: Shell limestone, sandstone
Grape varieties: 45% Müller-Thurgau,
20% Silvaner, 7% Scheurebe, 4%
each of Kerner, Weißburgunder and
Spätburgunder, 16% other varieties
Average yield: 76 hl/ha
Best vintages: 2001, 2002, 2003

Thüngersheim is located downriver from Würzburg, on the right side of the Main river. The largest wine-growing community in the Würzburg district is home to one of the leading co-operatives in Franken. The members have been eagerly collecting medals and trophies at Bavarian and national wine competitions for many years. They focus especially on maintaining stocks of mature wines. Their support for organic vineyard practices is remarkable, and is further strengthened by the building of the organic group "Terra Thu." The best wines of the 2003 vintage are two dry Weißburgunder wines.

2002 Thüngersheimer Johannisberg
Grauer Burgunder Spätlese trocken
12.5%, ♀ till 2007   **85**

2002 Retzbacher Benediktusberg
Riesling Spätlese trocken
11%, ♀ till 2007   **86**

2003 Thüngersheimer Johannisberg
Weißer Burgunder Spätlese trocken
13%, ♀ till 2009   **86**

2002 Thüngersheimer Johannisberg
Weißer Burgunder Spätlese trocken
Barrique
12.5%, ♀ till 2009   **87**

2003 Retzbacher Benediktusberg
Scheurebe Spätlese
12.5%, ♀ till 2009   **83**

2002 Laudenbacher Schloss
Riesling Spätlese
11.5%, ♀ till 2007   **87**

2002 Thüngersheimer Ravensburg
Bacchus Auslese
9.5%, ♀ till 2010   **87**

———— Red wines ————

2003 Thüngersheimer Ravensburg
Domina Spätlese trocken
13%, ♀ till 2009   **83**

2003 Thüngersheimer Ravensburg
Spätburgunder Spätlese trocken
13.5%, ♀ till 2008   **83**

2003 Thüngersheimer Johannisberg
Regent Spätlese trocken
13%, ♀ till 2008   **85**

2001 Thüngersheimer Ravensburg
Dornfelder trocken
13.5%, ♀ till 2006   **86**

2000
RETZBACHER
BENEDIKTUSBERG
Müller-Thurgau   Winzergenossenschaft Thüngersheim eG
trocken   D-97291 Thüngersheim
Qualitätswein

The wines: **100** Perfect · **95–99** Outstanding · **90–94** Excellent · **85–89** Very good · **80–84** Good · **75–79** Average

231

Franken

WEINGUT WOLFGANG WELTNER

Owner: Wolfgang Weltner
Winemaker: Paul Weltner
97348 Rödelsee,
Wiesenbronner Straße 17
Tel. (0 93 23) 36 46, Fax 38 46
e-mail: weingut.weltner@t-online.de
*Directions: A 3 Würzburg–Nürnberg,
Kitzingen or Schweinfurt-Wiesentheid
exit, at town limit in direction of
Schwanberg, last house on left*
Sales: Renate Weltner
Opening hours: Mon.–Sat. 08:00 to
18:00 hours, Sun. by appointment
History: Winemaking in family since
1553

Vineyard area: 6.8 hectares
Annual production: 45,000 bottles
Top sites: Rödelseer Küchen-
meister and Schwanleite,
Iphöfer Julius-Echter-Berg
Soil types: Gypsum with red marl,
clay and reed sandstone layers
Grape varieties: 42% Silvaner,
20% Müller-Thurgau, 10% Riesling,
8% Scheurebe, 6% Weißbur-
gunder, 14% other varieties
Average yield: 64 hl/ha
Best vintages: 2001, 2002, 2003
Member: VDP

Paul Weltner in Rödelsee is a shy man who took over responsibility in the cellar from his father a few years ago, and is producing a solid quality that is beginning to attract attention. His good training, which he received from the wine school at Weinsberg and from Rebholz in the Pfalz, is evident in the wines. Our favorite of the 2001 range was an extraordinary, not quite dry Riesling Spätlese from the Küchenmeister vineyard. Then in 2002 we particularly liked a dry Weißburgunder (Pinot Blanc) Spätlese from the Iphöfer Julius-Echter-Berg. And in 2003 the two "Große Gewächse" (First Growths) of Weißburgunder and Silvaner are at the top of the range.

2003 Rödelseer Küchenmeister
Silvaner Kabinett trocken
13%, ♀ till 2006 — 83

2003 Iphöfer Julius-Echter-Berg
Silvaner Spätlese trocken
13.5%, ♀ till 2007 — 84

2003 Silvaner Spätlese trocken
14%, ♀ till 2008 — 85

2003 Rödelseer Küchenmeister
Riesling Spätlese trocken
13.5%, ♀ till 2008 — 85

2002 Rödelseer Küchenmeister
Silvaner Spätlese trocken Barrique
13%, ♀ till 2008 — 85

2002 Iphöfer Julius-Echter-Berg
Silvaner Kabinett trocken
12%, ♀ till 2006 — 86

2003 Rödelseer Küchenmeister
Silvaner trocken "Großes Gewächs"
14%, ♀ till 2009 — 86

2003 Iphöfer Julius-Echter-Berg
Weißer Burgunder "Großes Gewächs"
14.5%, ♀ till 2009 — 86

2002 Iphöfer Julius-Echter-Berg
Weißer Burgunder Spätlese trocken
13%, ♀ till 2007 — 87

2002 Rödelseer Küchenmeister
Riesling Spätlese trocken
13%, ♀ till 2007 — 88

2003 Rödelseer Schwanleite
Scheurebe Spätlese
12%, ♀ till 2009 — 85

Franken

WEINGUT
HANS WIRSCHING

Owner: Dr. Heinrich Wirsching
Manager: Dr. Uwe Matheus
Administrator: Hubert Bäuerlein
Winemaker: Werner Probst
97346 Iphofen, Ludwigstraße 16
Tel. (0 93 23) 8 73 30, Fax 87 33 90
e-mail: wirsching@t-online.de
Internet: www.wirsching.de
Directions: A 3 Würzburg–Nürnberg,
Kitzingen or Wiesentheid exit
Sales: Armin Huth, Dr. Uwe Matheus
Opening hours: Mon.–Sat. 08:00 to
18:00 hours, Sun. 09:30 to 12:30 hours
History: Vineyards family-owned since
1630
Worth seeing: Old winery building and
vaulted cellar

> Vineyard area: 72 hectares
> Annual production: 490,000 bottles
> Top sites: Iphöfer Julius-Echter-
> Berg, Kalb and Kronsberg
> Soil types: Gypsum and red marl
> with layers of reed sandstone
> Grape varieties: 38% Silvaner,
> 20% Riesling, 8% each of Müller-Thur-
> gau and Weißburgunder, 7% each of
> Spätburgunder and Dornfelder,
> 5% Scheurebe, 7% other varieties
> Average yield: 58 hl/ha
> Best vintages: 2000, 2001, 2002
> Member: VDP, Deutsches
> Barrique Forum

This winery in Iphofen, one of the largest privately-owned wine estates in Germany, has invested heavily in cellar technology, and it shows in a significant improvement in the wines produced. Dr. Heinrich Wirsching, the far-sighted and likeable head of the operation, intends to be even more strictly selective at harvest time in order to further improve quality. The range here is very large, and of the top wines presented for tasting we again saw a homogeneously high standard, with the highlights being the Riesling and Silvaner wines.

2003 Iphöfer Kronsberg
Weißer Burgunder Spätlese trocken "S"
15%, ♀ till 2008 — **85**

2003 Iphöfer Julius-Echter-Berg
Grauer Burgunder Auslese trocken
16.5%, ♀ till 2009 — **86**

2003 Iphöfer Kronsberg
Scheurebe Spätlese trocken
14.5%, ♀ till 2009 — **86**

2003 Iphöfer Julius-Echter-Berg
Silvaner trocken "Großes Gewächs"
14.5%, ♀ till 2009 — **86**

2003 Iphöfer Julius-Echter-Berg
Riesling trocken "Großes Gewächs"
14%, ♀ till 2009 — **86**

2003 Iphöfer Julius-Echter-Berg
Riesling Spätlese trocken "S"
14%, ♀ till 2009 — **86**

2003 Iphöfer Julius-Echter-Berg
Silvaner Spätlese trocken "S"
14%, ♀ till 2009 — **86**

2002 Iphöfer Julius-Echter-Berg
Riesling Spätlese trocken "S"
13%, ♀ till 2007 — **88**

2002 Iphöfer Julius-Echter-Berg
Silvaner Spätlese trocken
"Großes Gewächs"
13%, ♀ till 2009 — **89**

2002 Iphöfer Julius-Echter-Berg
Riesling trocken "Großes Gewächs"
13%, ♀ till 2009 — **89**

2002 Rieslaner
Trockenbeerenauslese
9.5%, ♀ till 2023 — **91**

2002 Iphöfer Julius-Echter-Berg
Riesling Eiswein
8%, ♀ till 2018 — **92**

The wines: **100** Perfect · **95–99** Outstanding · **90–94** Excellent · **85–89** Very good · **80–84** Good · **75–79** Average

233

WEINGUT ZEHNTHOF

Owner: Luckert family
Manager: Wolfgang Luckert
Winemaker: Ulrich Luckert
97320 Sulzfeld, Kettengasse 3–5
Tel. (0 93 21) 2 37 78, Fax 50 77
e-mail: Luckert@weingut-zehnthof.de
Internet: www.weingut-zehnthof.de
Directions: A 3 Würzburg–Nürnberg,
Biebelried or Kitzingen exit
Sales: Wolfgang Luckert
Opening hours: Mon.–Sat. 08:00 to
18:00 hours
Worth seeing: Interesting cellar layout

Vineyard area: 12 hectares
Annual production: 70,000 bottles
Top sites: Sulzfelder Cyriakus-
berg and Maustal
Soil types: Shell limestone
Grape varieties: 40% Silvaner, 20%
Müller-Thurgau, 10% each of Riesling
and Weißburgunder, 5% Kerner,
15% other varieties
Average yield: 71 hl/ha
Best vintages: 2000, 2001, 2002
Member: VDP

The former tithe barn of the prince bishops was acquired by the Luckert family
in the late Seventies, and has since given
the name to this family operation. Silvaner and Müller-Thurgau are the preferred
grape varieties here, although Wolfgang
Luckert also shines with his Riesling,
Pinot Blanc and Chardonnay. He plans
to extend his involvement in red wine, he
has planted Frühburgunder and Merlot.
The red blend "Grand Noir," presented
for the first time, not only has a deep
color, but is also convincing as a balanced composition with a judicious use
of barriques. White wines are fermented
in temperature-controlled stainless steel
tanks, the wines are then mostly matured
in large oak vats. Usually the Chardonnay and Weißburgunder (Pinot Blanc) are
particularly good, but in the 2003 vintage a dry Riesling Auslese is the highlight of the range.

2003 Sulzfelder Cyriakusberg
Chardonnay Spätlese trocken
14.5%, ♀ till 2009 — **85**

2003 Sulzfelder Maustal
Silvaner Auslese trocken
15%, ♀ till 2011 — **85**

2003 Sulzfelder Cyriakusberg
Weißer Burgunder Auslese trocken
15%, ♀ till 2011 — **86**

2003 Sulzfelder Maustal
Riesling Auslese trocken
14.5%, ♀ till 2011 — **86**

2002 Sulzfelder Cyriakusberg
Riesling Spätlese trocken
12.5%, ♀ till 2007 — **87**

2002 Sulzfelder Maustal
Rieslaner Auslese trocken
14%, ♀ till 2013 — **87**

2002 Sulzfelder Cyriakusberg
Chardonnay Spätlese trocken
12.5%, ♀ till 2007 — **88**

2002 Sulzfelder Cyriakusberg
Weißer Burgunder Spätlese trocken
13%, ♀ till 2007 — **88**

2003 Sulzfelder Maustal
Rieslaner Auslese
11.5%, ♀ till 2011 — **86**

2003 Sulzfelder Cyriakusberg
Riesling Trockenbeerenauslese
11%, ♀ till 2025 — **89**

——— Red wines ———

2002 "Grand Noir" trocken
14%, ♀ till 2008 — **85**

2001 Spätburgunder trocken ***
13.5%, ♀ till 2006 — **86**

Other recommended producers

Weingut Baldauf

97729 Ramsthal, Hauptstraße 42
Tel. (0 97 04) 15 95, Fax 76 55

Gerald and Ralf Baldauf have their vineyards in the Saale valley in Franken. Here, good white wines as well as Dornfelder and Spätburgunder (Pinot Noir) are grown. The highlights of the 2003 vintage range are some remarkable botrytis dessert Scheurebe wines: Eiswein (89 points) and Trockenbeerenauslese (90).

Winzerhof Burrlein

97320 Mainstockheim, Schlossstraße 20
Tel. (0 93 21) 55 78, Fax 55 10
e-mail: mail@winzerhof-burrlein.de

At 35 hectares, this is quite a large operation, and is also one of the founder members of the federal association of organic wine producers. Following on a good range of 2002 wines, the 2003 range left much to be desired. The best of the lot is a dry Weißburgunder (Pinot Blanc) Spätlese (84 points).

Weingut Edelhof

97236 Randersacker, Herrengasse 2
Tel. (09 31) 70 96 02, Fax 70 86 71
e-mail: info@Weingut-Edelhof.de

Rüdiger and Katharina König have stylishly restored the 17th century Edelhof. The wines of the 2002 and 2003 vintages are of good quality. The highlights are a dry Traminer Spätlese (85 points) and two exceptionally clean red wines (85 and 86) from the "Ewig Leben" vineyard.

Bocksbeutelhof – Winzergenossenschaft Escherndorf

97332 Escherndorf, Astheimer Straße 6
Tel. (0 93 81) 80 33 10, Fax 80 33 11
e-mail: info@bocksbeutel-hof.de

In 1997, nine wine-growers in Escherndorf split off from the regional co-operative. By now, they have 30 hectares of vineyards. We tasted quite good wines of the 2002 vintage, and even better of 2003. The best are the dry Riesling and Silvaner from the Lump vineyard (84 to 86 points).

Weingut Schloss Frankenberg

97215 Weigenheim, Schloss Frankenberg
Tel. (0 93 39) 9 71 40, Fax 97 14 17
e-mail: buerofrankenberg@aol.com

The Schloss Frankenberg castle at the foot of the southern Steigerwald mountains was built in the 13th century. Today Baron Carl Lerchenfeld runs the operation with considerable passion. In terms of wine-making, he works closely with the domaine office in Castell. In 2003, the best wines were the Silvaner (83 points) and Riesling (81) Spätlese wines.

Weingut Freihof

97334 Sommerach, Maintorstraße 4
Tel. (0 93 81) 67 91, Fax 60 80
e-mail: info@weingut-freihof.de

At this freehold farm dating to the 14th century, Hubert and Manuela Kram have decided to focus on producing good quality wines. Their fresh 2003 Silvaner, Riesling and Pinot Blanc wines from the Sommerach and Nordheim sites have convinced us. But our favorite is the Katzenkopf Traminer Spätlese (85 points).

Weingut Clemens Fröhlich

97332 Volkach-Escherndorf,
Bocksbeutelstraße 19
Tel. (0 93 81) 17 76, Fax 61 63
e-mail: info@weingut-froehlich.de

Clemens Fröhlich and his wife Ingrid have 4.5 hectares of vineyard in Escherndorf, most of it on steep slopes. The 2003 range is quite attractive. A phalanx of dry Spätlese wines from the Fürstenberg and Lump sites is rated up to 85 points.

Weingut Giegerich

63868 Großwallstadt, Weichgasse 19
Tel. (0 60 22) 65 53 55, Fax 65 53 66
e-mail: info@weingut-giegerich.de

The winery run by Klaus and Helga Giegerich is located on six hectares of multi-colored sandstone soils in the area between the Spessart and Odenwald forests. The highlights of the 2003 range are a Rücker Schalk Silvaner Spätlese (85 points) and a Großwallstadter Lützelta-lerberg Spätburgunder (Pinot Noir, 84).

Franken

Weingut Martin Göbel

97236 Randersacker, Friedhofstraße 9
Tel. (09 31) 70 93 80, Fax 4 67 77 21
e-mail: info@weingut-martin-goebel.de

This winery in the town centre of Randersacker has a long tradition going back more than 400 years. Following on some problems in the 2000 and 2001 vintages, there was a slight improvement in 2002. This time round, we tasted a homogeneous range of mainly 2003 vintage wines, headed up by a 2002 Frühburgunder Spätlese trocken (85 points).

Weingut Hans-Jürgen Hart

Thüngersheim, Veitshöchheimer Str. 24
Tel. (0 93 64) 96 37, Fax 65 44

Hans-Jürgen Hart plants a wide variety of vines on a total of seven hectares in Thüngersheim and Retzbach. The best wines of the extremely ripe 2003 vintage are the botrytis dessert wines of Huxelrebe and Gewürztraminer. The Bacchus in liter bottles (83 points) is also well made.

Weingut Höfling

97776 Eußenheim, Kellereigasse 14
Tel. (0 93 53) 76 32, Fax 12 64
e-mail: weingut-hoefling@t-online.de

The wine-producing village of Eußenheim is located north of Würzburg in a side valley of the Main river. The Höfling winery creates a positive impression again with the 2003 vintage, presenting solid wines that represent good value for money. The highlights are two botrytis dessert Kerner wines (Auslese and Beerenauslese, 86 and 87 points).

Weingut A. F. Kreglinger

97340 Segnitz, Rathausstraße 2
Tel. (0 93 32) 14 22, Fax 48 45
e-mail: weingut.kreglinger@t-online.de

Müller-Thurgau, Silvaner and Bacchus are the dominant varieties on this ten-hectare estate. Last year, we tasted good 2002 white wines and 2001 red wines. The best of the 2003 range is a Gewürztraminer Spätlese from the Segnitzer Pfaffensteig site (87 points). However, the 2002 red wines are not nearly as good.

Weingut Wolfgang Kühn

63913 Klingenberg, Ludwigstraße 29
Tel. (0 93 72) 31 69, Fax 1 23 65

Wolfgang Kühn initially studied food technology at the Weihenstephan institute. Then, in the Eighties, he took over a small winery in his home town, and has specialized in red wine. The best wine this year is a solid 2003 Klingenberger Schlossberg Frühburgunder Auslese trocken (84 points).

Weingut Ewald Neder

97729 Ramsthal, Urbanusweg 5
Tel. (0 97 04) 56 92, Fax 74 69

Ramsthal is located in the valley of the Saale river in Franken. Ewald Neder is one of the few brave souls to make wine in this area. The best wines in the range this year were two dry Kerner Spätlese wines, one of 2003, the other a barrique-matured version from 2002. Both are from the St. Klausen site, and rated 85 points.

Weingut Bruno Reiss

97080 Würzburg, Unterdürrbacher Str. 182
Tel. (09 31) 9 46 00, Fax 96 04 08
e-mail: info@weingut-reiss.com

All the wines we tasted from the 2003 vintage here, sourced from the best Würzburg sites and from the Thüngersheimer Scharlachberg, were of good quality. The best of dry wines are a Scharlachberg Riesling Spätlese and a Würzburger Pfaffenberg Weißburgunder (Pinot Blanc) Auslese (both rated 86 points).

Weingut Markus Schneider

97332 Volkach, Mittlere Zwingergasse 16
Tel. (0 93 81) 46 76, Fax 45 85
e-mail: schneidervolkach@aol.com

Markus Schneider is the third generation to run the family winery in Volkach, which has 6.5 hectares of vineyard. Before taking the reins, he gained experience in other wineries, including that of top producer Horst Sauer. The highlights of the 2003 range of wines are a dry Kerner Spätlese and a dry Riesling Spätlese, both from the Volkacher Ratsherr site, and both rated 85 points.

Weingut Graf von Schönborn – Schloss Hallburg

97332 Volkach
Tel. (0 93 81) 24 15, Fax 37 80
e-mail: schlosshallburg@schoenborn.de

Estate manager Georg Hühnerkopf is in charge here, producing expressive wines, particularly from the Hallburger Schlossberg, which is a monopole vineyard. The wine we liked best was the 2003 dry Silvaner Spätlese (84 points).

Winzerhof Stahl

97215 Auernhofen, Lange Dorfstraße 21
Tel. (0 98 48) 9 68 96, Fax 9 68 98
e-mail: mail@vinzerhof-stahl.de

The Frankonian part of the Tauber valley is almost unknown, occasionally producing elegant, racy white wines, such as those made at the Stahl winery. We particularly liked the "Tauber-Edition" blend as well as a barrique-matured Domina red wine. We can also recommend a Pinot Meunier sparkling wine as well as plum and yellow plum distillates.

Weingut Otmar Zang

97334 Sommerach, Zum Katzenkopf 2
Tel. (0 93 81) 92 78, Fax 92 80
e-mail: info@weingut-zang.de
Internet: www.weingut-zang.de

Otmar and Adelheid Zang are in charge of this ambitious winery, located in an attractive complex in Sommerach. We were enthusiastic about the 2003 dry Silvaner Spätlese (86 points). The 2003 dry Spätburgunder (Pinot Noir) proves that they are also capable of making good red wines (85).

Weingut Weinkellerei Zehntkeller

97346 Iphofen, Bahnhofstraße 12
Tel. (0 93 23) 84 40, Fax 84 41 23
e-mail: zehntkeller@romantikhotels.com

The winery is attached to an attractive Romantik hotel, and has yet again produced a harmonious range of white wines from the 2003 vintage. However, the best wines in our opinion were two red wines, a Spätburgunder (Pinot Noir) and a Dornfelder, both from the 2002 vintage.

Other wineries tasted

- Poth, Röttingen
- Engelhardt, Röttingen
- Werner Emmerich, Iphofen
- Hans Bunzelt, Nordheim

Recommended by our wine producers

Hotels and inns

Bürgstadt: Adler, Weinhaus Stern
Dettelbach: Grüner Baum
Frickenhausen: Meintzinger
Geiselwind: Landhotel Krone
Iphofen: Zehntkeller
Kreuzwertheim: Herrnwiesen
Bad Mergentheim: Victoria
Ochsenfurt: Bären
Rödelsee: Tante Paula
Sommerach: Villa Sommerach
Sommerhausen: Steinmann-Pastoriushaus
Sulzfeld: Stern
Volkach: Schwane
Wertheim: Bestenheider Stuben
Würzburg: Stadt Mainz

Gourmet restaurants

Klingenberg: Zum Alten Rentamt
Bad Mergentheim: Zirbelstube im Hotel Victoria
Sommerhausen: Philipp

Restaurants, wine bars und winery facilities

Bürgstadt: Weinhaus Stern
Castell: Weinstall
Dettelbach: Himmelstoß
Iphofen: Iphöfer Kammer
Laudenbach: Goldner Engel
Mainbernheim: Falken
Marktbreit: Alter Esel
Nordheim: Weinstube Christ
Volkach: Schwane
Würzburg: Backöfele, Bürgerspital, Nikolaushof, Schiffbäuerin, Stachel, Weinstein

Hessische Bergstraße

Front runners get company

...area of Hessische Bergstraße ...ield of only 65 hl/ha in 2003, ...below the national average, while the percentage of predicate wines recorded was over 90, the highest figure in Germany. In spite of this, most of the wines presented were not particularly convincing. While the top botrytis dessert wines were among the finest we have ever tasted in this region, the dry wines were lacking in character. Many of the wines have alcoholic weight without freshness or acidity to balance them.

The state domaine continues to set the standard for the Hessische Bergstraße. Volker Hörr's work is exemplary and meticulous, yet, apart from an outstanding Trockenbeerenauslese even his range of wines did not quite come up to the standard of previous vintages. The second rank of producers is made up of the Simon-Bürkle estate as well as the winery of the town of Bensheim, whose wine-

maker Volker Dingeldey also spends some of his time working in his own winery, which also produces decent quality. Most of the many small vineyard parcels are worked by part-time producers, who deliver their grapes to the local co-operative for marketing.

While older growers are giving up some of the steepest slopes, which are extremely difficult to cultivate, it is encouraging to see some up-and-coming young producers, such as Hanno Rothweiler, jumping into the breach here.

Fortunately, new ambitious producers are making themselves known, such as the Heinrich Freiberger estate in Heppenheim, Mohr in Bensheim and Seitz in Auerbach. Even the Odenwälder Winzergenossenschaft, the co-operative in Groß-Umstadt, appears to be on an upward trend.

For nearly two decades the Hessische Bergstraße was the smallest wine-grow-

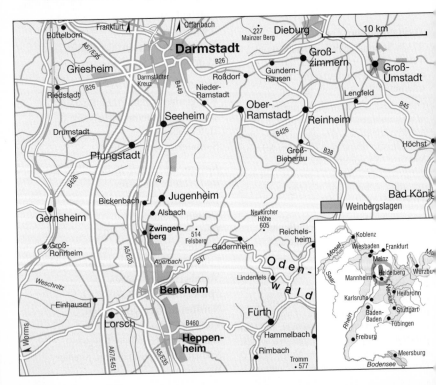

ing area in Germany, until re-unification added the Sachsen and Saale-Unstrut areas to the total. The region, which lies between Darmstadt and Heppenheim, and covers only 450 hectares, was only established in 1971, following on the insistence by authorities in the federal state of Baden that the Bergstraße vineyards on their side of the border should be incorporated in Baden. The Rheingau showed no interest in claiming the other portion of this region, so a separate region was established.

The region to the east of the Rhine, between Heidelberg and Darmstadt has always been particularly favoured by the sun. When other areas are still in the grip of late winter frost, the first almond blossoms can be seen here, on the western foothills of the Odenwald forest. In the words of Emperor Joseph II, "this is where Germany becomes more like Italy!". It thus comes as no surprise that the most demanding white grape variety, the slow-ripening Riesling, covers more than half the vineyard area on the Hessische Bergstraße. This is followed by Müller-Thurgau. Both producers and consumers showing an increasing interests in Pinot Blanc and Pinot Gris (Weißburgunder, Grauburgunder). In fact, these varieties often fare even better than Riesling on the lower slopes with their deep loess soils. Red wines are also on the increase.

The producers of the Hessische Bergstraße have no problem selling their wines. Much of the production is consumed in the nearby urban areas of Mannheim and Heidelberg, but the lion's share of each vintage is drunk at home, in the region. There are many tourists and visitors to the Hessische Bergstraße, which is also a popular destination for weekend trips within easy reach of the Rhein-Main area, particularly so during the wine festivals held in the medieval town of Heppenheim (late June) and in Bensheim (early September). Very few people, however, are familiar with the "Odenwälder Weininsel" (wine island), an area of only 50 hectares in the north-east, near Groß-Umstadt, which is also part of this winegrowing region.

239

BERGSTRÄSSER WINZER EG

General manager: Otto Guthier
Winemaker: Hans-Jürgen Weber,
Gerhard Weiß
64646 Heppenheim, Darmstädter Str. 56
Tel. (0 62 52) 79 94 11, Fax 79 94 50
e-mail:
Bergstraesser-Winzer@t-online.de
Directions: A 5 Heppenheim exit, direction of city center, turn left direction of Darmstadt, on the left after 2 kilometers
Opening hours: Mon.–Fri. 08:00 to 19:00 hours, Sat. 08:30 to 16:00 hours Sun. 10:00 to 15:00 hours
Restaurant and wine bar: Winzerkeller

Vineyard area: 265 hectares
Number of members: 500
Annual production: 1.8 mill. bottles
Top sites: Heppenheimer
Stemmler and Steinkopf,
Bensheimer Kalkgasse
Soil types: Loess-clay, granite and
decomposed sandstone
Grape varieties: 53% Riesling,
10% Spätburgunder, 9% Müller-
Thurgau, 28% other varieties
Average yield: 78 hl/ha
Best vintages: 1999, 2002, 2003

Approximately 500 members of this co-operative work significantly more than half the total area of 450 hectares available in this region. We generally see only a small section of the almost two million bottles produced here. In the previous vintage, the co-operative farmers of the Bergstraße had already shown that they intended to raise their sights, as evident, for instance, in the Classic and Selection wines. The range of 2003 vintage wines has continued this development of quality. The Riesling is the most important variety here, but for the first time the winery has also presented a few attractive red wines. A solid, reliable producer that can only enhance the reputation of co-operative wineries. Our congratulations on their 100th anniversary.

2003 Riesling Classic
11.5%, ♀ till 2006 **83**

2003 Heppenheimer Stemmler
Riesling Spätlese trocken "Starkenberg"
12.5%, ♀ till 2007 **84**

2003 Heppenheimer Stemmler
Riesling Spätlese trocken
"Jubiläumswein"
12.5%, ♀ till 2007 **85**

2003 Heppenheimer Maiberg
Riesling Selection
12.5%, ♀ till 2008 **86**

2003 Heppenheimer Schlossberg
Gewürztraminer Spätlese
8.5%, ♀ till 2007 **86**

2002 Heppenheimer Maiberg
Riesling Eiswein
6.5%, ♀ till 2015 **89**

2003 Heppenheimer Maiberg
Riesling Eiswein
6.5%, ♀ till 2015 **89**

2003 Heppenheimer Maiberg
Riesling Trockenbeerenauslese
6%, ♀ till 2025 **91**

——— Red wines ———

2003 Spätburgunder Classic
13.5%, ♀ till 2006 **83**

2003 Auerbacher Höllberg
Spätburgunder trocken
13%, ♀ till 2007 **84**

2003 St. Laurent trocken
13.5%, ♀ till 2006 **85**

2002 Laudenbacher Sonnberg
Spätburgunder Spätlese trocken Barrique
13%, ♀ till 2007 **85**

WEINGUT ROTHWEILER

Owner and manager: Hanno Rothweiler
64625 Bensheim, Ludwigstraße 55
Tel. (0 62 51) 7 65 69, **Fax** 7 65 69
e-mail: mail@weingut-rothweiler.de
Internet: www.weingut-rothweiler.de
*Directions: From South: A 5, Bensheim
exit, continue through Bensheim, in suburb of Auerbach, parallel to B 3;
from North: A 5, Zwingenberg exit, to
Auerbach*
Sales: Hanno Rothweiler
Opening hours: Mon.–Fri. 17:00 to
19:00 hours, Sat. 10:00 to 13:00 hours
and by appointment

Vineyard area: 3.5 hectares
Annual production: 35,000 bottles
Top sites: Auerbacher Fürsten-
lager, Zwingenberger Steingeröll
Soil types: Decomposed granite,
deep loess-clay
Grape varieties: 47% Riesling,
12% Grauburgunder, 10% St. Laurent,
8% each of Silvaner and Regent,
4% Chardonnay, 11% other varieties
Average yield: 67 hl/ha
Best vintages: 2001, 2002

Hanno Rothweiler was born in 1960, and
completed his studies at the viticultural
college in Oppenheim with a master's diploma. Until 1994 he was responsible as
vineyard manager for the Bensheim city
wine estate. He started producing his own
wines, initially as a side-line, in 1983,
then had the courage to go into business
on his own in the mid-Nineties. Most of
his vineyards are in particularly steep
sites that have been abandoned by other,
older producers. In the 2002 vintage he
switched over completely to synthetic
closures, which goes well with the modern label, showing the name Rothweiler
upside down. Here too, the Gewürztraminer coped well with the hot conditions in
2003 – and the red wines, too, show good
potential. No surprise then that ex-presi-
dent Johannes Rau ordered the Sankt
Laurent to be served at a state reception.

2003 Bensheimer Wo
Riesling trock
12.5%, ♀ till 2006

2003 Auerbacher Für
Riesling Kabinett t
12%, ♀ till 2006   82

2003 Auerbacher Fürstenlager
Riesling Spätlese halbtrocken
12%, ♀ till 2007   84

2003 Auerbacher Fürstenlager
Gewürztraminer
11.5%, ♀ till 2008   84

—— Red wines ——

2003 Alsbacher Schöntal
St. Laurent trocken
13%, ♀ till 2007   83

2002 Auerbacher Fürstenlager
Dornfelder trocken
13%, ♀ till 2007   84

2002 Auerbacher Fürstenlager
St. Laurent trocken Barrique
13%, ♀ till 2007   84

2003 Auerbacher Fürstenlager
trocken "Dakapo"
12.5%, ♀ till 2007   84

2003 Auerbacher Fürstenlager
St. Laurent trocken
13%, ♀ till 2008   86

*hessische
bergstraße*
qualitätswein b.a.

*auerbacher
fürstenlager
dakapo*

2003

erzeugerabfüllung weingut rothweiler
d-64625 bensheim - auerbach

a.p.nr. 5001600404

0,75 l   12,5%vol

WeinGut!
Rothweiler

The wines: **100** Perfect · **95–99** Outstanding · **90–94** Excellent · **85–89** Very good · **80–84** Good · **75–79** Average

WEINGUT SIMON-BÜRKLE

Owner: Dagmar Simon and
Wilfried Bürkle
Winemaker: Lisa Edling
64673 Zwingenberg,
Wiesenpromenade 13
Tel. (0 62 51) 7 64 46, Fax 78 86 41
e-mail: info@simon-buerkle.de
Internet: www.simon-buerkle.de
*Directions: A 5 Walldorf–Frankfurt,
Zwingenberg exit*
Sales: Dagmar Simon, Carmen Bauer
Opening hours: Mon.–Fri. 09:00 to
12:00 hours and 15:00 to 18:00 hours
Sat. 09:00 to 13:00 hours
Restaurant: "Piano" in historical town
center of Zwingenberg, Am Obertor 6,
daily 18:00 to 1:00 hours, Sun. and pub-
lic holidays 12:00 to 1:00 hours
Specialties: Regional cuisine

Vineyard area: 12 hectares
Annual production: 80,000 bottles
Top sites: Zwingenberger Alte
Burg and Steingeröll, Auerbacher
Fürstenlager and Höllberg
Soil types: Deep loess-clay on
decomposed granite
Grape varieties: 42% Riesling, 21%
Pinot varieties, 16% red varieties,
21% other varieties
Average yield: 65 hl/ha
Best vintages: 2000, 2001, 2003

Following completion of their studies at
the college in Weinsberg, Kurt Simon
and Wilfried Bürkle established this winery in Zwingenberg in 1991. Since then
the vineyard area has been expanded, a
restaurant and wine bar has been opened,
and a federal honors award has come
their way too. Since the death of Kurt
Simon in the spring of 2003, his widow
Dagmar continues to run the winery together with Wilfried Bürkle. 2003 is certainly the best vintage we have tasted
here in a long time. The Pinot varieties
are hearty and refreshing, and the whole
range is crowned by an excellent
Trockenbeerenauslese.

2003 Zwingenberger Steingeröll
Silvaner Kabinett trocken
12.5%, ♀ till 2006 — 81

2003 Riesling trocken
12.5%, ♀ till 2006 — 82

2003 Auerbacher Höllberg
Weißer Burgunder Spätlese trocken
12.5%, ♀ till 2006 — 83

2003 Auerbacher Höllberg
Chardonnay Spätlese trocken
14.5%, ♀ till 2006 — 83

2003 Zwingenberger Steingeröll
Riesling Spätlese trocken
12.5%, ♀ till 2007 — 84

2003 Auerbacher Höllberg
Grauer Burgunder Auslese trocken
14.5%, ♀ till 2008 — 86

2003 Zwingenberger Steingeröll
Riesling Trockenbeerenauslese
8.5%, ♀ till 2018 — 92

——— Red wines ———

2003 Auerbacher Höllberg
St. Laurent trocken
12%, ♀ till 2007 — 83

2001 Auerbacher Höllberg
Cabernet Sauvignon trocken
13%, ♀ till 2007 — 85

2003 Zwingenberger Alte Burg
Spätburgunder Auslese trocken
14%, ♀ till 2010 — 87

HESS. STAATSWEINGÜTER DOMAINE BERGSTRASSE

Owner: Federal state of Hessen
Manager: Volker Hörr
Administrator: Markus Volk
Winemaker: Thomas Löffler
64625 Bensheim, Grieselstraße 34–36
Tel. (0 62 51) 31 07, Fax 6 57 06
e-mail:
bergstrasse@staatsweingueterhessen.de
Directions: A 5, Bensheim exit, in direction of Lindenfels, turn right at church into plane-tree avenue
Sales: Volker Hörr, Ms. Stanzel
Opening hours: Mon.–Thur. 07:30 to 12:00 hours and 13:30 to 17:00 hours, Fri. to 18:00 hours, Sat. 09:00 to 12:00 hours
History: Founded in 1904 by Grand Duke von Hessen und bei Rhein
Worth seeing: Cross-vaulted cellar, vinotheque in barrel-vault cellar
Worth a visit: Wine auction in fall

Vineyard area: 38 hectares
Annual production: 240,000 bottles
Top sites: Heppenheimer Centgericht (monopole) and Steinkopf, Schönberger Herrnwingert (monopole), Bensheimer Kalkgasse
Soil types: Loess-clay, sandstone, gravel and decomposed granite
Grape varieties: 65% Riesling, 11% Weißburgunder, 9% Grauburgunder, 6% Spätburgunder, 9% other varieties
Average yield: 57 hl/ha
Best vintages: 1999, 2001, 2003
Member: VDP

When Hörr presented his first range of wines, from the 2001 vintage, it was evident that he knew how to follow in the footsteps of his predecessor. In the 2002 vintage, however, his top botrytis dessert wines did not live up to the standard set in the preceding vintages. Now, Hörr has made up for some lost ground in 2003 by producing a Trockenbeerenauslese that will go down in the annals of this estate. The new wine tasting room is located directly next to the manor-house.

2003 Heppenheimer Cen
Riesling Kabinett troc
12.5%, ♀ till 2006

2003 Heppenheimer St
Chardonnay Spätlese trocken
↗ auction wine, 13.5%, ♀ till 2006 · **83**

2003 Bensheimer Kalkgasse
Riesling Kabinett trocken
11.5%, ♀ till 2006 · **84**

2003 Heppenheimer Steinkopf
Riesling Spätlese trocken
13.5%, ♀ till 2007 · **86**

2003 Heppenheimer Centgericht
Ruländer Auslese
8.5%, ♀ till 2010 · **86**

2003 Schönberger Herrnwingert
Weißer Burgunder Auslese
9%, ♀ till 2012 · **88**

2003 Heppenheimer Centgericht
Riesling Eiswein
8%, ♀ till 2018 · **89**

2003 Bensheimer Kalkgasse
Riesling Beerenauslese
11.5%, ♀ till 2017 · **90**

2003 Heppenheimer Centgericht
Riesling Trockenbeerenauslese
7.5%, ♀ till 2035 · **94**

The wines: **100** Perfect · **95–99** Outstanding · **90–94** Excellent · **85–89** Very good · **80–84** Good · **75–79** Average

WEINGUT DER STADT BENSHEIM

Owner: City of Bensheim
Lessee: Axel Seiberth
Manager: Axel Seiberth
Administrator: Volker Dingeldey
64625 Bensheim, Darmstädter Str. 6
Tel. (0 62 51) 58 00 17, Fax 6 49 70
e-mail:
mail@weingut-der-stadt-bensheim.de
Internet:
www.weingut-der-stadt-bensheim.de
Directions: Located on the B 3
Sales: Axel Seiberth and Tanja Erdmann
Opening hours: Mon.–Fri. 08:00 to
12:00 hours and 13:00 to 16:30 hours
Sat. 10:00 to 12:00 hours
Restaurant: Kirchberghäuschen right in
the middle of the vineyards
Tue.–Sun. 11:00 to 21:00 hours

Vineyard area: 13 hectares
Annual production: 100,000 bottles
Top sites: Bensheimer Kalkgasse and
Kirchberg, Auerbacher Fürstenlager
Soil types: Decomposed limestone
rock, clay, loess
Grape varieties: 60% Riesling,
14% Rotberger, 20% Grau-, Weiß-
and Spätburgunder, Chardonnay and
Regent, 6% Dornfelder
Average yield: 71 hl/ha
Best vintages: 1999, 2001, 2003

The city of Bensheim employed its own
wine cooper as early as 1504. The jewel
of vineyards owned by the city winery is
the well-known Kalkgasse site. Yields
are seldom high here, which is reflected
in the concentration of the wines. A positive aspect noted in recent years is that of
this estate, which is now leased by Axel
Seiberth, even the more basic quality
wines are always reliably good. Following
on from the good work we saw here in
2001, however, the young wines of the
2002 vintages were not quite up to standard. In 2003, the medium-quality wines
have improved, but the highlights are not
sparkling as brightly as they used to be.

2003 Bensheimer Kalkgasse
Weißer Burgunder trocken
12%, ♀ till 2006   80

2003 Auerbacher Fürstenlager
Riesling trocken
12%, ♀ till 2006   82

2003 Bensheimer Kalkgasse
Grauer Burgunder trocken
12.5%, ♀ till 2006   82

2002 Bensheimer Kalkgasse
Riesling Kabinett trocken
12%, ♀ till 2006   83

2003 Bensheimer Kalkgasse
Riesling Kabinett trocken
12%, ♀ till 2007   84

2003 Bensheimer Kirchberg
Riesling Spätlese trocken
12%, ♀ till 2007   85

2003 Bensheimer Kirchberg
Riesling Kabinett halbtrocken
11%, ♀ till 2007   83

2003 Bensheimer Kirchberg
Riesling Kabinett
9.5%, ♀ till 2007   84

2003 Bensheimer Kalkgasse
Riesling Spätlese
9%, ♀ till 2008   85

2001 Bensheimer Kalkgasse
Riesling Spätlese
9%, ♀ till 2006   86

2002 Bensheimer Kalkgasse
Riesling Auslese
12%, ♀ till 2008   87

2003 Bensheimer Kalkgasse
Riesling Auslese
12%, ♀ till 2009   87

HESSISCHE BERGSTRASSE

2003
BENSHEIMER KIRCHBERG
Riesling Spätlese
trocken
Qualitätswein mit Prädikat
Amtliche Prüfnummer
50 012 005 04
12%vol   ERZEUGERABFÜLLUNG
WEINGUT DER STADT BENSHEIM
D-64625 BENSHEIM   75 cl

The estates: ♛♛♛♛♛ World's finest · ♛♛♛♛ Germany's best · ♛♛♛ Very good · ♛♛ Good · ♛ Reliable

Other recommended producers

Weingut Brücke-Ohl

64823 Groß-Umstadt,
Georg-August-Zinn-Straße 23
Tel. (0 60 78) 7 43 74, Fax 7 48 80

We first came across the wines of this winery in the Northern section of the Bergstraße with the 2001 vintage. Since then, quality has improved each year. The highlight of the range of 2003 vintage wines is a juicy Gewürztraminer from the Groß-Umstadter Steingerück site. If the trend continues, we will soon have more to report on this winery.

Weingut Volker Dingeldey

64625 Bensheim-Gronau, Hintergasse 28
Tel. (0 62 51) 3 98 16, Fax 78 06 78
e-mail:
weingutvolkerdingeldey@t-online.de

Volker Dingeldey has a day job as wine-maker at the Stadt Bensheim estate. In addition, he produces attractive wines at his own estate. The wines in liter bottles provide good value for money, and even the Dornfelder here is quite an attractive wine.

Other wineries tasted

- Edling, Groß-Umstadt
- Heinrich Freiberger, Heppenheim
- Mohr, Bensheim
- Odenwälder Winzergenossenschaft, Groß-Umstadt
- Tobias Georg Seitz, Bensheim-Auerbach

Recommended by our wine producers

Hotels and inns

Bensheim: Alleehotel Europa
Bensheim-Auerbach: Poststuben
Birkenau: Drei Birken
Heppenheim: Mercure, Goldener Engel
Zwingenberg: Zur Bergstraße

Restaurants and wine bars

Bensheim: Walderdorffer Hof, Hahnmühle
Bensheim-Auerbach: Blauer Aff – Weinstube Scherer
Birkenau: Drei Birken
Fischbachtal: Landhaus Baur
Heppenheim: Bistro Filou, Winzerkeller
Lampertheim: Geos Stube im Waldschlöss'l
Mannheim: Doblers l'Epi d'Or, da Gianni, Grissini, Kopenhagen
Reichelsheim: Treusch im Schwanen
Schriesheim: Strahlenberger Hof, Goldener Hirsch
Weinheim-Lützelsachsen: Winzerstube
Zwingenberg: Weinstube Piano

Major and minor vintages on the Hessische Bergstraße

Vintage	Rating
2003	♉♉
2002	♉♉
2001	♉♉♉
2000	♉♉
1999	♉♉♉
1998	♉♉♉
1997	♉♉♉
1996	♉♉♉♉
1995	♉♉♉
1994	♉♉♉

Vintage rating:

♉♉♉♉♉ : Excellent vintage

♉♉♉♉ : Very good vintage

♉♉♉ : Good vintage

♉♉ : Average vintage

♉ : Poor vintage

"Starvation islands" and thirsty vines

The term "starvation islands" dates back to the time when ships were towed by ferrymen with ropes through the narrow Mittelrhein valley. When the water level was low, stony islands appeared in the river, and shipping had to be stopped. As a result, the ferrymen had no work, and suffered hunger or even starvation.

In 2003, the level of the Rhine was the lowest ever recorded. However, there are no more ferrymen, and nobody has to go hungry anymore. But the vines on the slopes on both sides of the river were extremely thirsty, as there was not enough water in the vineyards. The vintage of the century? Most certainly an unusual and extreme vintage, such as only occurs perhaps once in a century. But does this necessarily mean outstanding quality? It is by now abundantly clear that the 2003 vintage was too hot and too dry for many vineyards. Wine producers faced enormous challenges, both in the vineyard and in the cellar. What everybody experienced were record must weights. Jochen Ratzenberger: "We did not harvest any grapes at below 90 degrees Oechsle." Jörg Lanius: "We bottled our 90-degree-Oechsle wines in liter bottles."

In other words, a vintage that only starts at the Spätlese or Auslese quality levels – and still has its problems. Too often, the wines are out of balance – too rich and opulent, too alcoholic, with too little acidity and elegance. To help cope with the conditions, producers were for the first time allowed to add acidity, as is common in southern Europe. Many of the top producers made little or no use of this option. And the surprising result: Most of the wines to which no acid has been added appear more natural and more balanced – exceptions prove the rule. It remains to be seen how the wines will present themselves in two or three years time.

The dry wines are rich and full-bodied – probably quite acceptable with food, but with little to entice one to enjoy a second or third glass. They simply lack the fresh, fruity and lively style that was so characteristic of the 2002 vintage.

In the 2003 vintage, there is no outstanding overall range of a particular producer, there is light and shade everywhere. In other words, the wine lover must look carefully to see, which wine at which winery is particularly good. It is noticeable that many wineries, previously dedicated to Riesling, now also have one or two red wines in their range, and some have considerably expanded the vineyard area planted to red varieties, for example Walter Perll and Goswin Lambrich. In our opinion, red wine can in no way be the savior for the Mittelrhein region, although it may make sense in some individual cases to provide a wider choice to one's loyal customers.

There have been no changes in the top group of producers with three and four bunch ratings. The key players who set the standard are still Weingart, Didinger, Müller and Thomas Perll in the Boppard area, as well as Jost and Ratzenberger in the Bacharach area. We would like to see the reticent Weingart get together with Müller and Didinger to put some pressure behind their move for acceptance into the VDP Mittelrhein, so that the leading producers can give new impetus to the small regional association.

There is room for improvement too for the so-called Mittelrhein Wine Festival held in Steeg, which in truth is only a local showcase for Bacharach and Oberwesel. As long as the top producers from Boppard and Leutesdorf are not represented, this event does not deserve its claim of representing the Mittelrhein.

It is more important than ever that restaurateurs and hoteliers, wine producers, and representatives of politics and culture all work together to increase the visibility of this region, which after all is a Unesco world cultural heritage site. This status represents an enormous opportunity for the small wine-growing area, whose vineyards cover only 500 hectares. If they can all work together, and increase their efforts to produce top quality, there may well be a glowing future for the Mittelrhein as a small but well-respected region.

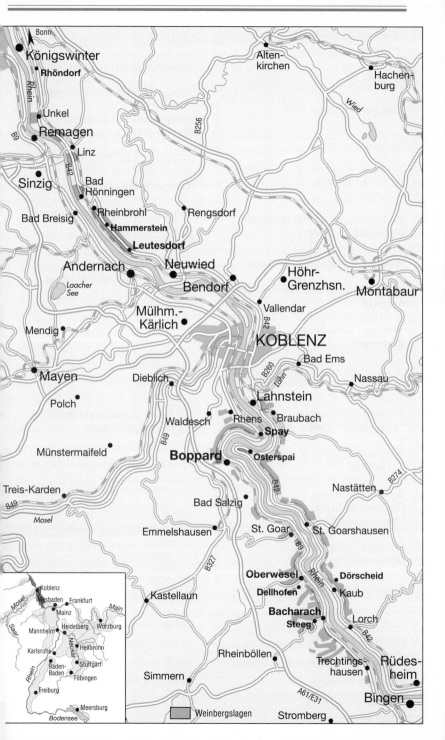

Mittelrhein

Weingut Weingart, Spay

Weingut Didinger, Osterspai

Weingut Toni Jost – Hahnenhof, Bacharach

Weingut Matthias Müller, Spay

Weingut August und Thomas Perll, Boppard

Weingut Ratzenberger, Bacharach

Weingut Fritz Bastian "Zum grünen Baum," Bacharach

Weingut Dr. Randolf Kauer, Bacharach

Wein- und Sektgut Goswin Lambrich, Oberwesel-Dellhofen

Weingut Lanius-Knab, Oberwesel

Weingut Toni Lorenz, Boppard

The best vineyard sites on the Mittelrhein

Bacharach: Hahn, Posten, Wolfshöhle

Engehöll: Bernstein

Oberwesel: Oelsberg

Steeg: St. Jost

Weingut Emmerich, Leutesdorf

Weingut Peter Hohn, Leutesdorf

Weingut Albert Lambrich, Oberwesel-Dellhofen

Weingut Mades, Bacharach-Steeg

Weingut Walter Perll, Boppard

Weingut Scheidgen, Hammerstein

Weingut Selt, Leutesdorf

Weingut Sonnenhang – Edelobst-Brennerei, Dörscheid

Major and minor vintages on the Mittelrhein

Vintage	Rating
2003	🍇🍇🍇
2002	🍇🍇🍇🍇
2001	🍇🍇🍇
2000	🍇🍇
1999	🍇🍇
1998	🍇🍇🍇
1997	🍇🍇🍇
1996	🍇🍇🍇🍇
1995	🍇🍇🍇
1994	🍇🍇🍇🍇

Vintage rating:

🍇🍇🍇🍇🍇 : Excellent vintage

🍇🍇🍇🍇 : Very good vintage

🍇🍇🍇 : Good vintage

🍇🍇 : Average vintage

🍇 : Poor vintage

WEINGUT FRITZ BASTIAN "ZUM GRÜNEN BAUM"

Owner: Friedrich Bastian
55422 Bacharach, Oberstraße 63
Tel. (0 67 43) 12 08, Fax 28 37
e-mail:
weingut-bastian-bacharach@t-online.de
Directions: A 61 Koblenz–Bingen, Rhein-böllen exit, in direction of Bacharach
Sales: Doris Bastian; during wine bar opening times, and by appointment
Restaurant: "Zum grünen Baum"
13:00 to 24:00 hours, closed Thu.
Specialties: Home-made sausages and ham
History: Winery founded 1697, buildings date from various periods (1421/1756/1825)

Vineyard area: 5.8 hectares
Annual production: 32,000 bottles
Top sites: Bacharacher Posten,
Wolfshöhle and Insel Heyles'en Werth
Soil types: Blue slate,
decomposed kaolin
Grape varieties: 80% Riesling,
10% Scheurebe, 5% Spätburgunder,
5% Portugieser
Average yield: 45 hl/ha
Best vintages: 1998, 2001, 2002
Member: VDP

In 2003, Friedrich Bastian picked every conceivable level of quality, from dry Riesling in liter bottles right up to the Trockenbeerenauslese. The vineyard on the island Heyles'en Werth, a monopole property, lies in the middle of the Rhine, which can be an advantage in a hot and dry vintage. The two "Große Gewächse" (First Growths) represent the best dry and off-dry wines respectively. We particularly liked the sweet Spätlese from the Bacharacher Posten vineyard, which has a firm acid structure. Bastian's Riesling Beerenauslese "Goldkapsel" (gold capsule) is certainly the best Beerenauslese in the region. He will present the Trockenbeerenauslese only next year. Overall, Bastian has coped well with the difficult 2003 vintage. He has one of the best two-bunch wineries.

2003 Bacharacher Insel Heyles'en Werth
Riesling trocken
12%, ♀ till 2006   83

2003 Bacharacher Wolfshöhle
Riesling trocken "Großes Gewächs"
14%, ♀ till 2008   85

2003 Bacharacher Wolfshöhle
Riesling halbtrocken
12.5%, ♀ till 2006   83

2003 Bacharacher Insel Heyles'en Werth
Riesling halbtrocken
11.5%, ♀ till 2007   84

2003 Bacharacher Posten
Riesling feinherb "Großes Gewächs"
13.5%, ♀ till 2008   86

2003 Riesling Kabinett
9%, ♀ till 2007   84

2003 Scheurebe Kabinett
9%, ♀ till 2007   84

2003 Bacharacher Insel Heyles'en Werth
Riesling Auslese Goldkapsel
10.5%, ♀ till 2009   85

2003 Bacharacher Posten
Riesling Spätlese
8%, ♀ till 2008   86

2002 Bacharacher Posten
Riesling Spätlese
8.5%, ♀ till 2007   87

2002 Bacharacher Posten
Riesling Auslese
8%, ♀ till 2008   89

2003 Bacharacher Posten
Riesling Beerenauslese Goldkapsel
7.5%, ♀ till 2015   93

The wines: **100** Perfect · **95–99** Outstanding · **90–94** Excellent · **85–89** Very good · **80–84** Good · **75–79** Average

WEINGUT DIDINGER

Owner: Jens Didinger
56340 Osterspai, Rheinuferstraße 13
Tel. (0 26 27) 5 12, Fax 97 12 72
e-mail: WeingutDidinger@web.de
Internet: www.weingut-didinger.de
Directions: From Koblenz via the B 42
in the direction of Rüdesheim
Sales: Didinger family
Restaurant: "Bopparder Hamm"
daily except Wed., from 15:00 hours

Vineyard area: 3.5 hectares
Annual production: 40,000 bottles
Top site: Bopparder Hamm
Feuerlay
Soil types: Decomposed slate
Grape varieties: 76% Riesling, 10%
Müller-Thurgau, 5% each of Dornfel-
der and Spätburgunder, 4% Kerner
Average yield: 85 hl/ha
Best vintages: 2000, 2001, 2002

Jens Didinger just keeps on getting better
each year. He presented a most impressive range in 2002. However, in 2003 even
he suffered from the heat and drouth,
although his wines are among the best in
the region. The range of points for his
wines this time is from 85 to 89. He was
specific about not adding acidity, and the
results prove that even without this measure it was possible to produce an exceptionally good range of wines in this year
of extremes. His off-dry Riesling Spätlese is a good and animating example. His
Feuerlay Trockenbeerenauslese, picked
at a must weight of 230 degrees Öchsle
and 380 g/l of residual sugar has a natural
acidity of 12.3 g/l: a wonderfully round
wine with caramel and honeyed notes,
lovely on the palate; unfortunately we
were not as happy with the nose. The
wine bar and restaurant have been completed, inviting the visitor to sample the
wines of the estate together with some
hearty dishes. The value-for-money ratio
remains unequalled. Given enough per-
sistence and ambition, Didinger can still
develop his potential.

2003 Bopparder Hamm Feuerlay
Riesling Spätlese trocken
12.5%, ♀ till 2007   **86**

2003 Bopparder Hamm Feuerlay
Riesling Spätlese trocken *
13%, ♀ till 2008   **88**

2002 Bopparder Hamm Feuerlay
Riesling Spätlese trocken *
13%, ♀ till 2007   **90**

2003 Bopparder Hamm Feuerlay
Riesling Spätlese halbtrocken *
12%, ♀ till 2008   **87**

2002 Bopparder Hamm Feuerlay
Riesling Spätlese halbtrocken *
12%, ♀ till 2006   **90**

2003 Bopparder Hamm Feuerlay
Riesling Spätlese *
8%, ♀ till 2009   **88**

2003 Bopparder Hamm Feuerlay
Riesling Spätlese – S –
9%, ♀ till 2010   **88**

2003 Bopparder Hamm Feuerlay
Riesling Auslese
9%, ♀ till 2012   **89**

2003 Bopparder Hamm Feuerlay
Riesling Trockenbeerenauslese
6%, ♀ till 2020   **89**

2002 Bopparder Hamm Feuerlay
Riesling Spätlese *
9%, ♀ till 2009   **90**

2002 Bopparder Hamm Feuerlay
Riesling Eiswein *
7.5%, ♀ till 2020   **93**

WEINGUT DIDINGER

MITTELRHEIN

2002
BOPPARDER HAMM FEUERLAY
RIESLING EISWEIN *

7,5 % vol   Qualitätswein mit Prädikat   0,375 l
Gutsabfüllung   A. P. Nr. 1 693 005 021 03
Weingut Didinger · D-56340 Osterspai · Tel. 0 26 27 / 5 12

WEINGUT EMMERICH

Owner: Gotthard Emmerich
Manager and winemaker:
Gotthard Emmerich
56599 Leutesdorf, Hauptstraße 80c
Tel. (0 26 31) 7 29 22, Fax 7 54 83
e-mail: weingut-emmerich@
leutesdorf-rhein.de
Internet: leutesdorf-rhein.de/
weingut-emmerich
Directions: A 3/A 48, Neuwied exit,
B 42 to Leutesdorf; A 59 in direction of
Königswinter, via B 42 to Leutesdorf
Sales: Rita and Gotthard Emmerich
Opening hours: Mon.–Sat. 09:00 to
19:00 hours, Sun. 11:00 to 13:00 hours
by appointment only at all times
Tasting room: With a view of the
world's biggest cold water geyser
Worth seeing: Winery directly at signposted vineyard tour, including steep
slopes, "Weinkul-Tour"

Vineyard area: 3 hectares
Annual production: 32,000 bottles
Top sites: Leutesdorfer
Rosenberg and Gartenlay
Soil types: Decomposed kaolin with
slate, and grey wacke
Grape varieties: 70% Riesling, 10%
each of Kerner and Weißburgunder,
5% each of Portugieser and Dornfelder
Average yield: 80 hl/ha
Best vintage: 2002

Gotthard Emmerich, who is head of the
Leutesdorf wine growers association,
likes to lead by example. Together with
Peter Hohn, who also runs a very solid
winery, he has created a blend called "Inspiration," a dry Riesling Classic rated at
83 points. Something we did not like a-
bout the Spätlese was the untypical bottle
shape. Even Emmerich has had to pay his
dues in the 2003 vintage, as evidenced by
the dry Hochgewächs wine from the
Rosenberg vineyard. Emmerich could still
improve his botrytis dessert wines. An
improvement next year would do the
rating of this winery a world of good.

2003 Leutesdorfer Gartenlay
Riesling Hochgewächs trocken
13%, ♀ till 2006 **82**

2002 Leutesdorfer Gartenlay
Riesling Hochgewächs trocken – 7 –
13%, ♀ till 2006 **83**

2002 Riesling Classic
12.5%, ♀ till 2006 **83**

2003 Cuvée "Inspiration"
Riesling Classic
13%, ♀ till 2006 **83**

2002 Leutesdorfer Gartenlay
Riesling Hochgewächs trocken – 18 –
13%, ♀ till 2006 **84**

2003 Leutesdorfer Gartenlay
Riesling Hochgewächs halbtrocken
12%, ♀ till 2006 **82**

2003 Leutesdorfer Rosenberg
Riesling Spätlese halbtrocken
13%, ♀ till 2006 **82**

2002 Leutesdorfer Gartenlay
Riesling Hochgewächs halbtrocken – 19 –
12%, ♀ till 2006 **83**

2002 Leutesdorfer Gartenlay
Riesling Hochgewächs
10.5%, ♀ till 2006 **83**

2002 Leutesdorfer Rosenberg
Riesling Auslese
7.5%, ♀ till 2008 **85**

The wines: **100** Perfect · **95–99** Outstanding · **90–94** Excellent · **85–89** Very good · **80–84** Good · **75–79** Average

251

WEINGUT PETER HOHN

Owner: Peter Hohn
56599 Leutesdorf, In der Gartenlay 50
Tel. (0 26 31) 7 18 17, Fax 7 22 09
e-mail: pHohn@t-online.de
Internet: www.leutesdorf-rhein.de/weingut-peter-hohn
*Directions: B 42 Koblenz–Bonn,
seven kilometers north of Neuwied*
Sales: Peter Hohn and Jeanette Schmidt
Opening hours: Mon.–Sun. by appointment
History: Family-owned since 1638
Worth a visit: "Summertime" event with music and food in the winery yard in July

Vineyard area: 3.5 hectares
Annual production: 40,000 bottles
Top sites: Leutesdorfer Rosenberg, Gartenlay and Forstberg
Soil types: Decomposed slate
Grape varieties: 62% Riesling, 13% Dornfelder, 10% each of Spätburgunder and Portugieser, 5% Kerner
Average yield: 83 hl/ha
Best vintages: 2002, 2003

Peter Hohn is back again. In the first issues of the Gault Millau guide he was the only wine producer from Leutesdorf on the Mittelrhein to be awarded a bunch of grapes. His overall good range of 2003 wines has ensured that he has regained this status. While there are no real highlights, there are also no weak wines in the range. There is one innovation, a blend made together with his colleague Gotthard Emmerich, a Riesling Classic called "Inspiration," rated 83 points. The off-dry wines as well as his Kerner Auslese were likewise enjoyable wines, and his fruity Riesling Spätlese achieved a respectable 84 point rating. His Riesling Classic even made it into the top ten in the country. Peter Hohn has recently acquired an additional two hectares of vineyard, and has a good base from which to build for the future. We recommend that he continues in the same vein.

2003 Leutesdorfer Forstberg
Riesling Hochgewächs trocken
12.5%, ♀ till 2006 · 80

2003 Leutesdorfer Rosenberg
Riesling Spätlese trocken "S"
13.5%, ♀ till 2006 · 82

2002 Leutesdorfer Forstberg
Riesling Hochgewächs trocken
12%, ♀ till 2006 · 83

2003 Cuvée "Inspiration"
Riesling Classic
13%, ♀ till 2006 · 83

2003 Riesling Classic
12.5%, ♀ till 2006 · 84

2003 Leutesdorfer
Riesling halbtrocken "J"
12.5%, ♀ till 2006 · 82

2003 Leutesdorfer Forstberg
Riesling Spätlese halbtrocken "J"
12.5%, ♀ till 2007 · 83

2003 Leutesdorfer Rosenberg
Riesling Spätlese
11%, ♀ till 2008 · 84

2002 Leutesdorfer
Riesling Spätlese
10%, ♀ till 2007 · 85

2003 Leutesdorfer Rosenberg
Kerner Beerenauslese
9%, ♀ till 2013 · 86

WEINGUT TONI JOST – HAHNENHOF

Owner: Peter Jost
55422 Bacharach am Rhein,
Oberstraße 14
Tel. (0 67 43) 12 16, Fax 10 76
e-mail: tonijost@debitel.net
Directions: A 61 Koblenz–Bingen,
Rheinböllen exit
Sales: Peter and Linde Jost
by appointment
Worth seeing: Old German tasting room
in picturesque old part of town

Vineyard area: 8.8 hectares
Annual production: 70,000 bottles
Top site: Bacharacher Hahn
Soil types: Decomposed Devon slate
Grape varieties: 85% Riesling,
15% Spätburgunder
Average yield: 58 hl/ha
Best vintages: 1995, 1996, 2001
Member: VDP

Josts best dry wine is a Bacharacher Hahn "Großes Gewächs" (First Growth) of the 2002 vintage, which Jost only submitted for tasting at a late stage. It has also become clear that the 2003 vintage has not produced absolutely top wines in the dry sector. Jost harvested everything, from the dry Riesling "Devon S" to the Trockenbeerenauslese from the Hahn vineyard. The Pinot Noirs are always of above-average quality for the Mittelrhein region, and are a regular part of the range. His Beerenauslese gold capsule is characterized by botrytis. The Trockenbeerenauslese from the Hahn vineyard was picked at a must weight of 257 degrees Öchsle, a record for the winery: a wine with an extremely spicy bouquet, a light touch of petrol, and great concentration, the top wine in the range. An annual highlight event here is a "floating wine tasting," held as part of the "Mittelrhein-Momente" series, and organized in conjunction with top chef Harald Kutsche from the "Zum Turm" hotel in Kaub on the other bank of the river.

2003 Bacharacher Hahn
Riesling Spätlese trocken
12%, ♀ till 2006   **84**

2003 "Devon S" Riesling trocken
12%, ♀ till 2006   **85**

2002 Bacharacher Hahn
Riesling Spätlese trocken
12%, ♀ till 2007   **88**

2002 Bacharacher Hahn
Riesling trocken "Großes Gewächs"
13%, ♀ till 2009   **90**

2003 Bacharacher Hahn
Riesling Spätlese feinherb
12%, ♀ till 2007   **85**

2003 Bacharacher Hahn
Riesling Spätlese
8.5%, ♀ till 2008   **88**

2003 Bacharacher Hahn
Riesling Beerenauslese Goldkapsel
11%, ♀ till 2015   **88**

2001 Bacharacher Hahn
Riesling Spätlese
9.5%, ♀ till 2008   **89**

2001 Bacharacher Hahn
Riesling Trockenbeerenauslese
7%, ♀ till 2018   **91**

2003 Bacharacher Hahn
Riesling Trockenbeerenauslese
7%, ♀ till 2020   **94**

——— Red wines ———

2002 Bacharacher Hahn
Spätburgunder trocken
13%, ♀ till 2007   **84**

2002 Bacharacher Hahn
Spätburgunder trocken Barrique
13%, ♀ till 2008   **85**

The wines: **100** Perfect · **95–99** Outstanding · **90–94** Excellent · **85–89** Very good · **80–84** Good · **75–79** Average

WEINGUT
DR. RANDOLF KAUER

Owner: Martina and Randolf Kauer
Manager: Dr. Randolf Kauer
55422 Bacharach, Mainzer Straße 21
Tel. (0 67 43) 22 72, Fax 9 36 61
e-mail: weingut-dr-kauer@t-online.de
Internet: www.weingut-dr-kauer.de
Directions: A 61 Koblenz–Bingen, Rhein-böllen exit, in direction of Bacharach
Sales: Martina Kauer
by appointment
Worth seeing: Cross-vaulted cellar at Schieferfelsen (slate rock)
Worth a visit: Culinary guided tour of town and events within the framework of "Mittelrhein-Momente"

Vineyard area: 3 hectares
Annual production: 20,000 bottles
Top sites: Bacharacher Kloster
Fürstental and Wolfshöhle,
Urbarer Beulsberg, Oberdiebacher
Fürstenberg, Oberweseler Oelsberg
Soil types: Decomposed kaolin-slate
Grape varieties: 90% Riesling,
10% Spätburgunder
Average yield: 51 hl/ha
Best vintages: 1998, 1999, 2001
Member: EcoVin

In his price list, Dr. Randolf Kauer specifies alcoholic strength, acidity and residual sugar for each wine, so that wine enthusiasts have ready access to the analytical data. In the 2003 vintage, as was to be expected, the levels of acidity were well below those of the previous vintage. This, according to Kauer himself, "makes for an early-drinking wine." In some cases, Kauer added some acidity to the must. We particularly liked his dry Riesling wines. Considering the vintage, Kauer has presented a remarkably lean and light-bodied range. His Beerenauslese, picked at a must weight of more than 150 degrees Öchsle is not in the top league for the region. Nevertheless, the Dr. Kauer winery is one of the best producers in the two-bunch category.

2003 Riesling trocken
12.5%, ♀ till 2006 — 82

2003 Riesling Kabinett trocken
12%, ♀ till 2006 — 82

2003 Bacharacher Wolfshöhle
Riesling Kabinett trocken
12.5%, ♀ till 2007 — 83

2003 Oberweseler Oelsberg
Riesling Spätlese trocken
12.5%, ♀ till 2007 — 84

2002 Bacharacher Kloster Fürstental
Riesling Kabinett trocken
11%, ♀ till 2006 — 85

2002 Urbarer Beulsberg
Riesling Spätlese trocken
11.5%, ♀ till 2006 — 85

2002 Oberweseler Oelsberg
Riesling Spätlese halbtrocken
11%, ♀ till 2006 — 85

2003 Oberdiebacher Fürstenberg
Riesling Spätlese
10%, ♀ till 2008 — 84

2001 Bacharacher Kloster Fürstental
Riesling Auslese
8.5%, ♀ till 2010 — 88

2001 Oberweseler Oelsberg
Riesling Auslese
9%, ♀ till 2012 — 89

WEINGUT
ALBERT LAMBRICH

Owner: Albert Lambrich
Winemaker: Albert Lambrich
55430 Oberwesel-Dellhofen,
In der Neuwies
Tel. (0 67 44) 82 76, Fax 71 16 07
e-mail:
info@weingut-albert-lambrich.de
Internet:
www.weingut-albert.lambrich.de
Directions: A 61 Koblenz–Bingen,
Laudert exit, in direction of Oberwesel
Sales: Lambrich family
Restaurant: Dellhofener Winzerstube,
Fri. from 18:00 hours, Sat. from 16:00
hours, Sun. from 15:00 hours

Vineyard area: 4.6 hectares
Annual production: 40,000 bottles
Top site: Oberweseler
Römerkrug
Soil types: Decomposed slate
Grape varieties: 70% Riesling,
12% Spätburgunder, 6% Müller-Thur-
gau, 6% Weiß- and Grauburgunder,
3% Dornfelder, 3% other varieties
Average yield: 70 hl/ha
Best vintages: 1999, 2001, 2002

Albert Lambrich is often perceived as
standing in the shadow of the well-known
Goswin Lambrich estate. He has thrown
his old label over board, and created a
really attractive, well designed new emblem. He has managed to overcome the
financial strains involved in building a
new winery with restaurant and wine bar
on the outskirts of Oberwesel-Dellhofen,
plus planting new vineyards, and now
plans to invest in stainless steel tanks
next. There is a slight touch of bitterness
and an almond aroma in many of his dry
2003 wines, particularly among the better
ones, certainly a result of the hot summer, which partly damaged some of the
grapes. Unfortunately Albert Lambrich
did not present any botrytis dessert wines
for tasting. His prices remain very consumer-friendly.

2003 Oberweseler Schloss Schönburg
Riesling Hochgewächs trocken
12%, ♀ till 2006   82

2003 Oberweseler Römerkrug
Riesling Spätlese trocken
12.5%, ♀ till 2006   82

2002 Oberweseler Römerkrug
Riesling Spätlese trocken
11.5%, ♀ till 2006   84

2003 Oberweseler Römerkrug
Riesling halbtrocken
11%, ♀ till 2006   80

2003 Oberweseler Schloss Schönburg
Riesling Hochgewächs halbtrocken
11%, ♀ till 2006   81

2003 Oberweseler Römerkrug
Riesling Spätlese halbtrocken
11.5%, ♀ till 2006   82

2002 Oberweseler Römerkrug
Riesling Spätlese halbtrocken
11%, ♀ till 2006   84

2003 Oberweseler Römerkrug
Riesling Spätlese
9%, ♀ till 2006   83

2002 Oberweseler Römerkrug
Riesling Spätlese
8%, ♀ till 2008   85

2001 Oberweseler Römerkrug
Riesling Auslese
9%, ♀ till 2008   87

The wines: **100** Perfect · **95–99** Outstanding · **90–94** Excellent · **85–89** Very good · **80–84** Good · **75–79** Average

WEIN- UND SEKTGUT GOSWIN LAMBRICH

Owner: Gerhard, Marita and
Christiane Lambrich
55430 Oberwesel-Dellhofen,
Auf der Kripp 3
Tel. (0 67 44) 80 66, Fax 80 03
e-mail: info@weingut-lambrich.de
Internet: www.weingut-lambrich.de
*Directions: A 61, coming from Mainz
Rheinböllen exit, coming from Koblenz
Laudert exit*
Sales: Lambrich family
Opening hours: By appointment
Restaurant: March to December,
Fri. 18:00 to 23:00, Sat. 16:00 to 23:00,
Sun. 15:00 to 23:00 hours

Vineyard area: 12 hectares
Annual production: 75,000 bottles
Top sites: Oberweseler Oelsberg,
St. Martinsberg, Bernstein
and Römerkrug
Soil types: Decomposed slate
Grape varieties: 65% Riesling,
15% Weißer Burgunder, 8% each of
Dornfelder and Spätburgunder,
4% Cabernet Dorsa
Average yield: 75 hl/ha
Best vintages: 1998, 2001, 2002

Gerhard Lambrich is the indefatigable chairman of the Mittelrhein wine growers association, and believes firmly in the future of the region. His vineyard area of more than 12 hectares makes him one of the largest producers in the area. Apart from the dominant variety Riesling he also grows Pinot Blanc and red varieties. In the 2002 vintage, the Riesling Classic and the dry Blauschiefer (blue slate) were each rated 85 points. This year, too, we preferred his dry wines to the off-dry ones. The two botrytized Auslese wines from the St. Martinsberg and the Oelsberg sites came in neck and neck. The Riesling Beerenauslese is the highlight of the range. The red wines – which make up a full 20 percent of the vineyard area – are reasonable.

2003 Oberweseler Römerkrug
Riesling Hochgewächs trocken
12%, ♀ till 2006 — **82**

2003 Riesling Classic
12%, ♀ till 2006 — **82**

2003 Dellhofener St. Wernerberg
Riesling Hochgewächs trocken
12.5%, ♀ till 2006 — **83**

2003 Oberweseler St. Martinsberg
Blauschiefer Riesling trocken
12%, ♀ till 2007 — **84**

2002 Riesling Classic
11.5%, ♀ till 2006 — **85**

2003 Oberweseler St. Martinsberg
Riesling Spätlese
9%, ♀ till 2007 — **85**

2003 Oberweseler St. Martinsberg
Riesling Auslese
8.5%, ♀ till 2008 — **85**

2003 Oberweseler Oelsberg
Riesling Auslese
8%, ♀ till 2008 — **85**

2003 Oberweseler St. Martinsberg
Riesling Beerenauslese
8.5%, ♀ till 2015 — **87**

2002 Oberweseler Oelsberg
Riesling Auslese
8%, ♀ till 2009 — **88**

2001 Oberweseler Oelsberg
Riesling Trockenbeerenauslese
9.5%, ♀ till 2018 — **89**

2002 Oberweseler Römerkrug
Riesling Eiswein
8%, ♀ till 2015 — **89**

The estates: ✝✝✝✝✝ World's finest · ✝✝✝✝ Germany's best · ✝✝✝ Very good · ✝✝ Good · ✝ Reliable

WEINGUT LANIUS-KNAB

Owner: Jörg Lanius
55430 Oberwesel, Mainzer Straße 38
Tel. (0 67 44) 81 04, Fax 15 37
e-mail:
Weingut.Lanius.Knab@t-online.de
Internet: www.lanius-knab.de
Directions: A 61 Koblenz–Bingen,
Laudert-Oberwesel exit
Sales: Jörg Lanius
Opening hours: Mon.–Fri. by appointment, Sat. 08:00 to 17:00 hours
Worth seeing: Belle Epoque house with double-storey vaulted cellar

---

Vineyard area: 6.7 hectares
Annual production: 35,000 bottles
Top sites: Engehöller Bernstein
and Goldemund, Oberweseler
Oelsberg
Soil types: Decomposed slate and
grey wacke
Grape varieties: 85% Riesling, 10%
Spätburgunder, 5% Müller-Thurgau
Average yield: 55 hl/ha
Best vintages: 2000, 2001, 2002
Member: VDP

The Lanius-Knab estate has for many years been one of the very good two-bunch wineries in the Mittelrhein region. It is particularly gratifying to note that the aromatics of his wines have improved significantly in comparison to the 2001 and 2002 vintages, bear in mind that it was not easy to make good wine in the extreme 2003 vintage. The high must weights led to some unusual decisions: "We filled wines with 90 degrees Öchsle in liter bottles." The addition of acid is "anathema" here. Lanius had tasted older vintages with low levels of acidity, and found that they had matured well. He has recently replanted the Oberweseler Oelsberg site, and thus did not present any wines for tasting, those submitted were all from the two top sites in Engehöll, the "Goldemund" and "Bernstein." Of the botrytized dessert wines in 2003, we preferred the Riesling Beerenauslese.

2003 Engehöller Bernstein
Riesling Spätlese trocken
12%, ♀ till 2006 — 84

2002 Engehöller Bernstein
Riesling trocken "Großes Gewächs"
12.5%, ♀ till 2006 — 86

2003 Engehöller Goldemund
Riesling Kabinett halbtrocken
11%, ♀ till 2007 — 83

2003 Engehöller Goldemund
Riesling Spätlese
9.5%, ♀ till 2008 — 83

2002 Engehöller Goldemund
Riesling Beerenauslese
7%, ♀ till 2016 — 89

2002 Engehöller Bernstein
Riesling Trockenbeerenauslese
6.5%, ♀ till 2018 — 89

2003 Engehöller Goldemund
Riesling Beerenauslese
7%, ♀ till 2015 — 89

2003 Engehöller Goldemund
Riesling Eiswein
8.5%, ♀ till 2015 — 89

2001 Engehöller Goldemund
Riesling Eiswein
8.5%, ♀ till 2014 — 90

2001 Engehöller Bernstein
Riesling Trockenbeerenauslese
8%, ♀ till 2018 — 90

2002 Oberweseler Oelsberg
Riesling Auslese
9%, ♀ till 2011 — 90

2002 Engehöller Goldemund
Riesling Eiswein
7%, ♀ till 2018 — 92

The wines: **100** Perfect · **95–99** Outstanding · **90–94** Excellent · **85–89** Very good · **80–84** Good · **75–79** Average

WEINGUT TONI LORENZ

Owner: Joachim Lorenz
Winemaker: Joachim Lorenz
56154 Boppard, Ablaßgasse 4
Tel. (0 67 42) 35 11, Fax 10 90 63
e-mail: info@lorenz-weine.de
Internet: www.lorenz-weine.de
Directions: A 61 Koblenz–Bingen,
Boppard exit
Sales: Lorenz family
Opening hours: Mon.–Fri. 08:00 to
19:30 hours, Sat. 08:00 to 18:00 hours
and by appointment
Worth seeing: 400-year-old cross-vaulted barrel cellar
Worth a visit: Mittelrhein Rally

Vineyard area: 3.8 hectares
Annual production: 30,000 bottles
Top sites: Bopparder Hamm
Feuerlay, Mandelstein and Fässerlay
Soil types: Decomposed slate
Grape varieties: 81% Riesling,
10% Spätburgunder, 7% Grauburgunder, 2% Müller-Thurgau
Average yield: 85 hl/ha
Best vintages: 2001, 2002, 2003

Joachim Lorenz has presented a 2003
vintage range of above-average quality.
One of the reasons for the overall good
impression may be that he submitted only
a single dry wine. However, the Feuerlay
Riesling Spätlese (with star) packs quite a
punch. We rated it at 85 points, which is a
higher rating than the botrytized Riesling
Auslese. Our suggestion to produce a
Beerenauslese wine was brought to fruition with the 2003 vintage. However, we
believe that this can and should still be
improved upon. Following on his marriage to Martina, who is the junior boss
at the "Zum Landsknecht" hotel in St.
Goar, the marketing of the wines has also
gained a new dynamic dimension. One of
the highlights is certainly the "Trio of
Dream Landscapes" (Terzett der Traumlandschaften) comprising Mittelrhein,
Rioja from Spain and Tokaj from Hungary.

2003 Bopparder Hamm Feuerlay
Riesling Spätlese trocken *
12.5%, ♀ till 2008   85

2001 Bopparder Hamm Feuerlay
Riesling Spätlese trocken
12%, ♀ till 2006   86

2003 Bopparder Hamm Feuerlay
Riesling Spätlese halbtrocken
11.5%, ♀ till 2007   83

2003 Bopparder Hamm Feuerlay
Riesling Spätlese halbtrocken *
12.5%, ♀ till 2008   85

2001 Bopparder Hamm Feuerlay
Riesling Auslese halbtrocken
12%, ♀ till 2007   86

2002 Bopparder Hamm Feuerlay
Riesling Spätlese feinherb
11%, ♀ till 2007   84

2003 Bopparder Hamm Riesling
10%, ♀ till 2008   83

2003 Bopparder Hamm Feuerlay
Riesling Auslese
8%, ♀ till 2010   84

2001 Bopparder Hamm Feuerlay
Riesling Auslese
10%, ♀ till 2007   87

2003 Bopparder Hamm Feuerlay
Riesling Beerenauslese
9.5%, ♀ till 2015   87

2001 Bopparder Hamm Feuerlay
Riesling Auslese
9%, ♀ till 2008   88

WEINGUT MADES

Owner: Helmut Mades
55422 Bacharach-Steeg,
Borbachstraße 35–36
Tel. (0 67 43) 14 49, Fax 31 24
Directions: A 61 Koblenz–Bingen,
Rheinböllen exit
Sales: Mades family
Opening hours: By appointment
Worth a visit: For wine tasting groups
of ten persons or more regional dishes
can be ordered
History: Family-owned since 1663
Worth seeing: Original half-timbered
house dating to 16th century

Vineyard area: 3.5 hectares
Annual production: 20,000 bottles
Top sites: Bacharacher Posten
and Wolfshöhle, Steeger St. Jost
Soil types: Decomposed Devon slate
Grape varieties: 100% Riesling
Average yield: 50 hl/ha
Best vintages: 1999, 2001, 2002
Member: VDP

Helmut Mades is a member of the VDP,
and works 3.5 hectares of vineyard in the
Steeg valley. Following on a significant
improvement in quality reported last
year, Mades was able in broad terms to
hold on to that level in this difficult vintage. Mades is an outspoken opponent of
adding acidity, he believes the acidity
binds too much potassium, resulting in
wines that are "empty and sour." The highlight among the dry wines is the outstanding "Großes Gewächs" (First Growth)
from the Posten vineyard. We particularly liked the Steeger St. Jost Beerenauslese, which has an excellent balance of
sweetness and acidity. At the top of the
list is a Trockenbeerenauslese picked at a
must weight of 220 degrees Öchsle, and a
whopping 360 g/l of residual sugar. This
is a very full-bodied and extremely sweet
wine. A further positive feature here is
that the price list includes older wines
going back to 1997.

2003 Steeger St. Jost
Riesling Spätlese trocken
12%, ♀ till 2006 — **81**

2003 Bacharacher Posten
Riesling Spätlese trocken
12%, ♀ till 2006 — **81**

2003 Bacharacher Posten
Riesling "Großes Gewächs"
13%, ♀ till 2008 — **86**

2003 Steeger St. Jost
Riesling Spätlese feinherb
12%, ♀ till 2006 — **83**

2003 Bacharacher Wolfshöhle
Riesling Spätlese
9%, ♀ till 2007 — **84**

2002 Bacharacher Wolfshöhle
Riesling Spätlese
9%, ♀ till 2007 — **85**

2003 Steeger St. Jost
Riesling Auslese
8%, ♀ till 2010 — **85**

2003 Bacharacher Posten
Riesling Auslese
9%, ♀ till 2010 — **85**

2001 Bacharacher Wolfshöhle
Riesling Spätlese
9%, ♀ till 2008 — **86**

2003 Steeger St. Jost
Riesling Beerenauslese
10%, ♀ till 2015 — **88**

2003 Bacharacher Posten
Riesling Trockenbeerenauslese
7%, ♀ till 2020 — **90**

WEINGUT MADES

MITTELRHEIN
2003
Steeger St. Jost
Riesling Beerenauslese
Gutsabfüllung
10.0% Vol. Qualitätswein mit Prädikat · A.P.Nr. 1 698 159 008 04 0,375 l
D-55422 Bacharach/Steeg am Rhein
Borbachstraße 35 · 36 · Telefon 06743/1449

The wines: **100** Perfect · **95–99** Outstanding · **90–94** Excellent · **85–89** Very good · **80–84** Good · **75–79** Average

259

WEINGUT
MATTHIAS MÜLLER

Owner: Matthias Müller family
Manager: Matthias Müller
56322 Spay, Mainzer Straße 45
Tel. (0 26 28) 87 41, Fax 33 63
e-mail:
weingut.matthias.mueller@t-online.de
Directions: A 61 Koblenz–Bingen,
Boppard exit
Sales: Marianne Müller
Opening hours: Mon.–Sat. all day
Sun. 10:00 to 18:00 hours
History: Winemaking for 300 years
Worth a visit: Outdoor wine festival on
first weekend in September

Vineyard area: 8.1 hectares
Annual production: 74,000 bottles
Top sites: Bopparder Hamm
Feuerlay, Mandelstein, Engelstein
and Ohlenberg
Soil types: Decomposed Devon slate
Grape varieties: 86% Riesling, 8%
Grauburgunder, 6% Spätburgunder
Average yield: 77 hl/ha
Best vintages: 1998, 2001, 2002

Last year we tasted wines that had undergone spontaneous fermentation here for the first time. A year later, all but one of these wines has gained significantly in stature. In the 2003 vintage, Müller has again shown a deft touch in handling natural yeasts. In our opinion, a Bopparder Hamm Mandelstein Riesling Hochgewächs with some fruity residual sugar, good mineral notes, fruit, natural acidity was well worth 87 points. The other wines in the range presented by Marianne and Matthias Müller were also good, but just as in the case of other producers in the area, the extreme vintage conditions meant that they did not quite live up to the standard set by previous vintages. However, in its category the off-dry Mandelstein Spätlese is unbeatable. Plans for the future are already in place: The Müllers are expanding their vineyard area in the Bopparder Hamm site step by step.

2003 Bopparder Hamm Feuerlay
Riesling Hochgewächs trocken
12.5%, ♀ till 2007 **85**

2003 Bopparder Hamm Engelstein
Riesling Spätlese trocken
12%, ♀ till 2007 **86**

2003 Bopparder Hamm Feuerlay
Riesling Spätlese halbtrocken
11.5%, ♀ till 2007 **85**

2003 Bopparder Hamm Mandelstein
Riesling Spätlese halbtrocken
12%, ♀ till 2008 **90**

2003 Bopparder Hamm Mandelstein
Riesling Hochgewächs
9%, ♀ till 2008 **87**

2003 Bopparder Hamm Engelstein
Riesling Auslese
8.5%, ♀ till 2012 **89**

2003 Bopparder Hamm Feuerlay
Riesling Beerenauslese
8%, ♀ till 2015 **89**

2003 Bopparder Hamm Feuerlay
Riesling Trockenbeerenauslese
8.5%, ♀ till 2020 **92**

2002 Bopparder Hamm Feuerlay
Riesling Auslese
8.5%, ♀ till 2012 **93**

2002 Bopparder Hamm Feuerlay
Riesling Eiswein – 22 –
8%, ♀ till 2018 **93**

2002 Bopparder Hamm Feuerlay
Riesling Eiswein – 8 –
8.5%, ♀ till 2020 **94**

WEINGUT AUGUST UND THOMAS PERLL

Owner: Thomas Perll
Winemaker: Thomas Perll
56154 Boppard, Oberstraße 77–81
Tel. (0 67 42) 39 06, Fax 8 17 26
e-mail: post@perll.de
Internet: www.perll.de
Directions: A 61 Koblenz–Bingen, Buchholz exit, 8 km in direction of Boppard; B 9, 20 kilometers south of Koblenz
Sales: Perll family
Opening hours: Mon.–Fri. 10:00 to 13:00 hours and 15:00 to 19:00 hours
Sat. 10:00 to 13:00 hours
by appointment

Vineyard area: 6.7 hectares
Annual production: 50,000 bottles
Top sites: Bopparder Hamm Mandelstein, Feuerlay, Ohlenberg and Fässerlay
Soil types: Decomposed Devon slate and grey wacke
Grape varieties: 80% Riesling, 7% Spätburgunder, 2% Weißburgunder, 11% other varieties
Average yield: 70 hl/ha
Best vintages: 2000, 2001, 2003

Junior boss and winemaker Thomas Perll has brought all his experience and ability to bear on the 2003 vintage, particularly in the botrytis dessert wines, and with good results. In comparison to the 2002 range, which we did not rate very highly, this vintage has been exceedingly successful, although top marks could not be awarded to dry wines, this was just a vintage-related factor. The dry wines were rather "Rubensian;" on the other hand, we liked the off-dry Auslese, which has exotic aromas and a long finish, very much. The Mandelstein Riesling Auslese has honey and caramel notes, and is absolutely underrated, it is practically as good as the Beerenauslese. Perll has also produced a Beerenauslese and a Trockenbeerenauslese in 2003, both of them of a high standard.

2003 Bopparder Hamm Fässerlay
Riesling Spätlese trocken
13%, ♀ till 2007   **84**

2003 Bopparder Hamm Mandelstein
Riesling Auslese trocken
13%, ♀ till 2008   **85**

2003 Bopparder Hamm Fässerlay
Riesling halbtrocken
11.5%, ♀ till 2007   **86**

2003 Bopparder Hamm Feuerlay
Riesling Spätlese halbtrocken
12.5%, ♀ till 2008   **87**

2003 Bopparder Hamm Mandelstein
Riesling Auslese halbtrocken
13%, ♀ till 2009   **88**

2003 Bopparder Hamm Mandelstein
Riesling Spätlese
9.5%, ♀ till 2009   **86**

2002 Bopparder Hamm Mandelstein
Riesling Spätlese – 38 –
9.5%, ♀ till 2008   **87**

2003 Bopparder Hamm Mandelstein
Riesling Auslese
10%, ♀ till 2010   **91**

2003 Bopparder Hamm Mandelstein
Riesling Beerenauslese
10.5%, ♀ till 2015   **92**

2003 Bopparder Hamm Mandelstein
Riesling Trockenbeerenauslese
11%, ♀ till 2020   **92**

Mittelrhein
2000er
Bopparder Hamm
Fässerlay
Riesling Spätlese
trocken
Qualitätswein mit Prädikat 0,75ℓ
Erzeugerabfüllung
A.P.Nr. 1 671 062 20 01   12% vol
Oberstraße 81 · D-56154 Boppard
Telefon (06742) 3906 · Fax 8 17 26
www.perll.de
STAMMHAUS PERLL
ANNO 1606 GEBAUT

The wines: **100** Perfect · **95–99** Outstanding · **90–94** Excellent · **85–89** Very good · **80–84** Good · **75–79** Average

WEINGUT WALTER PERLL

Owner: Walter Perll
Manager: Walter Perll sen.
Winemaker: Walter Perll jun.
56154 Boppard, Ablaßgasse 11
Tel. (0 67 42) 36 71, Fax 30 23
Internet: www.walter-perll.de
Directions: A 61 Koblenz–Bingen,
Boppard exit, in Boppard turn up
towards left 100 meters before ferry
Sales: Doris Perll
Opening hours: Mon.–Fri. 09:00 to
12:00 and 14:00 to 18:00 hours, Sat.
09:00 to 14:00, Sun. 10:00 to 12:00
hours, and by appointment
Tasting room: In new building, with
Mediterranean character

Vineyard area: 6 hectares
Annual production: 40,000 bottles
Top sites: Bopparder Hamm Mandel-
stein, Feuerlay, Ohlenberg, Fässerlay
Soil types: Decomposed Devon slate,
partly grey wacke
Grape varieties: 80% Riesling,
20% red and other varieties
Average yield: 60 hl/ha
Best vintages: 1995, 1996, 2001

Both father and son are called Walter, and
work together in this winery, with the son
due to move into the new building soon,
with its nicely decorated tasting facility.
A great deal has been invested in expanding the vineyard area, in cellar technology and in the buildings. Based on the
owner's training in Bad Kreuznach as
well as on the potential of the vineyards,
this winery continues to underperform.
Red wines make up almost 20 percent of
the total, and this share is still increasing.
Unfortunately Walter Perll did not submit
his Bopparder Hamm Mandelstein Spätburgunder (Pinot Noir), picked at 120
degrees Öchsle and matured in barriques.
The standard of the range is on the same
level as the previous vintage. His Bopparder Hamm Mandelstein Riesling Auslese
(one star) was actually an Eiswein with a
Beerenauslese character.

2003 Bopparder Hamm Fässerlay
Riesling trocken
12%, ♀ till 2005 **79**

2003 Bopparder Hamm Mandelstein
Riesling Spätlese trocken
12%, ♀ till 2006 **81**

2003 Bopparder Hamm Mandelstein
Riesling Kabinett halbtrocken
12%, ♀ till 2005 **81**

2003 Bopparder Hamm Feuerlay
Riesling Spätlese halbtrocken
12%, ♀ till 2006 **82**

2003 Bopparder Hamm Mandelstein
Riesling Spätlese
9%, ♀ till 2007 **83**

2001 Bopparder Hamm Fässerlay
Riesling Spätlese
7.5%, ♀ till 2006 **85**

2001 Bopparder Hamm Fässerlay
Riesling Auslese
8%, ♀ till 2008 **85**

2003 Bopparder Hamm Mandelstein
Riesling Auslese *
7%, ♀ till 2009 **85**

2001 Bopparder Hamm Mandelstein
Riesling Eiswein
7%, ♀ till 2013 **89**

2002 Bopparder Hamm Mandelstein
Riesling Eiswein
7.5%, ♀ till 2015 **89**

WEINGUT
RATZENBERGER

Owner: Ratzenberger family
Administrator: Jochen Ratzenberger jr.
55422 Bacharach, Blücherstraße 167
Tel. (0 67 43) 13 37, Fax 28 42
e-mail:
weingut-ratzenberger@t-online.de
Internet: www.weingut-ratzenberger.de
Directions: A 61 Koblenz–Bingen, Rhein-böllen exit, in direction of Bacharach
Sales: Jochen Ratzenberger
Opening hours: Mon.–Sat. 09:00 to
18:00 hours by appointment
Worth seeing: Historic cross-vaulted cellar, winery building in Belle Epoque style

---

Vineyard area: 9.8 hectares
Annual production: 80,000 bottles,
incl. 10,000 bottles sparkling wines
Top sites: Steeger St. Jost,
Bacharacher Posten and Wolfshöhle
Soil types: Decomposed Devon slate
Grape varieties: 75% Riesling,
15% Spätburgunder, 5% each of
Grauburgunder and Rivaner
Average yield: 58 hl/ha
Best vintages: 1999, 2001, 2002
Member: VDP

We particularly praised Ratzenberger in 2002 for his crystal-clear wines with lots of fruit and good acidity. We also liked the pronounced mineral notes. The 2003 vintage is a far cry from this assessment. Of the dry wines, the creamy Steeger St. Jost Riesling Spätlese was still the best. In addition, the Grauburgunder (Pinot Gris), a rarity in this region, is enjoyable to drink. Our expectations were not fulfilled in the case of the off-dry wines. In the noble sweet category, the estate has produced two Eisweins, which can be distinguished only through the difference in control number and bottle size. Ratzenberger remains an absolutely top producer in terms of its potential. We sincerely hope that the next vintage will again be of the good quality seen in the 2002 wines.

2003 Bacharacher
Grauer Burgunder trocken
13%, ♀ till 2006 **85**

2003 Steeger St. Jost
Riesling Spätlese trocken
12%, ♀ till 2007 **86**

2002 Steeger St. Jost
Riesling Spätlese trocken
11.5%, ♀ till 2006 **87**

2002 Bacharacher Posten
Riesling Spätlese halbtrocken
11.5%, ♀ till 2007 **87**

2003 Bacharacher Wolfshöhle
Riesling Spätlese *
9%, ♀ till 2010 **86**

2003 Bacharacher Wolfshöhle
Riesling Auslese
8%, ♀ till 2013 **87**

2003 Bacharacher Kloster Fürstental
Riesling Eiswein – 11 –
7%, ♀ till 2015 **90**

2002 Bacharacher Wolfshöhle
Riesling Trockenbeerenauslese
7%, ♀ till 2019 **92**

2003 Bacharacher Kloster Fürstental
Riesling Eiswein – 1 –
7%, ♀ till 2020 **92**

2002 Bacharacher Kloster Fürstental
Riesling Eiswein **
7%, ♀ till 2020 **94**

RATZENBERGER

2002er
Steeger St. Jost
Riesling Spätlese trocken
Qualitätswein mit Prädikat
A. P. Nr. 1 698 179 11 03
Gutsabfüllung
alc. 11.5% by vol.   Mittelrhein   ℮ 750 ml
Weingut Ratzenberger · D-55422 Bacharach

The wines: **100** Perfect · **95–99** Outstanding · **90–94** Excellent · **85–89** Very good · **80–84** Good · **75–79** Average

263

WEINGUT SCHEIDGEN

Owner and manager: Georg Scheidgen
Winemaker: Georg Scheidgen
56598 Hammerstein, Hauptstraße 10
Tel. (0 26 35) 23 29, Fax 60 82
e-mail: winzer@weingut-scheidgen.de
Internet: weingut-scheidgen.de
*Directions: A 59 to Königsmünster, B 42
to Linz and Hammerstein; A 3/A 61 to Koblenz, B 42 to Neuwied and Hammerstein*
Sales: Birgit Lülsdorf, Georg Scheidgen
Opening hours: Mon.–Fri. 08:00 to
19:00 hours, Sat. u. Sun. 10:00 to 18:00
hours and by appointment
History: Winemaking in the family for
seven generations
Worth seeing: Vaulted cellar of quarry
stone

Vineyard area: 11.5 hectares
Annual production: 120,000 bottles
Top sites: Hammersteiner in
den Layfelsen and Schlossberg,
Leutesdorfer Gartenlay
Soil types: Decomposed slate and
grey wacke
Grape varieties: 40% Riesling,
16% Müller-Thurgau, 12% Weißburgunder, 8% Spätburgunder, 7% Grauburgunder, 6% each of Portugieser
and Dornfelder, 5% other varieties
Average yield: 94 hl/ha
Best vintage: 2002

The Scheidgen estate has produced particularly good dry wines in the difficult 2003 vintage, and this has been achieved without the addition of acidity. Last year, we preferred the Weißburgunder to the Grauburgunder, this year it is the other way around. We also liked the powerful off-dry Riesling Auslese. Going to the sweet Auslese wines, the Kerner is significantly better than the Riesling. Scheidgen has invested in mechanical care of the vineyards, as well as in modern cellar technology including a red wine fermenting tank. However, he continues to employ a confusing multitude of bottle shapes, colors and labels designed.

2003 Leutesdorfer Rosenberg
Riesling Hochgewächs trocken
12%, ♀ till 2006 — **82**

2003 Hammersteiner Hölle
Weißer Burgunder trocken
13%, ♀ till 2006 — **82**

2003 Hammersteiner Schlossberg
Riesling Spätlese trocken
13%, ♀ till 2007 — **83**

2003 Hammersteiner Hölle
Grauer Burgunder trocken
13%, ♀ till 2007 — **83**

2002 Hammersteiner Hölle
Weißer Burgunder trocken
12%, ♀ till 2006 — **84**

2003 Hammersteiner In den Layfelsen
Riesling Auslese halbtrocken
13%, ♀ till 2006 — **83**

2002 Hammersteiner In den Layfelsen
Riesling Hochgewächs halbtrocken
12.5%, ♀ till 2005 — **84**

**2003 Hammersteiner
Burg Hammerstein**
Kerner Auslese
10.5%, ♀ till 2010 — **83**

2002 Hammersteiner
Riesling Auslese
8%, ♀ till 2008 — **86**

WEINGUT SELT

Owner: Horst Peter Selt
56599 Leutesdorf, Zehnthofstraße 22
Tel. (0 26 31) 7 51 18, Fax 7 73 52
*Directions: A 59 to Königswinter, B 42
to Linz and Leutesdorf; A 3/A 61 to Ko-
blenz, B 9 or B 42 to Neuwied, B 42 to
Leutesdorf*
Sales: Frau Tilgen-Selt
Opening hours: Sat. 09:00 to 18:00
hours and by appointment
History: Winemaking in the family
since 1736
Worth a visit: Wine festival "Wein- und
Sektfrühling" on 1st weekend in June,
"Medieval festival" in September

Vineyard area: 3 hectares
Annual production: 30,000 bottles
Top sites: Leutesdorfer Gartenlay,
Forstberg and Rosenberg
Soil types: Decomposed slate and
grey wacke, partly with pumice
Grape varieties: 70% Riesling,
7% each of Kerner and Dornfelder,
6% Weißburgunder, 5% each of
Rivaner and Portugieser
Average yield: 85 hl/ha
Best vintages: 2001, 2002, 2003

The Selt winery has specialized in dry
wines and presented a good range of
2003. The decision not to add acidity has
paid off here. Selt's Leutesdorfer Forstberg is proof that excellent Rivaner can
be produced on the Mittelrhein. The 14
percent alcohol of his Riesling Spätlese
may be a bit over the top. The outstanding
highlight of the range is the dry Riesling
Kabinett from the Leutesdorfer Gartenlay
vineyard. The strengths of the Selt winery
are clearly in the dry and off-dry field.
This is one of the top wineries in Leutesdorf. Selt has already invested in the
purchase and restoration of an historical
building in order to complete the winery
surroundings, next he intends to increase
the size of his Riesling vineyards.

2003 Leutesdorfer Forstberg
Rivaner trocken
13%, ♀ till 2006 — **82**

2003 Leutesdorfer Forstberg
Riesling trocken
12.5%, ♀ till 2006 — **82**

2003 Leutesdorfer Forstberg
Riesling Spätlese trocken
14%, ♀ till 2006 — **83**

2002 Riesling "S" trocken
12%, ♀ till 2006 — **85**

2002 Leutesdorfer Forstberg
Riesling Spätlese trocken
12%, ♀ till 2006 — **85**

2003 Leutesdorfer Gartenlay
Riesling Kabinett trocken
12.5%, ♀ till 2007 — **86**

2003 Leutesdorfer Rosenberg
Riesling Kabinett halbtrocken
12%, ♀ till 2006 — **82**

2002 Leutesdorfer Gartenlay
Riesling Auslese halbtrocken
12.5%, ♀ till 2006 — **85**

2001 Leutesdorfer Gartenlay
Riesling Auslese
9%, ♀ till 2009 — **87**

2001 Leutesdorfer Forstberg
Riesling Beerenauslese
11%, ♀ till 2012 — **90**

The wines: **100** Perfect · **95–99** Outstanding · **90–94** Excellent · **85–89** Very good · **80–84** Good · **75–79** Average

265

WEINGUT SONNENHANG – EDELOBST-BRENNEREI

Owner and manager:
Heinz-Uwe and Andrea Fetz
56348 Dörscheid
Tel. (0 67 74) 15 48, Fax 82 19
Directions: B 42 to Kaub, about 3 kilometers to Dörscheid, on the hill
Sales: Heinz-Uwe and Andrea Fetz,
Opening hours: Mon. and Wed.–Fri. 09:00 to 12:00 and 13:00 to 19:00 hours; Sat. and Sun. 10:00 to 12:00 and 13:00 to 15:00 hours, by appointment
Restaurant: Landgasthaus Blücher, closed Tue., Tel. (0 67 74) 2 67
Worth seeing: New spirits distillery
Worth a visit: Echo on the Loreley plateau, menu accompanied by spirits

---

Vineyard area: 3.7 hectares
Annual production: 35,000 bottles
Top site: Kauber Backofen
Soil types: Slate, grey wacke
Grape varieties: 74% Riesling, 10% Spätburgunder, 7% Grauburgunder, 5% Müller-Thurgau, 4% Weißburgunder
Average yield: 75 hl/ha
Best vintages: 1998, 2000, 2002

Heinz-Uwe Fetz has invested heavily in his distillery, and is producing high quality spirits. The same can not be said unreservedly of his range of 2003 wines. Conditions were extremely dry in Dörscheid, why Fetz is marketing all his products except for a single Auslese as basic quality wines. Now that is what we call honest, and we respect it. Overall, the wines represent good value for money. His only predicate quality wine is a Wolfsnack Riesling Auslese. His Spätburgunder has an alcohol content of 15 percent by volume, which we feel is rather more than it should have. Fetz is one of the few wine producers on the right bank of the Rhine to care about maintaining the vineyards. The "Landgasthaus Blücher" restaurant run by his brother offers good cuisine to go with the wines and spirits.

2003 Riesling trocken
12%, ♀ till 2006 — 81

2003 Riesling Classic
11.5%, ♀ till 2006 — 81

2002 Riesling Classic
12%, ♀ till 2005 — 83

2003 Riesling feinherb
11.5%, ♀ till 2006 — 82

2002 Kauber Backofen
Riesling Spätlese
9%, ♀ till 2007 — 85

2003 Dörscheider Wolfsnack
Riesling Auslese
9.5%, ♀ till 2009 — 86

2002 Kauber Backofen
Riesling Eiswein
6.5%, ♀ till 2013 — 89

2002 Dörscheider Wolfsnack
Riesling Eiswein
7.8%, ♀ till 2015 — 90

——— Red wines ———

2002 Spätburgunder trocken
15%, ♀ till 2008 — 83

2001 Spätburgunder
trocken Barrique
14%, ♀ till 2007 — 84

2002 Spätburgunder
trocken Barrique
14.5%, ♀ till 2008 — 85

View of one of the many attractive half-timbered houses in Bacharach on the Mittel-rhein.
Photo: DWI/Hartmann

WEINGUT WEINGART

Owner: Florian Weingart family
Manager: Florian Weingart
Winemaker: Florian Weingart
56322 Spay, Mainzer Straße 32
Tel. (0 26 28) 87 35, Fax 28 35
e-mail: mail@weingut-weingart.de
Internet: www.weingut-weingart.de
Directions: A 61 Koblenz–Bingen,
Boppard exit; B 9 Koblenz–Boppard,
Spay exit
Sales: Ulrike Weingart
Opening hours: Mon.–Sat. 09:00 to
20:00 hours, Sun. 14:00 to 19:00 hours
by appointment
Vacation apartments: In historic half-
timbered house, directly on the Rhine

Vineyard area: 10 hectares
Annual production: 75,000 bottles
Top sites: Bopparder Hamm
Engelstein, Feuerlay and Ohlenberg,
Schloss Fürstenberg
Soil types: Decomposed Devon slate
Grape varieties: 93% Riesling, 5%
Spätburgunder, 2% Grauburgunder
Average yield: 58 hl/ha
Best vintages: 1998, 2001, 2002

Florian Weingart was a rising star for the Mittelrhein region last year, and he remains among the top producers of the region. The basic philosophy of the winery is based on selection of grapes in the best sites, and extremely low yields, sometimes well below 50 hectoliters per hectare. However, even Weingart had to realize that the extremely hot and dry 2003 vintage was an exceptional one, and limited the potential of what even he could achieve. Compared to the wines of the 2002 vintage, the dry 2003 wines cannot quite achieve the same level. As is the case in other wineries, these wines are characterized more by opulence and power than by elegance, mineral notes. Florian Weingart was one of the few top producers to make use of the special dispensation on acidity, and added some acidity to the must in some cases, depend-

ing on the pH-value. While we are certain that many producers have made excellent wines without adding acidity, we must also concede that Weingart has done it very well. Whether these wines will have any advantages later in their maturation cycle remains to be seen. What can already be said is that in the 2003 vintage wines with some residual sugar tend overall to be better than their dry counterparts. This is demonstrated very clearly by his Schloss Fürstenberg Riesling Spätlese, rated an excellent 89 points. In 2003 the estate has bottled no fewer than five different Auslese wines, three of them from the Feuerlay vineyard. Using the same vineyard designation, Weingart distinguished them by adding either one or two stars to the label. The one-star Auslese is riper, and characterized by botrytis, while the two-star Auslese is fresher, and has more clarity of fruit: two wines with very different styles. Best wine in the whole region is his two-star Auslese from the Feuerlay site. As in the previous vintage, Weingart has again harvested a Riesling Trockenbeerenauslese. Its rating of 98 points makes this not only the highest-rated wine in the Mittelrhein region, but also puts it in the absolute top group of German botrytis dessert wines. In spite of this, Florian Weingart has kept the price of this wine, of which only 200 bottles are available, delightfully low. Overall, this is a top-class estate, providing its wines at very consumer-friendly prices. We look forward with interest to seeing how his two new projects in Boppard and Spay, which employ new viticultural methods, will develop, and wait in eager anticipation of the maiden vintages from there.

2003 Riesling Kabinett trocken
11.5%, ♀ till 2006 **85**

2003 Riesling
Hochgewächs trocken
12%, ♀ till 2006 **86**

2003 Schloss Fürstenberg
Riesling Spätlese trocken
13%, ♀ till 2007 **86**

2002 Bopparder Hamm Feuerlay
Riesling Spätlese trocken
12%, ♀ till 2006   **87**

2002 Bopparder Hamm Ohlenberg
Riesling Spätlese trocken
12%, ♀ till 2006   **87**

2003 Bopparder Hamm Ohlenberg
Riesling Spätlese trocken
12%, ♀ till 2007   **87**

2003 Bopparder Hamm Feuerlay
Riesling Spätlese trocken
12%, ♀ till 2008   **88**

2002 Bopparder Hamm Feuerlay
Riesling Spätlese trocken *
12.5%, ♀ till 2007   **90**

2003 Riesling
Hochgewächs halbtrocken
11.5%, ♀ till 2007   **85**

2003 Riesling Kabinett halbtrocken
11.5%, ♀ till 2007   **87**

2003 Bopparder Hamm Feuerlay
Riesling Spätlese halbtrocken
11.5%, ♀ till 2008   **87**

2002 Bopparder Hamm Ohlenberg
Riesling Spätlese halbtrocken
11%, ♀ till 2008   **89**

2003 Schloss Fürstenberg
Riesling Spätlese halbtrocken
11.5%, ♀ till 2008   **89**

2002 Bopparder Hamm Ohlenberg
Riesling Spätlese halbtrocken *
12.5%, ♀ till 2008   **90**

2003 Bopparder Hamm Feuerlay
Grauer Burgunder Spätlese feinherb
13%, ♀ till 2007   **82**

2002 Schloss Fürstenberg
Riesling Hochgewächs
8.5%, ♀ till 2006   **86**

2003 Bopparder Hamm Feuerlay
Riesling Spätlese
7.5%, ♀ till 2009   **87**

2003 Schloss Fürstenberg
Riesling Auslese
8.5%, ♀ till 2010   **87**

2002 Bopparder Hamm Ohlenberg
Riesling Spätlese
9.5%, ♀ till 2008   **88**

2003 Bopparder Hamm Feuerlay
Riesling Auslese
10.5%, ♀ till 2010   **88**

2002 Bopparder Hamm Feuerlay
Riesling Spätlese
9%, ♀ till 2009   **89**

2001 Schloss Fürstenberg
Riesling Hochgewächs
9%, ♀ till 2008   **90**

2003 Schloss Fürstenberg
Riesling Spätlese
8%, ♀ till 2009   **90**

2003 Bopparder Hamm Feuerlay
Riesling Auslese *
8%, ♀ till 2012   **90**

2003 Schloss Fürstenberg
Riesling Auslese *
7%, ♀ till 2017   **90**

2003 Bopparder Hamm Feuerlay
Riesling Auslese **
8%, ♀ till 2015   **91**

2002 Schloss Fürstenberg
Riesling Eiswein
7.5%, ♀ till 2017   **92**

2002 Bopparder Hamm Feuerlay
Riesling Auslese
7%, ♀ till 2015   **92**

2002 Bopparder Hamm
Riesling Trockenbeerenauslese
6%, ♀ till 2025   **96**

2003 Bopparder Hamm
Riesling Trockenbeerenauslese
5.5%, ♀ till 2030   **98**

The wines: **100** Perfect · **95–99** Outstanding · **90–94** Excellent · **85–89** Very good · **80–84** Good · **75–79** Average

Mittelrhein

Weingut Broel

53604 Rhöndorf, Karl-Broel-Straße 3
Tel. (0 22 24) 26 55, Fax 26 55

This is the most northerly winery in the Mittelrhein region. Karl-Heinz Broel cultivates 2.5 hectares of vines at the foot of the Drachenfels. The late Chancellor Konrad Adenauer was a frequent visitor here. The wine we liked best was the 2003 Drachenfels Riesling Auslese (83 points).

Weingut Eisenbach-Korn

55413 Oberheimbach, Kirchstraße 23
Tel. (0 67 43) 60 81, Fax 96 06
e-mail: eisenbach-korn@oberheimbach.de

This winery is located close to Bingen. The multitude of bottles and labels is confusing. The highlights of the range are the sweet Riesling Spätlese and the 2002 Spätburgunder (Pinot Noir) Barrique.

Weingut Fendel

55413 Niederheimbach, Rheinstraße 79
Tel. (0 67 43) 68 29, Fax 64 08

Ferdinand and Jens Fendel tend some 11 hectares of vineyard, some of them on the right bank of the Rhine, in the Rheingau. Riesling makes up 80 percent of the vineyards, in addition Pinot Gris and Pinot Blanc as well as some red varieties are grown. The cellar hewn from rock is worth a visit. The wine we liked best was the Riesling Kabinett halbtrocken (off-dry – 84 points).

Weingut Karl Heidrich

55422 Bacharach, Oberstraße 16–18
Tel. (0 67 43) 9 30 60, Fax 9 30 61
e-mail: karlheidrich@yahoo.de
Internet: www.weingut-karl-heidrich.de

Together with his wife Susanne, Markus Heidrich runs the winery in Bacharach, with 4.5 hectares of vineyards as well as a vinotheque and the restaurant "Zum Weinkrug." The quality is decent. His dry Silvaner Spätlese, with 13 percent alcohol, is reminiscent of a Grüne Veltliner from the Wachau in Austria. Highlight is the dry Riesling Auslese (83 points).

Weingut Weinhaus Heilig Grab

56154 Boppard, Zelkesgasse 12
Tel. (0 67 42) 23 71, Fax 8 12 20
e-mail: WeinhausHeiligGrab@t-online.de
Internet: www.heiliggrab.de

Rudolf Schoeneberger is a busy man, and markets his wines primarily through the oldest wine bar/restaurant in Boppard, which has a chestnut garden that attracts droves of visitors, particularly in summer. The range of 2003 vintage wines he has presented is of basic quality, the addition of acidity did not work out particularly well. The best wine in our opinion is the Feuerlay Riesling Auslese (83 points).

Stadtweingut Bad Hönningen

53557 Bad Hönningen, Hauptstraße 182
Tel. (0 26 35) 31 16, Fax 64 77
e-mail: info@stadtweingut.de

The estate of the town of Bad Hönningen is run by Ruth and Bernhard Schneider, and is located in the extreme north of the growing region. They have presented quite an attractive range of 2003 vintage wines. The exotic dry Gewürztraminer is remarkable, and we also liked the Riesling Classic. We look forward with interest to see what effect the entry of son Sebastian into the business will have – he trained at the famous Dönnhoff estate on the Nahe.

Weingut Königshof

56154 Boppard, Rheinallee 43
Tel. (0 67 42) 23 30, Fax 18 00
e-mail: baudobriga@rz-online.de

This year, the Königshof winery in Boppard submitted not a single dry wine, but sent a total of four sweet Spätlese wines instead. The wine we liked best in the range is the Feuerlay Riesling Auslese (84 points).

Weingut Mohr & Söhne

56599 Leutesdorf,
Krautsgasse 16/Hauptstraße 12
Tel. (0 26 31) 7 21 11 und 7 15 29,
Fax 7 57 31
e-mail: weingut-mohr@t-online.de

The estate owned by the brothers Martin and Georg Mohr covers seven hectares, making it one of the larger operations in

Leutesdorf. Apart from Riesling, Gewürz-traminer, Pinot Gris and Pinot Noir are also produced. The wine we liked best is the Kerner Spätlese (83 points). A specialty listed by Mohr is his 1999 Riesling Eiswein, which has low residual sugar, is deep-toned and reminiscent of sherry.

Weingut Hermann Ockenfels

56599 Leutesdorf, Oelbergstraße 3
Tel. (0 26 31) 7 25 93, Fax 97 93 96
e-mail: lreblaus@aol.com
Internet: www.leutesdorf-rhein.de

The 2003 vintage with its often overripe grapes obviously caused a lot of problems at the Ockenfels winery. The range is acceptable, but has no highlights. As in the previous vintage, the wines labeled "Hochgewächs" are generally better than the predicate wines.

Weingut Bernhard Praß

55422 Bacharach-Steeg,
Blücherstraße 132
Tel. (0 67 43) 15 85, Fax 32 60
e-mail: Weingut-Prass@t-online.de

Bernhard Praß has presented a good range of 2003 vintage wines. The wines we liked best were the Riesling Classic as well as the Wolfshöhle Riesling Auslese. We would also have liked to taste a botrytis dessert wine, such as a Beerenauslese or Trockenbeerenauslese, which would certainly have been possible in the 2003 vintage.

Weingut Villa Riesling

55413 Manubach, In der Grube 4
Tel. (0 67 43) 94 76 41, Fax 94 76 43
e-mail: villa.riesling@t-online.de

Lars Dalgaard hails from Denmark, and is a passionate newcomer in this region, located directly next to the Dr. Randolf Kauer winery. He works minuscule areas in the Oberdiebacher Fürstenberg and Manubacher Mönchswingert sites. It is evident in the tasting that he added acidity to the must. We preferred the dry wines to the botrytis dessert wines. The Danish owner will still have to work very hard if he wants the quality presented in the bottle to justify the high prices being asked.

Weingut Volk

56322 Spay, Koblenzer Straße 6
Tel. (0 26 28) 82 90, Fax 98 74 16
e-mail: info@weingutvolk.de

Jürgen and Heidi Volk from Spay work about 3.3 hectares of the Bopparder Hamm vineyard. They presented an acceptable range of wines in 2003. The Riesling quality wine from the Bopparder Hamm site in the liter bottle represents good value for money.

Other wineries tasted

- Werner Bork, Bacharach-Steeg
- Reinhard u. Brigitte Brück, Bach.-Steeg
- Karl Hugemann, Leutesdorf
- Ewald Kemmer, Bacharach-Steeg
- Winzergenossenschaft Loreley, Bornich
- Manfred Müller, Königswinter
- Thomas Nudig, Bacharach-Steeg
- Rebstock – Thomas Heidrich, Bacharach

Recommended by our wine producers

Hotels und inns
Bacharach-Henschhausen: Landhaus Delle
Bacharach: Rhein-Hotel
Braubach: Weißen Schwanen
Dörscheid: Landgasthaus Blücher
Lahnstein: Dorint Rhein Lahn
Oberwesel: Schönburg
St. Goar: Schlosshotel und Villa Rheinfels, Landsknecht
Spay: Alter Posthof
Unkel: Rheinhotel Schulz

Restaurants, wine bars and winery facilities
Bacharach: Zum grünen Baum, Zum Rebstock – Thomas Heidrich, Weingut Karl Heidrich, Altes Haus
Boppard: Heilig Grab, Fondels Mühle
Boppard-Hirzenach: Hirsch
Kaub: Hotel-Restaurant Zum Turm
Neuwied: Parkrestaurant Nodhausen
Oberwesel: Historische Weinwirtschaft
Osterspai: Didinger – Bopparder Hamm
Urbar: Chiaro im Klostergut Besselich

Mosel-Saar-Ruwer

The year of superlatives

Is 2003 really the year of superlatives on the Mosel? With regard to weather data it certainly is. Every single parameter main-

tained since the beginning of official documentation saw the record broken in 2003. Whether it was the highest number

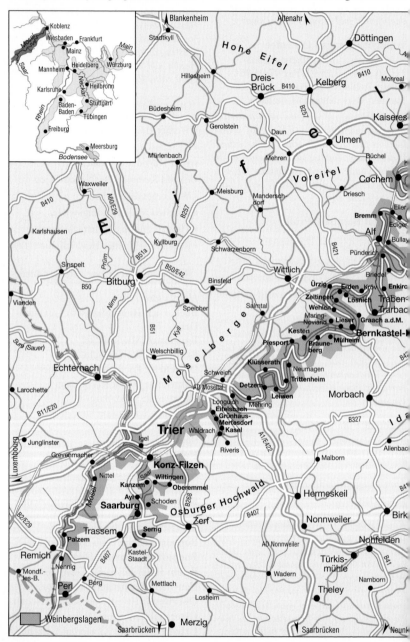

of sunshine hours recorded, the hottest summer, the hottest day or the hottest night – all these records fell in 2003. Accordingly, the progress of vegetative development was determined by these ex-

traordinary records. Early development of shoots, extremely early flowering and a consistent premature maturation period were the results. Where there was sufficient water available to ensure the vine had an adequate supply throughout the summer, the vines could be nursed to optimum physiological ripeness. This was a year in which old or ungrafted vines as well as those sites with an abundant water supply were clearly favored. In these vineyards, the producer was rewarded with perfectly ripened grapes, with must weights that were always at least at Spätlese levels.

However, only few producers managed to transform this ideal raw material into really great dry Riesling wines. Most of these wines are characterized by excessively high alcohol levels, which are not sufficiently balanced by appropriate levels of acidity or concentrated fruit. As a result, many of these dry wines appear dull, blunt, tart and not at all typical of Riesling. Looking at the top quality levels, "Erstes Gewächs" or "Großes Gewächs," known on the Mosel as "Erste Lage" (all mean First Growth), again only a handful of dry wines from the Mosel, Saar and Ruwer can compete with their counterparts from other regions.

On the other hand, the smooth, palate-pleasing wines in the off-dry or fruity categories are characterized by rich fruit and a smooth opulence that is much more pleasing, and in their style, which is so characteristic of this vintage, represent a category on their own.

With the benefit of hindsight, one could say that the preliminary accolades expressed with regard to this vintage long before the wines were ever made were over-optimistic, ...if only there were not quite a number of classic botrytis dessert Riesling wines that can quite credibly be described as wines of the century.

It has been a long time since we were last privileged to taste such an array of high-quality Beerenauslese wines, characterized by ripe and clear botrytis. Above these tower the monumental Trockenbeerenauslese wines, the best of which bear promise of virtually an unlimited maturation potential. It was certainly not easy to achieve the correct balance of extremely ripe, but very healthy grapes, with the appropriate amount of botrytis-infected grapes. Some producers have referred to the famous botrytis vintage of 1976 by comparison – although that differed in that botrytised grapes could be picked from the vine without any selection process. We would rather tend to side with the assessment of top producers such as Dr. Manfred Prüm or Egon Müller, who state that the 2003 vintage reminds them most of 1959.

However, it is the Spätlese and Auslese wines that are normally the best representatives of this region, and far too many wines in these categories were of somewhat ambiguous quality. Many wines came across with such uniformly high levels of acidity that it became impossible to discern the typical vineyard site characteristics. By contrast, many of these Riesling wines also show a dense structure, as well as mouthfilling ripe, yellow fruits and a persistent long finish that is extremely enjoyable. These wines are the best ambassadors of this vintage. For this reason, we were happy for the first time ever to award the dream score of 99 points to an Auslese wine.

Once again, it is mainly in the midfield that there have been some changes in the ratings of individual producers. A total of five producers have been upgraded to three-bunch status, confirming the determination shown by many wineries in this area to rise into the top echelons. More specifically, these are: Joh. Haart in Piesport, S. A. Prüm in Wehlen, both of the Thanisch wineries – Wwe. Dr. Thanisch Erben Müller-Burggraef as well as Erben Thanisch, both in Bernkastel-Kues, and Forstmeister Geltz-Zilliken in Saarburg.

Last year, we were unable to taste the ranges of Lauer in Ayl and of Dr. Wagner in Saarburg, partly because of late arrival, we have found them well worthy of their two-bunch status this year.

Last year the Jos. Christoffel jun. Winery in Ürzig managed to come from nowhere straight on a bunch rating. This year, another winery in Ürzig, that of Karl Erbes,

achieved the same status, earning its first bunch on the strength of its classic fruity Riesling wines. One bunch each was also awarded this year to the Melsheimer estate in Reil, which is dedicated to organic methods, as well as to Bert Simon from the Herrenberg estate in Serrig, whose concentrated and well-structured sweet Rieslings impressed us.

The so-called great vintage has ensured that the rising demand for Riesling wines from the Mosel, Saar and Ruwer areas continues unabated. That the producers in this region are serious in their pursuit of high quality is reflected in their growing purchases of vineyard sites in the best locations. This trend in the direction of superlative quality is also reflected in the results of the annual auctions. Both the strongly traditional Bernkasteler Ring as well as the "Große Ring" auction of the regional VDP association have enjoyed considerable price increases. The most recent example was a Trockenbeerenauslese of the renowned Fritz Haag winery in Brauneberg, which fetched the respectable price of 2,250 Euros per bottle on auction.

Major and minor vintages in the Mosel-Saar-Ruwer region

Vintage	Rating
2003	♣♣♣♣♣
2002	♣♣♣♣
2001	♣♣♣♣
2000	♣♣♣
1999	♣♣♣♣
1998	♣♣♣♣
1997	♣♣♣♣
1996	♣♣♣♣
1995	♣♣♣♣
1994	♣♣♣♣♣

Vintage rating:

♣♣♣♣♣ : Excellent vintage

♣♣♣♣ : Very good vintage

♣♣♣ : Good vintage

♣♣ : Average vintage

♣ : Poor vintage

The leading producers in the Mosel-Saar-Ruwer region

**Weingut Fritz Haag –
Dusemonder Hof, Brauneberg**

Weingut Dr. Loosen, Bernkastel

**Weingut Egon Müller –
Scharzhof, Wiltingen**

**Weingut Joh. Jos. Prüm,
Bernkastel-Wehlen**

**Weingut
Joh. Jos. Christoffel Erben, Ürzig**

**Weingut Grans-Fassian,
Leiwen**

**Weingut Reinhold Haart,
Piesport**

**Weingut Heymann-Löwenstein,
Winningen**

**Weingut Karthäuserhof,
Trier-Eitelsbach**

**Weingut
Reinhard und Beate Knebel,
Winningen**

Weingut Schloss Lieser, Lieser

**Weingut Markus Molitor,
Bernkastel-Wehlen**

Weingut Sankt Urbans-Hof, Leiwen

**Weingut Selbach-Oster,
Zeltingen**

**Weingut Erben von Beulwitz,
Mertesdorf**

**Weingut Clüsserath-Eifel,
Trittenheim**

**Weingut Clüsserath-Weiler,
Trittenheim**

**Weingut Franz-Josef Eifel,
Trittenheim**

Weingut Joh. Haart, Piesport

Weingut Kurt Hain, Piesport

Weinhof Herrenberg, Schoden

**Weingut von Hövel,
Konz-Oberemmel**

**Weingut Carl August
Immich – Batterieberg, Enkirch**

**Weingut Karlsmühle,
Mertesdorf**

Weingut Kees-Kieren, Graach

**Weingut Reichsgraf von
Kesselstatt, Morscheid**

Weingut Kirsten, Klüsserath

Weingut Carl Loewen, Leiwen

**Weingut Mönchhof –
Robert Eymael, Ürzig**

Weingut von Othegraven, Kanzem

Weingut Paulinshof, Kesten

**Weingüter Dr. Pauly-Bergweiler
und Peter Nicolay, Bernkastel-Kues**

**Weingut S. A. Prüm,
Bernkastel-Wehlen**

**Weingut Johann Peter Reinert,
Kanzem**

**Weingut Max Ferd. Richter,
Mülheim**

Weingut Josef Rosch, Leiwen

Weingut Schloss Saarstein, Serrig

Weingut Willi Schaefer, Graach

Weingut Heinz Schmitt, Leiwen

**Gutsverwaltung von
Schubert – Maximin Grünhaus,
Mertesdorf**

**Weingut Wwe. Dr. H. Thanisch –
Erben Müller-Burggraef,
Bernkastel-Kues**

Weingut Wwe. Dr. H. Thanisch –
Erben Thanisch, Bernkastel-Kues

Weingut Vollenweider,
Traben-Trarbach

Weingüter Wegeler – Gutshaus
Bernkastel, Bernkastel-Kues

Weingut Dr. F. Weins-Prüm,
Bernkastel-Wehlen

Weingut Forstmeister Geltz –
Zilliken, Saarburg

Bischöfliche Weingüter, Trier

Weingut Brauneberger Hof,
Brauneberg

Weingut Clemens Busch, Pünderich

Weingut Jos. Christoffel Jun.,
Ürzig

Weingut Ansgar Clüsserath,
Trittenheim

Weingut Ernst Clüsserath,
Trittenheim

Weingut Stephan Ehlen,
Erden

Weingut Reinhold Franzen, Bremm

Weingut Franz Friedrich-Kern,
Bernkastel-Wehlen

Weingut Leo Fuchs, Pommern

Weingut Willi Haag, Brauneberg

Weingut Freiherr von
Heddesdorff, Winningen

Weingut Heribert Kerpen,
Bernkastel-Wehlen

Weingut Sybille Kuntz,
Bernkastel-Lieser

Weingut Peter Lauer –
Weinhaus Ayler Kupp, Ayl

Lubentiushof
Weingut Andreas Barth, Niederfell

Weingut Alfred Merkelbach
Geschw. Albertz-Erben, Ürzig

Weingut Meulenhof, Erden

Weingut Milz –
Laurentiushof, Trittenheim

Weingut Molitor – Rosenkreuz,
Minheim

Weingut Martin Müllen,
Traben-Trarbach

Weingut Walter Rauen, Detzem

Weingut F. J. Regnery, Klüsserath

Weingut Andreas Schmitges,
Erden

Weingut Studert-Prüm –
Maximinhof, Bernkastel-Wehlen

Weingut Vereinigte Hospitien, Trier

Weingut van Volxem, Wiltingen

Weingut Dr. Heinz Wagner,
Saarburg

Weingut Weller-Lehnert, Piesport

Weingut Bastgen, Monzel

Weingut Blees-Ferber, Leiwen

Weingut Heribert Boch,
Trittenheim

Weingut Bernhard Eifel,
Trittenheim

Weingut Eifel-Pfeiffer, Trittenheim

Weingut Karl Erbes, Ürzig

Weingut Fries, Winningen

Weingut Herrenberg –
Bert Simon, Serrig

Weingut Rüdiger Kröber, Winningen

Weingut Lehnert-Veit, Piesport

Weingut Melsheimer, Reil

Weingut Philipps-Eckstein, Graach-Schäferei

Weingut Piedmont, Konz-Filzen

Weingut Familie Rauen, Thörnich

Weingut Reh, Schleich

Weingut Hans Resch, Wiltingen

Weingut Reuscher-Haart, Piesport

Weingut Richard Richter, Winningen

Weingut Römerhof, Riol

Weingut Martin Schömann, Zeltingen-Rachtig

Weingut Später-Veit, Piesport

Weingut Peter Terges, Trier

Classification of producers

Highest rating,
for world-class wine producers

Excellent producers counted
as among the best in Germany

Very good producers
who have been making consistently
high quality wines for many years

Good producers who do better
than make just everyday wines

Reliable producers making
decent standard qualitiy wines

The best vineyard sites in the Mosel-Saar-Ruwer region *

Mosel

Bernkastel: Doctor, Lay, Graben, Badstube

Brauneberg: Juffer-Sonnenuhr, Juffer

Dhron: Hofberg

Erden: Treppchen, Prälat

Graach: Himmelreich, Domprobst

Hatzenport: Kirchberg

Leiwen: Laurentiuslay

Lieser: Niederberg Helden

Piesport: Goldtröpfchen, Domherr

Trittenheim: Apotheke, Felsenkopf, Leiterchen

Ürzig: Würzgarten

Wehlen: Sonnenuhr

Winningen: Uhlen, Röttgen

Wintrich: Ohligsberg

Zeltingen: Sonnenuhr

Saar

Ayl: Kupp

Filzen: Pulchen

Kanzem: Altenberg

Oberemmel: Hütte

Ockfen: Bockstein

Saarburg: Rausch

Serrig: Herrenberg, Würtzberg, Schloss Saarstein, Schloss Saarfelser Schlossberg

Wawern: Herrenberg

Wiltingen: Scharzhofberg, Braune Kupp, Hölle

Ruwer

Eitelsbach: Karthäuserhofberg

---

* Source: VDP Mosel-Saar-Ruwer

WEINGUT BASTGEN

Owner: Mona Bastgen and Armin Vogel
Vineyard manager: Mona Bastgen
Winemaker: Armin Vogel
54518 Monzel, Hofstraße 18
Tel. (0 65 35) 93 30 92, Fax 15 79
e-mail: info@weingut-bastgen.de
Internet: www.weingut-bastgen.de
Directions: A 48/1, Wittlich or Salmtal exit
Sales: Mona Bastgen and Armin Vogel by appointment

Vineyard area: 4.5 hectares
Annual production: 30,000 bottles
Top sites: Kestener Paulinshofberger, Brauneberger Juffer-Sonnenuhr, Kueser Weisenstein
Soil types: Decomposed slate, sand and loess
Grape varieties: 75% Riesling, 15% Weißburgunder, 5% Müller-Thurgau, 5% red varieties
Average yield: 60 hl/ha
Best vintages: 2001, 2002, 2003
Member: Bernkasteler Ring

Mona Bastgen and Armin Vogel run this winery in Monzel on the Mittelmosel. Not far from Bernkastel and Kues, this is where you find one top vineyard with steep slopes and slates soils next to the other. As Mona Bastgen states: "Wine is one of the few remaining natural products that man produces on an individual basis." Armin Vogel: "From carefully tending the vines through to minimal intervention in the cellar – we put in a lot of manual work and care to produce authentic wines." The 2003 range presented by this winery shows that they are continually getting better at achieving this goal. The Spätlese from Kesten is without a doubt the best of the dry Rieslings. The heart of the range consists of three very good fruity Spätlese wines, while the flagship of the range is the extremely good Kestener Paulinshofberger Auslese.

2003 Riesling trocken
11.5%, ♀ till 2006 — 82

2003 "Blauschiefer"
Riesling Kabinett trocken
12.5%, ♀ till 2006 — 83

2003 Kestener Paulinshofberger
Riesling Spätlese trocken
13%, ♀ till 2008 — 86

2003 Kestener Paulinshofberger
Riesling Kabinett
11%, ♀ till 2007 — 83

2003 Kueser Weisenstein
Riesling Spätlese
13.5%, ♀ till 2008 — 84

2003 Kestener Paulinshofberger
Riesling Kabinett "Auf den Felsen"
9.5%, ♀ till 2007 — 84

2003 Kestener Paulinshofberger
Riesling Spätlese
8.5%, ♀ till 2008 — 85

2003 Brauneberger Juffer-Sonnenuhr
Riesling Spätlese
12.5%, ♀ till 2008 — 86

2003 Kestener Paulinshofberger
Riesling Auslese
10%, ♀ till 2010 — 89

The estates: ✦✦✦✦✦ World's finest · ✦✦✦✦ Germany's best · ✦✦✦ Very good · ✦✦ Good · ✦ Reliable

WEINGUT
ERBEN VON BEULWITZ

Owner: Herbert Weis
Manager and winemaker:
Herbert Weis
54318 Mertesdorf, Eitelsbacher Weg 4
Tel. (06 51) 9 56 10, Fax 9 56 11 50
e-mail: info@von-beulwitz.de
Internet: www.von-beulwitz.de
Directions: A 48, Kenn-Ruwertal exit,
in direction of Mertesdorf
Sales: Anytime
Wine bar: "Von Beulwitz," daily from
10:00 to 22:00 hours
Restaurant: "Vinum," daily from 10:00
to 14:00 and 18:00 to 22:00 hours
Specialties: Beef brawn, local venison,
pike-perch

Vineyard area: 6.2 hectares
Annual production: 48,000 bottles
Top sites: Kaseler Nies'chen and
Kehrnagel, Eitelsbacher Marienholz
Soil types: Decomposed slate
Grape varieties: 90% Riesling,
5% each of Weißburgunder and
Spätburgunder
Average yield: 53 hl/ha
Best vintages: 1999, 2000, 2003
Member: Bernkasteler Ring

The Erben von Beulwitz winery was already collecting awards at the Paris world exhibition in 1867. However, the current owner Herbert Weis, who took over the property in Kasel in 1982, does not have to refer to the past. There has been practically no weak vintage here since 1995. Among the 2002 wines there were a few that did not quite have the class shown in previous vintages. The 2003 vintage was most enjoyable, with the sweet wines showing a rich fruity spectrum. The wine we particularly liked here is the Spätlese, picked from 100-year-old ungrafted vines. The winery business is augmented by a first-class hotel and restaurant located in Mertesdorf. A vinotheque has recently been added to the restaurant, where the estate's wines are available.

2003 Kaseler Nies'chen
Riesling Kabinett
9.5%, ♀ till 2008 — 87

2001 Kaseler Nies'chen
Riesling Auslese ****
7.5%, ♀ till 2009 — 88

2003 Kaseler Nies'chen
Riesling Spätlese * – 6 –
8%, ♀ till 2009 — 89

2003 Kaseler Nies'chen
Riesling Spätlese Alte Reben – 7 –
⤳ auction wine, 8.5%, ♀ till 2009 — 89

2003 Kaseler Nies'chen
Riesling Auslese ** – 5 –
8%, ♀ till 2010 — 90

2002 Kaseler Nies'chen
Riesling Spätlese *** Alte Reben
⤳ auction wine, 8%, ♀ till 2009 — 90

2002 Kaseler Nies'chen
Riesling Auslese lange Goldkapsel
⤳ auction wine, 7.5%, ♀ till 2009 — 90

2003 Kaseler Nies'chen
Riesling Auslese *** – 4 –
8.5%, ♀ till 2010 — 91

2003 Kaseler Nies'chen
Riesling Eiswein – 3 –
7.5%, ♀ till 2012 — 92

2003 Kaseler Nies'chen
Riesling Eiswein – 1 –
⤳ auction wine, 8.5%, ♀ till 2012 — 93

2003 Kaseler Nies'chen
Riesling Beerenauslese – 23 –
⤳ auction wine, 7.5%, ♀ till 2010 — 93

Produce of Germany
Gutsabfüllung
Alc. 8,5 % by vol.
750 ml

Erben von Beulwitz
MOSEL-SAAR-RUWER
2003er Kaseler Nies'chen
Riesling Spätlese-Alte Reben
Qualitätswein mit Prädikat
A.P.-Nr. 3 519 004-07-04

The wines: **100** Perfect · **95–99** Outstanding · **90–94** Excellent · **85–89** Very good · **80–84** Good · **75–79** Average

279

BISCHÖFLICHE WEINGÜTER

Owner: Bishop's theological seminary, Hohe Domkirche
Estate director: Wolfgang Richter
Winemaker: Johannes Becker
54290 Trier, Gervasiusstraße 1
Tel. (06 51) 14 57 60, Fax 4 02 53
e-mail: info@bwgtrier.de
Internet: www.bwgtrier.de
Directions: Trier city center, near Kaiserthermen (Roman baths) and cloth factory (Tuchfabrik)
Sales: Erwin Engel
Opening hours: Mon.–Fri. 09:00 to 17:00 hours
Worth seeing: 400-year-old vaulted barrel cellar

Vineyard area: 106 hectares
Annual production: 800,000 bottles
Top sites: Scharzhofberger, Erdener Treppchen and Prälat, Kaseler Nies'chen, Ayler Kupp, Kanzemer Altenberg
Soil types: Devon slate, grey wacke, decomposed slate
Grape varieties: 96% Riesling, 3% Spätburgunder, 1% St. Laurent
Average yield: 67 hl/ha
Best vintages: 1997, 1999, 2003

The formerly independent church-owned wineries of the Hohe Domkirche and the theological seminary own property on the Mittelmosel, the Ruwer and Saar. They have no less than six hectares of the legendary Scharzhofberg vineyard. The list of top-class vineyard holdings is almost endless, as are the passages through the extensive barrel cellars located below the city center of Trier. While the 2001 vintage was a mixed bag, the 2002 range was characterized by a high level of acidity, a result of high yields. This year we can report that the situation is improving, the wines of the 2003 vintage show more concentration and body. We particularly liked the invigorating Nies'chen Auslese.

2003 Scharzhofberger
Riesling Spätlese trocken
12.5%, ♀ till 2006   **82**

2003 Ayler Kupp
Riesling Kabinett halbtrocken
11.5%, ♀ till 2006   **83**

2003 Eitelsbacher Marienholz
Riesling Kabinett
9.5%, ♀ till 2008   **84**

2003 Scharzhofberger
Riesling Kabinett
9.5%, ♀ till 2008   **85**

2002 Kaseler Nies'chen
Riesling Spätlese
8.5%, ♀ till 2008   **86**

2003 Kanzemer Altenberg
Riesling Spätlese
9%, ♀ till 2008   **86**

2002 Erdener Prälat
Riesling Spätlese
8%, ♀ till 2008   **87**

2003 Ayler Kupp Riesling Auslese
9%, ♀ till 2009   **88**

2003 Kaseler Kehrnagel
Riesling Auslese
9%, ♀ till 2009   **89**

2001 Erdener Treppchen
Riesling Auslese Goldkapsel
8%, ♀ till 2010   **89**

2001 Kaseler Nies'chen
Riesling Auslese Goldkapsel
7.5%, ♀ till 2010   **89**

2003 Scharzhofberger
Riesling Auslese Goldkapsel
9%, ♀ till 2010   **89**

2003 Kaseler Nies'chen
Riesling Auslese Goldkapsel
9%, ♀ till 2010   **90**

The estates: ⁑⁑⁑⁑⁑ World's finest · ⁑⁑⁑⁑ Germany's best · ⁑⁑⁑ Very good · ⁑⁑ Good · ⁑ Reliable

WEINGUT BLEES-FERBER

Owner and manager:
Stefan Blees
54340 Leiwen, Liviastraße 1a
Tel. (0 65 07) 31 52, Fax 84 06
e-mail:
weingut-blees-ferber@t-online.de
Internet: www.blees-ferber.de
Directions: A 48, Föhren exit;
A 1 Mehring exit; the winery is outside
the village limits, on the right, among the
vineyards
Sales: Stefan and Karl Blees
by appointment
Guest house: With modern apartments
Worth seeing: Beautiful view of the
Mosel

Vineyard area: 7.5 hectares
Annual production: 50,000 bottles
Top sites: Piesporter Gärtchen
(monopole) and Goldtröpfchen,
Trittenheimer Apotheke and Altärchen, Leiwener Laurentiuslay
Soil types: Decomposed slate
Grape varieties: 86% Riesling,
6% Müller-Thurgau, 4% each of Spät- and Weißburgunder
Average yield: 77 hl/ha
Best vintages: 2001, 2002, 2003

Stefan Blees took over responsibility for this family operation once he had completed his training in the mid-Nineties, thus becoming the third generation in charge. The acquisition of another winery brought in holdings in the top-class Piesporter Goldtröpfchen vineyard, as well as sole ownership of the tiny Gärtchen site. Together with his father Karl, Stefan Blees has set his sights on producing top-quality Mosel wines, and it appears he is moving closer to that goal. The 2003 range continues seamlessly from the good work done in 2001 and 2002. The wines are characterized by a refreshing acidity, and are very well balanced. The wine we liked best was the Trittenheimer Apotheke Riesling Trockenbeerenauslese.

2003 Piesporter Gärtchen
Riesling Spätlese halbtrocken
12.5%, ♀ till 2007 — **82**

2003 Leiwener Laurentiuslay
Riesling Kabinett
9%, ♀ till 2007 — **83**

2003 Piesporter Goldtröpfchen
Riesling Spätlese
9.5%, ♀ till 2007 — **83**

2002 Piesporter Goldtröpfchen
Riesling Spätlese
9%, ♀ till 2008 — **85**

2003 Trittenheimer Apotheke
Riesling Spätlese
8.5%, ♀ till 2009 — **85**

2003 Leiwener Klostergarten
Riesling Auslese
7%, ♀ till 2010 — **85**

2001 Piesporter Gärtchen
Riesling Auslese
8%, ♀ till 2008 — **86**

2003 Piesporter Gärtchen
Riesling Auslese
8.5%, ♀ till 2010 — **86**

2003 Leiwener Klostergarten
Riesling Eiswein
8%, ♀ till 2012 — **88**

2001 Leiwener Klostergarten
Riesling Eiswein
8%, ♀ till 2010 — **89**

2002 Leiwener Klostergarten
Riesling Eiswein
7.5%, ♀ till 2010 — **89**

2003 Trittenheimer Apotheke
Riesling Trockenbeerenauslese
8%, ♀ till 2015 — **90**

The wines: **100** Perfect · **95–99** Outstanding · **90–94** Excellent · **85–89** Very good · **80–84** Good · **75–79** Average

281

WEINGUT HERIBERT BOCH

Owner and manager:
Michael Boch
54349 Trittenheim,
Moselweinstraße 62
Tel. (0 65 07) 27 13, Fax 67 95
e-mail: Weingut.Boch@t-online.de
Directions: A 1 from north, Föhren exit;
A 1 from south, Mehring exit
Sales: Anne Boch
Opening hours: Mon.–Fri. 09:00 to
19:00 hours, Sat. 10:00 to 19:00 hours
and by appointment

Vineyard area: 4.95 hectares
Annual production: 40,000 bottles
Top sites: Trittenheimer
Apotheke and Altärchen
Soil types: Decomposed slate,
Devon slate with loess
Grape varieties: 56% Riesling,
22% Spätburgunder, 10% Müller-
Thurgau, 5% Kerner, 4% Cabernet
Sauvignon, 3% Bacchus
Average yield: 75 hl/ha
Best vintages: 2002, 2003

A qualified winemaker and a lady with a business degree: the ideal combination to run a winery. Winemaker Michael Boch is responsible for the vineyards and cellar, while his wife Anne looks after the accounts and sales. The winery has almost five hectares in the renowned Trittenheim vineyards. All started with the acquisition of a very small winery in 1989. Additional land in the best sites was acquired step by step. What is perhaps most unusual for a Mosel winery is that more than a quarter of the vineyards is planted to red varieties. We showed our appreciation for the quality of wines produced here by awarding a bunch of grapes last year, and the range of 2003 wines presented has confirmed that this was justified. We particularly liked the Trittenheimer Apotheke Beerenauslese, while the 2002 Spätburgunder (Pinot Noir) is arguably the best Boch has ever produced.

2003 Trittenheimer Apotheke
Riesling Spätlese trocken
13.5%, ♀ till 2008 **83**

2003 Trittenheimer Apotheke
Riesling Spätlese halbtrocken
12.5%, ♀ till 2008 **83**

2003 Trittenheimer Altärchen
Riesling Kabinett
10.5%, ♀ till 2007 **82**

2003 Trittenheimer Apotheke
Riesling Spätlese
10%, ♀ till 2008 **84**

2002 Trittenheimer Apotheke
Riesling Auslese
8%, ♀ till 2008 **86**

2002 Trittenheimer Apotheke
Riesling Eiswein
8.5%, ♀ till 2009 **87**

2003 Trittenheimer Apotheke
Riesling Auslese
9.5%, ♀ till 2010 **87**

2003 Trittenheimer Apotheke
Riesling Beerenauslese
9.5%, ♀ till 2015 **89**

———— Red wine ————

2002 Trittenheimer Altärchen
Spätburgunder trocken
12%, ♀ till 2008 **83**

2002er
Trittenheimer Apotheke
RIESLING KABINETT
Halbtrocken

WEINGUT
heRIBERT Boch

WEINORT TRITTENHEIM

0,75 l
11,0 % vol

D-54349 Trittenheim / Mosel
MOSEL-SAAR-RUWER
GUTSABFÜLLUNG
QUALITÄTSWEIN MIT PRÄDIKAT
Amtliche Prüfnummer 2 607 314 06 03

Typical steep slopes along the Mosel in winter, dominated by the towers of the Beilstein castle ruins.
Photo: DWI/Hartmann

WEINGUT BRAUNEBERGER HOF

Owner and manager:
Martin Conrad
54472 Brauneberg, Moselweinstr. 133
Tel. (0 65 34) 9 39 80, Fax 93 98 55
e-mail: info@braunebergerhof.de
Internet: www.braunebergerhof.de
*Directions: A 1/A 48 Koblenz–Trier,
Wittlich exit, in direction of Bernkastel-
Kues, via Mülheim to the B 53 in direc-
tion of Trier to Brauneberg*
Sales: Martin Conrad
Opening hours: Mon.–Fri. 09:00 to
19:00 hours, Sat. and Sun. 10:00 to
15:00 hours by appointment
Restaurant: In Brauneberger Hof Hotel
Fri.–Wed. from 18:00 to 22:00 hours
Specialties: Fresh eel or pike-perch from
the Mosel
History: Winery first documented in 1558
Worth seeing: Vaulted cellar dating
to 1750

Vineyard area: 3.3 hectares
Annual production: 26,000 bottles
Top sites: Brauneberger
Juffer and Juffer-Sonnenuhr
Soil types: Decomposed gray slate
Grape varieties: 95% Riesling,
5% Weißburgunder
Average yield: 70 hl/ha
Best vintages: 2001, 2002, 2003
Member: Bernkasteler Ring

The Conrad family has been involved in winemaking on the Mosel for more than 400 years. The ancient Roman cellar facility dating to the 3rd century is not the only thing worth seeing here. The range of 2003 vintage wines is the best the young winemaker Martin Conrad has produced since he joined his parents business in 1998. The wines are characterized by a refreshing acidity, they are both spicy and harmonious. Although the share of dry wines is increasing each year, we were again most impressed by his fruity sweet wines – so much so that we have added a second bunch of grapes to the rating.

2003 Veldenzer Kirchberg
Riesling trocken
12%, ♀ till 2006 — **83**

2003 Brauneberger Juffer
Riesling trocken Goldkapsel
12.5%, ♀ till 2007 — **86**

2003 Brauneberger Juffer-Sonnenuhr
Riesling trocken Goldkapsel
12.5%, ♀ till 2008 — **87**

2003 Mülheimer Sonnenlay
Riesling halbtrocken
11%, ♀ till 2008 — **84**

2003 Brauneberger Juffer
Riesling halbtrocken
11.5%, ♀ till 2008 — **84**

2003 Brauneberger Juffer
Riesling halbtrocken Goldkapsel
11.8%, ♀ till 2008 — **85**

2003 Brauneberger Juffer
Riesling Spätlese
9%, ♀ till 2008 — **85**

2003 Brauneberger Juffer-Sonnenuhr
Riesling Auslese
9.5%, ♀ till 2010 — **88**

2003 Brauneberger Juffer-Sonnenuhr
Riesling Beerenauslese
8.5%, ♀ till 2012 — **91**

2003 Brauneberger Juffer-Sonnenuhr
Riesling Trockenbeerenauslese
8.5%, ♀ till 2015 — **93**

The estates: ♯♯♯♯♯ World's finest · ♯♯♯♯ Germany's best · ♯♯♯ Very good · ♯♯ Good · ♯ Reliable

WEINGUT CLEMENS BUSCH

Owner: Clemens and Rita Busch
Manager: Clemens Busch
Administration: Uwe Jostock and Clemens Busch
Winemaker: Clemens Busch
56862 Pünderich, Kirchstraße 37
Tel. (0 65 42) 2 21 80, Fax 90 07 20
e-mail: weingut@clemens-busch.de
Directions: A 61, Rheinböllen exit, in direction of Zell; A 48, Wittlich exit, in direction of Zell
Sales: By appointment
Worth seeing: Vaulted cellar, original winery building – half-timbered house dating to 1663

Vineyard area: 9.7 hectares
Annual production: 55,000 bottles
Top site: Pündericher Marienburg
Soil types: Stony decomposed slate, red Devon slate, sandy clay with fossils
Grape varieties: 92% Riesling, 5% Müller-Thurgau, 3% Spätburgunder
Average yield: 59 hl/ha
Best vintages: 2001, 2002, 2003
Member: EcoVin

Clemens Busch was running this winery since 1985, and switched to organic practices. This includes severe pruning and selective harvesting, in the cellar Busch is increasingly fermenting his musts in temperature-controlled stainless steel tanks, though he has no plans to through out his oak barrels. Most of the wines are fermented dry, and the majority of sales go to the retail trade as well as to private consumers. We have noted a distinctly positive trend here in recent years. In 2002, Busch prodced particularly attractive dry Riesling wines. The 2003 wines, too, have a lot of character, and their concentrated spicy style reminds us of dry Rieslings from the Lower Mosel. He is equally at home in the fruity category, as shown by the concentrated structure of his harmonious Spätlese and Auslese wines.

2003 Pündericher Marienburg
Riesling Spätlese trocken **
12.5%, ♀ till 2008   87

2001 Pündericher Marienburg
Riesling Spätlese
7.5%, ♀ till 2008   87

2003 Pündericher Marienburg
Riesling Kabinett
7.5%, ♀ till 2009   87

2002 Pündericher Marienburg
Riesling Auslese ***
7%, ♀ till 2010   88

2003 Pündericher Marienburg
Riesling Kabinett "Fahrlay"
12.5%, ♀ till 2008   88

2003 Pündericher Marienburg
Riesling Spätlese "Weißenberg"
12.5%, ♀ till 2009   89

2003 Pündericher Marienburg
Riesling Spätlese
8.5%, ♀ till 2010   90

2001 Pündericher Marienburg
Riesling Beerenauslese
6.5%, ♀ till 2012   91

2003 Pündericher Marienburg
Riesling Auslese
7%, ♀ till 2014   92

2003 Pündericher Marienburg
Riesling Auslese ***
7.5%, ♀ till 2015   92

2001 Pündericher Marienburg
Riesling Trockenbeerenauslese
6%, ♀ till 2018   94

The wines: **100** Perfect · **95–99** Outstanding · **90–94** Excellent · **85–89** Very good · **80–84** Good · **75–79** Average

WEINGUT JOH. JOS. CHRISTOFFEL ERBEN

Owner: Robert Eymael
Manager: Robert Eymael
Administration: Volker Besch
Winemaker: Hans Leo Christoffel
54539 Ürzig, Mönchhof
Tel. (0 65 32) 9 31 64, Fax 9 31 66
e-mail: moenchhof.eymael@t-online.de
Directions: Via the B 53
Sales: At Mönchhof estate
by appointment

Vineyard area: 3.5 hectares
Annual production: 30,000 bottles
Top sites: Erdener Treppchen,
Ürziger Würzgarten
Soil types: Decomposed Devon slate,
lower new red sandstone
Grape varieties: 100% Riesling
Average yield: 65 hl/ha
Best vintages: 1998, 2000, 2002
Member: VDP

There was an important change here in 2001: Hans Leo Christoffel, who had formally reached retirement age at 65, leased out his 2.2 hectares of vineyard to Robert Eymael, a colleague from Ürzig. The substance of the vineyard area is to be retained, the wines are vinified separately, with their own label and winery number. However, the administration and sales run exclusively via the Mönchhof winery, owned by Robert Eymael. It was of particular importance for Eymael to be able to refer to Christoffel for advice and assistance in future, in order to retain the specific style of the wines, and thus Christoffel has gone into what he calls active retirement. The wines are vinified in a separate section of the Mönchhof cellars. The vineyards owned by the Christoffel family may not be large, but they are among the best. The vines are mostly ungrafted, and trained on the traditional single-pole trellises on steep, slate-covered slopes in the top vineyards Erdener Treppchen and Ürziger Würzgarten. Even in the last years of his independent operation, Christoffel was still busy planting ungrafted vines in the Treppchen vineyard – at his own risk, and totally unsubsidized. Christoffel is particularly proud of his dry wines, and it is true that they can be remarkable in a good vintage, but it is really the delicately fruity and botrytized Riesling wines that show the true potential of the vineyards. In his top vineyard Ürziger Würzgarten Christoffel distinguishes among as many as five different Auslese wines, which he designates with different numbers of stars. The decade of the Nineties was one long success story for Christoffel, and his 2000 vintage range was also well above the average for the region. Following on a slight dip in quality in 2001, the 2002 vintage wines again shone in their usual quality. Finesse, elegance and a generally light style were the major attributes of an excellent 2002 range. Exemplary to see how delicacy, breeding and dense mineral Riesling fruit were meshed together in perfect harmony. This was achieved only partially in 2003, a slightly piquant acidity, which appears to have been added, sets the tone, giving the wines a slightly blunt finish. At times of tasting the range, the wines lacked clarity of fruit, and were rather uniform in style. Only time will tell to what extent the acidity will integrate with the typical Riesling fruit. Whereas the 2002 vintage produced Auslese wines designated with three and four stars, which had the style of elegant Beerenauslese wines, we were shown only two-star Auslese wines from the 2003 vintage.

2002 Ürziger Würzgarten
Riesling Kabinett trocken
10.5%, ♀ till 2006   **85**

2002 Ürziger Würzgarten
Riesling Auslese trocken
12%, ♀ till 2007   **85**

2002 Ürziger Würzgarten
Riesling Spätlese trocken
11.5%, ♀ till 2007   **86**

2003 Ürziger Würzgarten
Riesling Spätlese halbtrocken
11.5%, ♀ till 2006   **83**

The estates: ♦♦♦♦♦ World's finest · ♦♦♦♦ Germany's best · ♦♦♦ Very good · ♦♦ Good · ♦ Reliable

2001 Ürziger Würzgarten
Riesling Kabinett
8%, ♀ till 2007   **84**

2001 Erdener Treppchen
Riesling Kabinett
8%, ♀ till 2007   **84**

2002 Erdener Treppchen
Riesling Kabinett
8%, ♀ till 2008   **85**

2003 Erdener Treppchen
Riesling Kabinett
8.5%, ♀ till 2007   **85**

2003 Ürziger Würzgarten
Riesling Kabinett
8.5%, ♀ till 2007   **85**

2001 Erdener Treppchen
Riesling Spätlese
8%, ♀ till 2009   **86**

2001 Ürziger Würzgarten
Riesling Auslese
8%, ♀ till 2012   **87**

2001 Ürziger Würzgarten
Riesling Spätlese
8%, ♀ till 2010   **88**

2001 Ürziger Würzgarten
Riesling Eiswein
8%, ♀ till 2010   **88**

2002 Erdener Treppchen
Riesling Spätlese
8%, ♀ till 2009   **88**

2001 Ürziger Würzgarten
Riesling Auslese *
8%, ♀ till 2010   **89**

2001 Ürziger Würzgarten
Riesling Auslese **
8%, ♀ till 2012   **89**

2001 Ürziger Würzgarten
Riesling Auslese ***
8%, ♀ till 2012   **89**

2002 Ürziger Würzgarten
Riesling Kabinett
8%, ♀ till 2009   **89**

2002 Erdener Treppchen
Riesling Auslese **
7.5%, ♀ till 2009   **89**

2003 Erdener Treppchen
Riesling Spätlese
8.5%, ♀ till 2010   **89**

2003 Ürziger Würzgarten
Riesling Auslese *
8.5%, ♀ till 2010   **89**

2001 Ürziger Würzgarten
Riesling Auslese **** Goldkapsel
⋎ auction wine, 8%, ♀ till 2012   **89**

2001 Erdener Treppchen
Riesling Auslese **
8%, ♀ till 2014   **90**

2002 Ürziger Würzgarten
Riesling Spätlese
8%, ♀ till 2009   **90**

2003 Ürziger Würzgarten
Riesling Spätlese
8.5%, ♀ till 2010   **90**

2003 Erdener Treppchen
Riesling Auslese **
8.5%, ♀ till 2010   **90**

2003 Ürziger Würzgarten
Riesling Auslese **
8.5%, ♀ till 2012   **91**

2002 Ürziger Würzgarten
Riesling Auslese ***
8%, ♀ till 2010   **92**

2002 Ürziger Würzgarten
Riesling Eiswein – 11 –
8%, ♀ till 2012   **92**

2002 Ürziger Würzgarten
Riesling Eiswein – 18 –
8%, ♀ till 2012   **92**

2002 Ürziger Würzgarten
Riesling Auslese ****
⋎ auction wine, 8%, ♀ till 2010   **93**

JOH. JOS. CHRISTOFFEL ERBEN
2002
ERDENER TREPPCHEN
RIESLING AUSLESE **
QUALITÄTSWEIN MIT PRÄDIKAT   GUTSABFÜLLUNG WEINGUT JOH. JOS. CHRISTOFFEL ERBEN · D-54539 ÜRZIG   PRODUCE OF GERMANY
750 ml e   MOSEL · SAAR · RUWER   alc.7.5% by vol
A.P.Nr. 2 602 041 009 03

The wines: **100** Perfect · **95–99** Outstanding · **90–94** Excellent · **85–89** Very good · **80–84** Good · **75–79** Average

Mosel-Saar-Ruwer

WEINGUT
JOS. CHRISTOFFEL JUN.

**Owner: Karl-Josef Christoffel
and Annekatrin Christoffel-Prüm
54539 Ürzig, Moselufer 1–3
Tel. (0 65 32) 21 13, Fax 10 50**
*Directions: A 48 Koblenz–Trier, Wittlich
exit, in direction of Traben-Trarbach*
Sales: By appointment only
History: Family has made wine here for
400 years

Vineyard area: 2 hectares
Annual production: 20,000 bottles
Top sites: Ürziger Würzgarten,
Erdener Prälat and Treppchen,
Wehlener Sonnenuhr
Soil types: Slate
Grape varieties: 100% Riesling
Average yield: 80 hl/ha
Best vintages: 2001, 2002, 2003

It was pure coincidence. We found this tiny winery, which so far has not made any waves in the German market. However, they have been producing typical Mosel Riesling of a very high quality here for decades. This is evidenced by a well-stocked rarities cellar, with wines up to 30 years old still available for sale – at very moderate prices. As with all good producers, the foundation for quality is to be found in the vineyards. Only Riesling is planted here, on ungrafted vines, with an average age of the vines of 40 years. The winery owns parcels of the best vineyards in Ürzig and Erden, while some of the best parcels of the former Prüm vineyards in Wehlen and Graach were added by marriage in the Fifties. Vinification is traditional, using only natural yeasts, and fermenting in large oak vats. The wines are matured there for at least six months before bottling. The result is a range of wines extremely expressive of their vineyard characters. All the wines of the 2002 vintage showed a gripping acidity. The 2003 vintage has a more full-bodied, rounded character, and is of at least the same high quality.

2002 Ürziger Würzgarten
Riesling Spätlese
7.5%, ♀ till 2010   89

2003 Ürziger Würzgarten
Riesling Spätlese
8.5%, ♀ till 2010   89

2001 Erdener Treppchen
Riesling Auslese ***
7.5%, ♀ till 2014   90

2003 Ürziger Würzgarten
Riesling Auslese
7.5%, ♀ till 2012   90

2002 Erdener Treppchen
Riesling Auslese ***
7.5%, ♀ till 2012   91

2001 Ürziger Würzgarten
Riesling Auslese ***
7.5%, ♀ till 2012   91

2003 Ürziger Würzgarten
Riesling Auslese **
7.5%, ♀ till 2012   91

2002 Erdener Prälat
Riesling Auslese ***
7.5%, ♀ till 2014   92

2001 Ürziger Würzgarten
Riesling Auslese ***
7.5%, ♀ till 2016   92

2003 Ürziger Würzgarten
Riesling Auslese ***
8%, ♀ till 2014   92

2003 Erdener Treppchen
Riesling Auslese ***
8%, ♀ till 2014   92

2003 Ürziger Würzgarten
Riesling Trockenbeerenauslese
9%, ♀ till 2025   94

The estates: ♟♟♟♟♟ World's finest · ♟♟♟♟ Germany's best · ♟♟♟ Very good · ♟♟ Good · ♟ Reliable

WEINGUT
ANSGAR CLÜSSERATH

Owner: Ansgar Clüsserath
Winemaker: Ansgar and
Eva Clüsserath
54349 Trittenheim, Spielestraße 4
Tel. (0 65 07) 22 90, Fax 66 90
e-mail: weingut@ansgar-cluesserath.de
*Directions: A 1 from north, Föhren exit;
A 1 from south, Mehring exit*
Sales: By appointment
Guest house: On the estate
History: Family tradition of wine-
making since the 17th century

Vineyard area: 3.9 hectares
Annual production: 30,000 bottles
Top sites: Trittenheimer Apotheke
and Altärchen, Neumagener Rosen-
gärtchen
Soil types: Slate, decomposed slate
Grape varieties: 89% Riesling,
5% Weißburgunder,
6% other varieties
Average yield: 76 hl/ha
Best vintages: 2001, 2002, 2003

Ever since the daughter of the house, Eva Clüsserath, has completed her studies in Geisenheim, she has been making her mark at the family winery. At this stage, her day job is still at the VDP offices in the Pfalz. However, on the weekends she helps her father in the Trittenheim winery, where he is responsible for managing the vineyards. She takes time of work for a few weeks in fall each year in order to work intensively on making the wines. She will most probably take over the entire business in a few years time. Her signature was evident in the 2001 vintage. The 2002 wines were virtually bursting with both power and elegance. The basic dry wines of the 2003 vintage are characterized by rather a weak fruit. However, the sweet wines produced here were typical of the vintage, with a pronounced fruity character, right up to a rich and yet elegant and well-balanced Beerenauslese. More of the same, please!

2003 Trittenheimer Apotheke
Riesling Spätlese trocken **
12%, ♀ till 2008 — **87**

2003 Trittenheimer Apotheke
Riesling Spätlese trocken ***
13%, ♀ till 2008 — **88**

2002 Trittenheimer Apotheke
Riesling Spätlese halbtrocken
11%, ♀ till 2007 — **86**

2003 Trittenheimer Apotheke
Riesling Kabinett
9%, ♀ till 2008 — **86**

2001 Trittenheimer Apotheke
Riesling Spätlese
8.5%, ♀ till 2007 — **88**

2002 Trittenheimer Apotheke
Riesling Spätlese
9%, ♀ till 2009 — **88**

2002 Trittenheimer Apotheke
Riesling Auslese
8.5%, ♀ till 2009 — **89**

2003 Trittenheimer Apotheke
Riesling Spätlese
9%, ♀ till 2010 — **90**

2003 Trittenheimer Apotheke
Riesling Auslese
8.5%, ♀ till 2012 — **91**

2003 Trittenheimer Apotheke
Riesling Beerenauslese
8%, ♀ till 2014 — **93**

W E I N G U T
ANSGAR CLÜSSERATH
2 0 0 1
RIESLING
SPÄTLESE
TRITTENHEIMER APOTHEKE
MOSEL SAAR RUWER
Alc. 8.5 % by Vol.
Qualitätswein mit Prädikat · Gutsabfüllung
A. R Nr. 2 607 269 5 02 · D-54349 Trittenheim
750 ml

The wines: **100** Perfect · **95–99** Outstanding · **90–94** Excellent · **85–89** Very good · **80–84** Good · **75–79** Average

WEINGUT
ERNST CLÜSSERATH

Owner: Ernst Clüsserath
Winemaker: Ernst Clüsserath
54349 Trittenheim, Moselweinstr. 67
Tel. (0 65 07) 26 07, Fax 66 07
e-mail:
weingut.ernst.cluesserath@t-online.de
Internet:
www.weingut-ernst-cluesserath.de
*Directions: A 1 from north, Föhren exit;
A 1 from south, Mehring exit*
Sales: Ernst and Heike Clüsserath
Opening hours: By appointment
Guest house and vacation apartments
History: Winemaking in the sixth
generation
Worth seeing: Vaulted cellar of slate

Vineyard area: 3 hectares
Annual production: 22,000 bottles
Top sites: Trittenheimer Apotheke
and Altärchen
Soil types: Decomposed slate
Grape varieties: 95% Riesling,
3% Müller-Thurgau, 2% Kerner
Average yield: 55 hl/ha
Best vintages: 2001, 2002, 2003
Member: Bernkasteler Ring

Ernst Clüsserath has already received a
number of important awards, ranging
from special state awards at regional level
up to the International Wine Challenge
and the Decanter Award, all of which dec-
orate the walls of the winery. For some
time now the off-dry wines produced here
have also been very good. We tasted very
attractive ranges here in the late Nineties.
While the vintage conditions led to a rather poor range in 2000, the 2001 range
was again much better. The 2002 range,
too, showed finesse and character. In the
2003 vintage the dry wines are characterized by caramel and spice, while the fruity
wines are elegant and delicate in style, a
real pleasure to drink. As in the previous
vintage, we can single out the Apotheke
Spätlese wine which obviously receives
special care from the winemaker.

2003 Trittenheimer Apotheke
Riesling Kabinett trocken
12%, ♀ till 2006 **83**

2003 Trittenheimer Apotheke
Riesling Spätlese trocken
13%, ♀ till 2006 **85**

2002 Trittenheimer Apotheke
Riesling Spätlese feinherb
11%, ♀ till 2008 **87**

2003 Trittenheimer Apotheke
Riesling Spätlese feinherb
12%, ♀ till 2008 **87**

2003 Trittenheimer Altärchen
Riesling Kabinett
10%, ♀ till 2007 **86**

2003 Trittenheimer Altärchen
Riesling Spätlese
9%, ♀ till 2008 **87**

2001 Trittenheimer Apotheke
Riesling Auslese – 22 –
↑ auction wine, 7.5%, ♀ till 2010 **88**

2002 Trittenheimer Apotheke
Riesling Spätlese
8%, ♀ till 2009 **89**

2003 Trittenheimer Apotheke
Riesling Spätlese
9%, ♀ till 2009 **89**

2003 Trittenheimer Apotheke
Riesling Auslese – 4 –
8.5%, ♀ till 2009 **90**

2003 Trittenheimer Apotheke
Riesling Auslese – 20 –
↑ auction wine, 8.5%, ♀ till 2010 **90**

2002 Trittenheimer Apotheke
Riesling Auslese
↑ auction wine, 9%, ♀ till 2010 **91**

WEINGUT CLÜSSERATH-EIFEL

Owner and manager: Gerhard Eifel
54349 Trittenheim, Moselweinstr. 39
Tel. (0 65 07) 9 90 00, **Fax** 9 90 02
e-mail: info@galerie.riesling.de
Internet: www.galerie-riesling.de
Directions: A 1 from north, Föhren exit;
A 1 from south, Mehring exit
Sales: Waltraud Eifel
Opening hours: Mon.–Fri. 09:00 to
18:00, Sat. 11:00 to 14:00 hours
Hotel/Restaurant: "Galerie Riesling"
Specialties: High-class cuisine
History: Founded 1760
Worth seeing: Fährfelsen promontory
with 100-year-old vines
Worth a visit: Trip around the world
with Riesling

Vineyard area: 3.8 hectares
Annual production: 30,000 bottles
Top sites: Trittenheimer Altärchen
and Apotheke, Neumagener Rosen-
gärtchen, Klüsserather Bruderschaft,
Leiwener Laurentiuslay
Soil types: Devon slate
Grape varieties: 100% Riesling
Average yield: 50 hl/ha
Best vintages: 2001, 2002, 2003
Member: Bernkasteler Ring

In 1993, Gerhard Eifel created an unmistakable logo for his winery: "Gale-
rie-Riesling" is stated on his bottle labels
– and this is also the name of the hotel
and restaurant located opposite the winery. Eifel goes on a world tour of Riesling each year. Following on after Paris,
Rome and Cape Town, he is headed for
Moscow in 2005. At home, Eifel has excellent material to work with, particularly
from the heart of the Apotheke vineyard,
where old vines are planted. The 2002
wines presented were of an even higher
quality than in the past, which led to the
third bunch of grapes being awarded. 2003
provides a seamless continuation. The
crowning glory of the range is a magnificent Trockenbeerenauslese.

2003 Trittenheimer Apotheke
Riesling feinherb
12%, ♀ till 2008 — 87

2003 Fährfels Riesling
12%, ♀ till 2008 — 87

2001 Trittenheimer Apotheke
Riesling Spätlese **
✔ auction wine, 8%, ♀ till 2008 — 88

2003 Trittenheimer Apotheke
Riesling Spätlese
9%, ♀ till 2009 — 88

2003 Trittenheimer Apotheke
Riesling Spätlese **
9.5%, ♀ till 2009 — 88

2003 Trittenheimer Apotheke
Riesling Goldkapsel "F"
12.5%, ♀ till 2008 — 88

2002 Trittenheimer Apotheke
Riesling Auslese *** "Celsius"
7.5%, ♀ till 2014 — 93

2003 Trittenheimer Apotheke
Riesling Beerenauslese **
9.5%, ♀ till 2018 — 94

2003 Trittenheimer Apotheke
Riesling Trockenbeerenauslese
7.5%, ♀ till 2020 — 97

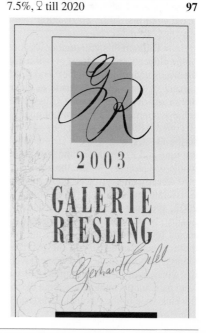

Mosel-Saar-Ruwer

WEINGUT CLÜSSERATH-WEILER

Owner: Helmut and Hilde Clüsserath
Manager and winemaker:
Helmut Clüsserath
54349 Trittenheim,
Haus an der Brücke
Tel. (0 65 07) 50 11, Fax 56 05
e-mail: helmut@cluesserath-weiler.de
Internet: www.cluesserath-weiler.de
Directions: A 1 from north, Föhren exit;
A 1 from south, Mehring exit
Sales: Hilde Clüsserath,
by appointment
Guest house: Comfortable rooms with a
view of the Mosel and Trittenheimer
Apotheke vineyard, large terrace
Worth seeing: Old cross-vaulted cellar,
Fährfels plateau with 100-year-old vines

Vineyard area: 5 hectares
Annual production: 40,000 bottles
Top sites: Trittenheimer Apotheke,
Mehringer Zellerberg
Soil types: Slate
Grape varieties: 100% Riesling
Average yield: 65 hl/ha
Best vintages: 1999, 2001, 2002

Helmut Clüsserath's grandfather was one of the pioneers on the Mosel of marketing his wines under his own label. Today, 85 percent of the wines are made in either dry or off-dry style, and the Clüsseraths achieve a remarkable standard of quality. His off-dry Rieslings, which they now describe as "fruchtig trocken (fruity dry)" are time and again among the best in the whole of Germany. While the 2001 vintage already showed very good quality, Clüsserath really showed off his ability in 2002, presenting wines of outstanding quality. Now, with the 2003 vintage, it seems to us that the dry wines are not quite as concentrated as in the previous vintage. At the higher predicate levels the wines gain in concentration, and we were particularly enthusiastic about the refreshing style of the Apotheke Auslese *.

2003 "Fährfels" Riesling trocken
12%, ♀ till 2008   **88**

2003 Mehringer Zellerberg
Riesling Spätlese fruchtig trocken "S"
12%, ♀ till 2007   **86**

2003 Trittenheimer Apotheke
Riesling Spätlese **
7.5%, ♀ till 2010   **89**

2001 Trittenheimer Apotheke
Riesling Spätlese *
8%, ♀ till 2010   **90**

2003 Trittenheimer Apotheke
Riesling Spätlese *
8%, ♀ till 2010   **90**

2001 Trittenheimer Apotheke
Riesling Eiswein
7%, ♀ till 2012   **91**

2002 Trittenheimer Apotheke
Riesling Eiswein
6.5%, ♀ till 2010   **91**

2003 Trittenheimer Apotheke
Riesling Auslese *
8.5%, ♀ till 2012   **92**

2003 Trittenheimer Apotheke
Riesling Auslese ***
8%, ♀ till 2015   **92**

2002 Trittenheimer Apotheke
Riesling Auslese **
7.5%, ♀ till 2010   **93**

The estates: ♦♦♦♦♦ World's finest · ♦♦♦♦ Germany's best · ♦♦♦ Very good · ♦♦ Good · ♦ Reliable

292

WEINGUT
STEPHAN EHLEN

Owner: Helma Justen
Winemaker: Stefan Justen
54492 Erden, Zur Kapelle 8
Tel. (0 65 32) 22 67, Fax 15 52
*Directions: A 48, Wittlich-Mitte exit, in
direction of Zeltingen, across the bridge,
then left, in Erden behind the church*
Sales: By appointment
History: Family involved in wine-
making since 1648
Worth seeing: Vaulted cellar

Vineyard area: 2.2 hectares
Annual production: 20,000 bottles
Top sites: Erdener Treppchen,
Lösnicher Försterlay
Soil types: Slate
Grape varieties: 100% Riesling
Average yield: 65 hl/ha
Best vintages: 2001, 2002, 2003
Member: Bernkasteler Ring

The house of quarried slate was built in
1889, and still dominates the slightly old-
fashioned label, symbolizing the 350
years of winemaking tradition in the Ehlen family. Stephan Ehlen has been amazingly consistent in recent years in producing elegant wines, particularly in the
fruity sweet sector. He has now, for reasons of age, handed over the operation to
the Justen family, owners of the Meulenhof winery. However, he will remain in
place to give advice and assistance. The
winery will continue to emphasize his
strong points, and produces only a marginal amount of off-dry wines, about 10 percent of the total. This comes as no surprise when you learn that 80 percent of the
production, mainly the fruity sweet wines,
is exported. Whereas the 2001 wines
were characterized by elegance and delicate fruit, we liked the 2002 range for its
spicy and at the same time powerful style.
Our favorite Riesling from the 2003 vintage was the Treppchen Spätlese Num-
mer –2–, which showed depth and length
typical of the vintage.

2002 Erdener Treppchen
Riesling Kabinett
9%, ♀ till 2007 **84**

2003 Erdener Treppchen
Riesling Kabinett
8.5%, ♀ till 2007 **84**

2003 Erdener Treppchen
Riesling Spätlese – 3 –
8.5%, ♀ till 2008 **85**

2001 Erdener Treppchen
Riesling Spätlese – 2 –
8.5%, ♀ till 2007 **86**

2001 Erdener Treppchen
Riesling Spätlese – 4 –
8%, ♀ till 2007 **86**

2002 Erdener Treppchen
Riesling Spätlese
8.5%, ♀ till 2008 **86**

2003 Erdener Treppchen
Riesling Spätlese – 2 –
8%, ♀ till 2008 **86**

2001 Lösnicher Försterlay
Riesling Auslese
8%, ♀ till 2008 **87**

2001 Erdener Treppchen
Riesling Auslese – 6 –
8%, ♀ till 2008 **88**

2001 Erdener Treppchen
Riesling Auslese – 7 –
8%, ♀ till 2010 **88**

2002 Erdener Treppchen
Riesling Auslese
8.5%, ♀ till 2010 **89**

2003 Erdener Treppchen
Riesling Beerenauslese
8.5%, ♀ till 2018 **92**

The wines: **100** Perfect · **95–99** Outstanding · **90–94** Excellent · **85–89** Very good · **80–84** Good · **75–79** Average

Mosel-Saar-Ruwer

WEINGUT BERNHARD EIFEL

Owner: Bernhard Eifel
Manager: Bernhard and
Marietta Eifel
54349 Trittenheim, Laurentiusstr. 17
Tel. (0 65 07) 59 72, Fax 64 60
e-mail: Bernhard.Eifel@t-online.de
Internet:
www.weingut-bernhard-eifel.de
*Directions: A 1 from north, Föhren exit;
A 1 from south, Mehring exit*
Sales: Mon.–Fri. 09:00 to 18:00 hours
Sat. and Sun. 10:00 to 14:00 hours
Guest house: On the estate
Restaurant: Stefan-Andres-Weinstube,
Wed.–Mon. from 18:00 to 24:00 hours,
closed Tue.
Specialties: Stuffed potatoes,
beef brawn, fried liver
History: Family-owned since 1634

Vineyard area: 5.8 hectares
Annual production: 40,000 bottles
Top sites: Schweicher Annaberg,
Longuicher Maximiner Herrenberg,
Trittenheimer Apotheke and Altärchen
Soil types: Slate with sandstone
and gray wacke, decomposed slate
Grape varieties: 94% Riesling,
3% Weißburgunder, 2% Müller-
Thurgau, 1% Kerner
Average yield: 70 hl/ha
Best vintages: 2001, 2002, 2003

The Bernhard Eifel wine estate and guest house have been run by Bernhard and Marietta Eifel with great passion and attention to detail for almost 30 years now. Alexandra, the daughter and regional wine princess in 2000 and 2001, greets guests in the beautifully appointed Stefan-Andres wine bar. Now that she has completed her studies in Geisenheim, she can join the business full-time. The 2003 vintage range is of a good, homogeneous quality, and slightly better than in 2001 and 2002. We again particularly liked the powerful Auslese from the Trittenheimer Altärchen vineyard.

2003 Trittenheimer Apotheke
Riesling Spätlese trocken
13%, ♀ till 2007   83

2003 Riesling
trocken
"Wurzelechte Reben vom roten Schiefer"
13%, ♀ till 2007   84

2003 Trittenheimer Altärchen
Riesling Spätlese halbtrocken
12%, ♀ till 2007   83

2001 Schweicher Annaberg
Riesling Spätlese
9.5%, ♀ till 2006   85

**2003 Longuicher
Maximiner Herrenberg**
Riesling Spätlese
9%, ♀ till 2008   85

2001 Schweicher Annaberg
Riesling Auslese
9.5%, ♀ till 2008   86

2002 Trittenheimer Apotheke
Riesling Auslese
10%, ♀ till 2008   86

2002 Trittenheimer Altärchen
Riesling Auslese
9%, ♀ till 2010   87

2003 Trittenheimer Apotheke
Riesling Auslese
10%, ♀ till 2010   87

2003 Trittenheimer Altärchen
Riesling Auslese
10.5%, ♀ till 2010   87

2003 Trittenheimer Altärchen
Riesling Auslese
9.5%, ♀ till 2010   88

2003 Trittenheimer Apotheke
Riesling Beerenauslese
11.5%, ♀ till 2012   90

The estates: ♛♛♛♛♛ World's finest · ♛♛♛♛ Germany's best · ♛♛♛ Very good · ♛♛ Good · ♛ Reliable

WEINGUT
FRANZ-JOSEF EIFEL

Owner: Franz-Josef Eifel
54349 Trittenheim,
Engelbert-Schue-Weg 2
Tel. (0 65 07) 7 00 09, Fax 71 39
e-mail: Info@FJEifel.de
Internet: www.FJEifel.de
Directions: A 1 from north, Föhren exit;
A 1 from south, Mehring exit
Sales: Franz-Josef Eifel
by appointment
Guest rooms: Six rooms on the estate

Vineyard area: 5 hectares
Annual production: 35,000 bottles
Top sites: Trittenheimer Apotheke,
Neumagener Rosengärtchen
Soil types: Slate, gravel, sand
Grape varieties: 94% Riesling,
4% Weißburgunder, 2% Rivaner
Average yield: 59 hl/ha
Best vintages: 1999, 2000, 2001

In a sense, the wines of this Trittenheim winery are absolutely unmistakable. Franz-Josef Eifel's fingerprint on the label of each bottle is intended to signify a personal guarantee of quality. Add to this the flourishing signature of the winemaker on the label, and you can deduce that this is a confident man – and he has every reason to be. In the Nineties, Franz-Josef Eifel simply kept on improving each year. We could not discern any faults whatsoever in the 2001 vintage range. Unfortunately, the same could not be said about the dry wines of the 2002 vintage. This year, too, the dry wines show a rather tired, delicately tart fruit. Admittedly, Eifel still plays on his strengths in the Spätlese and Auslese wines, but these, too, do not quite achieve the delicate style of the Eiswein produced in the previous vintage. Our favorite this year was the Altärchen Auslese, which reflects the vintage character in its tremendous concentration and ripe berry notes.

2001 Trittenheimer Apotheke
Riesling Spätlese trocken
12.5%, ♀ till 2006   **87**

2001 Trittenheimer Apotheke
Riesling Auslese feinherb
12%, ♀ till 2008   **88**

2002 Trittenheimer Apotheke
Riesling Spätlese *
7.5%, ♀ till 2008   **88**

2001 Trittenheimer Apotheke
Riesling Spätlese
8%, ♀ till 2010   **89**

2001 Trittenheimer Apotheke
Riesling Auslese *
7.5%, ♀ till 2012   **89**

2003 Trittenheimer Apotheke
Riesling Spätlese
8%, ♀ till 2010   **89**

2003 Trittenheimer Apotheke
Riesling Auslese
8%, ♀ till 2008   **89**

2002 Trittenheimer Altärchen
Riesling Auslese
7.5%, ♀ till 2009   **91**

2003 Trittenheimer Altärchen
Riesling Auslese
8.5%, ♀ till 2010   **91**

2002 Trittenheimer Altärchen
Riesling Eiswein
7.5%, ♀ till 2012   **93**

The wines: **100** Perfect · **95–99** Outstanding · **90–94** Excellent · **85–89** Very good · **80–84** Good · **75–79** Average

295

WEINGUT EIFEL-PFEIFFER

Owner: Heinz and Brigitte Eifel
Manager: Heinz Eifel
Winemaker: Anne Eifel
54349 Trittenheim,
Moselweinstraße 70
Tel. (0 65 07) 92 62 14 und 92 62 15,
Fax 92 62 30
e-mail: info@eifel-pfeiffer.de
Internet: www.eifel-pfeiffer.de
*Directions: A 1 from north, Föhren exit;
A 1 from south, Mehring exit*
Sales: Brigitte and Anne Eifel
by appointment
History: Winemaking in the family
since 1642

Vineyard area: 8 hectares
Annual production: 70,000 bottles
Top sites: Trittenheimer Apotheke,
Graacher Domprobst and Himmel-
reich, Wehlener Sonnenuhr
Soil types: Slate, decomposed slate
Grape varieties: 98% Riesling,
2% other varieties
Average yield: 76 hl/ha
Best vintages: 2001, 2002, 2003

Two generations work together in this family operation in Trittenheim. Whereas father Heinz Eifel is responsible for managing the vineyards, daughter Anne has completed her studies in Geisenheim, and gained some international experience, and has now found her place in the cellar. Although Heinz Eifel continues to run the operation as a whole, the wines are increasingly showing the signature of Anne Eifel. The winery owns top-rated vineyards in Trittenheim, Graach and Wehlen, with about three hectares still planted to ungrafted vines, of which more than half are between 50 and 90 years old. The strength of the Eifel family lies without a doubt in the production of fruity sweet wines, and there was no lack of these in the hot 2003 vintage. At the top of the range are two Riesling Trockenbeerenauslese wines, with the Wehlener Sonnenuhr being our favorite.

2003 Trittenheimer Apotheke
Riesling Spätlese trocken
13%, ♀ till 2008 — **83**

2001 Trittenheimer Altärchen
Riesling Kabinett
8%, ♀ till 2005 — **84**

2003 Wehlener Sonnenuhr
Riesling Spätlese
9%, ♀ till 2008 — **84**

2002 Trittenheimer Apotheke
Riesling Spätlese
8%, ♀ till 2008 — **85**

2002 Wehlener Sonnenuhr
Riesling Spätlese
8%, ♀ till 2008 — **85**

2003 Trittenheimer Apotheke
Riesling Auslese
8.5%, ♀ till 2010 — **85**

2002 Trittenheimer Altärchen
Riesling Auslese
7.5%, ♀ till 2009 — **86**

2003 Wehlener Sonnenuhr
Riesling Beerenauslese
8.5%, ♀ till 2015 — **86**

2002 Trittenheimer Altärchen
Riesling Eiswein
9%, ♀ till 2008 — **87**

2003 Trittenheimer Apotheke
Riesling Trockenbeerenauslese
7.5%, ♀ till 2015 — **87**

2003 Wehlener Sonnenuhr
Riesling Trockenbeerenauslese
7.5%, ♀ till 2015 — **88**

WEINGUT
Eifel-Pfeiffer
D-54349 TRITTENHEIM

2001er
RIESLING KABINETT

The estates: ✸✸✸✸✸ World's finest · ✸✸✸✸ Germany's best · ✸✸✸ Very good · ✸✸ Good · ✸ Reliable

WEINGUT KARL ERBES

Owner and Manager: Stefan Erbes
54539 Ürzig, Würzgartenstraße 25
Tel. (0 65 32) 21 23, Fax 14 17
e-mail: info@karlerbes.com
Internet: www.karlerbes.com
Directions: Via the B 53
Sales: Stefan Erbes
Opening hours: Mon.–Fri. 09:00 to
17:00 hours and by appointment
Karl and Ursula Erbes
Wine tasting room, Moseluferstraße 29
Restaurant: In the wine bar during
October, from 11:00 to 20:00 hours
Specialties: Onion tart

Vineyard area: 4 hectares
Annual production: 40,000 bottles
Top sites: Ürziger Würzgarten,
Erdener Treppchen
Soil types: Decomposed Devon slate
Grape varieties: 100% Riesling
Average yield: 78 hl/ha
Best vintage: 2003

Following on our new discovery of Jos. Christoffel jun. last year, we were surprised to find another winery in Ürzig that produced an excellent vintage collection, with wines holding up the Riesling tradition of fruity botrytized wines with their typical fructose sweetness. The four hectares of vineyard are planted completely with ungrafted vines, and are almost all located in the commune of Ürzig, only 0.3 hectares of the Erdener Treppchen site are in the commune of Erden. In the past, some 70 percent of the production was exported, mainly to Japan, the USA and Great Britain. If the number of domestic fans for this clean and refreshing invigorating style of Riesling can be increased, this ratio may change. We certainly like the style, and are sufficiently confident to award the first bunch of grapes spontaneously. We can particularly recommend the Würzgarten Auslese ***, which has a delicate fruity note and an elegant berry aroma. The Spätlese is a real bargain!

2003 Ürziger Würzgarten
Riesling Spätlese trocken
12.5%, ♀ till 2006 — **84**

2003 Ürziger Würzgarten
Riesling Spätlese halbtrocken
12%, ♀ till 2006 — **85**

2003 Ürziger Würzgarten
Riesling Kabinett
8.5%, ♀ till 2009 — **86**

2003 Ürziger Würzgarten
Riesling Spätlese
8.5%, ♀ till 2010 — **88**

2003 Ürziger Würzgarten
Riesling Auslese *
8.5%, ♀ till 2011 — **89**

2003 Ürziger Würzgarten
Riesling Auslese **
7.5%, ♀ till 2012 — **90**

2003 Ürziger Würzgarten
Riesling Auslese ***
7%, ♀ till 2014 — **91**

2003 Ürziger Würzgarten
Riesling Eiswein
7%, ♀ till 2012 — **91**

2003 Ürziger Würzgarten
Riesling Beerenauslese
7.5%, ♀ till 2015 — **92**

2003 Ürziger Würzgarten
Riesling Auslese *** Goldkapsel
8%, ♀ till 2014 — **92**

The wines: **100** Perfect · **95–99** Outstanding · **90–94** Excellent · **85–89** Very good · **80–84** Good · **75–79** Average

297

WEINGUT
REINHOLD FRANZEN

Owner: Ulrich Franzen
56814 Bremm, Gartenstraße 14
Tel. (0 26 75) 4 12, Fax 16 55
e-mail: info@weingut-franzen.de
Internet: www.weingut-franzen.de
Directions: Coming from Koblenz,
Bremm is 50 km up the Mosel, between
Cochem and Zell
Sales: Iris and Ulrich Franzen
by appointment
Worth a visit: Climbing tour in
the steepest vineyard in Europe

Vineyard area: 6 hectares
Annual production: 40,000 bottles
Top sites: Bremmer Calmont,
Neefer Frauenberg
Soil types: Devon slate with layers of
quartzite
Grape varieties: 75% Riesling,
10% Weißburgunder, 5% Elbling,
5% Spätburgunder, 5% other varieties
Average yield: 60 hl/ha
Best vintages: 2001, 2002, 2003
Member: Bernkasteler Ring

---

95 percent of the production here is dry Riesling, which makes him something of a specialist in this rare category in the Mosel region. Ulrich Franzen harvests some of his best Rieslings on the terraced slate-covered soils of the Bremmer Calmont vineyard, the steepest vineyard in Europe. He has recently laid an additional 550 meters of monorail track here to work the site even more effectively. In addition to Riesling vines, Franzen also plans to plant peach and fig trees. He is rigorous in ignoring the German predicate system, his best wines are identified by a gold capsule. In 2001 we actually preferred his basic wines, but in 2002 the Frauenberg gold capsule set the standard. The 2003 wines are more concentrated and have a delicate spicy note. A real treat to drink again this year: the "Calidus Mons," a combination of spice and delicate mellowness.

2003 Neefer Frauenberg Riesling trocken 12%, ♀ till 2006	85
2003 Bremmer Calmont Riesling trocken 12%, ♀ till 2006	85
2002 Neefer Frauenberg Riesling trocken Goldkapsel 13%, ♀ till 2008	87
2003 Neefer Frauenberg Riesling trocken Goldkapsel 12.5%, ♀ till 2008	87
2001 "Calidus Mons" Riesling 12.5%, ♀ till 2008	88
2003 "Calidus mons" Riesling 13%, ♀ till 2009	88
2003 Bremmer Calmont Riesling Auslese ↗ auction wine, 9.5%, ♀ till 2010	89
2002 Riesling Eiswein ↗ auction wine, 7%, ♀ till 2012	92

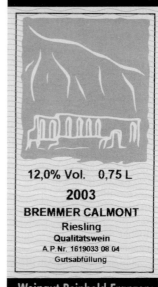

WEINGUT
FRANZ FRIEDRICH-KERN

Owner: Familie Friedrich
Manager and winemaker:
Franz-Josef Friedrich
54470 Bernkastel-Wehlen,
Hauptstraße 98
Tel. (0 65 31) 31 56, Fax 77 06
e-mail: ffkern@aol.com
Internet: www.friedrich-kern.de
Directions: From Bernkastel-Kues up
the left bank of the Mosel to Wehlen, in
the center of town opposite the church
Sales: Mechtilde Friedrich
Opening hours: Mon.–Sat. 10:00 to
18:00 hours and by appointment
Restaurant: Ascension Day to Pente-
cost, mid-July to October
daily from 11:00 hours, closed Wed.
Specialties: Local cheeses, smoked trout
from the Eifel region
History: Winemaking since 1753
Worth seeing: Historical estate buildings with vaulted cellar

---

Vineyard area: 4.5 hectares
Annual production: 40,000 bottles
Top sites: Wehlener Sonnenuhr,
Zeltinger Sonnenuhr, Zeltinger and
Graacher Himmelreich, Bernkasteler
Bratenhöfchen
Soil types: Stony clay on kaolin-slate,
decomposed kaolin-slate
Grape varieties: 95% Riesling,
5% other varieties
Average yield: 68 hl/ha
Best vintages: 1998, 1999, 2002

Some of the best vineyard sites of the
Mittelmosel provide the foundation for
this family operation, and Franz-Josef
Friedrich still intends to increase his
share of the Sonnenuhr and Himmelreich
sites in the years to come. Following on
two rather heterogeneous ranges in 2000
and 2001, the dry wines in 2002 were
more concentrated and more intense. The
2003 vintage does not follow on well
from this, the dry wines are simply too
acidic, and appear rather rustic in style.

The only exception is the Eiswein – its
gripping Riesling fruit and attractive mellow style make this a great wine.

2003 Wehlener Sonnenuhr
Riesling trocken "S"
13%, ♀ till 2006   83

2003 Bernkasteler Johannisbrünnchen
Riesling Kabinett
8.5%, ♀ till 2008   85

2003 Graacher Himmelreich
Riesling Spätlese
7.5%, ♀ till 2009   86

2003 Wehlener Sonnenuhr
Riesling Spätlese
8%, ♀ till 2009   86

2001 Wehlener Sonnenuhr
Riesling Spätlese
8%, ♀ till 2008   87

2003 Zeltinger Himmelreich
Riesling Auslese Goldkapsel
7.5%, ♀ till 2008   87

2003 Wehlener Sonnenuhr
Riesling Auslese
8.5%, ♀ till 2010   88

2002 Wehlener Sonnenuhr
Riesling Auslese Goldkapsel
8%, ♀ till 2010   88

2002 Zeltinger Himmelreich
Riesling Auslese Goldkapsel
8%, ♀ till 2010   88

2002 Zeltinger Himmelreich
Riesling Eiswein
7%, ♀ till 2010   90

2003 Zeltinger Himmelreich
Riesling Eiswein
7.5%, ♀ till 2020   94

The wines: **100** Perfect · **95–99** Outstanding · **90–94** Excellent · **85–89** Very good · **80–84** Good · **75–79** Average

299

WEINGUT FRIES

Owner: Reiner and Anke Fries
56333 Winningen, Bachstraße 66
Tel. (0 26 06) 26 86, Fax 20 00 16
e-mail: info@weingut-fries.de
Internet: www.weingut-fries.de
Directions: A 61, Koblenz-Metternich
exit, in direction of Winningen
Sales: Anke and Reiner Fries
Mon. to Sun. by appointment
History: Winemaking in the eighth
generation
Worth seeing: 300-year-old vaulted
cellar, historical tasting room in former
stables

Vineyard area: 6.2 hectares
Annual production: 50,000 bottles
Top sites: Winninger Uhlen and
Röttgen
Soil types: Decomposed slate
Grape varieties: 68% Riesling,
23% Spätburgunder, 5% Weißbur-
gunder, 4% other varieties
Average yield: 69 hl/ha
Best vintages: 2001, 2002, 2003

Reiner Fries is a qualified enological engineer, and together with wife Anke runs
the six hectares of vineyard and the winery in Winningen. About a quarter of his
vineyard area is located in the top-class
Uhlen and Röttgen vineyards, and it is
from these steep terraces that he regularly
picks his best wines. In the cellar, stainless steel tanks dominate the scene, and
the proportion of dry and off-dry wines
produced here is on the increase. For
these wines, Fries has for some time
done away with the traditional predicate
designations, as Spätlese and Auslese.
Instead, these wines now all carry the uniform designation "Apollo-Terrassen." An
unusual feature for a Mosel winery is the
high percentage of red wines here. The
2002 range was good, and the 2003 vintage leads on seamlessly from there. The
2002 Spätburgunder (Pinot Noir) matured in barriques is also quite good.

2003 "Apollo-Terrassen"
Riesling trocken
12%, ♀ till 2006   81

2002 Winninger Uhlen
Riesling trocken
12.5%, ♀ till 2007   84

2002 "Apollo-Terrassen"
Riesling feinherb
12%, ♀ till 2007   84

2002 Winninger Röttgen
Riesling Spätlese
9.5%, ♀ till 2008   84

2003 Winninger Röttgen
Riesling Spätlese
9.5%, ♀ till 2008   84

2001 Winninger Röttgen
Riesling Auslese
9%, ♀ till 2010   86

2003 Winninger Röttgen
Riesling Auslese
10%, ♀ till 2009   86

2002 Winninger Domgarten
Riesling Eiswein
10.5%, ♀ till 2008   87

2003 Winninger Röttgen
Riesling Beerenauslese
10%, ♀ till 2012   88

———— Red wine ————

2002 Spätburgunder Barrique
13.5%, ♀ till 2010   83

FRIES
APOLLO-TERRASSEN
RIESLING
TROCKEN
2003

WEINGUT LEO FUCHS

Owner and manager:
Bruno Fuchs
56829 Pommern, Hauptstraße 3
Tel. (0 26 72) 13 26, Fax 13 36
e-mail: leo-fuchs@t-online.de
Internet: www.leo-fuchs.de
Directions: A 61, Koblenz-Metternich
exit, to Winningen, B 416 to Treis-Kar-
den, then on the B 49 to Pommern
Sales: Bruno and Brunhilde Fuchs
by appointment
Worth seeing: Manor-house with barrel
cellar, courtyard with baking house

Vineyard area: 5 hectares
Annual production: 45,000 bottles
Top sites: Pommerner Zeisel,
Goldberg, Sonnenuhr and Rosenberg,
Klottener Burg Coraidelsteiner
Soil types: Gray wacke and slate
Grape varieties: 80% Riesling,
12% Rivaner, 8% Chardonnay
Average yield: 70 hl/ha
Best vintages: 2000, 2001, 2002

Bruno Fuchs brings great enthusiasm to his Riesling vines in the steep decomposed slate slopes of Pommern. Healthy grapes picked from old vines are the foundation for the standard of quality, which has been improving in recent years. No expense has been spared in bringing modern technology to the cellar. The investment includes a cellar full of stainless steel tanks. Some 60 percent of the range is now fermented dry, and this share is increasing. The 2001 range presented by Fuchs was good across the board, with a refreshing style, and he was awarded the second bunch of grapes for this. The 2002 vintage wines were characterized by a richness typical of the vintage, and by contrast the 2003 range shows lots of acidity. We are not enthusiastic about the rather tart dry Rieslings this year, the more so since Fuchs shows in his Zeisel Beerenauslese that it is possible to balance berry notes and acidity successfully.

2001 "Vom grauen Schiefer"
Riesling trocken
12.5%, ♀ till 2005 — **83**

2002 "Vom grauen Schiefer"
Riesling Hochgewächs halbtrocken
11.5%, ♀ till 2006 — **84**

2003 "Von alten Reben"
Riesling Spätlese feinherb
10.5%, ♀ till 2008 — **83**

2003 Pommerner Zeisel
Riesling Spätlese
8%, ♀ till 2009 — **85**

2002 Pommerner Zeisel
Riesling Spätlese
7.5%, ♀ till 2007 — **86**

2001 Pommerner Zeisel
Riesling Auslese ***
8%, ♀ till 2010 — **87**

2003 Pommerner Zeisel
Riesling Auslese ***
8%, ♀ till 2010 — **90**

2003 Pommerner Zeisel
Riesling Beerenauslese
8%, ♀ till 2012 — **91**

2003 "Vom grauen Schiefer"
Riesling Trockenbeerenauslese
9%, ♀ till 2015 — **91**

LEO FUCHS

2003er RIESLING
VOM GRAUEN SCHIEFER
Qualitätswein - trocken
ERZEUGERABFÜLLUNG
Amtliche Prüfnummer 1 907 320 9 04
alc. 12,5% vol ℮ 0,75 L
WEINGUT LEO FUCHS
D-56829 POMMERN/MOSEL
MOSEL-SAAR-RUWER

The wines: **100** Perfect · **95–99** Outstanding · **90–94** Excellent · **85–89** Very good · **80–84** Good · **75–79** Average

WEINGUT GRANS-FASSIAN

Owner and winemaker:
Gerhard Grans
54340 Leiwen, Römerstraße 28
Tel. (0 65 07) 31 70, Fax 81 67
e-mail: weingut@grans-fassian.de
Internet: www.grans-fassian.de
Directions: A 48 Koblenz–Trier,
Schweich exit, in direction of Leiwen
Sales: Gerhard and Doris Grans
by appointment
Restaurant: Alexander Oos,
Mosel promenade 4 in Trittenheim,
closed Mon. and Tue.,
Tel. (0 65 07) 70 28 03, Fax 70 28 04,
e-mail: wein-tafelhaus@t-online.de
Internet: www.wein-tafelhaus.de
History: Family-owned since 1624

Vineyard area: 9.6 hectares
Annual production: 80,000 bottles
Top sites: Trittenheimer Apotheke,
Leiwener Laurentiuslay, Piesporter
Goldtröpfchen, Drohn Hofberger
Soil types: Devon slate
Grape varieties: 89% Riesling,
11% Pinot varieties
Average yield: 74 hl/ha
Best vintages: 1999, 2002, 2003
Member: VDP

When Gerhard Grans took over responsibility in the winery in the early Eighties, this was still the heyday of newly-developed grape varieties, and this trend did not completely pass by the wineries in Leiwen. After that, Gerhard Grans made a name for himself quickly among the Young Winemakers of Leiwen, of which group he is a founder member. He and his colleagues were determined to get away from the image of producing only sweet must, and wanted to be independent of the large wholesale cellars. They have all succeeded in this, Gerhard Grans particularly so, as he has succeeded in establishing his estate as one of the leading producers in the region. Most recently he has been rewarded with the long-overdue acceptance into the regional VDP association

for the Mosel, Saar and Ruwer regions. Gerhard Grans produces Riesling wines with piquant acidity and an elegant, polished finish. The dry wines make up around half the production, and are often attractive for their body and structure, although they lack sometimes a little elegance. The best wines of the 1998 vintage were reminiscent of the glory days in the late Eighties. The 1999 vintage, too, revealed practically no poor wines. In fact, considering the relatively difficult vintage conditions, the range could even be described as excellent. At the time we tasted every wine in the range, and did not find a single poor wine, while the botrytized specialties were among the best examples of this style on the Mosel. However, the 2000 vintage did not live up to the standard set by the two preceding vintages. The wines tended to be middle-weight, and mostly lacked the depth for which this winery in particular is normally famous. In 2001, the dry wines were still on the weak side, although the remainder of the range was quite good, though not exciting. Last year, Gerhard Grans pulled it all together again. The dry wines had both elegance and body, and the elegant fruity and botrytized wines lived up to their reputation. The fruity Spätlese wines presented by Grans were among the best produced that year in Germany. It thus came as no surprise that Grans surpassed almost all the other entrants in our national taste-off. This year, his Apotheke Spätlese is not quite on a par with that of the previous vintage. But then, his rich and absolutely wonderful Trockenbeerenauslese surpasses even the best wines of recent years. A truly classical representative of this elegant botrytis vintage! The estate's own wine bar on the banks of the Mosel in Trittenheim is the best location for tasting some of the wines. The name "Wein- und Tafelhaus" designates the country restaurant and inn run by Alexander Oos and his wife Daniela.

2002 Riesling trocken
12%, ♀ till 2006   **82**

2003 Riesling trocken
12.5%, ♀ till 2006   **82**

2002 Drohn Hofberger
Spätlese trocken
12.5%, ♀ till 2006   **85**

2003 Drohn Hofberger
Riesling Spätlese trocken
12.5%, ♀ till 2006   **87**

2002 Leiwener Laurentiuslay
Riesling Spätlese trocken "S"
12.5%, ♀ till 2006   **88**

2002 Riesling
feinherb "Catherina"
12.5%, ♀ till 2006   **84**

2003 Trittenheimer
Riesling Kabinett
10%, ♀ till 2008   **85**

2001 Trittenheimer
Riesling Kabinett
8%, ♀ till 2008   **87**

2001 Piesporter Goldtröpfchen
Riesling Spätlese
8%, ♀ till 2010   **87**

2002 Piesporter
Riesling Kabinett
8%, ♀ till 2007   **87**

2001 Trittenheimer Apotheke
Riesling Spätlese
8%, ♀ till 2010   **88**

2001 Trittenheimer Apotheke
Riesling Auslese
7.5%, ♀ till 2012   **88**

2001 Piesporter Goldtröpfchen
Riesling Auslese
8%, ♀ till 2012   **88**

2003 Leiwener Laurentiuslay
Riesling Spätlese "S"
12%, ♀ till 2009   **88**

2002 Trittenheimer Apotheke
Riesling Spätlese – 12 –
8%, ♀ till 2009   **89**

2003 Drohn Hofberger
Riesling Spätlese
8.5%, ♀ till 2009   **89**

2003 Trittenheimer Apotheke
Riesling Auslese
8%, ♀ till 2012   **89**

2001 Trittenheimer Apotheke
Riesling Auslese Goldkapsel
↗ auction wine, 8%, ♀ till 2012   **89**

2003 Trittenheimer Apotheke
Riesling Spätlese
8.5%, ♀ till 2010   **90**

2003 Piesporter Goldtröpfchen
Riesling Auslese
8.5%, ♀ till 2010   **90**

2002 Drohn Hofberger
Riesling Spätlese
8%, ♀ till 2010   **91**

2002 Piesporter Goldtröpfchen
Riesling Spätlese
8%, ♀ till 2010   **91**

2001 Leiwener Laurentiuslay
Riesling Eiswein Goldkapsel
↗ auction wine, 6.5%, ♀ till 2015   **91**

2002 Trittenheimer Apotheke
Riesling Auslese Goldkapsel
↗ auction wine, 7%, ♀ till 2010   **91**

2002 Trittenheimer Apotheke
Riesling Beerenauslese
↗ auction wine, 6.5%, ♀ till 2012   **92**

2001 Trittenheimer Apotheke
Riesling Beerenauslese Goldkapsel
↗ auction wine, 6.5%, ♀ till 2015   **92**

2003 Trittenheimer Apotheke
Riesling Auslese lange Goldkapsel
↗ auction wine, 7%, ♀ till 2012   **92**

2002 Trittenheimer Apotheke
Riesling Spätlese
↗ auction wine, 8%, ♀ till 2010   **93**

2003 Trittenheimer Apotheke
Riesling Trockenbeerenauslese
↗ auction wine, 6.5%, ♀ till 2020   **95**

GRANS-FASSIAN

2001
Piesporter Goldtröpfchen
Riesling - Auslese

The wines: **100** Perfect · **95–99** Outstanding · **90–94** Excellent · **85–89** Very good · **80–84** Good · **75–79** Average

WEINGUT FRITZ HAAG – DUSEMONDER HOF

Owner: Wilhelm Haag
54472 Brauneberg,
Dusemonder Straße 44
Tel. (0 65 34) 4 10, Fax 13 47
e-mail: weingut-fritz-haag@t-online.de
Internet: www.weingut-fritz-haag.de
Directions: A 48 Koblenz–Trier, Salmtal
exit, in direction of Bernkastel-Mülheim,
B 53 to Brauneberg
Sales: Ilse Haag by appointment
History: Family-owned since 1605

Vineyard area: 7.5 hectares
Annual production: 65,000 bottles
Top sites: Brauneberger Juffer-
Sonnenuhr and Juffer
Soil types: Slate
Grape varieties: 100% Riesling
Average yield: 65 hl/ha
Best vintages: 2001, 2002, 2003
Member: VDP

The Dusemonder Hof winery was first mentioned in documents dated 1605. To further enhance the reputation of such world-famous vineyard sites as the "Brauneberger Juffer-Sonnenuhr" and the "Brauneberger Juffer," Dusemond was renamed as Brauneberg in 1925. In accordance with tradition, the Fritz Haag winery, which has 7.5 hectares of vineyards and is managed today by Wilhelm Haag, carries the additional designation "Dusemonder Hof." The exceptional Juffer-Sonnenuhr site, which is approximately ten hectares in size, lies at the center of the Brauneberg slopes. The hillside is shaped in such a way that a large flat parabolic dish is created, which can store the sun's energy no matter which direction it is coming from. Below this lies the Mosel river, which also stores heat, and above it are steep cliffs. Over the years we have not tired of praising the consistently high standard of quality of this winery. From the basic dry Riesling right up to the top botrytis wines,

the wines produced by Haag are always as of from the same mold. This is no chance occurrence, as few winemakers in the Mosel valley show the level of dedication to their work that Wilhelm Haag does. His success is based on the top Brauneberger Juffer-Sonnenuhr site, where Haag has extensive holdings, having secured the very best parcels here over time. As of 2005 Haag will be supported by his son Oliver, who has already created a good name for himself as winemaker and manager at the Wegeler winery in the Rheingau. He will in future be running his parents' operation in Brauneberg. Our enthusiasm for the elegantly fruity Riesling wines of this estate is unbroken: In 2001, Haag was able to present a whole phalanx of Auslese wines, with and without gold capsule, which included the Number 12, with aromas of an exotic fruit cocktail, and one of the five best Auslese wines of the vintage. The highlight of the range, without a doubt, was the Trockenbeerenauslese, with its aroma of apricots and peaches, a real fruit concentrate with an almost never-ending finish. In 2002 we again had to draw on our full range of superlative descriptive words to describe a fireworks of Auslese wines that was virtually unparalleled. Wines full of tension, with concentrated fruit, but without being heavy or clumsy, pure delicacy, and that in a vintage that was not particularly ideal for Auslese wines. This showed again the ability and class of this exceptional winemaker, who has yet again excited us with his filigree range of 2003 wines. All of the wines are characterized by a superb acid-driven structure, which underlines the elegance typical of Mosel wines to a degree which was achieved by few producers in this extreme vintage. We tasted seven Auslese wines, which simply sparkled with racy, minerally fruity notes, while there were exuberant berry notes in the Goldkapsel – 9 – and the Lange Goldkapsel (long gold capsule), the latter of which is the crowning glory of the range.

The estates: 🍇🍇🍇🍇🍇 World's finest · 🍇🍇🍇🍇 Germany's best · 🍇🍇🍇 Very good · 🍇🍇 Good · 🍇 Reliable

2003 Brauneberger Juffer-Sonnenuhr
Riesling Spätlese trocken
12%, ♀ till 2006 **88**

2002 Brauneberger Juffer-Sonnenuhr
Riesling Kabinett
8%, ♀ till 2008 **87**

2001 Brauneberger Juffer-Sonnenuhr
Riesling Spätlese – 7 –
8%, ♀ till 2008 **88**

2001 Brauneberger Juffer-Sonnenuhr
Riesling Auslese – 6 –
8%, ♀ till 2014 **89**

2003 Brauneberger Juffer
Riesling Spätlese
8%, ♀ till 2009 **89**

2001 Brauneberger Juffer-Sonnenuhr
Riesling Auslese – 10 –
8%, ♀ till 2015 **90**

2002 Brauneberger Juffer-Sonnenuhr
Riesling Spätlese – 7 –
8%, ♀ till 2009 **90**

2002 Brauneberger Juffer-Sonnenuhr
Riesling Auslese – 6 –
8%, ♀ till 2011 **90**

2001 Brauneberger Juffer-Sonnenuhr
Riesling Beerenauslese
7%, ♀ till 2015 **91**

2002 Brauneberger Juffer-Sonnenuhr
Riesling Auslese – 10 –
7.5%, ♀ till 2014 **91**

2001 Brauneberger Juffer-Sonnenuhr
Riesling Auslese Goldkapsel – 9 –
7.5%, ♀ till 2016 **91**

2001 Brauneberger Juffer-Sonnenuhr
Riesling Spätlese – 14 –
↗ auction wine, 7%, ♀ till 2012 **92**

2002 Brauneberger Juffer-Sonnenuhr
Riesling Spätlese – 14 –
↗ auction wine, 7.5%, ♀ till 2011 **92**

2003 Brauneberger Juffer-Sonnenuhr
Riesling Auslese – 6 –
8%, ♀ till 2012 **92**

2002 Brauneberger Juffer-Sonnenuhr
Riesling Auslese Goldkapsel – 9 –
7.5%, ♀ till 2015 **92**

2003 Brauneberger Juffer-Sonnenuhr
Riesling Auslese Goldkapsel
↗ auction wine, 7.5%, ♀ till 2014 **92**

2003 Brauneberger Juffer-Sonnenuhr
Riesling Auslese – 10 –
7%, ♀ till 2012 **93**

2003 Brauneberger Juffer-Sonnenuhr
Riesling Spätlese – 14 –
↗ auction wine, 7%, ♀ till 2012 **93**

2003 Brauneberger Juffer-Sonnenuhr
Riesling Auslese Goldkapsel – 9 –
7.5%, ♀ till 2012 **93**

2003 Brauneberger Juffer-Sonnenuhr
Riesling Auslese Goldkapsel – 13 –
↗ auction wine, 7%, ♀ till 2014 **93**

2001 Brauneberger Juffer-Sonnenuhr
Riesling Auslese Goldkapsel – 12 –
7.5%, ♀ till 2015 **94**

2002 Brauneberger Juffer-Sonnenuhr
Riesling Auslese Goldkapsel – 12 –
7.5%, ♀ till 2015 **94**

2002 Brauneberger Juffer-Sonnenuhr
Riesling Auslese Goldkapsel – 13 –
↗ auction wine, 7%, ♀ till 2015 **94**

2003 Brauneberger Juffer-Sonnenuhr
Riesling Auslese Goldkapsel – 12 –
7%, ♀ till 2014 **94**

2002 Brauneberger Juffer-Sonnenuhr
Riesling Auslese lange Goldkapsel – 15 –
↗ auction wine, 7%, ♀ till 2015 **94**

2001 Brauneberger Juffer-Sonnenuhr
Riesling Trockenbeerenauslese
↗ auction wine, 7%, ♀ till 2025 **95**

2003 Brauneberger Juffer-Sonnenuhr
Riesling Auslese lange Goldkapsel
↗ auction wine, 7%, ♀ till 2015 **96**

MOSEL·SAAR·RUWER

FRITZ HAAG
2001
Brauneberger Juffer-Sonnenuhr
Riesling - Auslese
Fuder 6
750 ml   A. P. Nr. 2 577 050 6 02   Alc. 7.5 % Vol.
Qualitätswein mit Prädikat - Gutsabfüllung
WEINGUT FRITZ HAAG · DUSEMONDER HOF · D-54472 BRAUNEBERG/MOSEL.

The wines: **100** Perfect · **95–99** Outstanding · **90–94** Excellent · **85–89** Very good · **80–84** Good · **75–79** Average

WEINGUT WILLI HAAG

Owner: Marcus Haag
Winemaker: Marcus Haag
54472 Brauneberg, Burgfriedenspfad 5
Tel. (0 65 34) 4 50, Fax 6 89
e-mail: info@willi-haag.de
Internet: www.willi-haag.de
*Directions: A 48 Koblenz–Trier, Salmtal
exit, in direction of Bernkastel-Mülheim,
B 53 to Brauneberg*
Sales: Marcus and Inge Haag
by appointment
History: Winemaking in the family
for 400 years
Worth seeing: Vaulted cellar

Vineyard area: 6 hectares
Annual production: 45,000 bottles
Top sites: Brauneberger Juffer-
Sonnenuhr and Juffer
Soil types: Devon slate
Grape varieties: 100% Riesling
Average yield: 55 hl/ha
Best vintages: 1995, 1997, 2001
Member: VDP

The former Ferdinand Haag estate was divided up among the sons Fritz and Willi in the early Sixties. While Fritz has always been the one in the limelight, the 1994 vintage helped to focus some attention on Willi Haag. Following on a slightly weaker phase in 1999 and 2000, the 2001 vintage shows a return to previous form. The 2002 did not quite reach the standard of the previous vintage. Looking to the 2003 vintage, the dry wines were not inspiring, their fruit simply lacks interest. In any case, dry wines are a minor concern here, with 80 percent of wines being made sweet, and 65 percent of total production being exported. The sweet wines in 2003 show an attractive style, although the piquant acidity occasionally dominates the elegant fruit.

2003 Brauneberger Juffer
Riesling Kabinett – 10 –
8.5%, ♀ till 2006 — **84**

2003 Brauneberger Juffer
Riesling – 3 –
9%, ♀ till 2008 — **84**

2003 Brauneberger Juffer
Riesling Spätlese
8.5%, ♀ till 2009 — **84**

2003 Brauneberger Juffer-Sonnenuhr
Riesling Spätlese
8.5%, ♀ till 2009 — **85**

2001 Brauneberger Juffer
Riesling Spätlese
8.5%, ♀ till 2010 — **86**

2003 Brauneberger Juffer-Sonnenuhr
Riesling Auslese
7.5%, ♀ till 2010 — **87**

2001 Brauneberger Juffer-Sonnenuhr
Riesling Auslese – 9 –
8.5%, ♀ till 2011 — **88**

2002 Brauneberger Juffer-Sonnenuhr
Riesling Auslese
8%, ♀ till 2009 — **88**

2001 Brauneberger Juffer-Sonnenuhr
Riesling Auslese – 10 –
⟁ auction wine, 8%, ♀ till 2013 — **89**

2002 Brauneberger Mandelgraben
Riesling Eiswein
⟁ auction wine, 9%, ♀ till 2011 — **89**

2003 Brauneberger Mandelgraben
Riesling Eiswein
8.5%, ♀ till 2012 — **91**

MOSEL·SAAR·RUWER

WILLI HAAG
2002ᵉʳ
Brauneberger Juffer
Riesling - Kabinett
QUALITÄTSWEIN MIT PRÄDIKAT
A. P. Nr. 2 577 049 ‖ 03
GUTSABFÜLLUNG

750 mle
alc. 8,5 % by vol
Weingut Willi Haag

Produce of
Germany
D-54472 Brauneberg

WEINGUT JOH. HAART

Owner: Gerd Haart
54498 Piesport,
Sankt-Michael-Straße 47
Tel. (0 65 07) 29 55, Fax 61 55
e-mail: joh.haart@t-online.de
Directions: A 48 Koblenz–Trier, Salmtal
exit, in direction of Piesport
Sales: Gerd and Elfriede Haart
Opening hours: Mon. to Fri. 08:00 to
19:00 hours
Sat. and Sun. 08:00 to 16:00 hours
History: The Haart family has been
making wine in Piesport since 1337
Worth seeing: Attractive old manor-
house built of slate

Vineyard area: 6 hectares
Annual production: 50,000 bottles
Top sites: Piesporter
Goldtröpfchen and Domherr
Soil types: Decomposed Devon slate
Grape varieties: 90% Riesling,
5% Müller-Thurgau, 5% Weiß- and
Spätburgunder
Average yield: 80 hl/ha
Best vintages: 2001, 2002, 2003

Riesling plays the leading role in this six-
hectare winery, run by Gerd Haart and his
wife Elfriede, who is also from a Piesport
winemaking family. Eighty percent of production is of fruity and botrytized wines.
Haart considers Pinot Blanc to be an
ideal complement, allowing him to make
more rounded wines. He intends to successively phase out the Müller-Thurgau.
He also plans to increase his vineyard
holdings in the Goldtröpfchen site. In
2001, Haart presented elegantly spicy,
minerally as well as mellow wines. The
2002 wines were good, with clean, piquant fruit in a classical style, heralding
the third bunch of grapes, which we were
happy to award this year. The tasting im-
pressions of the attractive 2003 range are
of spicy, yeasty notes, balanced acidity,
rich and soft at the same time – an enjoyable tasting.

2001 Piesporter Goldtröpfchen
Riesling Spätlese – 22 –
8%, ♀ till 2009 **87**

2002 Piesporter Goldtröpfchen
Riesling Kabinett – 19 –
8%, ♀ till 2007 **87**

2003 Piesporter Falkenberg
Riesling Spätlese – 11 –
8%, ♀ till 2008 **87**

2002 Piesporter Goldtröpfchen
Riesling Spätlese
8%, ♀ till 2008 **88**

2003 Piesporter Goldtröpfchen
Riesling Spätlese – 7 –
8%, ♀ till 2009 **88**

2001 Piesporter Goldtröpfchen
Riesling Auslese
8%, ♀ till 2010 **89**

2002 Piesporter Goldtröpfchen
Riesling Auslese
8%, ♀ till 2009 **89**

2003 Piesporter Goldtröpfchen
Riesling Auslese
8.5%, ♀ till 2009 **89**

2003 Piesporter Goldtröpfchen
Riesling Beerenauslese – 24 –
7%, ♀ till 2012 **91**

2003 Piesporter Treppchen
Riesling Eiswein – 23 –
8%, ♀ till 2012 **91**

2003 Piesporter Goldtröpfchen
Riesling Trockenbeerenauslese – 25 –
6%, ♀ till 2014 **93**

The wines: **100** Perfect · **95–99** Outstanding · **90–94** Excellent · **85–89** Very good · **80–84** Good · **75–79** Average

307

WEINGUT
REINHOLD HAART

Owner: Theo Haart
54498 Piesport, Ausoniusufer 18
Tel. (0 65 07) 20 15, Fax 59 09
e-mail: info@haart.de
Internet: www.haart.de
Directions: A 48 Koblenz–Trier, Salmtal exit, down into the Mosel valley
Sales: Theo and Edith Haart
Opening hours: Mon.–Sat.
by appointment
History: Winemaking in the family documented since 1337

Vineyard area: 6 hectares
Annual production: 50,000 bottles
Top sites: Piesporter Gold-tröpfchen, Wintricher Ohligsberg, Drohn Hofberger
Soil types: Decomposed kaolin-slate
Grape varieties: 100% Riesling
Average yield: 60 hl/ha
Best vintages: 2001, 2002, 2003
Member: VDP

Winemaker Theo Haart from Piesport is one of the quiet men in the region, a man who does little to draw attention to his own achievements. However, he has very definite ideas of how his wines should taste. Haart produces exclusively Riesling wines from his top sites in Piesport and Wintrich, and is strongly focussed on the concept of terroir. His wines always have an elegant bouquet as well as a complex palate, are always clearly products of the red slate soils in Piesport. A look in to history shows the Haarts have been concerned about producing good quality for a long time. The parish priest of Piesport, Johannes Hau, managed to convince the citizens of Piesport in 1763 that they should henceforth plant only the noble Riesling vine. It is for this reason that the designation "Piesporter" was for a long time synonymous with high-quality Riesling wine. Hau himself sold selected vines from his parish vineyard to many other towns along the Mosel, and thus

made a valuable contribution to the spread of Riesling. The vineyard, from which this "missionary work" was conducted is today part of the Haart family holdings. Theo Haart still selects the very best old vines from here to propagate the best new Riesling vines for his own vineyards. In time, Theo Haart has trebled his holdings in the Piesporter Goldtröpfchen vineyard to a respectable 4.5 hectares. Haart uses only natural yeasts, in order to support the typical style of his wines. He does not pay a great deal of attention to the production of dry Riesling, and this accounts for only five percent of his output. In fact, he does not particularly like the description "halbtrocken" (off-dry) either, which led him to an innovative name: He produces a trendy, very tasty wine that he claims can be enjoyed on the terrace in summer or pretty much with any type of food, and has called this "Haart to Heart," clearly with an eye to his English-speaking customers – after all, three-quarters of his production is exported. The neck-bands with their "Mickey Mouse ears" were re-introduced with the 1988 vintage, but actually go back to a tradition from the first half of the twentieth century. The 2000 vintage produced two outstanding Goldtröpfchen wines: the noble Beerenauslese and the minerally Kabinett. The 2001 range was very good, and Haart presented minerally and invigorating wines. The 2002 vintage character meant that Haart was unable to produce a delicacy such as the 2001 Trockenbeerenauslese, but his wines were nevertheless classical in style, and most enjoyable. Indeed, enjoyment was also the keyword for the 2003 vintage tasted this year: the range – a clear house style, providing perfect balance of concentrated ripe fruit and elegant acidity. The outstanding wine of the 2002 vintage was the Ohligsberg Auslese, while this year it is the Spätlese from the same vineyard, although we do not doubt that this could easily have been declared as an Auslese too.

The estates: World's finest · Germany's best · Very good · Good · Reliable

308

2003 Piesporter Goldtröpfchen
Riesling trocken
13%, ♀ till 2005   **89**

2001 Riesling
11.5%, ♀ till 2005   **82**

2002 "Haart to Heart" Riesling
10%, ♀ till 2007   **84**

2003 "Haart to Heart" Riesling
11%, ♀ till 2007   **84**

2002 Piesporter Goldtröpfchen
Riesling Kabinett
8.5%, ♀ till 2008   **87**

2003 Piesporter
Riesling Kabinett
8.5%, ♀ till 2008   **87**

2000 Piesporter Goldtröpfchen
Riesling Kabinett
8.5%, ♀ till 2005   **88**

2001 Piesporter Goldtröpfchen
Riesling Kabinett
8.5%, ♀ till 2007   **88**

2001 Drohn Hofberger
Riesling Spätlese
8%, ♀ till 2008   **89**

2002 Piesporter Goldtröpfchen
Riesling Auslese
7.5%, ♀ till 2010   **89**

2001 Piesporter Domherr
Riesling Auslese
7.5%, ♀ till 2012   **90**

2002 Drohn Hofberger
Riesling Spätlese
7%, ♀ till 2009   **90**

2002 Piesporter Goldtröpfchen
Riesling Spätlese
7%, ♀ till 2009   **90**

2002 Piesporter Goldtröpfchen
Riesling Beerenauslese
↗ auction wine, 7%, ♀ till 2010   **90**

2003 Piesporter
Riesling Spätlese
8%, ♀ till 2012   **90**

2001 Piesporter Goldtröpfchen
Riesling Spätlese
8.5%, ♀ till 2010   **91**

2003 Dhron Hofberger
Riesling Spätlese
7.5%, ♀ till 2012   **91**

2003 Piesporter Goldtröpfchen
Riesling Spätlese
7.5%, ♀ till 2012   **91**

2000 Piesporter Goldtröpfchen
Riesling Beerenauslese
↗ auction wine, 8%, ♀ till 2012   **92**

2001 Piesporter Goldtröpfchen
Riesling Auslese
8%, ♀ till 2012   **92**

2002 Wintricher Ohligsberg
Riesling Auslese
7%, ♀ till 2012   **92**

2003 Wintricher Ohligsberg
Riesling Spätlese
7.5%, ♀ till 2012   **92**

2003 Piesporter Domherr
Riesling Auslese
8%, ♀ till 2014   **92**

2001 Piesporter Goldtröpfchen
Riesling Auslese Goldkapsel
↗ auction wine, 7.5%, ♀ till 2015   **93**

2003 Piesporter Goldtröpfchen
Riesling Auslese Goldkapsel
↗ auction wine, 7.5%, ♀ till 2015   **93**

2003 Piesporter Goldtröpfchen
Riesling Auslese
7.5%, ♀ till 2014   **94**

2001 Piesporter Goldtröpfchen
Riesling Trockenbeerenauslese
↗ auction wine, 8%, ♀ till 2020   **95**

The wines: **100** Perfect · **95–99** Outstanding · **90–94** Excellent · **85–89** Very good · **80–84** Good · **75–79** Average

WEINGUT KURT HAIN

Owner: Gernot Hain
54498 Piesport, Am Domhof 5
Tel. (0 65 07) 24 42, **Fax** 68 79
e-mail: weingut-hain@t-online.de
Internet:
www.piesportergoldtroepfchen.de
*Directions: A 48 Koblenz–Trier, Salmtal
exit, in direction of Klausen-Piesport;
close to the Mosel bridge*
Sales: Gernot and Susanne Hain
Opening hours: Mon.–Sun. 09:00 to
20:00 hours
Hotel and restaurant: "Piesporter
Goldtröpfchen"
Mon.–Sun. 12:00 to 21:00 hours
Specialties: Regional cuisine
History: Winemaking in the family
since 1600
Worth seeing: 200-year-old vaulted cellar

Vineyard area: 5.5 hectares
Annual production: 40,000 bottles
Top sites: Piesporter Gold-
tröpfchen and Domherr
Soil types: Kaolin-slate, partly decom-
posed
Grape varieties: 85% Riesling,
5% each of Weißburgunder, Spätbur-
gunder and Rivaner
Average yield: 70 hl/ha
Best vintages: 2001, 2002, 2003

Gernot Hain runs to build on the foundation provided by his father's achievements. The elder Hain had built up a
hotel, and had purchased vineyard parcels
in the best Piesport sites, creating a solid
base for the winery. In his deep vaulted
cellar Gernot Hain makes his wine in a
particularly reductive style, which shows
off the specific character of the clay-slate
soils in Piesport. Following on his impressive range of 2001 wines, Hain again
improved on this in 2002. The 2003 range
is completely homogeneous: full-bodied
dry wines with soft fruit, as well as rich,
expansive sweet wines. We particularly
liked the elegant botrytis note of the
Goldtröpfchen Auslese Goldkapsel.

2003 Piesporter Domherr
Riesling Spätlese trocken
13.5%, ♀ till 2006   85

2003 Piesporter Goldtröpfchen
Riesling Kabinett halbtrocken
13%, ♀ till 2006   85

2002 Piesporter Goldtröpfchen
Riesling Spätlese – 13 –
8%, ♀ till 2009   88

2002 Piesporter Goldtröpfchen
Riesling Auslese
8%, ♀ till 2009   88

2001 Piesporter Falkenberg
Riesling Eiswein
7%, ♀ till 2012   89

2003 Piesporter Goldtröpfchen
Riesling Spätlese – 12 –
8.5%, ♀ till 2009   89

2003 Piesporter Goldtröpfchen
Riesling Auslese
8.5%, ♀ till 2009   89

2003 Piesporter Domherr
Riesling Auslese
8%, ♀ till 2009   89

2003 Piesporter Goldtröpfchen
Riesling Spätlese – 13 –
8.5%, ♀ till 2009   90

2003 Piesporter Goldtröpfchen
Riesling Beerenauslese
8%, ♀ till 2009   90

2003 Piesporter Goldtröpfchen
Riesling Auslese Goldkapsel
7.5%, ♀ till 2012   91

2003 Piesporter Goldtröpfchen
Riesling Trockenbeerenauslese
6.5%, ♀ till 2015   93

WEINGUT
KURT HAIN

2000
Piesporter Goldtröpfchen
Riesling Kabinett halbtrocken

Gutsabfüllung
Qualitätswein mit Prädikat
D-54498 Piesport · Domhof 5   Mosel-Saar-Ruwer   10,0 % vol 0,75 l
                                                                  A. P. Nr. 2 596 438 8 01

The estates: ♕♕♕♕♕ World's finest · ♕♕♕♕ Germany's best · ♕♕♕ Very good · ♕♕ Good · ♕ Reliable

WEINGUT FREIHERR VON HEDDESDORFF

Owner: Andreas von Canal
56333 Winningen, Am Moselufer 10
Tel. (0 26 06) 96 20 33, Fax 96 20 34
e-mail: Weingut@vonHeddesdorff.de
Internet: www.vonHeddesdorff.de
*Directions: From Koblenz via the B 416,
A 61 Koblenz-Metternich exit*
Sales: Andreas von Canal
Opening hours: Mon.–Fri. 09:00 to
18:00 hours
Weekends: By appointment only
Vacation apartments: On the estate
Worth seeing: 1000-year-old original
building, three-storey main structure
with slender crenellated towers on the
eastern corners

Vineyard area: 4.6 hectares
Annual production: 40,000 bottles
Top sites: Winninger Uhlen,
Röttgen and Brückstück
Soil types: Slate
Grape varieties: 100% Riesling
Average yield: 55 hl/ha
Best vintages: 1999, 2000, 2001

Andreas von Canal in Winningen decided many years ago to opt for the production of quality wines. Vineyard holdings in the best sites as well as low yields provide the right conditions for this. Vines are rigorously pruned to obtain the best results from Riesling. After long periods on the lees Andreas von Canal wants to retain the freshness and fruit of his wines with early bottling. The 2000 wines were clean, and the 2001 followed on from this with good structure and complex aromas. The 2002 range was not quite of the same quality. Looking to the 2003 vintage, we would have liked to report that Canal has improved his quality – alas, we cannot. The range is roughly of the same standard as that of 2002, and there is not a single really enjoyable wine in the range, the aromas of all the Rieslings are simply too tart and rough. We would really like to see an improvement here.

2003 Winninger Uhlen
Riesling Kabinett trocken
11.5%, ♀ till 2006 — **83**

2003 Winninger Uhlen
Riesling Spätlese trocken
12.5%, ♀ till 2006 — **83**

2003 Winninger Röttgen
Riesling Spätlese halbtrocken
12%, ♀ till 2007 — **83**

2003 Winninger Uhlen
Riesling Kabinett
9.5%, ♀ till 2008 — **84**

2001 Winninger Uhlen
Riesling Kabinett
9.5%, ♀ till 2006 — **85**

2003 Winninger Röttgen
Riesling Spätlese
9.5%, ♀ till 2008 — **85**

2002 Winninger Uhlen
Riesling Kabinett
9%, ♀ till 2008 — **86**

2003 Winninger Uhlen
Riesling Auslese
9%, ♀ till 2008 — **86**

2001 Winninger Röttgen
Riesling Spätlese
8.5%, ♀ till 2010 — **88**

2001 Winninger Domgarten
Riesling Eiswein
8%, ♀ till 2012 — **88**

2001 Winninger Röttgen
Riesling Auslese
8%, ♀ till 2012 — **89**

The wines: **100** Perfect · **95–99** Outstanding · **90–94** Excellent · **85–89** Very good · **80–84** Good · **75–79** Average

311

WEINGUT HERRENBERG – BERT SIMON

Owner: Bert Simon
Manager and winemaker: Bert Simon
54455 Serrig, Römerstraße 63
Tel. (0 65 81) 22 08, Fax 22 42
e-mail:
bert.simon@weingut-herrenberg.de
Internet: www.bertsimon.de
Directions: B 51 Trier–Saarbrücken, Saarburg, Serrig
Sales: Mrs. Thinnes and Bert Simon
Opening hours: Mon.–Fri. 08:00 to 19:00 hours, by appointment
History: Established 1897 by Prussian minister of agriculture von Schorlemer, family-owned since 1968
Worth seeing: Double-storey vaulted cellar

Vineyard area: 16 hectares
Annual production: 100,000 bottles
Top sites: Serriger Herrenberg and Würtzberg (both monopole)
Soil types: Slate, gray wacke, gravel with clay
Grape varieties: 70% Riesling, 20% Weißburgunder, 5% Spätburgunder, 5% other varieties
Average yield: 58 hl/ha
Best vintages: 1999, 2002, 2003
Member: VDP

This winery in Serrig has been owned by Bert Simon since 1968. The winery was established by the Prussian minister of agriculture, Baron von Schorlemer, in 1897. The 16 hectares of vineyard owned today are spread over three monopole (i.e. owned solely by this winery) vineyards, the Serriger Herrenberg and Würtzberg, as well as the Kastel-Staadter Maximiner Prälat. More than two-thirds of this area is planted to Riesling, while the Pinot varieties (twenty percent) also play an important role, and are almost all fermented dry. Special attention is also paid to elegant fruity and botrytized wines, with exports making up a hefty 50 percent of total sales of these wines. It is

these elegant Rieslings that have earned Simon his first bunch of grapes this year: dense, concentrated wines with good maturation potential. We hope that Simon will live up to this standard in the years to come.

2003 Serriger Würtzberg
Riesling Spätlese halbtrocken
11.5%, ♀ till 2006 — **78**

2003 Serriger Würtzberg
Riesling Spätlese
9%, ♀ till 2008 — **83**

2003 Serriger Herrenberg
Müller-Thurgau Beerenauslese
7.5%, ♀ till 2010 — **86**

2003 Weißer Burgunder
Beerenauslese
9.5%, ♀ till 2012 — **88**

2003 Serriger Herrenberg
Riesling Auslese
7.5%, ♀ till 2009 — **89**

2003 Serriger Würtzberg
Riesling Auslese – 3 –
8%, ♀ till 2010 — **90**

2003 Serriger Würtzberg
Riesling Beerenauslese
9%, ♀ till 2012 — **90**

2003 Serriger Herrenberg
Riesling Beerenauslese
7.5%, ♀ till 2012 — **91**

2003 Serriger Würtzberg
Riesling Auslese Goldkapsel
8.5%, ♀ till 2012 — **91**

2003 Serriger Herrenberg
Riesling Trockenbeerenauslese
7%, ♀ till 2020 — **92**

The estates: ♛♛♛♛♛ World's finest · ♛♛♛♛ Germany's best · ♛♛♛ Very good · ♛♛ Good · ♛ Reliable

WEINHOF HERRENBERG

Owner: Claudia Loch
54441 Schoden, Hauptstraße 80–82
Tel. (0 65 81) 12 58, Fax 99 54 38
e-mail: post@naturwein.com
Internet: www.lochriesling.de
Directions: From Trier via Konz on the right bank of the Saar, in the center of Schoden
Sales: Claudia and Manfred Loch, anytime by appointment

Vineyard area: 3 hectares
Annual production: 13,000 bottles
Top sites: Wiltinger Schlangen-graben, Schodener Herrenberg and Ockfener Bockstein
Soil types: Slate and Devon-slate
Grape varieties: 98% Riesling, 2% Müller-Thurgau
Average yield: 32 hl/ha
Best vintages: 2001, 2002, 2003
Member: EcoVin

Claudia and Manfred Loch purchased the first 1200 square meters of vineyard area in 1992, in the following year they were given another 30 are by their parents. Pride of place belongs to a parcel in the Wiltinger Schlangengraben with 100-year-old ungrafted vines. Three-quarters of the wines are fermented dry. The beautiful botrytized wines of the 1999 vintage outshone everything the Lochs had produced so far, only to excel themselves with an amazing 2000 vintage range that produced tasty, clean wines in a difficult vintage. There was nothing to complain about it in the 2001 vintage. When we noted a slight improvement last year, the awarding of the third bunch of grapes was a foregone conclusion. We tasted full-bodied, dry, concentrated sweet wines. Full body, paired with slightly tart fruit, is also the attribute that best characterizes the dry Riesling of the 2003 vintage. The elegant Bockstein Auslese Goldkapsel with its noble berry notes sets the high standard. Nothing similar was presented in the previous vintage.

2003 Wiltinger Schlangengraben
Riesling trocken Alte Reben
13%, ♀ till 2008   **86**

2003 Schodener Herrenberg
Riesling trocken "Quasaar"
13%, ♀ till 2008   **86**

2003 Ockfener Bockstein Riesling
13.5%, ♀ till 2009   **86**

2001 Schodener Herrenberg
Riesling Spätlese
8.5%, ♀ till 2010   **88**

2002 Ockfener Bockstein
Riesling Spätlese
7.5%, ♀ till 2008   **88**

2002 Wiltinger Schlangengraben
Riesling Auslese
8.5%, ♀ till 2010   **89**

2003 Schodener Herrenberg
Riesling Auslese
8%, ♀ till 2010   **90**

2003 Ockfener Bockstein
Riesling Auslese Goldkapsel
8.5%, ♀ till 2015   **92**

2002 Schodener Herrenberg
Riesling Trockenbeerenauslese
7%, ♀ till 2020   **93**

2003 Schodener Herrenberg
Riesling Beerenauslese
8%, ♀ till 2014   **93**

2003 Schodener Herrenberg
Riesling Trockenbeerenauslese
7.5%, ♀ till 2020   **93**

The wines: **100** Perfect · **95–99** Outstanding · **90–94** Excellent · **85–89** Very good · **80–84** Good · **75–79** Average

WEINGUT HEYMANN-LÖWENSTEIN

**Owner: Reinhard Löwenstein
and Cornelia Heymann-Löwenstein**
56333 Winningen, Bahnhofstraße 10
Tel. (0 26 06) 19 19, Fax 19 09
e-mail:
weingut@heymann-loewenstein.com
Internet:
www.heymann-loewenstein.com
*Directions: A 61, Koblenz-Metternich
exit, in direction of Winningen, main
road to railroad track, left into Bahnhofstraße*
Sales: By appointment
Worth seeing: Vaulted cellar, terraced
vineyards with dry-bag walls

Vineyard area: 14 hectares
Annual production: 90,000 bottles
Top sites: Winninger Uhlen
and Röttgen, Hatzenporter Kirchberg
and Stolzenberg
Soil types: Decomposed soils of va-
rious Devon slate types
Grape varieties: 99% Riesling,
1% other varieties
Average yield: 51 hl/ha
Best vintages: 2001, 2002, 2003
Member: VDP

Reinhard Löwenstein describes Riesling
as "this ancient variety with its virtually
unbelievable vitality," and has been a vol-
uble supporter of this variety, and of the
concept of terroir, for many years. He expresses clearly his opinion that the production of the filigreed, elegant Mosel
Riesling style is only possible because of
the marginal climate. Whereas grapes in
the south may be ripe after only 100 days,
here in the north berries have up to 160
days "to develop their subtle aromas
gently and at their own pace." The vines
grow on terraced vineyards that appear
stuck to the rock cliffs above the river
valley like swallows' nests. These ecolo-
gical niches not only provide space for
the Riesling grapes to mature, they provide a home for a Mediterranean fauna,
including such illustrious examples as
"Apollo winingensis," a rare butterfly that
occurs in only four locations north of the
Alps. Indeed, the ever-improving quality
and character of wines produced by
Löwenstein has for long brought forth a
joyous song from the multi-colored types
of slate found here. He produced very
good ranges in 1995 and 1996, only to excel himself in 1997. The 1998 vintage
again presented a cornucopia of enchanting botrytis dessert wines. The 1999
wines had an astonishing concentration,
high levels of extract. The top Winningen
sites Röttgen and Uhlen have been producing top wines of remarkable quality
for many years. Löwenstein labels the
opulent Auslese wines, which are often
picked at must weights between 130 and
150 degrees Oechsle, as well as the top
dry wines produced from these sites, with
the old names given to individual parcels
of land, such as "Blaufüßer Lay," "Laubach" and "Roth Lay," to draw attention
to the different types of soils found there
– in part, the name indicate the color of
the slate that dominates there (Blau =
blue, Roth = red). The outstanding wines
of the 2001 vintage were a wonderful
Beerenauslese as well as a magnificent
Trockenbeerenauslese produced from the
red slate soils of the "Roth Lay." The dry
Riesling wines produced by Löwenstein
in 2002 were among the most elegant
wines in this class in the region. And
the highly concentrated and yet exceptionally clear Trockenbeerenauslese was
among the three best botrytis dessert
wines of the vintage. The excellent quality
wines of the 2003 vintage are dominated
by a soft, sweetish and full fruit, giving
the wines an intense mellow character.
They represent an impressive reflection
of the vintage character. The botrytis
wines too, in their pure, quite structured
style are perfect representatives of the
vintage. They were perhaps not quite as
concentrated as the top wines of the previous vintage, but in all fairness it must
be mentioned that some wines had not yet
been bottled at the time of tasting.

2001 Hatzenporter Stolzenberg
Riesling
13%, ♀ till 2005 — **84**

2001 "Schieferterrassen"
Riesling
12.5%, ♀ till 2005 — **85**

2002 "Von blauem Schiefer"
Riesling
12.5%, ♀ till 2007 — **86**

2002 Winninger Röttgen Riesling
13%, ♀ till 2008 — **87**

2001 Winninger Uhlen
Riesling "Blaufüßer Lay"
13%, ♀ till 2007 — **87**

2002 Winninger Uhlen
Riesling "Blaufüßer Lay"
13%, ♀ till 2008 — **87**

2001 Winninger Röttgen Riesling
13%, ♀ till 2007 — **88**

2001 Winninger Röttgen
Riesling Auslese
10.5%, ♀ till 2008 — **88**

2003 "Schieferterrassen"
Riesling
12.5%, ♀ till 2007 — **88**

2001 Winninger Uhlen
Riesling "Roth Lay"
13%, ♀ till 2008 — **88**

2003 "Vom blauen Schiefer"
Riesling
12.5%, ♀ till 2009 — **89**

2003 Hatzenporter Kirchberg
Riesling
12.5%, ♀ till 2010 — **89**

2001 Winninger Uhlen
Riesling "Laubach"
13%, ♀ till 2009 — **89**

2002 Winninger Uhlen
Riesling "Roth Lay"
13%, ♀ till 2008 — **89**

2002 Winninger Uhlen
Riesling "Laubach"
13%, ♀ till 2009 — **90**

2001 Winninger Uhlen
Riesling Auslese "Roth Lay"
⟡ auction wine, 7.5%, ♀ till 2012 — **90**

2003 Winninger Röttgen Riesling
12.5%, ♀ till 2011 — **91**

2000 Winninger Röttgen
Riesling Beerenauslese
6%, ♀ till 2015 — **93**

2003 "Schieferterrassen"
Riesling Auslese
7%, ♀ till 2018 — **93**

2000 "Schieferterrassen"
Riesling Trockenbeerenauslese
6%, ♀ till 2020 — **94**

2003 Winninger Röttgen
Riesling Auslese
⟡ auction wine, 7%, ♀ till 2020 — **94**

2001 Winninger Uhlen
Riesling Beerenauslese "Roth Lay"
7%, ♀ till 2015 — **94**

2001 Winninger Uhlen
Riesling Trockenbeerenauslese
"Roth Lay"
6.5%, ♀ till 2022 — **94**

2002 "Schieferterrassen"
Riesling Eiswein
7.5%, ♀ till 2020 — **95**

2003 Winninger Uhlen
Riesling Trockenbeerenauslese
"Roth Lay"
6%, ♀ till 2025 — **95**

2002 "Von blauem Schiefer"
Riesling Trockenbeerenauslese
7.5%, ♀ till 2020 — **99**

The wines: **100** Perfect · **95–99** Outstanding · **90–94** Excellent · **85–89** Very good · **80–84** Good · **75–79** Average

WEINGUT VON HÖVEL

Owner: Eberhard von Kunow
Winemaker: Hermann Jäger
54329 Konz-Oberemmel,
Agritiusstraße 5
Tel. (0 65 01) 1 53 84, Fax 1 84 98
e-mail: weingutvonhoevel@t-online.de
*Directions: B 51 in direction of Konz, in
Konz continue in direction of Oberemmel*
Sales: Eberhard von Kunow
by appointment
History: Estate of St. Maximin abbey,
family-owned since 1803
Worth seeing: Old abbey estate buildings, abbey cellar dating to 12th century

---

Vineyard area: 10 hectares
Annual production: 50,000 bottles
Top sites: Oberemmeler Hütte
(monopole), Scharzhofberger,
Kanzemer Hörecker (monopole)
Soil types: Devon slate
Grape varieties: 100% Riesling
Average yield: 48 hl/ha
Best vintages: 1999, 2002, 2003
Member: VDP

Eberhard von Kunow, the owner of this winery with its long tradition, also owns just on three hectares of the famous Scharzhofberg vineyard, but he regularly picks his best wines from the five-hectare monopole site Oberemmeler Hütte. Faced with the filigree structure and the sometimes overwhelming acidity of his Riesling wines, it is surely a good thing that only about five percent of the wines here are fermented dry. He produced a very attractive range in the difficult 2000 vintage, and the 2001 range was of a similar standard. In 2002 we reported a significant improvement in the higher quality wines. Based on the vintage character, the 2003 wines from Auslese level up have richer fruit aromas than their counterparts of the previous vintage. Fans of the crisp Saar style will enjoy the acidic Spätlese wines. Our own favorite is the Hütte Auslese, which has subtle slate notes and a well-integrated acidity.

2003 Oberemmeler Hütte
Riesling Kabinett
8%, ♀ till 2009 — 85

2003 Oberemmeler Hütte
Riesling Spätlese
8.5%, ♀ till 2009 — 86

2003 Scharzhofberger
Riesling Spätlese
8%, ♀ till 2009 — 87

2002 Scharzhofberger
Riesling Spätlese
7.5%, ♀ till 2008 — 88

2003 Scharzhofberger
Riesling Auslese
7.5%, ♀ till 2010 — 88

2001 Oberemmeler Hütte
Riesling Auslese *
7.5%, ♀ till 2010 — 89

2003 Oberemmeler Hütte
Riesling Auslese
8%, ♀ till 2010 — 90

2003 Oberemmeler Hütte
Riesling Auslese *
8.5%, ♀ till 2011 — 90

2003 Oberemmeler Hütte
Riesling Auslese Goldkapsel
⇗ auction wine, 8.5%, ♀ till 2012 — 90

2003 Kanzemer Hörecker
Riesling Auslese *
8.5%, ♀ till 2011 — 91

2002 Oberemmeler Hütte
Riesling Auslese lange Goldkapsel
⇗ auction wine, 8%, ♀ till 2012 — 92

2002 Oberemmeler Hütte
Riesling Eiswein
7%, ♀ till 2012 — 93

The estates: ✦✦✦✦✦ World's finest · ✦✦✦✦ Germany's best · ✦✦✦ Very good · ✦✦ Good · ✦ Reliable

WEINGUT CARL AUGUST IMMICH – BATTERIEBERG

Owner: Gert Basten
Winemaker: Konstantin Weiser
56850 Enkrich, Im Alten Tal 2
Tel. (0 65 41) 8 30 50, Fax 83 05 16
e-mail: info@batterieberg.de
Internet: www.batterieberg.de
Directions: A 48 Koblenz–Trier, Wittlich exit, in direction of Traben-Trarbach
Sales: Gert and Birgit Basten
Opening hours: Mon.–Fri. 09:00 to 18:00 hours, Sat. and Sun. by appointment
History: Winemaking since 1425
Worth seeing: Medieval "Escheburg" castle, 1000-year-old cellar with remaining foundation of Roman columns in old barrel cellar
Worth a visit: Wine tastings and gourmet dinners in grand hall of castle

---

Vineyard area: 4.5 hectares
Annual production: 25,000 bottles
Top sites: Enkircher Batterieberg and Steffensberg
Soil types: Blue Devon slate, partly red slate
Grape varieties: 100% Riesling
Average yield: 45 hl/ha
Best vintages: 2001, 2002, 2003

Georg-Heinrich Immich used countless dynamite charges in the 19th century to blast the massive slate formations of the Batterieberg into submission, and to plant vines there. In the Nineties, Gert Basten invested heavily in the vineyards and cellar. The wines are all fermented with temperature control, whether in stainless steel tanks or oak barrels, a few are matured in large barrels for few months. Recently, two hectares of excellent land in the Enkircher Zeppwingert site have been acquired. The fruity sweet wines showed an improvement in the 2001 vintage. Last year, the dry Riesling wines were also improved, and earned the winery its third bunch of grapes. This is impressively confirmed in 2003, particularly by the concentrated characterful dry Rieslings.

2003 Enkircher Batterieberg
Riesling trocken
13%, ♀ till 2006 — **84**

2003 "Alte Reben"
Riesling trocken
12%, ♀ till 2006 — **87**

2003 Enkircher Steffensberg
Riesling Spätlese halbtrocken
12%, ♀ till 2008 — **87**

2003 Enkircher Batterieberg
Riesling Spätlese feinherb
12.5%, ♀ till 2008 — **89**

2003 Riesling Kabinett
10%, ♀ till 2008 — **86**

2003 Riesling Spätlese
9.5%, ♀ till 2009 — **88**

2003 Enkircher Batterieberg
Riesling Spätlese
9.5%, ♀ till 2010 — **89**

2002 Enkircher Batterieberg
Riesling Spätlese
7%, ♀ till 2009 — **90**

2001 Enkircher Batterieberg
Riesling Beerenauslese
7.5%, ♀ till 2020 — **92**

2003 Riesling Auslese
7.5%, ♀ till 2012 — **92**

2003 Enkircher Batterieberg
Riesling Auslese
8%, ♀ till 2012 — **92**

2002 Riesling Auslese
7%, ♀ till 2010 — **93**

2002 Enkircher Steffensberg
Riesling Eiswein
7%, ♀ till 2012 — **95**

MOSEL · SAAR · RUWER
RIESLING
BATTERIEBERG
CARL AUG.
J.MMICH-BATTERIEBERG
ENKIRCH a.d.Mosel
2001
RIESLING
KABINETT
750 ML
ALC. 8% VOL

The wines: **100** Perfect · **95–99** Outstanding · **90–94** Excellent · **85–89** Very good · **80–84** Good · **75–79** Average

317

WEINGUT KARLSMÜHLE

Owner: Peter Geiben
Manager and winemaker:
Peter Geiben
54318 Mertesdorf, Im Mühlengrund 1
Tel. (06 51) 51 24, Fax 5 61 02 96
e-mail:
anfrage@weingut-karlsmuehle.de
Internet: www.weingut-karlsmuehle.de
Directions: A 48 Koblenz–Trier,
Kenn-Ruwertal exit, in direction of Mer-
tesdorf, between Mertesdorf and Kasel
Sales: Mon.–Fri. 08:00 to 17:00 hours
Sat. and Sun. by appointment
Restaurant: In hotel,
Tue.–Sun. 12:00 to 24:00 hours
Specialties: Trout in Riesling
Worth seeing: 600-year-old former
stone mill

Vineyard area: 13.5 hectares
Annual production: 65,000 bottles
Top sites: Lorenzhöfer Felslay
and Mäuerchen (monopole),
Kaseler Nies'chen and Kehrnagel
Soil types: Kaolin-slate
Grape varieties: 90% Riesling,
3% Spätburgunder, 2% each of
Müller-Thurgau, Weißburgunder
and Kerner, 1% Elbling
Average yield: 55 hl/ha
Best vintages: 1997, 1998, 1999

The Geiben family has been making wine in the Ruwer valley since Napoleonic times. The monopole vineyard sites Lorenzhöfer Mäuerchen and Felslay are at the heart of the operation. In 1994 Geiben purchased top sites in Kasel from the former Patheiger winery, and has been selling the wines produced there under a separate label ever since. Now he has purchased the Timpert winery, where 1.5 hectares have been newly planted with Riesling vines. The vintages from 2000 onward have shown a decline in quality. In 2003, many wines have a steely acidity, which tends to diminish the fruit. The attractive Spätlese is a typical representative of the vintage.

2003 Kaseler Nies'chen
Riesling Kabinett feinherb
11%, ♀ till 2007 — **84**

2003 Kaseler Nies'chen
Riesling Kabinett
9%, ♀ till 2008 — **86**

2003 Lorenzhöfer Mäuerchen
Riesling Kabinett
8.5%, ♀ till 2005 — **87**

2003 Kaseler Nies'chen
Riesling Spätlese
9%, ♀ till 2009 — **88**

2003 Lorenzhöfer
Riesling Auslese lange Goldkapsel
7.5%, ♀ till 2010 — **88**

2002 Lorenzhöfer
Riesling Auslese Goldkapsel
7%, ♀ till 2008 — **89**

2001 Lorenzhöfer
Riesling Auslese lange Goldkapsel
8.5%, ♀ till 2012 — **89**

2003 Lorenzhöfer
Riesling Auslese lange Goldkapsel
8%, ♀ till 2010 — **89**

2003 Lorenzhöfer
Riesling Beerenauslese
8.5%, ♀ till 2012 — **90**

2002 Lorenzhöfer
Riesling Eiswein
7%, ♀ till 2010 — **91**

2003 Lorenzhöfer
Riesling Eiswein
8.5%, ♀ till 2014 — **91**

Mono-rack rail: The extremely steep slopes along the Mosel river can in some cases only be worked with the assistance of such a miniature funicular rail system.   Photo: DWI

WEINGUT
KARTHÄUSERHOF

Owner and manager:
Christoph Tyrell
Administrator and winemaker:
Ludwig Breiling
54292 Trier-Eitelsbach, Karthäuserhof
Tel. (06 51) 51 21, Fax 5 35 57
e-mail: mail@karthaeuserhof.com
Internet: www.karthaeuserhof.com
Directions: A 48, Kenn exit, in Ruwer
at Brunnenplatz in direction of Eitelsbach;
from Hunsrück B 52, Mertesdorf exit;
from Luxembourg B 51 Bitburg,
B 52 Mertesdorf exit
Sales: Christoph Tyrell
Opening hours: Mon.–Fri. 08:00 to
12:00 and13:00 to 17:00 hours
Weekend by appointment
History: Prince elector Balduin of
Luxembourg presented this estate
to Carthusian monks in 1335
Worth seeing: Moated castle dating to
13th century, historical tasting room
with Delft tiles, park

Vineyard area: 19 hectares
Annual production: 150,000 bottles
Top site: Eitelsbacher
Karthäuserhofberg
Soil types: Decomposed Devon slate
Grape varieties: 93% Riesling,
7% Weißburgunder
Average yield: 55 hl/ha
Best vintages: 2001, 2002, 2003
Member: VDP

This exemplary winery in the Ruwer valley has a long tradition. Ever since Christoph Tyrell took over the reins here, the quality has been continuously improved. After a short breather, the estate came back to form among the top wineries of the region with an outstanding 1999 range. From the botrytis dessert wines to the top-class dry Auslese "S," one wine was better than the next. And talking about dry Riesling, when conditions are right, there is nobody in the region who can match Tyrell's form in this category. He demonstrated this by presenting two outstanding dry Auslese wines in 2001. The 2000 vintage, which did not provide the same climatic conditions, was of necessity not of the same high standard. However, Tyrell made up for this by presenting a range that was of high quality all round in 2001. Then in 2002 we gained the impression that he had decided to play with the really big boys in future. The whole range was so wonderfully sculpted, so elegant and had such minerality, all in a class that we have not seen here before. The same can be said of the latest vintage collection. This time we particularly liked the elegant and classy Auslese "S." It is no surprise that the dry wines here are particularly good each year, as Tyrell lavishes particular attention on them. But in the case of the fruity and sweet botrytis wines as well, Tyrell remains true to his quest for the highest quality, and to his own style. All of the 2003 wines are characterized by both clarity and elegance on the one hand, and by a vintage-related concentration and mellow, full-bodied style on the other. The most enchanting example of this balance is the Auslese Nr. 45, with a long gold capsule. Summarizing all this, Tyrell is a worthy "Producer of the year 2005." The name Karthäuserhof dates back to the Middle Ages, at a time when the order of the holy Bruno of Chartreuse was spreading all over Europe. In 1335 Prince Elector Balduin of Luxembourg donated properties in Eitelsbach, at the confluence of the Ruwer and Mosel rivers, to the monks. When church property was secularized, the current family acquired ownership in 1811, and Christoph Tyrell is now the sixth generation to run this winery. In fact, he is a trained lawyer, but took over the property from his father in the late Eighties, at which stage the winery was in a rather delapidated state. The estate buildings themselves are beautiful, and are located in truly idyllic surroundings. It is hardly possible to imagine better country living anywhere in Germany.

2003 Eitelsbacher Karthäuserhofberg
Riesling Spätlese trocken
12%, ♀ till 2006   **88**

2001 Eitelsbacher Karthäuserhofberg
Riesling Auslese trocken "S"
12%, ♀ till 2008   **89**

2002 Eitelsbacher Karthäuserhofberg
Riesling Auslese trocken
12%, ♀ till 2007   **90**

2003 Eitelsbacher Karthäuserhofberg
Riesling Auslese trocken
13%, ♀ till 2007   **90**

2003 Eitelsbacher Karthäuserhofberg
Riesling Auslese trocken "S"
13%, ♀ till 2008   **91**

2003 Eitelsbacher Karthäuserhofberg
Riesling Kabinett
10%, ♀ till 2008   **87**

2001 Eitelsbacher Karthäuserhofberg
Riesling Spätlese
8.5%, ♀ till 2010   **88**

2003 Eitelsbacher Karthäuserhofberg
Riesling Spätlese
9.5%, ♀ till 2009   **89**

2001 Eitelsbacher Karthäuserhofberg
Riesling Eiswein – 41 –
7.5%, ♀ till 2015   **91**

2003 Eitelsbacher Karthäuserhofberg
Riesling Auslese
8.5%, ♀ till 2011   **91**

2003 Eitelsbacher Karthäuserhofberg
Riesling Auslese – 24 –
8.5%, ♀ till 2014   **91**

2001 Eitelsbacher Karthäuserhofberg
Riesling Auslese Goldkapsel – 43 –
↗ auction wine, 7.5%, ♀ till 2015   **91**

2001 Eitelsbacher Karthäuserhofberg
Riesling Eiswein – 39 –
7%, ♀ till 2015   **92**

2003 Eitelsbacher Karthäuserhofberg
Riesling Eiswein
↗ auction wine, 7.5%, ♀ till 2015   **92**

2002 Eitelsbacher Karthäuserhofberg
Riesling Auslese Goldkapsel – 53 –
8%, ♀ till 2010   **92**

2001 Eitelsbacher Karthäuserhofberg
Riesling Auslese – 33 –
7.5%, ♀ till 2015   **93**

2002 Eitelsbacher Karthäuserhofberg
Riesling Auslese – 33 –
8%, ♀ till 2010   **93**

2003 Eitelsbacher Karthäuserhofberg
Riesling Auslese – 18 –
7.5%, ♀ till 2014   **93**

2003 Eitelsbacher Karthäuserhofberg
Riesling Auslese – 30 –
8%, ♀ till 2014   **93**

2003 Eitelsbacher Karthäuserhofberg
Riesling Auslese – 38 –
7.5%, ♀ till 2014   **93**

2003 Eitelsbacher Karthäuserhofberg
Riesling Auslese – 43 –
7.5%, ♀ till 2014   **93**

2003 Eitelsbacher Karthäuserhofberg
Riesling Beerenauslese – 39 –
↗ auction wine, 6.5%, ♀ till 2015   **94**

2002 Eitelsbacher Karthäuserhofberg
Riesling Auslese lange Goldkapsel – 52 –
9%, ♀ till 2012   **94**

2003 Eitelsbacher Karthäuserhofberg
Riesling Auslese lange Goldkapsel – 33 –
9.5%, ♀ till 2015   **94**

2002 Eitelsbacher Karthäuserhofberg
Riesling Eiswein – 48 –
6.5%, ♀ till 2015   **95**

2002 Eitelsbacher Karthäuserhofberg
Riesling Eiswein – 55 –
6%, ♀ till 2020   **96**

2003 Eitelsbacher Karthäuserhofberg
Riesling Auslese lange Goldkapsel – 45 –
↗ auction wine, 8.5%, ♀ till 2017   **96**

The wines: **100** Perfect · **95–99** Outstanding · **90–94** Excellent · **85–89** Very good · **80–84** Good · **75–79** Average

WEINGUT KEES-KIEREN

Owner: Ernst-Josef and Werner Kees
Administration: Werner Kees
Winemaker: Ernst-Josef Kees
54470 Graach, Hauptstraße 22
Tel. (0 65 31) 34 28, **Fax** 15 93
e-mail: weingut@kees-kieren.de
Internet: www.kees-kieren.de
Directions: A 48, Wittlich exit,
in direction of Bernkastel-Kues via
Zeltingen or A 61, Rheinböllen exit,
B 50 in direction of Bernkastel
Sales: Ernst-Josef, Werner and
Gerlinde Kees
Opening hours: Mon.–Sat. 09:00 to
18:00 hours, Sun. and public holidays
by appointment
Restaurant: Pentecost and Corpus
Christi (tasting of young wines)
History: Family-owned since 1648
Worth seeing: Vaulted cellar dating
to 1826

Vineyard area: 5.5 hectares
Annual production: 50,000 bottles
Top sites: Graacher Domprobst
and Himmelreich, Erdener Treppchen,
Kestener Paulinshofberger
Soil types: Devon slate
Grape varieties: 90% Riesling,
5% Kerner, 3% Müller-Thurgau
and 2% Spätburgunder
Average yield: 69 hl/ha
Best vintages: 2001, 2002, 2003
Member: Bernkasteler Ring

Ernst-Josef and Werner Kees have for many years been highly successful at state wine shows, and have been rewarded with the rare honor prize in gold. Whatever one may think about such awards, one thing is clear: We have been tasting Riesling wines of constantly high quality here over a long period of time. We really enjoyed the tasting of 2001 wines, and that was repeated on a similarly high level last year. The dry Riesling wines of the 2003 vintage are dominated by rather tart fruit. On the other hand, the sweet botrytis wines are extremely enjoyable.

2002 Erdener Treppchen
Riesling Kabinett *
8.5%, ♀ till 2008 — 87

2002 Kestener Paulinshofberger
Riesling Spätlese *
7.5%, ♀ till 2008 — 88

2001 Erdener Treppchen
Riesling Spätlese **
↗ auction wine, 8%, ♀ till 2010 — 89

2002 Erdener Treppchen
Riesling Spätlese **
8%, ♀ till 2009 — 90

2003 Graacher Himmelreich
Riesling Auslese **
8%, ♀ till 2010 — 91

2001 Graacher Himmelreich
Riesling Eiswein
7%, ♀ till 2015 — 92

2002 Graacher Domprobst
Riesling Auslese ***
8%, ♀ till 2010 — 92

2002 Graacher Himmelreich
Riesling Eiswein
7.5%, ♀ till 2012 — 92

2003 Graacher Domprobst
Riesling Auslese ***
↗ auction wine, 8.5%, ♀ till 2012 — 92

2003 Graacher Himmelreich
Riesling Beerenauslese
8%, ♀ till 2015 — 95

2003 Graacher Himmelreich
Riesling Trockenbeerenauslese
6.5%, ♀ till 2020 — 95

WEINGUT KEES-KIEREN
D-54470 GRAACH
2003
GRAACHER HIMMELREICH
RIESLING - AUSLESE**
Gutsabfüllung
MOSEL SAAR RUWER   750 ml

WEINGUT HERIBERT KERPEN

Owner: Martin Kerpen
54470 Bernkastel-Wehlen, Uferallee 6
Tel. (0 65 31) 68 68, Fax 34 64
e-mail: weingut-kerpen@t-online.de
Internet: www.weingut-kerpen.com
Directions: A 48 Koblenz–Trier, Wittlich exit, in direction of Bernkastel-Kues, at center of town go to bank of Mosel
Sales: Mon.–Fri. 08:00 to 18:00 hours
Sat. 09:00 to 16:00 hours, Sun., public holidays and evenings by appointment
History: Winemaking for eight generations
Worth seeing: Belle Epoque house on banks of Mosel, old basket press
Worth a visit: Wine and culture week from Ascension Day to Pentecost

Vineyard area: 6 hectares
Annual production: 45,000 bottles
Top sites: Wehlener Sonnenuhr, Graacher Domprobst and Himmelreich, Bernkasteler Bratenhöfchen
Soil types: Devon slate
Grape varieties: 100% Riesling
Average yield: 63 hl/ha
Best vintages: 1995, 2001, 2003
Member: Bernkasteler Ring

Martin Kerpen is one of the reliable producers in Wehlen, his vineyard holdings in Wehlen, Bernkastel and Graach providing an excellent foundation for this. While the Kerpen family was producing 70 percent of dry or off-dry wines in the early Seventies, this has now shifted to a point where two-thirds of total production is of sweet and botrytized wines. While in the previous vintage we were still shown Classic and Selection wines in claret bottles (Bordeaux-style), this year's range had a positively traditional appearance. We have not tasted such elegant wines here for a long time, and hope that this trend continues. Our memory of the Domprobst Beerenauslese * brings forth a sigh of contentment.

2001 Wehlener Sonnenuhr
Riesling Spätlese *
☞ auction wine, 7.5%, ♀ till 2008 — 86

2002 Wehlener Sonnenuhr
Riesling Spätlese *
☞ auction wine, 7.5%, ♀ till 2007 — 86

2003 Bernkasteler Bratenhöfchen
Riesling Spätlese
8%, ♀ till 2009 — 87

2003 Wehlener Sonnenuhr
Riesling Spätlese *
7.5%, ♀ till 2010 — 89

2003 Wehlener Sonnenuhr
Riesling Auslese
7.5%, ♀ till 2010 — 89

2003 Wehlener Sonnenuhr
Riesling Auslese **
8%, ♀ till 2012 — 90

2003 Wehlener Sonnenuhr
Riesling Auslese ***
7%, ♀ till 2012 — 92

2003 Wehlener Sonnenuhr
Riesling Beerenauslese
7.5%, ♀ till 2015 — 92

2003 Graacher Domprobst
Riesling Beerenauslese *
7.5%, ♀ till 2015 — 92

2003 Wehlener Sonnenuhr
Riesling Trockenbeerenauslese
6.5%, ♀ till 2020 — 93

The wines: **100** Perfect · **95–99** Outstanding · **90–94** Excellent · **85–89** Very good · **80–84** Good · **75–79** Average

323

WEINGUT REICHSGRAF VON KESSELSTATT

Owner: Günther Reh family
General manager:
Annegret Reh-Gartner
Manager and winemaker:
Bernward Keiper
54317 Morscheid,
Schlossgut Marienlay
Tel. (0 65 00) 9 16 90, Fax 91 69 69
e-mail: weingut@kesselstatt.de
Internet: www.kesselstatt.com
Directions: A 602, Kenn/Ruwer exit, in
direction of Ruwertal, through Kasel and
Waldrach, signs to Schloss Marienlay
Sales: Annegret Reh-Gartner,
Andrea Galli
Restaurant: Palais Kesselstatt
Liebfrauenstraße 10, 54290 Trier
Tel. (06 51) 4 02 04, Fax 4 23 08
Mon.–Sun. 11:00 to 24:00 hours
Specialties: Regional cuisine
Estate hotel: Balduinstraße 1, 54347
Neumagen-Dhron, Tel. (0 65 07) 20 35
History: 1377 Friedrich von Kesselstatt
was administrator of bishop elector's
cellars in Trier, recent 650th anniversary
Worth seeing: Palais Kesselstatt (1745)

Vineyard area: 40 hectares
Annual production: 280,000 bottles
Top sites: Josephshöfer (monopole),
Wehlener Sonnenuhr, Bernkasteler
Doctor, Piesporter Goldtröpfchen,
Scharzhofberger, Brauneberger Juf-
fer-Sonnenuhr
Soil types: Decomposed Devon slate
Grape varieties: 100% Riesling
Average yield: 50 hl/ha
Best vintages: 2001, 2002, 2003

This winery has a long tradition, and
owns parcels of the most famous vineyard sites of Mosel, Saar and Ruwer. It
is run by Annegret Reh and her husband
Gerhard Gartner. The vineyard holdings
have been successively reduced in recent
years. While the pleasing wines of the
2001 were responsible for regaining the
third bunch of grapes, the 2002 provided

strong evidence of this winery's comeback. This year we again tasted a homogeneous range at a very high level, and
even brilliant in parts.

2003 Josephshöfer
Riesling Spätlese trocken ***
13%, ♀ till 2008   **89**

2001 Kaseler Nies'chen
Riesling Spätlese
8%, ♀ till 2009   **88**

2003 Ockfener Bockstein
Riesling Kabinett
8.5%, ♀ till 2009   **89**

2003 Josephshöfer
Riesling Spätlese
8%, ♀ till 2011   **89**

2001 Scharzhofberger
Riesling Auslese lange Goldkapsel – 10 –
8%, ♀ till 2011   **89**

2003 Brauneberger Juffer-Sonnenuhr
Riesling Spätlese
8%, ♀ till 2011   **90**

2003 Wehlener Sonnenuhr
Riesling Auslese lange Goldkapsel – 8 –
7.5%, ♀ till 2012   **91**

2003 Scharzhofberger
Riesling Beerenauslese – 25 –
7.5%, ♀ till 2015   **93**

2002 Josephshöfer
Riesling Auslese lange Goldkapsel – 6 –
7.5%, ♀ till 2012   **93**

2003 Scharzhofberger
Riesling Auslese lange Goldkapsel – 10 –
7.5%, ♀ till 2014   **93**

2002 Scharzhofberger
Riesling Eiswein – 18 –
8%, ♀ till 2020   **95**

REICHSGRAF von KESSELSTATT

2001 KASELER RIESLING
TROCKEN

WEINGUT KIRSTEN

Owner: Bernhard Kirsten
54340 Klüsserath, Krainstraße 5
Tel. (0 65 07) 9 91 15, Fax 9 91 13
e-mail: mail@weingut-kirsten.de
Internet: www.weingut-kirsten.de
Directions: A 48, Föhren exit
Sales: Bernhard Kirsten
by appointment

Vineyard area: 8 hectares
Annual production: 40,000 bottles
Top sites: Klüsserather
Bruderschaft, Pölicher Held,
Köwericher Laurentiuslay
Soil types: Decomposed slate
Grape varieties: 95% Riesling,
5% Weißburgunder
Average yield: 55 hl/ha
Best vintages: 2001, 2002, 2003

Bernhard Kirsten has most of his vineyards located right in front of his house door: He owns a respectable 5.5 hectares of the well-known Klüsserather Bruderschaft site. For the future, he plans to acquire a few more parcels with old vines. In the cellar, Kirsten is not averse to modern methods such as whole-bunch pressing and must oxidation. Apart from this, his approach is fairly traditional. The Riesling is usually made reductively in stainless steel tanks, with some small quantities also being made in oak barrels. Low yields lead to the production of markedly concentrated wines. In 2001 we particularly liked the lively, minerally Spätlese wines, while the 2002 range impressed overall, presenting wines that have finesse, spice and depth. Of the 2003 range, we particularly liked the Bruderschaft "Herzstück" Spätlese, as it shows a perfect balance of elegant fruit and tremendous concentration. The "Eisbeer," too, kept the promise this year that it had already suggested last year. Thus, the very well-made dry Rieslings rounded off an impressively strong range. We are already looking forward to next year.

2003 Trittenheimer Laurentiuslay
Riesling Spätlese trocken
12.5%, ♀ till 2007 **87**

2003 Klüsserather Bruderschaft
Riesling Spätlese trocken "Herzstück"
12.5%, ♀ till 2007 **88**

2003 Klüsserather Bruderschaft
Riesling Spätlese trocken Alte Reben
13%, ♀ till 2007 **89**

2003 Riesling
Spätlese "Pfarrwingert"
12.5%, ♀ till 2008 **89**

2001 Klüsserather Bruderschaft
Riesling Auslese "S"
8.5%, ♀ till 2010 **89**

2003 Pölicher Held
Riesling Auslese
8.5%, ♀ till 2010 **90**

2003 Klüsserather Bruderschaft
Riesling Spätlese "Herzstück"
7.5%, ♀ till 2010 **91**

2002 "Eisbeer"
Riesling Beerenauslese
8%, ♀ till 2012 **92**

2003 Klüsserather Bruderschaft
Riesling Auslese
7.5%, ♀ till 2012 **92**

2003 "Eisbeer"
Riesling Beerenauslese
8.5%, ♀ till 2015 **94**

The wines: **100** Perfect · **95–99** Outstanding · **90–94** Excellent · **85–89** Very good · **80–84** Good · **75–79** Average

WEINGUT REINHARD UND BEATE KNEBEL

Owner: Beate Knebel
56333 Winningen,
August-Horch-Straße 24
Tel. (0 26 06) 26 31, Fax 25 69
e-mail: info@weingut-knebel.de
Directions: A 61, Koblenz-Metternich
exit, in direction of Winningen
Sales: By appointment

Vineyard area: 7 hectares
Annual production: 45,000 bottles
Top sites: Winninger Uhlen,
Röttgen and Brückstück
Soil types: Decomposed slate,
blue slate
Grape varieties: 97% Riesling,
3% Weißburgunder
Average yield: 54 hl/ha
Best vintages: 2001, 2002, 2003
Member: Bernkasteler Ring

When the news of Reinhard Knebels suicide spread at the end of September 2004, it came as a complete surprise even to those who had met him recently. We had tasted his range together with him only a few days before his death, and there was nothing to indicate that this highly sensitive winemaker was going to take his own life shortly thereafter. Looking from the outside, there was not the slightest reason for this. Beate and Reinhard Knebel have built their business from humble beginnings, starting with 2.7 hectares of vineyards, adding carefully selected top Winningen vineyard parcels to move up quickly into the top ranks of Mosel producers. The fairly basic winery buildings were redecorated with considerable good taste. In family terms, too, the future appeared secure. The oldest son is studying chemistry, while his younger brother has commenced enology studies at Geisenheim. Once the first shock had been digested, Beate Knebel decided to continue with business. With the assistance of consultant Gernot Kollmann, the fall of 2004 and the vinification in the style intended by Reinhard Knebel look likely to be mastered. Kollmann, who was largely responsible for the renaissance of the van Volxem winery on the Saar, will also assist in finding a new general manager. But the footsteps to be filled are large ones. Knebel has left a magnificent legacy in his 2003 vintage wines. Even in the years before that, there were no weak links in the range of wines. In 1999, the Knebels presented the best, and very homogeneous, range of all producers in Winningen. We were able to sing their praises just as loudly with respect to the 2000 vintage. At the time, we were happy to award the fourth bunch of grapes to the Knebels. Reinhard Knebel was not a man to rest on the laurels of the previous vintage, and presented a brilliant range of 2001 wines. The result: The Winninger Bruchstück Spätlese took top honors as "Wine of the Year" in the off-dry Riesling category. It was specifically these dry and off-dry wines that confirmed the outstanding reputation of the winery in 2002, as the vineyards in Winningen are ideally suited to give Riesling the power and intensity it can sometimes lack. The 2002 Uhlen Spätlese has a mineral note and well-integrated acidity, and remains a classical example of this. Knebel again confirmed his position as an all-round talent by presenting a very homogeneous range of 2003 vintage wines. The dry wines are mellow, concentrated, the off-dry wines have good clarity of fruit, and the Spätlese and Auslese wines have concentrated, dense fruit, showing off what could be achieved in this vintage if the grapes were handled correctly. Certainly, at this winery one would be correct to refer to the "vintage of the century." And to a great legacy.

2003 Winninger Uhlen
Riesling trocken
12.5%, ♀ till 2006　　　　　　**87**

2002 Winninger Uhlen
Riesling Spätlese trocken
13%, ♀ till 2007　　　　　　**90**

The estates: ⬥⬥⬥⬥⬥ World's finest · ⬥⬥⬥⬥ Germany's best · ⬥⬥⬥ Very good · ⬥⬥ Good · ⬥ Reliable

2003 Winninger Röttgen
Riesling Spätlese trocken
13%, ♀ till 2008   90

2003 Winninger Uhlen
Riesling Spätlese trocken
13%, ♀ till 2008   90

2003 Winninger Hamm
Riesling Kabinett halbtrocken
11.5%, ♀ till 2007   87

2003 Winninger Brückstück
Riesling halbtrocken
11.5%, ♀ till 2008   88

2003 Winninger Brückstück
Riesling Spätlese halbtrocken
12%, ♀ till 2008   88

2001 Winninger Brückstück
Riesling Spätlese halbtrocken
11.5%, ♀ till 2008   89

2002 Winninger Brückstück
Riesling Spätlese halbtrocken
12%, ♀ till 2007   89

2002 Winninger Röttgen
Riesling Auslese
8%, ♀ till 2010   88

2003 Winninger Röttgen
Riesling Spätlese
9%, ♀ till 2010   88

2002 Winninger Röttgen
Riesling Spätlese
7.5%, ♀ till 2009   90

2001 Winninger Uhlen
Riesling Auslese
☛ auction wine, 8%, ♀ till 2015   91

2003 Winninger Röttgen
Riesling Auslese
8%, ♀ till 2010   91

2001 Winninger Röttgen
Riesling Spätlese "Alte Reben" – 10 –
7.5%, ♀ till 2012   91

2001 Winninger Röttgen
Riesling Eiswein
9%, ♀ till 2015   92

2002 Winninger Röttgen
Riesling Auslese
☛ auction wine, 8%, ♀ till 2012   92

2002 Winninger Röttgen
Riesling Beerenauslese
8%, ♀ till 2012   92

2003 Winninger Röttgen
Riesling Spätlese "Alte Reben"
8.5%, ♀ till 2010   92

2001 Winninger Röttgen
Riesling Beerenauslese
8%, ♀ till 2020   93

2002 Winninger Röttgen
Riesling Eiswein
8%, ♀ till 2015   93

2003 Winninger Röttgen
Riesling Auslese
☛ auction wine, 8%, ♀ till 2012   93

2003 Winninger Röttgen
Riesling Eiswein
8.5%, ♀ till 2014   93

2002 Winninger Röttgen
Riesling Eiswein
7.5%, ♀ till 2015   94

2003 Winninger Röttgen
Riesling Beerenauslese
8%, ♀ till 2014   94

2000 Winninger Röttgen
Riesling Trockenbeerenauslese
6.5%, ♀ till 2020   95

2003 Winninger Röttgen
Riesling Trockenbeerenauslese
7%, ♀ till 2020   97

R I E S L I N G

2003er WINNINGER RÖTTGEN   SPÄTLESE
QUALITÄTSWEIN MIT PRÄDIKAT   ALTE REBEN
1500 ML   MOSEL SAAR RUWER   ALC.8.5%BY. VOL

WEINGUT REINHARD UND BEATE KNEBEL   AUGUST-HORCH-STR. 24
D-56333 WINNINGEN/MOSEL   A.P.NR. 1 658 069 10 04

The wines: **100** Perfect · **95–99** Outstanding · **90–94** Excellent · **85–89** Very good · **80–84** Good · **75–79** Average

Mosel-Saar-Ruwer

WEINGUT RÜDIGER KRÖBER

Owner and manager: Rüdiger Kröber
56333 Winningen, Hahnenstraße 14
Tel. (0 26 06) 3 51, Fax 26 00
e-mail: info@weingut-kroeber.de
Internet: www.weingut-kroeber.de
*Directions: A 61, Koblenz-Metternich
exit, turn right in Winningen center*
Sales: Ute and Rüdiger Kröber
Opening hours: Mon.–Sat. 09:00 to
18:00 hours, Sun. by appointment
Worth seeing: Beautiful view of Mosel
valley when doing vineyard tasting in
Winninger Röttgen

Vineyard area: 6 hectares
Annual production: 42,000 bottles
Top sites: Winninger Uhlen
and Röttgen
Soil types: Decomposed slate
Grape varieties: 92% Riesling,
3% each of Spätburgunder and
Dornfelder, 2% Müller-Thurgau
Average yield: 62 hl/ha
Best vintages: 2001, 2002, 2003

Rüdiger Kröber is yet another wine producer intent on making high-quality wines in Winningen. Father W. Kröber is a cooper, and was working in his trade until 1964, when he decided to become a full-time winemaker. Son Rüdiger and his wife Ute took over the business in 1991. The 2001 wines here represented a significant improvement on the wines of the previous year. While the dry Rieslings at that time were only moderately good, he was able to show in his 2002 wines what potential lies in the Winningen vineyards. The dry wines were really enjoyable, leading us to award the first bunch of grapes last year. Kröber has shown with his 2003 wines that he is not content to rest on his laurels, and has made another step forward. Only the botrytis wines could still do with some fine-tuning. Our recommendation: the Hamm Spätlese halbtrocken, which is very powerful and has a bouquet of ripe pears.

2002 Winninger Uhlen
Riesling Spätlese trocken
13%, ♀ till 2006 — 85

2003 Winninger Uhlen
Riesling trocken
13%, ♀ till 2006 — 85

2003 Winninger Röttgen
Riesling Spätlese trocken
12.5%, ♀ till 2007 — 85

2003 Winninger Uhlen
Riesling Spätlese trocken
13%, ♀ till 2008 — 86

2003 Winninger Hamm
Riesling Spätlese halbtrocken
12.5%, ♀ till 2009 — 88

2002 Winninger Hamm
Riesling Spätlese feinherb
12%, ♀ till 2007 — 85

2002 Winninger Röttgen
Riesling Spätlese
9.5%, ♀ till 2007 — 86

2002 Winninger Röttgen
Riesling Auslese
8%, ♀ till 2008 — 87

2003 Winninger Röttgen
Riesling Kabinett
9.5%, ♀ till 2010 — 87

2003 Winninger Röttgen
Riesling Auslese
8.5%, ♀ till 2010 — 87

2003 Winninger Röttgen
Riesling Beerenauslese
9%, ♀ till 2010 — 89

The estates: ✠✠✠✠✠ World's finest · ✠✠✠✠ Germany's best · ✠✠✠ Very good · ✠✠ Good · ✠ Reliable

WEINGUT SYBILLE KUNTZ

Owner and manager: Sybille Kuntz and Markus Kuntz-Riedlin
54470 Bernkastel-Lieser,
Moselstraße 25
Tel. (0 65 31) 9 10 00 und 9 10 03,
Fax 9 10 01
e-mail: weingut@sybillekuntz.de
Internet: www.sybillekuntz.de
Directions: A 61, Rheinböllen exit, via Hunsrückhöhenstraße; A 48, Wittlich exit
Sales: Wine shop Moselstraße 25
Opening hours: Mon.–Fri. 09:00 to 12:00 hours and 13:00 to 17:00 hours
Wine cellar Paulsstraße 48
by appointment

Vineyard area: 6 hectares
Annual production: 40,000 bottles
Top sites: Lieser Niederberg Helden, Wehlener Sonnenuhr
Soil types: Decomposed Devon slate, quartz
Grape varieties: 100% Riesling
Average yield: 55 hl/ha
Best vintages: 2001, 2002, 2003

Sybille Kuntz is proud of the corporate identity of her operation in Lieser, which has received several awards for its overall image. The convincing presentation is backed up by a range of wines that has consistently improved in recent years. The foundation for the concentrated minerally Rieslings can be found in the mostly ungrafted vines planted on some of the best vineyard sites. Both Sybille Kuntz and her husband Markus Kuntz-Riedlin share winemaking responsibility. Additional investment in the cellar is planned, in particular for temperature-controlled stainless steel tanks. By now the winery has converted almost totally to the production of dry wines, with only five percent still being made in a fruity or botrytized style. And it is the dry wines that we also liked best in the 2003 vintage. The best among equals this year is the Niederberg Helden Auslese, which has mellow fruit and typical spiciness.

2002 "Quadrat Gold"
Riesling trocken
13%, ♀ till 2006   85

2003 "Gold-Quadrat"
Riesling trocken
13.5%, ♀ till 2006   86

2003 "Dreistern"
Riesling trocken
13.5%, ♀ till 2007   87

2001 Lieser Niederberg Helden
Riesling Spätlese trocken "Dreistern"
13.5%, ♀ till 2006   87

2002 Lieser Niederberg Helden
Riesling trocken "Dreistern"
12.5%, ♀ till 2006   87

2003 Lieser Niederberg Helden
Riesling Spätlese trocken "Dreistern"
14%, ♀ till 2008   87

2003 Wehlener Sonnenuhr
Riesling Auslese feinherb
14%, ♀ till 2008   88

2003 Lieser Niederberg Helden
Riesling Auslese feinherb Goldkapsel
14%, ♀ till 2008   88

2000 Lieser Niederberg Helden
Riesling Trockenbeerenauslese
7.5%, ♀ till 2014   89

2003 Lieser Niederberg Helden
Riesling Auslese Goldkapsel ***
8.5%, ♀ till 2012   90

The wines: **100** Perfect · **95–99** Outstanding · **90–94** Excellent · **85–89** Very good · **80–84** Good · **75–79** Average

329

WEINGUT PETER LAUER
WEINHAUS AYLER KUPP

Owner: Julia and Peter Lauer
Manager and winemaker: Peter Lauer
54441 Ayl, Trierer Straße 49
Tel. (0 65 81) 30 31, Fax 23 44
e-mail: Ayler-kupp@t-online.de
Internet: www.riesling-weine.de
Directions: From Trier via the B 51 to Ayl;
from Saarbrücken: A 61 to Merzig, via
the B 51 to Mettlach, Saarburg, Ayl
Sales: Julia and Peter Lauer
Tue.–Sat. 15:00 to 22:00 hours
Sun. and Mon. by appointment
Restaurant: Wine house "Ayler Kupp"
Wine bistro open from 15:00 hours
through to 24:00 hours, food to 21:00 hours
Sun. from 12:00 hours, closed Mon.
Specialties: Marinated slices of boiled
beef, homemade potato soup with small
delicacies

Vineyard area: 5 hectares
Annual production: 30,000 bottles
Top site: Ayler Kupp
Soil types: Brown limonite soil regusol
on decomposed slate
Grape varieties: 100% Riesling
Average yield: 70 hl/ha
Best vintages: 2001, 2002, 2003

Peter Lauer has his own internal classification of wines, and he has introduced
some changes for the 2003 vintage. Wines
from the best parcels of the Ayler Kupp
and Saar Feilser sites will be designated
"Selection Gold." The estate wines form
the foundation of the range. This means
Lauer has now more clearly defined the
profile of his top sites, and remains true to
his principle of labeling by barrel. Last
year he bottled his wines so late that we
were unable to taste the 2002 range, we
are happy to report that this year we found
concentrated dry Rieslings with ripe and
at the same time clean fruit in the 2003
wines. The 2002 wines have crisp acidity, and are not as concentrated, but for
all that are just as good as the new vintage.

2003 Ayler Kupp
Riesling Kabinett trocken – 25 –
11.5%, ♀ till 2006   86

2003 Ayler Kupp
Riesling Spätlese trocken – 10 –
11.5%, ♀ till 2006   87

2003 Ayler Kupp
Riesling Kabinett halbtrocken – 11 –
11%, ♀ till 2007   86

2002 Ayler Kupp
Riesling Kabinett feinherb – 16 –
10.5%, ♀ till 2007   87

2003 Ayler Kupp
Riesling Kabinett feinherb – 4 –
11%, ♀ till 2008   88

2002 Ayler Kupp
Riesling Kabinett – 17 –
9.5%, ♀ till 2006   84

2002 Ayler Kupp
Riesling Spätlese – 13 –
10%, ♀ till 2008   86

2001 Ayler Kupp
Riesling Spätlese – 6 –
9%, ♀ till 2010   87

2003 Saar Feilser
Riesling Spätlese – 1 –
10%, ♀ till 2008   87

2002 Saar Feilser
Riesling Spätlese – 14 –
8.5%, ♀ till 2009   87

WEINGUT LEHNERT-VEIT

Owner: Erich Lehnert
Manager and winemaker:
Erich Lehnert
54498 Piesport, In der Dur 6–10
Tel. (0 65 07) 21 23, Fax 71 45
e-mail: weingut-lv@gmx.net
Internet: www.weingut-lv.de
Directions: A 48, Salmtal-Piesport exit
Sales: Ingrid and Erich Lehnert
Opening hours: Mon.–Fri. 09:00 to
17:00 hours, Sat. 10:00 to 13:00 hours
Wine bar Moselgarten: May to Oct.,
11:00 to 21:00 hours
Specialties: Typical regional cuisine
Worth seeing: Roman wine press from
the 4th century, old plague cross owned
by family

Vineyard area: 6.8 hectares
Annual production: 40,000 bottles
Top sites: Piesporter Goldtröpf-
chen, Falkenberg and Treppchen
Soil types: Decomposed kaolin-slate
Grape varieties: 70% Riesling,
20% Müller-Thurgau, 5% each of
Spätburgunder and other varieties
Average yield: 67 hl/ha
Best vintages: 2001, 2002, 2003
Member: Bernkasteler Ring

There are not many producers in the Mosel region who ferment more than half their production dry, Erich Lehnert is one of these exceptions. On the other hand, we would actually prefer to see more of his fruity and botrytized wines, which we feel he does best, although the dry Goldtröpfchen Spätlese is particularly good this year. Most of his vineyards are in the Piesporter Treppchen site. His parcels of the Falkenberg and Goldtröpfchen sites are planted only with Riesling vines. Following on good ranges in the 2001 and 2002 vintages, the 2003 collection is again very good. The exotic touch of the Trockenbeerenauslese is unusual. We particularly recommend you to enjoy the estate wines in the attractive wine bar, open from May to October.

2002 Piesporter Goldtröpfchen
Riesling Auslese trocken
12%, ♀ till 2006 — **84**

2003 Piesporter Goldtröpfchen
Riesling Spätlese trocken
13%, ♀ till 2008 — **85**

2002 Piesporter Goldtröpfchen
Riesling Spätlese halbtrocken
11%, ♀ till 2007 — **85**

2003 Piesporter Goldtröpfchen
Riesling Spätlese
9%, ♀ till 2008 — **85**

2001 Piesporter Goldtröpfchen
Riesling Eiswein
9%, ♀ till 2008 — **86**

2002 Piesporter Goldtröpfchen
Riesling Spätlese
8.5%, ♀ till 2007 — **86**

2003 Piesporter Goldtröpfchen
Riesling Auslese
9.5%, ♀ till 2010 — **86**

2001 Piesporter Goldtröpfchen
Riesling Spätlese Goldkapsel
8%, ♀ till 2008 — **86**

2000 Piesporter Goldtröpfchen
Riesling Spätlese
8.5%, ♀ till 2005 — **87**

2002 Piesporter Goldtröpfchen
Riesling Spätlese **
8.5%, ♀ till 2009 — **87**

2003 Piesporter Goldtröpfchen
Riesling Trockenbeerenauslese
10%, ♀ till 2015 — **89**

Weingut
LEHNERT-VEIT
2003
PIESPORTER GOLDTRÖPFCHEN
RIESLING AUSLESE

GUTSABFÜLLUNG
Product of Germany
Qualitätswein mit Prädikat · L-A. P. Nr. 2 596 291 3 04

MOSEL-SAAR-RUWER
D-54498 PIESPORT/MOSEL
alc. 9,5 % by vol   500 ml

The wines: **100** Perfect · **95–99** Outstanding · **90–94** Excellent · **85–89** Very good · **80–84** Good · **75–79** Average

WEINGUT SCHLOSS LIESER

Owner: Thomas Haag
54470 Lieser, Am Markt 1
Tel. (0 65 31) 64 31, Fax 10 68
e-mail: info@weingut-schloss-lieser.de
Internet: www.weingut-schloss-lieser.de
Directions: A 48, Wittlich-Salmtal exit, in direction of Mülheim-Lieser, on left bank of Mosel
Sales: Thomas Haag
by appointment
History: Estate was formerly owned by Baron von Schorlemer

Vineyard area: 7 hectares
Annual production: 50,000 bottles
Top sites: Lieser Niederberg Helden and Schlossberg, Graacher Domprobst and Himmelreich, Brauneberger Juffer-Sonnenuhr
Soil types: Decomposed slate
Grape varieties: 100% Riesling
Average yield: 55 hl/ha
Best vintages: 2001, 2002, 2003
Member: VDP

The village of Lieser lies at the heart of the Middle Mosel, its visible emblem is the mighty Schloss Lieser palace, built in the late 19th century of massive grey slate, once the home of the Baron von Schorlemer. The wine estate "Schloss Lieser" was built in close proximity in 1904, and immediately started producing some of the best wines of the region. The estate was sold in the 1970's, changed hands several times, which led to a decline in quality. Shortly before the 1992 harvest the estate was taken over by Thomas Haag, who acted as general manager and winemaker. He found the estate in poor condition, with no stocks of bottled wine and no regular customers. It took him five years of hard work until he was able to acquire the estate in 1997, and he now owns seven hectares of vineyards in Lieser, Graach, Bernkastel and most recently in Brauneberg. If the opportunity arises, Haag intends to purchase addi-

tional top-quality vineyard parcels in the years to come. Until now, only his top site "Lieser Niederberg Helden" has appeared on the label, all other wines have been sold as estate wines. 2003 is the first year in which he is also marketing a wine from the Brauneberger Juffer-Sonnenuhr site as such. It is a real pleasure to see and taste how positively this estate has developed under Haag's guiding hand. Right from the beginning, he brought all the knowledge of his studies at Geisenheim as well as a great deal of enthusiasm to the job at hand. Even more important, no doubt, was the background he received from his father Wilhelm Haag, recognized as one of the best winemakers of the Mosel region in the past few decades. Although Lieser is only a few kilometers away from his home of Brauneberg, the wines are quite different in character. Thomas Haag manages to produce wines with a very definite terroir character, particularly from the top vineyard Niederberg Helden. He presented excellent ranges of the 1997 to 1999 vintages, and even that of the 2000 vintage was of remarkably high quality. 2001 was a particularly good year for Thomas Haag, who produced minerally, clean Kabinett wines, concentrated Spätlese wines with elegant fruit, right up to a tremendous set of Auslese and botrytized wines – a wonderful range across the board. The style of the 2002 range was characterized by elegant mellow fruit. Haag himself describes the 2003 vintage as that with the highest must weight for decades, while still producing elegant, even filigree wines. The results are well worth tasting: Riesling wines with ripe and well-balanced acidity, lots of concentration and low alcohol levels, classics of the vintage in the best sense possible. The outstanding highlight is the Niederberg Helden Auslese ***, an auction wine with tremendous depth and an elegant berry note.

2002 Riesling Spätlese trocken
11.5%, ♀ till 2006 **85**

2002 Riesling Kabinett
9%, ♀ till 2006   **87**

2003 Riesling Kabinett
9.5%, ♀ till 2008   **87**

2001 Lieser Niederberg Helden
Riesling Spätlese
8.5%, ♀ till 2010   **88**

2003 Lieser Niederberg Helden
Riesling Spätlese
9%, ♀ till 2009   **88**

2001 Lieser Niederberg Helden
Riesling Spätlese
↗ auction wine, 8%, ♀ till 2012   **89**

2001 Lieser Niederberg Helden
Riesling Auslese
8%, ♀ till 2012   **89**

2001 Lieser Niederberg Helden
Riesling Auslese **
8%, ♀ till 2012   **89**

2002 Lieser Niederberg Helden
Riesling Spätlese
8.5%, ♀ till 2009   **89**

2002 Lieser Niederberg Helden
Riesling Spätlese
↗ auction wine, 7.5%, ♀ till 2010   **90**

2002 Lieser Niederberg Helden
Riesling Auslese
8%, ♀ till 2009   **90**

2003 Brauneberger Juffer-Sonnenuhr
Riesling Spätlese
8%, ♀ till 2009   **90**

2001 Lieser Niederberg Helden
Riesling Auslese *
7.5%, ♀ till 2014   **91**

2002 Lieser Niederberg Helden
Riesling Auslese **
7.5%, ♀ till 2010   **91**

2002 Brauneberger Juffer-Sonnenuhr
Riesling Auslese
8%, ♀ till 2010   **91**

2003 Lieser Niederberg Helden
Riesling Spätlese
↗ auction wine, 7.5%, ♀ till 2010   **91**

2002 Lieser Niederberg Helden
Riesling Auslese ***
7.5%, ♀ till 2012   **92**

2003 Lieser Niederberg Helden
Riesling Auslese
7.5%, ♀ till 2011   **92**

2003 Lieser Niederberg Helden
Riesling Auslese **
8%, ♀ till 2012   **92**

2002 Lieser Niederberg Helden
Riesling Auslese Goldkapsel
↗ auction wine, 7%, ♀ till 2012   **92**

2001 Lieser Niederberg Helden
Riesling Auslese ***
7.5%, ♀ till 2015   **93**

2001 Lieser Niederberg Helden
Riesling Beerenauslese – 12 –
7%, ♀ till 2017   **93**

2003 Lieser Niederberg Helden
Riesling Auslese ***
7.5%, ♀ till 2014   **93**

2001 Lieser Niederberg Helden
Riesling Auslese *** lange Goldkapsel
↗ auction wine, 7%, ♀ till 2015   **93**

2001 Lieser Niederberg Helden
Riesling Beerenauslese – 13 –
↗ auction wine, 7%, ♀ till 2018   **94**

2002 Brauneberger Juffer-Sonnenuhr
Riesling Auslese Goldkapsel
7%, ♀ till 2012   **94**

2003 Lieser Niederberg Helden
Riesling Auslese Goldkapsel***
↗ auction wine, 7.5%, ♀ till 2015   **94**

WEINGUT

SCHLOSS LIESER

LIESER
NIEDERBERG HELDEN
RIESLING AUSLESE★★★

2001

QUALITÄTSWEIN MIT PRÄDIKAT · L.A.P.NR. 2 589314 10 02
GUTSABFÜLLUNG WEINGUT SCHLOSS LIESER · D-54470 LIESER/MOSEL
MOSEL·SAAR·RUWER
Alc. 7.5% by Vol.   PRODUCE OF GERMANY   750 ml

The wines: **100** Perfect · **95–99** Outstanding · **90–94** Excellent · **85–89** Very good · **80–84** Good · **75–79** Average

WEINGUT CARL LOEWEN

Owner: Karl Josef Loewen
54340 Leiwen, Matthiasstraße 30
Tel. (0 65 07) 30 94, Fax 80 23 32
e-mail: mail@weingut-loewen.de
Internet: www.weingut-loewen.de
Directions: A 48, Leiwen exit, in direction of Leiwen, in center of town
Sales: Edith and Karl Josef Loewen
Opening hours: Mon.–Fri. by appointment, Sat. 13:00 to 16:00 hours
History: Winemaking since 1803

Vineyard area: 7.8 hectares
Annual production: 67,000 bottles
Top sites: Leiwener Laurentiuslay,
Thörnicher Ritsch, Detzemer
Maximiner Klosterlay
Soil types: Devon slate, light decomposed slate
Grape varieties: 94% Riesling,
4% Weißburgunder,
2% Müller-Thurgau
Average yield: 70 hl/ha
Best vintages: 1999, 2001, 2002

When church property was secularized some 200 years ago, the predecessors of Karl Josef Loewen acquired the Maximiner Klosterlay in Detzem. Loewen himself purchased a parcel of the extremely steep top site Leiwener Laurentiuslay, and parts of the Thörnicher Ritsch. One of his main objectives is to produce small-berried grapes, as he is firmly convinced that these produce a more elegant fruit aroma than do large grapes. His ideal Riesling is strongly expressive, while having a lean, elegant body and a long finish. Dry wines make up around 70 percent of his portfolio. Following on from a good vintage range in 2001, the 2002 range presented with elegantly spicy, concentrated and characterful wines. The dry Rieslings of the 2003 vintage do not quite come up to the level of their predecessors. The Spätlese and Auslese wines are of similar quality as those of 2002, and the deep, expressive Ritsch Auslese best reflects the vintage character.

2003 "Varidor" Riesling trocken
12.5%, ♀ till 2006 — 85

2003 Riesling trocken Alte Reben
12.5%, ♀ till 2007 — 85

2003 Leiwener Laurentiuslay
Riesling trocken Alte Reben
12.5%, ♀ till 2007 — 85

2002 Leiwener Laurentiuslay
Riesling trocken Alte Reben
12.5%, ♀ till 2006 — 86

2003 Leiwener Laurentiuslay
Riesling Spätlese
8.5%, ♀ till 2009 — 85

2003 Thörnicher Ritsch
Riesling Spätlese
9%, ♀ till 2009 — 86

2001 Thörnicher Ritsch
Riesling Spätlese
8.5%, ♀ till 2010 — 88

2003 Leiwener Laurentiuslay
Riesling Auslese
8.5%, ♀ till 2010 — 88

2002 Leiwener Laurentiuslay
Riesling Auslese
8.5%, ♀ till 2008 — 89

2003 Thörnicher Ritsch
Riesling Auslese
9%, ♀ till 2011 — 89

2003 Leiwener Laurentiuslay
Riesling Beerenauslese
8%, ♀ till 2011 — 89

2001 Leiwener Klostergarten
Riesling Eiswein
7.5%, ♀ till 2015 — 90

2002 Leiwener Klostergarten
Riesling Auslese
7.5%, ♀ till 2012 — 91

2003 Thörnicher Ritsch
Riesling Beerenauslese
9%, ♀ till 2012 — 91

2003
LEIWENER LAURENTIUSLAY
RIESLING
> ALTE REBEN <
TROCKEN
CARL LOEWEN   D-54340 LEIWEN/MOSEL

Picturesque fall view over vineyards to one of the many loops on the Mosel river.
Photo: DWI

WEINGUT DR. LOOSEN

Owner: Ernst F. Loosen
Winemaker: Bernhard Schug
54470 Bernkastel, St. Johannishof
Tel. (0 65 31) 34 26, Fax 42 48
e-mail: vertrieb@drloosen.de
Internet: www.drloosen.de
Directions: A 48 Koblenz–Trier,
Wittlich exit, on the B 53, one km outside
of Bernkastel, downriver
Sales: By appointment only

Vineyard area: 12 hectares
Annual production: 70,000 bottles
Top sites: Bernkasteler Lay,
Erdener Treppchen and Prälat, Weh-
lener Sonnenuhr, Ürziger Würzgarten
Soil types: Devon slate and
lower new red sandstone
Grape varieties: 100% Riesling
Average yield: 70 hl/ha
Best vintages: 2001, 2002, 2003
Member: VDP

"All of the great winemakers I have met
have a clear vision of what their wine
should be," says Ernst Loosen. Their
overall concept is that on the one hand the
terroir takes precedence over technology,
and that grape quality is more important
than quantity. "That is precisely the type
of wine production I am trying to implement at Dr. Loosen. My aim is to produce
wines that are concentrated and complex,
and that reflect their origin," this is Ernst
Loosen's creed. Few other winemakers
have been as straightforward as he in following this objective. For a long time, his
wines were better known outside Germany than at home, and even today two-
thirds of his production is exported. In the
cellar, Bernhard Schug is responsible for
putting Ernst Loosen's ideals into practice: slow fermentation using natural
yeasts, no fining, and as little racking and
handling as possible. The 1993 vintage
first established Ernst Loosen among the
top Mosel producers. The 1995 vintage
was rich and full-bodied, and also had a
brilliantly crisp acidity. The 1996 vintage

was similar in structure. Loosen achieved
a new high level with a virtually perfect
1997 vintage range, which was continued
brilliantly in 1998 with a tremendous
range of botrytis dessert wines. In 1999,
even the dry wines turned out significantly better than in the previous years. Nevertheless, the fruity wines remain Loosen's real domain, making up 70 percent
of total production. The 1999 range was
of a uniformly very high standard here,
from the delicately structured Kabinett
through the juicy Spätlese wines up to the
huge range of Auslese wines. The 2000
vintage wines did not quite reach this tremendously high standard, but one must
stress that Loosen nevertheless produced
a very respectable range of wines in
this difficult vintage. In 2001, he again
presented a collection that can only be
described as outstanding. And yet again,
2002 brought us another superb range.
These wines have a compact style with
concentrated, dense fruit, supported by
subtle mineral notes that always maintain
a lightness, and which gives the wines
tremendous maturation potential. These
are not upfront wines, in their youthful
stages they appear to be resting within
themselves. 2003 provides a seamless
continuation of the performance in previous years. Because of the vintage character, the style is a little changed. The
wines are characterized by even more
rich fruit, which even has hints of caramel. We do very slightly miss the really
refreshing moments, but one of the best
and most typical Eisweins of the regions
can only leave us satisfied with yet
another good vintage courtesy of Ernst
Loosen.

2003 Ürziger Würzgarten
Riesling trocken Alte Reben
12.5%, ♀ till 2007 **87**

2003 Erdener Treppchen
Riesling trocken Alte Reben
12.5%, ♀ till 2007 **88**

2003 Wehlener Sonnenuhr
Riesling Kabinett
8.5%, ♀ till 2008 **87**

The estates: 🍇🍇🍇🍇🍇 World's finest · 🍇🍇🍇🍇 Germany's best · 🍇🍇🍇 Very good · 🍇🍇 Good · 🍇 Reliable

2003 Erdener Treppchen
Riesling Kabinett
8.5%, ♀ till 2005 — 87

2003 Wehlener Sonnenuhr
Riesling Spätlese
8%, ♀ till 2010 — 89

2002 Wehlener Sonnenuhr
Riesling Spätlese
7.5%, ♀ till 2008 — 90

2002 Ürziger Würzgarten
Riesling Spätlese
7.5%, ♀ till 2009 — 90

2002 Wehlener Sonnenuhr
Riesling Auslese
7.5%, ♀ till 2010 — 90

2002 Erdener Prälat
Riesling Auslese
7.5%, ♀ till 2010 — 90

2003 Erdener Treppchen
Riesling Spätlese
8%, ♀ till 2010 — 90

2002 Ürziger Würzgarten
Riesling Spätlese
↑ auction wine, 7.5%, ♀ till 2009 — 91

2002 Erdener Treppchen
Riesling Auslese
7.5%, ♀ till 2010 — 91

2002 Ürziger Würzgarten
Riesling Auslese
7.5%, ♀ till 2010 — 91

2003 Erdener Treppchen
Riesling Auslese
8.5%, ♀ till 2012 — 91

2003 Ürziger Würzgarten
Riesling Auslese
8%, ♀ till 2013 — 91

2002 Ürziger Würzgarten
Riesling Auslese Goldkapsel
7.5%, ♀ till 2012 — 91

2003 Wehlener Sonnenuhr
Riesling Auslese
8%, ♀ till 2013 — 92

2003 Erdener Prälat
Riesling Auslese
8.5%, ♀ till 2015 — 92

2001 Erdener Prälat
Riesling Auslese Goldkapsel
7.5%, ♀ till 2014 — 92

2002 Erdener Treppchen
Riesling Auslese Goldkapsel
7.5%, ♀ till 2015 — 92

2003 Wehlener Sonnenuhr
Riesling Auslese Goldkapsel
8%, ♀ till 2015 — 92

2001 Erdener Prälat
Riesling Eiswein
6.5%, ♀ till 2018 — 93

2002 Bernkasteler Lay
Riesling Eiswein
6.5%, ♀ till 2018 — 93

2001 Wehlener Sonnenuhr
Riesling Auslese Goldkapsel
↑ auction wine, 7.5%, ♀ till 2012 — 93

2002 Erdener Prälat
Riesling Auslese Goldkapsel
7.5%, ♀ till 2012 — 93

2003 Ürziger Würzgarten
Riesling Auslese Goldkapsel
8%, ♀ till 2015 — 93

2001 Ürziger Würzgarten
Riesling Trockenbeerenauslese
6.5%, ♀ till 2024 — 94

2002 Erdener Treppchen
Riesling Eiswein
6%, ♀ till 2015 — 94

2003 Bernkasteler Lay
Riesling Eiswein
6.5%, ♀ till 2020 — 94

2003 Erdener Prälat
Riesling Auslese Goldkapsel
8%, ♀ till 2018 — 94

DR. LOOSEN

2002
Ürziger Würzgarten
Riesling Spätlese

QUALITÄTSWEIN MIT PRÄDIKAT · PRODUCE OF GERMANY
ERZEUGERABFÜLLUNG: WEINGUT DR. LOOSEN · D-54470 BERNKASTEL/MOSEL
A. P. NR. 2 576 162 17 03

alc. 7.5% by vol   Mosel·Saar·Ruwer   750 ml ℮

The wines: **100** Perfect · **95–99** Outstanding · **90–94** Excellent · **85–89** Very good · **80–84** Good · **75–79** Average

LUBENTIUSHOF
WEINGUT ANDREAS BARTH

Owner and manager: Andreas Barth
56332 Niederfell, Kehrstraße 16
Tel. (0 26 07) 81 35, Fax 84 25
e-mail: weingut@lubentiushof.de
Internet: www.lubentiushof.de
Directions: A 61, Koblenz-Moselweiß/
Dieblich exit, on the B 49 two kilometers
upstream in direction of Cochem
Sales: By appointment

Vineyard area: 4.6 hectares
Annual production: 20,000 bottles
Top sites: Gondorfer Gäns,
Koberner Uhlen
Soil types: Slate with sandstone and
quartzite, decomposed slate
Grape varieties: 90% Riesling,
6% Spätburgunder,
4% other varieties
Average yield: 34 hl/ha
Best vintages: 2001, 2002, 2003

When Andreas Barth took over the Lubentiushof in 1994, around 1.5 hectares of old Riesling vines in the terraced Gonsdorfer Gäns site were pretty much the only asset he had to build on. Everything else had to be newly purchased, the complete cellar installation, as well as the monorack rail in the vineyards, allowing him to replant the overgrown vineyards on the terraced slopes above the Mosel river. Andreas Barth was first listed in this guide as a result of his good range of 1998 vintage wines. His dry Riesling wines benefit from low yields – this style makes up 80 percent of his production, which is not typical of the Mosel region. The 2001 vintage produced concentrated juicy wines with a long finish, earning him the second bunch of grapes. The 2002 vintage was similar in style. The 2003 wines are also characterized by a combination of elegance and substance, coupled with a striking yeasty note. The best wine of the vintage is a full-bodied Gondorfer Schlossberg Auslese, which in style is very close to a Beerenauslese.

2003 Gondorfer Gäns
Riesling trocken
12.5%, ♀ till 2006   85

2003 Gondorfer Gäns
Riesling trocken Goldkapsel
12.5%, ♀ till 2006   86

2003 Koberner Weißenberg
Riesling Spätlese
10%, ♀ till 2008   87

2001 Gondorfer Gäns
Riesling Auslese
8%, ♀ till 2007   88

2003 Koberner Uhlen
Riesling Auslese
9.5%, ♀ till 2009   88

2003 Gondorfer Gäns
Riesling Beerenauslese
7%, ♀ till 2007   88

2002 Gondorfer Schlossberg
Riesling Eiswein
7%, ♀ till 2012   92

2003 Gondorfer Schlossberg
Riesling Auslese
7.5%, ♀ till 2012   92

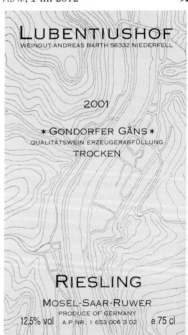

The estates: ♛♛♛♛♛ World's finest · ♛♛♛♛ Germany's best · ♛♛♛ Very good · ♛♛ Good · ♛ Reliable

WEINGUT MELSHEIMER

Owner: Eberhard and
Thorsten Melsheimer
Manager and winemaker:
Thorsten Melsheimer
56861 Reil, Dorfstraße 21
Tel. (0 65 42) 24 22, Fax 12 65
e-mail:
Thorsten.Melsheimer@t-online.de
Internet: www.melsheimer-riesling.de
Directions: A 61, Rheinböllen exit, in direction of Zell; A 48, Wittlich exit, in direction of Zell
Sales: Melsheimer family
Opening hours: Mon.–Sat. from 09:00 to 11:00 hours and from 14:00 to 18:00 hours, Sun. from 10:00 to 13:00 hours by appointment
Guest house: Stylishly decorated "Altes Burghaus" (1517) in Pünderich
History: Family-owned estate for more than 200 years

Vineyard area: 10 hectares
Annual production: 60,000 bottles
Top site: Reiler Mullay-Hofberg
Soil types: Blue-black and red slate
Grape varieties: 100% Riesling
Average yield: 37 hl/ha
Best vintage: 2003
Member: EcoVin

This estate in Reil has ten hectares of vineyards, and is run by Eberhard Melsheimer and his son Thorsten, who has been responsible for the vineyards and cellar since 1995. During the Eighties, father Eberhard converted the vineyards to organic practices. Three-quarters of the vineyards are in the Reiler Mullay-Hofberg, a site for which Thorsten Melsheimer feels himself to be particularly responsible, since he is the only one remaining in the village who is still prepared to cultivate this extremely steep vineyard. His wines are characterized by a soft style, which here and there lacks a little elegance. The Trockenbeerenauslese is an excellent wine.

2003 Reiler Mullay-Hofberg
Riesling trocken
13%, ♀ till 2006 — **82**

2003 Reiler Mullay-Hofberg
Riesling Spätlese trocken
13%, ♀ till 2006 — **82**

2003 Reiler Mullay-Hofberg "Schäf"
Riesling Spätlese
8%, ♀ till 2008 — **85**

2003 Reiler Mullay-Hofberg "Pfefferberg"
Riesling Spätlese
8%, ♀ till 2008 — **86**

2003 Reiler Mullay-Hofberg
Riesling Spätlese – 65 –
8%, ♀ till 2009 — **87**

2003 Reiler Mullay-Hofberg
Riesling Auslese – 66 –
8%, ♀ till 2009 — **88**

2003 Reiler Mullay-Hofberg
Riesling Auslese – 61 –
9%, ♀ till 2009 — **88**

2003 Reiler Mullay-Hofberg
Riesling Beerenauslese – 68 –
9.5%, ♀ till 2010 — **89**

2003 Reiler Mullay-Hofberg
Riesling Trockenbeerenauslese
6.5%, ♀ till 2020 — **93**

2003er
Reiler Mullay-Hofberg
Riesling Spätlese

Mosel-Saar-Ruwer

The wines: **100** Perfect · **95–99** Outstanding · **90–94** Excellent · **85–89** Very good · **80–84** Good · **75–79** Average

WEINGUT ALFRED MERKELBACH GESCHW. ALBERTZ-ERBEN

Owner: Alfred and Rolf Merkelbach
54539 Ürzig, Brunnenstraße 11
Tel. (0 65 32) 45 22, Fax 28 89
Directions: Via the B 53
Sales: Alfred Merkelbach
Opening hours: Mon.–Fri. 08:00 to
19:00 hours, Sat. 10:00 to 18:00 hours,
by appointment

Vineyard area: 1.9 hectares
Annual production: 17,000 bottles
Top sites: Ürziger Würzgarten,
Erdener Treppchen, Kinheimer
Rosenberg
Soil types: Slate
Grape varieties: 100% Riesling
Average yield: 90 hl/ha
Best vintages: 2001, 2002, 2003
Member: Bernkasteler Ring

One could gain the impression that time was stopped at the end of the Sixties in this winery in Ürzig. The Merkelbach brothers, whose winery is in a side-street down towards the river, are firm believers in tradition, though for the future they are considering the purchase of a yeast filter for clarifying the musts. They have never considered cultivating anything other than Riesling vines. The two bachelors have 1.2 hectares in the Ürziger Würzgarten vineyard, with vines – 40 years old on average – being trained up individual poles. Whereas yields were often above 100 hectoliters per hectare in the early Nineties, recently yields have been somewhat reduced, and are now still around 90 hl/ha. This has not prevented the Merkelbach brothers from producing wines in 2002 that were just as good as those of the 2001 vintage. The wines of the 2003 vintage are of even better quality than before, with more concentration and structure, particularly in the Auslese wines. Whereas the Spätlese wines are dominated by acidity at this stage, the Auslese wines show off an elegant spicy slate character.

2003 Ürziger Würzgarten
Riesling Kabinett
8.5%, ♀ till 2008 — **86**

2001 Erdener Treppchen
Riesling Auslese
8.5%, ♀ till 2012 — **87**

2001 Ürziger Würzgarten
Riesling Auslese – 17 –
8%, ♀ till 2012 — **87**

2001 Ürziger Würzgarten
Riesling Auslese – 16 –
8%, ♀ till 2012 — **87**

2002 Ürziger Würzgarten
Riesling Spätlese – 10 –
8.5%, ♀ till 2009 — **87**

2002 Ürziger Würzgarten
Riesling Auslese – 16 –
8%, ♀ till 2010 — **87**

2003 Erdener Treppchen
Riesling Spätlese
8%, ♀ till 2009 — **87**

2003 Ürziger Würzgarten
Riesling Spätlese – 2 –
8%, ♀ till 2010 — **88**

2003 Ürziger Würzgarten
Riesling Spätlese – 12 –
8.5%, ♀ till 2010 — **88**

2003 Ürziger Würzgarten
Riesling Auslese – 15 –
9%, ♀ till 2010 — **88**

2003 Ürziger Würzgarten
Riesling Auslese – 18 –
8.5%, ♀ till 2011 — **88**

2003 Ürziger Würzgarten
Riesling Auslese – 14 –
8%, ♀ till 2010 — **89**

WEINGUT MEULENHOF

Owner: Stefan Justen
Manager and winemaker: Stefan Justen
54492 Erden, Zur Kapelle 8
Tel. (0 65 32) 22 67, Fax 15 52
e-mail: meulenhof@web.de
Directions: A 48 Koblenz–Trier, Wittlich exit, in direction of Bernkastel-Kues/Zeltingen, turn left in Zeltingen in direction of Erden
Sales: By appointment
History: First documented mention of Meulenhof in 1337, as security of Count von Sponheim, from 1477 owned by Cistercian abbey Machern
Worth seeing: Roman wine press complex in Erdener Treppchen vineyard, own distillery

---

Vineyard area: 4.5 hectares
Annual production: 35,000 bottles
Top sites: Erdener Prälat and Treppchen, Wehlener Sonnenuhr
Soil types: Decomposed slate and lower new red sandstone
Grape varieties: 78% Riesling, 13% Müller-Thurgau, 9% Kerner
Average yield: 72 hl/ha
Best vintages: 1995, 1997, 2001
Member: Bernkasteler Ring

For Stefan Justen it is not enough to go through his vineyards several times to pick grapes at optimum ripeness, he sometimes even picks vine by vine. The Riesling wines here can be quite full-bodied and powerful, with a noticeable touch of residual sugar. He seems to have lost a little of his drive since the late Nineties. Then the 2001 range showed that the winemaker was again trying to achieve more finesse and elegance. Unfortunately, the 2002 vintage that followed, bringing ripe fruit aromas, did not help him in his endeavors. The wines of the 2003 vintage lack harmony to a greater or lesser degree, and are tart. The Erdener Treppchen Auslese Nr. 12 has an attractive mellow character, and is the only exception in this vintage.

2003 Erdener Treppchen
Riesling Spätlese – 2 –
8.5%, ♀ till 2008   **85**

2003 Erdener Treppchen
Riesling Auslese – 15 –
9%, ♀ till 2008   **85**

2003 Wehlener Sonnenuhr
Riesling Spätlese
9%, ♀ till 2009   **86**

2003 Erdener Treppchen
Riesling Spätlese – 4 –
8%, ♀ till 2009   **87**

2003 Erdener Prälat
Riesling Auslese
9%, ♀ till 2009   **87**

2001 Erdener Treppchen
Riesling Auslese – 15 –
8.5%, ♀ till 2010   **88**

2002 Erdener Prälat
Riesling Auslese
8%, ♀ till 2009   **88**

2003 Wehlener Sonnenuhr
Riesling Auslese
8.5%, ♀ till 2010   **88**

2002 Erdener Bußlay
Riesling Eiswein
8%, ♀ till 2012   **89**

2003 Erdener Treppchen
Riesling Auslese – 12 –
8%, ♀ till 2010   **89**

2003 Erdener Treppchen
Riesling Beerenauslese
8%, ♀ till 2015   **90**

The wines: **100** Perfect · **95–99** Outstanding · **90–94** Excellent · **85–89** Very good · **80–84** Good · **75–79** Average

341

WEINGUT MILZ – LAURENTIUSHOF

Owner: Markus Milz
Administrator and winemaker:
Thomas Hermes
54349 Trittenheim, Moselstraße 7
Tel. (0 65 07) 23 00, Fax 56 50
e-mail: milz-laurentiushof@t-online.de
Directions: A 48, Föhren exit, in direction of Trittenheim
Sales: Markus Milz, Elke Meißner
by appointment only
History: Winemaking in the family since 1520
Worth seeing: Cellar dating to 1680

Vineyard area: 5.4 hectares
Annual production: 30,000 bottles
Top sites: Trittenheimer Leiterchen and Felsenkopf (both monopole), Trittenheimer Apotheke, Drohn Hofberger, Neumagener Nusswingert
Soil types: Decomposed slate
Grape varieties: 97% Riesling, 3% Weißburgunder
Average yield: 48 hl/ha
Best vintages: 1997, 1998, 2003
Member: VDP

The Milz family looks back on a winemaking tradition spanning several centuries. Some of the vineyards held today were formerly owned by the knights of Warsberg and the Counts of Hunolstein. Markus Milz is particularly proud of three pure slate vineyards that are held exclusively: the Trittenheimer Leiterchen and Felsenkopf as well as the Neumagener Nusswingert. The 1998 vintage was outstandingly good here, a standard that has not been achieved again in the years since. The wines of the 2002 vintage were a little too tart. The 2003 vintage shows that things are looking up again in terms of quality. We very much liked the Spätlese and Auslese wines, which have harmonious fruit and an elegant touch of carbon dioxide. The best of the lot is the Apotheke Auslese auction wine.

2003 Trittenheimer Apotheke
Riesling Spätlese trocken
13%, ♀ till 2007 **86**

2003 Trittenheimer Apotheke
Riesling Spätlese halbtrocken
13%, ♀ till 2008 **85**

2003 Neumagener Nusswingert
Riesling Kabinett feinherb
11%, ♀ till 2008 **85**

2003 Trittenheimer Felsenkopf
Riesling Spätlese
9%, ♀ till 2009 **88**

2001 Trittenheimer Apotheke
Riesling Eiswein
8%, ♀ till 2014 **89**

2003 Trittenheimer Leiterchen
Riesling Spätlese
9%, ♀ till 2009 **89**

2003 Trittenheimer Apotheke
Riesling Auslese
8.5%, ♀ till 2010 **89**

2002 Trittenheimer Apotheke
Riesling Eiswein
9%, ♀ till 2010 **90**

2003 Trittenheimer Apotheke
Riesling Auslese
↑ auction wine, 9.5%, ♀ till 2010 **90**

2003 Trittenheimer Apotheke
Riesling Beerenauslese
9.5%, ♀ till 2012 **91**

WEINGUT MÖNCHHOF – ROBERT EYMAEL

Owner: Robert Eymael
Administrator: Volker Besch
Winemaker: Robert Eymael
and Volker Besch
54539 Ürzig, Mönchhof
Tel. (0 65 32) 9 31 64, Fax 9 31 66
e-mail: moenchhof.eymael@t-online.de
Internet: www.moenchhof.de
*Directions: A 48 Koblenz–Trier, Wittlich
exit, in direction of Traben-Trarbach*
Sales: Robert Eymael, Volker Besch
Opening hours: Mon.–Fri. 09:00 to
16:00 hours, weekend by appointment
Guest rooms: In country-house style
History: Winemaking at Mönchhof
since 1177, either by monks or Himmerod abbey. Family-owned by the
Eymaels since 1804
Worth seeing: Medieval vaulted cellar,
main building is a historic monument

Vineyard area: 10 hectares
Annual production: 70,000 bottles
Top sites: Ürziger Würzgarten,
Erdener Treppchen and Prälat
Soil types: Devon slate, clay with
slate and sandstone
Grape varieties: 100% Riesling
Average yield: 55 hl/ha
Best vintages: 1998, 1999, 2002
Member: VDP

This traditional winery has been run by
Robert Eymael since the mid-Nineties.
The front of the Mönchhof building has
been tastefully restored, and there are
now five exclusive guest rooms on the
estate. Initially under his guidance, the
quality of wines improved, with the 1999
vintage marking the high point of this development. We tasted a number of excellent, elegantly fruity 2002 Spätlese and
Auslese wines, such as only few winemakers produced in that vintage. While
we were able to taste the individual vintage characteristics in the 2002 wines,
the 2003 wines have an acidic note that
makes them all taste much the same.

2003 Ürziger Würzgarten
Riesling Kabinett
9%, ♀ till 2008 — 84

2003 Erdener Treppchen
Riesling Spätlese
8.5%, ♀ till 2009 — 86

2003 Ürziger Würzgarten
Riesling Spätlese
8.5%, ♀ till 2009 — 87

2003 Ürziger Würzgarten
Riesling Auslese
8%, ♀ till 2010 — 88

2003 Erdener Treppchen
Riesling Auslese
8%, ♀ till 2010 — 88

2003 Erdener Prälat
Riesling Auslese
8%, ♀ till 2010 — 89

2002 Ürziger Würzgarten
Riesling Spätlese
8%, ♀ till 2008 — 91

2002 Ürziger Würzgarten
Riesling Auslese
8%, ♀ till 2010 — 91

2002 Erdener Prälat
Riesling Auslese
8%, ♀ till 2012 — 92

2003 Erdener Prälat
Riesling Trockenbeerenauslese
6.5%, ♀ till 2018 — 92

2002 Ürziger Würzgarten
Riesling Eiswein
8%, ♀ till 2015 — 93

2002 Erdener Prälat
Riesling Auslese Goldkapsel
➶ auction wine, 8%, ♀ till 2015 — 93

The wines: **100** Perfect · **95–99** Outstanding · **90–94** Excellent · **85–89** Very good · **80–84** Good · **75–79** Average

343

WEINGUT MOLITOR – ROSENKREUZ

Owner: Achim Molitor
**54518 Minheim near Piesport,
Am Rosenkreuz 1**
Tel. (0 65 07) 99 21 07, Fax 99 21 09
*Directions: A 48 Koblenz–Trier,
Salmtal exit, down into Mosel valley*
Sales: Achim Molitor
by appointment
Restaurant: In Bernkastel,
Karlstraße 1, Tel. (0 65 31) 97 39 90

Vineyard area: 5.2 hectares
Annual production: 36,000 bottles
Top sites: Piesporter Gold-
tröpfchen, Wintricher Ohligsberg
Soil types: Devon slate
Grape varieties: 92% Riesling,
8% Spätburgunder
Average yield: 54 hl/ha
Best vintages: 2001, 2002, 2003

The meteoric rise of Markus Molitor has ensured that the Molitor name is now well-known in the Mosel region. A few years ago we added a further winery with this name to the guide, that of Markus Molitor's brother. Achim Molitor, an enologist, worked in the wine trade in Switzerland for many years, and returned to the Mosel in 1995 to take over a small winery in Minheim near Piesport. He has purchased additional vineyards with old vines in Wintrich, and now has more than five hectares of top-quality vineyards. Initially the wines were made and matured at brother Markus's cellar at Haus Klosterberg in Wehlen, an own small winery was built in Minheim in 1998, working along the same principles. We were highly enthusiastic about the 1999 vintage, and added a second bunch of grapes to the rating in 2001, a decision which was confirmed by the good quality of the 2002 wines. The 2003 range is characterized by lots of power and spice. All of the wines have gained in stature, which is particularly apparent in the still youthful and impetuous Grafenberg Spätlese.

2003 Wintricher Ohligsberg
Riesling Spätlese trocken
13%, ♀ till 2006   **86**

2003 Piesporter Goldtröpfchen
Riesling Spätlese feinherb
11.5%, ♀ till 2008   **86**

2001 Piesporter Goldtröpfchen
Riesling Spätlese
7.5%, ♀ till 2008   **88**

2002 Piesporter Falkenberg
Riesling Eiswein
8.5%, ♀ till 2010   **88**

2003 Piesporter Goldtröpfchen
Riesling Spätlese
8%, ♀ till 2009   **88**

**2003 Bernkasteler Kurfürstlay,
Honigberg**
Riesling Auslese
9%, ♀ till 2009   **88**

2003 Piesporter Grafenberg
Riesling Spätlese
7.5%, ♀ till 2010   **89**

2003 Wintricher Großer Herrgott
Riesling Eiswein
7%, ♀ till 2011   **89**

2003 Piesporter Falkenberg
Riesling Eiswein
7.5%, ♀ till 2012   **89**

2003 Wintricher Großer Herrgott
Riesling Beerenauslese
9%, ♀ till 2012   **90**

2003 Wintricher Ohligsberg
Riesling Beerenauslese
8.5%, ♀ till 2015   **91**

2003 Wintricher Großer Herrgott
Riesling Trockenbeerenauslese
7%, ♀ till 2020   **92**

WEINGUT
MARKUS MOLITOR

Owner: Markus Molitor
Manager and winemaker:
Markus Molitor
54470 Bernkastel-Wehlen,
Klosterberg (mail: 54492 Zeltingen)
Tel. (0 65 32) 39 39, Fax 42 25
e-mail:
weingut.markus.molitor@t-online.de
Internet: www.wein-markus-molitor.de
Directions: A 48, Wittlich exit, in direc-
tion of Zeltingen
Sales: Molitor family and Anna Thoma
Opening hours: Mon.–Fri. 08:00 to
18:00 hours, Sat. and Sun. 11:00 to
18:00 hours, by appointment
Worth seeing: Old slate vaulted cellar
and rock-hewn cellar

Vineyard area: 38 hectares
Annual production: 270,000 bottles
Top sites: Zeltinger Sonnenuhr
and Schlossberg, Wehlener Sonnen-
uhr, Graacher Domprobst,
Bernkasteler Badstube, Lay and
Graben, Ürziger Würzgarten,
Erdener Treppchen
Soil types: Blue Devon slate, decom-
posed slate
Grape varieties: 92% Riesling, 5%
Spätburgunder, 3% Weißburgunder
Average yield: 45 hl/ha
Best vintages: 2001, 2002, 2003
Member: Bernkasteler Ring

Since taking over the winery from his
father in 1984, Markus Molitor has increased the vineyard area by more than
1000 percent, from three to an almost unbelievable 36 hectares now. The latest
parcels to be added were in the Nieder-
menninger Herrenberg on the Saar. While
some observers in the region simply
shake their heads in astonishment at such
entrepreneurial drive, Molitor is now considering rationalizing his vineyard holdings, and expanding his cellar capacity to
cope with the new dimensions. In any case,
the holdings in more than 20 different

vineyard sites between Traben-Trarbach
and Bernkastel give the young winemaker
plenty of scope to produce top-quality
botrytis dessert wines. And these wines
have in recent years been just as impressive as the Haus Klosterberg building itself, which is visible from as far away as
the Zeltingen bridge. The harvest is always
carried out very late, and the reward is a
multitude of Auslese as well as Beerenauslese and Trockenbeerenauslese wines.
Even in a difficult vintage such as
2002, Molitor worked hard to make the
most of what nature had provided. While
there were one or two slightly weaker dry
or off-dry wines in 2001, the bulk of the
higher quality Rieslings were clean, racy,
full-bodied and even substantial. Although Molitor was worried in October
2002 about the conditions, which he
thought would prevent the production of
top-quality wines, the wines he presented
were clear evidence of how much work he
must have put into them. The impressive
range of 2001 Pinot Noir wines presented
came as a surprise. Based on the vintage
character, the 2002 vintage Pinot Noirs
were not quite as good. In 2002, Molitor's
strengths were quite clearly to be found in
the botrytized wines, their depth and baroque body put them in a class above
those of the previous vintage. The naturally sweet wines showed exotic fruit and a
mellow elegance. The 2003 vintage is just
right for the preferred house style: mellow, intense, spicy, yeasty naturally sweet
wines. Of course, Molitor makes full use
of such a vintage to produce the full spectrum of top-quality Riesling. However,
some of the Trockenbeerenauslese wines
were still fermenting at the time of our
tastings. For the moment, we must make
do with the excellent Domprobst Eiswein,
which has extremely elegant ripe notes
in the style of a Beerenauslese. We were
able to taste 42 of the total of 62 different
wines from the 2003 vintage bottled.

2003 Wehlener Sonnenuhr
Riesling Auslese trocken **
12.5%, ♀ till 2008   **89**

The wines: **100** Perfect · **95–99** Outstanding · **90–94** Excellent · **85–89** Very good · **80–84** Good · **75–79** Average

2002 Wehlener Klosterberg
Riesling Spätlese feinherb
11%, ♀ till 2006 90

2002 Wehlener Klosterberg
Riesling Eiswein
6.5%, ♀ till 2012 93

2003 Graacher Domprobst
Riesling Auslese feinherb **
12.5%, ♀ till 2010 90

2002 Wehlener Klosterberg
Riesling Eiswein *
↗ auction wine, 6.5%, ♀ till 2012 ... 93

2003 Wehlener Klosterberg
Riesling Spätlese feinherb
11.5%, ♀ till 2010 91

2003 Wehlener Sonnenuhr
Riesling Auslese **
8%, ♀ till 2015 93

2003 Wehlener Sonnenuhr
Riesling Spätlese
8%, ♀ till 2010 90

2003 Zeltinger Sonnenuhr
Riesling Auslese **
7.5%, ♀ till 2015 93

2003 Niedermenniger Herrenberg
Riesling Spätlese
9%, ♀ till 2011 90

2002 Zeltinger Sonnenuhr
Riesling Trockenbeerenauslese *
↗ auction wine, 7%, ♀ till 2012 94

2002 Zeltinger Sonnenuhr
Riesling Spätlese – 23 –
↗ auction wine, 7.5%, ♀ till 2012 ... 91

2003 Wehlener Sonnenuhr
Riesling Beerenauslese *
7%, ♀ till 2022 94

2003 Zeltinger Sonnenuhr
Riesling Spätlese – 22 –
8%, ♀ till 2010 91

2003 Zeltinger Sonnenuhr
Riesling Auslese ***
↗ auction wine, 7.5%, ♀ till 2020 ... 95

2003 Zeltinger Schlossberg
Riesling Auslese *
7.5%, ♀ till 2012 91

2003 Graacher Domprobst
Riesling Eiswein
7.5%, ♀ till 2020 95

2001 Zeltinger Sonnenuhr
Riesling Auslese ***
↗ auction wine, 7.5%, ♀ till 2020 ... 92

2002 Zeltinger Sonnenuhr
Riesling Auslese ** – 28 –
↗ auction wine, 7.5%, ♀ till 2012 ... 92

2003 Zeltinger Sonnenuhr
Riesling Spätlese – 23 –
↗ auction wine, 7.5%, ♀ till 2014 ... 92

2003 Ürziger Würzgarten
Riesling Auslese **
9%, ♀ till 2014 92

2003 Bernkasteler Graben
Riesling Auslese **
7.5%, ♀ till 2013 92

2003 Niedermenniger Herrenberg
Riesling Auslese ***
7.5%, ♀ till 2016 92

2001 Zeltinger Sonnenuhr
Riesling Spätlese – 23 –
↗ auction wine, 7.5%, ♀ till 2014 ... 93

HAUS KLOSTERBERG

MARKUS MOLITOR

2001
Bernkasteler Lay
Spätlese
Riesling Trocken

MOSEL · SAAR · RUWER

Gutsabfüllung
Weingut Markus Molitor
D-54470 Bernkastel-Wehlen

Product of Germany
A.P.Nr. 2 576 609 50 02
Qualitätswein mit Prädikat

750 ml   ALC. 11,5 % BY VOL.

WEINGUT
MARTIN MÜLLEN

Owner: Martin Müllen
56841 Traben-Trarbach,
Alte Marktstraße 2
Tel. (0 65 41) 94 70, Fax 81 35 37
e-mail: MartinMuellen@t-online.de
Internet: www.weingutmuellen.com
Directions: A 48, Wittlich exit, in direction
of Traben-Trarbach; A 61, Rheinböllen
exit, B 50 in direction of Traben-Trarbach;
from Hahn airport 20 min. by shuttle bus
Sales: Martin and Susanne Müllen
Opening hours: Mon.–Sat. by appointment
Worth a visit: Guided tour of terraces in
Trarbacher Hühnerberg vineyard

Vineyard area: 4.4 hectares
Annual production: 35,000 bottles
Top sites: Kröver Steffensberg,
Letterlay and Paradies, Kinheimer
Rosenberg, Trarbacher Hühnerberg
Soil types: Lower new red sandstone
and Devon slate
Grape varieties: 84% Riesling,
6% Rivaner, 4% Dornfelder, 3% each
of Weiß- and Spätburgunder
Average yield: 69 hl/ha
Best vintages: 2001, 2002, 2003

Some twelve years after going into business on his own, Martin Müllen can already look back on a tremendous growth and development. The young viticultural technician is aiming at owning five hectares of vineyard. 1998 he bought a winery building, and in 2000 added a parcel of the Trarbacher Hühnerberg vineyard, which is listed in a vineyard map of 1897 as a "Erstes Gewächs" (First Growth). Following on quite an attractive 2000 range, Müllen pulled all the stops in 2001, easily gaining his second bunch of grapes, and confirmed this achievement with his 2002 range. While the wines were already characterized by clean fruit in the previous vintage, depth and spice were added to this in 2003. The wines provide a whole bouquet of aromas.

2003 Kröver Letterlay
Riesling Spätlese halbtrocken
12.5%, ♀ till 2007 — **87**

2001 Trarbacher Hühnerberg
Riesling
8%, ♀ till 2008 — **87**

2001 Kröver Letterlay
Riesling Auslese
9.5%, ♀ till 2015 — **88**

2002 Trarbacher Hühnerberg
Riesling Auslese
8%, ♀ till 2010 — **88**

2003 Kröver Paradies "Jippi"
Riesling Spätlese **
8%, ♀ till 2010 — **89**

2002 Trarbacher Hühnerberg
Riesling Eiswein
7.5%, ♀ till 2012 — **90**

2003 Kröver Paradies "Retsch"
Riesling Spätlese **
8%, ♀ till 2010 — **90**

2003 Trarbacher Hühnerberg
Riesling Spätlese
8%, ♀ till 2012 — **90**

2003 Trarbacher Hühnerberg
Riesling Auslese
7.5%, ♀ till 2012 — **91**

2003 Trarbacher Hühnerberg
Riesling Auslese *
7.5%, ♀ till 2015 — **92**

2003 Trarbacher Hühnerberg
Riesling Beerenauslese
7%, ♀ till 2017 — **94**

The wines: **100** Perfect · **95–99** Outstanding · **90–94** Excellent · **85–89** Very good · **80–84** Good · **75–79** Average

347

WEINGUT EGON MÜLLER – SCHARZHOF

Owner: Egon Müller
Winemaker: Stefan Fobian
54459 Wiltingen, Scharzhof
Tel. (0 65 01) 1 72 32, Fax 15 02 63
e-mail: egon@scharzhof.de
Internet: www.scharzhof.de
Directions: From Trier via Konz in direction of Wiltingen–Oberemmel
Sales: No sales to the public
Tastings: By appointment only
History: Family-owned since 1797
Worth seeing: Scharzhof, park

Vineyard area: 8 hectares
Le Gallais: 4 hectares
Annual production: 70,000 bottles
Top sites: Scharzhofberger,
Wiltinger Braune Kupp (monopole)
Soil types: Decomposed slate
Grape varieties: 98% Riesling,
2% other varieties
Average yield: 45 hl/ha
Best vintages: 1997, 1999, 2003
Member: VDP

Many of the botrytis wines of this estate have long since become legends. Back in the 19th century, this winery was already collecting awards and medals, mainly from outside Germany, and made a name for itself that remains among the very best today. So far, Egon Müller has not revealed himself to be a top producer of dry wines. This has now changed, with wines produced from vineyards owned by his wife's family. Some 40 hectares of vines are grown on the property surrounding the château of Baron Ullmann in Slovakia, on the border to Hungary, located between Vienna and Budapest. Last year we tasted a 2002 from there that showed ripe fruit, and had the style of a powerful Riesling, the 2003 vintage has a stature reminiscent of a full-bodied "Smaragd" wine from the Wachau in Austria. At home in the Saar region, Müller looks back on a series of outstanding vintages in the late Nineties. The 1997 wines had lots of substance, while Egon Müller IV considers the 1999 vintage to be "the best and most elegant I have ever harvested." Müller owns a remarkable seven hectares in the best sections of the famous Scharzhofberg, and slightly more than half that in the Wiltinger Braune Kupp, with the wines from there being marketed under the "Le Gallais" label. The fabulous high-predicate wines, outstanding Eisweins and breathtaking Trockenbeerenauslese wines show clearly that there is hardly another producer in Germany who could improve on the wines in this category. Egon Müller's father already regularly achieved record prices for such wines at the renowned auctions of the VDP Großer Ring held in Trier each year. The 2000 vintage saw a new winemaker taking over in the cellar, Stefan Fobian came to take over from Horst Frank, who had worked here successfully for decades. The 2001 wines were partly characterized by a hearty acidity, which is typical of the vintage. The wines of the 2002 vintage tasted were of a different stature altogether: Even the Kabinett wines exuded an opulence we had not expected here. It should have been no surprise, since the Kabinett wines had the must weights as the Spätlese wines – never below 90 degrees Oechsle. The Spätlese wines also showed this richness, typical of the vintage, and an Eiswein crowned this formidable range. The wines Müller showed us on the occasion of our visit this year were, quite simply, fantastic. The wines have an entirely noble, very self-assured style that we have not encountered here before. Müller himself refers to it as a relatively easy year for him, with the harvest starting earlier than ever before, compares the style of these wines with that of the legendary 1959 vintage. Our reward to him is the crown we can happily award him for the best Auslese of the vintage, rated at 99 points! The Trockenbeerenauslese wines were still fermenting at the time of our tasting, and will no doubt be a topic of discussion for a long time to come.

The estates: ❀❀❀❀❀ World's finest · ❀❀❀❀ Germany's best · ❀❀❀ Very good · ❀❀ Good · ❀ Reliable

2002 Scharzhofberger
Riesling Kabinett – 9 –
9.5%, ♀ till 2008   87

2002 Wiltinger Braune Kupp
Riesling Spätlese "Le Gallais"
9%, ♀ till 2008   87

2002 Scharzhofberger
Riesling Kabinett – 10 –
9.5%, ♀ till 2009   88

2002 Scharzhofberger
Riesling Spätlese – 13 –
↗ auction wine, 8.5%, ♀ till 2012   89

2003 Scharzhofberger
Riesling Kabinett – 15 –
9.5%, ♀ till 2010   89

2001 Scharzhofberger
Riesling Spätlese – 7 –
8%, ♀ till 2009   90

2001 Scharzhofberger
Riesling Auslese Goldkapsel
7.5%, ♀ till 2010   90

2001 Wiltinger Braune Kupp
Riesling Auslese Goldkapsel
"Le Gallais"
8%, ♀ till 2009   90

2003 Wiltinger Braune Kupp
Riesling Spätlese "Le Gallais" – 6 –
9%, ♀ till 2010   90

2003 Scharzhofberger
Riesling Kabinett – 3 –
↗ auction wine, 9%, ♀ till 2012   91

2003 Wiltinger Braune Kupp
Riesling Spätlese "Le Gallais" – 19 –
↗ auction wine, 9%, ♀ till 2012   91

2003 Scharzhofberger
Riesling Spätlese – 16 –
9%, ♀ till 2015   92

2003 Scharzhofberger
Riesling Spätlese – 8 –
9%, ♀ till 2015   92

2001 Wiltinger Braune Kupp
Riesling Beerenauslese "Le Gallais"
6%, ♀ till 2015   92

2001 Scharzhofberger
Riesling Trockenbeerenauslese
6%, ♀ till 2020   93

2003 Scharzhofberger
Riesling Spätlese – 14 –
9%, ♀ till 2017   93

2003 Scharzhofberger
Riesling Spätlese – 17 –
9%, ♀ till 2015   93

2003 Scharzhofberger
Riesling Auslese – 11 –
8.5%, ♀ till 2017   93

2000 Scharzhofberger
Riesling Auslese Goldkapsel – 9 –
7.5%, ♀ till 2020   93

2003 Scharzhofberger
Riesling Spätlese – 21 –
↗ auction wine, 9%, ♀ till 2017   94

2002 Scharzhofberger
Riesling Auslese Goldkapsel – 14 –
↗ auction wine, 8%, ♀ till 2015   94

2003 Wiltinger Braune Kupp
Riesling Auslese Goldkapsel
"Le Gallais" – 24 –
↗ auction wine, 8.5%, ♀ till 2020   94

2000 Scharzhofberger
Riesling Trockenbeerenauslese
6%, ♀ till 2030   95

2003 Scharzhofberger
Riesling Auslese – 22 –
7.5%, ♀ till 2020   95

2003 Scharzhofberger
Riesling Auslese Goldkapsel – 25 –
↗ auction wine, 8.5%, ♀ till 2025   98

2002 Scharzhofberger
Riesling Eiswein – 15 –
↗ auction wine, 6%, ♀ till 2025   99

2003 Scharzhofberger
Riesling Auslese Goldkapsel – 26 –
↗ auction wine, 7.5%, ♀ till 2025   99

The wines: **100** Perfect · **95–99** Outstanding · **90–94** Excellent · **85–89** Very good · **80–84** Good · **75–79** Average

WEINGUT VON OTHEGRAVEN

Owner and manager: Dr. Heidi Kegel
Administrator: Swen Klinger
Winemaker: Andreas Barth
54441 Kanzem, Weinstraße 1
Tel. (0 65 01) 15 00 42, Fax 1 88 79
e-mail: von-othegraven@t-online.de
Internet: www.von-othegraven.de
Directions: From Trier via Konz to
Kanzem on right bank of Saar, straight
on from the Saar bridge
Sales: Dr. Heidi Kegel
Opening hours: Mon.–Fri. 08:00 to
17:00 hours and by appointment
History: Privately owned since 16th
century
Worth seeing: Park with beautiful old
trees

Vineyard area: 8.5 hectares
Annual production: 50,000 bottles
Top sites: Kanzemer Altenberg, Wiltinger Kupp, Ockfener Bockstein
Soil types: Decomposed Devon slate with quartzite, iron, gray wacke, clay
Grape varieties: 100% Riesling
Average yield: 47 hl/ha
Best vintages: 2001, 2002, 2003
Member: VDP

This winery has a long tradition, and is located in idyllic surroundings at the foot of the Kanzem hill. After many years of changing fortunes, it is currently experiencing a renaissance under the sensitive guidance of Dr. Heidi Kegel. The wines are again finding the level of the glorious Sixties and Seventies, when Maria von Othegraven presented one lovely vintage after another. After producing the probably best dry Saar wines in 1999, the winery has now impressively repeated this achievement. While new standards were set in 2002 with regard to the sweet Spätlese wines, in this vintage it is the elegant and at the same time concentrated Auslese wines that remind of earlier times. An excellent example is the Altenberg Auslese Nr. 15.

2003 Kanzemer Altenberg
Riesling Spätlese – 11 –
9.5%, ♀ till 2009 **88**

2003 Kanzemer Altenberg
Riesling Spätlese – 12 –
10%, ♀ till 2010 **89**

2003 Kanzemer Altenberg
Riesling Spätlese – 13 –
10%, ♀ till 2010 **90**

2003 Kanzemer Altenberg
Riesling Spätlese – 14 –
↗ auction wine, 10%, ♀ till 2012 **90**

2003 Kanzemer Altenberg
Riesling Auslese – 16 –
9.5%, ♀ till 2011 **91**

2003 Kanzemer Altenberg
Riesling Auslese – 17 –
↗ auction wine, 9.5%, ♀ till 2010 **91**

2003 Kanzemer Altenberg
Riesling Auslese Goldkapsel – 18 –
↗ auction wine, 9%, ♀ till 2012 **91**

2003 Kanzemer Altenberg
Riesling Auslese – 15 –
9%, ♀ till 2012 **92**

2002 Kanzemer Altenberg
Riesling Auslese Goldkapsel – 13 –
8.5%, ♀ till 2014 **92**

2003 Kanzemer Altenberg
Riesling Auslese lange Goldkapsel – 19 –
↗ auction wine, 8%, ♀ till 2014 **93**

WEINGUT PAULINSHOF

**Owner: Klaus Jüngling
and Oliver Jüngling
Winemaker: Oliver Jüngling
54518 Kesten, Paulinstraße 14
Tel. (0 65 35) 5 44, Fax 12 67
e-mail: paulinshof@t-online.de
Internet: www.paulinshof.de**
Directions: A 48/1, Wittlich or Salmtal exit
Sales: Klaus and Christa Jüngling
Opening hours: Mon.–Fri. 08:00 to
18:00 hours, Sat. 09:00 to 17:00 hours
and by appointment
History: First documented mention in 936
Worth seeing: Former estate of St. Pau-
lin church in Trier, buildings and cellar
dating to 1716 and 1770
Worth a visit: Wine tastings in former
court chapel

Vineyard area: 8 hectares
Annual production: 75,000 bottles
Top sites: Brauneberger Kammer
(monopole), Juffer-Sonnenuhr and
Juffer, Kestener Paulinshofberger
Soil types: Decomposed slate
Grape varieties: 96% Riesling,
4% Müller-Thurgau
Average yield: 60 hl/ha
Best vintages: 2001, 2002, 2003
Member: Bernkasteler Ring

This winery has an idyllic location in the
old church precinct, and has been run by
the Jüngling family since 1969. The vineyard holdings have been gradually extended, with some parcels in Brauneberg
acquired from the old Bergweiler property. The stylish labels bear the coat of
arms of the Sankt Paulin collegiate
church. Son Oliver has joined the team as
of early 2003. The 2002 range covered a
wide spectrum, from fully-bodied dry
wines to Spätlese wines with attractive
clear fruit. The powerful style of the dry
2003 wines shows the vintage character
at its best, although they are still at an early stage of development. We particularly
liked the invigorating fruit of the sweet
Juffer Auslese.

2002 Kestener Paulinshofberger
Riesling Auslese trocken
12.5%, ♀ till 2006 **86**

2003 Brauneberger Kammer
Riesling Auslese trocken
13.5%, ♀ till 2006 **86**

2003 Brauneberger Kammer
Riesling Spätlese feinherb
12.5%, ♀ till 2008 **86**

2003 Brauneberger Kammer
Riesling Auslese feinherb
13%, ♀ till 2008 **88**

2003 Kestener Paulinsberg
Riesling Spätlese
9%, ♀ till 2009 **86**

2001 Brauneberger Juffer
Riesling Spätlese
9%, ♀ till 2008 **87**

2001 Kestener Paulinshofberger
Riesling Auslese
7.5%, ♀ till 2010 **89**

2003 Kestener Paulinshofberger
Riesling
13.5%, ♀ till 2009 **89**

2001 Brauneberger Juffer-Sonnenuhr
Riesling Beerenauslese
8%, ♀ till 2012 **90**

2003 Brauneberger Juffer
Riesling Auslese
10%, ♀ till 2010 **90**

2002 Brauneberger Juffer-Sonnenuhr
Riesling Auslese "Fels" – 26 –
9%, ♀ till 2009 **90**

2002 Brauneberger Juffer-Sonnenuhr
Riesling Beerenauslese
9%, ♀ till 2010 **91**

The wines: **100** Perfect · **95–99** Outstanding · **90–94** Excellent · **85–89** Very good · **80–84** Good · **75–79** Average

WEINGÜTER DR. PAULY-BERGWEILER UND PETER NICOLAY

Owner: Dr. Peter Pauly
Administrator and winemaker: Edmund Licht
54470 Bernkastel-Kues, Gestade 15
Tel. (0 65 31) 30 02, Fax 72 01
e-mail: info@pauly-bergweiler.com
Internet: www.pauly-bergweiler.com
Directions: Via the B 53 and the Eifel autobahn, Bernkastel-Kues exit
Sales: Pauly family and Monika Schmitt
Opening hours: Mon.–Sat. 10:00 to 18:00 hours, Sun. by appointment only
Worth seeing: Formidable manor-house with small private chapel, large vaulted cellars and baroque hall for wine tastings

---

Vineyard area: 14 hectares
Annual production: 110,000 bottles
Top sites: Bernkasteler alte Badstube am Doctorberg, Wehlener Sonnenuhr, Graacher Himmelreich, Brauneberger Juffer-Sonnenuhr, Ürziger Goldwingert (monopole), Erdener Treppchen and Prälat
Soil types: Decomposed slate, lower new red sandstone
Grape varieties: 90% Riesling, 3% Müller-Thurgau, 7% Spätburgunder
Average yield: 60 hl/ha
Best vintages: 2001, 2002, 2003
Member: Bernkasteler Ring

The unusual background to this winery is that the vineyard holdings in the very best Middle Mosel sites go back to four old winemaking families. The slightly more spicy wines of the Peter Nicolay estate are marketed under an own label, and are an ideal complement to the Bernkastel wines. Clean fruit character, coupled with a racy style, would be the brief description for the style of the 2002 vintage wines. Following the taste profile of the previous vintage, the 2003 Riesling wines in many cases have an expressive acidity. 70 percent of the wines are sweet in style, 65 percent of production is exported.

2003 Graacher Himmelreich
Riesling Auslese
8%, ♀ till 2010 — **88**

2001 Bernkasteler alte Badstube am Doctorberg
Riesling Spätlese
8%, ♀ till 2012 — **89**

2002 Bernkasteler alte Badstube am Doctorberg
Riesling Spätlese – 9 –
7%, ♀ till 2009 — **89**

2003 Ürziger Goldwingert
Riesling Spätlese
8.5%, ♀ till 2009 — **89**

2003 Brauneberger Juffer-Sonnenuhr
Riesling Auslese
8%, ♀ till 2005 — **89**

2003 Erdener Prälat
Riesling Auslese
9%, ♀ till 2011 — **90**

2003 Bernkasteler alte Badstube am Doctorberg
Riesling Auslese
8%, ♀ till 2010 — **91**

2002 Bernkasteler Badstube
Riesling Eiswein
↗ auction wine, 8.5%, ♀ till 2012 — **92**

2002 Ürziger Würzgarten
Riesling Eiswein
↗ auction wine, 9%, ♀ till 2018 — **92**

2003 Bernkasteler Badstube
Riesling Beerenauslese
↗ auction wine, 9%, ♀ till 2015 — **92**

2000 Graacher Himmelreich
Riesling Eiswein
8.5%, ♀ till 2015 — **93**

Dr. Pauly-Bergweiler
Bernkasteler alte Badstube
am Doctorberg
2001 Riesling Auslese

WEINGUT
PHILIPPS-ECKSTEIN

Owner and manager: Patrick Philipps
Winemaker: Hans and
Patrick Philipps
54470 Graach-Schäferei,
Panoramastraße 11
Tel. (0 65 31) 65 42, Fax 45 93
e-mail:
info@weingut-philipps-eckstein.de
Internet:
www.weingut-philipps-eckstein.de
Directions: A 1/A 48, Wittlich exit, in
direction of Zeltingen, in Graach turn at
the church in direction of Schäferei sub-
urb, 2nd house on left after 2 kilometers
Sales: Patrick Philipps
Opening hours: Mon.–Fri. 08:30 to
22:00 hours
Sat. and Sun. 09:30 to 22:00 hours
Restaurant/Wine bar: 10:30 to 22:30
hours daily
Specialties: Vintner's steak, onion tart

Vineyard area: 3 hectares
Annual production: 30,000 bottles
Top sites: Graacher Domprobst
and Himmelreich
Soil types: Slate
Grape varieties: 93% Riesling,
5% Spätburgunder, 2% Dornfelder
Average yield: 84 hl/ha
Best vintages: 2001, 2002, 2003

This winery is located high above the
town of Graach, in the suburb of Schäferei,
together with its guest house as well as
restaurant and wine bar. Patrick Philipps,
who runs this small family operation, has
produced a 2003 range that is good across
the board. While we criticized a slight
lack of body and concentration in the dry
and off-dry wines tasted last year, we
were in for a positive surprise this year.
Not only the dry wines were convincing,
but the elegant fruity wines too, and we
particularly liked the Domprobst Spätlese
***, which is both elegant and powerful,
with a touch of exotic fruit.

2003 Graacher Domprobst
Riesling Kabinett halbtrocken
10.5%, ♀ till 2007 **84**

2003 Graacher Domprobst
Riesling Kabinett
9.5%, ♀ till 2007 **84**

2001 Graacher Domprobst
Riesling Spätlese
8%, ♀ till 2006 **85**

2001 Graacher Himmelreich
Riesling Spätlese
8%, ♀ till 2006 **85**

2003 Graacher Himmelreich
Riesling Spätlese ***
8%, ♀ till 2008 **85**

2003 Graacher Himmelreich
Riesling Auslese **
8%, ♀ till 2010 **85**

2002 Graacher Domprobst
Riesling Spätlese ***
8%, ♀ till 2008 **86**

2003 Graacher Domprobst
Riesling Spätlese ***
9%, ♀ till 2008 **86**

2003 Graacher Domprobst
Riesling Auslese ***
7.5%, ♀ till 2010 **87**

2001 Graacher Himmelreich
Riesling Eiswein
8%, ♀ till 2010 **89**

2003 Graacher Domprobst
Riesling Beerenauslese
9.5%, ♀ till 2012 **89**

2002 Graacher Himmelreich
Riesling Eiswein
8%, ♀ till 2010 **90**

The wines: **100** Perfect · **95–99** Outstanding · **90–94** Excellent · **85–89** Very good · **80–84** Good · **75–79** Average

WEINGUT PIEDMONT

Owner: Claus and Monika Piedmont
Winemaker: Albert Permesang
54329 Konz-Filzen, Saartal 1
Tel. (0 65 01) 9 90 09, Fax 9 90 03
e-mail: piedmont.weingut@t-online.de
Directions: From Trier to Konz, after
three kilometers on right bank of Saar
Sales: By appointment
Worth seeing: Winery building of
Maximin abbey dating to 1698, family-
owned since 1881
Worth a visit: Wine tastings high above
the Saar, e.g. at the Schinkel monument
for the king of Bohemia, wine picnic in
courtyard and garden for up to 35 people

Vineyard area: 4.5 hectares
Annual production: 30,000 bottles
Top site: Filzener Pulchen
Soil types: Devon slate
Grape varieties: 90% Riesling,
10% Weißburgunder
Average yield: 52 hl/ha
Best vintages: 1999, 2002, 2003
Member: VDP

Claus Piedmont now bottles only half a
dozen wines each vintage. This makes his
price-list easy to follow. In addition,
Piedmont has hit upon an idea for the
light style of his Saar wines, targeting
health-conscious consumers. The bouquet of the wines is reminiscent of flint-
stone and grapefruit, and to retain their
freshness they are bottled early, in the
spring following the harvest. The focus of
production is on delicately fruity Rieslings with a moderate residual sugar level. Following on several weaker vintages, the total range of six wines showed
some improvement in the 2002 vintage.
The 2003 range of wines tasted was much
better, and the wines benefited particularly from the ripe vintage character. We
noted more depth in the dry wines, and
more body in the sweeter wines, without
compromising the typical fruit. The Pulchen Auslese is very elegant, with a long
finish. More of the same, please.

2002 Filzener Urbelt
Riesling Kabinett trocken
11%, ♀ till 2005 — **82**

2003 Weißer Burgunder trocken
12.5%, ♀ till 2006 — **84**

2003 Filzener
Riesling Kabinett trocken
12%, ♀ till 2006 — **84**

2003 Filzener Pulchen
Riesling Spätlese trocken
13%, ♀ till 2006 — **85**

2002 Filzener Pulchen
Riesling Kabinett
9%, ♀ till 2005 — **82**

2002 Filzener Pulchen
Riesling Kabinett – 3 –
9.5%, ♀ till 2005 — **83**

2002 Filzener Pulchen
Riesling Spätlese
8.5%, ♀ till 2007 — **84**

2002 Filzener Pulchen
Riesling Auslese
9.5%, ♀ till 2008 — **85**

2003 Filzener Pulchen
Riesling Kabinett – 3 –
12%, ♀ till 2007 — **85**

2003 Filzener Pulchen
Riesling Spätlese
9.5%, ♀ till 2009 — **88**

2003 Filzener Pulchen
Riesling Auslese
9%, ♀ till 2011 — **91**

MOSEL SAAR RUWER

PIEDMONT

2001
Filzener Urbelt Riesling
Kabinett
trocken

9.5% / vol   750 ml

Gutsabfüllung Weingut Piedmont, D-54329 Filzen/Saar
Qualitätswein mit Prädikat   A. P. Nr. 3 525 017 1 02

WEINGUT JOH. JOS. PRÜM

**Owner: Dr. Manfred and
Wolfgang Prüm
Manager and winemaker:
Dr. Manfred Prüm
54470 Bernkastel-Wehlen,
Uferallee 19
Tel. (0 65 31) 30 91, Fax 60 71**
*Directions: From Bernkastel-Kues as far
as Wehlen on the left bank of the Mosel,
in the center of town turn right in direc-
tion of Mosel bridge, to Uferallee*
Sales: By appointment only
History: Founded 1911 following in
heritance split of old Prüm operation
Worth seeing: Manor-house, which has
grown over centuries

Vineyard area: 19 hectares
Annual production: 130,000 bottles
Top sites: Wehlener Sonnenuhr,
Graacher Himmelreich, Zeltinger
Sonnenuhr, Bernkasteler Lay and
Badstube
Soil types: Slate
Grape varieties: 100% Riesling
Average yield: 60 hl/ha
Best vintages: 2001, 2002, 2003
Member: VDP

This winery has for decades been by common consent one of the exceptional producers of top-quality wine in Germany.
More than half the vineyard holdings are
distributed among the best parcels of the
top sites Wehlener Sonnenuhr and Graacher Himmelreich, where Dr. Manfred
Prüm regularly produces top-class botrytis wines. His wines are amazingly
long-lived, and he usually leaves them
some residual sugar and a little natural
carbon dioxide. The owner tends not to
speak much about the details of vinification, although he surely has nothing to
hide in this regard; visitors are simply not
allowed into the well-cooled cellar. The
wines of the 1999 vintage were very good
across the board, and reminded us of the
extremely elegant style of the 1997 wines.
Both the classic Spätlese wines and the

Ausleses with gold capsule were among
the exceptional wines of that vintage. In
the 2000 vintage, Prüm remained true to
his own inimitable style. This difficult
vintage demanded every bit of ability
from wine producers on the Mosel, and
his wines are among the highlights of the
vintage. For the third time in only four
years, this renowned winery produced the
best Riesling Spätlese in the whole of
Germany. The millennium vintage was
crowned by a fabulous Trockenbeerenauslese, the botrytized grapes for which
were picked at a must weight of almost
200 degrees Oechsle. While Prüm was unable to repeat production of such an exceptional wine in 2001, he did again make
the "Spätlese of the year," his 2001 Wehlener Sonnenuhr Nr. 16. Prüm considers
the 2002 vintage to be on the whole more
elegant. A great deal of work was involved in selecting the grapes for the high-
quality Auslese wines, and the quantities
of these produced were much smaller than
in the previous vintage. As botrytis did
not develop, it was impossible to produce
a Beerenauslese wine. The Sonnenuhr
Kabinett has a slightly smoky aroma and
an extremely elegant style, and is one of
the best in its class. In his favorite category, the Spätlese wines, Prüm again presented us with one of the most elegant examples of the entire vintage, his Wehlener
Sonnenuhr Spätlese Nr. 18. In addition,
his Himmelreich Lange Goldkapsel Auslese (long gold capsule, sold on auction)
was selected as our best Auslese of the
2002 vintage. It appears Prüm has established an almost statutory right to collect
at least one title each year. How else can
we explain that in 2003 he again collected
the title for the best "Spätlese of the
year?" This wine was so intense and at
the same time so elegant that we simply
could not ignore it for the award. Prüm
himself compares the 2003 vintage to that
of 1997, "just a touch better." He believes
that in such exceptional vintages nature
helps itself, providing for more piquant
and mineral notes in the wines.

The wines: **100** Perfect · **95–99** Outstanding · **90–94** Excellent · **85–89** Very good · **80–84** Good · **75–79** Average

2001 Bernkasteler Badstube
Riesling Spätlese
8%, ♀ till 2010   89

2002 Wehlener Sonnenuhr
Riesling Kabinett
8%, ♀ till 2010   89

2002 Graacher Himmelreich
Riesling Spätlese
8%, ♀ till 2010   89

2003 Wehlener
Riesling Kabinett – 14 –
9%, ♀ till 2010   89

2001 Graacher Himmelreich
Riesling Spätlese
8%, ♀ till 2010   90

2001 Graacher Himmelreich
Riesling Auslese
7.5%, ♀ till 2015   90

2002 Wehlener Sonnenuhr
Riesling Spätlese
7.5%, ♀ till 2012   90

2001 Wehlener Sonnenuhr
Riesling Auslese – 20 –
7.5%, ♀ till 2017   91

2001 Wehlener Sonnenuhr
Riesling Auslese – 21 –
⟰ auction wine, 8%, ♀ till 2017   91

2002 Graacher Himmelreich
Riesling Auslese
7.5%, ♀ till 2012   91

2003 Wehlener Sonnenuhr
Riesling Spätlese – 18 –
8%, ♀ till 2015   91

2003 Graacher Himmelreich
Riesling Auslese – 29 –
8%, ♀ till 2015   91

2001 Wehlener Sonnenuhr
Riesling Auslese Goldkapsel
⟰ auction wine, 7.5%, ♀ till 2017   91

2002 Wehlener Sonnenuhr
Riesling Spätlese – 18 –
⟰ auction wine, 7.5%, ♀ till 2014   92

2002 Wehlener Sonnenuhr
Riesling Auslese – 19 –
⟰ auction wine, 7%, ♀ till 2015   92

2003 Graacher Himmelreich
Riesling Spätlese – 8 –
8%, ♀ till 2015   92

2003 Wehlener Sonnenuhr
Riesling Spätlese – 6 –
8%, ♀ till 2015   92

2001 Wehlener Sonnenuhr
Riesling Spätlese – 17 –
7.5%, ♀ till 2014   93

2001 Wehlener Sonnenuhr
Riesling Eiswein
7%, ♀ till 2020   93

2003 Wehlener Sonnenuhr
Riesling Auslese – 7 –
7.5%, ♀ till 2018   93

2003 Wehlener Sonnenuhr
Riesling Auslese Goldkapsel – 24 –
⟰ auction wine, 7%, ♀ till 2020   93

2001 Wehlener Sonnenuhr
Riesling Auslese lange Goldkapsel
⟰ auction wine, 8%, ♀ till 2020   93

2001 Wehlener Sonnenuhr
Riesling Spätlese – 16 –
7.5%, ♀ till 2016   94

2000 Wehlener Sonnenuhr
Riesling Trockenbeerenauslese
⟰ auction wine, 7%, ♀ till 2025   95

2003 Wehlener Sonnenuhr
Riesling Spätlese – 22 –
7.5%, ♀ till 2015   95

2003 Wehlener Sonnenuhr
Riesling Auslese – 23 –
⟰ auction wine, 7%, ♀ till 2018   95

2002 Graacher Himmelreich
Riesling Auslese lange Goldkapsel
7.5%, ♀ till 2015   95

2003 Wehlener Sonnenuhr
Riesling Auslese lange Goldkapsel – 25 –
⟰ auction wine, 7.5%, ♀ till 2020   96

Erzeugerabfüllung
Weingut
Joh. Jos. Prüm
D-54470 Wehlen/Mosel

Produce of Germany
ALC. 7.5% by vol
A.P.Nr. 2 576 611 25 02
750 ml
R i e s l i n g
Mosel-Saar-Ruwer
Qualitätswein
mit Prädikat

Joh. Jos. Prüm
2001
Wehlener Sonnenuhr
Spätlese

The estates: ♛♛♛♛♛ World's finest · ♛♛♛♛ Germany's best · ♛♛♛ Very good · ♛♛ Good · ♛ Reliable

WEINGUT S. A. PRÜM

Owner: Raimund Prüm
Administrator: Gerd Faber
Winemaker: Thomas Jacoby
54470 Bernkastel-Wehlen,
Uferallee 25–26
Tel. (0 65 31) 31 10, Fax 85 55
e-mail: info@sapruem.com
Internet: www.sapruem.com
*Directions: A 48, Wittlich exit,
in direction of Bernkastel-Wehlen, follow
signs, located directly on river banks*
Sales: Mon.–Sat. 10:00 to 12:00 hours
and 14:00 to 18:00 hours, Sat. 10:00 to
16:00 hours, Sun. by appointment
Restaurant: Used for numerous events
in historic location
Guest house: Eight rooms at estate
Worth a visit: Open days at cellar over
Ascension Day weekend,
wine festival late September

Vineyard area: 16.5 hectares
Annual production: 120,000 bottles
Top sites: Wehlener Sonnenuhr,
Bernkasteler Lay and Graben, Graa-
cher Himmelreich and Domprobst
Soil types: Devon slate
Grape varieties: 90% Riesling,
10% Weißburgunder
Average yield: 55 hl/ha
Best vintages: 2001, 2002, 2003
Member: VDP

Raimund Prüm has a wonderful facility in Wehlen, directly on the Mosel river, where he can concentrate fully on his wine-making. After a decline in form we saw an improvement in the 2000 vintage. The 2001 Riesling wines followed on from this. The basic wines presented last year were a bit of a mixed bag. However, the better qualities showed good concentration. We were sincerely pleased to see the improvement evident in the dry 2003 wines. We have rarely tasted wines with such elegance and such concentration here. As the botrytis wines, too, showed a leap forward in quality, we have awarded the third bunch of grapes.

2003 Bernkasteler Lay
Riesling trocken "Erste Lage"
12.5%, ♀ till 2006 — **87**

2003 Wehlener Sonnenuhr
Riesling Kabinett
9%, ♀ till 2008 — **86**

2003 Wehlener Sonnenuhr
Riesling Spätlese Alte Reben
12.5%, ♀ till 2006 — **86**

2003 Wehlener Sonnenuhr
Riesling Spätlese
9.5%, ♀ till 2009 — **87**

2001 Wehlener Sonnenuhr
Riesling Auslese
8%, ♀ till 2010 — **88**

2001 Graacher Domprobst
Riesling Auslese Goldkapsel – 45 –
↗ auction wine, 8%, ♀ till 2010 — **88**

2001 Graacher Domprobst
Riesling Eiswein – 44 –
8%, ♀ till 2010 — **90**

2002 Graacher Domprobst
Riesling Beerenauslese – 62 –
8%, ♀ till 2010 — **90**

2003 Graacher Domprobst
Riesling Auslese – 8 –
↗ auction wine, 8.5%, ♀ till 2010 — **90**

2003 Wehlener Sonnenuhr
Riesling Auslese – 17 –
8.5%, ♀ till 2012 — **92**

2003 Wehlener Sonnenuhr
Riesling Auslese Goldkapsel – 20 –
↗ auction wine, 8%, ♀ till 2012 — **92**

2003 Wehlener Sonnenuhr
Riesling Beerenauslese – 41 –
↗ auction wine, 8%, ♀ till 2014 — **93**

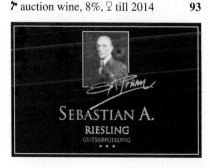

SEBASTIAN A.
RIESLING
GUTSABFÜLLUNG

WEINGUT FAMILIE RAUEN

Owner: Harald Rauen
54340 Thörnich, Hinterm Kreuzweg 5
Tel. (0 65 07) 34 03, Fax 83 82
e-mail:
Weingut.Familie-Rauen@t-online.de
Directions: A 1/A 48 Koblenz–Trier,
Föhren exit
Sales: Maria Rauen, by appointment
Worth a visit: Wine festival second
weekend in September

Vineyard area: 7.5 hectares
Annual production: 65,000 bottles
Top sites: Detzemer Maximiner
Klosterlay, Thörnicher St. Michael
Soil types: Decomposed slate, gravel
Grape varieties: 71% Riesling, 8% Mül-
ler-Thurgau, 7% each of Spätburgun-
der, Dornfelder and Weißburgunder
Average yield: 80 hl/ha
Best vintages: 2001, 2002, 2003

When Harald Rauen took over the business from his father in 1982, most of the
wine was still sold in bulk. Today, more
than two-thirds of the production is sold
via the specialist retail trade – unusual for
a family winery of this size. Harald Rau-
en prefers to concentrate on the vineyards
and the cellar, rather than to spend his
time selling wine to consumers by the
bottle. He, too, has had red varieties in his
vineyard for some time. The 2001 range
was clean as a whistle, and helped Rauen
earn his first bunch of grapes. While we
were not that enthusiastic about the dry
2002 Rieslings, we liked the sweeter
wines all the more. Generally, however,
Rauen ferments 80 to 90 percent of his
production dry. However, the extremely
ripe grapes harvested in 2003 constitute
an exception, and only around 60 percent
of the wines were made in a dry style.
That Rauen was right to make this decision is evidenced by the Auslese wines as
well as the Beerenauslese, which were
particularly good in this vintage. His dry
wines, too, are better than those of the
previous vintage.

2003 Detzemer Würzgarten
Riesling Kabinett trocken
12%, ♀ till 2006   82

2003 Detzemer Maximiner Klosterlay
Riesling Spätlese trocken
12%, ♀ till 2008   84

2003 Detzemer Würzgarten
Riesling Kabinett halbtrocken
12%, ♀ till 2006   82

2003 Detzemer Maximiner Klosterlay
Riesling Spätlese halbtrocken
12%, ♀ till 2008   83

2003 Detzemer Würzgarten
Riesling
10%, ♀ till 2006   82

2001 Detzemer Maximiner Klosterlay
Riesling Spätlese
9%, ♀ till 2007   86

2003 Detzemer Maximiner Klosterlay
Riesling Auslese
7%, ♀ till 2010   87

2002 Thörnicher St. Michael
Riesling Auslese
10%, ♀ till 2009   89

2003 Thörnicher St. Michael
Riesling Auslese
7%, ♀ till 2010   89

2002 Detzemer Würzgarten
Riesling Eiswein
9%, ♀ till 2012   90

2003 Detzemer Maximiner Klosterlay
Riesling Beerenauslese
7%, ♀ till 2012   90

2003 Detzemer Würzgarten
Riesling Eiswein
7%, ♀ till 2010   91

The estates: ����� World's finest · ���� Germany's best · ��� Very good · �� Good · � Reliable

WEINGUT WALTER RAUEN

Owner: Walter and Irmtrud Rauen
Winemaker: Stefan Rauen
54340 Detzem, Im Würzgarten
Tel. (0 65 07) 32 78, Fax 83 72
e-mail: info@weingut-rauen.de
Internet: www.weingut-rauen.de
Directions: A 48, Föhren exit,
A 1 Mehring exit.

The winery is located among the vine-
yards above the town of Detzem
Sales: By appointment
Wine tasting room: With stunning view
of Mosel valley
History: Built on ruins of old Roman road
linking Trier with Bingen, at milepost ten

Vineyard area: 9.6 hectares
Annual production: 95,000 bottles
Top sites: Detzemer Maximiner
Klosterlay and Würzgarten,
Thörnicher Ritsch, Pölicher Held
Soil types: Decomposed slate,
sandy gravel
Grape varieties: 68% Riesling,
10% each of Spätburgunder and
Weißburgunder, 8% Müller-
Thurgau, 4% other varieties
Average yield: 78 hl/ha
Best vintages: 1998, 2001, 2002

The winery lies in the middle of the slate-dominated Würzgarten vineyard, and that is also the address given. Son Stefan has been running the business for a number of years, we first noted his positive influence in the 1996 range. A very clean range was presented in 2001. The basic wines of the 2002 vintage were elegant and delicately spicy, while the predicate wines from Spätlese up were characterized by botrytis. This year, too, we particularly liked the deeply structured sweet Riesling wines. Unfortunately the dry wines do not live up to the 2002 vintage in quality. They showed dull fruit, and were not particularly enjoyable. Investments have recently been made in building a cellar as well as a new wine tasting room.

2003 Thörnicher Ritsch
Riesling Spätlese trocken
12%, ♀ till 2006   83

2002 Detzemer Maximiner Klosterlay
Riesling Spätlese trocken
11.5%, ♀ till 2006   85

2001 Thörnicher
Riesling Spätlese trocken
11.5%, ♀ till 2005   86

2002 Thörnicher Ritsch
Riesling Spätlese halbtrocken
11%, ♀ till 2008   86

2003 Detzemer Maximiner Klosterlay
Riesling Spätlese
10%, ♀ till 2008   86

2001 Detzemer Maximiner Klosterlay
Riesling Spätlese
10%, ♀ till 2008   87

2002 Detzemer Maximiner Klosterlay
Riesling Auslese ***
10%, ♀ till 2007   87

2003 Detzemer Maximiner Klosterlay
Riesling Auslese ***
10%, ♀ till 2008   88

2002 Detzemer Würzgarten
Riesling Eiswein
9%, ♀ till 2012   89

2003 Detzemer Maximiner Klosterlay
Riesling Spätlese *
10%, ♀ till 2009   89

2003 Detzemer Maximiner Klosterlay
Riesling Auslese
10%, ♀ till 2009   89

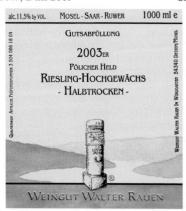

alc.11,5% by VOL.   MOSEL - SAAR - RUWER   1000 ml e

GUTSABFÜLLUNG

2003ER

PÖLICHER HELD
RIESLING-HOCHGEWÄCHS
- HALBTROCKEN -

WEINGUT WALTER RAUEN

The wines: **100** Perfect · **95–99** Outstanding · **90–94** Excellent · **85–89** Very good · **80–84** Good · **75–79** Average

359

WEINGUT F. J. REGNERY

Owner: Peter Regnery
54340 Klüsserath, Mittelstraße 39
Tel. (0 65 07) 46 36, Fax 30 53
e-mail: mail@weingut-regnery.de
Internet: www.weingut-regnery.de
Directions: A 48/A 1, Föhren exit,
in direction of Klüsserath
Sales: Franz-Josef Regnery
by appointment
History: Bottled wine sold here since
the "vintage of the century" 1921

Vineyard area: 5.5 hectares
Annual production: 40,000 bottles
Top site: Klüsserather Bruder-
schaft
Soil types: Slate
Grape varieties: 75% Riesling,
25% Spätburgunder
Average yield: 69 hl/ha
Best vintages: 2000, 2001, 2002
Member: Bernkasteler Ring

Peter Regnery is no normal Mosel winemaker. To begin with, there is the fact
that a quarter of his vines are red – Pinot
Noir, which he again submitted for our
tasting. In addition, no less than 70 percent
of his wines are fermented dry – a share
that would be appropriate in Baden or the
Pfalz region. These dry Riesling wines
were really good last year: mellow, characterful wines. Unfortunately, the same
cannot be said of the 2003 vintage. Only
the Bruderschaft Spätlese trocken reminds us a little of the quality seen in the
previous vintage. The other dry Rieslings
are too tart and downright sour. When it
comes to the sweet Spätlese and Auslese
wines, Regnery is in his element, in spite
of the slightly higher alcohol levels. The
Bruderschaft Auslese this year is a particularly elegant example of his style,
and has concentrated fruit as well as a
rounded, mellow finish. This estate started
marketing its bottled wines as early as
1921.

2003 Klüsserather Bruderschaft
Riesling Spätlese trocken
13.5%, ♀ till 2006   **83**

2002 Klüsserather Bruderschaft
Riesling Selection
12.5%, ♀ till 2006   **85**

2002 Klüsserather Bruderschaft
Riesling Auslese trocken
⟶ auction wine, 12.5%, ♀ till 2007   **87**

2003 Klüsserather Bruderschaft
Riesling Spätlese halbtrocken
12.5%, ♀ till 2008   **84**

2003 Klüsserather Bruderschaft
Riesling Spätlese
10.5%, ♀ till 2008   **85**

2002 Klüsserather Bruderschaft
Riesling Auslese
⟶ auction wine, 8.5%, ♀ till 2010   **87**

2003 Klüsserather Bruderschaft
Riesling Auslese
11%, ♀ till 2010   **88**

2002 Klüsserather Bruderschaft
Riesling Eiswein
10.5%, ♀ till 2012   **89**

2003 Klüsserather Bruderschaft
Riesling Beerenauslese
13%, ♀ till 2012   **91**

——————— Red wines ———————

2002 Klüsserather Bruderschaft
Spätburgunder trocken
13.5%, ♀ till 2006   **80**

2002 Spätburgunder
trocken Barrique
13%, ♀ till 2006   **83**

WEINGUT REH

Owner: Winfried and Sigrid Reh
Manager and winemaker:
Winfried Reh
54340 Schleich, Weierbachstraße 12
Tel. (0 65 07) 9 91 10, Fax 9 91 11
e-mail: weingut-reh@t-online.de
Directions: From north A 1/ A 48, Föhren
exit; from south A 60, Mehring exit
Sales: Winfried and Sigrid Reh
by appointment
Worth seeing: Vaulted cellar, vineyard
terrace with old slate steps (350 steps)

Vineyard area: 6.8 hectares
Annual production: 35,000 bottles
Top sites: Mehringer Blattenberg
and Zellerberg
Soil types: Devon-slate, slate and
sand, decomposed kaolin-slate
Grape varieties: 80% Riesling,
5% each of Weiß- and Spätbur-
gunder, 10% other varieties
Average yield: 55 hl/ha
Best vintages: 2001, 2002, 2003

After completing his training as a winemaker, Winfried Reh initially gained experience working at the two large wineries in Trier, the Friedrich-Wilhelm-
Gymnasium and the Vereinigte Hospiti-
en. He only started bottling and marketing his own wines in the mid-Eighties.
Reh now concentrates on his Riesling
vineyards, which are located in some excellent sites. Following on investments in
stainless steel tanks and a new press in recent years, he has now also added a new
winery building. We were not particularly impressed with the dry wines in the
2000 vintage, and the same had to be said
of the 2001 wines. The botrytis desert
wines, on the other hand, were already
worthy of a two-bunch rating. In 2003 it
is again the elegant fruity wines that are
attractive. Both the Beerenauslese and
the Trockenbeerenauslese from the Mehringer Blattenberg site are lively as well
as concentrated. The quality of the dry
wines has also improved now.

2003 Mehringer Blattenberg
Riesling Spätlese trocken
13.5%, ♀ till 2007 · · · · · · · · · · · · **83**

2001 Riesling Spätlese
9%, ♀ till 2006 · · · · · · · · · · · · **84**

2003 Mehringer Zellerberg
Riesling Spätlese
9.5%, ♀ till 2008 · · · · · · · · · · · · **85**

2003 Mehringer Zellerberg
Riesling Spätlese "S"
10%, ♀ till 2008 · · · · · · · · · · · · **86**

2001 Riesling Spätlese "S"
9%, ♀ till 2007 · · · · · · · · · · · · **87**

2002 Mehringer Zellerberg
Riesling Spätlese "S"
9%, ♀ till 2008 · · · · · · · · · · · · **87**

2001 "Zenit" Riesling Auslese
9.5%, ♀ till 2008 · · · · · · · · · · · · **88**

2003 Mehringer Blattenberg
Riesling Auslese "Zenit"
10%, ♀ till 2010 · · · · · · · · · · · · **88**

2001 Riesling Beerenauslese
11%, ♀ till 2010 · · · · · · · · · · · · **89**

2003 Mehringer Blattenberg
Riesling Beerenauslese
10.5%, ♀ till 2010 · · · · · · · · · · · · **89**

2002 Pölicher Held
Riesling Eiswein *
7%, ♀ till 2012 · · · · · · · · · · · · **90**

2003 Mehringer Blattenberg
Riesling Trockenbeerenauslese
10%, ♀ till 2012 · · · · · · · · · · · · **90**

2003 Pölicher Held
Riesling Eiswein
8.5%, ♀ till 2012 · · · · · · · · · · · · **90**

The wines: **100** Perfect · **95–99** Outstanding · **90–94** Excellent · **85–89** Very good · **80–84** Good · **75–79** Average

WEINGUT
JOHANN PETER REINERT

Owner: Johann Peter Reinert
54441 Kanzem, Alter Weg 7a
Tel. (0 65 01) 1 32 77, Fax 15 00 68
e-mail: kontakt@weingut-reinert.de
Internet: www.weingut-reinert.de
Directions: From Trier via the B 51 to Konz, third Konz exit, past the Saar to Kanzem
Sales: Annetrud and J. P. Reinert
Opening hours: By appointment
History: Family-owned since 1813

Vineyard area: 4.4 hectares
Annual production: 31,000 bottles
Top sites: Ayler Kupp,
Kanzemer Altenberg, Wiltinger
Schlossberg and Schlangengraben
Soil types: Slate
Grape varieties: 74% Riesling,
8% Regent, 6% each of Elbling
and Weißburgunder, 3% each of Riva-
ner and Ortega
Average yield: 60 hl/ha
Best vintages: 2001, 2002, 2003
Member: Bernkasteler Ring

Johann Peter Reinert has for some years now been one of the top wine producers in Kanzem. As proof of this he can point to a number of highly-rated awards and trophies that he has won. The Reinerts intend to focus even more strongly on top-quality wines in future, and also want to increase their holdings in the best vineyard sites. The replanting of the steep Wiltinger Schlossberg site has been completed. The 2001 range showed clearly the delicate fruit and acidity typical of good Saar wines, this was followed by the 2002 wines that added concentration to the previous year's level, and we did not hesitate to award the third bunch of grapes. This high standard is confirmed by the 2003 wines presented, with Reinert showing us some classic representatives. A particularly good example is the Altenberg Auslese***, which is very rich and has great length on the finish.

2003 Wawerner Ritterpfad
Riesling Kabinett
10%, ♀ till 2008   **85**

2001 Kanzemer Altenberg
Riesling Spätlese
7.5%, ♀ till 2008   **86**

2003 Wawerner Ritterpfad
Riesling Spätlese
9.5%, ♀ till 2008   **87**

2001 Wiltinger Schlossberg
Riesling Auslese **
↗ auction wine, 7.5%, ♀ till 2010   **88**

2002 Wiltinger Klosterberg
Riesling Auslese
↗ auction wine, 7.5%, ♀ till 2009   **89**

2003 Wiltinger Schlangengraben
Riesling Auslese
8%, ♀ till 2009   **89**

2003 Kanzemer Sonnenberg
Riesling Auslese
7.5%, ♀ till 2010   **90**

2003 Wiltinger Klosterberg
Riesling Auslese **
7.5%, ♀ till 2009   **90**

2003 Ayler Kupp
Riesling Auslese **
↗ auction wine, 8%, ♀ till 2010   **91**

2003 Kanzemer Altenberg
Riesling Auslese *** Alte Reben
↗ auction wine, 7%, ♀ till 2012   **91**

2003 Kanzemer Altenberg
Riesling Beerenauslese Alte Reben
↗ auction wine, 7.5%, ♀ till 2012   **91**

2002 Wiltinger Schlangengraben
Riesling Eiswein
7.5%, ♀ till 2012   **92**

MOSEL · SAAR · RUWER
QUALITÄTSWEIN MIT PRÄDIKAT
Amtliche Prüfungsnummer 3 518 048 04 04
Product of Germany · white wine

2003er
Kanzemer Sonnenberg
Riesling Spätlese halbtrocken
750 ml   ERZEUGERABFÜLLUNG   alc. 11,5% by vol.

Weingut Johann Peter Reinert
D-54441 KANZEM/SAAR

The estates: ✿✿✿✿✿ World's finest · ✿✿✿✿ Germany's best · ✿✿✿ Very good · ✿✿ Good · ✿ Reliable

WEINGUT HANS RESCH

Owner: Franz-Andreas Resch
54459 Wiltingen, Kirchstraße 29
Tel. (0 65 01) 1 64 50, Fax 1 45 86
e-mail: info@weingut-resch.de
Directions: From Trier via Konz,
in direction of Saarburg to Wiltingen,
in the old center of town, near church
Sales: Monika and Franz-Andreas
Resch, Mon.–Sat. by appointment
History: Founded 1873 by the widow
Anna Lioba Resch
Worth seeing: Vaulted cellar dating to
18th century

Vineyard area: 6.6 hectares
Annual production: 38,000 bottles, including 6,000 bottles sparkling wine
Top sites: Scharzhofberger, Wiltinger Rosenberg, Klosterberg and Schlangengraben
Soil types: Devon slate, partly with alluvial sand
Grape varieties: 85% Riesling, 5% each of Chardonnay, Weiß- and Spätburgunder
Average yield: 57 hl/ha
Best vintages: 1998, 2001, 2003

Franz-Andreas Resch has a business degree, and made his name as a marketing expert in a Luxembourg advertising agency. However, in 1991 he returned to take over his father's winery. Last year, a very attractive and spacious new guest house was added to the complex. To date, Resch has focused his attention on the Wiltinger Klosterberg, and he has acquired more than half a hectare of the best parcels of this site in recent years. However, he then created a prominent competitor in-house, the 1000 square meters of the famous Scharzhofberg site that he acquired at an astronomical price. In the past few years his best wine has always come from this site. Apart from this, the 2002 wines have a fairly simple structure. The 2003 range is good, although the dry wines could do with a little more elegance. The wines from the Wiltinger Klosterberg are good,

but as in the past few years the best wine is from the Scharzhofberg site.

2003 Wiltinger Klosterberg
Riesling Spätlese trocken
11.5%, ♀ till 2008 — 82

2003 Wiltinger Rosenberg
Riesling Kabinett halbtrocken
10.5%, ♀ till 2008 — 82

2001 Wiltinger Rosenberg
Riesling Auslese feinherb
10.5%, ♀ till 2007 — 84

2002 Wiltinger Klosterberg
Riesling Spätlese feinherb "Newton"
10.5%, ♀ till 2008 — 84

2003 Wiltinger Klosterberg
Riesling Kabinett
9.5%, ♀ till 2007 — 83

2002 Wiltinger Klosterberg
Riesling Spätlese
10.5%, ♀ till 2008 — 84

2003 Wiltinger Klosterberg
Riesling Eiswein
9%, ♀ till 2012 — 84

2003 Wiltinger Klosterberg
Riesling Auslese
9%, ♀ till 2007 — 84

2003 Wiltinger Rosenberg
Riesling Spätlese
10.5%, ♀ till 2008 — 84

2002 Scharzhofberger
Riesling Spätlese
10%, ♀ till 2008 — 85

2003 Scharzhofberger
Riesling Auslese
9.5%, ♀ till 2010 — 86

2001 Scharzhofberger
Riesling Spätlese
8%, ♀ till 2010 — 87

The wines: **100** Perfect · **95–99** Outstanding · **90–94** Excellent · **85–89** Very good · **80–84** Good · **75–79** Average

WEINGUT REUSCHER-HAART

Owner: Franz-Hugo Schwang
Manager: Mario Schwang
54498 Piesport,
Sankt-Michael-Straße 20–22
Tel. (0 65 07) 24 92, Fax 56 74
e-mail:
info@weingut-reuscher-haart.de
Internet:
www.weingut-reuscher-haart.de
Directions: A 1/48, Salmtal exit, via the B 53 to Piesport, in Alt-Piesport on the left bank of the Mosel
Sales: Anytime by appointment
History: Winemaking in the family since 1337
Worth a visit: Tour through the Piesport vineyards including visit to the Roman wine press complex

---

Vineyard area: 4.5 hectares
Annual production: 34,000 bottles
Top sites: Piesporter Gold-
tröpfchen, Domherr and Falkenberg
Soil types: Slate
Grape varieties: 90% Riesling,
8% Rivaner, 2% Regent
Average yield: 60 hl/ha
Best vintages: 2001, 2002, 2003

This small winery has substantial holdings in the best Piesport vineyards. Franz-Hugo Schwang changed from traditional single-pole to wire-frame trellisses. In the meantime, the average yield has settled down at a moderate level of 60 hectoliters per hectare. The method of vinification was changed, the wines are now kept on the lees for an extended period to give it a longer period of maturation. The 2002 wines were of much the same quality as those of the 2001 vintage, and we particularly liked the slightly nervous Goldtröpfchen Kabinett wines with their mineral notes. Rich fruit, but not lacking in elegance – these are the attributes of the sweet 2003 Rieslings. We very much enjoyed the mellow elegance of the Goldtröpfchen Auslese.

2003 Piesporter Goldtröpfchen
Riesling Spätlese trocken
13.5%, ♀ till 2006   82

2003 Piesporter Domherr
Riesling Spätlese trocken
14%, ♀ till 2006   82

2001 Piesporter Goldtröpfchen
Riesling Kabinett – 7 –
9%, ♀ till 2007   84

2003 Piesporter Treppchen
Riesling
9%, ♀ till 2007   84

2002 Piesporter Goldtröpfchen
Riesling Kabinett – 6 –
8%, ♀ till 2007   85

2002 Piesporter Goldtröpfchen
Riesling Kabinett
8%, ♀ till 2007   85

2001 Piesporter Goldtröpfchen
Riesling Kabinett – 6 –
8%, ♀ till 2008   86

2003 Piesporter Goldtröpfchen
Riesling Kabinett
9%, ♀ till 2008   86

2002 Piesporter Goldtröpfchen
Riesling Spätlese
8.5%, ♀ till 2008   87

2003 Piesporter Goldtröpfchen
Riesling Spätlese
10.5%, ♀ till 2009   87

2001 Piesporter Goldtröpfchen
Riesling Spätlese
8.5%, ♀ till 2010   88

2003 Piesporter Goldtröpfchen
Riesling Auslese
8%, ♀ till 2010   90

Piesporter Goldtröpfchen
Riesling - Spätlese
2002
750ml   GUTSABFÜLLUNG   ALC 8,5%VOL
A. P. Nr 2 596 420 10 03   WEINGUT REUSCHER-HAART   MOSEL-SAAR-RUWER
QUALITÄTSWEIN MIT PRÄDIKAT   D-54498 PIESPORT/MOSEL   PRODUCT OF GERMANY

The estates: ✚✚✚✚✚ World's finest · ✚✚✚✚ Germany's best · ✚✚✚ Very good · ✚✚ Good · ✚ Reliable

WEINGUT
MAX FERD. RICHTER

**Owner: Ökonomierat Horst Richter
and Dr. Dirk Richter**
Administrator: Werner Franz
Winemaker: Walter Hauth
54486 Mülheim/Mosel, Hauptstr. 37/85
Tel. (0 65 34) 93 30 03, Fax 12 11
e-mail: weingut@maxferdrichter.com
Internet: www.maxferdrichter.com
*Directions: A 1/A 48, from Trier Salmtal
exit, from Koblenz Wittlich exit, in direction of Mülheim, at end of town turn in
direction of Bernkastel-Kues*
Sales: Dr. Dirk Richter
and Anneliese Hauth
Opening hours: Mon.–Fri. 09:00 to
18:00 hours, Sat. 09:00 to 13:00 hours
and by appointment
History: Family-owned since 1680
Worth seeing: Baroque manor-house,
French garden, barrel cellar dating to
1880

Vineyard area: 15 hectares
Annual production: 120,000 bottles
Top sites: Brauneberger Juffer
and Juffer-Sonnenuhr, Wehlener
Sonnenuhr, Graacher Domprobst
Soil types: Decomposed kaolin-slate
Grape varieties: 95% Riesling,
5% other varieties
Average yield: 60 hl/ha
Best vintages: 2000, 2001, 2002

This operation goes back to a merchant
house founded in 1680, which is still active. The share of fruity sweet wines exported in recent years has grown to more
than 80 percent, the main markets are the
USA and Japan. This winery, which has a
long tradition, houses one of the largest
barrel cellars in the Middle Mosel region.
The 2001 range was good, and the 2002
wines were elegant right across the board,
with a spicy note. The 2003 range has left
a mixed impression. Some of the wines
have rather dull fruit, others have excessively high acidity, the wines are not particularly harmonious.

2002 Wehlener Sonnenuhr
Riesling Kabinett
8%, ♀ till 2008 **86**

2003 Brauneberger Juffer
Riesling Kabinett
8.5%, ♀ till 2008 **86**

2003 Graacher Himmelreich
Riesling Spätlese
9%, ♀ till 2008 **86**

2003 Brauneberger Juffer-Sonnenuhr
Riesling Spätlese
9%, ♀ till 2009 **87**

2002 Brauneberger Juffer-Sonnenuhr
Riesling Spätlese
8%, ♀ till 2009 **88**

2003 Brauneberger Juffer-Sonnenuhr
Riesling Auslese
9%, ♀ till 2009 **89**

2002 Brauneberger Juffer-Sonnenuhr
Riesling Auslese ** – 40 –
8%, ♀ till 2011 **90**

2002 Brauneberger Juffer-Sonnenuhr
Riesling Auslese
8.5%, ♀ till 2010 **91**

2003 Veldenzer Elisenberg
Riesling Auslese ***
9%, ♀ till 2012 **91**

2002 Mülheimer Helenenkloster
Riesling Eiswein
9%, ♀ till 2018 **93**

2001 Mülheimer Helenenkloster
Riesling Eiswein
9.5%, ♀ till 2015 **95**

2001 Mülheimer Helenenkloster
Riesling Eiswein **
8%, ♀ till 2020 **100**

The wines: **100** Perfect · **95–99** Outstanding · **90–94** Excellent · **85–89** Very good · **80–84** Good · **75–79** Average

365

WEINGUT RICHARD RICHTER

Owner: Thomas and Claus-Martin Richter
56333 Winningen, Marktstraße 19
Tel. (0 26 06) 3 11, Fax 14 57
e-mail: info@weingut-richter.net
Internet: www.weingut-richter.net
Directions: A 61, Koblenz-Metternich exit, in direction of Winningen
Sales: Richter family
Opening hours: Mon.–Fri. 08:00 to 18:00 hours and by appointment

---

Vineyard area: 6 hectares
Annual production: 45,000 bottles
Top sites: Winninger Brückstück, Uhlen and Röttgen
Soil types: Decomposed Devon slate, partly with pumice
Grape varieties: 90% Riesling, 8% Spätburgunder, 2% Chardonnay
Average yield: 65 hl/ha
Best vintages: 2001, 2002, 2003

This was at one stage the best-known winery in Winningen, collecting prizes and medals by the dozen in the Sixties and Seventies. Claus-Martin and Thomas Richter are intent on continuing this tradition, and received five state honor awards in succession in recent years. They also did well at the latest awards, collecting no fewer than eleven gold medals. Successes such as these help to guarantee the continued existence of the terraced vineyards they own. The 2000 and 2001 vintages were of roughly the same quality, while the 2002 showed a slight upward trend, particularly among the dry and off-dry Riesling wines. The wines are elegantly spicy, and have a delicate slate note. Most bottles are closed with a well-disguised crown closure. The 2003 vintage indicates a further improvement in quality. Particularly the wines from the Winninger Brückstück site show a clear structure and typical terroir aromas. Unfortunately, none of the botrytis dessert wines were again available for tasting.

2002 Felsterrassen
Riesling trocken
12.5%, ♀ till 2007 — **84**

2002 Winninger Uhlen
Riesling Spätlese trocken
12.5%, ♀ till 2007 — **86**

2003 Winninger Brückstück
Riesling Kabinett halbtrocken
11%, ♀ till 2007 — **84**

2003 Winninger Domgarten
Riesling halbtrocken
11%, ♀ till 2007 — **84**

2002 Winninger Brückstück
Riesling Spätlese halbtrocken
11.5%, ♀ till 2008 — **85**

2003 Winninger Brückstück
Riesling Spätlese
10%, ♀ till 2008 — **84**

2003 Winninger Brückstück
Riesling Kabinett
9.5%, ♀ till 2006 — **84**

2001 Winninger Röttgen
Riesling Spätlese
8.5%, ♀ till 2008 — **85**

2003 Winninger Röttgen
Riesling Spätlese
9%, ♀ till 2008 — **85**

2001 Winninger Röttgen
Riesling Beerenauslese
11.5%, ♀ till 2010 — **86**

2002 Winninger Röttgen
Riesling Auslese
8.5%, ♀ till 2008 — **86**

2003 Winninger Röttgen
Riesling Auslese
8.5%, ♀ till 2009 — **86**

WEINGUT RÖMERHOF

Owner and manager:
Irmgard and Franz Peter Schmitz
Winemaker: Franz Peter Schmitz
54340 Riol, Burgstraße 2
Tel. (0 65 02) 21 89, Fax 2 06 71
e-mail: mail@weingut-roemerhof.de
Internet: www.weingut-roemerhof.de
Directions: A 1/A 48 Koblenz–Trier, to
Autobahndreieck Moseltal branch-off,
Fell-Longuich exit, two kilometers to Riol
Sales: Irmgard and Franz Peter Schmitz
by appointment
Worth seeing: Old slate vaulted cellar
with rarities

Vineyard area: 7 hectares
Annual production: 40,000 bottles
Top sites: Mehringer Zellerberg
and Blattenberg, Longuicher Maxi-
miner Herrenberg
Soil types: Decomposed slate
Grape varieties: 64% Riesling,
22% Spätburgunder, 7% Frühbur-
gunder, 7% other varieties
Average yield: 60 hl/ha
Best vintages: 2001, 2002

The Schmitz family is at home in Riol,
which was called Rigodulum in Roman
times, producing wines of reliable quality
as well as sparkling wine and distillates.
Winemaking has been carried on at the
Römerhof for generations, but Schmitz decided in the late Eighties to focus on quality, has specifically added steep vineyard
slopes to his holdings. The yields are kept
relatively low, the grapes are selectively
hand-picked, and minimal intervention in
the cellar is part of the philosophy. The
2001 range was solid across the board.
While some of the 2002 wines are a little
lacking in elegance, they revealed plenty
of extract and intense fruit. A further top
vineyard site has been added through the
purchase of a parcel in the Mehringer Blattenberg. The 2003 vintage is not quite of
the same high quality as the 2002 wines.
Only the Zellerberg Auslese reveals the
quality potential that is available here.

2003 Mehringer Zellerberg
Riesling Spätlese trocken
13%, ♀ till 2007   **82**

2002 Mehringer Zellerberg
Riesling Spätlese trocken
12.5%, ♀ till 2006   **84**

2003 Mehringer Zellerberg
Riesling Spätlese halbtrocken Alte Reben
13%, ♀ till 2008   **83**

2002 Mehringer Zellerberg
Riesling Spätlese halbtrocken
"Felsenterrassen"
12%, ♀ till 2007   **85**

2002 Mehringer Zellerberg
Riesling Spätlese feinherb "Selection"
12%, ♀ till 2006   **85**

2003 Mehringer Zellerberg
Riesling Spätlese
8.5%, ♀ till 2008   **83**

2003 Mehringer Zellerberg
Riesling Spätlese – 1 –
8.5%, ♀ till 2008   **83**

2003 Mehringer Zellerberg
Riesling Auslese
7.5%, ♀ till 2008   **85**

2002 Mehringer Zellerberg
Riesling Spätlese – 1 –
9%, ♀ till 2009   **88**

2002 Mehringer Zellerberg
Riesling Eiswein
7%, ♀ till 2012   **88**

The wines: **100** Perfect · **95–99** Outstanding · **90–94** Excellent · **85–89** Very good · **80–84** Good · **75–79** Average

367

WEINGUT JOSEF ROSCH

Owner: Werner Rosch
54340 Leiwen, Mühlenstraße 8
Tel. (0 65 07) 42 30, Fax 82 87
e-mail:
weingut-josef-rosch@t-online.de
Directions: A 48 Koblenz–Trier,
Leiwen exit, A1 Mehring exit
Sales: By appointment

Vineyard area: 5.5 hectares
Annual production: 46,000 bottles
Top sites: Leiwener Laurentiuslay,
Trittenheimer Apotheke, Klüsserather
Bruderschaft
Soil types: Slate
Grape varieties: 100% Riesling
Average yield: 63 hl/ha
Best vintages: 2001, 2002, 2003

This is one of those formerly young wine-makers of Leiwen who called for a revolution in quality in the Eighties. Werner Rosch first attracted attention at national level for his 1988 wines. A dry Riesling came out on top in a major tasting. The wines of the 1990 vintage were even better, assuring his breakthrough. From then on it was all an upward trend, the temporary peak being reached with the excellent 1995 vintage. Rosch was not quite able to maintain that high standard in the years that followed. The 1998 vintage was a mixed bag, and the 1999 wines showed a similar lack of homogeneity. Then in 2000 we reported a clear improvement in quality. In 2001 Werner Rosch had clearly returned to the standard of a three-bunch rating. This high standard was confirmed by a homogeneous range last year, with the range covering a spectrum from soft smoky fruit to gripping crisp acidity. The wines of the latest vintage 2003 fit in seamlessly. The highlights of the range are extremely elegant botrytis Rieslings with currently some yeasty notes.

2003 Leiwener Klostergarten
Riesling trocken
12.5%, ♀ till 2006 — 85

2003 Riesling
Spätlese trocken Selection
13%, ♀ till 2006 — 85

2002 "Selection J.R."
Riesling Spätlese trocken
12%, ♀ till 2006 — 86

2003 "J.R. Junior" Riesling
12%, ♀ till 2008 — 86

2001 Trittenheimer Apotheke
Riesling Spätlese ***
8.5%, ♀ till 2010 — 88

2003 Trittenheimer Apotheke
Riesling Spätlese
8.5%, ♀ till 2010 — 89

2001 Trittenheimer Apotheke
Riesling Beerenauslese
7%, ♀ till 2015 — 90

2002 Leiwener Klostergarten
Riesling Auslese
8.5%, ♀ till 2010 — 90

2003 Trittenheimer Apotheke
Riesling Auslese
8.5%, ♀ till 2012 — 90

2003 Trittenheimer Apotheke
Riesling Spätlese ***
9%, ♀ till 2012 — 91

2002 Leiwener Klostergarten
Riesling Eiswein
7%, ♀ till 2015 — 92

2003 Leiwener Klostergarten
Riesling Auslese
8.5%, ♀ till 2013 — 92

2003 Leiwener Klostergarten
Riesling Eiswein
8%, ♀ till 2020 — 94

WEINGUT
SCHLOSS SAARSTEIN

Owner: Christian Ebert
Manager and winemaker:
Christian Ebert
54455 Serrig
Tel. (0 65 81) 23 24, Fax 65 23
e-mail: Weingut@Saarstein.de
Internet: www.saarstein.de
Directions: B 51 Trier–Saarburg–Serrig
Sales: Andrea Ebert
by appointment
Worth seeing: Château built at turn of
century, terrace above the Saar

Vineyard area: 11 hectares
Annual production: 60,000 bottles
Top site: Serriger Schloss
Saarsteiner
Soil types: Decomposed slate
Grape varieties: 93% Riesling, 6%
Weißburgunder, 1% other varieties
Average yield: 55 hl/ha
Best vintages: 1999, 2002, 2003
Member: VDP

Dieter Ebert purchased the manor-house,
which had been built at the turn of the century, in 1956, together with the monopole
Serriger Schloss Saarstein vineyard site.
His son Christian took over the helm in
the mid-Eighties, and is supported by his
charming wife Andrea, who hails from the
Wirsching winery in Iphofen in Franken.
The musts are increasingly being fermented in stainless steel tanks. The dry wines
are always characterized by high acidity,
and make up half the production. Schloss
Saarstein produced a whole series of good
vintages in the Nineties, and he was able
to find this level of quality again with the
2002 Riesling wines. While the dry wines
in 2002 were characterized by strong
mineral notes, a ripe fruit dimension has
been added this year. Because of the vintage character, Eberts 2003 Eiswein is not
as great as its predecessor, but is among
the best that was made in this category.
The Beerenauslese is one of the best in
the country.

2002 Riesling Spätlese trocken
12%, ♀ till 2007   **87**

2003 Serriger Schloss Saarsteiner
Riesling Kabinett
8.5%, ♀ till 2008   **87**

2003 Serriger Schloss Saarsteiner
Riesling Spätlese
8.5%, ♀ till 2010   **89**

2003 Serriger Schloss Saarsteiner
Riesling Auslese
8%, ♀ till 2012   **91**

2003 Serriger Schloss Saarsteiner
Riesling Auslese Goldkapsel
7.5%, ♀ till 2015   **92**

2002 Serriger Schloss Saarsteiner
Riesling Auslese lange Goldkapsel
⟶ auction wine, 9.5%, ♀ till 2012   **93**

2003 Serriger Schloss Saarsteiner
Riesling Eiswein
6%, ♀ till 2020   **94**

2003 Serriger Schloss Saarsteiner
Riesling Auslese lange Goldkapsel
⟶ auction wine, 8%, ♀ till 2018   **94**

2003 Serriger Schloss Saarsteiner
Riesling Beerenauslese
⟶ auction wine, 6%, ♀ till 2020   **95**

2002 Serriger Schloss Saarsteiner
Riesling Eiswein
7%, ♀ till 2020   **96**

2003
SCHLOSS SAARSTEIN

RIESLING

Mosel Saar Ruwer · Qualitätswein · trocken
Gutsabfüllung · D-54455 Serrig
A. P. Nr. 3555014304 · Alc. 11.5% BY VOL. · 750 ml

The wines: **100** Perfect · **95–99** Outstanding · **90–94** Excellent · **85–89** Very good · **80–84** Good · **75–79** Average

WEINGUT
SANKT URBANS-HOF

Owner: Nik Weis
Manager: Nik Weis
Administrator: Hermann Jostock
Winemaker: Rudolf Hoffmann
54340 Leiwen, Urbanusstraße 16
Tel. (0 65 07) 9 37 70, Fax 93 77 30
e-mail: St.Urbans-Hof@t-online.de
Internet: www.urbans-hof.de
Directions: A 48, Bekond exit,
Leiwen or A 1, Mehring exit, in direction
of Büdlicher Brück
Sales: Nik and Daniela Weis, Rudolf
Hoffmann, Rosi Marx
Opening hours: Mon.–Fri. 09:00 to
18:00 hours, Sat. 09:00 to 17:00 hours
Sun. and public holidays by appointment
Restaurant: Landhaus St. Urban
Thur.–Mon. 12:00 to 14:00 hours
and 18:00 to 22:00 hours
Closed Tue. and Wed.
Specialties: Top-class regional cuisine
by chef Harald Rüssel

Vineyard area: 38 hectares
Annual production: 250,000 bottles
Top sites: Leiwener Laurentiuslay,
Piesporter Goldtröpfchen, Ockfener
Bockstein, Schodener Saarfeilser
Marienberg
Soil types: Devon slate
Grape varieties: 95% Riesling,
5% other varieties
Average yield: 64 hl/ha
Best vintages: 1999, 2000, 2003
Member: VDP

This family winery has seen a dynamic development in the past decade. The foundation was laid by Nicolaus Weis, who built the business on a rise overlooking Leiwen in 1947. He was by training a master shoemaker, and until after World War II had worked a few vineyards that had been owned by the family for centuries as a side-line. He was also a politician who had the interests of the wine industry in general at heart, and for his activities Nicolaus Weis was given the title of Ökonomierat, or economic councilor. His son Hermann Weis, one of the sponsors of the young winemakers association in Leiwen, and one of the most successful vine grafters in Germany, has purchased additional vineyards on the Saar, almost doubling the original holdings of 20 hectares. For a few years now his hard-working son Nik has been running the business. The past few vintages here have been outstanding, each new one better than the previous one. Only a handful of Mosel vineyards could present such a homogeneous high level of quality across the board at the end of the Nineties. The Eisweins, in particular, are often among the best examples of their style in the whole region. It would be helpful to indicate the style on the label, to distinguish the dry and off-dry Riesling wines from the fruity ones. The only limited means one has of distinguishing them is to look at the alcohol levels. Considering the difficult vintage conditions, the 2000 range was little short of fantastic, followed by a good to very good range in 2001, in which the Spätlese wines were particularly good. Looking to the 2002 vintage, the most enjoyable wines were the lively, fresh, fruity Spätlese wines, while the Auslese wines were in some cases baroque, and less enjoyable. The wines have a yeasty note this year, and are all characterized by the concentrated and at the same time soft fruit that is typical of the vintage. The only exception is the Ockfener Bockstein from the Saar, which has a little more acidity. The familiar expansive style of the wines is in this vintage paired in an attractive way with a yeasty spice and mellowness found only in very ripe vintages. The pinnacle of the range is the Goldtröpfchen Beerenauslese, which combines the best features of the vintage: an elegant botrytis note and an intense, long finish.

2003 Leiwener Laurentiuslay
Riesling Spätlese trocken
12.5%, ♀ till 2007   88

2003 Wiltinger
Riesling Kabinett feinherb
10.5%, ♀ till 2008   8

2003 Ockfener Bockstein
Riesling Spätlese feinherb
12%, ♀ till 2009   **91**

2002 Ockfener Bockstein
Riesling Spätlese
7.5%, ♀ till 2009   **88**

2002 Ockfener Bockstein
Riesling Auslese
7.5%, ♀ till 2010   **88**

2001 Piesporter Goldtröpfchen
Riesling Spätlese
8%, ♀ till 2010   **89**

2002 Saarfeilser
Riesling Spätlese
8%, ♀ till 2008   **89**

2002 Leiwener Laurentiuslay
Riesling Spätlese
↗ auction wine, 8%, ♀ till 2009   **89**

2002 Piesporter Goldtröpfchen
Riesling Auslese
7.5%, ♀ till 2011   **89**

2003 Ockfener Bockstein
Riesling Kabinett
10%, ♀ till 2009   **89**

2003 Ockfener Bockstein
Riesling Auslese
9%, ♀ till 2009   **89**

2001 Ockfener Bockstein
Riesling Auslese
7.5%, ♀ till 2012   **90**

2003 Piesporter Goldtröpfchen
Riesling Spätlese
8.5%, ♀ till 2010   **90**

2003 Leiwener Laurentiuslay
Riesling Spätlese
↗ auction wine, 9%, ♀ till 2009   **90**

2003 Ockfener Bockstein
Riesling Eiswein
6.5%, ♀ till 2012   **90**

2003 Ockfener Bockstein
Riesling Auslese Goldkapsel
↗ auction wine, 9%, ♀ till 2010   **90**

2001 Leiwener Laurentiuslay
Riesling Spätlese
↗ auction wine, 9%, ♀ till 2010   **91**

2001 Piesporter Goldtröpfchen
Riesling Auslese
9%, ♀ till 2010   **91**

2002 Ockfener Bockstein
Riesling Eiswein
6.5%, ♀ till 2015   **91**

2001 Ockfener Bockstein
Riesling Auslese Goldkapsel
↗ auction wine, 8.5%, ♀ till 2012   **91**

2001 Leiwener Klostergarten
Riesling Eiswein
6%, ♀ till 2018   **92**

2002 Ockfener Bockstein
Riesling Eiswein
↗ auction wine, 6.5%, ♀ till 2020   **92**

2003 Ockfener Bockstein
Riesling Spätlese
8%, ♀ till 2010   **92**

2003 Piesporter Goldtröpfchen
Riesling Auslese
8.5%, ♀ till 2010   **92**

2003 Ockfener Bockstein
Riesling Auslese – 43 –
8.5%, ♀ till 2012   **92**

2002 Ockfener Bockstein
Riesling Auslese lange Goldkapsel
↗ auction wine, 7.5%, ♀ till 2014   **93**

2003 Piesporter Goldtröpfchen
Riesling Beerenauslese
8%, ♀ till 2020   **94**

MOSEL SAAR RUWER
Estate bottled
Qualitätswein mit Prädikat
White Wine Product of Germany
A. P. Nr. 3 529 290 029 03
6.5% alc./vol.
375 ml
EISWEIN
2002
OCKFENER BOCKSTEIN
Riesling EISWEIN
WEINGUT
St. URBANS-HOF
OEKONOMIERAT NIC. WEIS
D-54340 LEIWEN / MOSEL

The wines: **100** Perfect · **95–99** Outstanding · **90–94** Excellent · **85–89** Very good · **80–84** Good · **75–79** Average

Rising star of the year 1997   # Mosel-Saar-Ruwer

WEINGUT
WILLI SCHAEFER

Owner: Willi Schaefer and
Christoph Schaefer
Winemaker: Christoph
and Willi Schaefer
54470 Graach, Hauptstraße 130
Tel. (0 65 31) 80 41, Fax 14 14
Directions: A 48, Wittlich exit, in direc-tion of Bernkastel-Kues
Sales: Schaefer family
Opening hours: Mon.–Fri. 09:00 to
12:00 hours and 14:00 to 18:00 hours
Sat. 10:00 to 12:00 hours
Sun. by appointment
History: Winemaking in the family
since 1590
Worth seeing: Rarities dating back to
1921 in cellar

Vineyard area: 3.2 hectares
Annual production: 30,000 bottles
Top sites: Graacher Domprobst
and Himmelreich
Soil types: Devon slate
Grape varieties: 100% Riesling
Average yield: 65 hl/ha
Best vintages: 1997, 1999, 2003
Member: VDP

Willi Schaefer from Graach experienced some tremendous successes in the Nineties, based on two hectares of the best parcels of the top Graach sites, the Himmelreich and Domprobst, as well as smaller holdings in the Sonnenuhr vineyard. However, things have taken a slight downturn since the end of the Nineties. The rather weak 2000 range represented the low point in this development, and the 2001 vintage was also rather mediocre. Schaefer showed a decent range in 2002, and has supported this considerably by his efforts in 2003. Whereas in the previous vintage the lively Spätlese wines set the standard of quality, in this vintage Schaefer has been particularly strong with his Auslese wines. The highlight is the Beerenauslese. Around half of the production continues to be exported.

2002 Graacher Domprobst
Riesling Kabinett
8%, ♀ till 2007 — **86**

2003 Graacher Domprobst
Riesling Kabinett
8%, ♀ till 2008 — **87**

2003 Graacher Himmelreich
Riesling Spätlese
8%, ♀ till 2008 — **87**

2002 Graacher Domprobst
Riesling Spätlese
↱ auction wine, 8%, ♀ till 2009 — **88**

2002 Graacher Domprobst
Riesling Auslese Goldkapsel
↱ auction wine, 7.5%, ♀ till 2010 — **88**

2003 Graacher Domprobst
Riesling Spätlese
8%, ♀ till 2009 — **89**

2003 Graacher Domprobst
Riesling Spätlese
↱ auction wine, 7.5%, ♀ till 2010 — **90**

2003 Graacher Domprobst
Riesling Auslese – 14 –
7.5%, ♀ till 2010 — **90**

2003 Graacher Himmelreich
Riesling Auslese
7.5%, ♀ till 2010 — **90**

2003 Graacher Domprobst
Riesling Auslese – 18 –
7.5%, ♀ till 2011 — **91**

2003 Graacher Domprobst
Riesling Auslese Goldkapsel
↱ auction wine, 7.5%, ♀ till 2011 — **92**

2003 Graacher Domprobst
Riesling Beerenauslese
7.5%, ♀ till 2015 — **93**

WEINGUT ANDREAS SCHMITGES

Owner: Andreas Schmitges
54492 Erden, Im Unterdorf 12
Tel. (0 65 32) 27 43, Fax 39 34
e-mail: info@schmitges-weine.de
Internet: www.schmitges-weine.de
Directions: A 48 Koblenz–Trier,
Zeltingen exit, 5 km in direction of
Traben-Trarbach, in center of town
Sales: Waltraud and Andreas Schmitges,
by appointment
History: Winemaking since 1744

Vineyard area: 8 hectares
Annual production: 80,000 bottles
Top sites: Erdener Treppchen
and Prälat
Soil types: Gray and blue slate, sandy
clay soils
Grape varieties: 80% Riesling,
20% Müller-Thurgau
Average yield: 78 hl/ha
Best vintages: 1999, 2001, 2002
Member: Bernkasteler Ring

"Our philosophy is that in the cellar we can at best maintain the quality we have picked in the vineyard." Andreas Schmitges calls this his commitment to controlled inactivity, referring to his policy of minimum intervention in the cellar, though this should not turn attention away from the fact that he and his wife Waltraud have achieved a great deal since taking over the winery in 1990. The first thing this marketing expert did was to create a totally new image. His credibility was improved by the fact that the contents of the bottles matched their sleek outward appearance. The 2001 vintage saw a jump in quality, earning the winery its second bunch of grapes. The fruity and botrytized wines of the 2002 vintages surpassed those of the previous vintages. However, the wines of the 2003 vintage were not as convincing, they are all characterized by a lemony acidity. The baroque Trockenbeerenauslese has an almost unlimited maturation potential.

2003 Erdener Prälat
Riesling Spätlese feinherb
11.5%, ♀ till 2008 — **84**

2003 Erdener Treppchen
Riesling Kabinett
8.5%, ♀ till 2008 — **84**

2002 Erdener Treppchen
Riesling Kabinett – 12 –
8%, ♀ till 2006 — **85**

2003 Erdener Treppchen
Riesling Spätlese
7.5%, ♀ till 2008 — **85**

2003 Erdener Treppchen
Riesling Auslese *
8%, ♀ till 2009 — **85**

2003 Erdener Prälat
Riesling Auslese **
7.5%, ♀ till 2010 — **87**

2001 Erdener Treppchen
Riesling Spätlese
8%, ♀ till 2009 — **88**

2002 Erdener Treppchen
Riesling Auslese
8%, ♀ till 2009 — **88**

2001 Erdener Treppchen
Riesling Auslese
7.5%, ♀ till 2010 — **89**

2001 Erdener Prälat
Riesling Auslese *
7.5%, ♀ till 2012 — **89**

2002 Erdener Treppchen
Riesling Spätlese – 17 –
7.5%, ♀ till 2008 — **89**

2002 Erdener Riesling Eiswein
7%, ♀ till 2012 — **91**

2003 Erdener Treppchen
Riesling Trockenbeerenauslese
⟶ auction wine, 6.5%, ♀ till 2018 — **94**

SCHMITGES
WEINBAU SEIT MDCCXLIV

2000
Erdener Treppchen
Riesling Spätlese

QUALITÄTSWEIN MIT PRÄDIKAT · A.P.Nr. 2582071801
WEINGUT HEINRICH SCHMITGES · D-54492 ERDEN
GUTSABFÜLLUNG · PRODUCE OF GERMANY
7,5% alc./vol.   Mosel-Saar-Ruwer   e 500 ml

The wines: **100** Perfect · **95–99** Outstanding · **90–94** Excellent · **85–89** Very good · **80–84** Good · **75–79** Average

WEINGUT HEINZ SCHMITT

Owner and manager: Heinz Schmitt
54340 Leiwen, Stephanusstraße 4
Tel. (0 65 07) 42 76, Fax 81 61
e-mail:
weingutheinzschmitt@t-online.de
Internet:
www.Weingut-Heinz-Schmitt.de
Directions: A 48, Leiwen exit or
A 1, Mehring exit
Sales: Silvi Schmitt, Heinz Schmitt,
Andreas Bender, by appointment

Vineyard area: 22 hectares
Annual production: 140,000 bottles
Top sites: Schweicher Annaberg,
Longuicher Maximiner Herrenberg,
Klüsserather Bruderschaft, Mehringer
Blattenberg, Trittenheimer Apotheke,
Köwericher Laurentiuslay
Soil types: Slate and decomposed
slate, red slate with sandstone and
gray wacke
Grape varieties: 90% Riesling,
5% Weißburgunder, 5% Rivaner
Average yield: 54 hl/ha
Best vintages: 1999, 2001, 2003

This winery in Leiwen has expanded its vineyard area dramatically in recent years. When Heinz Schmitt took over the operation in 1983, he had only 3.5 hectares of vineyard. This has now grown to a total of 22 hectares. At the same time, he has achieved something only a few of his colleagues can claim, in that he has maintained the quality of his wines at a high level in spite of this rapid growth, collecting his third bunch of grapes two years ago, an achievement which he confirmed by a good performance last year. The dry Riesling wines still lack a bit more depth, but Schmitt makes up this liability with a whole palette of rich Spätlese and Auslese wines. We were impressed with how well the 2003 wines, from ungrafted vines, express the whole character of the vintage in their depth and expressiveness.

2003 Longuicher Maximiner Herrenberg
Riesling Spätlese
9.5%, ♀ till 2008 — 87

2003 Köwericher Laurentiuslay
Riesling Spätlese
8.5%, ♀ till 2009 — 89

2002 Mehringer Blattenberg
Riesling Auslese "Wurzelechte Reben"
7.5%, ♀ till 2009 — 89

2003 Neumagener Rosengärtchen
Riesling Auslese "Wurzelechte Reben"
10%, ♀ till 2009 — 89

2003 Trittenheimer Apotheke
Riesling Spätlese "Wurzelechte Reben"
8.5%, ♀ till 2010 — 89

2003 Schweicher Annaberg
Riesling Auslese – 1 –
8%, ♀ till 2010 — 90

2003 Schweicher Annaberg
Riesling Auslese – 4 –
7.5%, ♀ till 2010 — 91

2003 Schweicher Annaberg
Riesling Auslese "Wurzelechte Reben"
8%, ♀ till 2012 — 92

2003 Schweicher Annaberg
Riesling Trockenbeerenauslese
10%, ♀ till 2020 — 93

MOSEL SAAR RUWER

Heinz
SCHMITT
Riesling

2000
KABINETT TROCKEN
Mehringer Zellerberg

Gutsabfüllung
Qualitätswein mit Prädikat -A.P.Nr. 3 529 179 12 01
Weingut Heinz Schmitt · stephanusstraße 4
D-54340 Leiwen/Mosel

750 ml — ALC.10.5% BY VOL

WEINGUT MARTIN SCHÖMANN

Owner and manager:
Martin Schömann
Winemaker: Bartho Kroth and
Martin Schömann
54492 Zeltingen-Rachtig, Uferallee 50
Tel. (0 65 32) 23 47, Fax 10 10
e-mail: M.Schoemann@t-online.de
Internet: www.schoemann-weine.de
Directions: A 1/A 48 Koblenz–Trier,
Wittlich exit
Sales: Martin and Helga Schömann
by appointment
History: Winemaking in the family
since the 16th century
Worth seeing: Old stalactite vaulted
cellar, attractive courtyard

Vineyard area: 6 hectares
Annual production: 50,000 bottles
Top sites: Zeltinger Sonnenuhr
and Himmelreich, Graacher Dom-
probst, Wintricher Großer Herrgott
Soil types: Decomposed Devon slate
Grape varieties: 90% Riesling,
10% Pinot varieties
Average yield: 70 hl/ha
Best vintages: 2001, 2002, 2003
Member: Vinum COS

Stephan Schömann founded a small merchant house in 1900 that was only dis-
banded in 1999. At that stage there were
already some own vineyard holdings in
good sites, and Martin Schömann has added to these selectively. For instance, he
has acquired another hectare in the Zeltinger Sonnenuhr. The businessman and
winemaker is assisted by Bartho Kroth
from Briedel, who gained international
experience in Canada. The 2001 and
2002 ranges showed very solid work.
Starting with the 2003 vintage, the designations Spätlese and Auslese are no
longer applied to dry and off-dry wines.
All of the wines of this vintage are of
the same standard as those of the 2002
vintage. The Zeltinger Himmelreich Eiswein is outstanding.

2003 Graacher Himmelreich
Riesling Kabinett
8.5%, ♀ till 2007   **83**

2003 Zeltinger Schlossberg
Riesling Spätlese
8.5%, ♀ till 2008   **83**

2001 Bernkasteler Johannisbrünnchen
Riesling
9.5%, ♀ till 2005   **84**

2002 Bernkasteler Johannisbrünnchen
Riesling Hochgewächs
9%, ♀ till 2006   **84**

2003 Bernkasteler Johannisbrünnchen
Riesling Spätlese
7.5%, ♀ till 2008   **84**

2003 Zeltinger Sonnenuhr
Riesling Spätlese **
8.5%, ♀ till 2009   **84**

2002 Zeltinger Sonnenuhr
Riesling Spätlese
8.5%, ♀ till 2007   **85**

2002 Zeltinger Sonnenuhr
Riesling Auslese
8.5%, ♀ till 2007   **85**

2003 Zeltinger Sonnenuhr
Riesling Auslese *
9%, ♀ till 2010   **85**

2001 Wintricher Großer Herrgott
Riesling Spätlese
8.5%, ♀ till 2007   **86**

2003 Zeltinger Sonnenuhr
Riesling Auslese **
7%, ♀ till 2010   **86**

2003 Zeltinger Himmelreich
Riesling Eiswein
8.5%, ♀ till 2012   **89**

M. SCHÖMANN

2001
Zeltinger Sonnenuhr
Riesling Kabinett trocken

GUTSABFÜLLUNG WEINGUT MARTIN SCHÖMANN · D-54492 ZELTINGEN/MOSEL
QUALITÄTSWEIN MIT PRÄDIKAT · A.P.NR. 2 606 292 035 05 · PRODUCE OF GERMANY

11,5% vol   *Mosel · Saar · Ruwer*   750 ml

The wines: **100** Perfect · **95–99** Outstanding · **90–94** Excellent · **85–89** Very good · **80–84** Good · **75–79** Average

GUTSVERWALTUNG VON SCHUBERT – MAXIMIN GRÜNHAUS

Owner: Dr. Carl-Ferdinand von Schubert
54318 Mertesdorf, Maximin Grünhaus
Tel. (06 51) 51 11, Fax 5 21 22
e-mail: info@vonSchubert.com
Internet: www.vonSchubert.com
Directions: A 48, Kenn/Trier-Ruwer exit, left into Ruwer valley after 3 km
Sales: Dr. Carl von Schubert
Opening hours: Mon.–Fri. 08:00 to 12:00 hours and 13:00 to 16:30 hours
Sat. 09:00 to 12:00 hours
by appointment only
History: First mentioned in documents 966, St. Maximin abbey, owned by von Schubert family since 1882
Worth seeing: Ensemble manor-house and "Cavalier" house and winery building with Gothic-style surrounding wall

---

Vineyard area: 34 hectares
Annual production: 200,000 bottles
Top sites: Maximin Grünhäuser Abtsberg and Herrenberg
Soil types: Blue (Abtsberg) and red (Herrenberg) Devon slate
Grape varieties: 97% Riesling, 3% other varieties
Average yield: 53 hl/ha
Best vintages: 1993, 1995, 1997

Under the guidance of Dr. Carl-Ferdinand von Schubert this beautifully located estate in Grünhaus has become a sought-after producer of elegant Ruwer Riesling. For many decades one could buy the wines with their distinctive Belle-Epoque-style label almost blind. However, this positive development appears to have turned around since the 1999 vintage. Unfortunately, the 2002 vintage did not mark a turning point in this development, and wines were characterized by tart fruit aromas. The latest vintage holds a slight promise of some improvement, as the botrytis dessert wines are of a better quality than in the previous vintage.

2003 Maximin Grünhäuser Abtsberg
Riesling Auslese trocken
13%, ♀ till 2006   **85**

2003 Maximin Grünhäuser Abtsberg
Riesling Kabinett
8%, ♀ till 2008   **86**

2002 Maximin Grünhäuser Abtsberg
Riesling Spätlese
7.5%, ♀ till 2008   **87**

2003 Maximin Grünhäuser Abtsberg
Riesling Auslese – 70 –
8%, ♀ till 2009   **87**

2002 Maximin Grünhäuser Abtsberg
Riesling Auslese – 93 –
7.5%, ♀ till 2009   **88**

2003 Maximin Grünhäuser Herrenberg
Riesling Spätlese
7.5%, ♀ till 2008   **88**

2003 Maximin Grünhäuser Abtsberg
Riesling Spätlese
8%, ♀ till 2009   **88**

2003 Maximin Grünhäuser Abtsberg
Riesling Auslese – 155 –
7.5%, ♀ till 2012   **89**

2003 Maximin Grünhäuser Abtsberg
Riesling Eiswein
7.5%, ♀ till 2015   **89**

2002 Maximin Grünhäuser Abtsberg
Riesling Eiswein – 211 –
7.5%, ♀ till 2012   **90**

2003 Maximin Grünhäuser Abtsberg
Riesling Beerenauslese
8%, ♀ till 2015   **90**

2003 Maximin Grünhäuser Abtsberg
Riesling Trockenbeerenauslese
8%, ♀ till 2020   **92**

WEINGUT
SELBACH-OSTER

Owner: Johannes Selbach
Winemaker: Klaus-Rainer Schäfer
and Hans Selbach
54492 Zeltingen, Uferallee 23
Tel. (0 65 32) 20 81, Fax 40 14
e-mail: info@selbach-oster.de
Internet: www.selbach-oster.de
Directions: A 48, Wittlich-Mitte exit, in
direction of Bernkastel-Kues, cross the
Mosel bridge at Zeltingen, turn right into
Uferallee, on river bank in center of town
Sales: Selbach family
Opening hours: By appointment
History: Winemaking in the family
since 1661

Vineyard area: 16 hectares
Annual production: 100,000 bottles
Top sites: Zeltinger Schlossberg
and Sonnenuhr, Wehlener Sonnen-
uhr, Graacher Domprobst
Soil types: Stony blue Devon slate, in
Graach partly with clay
Grape varieties: 97% Riesling,
3% Weißburgunder
Average yield: 70 hl/ha
Best vintages: 2000, 2001, 2003

For many years father and son have
worked together in rare harmony in this
top winery. The harmonious co-operation
of Hans and Johannes Selbach is also reflected in the character of their wines. The
Selbach family has always worked as a
team. The great-grandfather of Johannes
owned a steam barge with which he
would transport the wine barrels via the
Mosel and Rhine rivers up to the North
Sea ports. The barrels in turn were made
by Matthias Oster, a cooper and paternal
great-grandfather. The family operation
developed along three lines: as a wine
estate, as a merchant house and whole-
saler, and as a commission agent. Now,
Johannes Selbach has taken over the wine
estate as his sole responsibility. This includes some of the best parcels in famous
steep slopes in Bernkastel, Graach, Weh-

len and Zeltingen, which are partly still
planted with very old ungrafted Riesling
vines. A little Pinot Blanc has been added
to this, which is still to be expanded
slightly, though not at the expense of
the Riesling vineyards. A lot has been invested in recent years in mechanizing the
work in the steepest slopes. In the cellar,
new large oak barrels are used every two
to three years. The wines are all of good
quality, with about half being made dry or
off-dry, and the other half fruity and
sweet. In future, the share of off-dry
wines is to be reduced, with more concentration on the dry and sweet segments.
Around two-thirds of the production today is exported. There was not a single
blemish on the high quality of the 2000
range, and the fruity wines were among
the best that could be produced in the
Mosel region in that vintage. The highlight was a tremendous Zeltinger Sonnenuhr Trockenbeerenauslese. The 2001
range set new standards. With this range
Johannes Selbach was knocking loudly,
unmistakably at the doors of the Mosel
equivalent of the Olympian heights. The
impressive crystal-clear style of that vintage was not quite as precise in the 2002
vintage. To hear Selbach speaking about
the 2003 vintage, he compares the development of the wines since bottling with a
change in musical key, "from minor at the
beginning to major at the present stage."
In this he is by no means implying that his
Riesling wines have already reached their
zenith, and continues, referring to the
wines as "roses whose blooms are still
closed." The fascinating aspect of the
Selbach wines is their light and playful
mineral note. This is particularly evident
in the "Schmitt" Auslese, a tiny parcel of
the Zeltinger Schlossberg. All in all, 2003
saw the production of a fantastic range of
botrytized Riesling wines here that is
sure to go down in the history books of
the estate.

2003 Zeltinger Schlossberg
Riesling Spätlese trocken *
12.5%, ♀ till 2006   **88**

---

he wines: **100** Perfect · **95–99** Outstanding · **90–94** Excellent · **85–89** Very good · **80–84** Good · **75–79** Average

2003 Zeltinger Sonnenuhr
Riesling Spätlese trocken *
12.5%, ♀ till 2006 — 89

2002 Zeltinger Schlossberg
Riesling Kabinett
9%, ♀ till 2007 — 87

2003 Zeltinger Schlossberg
Riesling Kabinett
9.5%, ♀ till 2007 — 87

2003 Wehlener Sonnenuhr
Riesling Kabinett
9%, ♀ till 2009 — 88

2002 Zeltinger Sonnenuhr
Riesling Spätlese * – 23 –
8.5%, ♀ till 2009 — 89

2003 Bernkasteler Badstube
Riesling Spätlese *
9%, ♀ till 2008 — 89

2003 Zeltinger Schlossberg
Riesling Spätlese
8.5%, ♀ till 2010 — 89

2002 Zeltinger Sonnenuhr
Riesling Spätlese * – 18 –
8%, ♀ till 2010 — 90

2003 Wehlener Sonnenuhr
Riesling Spätlese
8.5%, ♀ till 2009 — 90

2003 Zeltinger Sonnenuhr
Riesling Spätlese *
9%, ♀ till 2008 — 90

2003 Zeltinger Sonnenuhr
Riesling Spätlese
9%, ♀ till 2010 — 90

2001 Zeltinger Sonnenuhr
Riesling Auslese *
8%, ♀ till 2012 — 91

2003 Zeltinger Sonnenuhr
Riesling Auslese
8.5%, ♀ till 2010 — 91

2002 Bernkasteler Badstube
Riesling Auslese **
8%, ♀ till 2012 — 92

2003 Zeltinger Sonnenuhr
Riesling Beerenauslese
7%, ♀ till 2018 — 92

2003 Wehlener Sonnenuhr
Riesling Auslese
8%, ♀ till 2012 — 92

2001 Zeltinger Sonnenuhr
Riesling Trockenbeerenauslese
7.5%, ♀ till 2025 — 93

2002 Bernkasteler Badstube
Riesling Eiswein
7.5%, ♀ till 2020 — 93

2003 Graacher Domprobst
Riesling Auslese *
9%, ♀ till 2012 — 93

2003 Zeltinger Sonnenuhr
Riesling Auslese ***
7.5%, ♀ till 2012 — 93

2003 Zeltinger Schlossberg
Riesling Auslese **
8%, ♀ till 2012 — 93

2002 Zeltinger Himmelreich
Riesling Eiswein *
7%, ♀ till 2020 — 94

2003 Zeltinger Himmelreich
Riesling Eiswein
7.5%, ♀ till 2024 — 94

2003 Zeltinger Sonnenuhr
Riesling Beerenauslese *
7%, ♀ till 2018 — 94

2003 Zeltinger Schlossberg
Riesling Auslese ***
8%, ♀ till 2012 — 94

2003 Zeltinger Schlossberg
Riesling Auslese "Schmitt"
8%, ♀ till 2014 — 94

ANNO 1661

SELBACH-OSTER

2003
ZELTINGER SONNENUHR
RIESLING BEERENAUSLESE

QUALITÄTSWEIN MIT PRÄDIKAT · PRODUCE OF GERMANY
GUTSABFÜLLUNG WEINGUT SELBACH-OSTER · D-54492 ZELTINGEN
L · A.P. NR. 2 606 319 032 04

MOSEL · SAAR · RUWER

alc. 8 % vol   375 ml e

The estates: ♛♛♛♛♛ World's finest · ♛♛♛♛ Germany's best · ♛♛♛ Very good · ♛♛ Good · ♛ Reliab.

WEINGUT SPÄTER-VEIT

Owner: Heinz Welter-Später
54498 Piesport, Brückenstraße 13
Tel. (0 65 07) 54 42, Fax 67 60
e-mail: Spaeter-Veit@t-online.de
Directions: A 1, Salmtal exit, in direc-
tion of Piesport, cross over Mosel bridge
there, 3rd house on left
Sales: Silvia and Heinz Welter
Opening hours: Mon.–Fri. 11:00 to
21:00, Sat. and Sun. 10:00 to 21:00 hours
Restaurant: June to October
daily from 11:00 hours
Specialties: Riesling cream soup,
smoked trout
History: Winemaking in the family
since more than 300 years
Worth seeing: Panorama terrace with
view of old part of Piesport

Vineyard area: 7.3 hectares
Annual production: 25,000 bottles
Top sites: Piesporter Goldtröpfchen
and Domherr, Wintricher Ohligsberg
Soil types: Slate and red slate
Grape varieties: 68% Riesling, 15%
Müller-Thurgau, 8% Spätburgunder,
7% Weißburgunder, 2% other varieties
Average yield: 65 hl/ha
Best vintages: 2001, 2002, 2003

Ever since his marriage to Silvia Später in
1988, Heinz Welter has been busy getting
rid of all the new grape varieties, prefer-
ing instead to concentrate on Riesling,
plus some Pinot Blanc and Pinot Noir.
The latter can produce remarkably good
wines here. Welter's success is based
mainly on his vineyard holdings in Piesport and Wintrich, with almost one and a
half hectares of the Piesporter Goldtröpfchen site. Welter's strength lies clearly in
the range of elegantly fruity Spätlese and
Auslese wines produced. In the 2003 vintage, his best wines were sourced from
the Piesporter Goldtröpfchen site. The
Auslese *** is full-bodied and concentrated, Beerenauslese has an enticing
honey-aroma. The yields here are quite
low by Mosel standards.

2003 Piesporter Goldtröpfchen
Riesling Spätlese halbtrocken
14%, ♀ till 2009 — **83**

2003 Piesporter Goldtröpfchen
Riesling Spätlese
9.5%, ♀ till 2008 — **84**

2001 Piesporter Domherr
Riesling Kabinett
9%, ♀ till 2007 — **85**

2003 Piesporter Goldtröpfchen
Riesling Auslese
9%, ♀ till 2010 — **85**

2001 Piesporter Goldtröpfchen
Riesling Auslese
9%, ♀ till 2008 — **86**

2002 Piesporter Goldtröpfchen
Riesling Spätlese – 34 –
8%, ♀ till 2008 — **86**

2003 Piesporter Goldtröpfchen
Riesling Auslese ***
9.5%, ♀ till 2012 — **86**

2002 Piesporter Goldtröpfchen
Riesling Auslese
8%, ♀ till 2009 — **87**

2003 Piesporter Goldtröpfchen
Riesling Beerenauslese
7.5%, ♀ till 2012 — **87**

——————— Red wine ———————

2002 Spätburgunder trocken
13%, ♀ till 2008 — **84**

The wines: **100** Perfect · **95–99** Outstanding · **90–94** Excellent · **85–89** Very good · **80–84** Good · **75–79** Average

379

WEINGUT STUDERT-PRÜM – MAXIMINHOF

Owner: Stephan and Gerhard Studert
Manager and winemaker:
Stephan and Gerhard Studert
54470 Bernkastel-Wehlen,
Hauptstraße 150
Tel. (0 65 31) 24 87, Fax 39 20
e-mail: info@studert-pruem.com
Internet: www.studert-pruem.com
Directions: From Bernkastel-Kues keep to left bank of Mosel, at entrance to Wehlen suburb
Sales: Mon.–Fri. 09:00 to 18:00 hours
Sat. 10:00 to 16:00 hours
Sun. by appointment
History: First mentioned as part of St. Maximin abbey 1256. Winemaking by Studert family since 1581
Worth seeing: The Maximinhof, part of former St. Maximin abbey

Vineyard area: 5 hectares
Annual production: 40,000 bottles
Top sites: Wehlener Sonnenuhr, Graacher Himmelreich and Domprobst, Bernkasteler Graben
Soil types: Devon slate
Grape varieties: 100% Riesling
Average yield: 60 hl/ha
Best vintages: 2001, 2002, 2003
Member: VDP

Ever since the merger between the Stephan Studert and Peter Prüm wineries, the combined company has been known as the Studert-Prüm estate. The brothers Stephan and Gerhard Studert presented a succession of good vintages in the Nineties. In the 2001 vintage the Trockenbeerenauslese produced was a real stunner. The 2002 vintage produced a very good range, characterized by the estate's typical dense structure, spice and opulent style. Only two botrytized Rieslings of the 2003 vintage were presented, and we particularly liked the delicate berry notes of the Auslese wine. The fruity Spätlese wines showed well, with soft and at the same time elegant notes.

2003 Bernkasteler Badstube
Riesling
11%, ♀ till 2008 — **84**

2003 Wehlener Sonnenuhr
Riesling Kabinett
10%, ♀ till 2008 — **85**

2003 Graacher Himmelreich
Riesling Kabinett
8.5%, ♀ till 2008 — **85**

2003 Graacher Himmelreich
Riesling Spätlese
8.5%, ♀ till 2009 — **87**

2001 Wehlener Sonnenuhr
Riesling Auslese **
7.5%, ♀ till 2010 — **89**

2003 Wehlener Sonnenuhr
Riesling Spätlese
9%, ♀ till 2010 — **89**

2002 Wehlener Sonnenuhr
Riesling Auslese lange Goldkapsel
⟩ auction wine, 8.5%, ♀ till 2010 — **89**

2003 Wehlener Sonnenuhr
Riesling Auslese
8.5%, ♀ till 2010 — **90**

2003 Wehlener Sonnenuhr
Riesling Beerenauslese
8.5%, ♀ till 2012 — **91**

2002 Wehlener Sonnenuhr
Riesling Trockenbeerenauslese
⟩ auction wine, 8.5%, ♀ till 2018 — **93**

2001 Wehlener Sonnenuhr
Riesling Trockenbeerenauslese
⟩ auction wine, 8.5%, ♀ till 2020 — **94**

WEINGUT PETER TERGES

Owner: Peter Terges
54295 Trier, Olewiger Straße 145
Tel. (06 51) 3 10 96, Fax 30 96 71
e-mail: peter-terges@web.de
Directions: A 48, Trier-Olewig exit
Sales: Mon.–Sun. by appointment

Vineyard area: 5 hectares
Annual production: 38,000 bottles
Top sites: Trierer Burgberg,
Deutschherrenberg and
Jesuitenwingert
Soil types: Slate and Devon slate
Grape varieties: 65% Riesling,
20% Weißburgunder, 10% Müller-
Thurgau, 5% Gewürztraminer
Average yield: 81 hl/ha
Best vintages: 1993, 1995, 1999

There is definitely no lack of wine here.
The current price list of this five-hectare
winery runs to more than a hundred items
all produced here, going back to the 1988
vintage. The 65 percent share of Riesling
is quite low for the region. Terges has a
special interest in Pinot Blanc, which by
now makes up a fifth of the vineyard area.
Two-thirds of the wines are produced in
fruity sweet style, and are mostly sold to
loyal private customers. Terges was particularly proud to receive the state honor
award in gold in 1998, a rare distinction.
However, his ambition to be one of the
best producers in the region received a
damper in his 2000 and 2001 ranges. The
dry wines of the 2002 vintage, too, were
of a fairly low standard. However, we are
firmly convinced, there is more potential
in this winery than Peter Terges has again
shown us with his 2003 range. Although
the standard overall is slightly better than
that of the previous vintage, we were
again only really convinced by the elegant fruity Riesling wines, particularly
those from the Deutschherrenberg vineyard.

2003 Trierer Burgberg
Weißer Burgunder Kabinett trocken
12.5%, ♀ till 2007 **81**

2003 Trierer Burgberg
Riesling trocken
11.5%, ♀ till 2007 **81**

2003 Trierer Burgberg
Riesling Spätlese halbtrocken
10%, ♀ till 2007 **83**

2003 Trierer Jesuitenwingert
Riesling Auslese halbtrocken
12.5%, ♀ till 2008 **83**

2003 Trierer Jesuitenwingert
Riesling Auslese
7.5%, ♀ till 2008 **84**

2003 Trierer Deutschherrenberg
Riesling Spätlese
9%, ♀ till 2008 **84**

2003 Trierer Jesuitenwingert
Riesling Spätlese
8.5%, ♀ till 2007 **85**

2003 Trierer Burgberg
Riesling Auslese
8%, ♀ till 2009 **85**

2002 Trierer Burgberg
Riesling Auslese
7%, ♀ till 2009 **86**

2002 Trierer Deutschherrenberg
Riesling Auslese Goldkapsel
7%, ♀ till 2010 **86**

2003 Trierer Deutschherrenberg
Riesling Auslese ***
7.5%, ♀ till 2010 **87**

2003 Trierer Deutschherrenberg
Riesling Beerenauslese
7.5%, ♀ till 2014 **89**

The wines: **100** Perfect · **95–99** Outstanding · **90–94** Excellent · **85–89** Very good · **80–84** Good · **75–79** Average

381

WEINGUT WWE. DR. H. THANISCH – ERBEN MÜLLER-BURGGRAEF

Owner: Margrit Müller-Burggraef
Director: Barbara Rundquist-Müller
Administrator and manager:
Christian Lintz
Winemaker: Edgar Schneider
54470 Bernkastel-Kues, Saarallee 24
Tel. (0 65 31) 75 70, Fax 79 10
e-mail: info@dr-thanisch.de
Internet: www.dr-thanisch.de
Directions: A 48, Wittlich exit, on the left bank of the Mosel in Bernkastel-Kues, in suburb of Kues
Sales: By appointment
History: Winemaking in the family since 1636, in the 4th generation of female hands
Worth seeing: Cellar hewn out of rock under Doctorberg vineyard

Vineyard area: 11 hectares
Annual production: 90,000 bottles
Top sites: Bernkasteler Doctor, Badstube and Lay, Wehlener Sonnenuhr, Graacher Himmelreich, Brauneberger Juffer-Sonnenuhr
Soil types: Decomposed kaolin-slate
Grape varieties: 90% Riesling, 5% Spätburgunder, 3% Dornfelder, 2% Weißburgunder
Average yield: 60 hl/ha
Best vintages: 2000, 2001, 2003

The Thanisch estate was run as a single entity until 1988. Differing views on how the business should be managed led to a split. In most cases, the vineyard parcels were cut in half vertically, and allocated to the two parties, the Thanisch descendants and the Müller-Burggraef descendants. The estate management is proud of the special state awards received in recent years. The 2002 vintage collection was not quite up to the standard of the 2001 vintage. The 2003 range shows a distinct improvement, making the best of the vintage characteristics. With its spicy slate aromas and persistent aromatics, this range was excellent across the board.

2002 Bernkasteler Badstube
Riesling Kabinett
9%, ♀ till 2008 — 85

2001 Bernkasteler Doctor
Riesling Auslese
9.5%, ♀ till 2009 — 87

2002 Bernkasteler Doctor
Riesling Spätlese
9%, ♀ till 2009 — 87

2003 Brauneberger Juffer-Sonnenuhr
Riesling Spätlese
9.5%, ♀ till 2008 — 87

2001 Bernkasteler Doctor
Riesling Spätlese
8.8%, ♀ till 2010 — 88

2003 Bernkasteler Lay
Riesling Auslese
9.5%, ♀ till 2009 — 88

2003 Bernkasteler Doctor
Riesling Spätlese
9%, ♀ till 2009 — 88

2003 Brauneberger Juffer-Sonnenuhr
Riesling Auslese
9.5%, ♀ till 2009 — 89

2003 Graacher Himmelreich
Riesling Auslese
9.5%, ♀ till 2009 — 89

2003 Wehlener Sonnenuhr
Riesling Auslese
9%, ♀ till 2010 — 90

2003 Bernkasteler Doctor
Riesling Auslese
9.5%, ♀ till 2011 — 91

2003 Bernkasteler Doctor
Riesling Trockenbeerenauslese
9%, ♀ till 2020 — 93

WEINGUT WWE. DR. H. THANISCH – ERBEN THANISCH

Owner: Sofia Thanisch-Spier
Technical manager: Olaf Kaufmann
54470 Bernkastel-Kues, Saarallee 31
Tel. (0 65 31) 22 82, Fax 22 26
Directions: A 48, Wittlich exit, on the left bank of the Mosel in Bernkastel-Kues, in suburb of Kues
Sales: Mon.–Sat. by appointment
History: Winemaking in the family since 1636, in the 4th generation of female hands
Worth seeing: Cellar hewn out of rock under the Doctor vineyard, manor-house dating to 1884

Vineyard area: 6.5 hectares
Annual production: 45,000 bottles
Top sites: Bernkasteler Doctor,
Lay and Badstube, Brauneberger
Juffer-Sonnenuhr
Soil types: Decomposed Devon slate
Grape varieties: 100% Riesling
Average yield: 63 hl/ha
Best vintages: 2001, 2002, 2003
Member: VDP

Until a few years ago, only fruity sweet wines were produced in this winery with its long tradition, and these were mainly produced for export. Even today, 75 percent of the production is exported. The viticulture in the steep slopes has been rationalized in recent years, and there are plans to invest in the winery buildings. The wines from the top Bernkasteler Doctor vineyard site, which command exceptionally high prices, have a special position here. The Erben Thanisch wines saw the peak of their development in the mid-Nineties. After that, the quality was no longer as reliable. We have noted a slight and gradual improvement again since the 2001 vintage, which has now been crowned by an excellent range from the 2003 vintage. Noble, elegant wines, imbued with compact fruit and piquant, well-integrated acidity were a pleasure to taste.

2003 Bernkasteler Badstube
Riesling Spätlese
8%, ♀ till 2008   87

2003 Bernkasteler Doctor
Riesling Kabinett
8.5%, ♀ till 2008   87

2001 Bernkasteler Doctor
Riesling Spätlese
8.5%, ♀ till 2010   88

2002 Bernkasteler Doctor
Riesling Spätlese
8%, ♀ till 2010   88

2001 Bernkasteler Doctor
Riesling Auslese
8%, ♀ till 2010   89

2002 Bernkasteler Doctor
Riesling Auslese
8.5%, ♀ till 2012   90

2003 Bernkasteler Doctor
Riesling Spätlese
8.5%, ♀ till 2010   90

2003 Bernkasteler Doctor
Riesling Auslese
8%, ♀ till 2012   92

2003 Bernkasteler Doctor
Riesling Auslese lange Goldkapsel – 20 –
➐ auction wine, 8.5%, ♀ till 2012   92

2003 Bernkasteler Doctor
Riesling Trockenbeerenauslese – 18 –
8%, ♀ till 2020   93

2003 Bernkasteler Doctor
Riesling Trockenbeerenauslese – 19 –
6.5%, ♀ till 2020   95

The wines: **100** Perfect · **95–99** Outstanding · **90–94** Excellent · **85–89** Very good · **80–84** Good · **75–79** Average

383

WEINGUT VEREINIGTE HOSPITIEN

Owner: Public Foundation
Manager: Joachim Arns
Winemaker: Klaus Schneider
54290 Trier, Krahnenufer 19
Tel. (06 51) 9 45 12 10, Fax 9 45 20 60
e-mail: weingut@vereinigtehospitien.de
Internet: www.vereinigtehospitien.de
Directions: On banks of Mosel in Trier, five minutes walk from city center
Sales: Heike Melchior
Opening hours: Mon.–Thur. 08:00 to 12:30 and 13:30 to 17:00 hours, Fri. 08:00 to 12:30 and 13:30 to 16:00 hours
History: Oldest recorded evidence of Riesling cultivation on Mosel (1464)
Worth seeing: Oldest wine cellar in Germany

Vineyard area: 25 hectares
Annual production: 150,000 bottles
Top sites: Scharzhofberger, Piesporter Goldtröpfchen, Kanzemer Altenberg, Serriger Schloss Saarfelser Schlossberg, Wiltinger Hölle
Soil types: Decomposed slate
Grape varieties: 88% Riesling, 4% each of Spät-, Grau- and Weißburgunder
Average yield: 57 hl/ha
Best vintages: 2001, 2002, 2003
Member: VDP

Where the administration of the Vereinigte Hospitien is located on the banks of the Mosel, the Romans used to store their regional wines in oak barrels – nothing much has changed in this regard. The Foundation itself goes back to an edict by Napoleon, and is the center of living and work for the sick, for handicapped and old people, and for children. The Foundation owns some of the best vineyard sites on the Middle Mosel and Saar rivers. Following on from a good 2001 vintage, the first fruits of recent investments can be seen in the 2002 vintage. From the 2003 vintage range we particularly liked the 2003 Goldtröpfchen Auslese which has a fresh, delicate, aromatic style.

2003 Scharzhofberger
Riesling Spätlese trocken
13%, ♀ till 2006 — 85

2002 Wiltinger Kupp
Riesling Spätlese trocken
11%, ♀ till 2005 — 86

2001 Piesporter Goldtröpfchen
Riesling Spätlese trocken
11%, ♀ till 2007 — 88

2003 Piesporter Goldtröpfchen
Riesling Kabinett
10.5%, ♀ till 2008 — 86

2003 Piesporter Goldtröpfchen
Riesling Spätlese
9.5%, ♀ till 2008 — 87

2003 Scharzhofberger
Riesling Spätlese
10%, ♀ till 2008 — 88

2002 Piesporter Goldtröpfchen
Riesling Auslese
8%, ♀ till 2010 — 89

2003 Piesporter Goldtröpfchen
Riesling Auslese
8.5%, ♀ till 2010 — 89

2003 Serriger Schloss Saarfelser Schlossberg
Riesling Auslese Goldkapsel
7%, ♀ till 2010 — 90

2002 Scharzhofberger
Riesling Eiswein
7.5%, ♀ till 2012 — 92

VEREINIGTE HOSPITIEN

2003
Piesporter Goldtröpfchen
Riesling
Spätlese

MOSEL-SAAR-RUWER

WEINGUT VOLLENWEIDER

Owner: Daniel Vollenweider
56841 Traben-Trarbach, Wolfer Weg 53
Tel. (0 65 41) 81 44 33, Fax 81 67 73
e-mail: mail@weingut-vollenweider.de
Internet: www.weingut-vollenweider.de
Directions: A 48, Wittlich exit, in direction of Traben-Trarbach;
A 61, Rheinböllen exit,
B 50 in direction of Traben-Trarbach
Sales: Only via retail trade
Visits by appointment

Vineyard area: 2 hectares
Annual production: 13,000 bottles
Top site: Wolfer Goldgrube
Soil types: Blue and red Devon slate
Grape varieties: 100% Riesling
Average yield: 42 hl/ha
Best vintages: 2001, 2002, 2003

Daniel Vollenweider is from Switzerland, and started off in the small village of Wolf in 2000, arduously working the Goldgrube vineyard, which has not yet been modernized. He managed to produce 3,500 bottles in his first vintage. This climbed to 8,000 bottles in 2001, and by now he is up to 13,000 bottles. There is plenty of space for his production in the three-storey rock cellar in Traben-Trarbach. When we first tasted this beginner's wines two years ago, we reported that we had never before been so impressed by a newcomer's first efforts, from somebody who was completely new to the wine industry. We proclaimed him as our "Discovery of the year 2003," which fortunately did not make him go and rest on his laurels. Instead, he invested both in his vineyards and in stainless steel tanks, and kept storming ahead, earning the third bunch of grapes. In the 2002 vintage, his strengths lay in his fruity Spätlese wines, which we cannot say again this year – we simply liked the two Auslese wines so much that they overshadowed the Spätleses. The Beerenauslese combines elegance and ripe fruit to one of the best wines produced in this category in 2003.

2003 Wolfer Goldgrube
Riesling Kabinett – 1 –
8.5%, ♀ till 2009 — **88**

2003 Wolfer Goldgrube
Riesling Spätlese – 3 –
8.5%, ♀ till 2009 — **88**

2003 Wolfer Goldgrube Reiler
Riesling Spätlese – 4 –
8.5%, ♀ till 2010 — **89**

2003 Wolfer Goldgrube
Riesling Auslese – 7 –
8.5%, ♀ till 2012 — **90**

2003 Wolfer Goldgrube
Riesling Spätlese Goldkapsel – 6 –
8.5%, ♀ till 2010 — **90**

2001 Wolfer Goldgrube
Riesling Auslese lange Goldkapsel – 7 –
7.5%, ♀ till 2012 — **90**

2002 Wolfer Goldgrube
Riesling Spätlese "Reiler"
8%, ♀ till 2010 — **91**

2001 Wolfer Goldgrube
Riesling Auslese – 8 –
6%, ♀ till 2016 — **92**

2003 Wolfer Goldgrube
Riesling Beerenauslese – 9 –
7.5%, ♀ till 2020 — **95**

2003 Wolfer Goldgrube
Riesling Auslese lange Goldkapsel – 8 –
8.5%, ♀ till 2015 — **95**

wolfer goldgrube

2001
riesling beerenauslese

qualitätswein mit prädikat
produce of germany
erzeugerabfüllung: weingut vollenweider
d-56841 traben-trarbach/mosel
a.p.nr. 2 576 801 08 02

mosel · saar · ruwer

alc 6.0% vol   e 375 ml

The wines: **100** Perfect · **95–99** Outstanding · **90–94** Excellent · **85–89** Very good · **80–84** Good · **75–79** Average

385

WEINGUT VAN VOLXEM

Owner and manager: Roman Niewodniczanski
Administrator: Hermann Tapp
Winemaker: Dominik Völk
54459 Wiltingen, Dehenstraße 2
Tel. (0 65 01) 1 65 10, Fax 1 31 06
e-mail: vanvolxem@t-online.de
Internet: www.vanvolxem.de
Directions: B 51 Konz exit, after 3 km in Wiltingen, near the church
Sales: Mon.–Sat. 08:00 to 19:00 hours by appointment
History: Winemaking here since 1700, estate re-established in 2000
Worth seeing: Buildings are a national monument, Belle-Epoque ball-room

---

Vineyard area: 20 hectares
Annual production: 135,000 bottles
Top sites: Wiltinger Gottesfuß, Kupp and Braunfels, Scharzhofberger, Kanzemer Altenberg
Soil types: Devon slate
Grape varieties: 96% Riesling, 4% Weißburgunder
Average yield: 34 hl/ha
Best vintages: 2000, 2003

The winery is located in the historical town center of Wiltingen, and was built on the foundations of a Roman farm complex. It was formerly owned by a Jesuit abbey in Luxembourg, and has owned parts of the most famous vineyards in Wiltingen since the early 18th century. The renaissance currently being experienced here is thanks to Roman Niewodniczanski, who took over the operation at the end of 1999. He got off to a good start with his 2000 vintage wines, and the 2001 wines followed on from this. In the last vintage, some of the wines had the structure and richness of more southerly wine-growing regions. The new vintage carries on in the same style. The residual sugar of the 2003 quality wines is an asset. They are dense and rich wines with a spicy character. The sweet Spätlese wines are of a very high standard.

2003 Wiltinger Riesling
11.5%, ♀ till 2008   86

2003 Wiltinger Braunfels Vols
Riesling
12%, ♀ till 2009   87

2003 Wiltinger Kupp Riesling
11.5%, ♀ till 2008   87

2003 Saar Riesling
Riesling Alte Reben
12%, ♀ till 2008   87

2003 Scharzhofberger Riesling
11.5%, ♀ till 2008   88

2002 Wiltinger Gottesfuß
Riesling Alte Reben
12.5%, ♀ till 2008   88

2001 Scharzhofberger
Riesling Eiswein
8.5%, ♀ till 2014   89

2003 Wiltinger Klosterberg Millichberg
Riesling
11.5%, ♀ till 2009   89

2003 Scharzhofberger Pergentsknopp
Riesling
11.5%, ♀ till 2010   89

2003 Scharzhofberger
Riesling Spätlese
9.5%, ♀ till 2012   89

2003 Saar Riesling
Riesling Spätlese Alte Reben
10%, ♀ till 2009   89

2003 Kanzemer Altenberg
Riesling Spätlese
9.5%, ♀ till 2015   90

2003 Wiltinger Gottesfuß
Riesling Alte Reben
11.5%, ♀ till 2010   91

SAAR   ABFÜLLER   VAN VOLXEM ROMAN

Saar Riesling 2003ER

VAN VOLXEM

The estates: ✦✦✦✦✦ World's finest · ✦✦✦✦ Germany's best · ✦✦✦ Very good · ✦✦ Good · ✦ Reliable

WEINGUT
DR. HEINZ WAGNER

Owner: Heinz Wagner
54439 Saarburg, Bahnhofstraße 3
Tel. (0 65 81) 24 57, Fax 60 93
e-mail: drwagner@t-online.de
Directions: Close to railway station in
Saarburg
Sales: Heinz and Ulrike Wagner
by appointment
History: Founded 1880, first wine and
sparkling wine cellar on the Saar
Worth seeing: Largest vaulted cellar in
the Saar region

Vineyard area: 9 hectares
Annual production: 60,000 bottles
Top sites: Saarburger Rausch
and Kupp, Ockfener Bockstein
Soil types: Deep slate
Grape varieties: 100% Riesling
Average yield: 60 hl/ha
Best vintages: 1997, 1999, 2003
Member: VDP

Heinz Wagner owns some excellent parcels of vineyard land in Saarburg and
Ockfen in the Saar region, in the core sections of the steepest vineyards. His dry
Riesling wines show off their unmistakable slate-dominated fresh mineral character, and are remarkable long-lived.
However, his ability really shines through
in the elegantly fruity Spätlese and Auslese wines. Here he can masterfully blend
the crisp acidity of Riesling with juicy,
fruity sweetness. He has done this particularly successfully in the 2003 vintage,
we tasted clean, classical Riesling wines
with clear fruit and good maturation
potential. While the wines were initially
a little undeveloped, they developed on
aeration, and gained in format. A no-frills
style, and a traditional range in the best
possible sense.

2003 Saarburger Kupp
Riesling trocken
12%, ♀ till 2006   **84**

2003 Saarburger Rausch
Riesling Kabinett trocken
11.5%, ♀ till 2006   **85**

2003 Saarburger Kupp
Riesling Spätlese trocken
11.5%, ♀ till 2006   **86**

2003 Saarburger Kupp
Riesling Kabinett halbtrocken
11.4%, ♀ till 2007   **85**

2003 Saarburger Kupp
Riesling Spätlese halbtrocken
12%, ♀ till 2007   **86**

2003 Ockfener Bockstein Riesling
9.5%, ♀ till 2008   **86**

2003 Saarburger Rausch
Riesling Kabinett
10%, ♀ till 2008   **87**

2003 Ockfener Bockstein
Riesling Kabinett
9.5%, ♀ till 2009   **88**

2003 Saarburger Rausch
Riesling Spätlese
9%, ♀ till 2010   **89**

2003 Ockfener Bockstein
Riesling Auslese
8.5%, ♀ till 2011   **90**

2003 Saarburger Rausch
Riesling Auslese
8.5%, ♀ till 2015   **91**

2003 Ockfener Bockstein
Riesling Auslese
➐ auction wine, 8.5%, ♀ till 2015   **92**

MOSEL-SAAR-RUWER   DR. WAGNER
Erzeuger-Abfüllung
Weingut
Dr. Heinz Wagner
gegründet 1880
D-54439 Saarburg
0,75 l
QUALITÄTSWEIN MIT PRÄDIKAT
alc. 8.5%vol.
A. P. Nr. 3 551 073 - 13 00
PRODUCE OF GERMANY
1999er
Ayler Kupp
Riesling Spätlese

The wines: **100** Perfect · **95–99** Outstanding · **90–94** Excellent · **85–89** Very good · **80–84** Good · **75–79** Average

WEINGÜTER WEGELER – GUTSHAUS BERNKASTEL

Owner: Rolf Wegeler family
Administrator: Norbert Breit
54470 Bernkastel-Kues, Martertal 2
Tel. (0 65 31) 24 93, Fax 87 23
e-mail: info@wegeler.com
Directions: From Bernkastel across the Mosel bridge, left at railway station
Sales: Norbert Breit, by appointment
History: First vineyards acquired 1890
Worth seeing: Wine cellar in Doctor vineyard, as well as historic cellar based on gravity-feed principle

---

Vineyard area: 15 hectares
Annual production: 100,000 bottles
Top sites: Bernkasteler Doctor, Wehlener Sonnenuhr
Soil types: Decomposed slate
Grape varieties: 100% Riesling
Average yield: 60 hl/ha
Best vintages: 1999, 2002, 2003
Member: VDP

For many years, this winery concentrated on producing sweet Riesling for the export market. Since the mid-Eighties, the Wegelers have been paying increasing attention to the dry style, which can be rewarded in good years with excellent dry Spätlese wines. In the meantime, the most important category of customers is the German restaurant trade, and almost two-thirds of the wines are fermented dry. In the mid-Nineties, the owners invested a lot of money in a sparkling new cellar filled with stainless-steel tanks, and also took on a highly-motivated new manager in the shape of Norbert Breit. The vineyard area was decreased to 15 hectares. The 1999 vintage marked the high point in the development of quality. Looking to the 2002 range, this consisted of some rather weak dry wines on the one hand, and some elegant fruity botrytis Rieslings one the other. In the 2003 vintage, the sweet wines still outshine their predecessors. Elegant, well integrated botrytis notes characterize the style of the wines.

2003 Wehlener Sonnenuhr
Riesling Spätlese trocken
12%, ♀ till 2006   84

2003 Bernkasteler Doctor
Riesling trocken
12.5%, ♀ till 2007   88

2003 Wehlener Sonnenuhr
Riesling Spätlese
8%, ♀ till 2009   87

2002 Bernkasteler Doctor
Riesling Spätlese
8%, ♀ till 2009   89

2003 Bernkasteler Doctor
Riesling Spätlese
8%, ♀ till 2010   89

2003 Wehlener Sonnenuhr
Riesling Auslese Goldkapsel
⟶ auction wine, 8%, ♀ till 2009   89

2003 Bernkasteler Doctor
Riesling Spätlese – 22 –
⟶ auction wine, 8%, ♀ till 2010   90

2003 Bernkasteler Doctor
Riesling Auslese
8%, ♀ till 2010   91

2003 Wehlener Sonnenuhr
Riesling Beerenauslese
7%, ♀ till 2015   92

2002 Bernkasteler Doctor
Riesling Eiswein
7%, ♀ till 2015   93

2003 Bernkasteler Doctor
Riesling Beerenauslese
7%, ♀ till 2015   95

2003 Bernkasteler Doctor
Riesling Trockenbeerenauslese
6%, ♀ till 2020   96

WEINGÜTER
WEGELER

2002
Bernkasteler
Doctor
Riesling Spätlese

The estates: ♣♣♣♣♣ World's finest · ♣♣♣♣ Germany's best · ♣♣♣ Very good · ♣♣ Good · ♣ Reliable

WEINGUT DR. F. WEINS-PRÜM

Owner: Bert Selbach
Manager and winemaker:
Bert Selbach
54470 Bernkastel-Wehlen,
Uferallee 20
Tel. (0 65 31) 22 70, Fax 31 81
Directions: From Bernkastel drive along
the left bank of the Mosel, in the center
of Wehlen turn right in direction of
Uferallee (avenue of river bank)
Sales: By appointment
Worth seeing: Old cross-vaulted cellar

Vineyard area: 4 hectares
Annual production: 32,000 bottles
Top sites: Wehlener Sonnenuhr,
Ürziger Würzgarten, Erdener Prälat,
Graacher Himmelreich and
Domprobst
Soil types: Slate
Grape varieties: 100% Riesling
Average yield: 63 hl/ha
Best vintages: 2001, 2002, 2003
Member: VDP

This winery is currently run by Bert Selbach, in buildings erected here in 1924 by Dr. Weins-Prüm. Selbach owns good vineyard parcels in Erden, Ürzig, Wehlen and Graach, as well as one hectare in Waldrach on the Ruwer. His current success is based mainly on his dry wines, which make up almost 90 percent of the production. The problems associated with the 2000 vintage were quite evident here, particularly in the basic wines. By contrast, the 2001 wines from Kabinett upward showed good quality. The 2002 Riesling wines gave Selbach an opportunity to shine in his role of fruity wine specialist. At the top of the range, the 2003 wines could not quite equal the high standard of the 2002 Eiswein, simply because the conditions for producing this level of quality were not ideal. We can quite happily sit back with a Prälat Auslese, which has pure soft and intense grapefruit aromas, and wait for next year.

2003 Wehlener Sonnenuhr
Riesling Kabinett
8%, ♀ till 2009   **86**

2003 Graacher Himmelreich
Riesling Spätlese
7.5%, ♀ till 2009   **87**

2003 Wehlener Sonnenuhr
Riesling Spätlese
8%, ♀ till 2009   **88**

2003 Erdener Prälat
Riesling Spätlese
7.5%, ♀ till 2009   **88**

2003 Wehlener Sonnenuhr
Riesling Auslese
7.5%, ♀ till 2010   **88**

2001 Erdener Prälat
Riesling Spätlese
7.5%, ♀ till 2010   **89**

2002 Erdener Prälat
Riesling Spätlese
7.5%, ♀ till 2009   **89**

2001 Wehlener Sonnenuhr
Riesling Auslese lange Goldkapsel
8%, ♀ till 2010   **89**

2003 Wehlener Sonnenuhr
Riesling Auslese Goldkapsel
8.5%, ♀ till 2012   **90**

2002 Graacher Himmelreich
Riesling Eiswein
7.5%, ♀ till 2012   **92**

2003 Erdener Prälat
Riesling Auslese
8%, ♀ till 2012   **92**

2002 Wehlener Sonnenuhr
Riesling Eiswein
6.5%, ♀ till 2015   **94**

The wines: **100** Perfect · **95–99** Outstanding · **90–94** Excellent · **85–89** Very good · **80–84** Good · **75–79** Average

WEINGUT
WELLER-LEHNERT

Owner: Jörg and Petra Matheus
Winemaker: Jörg Matheus
54498 Piesport,
St.-Michael-Straße 27–29
Tel. (0 65 07) 24 98, Fax 67 66
e-mail: info@weller-lehnert.de
Internet: www.weller-lehnert.de
Directions: A 48, Koblenz–Trier, Salmtal exit, down into Mosel valley
Sales: By appointment
History: Winemaking in the family since eight generations

Vineyard area: 8 hectares
Annual production: 40,000 bottles
Top sites: Piesporter Goldtröpfchen,
Domherr and Treppchen,
Dhron Hofberger
Soil types: Decomposed slate
Grape varieties: 80% Riesling,
6% each of Weißburgunder and Spätburgunder, 4% Dornfelder, 2% each
of Cabernet Sauvignon and Rivaner
Average yield: 62 hl/ha
Best vintages: 2001, 2002, 2003
Member: Bernkasteler Ring

Together with her husband Jörg, Petra Matheus has built new winery facilities, guest rooms as well as a distillery. Following on appropriate investments in the cellar, the 2002 vintage saw a shift to whole-bunch pressing, partial de-stemming and long periods on the lees. The vineyard yields have been kept relatively low here for many years. The 2000 vintage range showed reliable good quality, and the 2001 wines were of approximately the same standard. The 2002 range saw an improved quality, particularly among the botrytis wines. The result of our tasting this year is a homogeneous range of good two-bunch standard. We like the slightly baroque style of the vintage, which here receives a very honest interpretation. Our favorite is the three-star Goldtröpfchen Auslese, with the aroma of ripe yellow fruits.

2003 Piesporter Domherr
Riesling Spätlese trocken
12.5%, ♀ till 2006   85

2003 Piesporter Goldtröpfchen
Riesling Kabinett
9%, ♀ till 2008   85

2001 Piesporter Goldtröpfchen
Riesling Spätlese
9%, ♀ till 2008   86

2003 Piesporter Goldtröpfchen
Riesling Spätlese – 24 –
9.5%, ♀ till 2009   87

2003 Piesporter Goldtröpfchen
Riesling Spätlese – 23 –
9.5%, ♀ till 2009   88

2003 Piesporter Goldtröpfchen
Riesling Auslese **
9%, ♀ till 2010   88

2001 Piesporter Treppchen
Riesling Eiswein – 1 –
6.5%, ♀ till 2015   89

2002 Piesporter Goldtröpfchen
Riesling Auslese ***
8.5%, ♀ till 2011   90

2002 Piesporter Treppchen
Riesling Eiswein – 12 –
9%, ♀ till 2012   90

2003 Piesporter Goldtröpfchen
Riesling Auslese ***
9%, ♀ till 2012   90

2002 Piesporter Treppchen
Riesling Eiswein – 13 –
9%, ♀ till 2014   91

WELLER-LEHNERT

2000
PIESPORTER GOLDTRÖPFCHEN
RIESLING - AUSLESE
* * *

WEINGUT FORSTMEISTER GELTZ – ZILLIKEN

Owner: Hans-Joachim Zilliken
Winemaker: Hans-Joachim Zilliken
54439 Saarburg, Heckingstraße 20
Tel. (0 65 81) 24 56, Fax 67 63
e-mail: info@zilliken-vdp.de
Internet: www.zilliken-vdp.de
Directions: B 51 resp. B 407 in direction of hospital, across the Laurentius bridge, first turn right after the tunnel, in direction of town center, 4th house on the right
Sales: By appointment
History: Ferdinand Geltz was chief forester to the Prussian royal family
Worth seeing: Deep vaulted cellars

Vineyard area: 10.5 hectares
Annual production: 60,000 bottles
Top sites: Saarburger Rausch, Ockfener Bockstein
Soil types: Devon slate and diabase
Grape varieties: 100% Riesling
Average yield: 50 hl/ha
Best vintages: 1997, 2002, 2003
Member: VDP

Without a doubt, the whole decade of the Nineties was a single success story for Hans-Joachim Zilliken. One good vintage just kept on following another. Zilliken has firmly established himself as one of the very best producers on the Saar. The fruity sweet predicate wines make up about 75 percent of the total production, and have always been the highlights of this winery. However, both 2000 and 2001 were not all that spectacular here. Then the 2002 vintage saw an improved quality right across the range. Now, in 2003, Zilliken has pulled all the stops, and well deserves to be awarded his third bunch of grapes. The crowning glory is a Trockenbeerenauslese that is almost without equal, setting a standard that combines power with elegance. Zilliken: "I have never seen anything like this produced in the Rausch vineyard." Our congratulations!

2003 Saarburger Rausch
Riesling Spätlese trocken
12.5%, ♀ till 2006 — **86**

2003 Saarburger Rausch
Riesling Kabinett
9%, ♀ till 2008 — **87**

2003 Ockfener Bockstein
Riesling Spätlese
8.5%, ♀ till 2009 — **89**

2003 Saarburger Rausch
Riesling Spätlese
8.5%, ♀ till 2009 — **89**

2003 Saarburger Rausch
Riesling Auslese
8.5%, ♀ till 2011 — **90**

2003 Saarburger Rausch
Riesling Spätlese
↗ auction wine, 8.5%, ♀ till 2010 — **90**

2002 Saarburger Rausch
Riesling Eiswein
↗ auction wine, 8%, ♀ till 2014 — **91**

2003 Saarburger Rausch
Riesling Auslese
↗ auction wine, 8%, ♀ till 2012 — **91**

2003 Saarburger Rausch
Riesling Auslese Goldkapsel
8%, ♀ till 2012 — **92**

2003 Saarburger Rausch
Riesling Auslese lange Goldkapsel
↗ auction wine, 8%, ♀ till 2015 — **94**

2003 Saarburger Rausch
Riesling Beerenauslese – 2 –
↗ auction wine, 8%, ♀ till 2020 — **95**

2003 Saarburger Rausch
Riesling Trockenbeerenauslese
↗ auction wine, 7.5%, ♀ till 2025 — **97**

The wines: **100** Perfect · **95–99** Outstanding · **90–94** Excellent · **85–89** Very good · **80–84** Good · **75–79** Average

Mosel-Saar-Ruwer

Weingut Becker-Steinhauer

54486 Mülheim, Hauptstraße 72
Tel. (0 65 34) 5 21, Fax 1 83 78

We can see a definite positive trend in the wines of the 2003 vintage presented by the Becker family. The dry wines are clean and clear, the elegantly fruity wines are concentrated and have substance. This appears to have been a vintage that was to the taste of the Beckers. If this trend continues next year, we will be happy to award that first bunch of grapes.

Weingut Josef Bernard-Kieren

54470 Graach, Hauptstraße 101
Tel. (0 65 31) 21 83, Fax 20 90

The Bernard-Kieren winery is on the right path. The current owner represents the 4th generation of the family. The best wines are sourced from the Graacher Himmelreich and Domprobst vineyards. The State honors prize was awarded to the winery in 2002, and we are confident that we will also soon be in a position to make complimentary remarks about the winery.

Weingut Klaus Berweiler-Merges und Sandra Berweiler

54340 Leiwen, Euchariusstraße 35
Tel. (0 65 07) 32 85, Fax 8 01 75

It seems the 2003 vintage was very much to Sandra Berweiler's liking. In particular the spontaneously fermented wines deserve special attention this year, and these are the forte of Sandra Berweiler. We particularly liked the Leiwener Klostergarten Auslese. More of the same, please!

Weingut Frank Brohl

56862 Pünderich, Zum Rosenberg 2
Tel. (0 65 42) 2 21 48, Fax 12 95

Frank Brohl is big on quality as well as on environmental concerns and organic farming. Overall, the 2003 vintage wines are well made, with the fruity-sweet and botrytis dessert wines clearly being the strong suit here. A Trockenbeerenauslese was bottled for the first time ever, and is rated at a respectable 85 points.

Weingut Deutschherren-Hof

54295 Trier, Olewiger Straße 181
Tel. (06 51) 3 11 13, Fax 3 04 63
e-mail: info@weingut-deutschherrenhof.de
Internet: www.weingut-deutschherrenhof.de

We are still convinced that the winery run by Marianne and Albert Oberbillig in Trier has the potential to be awarded a bunch of grapes eventually. The 2003 vintage wines were quite decent across the board, although the dry wines were again rather weak. The best of the range is a Trierer Jesuitenwingert Auslese. A restaurant is also available at the estate.

Stiftung Friedrich-Wilhelm-Gymnasium

54290 Trier, Weberbach 75
Tel. (06 51) 97 83 00, Fax 4 54 80
e-mail: trierwg@aol.com
Internet: www.fwg-weingut-trier.com/fwg.htm und www.fwgtrier.de

A Jesuit college was founded here in 1561, leading to the "Friedrich-Wilhelm-Gymnasium" high school as well as the "Stiftung Friedrich-Wilhelm-Gymnasium," the winery managed by a foundation, which exist today. Although this traditional winery owns some excellent vineyard parcels, they have not yet made it back into the grape-bunch ratings. Looking at the 2003 range, we were impressed by the Graacher Domprobst Auslese (87 points).

Weingut Albert Gessinger

54492 Zeltingen-Rachtig, Moselstraße 9
Tel. (0 65 32) 23 69, Fax 15 78

We liked the 2002 range of wines here so much, it would have given us great pleasure to award Albert Gessinger his first bunch of grapes. Unfortunately, the 2003 wines do not show any improvement, both the dry and off-dry wines are simply too weak. However, we continue to believe in the potential of this winery.

Klostergut Himmeroder Hof

54518 Kesten, Am Herrenberg 1
Tel. (0 65 35) 71 43, Fax 15 21

The Himmeroder Hof winery run by Rainer Licht is located in Kesten. This year,

Mosel-Saar-Ruwer

it is again the dry wines that are particularly good. The range is headed up by a dry Brauneberger Juffer Auslese (85 points). The Kerner Auslese, too, is very interesting.

Weingut Hoffmann-Simon

54498 Piesport, Kettergasse 24
Tel. (0 65 07) 50 25 and 50 26,
Fax 99 22 27
e-mail: weingut@hoffmann-simon.de
Internet: www.hoffmann-simon.de

The strong suit of this winery, which has around ten hectares of vineyard in Piesport, is once again the range of elegantly fruity wines. The transition from the good 2002 vintage to 2003 is seamless. This year, we also found the dry wines to be improved. We like the dry Klüsserather Bruderschaft Spätlese (84 points).

Weingut Klaus Junk

54340 Leiwen, Euchariusstraße 23
Tel. (0 65 07) 43 49, Fax 48 83

Though the winery, which is located in Leiwen, has only 6.5 hectares of vineyard, these are spread around ten different communes on the Mosel and Ruwer rivers. Claus Junk jr. studied red wine production under Wolfgang Hehle, on the Ahr, as well as in Burgundy. However, he did not present any of his reds to us this year, so we are looking forward with anticipation to the 2003 vintage due out next year. The wine we liked best was a Laurentiuslay Spätlese "Alte Reben" (old vines) rated at 86 points.

Weingut Albert Kallfelz

56856 Zell-Merl, Hauptstraße 60–62
Tel. (0 65 42) 9 38 80, Fax 93 88 50
e-mail: info@kallfelz.de
Internet: www.kallfelz.de

This formerly family-owned winery has now broken through the "sound barrier" by exceeding 40 hectares of vineyard, making it one of the biggest wineries in the Mosel-Saar-Ruwer region. Large quantities of dry and off-dry wines are produced and bottled here, however the quality in recent vintages has not been up to the standard of earlier years.

Weingut Köwerich

54340 Leiwen, Reichgasse 7
Tel. (0 65 07) 42 82, Fax 30 37
e-mail: weingut.koewerich@t-online.de

Last year, we criticized the lack of freshness in the basic wines of the Köwerich winery, hoping this would be remedied in the next vintage. Unfortunately, the 2003 vintage is not really predestined for this, and the dry wines again lack freshness and elegance. The fruity wines are different and are, as last year, headed towards being awarded a bunch of grapes.

Stiftungsweingüter Langguth Erben

56841 Traben-Trarbach,
Rißbacherstraße 31
Tel. (0 65 41) 1 72 43, Fax 22 95

This traditional winery in Traben-Trarbach has a history going back more than 200 years, with vineyard holdings in such famous sites as the Piesporter Goldtröpfchen or the Wehlener Sonnenuhr. The 2003 range is well made across the board, we particularly liked the Piesporter Goldtröpfchen Auslese.

Weingut Lenz-Dahm

56862 Pünderich, Hauptstraße 3
Tel. (0 65 42) 2 29 50, Fax 2 14 87
e-mail: lenz-dahm@lenz-dahm.de
Internet: www.lenz-dahm.de

Heinrich Lenz-Dahm was already busy building a reputation mainly based on dry Riesling in the Seventies, at a time when the Mosel was awash with sweet wines made from new grape varieties and "improved" with sugar concentrate. The current owners feel obliged to continue this tradition. The 2003 wines are sadly lacking in elegance. The three-star Pündericher Marienburg Auslese (86 points) is the only wine of the vintage to show at least some of the potential available from this site.

Weingut Gunther Matheus

54498 Piesport, Auf der Kaub 34
Tel. (0 65 07) 51 38, Fax 99 22 28
e-mail: weingut-matheus@t-online.de

The quality base for this Piesport winery can be found in vineyard holdings in re-

nowned sites such as the Dhron Hofberger, Wintricher Ohligsberg and Piesporter Goldtröpfchen. In the 2003 vintage, we particularly liked the minerally, racy style of the Goldtröpfchen Auslese. Given a little more finesse, this winery could be heading toward a higher rating.

Weingut Rebenhof – Johannes Schmitz

54539 Ürzig, Hüwel 2–3
Tel. (0 65 32) 45 46, Fax 15 65
e-mail: genuesse@rebenhof.de
Internet: www.rebenhof.de

This year, Johannes Schmitz has presented a really attractive range. Gone are the rather rustic dry wines we tasted here only last year, from the 2002 vintage. All of the wines we tasted were sourced from the Ürziger Würzgarten site, and we particularly liked the Auslese No. 12.

Weingut Edmund Reverchon

54329 Konz-Filzen, Saartalstraße 2–3
Tel. (0 65 01) 92 35 00, Fax 92 35 09
e-mail: edmund.reverchon@t-online.de
Internet: www.weingut-reverchon.de

Although we would dearly like to see the Reverchon winery regain its bunch of grapes rating, the 2003 vintage range showed that we were justified in downgrading the winery two years ago. Looking at the 2003 vintage, only the botrytis dessert wines were attractive, while the dry wines lacked elegance and structure.

Weingut Freiherr von Schleinitz

56330 Kobern-Gondorf, Kirchstraße 17
Tel. (0 26 07) 97 20 20, Fax 97 20 22
e-mail: weingut@vonschleinitz.de
Internet: www.vonschleinitz.de

Konrad Hähn has thrown out the traditional oak vats, and opted for stainless steel and synthetic tanks instead. The winemaker hopes to retain freshness and fruit by bottling his wines early. Unfortunately, we did not find much of this in the 2003 wines. The dry wines lack elegance, and even the sweet Koberner Weißenberg Spätlese did not manage to rise above 80 points. We were not able to taste any Auslese or Beerenauslese wines this year.

Weingut Schmitt Erben

54349 Trittenheim, Moselweinstraße 43
Tel. (0 65 07) 70 17 36, Fax 70 17 38
e-mail: info@weingut-schmitt-erben.de

Niko Schmitt completed his training as a technician in Weinsberg, which included practical work at the Dr. Crusius winery, before taking over his parents' operation, which has 2.2 hectares of vineyard, all in the Trittenheimer Altärchen and Apotheke sites. Schmitt presented a small range of well-made wines from the 2003 vintage, headed up by a mouth-filling, rounded Apotheke Spätlese (85 points).

Weingut Gebrüder Simon

54492 Lösnich, Hauptstraße 6
Tel. (0 65 32) 21 30, Fax 9 43 69
e-mail: weingut@gebrueder-simon.de

The vineyard parcels from which Ingo Simon sources his grapes are mainly in the well-known steep Erdener Treppchen, Lösnicher Försterlay and Kinheimer Rosenberg sites. Unfortunately, the 2003 wines he has produced are lacking a little in acidity, so that they all appear a bit plump and tired. As in the previous vintage, our favorite wine was the Eiswein.

Weingut St. Nikolaus-Hof

54340 Leiwen, Mühlenstraße 44
Tel. (0 65 07) 81 07, Fax 80 28 21

Last year, we stated that Klaus Schweicher was headed in the right direction. We like the elegant fruity wines he produced in 2003, even the dry wines were of decent quality. We particularly like the Leiwener Klostergarten Hochgewächs.

Weingut Ludwig Thanisch und Sohn

54470 Lieser, Moselstraße 56
Tel. (0 65 31) 82 27, Fax 82 94
e-mail: info@thanisch.de

This family winery is located on the Mosel promenade, surrounded by steep vineyards. As in the 2002 vintage, we were again particularly attracted to the sweet wines, such as the Lieser Niederberg Helden Auslese (85 points). Also, just as last year, the dry wines lacked body and power.

Weingut Karl und Maria Willems

54329 Konz, Mühlenstraße 13
Tel. (0 65 01) 1 58 16, Fax 15 03 87

Maria and Karl Willems appear to be open for new ideas. Certainly, the second vintage of the wine called "Fusion II" is an attractive wine. Here, daughter Carolin has taken an unusual direction, and together with Jürgen Hofmann from Appenheim (Rheinhessen) has produced a "Rhein-Mosel wine." A new and interesting product!

Other wineries tasted

- Altenhofen, Ayl
- Weingut Bauer, Mülheim
- Werner Clemens, Ellenz-Poltersdorf
- Clüsserath-Hilt, Trittenheim
- Cusanus Hofgut, Bernkastel
- Markus Fries, Maring-Noviand
- Theo Grumbach, Lieser
- Hobe-Gelting, Schloss Thorn
- Hubertushof, Lieser
- Kanzlerhof, Pölich
- Klaus Lotz, Erden
- Hermann Ludes, Thörnich
- Gebr. Ludwig, Thörnich
- Peter Mertes, Kanzem
- Kirchengut Wolf, Traben-Trarbach

Recommended by our wine producers

Hotels and inns

Ayl: Ayler Kupp
Bernkastel-Kues: Bären, Doctor-Weinstuben, Post
Dieblich: Pistono
Dreis: Waldhotel Sonnora
Kobern-Gondorf: Höreth, Simonis
Konz: Römerstuben
Leiwen: Zummethof
Mertesdorf: Karlsmühle, Weis
Mülheim: Richtershof
Naurath: St. Urban

Neumagen-Dhron: Anker, Kesselstatt
Ochtendung: Gutshof Arosa
Piesport: Winzerhof
Saarburg: Saarburger Hof, Villa Keller
Sitzerath: Landgasthof Paulus
Traben-Trarbach: Bellevue, Moselschlösschen
Trier: Villa Hügel, Eurener Hof, Römischer Kaiser
Trittenheim: Krone Riesling
Wehlen: Gästehaus S.A. Prüm
Zeltingen: Nicolay, St. Stephanus

Gourmet restaurants

Dreis: Waldhotel Sonnora
Naurath: Landhaus St. Urban
Perl-Nennig: Schloss Berg
Trier: Weinhaus Becker

Restaurants, wine bars and winery facilities

Alken: Burg Thurant
Ayl: Weinhaus Ayler Kupp
Bernkastel: Doctor-Weinstuben, Ratskeller
Bescheid: Malerklause
Brauneberg: Brauneberger Hof
Daufenbach: Mühlenberg
Dieblich: Halferschenke
Kobern-Gondorf: Alte Mühle Höreth
Mertesdorf: Weis
Saarburg: Saarburger Hof, Villa Keller, Weinschmecker
Serrig: Wagner
Traben-Trarbach: Alte Zunftscheune
Trier: Bagatelle, Palais Kesselstatt, Schlemmereule, Schloss Monaise
Trittenheim: Wein- und Tafelhaus, Stefan-Andres, Galerie Riesling
Ürzig: Moselschild
Winningen: Höreth-Schaaf
Zell: Gutsschänke Till
Zeltingen: Weinstein im St. Stephanus

First Growth comes to the Nahe

There is cause to celebrate in the Nahe region: at last the "Grosse Gewächs" (First Growth) has arrived. A more suitable vintage could not have been chosen for this purpose. Four of the leading producers – Crusius, Diel, Dönnhoff and Prinz zu Salm-Dalberg – have all produced the best dry Riesling wines in a long time.

It really was a magnificent vintage on the Nahe, particularly the Spätlese and Beerenauslese wines were exciting. Many producers have called it their vintage of a lifetime. Where after the hot summer many had expected problems with acidity or high alcohols, these were only experienced in a few cases. Where acidity was added, this was in most cases already added to the must in moderate quantities.

It was not a good year for Eiswein. This rare specialty has become something of a feature of the Nahe region in recent years. But the top producers do not go out of their way to force the production of Eiswein at any cost. Harald Hexamer, a specialist for this rarity, has a wine in his cellar that he would be able to sell as Eiswein, but which does not come up to his own high standards, and will thus not be sold as such. Werner Schönleber, too, who last year achieved a perfect score of 100 points with an Eiswein gold capsule, this year presented a Trockenbeerenauslese as the flagship of his range. This producer in Monzingen has been ahead of the competition for three years, but this year Helmut Dönnhoff has presented the best range of wines, by the closest possible margin (bearing in mind that wines from the Diel estate are not rated). In particular, Dönnhoffs virtual parade of Spätlese wines is fascinating. It comes as no surprise to here that this top winery constantly displays the "Sold out" sign. Helmut Dönnhoff is not the man to brag about his achievements, but if you speak to him you can sense that he thinks the 2003 vintage is one of the best he has ever produced.

Apart from the ranges presented by the five-bunch producers, that presented by

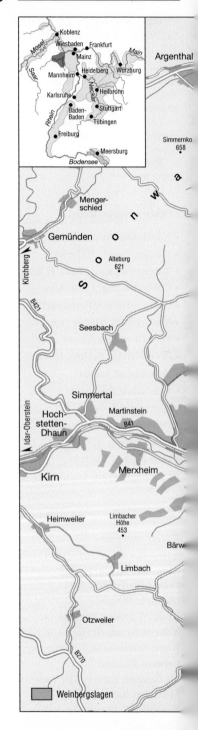

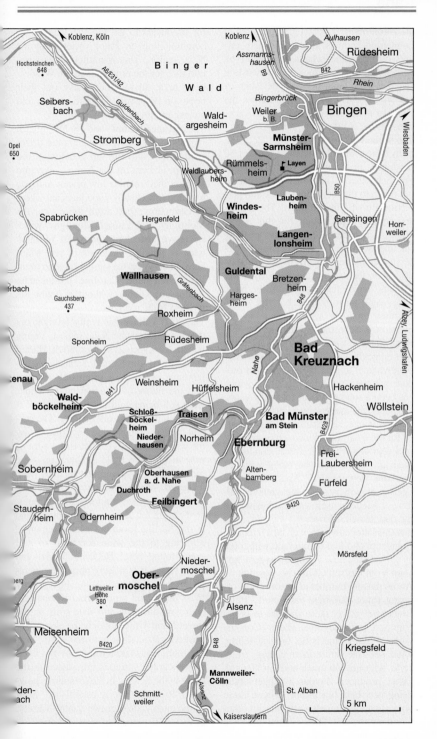

Koblenz, Köln

Koblenz

Assmanns-
hausen

Aulhausen

Rüdesheim

Hochsteinchen
648

A6/E31/42

B i n g e r

W a l d

B9

B42

Rhein

Seibers-
bach

Guldenbach

Waldal-
gesheim

Bingerbrück

Weiler
b. B.

Bingen

Opel
650

Stromberg

Münster-
Sarmsheim

Wiesbaden

Waldlaubers-
heim

Rümmels-
heim

Layen

B50

Spabrücken

Hergenfeld

Windes-
heim

Lauben-
heim

Gensingen

Horr-
weiler

Langen-
lonsheim

Wallhausen

Gräfenbach

Guldental

Bretzen-
heim

B48

rbach

Gauchsberg
437

Roxheim

Harges-
heim

Sponheim

Rüdesheim

Nahe

Bad
Kreuznach

Alzey, Ludwigshafen

enau

Weinsheim

B41

Hüffelsheim

Hackenheim

Wald-
böckelheim

Schloß-
böckel-
heim

Traisen

Bad Münster
am Stein

Wöllstein

Nieder-
hausen

Norheim

Ebernburg

B428

Sobernheim

Oberhausen
a. d. Nahe

Alten-
bamberg

Frei-
Laubersheim

Staudern-
heim

Duchroth

Feilbingert

Fürfeld

Odernheim

B420

Nieder-
moschel

Mörsfeld

berg

Ober-
moschel

Lettweiler
Höhe
380

Alsenz

Meisenheim

B420

B48

Kriegsfeld

den-
ach

Schmitt-
weiler

Mannweiler-
Cölln

Alsenz

St. Alban

5 km

Kaiserslautern

the Bürgermeister Schweinhardt estate in Langenlonsheim is also particularly impressive. No matter whether it is a botrytis dessert wine – the Trockenbeerenauslese Goldkapsel is fantastic –, dry Riesling or red wines, every single wine across the board from this respectably-sized (33 hectares) estate is fully convincing.

The second producer to be upgraded, and even to rise into the ranks of the top 50 producers in Germany, is the Schäfer-Fröhlich winery. This development can be put down to the meticulous work and perfectionism of Tim Fröhlich. The results are never good enough for this active young winemaker, he is always pushing for improvements. Two other ranges deserve special mention. We were enthusiastic about the wines presented by Peter Crusius, across the board from the basic wines right up to the top botrytis wines. Another producer worthy of a special mention is Sebastian Schäfer of the Joh. Bapt. Schäfer winery, who presented the best range this producer has ever shown.

A newcomer among the bunch-rated producers is the Carl Adelseck estate, which has been a solid producer for many years. This year, the range showed just that extra touch of quality and character that is required for the awarding of a bunch of grapes.

In a year of such good overall conditions there are unlikely to be many wineries that are downgraded. Apart from the Lötzbeyer winery only the Gutsverwaltung at Niederhausen were each demoted by one bunch. However, we anticipate that this latter case may well be a temporary hiccup, and that an upgrade will come as soon as the new young manager Christian Vogt has settled into his position.

An increasing number of producers is offering Pinot varieties, particularly Pinot Blanc, but as yet there appears to be no common regional style. Peter Crusius, whose Pinot Blanc is his biggest-selling wine, sees the future in an elegant fruity style, with not too much body or alcohol. Other producers favour a bigger style, using new oak, but in our opinion these wines cannot compete with those of other Germany regions. There is a definite need for producers to get together and find a common line on Pinot varieties in the Nahe region. This is particularly of importance for the producers in the Windesheim area, all of whom have put their hopes on Pinot varieties, and need to find a clear and recognisable profile.

The Kruger-Rumpf and Schweinhardt wineries have this year catapulted themselves right into the top echelon of red wine producers on the Nahe. Take into account their relative low prices, and you will find few equally good buys anywhere in Germany. Apart from these two, the Montigny and Emrich-Montigny wineries have also done their best to show what is possible in terms of red wines here. In addition we simply have to mention the red blend "Caroline" produced by Schlossgut Diel – without a doubt the greatest Nahe red wine.

The 2003 vintage has really brought out the dynamics of the Nahe region. Young winemakers such as Tim Fröhlich, Harald Hexamer, Martin Korrell, Sebastian Schäfer have given us a promising glimpse into the future of a region whose wines were still being sold as "Rhine wines" at the beginning of the last century. The current borders of the region were only set by the wine law of 1971. That is not a lot of time in which to build a reputation – the more cause to applaud that this has been achieved. Many promotional brochures on German wine for a long time perpetuated a common error, describing the Nahe as the "tasting room of German regions," referring to the wide spectrum of soil types found here: Between Monzingen and Traisen it is mainly porphyry, melaphyry and layered sandstone, then mainly loess and claim around Bad Kreuznach, and clay, quartzite and slate soils on the lower Nahe. Unfortunately the essentially positive association with the term "tasting room" was taken too far by the flood of new grape varieties introduced to the Nahe in the Sixties. In the meantime, however, Riesling has re-established itself as the most widely grown quality variety, covering 25 percent of vineyard area.

**The leading producers
in the Nahe region**

**Weingut Hermann Dönnhoff,
Oberhausen**

**Weingut Emrich-Schönleber,
Monzingen**

**Weingut Schäfer-Fröhlich,
Bockenau**

Weingut Dr. Crusius, Traisen

**Weingut Göttelmann,
Münster-Sarmsheim**

Weingut Hexamer, Meddersheim

**Weingut Korrell – Johanneshof,
Bad Kreuznach-Bosenheim**

**Weingut Kruger-Rumpf,
Münster-Sarmsheim**

**Weingut Prinz zu Salm-Dalberg –
Schloss Wallhausen, Wallhausen**

**Weingut Bürgermeister
Willi Schweinhardt Nachf.,
Langenlonsheim**

Weingut Tesch, Langenlonsheim

**Wein- und Sektgut
Karl-Kurt Bamberger
& Sohn, Meddersheim**

**Weingut Hahnmühle,
Mannweiler-Cölln**

**Weingut Lindenhof –
Martin Reimann, Windesheim**

Weingut Mathern, Niederhausen

Weingut Montigny, Laubenheim

**Gutsverwaltung Niederhausen-
Schlossböckelheim, Niederhausen**

**Weingut Joh. Bapt. Schäfer,
Burg Layen**

**Weingut Jakob Schneider,
Niederhausen**

**Staatsweingut Bad Kreuznach,
Bad Kreuznach**

**Weingut Carl Adelseck,
Münster-Sarmsheim**

**Weingut Edelberg,
Weiler bei Monzingen**

**Weingut Emrich-Montigny,
Bad Kreuznach-Planig**

**Weingut Anton Finkenauer,
Bad Kreuznach**

**Weingut Gebrüder Kauer,
Windesheim**

**Weingut Klostermühle,
Odernheim**

Weingut Lötzbeyer, Feilbingert

**Weingut Rapp,
Bad Münster am Stein-Ebernburg**

**Weingut Michael Rohr,
Raumbach**

**Weingut Erich Schauß & Sohn,
Monzingen**

Weingut Schmidt, Obermoschel

**Weingut Meinolf Schömehl,
Dorsheim**

**Weingut Wilhelm Sitzius,
Langenlonsheim**

Note:

The Schlossgut Diel estate, Burg Layen,
is not rated, as Armin Diel, the owner, is
editor in chief of the Gault Millau Wine-
Guide.

Nahe

Altenbamberg: Rotenberg
Bockenau: Felseneck
Dorsheim: Burgberg, Goldloch, Pittermännchen
Langenlonsheim: Königsschild, Löhrer Berg, Rothenberg
Laubenheim: Karthäuser, Krone, St. Remigiusberg
Monzingen: Frühlingsplätzchen, Halenberg
Münster-Sarmsheim: Dautenpflänzer, Kapellenberg, Pittersberg, Rheinberg
Niederhausen: Felsensteyer, Hermannsberg, Hermannshöhle, Kertz, Steinberg
Norheim: Dellchen, Kirschheck
Oberhausen: Brücke, Leistenberg
Roxheim: Berg
Schloßböckelheim: Felsenberg, Kupfergrube
Traisen: Bastei, Rotenfels
Wallhausen: Felseneck, Johannisberg

* Source: VDP Nahe-Ahr

Major and minor vintages in the Nahe region

Vintage	Rating
2003	♛♛♛♛
2002	♛♛♛♛
2001	♛♛♛♛
2000	♛♛♛
1999	♛♛♛
1998	♛♛♛♛
1997	♛♛♛
1996	♛♛♛♛
1995	♛♛♛♛
1994	♛♛♛♛

Vintage rating:

♛♛♛♛♛ : Excellent vintage

♛♛♛♛ : Very good vintage

♛♛♛ : Good vintage

♛♛ : Average vintage

♛ : Poor vintage

Recommended by our wine producers

Hotels and inns

Guldental: Kaiserhof
Kirn: Parkhotel
Bad Kreuznach: Inselhotel, Mühlentor
Bad Kreuznach-Bosenheim: Alter Bauernhof
Langenlonsheim: Kleines Landhaus
Meisenheim: Hotel am Markt
Bad Münster-Ebernburg: Rapp
Münster-Sarmsheim: Münsterer Hof, Trollmühle
Niederhausen: Gästehaus Maurer
Obermoschel: Schlosshotel
Schloßböckelheim: Niederthäler Hof
Simmertal: Felsengarten
Bad Sobernheim: Bollants im Park, Maasberg Therme
Stromberg: Lafers Stromburg, Land- und Golfhotel

Gourmet restaurants

Hackenheim: Metzlers Gasthof
Bad Kreuznach: Im Gütchen
Stromberg: Lafers Le Val d'Or

Restaurants, wine bars and winery facilities

Altenbamberg: Altenbaumburg
Guldental: Kaiserhof
Hackenheim: Metzlers Weinstube
Bad Kreuznach: Dienheimer Hof, Weinstube im Brückenhaus
Bad Kreuznach-Bosenheim: Johanneshof
Meddersheim: Lohmühle, Zur Traube
Münster-Sarmsheim: Göttelmann, Kruger-Rumpf
Bad Sobernheim: Hist. Hermannshof
Staudernheim: Bacchusstuben
Stromberg: Alte Gerberei, Lafers Turmstube

WEINGUT CARL ADELSECK

Owner: Carl-Günther and Jens Adelseck
Manager: Carl-Günther Adelseck
Winemaker: Jens Adelseck
55424 Münster-Sarmsheim, Saarstr. 41
Tel. (0 67 21) 9 74 40, Fax 97 44 22
e-mail: info@adelseck.de
Internet: www.adelseck.de
Directions: A 61, Dorsheim exit,
B 48 in direction of Bingen
Sales: Dagmar Adelseck
by appointment
History: Family winemaking tradition
goes back to the 11th century
Worth seeing: 17th-century vaulted cellar

Vineyard area: 10 hectares
Annual production: 95,000 bottles
Top sites: Münsterer Dauten-
pflänzer and Pittersberg, Lauben-
heimer Karthäuser and Fuchsen
Soil types: Slate, porphyry, loess-clay
Grape varieties: 45% Riesling, 16%
Spätburgunder, 8% Dornfelder,
7% each of Scheurebe and Portugie-
ser, 17% other varieties
Average yield: 74 hl/ha
Best vintages: 2002, 2003

We have been keeping an eye on the Carl
Adelseck winery for a number of years,
as the quality improved from year to year.
The 2003 vintage has given the brothers
Jens and Carl-Günther Adelseck a range
of wines that convinced us to award them
the first bunch of grapes. The winery can
look back on a long tradition – the first
mention of the Adelseck family name refers to a cooper living in the Bingen area
in the 11th century. However, the wines
produced here today are modern in style,
in the best sense of the word. Clean and
with clear fruit, well-balanced, and, in the
case of the red wines, characterized by
strong wood notes. Particularly the red
wines reveal the international view taken
by the winery, which also includes an im-
porting company and a wholesale division. This winery has made an impressive breakthrough with the 2003 vintage.

2003 Riesling trocken
12.5%, 1.0 liter, ♀ till 2006 — **78**

2003 Riesling trocken
12.5%, ♀ till 2006 — **80**

2003 Sarmsheimer Liebehöll
Riesling Spätlese trocken
12.5%, ♀ till 2006 — **81**

2003 Münsterer Pittersberg
Riesling trocken
12.5%, ♀ till 2006 — **82**

2003 Münsterer Dautenpflänzer
Riesling trocken Selection
12.5%, ♀ till 2006 — **83**

2003 Laubenheimer Karthäuser
Riesling trocken Selection
12.5%, ♀ till 2006 — **84**

2003 Laubenheimer Vogelsang
Riesling halbtrocken
12.5%, ♀ till 2006 — **80**

2003 Münsterer Riesling Kabinett
10%, ♀ till 2006 — **82**

2002 Laubenheimer Karthäuser
Riesling Selection
13%, ♀ till 2006 — **84**

2003 Laubenheimer Fuchsen
Riesling Auslese
8%, ♀ till 2009 — **86**

——— Red wines ———

2002 Münsterer Dautenpflänzer
Spätburgunder Selection
13%, ♀ till 2007 — **84**

2002 Münsterer Dautenpflänzer
Spätburgunder trocken
13.5%, ♀ till 2007 — **85**

2002 Dornfelder trocken Barrique
13.5%, ♀ till 2008 — **86**

he wines: **100** Perfect · **95–99** Outstanding · **90–94** Excellent · **85–89** Very good · **80–84** Good · **75–79** Average

401

WEIN- UND SEKTGUT KARL-KURT BAMBERGER & SOHN

Owner: Bamberger family
Winemaker: Heiko Bamberger
55566 Meddersheim, Römerstraße 10
Tel. (0 67 51) 26 24, Fax 21 41
e-mail: kontakt@weingut-bamberger.de
Internet: www.weingut-bamberger.de
*Directions: From Bad Kreuznach via the
B 41, Meddersheim exit*
Opening hours: Mon.–Sat. 09:00 to
19:00 hours, Sun. by appointment
Worth seeing: Sparkling wine production
in remuage cellar, small house in vineyards

Vineyard area: 10.5 hectares
Annual production: 75,000 bottles,
incl. 10,000 bottles sparkling wine
Top sites: Monzinger Frühlingsplätzchen, Meddersheimer Altenberg
and Rheingrafenberg, Schlossböckelheimer Königsfels
Soil types: Gravel, decomposed new
red sandstone and clay, porphyry
Grape varieties: 50% Riesling,
25% red varieties, 10% Grau- and
Weißburgunder, 5% Gewürztraminer,
10% other varieties
Average yield: 68 hl/ha
Best vintages: 2001, 2002, 2003

This family winery on the Middle Nahe
near Bad Sobernheim has for many years
been an extremely reliable producer of
sparkling wines. In the meantime, the
whole range has come to shine – just like
the stainless steel tanks in the cellar. The
wines are clean and racy, with some
strong points in the fruity sector, with impressive Spätlese and Auslese wines. The
2003 range was the third successive good
range in a row we have tasted. Pleasantly
clean fruit and an attractive freshness
characterize the wines here, in this vintage they have a lovely quaffing style.
The highlight of the vintage for the Bam-
bergers in the botrytis dessert section is
a fascinating Beerenauslese.

2003 Schlossböckelheimer Königsfels
Riesling Spätlese trocken
13%, ♀ till 2006   82

2003 Schlossböckelheimer Königsfels
Riesling Spätlese halbtrocken
12.5%, ♀ till 2006   83

2003 Meddersheimer Altenberg
Riesling Spätlese
7.5%, ♀ till 2007   85

2002 Meddersheimer Altenberg
Riesling Spätlese *
7%, ♀ till 2008   86

2003 Meddersheimer Altenberg
Riesling Spätlese *
8.5%, ♀ till 2008   87

2003 Meddersheimer Rheingrafenberg
Riesling Auslese *
7.5%, ♀ till 2009   88

2002 Sobernheimer Marbach
Riesling Auslese *
8%, ♀ till 2009   88

2003 Meddersheimer Rheingrafenberg
Riesling Eiswein
6.5%, ♀ till 2010   89

2003 Meddersheimer Altenberg
Riesling Beerenauslese
6.5%, ♀ till 2012   90

NAHE

2003er

RIESLING SPÄTLESE

TROCKEN

Schlossböckelheimer Königsfels

QUALITÄTSWEIN MIT PRÄDIKAT
GUTSABFÜLLUNG
A. P. Nr. 7 745 067 08 04

0,75 L   13% vol

WEIN- UND SEKTGUT
KARL-KURT BAMBERGER & SOHN
D-55566 Meddersheim
Telefon 0 67 51 / 26 24

The estates: ✲✲✲✲✲ World's finest · ✲✲✲✲ Germany's best · ✲✲✲ Very good · ✲✲ Good · ✲ Reliabl

WEINGUT DR. CRUSIUS

Owner: Dr. Peter Crusius
55595 Traisen, Hauptstraße 2
Tel. (06 71) 3 39 53, Fax 2 82 19
e-mail: weingut-crusius@t-online.de
Internet: www.weingut-crusius.de
Directions: A 61, Waldlaubersheim exit,
in direction of Bad Münster; A 61, Bad
Kreuznach exit, B 41, Bad Münster exit
Opening hours: Mon.–Sat. 09:00 to
17:00 hours, by appointment
History: Documents show family resident in Traisen since 1586, as wine producers and village mayors
Worth seeing: Unique vineyard site
"Traiser Bastei" at foot of Roten-
felsen rock formation, vaulted cellar,
courtyard has Mediterranean flair

Vineyard area: 15 hectares
Annual production: 100,000 bottles
Top sites: Traiser Bastei and Roten-
fels, Schlossböckelheimer Felsen-
berg, Niederhäuser Felsensteyer,
Norheimer Kirschheck
Soil types: Volcanic and
decomposed slate, gravelly clay
Grape varieties: 65% Riesling,
20% Weißburgunder, 5% each of
Spätburgunder and Müller-Thurgau,
5% other varieties
Average yield: 60 hl/ha
Best vintages: 2000, 2002, 2003
Member: VDP

Peter Crusius has been modernizing the
winery carefully in recent years: new labels and price lists, a few new grape varieties and a few barrique barrels. In this
process, he has retained all the good old
positive characteristics, and added a few
new ones. What has remained is the concentrated Crusius style, which his father
Hans had already established, and which
helped to establish the winery among
the top producers of the region. The new
vintage is the best for some years. This
stretches from wonderful basic wines to
absolutely magnificent wines that are
among the best of the vintage.

2003 Traiser Rotenfels
Riesling Spätlese trocken
13.5%, ♀ till 2009   86

2003 Traiser Bastei
Riesling Spätlese trocken
13%, ♀ till 2009   87

2002 Traiser Bastei
Riesling Spätlese trocken
12%, ♀ till 2008   88

2003 Norheimer Kirschheck
Riesling trocken "Großes Gewächs"
13%, ♀ till 2012   92

2003 Traiser Rotenfels
Riesling Spätlese Goldkapsel
11%, ♀ till 2010   89

2003 Niederhäuser Felsensteyer
Riesling Spätlese
9%, ♀ till 2012   90

2003 Norheimer Kirschheck
Riesling Beerenauslese
9.5%, ♀ till 2016   90

2003 Traiser Rotenfels
Riesling Spätlese
9%, ♀ till 2012   91

2002 Norheimer Kirschheck
Riesling Spätlese
7%, ♀ till 2010   91

2002 Traiser
Riesling Auslese Goldkapsel
⤳ auction wine, 8%, ♀ till 2014   91

2003 Traiser Rotenfels
Riesling Trockenbeerenauslese
9.5%, ♀ till 2020   93

2003 Traiser Rotenfels
Riesling Auslese Goldkapsel
9.5%, ♀ till 2014   93

NAHE
2003er
Traiser Rotenfels
Riesling Auslese
QUALITÄTSWEIN MIT PRÄDIKAT

WEINGUT DR. CRUSIUS
alc 9,5% vol.   Gutsabfüllung · Produce of Germany · D-55595 Traisen · A. P. Nr. 7 775 009 020 04   750 ml

---

The wines: **100** Perfect · **95–99** Outstanding · **90–94** Excellent · **85–89** Very good · **80–84** Good · **75–79** Average

SCHLOSSGUT DIEL

Owner: Armin Diel
Winemaker: Christoph J. Friedrich
55452 Burg Layen
Tel. (0 67 21) 9 69 50, **Fax** 4 50 47
e-mail: info@schlossgut-diel.com
Internet: www.schlossgut-diel.com
Directions: A 61, Dorsheim exit,
in direction of Burg Layen (500 meters)
Sales: Bernd Benz
Opening hours: Mon.–Thur. 08:00 to
17:00 hours, Fri. 08:00 to 14:00 hours
Tastings by appointment
History: Burg Layen (12th century),
owned by Diel family since 1802
Worth seeing: Ruins of Burg Layen
castle, artistically designed tank cellar,
historic vaulted cellar

Vineyard area: 16 hectares
Annual production: 90,000 bottles
Top sites: Dorsheimer Goldloch,
Pittermännchen and Burgberg
Soil types: Gravelly clay with slate
Grape varieties: 70% Riesling,
30% Pinot varieties
Average yield: 45 hl/ha
Best vintages: 2001, 2002, 2003
Member: VDP,
Deutsches Barrique Forum

If you travel along the A 61 autobahn near Dorsheim, you will notice the prominent place taken by the old fortifications of Burg Layen. The owner, Armin Diel, occupies a similarly prominent position in the Nahe region – he is chairman of the VDP, and a truly cosmopolitan representative in the world of wine. Diel sets high standards for himself and for the wines he produces. With the 2002 vintage, Diel celebrated the 200th anniversary of the wine estate. In addition to presenting excellent dry and fruity Rieslings, he has produced some charming Pinot Blancs, as well as a bottle-fermented sparkling wine and – for the first time – he has presented a remarkable red wine that bears the name of his daughter Caroline. Diel has thus presented top wines, among the best in the region, in each of the disciplines in which he is active. The range of 2003 vintage wines is by no means of a lesser quality than its predecessor, quite the contrary, the level of the previous vintage has even been exceeded. For instance, the three First Growths show a concentration and individual character that places them clearly among the outstanding wines in the whole of Germany: the Pittermännchen, with herbs and spices, and dominated by gray slate, the Goldloch, full-bodied and firmly bursting with honey aromas, while the wines from the Burgberg vineyard are always characterized by mineral notes and citrus aromas. Armin Diel and winemaker Christoph Friedrich have shown their mastery of blended wines consistently over a period of many years. This is evidenced by the cult status enjoyed in leading German restaurants of the "Victor," a blend of white Pinot varieties named after Diel's son. And the "little brother" of this wine, named tongue-in-cheek "Diel de Diel," makes a hot summer's day more bearable. Armin Diel is certainly not resting on his laurels, as is evidenced by the latest challenge he has taken on: He has since the 2003 vintage been involved in a joint venture with a small, but high-profile winery in Washington State, specializing in Riesling production. The results should be more than just satisfactory for the global player Armin Diel, and rightly so. (Text: Carsten Henn)

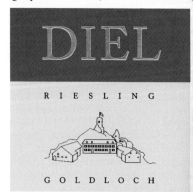

The restored castle tower of the Layen ruin rises directly behind the Schlossgut Diel winery, and is visible to visitors from afar.

405

WEINGUT HERMANN DÖNNHOFF

Owner: Helmut Dönnhoff
55585 Oberhausen, Bahnhofstraße 11
Tel. (0 67 55) 2 63, Fax 10 67
e-mail: weingut@doennhoff.com
Internet: www.doennhoff.com
Directions: A 61, Bad Kreuznach exit,
on B 41 to Bad Münster a. St. via
Norheim–Niederhausen–Oberhausen
Sales: By appointment
History: Winemaking in the family since 1750
Worth seeing: Beautiful view of top vineyard sites of Niederhausen and Schlossböckelheim

---

Vineyard area: 16 hectares
Annual production: 100,000 bottles
Top sites: Niederhäuser Hermanns-höhle, Oberhäuser Brücke (mono-pole), Schlossböckelheimer Felsen-berg and Kupfergrube, Norheimer Kirschheck and Dellchen
Soil types: Gray slate, porphyry as well as melaphyry and decom-posed volcanic formation
Grape varieties: 75% Riesling, 25% Weiß- and Grauburgunder
Average yield: 50 hl/ha
Best vintages: 2001, 2002, 2003
Member: VDP

Helmut Dönnhoff has attained a status in the German wine industry that can perhaps be compared only to that of Egon Müller. The wines as well as the wine-maker are legendary, virtually a national heritage. It is a long road to this posi-tion, and Helmut Dönnhoff took this path by virtue of hard work, and in all humili-ty, as is his style, always expressing a spe-cial enthusiasm for the wine. This honest love of wine is the key required to under-stand the liquid masterpieces produced at Oberhausen. The grand master of Nahe wines works meticulously on his wines, and shies away from generalizations or standard recipes. To him, a vintage is not just a simple combination of must weights or acidity levels. Dönnhoff clas-sifies the wines according to their whole ripening profile – and this can be tasted in the wines he makes. Just like the often mentioned terroir, which is so convenient for marketing purposes. Helmut Dönn-hoff actually does manage to bring it to the bottle, whether it is from the legen-dary Niederhäuser Hermannshöhle site, or from the Oberhäuser Brücke, which he owns in its entirety. It is from the decom-posed gray slate soils of the latter site that his Eiswein is produced, which by now virtually has cult status. In the 2003 vin-tage, which was not really pre-ordained for the production of this specialty, Dönnhoff was one of the very few, be-cause of this specific site, who was able to produce a convincing Eiswein. In terms of vineyards, the very best is just about good enough for Dönnhoff. He has ex-panded his little treasure-trove of top vineyards in recent years by systemati-cally acquiring some of the best parcels of land in Norheim and Schlossböckelheim. Not much has changed in the cellar for many years. Dönnhoff is a traditionalist, and a true master of producing Riesling in classical large oak vats. The international press heaps praise on him for this ability. This will not be much different with re-gard to the 2003 vintage, as this is even better than the two very good vintages preceding it. There is a unique parade of fruity Spätlese wines, the highlights this year are the Dellchen, with its vibrating acidity, and of course the enormous gold capsule wine from the Hermannshöhle site. The most pleasant surprise is the "Großes Gewächs" (First Growth). Never before has Helmut Dönnhoff presented such an outstanding dry wine, virtually a minerally monument. Consumers have grown used to – what a luxury – excep-tional Auslese wines from the Oberhäu-ser Brücke site in recent years, and the 2003 vintage is no exception. The only disappointment for the countless Dönn-hoff fans is that the most popular wine are sold out at the winery in no time.

2003 Niederhäuser Hermannshöhle
Riesling trocken "Großes Gewächs"
13.5%, ♀ till 2010 **93**

2002 Norheimer Dellchen
Riesling Spätlese
8.5%, ♀ till 2010 **87**

2002 Niederhäuser Hermannshöhle
Riesling Spätlese
8.5%, ♀ till 2013 **89**

2001 Schlossböckelheimer Kupfergrube
Riesling Spätlese
9%, ♀ till 2008 **89**

2001 Oberhäuser Brücke
Riesling Spätlese
9%, ♀ till 2009 **89**

2003 Schlossböckelheimer Felsenberg
Riesling Spätlese
9%, ♀ till 2012 **90**

2003 Oberhäuser Brücke
Riesling Spätlese
8.5%, ♀ till 2012 **90**

2003 Niederhäuser Hermannshöhle
Riesling Spätlese
8.5%, ♀ till 2012 **90**

2002 Norheimer Kirschheck
Riesling Spätlese
8.5%, ♀ till 2012 **90**

2002 Oberhäuser Brücke
Riesling Spätlese
8.5%, ♀ till 2012 **90**

2001 Niederhäuser Hermannshöhle
Riesling Spätlese
9%, ♀ till 2011 **90**

2001 Oberhäuser Brücke
Riesling Auslese
8.5%, ♀ till 2012 **90**

2001 Niederhäuser Hermannshöhle
Riesling Auslese – 18 –
8.5%, ♀ till 2012 **90**

2002 Niederhäuser Hermannshöhle
Riesling Auslese Goldkapsel
8.5%, ♀ till 2015 **90**

2003 Oberhäuser Leistenberg
Riesling Auslese
8.5%, ♀ till 2016 **91**

2001 Oberhäuser Brücke
Riesling Auslese – 19 –
↗ auction wine, 8.5%, ♀ till 2015 **91**

2003 Niederhäuser Hermannshöhle
Riesling Auslese Goldkapsel
8.5%, ♀ till 2018 **91**

2001 Schlossböckelheimer Felsenberg
Riesling Spätlese "Türmchen"
↗ auction wine, 8.5%, ♀ till 2011 **91**

2003 Norheimer Dellchen
Riesling Spätlese
8.5%, ♀ till 2014 **92**

2003 Niederhäuser Hermannshöhle
Riesling Spätlese Goldkapsel
↗ auction wine, 8%, ♀ till 2015 **92**

2003 Oberhäuser Brücke
Riesling Eiswein
8%, ♀ till 2022 **93**

2003 Oberhäuser Brücke
Riesling Beerenauslese
↗ auction wine, 8%, ♀ till 2020 **93**

2001 Oberhäuser Brücke
Riesling Beerenauslese
↗ auction wine, 8.5%, ♀ till 2020 **93**

2002 Oberhäuser Brücke
Riesling Auslese Goldkapsel
↗ auction wine, 8.5%, ♀ till 2018 **93**

2001 Oberhäuser Brücke
Riesling Eiswein
8%, ♀ till 2020 **94**

2002 Oberhäuser Brücke
Riesling Eiswein
7.5%, ♀ till 2025 **96**

2003 Oberhäuser Brücke
Riesling Auslese Goldkapsel
↗ auction wine, 8.5%, ♀ till 2020 **96**

DÖNNHOFF
Oberhäuser Brücke
Riesling Spätlese
2001

ERZEUGERABFÜLLUNG
WEINGUT HERMANN DÖNNHOFF D-55585 OBERHAUSEN/NAHE
QUALITÄTSWEIN MIT PRÄDIKAT A. P. Nr. 7753040902
PRODUCE OF GERMANY.

alc 9.0 % vol.   NAHE   750 ml e

he wines: **100** Perfect · **95–99** Outstanding · **90–94** Excellent · **85–89** Very good · **80–84** Good · **75–79** Average

407

WEINGUT EDELBERG

Owner: Willi Ebert and son
Manager: Willi Ebert
Winemaker: Peter and Michael Ebert
55627 Weiler bei Monzingen,
Gonratherhof 3
Tel. (0 67 54) 2 24, Fax 94 58 81
e-mail: WeingutEdelberg@t-online.de
Directions: B 41 in direction of Idar-Oberstein, first exit after Monzingen, to Weiler-Gonratherhof
Sales: Ebert family
Opening hours: Mon.–Fri. 09:00 to 19:00 hours, Sat. and Sun. 10:00 to 20:00 hours
Restaurant: Sat. from 17:00 hours, Sun. open from 11:00 hours
Worth a visit: Walks and hikes around the Gonratherhof

Vineyard area: 7.4 hectares
Annual production: 35,000 bottles
Top sites: Weilerer Herrenzehntel, Meddersheimer Rheingrafenberg
Soil types: Decomposed upper red sandstone and clay, gravel and stone
Grape varieties: 64% Riesling, 9% Dornfelder, 8% Müller-Thurgau, 5% each of Spätburgunder and Kerner, 9% other varieties
Average yield: 67 hl/ha
Best vintages: 2001, 2002, 2003

Willi Ebert is a contented father, blessed as he is with two sons, Peter and Michael, both of whom work hard in the winery. Willi Ebert proclaims the formula of all successful winemakers: The foundation for good wine is laid in the vineyard. In his own words, that is how they managed to achieve their improvement in quality in the 2002 vintage. The technology available in the cellar – stainless steel tanks, temperature control – also help in this regard. Another important factor here is the tasting of wines made by other producers, looking further than the boundaries of one's own estate. A 2003 wine we can particularly recommend: the juicy Weilerer Heiligenberg Spätlese, with its exotic aromas.

2003 Riesling Classic
12%, ♀ till 2006   82

2002 Meddersheimer Rheingrafenberg
Riesling Selection
13%, ♀ till 2006   84

2003 Meddersheimer Rheingrafenberg
Riesling halbtrocken "No. 13"
12%, ♀ till 2006   82

2003 Weilerer Herrenzehntel
Riesling Spätlese halbtrocken
12%, ♀ till 2007   83

2003 Weilerer Herrenzehntel
Riesling Kabinett
9.5%, ♀ till 2006   83

2003 Meddersheimer Altenberg
Gewürztraminer Spätlese
8.5%, ♀ till 2007   84

2003 Weilerer Heiligenberg
Riesling Spätlese
8%, ♀ till 2007   85

2002 Weilerer Herrenzehntel
Riesling Auslese
10.5%, ♀ till 2007   85

2003 Weilerer Herrenzehntel
Riesling Beerenauslese
7.5%, ♀ till 2012   88

2002 Weilerer Herrenzehntel
Riesling Eiswein
8%, ♀ till 2014   90

WEINGUT EMRICH-MONTIGNY

Owner: Ursula Emrich-Montigny and Steffen Montigny
Winemaker: Steffen Montigny
55545 Bad Kreuznach-Planig, Burgundenstraße 1–3
Tel. (06 71) 6 58 35, Fax 6 35 35
e-mail: weingut@emrich-montigny.de
Internet: www.emrich-montigny.de
Directions: A 61, Bad Kreuznach exit, continue to Planig exit, in center of town
Sales: Ursula Emrich-Montigny
Opening hours: Mon.–Fri. 09:00 to 18:00 hours, Sat. 09:00 to 16:00 hours and by appointment
History: Winemaking since 300 years
Worth seeing: Old estate with large walnut tree in courtyard
Worth a visit: Wine tasting days in May, wine festival in the courtyard

---

Vineyard area: 11 hectares
Annual production: 100,000 bottles
Top sites: Planiger Katzenhölle and Römerhelde, Kreuznacher Forst
Soil types: Old terrace rubble with new upper red sandstone
Grape varieties: 21% Riesling, 20% Grauburgunder, 15% Spätburgunder, 11% Portugieser, 7% Dornfelder, 6% Chardonnay, 5% Dunkelfelder, 15% other varieties
Average yield: 86 hl/ha
Best vintages: 2002, 2003

While Sascha Montigny continued to run his parents' winery in Laubenheim, his brother Steffen in 1985 took over the 300-year-old winery of his in-laws in Planig, a suburb of Bad Kreuznach. Together they organize tastings of young wines, travel to other growing areas, and both use the machinery and equipment available. Steffen Montigny sees his own strengths particularly with the Pinot varieties. He was awarded the first bunch of grapes last year, and his 2003 wines vindicated this decision. Only his Riesling wines have not reached the high standard.

2003 Planiger Römerhelde
Chardonnay trocken
12.5%, ♀ till 2006 — **82**

2003 Planiger Katzenhölle
Grauer Burgunder Auslese trocken
14%, ♀ till 2007 — **83**

2003 Kreuznacher
Spätburgunder Auslese trocken
"Blanc de Noir"
13%, ♀ till 2007 — **84**

2003 Kreuznacher Forst
Riesling Spätlese
9%, ♀ till 2007 — **83**

——— Red wines ———

2003 Kreuznacher
Spätburgunder trocken
13%, ♀ till 2007 — **83**

2002 Kreuznacher "Solitaire Cuvée"
trocken Barrique
13%, ♀ till 2009 — **85**

2001 Kreuznacher
Cabernet Sauvignon trocken Barrique
13.5%, ♀ till 2009 — **86**

2002 Kreuznacher
Dornfelder trocken Barrique
13.5%, ♀ till 2007 — **86**

2001 "Cuvée Solitaire"
trocken Barrique
13%, ♀ till 2008 — **86**

The wines: **100** Perfect · **95–99** Outstanding · **90–94** Excellent · **85–89** Very good · **80–84** Good · **75–79** Average

409

WEINGUT EMRICH-SCHÖNLEBER

Owner: Hannelore and Werner Schönleber
Manager and winemaker:
Werner Schönleber
55569 Monzingen, Naheweinstraße 10a
Tel. (0 67 51) 27 33, Fax 48 64
e-mail:
weingut@emrich-schoenleber.com
Internet: www.emrich-schoenleber.com
Directions: B 41, Monzingen exit, in direction of town center, Soonwaldstraße
Opening hours: Mon.–Fri. 08:00 to 12:00 and 13:30 to 18:00 hours, Sat. 09:00 to 12:00 and 13:30 to 16:00 hours by appointment only
History: Winemaking in family for more than 250 years

Vineyard area: 14 hectares
Annual production: 110,000 bottles
Top sites: Monzinger Halenberg and Frühlingsplätzchen
Soil types: Mixture of various types of slate and quartzite
Grape varieties: 76% Riesling, 9% Grauburgunder, 5% Weißburgunder, 10% other varieties
Average yield: 63 hl/ha
Best vintages: 2001, 2002, 2003
Member: VDP

Werner Schönleber is one of the most self-critical winemakers in Germany. He does not easily accept praise for his wines. He will always question such comments, analyze whether it matches his own assessment, and say so openly if this is not the case. This slightly distanced approach to that which is most important in his life has made it possible for him to be where he is today: at the pinnacle of producers in the region. Werner Schönleber started out with only two hectares of vineyard in the late Sixties, and has over the years developed first his dry Riesling wines, then his Pinots, finally the Eisweins to the level that he had envisaged. Small, well-reasoned steps, and lots of work on the details are what have ensured lasting success. There are simply no slip-ups here, even on the most basic wines. He has revived the reputation of the Monzinger Frühlingsplätzchen and Halenberg sites, it is his wines that have shown the potential of these vineyards. He has gradually added to his holdings in the best parcels of land. His key variety is Riesling, and this variety often produces particularly elegant wines here, with floral aromas on the nose and mineral notes on the palate. In the past three vintages, this winery has produced the best range of wines in the Nahe region, the botrytis dessert wines are among the best in Germany. Last year, he was not only awarded the fifth bunch of grapes, his Eiswein gold capsule was also rated a perfect 100 points, a rating that has been awarded only five times in eleven years. As Werner Schönleber explains, the 2003 vintage is the most unusual vintage he has experienced in the past 40 years. The spice is a little more creamy, the fruity acid is a little softer, and all-round they are simply "darn good." In the opinion of Schönleber, and many others, 2003 simply was not a year for Eiswein; instead he has for the first time produced a Trockenbeerenauslese from the Halenberg site. Yet again, Monzingen has produced one of the very best botrytis dessert wines in Germany. There is no secret behind the quality produced here, only meticulous work: late hand-picking, often selective, gentle pressing, cool fermentation. It is not unusual for his Riesling wines, which undergo spontaneous fermentation in large oak vats and maturation in stainless steel tanks, to undergo a closed phase in the summer after the harvest. They make up for this by developing beautifully in the fall. And over the years the Schönleber wines have proven convincingly how well they can mature. It is definitely worth the wait!

2003 Monzinger Halenberg
Riesling Spätlese trocken
13%, ♀ till 2009   88

2001 Monzinger Halenberg
Riesling Spätlese trocken
12.5%, ♀ till 2006   **88**

2002 Monzinger Halenberg
Riesling Spätlese trocken
12.5%, ♀ till 2008   **89**

2003 Monzinger Halenberg
Riesling trocken "Großes Gewächs"
13%, ♀ till 2012   **90**

2002 Monzinger Halenberg
Riesling Auslese trocken
12.5%, ♀ till 2010   **92**

2001 Monzinger Halenberg
Riesling Auslese trocken
12.5%, ♀ till 2007   **92**

2003 Monzinger Halenberg
Riesling Spätlese halbtrocken
12%, ♀ till 2010   **89**

2002 Monzinger Halenberg
Riesling Spätlese halbtrocken
11.5%, ♀ till 2010   **89**

2001 Monzinger Halenberg
Riesling Spätlese halbtrocken
11.5%, ♀ till 2008   **89**

2003 Monzinger Frühlingsplätzchen
Riesling Kabinett
11%, ♀ till 2008   **87**

2001 Monzinger Halenberg
Riesling Spätlese
9.5%, ♀ till 2008   **88**

2002 Monzinger Frühlingsplätzchen
Riesling Spätlese – 16 –
9.5%, ♀ till 2011   **89**

2003 Monzinger Frühlingsplätzchen
Riesling Spätlese
10%, ♀ till 2012   **90**

2003 Monzinger Halenberg
Riesling Auslese
9.5%, ♀ till 2015   **90**

2002 Monzinger Frühlingsplätzchen
Riesling Auslese
9%, ♀ till 2014   **90**

2002 Monzinger Halenberg
Riesling Spätlese
9.5%, ♀ till 2012   **90**

2003 Monzinger Halenberg
Riesling Spätlese
10.5%, ♀ till 2012   **91**

2002 Monzinger Halenberg
Riesling Auslese
9.5%, ♀ till 2014   **91**

2003 Monzinger Frühlingsplätzchen
Riesling Auslese Goldkapsel
↗ auction wine, 10%, ♀ till 2016   **92**

2001 Monzinger Halenberg
Riesling Auslese *** Goldkapsel
↗ auction wine, 9%, ♀ till 2016   **92**

2002 Monzinger Frühlingsplätzchen
Riesling Spätlese "Rutsch"
↗ auction wine, 9.5%, ♀ till 2014   **92**

2001 Monzinger Halenberg
Riesling Eiswein
8%, ♀ till 2020   **93**

2003 Monzinger Halenberg
Riesling Beerenauslese
9%, ♀ till 2022   **94**

2002 Monzinger Halenberg
Riesling Auslese Goldkapsel
↗ auction wine, 8%, ♀ till 2016   **94**

2003 Monzinger Halenberg
Riesling Trockenbeerenauslese
↗ auction wine, 8%, ♀ till 2030   **96**

2002 Monzinger Halenberg
Riesling Eiswein
7%, ♀ till 2025   **96**

2002 Monzinger Halenberg
Riesling Eiswein Goldkapsel
↗ auction wine, 7%, ♀ till 2030   **100**

Emrich-Schönleber

Nahe

2002

Monzinger Frühlingsplätzchen

Riesling Spätlese trocken

alc. 12% vol   Qualitätswein mit Prädikat   750 ml
Gutsabfüllung · A. P. Nr. 7 748 066 17 03
Produce of Germany · D-55569 Monzingen an der Nahe

The wines: **100** Perfect · **95–99** Outstanding · **90–94** Excellent · **85–89** Very good · **80–84** Good · **75–79** Average

WEINGUT ANTON FINKENAUER

Owner and winemaker:
Hans-Anton Finkenauer
55543 Bad Kreuznach,
Rheingrafenstraße 15
Tel. (06 71) 6 22 30, Fax 6 22 10
Directions: A 61, Bad Kreuznach exit, in direction of Bad Münster, turn left at parking arcade into Rheingrafenstraße
Sales: Finkenauer family
Opening hours: Mon.–Fri. 08:30 to 18:30 hours or by appointment
History: Winemaking in the family for more than 250 years

Vineyard area: 8.5 hectares
Annual production: 60,000 bottles
Top sites: Kreuznacher
Kahlenberg and Brückes
Soil types: Decomposed sandstone, sandy clay
Grape varieties: 57% Riesling, 14% Müller-Thurgau, 10% Grauburgunder, 9% Spätburgunder, 10% other varieties
Average yield: 94 hl/ha
Best vintages: 1999, 2002, 2003

The Anton Finkenauer winery is a timeless place. Very little has changed here in recent years, except that the importance of Pinot Noir has grown. A solid, classical style of wine is made here, a style that has always had its adherents. And there are always highlights to be found in the range of wines presented. This year it is particularly the juicy Hinkelstein Beerenauslese that we liked, but in fact the whole range of wines, whether dry or sweet, is of very good quality. And what is particularly important for customers: There are no negative surprises. Another point that must be stressed is that the pricing is very reasonable. In the first quarter of the last century, Anton and Carl Finkenauer ran a mutual winery, the brothers going separate paths in 1925. Ever since then, the capital of the Nahe region, Bad Kreuznach, has had two Finkenauer wineries.

2003 Kreuznacher Hinkelstein
Riesling Spätlese trocken
13%, ♀ till 2007 — 83

2002 Kreuznacher Rosenberg
Riesling Kabinett trocken
11.5%, ♀ till 2006 — 83

2002 Kreuznacher Hinkelstein
Riesling Spätlese trocken
12%, ♀ till 2006 — 83

2002 Kreuznacher Kahlenberg
Riesling Spätlese trocken
12.5%, ♀ till 2006 — 84

2003 Kreuznacher Osterhöll
Riesling Auslese trocken
13.5%, ♀ till 2008 — 85

2002 Kreuznacher Hinkelstein
Riesling Spätlese halbtrocken
11.5%, ♀ till 2006 — 82

2003 Kreuznacher Hinkelstein
Riesling Spätlese
10%, ♀ till 2007 — 84

2003 Kreuznacher Kahlenberg
Riesling Auslese
9.5%, ♀ till 2008 — 84

2002 Kreuznacher Kahlenberg
Riesling Spätlese
9%, ♀ till 2006 — 84

2003 Kreuznacher Hinkelstein
Riesling Auslese
9%, ♀ till 2009 — 85

2003 Kreuznacher Forst
Grauer Burgunder Beerenauslese
7.5%, ♀ till 2014 — 87

2003 Kreuznacher Hinkelstein
Riesling Beerenauslese
7%, ♀ till 2014 — 88

ANTON FINKENAUER
2002
Kreuznacher Kahlenberg
Riesling Spätlese
trocken
Gutsabfüllung
12,5%vol — Nahe — 750 ml
Qualitätswein mit Prädikat · A.P. Nr. 7 710 034 013 03 · Weingut Anton Finkenauer · 55543 Bad Kreuznach

---

The estates: ♦♦♦♦♦ World's finest · ♦♦♦♦ Germany's best · ♦♦♦ Very good · ♦♦ Good · ♦ Reliable

WEINGUT GÖTTELMANN

Owner: Ruth Göttelmann-Blessing, Götz Blessing
55424 Münster-Sarmsheim,
Rheinstraße 77
Tel. (0 67 21) 4 37 75, Fax 4 26 05
e-mail: goettelmannWein@aol.com
*Directions: A 61, Dorsheim exit,
in direction of Münster-Sarmsheim*
Sales: Blessing family
Opening hours: Mon.–Sun. 10:00 to
20:00 hours, by appointment only
Restaurant: May to early Aug.,
mid-Sept. to early Nov.
Wed.–Sat. 18:00 to 24:00, Sun. and
public holidays 16:00 to 23:00 hours
Specialties: Baked "vineyard knots,"
"brick" cheese

Vineyard area: 13 hectares
Annual production: 85,000 bottles
Top sites: Münsterer Dauten-
pflänzer, Pittersberg and Rheinberg
Soil types: Decomposed slate, loess
Grape varieties: 66% Riesling,
12% Weiß- and Grauburgunder,
6% Spätburgunder, 4% Silvaner,
12% other varieties
Average yield: 60 hl/ha
Best vintages: 2001, 2002, 2003

There are few winemakers in the Nahe region who work as diligently at improving the quality of their wines as the likeable Götz Blessing. Thus it is that virtually each vintage range is better than that preceding it. Another positive aspect: the pricing of the wines, a real attraction for price-conscious wine lovers. Three quarters of the wines are fermented dry, although we feel the real strengths of the winery are the fruity wines. In opinion of the winemaker, the 2003 vintage is regarded as the vintage of the century, and the Trockenbeerenauslese produced is the greatest wine since 1971. All of the wines are characterized by high must weights in the Spätlese range, even the most basic wines in liter bottles, and all wines are very full-bodied.

2003 Münsterer Kapellenberg
Riesling Spätlese trocken
12.5%, ♀ till 2008 — **86**

2002 Münsterer Dautenpflänzer
Riesling trocken Selection
13%, ♀ till 2006 — **88**

2003 Münsterer Rheinberg
Riesling Spätlese
8.5%, ♀ till 2010 — **88**

2003 Münsterer Dautenpflänzer
Riesling Spätlese *
8%, ♀ till 2010 — **89**

2003 Münsterer Dautenpflänzer
Riesling Spätlese **
7.5%, ♀ till 2012 — **89**

2002 Münsterer Rheinberg
Riesling Spätlese
8%, ♀ till 2009 — **89**

2003 Münsterer Pittersberg
Riesling Auslese
8%, ♀ till 2013 — **90**

2003 Münsterer Rheinberg
Riesling Auslese ***
8%, ♀ till 2014 — **91**

2002 Münsterer Rheinberg
Riesling Eiswein
7.5%, ♀ till 2014 — **92**

2003 Münsterer Rheinberg
Riesling Trockenbeerenauslese
7%, ♀ till 2020 — **94**

WEINGUT

GÖTTELMANN

2002
Münsterer Kapellenberg
Riesling Spätlese trocken
Qualitätswein mit Prädikat
Gutsabfüllung · A. P. Nr. 7 702 028 015 03
Product of Germany
12,5% vol   Nahe   0,75 l
WEINGUT GÖTTELMANN · D-55424 MÜNSTER-SARMSHEIM

The wines: **100** Perfect · **95–99** Outstanding · **90–94** Excellent · **85–89** Very good · **80–84** Good · **75–79** Average

WEINGUT HAHNMÜHLE

Owner: Peter and Martina Linxweiler
67822 Mannweiler-Cölln,
Alsenzstraße 25
Tel. (0 63 62) 99 30 99, Fax 44 66
e-mail: info@weingut-hahnmuehle.de
Internet: www.weingut-hahnmuehle.de
Directions: A 61, Gau-Bickelheim exit, via
B 420 / B 48 in direction of Kaiserslau-
tern, left over bridge at town exit
Opening hours: Mon.–Fri. 08:00 to
19:00 hours, Sat. 08:00 to 17:00 hours
History: The Hahnmühle is a water mill
dating to the 13th century, and has been
owned by the family since 1898

Vineyard area: 11.2 hectares
Annual production: 70,000 bottles
Top sites: Oberndorfer Beutel-
stein, Alsenzer Elkersberg
Soil types: Decomposed sandstone
and slate
Grape varieties: 50% Riesling,
12% each of Weißburgunder and
Silvaner, 6% each of Traminer and
Chardonnay, 9% Spätburgunder,
5% other varieties
Average yield: 50 hl/ha
Best vintages: 2000, 2002, 2003
Member: Naturland

The Linxweiler family are among the
most dedicated followers of organic practices. Their winery is located in the ruggedly romantic Alsenz valley. The Hahnmühle wines are characterized by elegance, mineral notes and concentration –
whether this can be attributed to the relatively low yields of around 50 hectoliters
per hectare, or the quality of the vineyard
sites, or the organic practices – surely all
factors play a part. The range of 2003 vintage wines presented was even better than
in the preceding years: Again, there is an
elegantly fruity Silvaner, the "Alisencia"
Riesling is more fascinating than ever,
and is among the best in the region, while
the Oberndorfer Beutelstein Chardonnay
delivers eloquent proof that this variety
does not need barrique treatment.

2003 "Fass 14"
Riesling trocken
12.5%, ♀ till 2007 — 83

2003 Oberndorfer Beutelstein
Silvaner Spätlese trocken
13%, ♀ till 2007 — 84

2003 Cöllner Rosenberg
Riesling & Traminer trocken
13%, ♀ till 2007 — 84

2003 Oberndorfer Beutelstein
Chardonnay trocken
14%, ♀ till 2007 — 85

2003 Oberndorfer Beutelstein
Riesling Spätlese trocken "Sandstein"
13.5%, ♀ till 2007 — 85

2002 Oberndorfer Beutelstein
Silvaner Spätlese trocken
12%, ♀ till 2007 — 86

2002 "Alisencia"
Riesling Spätlese trocken
12%, ♀ till 2007 — 86

2003 "Alisencia"
Riesling Spätlese trocken
12.5%, ♀ till 2008 — 87

2003 Oberndorfer Beutelstein
Riesling & Traminer Spätlese feinherb
9.5%, ♀ till 2008 — 86

2003 Oberndorfer Beutelstein
Riesling Spätlese
9.5%, ♀ till 2008 — 86

2003 Oberndorfer Beutelstein
Riesling Auslese
9%, ♀ till 2010 — 86

2002 Cöllner Rosenberg
Riesling Eiswein
9%, ♀ till 2012 — 88

2003
Cöllner Rosenberg
Riesling + Traminer
trocken
Qualitätswein

Gutsabfüllung · A. P. Nr. 7 786 010 5 04
Weingut Hahnmühle, P.+M. Linxweiler
D-67822 Mannweiler-Cölln
DE-022-Öko Kontrollstelle
Product of Germany
0,75 l
13,0% vol
NAHE

WEINGUT HEXAMER

Owner: Harald Hexamer
55566 Meddersheim,
Sobernheimer Straße 3
Tel. (0 67 51) 22 69, Fax 9 47 07
e-mail: weingut-hexamer@t-online.de
Internet: www.weingut-hexamer.de
Directions: From Bad Kreuznach via the
B 41, Meddersheim exit
Sales: Hexamer family
Opening hours: Mon.–Fri. 08:00 to
19:00 hours, Sat. 08:00 to 17:00 hours

Vineyard area: 13.2 hectares
Annual production: 75,000 bottles
Top sites: Meddersheimer
Rheingrafenberg and Altenberg,
Sobernheimer Marbach
Soil types: Gravelly stone, decompo-
sed upper red sandstone, quartzite,
decomposed multi-colored sandstone
Grape varieties: 58% Riesling,
15% Spätburgunder, 7% Weiß-
burgunder, 5% Müller-Thurgau,
3% Frühburgunder, 2% Gewürztrami-
ner, 10% other varieties
Average yield: 64 hl/ha
Best vintages: 1999, 2000, 2002

Last year, this estate presented an outstanding range of wines, on the basis of
which we awarded the third bunch of
grapes. Harald Hexamer's 2003 range confirms this rating, although the dry wines
were not quite as brilliant as they were in
the previous vintage. However, his favorites are in any case the fruity wines,
which are always balanced by a fresh,
racy acidity. This is an individual characteristic, keeping the wines lively and
refreshing. Harald Hexamer took over
his parents' winery in 1999, and has improved quality in a very short time. The
highlights each year are Eisweins that
are almost unparalleled in brilliance and
an explosive acidity. In the 2003 vintage
Hexamer did not produce an Eiswein –
a Hexamer Eiswein simply has to be an excellent one, or not at all. Would that all
producers had such a long-term attitude!

2003 Meddersheimer Rheingrafenberg
Riesling Spätlese trocken "Eisendell"
12%, ♀ till 2006 **83**

2003 Meddersheimer Rheingrafenberg
Riesling Spätlese trocken
13%, ♀ till 2007 **85**

2002 Meddersheimer Rheingrafenberg
Riesling Spätlese trocken
13%, ♀ till 2006 **86**

2003 Sobernheimer Marbach
Riesling Spätlese
8.5%, ♀ till 2009 **88**

2002 Meddersheimer Rheingrafenberg
Riesling Auslese "Minus 7 Grad Celsius"
7.5%, ♀ till 2009 **88**

2003 Meddersheimer Rheingrafenberg
Riesling Spätlese *
7.5%, ♀ till 2009 **89**

2003 Meddersheimer Rheingrafenberg
Riesling Auslese
7.5%, ♀ till 2012 **90**

2003 Meddersheimer Rheingrafenberg
Riesling Beerenauslese
8%, ♀ till 2016 **90**

2003 Meddersheimer Rheingrafenberg
Riesling Auslese *
8%, ♀ till 2012 **91**

2002 Meddersheimer Rheingrafenberg
Riesling Eiswein
6.5%, ♀ till 2016 **91**

2002 Sobernheimer Marbach
Riesling Eiswein
6%, ♀ till 2018 **92**

NAHE

2000ER RIESLING HOCHGEWÄCHS
MEDDERSHEIMER ALTENBERG
Qualitätswein
0,75 l   Erzeugerabfüllung · A. P. Nr. 7 745 028 001 01   8,5% vol
WEINGUT HELMUT HEXAMER   D-55566 MEDDERSHEIM

The wines: **100** Perfect · **95–99** Outstanding · **90–94** Excellent · **85–89** Very good · **80–84** Good · **75–79** Average

415

WEINGUT
GEBRÜDER KAUER

Owner: Christoph and Markus Kauer
Winemaker: Christoph Kauer
55452 Windesheim,
Bürgermeister-Dielhenn-Straße 1
Tel. (0 67 07) 2 55, Fax 5 17
e-mail:
info@weingut-gebrueder-kauer.de
Internet:
www.weingut-gebrueder-kauer.de
*Directions: A 61, Windesheim exit,
the winery is in the center of town*
Sales: Markus Kauer
Opening hours: Mon.–Fri. 09:00 to
19:00 hours, Sat. 09:00 to 15:00 hours
by appointment
History: Family-owned for 300 years

Vineyard area: 9 hectares
Annual production: 80,000 bottles
Top sites: Windesheimer Römer-
berg, Rosenberg and Saukopf
Soil types: Lower new red sandstone,
sandy clay
Grape varieties: 25% Riesling, 20%
Weißburgunder, 15% each of Müller-
Thurgau and Spätburgunder, 5%
Grauburgunder, 20% other varieties
Average yield: 68 hl/ha
Best vintages: 2000, 2001, 2002

The old wine-growing village of Windesheim appears to be a good place for Pinot
grapes. The estate owned by the Kauer
brothers has specialized in these wines,
although the Rieslings made here can be
just as good. The improvement began in
1999, when Christoph Kauer took over
responsibility in the cellar. Following on
a good homogeneous range in the previous vintage, the 2003 wines were not
quite as convincing, with many wines
coming over as being too sweet. Their barrique-matured Weißburgunder once again
provides proof that they know how to
handle new wood. The sparkling wines,
too, are always good. However, you need
a magnifying glass to discover the taste
designation on the label.

2003 Silvaner trocken
12%, ♀ till 2006   81
2003 Riesling Classic
12%, ♀ till 2006   81
2003 Grauer Burgunder trocken
13.5%, ♀ till 2006   82
2002 Riesling
Hochgewächs trocken
12%, ♀ till 2006   82
2003 Riesling
Spätlese trocken "S"
12%, ♀ till 2006   82
2002 Riesling Spätlese trocken
12%, ♀ till 2006   84
2002 Weißer Burgunder trocken
12.5%, ♀ till 2006   84
2003 Weißer Burgunder
trocken Barrique
14.5%, ♀ till 2008   85
2002 Weißer Burgunder
trocken "S"
13%, ♀ till 2007   85
2002 "Cuvée Pinot"
trocken Barrique
13%, ♀ till 2007   86
2003 Riesling Spätlese feinherb
12%, ♀ till 2007   83
2002 Riesling Spätlese feinherb
11.5%, ♀ till 2006   83
2002 Riesling Classic
11.5%, ♀ till 2006   83
2003 Riesling Spätlese
8%, ♀ till 2008   85

——————— Red wine ———————

2002 Spätburgunder Weißherbst
trocken "Blanc de Noir" Barrique
13.5%, ♀ till 2007   84

WEINGUT KLOSTERMÜHLE

**Owner: Dr. Peter Becker,
Christian Held, Dr. Michael Ritzau,
Dr. Martin Riedel
General manager: Christian Held
Manager and winemaker: Thomas Zenz
55571 Odernheim, Am Disibodenberg
Tel. (0 67 55) 3 19, Fax 3 20
e-mail: mail@claretum.de
Internet: www.claretum.de**
*Directions: A 61, Bad Kreuznach exit, B
41, Waldböckelheim exit, in direction of
Staudernheim, on left before Odernheim*
Sales: Charlotte Held
Opening hours: Mon.–Fri. 09:00 to
18:00 hours and by appointment
Worth seeing: Ruins of Disibodenberg
abbey
Worth a visit: Ride on hand-operated
railway trolley, culinary wine tastings

Vineyard area: 11 hectares
Annual production: 70,000 bottles
Top sites: Odernheimer Kloster Di-
sibodenberg and Montfort (monopole)
Soil types: Decomposed kaolin-slate
and sandstone
Grape varieties: 36% Spätburgunder,
25% Grauburgunder, 22% Riesling,
9% Weißburgunder, 4% Frühburgun-
der, 3% Chardonnay, 1% Silvaner
Average yield: 50 hl/ha
Best vintages: 2001, 2002, 2003

Christian Held is a lawyer by training.
Together with three partners, he took
over the Klostermühle Odernheim in
1993. The mill was formerly the working
farm of the historically significant abbey
of Disibodenberg (Hildegard of Bingen).
In doing this, Held not only saved a section of steep vineyard slopes on the middle Nahe, he also helped to continue an
unusual tradition in this region: The fact
that almost three-quarters of the vineyard
area is planted to Pinot vines. Almost all
wines are fermented dry. The 2003 vintage is the third good range in succession,
the highlight is the Trockenbeerenauslese with an orange citrus nose.

2002 Grauer Burgunder
trocken Barrique
14%, ♀ till 2007 · · · · · · · · · · **84**

2002 Chardonnay & Weißer Burgunder
trocken Barrique
14%, ♀ till 2008 · · · · · · · · · · **85**

2001 Chardonnay & Weißburgunder
trocken Barrique
13.5%, ♀ till 2007 · · · · · · · · · · **85**

**2003 Odernheimer
Kloster Disibodenberg**
Riesling Auslese
8%, ♀ till 2008 · · · · · · · · · · **85**

2002 "Henriette Elisabeth"
Grauer Burgunder Auslese
9%, ♀ till 2009 · · · · · · · · · · **86**

**2003 Odernheimer
Kloster Disibodenberg**
Riesling Trockenbeerenauslese
8.5%, ♀ till 2012 · · · · · · · · · · **88**

**2002 Odernheimer
Kloster Disibodenberg**
Riesling Eiswein
9%, ♀ till 2010 · · · · · · · · · · **88**

——————— Red wines ———————

2002 Spätburgunder
trocken Barrique
14%, ♀ till 2008 · · · · · · · · · · **84**

2001 Spätburgunder
trocken Barrique "Unser bestes Fass"
13.5%, ♀ till 2007 · · · · · · · · · · **86**

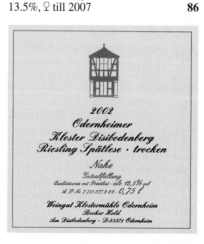

*2002
Odernheimer
Kloster Disibodenberg
Riesling Spätlese · trocken
Nahe
Gutsabfüllung
Qualitätswein mit Prädikat · alc 12,5% vol
A.P.Nr 7 733 077 3 03 · 0,75 l
Weingut Klostermühle Odernheim
Becker Held
Am Disibodenberg · D-55571 Odernheim*

The wines: **100** Perfect · **95–99** Outstanding · **90–94** Excellent · **85–89** Very good · **80–84** Good · **75–79** Average

417

WEINGUT KORRELL – JOHANNESHOF

Owner: Wilfried and Martin Korrell
Winemaker: Martin Korrell
55545 Bad Kreuznach-Bosenheim,
Parkstraße 4
Tel. (06 71) 6 36 30, Fax 7 19 54
e-mail: weingut-korrell@t-online.de
Internet: www.weingut-korrell.de
Directions: A 61, Bad Kreuznach exit,
left at first traffic light to Bosenheim
Opening hours: Mon.–Fri. 10:00 to
12:00 hours and 14:00 to 18:00 hours,
Sat. 10:00 to 12:00 and 14:00 to 16:00
hours, and by appointment
Wine bar: Rotzinek family
Specialties: German-Bohemian cuisine
History: Winemaking since 1760,
family coat of arms since 1483

Vineyard area: 20.9 hectares
Annual production: 145,000 bottles
Top sites: Kreuznacher Paradies
and St. Martin
Soil types: Marl with shell limestone,
gravel with kaolin, loess, sandstone
Grape varieties: 45% Riesling, 10%
each of Spätburgunder, Grauburgun-
der, Weißburgunder and Portugieser,
15% other varieties
Average yield: 65 hl/ha
Best vintages: 2001, 2002, 2003

The folks at the Korrell estate are well aware of the importance of appearances. There were many changes, until the current appealing blue label design was found. The decisive turning point in the development of the wine quality of this family winery was the addition of son Martin to the business. The 2003 vintage range is the third exemplary range in succession. There are plans to improve the quality by handling the grapes even more carefully. The wonderfully clear and fruity Gelbe Muskateller deserves special attention. A Trockenbeerenauslese wine represents the highlight of the botrytis dessert wines. Just as enjoyable is the Riesling Auslese with passion fruit aromas.

2003 Grauer Burgunder trocken
12.5%, ♀ till 2006 — **83**

2003 Riesling trocken
12%, ♀ till 2006 — **84**

2003 Kreuznacher St. Martin
Riesling trocken "Johannes K."
12%, ♀ till 2007 — **85**

2003 "Johannes K."
Chardonnay trocken
13.5%, ♀ till 2008 — **86**

2003 Kreuznacher Paradies
Riesling trocken "Großes Gewächs"
13%, ♀ till 2008 — **87**

2003 Kreuznacher St. Martin
Riesling Spätlese
7.5%, ♀ till 2008 — **86**

2003 Kreuznacher St. Martin
Riesling Auslese
7.5%, ♀ till 2010 — **87**

2003 Muskateller
8%, ♀ till 2007 — **87**

2002 Kreuznacher St. Martin
Riesling Spätlese
9%, ♀ till 2008 — **87**

2003 Kreuznacher Paradies
Riesling Eiswein
6%, ♀ till 2013 — **89**

2003 Kreuznacher Paradies
Riesling Trockenbeerenauslese
6.5%, ♀ till 2015 — **90**

2002 Kreuznacher St. Martin
Riesling Auslese
7.5%, ♀ till 2011 — **90**

2001 Kreuznacher Paradies
Riesling Eiswein "Johannes K."
7.5%, ♀ till 2020 — **92**

WEINGUT KRUGER-RUMPF

Owner: Stefan and Cornelia Rumpf
Manager: Stefan Rumpf
55424 Münster-Sarmsheim,
Rheinstraße 47
Tel. (0 67 21) 4 38 59, Fax 4 18 82
e-mail: info@kruger-rumpf.com
Internet: www.Kruger-rumpf.com
Directions: A 61, Dorsheim exit, B 48
in direction of Bingen, on main road in
Münster-Sarmsheim
Opening hours: Mon.–Sat. 09:00 to
19:00 hours, Sun. 16:00 to 20:00 hours
Restaurant: 17:00 to 23:00 hours
Sun. and public holidays from 16:00
hours, Closed Mon.
Specialties: Good home cooking
Worth seeing: Historical residential
house, pretty courtyard with old Nahe
cobblestones

Vineyard area: 19.5 hectares
Annual production: 140,000 bottles
Top sites: Münsterer Dauten-
pflänzer, Pittersberg and Rheinberg,
Dorsheimer Goldloch and Burgberg,
Binger Scharlachberg
Soil types: Slate, volcanic soil
Grape varieties: 65% Riesling,
10% each of Silvaner and Weißbur-
gunder, 5% each of Chardonnay,
Grau- and Spätburgunder
Average yield: 60 hl/ha
Best vintages: 2000, 2001, 2002
Member: VDP

We were again able to taste two very
good First Growths made by Stefan
Rumpf, although they were not quite as
brilliant as those of 2002. On the other
hand, the Pinot Noir he presented was
absolutely outstanding. It is the best red
wine of 2002 vintages in the Nahe region,
with an elegant, almost nervous body and
perfectly judged use of oak. There is no
doubt this winery is characterized by its
versatility. Be it Pinot or Riesling, red or
white, Stefan Rumpf produces above-
average quality in all the categories.

2003 Münsterer Pittersberg
Riesling trocken "Großes Gewächs"
13%, ♀ till 2009 **87**

2003 Münsterer Dautenpflänzer
Riesling trocken "Großes Gewächs"
13%, ♀ till 2009 **88**

2002 Münsterer Pittersberg
Riesling trocken "Großes Gewächs"
12%, ♀ till 2008 **90**

2002 Münsterer Dautenpflänzer
Riesling trocken "Großes Gewächs"
12.5%, ♀ till 2008 **90**

2003 Münsterer Kapellenberg
Riesling Kabinett
9.5%, ♀ till 2008 **87**

2003 Münsterer Pittersberg
Riesling Spätlese
8.5%, ♀ till 2009 **87**

2003 Münsterer Dautenpflänzer
Riesling Auslese
8.5%, ♀ till 2010 **88**

2002 Münsterer Pittersberg
Riesling Spätlese
8.5%, ♀ till 2010 **89**

2002 Münsterer Pittersberg
Riesling Eiswein
9.5%, ♀ till 2014 **90**

———— Red wines ————

2002 Spätburgunder trocken "M"
13%, ♀ till 2008 **87**

2002 Spätburgunder trocken "R"
13%, ♀ till 2008 **89**

The wines: **100** Perfect · **95–99** Outstanding · **90–94** Excellent · **85–89** Very good · **80–84** Good · **75–79** Average

419

WEINGUT LINDENHOF – MARTIN REIMANN

Owner: Martin Reimann
Winemaker: Martin Reimann
55452 Windesheim, Lindenhof
Tel. (0 67 07) 3 30, Fax 83 10
e-mail: weingut.lindenhof@t-online.de
Internet: www.weingutlindenhof.de
Directions: A 61, Windesheim exit,
in Windesheim follow winery signs
Opening hours: Mon.–Fri. 08:00 to
12:00 hours and 14:00 to 18:00 hours
Sat. 10:00 to 16:00 hours
and by appointment

Vineyard area: 9.5 hectares
Annual production: 55,000 bottles
Top sites: Windesheimer Fels,
Römerberg and Rosenberg
Soil types: Gray slate, decomposed
red sandstone, sandy clay
Grape varieties: 35% Riesling,
22% Weißburgunder, 21%
Spätburgunder, 5% each of Gewürz-
traminer and Chardonnay, 2% Dorn-
felder, 10% other varieties
Average yield: 58 hl/ha
Best vintages: 1999, 2001, 2002

Martin Reimann has done his homework. This refers to the strict restriction of yields, involving thinning out the Pinot varieties and a selective hand-picking procedure at harvest time. Both Pinot Noir and Pinot Blanc wines can be very good here, and the Rieslings are of the same high quality. The wines Martin Reimann makes are unpretentious in the best sense of the word, and excellent partners with food. The fruit is always clearly presented, and the structure well-balanced. The 2003 vintage range is the third good range in succession that Reimann has presented. However, unfortunately in this vintage the wines are a little lacking in personality. We would be happy to see the endeavors for better quality further intensified here, mainly to find out what Windesheim can still produce in the real top echelons.

2003 Weißer Burgunder
Spätlese trocken
13%, ♀ till 2006   82

2003 Riesling Spätlese trocken
13%, ♀ till 2007   84

2002 Weißer Burgunder
Spätlese trocken
12.5%, ♀ till 2006   84

2003 Weißer Burgunder
Spätlese trocken Goldkapsel Barrique
14%, ♀ till 2008   84

2002 Riesling Spätlese trocken
12.5%, ♀ till 2006   85

2002 Weißer Burgunder
Spätlese trocken Barrique
13.5%, ♀ till 2007   85

2003 Riesling
Spätlese trocken Goldkapsel
13.5%, ♀ till 2007   85

2003 Weißer Burgunder
Spätlese trocken Goldkapsel
13.5%, ♀ till 2008   85

2002 Riesling Spätlese
9%, ♀ till 2006   84

2003 Riesling
Spätlese Goldkapsel
9%, ♀ till 2008   86

2002 Riesling
Spätlese Goldkapsel
8.5%, ♀ till 2007   86

2002 Riesling Eiswein
7%, ♀ till 2010   87

———— Red wines ————

2002 Spätburgunder trocken
12.5%, ♀ till 2007   83

2002 Spätburgunder
Auslese trocken Barrique
14.5%, ♀ till 2008   86

2 0 0 2
RIESLING
Spätlese
WEINGUT LINDENHOF . M. REIMANN . WINDESHEIM . NAHE
LINDENHOF

WEINGUT LÖTZBEYER

Owner: Adolf Lötzbeyer
67824 Feilbingert, Kirchstraße 6
Tel. (0 67 08) 22 87, Fax 46 67
*Directions: A 61, Bad Kreuznach exit,
B 48 to Bad Münster am Stein-Ebern-
burg, in direction of Obermoschel*
Opening hours: Mon.–Fri. 09:00 to
18:00 hours, Sat. and Sun. 10:00 to
13:00 hours by appointment
History: Founded 1880

Vineyard area: 6.2 hectares
Annual production: 50,000 bottles
Top sites: Norheimer Dellchen,
Niederhäuser Rosenberg
Soil types: Volcanic soils and basalt
Grape varieties: 65% Riesling,
11% each of Bacchus and Scheurebe,
4% Portugieser, 3% each of Grau-
burgunder, Huxelrebe and Kerner
Average yield: 48 hl/ha
Best vintages: 1998, 1999, 2002

Feilbingert is hardly the center of the Nahe wine industry, nevertheless Adolf
Lötzbeyer attracted attention in the United States more than a decade ago, when
critic Robert Parker praised his wines.
That certainly helps to explain the high
share of export sales here, although exports to the US market have declined a
little. However, the Japanese continue to
enjoy Lötzbeyer's wines. We were not altogether happy with the range of 2003
wines presented, there is an aroma of
herbs and spices that is present in all the
wines. In addition, the quality of the Auslese wines is much too close to that of the
Spätlese wines. There is a good grapy
Feilbingerter Königsgarten Eiswein, but
on its own this is not enough to keep the
winery on the road to success. The estate
used to be extremely reliable as a producer of good fruity wines, and we sincerely hope that Lötzbeyer will return to form
soon. We have fond memories of very
good Spätlese and Auslese wines, as well
as of botrytis dessert wines that were
among the best in the region.

2002 Norheimer Oberberg
Riesling Spätlese trocken
11%, ♀ till 2007 — **86**

2003 Riesling Auslese
9%, ♀ till 2007 — **82**

2003 Norheimer Dellchen
Riesling Auslese
8%, ♀ till 2007 — **83**

2003 Feilbingerter Königsgarten
Scheurebe Auslese
9.5%, ♀ till 2007 — **83**

2002 Feilbingerter Königsgarten
Bacchus
10.5%, ♀ till 2008 — **85**

2002 Niederhäuser Pfaffenstein
Riesling Spätlese
8.5%, ♀ till 2008 — **85**

2003 Feilbingerter Königsgarten
Riesling Eiswein
7.5%, ♀ till 2012 — **87**

2002 Feilbingerter Königsgarten
Riesling Eiswein
7.5%, ♀ till 2014 — **90**

2001
Feilbingerter
Königsgarten
Riesling

Eiswein

Nahe

e 375 ml · alc. 9. 5 % vol.
A.P.-Nr. 7 725 072 025 02

Erzeugerabfüllung Weingut Lötzbeyer D-67824 Feilbingert
Telefon: 0 67 08-22 87 Qualitätswein mit Prädikat

The wines: **100** Perfect · **95–99** Outstanding · **90–94** Excellent · **85–89** Very good · **80–84** Good · **75–79** Average

421

WEINGUT MATHERN

Owner: Gloria Mathern
Administrator and winemaker:
Sabine Habenicht
55585 Niederhausen, Winzerstraße 7
Tel. (0 67 58) 67 14, Fax 81 09
e-mail: info@weingut-mathern.de
Internet: www.weingut-mathern.de
Directions: A 61, Bad Kreuznach exit,
via B 41 to Bad Münster exit, in direction
of Hüffelsheim, then left to Niederhausen
Sales: By appointment
Worth seeing: Was awarded "Golden
Vine" in 1981 as most attractive winery
building in the Nahe region

Vineyard area: 11 hectares
Annual production: 100,000 bottles
Top sites: Niederhäuser Her-
mannshöhle, Rosenberg, Felsenstey-
er, Kertz and Rosenheck, Norheimer
Dellchen and Kirschheck
Soil types: Porphyry and slate
Grape varieties: 70% Riesling, 11%
Dornfelder, 7% Müller-Thurgau, 6%
Weißburgunder, 6% other varieties
Average yield: 80 hl/ha
Best vintages: 1998, 1999, 2000

Following on the death of Helmut Mathern, Sabine Habenicht took on the running of the winery in July 2003, a difficult legacy. Following on an interim vintage, the 2003 vintage has now given her
an opportunity to display her ability. She
worked at one stage at the Finkenauer
winery in Bad Kreuznach, and can now
rely on the resources provided by Mathern's portfolio of very good Niederhausen vineyard sites. The range shows good
quality, although it is not of the same high
standard as that achieved by Helmut Mathern in his heyday. Certainly, more is
possible in the dry segment. The best
wine is the elegant Norheimer Kirschheck
Riesling Auslese "Luisa." We were not
all that impressed with the blend of Riesling and Pinot Blanc. Is a blend of these
varieties really necessary?

2003 Niederhäuser Rosenberg
Riesling Spätlese trocken
"50 Jahre alte Rebstöcke"
12.5%, ♀ till 2007 — **83**

2003 Niederhäuser Kertz
Riesling Spätlese
9%, ♀ till 2007 — **84**

2003 Niederhäuser Hermannshöhle
Riesling Spätlese
9%, ♀ till 2007 — **85**

2003 Niederhäuser Rosenberg
Riesling Auslese
9%, ♀ till 2008 — **85**

2003 Niederhäuser Rosenheck
Riesling Auslese "Henning"
9%, ♀ till 2008 — **85**

2001 Niederhäuser Rosenheck
Riesling Spätlese
7.5%, ♀ till 2006 — **86**

2003 Niederhäuser Rosenberg
Riesling Beerenauslese "HM"
9%, ♀ till 2010 — **86**

2003 Norheimer Kirschheck
Riesling Auslese "Luisa"
8.5%, ♀ till 2008 — **86**

2001 Niederhäuser Rosenberg
Riesling Spätlese
7.5%, ♀ till 2006 — **87**

2001 Niederhäuser Rosenberg
Riesling Auslese
8%, ♀ till 2008 — **88**

WEINGUT MATHERN

2000

Niederhäuser Rosenberg

Riesling Spätlese

Qualitätswein mit Prädikat

A.P.-Nr.7 750 043 18 01

alc.9 % vol   Gutsabfüllung   750 ml

Winzermeister Helmut Mathern
D-55585 Niederhausen/Nahe · Tel. 06758/6714

NAHE

The estates: ♦♦♦♦♦ World's finest · ♦♦♦♦ Germany's best · ♦♦♦ Very good · ♦♦ Good · ♦ Reliabl

WEINGUT MONTIGNY

Owner: Sascha Montigny
55452 Laubenheim, Weidenpfad 46
Tel. (0 67 04) 14 68, Fax 16 02
e-mail: sascha.montigny@montigny.de
Internet: www.montigny.de
Directions: A 61, Dorsheim exit, in direction of Laubenheim, in Laubenheim turn tight in direction of Bad Kreuznach, right at town exit
Sales: Sascha Montigny
Opening hours: Mon.–Sat. 14:00 to 18:00 hours by appointment

Vineyard area: 5.7 hectares
Annual production: 50,000 bottles
Top site: Laubenheimer Karthäuser
Soil types: Decomposed red sandstone with clay, loess
Grape varieties: 25% Riesling, 20% Spätburgunder, 13% Portugieser, 11% Grauburgunder, 8% Sankt Laurent, 5% Weißburgunder, 18% other varieties
Average yield: 80 hl/ha
Best vintage: 2000, 2001, 2002

For a long time now, the Nahe region has needed an estate such as this. A winery that proves each year just what is possible in this region in the red wine segment. The business was founded in the late Fifties by Waltraud and Rudolf Montigny as a vine-grafting operation, the first own wines were made in 1962. However, the marketing of bottled wine only gained in importance in the Nineties. When son Sascha took over the business in 1994, he closed down the grafting side. The white wines continue to be of reliable quality, and the red wines are in any case well known for their consistently convincing quality. The "Cuvée Mariage" is again one of the best Nahe red wines of the vintage. In future, red vines will also be found in the Karthäuser, the best vineyard site. Frühburgunder (early-ripening clone of Pinot Noir) has recently been planted. Sascha continues to work on the gradual improvement of his wines.

2003 Laubenheimer Karthäuser
Grauer Burgunder trocken
14%, ♀ till 2006 **83**

2003 Laubenheimer
Weißer Burgunder trocken
13.5%, ♀ till 2006 **84**

2002 Laubenheimer Karthäuser
Riesling Spätlese halbtrocken
11.5%, ♀ till 2006 **84**

2003 Laubenheimer Karthäuser
Riesling Spätlese
8.5%, ♀ till 2006 **83**

——————— Red wines ———————

2001 Spätburgunder
trocken Barrique
13%, ♀ till 2007 **85**

2001 Sankt Laurent
trocken Barrique
13%, ♀ till 2007 **85**

2002 St. Laurent
trocken Barrique "R"
13.5%, ♀ till 2008 **85**

2002 Spätburgunder
trocken Barrique "R"
14%, ♀ till 2009 **86**

2002 "Cuvée Mariage"
trocken Barrique
13.5%, ♀ till 2009 **87**

2001 "Cuvée Mariage"
trocken Barrique
13.5%, ♀ till 2008 **87**

Montigny
2003
Laubenheimer Karthäuser
Grauburgunder trocken
Qualitätswein

Gutsabfüllung
Weingut Sascha Montigny
D-55452 Laubenheim/Nahe
Nahe www.montigny.de
alc.14,0% vol A.P.Nr. 7 740 037 02 04 0,75 l

The wines: **100** Perfect · **95–99** Outstanding · **90–94** Excellent · **85–89** Very good · **80–84** Good · **75–79** Average

GUTSVERWALTUNG NIEDERHAUSEN-SCHLOSSBÖCKELHEIM

Owner: Erich Maurer family
Manager and winemaker: Christian Vogt
Administrator: Hartmut Günther
55585 Niederhausen
Tel. (0 67 58) 9 25 00, Fax 92 50 19
e-mail: info@riesling-domaene.de
Internet: www.riesling-domaene.de
Directions: Bad Kreuznach–Norheim,
turn right after Niederhausen
Sales: Werner Bumke, Gudrun Maurer
Opening hours: Mon.–Fri. 08:00 to
18:00 hours, Sat. 10:00 to 16:00 hours
Sun. 10:00 to 16:00 hours (May–Oct.)
History: Founded as model farm by
Prussian state in 1902
Worth seeing: Belle Epoque building
among the vineyards

> Vineyard area: 34 hectares
> Annual production: 200,000 bottles
> Top sites: Niederhäuser Her-
> mannsberg and Hermannshöhle,
> Schlossböckelheimer Kupfergrube
> and Felsenberg, Traiser Bastei
> Soil types: Volcanic, gray slate and
> lower new red sandstone
> Grape varieties: 90% Riesling,
> 3% each of Spätburgunder and Weiß-
> burgunder, 4% other varieties
> Average yield: 58 hl/ha
> Best vintages: 1999, 2001, 2002
> Member: VDP

Last year, the Maurer family presented
Christian Vogt, at 28 an exceptionally
young successor for Kurt Gabelmann,
who had left the winery. The young graduate of the wine school at Weinsberg hails
from the Mosel, and the 2003 vintage was
the first he has produced on his own. Unfortunately we were not particularly impressed by the wines, and have decided to
downgrade the winery. It will no doubt
take some time for Vogt to really get
to grips with the portfolio of top-class
vineyard sites available to him. The first
signs of this are already evident.

2003 Schlossböckelheimer Kupfergrube
Riesling Spätlese trocken
12.5%, ♀ till 2007   **84**

2003 Niederhäuser Hermannshöhle
Riesling Spätlese
8%, ♀ till 2007   **84**

2003 Niederhäuser Hermannsberg
Riesling Auslese
9.5%, ♀ till 2008   **87**

2002 Niederhäuser Hermannshöhle
Riesling Spätlese
9%, ♀ till 2008   **87**

2003 Niederhäuser Hermannsberg
Riesling Eiswein
6%, ♀ till 2012   **88**

2002 Niederhäuser Hermannshöhle
Riesling Spätlese Goldkapsel
7.5%, ♀ till 2009   **88**

2002 Schlossböckelheimer Kupfergrube
Riesling Auslese
8.5%, ♀ till 2010   **89**

2002 Niederhäuser Hermannsberg
Riesling Eiswein
8%, ♀ till 2012   **89**

2003 Niederhäuser Hermannsberg
Riesling Trockenbeerenauslese
7%, ♀ till 2014   **90**

GUTSVERWALTUNG
NIEDERHAUSEN
SCHLOSSBÖCKELHEIM

2003
Schloßböckelheimer
Kupfergrube
RIESLING SPÄTLESE
NAHE   TROCKEN

L.-A.P.Nr. 7 750 053 035 04
Qualitätswein mit Prädikat
D - 55585 Niederhausen
Gutsabfüllung
Product of Germany
alc. 12,5 % vol.
e 750 ml

WEINGUT RAPP

Owner: Walter Rapp
Winemaker: Walter Rapp
55583 Bad Münster a. St.-Ebernburg,
Schlossgartenstraße 74
Tel. (0 67 08) 23 12, Fax 30 74
e-mail: info@weingut-rapp.de
Internet: www.weingut-rapp.de
Directions: Via Bad Kreuznach to
Ebernburg, at town exit
(Schlossgartenstraße) next to entrance
to Ebernburg castle
Opening hours: Mon.–Sat. as well as
Sunday morning
Guest house: At winery
Worth a visit: Summer Night Jazz on
2nd weekend in August

Vineyard area: 8 hectares
Annual production: 55,000 bottles
Top sites: Ebernburger Schloss-
berg, Erzgrube and Stephansberg,
Altenbamberger Rotenberg
Soil types: Porphyry, slate, sandstone,
gravel, loess-clay
Grape varieties: 48% Riesling, 9%
Grauburgunder, 8% each of Müller-
Thurgau and Spätburgunder,
6% each of Dornfelder and Scheu-
rebe, 5% Weißburgunder, 4% each of
Silvaner and Kerner, 2% Portugieser
Average yield: 65 hl/ha
Best vintages: 1997, 2000, 2003

The best wines of this estate are labeled
"Porphyr," a sign for the attention and respect paid to the local terroir. This volcanic stone formation in the Ebernburg
vineyards is responsible for the elegant
mineral note found in the wines produced here. The Rapp winery is a family business, and son Walter has by now pretty
much taken over responsibility in the
cellar. Following on three preceding vintages that had a rather mixed bag of quality, the 2003 vintage range represents a distinct improvement. The wine we enjoyed most was the lovely off-dry Schlossberg Spätlese, which has an attractive
balance of mineral and fruity notes.

2002 Altenbamberger Rotenberg
Riesling Spätlese trocken
11%, ♀ till 2006   82

2002 Ebernburger Schlossberg
Riesling Spätlese trocken
12%, ♀ till 2006   83

2003 Altenbamberger Rotenberg
Riesling Spätlese trocken
12%, ♀ till 2007   84

2002 Ebernburger Schlossberg
Riesling Spätlese trocken "Porphyr"
12%, ♀ till 2007   84

2002 Altenbamberger Rotenberg
Riesling Spätlese halbtrocken
10.5%, ♀ till 2006   83

2002 Ebernburger Schlossberg
Riesling Spätlese halbtrocken "Porphyr"
11%, ♀ till 2006   84

2003 Ebernburger Stephansberg
Riesling Auslese halbtrocken "Porphyr"
12%, ♀ till 2008   85

2003 Ebernburger Schlossberg
Riesling Spätlese halbtrocken "Porphyr"
12%, ♀ till 2007   86

2003 Ebernburger Luisengarten
Scheurebe Auslese
12%, ♀ till 2006   83

2001 Altenbamberger Rotenberg
Riesling Spätlese
8%, ♀ till 2006   84

2003 Altenbamberger Rotenberg
Riesling Auslese
10%, ♀ till 2008   86

The wines: **100** Perfect · **95–99** Outstanding · **90–94** Excellent · **85–89** Very good · **80–84** Good · **75–79** Average

425

WEINGUT MICHAEL ROHR

Owner and manager: Michael Rohr
55592 Raumbach, Hauptstraße 104
Tel. (0 67 53) 28 27, Fax 62 78
e-mail: info@weingut-rohr.de
Internet: www.weingut-rohr.de
*Directions: B 41, Waldböckelheim exit,
to Meisenheim, one kilometer from the
B 420 to Raumbach*
Sales: Monika Rohr
Opening hours: Mon.–Fri. 09:00 to
18:00 hours, weekends by appointment
Worth seeing: Beautiful view from cottage in vineyards over Glan valley and
North Pfalz mountains

Vineyard area: 4.5 hectares
Annual production: 55,000 bottles
Top sites: Raumbacher
Schwalbennest and Schlossberg,
Meisenheimer Obere Heimbach
Soil types: Slate with sandy clay
Grape varieties: 50% Riesling, 11%
Müller-Thurgau, 10% each of Dornfelder and Weißburgunder, 7% Kerner,
6% Spätburgunder, 6% other varieties
Average yield: 90 hl/ha
Best vintages: 2000, 2001, 2002

Michael Rohr has practically single-handedly managed to return the name of Raumbach to the attention of Nahe wine enthusiasts. The steep vineyard slopes found there have the potential to produce great wines, the necessary skills in the cellar are also available: exclusively hand-picked grapes, slow fermentation, reductive maturation. The winery, with only 4.5 hectares of vineyards, has been in operation since 1950. While the estate is capable of producing excellent top-class botrytis dessert wines, these were noticeable by their absence in both 2002 and 2003. The so-called "small" wines are of a good standard. However, there is a lack of highlights. The best wines presented were off-dry Auslese as well as the dry Weißburgunder (Pinot Blanc) Auslese, both from the Schlossberg site. However, neither of these was really outstanding.

2003 Meisenheimer Obere Heimbach
Weißer Burgunder Spätlese trocken
13.5%, ♀ till 2006   **82**

2003 Raumbacher Schwalbennest
Riesling Kabinett trocken
12%, ♀ till 2006   **82**

2003 Raumbacher Schwalbennest
Riesling Spätlese trocken
12.5%, ♀ till 2006   **83**

2003 Raumbacher Schlossberg
Weißer Burgunder Auslese trocken
Barrique
14%, ♀ till 2007   **84**

2003 Raumbacher Schwalbennest
Riesling Spätlese halbtrocken
12.5%, ♀ till 2006   **83**

2003 Raumbacher Schlossberg
Riesling Auslese halbtrocken
13%, ♀ till 2008   **84**

2003 Raumbacher Schlossberg
Riesling Spätlese feinherb "Alte Reben"
13%, ♀ till 2007   **82**

2003 Raumbacher Schlossberg
Kerner Spätlese
11.5%, ♀ till 2006   **82**

2003 Raumbacher Schwalbennest
Riesling Spätlese
11%, ♀ till 2006   **83**

2001 Raumbacher Schwalbennest
Riesling Spätlese
10.5%, ♀ till 2006   **85**

2001 Raumbacher Schwalbennest
Riesling Auslese
9.5%, ♀ till 2006   **85**

2001 Raumbacher Schlossberg
Riesling Eiswein
7.5%, ♀ till 2009   **87**

WEINGUT
Rohr
2002ER
WEISSER BURGUNDER
TROCKEN
Meisenheimer Obere Heimbach
alc 12,5% vol   NAHE   750 ml

PRINZ ZU SALM-DALBERG
SCHLOSS WALLHAUSEN

Owner: Michael Prinz zu Salm-Salm
Manager and winemaker:
Markus Leyendecker
55595 Wallhausen, Schlossstraße 3
Tel. (0 67 06) 94 44 11, Fax 94 44 24
e-mail: salm.dalberg@salm-salm.de
Internet: www.salm-salm.de
Directions: A 61, Waldlaubersheim exit,
turn left over bridge at town exit
Opening hours: Mon.–Fri. 08:00 to 17:00
hours, Sat. and Sun. by appointment
History: First documented 1200; oldest
winery in Germany in family hands
without interruption
Worth seeing: Schloss Wallhausen
castle, vaulted cellar (1565), ruins of
Dalburg castle

Vineyard area: 12.5 hectares
Annual production: 70,000 bottles
Top sites: Wallhäuser Johannis-
berg and Felseneck, Roxheimer Berg
Soil types: Lower new red sandstone,
green slate
Grape varieties: 60% Riesling,
20% Spätburgunder, 4% Silvaner,
5% Müller-Thurgau, 6% Grau- and
Weißburgunder, 5% other varieties
Average yield: 40 hl/ha
Best vintages: 1999, 2000, 2003
Member: VDP, Naturland

The key vineyard site here is the Wallhäuser Felseneck, the only one known in
the world to feature green slate. This too
is part of the exemplary new concept put
forward by Michael Prinz zu Salm-Salm.
In the long run, he plans to produce only
a single wine from each vineyard site, a
wine that is intended to reflect the best of
each terroir. In the case of the Johannisberg site, the dry Spätlese is the best-
suited wine type, and has already been
identified. The Johannisberg and the Roxheimer Berg sites in this vintage produced First Growths such as we have never
tasted here before. The only wines we can
criticize a little are the basic ones.

2003 Wallhäuser Johannisberg
Riesling "Großes Gewächs"
12.5%, ♀ till 2008   **87**

2003 Roxheimer Berg
Riesling "Großes Gewächs"
12.5%, ♀ till 2008   **89**

2003 Schloss Wallhausen
Riesling Kabinett
10.5%, ♀ till 2006   **83**

2003 Roxheimer Berg
Riesling Spätlese
9.5%, ♀ till 2008   **85**

2003 Wallhäuser Felseneck
Riesling Spätlese
9.5%, ♀ till 2009   **87**

2003 Wallhäuser Johannisberg
Riesling Auslese
8.5%, ♀ till 2009   **88**

2002 Wallhäuser Felseneck
Riesling Spätlese
8%, ♀ till 2009   **88**

2002 Schloss Wallhausen
Riesling Eiswein
6.5%, ♀ till 2011   **88**

2002 Wallhäuser Felseneck
Riesling Eiswein
6.5%, ♀ till 2013   **90**

2001 Schloss Wallhausen
Riesling Eiswein
6.5%, ♀ till 2012   **90**

2003

BERG
ROXHEIM

SPÄTLESE

Schloss Wallhausen
Prinz zu Salm-Dalberg'sches Weingut

The wines: **100** Perfect · **95–99** Outstanding · **90–94** Excellent · **85–89** Very good · **80–84** Good · **75–79** Average

WEINGUT
JOH. BAPT. SCHÄFER

Owner: Sebastian Schäfer
Winemaker: Sebastian Schäfer
55452 Burg Layen, Burg Layen 8
Tel. (0 67 21) 4 35 52, Fax 4 78 41
Directions: A 61, Dorsheim exit, at Burg Layen after 500 meters
Sales: By appointment
Worth seeing: Vaulted cellar more than 100 years old, with oak barrels

---

Vineyard area: 6 hectares
Annual production: 40,000 bottles
Top sites: Dorsheimer Goldloch and Pittermännchen
Soil types: Gravelly clay and decomposed slate with heavy gravel
Grape varieties: 50% Riesling, 15% Spätburgunder, 10% Weißburgunder, 5% each of Scheurebe and Dornfelder, 15% other varieties
Average yield: 60 hl/ha
Best vintages: 2001, 2002, 2003

The 2003 vintage range presented by Sebastian Schäfer is a magnificent one. Certainly it is the best vintage in the history of the winery, and there are very few other producers in the Nahe region that can match this. In particular the botrytis dessert wines are all absolutely excellent, crowned by an awe-inspiring Trockenbeerenauslese Goldkapsel. There is no doubt that the young viticultural technician is one of the great talents in the Nahe region. He has been in charge of the estate since 1997, and gaining experience, he just keeps on getting better each year. In the cellar, each wine is tasted every day. This is an effort that pays off, and the same can be said of the investment in recent years in new stainless steel tanks, as well as in the acquisition of an additional two hectares of vineyard area. Now Sebastian Schäfer can select even more effectively at harvest time. He already has parcels in excellent vineyard sites. We are confident in predicting that a lot more will be heard from this estate in future.

2003 Riesling Classic
14%, ♀ till 2007 — **86**

2003 Dorsheimer Pittermännchen
Riesling Kabinett
8%, ♀ till 2007 — **86**

2003 Scheurebe Spätlese
9.5%, ♀ till 2008 — **86**

2002 Riesling Classic
12%, ♀ till 2006 — **87**

2003 Dorsheimer Pittermännchen
Riesling Spätlese
8.5%, ♀ till 2008 — **88**

2002 Dorsheimer Pittermännchen
Riesling Spätlese
8.5%, ♀ till 2008 — **89**

2003 Dorsheimer Pittermännchen
Riesling Auslese Goldkapsel
8%, ♀ till 2012 — **89**

2003 Dorsheimer Goldloch
Riesling Beerenauslese
7%, ♀ till 2016 — **90**

2003 Dorsheimer Goldloch
Riesling Eiswein
6.5%, ♀ till 2014 — **91**

2001 Dorsheimer Goldloch
Riesling Auslese Goldkapsel
7.5%, ♀ till 2012 — **91**

2003 Dorsheimer Pittermännchen
Riesling Trockenbeerenauslese
6%, ♀ till 2018 — **92**

2003 Dorsheimer Pittermännchen
Riesling Trockenbeerenauslese Goldkapsel
6%, ♀ till 2020 — **96**

Weingut Joh.Bapt.Schäfer
D-55452 Burg Layen · Telefon (0 67 21) 4 35 52 · Fax 4 78 41

2002
Dorsheimer Pittermännchen
Riesling Spätlese

Nahe
8,5 % vol

Gutsabfüllung
A. P. Nr. 7 763 075 008 03

Qualitätswein
mit Prädikat
0,75 l

The unique vineyard site Traiser Bastei at the foot of the Rotenfelsen rock formation, the highest steep slope north of the Alps.   *Photo: DWI/Dieth*

WEINGUT
SCHÄFER-FRÖHLICH

Owner: Hans, Karin, Tim and Meike Fröhlich
Manager: Hans Fröhlich
Winemaker: Tim and Karin Fröhlich
55595 Bockenau, Schulstraße 6
Tel. (0 67 58) 65 21, Fax 87 94
e-mail:
info@weingut-schaefer-froehlich.de
Directions: B 41, at Waldböckelheim
turn off to right, towards Bockenau
Sales: Karin and Meike Fröhlich
Opening hours: Mon.–Fri. 09:00 to
12:00 hours and 13:00 to 18:00 hours,
Sat. 08:00 to 12:00 hours
and 13:00 to 16:00 hours
by appointment only
History: Winemaking in the family
since 1800

Vineyard area: 11 hectares
Annual production: 70,000 bottles
Top sites: Schlossböckelheimer
Felsenberg, Bockenauer Felseneck,
Monzinger Frühlingsplätzchen
and Halenberg
Soil types: Porphyry, melaphyry and
decomposed volcanic formation, mix-
ture of lower new red sandstone and
Devon slate
Grape varieties: 58% Riesling, 26%
Pinot varieties, 16% other varieties
Average yield: 50 hl/ha
Best vintages: 2001, 2002, 2003
Member: VDP

The perfectionism found here is all-em-
bracing, and extends to all aspects of
wine production, to an extent probably
found nowhere else in the Nahe region.
Tim Fröhlich took over responsibility in
the cellar in 1995, since then the estate
has been going from strength to strength.
Tim Fröhlich is a serious man for one so
young (his surname means "happy" in
German), very firmly concentrated on his
work and on the wines he produces.
Asked where he foresees improving his
work in the years to come, in the vineyard
or in the cellar, his spontaneous reply is
"everywhere." In spite of the high level of
quality already achieved, he intends to
look in all directions for opportunities to
improve. A cool thinker, who is self-critical, and questions all he does. His wines
appear to be a reflection of their maker:
clear and with no frills, extremely strong
mineral notes, with no room for false
compromises. The ideal embodiment of
this philosophy are the brilliant botrytis
dessert wines, which each year are among
the best produced anywhere in Germany
in this category. Last year, a gold capsule
Eiswein was rated at a phantastic 97
points, this year a wonderfully creamy
Trockenbeerenauslese has also achieved
a dream score. However, these wines
should not draw attention away from the
other wines produced here: the concentrated, straight-as-a die style of the
"Große Gewächse" (First Growths), or
the beautifully mellow Pinot wines, of a
quality unequalled by any other producer
in the region. The incredible mineral
backbone of the wines made here meant
that even in a vintage such as 2003 there
was no need to add acidity, every wine
was refreshing and invigorating. All these
wonderful wines would not be possible
without the support of the family. Tim
Fröhlich's parents and his sister together
make up a powerful dream team in vinous
matters. The vineyard holdings have been
increased by three hectares in the past
few years, and this has also been beneficial in giving more choice in the selection
of top-class wines. We are very happy to
award the fourth bunch of grapes this
year, which means this family winery is
now among the very best producers in
Germany. We gladly express our congratulations, and raise our glasses to the
"Rising star of the year 2005."

2002 Bockenauer
Weißer Burgunder trocken Barrique
15%, ♀ till 2008 **86**

2003 Bockenauer
Weißer Burgunder trocken "S"
14.5%, ♀ till 2008 **86**

2003 Schlossböckelheimer Felsenberg
Riesling Spätlese trocken
13%, ♀ till 2008   **87**

2002 Monzinger Halenberg
Riesling Spätlese trocken
12.5%, ♀ till 2007   **87**

2001 Schlossböckelheimer Felsenberg
Riesling trocken "Erstes Gewächs"
13%, ♀ till 2006   **88**

2003 Monzinger Frühlingsplätzchen
Riesling trocken "Großes Gewächs"
13.5%, ♀ till 2008   **89**

2003 Monzinger Halenberg
Riesling trocken "Großes Gewächs"
13%, ♀ till 2008   **90**

2002 Bockenauer Felseneck
Riesling Spätlese halbtrocken
11.5%, ♀ till 2006   **86**

2003 Bockenauer Felseneck
Riesling Spätlese
10%, ♀ till 2008   **87**

2002 Monzinger Frühlingsplätzchen
Riesling Spätlese
8.5%, ♀ till 2008   **87**

2003 Monzinger Halenberg
Riesling Spätlese
10%, ♀ till 2009   **88**

2002 Monzinger Halenberg
Riesling Spätlese
8.5%, ♀ till 2008   **88**

2002 Bockenauer Felseneck
Riesling Spätlese Goldkapsel
7.5%, ♀ till 2009   **88**

2003 Bockenauer Felseneck
Riesling Auslese
9%, ♀ till 2010   **89**

2002 Bockenauer Felseneck
Riesling Auslese
7%, ♀ till 2010   **89**

2001 Bockenauer Felseneck
Riesling Spätlese Goldkapsel
9%, ♀ till 2008   **89**

2003 Bockenauer Felseneck
Riesling Spätlese Goldkapsel
9%, ♀ till 2009   **90**

2001 Bockenauer Felseneck
Riesling Auslese Goldkapsel
8%, ♀ till 2010   **90**

2003 Bockenauer Felseneck
Riesling Auslese Goldkapsel
9%, ♀ till 2012   **91**

2001 Bockenauer Felseneck
Riesling Eiswein Goldkapsel
7%, ♀ till 2014   **91**

2003 Monzinger Frühlingsplätzchen
Riesling Beerenauslese
7.5%, ♀ till 2016   **92**

2001 Bockenauer Felseneck
Riesling Beerenauslese
⋎ auction wine, 7%, ♀ till 2012   **92**

2002 Bockenauer Felseneck
Riesling Auslese Goldkapsel
⋎ auction wine, 8%, ♀ till 2011   **92**

2002 Bockenauer Felseneck
Riesling Eiswein
⋎ auction wine, 6%, ♀ till 2020   **93**

2003 Bockenauer Felseneck
Riesling Trockenbeerenauslese – 30 –
⋎ auction wine, 6.5%, ♀ till 2024   **95**

2002 Bockenauer Felseneck
Riesling Eiswein Goldkapsel
6%, ♀ till 2022   **97**

2003 Bockenauer Felseneck
Riesling Trockenbeerenauslese
Goldkapsel – 31 –
6%, ♀ till 2028   **98**

The wines: **100** Perfect · **95–99** Outstanding · **90–94** Excellent · **85–89** Very good · **80–84** Good · **75–79** Average

WEINGUT
ERICH SCHAUSS & SOHN

Owner: Edgar und Elmar Schauß
Winemaker: Elmar Schauß
55569 Monzingen, Römerstraße 5 + 12
Tel. (0 67 51) 28 82, Fax 68 60
e-mail: weingut-schauss@web.de
Internet: www.weingut-schauss.de
Directions: On the B41 from Bad Kreuz-
nach, in direction of Kirn
Sales: Schauß family
Opening hours: Mon.–Fri. 08:00 to
19:30 hours, Sat. 09:00 to 18:00 hours
Sun. 10:00 to 17:00 hours
History: Winery founded 1800

Vineyard area: 12.5 hectares
Annual production: 100,000 bottles
Top sites: Monzinger Halenberg
and Frühlingsplätzchen
Soil types: Mixture of slate, quartzite
and basalt, lower new red sandstone
Grape varieties: 42% Riesling,
31% red varieties, 6% Müller-Thurgau,
8% Grau- and Weißburgunder,
13% other varieties
Average yield: 62 hl/ha
Best vintages: 2001, 2002, 2003

The family winery is located next to the old town mill, and never before have such good wines been produced here as in the 2002 and 2003 vintages. The Riesling wines, in particular, are very good. There is a good reason for this. There are significant holdings in the best local vineyard sites, and 30 percent of the Riesling vines are 30 years or older. Some decisive innovative impulses have come from Elmar Schauß, who completed his winemaking studies and took over the management of the operation four years ago. 2003 was the first vintage in which a Trockenbeerenauslese wine has been produced – and indeed two such wines were made. "The vintage was simply pre-destined for botrytis dessert wines" says the owner proudly, confident of the quality of his top-class botrytis wines, which have an incredible acidity.

2003 Monzinger Rosenberg
Riesling Spätlese trocken
12%, ♀ till 2006   **83**

2002 Monzinger Frühlingsplätzchen
Riesling Auslese **
9%, ♀ till 2008   **87**

2003 Monzinger Halenberg
Riesling Auslese **
8%, ♀ till 2009   **88**

2003 Monzinger Halenberg
Riesling Beerenauslese
7.5%, ♀ till 2012   **88**

2003 Monzinger Halenberg
Riesling Eiswein
7%, ♀ till 2012   **88**

2003 Monzinger Frühlingsplätzchen
Riesling Trockenbeerenauslese
7%, ♀ till 2014   **89**

2003 Monzinger Frühlingsplätzchen
Spätburgunder Weißherbst
Trockenbeerenauslese
7.5%, ♀ till 2014   **89**

2002 Monzinger Halenberg
Riesling Eiswein
8.5%, ♀ till 2012   **89**

2002 Monzinger Halenberg
Riesling Eiswein ***
8.5%, ♀ till 2016   **92**

WEINGUT Schauß & SOHN

2002
SPÄTBURGUNDER WEISSHERBST
SPÄTLESE FEINHERB
MONZINGER FRÜHLINGSPLÄTZCHEN

NAHE

Qualitätswein mit Prädikat · Gutsabfüllung
12,5% vol   A. P. Nr. 7 748 062 17 03 · Product of Germany   750 ml
RÖMERSTRASSE 12 · D-55569 MONZINGEN · TEL 0 67 51-28 82

The estates: World's finest · Germany's best · Very good · Good · Reliable

WEINGUT SCHMIDT

Owner: Andreas Schmidt
Winemaker: Andreas Schmidt
67823 Obermoschel, Luitpoldstraße 24
Tel. (0 63 62) 12 65, Fax 41 45
e-mail:
weingut-schmidt@otelo-online.de
Internet: www. weingut-schmidt.net
*Directions: A 61, Gau-Bickelheim exit,
via the B 420*
Sales: Schmidt family
Opening hours: Mon.–Sat. 08:00 to
18:00 hours, Sun. by appointment

Vineyard area: 19 hectares
Annual production: 250,000 bottles
Top sites: Obermoscheler Silberberg
and Schlossberg, Norheimer Dellchen
Soil types: Slate, volcanic soil
Grape varieties: 59% Riesling, 8%
each of Müller-Thurgau and Silvaner,
12% red varieties, 4% Kerner, 6%
Grauburgunder, 3% other varieties
Average yield: 63 hl/ha
Best vintages: 1997, 2001, 2003

This is the largest winery in the Alsenz valley, which lies to the south of the Nahe. Herbert and Andreas Schmidt own 16 hectares of vineyards, and additionally take in grapes from a few contract growers. Their own vineyards are mostly steep slopes that are difficult to work, and here the brothers look particularly for a good humus content of the soils. The vintage often only ends around the middle of November, as the Schmidts try to nurture every bit of ripeness possible in the grapes. A lot of changes have been implemented in both the vineyards and the cellar recently in an endeavor to improve quality. A new winery facility is planned for construction in 2005. This year's range is characterized by quite a marked acidity. The wines we liked best were the racy, fruity Schlossberg Spätlese, as well as the Gewürztraminer Auslese, which is reminiscent of Alsace wines. The two Trockenbeerenauslese wines lacked clarity, and did not convince us.

2003 Obermoscheler Silberberg
Riesling trocken
12%, ♀ till 2006 **81**

2003 Obermoscheler Silberberg
Riesling Kabinett trocken
12%, ♀ till 2006 **82**

2003 Obermoscheler Silberberg
Riesling Spätlese trocken
13%, ♀ till 2006 **82**

2003 Obermoscheler Geißenkopf
Weißer Burgunder trocken Selection
14%, ♀ till 2006 **82**

2003 Obermoscheler Sonnenplätzchen
Grauer Burgunder trocken Selection
14%, ♀ till 2007 **83**

2003 Obermoscheler Silberberg
Riesling trocken Selection
13.5%, ♀ till 2007 **83**

2003 Obermoscheler Schlossberg
Riesling Spätlese
9.5%, ♀ till 2007 **84**

2003 Obermoscheler Geißenkopf
Gewürztraminer Auslese
11.5%, ♀ till 2009 **86**

2003 Obermoscheler Silberberg
Riesling Trockenbeerenauslese – 17 –
6.5%, ♀ till 2012 **86**

2003 Obermoscheler Silberberg
Riesling Trockenbeerenauslese – 16 –
9%, ♀ till 2013 **87**

Weingut
SCHMIDT

NAHE
2002
OBERMOSCHELER
SILBERBERG
RIESLING
TROCKEN
Qualitätswein b. A. · A.P. Nr. 7 785 033 14 03
GUTSABFÜLLUNG
Weingut SCHMIDT · D-87823 Obermoschel/Nahe
750 ml   alc.12.0 % vol

The wines: **100** Perfect · **95–99** Outstanding · **90–94** Excellent · **85–89** Very good · **80–84** Good · **75–79** Average

433

WEINGUT
JAKOB SCHNEIDER

Owner: Jakob Schneider
55585 Niederhausen, Winzerstraße 15
Tel. (0 67 58) 9 35 33, Fax 9 35 35
e-mail: info@schneider-wein.de
Internet: www.schneider-wein.de
*Directions: From Bad Kreuznach via
Bad Münster and Norheim to Nieder-
hausen, turn right to center of town*
Opening hours: Mon.–Sat. 08:00 to
19:00 hours and by appointment
History: Winemaking since 1575
Worth seeing: Vaulted cellar with oak
barrels, vineyard walks

Vineyard area: 13 hectares
Annual production: 85,000 bottles
Top sites: Niederhäuser
Hermannshöhle and Klamm,
Norheimer Dellchen and Kirschheck
Soil types: Volcanic soil, slate
Grape varieties: 88% Riesling,
4% red varieties, 8% other varieties
Average yield: 58 hl/ha
Best vintages: 2000, 2001, 2002

Jakob Schneider owns almost two hectares of the legendary Niederhäuser Hermannshöhle site, making him one of the
largest holders here. In other respects too,
this winery has a portfolio of top-class
vineyard parcels on the middle Nahe second to none. Hail damage reduced the
yield of the vineyards in 2003 to a minuscule 28 hl/ha. This was at least partly
made up by a wine such as the Trockenbeerenauslese, which was picked at a
must weight of 220 degrees of Oechsle.
Since last year Jakob Schneider junior –
who lends his name each year to the best
Auslese of the winery – has been studying
winemaking in Geisenheim. He has already been responsible for innovations
such as the purchase of a new tank press
and the installation of air-conditioning
for the cellar. The style of the wines can
only be termed classic, while the prices are
particularly consumer-friendly.

2003 Niederhäuser Hermannshöhle
Riesling Spätlese trocken
12.5%, ♀ till 2006 82

2003 Niederhäuser Rosenheck
Riesling Spätlese trocken
13%, ♀ till 2006 83

2003 Niederhäuser Kertz
Riesling Spätlese halbtrocken
11.5%, ♀ till 2006 82

2003 Niederhäuser Klamm
Riesling Spätlese
10.5%, ♀ till 2007 83

2003 Norheimer Kirschheck
Riesling Spätlese
10%, ♀ till 2007 84

2003 Norheimer Dellchen
Riesling Auslese
9%, ♀ till 2008 86

2003 Niederhäuser Hermannshöhle
Riesling Spätlese "Edith-Elisabeth"
9%, ♀ till 2008 86

2003 Niederhäuser Hermannshöhle
Riesling Auslese "Junior"
9%, ♀ till 2010 88

2002 Niederhäuser Hermannshöhle
Riesling Auslese "Junior"
8.5%, ♀ till 2010 89

2003 Niederhäuser Hermannshöhle
Riesling Trockenbeerenauslese
7%, ♀ till 2018 91

2002 Niederhäuser Hermannshöhle
Riesling Eiswein "Magnus"
6.5%, ♀ till 2016 92

Anno 1575

NAHE   NAHE

2003er
Niederhäuser Rosenheck
Riesling Spätlese trocken
Qualitätswein mit Prädikat
A. P. Nr. 7 750 052 25 04
GUTSABFÜLLUNG
alc. 13 by % vol.   Product of Germany   e 750 ml
WEINGUT JAKOB SCHNEIDER
D 55585 NIEDERHAUSEN · Tel. 06758/93533 und 6701

WEINGUT
MEINOLF SCHÖMEHL

**Owner: Hartmut Hahn
and Elke Schömehl-Hahn**
55452 Dorsheim, Binger Straße 2
Tel. (0 67 21) 4 56 75, Fax 4 86 23
e-mail: weingut@schoemehl.de
Internet: www.schoemehl.de
*Directions: A 61, Dorsheim exit, in
center of town*
Sales: Schömehl and Hahn families
Opening hours: Mon.–Sat. 09:00 to
18:00 hours and by appointment

Vineyard area: 11 hectares
Annual production: 90,000 bottles
Top sites: Dorsheimer Burgberg,
Goldloch and Pittermännchen, Lau-
benheimer Karthäuser and Fuchsen
Soil types: Stony, gravelly clay on
layered lower new red sandstone,
decomposed sandstone, gravel
Grape varieties: 43% Riesling, 12%
Müller-Thurgau, 7% each of Silvaner
and Portugieser, 6% Spätburgunder,
5% Dornfelder, 20% other varieties
Average yield: 92 hl/ha
Best vintages: 2001, 2002

Because of its top-class vineyards, Dorsheim is famous well beyond the borders
of the region, but until now none of the
wineries in the village itself have been
deemed worthy of grape-bunch status by
this guide. Now, Hartmut Hahn and Elke
Schömehl-Hahn have changed this. The
2001 range was most convincing, the
2002 range not quite as good but still on a
high level. In 2003, the wines lack clarity
and brilliance, and there are no real highlights of the vintage. Hartmut Hahn plans
to concentrate increasingly on red wine,
and wants to instal a separate cellar for
this specific purpose. The white wines,
too, will no doubt benefit from the plans
to expand the stainless steel tank capac-
ty. Hahn has recently purchased additional parcels in the famous Dorsheimer
Pittermännchen and Goldloch sites, and
this, too, is bound to improve quality.

2003 Riesling Classic
12%, ♀ till 2006 — **81**

2003 Dorsheimer Pittermännchen
Riesling Kabinett halbtrocken
11%, ♀ till 2006 — **82**

2003 Dorsheimer Burgberg
Riesling Spätlese halbtrocken
11.5%, ♀ till 2006 — **82**

2003 Laubenheimer Karthäuser
Riesling Spätlese halbtrocken
12%, ♀ till 2006 — **83**

2002 Laubenheimer Karthäuser
Riesling Spätlese halbtrocken
11%, ♀ till 2006 — **84**

2001 Dorsheimer Burgberg
Riesling Spätlese halbtrocken
11%, ♀ till 2006 — **85**

2003 Laubenheimer Karthäuser
Riesling Auslese
7.5%, ♀ till 2008 — **84**

2002 Laubenheimer Karthäuser
Riesling Auslese
9%, ♀ till 2007 — **85**

2001 Dorsheimer Goldloch
Riesling Spätlese
8.5%, ♀ till 2006 — **86**

2002 Laubenheimer Karthäuser
Riesling Eiswein
6.5%, ♀ till 2011 — **88**

The wines: **100** Perfect · **95–99** Outstanding · **90–94** Excellent · **85–89** Very good · **80–84** Good · **75–79** Average

435

WEINGUT BÜRGERMEISTER WILLI SCHWEINHARDT NACHF.

Owner: Wilhelm and Axel Schweinhardt
Winemaker: Axel Schweinhardt
55450 Langenlonsheim,
Heddesheimer Straße 1
Tel. (0 67 04) 9 31 00, Fax 93 10 50
e-mail: info@schweinhardt.de
Internet: www.schweinhardt.de
Directions: A 61, Dorsheim or Bad Kreuznach/Langenlonsheim exit
Opening hours: Mon.–Fri. 09:00 to 12:00 hours and 13:00 to 18:00 hours
Sat. 10:00 to 12:00 hours
and by appointment
Worth seeing: Distillery, visitors courtyard from turn of 20th century, old vaulted cellar with barrique barrels

---

Vineyard area: 33 hectares
Annual production: 150,000 bottles
Top sites: Langenlonsheimer Rothenberg, Löhrer Berg and Königsschild
Soil types: Decomposed sandstone, gravel, rubble and loess
Grape varieties: 35% Riesling, 20% Grau- and Weißburgunder as well as Chardonnay, 20% red varieties, 25% other varieties
Average yield: 55 hl/ha
Best vintages: 1998, 2002, 2003

The Wilhelm Schweinhardt winery is one of the largest wineries in the Nahe region, and one which has all the modern technology installed. The barrique cellar located below the winery is beautiful. A distillery is located in the attractive and well-kept courtyard of the former Pies winery, producing reliably good distilled products. Schweinhardt presented a fantastic range this year. Concentrated dry white wines, elegant reds, and the highlight is a Trockenbeerenauslese Goldkapsel that compares with the best in Germany. We raise our hat to this performance. We are happy to award the third bunch of grapes for this.

2003 Langenlonsheimer Löhrer Berg
Riesling Spätlese trocken
13%, ♀ till 2007   86

2003 Langenlonsheimer Rothenberg
Riesling Spätlese trocken
12.5%, ♀ till 2008   88

2003 Langenlonsheimer Rothenberg
Riesling Spätlese halbtrocken
12.5%, ♀ till 2008   87

2002 Langenlonsheimer Rothenberg
Riesling Auslese
9.5%, ♀ till 2008   87

2003 Langenlonsheimer Königsschild
Riesling Spätlese
9%, ♀ till 2008   88

2003 Langenlonsheimer Königsschild
Riesling Trockenbeerenauslese
9%, ♀ till 2016   90

2003 Langenlonsheimer Königsschild
Riesling Trockenbeerenauslese Goldkapsel
6.5%, ♀ till 2020   95

——————— Red wines ———————

2001 Frühburgunder
trocken Barrique
13.5%, ♀ till 2007   85

2002 Langenlonsheimer
Spätburgunder Auslese trocken
13.5%, ♀ till 2008   86

2002 Frühburgunder
Auslese trocken
14%, ♀ till 2008   88

2002

Weißer Burgunder
Spätlese trocken

Langenlonsheimer Löhrer Berg

BÜRGERMEISTER WILLI
SCHWEINHARDT
LANGENLONSHEIM NAHE

WEINGUT
WILHELM SITZIUS

Owner: Sonja and Wilhelm Sitzius
Winemaker: Wilhelm Sitzius
55450 Langenlonsheim,
Naheweinstraße 87
Tel. (0 67 04) 13 09, Fax 27 81
e-mail: weingut@sitzius.de
Directions: A 61, Dorsheim exit,
via Laubenheim to Langenlonsheim
Opening hours: Mon.–Fri. 09:30 to
18:00, Sat. 09:30 to 16:00 hours,
Sun. by appointment
Restaurant: With Mediterranean court-
yard, March to Oct. Fri. and Sat. from
18:00 hours, Sun. from 17:00 hours
History: Winemaking here since 1560

Vineyard area: 15 hectares
Annual production: 90,000 bottles
Top sites: Niederhäuser
Hermannshöhle, Langenlonsheimer
Königsschild, Löhrer Berg and
Rothenberg, Oberhäuser Leistenberg
Soil types: Volcanic soil, slate, red
sandstone, melaphyry, gravelly clay
Grape varieties: 60% Riesling,
30% white and red Pinot varieties,
10% other varieties
Average yield: 70 hl/ha
Best vintages: 1998, 2000, 2003

The Sitzius family has lived in Langenlonsheim since the 16th century, and currently the tenth generation is involved in
winemaking. However, all this tradition
does not mean that one is opposed to innovation. A new cellar facility has been
built in recent years, bringing with it temperature-controlled stainless steel tanks.
A restaurant and wine bar was added in
2003. The new vintage gives the estate an
opportunity to present a solid range. The
most attractive wine is the concentrated
Laubenheimer Krone Scheurebe Spätlese,
which shows just what this often underrated variety can produce. Unfortunately
we were denied the pleasure of tasting any
botrytis dessert wines, which Wilhelm
Sitzius knows how to make so well.

2003 Oberhäuser Kieselberg
Riesling Spätlese trocken
13%, ♀ till 2006 — **83**

2003 Chardonnay trocken
13.5%, ♀ till 2006 — **83**

2002 Langenlonsheimer Königsschild
Riesling Spätlese trocken
"Sitzius Selektion"
12%, ♀ till 2006 — **84**

2003 Silvaner
12.5%, ♀ till 2006 — **80**

2003 Weißer Burgunder Spätlese
13.5%, ♀ till 2006 — **84**

2003 Laubenheimer Krone
Scheurebe Spätlese
9.5%, ♀ till 2007 — **86**

2002 Riesling Eiswein
7%, ♀ till 2012 — **88**

——— Red wines ———

2003 Spätburgunder
trocken Selection
13.5%, ♀ till 2007 — **83**

2002 Spätburgunder
Auslese trocken
13.5%, ♀ till 2007 — **84**

2001 Spätburgunder
Auslese trocken
13%, ♀ till 2006 — **84**

The wines: **100** Perfect · **95–99** Outstanding · **90–94** Excellent · **85–89** Very good · **80–84** Good · **75–79** Average

437

STAATSWEINGUT BAD KREUZNACH

Owner: Federal state of Rheinland-Pfalz
Administrator: Alfred Krolla
Winemaker: Rainer Gies
55545 Bad Kreuznach,
Rüdesheimer Straße 68
Tel. (06 71) 82 03 30, Fax 82 03 01
e-mail: info@staatsweingut.de
Internet: www.staatsweingut.de
Directions: B 41, Kreuznach-Nord exit
Sales: Elfriede Gerhart
Opening hours: Mon.–Thur. 09:00 to
12:30 hours and 14:00 to 17:00 hours
Fri. 09:00 to 14:30 hours
Worth seeing: Building in historical
Belle Epoque style, vaulted cellar

Vineyard area: 19 hectares
Annual production: 120,000 bottles
Top sites: Kreuznacher Kahlen-
berg, Forst, Hinkelstein and Vogel-
sang, Norheimer Kafels
Soil types: Gravel on terraces, loess-
clay, sandy clay on kaolin, porphyry
Grape varieties: 45% Riesling, 13%
Müller-Thurgau, 9% Silvaner, 17%
red varieties, 5% Weißburgunder,
11% other varieties
Average yield: 70 hl/ha
Best vintages: 2001, 2002, 2003

The "Provincial Educational Institution"
was founded in 1900, and the state winery
that grew out of this has been instrumen-
tal in shaping the development of the
wine industry in the Nahe region for the
past 105 years. The viticultural college includes 19 hectares of vineyards, which are
planted to a whole host of varieties in addition to Riesling, as can be expected at a
school where experimentation is part of
the philosophy. In 2003, as in other vintages, the wines leaving the best impression are from the Norheimer Kafels, with
their distinct terroir character. In addition
the red wines, for which the winery has
built up an excellent reputation, are good.
The botrytis dessert wines crown a very
good range across the board.

2003 Kreuznacher Kahlenberg
Riesling Spätlese trocken
13%, ♀ till 2006   83

2002 Kreuznacher Kahlenberg
Riesling Auslese trocken
12.5%, ♀ till 2007   87

2003 Kreuznacher Kahlenberg
Riesling Spätlese halbtrocken
12.5%, ♀ till 2006   83

2003 Kreuznacher Kahlenberg
Riesling Spätlese
10%, ♀ till 2008   85

2002 Norheimer Kafels
Riesling Spätlese
8.5%, ♀ till 2008   87

2003 Norheimer Kafels
Riesling Spätlese
9.5%, ♀ till 2009   88

2003 Norheimer Kafels
Riesling Auslese
10%, ♀ till 2010   88

2003 Kreuznacher Kahlenberg
Riesling Beerenauslese
9%, ♀ till 2014   89

2003 Norheimer Kafels
Riesling Trockenbeerenauslese
8%, ♀ till 2018   91

——————— Red wines ———————

2002 Kreuznacher Hinkelstein
Domina trocken
13.5%, ♀ till 2008   85

2002 "Prestige" trocken Barrique
14%, ♀ till 2008   86

Staatsweingut
Bad Kreuznach

2001
Norheimer Kafels
RIESLING AUSLESE
NAHE

WEINGUT TESCH

Owner: Hartmut Tesch
Manager: Hartmut Tesch
and Dr. Martin Tesch
55450 Langenlonsheim,
Naheweinstraße 99
Tel. (0 67 04) 9 30 40, Fax 93 04 15
e-mail: info@weingut-tesch.de
Internet: www.weingut-tesch.de
Directions: A 61, Langenlonsheim exit
Sales: Mon.–Fri. by appointment
History: Family-owned since 1723

Vineyard area: 18.8 hectares
Annual production: 140,000 bottles
Top sites: Laubenheimer Karthäuser
and St. Remigiusberg, Langenlons-
heimer Königsschild and Löhrer Berg
Soil types: Red sandstone, clay-kao-
lin, clay with red rubble, loess
Grape varieties: 84% Riesling,
8% each of Weiß- and Spätburgunder
Average yield: 65 hl/ha
Best vintages: 1998, 1999, 2000
Member: VDP

You can either love or hate the new labels of this winery – but nobody is indifferent to them. That is a reaction Martin Tesch expected, and it will not sway him. He is extremely conscious of vineyard character, one of the most dedicated terroir-ists in Germany. His range includes five dry Riesling Spätlese wines, all the grapes being picked at the same time, and all the wines were similarly vinified. What speaks to you is the terroir. The vineyards were in a time warp for 20 years, no fashions or trends have left their mark here. That is one of the reasons the average age of the vineyards is around 30 years. Martin Tesch is aware that his Rieslings will polarize consumers. This year, we were not completely happy with the wines. In addition one must ask the question whether it makes sense to completely ig-nore the botrytis dessert segment in a ripe vintage like 2003, which is tailor-made for this style of wine – a Riesling style that Tesch works with very well!

2003 "Unplugged"
Riesling Kabinett trocken
12%, ♀ till 2006   83

2003 Langenlonsheimer Königsschild
Riesling Spätlese trocken
12.5%, ♀ till 2007   83

2003 "Deep Blue" trocken
13%, ♀ till 2006   83

2003 Langenlonsheimer Löhrer Berg
Riesling Spätlese trocken
12.5%, ♀ till 2007   84

2003 Laubenheimer Krone
Riesling Spätlese trocken
12.5%, ♀ till 2007   84

2003 Laubenheimer Karthäuser
Riesling Spätlese trocken
12.5%, ♀ till 2008   86

2003 Laubenheimer St. Remigiusberg
Riesling Spätlese trocken
12.5%, ♀ till 2008   87

2003 Laubenheimer St. Remigiusberg
Riesling trocken "Großes Gewächs"
➤ auction wine, 12.5%, ♀ till 2008   87

2002 Laubenheimer Karthäuser
Riesling Spätlese trocken
12.5%, ♀ till 2008   89

2002 Laubenheimer St. Remigiusberg
Riesling Spätlese trocken
➤ auction wine, 12.5%, ♀ till 2008   89

2002 Langenlonsheimer Löhrer Berg
Riesling Trockenbeerenauslese
6%, ♀ till 2016   92

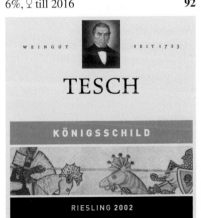

The wines: **100** Perfect · **95–99** Outstanding · **90–94** Excellent · **85–89** Very good · **80–84** Good · **75–79** Average

439

Nahe

Weingut Theodor Enk

55452 Dorsheim, Weinbergstraße 13
Tel. (0 67 21) 4 54 70, Fax 4 78 84

Last year, we predicted a positive devlop-
ment here, and Steffen Enk has confirmed
this in the shape of his 2003 range of
wines. Yet again, our favorite wine was
the Laubenheimer Karthäuser Weißbur-
gunder (Pinot Blanc) Spätlese (83 points).
The Rieslings are clean and typical of the
variety, but we are mystified as to why
they should be presented in Burgundy
bottles. With reference to the red wines,
there is ample scope for improvement.

Weingut Georg Forster

55452 Rümmelsheim,
Burg Layer Straße 20
Tel. (0 67 21) 4 51 23, Fax 49 87 77
e-mail: mail@georgforster.de
Internet: www.georgforster.de

The Georg Forster winery focuses on red
wine: Pinot Noir, Dornfelder and Regent,
and organic viticulture is practised. This
was the best range we have ever tasted
here. At last, the wines are harmonious,
and not dominated by acidity. The high-
lights of the range are the barrel-matured
2002 Regent trocken (dry – 83 points)
and the juicy 2003 Johannisberg Riesling
Auslese (83 points).

Weingut Albert Gälweiler

55595 Sankt Katharinen, Mühlenstraße 6
Tel. (0 67 06) 4 05, Fax 67 86

The best new discovery is located in St.
Katharinen. Albert Gälweiler is the fa-
ther, and he works closely with his sons
Andreas and Dr. Leo Gälweiler. The
declared objective is "individual wines
with an unmistakable character." Both,
the packaging and the bottle contents are
convincing, the wines are full-bodied and
clean. The wines we liked best are the
2002 St. Kathariner Fels Spätburgunder
(Pinot Noir – 85 points) and the dry 2003
Grauburgunder (Pinot Gris – 83 points),
showing they can make good white wines
too.

Weingut Graf-Binzel

55450 Langenlonsheim,
Naheweinstraße 164
Tel. (0 67 04) 13 25, Fax 28 90
e-mail: weingut@graf-binzel.de
Internet: www.graf-binzel.de

Andreas Binzel, who works closely wi
his father Helmut Binzel in running th
winery, has spent time in South Afric
California, Chile and New Zealand, o
serving winemaking practices there. Th
2003 vintage here has brought forth
convincing range of wines, headed up b
a Huxelrebe Beerenauslese (86 points
We even slightly preferred the incredib
creamy Langenlonsheimer Königsschi
*Auslese ** (86 points).*

Weingut Königswingert

55452 Guldental, Naheweinstraße 44
Tel. (0 67 07) 87 65, Fax 82 13
e-mail: info@koenigswingert.de
Internet: www.koenigswingert.de

Regrettably, there are hardly any win
makers in the Guldental valley who ma
age to make more than basic wines her
in spite of the recognized potential of th
area. The Königswingert winery is an e.
ception. The strong suits here are the of
dry and fruity wines. This year, Greg
Zimmermann even managed to preser
an excellent botrytis dessert wine, th
Guldentaler Hipperich Riesling Trocke
beerenauslese (90 points).

Weingut Kronenbergerhof –
Erhard Eckes

55595 Wallhausen, Steingasse 1
Tel. (0 67 06) 4 40, Fax 65 00

The philosophy followed by Andreas ar
Bernhard Eckes includes severe prunir
in the vineyard, followed by rigoro
clarification and temperature-controlle
fermentation in the cellar. The focus is c
Pinot varieties. However, this year the tw
wines we liked best were both Riesling
the Wallhäuser Pastorenberg Spätlese, c
well as the fantastic Eiswein from the sam
site. This is one of the very few good Ei
weins from the Nahe in this vintage, and
real bargain.

Weingut Lersch

55450 Langenlonsheim, Cramerstraße 34
Tel. (0 67 04) 12 36, Fax 96 29 59

Jürgen Lersch and his son Thomas cultivate five hectares of vineyard. An historic specialty here are the wines made from the "Senator" grape, which was first bred by the grandfather. Last year, an Eiswein (12 percent alcohol) was produced for the first time. Even the 10.5 percent strength of this year's Eiswein (86 points) are more than enough. The best wines of the 2003 vintage: the Steinchen Scheurebe Spätlese and the dry Silvaner Auslese.

Weingut Werner Marx

55452 Windesheim, Im Setzling 6
Tel. (0 67 07) 3 16, Fax 16 69
e-mail: weingut.marx@t-online.de

As one could expect in Windesheim, Rainer and Werner Marx have turned their attention to Pinot varieties (50 percent of vineyard area). However, in this vintage the Pinot wines were a little too rustic, leaving two Rieslings as the highlights of the range: the fruity Schweppenhäuser Schlossgarten Spätlese (84 points) and the fruity Auslese from the same site (85). The wines are slowly gaining a reputation for good quality – no less than three times wines from the Marx winery have made it into the final round for the Chamber of Commerce wine of the year.

Weinhof Mayer

55545 Bad Kreuznach-Bosenheim,
Rheinhessenstraße 71
Tel. (06 71) 8 95 91 60, Fax 7 96 42 46
e-mail: info@weinhof-mayer.de

Gernot Mayer began bottling the wines produced from his six hectares of vineyard in 1998. The intention is to gradually increase this share to 100 percent. The range of 2003 vintage wines is not particularly convincing. The best wine in the range was the 2003 Chardonnay, rated 81 points. Other wines were considerably weaker, such as the 2003 dry Rivaner or the 2003 Portugieser Rosé, both of which scored 78 points. In future, the focus is to be on Riesling and red wine.

Weingut Meinhard

55545 Bad Kreuznach-Winzenheim,
Kirchstraße 13
Tel. (06 71) 4 30 30, Fax 4 30 06

Steffen Meinhard intends to increase the share of Pinot varieties. This year, he presented a solid range, the highlight of which is the dry Kreuznacher St. Martin Grauburgunder (Pinot Gris) Spätlese "Select" (83 points). On the other hand, we did not like the Grauburgunder Classic at all (77). We must repeat the criticism made last year, that the deep soils around Bad Kreuznach have much greater potential than is reflected in the wines of this producer.

Weingut Poss

55452 Windesheim, Goldgrube 20–22
Tel. (0 67 07) 3 42, Fax 83 32
e-mail: info@weingut-poss.de

This year, we have made yet another pleasant discovery in Windesheim. The Poss winery has – as is to be expected here – decided to concentrate on Pinot varieties. The range shows a good homogeneous level of quality, the best wine is the dry Windesheimer Fels Grauburgunder (Pinot Gris) Spätlese (84 points). What most of the wines still lack is typical varietal and terroir character, many of the wines taste similar, and one would wish for a little more personality. Nevertheless: There is growing potential here!

Weingut Michael Schäfer

55452 Burg Layen, Hauptstraße 15
Tel. (0 67 21) 4 30 97 und 4 55 93,
Fax 4 20 31

More than half the wine produced here is exported. No wonder, then, that the focus is on a traditional fruity style. This type of wine – unlike the dry versions – can be quite successful here. We particularly liked the 2003 Burg Layer Rothenberg Riesling Spätlese (84 points). The best wine of the vintage is an exotic one: the Langenlonsheimer Steinchen Weißburgunder (Pinot Blanc) Beerenauslese (86). We would like to see the label designs showing a similarly clear signature as does the range of wines.

Nahe

Weingut Kurt Schild

55595 St. Katharinen, Klosterstraße 7
Tel. (0 67 06) 4 47, Fax 62 98

Thomas Schild works seven hectares of vineyard. The self-confessed Riesling fan and enthusiastic mountain biker took over the winery from his father Kurt 21 years ago. This year, only the racy, fruity Kreuznacher Hofgarten Riesling Spätlese (83 points) was in any way convincing. All the other wines in the range were significantly less good than those of the previous vintage. Both, the cellar and the storage facility of the winery, have been newly built recently.

Weingut Rudolf Sinß

55452 Windesheim, Hauptstraße 18
Tel. (0 67 07) 2 53, Fax 85 10

The Sinß winery is located in Windesheim, which already tells you which varieties are favoured here: the Pinots. In terms of quality, this estate comes in third place in the town. This year's vintage range shows a clearly defined style, and all the wines are invigorating. The highlights are the dry Weißburgunder (Pinot Blanc) Spätlese as well as the dry Grauburgunder (Pinot Gris) Auslese from the Windesheimer Rosenberg site (both 84 points). Successful sparkling wines (Sekt) are also produced here, the 2002 Weißburgunder Sekt Brut was rated 83 points. This is a winery worth watching.

Weingut Udo Weber

55569 Monzingen, Soonwaldstraße 41
Tel. (0 67 51) 32 78, Fax 20 76

We have noted in recent years that the fruity wines Udo Weber in Monzingen produces are consistently better than his dry wines. This year, all that is different, with neither of the two categories being particularly convincing. The best wines of the range are the Monzinger Frühlingsplätzchen Riesling Auslese Goldkapsel (84 points) and the dry Bad Sobernheimer Marbach Riesling Spätlese (83). Particularly weak: the dry Rivaner (76). Perhaps they just did not know how to cope with the extreme vintage.

Weingut Wilhelmy

55450 Langenlonsheim,
Untere Grabenstraße 29
Tel. (0 67 04) 15 50, Fax 15 02

In recent years, this winery in Langenlonsheim has been among the best of the "other recommended producers" in the Nahe region. However, when referring to the 2003 vintage, there is no sign of a consistently good range with body and a individual style. The best wines are the most basic ones: a dry Langenlonsheimer Löhrer Berg Riesling Qualitätswein (quality wine – 82 points) and a clean Langenlonsheimer Steinchen Portugieser Rosé Qualitätswein (81). Unfortunately, we did not find any outstandingly good wines in the range.

Weingut Im Zwölberich

55445 Langenlonsheim, Schützenstr. 14
Tel. (0 67 04) 92 00, Fax 9 20 40
e-mail: zwoelberich@t-online.de

The "Im Zwölberich" winery brings together apparently irreconcilable extremes: Prices that are more befitting of a four-bunch star winery being charged for wines that occasionally have some very strange aromas, such as moss. The alleged answer to this is the term "biodynamics," and prominent membership in the Demeter organic association. We have never before seen such a good, convincing range from this winery as in this vintage. The highlights are a dry Langenlonsheimer Steinchen Riesling Auslese (84 points) as well as a Ruländer (Pinot Gris) Trockenbeerenauslese from the same site (86). More of the same, please.

Other wineries tasted

- Konrad Closheim, Langenlonsheim
- Wolfgang Eckes, Windesheim
- Emmerich-Koebernik, Waldböckelheim
- Hehner-Kiltz, Waldböckelheim
- Heinrich Schmidt, Windesheim
- Wolfgang Schneider, Guldental
- Von Racknitz, Odernheim

Pfalz

A year for Gewürztraminer

The band of vineyards that makes up the Pfalz (Palatinate) stretches from the southern limits of Rheinhessen near Worms down to the French border at Wissembourg, following the contours of the Pfälzer Wald forest, covering some 23,000 hectares of vineyard area. This makes the Pfalz the second-largest wine-growing region in Germany. An area in which figs and almonds ripen each year must also provide favorable conditions for grape vines, a fact first noticed by the Romans 2,000 years ago. The location to the east of the Haardt mountains is protected from the wind, experiencing adequate rainfall in normal years, although a drouth was in evidence in the dry summer of 2003, overall it is a rather temperate climate. The soils offer many permutations: From loess and decomposed layered sandstone through to isolated islands of shell limestone, marl, granite, porphyry and clay-slate, the vineyards of the region exhibit a wide range of soil structures, which is also reflected in the character of the wines.

Only two decades ago, the Pfalz was regarded, with very few exceptions, as a supplier of basic quaffing wines. In the meantime, the producers between have managed to move into the top ranks of dry Riesling as well as Pinot Noir and even white Pinot varieties. The phalanx of top Pfalz producers regularly shines in our lists of top-ranked wineries in these categories. There is hardly another region that has shown such dynamic development in the past 15 years. This is based not only on the performances of a few outstanding producers. Each year the base of good producers rated with one or two bunches increases.

Perhaps the key element in the success of the Pfalz has been the degree of co-operation between producers, as well as their willingness to encourage young producers. Examples such as Hans-Günther Schwarz or the "Five Friends" from the southern Pfalz are respected and emulated. They, in turn, are happy to pass on their knowledge and experience.

The 2003 vintage was particularly difficult for producers in the Pfalz region. The severe drouth led to vines in many sites being stressed, which has noticeable negative effects on the freshness und fruitiness of the wines. Particularly in the top Riesling sites in the area between Neustadt and Wachenheim producers found it extremely difficult to match the high standard of the previous vintage.

The only way of combating the drouth was by irrigation, which in many cases is difficult to implement. Those producers who tackled this problem early and seriously were rewarded. A prime example for this is the Weegmüller estate in Neustadt-Haardt, which managed to produce brilliantly clear wines in spite of the extreme drouth. In the southern Pfalz, too, a number of young winemakers presented wines with greater concentration and personality. We noticed significant improvement in a number of winemakers all aged around 30: at the Ullrichshof, the Immengarten Hof, the Karl Pfaffmann and at the Kranz winery. With some of their wines these young producers are already exceeding the level of quality shown by some of the "Große Gewächs." The leading producers were likewise unable to escape the effect of the drought. The volumes produced of top dry wines were reduced, and many did not achieve their usual quality. The wineries that coped best with this vintage were Knipser and Bürklin-Wolf. The Ökomomierat Rebholz winery, too, has among the best wines in all relevant categories in its cellars.

Looking at varieties, both Riesling and red grapes continue to make progress in the region. But it was Gewürztraminer that presented the largest number of positive surprises in 2003. Rarely have we been fortunate enough to taste so many crystal-clear, powerful and typical Traminer wines. By contrast, fewer botrytis wines than usual were presented. On the positive side, the healthy grapes yielded excellent wines at the highest categories, resulting in Trockenbeerenauslese wines of rare purity and brilliance.

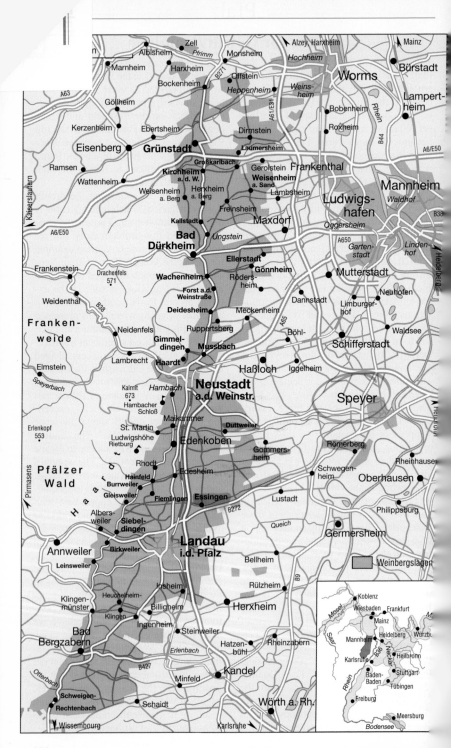

**The leading producers
in the Pfalz region**

Weingut Ökonomierat Rebholz,
Siebeldingen

Weingut Geheimer Rat
Dr. von Bassermann-Jordan,
Deidesheim

Weingut Dr. Bürklin-Wolf,
Wachenheim

Weingut A. Christmann,
Gimmeldingen

Weingut Knipser, Laumersheim

Weingut Koehler-Ruprecht,
Kallstadt

Weingut Georg Mosbacher, Forst

Weingut Müller-Catoir, Haardt

Weingut Dr. Wehrheim, Birkweiler

Weingut Friedrich Becker,
Schweigen

Weingut Bergdolt, Duttweiler

Weingut Bernhart, Schweigen

Weingut Josef Biffar, Deidesheim

Weingut Reichsrat von Buhl,
Deidesheim

Weingut Dr. Deinhard, Deidesheim

Weingut Ökonomierat
Johannes Kleinmann, Birkweiler

Weingut Münzberg,
Landau-Godramstein

Weingut Pfeffingen –
Fuhrmann-Eymael, Bad Dürkheim

Weingut Karl Schaefer,
Bad Dürkheim

Weingut Siegrist, Leinsweiler

Weingut Ullrichshof –
Familie Faubel, Maikammer

Weingut Weegmüller,
Neustadt-Haardt

Weingut Wilhelmshof, Siebeldingen

Weingut J. L. Wolf, Wachenheim

Weingut Acham-Magin, Forst

Weingut Benderhof, Kallstadt

Weingut Brenneis-Koch,
Bad Dürkheim-Leistadt

Weingut Darting, Bad Dürkheim

Weingut Eymann, Gönnheim

Weingut Winfried Frey & Söhne,
Essingen

Weingut Karl-Heinz Gaul,
Grünstadt-Sausenheim

Weingut Gies-Düppel, Birkweiler

Weingut Walter Hensel,
Bad Dürkheim

Weingut Christian Heußler, Rhodt

Wein- und Sektgut
Immengarten Hof, Maikammer

Weingut Jülg,
Schweigen-Rechtenbach

Weingut Karl Heinz Kaub,
Neustadt-Haardt

Weingut Familie Kranz, Ilbesheim

Weingut Philipp Kuhn,
Laumersheim

Weingut Leiningerhof, Kirchheim

Weingut Lergenmüller, Hainfeld

Weingut Lucashof –
Pfarrweingut, Forst

Weingut Herbert Meßmer,
Burrweiler

Stiftsweingut Frank Meyer,
Klingenmünster

Weingut Theo Minges, Flemlingen

Pfalz

Weingut Eugen Müller, Forst

Weingut Petri, Herxheim am Berg

Weingut Karl Pfaffmann,
Walsheim

Weinhof Scheu,
Schweigen-Rechtenbach

Weingut Egon Schmitt,
Bad Dürkheim

Weingut Schumacher,
Herxheim am Berg

Weingut Siener, Birkweiler

Weingut Heinrich Spindler, Forst

Weingut Ackermann, Ilbesheim

Weingut G. Beck, Schweigen

Weingut Borell-Diehl, Hainfeld

Weingut Castel Peter,
Bad Dürkheim

Weingut Dengler-Seyler,
Maikammer

Weingut Fader – Kastanienhof,
Rhodt

Weingut Fitz-Ritter, Bad Dürkheim

Weingut Ludwig Graßmück,
Birkweiler

Weingut Ernst Karst und Sohn,
Bad Dürkheim

Weingut Kaßner-Simon,
Freinsheim

Weingut Gerhard Klein, Hainfeld

Weingut Bernhard Koch, Hainfeld

Weingut Jürgen Leiner, Ilbesheim

Weingut Lidy, Frankweiler

Weingut Ludi Neiss, Kindenheim

Weingut Pfirmann,
Landau-Wollmesheim

Weingut Jakob Pfleger,
Herxheim am Berg

Weingut Peter Stolleis
– Carl-Theodor-Hof,
Neustadt an der Weinstraße

Vier Jahreszeiten Winzer EG,
Bad Dürkheim

Weingut Wageck-Pfaffmann,
Bissersheim

Weingut Wegner, Bad Dürkheim

Weingut Weik, Neustadt-Mußbach

Weingut Wilker,
Pleisweiler-Oberhofen

Weingut August Ziegler,
Maikammer

Weingut Zimmermann,
Wachenheim

The best vineyard sites in the Pfalz region *

Birkweiler: Kastanienbusch, Mandelberg

Deidesheim: Grainhübel, Kalkofen, Hohenmorgen, Langenmorgen, Kieselberg, Paradiesgarten

Dirmstein: Mandelpfad "Himmelsrech"

Bad Dürkheim: Michelsberg

Duttweiler: Kalkberg

Forst: Ungeheuer, Jesuitengarten, Freundstück, Kirchenstück, Pechstein

Gimmeldingen: Mandelgarten

Godramstein: Münzberg "Schlangenpfiff"

Großkarlbach: Burgweg "Im großen Garten"

Kirrweiler: Mandelberg

Königsbach: Idig

Laumersheim: Mandelberg "Steinbuckel"

Leinsweiler: Sonnenberg

Ruppertsberg: Reiterpfad, Gaisböhl

Schweigen: Sonnenberg "Kammerberg"

Siebeldingen: Im Sonnenschein

Ungstein: Herrenberg, Weilberg

Wachenheim: Gerümpel

---

* Source: VDP Pfalz

WEINGUT ACHAM-MAGIN

Owner: Anna-Barbara Acham
Manager: Vinzenz Troesch
Winemaker: Anna-Barbara Acham
and Rudolf Becker
67147 Forst, Weinstraße 67
Tel. (0 63 26) 3 15, Fax 62 32
e-mail: info@acham-magin.de
Internet: www.acham-magin.de
Directions: From Neustadt/Weinstraße
or from Bad Dürkheim via the new B 271
Sales: Anna-Barbara Acham
Opening hours: Mon.–Sat. 09:00 to
12:00 and 15:00 to 21:00, Sun. 11:00 to
13:00 hours, and by appointment
Restaurant: Since 1712, inn kept by
bishop of Speyer
Wed.–Sat. 16:00 to 23:00 hours
Specialties: Home-made roast pork, venison
Worth seeing: Baroque house, vaulted
sandstone cellar (18th century)

Vineyard area: 6.5 hectares
Annual production: 45,000 bottles
Top sites: Ruppertsberger Reiter-
pfad, Deidesheimer Mäushöhle,
Forster Musenhang, Pechstein,
Ungeheuer and Kirchenstück
Soil types: Sandy clay with limestone
and basalt layers
Grape varieties: 75% Riesling, 8%
Spätburgunder, 7% Weißburgunder,
10% other varieties
Average yield: 66 hl/ha
Best vintages: 2000, 2001, 2002
Member: VDP

In the difficult 2000 vintage, the wines
here were unusually clear, and were followed in 2001 by Rieslings that were brilliantly clean, concentrated and had mineral notes. The 2002 vintage brought remarkable First Growths. This positive assessment can be applied to 2003 only
with limitations, as the drouth caused
particularly severe damage in the area
around Forst. The wines are very variable. In a number of cases, we would have
preferred to see more residual sugar rather than excessively high alcohol levels.

2003 Deidesheimer Herrgottsacker
Riesling Kabinett trocken
11.5%, ♀ till 2007   **84**

2003 Forster Ungeheuer
Riesling Spätlese trocken
13%, ♀ till 2007   **85**

2003 Forster Kirchenstück
Riesling Spätlese trocken
"Großes Gewächs"
13.5%, ♀ till 2008   **86**

2003 Forster Musenhang
Riesling Spätlese trocken
13%, ♀ till 2008   **87**

2002 Forster Pechstein
Riesling Spätlese trocken
12.5%, ♀ till 2007   **88**

2003 Ruppertsberger Reiterpfad
Riesling Spätlese trocken
"Großes Gewächs"
13%, ♀ till 2009   **88**

2001 Ruppertsberger Reiterpfad
Riesling trocken "Großes Gewächs"
13%, ♀ till 2008   **89**

2002 Ruppertsberger Reiterpfad
Riesling Spätlese trocken
"Großes Gewächs"
13%, ♀ till 2008   **90**

2001 Forster Kirchenstück
Riesling trocken "Großes Gewächs"
13%, ♀ till 2008   **91**

2002 Forster Kirchenstück
Riesling Spätlese trocken
"Großes Gewächs"
12.5%, ♀ till 2010   **91**

The wines: **100** Perfect · **95–99** Outstanding · **90–94** Excellent · **85–89** Very good · **80–84** Good · **75–79** Average

WEINGUT ACKERMANN

Owner: Karl-Heinz Ackermann
Winemaker: Frank Ackermann
76831 Ilbesheim, Oberdorfstraße 40
Tel. (0 63 41) 3 06 64, Fax 3 25 47
e-mail: email@Weingut-Ackermann.de
Internet: www.weingut-ackermann.de
Directions: A 65, Landau-Süd exit, in direction of Klingenmünster, 6 kilometers past Landau, winery is on south-western border of Ilbesheim
Sales: Ackermann family
Opening hours: Mon.–Sat. by appointment

Vineyard area: 12.5 hectares
Annual production: 50,000 bottles
Top sites: Ilbesheimer Rittersberg and Leinsweiler Sonnenberg
Soil types: Shell limestone, loess-clay, decomposed sandstone
Grape varieties: 16% Riesling, 14% Dornfelder, 12% Müller-Thurgau, 7% each of Spätburgunder and Portugieser, 6% each of Grau- and Weißburgunder, 5% each of Schwarzriesling and Regent, 22% other varieties
Average yield: 80 hl/ha
Best vintages: 2002, 2003

Young Frank Ackermann is one of the new generation of winemakers in the Pfalz, who build on what's been achieved by their elders, and go a step further. In the wines of the 2002 vintage, we were particularly impressed by the clarity and the expressive character of the dry white wines, while in 2003 Ackermann has again produced a very good Riesling Spätlese as well as an outstanding Eiswein. In particular, though, the young winemaker has now shown that he is capable of making much better red wines than in the past. The Dornfelder is full of character, and brimming with black berry fruit, while the Spätburgunder (Pinot Noir) is complex and multi-layered. And if you would like to do an extensive tasting of the distilled spirits produced by father Karl-Heinz, we recommend you staying over at the guest apartment.

2003 Leinsweiler Sonnenberg
Riesling Kabinett trocken
12.5%, ♀ till 2006 — 81

2002 Grauer Burgunder
trocken Classic
12.5%, ♀ till 2006 — 84

2003 Ilbesheimer Rittersberg
Riesling Spätlese trocken
13.5%, ♀ till 2006 — 86

2002 Riesling Spätlese trocken
13%, ♀ till 2007 — 87

2002 Chardonnay Spätlese trocken
13%, ♀ till 2006 — 87

2002 Riesling
Spätlese trocken "S"
11%, ♀ till 2008 — 87

2002 Riesling halbtrocken
11.5%, ♀ till 2006 — 85

2003 Göcklinger Kaiserberg
Weißer Burgunder Eiswein
8%, ♀ till 2012 — 89

——— Red wines ———

2002 Spätburgunder Weißherbst
Kabinett halbtrocken "FreeRun"
12%, ♀ till 2006 — 85

2003 Kabinett
"Blanc de Noirs freerun"
13%, ♀ till 2006 — 84

2002 Ilbesheimer Rittersberg
Dornfelder trocken "Nr. 1"
14%, ♀ till 2008 — 88

2002 Ilbesheimer Rittersberg
Spätburgunder trocken "Nr. 1"
14.5%, ♀ till 2008 — 88

Picturesque wine-growing villages adorned with flowers and vines, such as Leinswei-der, shown here, are typical of the Pfalz region.   Photo: DWI/Hartmann

449

WEINGUT GEHEIMER RAT DR. VON BASSERMANN-JORDAN

Owner: Achim Niederberger
General manager: Gunther Hauck (commercial), Ulrich Mell (technical)
67146 Deidesheim, Kirchgasse 10
Tel. (0 63 26) 60 06, Fax 60 08
e-mail: hauck@bassermann-jordan.de
Internet: www.bassermann-jordan.de
Directions: On the Weinstraße between Neustadt and Bad Dürkheim
Sales: Ulrich Krack, Sebastian Wandt, Silke Wolz
Opening hours: Mon.–Fri. 08:00 to 12:00 hours and 13:00 to 18:00 hours
Sat. and Sun. 10:00 to 15:00 hours
History: Family-owned since 1718
Worth seeing: Centuries-old vaulted cellar with unique wine museum

Vineyard area: 46 hectares
Annual production: 350,000 bottles
Top sites: Deidesheimer Grain-hübel, Hohenmorgen and Kalkofen, Forster Kirchenstück, Ungeheuer, Pechstein and Jesuitengarten, Ruppertsberger Reiterpfad
Soil types: Decomposed sandstone with porphyry, loess and decomposed basalt
Grape varieties: 90% Riesling, 10% other varieties
Average yield: 50 hl/ha
Best vintages: 2001, 2002, 2003
Member: VDP

After many generations of being a family business, 2002 saw the majority of the share capital of this monument of German wine history pass into new hands. Gabriele von Bassermann-Jordan has sold her shares to an entrepreneur in Neustadt. Before Margrit von Bassermann-Jordan and her daughter Gabriele were for a few years the two ladies at the helm of the estate, a long succession of highly respected men had left their mark on the family and estate history. In this, their activities stretched far beyond the borders of Deidesheim. They sat in the Reichstag, the German parliament (Ludwig Andreas Jordan), participated in drafting the first German wine law (Dr. Ludwig von Bassermann-Jordan) or wrote the standard text on the history of the wine industry (Dr. Friedrich von Bassermann-Jordan). Over the centuries they built up a wine empire that can best be understood if you go underground in Deidesheim. Among all the wine cellars of estates in Germany, that of Bassermann-Jordan holds a special place. The mighty walls are of natural stone, and are up to 3.40 meters (11 feet) thick. Step by step, neighboring facilities, such as the cellar chapel or the tithe farm of the prince bishop of Speyer were integrated. The medieval Dirmstein knights' cellar was also added. Memorabilia on the history of winemaking were accumulated over a period of decades. Greek drinking bowls stand next to Roman amphorae, patrons of wine greet the visitor in the shape of wood sculptures, and a 500-year-old cross shows Christ in the wine cellar. The museum of old wines is also unique, it goes back to 100 A.D., and includes treasures of 1706, 1811, as well as all vintages since 1880. After a weaker period in the Eighties, the fortunes have been on the rise again thanks to winemaker Ulrich Mell. Ever since he joined the winery, he has produced crystal-clear, modern Riesling wines here. In the difficult 2000 vintage, Mell managed to achieve a quality that only few others could match. Both 2001 and 2002 were thoroughly convincing, with not a single weak wine in sight. In the 2003 vintage, too, Mells wines are among the best in the Pfalz region, although it simply was not possible in this core region of the Mittelhaardt to fully compensate for the ravages of the extreme summer heat and drouth; nothing matters the effort. Nevertheless, in both the dry Riesling and botrytis dessert segments, top scores were again achieved. The vineyard area is to be increased by eight hectares in the coming years.

2003 Forster Jesuitengarten
Riesling Spätlese trocken
13%, ♀ till 2008   86

2001 Deidesheimer Mäushöhle
Riesling Kabinett trocken
11.5%, ♀ till 2006   87

2001 Ruppertsberger Hoheburg
Riesling Spätlese trocken
13%, ♀ till 2006   88

2002 Forster Jesuitengarten
Riesling Spätlese trocken
13%, ♀ till 2007   88

2002 Weißer Burgunder/Chardonnay
trocken
13.5%, ♀ till 2008   88

2002 Deidesheimer Hohenmorgen
Riesling Spätlese trocken
"Großes Gewächs"
13%, ♀ till 2007   88

2001 Deidesheimer Hohenmorgen
Riesling Spätlese trocken
"Großes Gewächs"
13%, ♀ till 2007   89

2002 Deidesheimer Kalkofen
Riesling Spätlese trocken
"Großes Gewächs"
13%, ♀ till 2007   89

2003 Deidesheimer Kalkofen
Riesling trocken "Großes Gewächs"
13%, ♀ till 2008   89

2001 Forster Jesuitengarten
Riesling Spätlese trocken
13%, ♀ till 2007   90

2001 Deidesheimer Kalkofen
Riesling Spätlese trocken
"Großes Gewächs"
12.5%, ♀ till 2007   90

2003 Forster Pechstein
Riesling trocken "Großes Gewächs"
13%, ♀ till 2008   90

2002 Forster Kirchenstück
Riesling Spätlese trocken
"Großes Gewächs"
13%, ♀ till 2008   91

2003 Deidesheimer Hohenmorgen
Riesling trocken "Großes Gewächs"
13%, ♀ till 2008   91

2002 Forster Pechstein
Riesling Spätlese trocken
"Großes Gewächs"
13%, ♀ till 2008   92

2003 Forster Kirchenstück
Riesling trocken "Großes Gewächs"
13%, ♀ till 2008   92

2001 Forster Kirchenstück
Riesling Spätlese trocken
"Großes Gewächs"
13%, ♀ till 2008   93

2001 Deidesheimer Kalkofen
Riesling Eiswein
10%, ♀ till 2020   91

2003 Rieslaner Auslese
9%, ♀ till 2010   91

2001 Ruppertsberger Reiterpfad
Riesling Trockenbeerenauslese
10%, ♀ 2008 till 2025   92

2002 Deidesheimer Leinhöhle
Riesling Beerenauslese
8.5%, ♀ till 2015   92

2003 Deidesheimer Mäushöhle
Riesling Beerenauslese
8%, ♀ till 2020   93

2000 Ruppertsberger Reiterpfad
Riesling Trockenbeerenauslese
9.5%, ♀ till 2020   94

2002 Forster Jesuitengarten
Riesling Trockenbeerenauslese
8.5%, ♀ till 2030   94

2003 Deidesheimer Kieselberg
Riesling Trockenbeerenauslese
7.5%, ♀ till 2025   95

The wines: **100** Perfect · **95–99** Outstanding · **90–94** Excellent · **85–89** Very good · **80–84** Good · **75–79** Average

WEINGUT G. BECK

Owner and manager: Gerhard Beck
76889 Schweigen-Rechtenbach,
Paulinerstraße 5
Tel. (0 63 42) 5 35, Fax 74 48
e-mail: weingut.beck@t-online.de
Internet: www.weingut-beck.de
Directions: A 65, Landau-Süd exit, in direction of Bad Bergzabern, Weißenburg
Sales: Gerhard Beck, Daniel Scheib
Opening hours: Mon.–Fri. by appointment, Sat. 09:00 to 12:00 hours and 14:00 to 18:00 hours
Restaurant: Easter to late June as well as September and October every Fri. and Sat. from 15:00 hours

---

Vineyard area: 13 hectares
Annual production: 75,000 bottles
Top site: Schweigener Sonnenberg
Soil types: Sand, partly heavy kaolin
Grape varieties: 20% Riesling, 14% Müller-Thurgau, 9% each of Gewürztraminer and Dornfelder, 7% each of Spätburgunder and Weißburgunder, 6% Silvaner, 28% other varieties
Average yield: 70 hl/ha
Best vintages: 2000, 2003

This family winery with a particularly wide range of wines has been bottling its own wines since 1958. The wines Gerhard Beck produces reflect a sense of tradition, but also a feel for the characteristic of each variety. There are no barriques in this cellar, just a few oak vats plus stainless steel tanks. The wines come over as being baroque and full-bodied, and a little soft in style. At the same time they are clear, and typical of their variety, even in the difficult 2000 vintage. In 2001, as well as in 2003, the Gewürztraminer wines, for which the estate has always had a good reputation, were outstanding. In 2002 and 2003 the wines were rather heavy and alcoholic, although those of 2003 are a little more polished. We would much prefer the Pinot Noirs to have a less deep color, and rather more varietal characteristics.

2003 Weißer Burgunder
Kabinett trocken
13.5%, ♀ till 2006 — **83**

2003 Grauer Burgunder
Spätlese trocken
14.5%, ♀ till 2006 — **84**

2003 Auxerrois Spätlese trocken
13.5%, ♀ till 2006 — **85**

2003 Chardonnay Spätlese trocken
13.5%, ♀ till 2006 — **85**

2001 Schweigener Sonnenberg
Gewürztraminer Spätlese trocken
13.5%, ♀ till 2006 — **88**

2002 Schweigener Sonnenberg
Gewürztraminer trocken Selection
14.5%, ♀ till 2006 — **88**

2001 Gewürztraminer
trocken Selection
14%, ♀ till 2006 — **90**

2003 Schweigener Sonnenberg
Muskateller Spätlese
12%, ♀ till 2008 — **83**

2003 Gewürztraminer Kabinett
12%, ♀ till 2006 — **85**

2003 Gewürztraminer Auslese
12%, ♀ till 2010 — **92**

WEINGUT
FRIEDRICH BECKER

Owner and manager: Friedrich Becker
Administrator: Gerard Paul
Winemaker: Stefan Dorst
76889 Schweigen, Hauptstraße 29
Tel. (0 63 42) 2 90, Fax 61 48
e-mail:
wein@weingut-friedrich-becker.de
Internet:
www.weingut-friedrich-becker.de
Directions: A 65, Landau-Süd exit,
in direction of Weißenburg
Sales: Helena Becker
Opening hours: Sat. 10:00 to 17:00
hours, Mon.–Fri. by appointment
Worth seeing: Courtyard, distillery

Vineyard area: 14.5 hectares
Annual production: 90,000 bottles
Top sites: Schweigener
Sonnenberg and Kammerberg
Soil types: Loess, kaolin, marl
Grape varieties: 60% Pinot varieties,
22% Riesling, 18% other varieties,
including Silvaner, Gewürztraminer,
Kerner and Müller-Thurgau
Average yield: 71 hl/ha
Best vintages: 1997, 2001, 2002
Member: VDP

Ever since his legendary 1989 vintage,
Friedrich Becker has been one of the best
red winemakers in Germany, and hardly
any other can look back on such a continuous series of great Pinot Noirs. The
Spätburgunder "Reserve" is a classic.
Ever since, the exceptional 1996 "Res.,"
which at the time was the best ever made
by this estate, we have been enthusiastic
about the red wines here practically every
year, especially by the latest release, the
magnificent 2002 "Res.," which just possibly may be even better than the 2001.
In the 2003 vintage, too, the standard of
the white wines remains well behind that
of the reds. It appears Becker had some
problems with the fermentation of Spätlese wines, which got stuck at a residual
sugar of around nine grams.

2003 Auxerrois Spätlese trocken
13%, ♀ till 2006   **86**

2001 Schweigener Sonnenberg
Grauer Burgunder Spätlese trocken
13.5%, ♀ till 2006   **88**

2003 Schweigener Sonnenberg
Riesling Spätlese trocken
"Großes Gewächs"
13%, ♀ till 2009   **89**

2001 Chardonnay
Tafelwein trocken Barrique
13%, ♀ till 2008   **90**

2003 Chardonnay trocken Barrique
14%, ♀ till 2008   **90**

2003 Riesling Auslese
10.5%, ♀ till 2012   **88**

2003 Gewürztraminer Spätlese
13.5%, ♀ till 2008   **88**

2002 Gewürztraminer Spätlese
12%, ♀ till 2007   **89**

2001 Schweigener Sonnenberg
Riesling Trockenbeerenauslese
8.5%, ♀ till 2015   **92**

——— Red wines ———

2001 Schweigener Sonnenberg
Spätburgunder "Großes Gewächs"
13%, ♀ till 2008   **90**

2002 Schweigener Kammerberg
Spätburgunder "Großes Gewächs"
13%, ♀ till 2010   **91**

2001 Spätburgunder
trocken "Res."
13.5%, ♀ till 2010   **93**

2002 Spätburgunder
trocken "Res."
13.5%, ♀ till 2012   **94**

Pfalz

Weingut Friedrich Becker
D-76889 Schweigen
2002

Auxerrois
Kabinett trocken
Qualitätswein mit Prädikat
Gutsabfüllung

A. P. Nr. 5 066 012 03 03   alc. 11,5% vol   0,75 ℓ

The wines: **100** Perfect · **95–99** Outstanding · **90–94** Excellent · **85–89** Very good · **80–84** Good · **75–79** Average

WEINGUT BENDERHOF

Owner and manager:
Otto Haaß, Karola Bender-Haaß
Winemaker: Otto Haaß
67169 Kallstadt, Neugasse 45
Tel. (0 63 22) 15 20, Fax 98 07 75
Directions: A 61 – A 6, in direction of
Kaiserslautern, Grünstadt exit
Sales: Karola Bender-Haaß
Opening hours: Mon.–Sat. 08:00 to
11:00 hours and 13:00 to 19:00 hours
and by appointment
History: Resident as winemaking family
in Kallstadt since the 17th century

Vineyard area: 9 hectares
Annual production: 70,000 bottles
Top sites: Kallstadter Saumagen,
Kreidekeller and Steinacker,
Herxheimer Himmelreich
Soil types: Loess-clay on limestone
Grape varieties: 33% Riesling, 12%
each of Spätburgunder and St. Lau-
rent, 11% Weißburgunder, 6%
Schwarzriesling, 5% each of Silvaner
and Scheurebe, 4% each of Regent
and Dornfelder, 8% other varieties
Average yield: 70 hl/ha
Best vintages: 2000, 2001

This winemaking family has been active
in Kallstadt since the 17th century. While
the focus is still on Riesling, Pinot Noir
and St. Laurent have caught up in importance. Otto Haaß says "by reminding ourselves of tradition we are trying to create
individualistic wines," and this is reflected in his Rieslings in a good vintage:
juicy, soft, classical representatives of the
Mittelhaardt region. A good Pinot Noir
has also been available for a number of
years. The 2001 vintage was very good.
In 2002, Selection wines were produced
for the first time, but the overall level
was only average. In the 2003 vintage, we
were particularly disappointed by the
white wines, which can at least in part be
attributed to the extremely dry conditions
of that summer. But we have faith in this
producer, and did not drop his rating.

2003 Kallstadter Steinacker
Grauer Burgunder trocken Barrique
15.5%, ♀ till 2007   **84**

2003 Kallstadter Kreidekeller
Riesling Kabinett trocken
12.5%, ♀ till 2006   **85**

2002 Kallstadter Saumagen
Riesling trocken Selection
13%, ♀ till 2006   **85**

2002 Herxheimer Himmelreich
Riesling trocken Selection
13%, ♀ till 2007   **86**

2001 Kallstadter Saumagen
Riesling Spätlese trocken
12.5%, ♀ till 2006   **87**

2001 Herxheimer Himmelreich
Riesling Spätlese trocken
12%, ♀ till 2006   **87**

2001 Kallstadter Kobnert
Gewürztraminer Spätlese trocken
12.5%, ♀ till 2006   **87**

2003 Herxheimer Honigsack
Scheurebe Trockenbeerenauslese
10.5%, ♀ till 2015   **89**

——————— Red wines ———————

2002 Kallstadter Steinacker
Spätburgunder trocken "Holzfassausbau"
13%, ♀ till 2008   **84**

2002 Kallstadter Kobnert
Regent trocken Barrique
13%, ♀ till 2008   **85**

2002 Kallstadter Steinacker
Spätburgunder trocken Selection Barrique
13.5%, ♀ till 2007   **86**

WEINGUT
BENDERHOF
2003
Weißburgunder

WEINGUT BERGDOLT

Owner: Rainer and Günther Bergdolt
Winemaker: Rainer Bergdolt
67435 Neustadt-Duttweiler,
Klostergut Sankt Lamprecht
Tel. (0 63 27) 50 27, Fax 17 84
e-mail: weingut-bergdolt-st.lamp-
recht@t-online.de
Internet: www.weingut-bergdolt.de
Directions: A 65, Neustadt-Süd exit
Sales: Mon.–Fri. 08:00 to 12:00 hours
and 13:30 to 18:00 hours
Sat. 10:00 to 16:00 hours
History: Formerly farm of Saint Lamp-
recht abbey, acquired by Jakob Bergdolt
in 1754

Vineyard area: 23 hectares
Annual production: 150,000 bottles
Top sites: Kirrweiler Mandelberg,
Duttweiler Kalkberg, Ruppertsberger
Reiterpfad
Soil types: Loess and sandy clay,
sandstone
Grape varieties: 35% Weißburgunder,
32% Riesling, 8% each of Char-
donnay and Spätburgunder, 6% each
of Silvaner and Kerner, 5% Dornfelder
Average yield: 66 hl/ha
Best vintages: 1999, 2001, 2003
Member: VDP, Deutsches Barrique
Forum

The winery of the St. Lamprecht abbey
has been documented since 1290. Rainer
and Günther Bergdolt are the eighth generation of this family to run the estate.
They have for long been counted among
the leading Pfalz producers of dry Pinot
Blanc, in some vintages even among the
best in Germany. The 2001 vintage was
very impressive, with clarity and a fresh
style. On the other hand, most of the 2002
vintage wines were less attractive. In the
2003 vintage, some of the wines show
clear evidence of the results of the
drouth experienced, although there are
also a few outstanding exceptions. The
two brilliant and clear botrytis dessert
wines are phenomenal.

2003 Weißer Burgunder
Spätlese trocken "sine nobilitas"
15%, ♀ till 2007   **86**

2003 Weißer Burgunder
Spätlese trocken St. Lamprecht
14%, ♀ till 2006   **88**

2001 Ruppertsberger Reiterpfad
Riesling trocken "Großes Gewächs"
12.5%, ♀ till 2007   **89**

2003 Kirrweiler Mandelberg
Weißer Burgunder Spätlese trocken
"Großes Gewächs"
13%, ♀ till 2008   **89**

2003 Ruppertsberger Reiterpfad
Riesling Spätlese trocken
"Großes Gewächs"
12.5%, ♀ till 2008   **89**

2002 Kirrweiler Mandelberg
Weißer Burgunder Spätlese trocken
"Großes Gewächs"
13%, ♀ till 2009   **91**

2001 Weißer Burgunder
Auslese trocken
14%, ♀ till 2008   **92**

2001 Kirrweiler Mandelberg
Weißer Burgunder trocken
"Großes Gewächs"
13.5%, ♀ till 2008   **92**

2002 Scheurebe Beerenauslese
8.5%, ♀ till 2014   **92**

2003 Duttweiler Kreuzberg
Riesling Beerenauslese
7%, ♀ till 2015   **92**

2003 Duttweiler Mandelberg
Weißer Burgunder Trockenbeerenauslese
7.5%, ♀ till 2020   **94**

The wines: **100** Perfect · **95–99** Outstanding · **90–94** Excellent · **85–89** Very good · **80–84** Good · **75–79** Average

455

WEINGUT BERNHART

Owner: Willi and Gerd Bernhart
Winemaker: Gerd Bernhart
76889 Schweigen, Hauptstraße 8
Tel. (0 63 42) 72 02, Fax 63 96
e-mail: weingut-bernhart@t-online.de
Internet: www.weingut-bernhart.de
Directions: A 65, Landau-Süd exit,
in direction of Weißenburg
Sales: Bernhart family
Opening hours: Fri. and Sat. 09:00 to
12:00 hours and 13:00 to17:00 hours
and by appointment

Vineyard area: 14.5 hectares
Annual production: 80,000 bottles
Top site: Schweigener Sonnenberg
Soil types: Loess-clay, sand, kaolin
and calcareous marl
Grape varieties: 20% Spätburgunder,
20% Riesling, 15% Weißburgunder,
10% Grauburgunder, 8% each of
Dornfelder and Portugieser,
19% other varieties
Average yield: 70 hl/ha
Best vintages: 2000, 2001, 2002
Member: VDP

This family winery has for many years
been in direct competition with Friedrich
Becker as to who produces the best quality in the large wine-growing community
of Schweigen. The family laid the foundation for the present winery when it
purchased vineyards in Weißenburg in
France in 1900. Willi Bernhart first started bottling and marketing his own wines
in 1972. Today he is assisted by his son
Gerd. The reductively made fruity white
wines have improved significantly in
recent years. It is an inevitable vintage
characteristic that the 2003 vintage is not
quite as good as the preceding vintages.
The red wines have been really good for
quite a few years, in particular the Pinot
Noirs. Their soft cinnamon style comes
through as well in the 2002 vintage. In
addition, very good reds are now being
produced from other varieties, even an
excellent Cabernet Sauvignon.

2003 Schweigener Sonnenberg
Gewürztraminer Spätlese trocken
14%, ♀ till 2008   86

2002 Schweigener Sonnenberg
Grauer Burgunder Spätlese trocken
13.5%, ♀ till 2006   87

2002 Schweigener Sonnenberg
Gewürztraminer Spätlese trocken
14%, ♀ till 2006   91

2002 Schweigener Sonnenberg
Chardonnay trocken "S"
13.5%, ♀ till 2007   92

———— Red wines ————

2002 Schweigener Sonnenberg
Spätburgunder Spätlese trocken "S"
13.5%, ♀ till 2008   88

2002 Schweigener Sonnenberg
Cabernet Sauvignon/Merlot trocken "S"
13.5%, ♀ till 2009   88

2002 Schweigener Sonnenberg
Spätburgunder Auslese trocken "S"
14%, ♀ till 2008   89

2002 Schweigener Sonnenberg
Spätburgunder Auslese trocken "R"
14%, ♀ till 2008   90

2001 Schweigener Sonnenberg
Spätburgunder Spätlese trocken "S"
13.5%, ♀ till 2008   90

2001 Schweigener Sonnenberg
Spätburgunder Auslese trocken "S"
13.5%, ♀ till 2008   90

Bernhart

2001
Weißburgunder
Spätlese trocken

Schweigener Sonnenberg · Gutsabfüllung
Qualitätswein mit Prädikat
13,5% vol   A. P. Nr. 5 066 014 12 02   0,75 L

Weingut   **Pfalz**   D-76889 Schweigen
Bernhart   Tel. (063 42) 72 02

WEINGUT JOSEF BIFFAR

Owner: Gerhard Biffar
Manager and winemaker:
Heiner Maleton
67146 Deidesheim,
Niederkirchener Straße 13
Tel. (0 63 26) 96 76 29, Fax 96 76 11
e-mail: info@josef-biffar.de
Internet: www.biffar.com
Directions: A 65, continue on the new
B 271 as far as the Deidesheim exit, keep
to the right after the 2nd roundabout
Sales: Uwe Gensheimer
Opening hours: Mon.–Fri. 09:00 to
12:00 and 13:00 to 17:30, Sat. 10:00 to
12:00 and 13:30 to 15:00 hours
and by appointment
History: The family moved from Lyon
to Deidesheim in 1739
Worth seeing: Attractive courtyard and
deep vaulted cellar

Vineyard area: 12 hectares
Annual production: 85,000 bottles
Top sites: Deidesheimer Grainhübel,
Kalkofen, Kieselberg and Mäushöhle,
Ruppertsberger Reiterpfad
Soil types: Decomposed sandstone
with loess, clay, basalt or limestone
Grape varieties: 79% Riesling, 14%
Weißburgunder, 7% other varieties
Average yield: 60 hl/ha
Best vintages: 2000, 2002, 2003
Member: VDP

The attractive winery complex dates to
1879, and is a national heritage monument. Now that the barrel cellar has been
renewed, and some other technical aspects have been modernized, the winery
is well-equipped. Hardly any other range
of Pfalz Rieslings of the 2003 vintage
was so unmarred by unpleasant vintage
characteristics, hardly any other range
showed more clear, brilliant Riesling
fruit. Whatever we tasted was virtually
free of flaws. The 2002 vintage was also
very convincing. With performances like
these, the estate is surely a candidate for
an even higher rating.

2003 Deidesheimer Mäushöhle
Riesling Kabinett trocken
12.5%, ♀ till 2006   **85**

2003 Ruppertsberger Nußbien
Riesling trocken
12%, ♀ till 2006   **87**

2003 Deidesheimer Mäushöhle
Riesling Spätlese trocken
12.5%, ♀ till 2007   **87**

2003 Wachenheimer Altenburg
Riesling Spätlese trocken
13%, ♀ till 2007   **87**

2002 Wachenheimer Altenburg
Riesling Spätlese trocken
13.5%, ♀ till 2007   **89**

2002 Deidesheimer Grainhübel
Riesling Spätlese trocken
"Großes Gewächs"
13.5%, ♀ till 2007   **89**

2002 Wachenheimer Gerümpel
Riesling Spätlese trocken
"Großes Gewächs"
13.5%, ♀ till 2007   **90**

2003 Deidesheimer Kalkofen
Riesling Spätlese
10%, ♀ till 2008   **86**

2002 Deidesheimer Kieselberg
Riesling Trockenbeerenauslese
9%, ♀ till 2025   **92**

2003 Deidesheimer Kieselberg
Riesling Beerenauslese
8.5%, ♀ till 2020   **92**

2003 Deidesheimer Mäushöhle
Riesling Auslese Goldkapsel
7.5%, ♀ till 2012   **92**

WEINGUT JOSEF BIFFAR

2003
RIESLING
TROCKEN

GUTSABFÜLLUNG JOSEF BIFFAR D-67146 DEIDESHEIM a. d. WEINSTRASSE
QUALITÄTSWEIN B. A. · A.P.Nr. 5 106 026 012 04 · PRODUCE OF GERMANY
alc. 12% vol   PFALZ   1 l e

The wines: **100** Perfect · **95–99** Outstanding · **90–94** Excellent · **85–89** Very good · **80–84** Good · **75–79** Average

WEINGUT BORELL-DIEHL

**Owner: Thomas Diehl
and Annette Borell-Diehl
Manager and winemaker: Thomas Diehl**
76835 Hainfeld, Weinstraße 47
Tel. (0 63 23) 98 05 30, Fax 98 05 70
e-mail: borell-diehl@t-online.de
Internet: www.weingut-borell-diehl.de
*Directions: A 65, Landau-Nord or Eden-
koben exit, in direction of Edesheim,
in Hainfeld town center*
Sales: Annette Borell-Diehl
Opening hours: Mon.–Sat. 08:00 to
12:00 hours and 13:00 to 18:00 hours
Worth seeing: Half-timbered house dating to 1619, Mediterranean courtyard

Vineyard area: 28.2 hectares
Annual production: 270,000 bottles
Top sites: Hainfelder Letten,
Edesheimer Forst
Soil types: Clay, sand, sandstone
Grape varieties: 16% each of Dornfel-
der and Riesling, 11% each of Grau-
and Spätburgunder, 7% each of Mül-
ler-Thurgau and Portugieser, 5% each
of Schwarzriesling, Regent and
St. Laurent, 17% other varieties
Average yield: 89 hl/ha
Best vintages: 2002, 2003

This is quite a large winery, located in an
attractively renovated winery building on
the Weinstraße. The proportion of Riesling has been further increased, showing
once again that there are some remarkable performances coming from the community of Hainfeld in the past few years.
Thomas Diehl's work is characterized
by very clean, clear wines. In the previous vintage, we had preferred the white
wines, whereas this year the reds managed to really bring out the varietal characteristics, even with Merlot and Cabernet.
The best red, however, is the remarkable
2002 Spätburgunder (Pinot Noir). By
performing at this level, Thomas Diehl
has fully vindicated the awarding of the
first bunch of grapes last year. Yet again,
our compliments on a job well done.

2003 Edesheimer Forst
Riesling Spätlese trocken
13%, ♀ till 2006 — 82

2003 Hainfelder Kapelle
Weißer Burgunder trocken
13%, ♀ till 2006 — 83

2003 Hainfelder Kirchenstück
Chardonnay Spätlese trocken
13.5%, ♀ till 2007 — 84

2003 Hainfelder Letten
Grauer Burgunder Spätlese trocken
14%, ♀ till 2006 — 84

2002 Flemlinger Vogelsprung
Auxerrois trocken
13%, ♀ till 2006 — 85

2002 Hainfelder Letten
Grauer Burgunder Spätlese trocken
13%, ♀ till 2006 — 86

2002 Hainfelder Letten
Gewürztraminer Spätlese
12%, ♀ till 2006 — 88

———— Red wines ————

2001 Flemlinger Herrenbuckel
Spätburgunder trocken Barrique
13%, ♀ till 2007 — 84

2001 Flemlinger Herrenbuckel
Spätburgunder Spätlese trocken
13%, ♀ till 2007 — 85

2001 Hainfelder Letten
Merlot trocken
15%, ♀ till 2008 — 85

2002 Flemlinger Herrenbuckel
Spätburgunder Spätlese trocken Alte Reben
13%, ♀ till 2008 — 86

458

Pfalz

WEINGUT BRENNEIS-KOCH

**Owner: Matthias Koch and
Verena Suratny GbR
Manager and winemaker:
Matthias Koch
67098 Bad Dürkheim-Leistadt,
Freinsheimer Straße 2
Tel. (0 63 22) 18 98, Fax 72 41
e-mail:**
matthias.koch@brenneis-koch.de
Internet: www.brenneis-koch.de
*Directions: Dürkheim-Zentrum North in
direction of Leistadt, right at town center*
Sales: Verena Suratny
Opening hours: By appointment
History: Established 1993 from the
merger of two wineries

Vineyard area: 9 hectares
Annual production: 55,000 bottles
Top sites: Leistadter Kirchenstück,
Kallstadter Steinacker and Saumagen
Soil types: Limestone boulders, lime-
stone-clay and gravelly sand
Grape varieties: 40% Riesling,
10% St. Laurent, 7% Spätburgunder,
6% each of Grau- and Weißburgun-
der, 5% each of Muskateller and Por-
tugieser, 21% other varieties
Average yield: 55 hl/ha
Best vintages: 2000, 2001, 2002
Member: Pfälzer Barrique Forum

In 1993 Matthias Koch brought together
the two wineries of Emil Brenneis (Leistadt) and Erhard Koch (Ellerstadt), and
can now draw on good Riesling as well as
red wine sites. This has given rise to a
modern winery that is active in barrique
maturation, and is also trying its hand at
varieties such as Nebbiolo, Merlot, Syrah
and Sauvignon Blanc. In recent years,
good results have been achieved with
white Pinot varieties as well as with modern, fruity and at the same time characterful Riesling wines. In 2002, the
Riesling wines were the strong suit of the
winery, in 2003 we were not convinced
by these. Only the typical, peppery Syrah
lived up to our expectations.

2003 Kallstadter Steinacker
Silvaner Kabinett trocken
12%, ♀ till 2006 **81**

2003 Kallstadter Saumagen
Riesling Spätlese trocken
12%, ♀ till 2006 **82**

2003 Leistadter Herzfeld
Riesling Kabinett trocken
12.5%, ♀ till 2006 **83**

2002 Chardonnay Spätlese trocken
13%, ♀ till 2007 **85**

2002 Kallstadter Steinacker
Riesling Spätlese trocken
13%, ♀ till 2006 **86**

2002 Riesling Spätlese trocken
13%, ♀ till 2006 **87**

2001 Leistadter Herzfeld
Riesling Spätlese trocken
13%, ♀ till 2006 **88**

2001 Riesling
Spätlese trocken "Domwein"
12.5%, ♀ till 2006 **89**

2003 Leistadter Kirchenstück
Muskateller Spätlese
12.5%, ♀ till 2007 **83**

2002 Riesling Spätlese "Export"
10.5%, ♀ till 2008 **83**

2002 Leistadter Kirchenstück
Muskateller
11.5%, ♀ till 2006 **84**

———— Red wines ————

2002 Spätburgunder trocken
13.5%, ♀ till 2008 **84**

2002 Dürkheimer Feuerberg
Syrah trocken
13.5%, ♀ till 2008 **86**

The wines: **100** Perfect · **95–99** Outstanding · **90–94** Excellent · **85–89** Very good · **80–84** Good · **75–79** Average

459

WEINGUT
DR. BÜRKLIN-WOLF

Owner: Bettina Bürklin-von Guradze, Christian von Guradze
General manager: Marc Halverscheid
Administrator: Bruno Sebastian
Winemaker: Fritz Knorr
67157 Wachenheim, Weinstraße 65
Tel. (0 63 22) 9 53 30, Fax 95 33 30
e-mail: bb@buerklin-wolf.de
Internet: www.buerklin-wolf.de
Directions: In the Mittelhaardt between Neustadt and Bad Dürkheim
Sales manager: Tom Benns
Advice and Sales:
Thur. and Fri. 11:00 to 18:00 hours
Sat. and Sun. 11:00 to 16:00 hours
Collections: Mon.–Wed. 08:00 to 17:00 hours
Restaurant: "Zur Kanne" in Deidesheim, Tel. (0 63 26) 9 66 00, closed Tue.
Wine tavern: Hofgut Ruppertsberg
Tel. (0 63 26) 98 20 97
History: Founded 1597
Worth seeing: Winery complex, vaulted cellar, English-style garden

---

Vineyard area: 90 hectares
Annual production: 600,000 bottles
Top sites: Forster Kirchenstück, Jesuitengarten, Pechstein and Ungeheuer, Ruppertsberger Reiterpfad and Gaisböhl, Deidesheimer Hohenmorgen, Langenmorgen and Kalkofen
Soil types: Basalt, limestone, terrace gravel, yellow-red-white sandstone
Grape varieties: 72% Riesling, 6% each of Spät- and Weißburgunder, 16% other varieties
Average yield: 65 hl/ha
Best vintages: 2001, 2002, 2003
Member: VDP

Christian von Guradze and his wife Bettina have taken this long-established winery into a new world. Most of the buildings in the extensive complex have been renovated, the three-hectare park with greenhouses has been completed, the old estate restaurant "Zur Kanne" was reopened under own management as an upper-class wine restaurant, the vinotheque is decorated with antiques, and sports an English expert who presents wine tastings – what more could you possibly want? Bürklin-Wolf has also been offering a comprehensive cultural program for a number of years, with summer opera and other events. All this provides the ideal framework for a presentation of the estate's wines. These too have improved significantly since 1990, quite apart from the fact that the range of wines on offer has been completely changed. Christian von Guradze was one of the movers behind the classification of vineyards in the Pfalz. His own wines are now presented in a completely new, absolutely clear classification system. The base is provided by the dry estate wines made from various varietals, the next step up are the Rieslings sourced from around the commune. The phalanx of high-quality dry Riesling wines, which is larger here than in any other winery in the Pfalz, is split into two levels of vineyard – labeled "A" and "B." The pinnacle of production is made up by the botrytis dessert wines, which may be made from several varieties. The white Pinot varieties as well as the Pinot Noir can also be remarkably good here. With the 2001 vintage, the team was able to produce very good wines in all categories, and 2002 was no different. Then in 2003 this winery on the Mittelhaardt was really able to show its ability: Hardly any of the wines shows traces of the dry vintage characteristics. The Rieslings are juicy and have clean fruit. And the Riesling Trockenbeerenauslese is again one of the best in the region. Following on four years of successful experiments with bio-dynamic organic methods in some sections of vineyards, an application was submitted in late September 2004 to convert the entire vineyard area to bio-dynamic viticultural practices. This puts the winery in a line with famous colleagues in Burgundy, in Alsace and on the Loire.

The estates: ✤✤✤✤✤ World's finest · ✤✤✤✤ Germany's best · ✤✤✤ Very good · ✤✤ Good · ✤ Reliable

2003 Riesling trocken
12.5%, ♀ till 2006 **85**

2003 Ruppertsberger
Riesling trocken
13%, ♀ till 2006 **85**

2003 Wachenheimer Altenburg
Riesling trocken "PC"
13%, ♀ till 2008 **86**

2003 Wachenheimer Böhlig
Riesling trocken "PC"
13%, ♀ till 2008 **87**

2003 Ruppertsberger Gaisböhl
Riesling trocken "Großes Gewächs"
13.5%, ♀ till 2007 **88**

2003 Forster Ungeheuer
Riesling trocken "Großes Gewächs"
13.5%, ♀ till 2008 **88**

2003 Wachenheimer Rechbächel
Riesling trocken "PC"
13%, ♀ till 2008 **88**

2003 Forster Pechstein
Riesling trocken "Großes Gewächs"
13.5%, ♀ till 2008 **89**

2003 Ruppertsberger Hoheburg
Riesling trocken "PC"
13%, ♀ till 2008 **89**

2002 Deidesheimer Hohenmorgen
Riesling trocken "Großes Gewächs"
13%, ♀ till 2007 **90**

2003 Deidesheimer Kalkofen
Riesling trocken "Großes Gewächs"
13.5%, ♀ till 2008 **90**

2003 Deidesheimer Hohenmorgen
Riesling trocken "Großes Gewächs"
13%, ♀ till 2008 **90**

2002 Ruppertsberger Gaisböhl
Riesling trocken "Großes Gewächs"
13%, ♀ till 2007 **91**

2003 Forster Jesuitengarten
Riesling trocken "Großes Gewächs"
13.5%, ♀ till 2008 **91**

2002 Forster Jesuitengarten
Riesling trocken "Großes Gewächs"
13%, ♀ till 2007 **92**

2003 Forster Kirchenstück
Riesling trocken "Großes Gewächs"
13.5%, ♀ till 2008 **92**

2002 Forster Kirchenstück
Riesling trocken "Großes Gewächs"
13.5%, ♀ till 2008 **94**

2002 Deidesheimer Kalkofen
Riesling Auslese
9.5%, ♀ till 2010 **91**

2002 Muskateller Beerenauslese
11%, ♀ till 2020 **92**

2002 Wachenheimer Gerümpel
Riesling Beerenauslese
9.5%, ♀ till 2020 **92**

2002 Ruppertsberger Gaisböhl
Riesling Trockenbeerenauslese
8.5%, ♀ till 2030 **93**

2002 Wachenheimer Goldbächel
Riesling Trockenbeerenauslese
9%, ♀ till 2030 **94**

2002 Wachenheimer Rechbächel
Riesling Trockenbeerenauslese
7.5%, ♀ till 2025 **94**

2003 Deidesheimer Gaisböhl
Riesling Trockenbeerenauslese
8.5%, ♀ till 2020 **95**

2002 Ruppertsberger Gaisböhl
Riesling Trockenbeerenauslese
Goldkapsel
7%, ♀ till 2040 **95**

——————— Red wines ———————

2001 Pinot Noir trocken "S"
13%, ♀ till 2007 **86**

2002 Pinot Noir trocken "S"
13.5%, ♀ till 2007 **87**

The wines: **100** Perfect · **95–99** Outstanding · **90–94** Excellent · **85–89** Very good · **80–84** Good · **75–79** Average

WEINGUT
REICHSRAT VON BUHL

**Owner: Reichsfreiherr Georg
Enoch von und zu Gutenberg
Lessee: Reichsrat von Buhl GmbH
Winery director: Stefan Weber
Vineyard manager: Werner Sebastian
Winemaker: Hubertus Meitzler
67146 Deidesheim, Weinstraße 16
Tel. (0 63 26) 9 65 00, Fax 96 50 24
e-mail: info@reichsrat-von-buhl.de
Internet: www.reichsrat-von-buhl.de**
*Directions: A 61, in direction of Bad
Dürkheim, Deidesheim exit*
Opening hours: Mon.–Fri. 08:00 to
12:00 and 13:00 to 18:00 hours
Sat., Sun. and public holidays 10:00 to
12:00 and 13:00 to 17:00 hours
Worth seeing: The entire complex is
a national monument, historical cellar,
grand manor-house for events

Vineyard area: 50 hectares
Annual production: 450,000 bottles
Top sites: Forster Freundstück,
Jesuitengarten, Pechstein, Kirchen-
stück and Ungeheuer, Deidesheimer
Kieselberg, Leinhöhle and Herrgotts-
acker, Ruppertsberger Reiterpfad
Soil types: Sandy clay, decomposed
limestone and basalt
Grape varieties: 88% Riesling,
4% Spätburgunder, 8% other varieties
Average yield: 50 hl/ha
Best vintages: 1996, 1998, 1999
Member: VDP

Millions were invested in this winery,
which has a long tradition, and in the
second half of the Nineties the brilliant
Rieslings produced here helped to regain
the estate's position among the top producers in Germany. However, since the
2000 vintage none of the vintages
has achieved the brilliance seen in the
previous years. While the 2003 vintage
range is a mixed bag, there are two outstanding wines: the Reiterpfad First
Growth as well as the magnificent Riesling Trockenbeerenauslese.

2003 Riesling
Kabinett trocken von Buhl
12%, ♀ till 2006   **83**

2003 Deidesheimer Kieselberg
Riesling Kabinett trocken
12%, ♀ till 2007   **84**

2003 Riesling
Spätlese trocken von Buhl
12%, ♀ till 2006   **84**

2003 Forster Ungeheuer
Riesling Spätlese trocken
12.5%, ♀ till 2007   **86**

2003 Forster Pechstein
Riesling Spätlese trocken
"Großes Gewächs"
12.5%, ♀ till 2008   **87**

2003 Deidesheimer Paradiesgarten
Riesling Spätlese trocken
"Großes Gewächs"
12.5%, ♀ till 2008   **87**

2003 Forster Kirchenstück
Riesling Spätlese trocken
"Großes Gewächs"
13%, ♀ till 2008   **88**

2002 Forster Pechstein
Riesling Spätlese trocken
"Großes Gewächs"
13%, ♀ till 2007   **89**

2003 Ruppertsberger Reiterpfad
Riesling Spätlese trocken
"Großes Gewächs"
12.5%, ♀ till 2009   **89**

2001 Forster Ungeheuer
Riesling Trockenbeerenauslese
6%, ♀ till 2025   **92**

2003 Forster Ungeheuer
Riesling Trockenbeerenauslese
7%, ♀ till 2040   **92**

2002ᵉʳ Pechſtein Forſt

The estates: ♣♣♣♣♣ World's finest · ♣♣♣♣ Germany's best · ♣♣♣ Very good · ♣♣ Good · ♣ Reliable

WEINGUT CASTEL PETER

Owner: Peter family
Winemaker: Karsten Peter
67098 Bad Dürkheim, Am Neuberg 2
Tel. (0 63 22) 58 99, Fax 6 79 78
e-mail: weingut-castel-peter@t-online.de
Directions: A 61, Kreuz Ludwigshafen exit, via A 650, in direction of Bad Dürkheim, "Am Neuberg" exit
Sales: Peter family
Opening hours: Mon.–Fri. 09:00 to 12:00 hours and 14:00 to 18:00 hours
Sat. 09:00 to 16:00 hours
by appointment
History: Winemaking in the family since 1774

Vineyard area: 11 hectares
Annual production: 80,000 bottles
Top sites: Dürkheimer Spielberg, Hochbenn and Steinberg
Soil types: Calcareous marl, sandy clay, loess, decomposed sandstone
Grape varieties: 38% Riesling, 15% each of Spätburgunder and St. Laurent, 10% each of Chardonnay and Weißburgunder, 12% other varieties
Average yield: 70 hl/ha
Best vintages: 2000, 2001, 2002
Member: Pfälzer Barrique Forum

The Peter family started making wine in 1774. Today, young Karsten Peter sees his challenge in finding the right balance of tradition and innovation. He regards terroir as the foundation of quality. He brings to his work practical experience gained all over the world. Overall, his wines do have a certain style. We again liked the white wines of this estate, particularly the clean, clear and light-bodied Rieslings, which show fresh, lively fruit even in the 2003 vintage. The white Pinot wines have their ups and downs. The mellow style of the reds, of which the 2002 vintage has now been presented, is still there, but it is now more juicy and harmonious. Just by way of interest, winemaker Wilfried Peter was the initiator of the Pfälzer Barrique Forum.

2003 Riesling trocken
12.5%, ♀ till 2006 — **80**

2003 Weißburgunder & Auxerrois
trocken **
12.5%, ♀ till 2006 — **81**

2002 Dürkheimer Hochbenn
Riesling trocken **
12.5%, ♀ till 2006 — **85**

2003 Chardonnay trocken
12.5%, ♀ till 2006 — **85**

2003 Dürkheimer Spielberg
Riesling trocken "Fingerprint" ***
13.5%, ♀ till 2008 — **85**

2002 Chardonnay trocken **
13%, ♀ till 2006 — **86**

2003 Dürkheimer Hochbenn
Riesling trocken **
12.5%, ♀ till 2007 — **86**

2003 Chardonnay
trocken "Fingerprint" ***
13.5%, ♀ till 2008 — **86**

2002 Riesling
trocken "Von den Terrassen" **
13%, ♀ till 2007 — **87**

2003 Riesling
trocken "Von den Terrassen" **
13%, ♀ till 2007 — **87**

——— Red wines ———

2002 Petit Noir trocken
13%, ♀ till 2008 — **82**

2001 St. Laurent trocken
13.5%, ♀ till 2006 — **83**

2002 St. Laurent trocken
13%, ♀ till 2008 — **84**

2001 St. Laurent
trocken "Fingerprint"
13%, ♀ till 2007 — **84**

The wines: **100** Perfect · **95–99** Outstanding · **90–94** Excellent · **85–89** Very good · **80–84** Good · **75–79** Average

463

WEINGUT A. CHRISTMANN

Owner and manager:
Steffen Christmann
Winemaker: Martin Eller
67435 Gimmeldingen,
Peter-Koch-Staße 43
Tel. (0 63 21) 6 60 39, Fax 6 87 62
e-mail: weingut.christmann@t-online.de
Internet: www.weingut-christmann.de
Directions: A 65, Neustadt-Nord exit, in Neustadt continue in direction of Gimmeldingen
Opening hours: Mon.–Fri. 09:00 to 11:30 hours and 14:00 to 17:00 hours
Sat. 09:00 to 12:00 hours
by appointment
Restaurant: Nett's Restaurant and Wine Bar, Wed.–Sun. from 17:00 hours,
also for tastings and wine sales
Worth seeing: Vaulted cellar dating to 1575

Vineyard area: 15 hectares
Annual production: 110,000 bottles
Top sites: Ruppertsberger Reiterpfad, Königsbacher Idig, Gimmeldinger Mandelgarten, Deidesheimer Hohenmorgen
Soil types: Clay, clay with sand, marl-limestone, decomposed sandstone
Grape varieties: 67% Riesling, 14% Spätburgunder, 8% Weißburgunder, 7% Grauburgunder, 4% other varieties
Average yield: 53 hl/ha
Best vintages: 2000, 2001, 2002
Member: VDP

This winery in Gimmeldingen has a long tradition, and has been among the three or four leading producers in the Pfalz since the mid-Nineties. The estate was founded by the winelovers Johann and Professor Dr. Ludwig Häusser who were part of the German democratic movement in the 1840's, and laid the foundation for the current winery in 1845. The current name was acquired by marriage in the early 20th century. Karl-Friedrich Christmann took over the business in 1965, and since his son Steffen joined the business in 1994 the winery has seen a remarkable development. Each year the wine-range presented here is a model example of reliability and good quality, even in difficult vintages such as 2000. In Steffen Christmann's view, this development is a direct result of the good teamwork practised. "The generations help and support each other. This results in an ideal combination of innovation and caution," explains Christmann who originally trained as a lawyer, but eventually found his love for wine. Two-thirds of the vineyard area are reserved for the key variety Riesling, and 85 percent of the wines are fermented dry. The real strength of the estate remains with the dry "Große Gewächse" (First Growths), which combine clarity and superb primary fruit with complexity, concentration and elegant spice. They set the standard in this category over several vintages, and matured very well in bottle, contrary to some expectations. And for the past two or three years the red and white Pinot variety wines produced by Christmann, as well as his botrytis dessert wines, have attained a standard remarkable even at national level. Christmann presented a whole phalanx of 90-point-wines from the 2001 and 2002 vintages, the highlights in 2002 were two excellent Trockenbeerenauslese wines. And again in 2002, two of his dry Rieslings were among the best produced in Germany. In the 2003 vintage, the vineyards between Neustadt and Forst suffered noticeably under the drouth. The "Große Gewächse" (First Growths) are still excellent, but the fruit and brilliance have suffered even here, despite undoubtedly Herculean efforts to achieve the best results possible. Christmann made the best of conditions that provided extreme ripeness with little botrytis, and made a magnificent, crystal-clear and brilliant Trockenbeerenauslese.

2003 Gimmeldinger Biengarten
Riesling Spätlese trocken
13%, ♀ till 2007   8●

2003 Ruppertsberger Reiterpfad
Riesling Spätlese trocken
"Großes Gewächs"
13.5%, ♀ till 2008   **88**

2003 Königsbacher Idig
Riesling Spätlese trocken
"Großes Gewächs"
13.5%, ♀ till 2008   **89**

2002 Grauer Burgunder
Spätlese trocken "SC"
13%, ♀ till 2006   **89**

2002 Ruppertsberger Reiterpfad
Riesling Spätlese trocken
"Großes Gewächs"
13%, ♀ till 2008   **90**

2003 Deidesheimer Hohenmorgen
Riesling Spätlese trocken
"Großes Gewächs"
13.5%, ♀ till 2008   **90**

2001 Chardonnay trocken "SC"
13.5%, ♀ till 2006   **90**

2002 Weißer Burgunder
Spätlese trocken "SC"
13%, ♀ till 2006   **90**

2002 Deidesheimer Hohenmorgen
Riesling Spätlese trocken
"Großes Gewächs"
13%, ♀ till 2008   **91**

2001 Deidesheimer Hohenmorgen
Riesling Spätlese trocken
"Großes Gewächs"
13%, ♀ till 2008   **92**

2002 Gimmeldinger Mandelgarten
Riesling Spätlese trocken
"Großes Gewächs"
13%, ♀ till 2008   **92**

2003 Gimmeldinger Mandelgarten
Riesling Spätlese trocken
"Großes Gewächs"
14%, ♀ till 2008   **92**

2001 Königsbacher Idig
Riesling Spätlese trocken
"Großes Gewächs"
3.5%, ♀ till 2008   **93**

2002 Königsbacher Idig
Riesling Spätlese trocken
"Großes Gewächs"
3%, ♀ till 2008   **93**

2003 Ruppertsberger Reiterpfad
Riesling Auslese
9%, ♀ till 2012   **91**

2001 Ruppertsberger Reiterpfad
Riesling Eiswein
11%, ♀ till 2020   **93**

2002 Königsbacher Idig
Riesling Trockenbeerenauslese
7%, ♀ till 2030   **93**

2002 Deidesheimer Hohenmorgen
Riesling Trockenbeerenauslese
7.5%, ♀ till 2030   **93**

2001 Ruppertsberger Reiterpfad
Riesling Auslese
9.5%, ♀ till 2010   **94**

2001 Königsbacher Idig
Riesling Trockenbeerenauslese
7.5%, ♀ till 2030   **95**

2003 Königsbacher Idig
Riesling Trockenbeerenauslese
7%, ♀ 2010 till 2035   **96**

———— Red wines ————

2002 Königsbacher Idig
Spätburgunder trocken
13.5%, ♀ till 2008   **88**

2001 Mußbacher Eselshaut
Spätburgunder trocken
13%, ♀ till 2008   **89**

2001 Königsbacher Ölberg
Spätburgunder trocken
13%, ♀ till 2006   **90**

2001 Königsbacher Idig
Spätburgunder trocken
"Großes Gewächs"
13%, ♀ till 2010   **90**

A. Christmann

2000
MANDELGARTEN
GIMMELDINGEN

WEINGUT DARTING

Owner: Helmut and Ella Darting
Manager and winemaker:
Helmut Darting
67098 Bad Dürkheim, Am Falltor 4
Tel. (0 63 22) 97 98 30 und 29 83, Fax
9 79 83 26
e-mail: weingut@darting.de
Internet: www.winesystem.com
Directions: From the A 61 to the A 650, direction of Trift suburb, via Triftweg road
Sales: Darting family
Opening hours: Mon.–Fri. 08:00 to 12:00 hours and 13:00 to 18:00 hours
Sat. to 16:00 hours

Vineyard area: 17 hectares
Annual production: 170,000 bottles
Top sites: Dürkheimer Michelsberg and Spielberg, Ungsteiner Herrenberg
Soil types: Calcareous marl and loess-clay, humous sand, clay
Grape varieties: 44% Riesling, 22% red varieties, 8% each of Spätburgunder and Weißburgunder, 6% Rieslaner, 5% Scheurebe, 7% other varieties
Average yield: 68 hl/ha
Best vintages: 1998, 2001, 2003
Member: Pfälzer Barrique Forum

Things have changed at the Darting winery – whereas for many years most of the wines here had some residual sugar, by now almost 70 percent of the wines are fermented dry. Helmut Darting brings good, accessible and harmonious wines to the bottle. This is particularly evident in a difficult vintage such as 2003, which he has mastered much better than many of his colleagues. Juicy, concentrated, fruit-dominated wines are the result, one that was not often achieved in this vintage. In previous years we have been quite critical because of the varying quality. In 2003, however, we found here one of the best Riesling Kabinett wines of the region, an elegant Gewürztraminer and a very good Huxelrebe Beerenauslese that has a honeyed nose. And the wines are inexpensive, as well!

2003 Wachenheimer Mandelgarten
Grauer Burgunder Kabinett trocken
12.8%, ♀ till 2006   83

2003 Dürkheimer Nonnengarten
Chardonnay Kabinett trocken
13%, ♀ till 2006   84

2002 Dürkheimer Spielberg
Riesling Kabinett trocken
12.5%, ♀ till 2006   85

2003 Dürkheimer Spielberg
Riesling Kabinett trocken
12.4%, ♀ till 2006   87

2003 Ungsteiner Herrenberg
Riesling Spätlese trocken
13.2%, ♀ till 2007   89

2003 Dürkheimer Nonnengarten
Gewürztraminer Kabinett
10.5%, ♀ till 2006   86

2002 Dürkheimer Steinberg
Muskateller Eiswein
9%, ♀ till 2012   90

2003 Forster Schnepfenflug
Huxelrebe Beerenauslese
9.9%, ♀ till 2012   90

———— Red wines ————

2003 Dürkheimer Feuerberg
Portugieser trocken
13%, ♀ till 2006   84

2001 Dürkheimer Feuerberg
St. Laurent trocken
12.5%, ♀ till 2006   85

2002 Dürkheimer Feuerberg
Spätburgunder trocken
13.2%, ♀ till 2006   85

WEINGUT DR. DEINHARD

Owner: Hoch family
Manager/Administrator: Heinz Bauer
Winemaker: Kurt Rathgeber
67146 Deidesheim, Weinstraße 10
Tel. (0 63 26) 2 21, Fax 79 20
e-mail: weingut@dr-deinhard.de
Directions: The winery is on the Weinstraße in Deidesheim
Sales: Heinz Bauer, Thomas Wagner
Opening hours: Mon.–Fri. 08:00 to 17:30 hours, Sat. 09:30 to 17:00 hours and by appointment
Worth a visit: Wine festival in courtyard under a huge sycamore, on 2nd and 3rd weekend in August
History: Founded 1849
Worth seeing: Manor-house in yellow and red sandstone, original tasting facility in former stables

---

Vineyard area: 35 hectares
Annual production: 240,000 bottles
Top sites: Deidesheimer Grainhübel, Kalkofen, Kieselberg, Langenmorgen and Mäushöhle, Ruppertsberger Reiterpfad and Linsenbusch, Forster Ungeheuer and Jesuitengarten
Soil types: Sandstone, basalt rubble, clay with sand, tertiary limestone, loess-clay
Grape varieties: 80% Riesling, 20% other varieties
Average yield: 67 hl/ha
Best vintages: 1998, 2001, 2002
Member: VDP

This estate was founded in 1849 by Friedrich Deinhard, of the Koblenz-based sparkling wine dynasty, and today has 35 hectares of vineyards. We have seen extremely variable quality here in recent years, and this has not changed with the arrival of the new winemaker Kurt Rathgeber. 2000 was particularly weak, while 2001 was good. The 2002 vintage range was brilliant, with not a single poor wine. The 2003 vintage now is reflecting both the tremendous drouth as well as poor judgement in acidifying the wines.

2003 Ruppertsberger Linsenbusch
Weißer Burgunder Spätlese trocken
13.5%, ♀ till 2006 — **85**

2003 Ruppertsberger Linsenbusch
Weißer Burgunder Kabinett trocken
13.5%, ♀ till 2006 — **86**

2003 Forster Ungeheuer
Riesling Spätlese trocken
12.5%, ♀ till 2007 — **86**

2003 Deidesheimer Grainhübel
Riesling Spätlese trocken
12.5%, ♀ till 2007 — **86**

2002 Forster Ungeheuer
Riesling Spätlese trocken
13%, ♀ till 2007 — **89**

2002 Forster Jesuitengarten
Riesling Spätlese trocken
"Großes Gewächs"
13%, ♀ till 2007 — **89**

2002 Deidesheimer Langenmorgen
Riesling Spätlese trocken
"Großes Gewächs"
13%, ♀ till 2007 — **91**

2003 Deidesheimer Herrgottsacker
Riesling Spätlese halbtrocken
11.5%, ♀ till 2008 — **87**

2003 Chardonnay Spätlese
14%, ♀ till 2007 — **86**

2003 Deidesheimer Kalkofen
Riesling Spätlese
10.5%, ♀ till 2010 — **86**

2003 Ruppertsberger Reiterpfad
Gewürztraminer Spätlese
12%, ♀ till 2008 — **88**

2002 Deidesheimer Herrgottsacker
Riesling Eiswein
11%, ♀ till 2015 — **89**

Weingut Dr. Deinhard
D-67146 DEIDESHEIM

PFALZ

Qualitätswein mit Prädikat · A.P.Nr. 510632701704
2003 Forster Ungeheuer
Riesling Spätlese trocken
alc.12,5% vol   GUTSABFÜLLUNG   750 mle

WEINGUT
DENGLER-SEYLER

Owner: Seyler family
Winemaker: Matthias Seyler
67487 Maikammer, Weinstraße Süd 6
Tel. (0 63 21) 51 03, Fax 5 73 25
e-mail: dengler-seyler@t-online.de
Internet: www.dengler-seyler.de
Directions: A 65, Edenkoben exit,
in town center of Maikammer
Sales: Julia, Eva and Matthias Seyler
Opening hours: Mon.–Sat. 08:00 to
18:00 hours, Sun. by appointment
Guest house/inn: "Zum Winzer"
Albers family, Tel. (0 63 21) 54 10
Tue.–Sun. 11:00 to 14:30, from 17:00 hours
Specialties: Seasonal cuisine
Worth seeing: Winery and baroque inn
with Mediterranean courtyard, vaulted
sandstone cellar 200 years old

Vineyard area: 11.2 hectares
Annual production: 90,000 bottles
Top sites: Maikammer Heiligen-
berg and Kirchenstück
Soil types: Clay with sand, sandy
clay with limestone layers
Grape varieties: 35% Riesling, 9%
each of Spät-, Weiß- and Grauburgun-
der, 8% Portugieser, 6% each of Silva-
ner and Dornfelder, 18% other varieties
Average yield: 89 hl/ha
Best vintage: 2002

This is one of the many wineries in the
Pfalz that have seen a significant improvement in quality brought about by
the new generation joining the business.
Matthias Seyler is improving his skills,
imparting not only clarity to his wines,
but also style in rising measure. Throughout the 2003 vintage range we liked the
mineral note of the wines, which indicates
the courage to "let things develop" in the
cellar. The Beerenauslese is convincingly
good, indicating that the winemaker's
ability extends to botrytis dessert wines.
If the Seylers continue in this vein, there
is no doubt they are hot candidates for the
awarding of another bunch of grapes.

2003 Maikammer Heiligenberg
Weißer Burgunder trocken
13%, ♀ till 2006   83

2003 Maikammer Kirchenstück
Chardonnay trocken
13.5%, ♀ till 2006   83

2003 Maikammer Heiligenberg
Riesling Kabinett trocken
12.5%, ♀ till 2006   84

2003 Maikammer Heiligenberg
Grauer Burgunder Spätlese trocken
14%, ♀ till 2006   85

2003 Maikammer Heiligenberg
Weißer Burgunder Spätlese trocken
14%, ♀ till 2006   86

2002 Maikammer Heiligenberg
Riesling Spätlese trocken
13%, ♀ till 2006   87

2003 Maikammer Heiligenberg
Riesling Spätlese trocken
13.5%, ♀ till 2007   87

2002 Maikammer Heiligenberg
Riesling Auslese
9%, ♀ till 2009   89

2003 Maikammer Heiligenberg
Riesling Beerenauslese
9.5%, ♀ till 2010   90

——————— Red wines ———————

2002 Maikammer Heiligenberg
trocken "Autumnus"
13.5%, ♀ till 2007   85

2000 Maikammer Heiligenberg
Spätburgunder trocken "Autumnus"
13.5%, ♀ till 2008   86

WEINGUT
DENGLER-SEYLER

PFALZ
2003

WEISSBURGUNDER
SPÄTLESE TROCKEN
MAIKAMMER HEILIGENBERG
14,0%vol   Qualitätswein mitPrädikat   0,751
Gutsabfüllung · A.P.Nr. 5 052 403 06 04
WEINSTRASSE SÜD 6 - D-67487 MAIKAMMER · TELEFON: 063 21 / 51 03

WEINGUT EYMANN

Owner: Rainer Eymann
Winemaker: Rainer Eymann
67161 Gönnheim, Ludwigstraße 35
Tel. (0 63 22) 28 08, Fax 6 87 92
e-mail: info@weinguteymann.de
Internet: www.weinguteymann.de
Directions: From the A 61, Kreuz
Ludwigshafen exit, via the A 650 in di-
rection of Bad Dürkheim, Gönnheim exit
Sales: Ingeborg Wagner-Eymann
Opening hours: Mon.–Fri. 08:00 to
12:00 hours and 13:00 to 19:00 hours
Sat. 10:00 to 19:00 hours
Restaurant: Wine Bar Eymann
Thur. and Fri. from 18:00 to 24:00 hours
Sat. from 17:00 to 24:00 hours

> Vineyard area: 16 hectares
> Annual production: 120,000 bottles
> Top site: Gönnheimer Sonnenberg
> Soil types: Limestone and loess
> Grape varieties: 35% Riesling,
> 12% Spätburgunder, 10% Weißbur-
> gunder, 8% each of Regent and Grau-
> burgunder, 7% St. Laurent, 4% each
> of Dornfelder, Chardonnay and Merlot,
> 8% other varieties
> Average yield: 68 hl/ha
> Best vintages: 1996, 1997, 2000

The Eymann name goes back to a farm
mentioned as early as 1350, called "Toreye," used today as a name for a selection of the finest wines. The Eymanns are
very environmentally conscious, and produced very clean, fruit-dominated wines
in the 2000 vintage. In the 2001 vintage,
we praised Eymann for two normally minor products, the perlé wine made from
Riesling grapes and the very attractive
Riesling in liter bottles. Unfortunately,
the 2002 vintage was a mixed bag, and
the same can be said of 2003. The elegant
Muskateller is the highlight of the vintage, which also produced a few solid
Classic wines. There are two interesting
reds from the 2002 vintage, and there is an
excellent 1998 Chardonnay Extra Brut
for lovers of sparkling wines.

2003 Riesling Classic
12%, ♀ till 2006 — **84**

2002 Gönnheimer Sonnenberg
Grauer Burgunder Spätlese trocken
"Toreye"
12.5%, ♀ till 2006 — **85**

2003 Gönnheimer Sonnenberg
Riesling Spätlese trocken "Toreye"
12.5%, ♀ till 2006 — **85**

2002 Gönnheimer Sonnenberg
Chardonnay trocken
13%, ♀ till 2006 — **86**

2002 Gönnheimer Sonnenberg
Weißer Burgunder Spätlese trocken
"Toreye"
13%, ♀ till 2006 — **86**

2003 Gönnheimer Sonnenberg
Muskateller Spätlese "Toreye"
12%, ♀ till 2007 — **89**

———— Red wines ————

2003 Gönnheimer Sonnenberg
St. Laurent trocken
13%, ♀ till 2006 — **84**

2002 Gönnheimer Sonnenberg
Portugieser trocken
13%, ♀ till 2006 — **85**

2002 Merlot trocken
13%, ♀ till 2006 — **85**

2001 Gönnheimer Mandelgarten
Dornfelder trocken
13%, ♀ till 2007 — **87**

2002 Gönnheimer Sonnenberg
Spätburgunder halbtrocken
13%, ♀ till 2007 — **86**

The wines: **100** Perfect · **95–99** Outstanding · **90–94** Excellent · **85–89** Very good · **80–84** Good · **75–79** Average

469

WEINGUT FADER – KASTANIENHOF

Owner and manager:
Karl-Heinz and Knut Fader
Winemaker: Knut Fader
76835 Rhodt, Theresienstraße 62
Tel. (0 63 23) 51 93, Fax 98 08 41
e-mail: weingut-fader@t-online.de
Internet: www.weingut-fader.de
Directions: A 65, Edenkoben exit, B 38
in direction of Landau, in Edenkoben
turn right toward Rhodt
Sales: Fader family
Opening hours: Mon.–Sat. 08:00 to
18:00 hours, Sun. 09:00 to 12:00 hours
History: Winemaking here since 1780
Worth seeing: Winery in an old sand-
stone building, historical chestnut avenue

Vineyard area: 14.3 hectares
Annual production: 150,000 bottles
Top sites: Rhodter Rosengarten,
Schlossberg and Klosterpfad
Soil types: Clay with sand and
kaolin-limestone
Grape varieties: 24% Riesling, 11%
Spätburgunder, 10% Grauburgunder,
8% Portugieser, 7% each of Dornfelder
and Weißburgunder, 6% Müller-Thur-
gau, 5% Gewürztraminer, 4% each of
Silvaner and Kerner, 14% other varieties
Average yield: 92 hl/ha
Best vintages: 2001, 2002, 2003

Rhodt is a winemaking village with long
tradition, the Theresienstraße is worth
seeing, as are the old sandstone arches,
as well as having one of the most attractive wine festivals. The wines of the
Fader estate have become distinctly more
modern in style in recent years. Ever
since Knut Fader has taken over the cellar, elegant, light-bodied Rieslings have
joined the full-bodied Pinot wines. Even
in the rather difficult 2003 vintage, he has
succeeded in producing a number of
typical Rieslings and Pinot wines, in
which the alcohol level is virtually imper-
ceptible. An amazing development is the
improvement in the red wines.

2003 Rhodter Schlossberg
Riesling Kabinett trocken
13%, ♀ till 2006 **84**

2003 Rhodter Schlossberg
Silvaner Spätlese trocken
13.5%, ♀ till 2006 **85**

2003 Rhodter Klosterpfad
Weißer Burgunder Spätlese trocken
14.5%, ♀ till 2006 **85**

2003 Rhodter Rosengarten
Grauer Burgunder Auslese trocken
15%, ♀ till 2006 **85**

2002 Rhodter Klosterpfad
Chardonnay Spätlese trocken
13%, ♀ till 2006 **86**

2003 Rhodter Schlossberg
Riesling Auslese trocken
14%, ♀ till 2006 **86**

2002 Rhodter Rosengarten
Gewürztraminer Spätlese trocken
13%, ♀ till 2006 **88**

2003 Rhodter Rosengarten
Gewürztraminer Spätlese trocken
14.5%, ♀ till 2006 **88**

2003 Rhodter Klosterpfad
Gewürztraminer Auslese
13%, ♀ till 2008 **87**

——————— Red wines ———————

2001 Rhodter Klosterpfad
Spätburgunder Spätlese trocken
13%, ♀ till 2007 **86**

2001 Rhodter Klosterpfad
Dornfelder trocken Barrique
13%, ♀ till 2007 **86**

2002 Rhodter Klosterpfad
Spätburgunder trocken Barrique
13%, ♀ till 2007 **8**

WEINGUT
FADER
KASTANIENHOF
2003 ER
CHARDONNAY
SPÄTLESE TROCKEN
RHODTER KLOSTERPFAD
14,5 % vol   Pfalz   0,75 L

The estates: ♟♟♟♟♟ World's finest · ♟♟♟♟ Germany's best · ♟♟♟ Very good · ♟♟ Good · ♟ Reliab

WEINGUT FITZ-RITTER

Owner: Konrad M. Fitz
Administrator: Christian Klein
Winemaker: Bernd Henninger
67098 Bad Dürkheim,
Weinstraße Nord 51
Tel. (0 63 22) 53 89, Fax 6 60 05
e-mail: info@fitz-ritter.de
Internet: www.fitz-ritter.de
Directions: A 61, Kreuz Ludwigshafen
exit, via A 650, in direction of Dürkheim
Sales: Ute Hoffmann, Steffen Becker
Opening hours: Mon.–Fri. 08:00 to
12:00 and 13:00 to 18:00, Sat. 09:00 to
13:00 hours, and by appointment
History: Family-owned since 1785
Worth seeing: Most beautiful garden of
the entire German Weinstraße

Vineyard area: 21 hectares
Annual production: 150,000 bottles
Top sites: Ungsteiner Herrenberg,
Dürkheimer Michelsberg, Spielberg,
Abtsfronhof and Hochbenn
Soil types: Sandy clay with limestone
Grape varieties: 65% Riesling, 6%
Spätburgunder, 5% Gewürztraminer,
4% Chardonnay, 20% other varieties
Average yield: 67 hl/ha
Best vintages: 2000, 2001, 2003
Member: VDP, Pfälzer Barrique Forum

What has happened here? The wines of
the 2003 vintage presented for tasting
was above average right across the board,
and much better than what we have seen
in previous vintages. We can only hope
that this long-established producer will
continue on the path of quality. Follow-
ng on a brief weak period, the 2000 and
2001 vintages had already heralded an
improvement. In 1832, at the "Hambacher Festival," "Red Fitz" was the speak-
er of the rebellious winemakers and
democrats. The pace is more restful today
in the stylish courtyard of the beautiful
manor-house, where the Fitz family adds
to the cultural life by presenting wine fes-
ivals, concerts and art exhibitions.

2001 Dürkheimer Abtsfronhof
Gewürztraminer Spätlese trocken
13%, ♀ till 2006   **84**

2002 Dürkheimer Spielberg
Chardonnay Spätlese trocken
12.5%, ♀ till 2006   **84**

2003 Dürkheimer Abtsfronhof
Gewürztraminer Spätlese trocken
13.5%, ♀ till 2006   **85**

2003 Dürkheimer Spielberg
Chardonnay Spätlese trocken
13%, ♀ till 2006   **86**

2002 Dürkheimer Spielberg
Chardonnay Spätlese trocken Barrique
13.5%, ♀ till 2008   **86**

2003 Michelsberg
Riesling Spätlese trocken
"Großes Gewächs"
13%, ♀ till 2007   **86**

2003 Ungsteiner Herrenberg
Riesling Spätlese trocken
13%, ♀ till 2007   **87**

2001 Dürkheimer Abtsfronhof
Riesling Spätlese halbtrocken
12%, ♀ till 2006   **85**

2003 Dürkheimer
Gewürztraminer Spätlese
11%, ♀ till 2008   **87**

2001 Dürkheimer Hochbenn
Riesling Eiswein
9.5%, ♀ till 2015   **89**

2003 Dürkheimer Hochbenn
Riesling Eiswein
10%, ♀ till 2015   **92**

he wines: **100** Perfect · **95–99** Outstanding · **90–94** Excellent · **85–89** Very good · **80–84** Good · **75–79** Average

471

WEINGUT
WINFRIED FREY & SÖHNE

Owner: Jürgen and Peter Frey
Winemaker: Jürgen Frey
76879 Essingen, Spanierstraße 9
Tel. (0 63 47) 82 24, Fax 72 90
e-mail: info@weingut-frey.com
Internet: www.weingut-frey.com
*Directions: Southern Weinstraße near
Landau*
Sales: Ursula Frey,
by appointment only
Guest house: For 50 persons
Worth seeing: Small wine museum

Vineyard area: 13 hectares
Annual production: 50,000 bottles
Top sites: Essinger Rossberg,
Sonnenberg and Osterberg
Soil types: Loess and sandy clay
Grape varieties: 30% Riesling, 15%
Grauburgunder, 10% each of Weißbur-
gunder, Portugieser, Dornfelder and
Chardonnay, 5% each of Gewürztra-
miner, Muskateller and Sankt Laurent
Average yield: 48 hl/ha
Best vintages: 1998, 2001, 2002

Winfried Frey owns rather mediocre and
unimportant vineyard sites in Essingen,
but has made an excellent reputation for
himself as a botrytis wine specialist. No
vineyard sites are mentioned on the labels. His son Jürgen has been responsible
for the cellar since 1995. We are pleased
to see that progress has been made in the
direction of producing exclusively botrytis dessert wines, as we were never
enthusiastic about the dry wines. There
were very good wines in 2001 and 2002,
ranging from Beerenauslese to Eiswein,
with a surprisingly large range of wines
from this latter category, bearing in mind
that 2002 was anything but a good vintage for Eiswein. Looking at the 2003
wines, they are (currently) lacking in
harmony because of excessive addition of
acidity. The Cabernet Sauvignon Eiswein
produced here must be a unique curiosity.

2003 Riesling Beerenauslese
6%, ♀ till 2012 — 82

2003 Ortega Beerenauslese
6.5%, ♀ till 2010 — 83

2003 Weißer Burgunder
Beerenauslese
6%, ♀ till 2012 — 86

2003 Chardonnay Eiswein
8%, ♀ till 2015 — 86

2003 Chardonnay Beerenauslese
6.5%, ♀ till 2012 — 88

2003 Riesling Eiswein
6.5%, ♀ till 2015 — 88

2003 Muskateller Eiswein
7.5%, ♀ till 2015 — 89

2003 Scheurebe Eiswein
6.5%, ♀ till 2015 — 89

2002 Riesling Eiswein
8.5%, ♀ till 2015 — 90

2002 Riesling
Trockenbeerenauslese
8.5%, ♀ till 2025 — 90

2002 Ortega Trockenbeerenauslese
8.5%, ♀ till 2025 — 91

——— Red wine ———

2002 Cabernet Sauvignon Eiswein
8.5%, ♀ till 2012 — 87

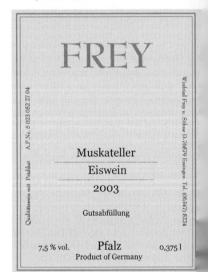

FREY

Muskateller

Eiswein

2003

Gutsabfüllung

7,5 % vol.   Pfalz   0,375 l
Product of Germany

Winfried Frey u. Söhne D-76879 Essingen Tel. (06347) 8224

A.P.Nr. 5 023 052 27 04

Qualitätswein mit Prädikat

WEINGUT
KARL-HEINZ GAUL

Owner and winemaker:
Karl-Heinz Gaul
67269 Grünstadt-Sausenheim,
Bärenbrunnenstraße 15
Tel. (0 63 59) 8 45 69, Fax 8 74 98
Directions: A 6 Mannheim–Saar-
brücken, Grünstadt exit
Sales: Rosemarie Gaul
Opening hours: Mon.–Fri. 08:00 to
12:00 hours and 13:00 to 18:00 hours
Sat. 09:00 to 15:00 hours

Vineyard area: 13.5 hectares
Annual production: 120,000 bottles
Top sites: Sausenheimer Honig-
sack, Asselheimer St. Stephan
Soil types: Limestone-rich marl with
sandy gravel and clay
Grape varieties: 35% Riesling, 10%
Weißburgunder, 9% Spätburgun-
der, 8% Portugieser, 7% each of
Sankt Laurent and Dornfelder, 6%
Schwarzriesling, 18% other varieties
Average yield: 77 hl/ha
Best vintages: 2001, 2002, 2003

This winery was created in 1993, when
the parents' estate, existed for generations, was split up. From the tasting
room of the winery, which lies amidst the
vineyards, you can look out over oleander
bushes that flower in twelve colors, with
some of them eighty years old, into the
sunset. Initially, the quality produced
here was very average. However, there
was a distinct change since the 1996 vintage. The 2001 vintage wines were so
good that we were able to award an additional bunch of grapes. The wines of the
2002 vintage were all clean and clear, and
of remarkably good quality. In the 2003
vintage we liked the very accessible,
amazingly fresh and fruity Rieslings best.
An example of this is the Riesling Classic, which is one of the best in the country. A whole series of well above average
dry wines was produced here.

2003 Sausenheimer K
Grauer Burgunder Spä
14%, ♀ till 2007

2003 Riesling (
12%, ♀ till 2006

2003 Sausenheimer Klostergarten
Riesling Spätlese trocken
12.5%, ♀ till 2007 — **86**

2003 Sausenheimer Honigsack
Weißer Burgunder Auslese trocken
14.5%, ♀ till 2007 — **86**

2002 Sausenheimer Honigsack
Weißer Burgunder Spätlese trocken
13%, ♀ till 2006 — **87**

2003 Sausenheimer Honigsack
Silvaner Spätlese trocken
13.5%, ♀ till 2006 — **87**

2003 Sausenheimer Hütt
Riesling Spätlese trocken
13%, ♀ till 2007 — **87**

2002 Sausenheimer Hütt
Gewürztraminer Spätlese trocken
13%, ♀ till 2006 — **88**

2003 Sausenheimer Honigsack
Riesling Spätlese trocken
13.5%, ♀ till 2007 — **88**

2003 Asselheimer St. Stephan
Riesling Beerenauslese
9.5%, ♀ till 2012 — **90**

2002 Sausenheimer Hütt
Riesling Eiswein
10%, ♀ 2006 till 2015 — **92**

GAUL

Weißer Burgunder
Spätlese trocken

2002 Sausenheimer Honigsack
Qualitätswein mit Prädikat · Erzeugerabfüllung
A.P.Nr.5 120 021 10 03

Weingut Karl-Heinz Gaul
D-67269 Grünstadt-Sausenheim
Tel.0 63 59 / 8 45 69

13% vol   Pfalz   0,75 L

WEINGUT GIES-DÜPPEL

Owner: Volker Gies
Manager and winemaker: Volker Gies
76831 Birkweiler, Am Rosenberg 5
Tel. (0 63 45) 91 91 56, Fax 91 91 57
e-mail: WeingutGies@aol.com
Directions: A 65, Landau-Nord exit;
B 10 in direction of Annweiler,
Birkweiler exit
Sales: Volker Gies
Opening hours: Mon.–Fri. 09:00 to
12:00 hours and 14:00 to 18:00 hours
Sat. 10:00 to 16:00 hours, by appointment

Vineyard area: 10.5 hectares
Annual production: 85,000 bottles
Top sites: Birkweiler Kastanien-
busch and Mandelberg, Siebeldinger
im Sonnenschein
Soil types: Sandstone, shell limestone,
lower new red sandstone, sandy clay
Grape varieties: 30% Riesling, 20%
Spätburgunder, 10% Weißburgunder,
8% each of Grauburgunder, Chardon-
nay and Silvaner, 6% each of Müller-
Thurgau and Dornfelder, 4% Auxerrois
Average yield: 68 hl/ha
Best vintages: 2001, 2002, 2003

This family has been involved in winemaking for four generations. However,
the wines have been remarkable since
young Volker Gies took over the helm
in 1999. He has reduced the yields, and
introduced more modern methods in the
cellar. All of a sudden, his Riesling wines
of the 2001 vintage were among the best
on offer in Birkweiler, a town that is not
lacking in good producers. In the 2003
vintage, intensive and on time irrigation
work in the vineyards has allowed the
herbal, spicy notes of the Kastanienbusch
site to become evident, as shown by
the excellent Riesling Spätlese. Following
on the critical comments we made last
year, the wines have now all shown more
concentration, and more courage on the
winemaker's part. The Pinot Noirs continue to improve.

2003 Weißer Burgunder
Kabinett trocken
13%, ♀ till 2006 — **85**

2003 Birkweiler Kastanienbusch
Riesling Kabinett trocken
12.5%, ♀ till 2006 — **85**

2003 Birkweiler Kastanienbusch
Weißer Burgunder Spätlese trocken
14%, ♀ till 2007 — **87**

2003 Birkweiler Mandelberg
Riesling Spätlese trocken
13.5%, ♀ till 2007 — **87**

2002 Birkweiler Kastanienbusch
Weißer Burgunder Spätlese trocken
13.5%, ♀ till 2006 — **88**

2003 Birkweiler Kastanienbusch
Riesling Spätlese trocken
12.5%, ♀ till 2008 — **88**

2002 Birkweiler Kastanienbusch
Riesling Spätlese
9%, ♀ till 2009 — **89**

——— Red wines ———

2002 Birkweiler Königsgarten
Spätburgunder trocken
13%, ♀ till 2008 — **86**

2002 Birkweiler Kastanienbusch
Spätburgunder trocken Barrique
13.5%, ♀ till 2008 — **87**

2001 Birkweiler Kastanienbusch
Spätburgunder trocken Barrique
13.5%, ♀ till 2008 — **89**

Pfalz

WEINGUT LUDWIG GRASSMÜCK

Owner and manager:
Markus Graßmück
76831 Birkweiler, Eichplatz 4
Tel. (0 63 45) 36 30, Fax 53 24
e-mail: wein@weingut-grassmueck.de
Internet: www.weingut-grassmueck.de
Directions: A 65, Landau-Nord exit,
B 10, Birkweiler exit
Sales: Else and Judith Graßmück
Opening hours: Mon.–Sat. 09:00 to
11:00 and 14:00 to 18:00, Sun. 09:00 to
11:00 hours, by appointment only
History: Winemaking here since 1667
Worth seeing: Attractive courtyard

Vineyard area: 11 hectares
Annual production: 90,000 bottles
Top sites: Birkweiler Mandelberg,
Kastanienbusch and Rosenberg
Soil types: Calcareous marl, lower
new red sandstone, kaolin, sandy clay
Grape varieties: 35% Riesling,
13% Weißburgunder, 7% Dornfelder,
6% Portugieser, 5% each of Silvaner,
Müller-Thurgau, Kerner, Chardonnay,
Huxelrebe and Cabernet, 9% other
varieties
Average yield: 85 hl/ha
Best vintages: 2001, 2002, 2003

The father handed over the reins to his son a few years ago at this family winery in the center of Birkweiler. Both of them have been making good wine for some time, as evidenced by the quality of mature vintages. The range is clean and with clear character, and there are no disappointments, at the same time there are no sensational wines either. The latest vintage 2003 is no exception. They are well-made, rounded wines, and none of them pretends to be any more than it is: pleasant wines made for drinking, with typical varietal character, of a good quality level for the southern Pfalz region. In this range, we particularly liked the Riesling wines. A new cosy wine tasting room is to be added in the near future.

2003 Birkweiler Rosenberg
Weißer Burgunder Spätlese trocken
14.5%, ♀ till 2006 — **84**

2003 Birkweiler Rosenberg
Grauer Burgunder Spätlese trocken
13.5%, ♀ till 2006 — **84**

2003 Birkweiler Rosenberg
Chardonnay Spätlese trocken
13.5%, ♀ till 2007 — **84**

2002 Birkweiler Mandelberg
Riesling Spätlese trocken
13%, ♀ till 2006 — **85**

2002 Birkweiler Rosenberg
Weißer Burgunder Kabinett trocken
12.5%, ♀ till 2006 — **85**

2002 Birkweiler Rosenberg
Weißer Burgunder Spätlese trocken
13%, ♀ till 2006 — **85**

2003 Birkweiler Kastanienbusch
Riesling Spätlese trocken
13%, ♀ till 2008 — **86**

2003 Nußdorfer Herrenberg
Kerner Spätlese halbtrocken
"Holzfassausbau"
14.5%, ♀ till 2007 — **85**

2002 Birkweiler Rosenberg
Huxelrebe Spätlese
12.5%, ♀ till 2006 — **85**

2002 Birkweiler Rosenberg
Huxelrebe Auslese
12.5%, ♀ till 2008 — **87**

2002 Birkweiler Rosenberg
Huxelrebe Beerenauslese
11.5%, ♀ till 2010 — **90**

The wines: **100** Perfect · **95–99** Outstanding · **90–94** Excellent · **85–89** Very good · **80–84** Good · **75–79** Average

475

WEINGUT
WALTER HENSEL

Owner: Hensel family
Winemaker: Thomas Hensel
67098 Bad Dürkheim, In den Almen 13
Tel. (0 63 22) 24 60, Fax 6 69 18
e-mail: henselwein@aol.com
Internet: www.weingut-hensel.de
Directions: A 61–A 650–B 37,
in direction of "In den Almen,"
close to airfield and camping site
Sales: Thomas Hensel
Opening hours: Mon.–Fri. 09:00 to
11:00 and 13:00 to 18:00, Sat. 09:00 to
11:00 and 13:00 to 16:00 hours
History: Winemaking for 300 years
Worth a visit: Summer wine festival in
July, must festival in October

Vineyard area: 16 hectares
Annual production: 125,000 bottles
Top sites: Dürkheimer Steinberg,
Nonnengarten, Fronhof and Spielberg
Soil types: Sand, sandstone, loess-
clay, decomposed limestone rock
Grape varieties: 30% Riesling, 25%
white Pinot varieties, 10% each of
Spätburgunder and St. Laurent,
9% Cabernet Sauvignon, 6%
Dornfelder, 10% other varieties
Average yield: 60 hl/ha
Best vintages: 1999, 2001, 2002
Member: Pfälzer Barrique Forum

Thomas Hensel took over the business in
1990 at the tender age of 20, since then
the estate has grown to 16 hectares of vineyard, and is continuously undergoing mod-
ernization. Hensel differs from his colleagues in the long time the white wines
spend on the lees, as well as with the
high-quality red blends matured in small
oak. In 2002, it appeared that a new door
had been opened with regard to the white
wines: The courage to leave in the natural
acidity, to give the wines character, and a
delightfully clean aroma. However, the
2003 vintage white wines appear to us to
be a little less accomplished.

2003 Dürkheimer Steinberg
Riesling trocken
12.5%, ♀ till 2006   82

2003 Dürkheimer Feuerberg
Riesling trocken
13.5%, ♀ till 2006   83

2003 Dürkheimer Nonnengarten
Gewürztraminer trocken
13.5%, ♀ till 2007   84

2001 Dürkheimer Schenkenböhl
Grauer Burgunder Spätlese trocken
13%, ♀ till 2006   86

2002 Dürkheimer Steinberg
Riesling Kabinett trocken
12%, ♀ till 2006   87

2002 Dürkheimer Feuerberg
Riesling Spätlese trocken
13%, ♀ till 2007   87

2002 Dürkheimer Nonnengarten
Chardonnay Kabinett trocken
12.5%, ♀ till 2006   87

2001 Dürkheimer Nonnengarten
Muskat-Ottonel Auslese
11.5%, ♀ till 2006   87

——— Red wines ———

2001 Dürkheimer Feuerberg
St. Laurent trocken
13%, ♀ till 2007   85

2002 Merlot trocken
13.5%, ♀ till 2009   85

2001 Spätburgunder
Spätlese trocken
13.5%, ♀ till 2007   86

2000 "Cuvée Ikarus" trocken
14%, ♀ till 2008   86

2002 Spätburgunder
Spätlese trocken
13.5%, ♀ till 2010   87

WEINGUT CHRISTIAN HEUSSLER

Owner and manager:
Herbert and Christian Heußler
Winemaker: Christian Heußler
76835 Rhodt, Mühlgasse 5
Tel. (0 63 23) 22 35 and 68 94,
Fax 98 05 33
e-mail: heussler-wein@t-online.de
Internet: www.heussler-wein.de
Directions: A 65, Edenkoben exit,
two kilometers past Rhodt
Sales: Heußler family
Opening hours: Mon.–Sat. 10:00 to
12:00 hours and 13:30 to 18:00 hours
Sun. and public holidays by appointment
History: Family-owned since 1748
Worth seeing: Old winery building dating to 1763, vaulted cellar dating to 1607

Vineyard area: 12 hectares
Annual production: 65,000 bottles
Top site: Rhodter Schlossberg
Soil types: Sandstone, lower new red
sandstone, limestone-loam, clay
Grape varieties: 30% Riesling,
8% each of Weißburgunder, Grauburgunder and Dornfelder, 6% Portugieser, 5% each of Spätburgunder and
Müller-Thurgau, 30% other varieties
Average yield: 72 hl/ha
Best vintages: 2002, 2003

It seems there is no stopping this young man on his way right to the top. We were quite delighted last year to discover the combination of modern applied technology and elegant varietal characteristics produced here. The 2003 vintage has brought a further improvement in quality, and consistently above-average wines. It is amazing how the tricky Muskateller turns out in almost a Rebholz style, and a basic Pinot Blanc provides tremendous quaffing enjoyment. Almost every single one of these elegant wines is a bargain buy. Bottled wine has only been available from this winery for the past eight years, yet already it is well worth the consumer's attention.

2002 Rhodter Ordensgut
Weißer Burgunder Spätlese trocken
13%, ♀ till 2006 — 85

2002 Rhodter Klosterpfad
Grauer Burgunder Spätlese trocken
13%, ♀ till 2006 — 85

2003 Rhodter Ordensgut
Weißer Burgunder trocken
13%, ♀ till 2006 — 85

2003 Rhodter Rosengarten
Grauer Burgunder Kabinett trocken
13.5%, ♀ till 2006 — 85

2002 Rhodter Schlossberg
Riesling Kabinett trocken
12%, ♀ till 2006 — 86

2003 Rhodter Schlossberg
Riesling Kabinett trocken
12.5%, ♀ till 2006 — 86

2003 Rhodter Schlossberg
Riesling Spätlese trocken
13.5%, ♀ till 2007 — 88

2003 Rhodter Rosengarten
Muskateller trocken
14%, ♀ till 2006 — 88

2002 Edenkobener
Schloss Ludwigshöhe
Riesling Spätlese halbtrocken
12.5%, ♀ till 2007 — 87

2003 Rhodter Klosterpfad
Gewürztraminer Spätlese
14%, ♀ till 2006 — 88

2003 Rhodter Schlossberg
Riesling Spätlese "RS"
9%, ♀ till 2008 — 90

he wines: **100** Perfect · **95–99** Outstanding · **90–94** Excellent · **85–89** Very good · **80–84** Good · **75–79** Average

477

WEIN- UND SEKTGUT IMMENGARTEN HOF

Owner: Höhn family
Manager: Hans, Gisela and Frank Höhn
Winemaker: Frank Höhn
67487 Maikammer, Marktstraße 62
Tel. (0 63 21) 5 94 00, Fax 5 74 37
e-mail: weingut.hoehn@t-online.de
Internet: www.immengarten-hof.de
Directions: A 65, Edenkoben exit, on L 516 to Maikammer; A 6, Speyer exit, on L 515 to Maikammer
Sales: Gisela Höhn
Opening hours: Mon.–Sat. 09:00 to 18:00 hours, Sun. 10:30 to 12:30 hours
Worth seeing: Turn-of-the-century style manor-house (built 1894)

Vineyard area: 12 hectares
Annual production: 100,000 bottles
Top sites: Maikammer Heiligen-berg and Kapellenberg, Hambacher Schlossberg, Diedesfelder Berg
Soil types: Sand with clay and loess
Grape varieties: 15% Dornfelder, 13% Riesling, 10% Portugieser, 8% Müller-Thurgau, 7% Spätburgunder, 6% each of Kerner and Heroldrebe, 5% St. Laurent, 30% other varieties
Average yield: 84 hl/ha
Best vintages: 2001, 2002, 2003
Member: Pfälzer Barrique Forum

This winery was a discovery in 2001, and the new vintage has surprised us yet again. The young Frank Höhn took over the helm here four years ago, and has gone to work with both ambition and a feeling for finesse and detail. The wines presented were again of improved quality. This time round, we were particularly impressed by the well-made aromatic varieties, as well as the concentrated, juicy red wines made from Blaufränkisch and from new crossings, and for this we are happy to award another bunch of grapes. The winery can draw on a cornucopia of vineyard sites and grape varieties, and space precludes us from listing more than a bare half of these here.

2002 Riesling Classic
12.5%, ♀ till 2006   **85**

2001 Maikammer Heiligenberg
Chardonnay Spätlese trocken
13.5%, ♀ till 2006   **86**

2003 Maikammer Heiligenberg
Chardonnay Spätlese trocken
13.5%, ♀ till 2006   **87**

2002 Maikammer Heiligenberg
Chardonnay Spätlese trocken
13.5%, ♀ till 2006   **88**

2003 Maikammer Heiligenberg
Muskateller Spätlese trocken
13.5%, ♀ till 2006   **88**

2003 Maikammer Mandelhöhe
Gewürztraminer Spätlese trocken
14%, ♀ till 2007   **89**

2003 Diedesfelder Berg
Gewürztraminer Spätlese
10.5%, ♀ till 2008   **87**

2003 Maikammer Heiligenberg
Riesling Auslese
9.5%, ♀ till 2012   **88**

———— Red wines ————

2002 Diedesfelder Berg
Cabernet Dorsa trocken Barrique
13%, ♀ till 2007   **86**

2002 Cabernet Cubin trocken
13.5%, ♀ till 2010   **87**

2002 "Cupido" trocken
13.5%, ♀ till 2008   **87**

2002 Blaufränkisch trocken
13.5%, ♀ till 2008   **87**

2002 Spätburgunder
trocken Barrique
12.5%, ♀ till 2009   **89**

WEINGUT JÜLG

Owner: Werner Jülg
Manager and winemaker: Werner Jülg
Administrator: Andreas Eck
76889 Schweigen-Rechtenbach,
Hauptstraße 1
Tel. (0 63 42) 91 90 90, Fax 91 90 91
e-mail: info@weingut-juelg.de
Internet: www.weingut-juelg.de
Directions: A 65, Kandel-Mitte exit, in
direction of Weißenburg
Sales: Mon.–Fri. by appointment
Sat. and Sun. 11:00 to 18:00 hours
Restaurant: 11:00 to 22:00 hours
Closed Thu. and Fri.
Specialties: Own production of cheese,
sausages and ham
Worth seeing: Large barrique and barrel
cellar, can be booked for festivities

Vineyard area: 17 hectares
Annual production: 130,000 bottles
Top site: Schweigener Sonnenberg
Soil types: Calcareous marl, kaolin,
loess
Grape varieties: 40% Weiß- and
Grauburgunder, 20% Riesling,
10% Spätburgunder, 5% each
of Schwarzriesling and St. Laurent,
20% other varieties
Average yield: 55 hl/ha
Best vintages: 2001, 2002, 2003

Peter and Werner Jülg took over this
well-established house with its wine bar
and good restaurant in the mid-Eighties.
Today Werner has 17 hectares of vineyard in production, and has recently
added a new fermentation cellar, while
his brother now owns a winery in Alsace.
From the 2001 vintage on, all the white
wines have a deep yellow color, and provide a successful combination of traditional style and clear fruit. In 2002, Jülg
produced remarkably good Pinot variety
wines in this style, with both character
and finess. In 2003, the white Pinot varieties have also gained a strong juicy character, while we were not particularly en-
husiastic about the reds.

2003 Schweigener Sonnenberg
Weißer Burgunder Spätlese trocken "S"
14%, ♀ till 2008   **85**

2003 Schweigener Sonnenberg
Grauer Burgunder Spätlese trocken
14%, ♀ till 2007   **86**

2003 Schweigener Sonnenberg
Riesling Spätlese trocken "S"
13.5%, ♀ till 2008   **86**

2002 Schweigener Sonnenberg
Muskateller Kabinett trocken
12%, ♀ till 2006   **87**

2002 Schweigener Sonnenberg
Weißer Burgunder Spätlese trocken
13%, ♀ till 2006   **87**

2002 Schweigener Sonnenberg
Grauer Burgunder trocken Selection "S"
13%, ♀ till 2006   **87**

2003 Schweigener Sonnenberg
Muskateller Spätlese "S"
14%, ♀ till 2006   **86**

2002 Schweigener Sonnenberg
Riesling Selection "S"
13%, ♀ till 2006   **87**

————— Red wines —————

2002 Schweigener Sonnenberg
Spätburgunder Spätlese trocken "R"
13.5%, ♀ till 2010   **84**

2001 Schweigener Sonnenberg
Spätburgunder trocken Selection "R"
14%, ♀ till 2008   **88**

The wines: **100** Perfect · **95–99** Outstanding · **90–94** Excellent · **85–89** Very good · **80–84** Good · **75–79** Average

479

WEINGUT ERNST KARST UND SOHN

Owner and manager: Manfred Karst
67098 Bad Dürkheim, In den Almen 15
Tel. (0 63 22) 28 62, Fax 6 59 65
e-mail: info@weingut-karst.de
Internet: www.weingut-karst.de
Directions: A 650, follow signs "Almen"
Sales: Mon.–Fri. 10:00 to 12:00 and
13:00 to 18:00, Sat. 09:00 to 17:00 hours
Restaurant: Weinrefugium, Schlacht-
hausstraße 1a, open Wed.–Mon. 17:00 to
24:00, Thur.–Sun. 12:00 to 14:00 hours,
closed Tue. and 1st Mon. of the month
Specialties: Light dishes from fresh in-
gredients
Guest house: On the estate
History: Winemaking here since 1765

Vineyard area: 11 hectares
Annual production: 80,000 bottles
Top sites: Dürkheimer Hochbenn, Rittergarten and Spielberg, Wachenheimer Mandelgarten
Soil types: Calcareous marl, loess-clay
Grape varieties: 35% Riesling, 20% Spätburgunder, 10% each of Weißburgunder, Portugieser and Dornfelder, 5% each of Grauburgunder, Gewürztraminer and Lemberger
Average yield: 68 hl/ha
Best vintages: 2001, 2002

Georg Karst, the great-grandfather of
Manfred Karst, was one of the co-found-
ers of the Dürkheim wine producers' association in the early 20th century. His
successors have flourished, and added to
the base, so that it was necessary to move
to the town border in 1970. The most interesting wines are made from Pinot varieties, and from Riesling. 2000 was not
an outstandingly good vintage. Pinots and
the blended red wine were the best of
the 2001 vintage. 2002 produced very
smooth, clean white wines. The 2003 vintage range is rather heterogeneous. While
we were not at all happy with the reds,
most of the baroque-style expansive
whites had fruit, and we liked this style.

2002 Dürkheimer Rittergarten
Riesling Kabinett trocken
12%, ♀ till 2006   82

2001 Dürkheimer Rittergarten
Riesling Kabinett trocken
11.5%, ♀ till 2006   84

2003 Wachenheimer Mandelgarten
Chardonnay Kabinett trocken
13%, ♀ till 2006   84

2003 Dürkheimer Spielberg
Chardonnay Spätlese trocken
13.5%, ♀ till 2007   85

2002 Riesling
Kabinett halbtrocken
11%, ♀ till 2006   83

2001 Dürkheimer Rittergarten
Riesling Spätlese halbtrocken
11%, ♀ till 2006   86

2003 Dürkheimer Hochbenn
Riesling Spätlese
11.5%, ♀ till 2006   83

2003 Dürkheimer Hochmess
Muskateller Kabinett
11.5%, ♀ till 2006   83

2003 Dürkheimer Nonnengarten
Gewürztraminer Spätlese
12%, ♀ till 2008   87

———— Red wines ————

2002 Dürkheimer Nonnengarten
St. Laurent trocken
12.5%, ♀ till 2006   84

2002 Wachenheimer Mandelgarten
Lemberger trocken
13%, ♀ till 2007   86

12,5%vol · 0,75 l
Karst
2001
Grauburgunder Spätlese trocken
Wachenheimer Königswingert
Gutsabfüllung
Pfalz
Weingut Ernst Karst+Sohn
In den Almen 15 · D-67098 Bad Dürkheim · Tel. 06322-2862

WEINGUT KASSNER-SIMON

Owner: Willi Heinrich and Rosemarie Simon
Manager: Willi Heinrich-Simon
Winemaker: Thomas Simon
67251 Freinsheim, Wallstraße 15
Tel. (0 63 53) 98 93 20, Fax 98 93 21
e-mail:
weingut-kassner-simon@t-online.de
Internet: www.kassner-simon.de
Directions: A 6, Grünstadt exit; A 650, Maxdorf exit; B 271, Bad Dürkheim-Bruch exit
Sales: Rosemarie Simon
Opening hours: Mon.–Sat. 13:00 to 19:00 hours, Sun. and public holidays 10:00 to 13:00 hours or by appointment

---

Vineyard area: 14 hectares
Annual production: 120,000 bottles
Top sites: Freinsheimer
Oschelskopf and Schwarzes Kreuz
Soil types: Clay with sand, sand
Grape varieties: 28% Riesling,
16% Portugieser, 8% each of Spätburgunder and Grauburgunder, 5% each of Dornfelder, Kerner, Rieslaner and Scheurebe, 20% other varieties
Average yield: 75 hl/ha
Best vintages: 2000, 2001, 2003

This winery was founded in 1949, and Thomas Simon already represents the young generation. "We are passionate about making wine," so says the family of itself, and has built itself a good reputation in the picturesque medieval town of Freinsheim. There is a whole bouquet of wine varieties available, with most wines being fermented dry. In 2001 we particularly noted the marked improvement in the quality of the reds. We were not quite as happy with the 2002 vintage, while the difficult 2003 vintage again brought about a very serious range, in which practically no wine was disappointing, although there were no outstanding highlights either. It is characteristic of the profile of this winery that the two wines we liked best are dry Spätlese wines.

2003 Freinsheimer Musikantenbuckel
Grauer Burgunder Spätlese trocken
14.5%, ♀ till 2006 — **83**

2003 Freinsheimer Schwarzes Kreuz
Riesling Spätlese trocken
13%, ♀ till 2007 — **85**

2001 Freinsheimer Oschelskopf
Riesling Spätlese trocken
12.5%, ♀ till 2006 — **86**

2003 Freinsheimer Musikantenbuckel
Weißer Burgunder Spätlese trocken
14%, ♀ till 2007 — **86**

2003 Freinsheimer Musikantenbuckel
Gewürztraminer Spätlese
11.5%, ♀ till 2007 — **82**

2002 Gewürztraminer Eiswein
9.5%, ♀ till 2015 — **90**

2002 Riesling Eiswein
10%, ♀ till 2015 — **91**

——————— Red wines ———————

2003 Freinsheimer Schwarzes Kreuz
Spätburgunder trocken
13%, ♀ till 2006 — **82**

2002 Freinsheimer Schwarzes Kreuz
Spätburgunder Spätlese trocken
13%, ♀ till 2008 — **84**

2001 Kirchheimer Steinacker
Portugieser trocken "Oporto"
13%, ♀ till 2008 — **86**

The wines: **100** Perfect · **95–99** Outstanding · **90–94** Excellent · **85–89** Very good · **80–84** Good · **75–79** Average

481

WEINGUT
KARL HEINZ KAUB

Owner: Karl Heinz Kaub
Manager and winemaker:
Karl Heinz Kaub
67433 Neustadt-Haardt,
Mandelring 55a
Tel. (0 63 21) 3 15 55, Fax 48 06 81
e-mail: KHKaubWeingut@t-online.de
Internet: www.weingut-kaub.de
Directions: A 65, Neustadt-Nord exit
Sales: Dorothea Kaub
Opening hours: Weekdays by appointment, Sat. 10:00 to 16:00 hours

---

Vineyard area: 5 hectares
Annual production: 45,000 bottles
Top sites: Haardter Herrenletten,
Herzog and Bürgergarten,
Mußbacher Eselshaut
Soil types: Sand, clay, decomposed
sandstone
Grape varieties: 44% Riesling,
28% Spätburgunder, 6% each of
Weiß- and Grauburgunder,
16% other varieties
Average yield: 65 hl/ha
Best vintages: 2000, 2001

One of the ancestors of this family was master chief at the royal court in Prague around 1600. Soon thereafter, the family moved to Haardt. Karl Heinz Kaub has planted almost exclusively Riesling and Pinot varieties on his five hectares of vineyard, on which he uses no insecticides or pesticides. The wines are matured in stainless steel tanks, barriques and large oak vats. This small operation presented a good range from the 2000 vintage. The 2001 range shone with a number of wines that had a distinct personality, and stood out clearly from the already good average standard. Both 2002 and 2003 were not quite as convincing, although Kaub continues to show a very good feeling for Riesling. The smoky, warm Spätburgunder (Pinot Noir) Spätlese is also remarkably good.

2003 Haardter Herzog
Riesling Kabinett trocken
12%, ♀ till 2006 — **84**

2003 Haardter Herrenletten
Riesling Spätlese trocken
13%, ♀ till 2007 — **85**

2002 Haardter Herzog
Weißer Burgunder Spätlese trocken
13%, ♀ till 2006 — **86**

2002 Haardter Herzog
Grauer Burgunder Spätlese trocken
13%, ♀ till 2006 — **87**

2003 Haardter Herzog
Grauer Burgunder Spätlese trocken
14%, ♀ till 2006 — **87**

2002 Haardter Herrenletten
Riesling Spätlese trocken
12%, ♀ till 2006 — **88**

2001 Haardter Herrenletten
Riesling Eiswein
9%, ♀ till 2012 — **90**

——————— Red wines ———————

2002 Haardter Mandelring
Blaufränkisch trocken
13.5%, ♀ till 2007 — **83**

2000 Haardter Mandelring
Sankt Laurent trocken
12.5%, ♀ till 2006 — **85**

2002 Haardter Bürgergarten
Spätburgunder Spätlese trocken
13%, ♀ till 2009 — **87**

WEINGUT GERHARD KLEIN

Owner: Sieglinde and Gerhard Klein
Winemaker: Thomas Fischer
76835 Hainfeld, Weinstraße 38
Tel. (0 63 23) 27 13, Fax 8 13 43
e-mail: klein-wein@t-online.de
Internet: weingut-gerhard-klein.de
Directions: A 65, Landau-Nord or Eden-
koben exit, in direction of Edesheim,
then toward Hainfeld
Sales: Klein family
Opening hours: Mon.–Fri. 08:00 to
18:00 hours, Sat. 09:00 to 16:00 hours
Restaurant: Four weeks in Sept./Oct.
always on Fri., Sat. and Sun.

Vineyard area: 16 hectares
Annual production: 150,000 bottles
Top sites: Hainfelder Letten
and Kapelle, Burrweiler Altenforst
Soil types: Heavy clay, loess
18% Spätburgunder, 12% Weißburgunder, 10% each of Grauburgunder and Müller-Thurgau, 8% Gewürztraminer, 7% Frühburgunder,
13% other varieties
Average yield: 84 hl/ha
Best vintages: 1998, 2001, 2002
Member: Pfälzer Barrique Forum

Gerhard Klein frequently delivers proof that many of the less well-known wineries of the southern Pfalz, not the least those from Hainfeld, deserve more attention. Winemaker Thomas Fischer makes wine in a classical Pfalz style, which is almost reminiscent of the Alsace. The winery makes no use of predicate designation, simply labeling its wines with an "S" or a "B." Following on from a slightly weaker 2000 vintage, 2001 was improved, showing the effect of reduced yields and a new press. This positive trend was continued in 2002. The 2003 vintage presents with many wines of a good average standard, an elegant 2002 Dornfelder and a remarkable Grauburgunder (Pinot Gris) from 2003.

2003 Burrweiler Altenforst
Riesling trocken "S"
13.5%, ♀ till 2007 — 85

2003 Hainfelder Letten
Weißer Burgunder trocken "S"
14.5%, ♀ till 2006 — 85

2003 Hainfelder Kirchenstück
Grauer Burgunder trocken "S"
14.5%, ♀ till 2006 — 88

2003 Hainfelder Kapelle
Riesling Spätlese
11%, ♀ till 2008 — 85

2002 Hainfelder Kapelle
Riesling Beerenauslese
9%, ♀ till 2012 — 89

2003 Hainfelder Kapelle
Riesling Trockenbeerenauslese
10%, ♀ till 2020 — 89

——— Red wines ———

2002 Spätburgunder trocken "S"
14%, ♀ till 2008 — 86

2001 St. Laurent trocken "B"
14%, ♀ till 2007 — 87

2002 Dornfelder trocken Barrique
13.5%, ♀ till 2008 — 87

2001 Frühburgunder trocken "S"
14%, ♀ till 2007 — 87

The wines: **100** Perfect · **95–99** Outstanding · **90–94** Excellent · **85–89** Very good · **80–84** Good · **75–79** Average

483

WEINGUT ÖKONOMIERAT JOHANNES KLEINMANN

Owner: Mathias Kleinmann
Winemaker: Mathias Kleinmann
76831 Birkweiler, Hauptstraße 17
Tel. (0 63 45) 35 47, Fax 77 77
e-mail: info@weingut-kleinmann.de
*Directions: From the A 65 via the B 10,
close to Landau-Nord*
Sales: Hannelore, Edith and
Mathias Kleinmann
Opening hours: Mon.–Fri. 09:00 to
12:00 and 14:00 to 18:00 hours,
Sat. 10:00 to 16:00 hours
History: The Kleinmann family came to
Birkweiler as coopers in 1733

Vineyard area: 11.5 hectares
Annual production: 100,000 bottles
Top sites: Birkweiler Kastanien-
busch, Mandelberg and Rosenberg
Soil types: Sandstone, decomposed
porphyry, chalky marl, red marl
Grape varieties: 20% each of Riesling,
Weißburgunder, Grauburgunder and
St. Laurent, 10% Spätburgunder,
10% other varieties
Average yield: 68 hl/ha
Best vintages: 2001, 2002, 2003

The grandfather of Karl-Heinz Kleinmann, state economic adviser Johannes
Kleinmann, already started selling his
own wine in bottles at the turn of the 20th
century. This grandson handed over the
reins at the winery to his son in 2002.
Apart from his own grapes, Kleinmann
also process the grapes produced by ten
part-time growers. Kleinmann's Pinot
Gris was already one of the best in the
Pfalz as in the early Nineties. Since then,
he has improved his standard significantly in virtually all departments. As has
been the case almost every year in recent
times, Kleinmann again presented a range
with a number of real highlights, wines
from the white Pinot varietals as well as
a brilliant Gewürztraminer. Of the red
wines, the top-quality Spätburgunder
(Pinot Noir) is particularly good.

2003 Birkweiler Mandelberg
Weißer Burgunder Kabinett trocken
13%, ♀ till 2006   **85**

2003 Birkweiler Rosenberg
Grauer Burgunder Kabinett trocken
13.5%, ♀ till 2006   **85**

2003 Birkweiler Rosenberg
Grauer Burgunder Spätlese trocken
14%, ♀ till 2006   **87**

2003 Birkweiler Rosenberg
Weißer Burgunder Spätlese trocken
15%, ♀ till 2006   **88**

2002 Birkweiler Kastanienbusch
Riesling Auslese trocken
13.5%, ♀ till 2007   **89**

2002 Birkweiler Mandelberg
Weißer Burgunder Spätlese trocken
14%, ♀ till 2007   **90**

2003 Birkweiler Mandelberg
Weißer Burgunder Spätlese trocken
"Signatur"
14%, ♀ till 2006   **90**

2003 Birkweiler Mandelberg
Gewürztraminer Spätlese
13%, ♀ till 2007   **88**

2002 Birkweiler Mandelberg
Gewürztraminer Auslese
14%, ♀ till 2007   **89**

——— Red wines ———

2002 Birkweiler Kastanienbusch
Spätburgunder Auslese trocken
"Signatur"
14.5%, ♀ till 2012   **88**

2001 Birkweiler Kastanienbusch
Spätburgunder Auslese trocken
13.5%, ♀ till 2008   **90**

WEINGUT KNIPSER

Owner and manager: Werner and Volker Knipser
Administrator: Stephan Knipser
Winemaker: Werner and Stephan Knipser
67229 Laumersheim, Hauptstr. 47–49
Tel. (0 62 38) 7 42 and 24 12, Fax 43 77
e-mail: mail@weingut-knipser.de
Internet: www.weingut-knipser.de
Directions: A 6 Mannheim–Saarbrücken, Grünstadt exit
Opening hours: Mon.–Fri. 08:00 to 12:00 hours and 14:00 to 18:00 hours
Sat. 10:00 to 16:00 hours
by appointment

Vineyard area: 27 hectares
Annual production: 200,000 bottles
Top sites: Laumersheimer Mandelberg and Kirschgarten, Großkarlbacher Burgweg, Dirmsteiner Mandelpfad
Soil types: Limestone and calcareous marl, partly with clay and loess top layer
Grape varieties: 22% Spätburgunder, 20% Riesling, 9% Chardonnay, 7% Sankt Laurent, 6% Dornfelder, 5% Cabernet Sauvignon, 4% Weißburgunder, 3% Grauburgunder, 24% other varieties
Average yield: 65 hl/ha
Best vintages: 1999, 2001, 2003
Member: VDP, Deutsches Barrique Forum

The origins of the Knipser family lie in South Tyrol, or Alto Adige as it is now known. A certain Gaudenz Knipser – a red wine is named after him today – was the city's master builder and member of the executive committee in Merano in 1573. It is also around this time that the family was awarded its coat-of-arms by archduke Ferdinand in Innsbruck in 1582, which the family still uses today. A grandson of the Gaudenz Knipser, Johann Georg Knipser, emigrated to the Pfalz in 1615. The family has been based in Laumersheim since 1876. Bottling and selling the own wines to consumers and restaurants were introduced in 1948, one of the first wine estates in the region to do so. The foundation for this now leading winery was laid by father Heinz in the Sixties. However, the rise in fortunes only began with his son Werner, a trained chemist, who took over responsibility in 1981, and today runs the business together with his brother Volker. Since then, the operation has grown steadily, and has achieved top marks in many fields, not just with its red wines. It is a sign of maturation that the brothers are now looking to reduce the range of wines made in future: Now that many different things have been proven, both to oneself and to others, one can now concentrate on the essentials. This new development will certainly be helped along by the brand-new, state-of-the-art cellar that has just been commissioned. Werner and Volker Knipser are pioneers of wine maturation in small oak barrels. In addition, they have proven that the grapes for top wines cannot only be grown on the slopes at the borders of the forest. Initially, they built quite a reputation for white wines matured in barriques, but now the focus is on red wines. The First Growths show that even the dry Rieslings here can be of outstanding quality. The wines made from white Pinot varieties are also all consistently good. The dry rosé proves that even in this category, which is often disregarded, wines full of character can be produced. In the 2003 vintage, the "Große Gewächse" again are of a standard that need not hide behind those from the famous sites of Forst and Deidesheim. The 2001 red wines currently available, particularly the Pinot Noirs, are among the best in Germany. The 2002 reds had not yet been bottled at the time of going to press, and were thus unable to participate in the final round of establishing the best wines of the vintage for the whole of Germany. However, we are convinced they would have scored well there, and look forward with great interest to tasting these wines next year.

The wines: **100** Perfect · **95–99** Outstanding · **90–94** Excellent · **85–89** Very good · **80–84** Good · **75–79** Average

2002 Chardonnay & Weißburgunder
Spätlese trocken
12.5%, ♀ till 2006   **87**

2003 Silvaner Auslese trocken
14%, ♀ till 2007   **88**

**2002 Großkarlbacher Burgweg
"Im großen Garten"**
Riesling trocken "Großes Gewächs"
13%, ♀ till 2007   **88**

**2003 Großkarlbacher Burgweg
"Im großen Garten"**
Riesling Spätlese trocken
"Großes Gewächs"
13.5%, ♀ till 2008   **88**

2001 Großkarlbacher Burgweg
Riesling Spätlese trocken
13%, ♀ till 2006   **89**

2002 Laumersheimer Mandelberg
Grauer Burgunder Spätlese trocken
13%, ♀ till 2006   **89**

2002 Dirmsteiner Mandelpfad
Riesling trocken "Großes Gewächs"
12.5%, ♀ till 2008   **89**

2001 Dirmsteiner Mandelpfad
Riesling Spätlese trocken
"Großes Gewächs"
13%, ♀ till 2006   **90**

**2002 Laumersheimer Mandelberg
"Steinbuckel"**
Riesling trocken "Großes Gewächs"
12.5%, ♀ till 2008   **90**

**2003 Dirmsteiner Mandelpfad
"Himmelsrech"**
Riesling Spätlese trocken
"Großes Gewächs"
13.5%, ♀ till 2008   **90**

**2003 Laumersheimer Mandelberg
"Steinbuckel"**
Riesling Spätlese trocken
"Großes Gewächs"
13.5%, ♀ till 2008   **90**

2003 Laumersheimer Kapellenberg
Riesling Spätlese
12.5%, ♀ till 2010   **85**

2003 Großkarlbacher Burgweg
Gelber Orléans Auslese
12.5%, ♀ till 2010   **85**

2003 Laumersheimer Kapellenberg
Riesling Auslese Goldkapsel
9%, ♀ till 2010   **87**

2003 Gewürztraminer & Riesling
Auslese
12.5%, ♀ till 2010   **88**

2003 Sauvignon Blanc
Trockenbeerenauslese
9%, ♀ till 2020   **89**

2003 Laumersheimer Kapellenberg
Riesling Trockenbeerenauslese
7%, ♀ till 2025   **91**

———— Red wines ————

2002 "Cuvée Rosé" trocken
12%, ♀ till 2006   **86**

2003 Cuvée rosé Spätlese trocken
13.5%, ♀ till 2007   **88**

2001 "Cuvée Gaudenz" trocken
13.5%, ♀ till 2007   **86**

2001 Spätburgunder trocken
13.5%, ♀ till 2008   **87**

2000 Großkarlbacher Burgweg
Spätburgunder trocken ***
13.5%, ♀ till 2008   **90**

2001 Großkarlbacher Burgweg
Spätburgunder Spätlese trocken
13%, ♀ till 2010   **90**

2001 "Cuvée X" trocken
13.5%, ♀ till 2008   **90**

2000 Großkarlbacher Burgweg
St. Laurent trocken Barrique
14%, ♀ till 2008   **91**

2001 Im großen Garten
Spätburgunder Spätlese trocken
"Großes Gewächs"
13.5%, ♀ till 2010   **92**

KNIPSER
2001
Im Großen Garten
Spätburgunder

The estates: ♛♛♛♛♛ World's finest · ♛♛♛♛ Germany's best · ♛♛♛ Very good · ♛♛ Good · ♛ Reliable

WEINGUT
BERNHARD KOCH

Owner and manager: Bernhard Koch
Winemaker: Bernhard Schwaab
76835 Hainfeld, Weinstraße 1
Tel. (0 63 23) 27 28, Fax 75 77
e-mail:
koch.bernhard-weingut@t-online.de
Directions: A 65, Edenkoben exit, on
B 38 in direction of Landau, in Edes-
heim turn right toward Hainfeld
Sales: Christine Koch and Klaus Gamber
Opening hours: Mon.–Sat. 09:00 to
12:00 hours and 13:30 to 18:00 hours
Sun. in pavilon 13:00 to 19:00 hours
Restaurant: In wine pavilion with light
dishes, Wed., Sat. and Sun. from 15:00
to 19:00 hours
Worth seeing: Cellar with 140 barriques

Vineyard area: 40 hectares
Annual production: 360,000 bottles
Top sites: Hainfelder Letten and
Kapelle, Burrweiler Altenforst
Soil types: Clay, calcareous marl,
sand and slate
Grape varieties: 25% Riesling,
15% each of Dornfelder and Spätbur-
gunder, 8% each of Weiß- and Grau-
burgunder, 29% other varieties
Average yield: 90 hl/ha
Best vintages: 2000, 2001, 2002

Bernhard Koch took over the small operation – 6.5 hectares of vineyard and a
small cellar – from his father in 1987.
Since then, he has given up the cellar, and
expanded the vineyards to 40 hectares. A
new cellar complex with lots of stainless
steel was essential to be able to process
a range of around 70 wines annually, of
which 14 were presented for tasting.
These wines are quite good in 2003, apart
from being very well priced, although
some show an unnaturally strong acidity.
Koch focuses on the strengths of large
operations, to be able to produce good
basic wines inexpensively. We liked the
Riesling in liter bottles, of which there are
almost 30,000 bottles available.

2003 Hainfelder Kapelle
Riesling Spätlese trocken
12.5%, ♀ till 2006   82

2003 Hainfelder Letten
Riesling Spätlese trocken
13.5%, ♀ till 2006   83

2003 Flemlinger Bischofskreuz
Weißer Burgunder Kabinett trocken
14.5%, ♀ till 2006   83

2002 Hainfelder Letten
Chardonnay Kabinett trocken
11.5%, ♀ till 2006   84

2003 Burrweiler Altenforst
Riesling Spätlese trocken Goldkapsel
14%, ♀ till 2006   84

2003 Flemlinger Bischofskreuz
Weißer Burgunder Spätlese trocken
14%, ♀ till 2006   85

2001 Hainfelder Letten
Chardonnay trocken Barrique
13.5%, ♀ till 2007   87

2001 Hainfelder Letten
Grauer Burgunder Spätlese trocken
13.5%, ♀ till 2006   88

2003 Riesling Classic
12%, ♀ till 2006   82

2003 Grauer Burgunder Classic
14%, ♀ till 2006   82

———— Red wines ————

2002 Merlot & Cabernet trocken
12%, ♀ till 2006   83

2001 Cabernet Sauvignon trocken
13.5%, ♀ till 2007   83

2002 Cabernet Sauvignon trocken
13%, ♀ till 2008   83

2001 Hainfelder Kapelle
Dornfelder trocken
13.5%, ♀ till 2006   84

2003
Hainfelder Kapelle
RIESLING
Kabinett trocken

Koch

The wines: **100** Perfect · **95–99** Outstanding · **90–94** Excellent · **85–89** Very good · **80–84** Good · **75–79** Average

487

WEINGUT KOEHLER-RUPRECHT

Owner and manager: Bernd Philippi
Administrator: Ulrich Meyer
Winemaker: Axel Heinzmann
67169 Kallstadt, Weinstraße 84
Tel. (0 63 22) 18 29, Fax 86 40
Directions: A 61–A 6, in direction of Kaiserslautern, Grünstadt exit
Sales: Bernd Philippi
Opening hours: Mon.–Fri. 09:00 to 11:30 hours and 13:00 to 17:00 hours or by appointment
Restaurant: Restaurant "Weincastell zum Weißen Roß," closed Mon. and Tue.
Specialties: High-class regional cuisine
History: Family-owned since 1680
Worth seeing: Historical winery complex with vaulted cellar dating to 1556

Vineyard area: 12.5 hectares
Annual production: 100,000 bottles
Top sites: Kallstadter Saumagen, Steinacker and Kronenberg
Soil types: Limestone detritus, sandy clay, partly with gravel
Grape varieties: 54% Riesling, 20% Spätburgunder, 8% Weißburgunder, 3% each of Chardonnay and Grauburgunder, 2% each of Dornfelder and Cabernet Sauvignon, 8% other varieties
Average yield: 68 hl/ha
Best vintages: 1997, 1998, 2002
Member: VDP, Deutsches Barrique Forum

Koehler-Ruprecht is surely one of the best-known, but also one of the most difficult wine producers in the Pfalz region. The wines are made in thoroughly traditional, but very individual style, which is concomitant with high risk, resulting to swings in quality, and sometimes it is difficult to assess the wines. When the top Rieslings from this producer go right, they are magnificent masterpieces. However, there are also fairly regularly unsuccessful attempts, which lead not only us to reconsider the rating for this estate. Bernd Philippi makes his best

wines from the grapes of the Kallstadter Saumagen. The Romans had a limestone quarry here, resulting in a south-facing bowl-shaped site, which opens up in an easterly direction towards the town. In this exceptional microclimate, both the Riesling and the Pinot varieties are able to reach full ripeness. In some vintages, the dry wines present with an almost baroque full-bodied style. As Philippi clarifies the musts stringently, and prefers small barrels for his Spätlese and Auslese wines, the wines often continue fermenting well into the summer following the harvest. The result are amazingly long-lived wines with body and power, but which can be rather eccentric in their youth. They need time to develop fully, such as the legendary 1990 Riesling Auslese trocken or the magnificent 1998 Auslese "R," which has only now been released for sale, and is perhaps the best dry Riesling made in Germany in the past 15 years. Just at the point when the swansong of most wines has faded away, Philippis masterpieces are just starting to shine. All the wines labeled with an "R" are only released for sale at a later stage. They are usually matured in barrique, and carry a "Philippi" label. The 1999 range appears rather heterogeneous, although there was some real class in the Rieslings from the Saumagen site. The 2000 Rieslings were heterogeneous as rarely before. In 2001 and 2002 there were again ups and downs, confirming our opinion that this is a winery with individual fantastic classics, and a lot of average wines. At the time of going to press, virtually none of the 2003 wines had been bottled. However, the 2002 dry Rieslings, which are now available, show remarkable class.

2003 Kallstadter
Riesling Kabinett trocken
12%, ♀ till 2007 — **84**

2002 "Philippi"
Weißer Burgunder trocken
13.5%, ♀ till 2007 — **85**

2000 Grauer Burgunder
Tafelwein trocken
13%, ♀ till 2006 — **86**

2001 Muskateller
Kabinett trocken
12%, ♀ till 2006   **86**

2002 Kallstadter Steinacker
Weißer Burgunder Spätlese trocken
13%, ♀ till 2006   **86**

2002 Kallstadter Saumagen
Riesling Kabinett trocken
12%, ♀ till 2007   **86**

2002 "Philippi"
Grauer Burgunder trocken
13.5%, ♀ till 2007   **86**

2002 "Philippi"
Chardonnay trocken
13.5%, ♀ till 2007   **86**

2000 Chardonnay
Tafelwein trocken
13%, ♀ till 2006   **87**

2002 Kallstadter Saumagen
Muskateller Kabinett trocken
11.5%, ♀ till 2006   **87**

2001 Kallstadter Saumagen
Riesling Spätlese trocken
13%, ♀ till 2006   **88**

2002 Kallstadter Saumagen
Riesling Spätlese trocken
12.5%, ♀ till 2008   **88**

2001 Kallstadter Saumagen
Riesling Auslese trocken
13.5%, ♀ till 2008   **90**

2002 Kallstadter Saumagen
Riesling Auslese trocken
13%, ♀ till 2010   **91**

2001 Kallstadter Saumagen
Riesling Spätlese trocken "R"
13%, ♀ till 2010   **91**

2001 Kallstadter Saumagen
Riesling Auslese trocken "R"
13.5%, ♀ till 2012   **92**

1998 Kallstadter Saumagen
Riesling Auslese trocken "R"
14%, ♀ till 2008   **95**

2002 Kallstadter Saumagen
Riesling Spätlese halbtrocken
11.5%, ♀ till 2006   **87**

2002 Kallstadter Steinacker
Gewürztraminer Spätlese
12.5%, ♀ till 2007   **85**

2001 "Philippi"
Chardonnay Tafelwein
13%, ♀ till 2006   **86**

2001 Kallstadter Saumagen
Riesling Auslese
10.5%, ♀ till 2008   **87**

2001 "Philippi"
Pinot Blanc Tafelwein
13%, ♀ till 2007   **87**

2002 Kallstadter Saumagen
Riesling Spätlese
11%, ♀ till 2008   **88**

2003 Kallstadter Saumagen
Riesling Auslese
10.5%, ♀ till 2012   **89**

2001 "Philippi"
Chardonnay Tafelwein "R"
13.5%, ♀ till 2007   **89**

2002 Kallstadter Saumagen
Riesling Auslese "R"
10%, ♀ till 2010   **91**

——— Red wines ———

2001 "Philippi"
Pinot Noir Tafelwein
13%, ♀ till 2008   **86**

2001 "Philippi"
Pinot Noir Tafelwein "R"
13%, ♀ till 2009   **92**

Koehler-Ruprecht

2002 KALLSTADTER SAUMAGEN
Riesling Spätlese
Erzeugerabfüllung Weingut Koehler-Ruprecht Bernd Philippi D-67169 Kallstadt
Qualitätswein mit Prädikat   A.P.Nr. 5123147060B   Produce of Germany
alc. 11,0 % by vol.   **PFALZ**   750 ml

The wines: **100** Perfect · **95–99** Outstanding · **90–94** Excellent · **85–89** Very good · **80–84** Good · **75–79** Average

WEINGUT FAMILIE KRANZ

Owner: Kranz family
Manager and winemaker: Boris Kranz
76831 Ilbesheim, Mörzheimer Str. 2
Tel. (0 63 41) 93 92 06, Fax 93 92 07
e-mail: weingut-kranz@t-online.de
Internet: www.weingut-kranz.de
Directions: A 65, Landau-Mitte exit, in
direction of Klingenmünster, winery out-
side town, opposite entrance to town, in
direction of Mörzheim
Sales: Lilo and Kerstin Kranz
Opening hours: Mon.–Thur. 08:00 to
12:00 hours, in the afternoons by appointment, Fri. 08:00 to 16:30 hours
Sat. 09:00 to 17:00 hours
Worth seeing: Terraced vineyards
below the "Kleine Kalmit"

Vineyard area: 17 hectares
Annual production: 85,000 bottles
Top sites: Ilbesheimer Kalmit
and Rittersberg
Soil types: Common snail limestone,
marl, loess, sloping clay
Grape varieties: 20% each of Riesling
and Spätburgunder, 15% each of
Weißburgunder, Müller-Thurgau and
Portugieser, 15% other varieties
Average yield: 84 hl/ha
Best vintages: 2001, 2002, 2003

Only last year we praised Boris Kranz for
his clean cellar technique, while at the
same time criticizing that his wines lacked character. It appears he has taken these
comments to heart. The new range he has
presented is impressive, even in the red
wines – no doubt this standard is worthy
of two bunches of grapes. The terroir and
the varietal characteristics are brought
out with equal sensitivity. Interesting
sites rich in limestone on the "Kleine
Kalmit" provide good potential. The
Pinot varieties are planted in the heavier
soils of the Seligmacher site, the Rieslings
at the "Kleine Kalmit." By the way: The
wine and fruit distillates produced by
father Robert Kranz can also be excellent,
particularly the Williams pear.

2002 Arzheimer Seligmacher
Weißer Burgunder & Chardonnay
Spätlese trocken "Fürstenweg"
13%, ♀ till 2006   86

2003 Arzheimer Seligmacher
Weißer Burgunder Kabinett trocken
13.5%, ♀ till 2006   87

2003 Arzheimer Seligmacher
Chardonnay trocken
14%, ♀ till 2008   87

2003 "Fürstenweg"
Weißer Burgunder Spätlese trocken
14.5%, ♀ till 2007   88

2002 Ilbesheimer Rittersberg
Riesling Spätlese trocken "Kalmit"
13%, ♀ till 2006   88

2003 "Kalmit"
Riesling Spätlese trocken
14%, ♀ till 2010   91

2003 "Hagedorn"
Silvaner Spätlese
14%, ♀ till 2006   87

——————— Red wines ———————

2003 Arzheimer Seligmacher
Spätburgunder Weißherbst Kabinett
trocken
13.5%, ♀ till 2006   86

2002 Ilbesheimer Rittersberg
Spätburgunder trocken
13.5%, ♀ till 2009   86

2002 "Kirchberg"
Spätburgunder Spätlese trocken
13.5%, ♀ till 2012   87

WEINGUT PHILIPP KUHN

Owner and winemaker: Philipp Kuhn
67229 Laumersheim,
Großkarlbacher Straße 20
Tel. (0 62 38) 6 56, Fax 46 02
e-mail: weingut-philipp-kuhn@gmx.de
Internet: www.weingut-philipp-kuhn.de
Directions: A 6 Mannheim–Saar-
brücken, Grünstadt exit
Sales: Kuhn family
Opening hours: Mon.–Fri. 09:00 to
12:00 hours and 13:00 to 18:00 hours
Sat. 10:00 to 12:00 hours
and 13:00 to 17:00 hours
and by appointment

Vineyard area: 13.5 hectares
Annual production: 95,000 bottles
Top sites: Laumersheimer
Kirschgarten and Mandelberg,
Großkarlbacher Burgweg,
Dirmsteiner Mandelpfad
Soil types: Sandy clay, partly with
gravel, on limestone underground
Grape varieties: 25% Riesling,
25% Spätburgunder and Cabernet
Sauvignon, 25% white Pinot varieties
and Chardonnay, 25% Dornfelder
and other red varieties
Average yield: 65 hl/ha
Best vintages: 2000, 2002, 2003

Actually, Philipp Kuhn wanted to study winemaking, but circumstances forced him to go into his parents' business straight after finishing high school, and he took over here in 1994. The estate built a reputation based on its fruit-dominated red wines. In the meantime, however, we consider the clean, often elegantly mineral whites to be even better. Kuhn showed a good performance in this department in the 2000 vintage. In 2002 and 2003 the standard was more than just good. The wines combine clarity and ripeness with, in some cases, mineral elements. Kuhn only presents his reds after two years, and the 2001 vintage presented now shows great variability among the wines.

2003 Großkarlbacher Burgweg
Riesling trocken
13.5%, ♀ till 2007   **84**

2003 Weißer Burgunder trocken
12.5%, ♀ till 2006   **84**

2003 Laumersheimer Kirschgarten
Weißer Burgunder trocken
14%, ♀ till 2006   **86**

2003 Laumersheimer Mandelberg
Grauer Burgunder trocken
14%, ♀ till 2006   **86**

2003 Laumersheimer Kirschgarten
Riesling trocken
13.5%, ♀ till 2006   **87**

2003 Dirmsteiner Mandelpfad
Chardonnay trocken
13.5%, ♀ till 2007   **87**

2002 Laumersheimer Kirschgarten
Riesling trocken
13%, ♀ till 2006   **88**

2002 Dirmsteiner Mandelpfad
Chardonnay trocken
13.5%, ♀ till 2006   **88**

——————— Red wines ———————

2001 "Luitmar" trocken
13.5%, ♀ till 2008   **85**

2000 Laumersheimer Mandelberg
Cabernet Sauvignon trocken Barrique
13.5%, ♀ till 2008   **86**

2001 Laumersheimer Kirschgarten
St. Laurent trocken
13.5%, ♀ till 2005   **87**

2001 Laumersheimer Kirschgarten
Spätburgunder trocken
13.5%, ♀ till 2008   **87**

The wines: **100** Perfect · **95–99** Outstanding · **90–94** Excellent · **85–89** Very good · **80–84** Good · **75–79** Average

491

WEINGUT JÜRGEN LEINER

Owner: Jürgen and Sven Leiner
Winemaker: Sven Leiner
76831 Ilbesheim, Arzheimer Straße 14
Tel. (0 63 41) 3 06 21, Fax 3 44 01
e-mail: weingut-leiner@t-online.de
Internet: www.weingut-leiner.de
*Directions: A 65, Landau-Süd exit, in
direction of Klingenmünster, 6 km past
Landau turn right toward Ilbesheim,
there it is directly next to the church*
Sales: Mon.–Sat. by appointment
Worth seeing: Historical barrel cellar

Vineyard area: 10 hectares
Annual production: 75,000 bottles
Top sites: Does not specify sites
Soil types: Loess and clay, decomposed colored sandstone,
kaolin with limestone
Grape varieties: 13% each of Grauburgunder and Dornfelder, 10% each
of Riesling, Müller-Thurgau, Spätburgunder and Portugieser,
6% each of Weißburgunder and
Silvaner, 22% other varieties
Average yield: 80 hl/ha
Best vintages: 2001, 2003

Ilbesheim is a picturesque wine-producing village with many romantic wine bars and restaurants. In recent years, the younger generation of winemakers here has ensured that significantly better wines are being produced. Young Sven Leiner could look to Hans-Günther Schwarz and Hansjörg Rebholz as his teachers, and obviously kept his eyes and ears open to learn as much as possible. Ever since he has taken over responsibility in his parents' winery, he has done quite well at putting this knowledge into practice, and is even experimenting with the Spanish grape variety Tempranillo. However, his strengths lie clearly with the white wines. In the 2003 vintage, he has once again presented individualistic Riesling wines with yeasty notes, as well as an extremely well-made Chardonnay.

2003 Riesling Kabinett trocken
11.5%, ♀ till 2006 — 81

2003 Riesling trocken
13%, ♀ till 2006 — 82

2003 Weißer Burgunder trocken
13%, ♀ till 2006 — 83

2001 Grauer Burgunder
Spätlese trocken
13%, ♀ till 2006 — 85

2003 Chardonnay trocken
13%, ♀ till 2006 — 85

2002 Weißer Burgunder
Spätlese trocken "Calvus Mons"
13%, ♀ till 2007 — 85

2001 Riesling Spätlese trocken
13%, ♀ till 2006 — 87

2002 Chardonnay trocken Barrique
13%, ♀ till 2008 — 87

2002 Riesling Spätlese
10%, ♀ till 2008 — 84

2002 Gewürztraminer Spätlese
12.5%, ♀ till 2006 — 87

2001 Gewürztraminer Auslese
14%, ♀ till 2006 — 90

––––––– Red wines –––––––

2002 Spätburgunder
trocken "Reserve"
13%, ♀ till 2007 — 81

2000 Spätburgunder trocken
13%, ♀ till 2007 — 83

2001 Dunkelfelder trocken
13%, ♀ till 2007 — 84

2002 "Curiosum" trocken
13%, ♀ till 2008 — 84

Weingut Jürgen Leiner

2001
Spätburgunder trocken
Gutsabfüllung
Pfalz

750ml — Qualitätswein b.A · A.P.Nr. 5042 149 1602
D-76831 Ilbesheim · Tel. 06341/30621 — 12.5% vol.

WEINGUT LEININGERHOF

Owner: Volker Benzinger
Winemaker: Volker Benzinger
67281 Kirchheim, Weinstraße Nord 24
Tel. (0 63 59) 13 39, Fax 23 27
e-mail: info@weingut-leiningerhof.de
Internet: www.leiningerhof.com
Directions: A 6, Grünstadt exit, in direc-
tion of Bad Dürkheim onto the B 271
Sales: Benzinger family
Opening hours: Mon.–Fri. 08:00 to
12:00 hours and 13:00 to 17:00 hours
and by appointment
Worth seeing: 400-year-old baroque win-
ery complex, double-storey vaulted cellar

Vineyard area: 13 hectares
Annual production: 100,000 bottles
Top sites: Bockenheimer
Schlossberg, Kirchheimer Geißkopf
Soil types: Loess-clay, decomposed
limestone soils
Grape varieties: 16% each of Riesling
and Grauer Burgunder, 13% Portugie-
ser, 8% each of Weißer Burgunder,
Dornfelder and Spätburgunder,
31% other varieties
Average yield: 80 hl/ha
Best vintages: 1999, 2000, 2002

The impressive 400-year-old baroque
residential house in the center of the village of Kirchheim serves as a reminder
of the feudal past of the Leiningerhof estate. In the cellar, modern techniques have
arrived, there is temperature control
during fermentation, and extended maturation on the lees. The 2000 vintage range
was surprisingly good, clean and clear.
Looking at the whites of the 2001 vintage, it would have been preferable to be
less safety-conscious, and to have allowed a bit more power to come through.
A little more courage was evident in the
2002 wines, and the entire range was good.
However, the 2003 whites are brittle and
tired, with no sign of the usual strengths.
Only the Grauburgunder Spätlese and
the 2002 Cabernet & Merlot are of the
usual standard.

2003 Kirchheimer Steinacker
Riesling Spätlese trocken
12.5%, ♀ till 2006   **83**

2002 Kirchheimer Geißkopf
Grauer Burgunder Spätlese trocken
13%, ♀ till 2006   **85**

2003 Kirchheimer Geißkopf
Grauer Burgunder Spätlese trocken
13.5%, ♀ till 2006   **86**

2002 Kirchheimer Steinacker
Riesling Spätlese trocken
12.5%, ♀ till 2006   **87**

2002 Kirchheimer Kreuz
Weißer Burgunder Spätlese trocken "SL"
12.5%, ♀ till 2006   **87**

2003 Kirchheimer Steinacker
Riesling Spätlese
10.5%, ♀ till 2007   **84**

———— Red wines ————

2003 Dornfelder trocken
13%, ♀ till 2007   **83**

2002 Kirchheimer Kreuz
Cabernet & Merlot trocken
14%, ♀ till 2008   **85**

2001 Kirchheimer Steinacker
Dornfelder trocken
13.5%, ♀ till 2007   **87**

2001 Kirchheimer Kreuz
Spätburgunder Spätlese trocken
13.5%, ♀ till 2007   **87**

2001 Kirchheimer Steinacker
Dornfelder trocken Barrique
13.5%, ♀ till 2008   **87**

2002 Kirchheimer Kreuz
Cabernet & Merlot trocken Barrique
13%, ♀ till 2008   **87**

2003
RIESLING AUSLESE
– FEINHERB –

The wines: **100** Perfect · **95–99** Outstanding · **90–94** Excellent · **85–89** Very good · **80–84** Good · **75–79** Average

WEINGUT LERGENMÜLLER

Owner: Lergenmüller family
Administrator: Dieter Hemberger
Winemaker: Jürgen Lergenmüller
76835 Hainfeld, Weinstraße 16
Tel. (0 63 41) 9 63 33, Fax 9 63 34
e-mail: info@lergenmueller.de
Internet: www.lergenmueller.de
Directions: A 65, Landau-Nord or Edenkoben exit
Sales: Lergenmüller family
Opening hours: Mon.–Fri. 09:00 to 18:00 hours, Sat. 09:00 to 17:00 hours Sun. 09:00 to 13:00 hours
Restaurant: Landhaus Herrenberg, from 17:00 to 23:00 hours, closed Thur. Tel. (0 63 41) 6 02 05, Fax 6 07 09
Specialties: High-class regional cuisine, culinary wine tastings
Worth seeing: Barrique cellar

Vineyard area: 80 hectares
Annual production: 600,000 bottles
Top sites: Hainfelder Kapelle and Letten, Godramsteiner Münzberg
Soil types: Calcareous marl and loess
Grape varieties: 10% each of Riesling, Müller-Thurgau, Spätburgunder, Weißburgunder and Dornfelder, 7% each of Grauburgunder, Chardonnay, Silvaner, Kerner and Portugieser, 15% other varieties
Average yield: 105 hl/ha
Best vintages: 1998, 2000, 2002

The Lergenmüller brothers, Stefan and Jürgen, have made a name for themselves with their exceptionally concentrated, even opulent red wines. The 2002 wines are deep red in color, and have their own style, the "Selektion LP" is remarkable, and of international class. Some progress has been made with the white wines, but the quality is highly variable, which is probably also related to the large size of the estate. In previous vintages, we liked the Rieslings from Burrweiler sites best, this time round it was the two Pinot wines that left the best impression.

2003 Weißer Burgunder
trocken "S"
13%, ♀ till 2006 **85**

2002 Burrweiler Schäwer
Riesling trocken
13.5%, ♀ till 2006 **87**

2003 Grauer Burgunder
trocken "S"
14%, ♀ till 2006 **87**

2002 Burrweiler St. Annaberg
Riesling trocken "Steinacker"
12.5%, ♀ till 2006 **87**

———— Red wines ————

2000 Merlot trocken
13.5%, ♀ till 2006 **85**

2000 St. Laurent trocken
13%, ♀ till 2006 **86**

2002 Dornfelder trocken
13.5%, ♀ till 2007 **87**

2002 Merlot trocken
13.5%, ♀ till 2008 **87**

2002 Cabernet Sauvignon trocken
13.5%, ♀ till 2008 **87**

2002 "Selektion LP" trocken
13.5%, ♀ till 2010 **90**

Pfalz

WEINGUT LIDY

Owner: Bertram Lidy
Winemaker: Bertram and Marcel Lidy
76833 Frankweiler,
Frankenburgstraße 6
Tel. (0 63 45) 34 72, Fax 52 38
e-mail: weingut-lidy@t-online.de
Internet: www.weingut-lidy.de
Directions: A 65, Edenkoben exit, in direction of Landau, turn onto Weinstraße at Edesheim, 6 km in southerly direction
Sales: Lidy family
Opening hours: Mon.–Fri. 09:00 to 12:00 and 13:00 to 17:00, Sat. 09:00 to 12:00 and 13:00 to 16:00 hours

---

Vineyard area: 18.5 hectares
Annual production: 200,000 bottles
Top site: Frankweiler Kalkgrube
Soil types: Limestone, marl, colored sandstone, red marl
Grape varieties: 32% Riesling, 15% Spätburgunder, 6% Weißburgunder, 5% each of Müller-Thurgau, Silvaner, Grauburgunder, Dornfelder and St. Laurent, 22% other varieties
Average yield: 75 hl/ha
Best vintages: 2002, 2003

A very good performance has earned Bertram Lidy his first bunch of grapes in this year. Some limestone-rich south-facing vineyards with good potential are available, but we believe even more can still be achieved in the vineyard. Lidy has learned well aspects such as brilliant color and lack of flaws, but as is the case with so many young winemakers, when forced to choose between cleanliness and character, he tends to err in favor of technical perfection. A little more body and substance would improve the quality of the white wines, in 2003 it was particularly the Gewürztraminer we liked. More than two thirds of the wines are fermented dry, and more than 90 percent of production is sold direct to consumers, the balance is sold to the restaurant trade. A distillery is attached to the winery.

2003 "Cuvée Nicolai"
Kabinett trocken
12%, ♀ till 2006 — **84**

2003 Frankweiler Kalkgrube
Weißer Burgunder Spätlese trocken
15%, ♀ till 2006 — **84**

2003 Frankweiler Kalkgrube
Riesling Kabinett trocken "SC"
13%, ♀ till 2007 — **86**

2003 Frankweiler Kalkgrube
Riesling Spätlese trocken "SC"
13.5%, ♀ till 2008 — **87**

2002 Frankweiler Kalkgrube
Riesling Spätlese trocken
12.5%, ♀ till 2006 — **88**

2003 Frankweiler Kalkgrube
Gewürztraminer Spätlese trocken
15%, ♀ till 2007 — **88**

2002 Frankweiler Kalkgrube
Gewürztraminer Spätlese
12.5%, ♀ till 2008 — **87**

——— Red wines ———

2003 Frankweiler Königsgarten
St. Laurent trocken
13%, ♀ till 2007 — **84**

2001 Frankweiler Kalkgrube
Spätburgunder trocken Barrique
13%, ♀ till 2007 — **85**

2001 Cabernet Dorsa trocken
13%, ♀ till 2008 — **86**

he wines: **100** Perfect · **95–99** Outstanding · **90–94** Excellent · **85–89** Very good · **80–84** Good · **75–79** Average

495

WEINGUT LUCASHOF – PFARRWEINGUT

Owner and manager: Klaus Lucas
Administrator: Hans Lucas
Winemaker: Klaus Lucas
67147 Forst, Wiesenweg 1a
Tel. (0 63 26) 3 36, Fax 57 94
e-mail: Weingut@Lucashof.de
Internet: www.lucashof.de
*Directions: On the Weinstraße B 271
between Neustadt and Bad Dürkheim*
Sales: Lucas family
Opening hours: Mon.–Fri. 08:00 to
12:00 hours and 13:00 to 19:00 hours
Sat. 08:00 to 16:00 hours
Sun. by appointment
Country hotel: Stylishly decorated, with
seven double rooms

Vineyard area: 16 hectares
Annual production: 130,000 bottles
Top sites: Forster Ungeheuer,
Pechstein, Musenhang and Stift,
Deidesheimer Herrgottsacker
Soil types: Loess-clay and sand,
basalt, decomposed sandstone
Grape varieties: 90% Riesling,
10% other varieties
Average yield: 75 hl/ha
Best vintages: 1996, 1998, 2001

The Lucashof estate, which also works
the vineyards of the Forster Pfarrweingut
(Forst parish church wine estate), was
founded by Edmund Lucas in the early
Sixties. His son Klaus and wife Christine
(from the Weis family of the Sankt Ur-
banshof winery on the Mosel), have been
running the business together for a number of years. In the meantime, a new cellar complex has been added, as well as an
attractive country hotel. The wines are
usually clear and attractive, although in
many cases they are on the lean side, and
a little impersonal in style. A little more
body, and a little less filtration in the cellar would have improved the Rieslings in
2002 and 2003. That the ability for better
things is available here is shown by the
magnificent 2003 Trockenbeerenauslese.

2003 Forster Ungeheuer
Riesling Kabinett trocken
12%, ♀ till 2006 — **81**

2003 Deidesheimer Herrgottsacker
Riesling Kabinett trocken
11.5%, ♀ till 2006 — **83**

2002 Forster Pechstein
Riesling Spätlese trocken
12.5%, ♀ till 2006 — **85**

2003 Forster Ungeheuer
Riesling Spätlese trocken
12.5%, ♀ till 2007 — **85**

2001 Forster Pechstein
Riesling Spätlese trocken
12.5%, ♀ till 2006 — **86**

2003 Forster Pechstein
Riesling Spätlese trocken
12.5%, ♀ till 2007 — **86**

2001 Forster Pechstein
Riesling Spätlese Goldkapsel
12.5%, ♀ till 2007 — **87**

2002 Forster Ungeheuer
Riesling Beerenauslese
8.5%, ♀ till 2014 — **89**

2003 Forster Ungeheuer
Riesling Trockenbeerenauslese
8%, ♀ till 2025 — **93**

——— Red wine ———

2003 Forster Stift
Spätburgunder trocken
13%, ♀ till 2007 — **81**

The estates: ♣♣♣♣♣ World's finest · ♣♣♣♣ Germany's best · ♣♣♣ Very good · ♣♣ Good · ♣ Reliable

WEINGUT
HERBERT MESSMER

Owner: Herbert and Gregor
Meßmer families
Manager: Gregor Meßmer
Administrator: Werner Sebastian
Winemaker: Michael Leibrecht
76835 Burrweiler, Gaisbergstraße 5
Tel. (0 63 45) 27 70, Fax 79 17
e-mail: messmer@weingut-messmer.de
Internet: www.weingut-messmer.de
Directions: A 65, Edenkoben exit, via
Edesheim and Hainfeld
Sales: Meßmer family
Opening hours: Mon.–Fri. 08:00 to
11:30 hours and 13:30 to 17:00 hours
Thur. by appointment to 19:00 hours
Sat. 09:00 to 14:00 hours
Vacation apartments: At winery

Vineyard area: 23 hectares
Annual production: 210,000 bottles
Top sites: Burrweiler Schäwer,
Schlossgarten and Altenforst
Soil types: Slate, sandy clay, loess,
sandstone and kaolin-marl, limestone
Grape varieties: 42% Riesling,
21% Spätburgunder, 11% Graubur-
gunder, 6% each of Weißburgunder,
Chardonnay and Sankt Laurent,
5% Gewürztraminer and Muskateller,
3% Cabernet Sauvignon
Average yield: 70 hl/ha
Best vintages: 1997, 1999, 2003
Member: VDP

It was 1960 that Herbert Meßmer decided
to go off on his own in the idyllic town of
Burrweiler. He has vines in his vineyards
that are of the perfect age, and the
Schäwer is the only vineyard in the Pfalz
that has slate soils. Today, his sons run
the estate, and after a few weak years the
range is back to its former level of quality. As recently as the 2002 vintage, there
was hardly a wine that was better than a
good average. In 2003, on the other hand,
the St. Laurent, Riesling and Grauburgunder are again very good, and the bot-
ytis dessert wines have a clear fruit.

2003 Grauer Burgunder
Spätlese trocken Barrique
14.5%, ♀ till 2007 **86**

2003 Burrweiler Schäwer
Riesling Spätlese trocken
13.5%, ♀ till 2008 **87**

2002 Burrweiler Schlossgarten
Grauer Burgunder Spätlese trocken
Selection
14%, ♀ till 2006 **87**

2003 Burrweiler Schlossgarten
Weißer Burgunder Spätlese trocken
"Großes Gewächs"
15.5%, ♀ till 2007 **88**

2003 Burrweiler Schlossgarten
Grauer Burgunder Spätlese trocken
14.5%, ♀ till 2007 **89**

2003 Muskateller Kabinett
13%, ♀ till 2007 **88**

2003 Burrweiler Altenforst
Rieslaner Beerenauslese
10.5%, ♀ till 2015 **88**

2003 Burrweiler Schäwer
Riesling Trockenbeerenauslese
9.5%, ♀ till 2025 **92**

——— Red wines ———

2002 Spätburgunder trocken
13%, ♀ till 2008 **86**

2002 St. Laurent trocken
13.5%, ♀ till 2008 **87**

2001 St. Laurent
trocken Selektion
13%, ♀ till 2008 **88**

The wines: **100** Perfect · **95–99** Outstanding · **90–94** Excellent · **85–89** Very good · **80–84** Good · **75–79** Average

497

STIFTSWEINGUT FRANK MEYER

Owner: Frank Meyer and
Manuela Cambeis-Meyer
Manager and winemaker: Frank Meyer
76889 Klingenmünster, Weinstraße 37
Tel. (0 63 49) 74 46, Fax 57 52
e-mail: stiftsweingut-meyer@t-online.de
*Directions: Weinstraße in direction of
Schweigen, in Klingenmünster past the
crossing in direction of Bad Bergzabern*
Sales: Manuela Cambeis-Meyer
and Frank Meyer
Opening hours: Sat. 09:00 to 17:00
hours, weekdays by appointment
Closed Sun. and public holidays
History: Winemaking at abbey since 1100
Worth seeing: Former Benedictine abbey with original barrel cellar, tasting
room in baroque house

Vineyard area: 8.5 hectares
Annual production: 70,000 bottles
Top site: Klingenmünster
Maria Magdalena
Soil types: Sandy clay, stony sand
Grape varieties: 30% Riesling,
30% Weiß- and Grauburgunder,
18% Spätburgunder, 10% Portugieser,
12% other varieties
Average yield: 75 hl/ha
Best vintages: 2001, 2002, 2003

Frank Meyer has developed his parents' winery, without abandoning such traditions as maturing Rieslings in large oak vats. Ever since he has moved to a very tastefully renovated baroque house on the Weinstraße, he appears to feel more free in his work, though it must be said that not all of his many experiments are successful. Meyer has his strengths with a clean, clear Riesling as well as with the Pinot varieties, whereby it is clear he is not always aiming at the greatest possible ripeness. This was a distinct benefit, and worked well, in the 2003 vintage. His Portugieser is pretty much regularly the best of his kind we have found in the Pfalz region.

2003 Klingenmünster Maria Magdalena
Weißer Burgunder Kabinett trocken
12.3%, ♀ till 2006 — **84**

2002 Klingenmünster Maria Magdalena
Riesling Spätlese trocken
12%, ♀ till 2006 — **85**

2003 Klingenmünster Maria Magdalena
Riesling Kabinett trocken
12.2%, ♀ till 2006 — **85**

2001 Klingenmünster Maria Magdalena
Grauer Burgunder Spätlese trocken
13%, ♀ till 2006 — **86**

2003 Klingenmünster Maria Magdalena
Weißer Burgunder Spätlese trocken
13.6%, ♀ till 2007 — **86**

2003 Klingenmünster Maria Magdalena
Riesling Spätlese feinherb
12.8%, ♀ till 2007 — **86**

2003 Rieslaner
Spätlese "edelsüß"
11%, ♀ till 2010 — **85**

———— Red wines ————

2002 Klingenmünster Maria Magdalena
Spätburgunder trocken
12.5%, ♀ till 2007 — **84**

2001 "Cuvée Nr. 37" trocken
14.1%, ♀ till 2010 — **85**

2001 Klingenmünster Maria Magdalena
Portugieser trocken
13%, ♀ till 2007 — **87**

STIFTSWEINGUT FRANK MEYER, WEINSTR. 37
D-76889 KLINGENMÜNSTER, TEL. 0 63 49/74 46, FAX 57 52
GUTSABFÜLLUNG, AP-NR. 5 049 099 25 01
QUALITÄTSWEIN

KLINGENMÜNSTERER
MARIA MAGDALENA
SPÄTBURGUNDER
ROTWEIN
trocken
2000

12.5 % Vol. 0.75l

2022

WEINGUT THEO MINGES

Owner and manager: Theo Minges
76835 Flemlingen, Bachstraße 11
Tel. (0 63 23) 9 33 50, Fax 9 33 51
Directions: A 65, Landau-Nord exit
Sales: Theo Minges
Opening hours: Mon.–Sat. 09:00 to 18:00 hours
Worth seeing: Tithing cellar dating to 15th century

Vineyard area: 23 hectares
Annual production: 150,000 bottles
Top sites: Gleisweiler Hölle, Flemlinger Vogelsprung
Soil types: Limestone, marl, loess-clay, sandstone
Grape varieties: 30% Riesling, 15% Spätburgunder, 10% each of Graburgunder and Dornfelder, 5% each of Weißburgunder, Chardonnay and St. Laurent, 20% other varieties
Average yield: 78 hl/ha
Best vintages: 2000, 2001, 2003

The vineyard holdings have increased by five hectares in recent years, making it definitely one of the larger operations in the Pfalz region. It was owned until the 16th century by the counts von der Layen. The Minges family has been running the business for the past six generations. For a long time, Theo Minges attracted attention only for a few individual wines, whereas some of the recent vintages have shown greater consistency and reliably good quality. Minges presented a thoroughly serious 2000 vintage range, and the 2001 collection also fulfilled all our expectations. 2002 was a little less exciting, although in this vintage there were already a number of elegant fruity-sweet Rieslings that were reminiscent of good wines from the Middle Mosel. These were also the strong points of the quite large and varied 2003 range. Unfortunately, we were again presented only with white wines for the tasting, the 2002 reds had not yet been bottled at the time of going to press.

2003 Gleisweiler Hölle
Riesling Spätlese trocken
13%, ♀ till 2007 — **85**

2003 "Buntsandstein"
Riesling Spätlese trocken
13%, ♀ till 2006 — **86**

2003 "Cuvée des fees" trocken
14%, ♀ till 2006 — **86**

2003 Böchinger Rosenkranz
Weißer Burgunder Spätlese trocken
15%, ♀ till 2006 — **86**

2002 Gleisweiler Hölle
Riesling Spätlese trocken
12.5%, ♀ till 2006 — **87**

2003 Gleisweiler Hölle
Riesling Spätlese
9.5%, ♀ till 2008 — **85**

2003 Gleisweiler Hölle
Scheurebe Spätlese
11.5%, ♀ till 2006 — **87**

2003 Gleisweiler Hölle
Riesling Spätlese Goldkapsel
9%, ♀ till 2010 — **89**

2002 Gleisweiler Hölle
Riesling Spätlese
9.5%, ♀ till 2008 — **90**

2002 Gleisweiler Hölle
Riesling Auslese Goldkapsel
8.5%, ♀ till 2015 — **90**

2003 Böchinger Rosenkranz
Riesling Eiswein
8%, ♀ till 2015 — **93**

Theo Minges
Pfalz
A.P.Nr. 5025 066 15 04
2003
Gleisweiler Hölle
Riesling
Spätlese · Trocken
750 ml e   alc. 13 % vol.
Produce of Germany
Gutsabfüllung Weingut Theo Minges · D-76835 Flemlingen/Pfalz
Qualitätswein mit Prädikat

The wines: **100** Perfect · **95–99** Outstanding · **90–94** Excellent · **85–89** Very good · **80–84** Good · **75–79** Average

WEINGUT
GEORG MOSBACHER

**Owner: Mosbacher and
Düringer families
Administrator and winemaker:
Jürgen Düringer
67147 Forst, Weinstraße 27
Tel. (0 63 26) 3 29, Fax 67 74
e-mail: Mosbacher@t-online.de
Internet: www.georg-mosbacher.de**
*Directions: On Deutsche Weinstraße
(B 271), between Neustadt and
Bad Dürkheim*
Sales: Sabine Mosbacher-Düringer
Opening hours: Mon.–Fri. 08:00 to
12:00 hours and 13:30 to 18:00 hours
Sat. 09:00 to 13:00 hours
Worth seeing: Vaulted cellar of sand-
stone dating to 18th century

Vineyard area: 14.2 hectares
Annual production: 110,000 bottles
Top sites: Forster Ungeheuer,
Freundstück and Pechstein, Deides-
heimer Mäushöhle and Kieselberg
Soil types: Decomposed sandstone
with limestone boulders, basalt and
kaolin
Grape varieties: 88% Riesling,
7% white varieties, 5% red varieties
Average yield: 60 hl/ha
Best vintages: 1996, 1998, 2001
Member: VDP

The Mosbacher family has been based in
Forst for more than 200 years. However,
the foundation for the production of high
quality wines was laid by Georg Mosbacher at the turn of the 20th century. The
first estate bottlings of wine date to 1920.
Today, Richard Mosbacher is in charge
of the business, which he runs together
with his daughter Sabine and son-in-law
Jürgen Düringer. In spite of the many
medals and prices he has won, he is humble about himself and his wines. Nevertheless, nobody would doubt the leading
role of this winery in Forst today. Richard
Mosbacher's long experience and the

well-founded education of the two young
people make a winning combination. The
best sites of Forst provide excellent conditions for the production of outstanding
Riesling wines – except for extreme vintages such as the dry 2003 vintage. The
share of Riesling is high at almost 90 percent, and the Mosbachers intend to keep it
this way. In addition, they plan to acquire
additional top vineyard sites, suitable for
the production of First Growths. At the
same time, there is no fear of experimentation here. For instance, Merlot has been
planted, and a Sauvignon Blanc is already
quite successful. However, it is particularly the Rieslings that speak for themselves. They are clean, typical of varieties,
with mineral notes and showing off their
terroir, these wines have for many years
been among the best the Pfalz has to
offer. The 1998 vintage was excellent,
although the Rieslings required some time
to develop. In the 1999 vintage, the First
Growths from the Freundstück and Ungeheuer sites were able to match the best of
previous vintages. The 2000 vintage was
a very difficult one. In the 2001 vintage,
the Riesling wines showed a superb class
of a level not seen for a long time. From
the Kabinett through the magnificent
"Große Gewächse" (First Growths) right
up to the outstanding Eiswein, these minerally and compact wines are typical of
the Mittelhaardt area, being enjoyable in
youth, but with the potential to develop
well for a few years. The 2002 vintage
did not present any really poor wines, but
at the same time the brilliance was not
quite what it had been in previous vintages. The same must be said, possibly as
a result of the drouth, of the 2003 vintage.
Just as in the previous vintage, the "Große
Gewächse," while being excellent wines
in their own right, were not among the
really top Rieslings in the Pfalz region.
However, the opportunity provided by
the vintage for the production of brilliant
clear botrytis dessert wines was fully implemented in the sensational Trockenbee
renauslese.

2003 Sauvignon Blanc trocken
12.5%, ♀ till 2006   85

2003 Deidesheimer Mäushöhle
Riesling Kabinett trocken
12%, ♀ till 2006   85

2002 Forster Stift
Riesling Spätlese trocken
13%, ♀ till 2006   86

2003 Forster Pechstein
Riesling Kabinett trocken
12%, ♀ till 2008   86

2003 Forster Musenhang
Riesling Spätlese trocken
13%, ♀ till 2008   86

2001 Deidesheimer Mäushöhle
Riesling Kabinett trocken
11.5%, ♀ till 2006   87

2001 Forster Pechstein
Riesling Kabinett trocken
12%, ♀ till 2006   87

2002 Forster Musenhang
Riesling Kabinett trocken
12%, ♀ till 2006   87

2002 Forster Pechstein
Riesling Spätlese trocken
12.5%, ♀ till 2007   87

2001 Forster Musenhang
Riesling Spätlese trocken
13%, ♀ till 2006   88

2003 Forster Stift
Riesling Spätlese trocken
13%, ♀ till 2008   88

2003 Deidesheimer Kieselberg
Riesling Spätlese trocken
"Großes Gewächs"
13%, ♀ till 2008   88

2001 Forster Stift
Riesling Spätlese trocken
13%, ♀ till 2006   89

2002 Deidesheimer Kieselberg
Riesling Spätlese trocken
"Großes Gewächs"
13%, ♀ till 2008   89

2002 Forster Ungeheuer
Riesling Spätlese trocken
"Großes Gewächs"
3%, ♀ till 2007   89

2002 Forster Freundstück
Riesling Spätlese trocken
"Großes Gewächs"
12.5%, ♀ till 2007   89

2003 Forster Freundstück
Riesling Spätlese trocken
"Großes Gewächs"
13%, ♀ till 2008   89

2003 Forster Ungeheuer
Riesling Spätlese trocken
"Großes Gewächs"
13%, ♀ till 2008   89

2001 Deidesheimer Kieselberg
Riesling Spätlese trocken
"Großes Gewächs"
13%, ♀ till 2006   92

2001 Forster Ungeheuer
Riesling Spätlese trocken
"Großes Gewächs"
13%, ♀ till 2006   94

2003 Deidesheimer Leinhöhle
Riesling Kabinett
11%, ♀ till 2010   86

2002 Forster Elster
Riesling Spätlese
11%, ♀ till 2008   88

2002 Forster Ungeheuer
Riesling Trockenbeerenauslese
8.5%, ♀ till 2030   91

2001 Forster Freundstück
Riesling Eiswein
9%, ♀ 2008 till 2020   92

2003 Deidesheimer Herrgottsacker
Riesling Trockenbeerenauslese
Goldkapsel
6.5%, ♀ till 2025   97

WEINGUT
GEORG MOSBACHER
FORST
PFALZ
Produce of Germany

2003
Gewürztraminer Spätlese
750 ml e   Qualitätswein mit Prädikat A.P.Nr. 5 112 066 020 04
Gutsabfüllung Weingut Georg Mosbacher D-67147 Forst   alc. 13%v vol

---

ne wines: **100** Perfect · **95–99** Outstanding · **90–94** Excellent · **85–89** Very good · **80–84** Good · **75–79** Average

501

WEINGUT EUGEN MÜLLER

Owner: Kurt and Stephan Müller
Winemaker: Jürgen Meißner
67147 Forst, Weinstraße 34a
Tel. (0 63 26) 3 30, Fax 68 02
e-mail:
weingut-eugen-mueller@t-online.de
Internet:
www.Weingut-Eugen-Mueller.de
Directions: On the Deutsche Weinstraße
between Neustadt and Bad Dürkheim
Sales: Elisabeth, Kurt and Stephan Müller
Opening hours: Mon.–Fri. 08:00 to
12:00 and 13:30 to 18:00, Sat. 09:00 to
16:00 hours, Sun. by appointment
Worth seeing: Cellar with 50 large vats

Vineyard area: 17 hectares
Annual production: 145,000 bottles
Top sites: Forster Kirchenstück,
Jesuitengarten, Ungeheuer,
Pechstein and Musenhang
Soil types: Limestone with clay, sand-
stone rubble with basalt and kaolin
Grape varieties: 77% Riesling,
10% Grau- and Weißburgunder,
13% red varieties
Average yield: 67 hl/ha
Best vintages: 1998, 2001, 2002

We are pleased to report that this renowned estate in Forst has returned to former level of quality. This is due at least in
part to considerable investment made in
the cellar. Another important factor is
Stephan Müller, who took over responsibility here in 2000, bringing in his German and international experience. He
showed straight off with a number of
Riesling wines of the 2001 vintage that he
knows what he is doing. In 2002, too, we
liked his individualistic Rieslings. 2003 is
a little weaker, due to the extreme conditions of the vintage, and he was not totally successful in managing the acidity, but
he has still managed to produce an elegant Trockenbeerenauslese. The reds of
the 2001 and 2002 vintages were presented recently, and we found them to
be very good.

2003 Forster Jesuitengarten
Riesling Kabinett trocken
12.5%, ♀ till 2006 — **83**

2003 Forster Kirchenstück
Riesling Spätlese trocken
12.5%, ♀ till 2007 — **85**

2003 Forster Ungeheuer
Riesling Spätlese trocken
12.5%, ♀ till 2007 — **86**

2002 Forster Kirchenstück
Riesling Auslese trocken
13.5%, ♀ till 2006 — **87**

2003 Forster Ungeheuer
Riesling Beerenauslese
10.5%, ♀ till 2012 — **88**

2002 Forster Ungeheuer
Scheurebe Eiswein
8%, ♀ 2006 till 2018 — **89**

2003 Forster Ungeheuer
Riesling Trockenbeerenauslese
10.5%, ♀ till 2020 — **90**

——— Red wines ———

2001 "Barrot C" trocken
13.5%, ♀ till 2007 — **86**

2002 Forster Musenhang
Spätburgunder trocken
13%, ♀ till 2007 — **86**

2001 "Barrot"
Dunkelfelder trocken
13%, ♀ till 2008 — **88**

WEINGUT
EUGEN MÜLLER

FORST

KIRCHENSTÜCK
FORST

WEINGUT MÜLLER-CATOIR

Owner: Jakob Heinrich Catoir
General manager: Jakob Heinrich
and Philipp David Catoir
Technical manager: Martin Franzen
Winemaker: Martin Franzen
67433 Haardt, Mandelring 25
Tel. (0 63 21) 28 15, Fax 48 00 14
e-mail: weingut@mueller-catoir.de
Internet: www.mueller-catoir.de
Directions: A 65, Neustadt-Nord exit,
right toward Haardt at 1st traffic light,
Haardter Schloss
Opening hours: Mon.–Fri. 08:00 to
12:00 hours and 13:00 to 17:00 hours
Closed on weekends
History: Winemaking since 1744
Worth seeing: 18th-century tasting
rooms, portal with columns, courtyard in
Mediterranean style, impressive facade
from turn of 20th century

Vineyard area: 20 hectares
Annual production: 135,000 bottles
Top sites: Haardter Herrenletten,
Bürgergarten, Herzog and Mandel-
ring, Gimmeldinger Mandelgarten
and Schlössel, Mußbacher Eselshaut
Soil types: From heavy loam to
gravelly loess
Grape varieties: 60% Riesling,
12% each of Rieslaner and Weißbur-
gunder, 7% Grauburgunder, 5% Mus-
kateller, 4% Scheurebe
Average yield: 55 hl/ha
Best vintages: 1998, 2000, 2001
Member: VDP

Müller-Catoir is one of the most impressive wineries in Germany. Visitors in
spring will see more than a thousand almond trees in full bloom, stretched out on
a south-facing slope that faces the Rhine
plain in front of the impressive facade of
the turn-of-the-century manor-house. The
imposing portal with its columns, the Mediterranean-style courtyard with gardens
as well as the majestic tasting rooms from
the 18th century combine in an ensemble
that is pretty much unique. Jakob Heinrich Catoir, who represents the eighth
generation of the family, shows great dedication in preserving this jewel. He has
recently allowed his son Phillipp David
to join the management team. The long-
serving administrator and general manager Hans-Günther Schwarz is given completely free rein. His wines show finesse
and grapey fruit that has influenced a
whole generation of young winemakers
in the Pfalz. This estate was the leading
winery in the Pfalz region, and stood in a
row with the best producers in Germany.
Then Schwarz retired after presenting his
magnificent 2001 vintage. His successor,
Martin Franzen, faced a new beginning,
working with a new team. This able and
likable young man had already shown his
mettle at the Schlossgut Diel winery in
the Nahe region, as well as at the Nägelsförst winery in Baden. The results of his
2002 vintage, his first at Müller-Catoir,
were sobering, to say the least. Franzen
hails from the Mosel, and produced a
range of delicate light wines that had
nothing in common with the accepted
Pfalz style. Now, a change in style need
not necessarily be such a bad thing, but
most of the wines lacked both opulence
and finesse. In spite of the drouth, the
2003 vintage was actually a step in the
right direction, as was the decision to join
the VDP association. Quite contrary to
the situation at most other estates, this
vintage actually produced more body and
better terroir characteristics than did the
preceding vintage, and this applies both
to the dry Rieslings and to the botrytis
dessert wines. That the new team is determined to pay more attention to the terroir
aspect is shown by the decision to split
the Bürgergarten site into three different
terroir-related dry Riesling Spätlese wines.
However, the aromatic varieties, which
used to be very strong here, as well as the
Rieslaner, are currently still suffering
from the change in style. An exception is
the dry Muskateller Spätlese, which is already showing more varietal character
and finesse.

the wines: **100** Perfect · **95–99** Outstanding · **90–94** Excellent · **85–89** Very good · **80–84** Good · **75–79** Average

2003 Haardter Herrenletten
Grauer Burgunder Spätlese trocken
14.5%, ♀ till 2007   **86**

2003 Mußbacher Eselshaut
Riesling trocken
12.5%, ♀ till 2006   **86**

2002 Gimmeldinger Mandelgarten
Riesling Spätlese trocken
12.5%, ♀ till 2006   **87**

2003 Haardter Bürgergarten
Muskateller Spätlese trocken
14%, ♀ till 2008   **87**

2003 Gimmeldinger Mandelgarten
Riesling Kabinett trocken
12.5%, ♀ till 2008   **87**

2003 Haardter Bürgergarten
Riesling Spätlese trocken "Im Breumel"
13.5%, ♀ till 2008   **87**

2003 Haardter Bürgergarten
Riesling Spätlese trocken "Im Aspen"
13.5%, ♀ till 2008   **88**

2003 Haardter Bürgergarten
Riesling Spätlese trocken "Im Gehren"
14%, ♀ till 2008   **89**

2001 Haardter Bürgergarten
Riesling Spätlese trocken
12.5%, ♀ till 2006   **91**

2001 Haardter Herrenletten
Grauer Burgunder Spätlese trocken
14%, ♀ till 2006   **91**

2001 Haardter Mandelring
Scheurebe Spätlese trocken
10.5%, ♀ till 2006   **92**

2002 Gimmeldinger Mandelgarten
Riesling Spätlese
8.5%, ♀ till 2007   **88**

2003 Haardter Herrenletten
Riesling Spätlese
9.5%, ♀ till 2010   **89**

2003 Gimmeldinger Schlössel
Rieslaner Auslese
10.5%, ♀ till 2010   **89**

2003 Haardter Bürgergarten
Rieslaner Auslese
10.5%, ♀ till 2010   **89**

2002 Mußbacher Eselshaut
Rieslaner Auslese
9%, ♀ till 2008   **90**

2003 Haardter Bürgergarten
Rieslaner Beerenauslese
8.5%, ♀ till 2010   **91**

2001 Haardter Mandelring
Scheurebe Spätlese
10.5%, ♀ till 2006   **92**

2003 Haardter Bürgergarten
Riesling Trockenbeerenauslese
7%, ♀ till 2015   **92**

2001 Mußbacher Eselshaut
Rieslaner Spätlese
12%, ♀ till 2008   **93**

2001 Mußbacher Eselshaut
Riesling Auslese
8%, ♀ till 2010   **94**

2001 Gimmeldinger Schlössel
Rieslaner Beerenauslese
9.5%, ♀ till 2015   **95**

2001 Mußbacher Eselshaut
Riesling Eiswein
9%, ♀ till 2030   **95**

2001 Mußbacher Eselshaut
Rieslaner Auslese
8.5%, ♀ till 2010   **95**

2001 Haardter Mandelring
Scheurebe Eiswein
10%, ♀ till 2030   **98**

2001 Mußbacher Eselshaut
Rieslaner Trockenbeerenauslese
9%, ♀ till 2030   **99**

Weingut
2209

seit 1744

Müller-Catoir
Gutsabfüllung · D-67433 Haardt · www.mueller-catoir.de

2002er Riesling trocken
Haardter Bürgergarten Kabinett
alc. 12,0 % vol. · Pfalz · 750 mle
Qualitätswein mit Prädikat · Amtl.Prüf.Nr. 51740790903

The estates: ♣♣♣♣♣ World's finest · ♣♣♣♣ Germany's best · ♣♣♣ Very good · ♣♣ Good · ♣ Reliabl

WEINGUT MÜNZBERG

Owner and manager:
Gunter and Rainer Keßler
76829 Landau-Godramstein, Hofgut
Tel. (0 63 41) 6 09 35, Fax 6 42 10
e-mail: wein@weingut-muenzberg.de
Internet: www.weingut-muenzberg.de
Directions: A 65, Landau-Nord exit onto
the B 10, in direction of Pirmasens,
Godramstein exit, winery outside town
in direction of Böchingen
Sales: Keßler family
Opening hours: Mon.–Fri. 08:00 to
12:00 hours and 14:00 to 18:00 hours
Sat. 09:00 to 16:00 hours
by appointment
Wine bistro: "5 Bäuerlein" at market-
place in Landau

Vineyard area: 14 hectares
Annual production: 100,000 bottles
Top site: Godramsteiner
Münzberg and Schneckenberg
Soil types: Limestone soils covered
with clay or sandy clay
Grape varieties: 26% Weißburgunder,
22% Riesling, 17% Spätburgunder,
9% Dornfelder, 8% Silvaner, 7% Char-
donnay, 6% Grauburgunder, 3% Mül-
ler-Thurgau, 2% Gewürztraminer
Average yield: 70 hl/ha
Best vintages: 2001, 2002, 2003
Member: VDP

The Keßler brothers, Gunter and Rainer,
have turned the attractively located farm
on the slopes of the Münzberg into a respectable winery producing excellent
quality. For many years, their particular
strength has lain in the powerful wines
made from white Pinot varieties, in particular the Pinot Blancs. The soils here
have good water-retentive qualities, and
thus had an advantage in the dry 2003 vintage. In addition, the brothers did just
about everything right in handling the
extreme conditions. The result: Good dry
Riesling wines, a significantly improved
use of barriques in the impressive Chardonnays, and a magnificent Gewürztraminer.

2003 Weißer Burgunder
Spätlese trocken
13.5%, ♀ till 2007   **87**

2003 Godramsteiner Münzberg "Schlangenpfiff"
Riesling Spätlese trocken
"Großes Gewächs"
13.5%, ♀ till 2008   **88**

2002 Chardonnay
Spätlese trocken Barrique
14%, ♀ till 2010   **89**

2003 Chardonnay Spätlese trocken
14.5%, ♀ till 2008   **90**

2002 Chardonnay Spätlese trocken
14%, ♀ till 2008   **91**

2002 Godramsteiner Münzberg "Schlangenpfiff"
Weißer Burgunder Spätlese trocken
"Großes Gewächs"
14%, ♀ till 2009   **92**

2003 Godramsteiner Münzberg "Schlangenpfiff"
Weißer Burgunder Spätlese trocken
"Großes Gewächs"
14.5%, ♀ till 2007   **92**

2002 Riesling Beerenauslese
10.5%, ♀ till 2015   **91**

2003 Gewürztraminer Spätlese
13.5%, ♀ till 2008   **91**

The wines: **100** Perfect · **95–99** Outstanding · **90–94** Excellent · **85–89** Very good · **80–84** Good · **75–79** Average

505

WEINGUT LUDI NEISS

Owner: Neiss family
Manager and winemaker:
Axel Neiss
67271 Kindenheim, Hauptstraße 91
Tel. (0 63 59) 43 27, Fax 4 04 76
e-mail: weingut-neiss@t-online.de
Directions: A 6, Grünstadt exit, via
Bockenheim to Kindenheim
Sales: Katja Neiss
Opening hours: Mon.–Fri. 09:00 to
17:00 hours, Sat. 10:00 to 15:00 hours
History: Winemaking since 1873

Vineyard area: 15 hectares
Annual production: 120,000 bottles
Top site: Kindenheimer Burgweg
Soil types: Clay soils with limestone
Grape varieties: 24% Riesling, 20%
Spätburgunder, 14% Dornfelder,
7% Portugieser, 6% Weißburgunder,
29% other varieties
Average yield: 75 hl/ha
Best vintage: 2003

This is yet another up-and-coming family winery in the northern part of the region. Neiss is one of the estates everybody is talking about. Perhaps that explains the exorbitant prices being charged for the very ordinary reds. At the same time, we have noted that Axel Neiss is working hard to improve his wine quality, which we would like to acknowledge by awarding the first bunch of grapes, based mainly on the fact that he has produced really good white wines in the difficult 2003 vintage. This is a modern winery with high expectations of itself, designer bottles, modern and very consumer-friendly labels, and the white wines prove that the winemaker knows his job. The reds are concentrated and fruity, but at least in their youth they tend to be tough, and perhaps too strongly dominated by wood. 90 percent of the wines are fermented dry. Around half the production is sold to loyal consumers, and an amazing 40 percent is sold via the retail trade.

2003 Silvaner trocken
12.5%, ♀ till 2006   82

2003 Kindenheimer Grafenstück
Weißer Burgunder trocken
13%, ♀ till 2006   83

2003 Kindenheimer Grafenstück
Chardonnay trocken
13%, ♀ till 2007   83

2003 Kindenheimer Burgweg
Riesling Spätlese trocken
13%, ♀ till 2007   86

2003 Bockenheimer Heiligenkirche
Riesling Spätlese trocken
13%, ♀ till 2006   87

2003 Kindenheimer Burgweg
Riesling trocken Alte Reben
14%, ♀ till 2007   87

——————— Red wines ———————

2002 Kindenheimer Grafenstück
Cabernet Sauvignon & Merlot trocken
13%, ♀ till 2008   80

2002 Kindenheimer Grafenstück
Frühburgunder trocken
13%, ♀ till 2007   82

2002 Kindenheimer Grafenstück
Dornfelder trocken
13%, ♀ till 2008   83

2002 "Cuvée N" trocken
13%, ♀ till 2008   85

2001 Kindenheimer Grafenstück
Spätburgunder trocken
13%, ♀ till 2008   85

NEISS

2003
Riesling
Spätlese trocken
Heiligenkirche

WEINGUT PETRI

Owner: Sigrun and Gerd Petri
Winemaker: Gerd Petri
67273 Herxheim/Berg, Weinstraße 43
Tel. (0 63 53) 23 45, Fax 41 81
e-mail: info@weingut-petri.de
Internet: www.weingut-petri.de
Directions: A 6 in direction of Kaisers-
lautern, Grünstadt exit, in direction of
Bad Dürkheim
Sales: Sigrun Petri
Opening hours: Mon.–Sat. 09:00 to
12:00 hours and 13:00 to 18:00 hours
Restaurant: Closed Mon.
Specialties: Regional Pfalz cuisine

Vineyard area: 11 hectares
Annual production: 100,000 bottles
Top sites: Herxheimer Himmelreich
and Honigsack, Kallstadter Saumagen
Soil types: Sandy clay, limestone-rich
loess-clay, decomposed limestone
Grape varieties: 41% Riesling,
14% Spätburgunder, 7% Grauburgun-
der, 6% Frühburgunder, 5% each of
Weißburgunder and St. Laurent,
22% other varieties
Average yield: 78 hl/ha
Best vintages: 2001, 2002, 2003

Gerd Petri represents the 13th generation of winemakers in the Petri family in Herxheim. When he took over the winery in 1977, after completing his studies in Geisenheim, the entire production was still sold in bulk. Petri has changed over gradually to marketing the wines in bottles. We have been tracking his development since 1995. In 1999, 2000 and 2001, there were a lot of good average-quality wines, plus a few remarkably good ones in the cellar. We tasted only very good white wines of the 2002 vintage, and some were even outstanding. Even in the difficult 2003 vintage, Petri has produced refreshing, fruit-dominated white wines of astonishing clarity, and dry Rieslings that are the equal of those from the very best producers. Unfortunately, the rustic reds are not of the same standard.

2001 Herxheimer Honigsack
Riesling Spätlese trocken
13%, ♀ till 2006   86

2003 Herxheimer Honigsack
Grauer Burgunder Spätlese trocken
13.5%, ♀ till 2006   86

2002 Kallstadter Saumagen
Riesling Spätlese trocken
13%, ♀ till 2007   87

2002 Herxheimer Honigsack
Grauer Burgunder Spätlese trocken
13.5%, ♀ till 2006   87

2003 Herxheimer Honigsack
Riesling Spätlese trocken
13%, ♀ till 2007   87

2003 Kallstadter Saumagen
Riesling Spätlese trocken
13.5%, ♀ till 2007   88

2001 Herxheimer Himmelreich
Chardonnay Spätlese trocken
12.5%, ♀ till 2007   89

2003 Herxheimer Himmelreich
Gewürztraminer Spätlese
14.5%, ♀ till 2008   85

2003 Herxheimer Honigsack
Scheurebe Spätlese
13.5%, ♀ till 2008   87

———— Red wines ————

2003 Frühburgunder
Spätlese trocken
13%, ♀ till 2007   82

2003 Herxheimer Himmelreich
St. Laurent trocken
13%, ♀ till 2007   83

2003 Merlot Spätlese trocken
14.5%, ♀ till 2007   84

PETRI

2003
RIESLING
Spätlese trocken

The wines: **100** Perfect · **95–99** Outstanding · **90–94** Excellent · **85–89** Very good · **80–84** Good · **75–79** Average

507

WEINGUT KARL PFAFFMANN

**Owner: Helmut Pfaffmann
and Markus Pfaffmann
Winemaker: Markus Pfaffmann
76833 Walsheim, Allmendstraße 1
Tel. (0 63 41) 6 18 56, Fax 6 26 09
e-mail:
info@weingut-karl-pfaffmann.de
Internet:
www.weingut-karl-pfaffmann.de**
*Directions: A 65, Landau-Nord exit,
in direction of Edesheim*
Sales: Sigrid Pfaffmann
Opening hours: Mon.–Fri. 08:00 to
12:00 hours and 13:00 to 18:00 hours
Sat. 08:00 to 16:00 hours
Sun. 10:00 to 12:00 hours
Closed for vacation 1st half of January

Vineyard area: 35 hectares
Annual production: 300,000 bottles
Top sites: Walsheimer Silber-
berg, Nußdorfer Herrenberg
Soil types: Sandy loess-clay
Grape varieties: 25% Riesling,
25% white Pinot varieties and Char-
donnay, 12% Spätburgunder,
10% Dornfelder, 8% Portugieser,
6% Silvaner, 14% other varieties
Average yield: 75 hl/ha
Best vintages: 2001, 2002, 2003

Two generations work hand in hand at the
Pfaffmann winery – Helmut Pfaffmann
and his son Markus. Their common aim
is quality. Certainly, since 1999 (at the
latest) they have been producing modern,
flawless, thoroughly convincing ranges –
not an easy task for an operation of this
size. Ever since 2002, Pfaffmann has be-
en astounding us with a series of amazing
sweet wines, which in this region are very
rarely as fresh, invigorating, clear and
low in alcohol as here. In 2003, the botrytis dessert wines are again among the
highlights, but not exclusively so. Riesling and Pinot Blanc have again produced
a number of remarkable wines.

2003 Nußdorfer Bischofskreuz
Weißer Burgunder Kabinett trocken
13%, ♀ till 2006   85

2003 Nußdorfer Herrenberg
Riesling Spätlese trocken
13.5%, ♀ till 2007   86

2003 Walsheimer Silberberg
Chardonnay Spätlese trocken
14%, ♀ till 2007   86

2003 Walsheimer Silberberg
Grauer Burgunder Spätlese trocken
14.5%, ♀ till 2007   87

2003 Walsheimer Silberberg
Riesling Spätlese trocken Selection
14%, ♀ till 2008   88

2003 Walsheimer Silberberg
Riesling Auslese
9%, ♀ till 2010   90

2003 Walsheimer Silberberg
Riesling Eiswein
9.5%, ♀ till 2012   91

2002 Walsheimer Silberberg
Riesling Eiswein
7.5%, ♀ till 2020   92

2002 Walsheimer Silberberg
Huxelrebe Beerenauslese
7.5%, ♀ till 2020   93

2003 Walsheimer Silberberg
Riesling Beerenauslese
9%, ♀ till 2015   94

WEINGUT PFEFFINGEN – FUHRMANN-EYMAEL

Owner: Doris Eymael
Manager: Doris and Jan Eymael
Winemaker: Rainer Gabel
67098 Bad Dürkheim, Pfeffingen
Tel. (0 63 22) 86 07, Fax 86 03
e-mail: Pfeffingen@t-online.de
Internet: www.pfeffingen.de
Directions: On the Weinstraße between
Bad Dürkheim and Ungstein
Sales: Doris and Jan Eymael
Opening hours: Mon.–Fri. 08:00 to
12:00 and 13:00 to 18:00, Sat. 09:00
to 12:00 and 13:00 to 17:00, Sun. 10:00
to 12:00 hours
Worth a visit: Culinary symposium in
May, wine festival in July, vineyard
happening in October

Vineyard area: 11.7 hectares
Annual production: 100,000 bottles
Top sites: Ungsteiner Herrenberg
and Weilberg
Soil types: Terra rossa, calcareous
marl, loess
Grape varieties: 55% Riesling, 12%
Scheurebe, 11% Gewürztraminer,
6% each of Spätburgunder and Weiß-
burgunder, 3% each of Chardonnay
and Silvaner, 4% other varieties
Average yield: 65 hl/ha
Best vintages: 2000, 2001, 2002
Member: VDP

The attractive winery complex set amidst
the vineyards is the life's work of Karl
Fuhrmann, whose daughter Doris now
runs the business, assisted since 2002 by
son Jan. Riesling and Scheurebe wines
have always been the strengths of this
estate. The typical Rieslings produced
here enchant by virtue of their aromas
of ripe apricots and yellow peaches. The
wines of the 2000 vintage were all first-
class, as were those of 2001 and 2002.
Tasting the 2003 vintage, we found fewer
highlights than usual, and sincerely hope
that this can only be attributed to the exceptional drouth experienced.

2003 Ungsteiner Herrenberg
Riesling Spätlese trocken
13.5%, ♀ till 2007 — **86**

2003 Ungsteiner Weilberg
Riesling Spätlese trocken
13%, ♀ till 2008 — **88**

2003 Ungsteiner Weilberg
Riesling Spätlese trocken
"Großes Gewächs"
13%, ♀ till 2008 — **89**

2002 Ungsteiner Weilberg
Riesling Spätlese trocken
"Großes Gewächs"
13%, ♀ till 2008 — **90**

2001 Ungsteiner Weilberg
Riesling Spätlese trocken
"Großes Gewächs"
13%, ♀ till 2008 — **91**

2003 Ungsteiner Herrenberg
Riesling Spätlese
11.5%, ♀ till 2010 — **87**

2003 Scheurebe Spätlese
11.5%, ♀ till 2008 — **88**

2003 Ungsteiner Nußriegel
Rieslaner Auslese
11%, ♀ till 2010 — **88**

2003 Ungsteiner Herrenberg
Scheurebe Auslese
10.5%, ♀ till 2010 — **90**

2002 Ungsteiner Herrenberg
Scheurebe Beerenauslese
9%, ♀ till 2012 — **92**

Weingut Pfeffingen
2003
Scheurebe
Spätlese
trocken

The wines: **100** Perfect · **95–99** Outstanding · **90–94** Excellent · **85–89** Very good · **80–84** Good · **75–79** Average

509

WEINGUT PFIRMANN

Owner: Otto Pfirmann
Manager: Otto and Jürgen Pfirmann
Winemaker: Jürgen Pfirmann
76829 Landau-Wollmesheim,
Wollmesheimer Hauptstraße 84
Tel. (0 63 41) 3 25 84, Fax 93 00 66
e-mail: info@weingut-pfirmann.de
Directions: A 65, Landau-Mitte exit, on
the L 509 in westerly direction to suburb
of Wollmesheim
Sales: Pfirmann family
Opening hours: Sat. 09:00 to 18:00
hours, and by appointment

Vineyard area: 11 hectares
Annual production: 60,000 bottles
Top site: Wollmesheimer Mütterle
Soil types: Clay with limestone and
shell limestone
Grape varieties: 20% Riesling,
14% Weißburgunder, 12% Spätbur-
gunder, 7% each of Grauburgunder
and Dornfelder, 5% each of Silvaner,
Chardonnay and St. Laurent,
25% other varieties
Average yield: 79 hl/ha
Best vintages: 2002, 2003

Wollmesheim is an attractive village, and this winery, which has been considerably modernized in the past few years, has surprised us with the first vintages of the young Jürgen Pfirmann. Reasons can be seen in the improved technical facilities, his enthusiasm and his close interaction with other ambitious young winemakers, and particularly his good enological training. The 2002 vintage saw him overcoming some initial weaknesses, showing great ability in handling the white Pinot varieties. He manages achieving the ideal combination of clean work in the cellar on the one hand, and retaining the substance of the fruit on the other. His wines of the 2003 vintage are also polished, and show good fruit, which was not automatic in this difficult vintage. He has also shown great feeling in the making of his remarkable and fruity Riesling Spätlese.

2003 Wollmesheimer Mütterle
Weißer Burgunder Spätlese trocken
14.5%, ♀ till 2006 — 84

2003 Grauer Burgunder
Kabinett trocken
12.5%, ♀ till 2006 — 84

2002 Wollmesheimer Mütterle
Silvaner Kabinett trocken
12%, ♀ till 2006 — 85

2002 Wollmesheimer Mütterle
Weißer Burgunder Kabinett trocken
12.5%, ♀ till 2006 — 85

2003 Wollmesheimer Mütterle
Riesling Spätlese trocken
14%, ♀ till 2007 — 86

2003 Wollmesheimer Mütterle
Spätlese trocken "Trio" Barrique
14%, ♀ till 2008 — 86

2002 Wollmesheimer Mütterle
Weißer Burgunder Spätlese trocken
13.5%, ♀ till 2006 — 87

2002 Wollmesheimer Mütterle
Chardonnay Spätlese trocken
13%, ♀ till 2006 — 88

2002 Wollmesheimer Mütterle
Riesling Spätlese
12%, ♀ till 2006 — 86

2003 Wollmesheimer Mütterle
Riesling Spätlese
9%, ♀ till 2008 — 88

——— Red wines ———

2003 Wollmesheimer Mütterle
Spätburgunder Weißherbst Kabinett
trocken
13%, ♀ till 2006 — 84

2001 St. Laurent trocken
13%, ♀ till 2008 — 84

WEINGUT
JAKOB PFLEGER

Owner: Roland Pfleger
Manager: Roland Pfleger
67273 Herxheim/Berg, Weinstraße 38
Tel. (0 63 53) 74 65, Fax 68 50
e-mail:
WeingutJPfleger@Compuserve.de
*Directions: On B 271 between Bad
Dürkheim and Grünstadt*
Sales: Roland Pfleger
Opening hours: Mon.–Fri. 08:00 to
12:00 hours and 13:00 to 18:00 hours
Sat. 09:00 to 16:00 hours
History: Family-owned since 1720

Vineyard area: 7.5 hectares
Annual production: 60,000 bottles
Top sites: Herxheimer Honigsack and
Kirchenstück, Kallstadter Steinacker,
Freinsheimer Musikantenbuckel
Soil types: Decomposed limestone,
clay, kaolin, sand
Grape varieties: 25% Riesling, 11%
each of Dornfelder and Spätburgun-
der, 9% Grauburgunder, 7% Portugie-
ser, 5% each of Chardonnay, St. Lau-
rent, Merlot, Cabernet Sauvignon and
Scheurebe, 12% other varieties
Average yield: 68 hl/ha
Best vintages: 1998, 1999, 2003
Member: Pfälzer Barrique Forum

This estate was changed from a mixed
farming operation to a pure winery only
in the late Fifties, yet by the Seventies
Pfleger was already one of the winemakers in the Pfalz region receiving the
most awards. He shifted his focus to the
reds and dry wines, and rightly regards
himself as a specialist for barrique-matured wines. In the past we have particularly liked the Dornfelder and the Chardonnay under the "Curator" label. Last
year it were the Rieslings we liked best. We
were able to taste only a small range of
2003 vintage wines, as some of the wines
had not yet been bottled. However, those
that we were able to taste were quite attractive.

2001 Chardonnay
trocken "Curator"
13.3%, ♀ till 2007   85

2003 Herxheimer Honigsack
Riesling Spätlese trocken
13%, ♀ till 2006   86

2003 Herxheimer Honigsack
Chardonnay Spätlese trocken
13%, ♀ till 2007   86

2002 Herxheimer Honigsack
Riesling Spätlese trocken
13%, ♀ till 2006   87

2003 Chardonnay
trocken "Curator"
13.5%, ♀ till 2010   87

2002 Freinsheimer Schwarzes Kreuz
Riesling Spätlese halbtrocken
12.5%, ♀ till 2006   87

2001 Herxheimer Honigsack
Riesling Spätlese
10.5%, ♀ till 2006   85

————— Red wines —————

2001 Spätburgunder
trocken "Curator"
13.5%, ♀ till 2008   84

2003 Freinsheimer Musikantenbuckel
St. Laurent trocken
12.5%, ♀ till 2007   85

2000 Dornfelder
trocken "Curator"
13%, ♀ till 2008   86

2001 St. Laurent
trocken "Curator"
13%, ♀ till 2007   86

The wines: **100** Perfect · **95–99** Outstanding · **90–94** Excellent · **85–89** Very good · **80–84** Good · **75–79** Average

511

WEINGUT ÖKONOMIERAT REBHOLZ

Owner: Hansjörg Rebholz
76833 Siebeldingen, Weinstraße 54
Tel. (0 63 45) 34 39, Fax 79 54
e-mail: wein@oekonomierat-rebholz.de
Internet: www.oekonomierat-rebholz.de
Directions: A 65 to Landau-Nord exit,
then on B 10 to Siebeldingen exit
Sales: Rebholz family by appointment
Opening hours: Mon.–Fri. 09:00 to
12:00 hours and 14:00 to 17:00 hours
Sat. 09:00 to 15:00 hours
History: Winemaking for more than 300
years

Vineyard area: 14 hectares
Annual production: 80,000 bottles
Top sites: Birkweiler Kastanien-
busch, Siebeldinger im Sonnenschein,
Albersweiler Latt
Soil types: Loess-clay, shell limestone,
decomposed sandstone, lower
new red sandstone
Grape varieties: 35% Riesling,
25% Spätburgunder, 25% Weiß- and
Grauburgunder as well as Chardon-
nay, 10% Gewürztraminer and
Muskateller, 5% other varieties
Average yield: 55 hl/ha
Best vintages: 2001, 2002, 2003
Member: VDP

This winery with long tradition has been one of the pioneers of top quality in the Pfalz for three generations. Hansjörg Rebholz, our "Producer of the year 2002" is a highly motivated man, and in the early years of his stewardship continued along the same path set by his father and grandfather: the production of very individualistic, uncompromisingly dry wines, which appear a little rough in their youth, only to develop better than anybody had expected, even those who have followed the fortunes of Rebholz over the years. They simply need enough time to blossom. Rebholz is thus quite right in releasing some of his wines for sale only at a later stage. For some years now, Rebholz has not been content to carry on what he has inherited from his forefathers. He travels internationally on a regular basis to gain experience, and is supported and motivated by his wife Birgit, and is now going gradually further, maintaining the Rebholz style while adding finesse and polish to his wines. Since 1998 he has raised his wines to a level of quality that deserves our admiration. He has worked his way into the top echelons of German producers; this applies not only to the red and white Pinot varieties, which are the strong suits of the southern Pfalz. Even his characteristic dry Rieslings are among the best in Germany – in years with adequate rain those from the Kastanienbusch site, in other vintages those from the Sonnenschein. Specialties such as Gewürztraminer or Muskateller are very good, indeed impressive each year, showing freshness and individual character from Kabinett right up to Auslese level. In every vintage since 1998 his dry wines have been among the best produced in Germany. In the extremely complicated 2000 vintage Rebholz presented masterpieces of unusual character. The white wines of the 2001 vintage surpassed those of 2000. On the 2002 vintage, Rebholz comments: "Certainly not an easy vintage," but is very happy with the results – and so are we. The drouth in 2003 may arguably have resulted in the production of fewer exceptional wines, but there is virtually no loss of quality overall. Yet again, Rebholz has presented us a phalanx of dry 90-point wines, impressively confirming his leading role both in the Pfalz and in Germany as a whole. The 2002 reds are equally magnificent. The barrique-matured Chardonnays are unsurpassed in Germany. As though this were the most natural thing in the world, he has in 2003 also produced a whole series of outstanding botrytis dessert wines, crowned by a really fabulous Trockenbeerenauslese.

2003 Weißer Burgunder
Spätlese trocken
14.5%, ♀ till 2008 **89**

2003 Riesling
Spätlese trocken "Buntsandstein"
13.5%, ♀ till 2008 **89**

2002 Riesling
Spätlese trocken "Rotliegend"
12%, ♀ till 2008 **90**

2001 "π no" Spätlese trocken
13%, ♀ till 2010 **91**

2002 "π no" Spätlese trocken
13%, ♀ till 2007 **91**

2003 Chardonnay trocken
15%, ♀ till 2010 **91**

2003 Siebeldinger im Sonnenschein
Riesling Spätlese trocken
"Großes Gewächs"
13.5%, ♀ till 2009 **91**

2002 Chardonnay Spätlese trocken
13%, ♀ till 2010 **92**

2001 Siebeldinger im Sonnenschein
Riesling Spätlese trocken
"Großes Gewächs"
13%, ♀ till 2008 **92**

2002 Birkweiler Kastanienbusch
Riesling Spätlese trocken
"Großes Gewächs"
12.5%, ♀ till 2008 **92**

2002 Siebeldinger im Sonnenschein
Weißer Burgunder Spätlese trocken
"Großes Gewächs"
13.5%, ♀ till 2007 **92**

2003 Birkweiler Kastanienbusch
Riesling Spätlese trocken
"Großes Gewächs"
13%, ♀ till 2010 **92**

2001 Siebeldinger im Sonnenschein
Weißer Burgunder Spätlese trocken
"Großes Gewächs"
13%, ♀ till 2006 **93**

2003 Siebeldinger im Sonnenschein
Weißer Burgunder Spätlese trocken
"Großes Gewächs"
14%, ♀ till 2010 **93**

2001 Birkweiler Kastanienbusch
Riesling Spätlese trocken
"Großes Gewächs"
13%, ♀ till 2008 **94**

2002 Gewürztraminer Spätlese
12.5%, ♀ till 2008 **90**

2003 Muskateller Spätlese
14.5%, ♀ till 2010 **90**

2003 Siebeldinger im Sonnenschein
Riesling Auslese
11.5%, ♀ till 2012 **90**

2003 Albersweiler Latt
Gewürztraminer Auslese
11.5%, ♀ till 2012 **90**

2002 Albersweiler Latt
Gewürztraminer Auslese
12%, ♀ till 2010 **93**

2003 Godramsteiner Münzberg
Muskateller Beerenauslese
10.5%, ♀ till 2015 **93**

2003 Siebeldinger im Sonnenschein
Riesling Trockenbeerenauslese
8%, ♀ till 2025 **96**

———— Red wines ————

2002 Siebeldinger im Sonnenschein
Spätburgunder Spätlese trocken
"Großes Gewächs"
13%, ♀ till 2010 **90**

2001 Siebeldinger im Sonnenschein
Spätburgunder Spätlese trocken
"Großes Gewächs"
13%, ♀ till 2010 **91**

2001 Siebeldinger im Sonnenschein
Spätburgunder Spätlese trocken
"Großes Gewächs" Gold
13.5%, ♀ till 2010 **92**

2002 Siebeldinger im Sonnenschein
Spätburgunder Spätlese trocken
"Großes Gewächs" Gold
13%, ♀ till 2012 **92**

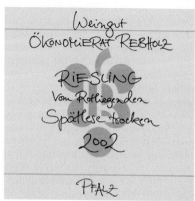

Weingut
ÖKONOMIERAT REBHOLZ

RIESLING
Vom Rotliegenden
Spätlese trocken
2002

PFALZ

The wines: **100** Perfect · **95–99** Outstanding · **90–94** Excellent · **85–89** Very good · **80–84** Good · **75–79** Average

WEINGUT KARL SCHAEFER

Owner: Gerda Lehmeyer
Administrator: Daniel Molitor
Winemaker: Günter Deeters
67098 Bad Dürkheim,
Weinstraße Süd 30
Tel. (0 63 22) 21 38, Fax 87 29
e-mail: info@weingutschaefer.de
Internet: www.weingutschaefer.de
Directions: At southern exit of Bad
Dürkheim in direction of Neustadt
Sales: Messrs. Koob and Sebastian
Opening hours: Mon.–Fri. 08:00 to
12:00 hours and 13:00 to 18:00 hours
Sat. 09:00 to 16:00 hours
History: Family-owned since 1843

Vineyard area: 16.5 hectares
Annual production: 80,000 bottles
Top sites: Dürkheimer Michels-
berg and Spielberg, Wachenheimer
Gerümpel and Fuchsmantel
Soil types: Limestone-rich clay, partly
with sand, marl, basalt
Grape varieties: 86% Riesling,
14% other varieties
Average yield: 65 hl/ha
Best vintages: 2000, 2001, 2003
Member: VDP

Gerda Lehmeyer runs this old-established
estate, and was supported by winemaker
Thorsten Rotthaus, who unfortunately is
no longer available full-time for health
reasons. Instead, Günter Deeters has
come, is busy interpreting the traditional
style of the house in his own manner.
He is the lord of the barrel cellar, which
still remains the heart of the renowned
estate. This cellar also provides the foundation for the typical Riesling style,
which matures slowly. Vintages such as
2000 or 2003 show clearly, what can be
achieved here even under difficult conditions. The new vintage has produced
some individualistic dry Rieslings full of
character, occasionally showing a slight
yeasty note. We look forward with anticipation how this will develop in bottle.

2003 Dürkheimer Spielberg
Riesling Spätlese trocken
13%, ♀ till 2008   87

2003 Wachenheimer Gerümpel
Riesling Spätlese trocken
13%, ♀ till 2008   87

2001 Forster Pechstein
Riesling Spätlese trocken
12%, ♀ till 2007   88

2001 Dürkheimer Michelsberg
Riesling Spätlese trocken
"Großes Gewächs"
12.5%, ♀ till 2006   88

2003 Dürkheimer Spielberg
Riesling Spätlese trocken *
12.5%, ♀ till 2010   89

2003 Dürkheimer Michelsberg
Riesling Spätlese trocken
"Großes Gewächs"
13.5%, ♀ till 2010   89

2002 Dürkheimer Michelsberg
Riesling Spätlese trocken
"Großes Gewächs"
12.5%, ♀ till 2008   90

2003 Forster Pechstein
Riesling Spätlese trocken
"Großes Gewächs"
13.5%, ♀ till 2010   90

2003 Ungsteiner Herrenberg
Riesling Spätlese
13%, ♀ till 2008   88

2003 Wachenheimer Gerümpel
Riesling Auslese
10%, ♀ till 2010   88

2003 Wachenheimer Fuchsmantel
Riesling Beerenauslese
9%, ♀ till 2020   90

Pfalz

WEINGUT KARL SCHAEFER
D-67098 BAD DÜRKHEIM
2002er
Dürkheimer Spielberg
Silvaner Kabinett trocken
Qualitätswein mit Prädikat
A. P. Nr. 5 160 256 07 03
12% vol   0,75 L

WEINHOF SCHEU

Owner: Günter and Klaus Scheu
Winemaker: Klaus Scheu
76889 Schweigen-Rechtenbach,
Hauptstraße 33
Tel. (0 63 42) 72 29, Fax 91 99 75
e-mail: weinhof.Scheu@t-online.de
Directions: A 65, Landau-Süd exit, in direction of Bad Bergzabern, Weißenburg
Sales: Günter and Klaus Scheu
Opening hours: Mon.–Fri. by appointment, Sat. and Sun. 10:00 to 18:00 hours

---

Vineyard area: 12 hectares
Annual production: 80,000 bottles
Top site: Schweigener
Sonnenberg
Soil types: Sandy clay, calcareous
marl and kaolin
Grape varieties: 30% Riesling,
25% Weißburgunder, 12% Grauburgunder, 8% each of Spätburgunder,
Müller-Thurgau and Gewürztraminer,
9% other varieties
Average yield: 72 hl/ha
Best vintages: 2000, 2001, 2003

Günter Scheu established his winery in the mid-Sixties. 30 years later, following completion of his training as a viticultural technician, his son Klaus took over the business. Since the mid-Nineties we have been tasting reliably good wines on a consistent level here, though they were never quite as good as they have turned out in the 2003 vintage. Klaus Scheu presented a solid, serious range of 2000 vintage wines, good for the difficult conditions. The 2001 vintage range was elegant, clean, with typical varietal characteristics. The wines of the 2002 vintage were too uniform and smooth for our taste. The 2003 range is remarkably good, showing a significant improvement, although the one or other dry wine would have even more character if it were less sweet. The tremendous botrytis dessert wines clearly show the signature of Hans-Günther Schwarz, who trained Scheu. We take our hat off to him.

2003 Schweigener Sonnenberg
Riesling Kabinett trocken
12.5%, ♀ till 2006   **85**

2003 Schweigener Sonnenberg
Weißer Burgunder Kabinett trocken
13%, ♀ till 2006   **85**

2002 Schweigener Sonnenberg
Weißer Burgunder trocken "GS"
13.5%, ♀ till 2006   **87**

2003 Schweigener Sonnenberg
Riesling trocken "GS"
14%, ♀ till 2007   **88**

2003 "Philipp Cuntz"
13.5%, ♀ till 2007   **86**

2003 Schweigener Sonnenberg
Scheurebe Auslese
10.5%, ♀ till 2008   **87**

2003 Schweigener Sonnenberg
Weißer Burgunder "GS"
14.5%, ♀ till 2008   **87**

2003 Schweigener Sonnenberg
Grauer Burgunder "GS"
15%, ♀ till 2008   **87**

2003 Schweigener Sonnenberg
Gewürztraminer "GS"
14.5%, ♀ till 2008   **91**

2003 Riesling Beerenauslese
8.5%, ♀ till 2015   **92**

2003 Rieslaner
Trockenbeerenauslese
9%, ♀ till 2020   **95**

---

he wines: **100** Perfect · **95–99** Outstanding · **90–94** Excellent · **85–89** Very good · **80–84** Good · **75–79** Average

515

WEINGUT EGON SCHMITT

Owner: Egon Schmitt family
Winemaker: Jochen Schmitt
67098 Bad Dürkheim, Am Neuberg 6
Tel. (0 63 22) 58 30, Fax 6 88 99
e-mail: info@weingut-egon-schmitt.com
Directions: B 271, Bad Dürkheim-Mitte exit, in direction of A 650; A 61, Bad Dürkheim exit (A 650), Wachenheim exit (turn right), left before town border, follow signs with logo "S"
Sales: Schmitt family
Opening hours: Mon.–Fri. 10:30 to 12:00 and 14:00 to 18:30, Sat. 09:00 to 15:30 hours, Wed. by appointment
Worth a visit: Wine festival on 2nd weekend in August, Jazz brunch with regional Pfalz cuisine

---

Vineyard area: 12.8 hectares
Annual production: 120,000 bottles
Top sites: Dürkheimer Spielberg and Hochbenn, Ungsteiner Herrenberg and Honigsäckel
Soil types: Decomposed limestone with clay, heavy loess, heat-retaining sandy soils, decomposed sandstone
Grape varieties: 30% Riesling, 15% white Pinot varieties, 10% Spätburgunder, 45% other red varieties
Average yield: 81 hl/ha
Best vintages: 2001, 2002, 2003

Jochen Schmitt is most respected for his red wines. His Regent is always one of the best in the country. However, improvements in the whites are becoming ever more evident. The white wines are characterized by typical varietal style and clarity, the substantial red blends are concentrated. The only surprising fact is that we are still waiting for a really good Pinot Noir. The dry whites have been improved since the 2002 vintage, and the "Ausblick" Riesling is again very good in 2003. It is true that Dürkheim sites experienced less heat stress than other areas in 2003, but that alone does not produce such outstanding clear botrytis dessert wines as those we have seen here.

2003 Grauer Burgunder trocken
13.5%, ♀ till 2006   **85**

2002 Dürkheimer Spielberg
Riesling Spätlese trocken
13%, ♀ till 2006   **86**

2003 Ungsteiner Herrenberg
Riesling Spätlese trocken "Ausblick"
13.5%, ♀ till 2008   **87**

2002 Ungsteiner Herrenberg
Riesling Spätlese trocken "Ausblick"
13.5%, ♀ till 2006   **90**

2003 Ungsteiner Herrenberg
Riesling Auslese
9.5%, ♀ till 2010   **89**

2003 Dürkheimer Fronhof
Rieslaner Auslese
8.5%, ♀ till 2008   **92**

2003 Dürkheimer Steinberg
Riesling Beerenauslese
9.5%, ♀ till 2012   **92**

——— Red wines ———

2000 Acolon trocken "Thor"
13.5%, ♀ till 2009   **86**

2001 Spätburgunder trocken "X"
13.5%, ♀ till 2008   **86**

2001 Dornfelder trocken "Taurus"
13.5%, ♀ till 2008   **87**

2001 "Duka XI" trocken
13.5%, ♀ till 2008   **88**

2001 Regent trocken Barrique
13%, ♀ till 2008   **88**

2002 Regent trocken Barrique
13.5%, ♀ till 2008   **88**

BAD DÜRKHEIM
SCHMITT
S
2003
„AUSBLICK"
RIESLING

WEINGUT SCHUMACHER

Owner: Annetrud Franke
Manager: Michael Acker
67273 Herxheim am Berg,
Hauptstraße 40
Tel. (0 63 53) 9 35 90, Fax 93 59 22
e-mail:
weingut-schumacher@t-online.de
Internet: www.schumacher-weine.de
Directions: A 6 Mannheim–Kaiserslautern, Grünstadt exit, on the Weinstraße in direction of Bad Dürkheim
Sales: By appointment
Worth seeing: Historical winery courtyard with 500-year-old vaulted cellar, terraced vineyard with view of Rhine plain

Vineyard area: 11 hectares
Annual production: 65,000 bottles
Top sites: Herxheimer Himmelreich, Kallstadter Saumagen
Soil types: Shell limestone, calcareous marl with loess, sandy clay, decomposed colored sandstone
Grape varieties: 44% Riesling, 21% Spätburgunder, 11% Portugieser, 10% Silvaner, 5% Scheurebe, 3% Weißburgunder, 6% other varieties
Average yield: 46 hl/ha
Best vintages: 2000, 2002, 2003

For many centuries, the monks held their guiding hands over the ancient village of Herxheim, and obtained their own wine supplies from the "small estate," which today is the Schumacher winery. This winery complex is impressive, with its 500-year-old vaulted cellar. However, it is primarily the well-tended Himmelreich vineyard site, completely enclosed by a five meter (18 feet) high wall, that is the heart and foundation of the current operation, which is focusing ever more strongly on Riesling. Michael Acker has been presenting juicy wines for a number of years. Although the 2001 vintage had some good botrytis dessert wines, overall we preferred the 2002 vintage. The 2003 vintage has no real weaknesses, but no really impressive highlights either.

2003 Herxheimer Himmelreich
Riesling Kabinett trocken
12%, ♀ till 2006 — **84**

2003 Herxheimer Himmelreich
Riesling Spätlese trocken
13%, ♀ till 2006 — **84**

2003 Herxheimer Himmelreich
Weißer Burgunder Spätlese trocken
13.5%, ♀ till 2007 — **85**

2003 Herxheimer Himmelreich
Grauer Burgunder Spätlese trocken
14%, ♀ till 2006 — **85**

2003 Herxheimer Himmelreich
Riesling Spätlese trocken "Garten"
13.5%, ♀ till 2007 — **87**

2003 Herxheimer Honigsack
Scheurebe Spätlese
13%, ♀ till 2006 — **87**

———— Red wines ————

2002 Spätburgunder trocken
13.5%, ♀ till 2008 — **86**

2001 Herxheimer Himmelreich
Spätburgunder Spätlese trocken
13.5%, ♀ till 2008 — **87**

2002 Herxheimer Himmelreich
Frühburgunder Spätlese trocken
14%, ♀ till 2007 — **87**

2001 Herxheimer Himmelreich
Frühburgunder Spätlese trocken
14%, ♀ till 2007 — **88**

WEINGUT
SCHUMACHER

2000
Auxerrois

ESTATE BOTTLED · GUTSABFÜLLUNG · PRODUCE OF GERMANY

WEINGUT SIEGRIST

Owner: Siegrist and Schimpf families
Manager: Bruno Schimpf
and Thomas Siegrist
Winemaker: Bruno Schimpf
76829 Leinsweiler, Am Hasensprung 4
Tel. (0 63 45) 13 09, Fax 75 42
e-mail: wein@weingut-siegrist.de
Internet: www.weingut-siegrist.de
*Directions: A 65, Landau-Nord exit, via
the B 10, "Deutsche Weinstraße" exit in
Leinsweiler*
Sales: Siegrist and Schimpf families
Opening hours: Mon.–Fri. 08:00 to
12:00 and 13:30 to 18:00, Sat. 09:00 to
16:00 hours, and by appointment
Restaurant: In restored national heritage tithing cellar (built 1555); daily from
17:00 hours, Sat. and Sun. from 12:00
hours, closed Tue., Tel. (0 63 45) 30 75

Vineyard area: 14.5 hectares
Annual production: 90,000 bottles
Top site: Leinsweiler Sonnenberg
Soil types: Calcareous marl, loess-clay, decomposed sandstone
Grape varieties: 25% Riesling,
17% Spätburgunder, 10% each of
Weißburgunder, Chardonnay, Dornfelder, 8% Silvaner, 5% each of Cabernet Sauvignon and Merlot, 3% Grauburgunder, 7% other varieties
Average yield: 70 hl/ha
Best vintages: 2000, 2001, 2002
Member: VDP,
Deutsches Barrique Forum

Thomas Siegrist is best known for his barrique-matured red wines. Son-in-law Bruno Schimpf has had a new, modern cellar at his disposal since 2002. The red wines of the 2001 vintage were the best we have ever tasted here. The wines of the 2002 vintage did not reach this high standard. The 2003 vintage presents a mixed bag of white wines, good fruity Rieslings stand next to rather hard Pinot wines. The 2002 Chardonnay is made in modern New World style and has exotic aromas, it is the highlight of the range.

2002 Wollmesheimer
Weißer Burgunder Spätlese trocken
13%, ♀ till 2006 — **85**

2003 Riesling Spätlese trocken
12.5%, ♀ till 2008 — **86**

2002 Riesling Spätlese trocken
12.5%, ♀ till 2006 — **87**

2002 Chardonnay Spätlese trocken
13%, ♀ till 2007 — **87**

2003 Leinsweiler Sonnenberg
Riesling Spätlese trocken
"Großes Gewächs"
13%, ♀ till 2008 — **87**

2001 Chardonnay
Spätlese trocken "sur lie"
13.5%, ♀ till 2008 — **89**

2002 Chardonnay
Spätlese trocken "sur lie"
13%, ♀ till 2008 — **89**

2002 Leinsweiler Sonnenberg
Riesling Spätlese trocken
"Großes Gewächs"
12.5%, ♀ till 2008 — **91**

—————— Red wines ——————

2001 "Bergacker" trocken
13%, ♀ till 2008 — **87**

**2001 Dornfelder trocken ** ∗∗
12.5%, ♀ till 2008 — **88**

**2001 Spätburgunder trocken ** ∗∗
12.5%, ♀ till 2007 — **88**

2001 Cabernet Sauvignon trocken
13%, ♀ till 2008 — **88**

**2002 Spätburgunder trocken ** ∗∗∗
13%, ♀ till 2010 — **88**

**2001 Spätburgunder trocken ** ∗∗∗
13%, ♀ till 2010 — **90**

WEINGUT SIEGRIST
LEINSWEILER · SÜDLICHE WEINSTRASSE
PFALZ
2001 WEISSBURGUNDER
SPÄTLESE TROCKEN
QUALITÄTSWEIN MIT PRÄDIKAT · GUTSABFÜLLUNG
A.P.NR. 5 081 045 05 02 · PRODUCE OF GERMANY
WEINGUT SIEGRIST · D-76829 LEINSWEILER
750 ml — alc. 13% vol

The estates: ⚜⚜⚜⚜⚜ World's finest · ⚜⚜⚜⚜ Germany's best · ⚜⚜⚜ Very good · ⚜⚜ Good · ⚜ Reliabl

Pfalz

WEINGUT SIENER

Owner and manager:
Peter and Sieglinde Siener
Winemaker: Peter Siener
76831 Birkweiler, Weinstraße 31
Tel. (0 63 45) 35 39, Fax 91 91 00
e-mail: weingut-siener@t-online.de
Directions: A 65, Landau-Nord exit, B 10
in direction of Annweiler, Birkweiler exit
Sales: Peter and Sieglinde Siener
Opening hours: Mon.–Fri. 08:00 to
12:00 hours and 14:00 to 18:00 hours
Sat. 09:00 to 16:00 hours
Worth seeing: Barrique cellar

Vineyard area: 8.5 hectares
Annual production: 60,000 bottles
Top sites: Birkweiler Kastanien-
busch and Mandelberg, Leinsweiler
Sonnenberg
Soil types: Red marl, sandstone,
calcareous marl, loess-clay
Grape varieties: 30% Riesling, 22%
Spätburgunder, 15% Grauburgunder,
10% Weißburgunder, 7% Silvaner, 5%
Müller-Thurgau, 11% other varieties
Average yield: 65 hl/ha
Best vintages: 2001, 2002, 2003

Peter Siener is now 30 years old, and is a member of a group of young winemakers in the Southern Pfalz that meet to exchange ideas and experiences, and organize mutual events under the heading of "Südpfalz Connexion." The son of this long-established winery in Birkweiler is in charge of both the vineyards and cellar, and produces a thoroughly convincing range of white wines, and each year there are some outstanding wines in the range. The 2002 collection provided more evidence that he is aiming for the stars. We liked practically all the whites of the 2003 vintage, the Riesling Spätlese "Rotschiefer" (red slate) is outstanding. The reds presented this year have good substance, but we feel they lack a little stability.

2003 Birkweiler Kastanienbusch
Riesling Spätlese trocken
13%, ♀ till 2007　　　　85

2003 Birkweiler Mandelberg
Weißer Burgunder Spätlese trocken
"Kalkgestein"
14%, ♀ till 2007　　　　85

2002 Birkweiler Kastanienbusch
Riesling Spätlese trocken
13%, ♀ till 2007　　　　87

2002 Birkweiler Mandelberg
Weißer Burgunder Spätlese trocken – 23 –
13.5%, ♀ till 2007　　　　87

2003 Birkweiler Kastanienbusch
Riesling Spätlese trocken "Rotschiefer"
13.5%, ♀ till 2008　　　　88

2001 Birkweiler Kastanienbusch
Riesling trocken "Rotschiefer"
11.5%, ♀ till 2008　　　　89

2003 Leinsweiler Sonnenberg
Riesling Auslese halbtrocken
13.5%, ♀ till 2008　　　　87

2003 Birkweiler Mandelberg
Chardonnay "S"
13%, ♀ till 2008　　　　89

———— Red wines ————

2003 Birkweiler Mandelberg
St. Laurent trocken
13%, ♀ till 2006　　　　84

2002 Birkweiler Kastanienbusch
Spätburgunder trocken "No. 1"
14%, ♀ till 2007　　　　84

he wines: **100** Perfect · **95–99** Outstanding · **90–94** Excellent · **85–89** Very good · **80–84** Good · **75–79** Average

519

WEINGUT
HEINRICH SPINDLER

Owner: Hans Spindler
Winemaker: Berthold Klöckner
67147 Forst, Weinstraße 44
Tel. (0 63 26) 2 80, Fax 78 77
e-mail: hch.spindler@t-online.de
Internet: www.spindler-weine.de
Directions: Via B 271 new coming from
Bad Dürkheim or Neustadt
Sales: Hans and Johanna Spindler
Opening hours: Mon.–Sat. 09:00 to
18:00 hours and by appointment
Restaurant: Hot meals
Tue. to Sat. from 11:30 to 21:30 hours
Specialties: Regional Pfalz cuisine,
seasonal (asparagus, venison)
History: Winemaking in family since 1620
Worth seeing: Vaulted cellar

Vineyard area: 13.5 hectares
Annual production: 100,000 bottles
Top sites: Forster Pechstein,
Freundstück, Kirchenstück,
Ungeheuer and Jesuitengarten,
Ruppertsberger Reiterpfad
Soil types: Sandy clay with basalt
and limestone
Grape varieties: 86% Riesling, 8%
Spätburgunder, 3% Weißburgunder,
2% Dornfelder, 1% Gewürztraminer
Average yield: 60 hl/ha
Best vintages: 2000, 2001, 2002

This long-established Riesling specialist
in the center of Forst was for many years
known only for its cosy restaurant and
wine bar. However, a few years ago Hans
Spindler thoroughly modernized his cellar, and now produces more modern, appealing wines. The advantages provided
by the top Forst sites are evident since the
2000 vintage. 2002 was another step in
the right direction, presenting above-
average, nicely contoured Riesling wines.
The hot 2003 vintage cannot quite live up
to this standard – the wines remain full-
bodied, but the damage the drouth did to
the fruit is unmistakable.

2003 Forster Ungeheuer
Riesling Kabinett trocken
12%, ♀ till 2006 — 83

2003 Riesling
Kabinett trocken "Philosophie"
12%, ♀ till 2006 — 83

2003 Forster Freundstück
Riesling Spätlese trocken
12%, ♀ till 2007 — 84

2003 Forster Jesuitengarten
Riesling Spätlese trocken
12.5%, ♀ till 2008 — 85

2003 Forster Kirchenstück
Riesling Spätlese trocken
12.5%, ♀ till 2007 — 86

2002 Forster Pechstein
Riesling Spätlese trocken
13%, ♀ till 2008 — 87

2002 Forster Ungeheuer
Riesling Spätlese trocken
13%, ♀ till 2007 — 88

2002 Forster Jesuitengarten
Riesling Spätlese trocken
12.5%, ♀ till 2007 — 88

2002 Forster Kirchenstück
Riesling Spätlese trocken
12.5%, ♀ till 2008 — 88

2003 Forster Pechstein
Riesling Auslese
8.5%, ♀ till 2012 — 87

2003 Forster Stift
Gewürztraminer Auslese
10%, ♀ till 2010 — 87

2001 Forster Ungeheuer
Riesling Auslese
10.5%, ♀ till 2008 — 90

WEINGUT Heinrich Spindler
Familienbesitz seit 1620

D-67147 Forst an der Weinstraße
2003
Forster Ungeheuer
Riesling Spätlese trocken

Qualitätswein mit Prädikat · L.A.P.Nr. 5 112 089 18 04
Gutsabfüllung
750 ml   PFALZ   alc. 12,5%vol

WEINGUT PETER STOLLEIS – CARL-THEODOR-HOF

Owner: Peter Stolleis
Administrator: Thomas Reuther
Winemaker: Elke Vetter
67435 Gimmeldingen-Mußbach,
Kurpfalzstraße 91–99
Tel. (0 63 21) 6 60 71, Fax 6 03 48
e-mail: weingut.p.stolleis@t-online.de
Internet: www.stolleis.de
Directions: Via the A 65 to Neustadt/W., in Mußbach continue in direction of Gimmeldingen into the Kurpfalzstraße
Sales: Peter Stolleis
Opening hours: Mon.–Fri. 08:00 to 17:00, Sat. 09:00 to 12:00 hours, and by appointment
Worth seeing: Sculptures dating to prince elector's time, largest vaulted cellar (1709), gardens with Southern flair

---

Vineyard area: 21 hectares
Annual production: 170,000 bottles
Top sites: Königsbacher Ölberg, Gimmeldinger Mandelgarten and Biengarten, Mußbacher Eselshaut
Soil types: Limestone-rich clay, decomposed sandstone
Grape varieties: 55% Riesling, 8% Spätburgunder, 6% Portugieser, 3% each of Rieslaner, Grauburgunder and Dornfelder, 22% other varieties
Average yield: 82 hl/ha
Best vintages: 2001, 2002

This is quite a large family operation, located in the attractive Karl-Theodor-Hof estate of the former prince elector. The family owns good vineyard sites between Deidesheim and Haardt. A positive trend was already evident in the 2001 vintage. The same applied in 2002, with juicy white Pinot varietal wines and hearty Rieslings in the Pfalz style. However, the team here obviously did not cope well with the tremendous drouth in 2003, which caused particularly severe damage in the area between Neustadt and Forst. The result is a range of unimpressive wines, lacking concentration.

2003 Gimmeldinger Mandelgarten
Riesling Kabinett trocken
12%, ♀ till 2006   83

2002 Gimmeldinger Mandelgarten
Riesling Spätlese trocken
12%, ♀ till 2006   84

2003 Ruppertsberger Nußbien
Riesling Kabinett trocken
12%, ♀ till 2006   84

2003 Gimmeldinger Mandelgarten
Riesling Spätlese trocken
12%, ♀ till 2007   84

2002 Ruppertsberger Nußbien
Riesling Kabinett trocken
12%, ♀ till 2006   85

2003 Chardonnay trocken
13%, ♀ till 2006   85

2003 Gimmeldinger Biengarten
Riesling Kabinett halbtrocken
11.5%, ♀ till 2006   84

2003 Königsbacher Ölberg
Riesling Spätlese
12%, ♀ till 2007   85

2002 Ruppertsberger Nußbien
Riesling Eiswein
9.5%, ♀ till 2015   89

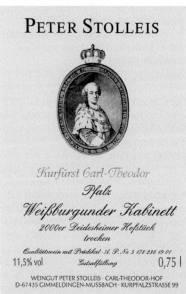

PETER STOLLEIS

Kurfürst Carl-Theodor
Pfalz
Weißburgunder Kabinett
2000er Deidesheimer Hofstück
trocken
Qualitätswein mit Prädikat · A. P. Nr. 5 178 238 19 01
11,5% vol   *Gutsabfüllung*   0,75 l
WEINGUT PETER STOLLEIS · CARL-THEODOR-HOF
D-67435 GIMMELDINGEN-MUSSBACH · KURPFALZSTRASSE 99

The wines: **100** Perfect · **95–99** Outstanding · **90–94** Excellent · **85–89** Very good · **80–84** Good · **75–79** Average

WEINGUT ULLRICHSHOF – FAMILIE FAUBEL

Owner: Faubel family
Winemaker: Gerd Faubel
67487 Maikammer, Marktstraße 86
Tel. (0 63 21) 50 48, Fax 5 73 88
e-mail: info@ullrichshof-faubel.de
Internet: www.ullrichshof-faubel.de
Directions: A 65, Edenkoben exit, in direction of Maikammer
Sales: Christa and Silke Faubel
Opening hours: Mon.–Fri. 08:00 to 12:00 and 13:00 to 18:00, Sat. 08:00 to 12:00 and 13:00 to 16:00 hours, and by appointment
Guest rooms: In country-house style
History: Winemaking since 1635
Worth seeing: Coach house, estate buildings of 1904, 100-year-old gingko tree

---

Vineyard area: 22 hectares
Annual production: 210,000 bottles
Top sites: Maikammer Heiligenberg and Kirchenstück, Haardter Herrenletten and Herzog
Soil types: Clay-loess, sandstone, limestone
Grape varieties: 25% Riesling, 30% white Pinot varieties, 15% Spätburgunder, 10% each of Dornfelder and Sankt Laurent, 10% other varieties
Average yield: 73 hl/ha
Best vintages: 2001, 2002, 2003

The Ullrichshof complex breathes Mediterranean flair in the summer months. The family leaves no doubt about their ambition to join the top ranks of Pfalz producers, and their efforts have met with some success. The 2000 vintage gave Gerd Faubel an opportunity to demonstrate how good wines can be made under difficult circumstances. We first awarded the third bunch of grapes for the 2001 vintage. The 2003 vintage, too, was convincing, the wines are accessible, round, but certainly concentrated. This applies to the white Pinot varieties as well as to the dry Rieslings and to the oustanding fruity sweet Gewürztraminer.

2002 Maikammer Heiligenberg
Weißer Burgunder Spätlese trocken
13.5%, ♀ till 2006   **87**

2003 Maikammer Heiligenberg
Riesling Spätlese trocken
13.5%, ♀ till 2007   **87**

2002 Gimmeldinger Kapellenberg
Riesling Spätlese trocken
12%, ♀ till 2006   **88**

2002 Maikammer Heiligenberg
Riesling Spätlese trocken
12.5%, ♀ till 2007   **88**

2003 Maikammer Kapellenberg
Silvaner Spätlese trocken
13.5%, ♀ till 2007   **88**

2003 Maikammer Kirchenstück
Weißer Burgunder Spätlese trocken
14%, ♀ till 2006   **88**

2002 Maikammer Kapellenberg
Weißer Burgunder Spätlese trocken
13.5%, ♀ till 2006   **89**

2002 Maikammer Heiligenberg
Gewürztraminer Spätlese trocken
13.5%, ♀ till 2006   **90**

2003 Maikammer Heiligenberg
Riesling Auslese trocken
14%, ♀ till 2009   **90**

2003 Maikammer Kapellenberg
Weißer Burgunder Spätlese trocken
13%, ♀ till 2009   **90**

2003 Maikammer Heiligenberg
Weißer Burgunder Spätlese
14.5%, ♀ till 2008   **87**

2003 Maikammer Heiligenberg
Gewürztraminer Spätlese
11.5%, ♀ till 2010   **90**

WEINGUT
ULLRICHSHOF
FAMILIE FAUBEL

2003
GEWÜRZTRAMINER
MAIKAMMER HEILIGENBERG

PFALZ

The estates: ♛♛♛♛♛ World's finest · ♛♛♛♛ Germany's best · ♛♛♛ Very good · ♛♛ Good · ♛ Reliable

VIER JAHRESZEITEN WINZER EG

Executive chairman:
Curt-Christian Stoffel
Manager and head of enology:
Walter Brahner
67098 Bad Dürkheim, Limburgstraße 8
Tel. (0 63 22) 9 49 00, Fax 94 90 37
e-mail: info@vj-wein.de
Internet: www.vj-wein.de
Directions: A 61, Kreuz Ludwigshafen
exit, via A 650, in direction of Dürkheim
Sales: Rüdiger Damian
Opening hours: Mon.–Fri. 09:00 to
17:00 hours, Sat. 08:30 to 12:30 hours
History: Founded 1900
Worth seeing: Barrel cellar, modern
grape-processing facility

Vineyard area: 360 hectares
Number of members: 180
Annual production: 3.2 mill. bottles
Top sites: Not mentioned
Soil types: Sandy clay, loess
Grape varieties: 35% Riesling, 18%
Portugieser, 8% Spätburgunder, 6%
Dornfelder, 5% Weißburgunder, 4%
each of Gewürztraminer, Silvaner and
Müller-Thurgau, 16% other varieties
Average yield: 80 hl/ha
Best vintages: 2000, 2001
Member: Pfälzer Barrique Forum

The co-operative in Dürkheim is equally
adept at making white or red wines, and
for some time now this winery has been
producing by far the best wines of any co-
operative in the Pfalz. As with most co-
operatives, the quality can vary quite a bit
from one wine to the next. That comes as
no surprise, considering the number of
different bottlings runs to 150 wines each
year. In terms of the 2001 vintage, we
rated the white wines highest, while things
went the other way in 2002. For the 2003
wines we awarded ratings ranging from
75 to 91 points, the highlights being surprisingly strong botrytis dessert wines as
well as the dry Riesling "Nr. 1," made in
the style of a First Growth.

2003 Weißer Burgunder &
Chardonnay trocken
14.5%, ♀ till 2007 — **85**

2002 Dürkheimer Fronhof
Riesling Auslese
11.5%, ♀ till 2007 — **86**

2003 Riesling "Nr. 1"
12%, ♀ till 2007 — **87**

2003 Forster Schnepfenpflug
Ortega Trockenbeerenauslese
9.5%, ♀ till 2020 — **88**

2003 Dürkheimer Hochmess
Scheurebe Eiswein
8.5%, ♀ till 2015 — **90**

2003 Dürkheimer Schenkenböhl
Huxelrebe Trockenbeerenauslese
10%, ♀ till 2025 — **91**

——————— Red wines ———————

2003 Spätburgunder
Spätlese trocken
13.5%, ♀ till 2007 — **81**

2002 Dürkheimer
Spätburgunder Spätlese trocken "Nr. 1"
13.5%, ♀ till 2008 — **84**

2001 Dürkheimer Feuerberg
St. Laurent trocken
13%, ♀ till 2008 — **86**

2002 Spätburgunder & Cabernet
& Merlot trocken "Nr. 1"
13.5%, ♀ till 2008 — **87**

The wines: **100** Perfect · **95–99** Outstanding · **90–94** Excellent · **85–89** Very good · **80–84** Good · **75–79** Average

523

WEINGUT
WAGECK-PFAFFMANN

Owner: Pfaffmann family
Manager: Gunter Pfaffmann
Winemaker: Frank Pfaffmann
67281 Bissersheim, Luitpoldstraße 1
Tel. (0 63 59) 22 16, Fax 8 66 68
e-mail: weingut@wageck-pfaffmann.de
Internet: www.wageck-pfaffmann.de
Directions: A 6, Grünstadt exit, via Kirch-
heim to Bissersheim, right at town exit
Sales: Thomas Pfaffmann
Opening hours: Mon.–Sat. 08:00 to
12:00 hours and 13:00 to 18:00 hours
Sun. 10:00 to 12:00 hours
and by appointment
Worth seeing: New barrique cellar

Vineyard area: 42 hectares
Annual production: 300,000 bottles
Top sites: Bissersheimer Gold-
berg, Großkarlbacher Burgweg
Soil types: Limestone-rich kaolin-marl,
loess-clay with gravel and sand
Grape varieties: 20% Riesling,
16% Portugieser, 13% Dornfelder,
7% Chardonnay, 6% each of Spät-
burgunder and Müller-Thurgau,
32% other varieties
Average yield: 95 hl/ha
Best vintages: 2002, 2003
Member: Pfälzer Barrique Forum

Don't be misled by the high average
yields recorded at this family winery, located on the most northerly point of the
Deutsche Weinstraße route. The wines
designated with two stars have yields of
only around 60 hectoliters per hectare,
and those with three stars only 40. The
fact that quality here has stabilized at a
high level is worth rewarding with a first
bunch of grapes. In spite of the difficult
vintage 2003, some good dry Rieslings
have been made here. The sweet Riesling
Auslese is brilliant and clear. The reds
have gained in structure. All these improvements have particularly benefited
the international varieties: The Cabernet
blends as well as the Merlot are excellent.

2003 Großkarlbacher Burgweg
Riesling trocken **
12.5%, ♀ till 2006   **82**

2001 Bissersheimer Goldberg
Chardonnay trocken *** Barrique
14%, ♀ till 2007   **84**

2002 Bissersheimer Goldberg
Riesling trocken ***
13%, ♀ till 2007   **85**

2002 Bissersheimer Goldberg
Chardonnay trocken *** Barrique
14.5%, ♀ till 2008   **86**

2003 Bissersheimer Goldberg
Riesling Auslese ***
8%, ♀ till 2010   **89**

——————— Red wines ———————

2002 Großkarlbacher Osterberg
Spätburgunder trocken ***
14%, ♀ till 2008   **83**

2001 Großkarlbacher Burgweg
Dornfelder trocken *** Barrique
14%, ♀ till 2008   **84**

2002 "Cuvée W" trocken
14%, ♀ till 2010   **86**

2002 Cabernet Sauvignon
trocken ***
14%, ♀ till 2008   **86**

2002 Merlot trocken *
14%, ♀ till 2008   **86**

Weingut
Wageck Pfaffmann

2003
GEWÜRZTRAMINER
TROCKEN
★★★

PFALZ

The estates: ✙✙✙✙✙ World's finest · ✙✙✙✙ Germany's best · ✙✙✙ Very good · ✙✙ Good · ✙ Reliable

WEINGUT WEEGMÜLLER

Owner: Stefanie Weegmüller-Scherr
Administrator: Richard Scherr
Winemaker: Stefanie Weegmüller-Scherr
67433 Neustadt-Haardt, Mandelring 23
Tel. (0 63 21) 8 37 72, Fax 48 07 72
e-mail: weegmueller-weine@t-online.de
Internet: www.weegmueller-weine.de
*Directions: A 65, Neustadt-Nord
(Lambrecht) exit, signs for Haardt*
Sales: Stefanie Weegmüller-Scherr
and Gabriele Weegmüller
Opening hours: Mon.–Fri. 08:00 to
12:30 and 13:30 to 17:00, Sat. 09:00 to
14:00 hours, and by appointment

Vineyard area: 15.2 hectares
Annual production: 110,000 bottles
Top sites: Haardter Herrenletten,
Herzog and Bürgergarten,
Mußbacher Eselshaut
Soil types: Sandy clay, marl with kaolin
Grape varieties: 60% Riesling,
6% Scheurebe, 5% each of Grauer
Burgunder, Weißer Burgunder, Ge-
würztraminer, Kerner and Dornfelder,
9% other varieties
Average yield: 70 hl/ha
Best vintages: 1998, 2002, 2003

This winery has been in existence since
1685, and Stefanie Weegmüller, together
with her husband Richard Scherr is the
12th generation to be in charge here. She
was only 25 when she took on the responsibility in the cellar. Following on a few
somewhat variable vintages, the couple
managed to improve a lot of things with
the 2002 vintage, and they got it all right
with the 2003 vintage. What we have
seen and tasted here is among the best
produced in the region. One of their decisions was to forego their annual vacation
in the hot, dry summer of 2003, and to ir-
rigate the vineyards instead. They have
been rewarded with brilliant, fruit-dominated wines, which have also been vinified in the cellar with just the right feel for
the character of each wine. An impressive
performance!

2003 Weißer Burgunder trocken
12.5%, ♀ till 2006 — **84**

2003 Haardter Herrenletten
Grauer Burgunder Spätlese trocken
13.5%, ♀ till 2007 — **85**

2003 Silvaner trocken
12.5%, ♀ till 2006 — **86**

2003 Haardter Mandelring
Riesling Kabinett trocken
12%, ♀ till 2007 — **87**

2003 Gimmeldinger Schlössel
Riesling Kabinett trocken
11.5%, ♀ till 2007 — **87**

2003 Haardter Herrenletten
Riesling Kabinett trocken
12.5%, ♀ till 2007 — **88**

2003 Haardter Herrenletten
Riesling Spätlese trocken "Alte Reben"
13%, ♀ till 2008 — **89**

2003 Haardter Bürgergarten
Gewürztraminer Spätlese trocken
"Alte Reben"
14.5%, ♀ till 2008 — **94**

2003 Haardter Bürgergarten
Riesling Spätlese
9.5%, ♀ till 2008 — **88**

2003 Haardter Mandelring
Scheurebe Auslese
9.5%, ♀ till 2010 — **89**

2002 Haardter Mandelring
Scheurebe Beerenauslese
8.5%, ♀ till 2020 — **94**

The wines: **100** Perfect · **95–99** Outstanding · **90–94** Excellent · **85–89** Very good · **80–84** Good · **75–79** Average

525

WEINGUT WEGNER

Owner and manager: Joachim Wegner
67098 Bad Dürkheim, Am Neuberg 4
Tel. (0 63 22) 98 93 27, Fax 98 93 28
e-mail: wegnerjf@yahoo.com
Internet: www.weingut-wegner.de
Directions: A 650, in direction of Bad
Dürkheim, in direction of "Am Neu-
berg," keep left
Sales: Joachim Wegner
Opening hours: Mon.–Fri. 09:00 to
12:00 hours and 13:00 to 19:00 hours
Sat. 09:00 to 17:00 hours
and by appointment
Worth a visit: Wine festival in court-
yard on 3rd weekend in August

Vineyard area: 8.5 hectares
Annual production: 80,000 bottles
Top sites: Ungsteiner Herren-
berg, Dürkheimer Fronhof
Soil types: Kaolin, clay with high pro-
portion of limestone, loess, sandy clay
Grape varieties: 35% Riesling,
20% Spätburgunder, 10% Dornfelder,
5% each of Kerner, Gewürztraminer,
Cabernet Sauvignon and Sauvignon
Blanc, 15% other varieties
Average yield: 85 hl/ha
Best vintages: 2002, 2003
Member: Pfälzer Barrique Forum

The father Karl Wegner was a member of
the local co-operative winery until 1978,
then he decided to go off on his own, and
moved slowly from selling bulk wine to
marketing his own bottled wine. Son Joachim Wegner has been working in the
family business since 1999, and took over
responsibility in 2003. Although we believe the winery is being a little optimistic
in its pricing, particularly for the reds, we
were sufficiently impressed with the previous vintage's wines to award a first
bunch of grapes. The 2003 vintage was
a mixed bag, with some less successful
wines, but also some very good ones,
such as the Chardonnay or the 2001 Merlot, or the modern, fresh, inexpensive
Riesling in liter bottles.

2003 Dürkheimer Feuerberg
Gewürztraminer Spätlese trocken
13.5%, ♀ till 2006   84

2002 Dürkheimer Schenkenböhl
Sauvignon Blanc Spätlese trocken
13%, ♀ till 2006   85

2002 Dürkheimer Feuerberg
Chardonnay Spätlese trocken
13%, ♀ till 2006   85

2003 Ungsteiner Herrenberg
Riesling Spätlese trocken
13.5%, ♀ till 2007   85

2001 Dürkheimer Schenkenböhl
Chardonnay Spätlese trocken
14%, ♀ till 2007   86

2003 Dürkheimer
Chardonnay Spätlese trocken
13%, ♀ till 2006   88

2003 Dürkheimer Feuerberg
Gewürztraminer Spätlese
11%, ♀ till 2006   85

2001 Dürkheimer Schenkenböhl
Eiswein "Aureus" Barrique
13.5%, ♀ till 2010   93

————— Red wines —————

2001 Dürkheimer Schenkenböhl
Spätburgunder trocken Barrique
13.5%, ♀ till 2008   85

2000 Dürkheimer Feuerberg
trocken "Cuvée Philipp"
13.5%, ♀ till 2008   85

2001 Dürkheimer Feuerberg
Merlot trocken Barrique
13.5%, ♀ till 2008   87

WEINGUT DR. WEHRHEIM

Owner and manager:
Karl-Heinz Wehrheim
Administrator: Patrick Christ
76831 Birkweiler, Weinstraße 8
Tel. (0 63 45) 35 42, Fax 38 69
e-mail: dr.wehrheim@t-online.de
Internet: www.weingut-wehrheim.de
Directions: A 65, Landau-Nord exit, via the B 10, Birkweiler exit
Sales: Wehrheim family
Opening hours: Mon.–Fri. 09:00 to 12:00 hours and 14:00 to 18:00 hours Sat. 10:00 to 16:00 hours, by appointment
Restaurant: 3. and 4. weekend in August and 1. weekend in September, Thur.–Sat. from 17:00, Sun. from 11:00 hours

---

Vineyard area: 12.5 hectares
Annual production: 80,000 bottles
Top sites: Birkweiler Kastanienbusch and Mandelberg
Soil types: Sandstone, porphyry, limestone-rich marl, sandy clay, shell limestone, lower new red sandstone
Grape varieties: 40% Riesling, 20% Weißburgunder, 12% Spätburgunder, 10% Silvaner, 8% Sankt Laurent, 10% other varieties
Average yield: 63 hl/ha
Best vintages: 2001, 2002, 2003
Member: VDP

The Wehrheim family winery has for a long time been one of the most respected producers of the Southern Weinstraße. A family atmosphere, and an accommodating attitude towards guests as well as attractive surroundings have always been part of the pleasant ambience of this family operation, in which currently three generations are at work. Dr. Heinz Wehrheim is still a pillar of daily business, even though he is over 80 years old. His son Karl-Heinz Wehrheim has been in charge of the business since 1990, is also busy on many other fronts, such as in the Pfalz VDP, as member of the "Five Friends" or in regional wine marketing. In spite of all these activities, he never forgets his responsibilities at home. He has always worked diligently at improving the quality of his wines, and invested in significant improvements in his cellar technology a few years ago, thus providing better facilities for the production of his top-quality white wines. The Pinot Noir, white Pinot varieties and Silvaner wines produced by Wehrheim have for a considerable time been acknowledged as being among the best in the Pfalz. The Rieslings have shown the most significant improvements since the 2000 vintage. The breakthrough for red wines came some time earlier. These red wines are characterized by balanced fruit and a fortuitous combination of length and harmony. In recent years, Wehrheim has come to focus strongly on the concept of terroir. Both the Rieslings and the Pinot varieties carry the soil type on the label, and he achieves extremely precise typical notes. The enormous ability at work here is shown in the 2000 vintage, as tremendous work effort went into this difficult vintage, with gratifying results, as quality was practically as good as in preceding vintages. In particular, the 2000 Spätburgunder (Pinot Noir): a prime example for outstanding work in a difficult vintage. The 2001 vintage presented by Karl-Heinz Wehrheim earned him the title of "Rising star of the year," and took him to the inner circle of top Pfalz producers. This high praise was fully vindicated by his 2002 vintage, and again by his 2003 range: In spite of the difficulties presented by the drouth, there is hardly any impact on the quality produced. The white Pinot wines, including the "Buntsandstein" Weißburgunder (colored sandstone Pinot Blanc) and "Keuper" (red marl) Chardonnay, which slot in below the magnificent First Growth are among the best wines in the Pfalz. Wehrheim also realized that the conditions were right for the production of excellent botrytis dessert wines and aromatic varieties, and produced outstanding Gewürztraminer and Muskateller wines as well as a superb Riesling Trockenbeerenauslese.

The wines: **100** Perfect · **95–99** Outstanding · **90–94** Excellent · **85–89** Very good · **80–84** Good · **75–79** Average

2003 Riesling
Spätlese trocken "Rotliegend"
12%, ♀ till 2008   87

2003 Weißer Burgunder
Spätlese trocken "Buntsandstein"
14%, ♀ till 2008   88

2002 Grauer Burgunder
Spätlese trocken "Keuper"
13.5%, ♀ till 2006   89

2002 Chardonnay
Spätlese trocken "Keuper"
13%, ♀ till 2008   89

2003 Chardonnay
Spätlese trocken "Keuper"
13.8%, ♀ till 2008   89

2002 Weißer Burgunder
Spätlese trocken "Buntsandstein"
13%, ♀ till 2006   90

2002 Birkweiler Kastanienbusch
Riesling Spätlese trocken
"Großes Gewächs"
13%, ♀ till 2008   90

2003 Birkweiler Kastanienbusch
Riesling trocken "Großes Gewächs"
13%, ♀ till 2010   90

2001 Birkweiler Kastanienbusch
Riesling trocken "Großes Gewächs"
13.5%, ♀ till 2008   91

2001 Grauer Burgunder
Spätlese trocken "Keuper"
14.5%, ♀ till 2006   91

2002 Weißer Burgunder
Spätlese trocken "Muschelkalk"
13.5%, ♀ till 2007   91

2001 Chardonnay
Spätlese trocken Barrique "Keuper"
14%, ♀ till 2006   92

2001 Birkweiler Mandelberg
Weißer Burgunder trocken
"Großes Gewächs"
14%, ♀ till 2006   92

2003 Birkweiler Mandelberg
Weißer Burgunder Spätlese trocken
"Großes Gewächs"
15%, ♀ till 2008   92

2002 Birkweiler Mandelberg
Weißer Burgunder Spätlese trocken
"Großes Gewächs"
14%, ♀ till 2007   93

2002 Riesling Spätlese
11%, ♀ till 2008   88

2003 Muskateller
Auslese "Keuper"
11.5%, ♀ till 2008   91

2001 Birkweiler Kastanienbusch
Riesling Eiswein
9.5%, ♀ 2006 till 2015   92

2003 Gewürztraminer
Auslese "Keuper"
11%, ♀ till 2008   92

2003 Birkweiler Kastanienbusch
Riesling Trockenbeerenauslese
7%, ♀ till 2025   93

———— Red wines ————

2001 "Cuvée Carolus" trocken
13%, ♀ till 2008   88

2001 Birkweiler Kastanienbusch
Spätburgunder Spätlese trocken
"Großes Gewächs"
13%, ♀ till 2008   91

2002 Birkweiler Kastanienbusch
Spätburgunder Spätlese trocken
"Großes Gewächs"
13.5%, ♀ till 2010   91

2000 Birkweiler Kastanienbusch
Spätburgunder trocken "Großes Gewächs"
13%, ♀ till 2010   92

WEINGUT

DR. WEHRHEIM

D-76831 BIRKWEILER WEINSTRASSE

WEISSER BURGUNDER
BUNTSANDSTEIN
2002

WEINGUT WEIK

Owner: Bernd Weik
Winemaker: Bernd Weik
67435 Neustadt-Mußbach,
Lutwizistraße 10
Tel. (0 63 21) 6 68 38, Fax 6 09 41
e-mail: weingut.weik@t-online.de
Internet: www.weingut-weik.de
Directions: A 65, Neustadt exit, after 400
meters in direction of Mußbach, turn
left in town center at war memorial
Sales: Mon.–Thur. by appointment
Fri. 13:00 to 18:00 hours
Sat. 10:00 to 16:00 hours
Restaurant: Weik's vinotheque and
restaurant in town, closed Thu.
Worth seeing: Historical winery complex

Vineyard area: 5.1 hectares
Annual production: 40,000 bottles
Top sites: Königsbacher Idig,
Haardter Herzog, Mußbacher
Eselshaut, Gimmeldinger Biengarten
Soil types: Clay-rich sand, loess, sand
Grape varieties: 35% Riesling,
16% Sauvignon Blanc, 10% each of
St. Laurent and Spätburgunder,
7% Weißburgunder, 5% Dornfelder,
17% other varieties
Average yield: 70 hl/ha
Best vintages: 1997, 1998, 2001

Bernd Weik's idyllic winery location in
Mußbach is close to the Eselshaut (don-
key's skin) vineyard, which makes up the
largest share of his vineyard holding.
Weik certainly knows the local scene
very well, but it seems he is content to put
in just enough effort to produce wines
slightly better than the (good) average.
His Riesling, which makes up almost a
third of his vineyards, and makes a good
dry Spätlese, has for many years been the
key varietal, next to the equally good
Sauvignon Blanc. Apart from these, we
have repeatedly tasted rather variable
quality here. The 2003 Riesling Beerenauslese Weik has produced is certainly not the best he is capable of, and the
reds are also nothing to crow about.

2003 Gimmeldinger Schlössel
Riesling Kabinett trocken
12%, ♀ till 2006 — **78**

2003 Weißer Burgunder
Kabinett trocken
13%, ♀ till 2006 — **82**

2003 Mußbacher Eselshaut
Chardonnay Spätlese trocken
13%, ♀ till 2007 — **83**

2003 Mußbacher Eselshaut
Riesling Kabinett trocken
12%, ♀ till 2006 — **84**

2003 Gimmeldinger Biengarten
Riesling Spätlese trocken
13.5%, ♀ till 2007 — **84**

2003 Mußbacher Eselshaut
Riesling Spätlese trocken
12.5%, ♀ till 2007 — **86**

2003 Mußbacher Eselshaut
Sauvignon Blanc Spätlese trocken
12.5%, ♀ till 2007 — **86**

2003 Mußbacher Eselshaut
Riesling Beerenauslese
10.5%, ♀ till 2010 — **87**

——— Red wine ———

2002 Haardter Bürgergarten
St. Laurent trocken
13%, ♀ till 2008 — **84**

The wines: **100** Perfect · **95–99** Outstanding · **90–94** Excellent · **85–89** Very good · **80–84** Good · **75–79** Average

529

WEINGUT WILHELMSHOF

Owner: Roth family
Manager: Herbert Roth
76833 Siebeldingen, Queichstraße 1
Tel. (0 63 45) 91 91 47, Fax 91 91 48
e-mail: mail@wilhelmshof.de
Internet: www.wilhelmshof.de
Directions: A 65, Landau-Nord exit, B 10
in direction of Pirmasens, Godramstein
exit to Siebeldingen, in center of town
Sales: Roth family
Opening hours: Mon.–Fri. 08:00 to
12:00 and 13:00 to 18:00, Sat. 09:00 to
17:00 hours, and by appointment
Worth seeing: Remuage cellar, guided
tour by appointment on Sat. at 10:00 hours

Vineyard area: 14 hectares
Annual production: 110,000 bottles,
incl. 40,000 bottles sparkling wine
Top site: Siebeldinger im
Sonnenschein, Frankweiler Kalkgrube
Soil types: decomposed sandstone,
shell limestone
Grape varieties: 33% Spätburgunder,
30% Riesling, 25% Weißburgunder,
10% Grauburgunder, 2% Dornfelder
Average yield: 65 hl/ha
Best vintages: 1999, 2000, 2002

Christa and Herbert Roth have had a good
reputation for classically-made sparkling
wine for some time. They produce around
half a dozen different sparkling wines,
the best is regularly the Blanc de Noirs, a
wine that can match many Champagnes.
With regard to the still wines, the last few
vintages have been rather variable. The
2000 vintage was difficult, yet Roth mastered the challenges impressively, while
the 2001 wines were less convincing.
Then in 2002 Herbert Roth was back on
form, producing racy Rieslings, as well as
a number of barrique-matured white Pinot wines that have only now been presented, as well as some good Pinot Noir
wines. The 2003 wines are extremely
brittle and unyielding and decidedly lack
fruit – they are miles away from the usual
high quality.

2003 Siebeldinger im Sonnenschein
Grauer Burgunder Spätlese trocken
13.5%, ♀ till 2006   83

2002 Siebeldinger im Sonnenschein
Grauer Burgunder Auslese trocken
Barrique
15%, ♀ till 2007   87

2002 Frankweiler Kalkgrube
Riesling Spätlese trocken
12.5%, ♀ till 2007   88

2002 Siebeldinger im Sonnenschein
Burgundercuvée trocken
14%, ♀ till 2010   89

2002 Siebeldinger im Sonnenschein
Weißer Burgunder Spätlese trocken
Barrique
13%, ♀ till 2008   89

2003 Frankweiler Kalkgrube
Riesling Beerenauslese
11%, ♀ till 2010   86

——— Red wines ———

2002 Siebeldinger im Sonnenschein
Spätburgunder trocken
"Alte Reben" Barrique
13%, ♀ till 2010   86

2002 Siebeldinger im Sonnenschein
Spätburgunder Spätlese trocken
13.5%, ♀ till 2006   88

2001 Siebeldinger im Sonnenschein
Spätburgunder Spätlese trocken
12.5%, ♀ till 2008   89

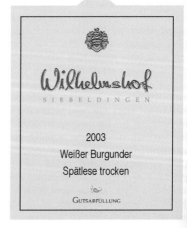

Wilhelmshof
SIEBELDINGEN

2003
Weißer Burgunder
Spätlese trocken

Gutsabfüllung

WEINGUT WILKER

Owner: Wilker family
Manager: Jürgen Wilker
Winemaker: Jürgen Wilker
and Michael Naab
76889 Pleisweiler-Oberhofen,
Hauptstraße 30
Tel. (0 63 43) 22 02, Fax 43 79
e-mail: weingut@wilker.de
Internet: www.wilker.de
*Directions: A 65, Landau-Süd exit, via
Bad Bergzabern to Pleisweiler-Oberhofen*
Sales: Mon.–Sat. 08:00 to 12:00 hours
and 14:00 to 18:00 hours
and by appointment
Restaurant: In Landhotel, Tel. 70 07 00,
Fri. and Sat. from 17:00 hours, Sun. and
public holidays from 11:30 hours
Specialties: Savory tarts at winery
History: Foundations of winery 1597

Vineyard area: 18 hectares
Annual production: 150,000 bottles
Top sites: Not mentioned on label
Soil types: Sandy loess, limestone
Grape varieties: 16% Riesling,
14% Dornfelder, 10% each of Spät-
burgunder, Grauburgunder and Trol-
linger, 8% each of Weißburgunder
and Portugieser, 6% Müller-Thurgau,
18% other varieties
Average yield: 93 hl/ha
Best vintages: 2000, 2002

It has not taken long for Jürgen Wilker to
turn his parent's business into an upward-
moving and expanded winery producing
clean, modern wines typical of their varieties. The recent opening of the new,
large country hotel has also added to the
image. However, the largest investment
in recent years has been in the cellar.
While we were not too happy with the
2001 vintage white wines, 2002 saw a return to previous form. The 2003 wines are
all technically flawless, and clean, but
should probably be drunk soon. The
wines could be even more expressive if
the fruit were more concentrated. The
Pinot Gris is headed in the right direction.

2003 Silvaner trocken
13%, ♀ till 2006 — **81**

2003 Riesling trocken
12%, ♀ till 2006 — **82**

2003 Riesling Classic
12%, ♀ till 2006 — **82**

2003 Weißer Burgunder
Spätlese trocken
13.5%, ♀ till 2006 — **85**

2003 Grauer Burgunder
Spätlese trocken
14%, ♀ till 2006 — **86**

——— Red wines ———

2003 Spätburgunder Weißherbst
trocken
13%, ♀ till 2006 — **84**

2002 Dornfelder trocken
13.5%, ♀ till 2007 — **82**

2002 Cuvée "Nr. 3" trocken
14%, ♀ till 2007 — **84**

2003 Dornfelder Classic
13%, ♀ till 2007 — **84**

2002 Frühburgunder
Spätlese trocken
13.5%, ♀ till 2006 — **87**

2001 "Cuvée Nr. 2"
trocken Barrique
14%, ♀ till 2010 — **87**

2001 Frühburgunder
Spätlese trocken Barrique
13.5%, ♀ till 2008 — **88**

---

the wines: **100** Perfect · **95–99** Outstanding · **90–94** Excellent · **85–89** Very good · **80–84** Good · **75–79** Average

531

WEINGUT J. L. WOLF

Owner: Ernst F. Loosen and Sturm family
Manager and winemaker: Günther Majer
67157 Wachenheim, Weinstraße 1
Tel. (0 63 22) 98 97 95, Fax 98 15 64
e-mail: J.L.Wolf@drloosen.de
Internet: www.drloosen.de
Directions: In the Mittelhaardt on the Weinstraße between Neustadt and Bad Dürkheim
Sales: Ernst Loosen, by appointment
Worth seeing: Villa Wolf with vaulted cellar, all a national heritage monument

---

Vineyard area: 10.5 hectares
Annual production: 70,000 bottles
Top sites: Forster Jesuitengarten, Ungeheuer and Pechstein, Deidesheimer Leinhöhle, Wachenheimer Belz (monopole), Ruppertsberger Hoheburg
Soil types: Sandy clay, basalt, volcanic formation
Grape varieties: 80% Riesling, 15% Grauburgunder, 5% Spätburgunder
Average yield: 65 hl/ha
Best vintages: 1999, 2000, 2002

The winery was first founded in 1645, but the Villa Wolf is a unique country house, built in 1843 according to the plans of architect Eisenlohr. When Ernst Loosen, of the Dr. Loosen winery in Bernkastel, took over the winery in 1996, the glory of the old days had faded, but a new positive development was begun. Loosen presented wines full of character from the 2000 vintage, in which many others battled to produce even a Spätlese. There were again very good dry Spätlese wines in 2001 and 2002. Even taking into account the specific problems of the hot and dry 2003 vintage, the wines this year are disappointing. There is no clear style here, nor any sign of the terroir character of the good vineyard sites. We must wonder whether this can be attributed to personnel changes in the cellar?

2003 Weißer Burgunder
trocken "Villa Wolf"
13%, ♀ till 2006   82

2003 Wachenheimer Gerümpel
Riesling Spätlese trocken
12%, ♀ till 2007   83

2003 Forster Ungeheuer
Riesling Spätlese trocken
12%, ♀ till 2007   85

2003 Forster Jesuitengarten
Riesling Spätlese trocken
12.5%, ♀ till 2007   85

2003 Wachenheimer Goldbächel
Riesling Spätlese trocken
11.5%, ♀ till 2006   86

2003 Forster Pechstein
Riesling Spätlese trocken
12%, ♀ till 2007   86

2002 Wachenheimer
Riesling trocken
12.5%, ♀ till 2006   87

2002 Forster Pechstein
Riesling Spätlese trocken
12.5%, ♀ till 2007   87

2002 Forster Ungeheuer
Riesling Spätlese trocken
12.5%, ♀ till 2007   88

2002 Wachenheimer Gerümpel
Riesling Spätlese trocken
12.5%, ♀ till 2007   88

2003 Forster Pechstein
Riesling Spätlese
10.5%, ♀ till 2008   80

——————— Red wine ———————

2001 Spätburgunder
trocken "J.L."
13.5%, ♀ till 2008   89

WEINGUT AUGUST ZIEGLER

Owner and manager:
Uwe and Harald Ziegler
Winemaker: Uwe Ziegler
67487 Maikammer, Bahnhofstraße 5
Tel. (0 63 21) 9 57 80, Fax 95 78 78
e-mail: aug.ziegler@t-online.de
Internet: www.august-ziegler.der
Directions: A 65, Edenkoben exit, on
L 516 to Maikammer; A 6, Speyer exit,
on L 515 via Kirrweiler to Maikammer
Sales: Harald Ziegler
Opening hours: Mon.–Fri. 08:00 to
18:00 hours, Sat. 09:00 to 15:00 hours
and by appointment
History: Winemaking in 8th generation
Worth seeing: National heritage winery
building from turn of 20th century

Vineyard area: 17 hectares
Annual production: 160,000 bottles
Top sites: Gimmeldinger Biengarten
and Mandelgarten, Alsterweiler Kapel-
lenberg, Maikammer Kirchenstück
Soil types: Decomposed sandstone,
clay with sand admixture
Grape varieties: 22% Riesling,
10% Spätburgunder, 8% each of
Weißburgunder and Dornfelder, 7%
each of Gewürztraminer and Por-
tugieser, 6% each of Scheurebe and
St. Laurent, 26% other varieties
Average yield: 75 hl/ha
Best vintages: 2001, 2002, 2003

Johann Adam Ziegler was a Swabian
journeyman tailor passing through Maikammer in 1717, who decided to stay by
virtue of his love for a local winemaker's
daughter. In 1894 the family built a manor-house that bears testimony to their
wealth. The vaulted cellar is impressive,
with both traditional oak vats and temperature-controlled stainless steel tanks.
The key strength of the Zieglers lies with
their Pinot wines, but the Rieslings, too,
are very good. Not only that: Yet again,
2003 has produced an outstanding Rieslaner Auslese.

2003 Maikammer Kirchenstück
Riesling Kabinett trocken
11.5%, ♀ till 2006   84

2003 Maikammer Heiligenberg
Sauvignon Blanc Spätlese trocken
14%, ♀ till 2006   84

2003 Gimmeldinger Biengarten
Riesling Kabinett trocken
12.5%, ♀ till 2006   86

2003 Kirrweiler Römerweg
Weißer Burgunder Kabinett trocken
14%, ♀ till 2006   86

2001 Maikammer Kirchenstück
Silvaner Kabinett trocken Barrique
14%, ♀ till 2007   86

2002 Kirrweiler Römerweg
Weißer Burgunder Spätlese trocken
13%, ♀ till 2006   87

2002 Maikammer Heiligenberg
Gewürztraminer Spätlese
12%, ♀ till 2007   86

2002 Gimmeldinger Meerspinne
Rieslaner Auslese
9.5%, ♀ till 2008   90

2003 Gimmeldinger Mandelgarten
Rieslaner Auslese
9.5%, ♀ till 2010   90

———— Red wines ————

2002 Gimmeldinger Schlössel
Merlot trocken
13%, ♀ till 2007   81

2002 Gimmeldinger Schlössel
Cabernet Franc trocken
13%, ♀ till 2008   83

---

he wines: **100** Perfect · **95–99** Outstanding · **90–94** Excellent · **85–89** Very good · **80–84** Good · **75–79** Average

533

WEINGUT ZIMMERMANN

Owner and manager:
Jürgen Zimmermann
67157 Wachenheim, Grabenstraße 5
Tel. (0 63 22) 23 84, Fax 6 51 60
e-mail: weingut-juergen-zimmermann
@t-online.de
*Directions: A 650 in direction of Bad Dürk-
heim, B 271 Wachenheim exit, follow signs*
Sales: Zimmermann family
Opening hours: Mon.–Fri. 9.:00 to
12:00 hours and 14:00 to 18:00 hours
Sat. 09:00 to 16:00 hours

Vineyard area: 10 hectares
Annual production: 80,000 bottles
Top sites: Wachenheimer
Gerümpel and Fuchsmantel
Soil types: decomposed sandstone
Grape varieties: 60% Riesling,
7% each of and Spätburgunder,
6% Grauburgunder, 4% Scheurebe,
16% other varieties
Average yield: 60 hl/ha
Best vintages: 2002, 2003

The assessment we made last year has
been confirmed: Here is somebody who
really knows how to handle the classical
varieties Riesling and Gewürztraminer.
The young winemaker even coped well
with the difficult, hot and dry 2003 vintage, in particular because he was able to
produce typical, fruit-dominated Riesling
wines from the lesser vineyard sites,
which experienced less heat damage.
Quite remarkable too is the very well-
balanced and delicately aromatic Gewürztraminer, which appears to have the potential for bottle maturation. Of course,
there is a reason for this good performance – the yields at around 60 hectoliters
on average are quite low, and the self-im-
posed restriction to classical varieties is also an advantage. In fact, the 2003 vintage
averaged a yield of only 43 hectoliters per
hectare. The results achieved with Pinot
varieties are not yet quite what we would
like to see, but that has not deterred us
from awarding the first bunch of grapes.

2003 Forster Schnepfenpflug
Riesling trocken
12%, ♀ till 2006 — 80

2003 Wachenheimer Luginsland
Riesling Kabinett trocken
12.5%, ♀ till 2006 — 80

2003 Wachenheimer Gerümpel
Riesling Spätlese trocken
13.5%, ♀ till 2006 — 82

2003 Weißer Burgunder
Spätlese trocken
14%, ♀ till 2006 — 82

2003 Grauer Burgunder
Spätlese trocken
14%, ♀ till 2006 — 82

2003 Wachenheimer Schlossberg
Riesling Spätlese trocken
13.5%, ♀ till 2006 — 84

2003 Wachenheimer Königswingert
Riesling Kabinett trocken
12.5%, ♀ till 2006 — 85

2003 Wachenheimer Königswingert
Riesling Spätlese trocken
13.5%, ♀ till 2007 — 85

2003 Wachenheimer Fuchsmantel
Riesling Spätlese trocken
13.5%, ♀ till 2007 — 85

2003 Gewürztraminer Spätlese
11%, ♀ till 2006 — 87

Other recommended producers

Weingut Michael Andres

67146 Deidesheim, Im Kathrinenbild 1
Tel. (0 63 26) 86 67, Fax 86 67
weingut.michaelandres@t-online.de

The winery has only around 3 hectares of vineyard. Michael Andres produces quite good Riesling and Pinot wines. Even better are the sparkling wines he makes together with his partner Mugler under the »Andres & Mugler« label, which are among the best in the Pfalz region.

Weingut Peter Argus

76835 Gleisweiler, Hauptstraße 23
Tel. (0 63 45) 91 94 24, Fax 91 94 25
e-mail: mail@argus-wein.de

Peter Argus surprised everybody by producing very good Pinot wines in the midNineties. In recent years he has presented some interesting wines, but also some less successful ones. His Pinot Gris wines are always worth a try, and we also liked his 2003 Chardonnay Spätlese.

Weingut Bärenhof

67098 Bad Dürkheim-Ungstein, Weinstr. 4
Tel. (0 63 22) 41 37, Fax 82 12
e-mail: weingut-baerenhof@t-online.de

Jürgen Bähr spent his apprentice years at the top Klaus Keller winery in Rheinhessen, and has now joined the family operation. However, the 2002 and 2003 vintages produced here appeared to us to be not as good as previous vintages, we feel too much of a good thing is being attempted in the cellar.

Weingut Gebrüder Bart

67098 Bad Dürkheim,
Kaiserslauterer Straße 42
Tel. (0 63 22) 18 54, Fax 18 88
e-mail: weingut-bart@t-online.de

This is a serious winery with a wide spectrum of grape varieties, but clearly focused on Riesling. Both the 2002 and 2003 ranges did not quite achieve the good quality of the 2001 vintage, although 2003 did produce a good Gewürztraminer as well as an elegant Eiswein.

Weingut Emil Bauer

76829 Landau-Nußdorf,
Walsheimer Straße 18
Tel. (0 63 41) 6 17 54, Fax 6 35 84

This winery is strong on red wines, although the dry Weißburgunder (Pinot Blanc) and Riesling wines are also usually good. The specialty here is unusual wines, such as the very good 1999 Cabernet Sauvignon (86 points) that was only recently released.

Weingut Bohnenstiel

67273 Herxheim am Berg, Weinstraße 77
Tel. (0 63 53) 9 11 86, Fax 9 11 96
e-mail: weingut.bohnenstiel@t-online.de
Internet: www.weingut-bohnenstiel.de

In spite of the difficult weather conditions, this family winery produced quite remarkable white wines in 2003, including a really attractive wine in liter bottles. We particularly liked the Classic, the dry Pinot Gris and the Chardonnay (all rated 85 points). Red wines are not yet the strong suit here.

Wein- und Sektgut Diehl

67483 Edesheim, Eisenbahnstraße 3a
Tel. (0 63 23) 93 89 30, Fax 9 38 93 38
e-mail: ad@diehl-wein.de
Internet: www.diehl-wein.de

A modern winery with a modern design. All the wines are very cleanly made, and reliable across the board. Of the 2002 (red) and 2003 vintage wines presented, we particularly liked a very typical Silvaner Spätlese, a rounded Auxerrois and the soft 2002 Pinot sparkling wine.

Weingut Wilhelm Gabel

67273 Herxheim am Berg, Weinstraße 45
Tel. (0 63 53) 74 62, Fax 9 10 19
e-mail: wein@weingut-gabel.de

As in previous years, this winery presented a serious range of wines with a few exceptionally good examples. The highlights are three very good botrytis dessert wines: two Scheurebe Eisweins and a Weißburgunder (Pinot Blanc) Trockenbeerenauslese. A Pinot Noir Selection was also rather attractive.

Weingut Gnägy

76889 Schweigen-Rechtenbach,
Müllerstraße 5
Tel. (0 63 42) 91 90 42, Fax 91 90 43
e-mail: weingut.gnaegy@t-online.de

This classic family winery produces well-made, fresh wines, which we again found attractive in 2003. One would not go wrong choosing any of the wines available, although they are not yet good enough for a higher rating. The 2002 Spätburgunder Barrique ist surprisingly good.

Weingut Peter Graeber

67480 Edenkoben, Schanzstraße 21
Tel. (0 63 23) 55 68, Fax 67 27
e-mail: info@weingut-graeber.de

Graeber has been a traditional winery with quite a good reputation. Every now and again, individual wines such as the very good 2000 "Il Pino" or the elegant 2003 Scheurebe Auslese show that there is considerable potential here. The 2003 vintage produced a range of clean but somewhat uninspiring wines.

Weingut Grimm & Sohn

76889 Schweigen, Pauliner Straße 9
Tel. (0 63 42) 71 06, Fax 2 49
e-mail: weingut.grimm-sohn@t-online.de

This winery produces fairly good wines, rather traditionally made, with particularly the Riesling and white Pinot wines being very attractive. The best wines of the 2003 vintage are a Gewürztraminer Spätlese, a powerful, juicy Weißburgunder as well as the perlé wine "Secco."

Weingut Bernd Grimm

76889 Schweigen, Bergstraße 2
Tel. (0 63 42) 91 90 45, Fax 91 90 46
e-mail: info@weingut-grimm.de

This winery is typical for the strong side of the Pfalz: Good family wineries with winemakers open to modern ideas, producing decent wines at a good price. Very clean whites were made again in 2003. This slightly lean style is quite appropriate for the Rieslings, while a well-made Grauburgunder Spätlese shows that a little more body can be a good thing.

Weingut Georg Henninger IV.

67169 Kallstadt, Weinstraße 93
Tel. (0 63 22) 22 77, Fax 6 28 61

This is an old, renowned family operation located in a beautiful half-timbered complex, which also houses an attractive country inn providing more than just good cooking. The wines are all made dry, and are produced by the Koehler-Ruprecht estate: traditionally made wines, bottled late, that require some time to develop. The cellar has vintages going back to 1992 available.

Weingut Julius Ferdinand Kimich

67142 Deidesheim, Weinstraße 54
Tel. (0 63 26) 3 42, Fax 98 04 14

Just as in days gone by, most of the wines are matured in large oak vats in the vaulted cellar. The main accent here is therefore on solid Riesling wines in the classic style. Only Kabinett quality wines of the 2003 vintage were submitted.

Weingut Bruno Leiner

76829 Landau-Wollmesheim,
Zum Mütterle 20
Tel. (0 63 41) 3 09 53, Fax 3 41 42

Bruno Leiner runs a large and well organized operation in the pretty town of Wollmesheim, producing solid wines typical of the southern Pfalz. The white wines appear to have gained in elegance and clarity in the 2003 vintage, such as the well-made Grauburgunder (Pinot Gris) Spätlese trocken (83 points) or the fresh Silvaner Spätlese trocken (82). In terms of red wines, Leiner concentrates on international and new cross-bred varieties.

Weingut Lingenfelder

67229 Großkarlbach, Hauptstraße 27
Tel. (0 62 38) 7 54, Fax 10 96

Ever since Rainer-Karl Lingenfelder joined his parents' business, things have been improving here. The ambitious winemaker concentrates particularly on Riesling and Scheurebe wines. Quite attractive, although generally no more than that, are his Silvaner, Scheurebe and Spätburgunder (Pinot Noir) wines.

Weingut Martinshof

76829 Landau-Nußdorf, Kirchhohl 20
Tel. (0 63 41) 6 12 46, Fax 6 24 48
e-mail: info@martinshof-heupel.de

Just like his father, young winemaker Martin Heupel concentrates on producing good, juicy wines from the white Pinot vines grown on the powerful sites around Nußdorf. Of the 2003 vintage, we also liked the juicy Riesling Kabinett trocken filled in liter bottles.

Weingut
Schlossberg Georg Naegele

67434 Neustadt-Hambach,
Schloss-Straße 27–29
Tel. (0 63 21) 28 80, Fax 3 07 08
e-mail: naegele-wein@t-online.de

In this winery in Hambach there have been marked improvements in the past two vintages, which includes the difficult 2003 vintage. The main focus is on Riesling, the best example is the dry Spätlese "Kirchberg" (84 points); the Riesling Eiswein is also attractive.

Weingut Rolf Pfaffmann

76833 Frankweiler, Am Stahlbühl
Tel. (0 63 45) 13 64, Fax 52 02
e-mail: R-T-Pfaffmann@t-online.de

Tina Pfaffmann has begun to make better use of the potential of the vineyards available here. The wines sometimes have a very specific character, and remain deeply colored and expansively baroque in style. Both good Silvaner and quite attractive Riesling wines are made this way. We remain skeptical with regard to the Pinots and the red wines here.

Weingut Pflüger

67098 Bad Dürkheim, Gutleutstraße 48
Tel. (0 63 22) 6 31 48, Fax 6 60 43
e-mail: info@pflueger-wein.de

Bernd Pflüger has been implementing organic viticultural practises since 1990, and in 2001 was awarded the European solar prize for agricultural operations. His wines are made in a traditional style, and always marked by stable acidity. In good cases, race and style are added.

Weingut Porzelt

76889 Klingenmünster, Steinstraße 91
Tel. (0 63 49) 81 86, Fax 39 50
e-mail: info@weingut-porzelt.de

Here, a young winemaker is forcing ahead with enthusiasm and drive, as well as well-made, very clear wines showing typical varietal characteristics. We tasted an excellent 2003 Silvaner Spätlese, very good Weißburgunder (Pinot Blanc) and attractive Rieslings; indeed, we found practically no weak points. We look forward to following the development here in future.

Weingut Probsthof

67433 Neustadt-Haardt, Probstgasse
Tel. (0 63 21) 63 15, Fax 6 02 15

A traditional winery, which in previous years has presented rather difficult wines. Recently, however, the number of attractive wines has increased, and it is particularly the Riesling wines of the 2002 and 2003 vintages that show up this positive tendency toward clean, modern aromas. We particularly liked the 2003 Muskateller Spätlese (86 points).

Weingut F. J. Rössler

67487 St. Martin, Maikammerer Str. 12
Tel. (0 63 23) 50 75, Fax 98 96 93

Sankt Martin is an attractive tourist destination. Here, Robert Schneider produces good dry Rieslings and Pinots as well as barrel-matured Dornfelder. In 2003 he also managed to produce a very good Gewürztraminer Auslese trocken (dry, 84 points), which is quite powerful.

Weingut Sauer

76833 Böchingen, Hauptstraße 44
Tel. (0 63 41) 6 11 75, Fax 6 43 80
e-mail: Heiner.Sauer.Biowein@gmx.de

Heiner Sauer has a good reputation among organic winemakers; apart from his vineyards in the Pfalz, he also runs a winery in Spain. His Pfalz wines made a significant leap forward in the 2003 vintage, they are more clear, more elegant, and more typical of their varieties. It looks as though a higher rating for this winery might be on the cards soon.

Pfalz

Weingut Schenk-Siebert

67269 Grünstadt-Sausenheim,
Leininger Straße 16
Tel. (0 63 59) 21 59, Fax 8 30 34
e-mail: schenk-siebert@t-online.de

This is a large, serious winery in the Leininger Land area, producing well-made wines which turned out quite fruity even in the drought-ridden 2003 vintage. We particularly liked the dry Riesling Spätlese (85 points).

Weingut Schneider

67158 Ellerstadt, Georg-Fitz-Straße 12
Tel. (0 62 37) 72 88, Fax 97 72 30
e-mail: weingut.schneider@t-online.de

This winery has generated quite a lot of positive discussion recently, the Riesling wines are clear and at the same time full-bodied, and are particularly well made.

Weingut Scholler

76831 Birkweiler, Alte Kirchstraße 7
Tel. (0 63 45) 35 29, Fax 85 35
e-mail: weingutscholler@t-online.de
Internet: www.weingut-scholler.de

After some ups and downs in quality, Scholler has found his way to interesting, clean wines of consistent serious quality. The strengths here are clearly with the white Pinots, and less so with red wines. If all the wines were as good as the 2003 dry Auslese wines of Riesling and Gewürztraminer (87 points), we would award the first bunch of grapes immediately.

Weingut Georg Siben Erben

67143 Deidesheim, Weinstraße 21
Tel. (0 63 26) 98 93 63, Fax 98 93 65
e-mail: siben_weingut@t-online.de
Internet: www.siben-weingut.de

For a long time, Wolfgang Georg Siben favored the classical style of vat-matured Riesling, that requires a long time to open up and develop. His son Andreas has attempted to modernize things, and produced attractive wines in 2003. He has made quite good Rieslings, not too alcoholic, including a very good dry estate Riesling bottled in liter bottles, as well as a very typical Weißburgunder (Pinot Blanc).

Weingut Siener – Dr. Wettstein

76833 Siebeldingen, Bengertstraße 1
Tel. (0 63 45) 95 45 40, Fax 95 45 42
e-mail: siener@t-online.de

This winery in Siebeldingen is a reliable producer of Riesling and Pinot wines. In the 2003 vintage, we again liked the dry Riesling Spätlese wines as well as the white Pinots.

Staatsweingut mit Johannitergut

67435 Neustadt-Mußbach, Breitenweg 71
Tel. (0 63 21) 67 13 19, Fax 67 12 22
e-mail: rberger.slfa@agrarinfo.rlp.de

In 2003 the state winery produced an interesting range of wines. While the dry white wines in some cases lacked balance, and had been worked on too hard in the cellar, the Riesling Trockenbeerenauslese (93 points) is one of the great botrytis dessert wines of the vintage. Our congratulations!

Weingut Georg Steiner – Johanneshof

76833 Siebeldingen
Tel. (0 63 45) 36 64, Fax 89 94
e-mail: georg.steiner@t-online.de

Georg Steiner has proved repeatedly that he is capable of making good wines, particularly in several vintages of his good dry Riesling Selection, and now also with a smoky, barrique-matured 2001 Spätburgunder (Pinot Noir). The 2003 wines are all very well made in terms of technical handling in the cellar, but the basic wines, in particular, lack concentration.

Weingut Stentz

76829 Landau-Mörzheim,
Mörzheimer Hauptstraße 47
Tel. (0 63 41) 3 01 21, Fax 3 45 65
e-mail: stentz@t-online.de
Internet: www.stentz.de

Ever since the younger generation has taken over at the helm, renovating and extending the complex (attractive guest rooms), many things have been improved, including the professional approach to marketing. Good, modern and clean white wines as well as an attractive 2003 Cuvée Nr.1 show the potential available here.

Weingut Theodorhof

76835 Hainfeld
Tel. (0 63 23) 50 34, Fax 98 04 30
e-mail: info@theodorhof.de

The family winery is located in the baroque village of Hainfeld, which boasts an increasing number of good producers. We particularly liked the Chardonnays, showing a deft use of oak, as well as the Riesling Hochgewächs and the reds of the 2002 vintage. The botrytis dessert wines are rather high in alcohol.

Weingüter Wegeler – Gutshaus Deidesheim

67146 Deidesheim, Weinstraße 10
Tel. (0 63 26) 2 21, Fax 79 20
e-mail: info@wegeler.com

This is the portion of the Dr. Deinhard winery that has been leased to Wegeler. We cannot really understand how it is that essentially the same grapes should produce significantly lesser wines here. The 2002 and 2003 vintages did not produce a single wine worth recommending.

Weingut Wolf

67098 Bad Dürkheim-Ungstein, Kirchstraße 28
Tel. (0 63 22) 15 01, Fax 98 08 29
e-mail: michael@weingut-wolf.de

This winery generally produces a reliable quality, and the 2003 vintage is as clean as ever. The wines we liked best were a very typical Grauburgunder Spätlese as well as two barrique-matured wines from the 2002 vintage, a ripe Dornfelder and a fruit-driven Cabernet Sauvignon.

Other wineries tasted

- Bach-Frobin, Niederkirchen
- Langenwalter-Gauglitz, Freinsheim
- Wein- und Sekthaus Möller, Hainfeld
- Rudi Möwes, Weyher
- Herbert Müller Erben, Neustadt-Haardt
- Kurt Mugler, Neustadt-Gimmeldingen
- Villa Pistoria, Bad Bergzabern
- Schädler, Maikammer
- Stern, Hochstadt

Recommended by our wine producers

Hotels and inns

Deidesheim: Deidesheimer Hof
Bad Dürkheim: Kurparkhotel
Herxheim-Hayna: Krone
Neuleiningen: Alte Pfarrey
Siebeldingen: Sonnenhof

Gourmet restaurants

Deidesheim: Schwarzer Hahn
Freinsheim: Luther
Herxheim-Hayna: Krone

Restaurants, wine bars and winery facilities

Deidesheim: Kanne
Forst: Acham-Magin
Frankweiler: Brand
Freinsheim: Freinsheimer Hof
Großkarlbach: Meurer, Karlbacher
Kallstadt: Weißes Ross, Henninger
Neustadt-Gimmeldingen: Netts
Neustadt-Mußbach: Eselsburg
Pleisweiler-Oberhofen: Holzappel
Schweigen: Jülg
Siebeldingen: Sonnenhof
Wartenberg: Scharffs Restaurant

Major and minor vintages in the Pfalz region

Vintage	Rating
2003	❀❀❀
2002	❀❀❀
2001	❀❀❀❀
2000	❀❀
1999	❀❀❀❀
1998	❀❀❀❀❀
1997	❀❀❀❀
1996	❀❀❀❀
1995	❀❀❀
1994	❀❀❀❀

Vintage rating:

❀❀❀❀❀	: Excellent vintage
❀❀❀❀	: Very good vintage
❀❀❀	: Good vintage
❀❀	: Average vintage
❀	: Poor vintage

Rheingau

A cornucopia of botrytis Riesling

The Rheingau has had a long wait for a vintage that deserves the title of "vintage of the century," and can legitimately claim to be the successor to the legendary 1976 vintage. This means no less than to be on a level with the 1971, 1959, 1945, 1937 and 1921 vintages, representing the best vintages of the last century. There is no doubt nature has been kind to wine producers in the Rheingau in the past 15 years: The last two vintages that were not quite up to par were 1987 and 1991, apart from these, the quality of the overall vintages in the Nineties always varied between good and very good. Now the waiting is over. The driest summer in human memory has given the Rheingau a veritable cornucopia of botrytis Riesling. There is hardly any self-respecting producer that did not produce a Beerenauslese or Trockenbeerenauslese in 2003, and that with a clarity and level of quality as has not been seen for decades. This can primarily be ascribed to the absence of botrytis cinerea, that unusual fungus that is mostly welcome, drying out the grapes and concentrating the fruit, but that can also add unpleasant nuances to both taste and smell of a wine. The extreme weather conditions in 2003 ensured that healthy grapes turned virtually to raisins, thus naturally concentrating both sugar and acidity. The wines produced from these grapes are among the highlights of this exceptional vintage, which also brought forth fabulous Auslese wines, opulent Spätlese wines, powerful dry Rieslings and perhaps the best red wines ever produced in the Rheingau.

This opulent vintage did, however, lead to a dearth of light quaffing wines: By the nature of things, there are very few basic quality wines, nor dry or off-dry Kabinett wines. To overcome this shortage, many producers generously declassified their wines, i.e. they are selling many wines as Kabinett, although their must weights would allow them to be classified as Spätlese or even Auslese wines. However, changing the label does not turn these powerful wines into sprightly, filigree Riesling, such as one might prefer to drink on an everyday basis. If you are looking for this lighter style of wine, you should ask the producer to look in his cellar for some 2001 or 2002 wines, which are still occasionally to be found. The Robert Weil estate certainly used the opportunity afforded by this vintage to firmly reclaim its place among the leading wine producers world wide. Incredibly a pair of botrytis wines produced by this star producer in Kiedrich achieved top marks of 100 points each, a feat never before recorded in the history of the Gault Millau Wine Guide.

A number of producers improved their rating by one bunch of grapes: the Fürst Löwenstein winery (up from two to

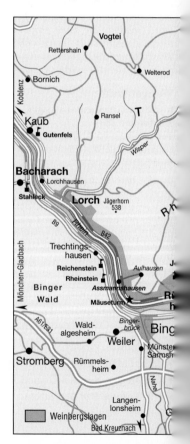

three bunches), then Altenkirch, Corvers-Kauter and Schloss Reinhartshausen (all now two bunches). The following appear for the first time in the list of leading producers: Lamm-Jung in Erbach, the estate of the bishop of Limburg in Rüdesheim and the Schamari mill, which also boasts one of the most attractive winery restaurants in the Rheingau. The Nineties in the Rheingau were characterised by investment in cellar technology, with many producers throwing out their synthetic tanks and oak vats in favor of temperature-controlled stainless steel tanks. Currently, the focus is on improving the local marketing infrastructure: Half of all producers are either thinking about establishing a vinotheque, or have already done so, some prime examples being Schloss Vollrads, or recently

the Johannishof winery in Johannisberg. A quarter of all producers wants to provide accommodation facilities, for example the Querbach estate in Oestrich-Winkel. This must be seen against a background of a rapidly developing culinary culture in the Rheingau, which has sprung up over the past decade, and is by now the envy of other wine regions. The Rheingau Culinary Week ("Rheingauer Schlemmerwoche"), which takes place in spring, a sort of communal culinary effort, as well as the "Rheingau Gourmet-Festival." Represent a valuable addition to the well-established "Rheingau Music-Festival," a major spectacle. The finale of oenological and culinary highlights takes place in November, in the shape of the "Glorreiche Tage," the glorious days reminiscent of their counterpart in Burgundy.

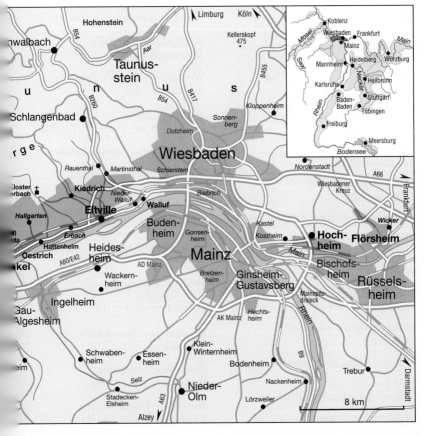

541

Rheingau

The leading producers
in the Rheingau region

Weingut Robert Weil, Kiedrich

**Weingut Georg Breuer,
Rüdesheim**

**Weingut August Kesseler,
Assmannshausen**

**Weingut Peter Jakob Kühn,
Oestrich-Winkel**

Weingut Josef Leitz, Rüdesheim

Weingut J. B. Becker, Walluf

**Domdechant Werner'sches
Weingut, Hochheim**

**Weingut Joachim Flick,
Flörsheim-Wicker**

**Weingut Prinz von Hessen,
Johannisberg**

**Schloss Johannisberg,
Johannisberg**

**Weingut Johannishof,
Johannisberg**

Weingut Jakob Jung, Erbach

Weingut Krone, Assmannshausen

**Weingut Franz Künstler,
Hochheim**

**Weingut Hans Lang,
Hattenheim**

**Weingut Fürst Löwenstein,
Hallgarten**

Weingut Prinz, Hallgarten

**Domänenweingut
Schloss Schönborn, Hattenheim**

Weingut Josef Spreitzer, Oestrich

**Weingut Schloss Vollrads,
Oestrich-Winkel**

**Weingüter Wegeler – Gutshaus
Oestrich, Oestrich-Winkel**

**Weingut Friedrich Altenkirch,
Lorch**

**Barth, Wein- und Sektgut,
Hattenheim**

**Weingut Dr. Corvers-Kauter,
Oestrich-Winkel**

**Weingut Toni Jost – Hahnenhof,
Bacharach**

Weingut Graf von Kanitz, Lorch

**Weingut
Baron zu Knyphausen, Erbach**

**Weingut Robert König,
Assmannshausen**

**Weingut Königin-Victoriaberg,
Oestrich-Winkel**

**Weingut Freiherr
Langwerth von Simmern, Eltville**

Weingut Heinz Nikolai, Erbach

**Weingut Wilfried Querbach,
Oestrich**

**Weingut Schloss Reinhartshausen,
Erbach**

**Weingut Balthasar Ress,
Hattenheim**

**Wein- und Sektgut
F. B. Schönleber,
Oestrich-Winkel**

**Weingut Speicher-Schuth,
Kiedrich**

**Hess. Staatsweingüter
Domaine Assmannshausen**

**Hessische Staatsweingüter
Kloster Eberbach, Eltville**

Bischöfliches Weingut, Rüdesheim

Diefenhardt'sches Weingut, Martinsthal

Weingut Friedrich Fendel, Rüdesheim

Weingut Alexander Freimuth, Marienthal

Weingut Hamm, Oestrich-Winkel

Weingut Lamm-Jung, Eltville-Erbach

Weingut Wilhelm Mohr Erben, Lorch

Weingut Detlev Ritter und Edler von Oetinger, Erbach

Weingut Johannes Ohlig, Oestrich-Winkel

Weingut W. J. Schäfer, Hochheim

Weingut Schamari-Mühle, Johannisberg

Classification of producers

Highest rating,
for world-class wine producers

Excellent producers counted
as among the best in Germany

Very good producers
who have been making consistently
high quality wines for many years

Good producers who do better
than make just everyday wines

Reliable producers making
decent standard qualitiy wines

The best vineyard sites in the Rheingau region *

Assmannshausen: Frankenthal, Höllenberg

Eltville: Langenstück, Rheinberg, Sonnenberg, Taubenberg, Kalbspflicht

Erbach: Hohenrain, Marcobrunn, Michelmark, Schlossberg, Siegelsberg, Steinmorgen

Flörsheim: Herrnberg

Geisenheim: Fuchsberg, Kläuserweg, Mäuerchen, Mönchspfad. Rothenberg

Hallgarten: Jungfer, Schönhell

Hattenheim: Engelmannsberg, Hassel, Mannberg, Nussbrunnen, Pfaffenberg, Schützenhaus, Wisselbrunnen

Hochheim: Domdechaney, Hofmeister, Hölle, Königin Viktoriaberg, Kirchenstück, Reichestal, Stein, Stielweg

Johannisberg: Hölle, Klaus

Kiedrich: Gräfenberg, Sandgrub, Wasseros

Kostheim: Weiß Erd

Lorch: Bodental-Steinberg, Kapellenberg, Krone, Pfaffenwies, Schlossberg

Lorchhausen: Seligmacher

Martinsthal: Langenberg, Rödchen, Wildsau

Mittelheim: Edelmann, St. Nikolaus

Oestrich: Doosberg, Lenchen

Rauenthal: Baiken, Gehrn, Rothenberg, Wülfen

Rüdesheim: Berg Roseneck, Berg Rottland, Berg Schlossberg, Bischofsberg, Drachenstein, Klosterlay, Magdalenenkreuz

Walluf: Berg Bildstock, Vitusberg, Walkenberg

Wicker: Mönchsgewann, Stein

Winkel: Gutenberg, Hasensprung, Jesuitengarten, Schlossberg

Official designations for parts of towns:

Schloss Johannisberg, Steinberg, Schloss Vollrads, Schloss Reichartshausen

---

* Source: VDP Rheingau

WEINGUT FRIEDRICH ALTENKIRCH

Owner: Franziska Breuer-Hadwiger
Managers: Stefan Breuer, Peter Weritz
65391 Lorch/Rheingau, Binger Weg 2
Tel. (0 67 26) 83 00 12, Fax 24 83
e-mail: info@weingut-altenkirch.de
Internet: www.weingut-altenkirch.de
Directions: B 42, between Rüdesheim and Loreley, at town entrance to Lorch, opposite the railway station
Sales: Stefan Breuer, Peter Weritz
by appointment
Restaurant: End of Sept. to mid-Nov., March to early May, Thu.–Sat. from 17:00 hours, Sun. from 15:00 hours
Specialties: Regional game and fish
History: Founded 1826, owned by Breuer family since 1934
Worth seeing: Historical vaulted cellar

Vineyard area: 16.5 hectares
Annual production: 100,000 bottles
Top sites: Lorcher Pfaffenwies, Bodental-Steinberg and Krone
Soil types: Grey slate, quartzite, loess
Grape varieties: 63% Riesling, 25% Spätburgunder, 6% each of Weißburgunder and Müller-Thurgau
Average yield: 52 hl/ha
Best vintages: 2001, 2002, 2003

This well-established winery in Lorch has been experiencing a renaissance since the late 90's. Here, too, the improvement came with a generation change. Stefan Breuer converted to temperature-controlled fermentation, among other innovations. The winery owns parcels of the best vineyard sites in Lorch, where grey slate and a combination of limestone and loess provide characterful wines. We particularly liked those wines that are dedicated to the winery's founder, Dr. Franz Breuer: For the 2003 vintage, this again includes a dry Spätlese, an excellent Weißburgunder as well as an opulent Beerenauslese. In addition, the Spätburgunder Weißherbst (Rosé) Auslese, with its whiff of smoked bacon, is very attractive!

2003 Riesling Kabinett trocken
12%, 1.0 liter, ♀ till 2006   **84**

2003 Riesling Kabinett trocken
12%, ♀ till 2006   **84**

2003 Lorcher Bodental-Steinberg
Riesling Kabinett trocken
11.5%, ♀ till 2007   **85**

2003 "Dr. Franz Breuer"
Weißer Burgunder trocken
13%, ♀ till 2007   **87**

2003 "Dr. Franz Breuer"
Riesling Spätlese trocken
12%, ♀ till 2008   **88**

2003 Lorcher Pfaffenwies
Riesling Spätlese feinherb
12%, ♀ till 2007   **86**

2003 Riesling Kabinett feinherb
11.5%, ♀ till 2008   **86**

2003 "Dr. Franz Breuer"
Riesling Spätlese
9.5%, ♀ till 2010   **88**

2003 "Dr. Franz Breuer"
Riesling Beerenauslese
7%, ♀ till 2015   **92**

————— Red wine —————

2003 "Dr. Franz Breuer"
Spätburgunder Weißherbst Auslese
9%, ♀ till 2010   **87**

BARTH
WEIN- UND SEKTGUT

Owner and manager: Norbert Barth
Winemaker: Stefan Thielen
65347 Eltville-Hattenheim, Bergweg 20
Tel. (0 67 23) 25 14, Fax 43 75
e-mail: Barth.Weingut@t-online.de
Internet: www.weingut-barth.de
Directions: B 42, Hattenheim exit
Sales: Marion and Norbert Barth
Opening hours: Mon.–Fri. 14:00 to
18:00 hours, Sat. 10:00 to 17:00 hours
and by appointment
Worth seeing: Traditional sparkling
wine production with fermentation in
bottle and manual riddling

Vineyard area: 10.5 hectares
Annual production: 80,000 bottles
Top sites: Hattenheimer
Wisselbrunnen and Hassel
Soil types: Loess-clay, kaolin, decomposed slate, tertiary marl
Grape varieties: 70% Riesling,
20% Spätburgunder, 5% Weißburgunder, 3% Cabernet Sauvignon,
2% other varieties
Average yield: 69 hl/ha
Best vintages: 1999, 2002, 2003
Member: VDP

The quality of this winery has shown a positive development in the past two years. One of the reasons may be seen in the transport of grapes, previously a manual affair, now handled by tipping palettes, followed by whole-bunch pressing. The wines we liked best was the First Growth from the Wisselbrunnen vineyard, the Spätlese from the Hassel, which is reminiscent of Williams pears, and the botrytized Auslese from the Schützenhaus site. Without wanting to promote the maturation of Riesling in small oak barriques, we again approached the opulent "Singularis" wine of the 2002 vintage with interest and great curiosity, and found it to be rather well made. Even the Cabernet Sauvignon, with its bell-pepper notes, is quite good here.

2002 "Singularis"
Riesling trocken Barrique
13%, ♀ till 2010   88

2003 Hattenheimer Wisselbrunnen
Riesling trocken Erstes Gewächs
12.5%, ♀ till 2008   88

2003 Hattenheimer Hassel
Riesling Spätlese
9.5%, ♀ till 2010   88

2003 Hattenheimer Schützenhaus
Riesling Eiswein
7%, ♀ till 2015   88

2002 Hattenheimer Schützenhaus
Riesling Trockenbeerenauslese
7%, ♀ till 2015   89

2003 Hattenheimer Wisselbrunnen
Riesling Beerenauslese
7.5%, ♀ till 2015   89

2003 Hattenheimer Schützenhaus
Riesling Auslese Goldkapsel
⮑ auction wine, 8%, ♀ till 2015   89

——————— Red wines ———————

2002 Spätburgunder
trocken Barrique
14%, ♀ till 2009   85

2002 Cabernet Sauvignon
trocken Barrique
14%, ♀ till 2010   86

WEINGUT J. B. BECKER

Owner: Maria and Hans-Josef Becker
Manager and winemaker:
Hans-Josef Becker
Administrator: Ulli Phillip
65396 Walluf, Rheinstraße 6
Tel. (0 61 23) 7 25 23, Fax 7 53 35
e-mail: h.j.becker@justmail.de
Directions: A 66, Walluf/Niederwalluf
exit, turn towards Rhine in center of town
Sales: Maria Becker
Opening hours: Mon.–Fri. 09:00 to
12:00 hours and 14:00 to 17:00 hours
Sat. and Sun. by appointment
Restaurant: "Der Weingarten" from
April to October, Mon.–Fri. 17:00 to
24:00, Sat. and Sun. 15:00 to 24:00 hours
Worth seeing: Ruins of Roman tower
fortifications

Vineyard area: 11.4 hectares
Annual production: 70,000 bottles
Top sites: Wallufer Walkenberg,
Eltviller Rheinberg
Soil types: Deep loess-clay
Grape varieties: 81% Riesling, 17%
Spätburgunder, 2% Müller-Thurgau
Average yield: 50 hl/ha
Best vintages: 2001, 2002, 2003

Hans-Josef Becker is a winemaker who
has very strong opinions on the style of
his wines, and is pretty much immune
to fashionable market trends. The one
exception this Walluf winery has made
since the 2002 vintage is the use of the
Vino-Lok glass closures. He still matures
his white wines in barrels for a full year
before bottling, and his red wines for two
years. As in the two previous vintages,
the range of wines he has produced in
2003 is thoroughly convincing right
across the board, in this case crowned by
several botrytis Riesling wines that really
stand out, showing a level of quality we
have not tasted here in a long time. It
is obvious that the wines are fermented
a little further than in other wineries:
"The main aim is to make food-friendly
wines!", is the winemaker's comment.

2003 Wallufer Walkenberg
Riesling Spätlese trocken
13%, ♀ till 2010   87

2001 Eltviller Sonnenberg
Riesling Spätlese trocken
12%, ♀ till 2007   89

2003 Wallufer Walkenberg
Riesling Spätlese trocken Alte Reben
13%, ♀ till 2012   89

2003 Wallufer Walkenberg
Riesling Auslese trocken
14%, ♀ till 2015   90

2003 Eltviller Sonnenberg
Riesling Spätlese
11.5%, ♀ till 2012   89

2002 Wallufer Walkenberg
Riesling Spätlese Alte Reben
12.5%, ♀ till 2010   89

2003 Wallufer Walkenberg
Riesling Spätlese
10.5%, ♀ till 2015   90

2003 Eltviller Rheinberg
Riesling Beerenauslese
14.5%, ♀ till 2018   90

2003 Eltviller Sonnenberg
Riesling Trockenbeerenauslese
12%, ♀ till 2020   91

2003 Wallufer Walkenberg
Riesling Trockenbeerenauslese
8%, ♀ till 2025   93

——————— Red wines ———————

2002 Wallufer
Spätburgunder Spätlese trocken
13.5%, ♀ till 2012   88

2002 Wallufer Walkenberg
Spätburgunder Spätlese trocken Alte Reben
13.5%, ♀ till 2015   88

750 ml   alc. 14,0% by vol.

SEIT   1893

J. B. BECKER
Rheingau
1999er Riesling Auslese trocken
Wallufer Walkenberg
A. P. Nr. 37030 011 00
Product of Germany
Qualitätswein mit Prädikat · Erzeugerabfüllung Weingut J. J. Becker, D-65396 Walluf

---

The estates: ♦♦♦♦♦ World's finest · ♦♦♦♦ Germany's best · ♦♦♦ Very good · ♦♦ Good · ♦ Reliable

BISCHÖFLICHES WEINGUT RÜDESHEIM

Owner: Limburg diocese
Manager: Jürgen Groh
Administrator: Carsten Weiland
Winemaker: Helmut Anthes
65385 Rüdesheim,
Marienthaler Straße 3
Tel. (0 67 22) 91 05 60, Fax 91 05 62
e-mail: pfarrgut@t-online.de
Internet: www.weingut.bistumlimburg.de
Directions: B 42, direction of the hospital, in the cellars of the Eibing church
Sales: Helmut Anthes
Opening hours: Mon.–Fri. 13:00 to 17:00 hours and by appointment
Worth seeing: Historical vaulted cellar

Vineyard area: 8 hectares
Annual production: 50,000 bottles
Top sites: Rüdesheimer Bischofs-
berg, Berg Schlossberg, Klosterlay
Soil types: Taunus quartzite, loess-clay
Grape varieties: 88% Riesling,
12% Spätburgunder
Average yield: 63 hl/ha
Best vintages: 2002, 2003

In the 60's and 70's, during the era of Reverend Moschhäuser, the church's winery in Rüdesheim was a respected supplier of truly dry wines. Even today, one wine each year is bottled as "classically dry," to keep alive the memory of that successful era. Ever since the merger with the Eibingen church winery in the 90's, the company has been trading as the Bischöfliches Weingut (bishop's wine estate). We found a very respectable range of wines, and have awarded a bunch of grapes to the winery. Among our favorites are the invigorating dry Riesling from the Berg Roseneck site, the elegantly fruity red wine from the Klosterlay, as well as the Riesling Beerenauslese, which has baroque proportions. In addition, the hearty Classic Riesling as well as the fruity Riesling from the Johannisberger Hölle site provide good quality.

2003 Riesling trocken
12%, ♀ till 2006 — **82**

2003 Rüdesheimer Kirchenpfad
Riesling trocken
12%, ♀ till 2006 — **83**

2003 Riesling Classic
12%, ♀ till 2007 — **83**

2003 Rüdesheimer Berg Roseneck
Riesling trocken
12%, ♀ till 2007 — **85**

2003 Johannisberger Erntebringer
Riesling feinherb
11%, ♀ till 2006 — **81**

2003 Johannisberger Hölle
Riesling
9%, ♀ till 2009 — **85**

2003 Riesling Auslese
8.5%, ♀ till 2012 — **88**

2003 Riesling Beerenauslese
13%, ♀ till 2015 — **89**

——— Red wine ———

2003 Rüdesheimer Klosterlay
Spätburgunder trocken
13%, ♀ till 2010 — **87**

Bischöfliches
Weingut
Rüdesheim
Bistum Limburg

2003
Riesling
CLASSIC

Qualitätswein b. A.
Erzeugerabfüllung
A. P. Nr. 24 068 007 04

Rheingau 0,75 l 12,0% vol

Bischöfliches Weingut · Marienthaler Straße 3 · D-65385 Rüdesheim · Rhein

---

The wines: **100** Perfect · **95–99** Outstanding · **90–94** Excellent · **85–89** Very good · **80–84** Good · **75–79** Average

547

WEINGUT GEORG BREUER

Owner: Familie Breuer
Manager: Heinrich Breuer
Winemaker: Hermann Schmoranz
65385 Rüdesheim, Grabenstraße 8
Tel. (0 67 22) 10 27, Fax 45 31
e-mail: info@georg-breuer.com
Internet: www.georg-breuer.com
www.ruedesheimer-schloss.com
Directions: On the B 42, at the cross-road in the center of Rüdesheim go in direction of Niederwald monument
Sales: Heinrich Breuer
Vinotheque: Open daily
May to Oct. 09:30 to 18:30 hours,
Nov. to April 10:00 to 16:30 hours
Restaurant: Rüdesheimer Schloss, Steingasse 10, May to Oct. daily 11:00 to 23:00 hours, Nov. to April closed on various days
Wine hotel: Rüdesheimer Schloss, open all year, closed Christmas to 6. January
Worth seeing: Historical vaulted cellar "Breuer's Kellerwelt," Grabenstraße 8

Vineyard area: 30 hectares
Annual production: 130,000 bottles
Top sites: Rüdesheim Berg Schlossberg, Berg Rottland, Berg Roseneck, Rauenthal Nonnenberg
Soil types: Taunus quartzite with layers of slate, stony, gravelly phyllite soils
Grape varieties: 80% Riesling, 11% Spätburgunder, 7% Grauburgunder, 2% other varieties
Average yield: 40 hl/ha
Best vintages: 1999, 2002, 2003
Member: Deutsches Barrique Forum

The unexpected death of Bernhard Breuer in May 2004 sent shock waves rippling throughout the German wine scene, and the feelings expressed at his funeral were unparalleled: Posthumously this son of Rüdesheim was given credit for many things left unsaid while he was still alive. This includes the reconciliation with the Rheingau VDP – Breuer fought even more vigorously than others for the introduction of the "Erstes Gewächs" (First Growth), but left the association some years ago mainly because he felt he was not receiving adequate support from his colleagues in his battle against new enological procedures, and apparently also because sections of his vineyards were excluded from First Growth status. Breuer's life's work is now being carried on by his brother Heinrich, as well as by winemaker Hermann Schmoranz and, apparently, the whole Breuer family. Of course, like anybody else we must wonder how things are to continue without the guiding strategic mind of Bernhard Breuer. Carrying on in the same vein will be made even more difficult by the fact that he has left the wine world an excellent 2003 vintage as his legacy, in which not only the full-bodied dry Rieslings, for which Breuer was particularly famous, are most convincing. This time, the botrytis dessert wines, too, are of a quality such as we have seen here only rarely. We preferred – only just – the Trockenbeerenauslese from the Berg Schlossberg vineyard to its counterpart from the Nonnenberg site. Talking about dry Rieslings: Our tasting this year entitled "Ten Years Later" proved once again that only very few German winemakers have devoted themselves to top-level dry Rieslings with the level of dedication that Bernhard Breuer showed: His two impressive entries from the 1994 vintage pulled off a double victory, taking first and second places in the tasting! We look forward with interest to see what the new era, beginning with the 2004 vintage, holds for this winery. A memorial stone donated by the VDP has been placed in the heart of the Rüdesheimer Berg vineyard, a visible reminder of the great winemaker Bernhard Breuer.

2003 "Sauvage" Riesling trocken
12.5%, ♀ till 2006 **85**

2003 Rauenthal "Estate"
Riesling trocken
12.5%, ♀ till 2006 **86**

2002 Rauenthal "Estate"
Riesling trocken
12%, ♀ till 2007 **87**

The estates: ✚✚✚✚✚ World's finest · ✚✚✚✚ Germany's best · ✚✚✚ Very good · ✚✚ Good · ✚ Reliable

2003 Rüdesheim "Estate"
Riesling trocken
12.5%, ♀ till 2008   **87**

2003 "Terra Montosa"
Riesling trocken
12.5%, ♀ till 2009   **87**

2002 Grauer Burgunder trocken
13.5%, ♀ till 2006   **88**

2003 Rüdesheim Berg Roseneck
Riesling trocken
13%, ♀ till 2008   **88**

2003 Grauer Burgunder trocken
13.5%, ♀ till 2010   **88**

2002 Rüdesheim Berg Roseneck
Riesling trocken
12.5%, ♀ till 2009   **89**

2003 Rauenthal Nonnenberg
Riesling trocken
13%, ♀ till 2012   **89**

2003 Rüdesheim Berg Rottland
Riesling trocken
13%, ♀ till 2010   **89**

2002 Grauer Burgunder
trocken "B"
13.5%, ♀ till 2008   **89**

2002 Rauenthal Nonnenberg
Riesling trocken
12.5%, ♀ till 2009   **90**

2003 Rüdesheim Berg Schlossberg
Riesling trocken
13%, ♀ till 2015   **91**

2002 Rüdesheim Berg Schlossberg
Riesling trocken
12.5%, ♀ till 2010   **92**

2003 Rüdesheim Bischofsberg
Riesling Auslese
10%, ♀ till 2014   **88**

2002 Rüdesheim Berg Rottland
Riesling Auslese Goldkapsel
8.5%, ♀ till 2010   **88**

2002 Rüdesheim Berg Schlossberg
Riesling Auslese Goldkapsel
8.5%, ♀ till 2012   **88**

2002 Rüdesheim Bischofsberg
Riesling Auslese Goldkapsel
8%, ♀ till 2014   **89**

2003 Rüdesheim Berg Rottland
Riesling Auslese Goldkapsel
10.5%, ♀ till 2015   **89**

2002 Rauenthal Nonnenberg
Riesling Beerenauslese
8%, ♀ till 2012   **90**

2003 Rauenthal Nonnenberg
Riesling Auslese Goldkapsel
9.5%, ♀ till 2014   **90**

2002 Rüdesheim Berg Schlossberg
Riesling Trockenbeerenauslese
7.5%, ♀ till 2016   **91**

2003 Rüdesheim Berg Schlossberg
Riesling Auslese Goldkapsel
8.5%, ♀ till 2016   **91**

2003 Rauenthal Nonnenberg
Riesling Trockenbeerenauslese
7.5%, ♀ till 2024   **93**

2003 Rüdesheim Berg Schlossberg
Riesling Trockenbeerenauslese
7%, ♀ till 2026   **94**

——— Red wines ———

2002 Spätburgunder trocken
13%, ♀ till 2010   **87**

2002 Spätburgunder trocken "B"
14%, ♀ till 2015   **89**

GEORG BREUER

NONNENBERG
MONOPOL

2001

RHEINGAU RIESLING

The wines: **100** Perfect · **95–99** Outstanding · **90–94** Excellent · **85–89** Very good · **80–84** Good · **75–79** Average

WEINGUT
DR. CORVERS-KAUTER

Owner: Matthias and Brigitte Corvers
Manager and winemaker:
Dr. Matthias Corvers
65375 Oestrich-Winkel,
Rheingaustraße 129
Tel. (0 67 23) 26 14, Fax 24 04
e-mail: info@corvers-kauter.de
Internet: www.corvers-kauter.de
Directions: B 42, Winkel/Mittelheim exit,
first right, on right after 800 meters
Sales: At winery, by appointment;
at vinotheque in old vaulted cellar
Opening hours: April to December
Fri. and Sat. 16:00 to 18:00 hours
Sun. 10:00 to 12:00 hours
Wine bar: May, June, Sept. to mid-Oct.,
Nov., Wed.–Fri. from 17:00, Sat. and
Sun. from 15:00 hours
Specialties: Regional cuisine
Worth seeing: 200-year-old renovated
manor-house and attractive vaulted cellar

Vineyard area: 11 hectares
Annual production: 80,000 bottles
Top sites: Rüdesheimer Berg
Roseneck, Rottland and Schlossberg
Soil types: Taunus quartzite with slate,
stony, gravelly phyllite, loess-clay
Grape varieties: 81% Riesling, 14%
Spätburgunder, 5% other varieties
Average yield: 65 hl/ha
Best vintages: 2001, 2003

When Brigitte and Dr. Matthias Corvers
got married in 1996, they also brought together two wineries, one from Rüdesheim
and one from Oestrich-Winkel. The 2001
wines were very interesting, the 2002 vintage did not quite live up to this standard. Now, the 2003 vintage has earned
the winery a second bunch of grapes. The
elegant and racy off-dry Kabinett from
the Berg Rottland site, the invigorating
Spätlese from the St. Nikloaus site, and
the spicy Auslese from the Hasensprung:
The wines are of remarkably good quality. The range is crowned by a majestic
Trockenbeerenauslese.

2003 Rüdesheimer Bischofsberg
Riesling trocken Erstes Gewächs
13.5%, ♀ till 2007 — **86**

2003 Rüdesheimer Berg Rottland
Riesling halbtrocken
13.5%, ♀ till 2007 — **85**

2003 Rüdesheimer Berg Roseneck
Riesling Kabinett halbtrocken
12.5%, ♀ till 2007 — **86**

2003 Rüdesheimer Drachenstein
Riesling Spätlese feinherb
12.5%, ♀ till 2008 — **87**

2003 Mittelheimer St. Nikolaus
Riesling Spätlese
10%, ♀ till 2014 — **88**

2002 Winkeler Gutenberg
Riesling Eiswein
6.5%, ♀ till 2012 — **89**

2003 Winkeler Hasensprung
Riesling Auslese
7.5%, ♀ till 2015 — **90**

2003 Oestricher Doosberg
Riesling Trockenbeerenauslese
8%, ♀ till 2020 — **93**

DIEFENHARDT'SCHES WEINGUT

Owner: Peter Seyffardt
Manager: Peter Nägler
Winemaker: Peter Seyffardt
65344 Martinsthal, Hauptstraße 11
Tel. (0 61 23) 7 14 90, Fax 7 48 41
e-mail: weingut@diefenhardt.de
Internet: www.diefenhardt.de
Directions: A 66, then on the B 42
and on to the B 260
Opening hours: Mon.–Fri. 09:00 to
12:00 hours and 14:00 to 18:00 hours
Sat. 10:00 to 17:00 hours
Wine bar: April to October
from 17:00 to 23:00 hours
Closed Sun. and Mon.
Worth seeing: Historical barrel cellar
dating back to the 17th century

Vineyard area: 16.6 hectares
Annual production: 100,000 bottles
Top sites: Martinsthaler Langen-
berg, Wildsau and Rödchen, Rauen-
thaler Rothenberg
Soil types: Loess on slate, red
phyllite slate, sandy
Grape varieties: 80% Riesling, 17%
Spätburgunder, 3% other varieties
Average yield: 76 hl/ha
Best vintages: 2000, 2001, 2003
Member: VDP

In the past few years, the quality produced here has been somewhat patchy:
While we found the wines of the 2001
vintage to be good, those of the 2002 vintage lacked elegance. The 2003 vintage
shows a marked improvement: From the
First Growth from the Langenberg vineyard through to the Auslese wines from
the same site, these are wines to be enjoyed. The two reds of the 2002 vintage,
too, are very attractive. Some events
of the Rheingau Music Festival are held
in the ever-popular restaurant and wine
bar. There is also a good reason why the
well-known chansonette Ulrike Neradt
often puts in performances there – she
hails from this winery in Martinsthal.

2003 Martinsthaler Langenberg
Riesling trocken Erstes Gewächs
12.5%, ♀ till 2007 — 88

2003 Martinsthaler Wildsau
Riesling Kabinett halbtrocken
11.5%, ♀ till 2006 — 83

2003 Rauenthaler Rothenberg
Riesling Spätlese
10.5%, ♀ till 2008 — 85

2001 Martinsthaler Langenberg
Riesling Spätlese
9%, ♀ till 2008 — 86

2003 Martinsthaler Langenberg
Riesling Auslese Goldkapsel
10.5%, ♀ till 2012 — 88

2003 Martinsthaler Langenberg
Riesling Auslese
8.5%, ♀ till 2014 — 89

2001 Martinsthaler Wildsau
Riesling Eiswein
9%, ♀ till 2015 — 90

——— Red wines ———

2002 Martinsthaler Rödchen
Spätburgunder trocken
13%, ♀ till 2009 — 86

2002 Martinsthaler Rödchen
Spätburgunder trocken "S"
13%, ♀ till 2012 — 87

The wines: **100** Perfect · **95–99** Outstanding · **90–94** Excellent · **85–89** Very good · **80–84** Good · **75–79** Average

551

DOMDECHANT WERNER'SCHES WEINGUT

Owner: Dr. Franz-Werner Michel
Administrator and winemaker:
Michael Bott
65234 Hochheim, Rathausstraße 30
Tel. (0 61 46) 83 50 37, Fax 83 50 38
e-mail:
weingut@domdechantwerner.com
Internet:
www.domdechantwerner.com
Directions: A 671, Hochheim-Süd exit,
direction Altstadt, after 100 meters turn
right, then right again into the vineyards
Opening hours: Mon.–Fri. 08:00 to
18:00 hours, Sat. 08:00 to 13:00 hours
by appointment
History: The father of Domdechant Dr.
Franz Werner bought the estate in 1780
Worth seeing: Old estate buildings, in
family ownership since 1780, manor-
house, historical vaulted cellar

Vineyard area: 12.3 hectares
Annual production: 90,000 bottles
Top sites: Hochheimer Domde-
chaney, Kirchenstück, Stein, Hölle
Soil types: Limestone, clay and loess
Grape varieties: 98% Riesling,
2% Spätburgunder
Average yield: 60 hl/ha
Best vintages: 1999, 2002, 2003
Member: VDP

Following on two lesser vintage ranges in
2000 and 2001, this winery in Hochheim
with its long tradition presented a significantly improved quality last year. With
regard to the 2003 vintage presented now,
we are enthusiastic about the quality,
and cannot remember ever having tasted
a more homogeneous good range here.
From the harmonious basic wines right
through to the excellent Spätlese and
Auslese wines from the Domdechaney
and Kirchenstück vineyards, we can recommend practically all the wines produced. In addition, the two Trockenbeerenauslese wines are really outstanding.
Two-thirds of the production is exported.

2003 Hochheimer Kirchenstück
Riesling Spätlese trocken
13%, ♀ till 2007 **86**

2003 Hochheimer Domdechaney
Riesling trocken Erstes Gewächs
13%, ♀ till 2008 **88**

2003 Hochheimer Hölle
Riesling Kabinett
8.5%, ♀ till 2010 **88**

2002 Hochheimer Domdechaney
Riesling Auslese
7.5%, ♀ till 2010 **89**

2003 Hochheimer Kirchenstück
Riesling Spätlese
8%, ♀ till 2012 **89**

2003 Hochheimer Kirchenstück
Riesling Auslese
7.5%, ♀ till 2012 **89**

2003 Hochheimer Domdechaney
Riesling Spätlese
8%, ♀ till 2015 **90**

2002 Hochheimer Kirchenstück
Riesling Eiswein
7.5%, ♀ till 2015 **91**

2003 Hochheimer Kirchenstück
Riesling Trockenbeerenauslese
6.5%, ♀ till 2025 **93**

2003 Hochheimer Domdechaney
Riesling Trockenbeerenauslese
↗ auction wine, 6%, ♀ till 2025 **96**

DOMDECHANT WERNER
2000er
Hochheimer Hölle
Riesling Kabinett
ERZEUGERABFÜLLUNG

R H E I N G A U

750 ml	alc 8.0 % vol
D 65239 Hochheim/M.	Produce of Germany
Qualitätswein mit Prädikat	A. P. Nr. 40 083 009 01

The estates: ✦✦✦✦✦ World's finest · ✦✦✦✦ Germany's best · ✦✦✦ Very good · ✦✦ Good · ✦ Reliable

WEINGUT
FRIEDRICH FENDEL

Owner: Fendel-Hetzert family
Manager and winemaker: Paul Hetzert
Administrators: Paul & Walter Hetzert
65385 Rüdesheim am Rhein,
Marienthaler Straße 46
Tel. (0 67 22) 9 05 70, Fax 90 57 66
e-mail: info@friedrich-fendel.de
Internet: www.friedrich-fendel.de
Directions: B 42, Rüdesheim direction of
St. Hildegard abbey, in Eibingen suburb
Sales: Walter Hetzert jun.
Opening hours: Mon.–Fri. 08:00 to
18:00 hours, Sat. 10:00 to 16:00 hours
and by appointment
Wine bar: Tue.–Fri. 16:00 to 24:00, Sat.,
Sun. and public holidays from 11:30 hours
Worth seeing: Vaulted cellar

Vineyard area: 10 hectares
Annual production: 95,000 bottles
Top sites: Rüdesheimer Berg
Schlossberg, Berg Roseneck,
Berg Rottland and Kirchenpfad
Soil types: Quartzite and phyllite slate,
sandstone and loess-clay
Grape varieties: 87% Riesling, 10%
Spätburgunder, 3% Weißburgunder
Average yield: 68 hl/ha
Best vintages: 2000, 2002, 2003
Member: VDP

Following on a rather patchy 2001 vintage, this estate last year presented wines of the 2002 vintage that marked a return to the high standards of the 1999 and 2000 vintages. Now the range of 2003 wines follows on from this high standard. The wines we liked best were the First Growth from the Klosterlay vineyard, as well as the surprisingly elegant fruity dry Auslese from the Berg Rottland site. Once again, the characterful dry Riesling "Fum Allerhinnerschde" (from the very back) is a very attractive wine. This historical brand, registered as long ago as 1903, describes the wines stored right at the back of the cellar, intended to honor this as the best wine in the cellar.

2003 Riesling trocken
12.5%, ♀ till 2006 **84**

2002 Riesling
trocken "Fum Allerhinnerschde"
12%, ♀ till 2006 **85**

2003 Riesling
trocken "Fum Allerhinnerschde"
13%, ♀ till 2007 **85**

2003 Rüdesheimer Berg Rottland
Riesling Auslese trocken
13%, ♀ till 2008 **86**

2003 Rüdesheimer Klosterlay
Riesling trocken Erstes Gewächs
13%, ♀ till 2008 **86**

2002 Rüdesheimer Berg Roseneck
Riesling Spätlese feinherb
12.5%, ♀ till 2006 **85**

2003 Rüdesheimer Kirchenpfad
Riesling "Josef Friedrich Fendel"
12.5%, ♀ till 2007 **83**

2003 Rüdesheimer Berg Schlossberg
Riesling Spätlese
12%, ♀ till 2008 **84**

2002 Rüdesheimer Berg Schlossberg
Riesling Spätlese
⤳ auction wine, 10%, ♀ till 2006 **85**

2003 Rüdesheimer Klosterlay
Riesling Kabinett
12%, ♀ till 2009 **86**

WEINGUT JOACHIM FLICK

Owner: Reiner Flick
65439 Flörsheim-Wicker, Straßenmühle
Tel. (0 61 45) 76 86, Fax 5 43 93
e-mail: info@flick-wein.de
Internet: www.flick-wein.de
Directions: A 66, Flörsheim-Weilbach exit; A 671, Hochheim-Nord exit
Opening hours: Mon.–Fri. 15:00 to 19:00 hours, Sat. 10:00 to 14:00 hours and by appointment
Wine bistro: "Flörsheimer Warte" open Sat. and Sun.
History: Winemaking here since 1775
Worth a visit: Winery festival on last weekend in August, Christmas market first December weekend
Worth seeing: Renovated sparkling wine cellar for events with up to 400 guests

---

Vineyard area: 14 hectares
Annual production: 120,000 bottles
Top sites: Wickerer Mönchs-gewann and Stein, Hochheimer Hölle
Soil types: Loess-clay, limestone
Grape varieties: 82% Riesling, 10% Spätburgunder, 4% each of Weiß- and Grauburgunder
Average yield: 70 hl/ha
Best vintages: 2001, 2002, 2003
Member: VDP

It has taken hard-working Reiner Flick only 20 years to expand the half a hectare of vineyard inherited from his father to a respectable area of 14 hectares. The most recent parcel to be added consisted of 2.7 hectares of the Wickerer Nonnenberg site, a vineyard that is first mentioned in documents dating back to 1281. Flick acquired the Straßenmühle as early as 1994, moved his residence to the complex, developed this to a beautiful ensemble of buildings. Following on the astoundingly good range of 2002 wines, Flick has taken another step forward in 2003. The elegantly spicy Erstes Gewächs (First Growth) is among the very best in the Rheingau, while the botrytis dessert wines surpass all their predecessors.

2003 Riesling Classic
12%, ♀ till 2007 — **84**

2003 Hochheimer Hölle
Riesling Spätlese trocken
13.5%, ♀ till 2008 — **87**

2003 Wickerer Mönchsgewann
Riesling trocken Erstes Gewächs
13%, ♀ till 2009 — **89**

2003 Wickerer Mönchsgewann
Riesling Spätlese
9.5%, ♀ till 2009 — **88**

2003 Hochheimer Hölle
Riesling Auslese
10%, ♀ till 2010 — **88**

2002 Wickerer Mönchsgewann
Riesling Auslese
7.5%, ♀ till 2010 — **90**

2002 Wickerer Mönchsgewann
Riesling Spätlese
↗ auction wine, 8.5%, ♀ till 2010 — **90**

2002 Wickerer Mönchsgewann
Riesling Beerenauslese
↗ auction wine, 6.5%, ♀ till 2025 — **92**

2003 Wickerer Stein
Riesling Trockenbeerenauslese
6.5%, ♀ till 2022 — **94**

2003 Hochheimer Hölle
Riesling Trockenbeerenauslese Goldkapsel
↗ auction wine, 6%, ♀ till 2030 — **96**

Joachim Flick

2002
Wickerer Mönchsgewann
RIESLING
Qualitätswein b. A.
A. P. Nr. 42017 011 02
RHEINGAU
13,0% vol   Gutsabfüllung   0,75 l
ERSTES 🏛 🏛 🏛 GEWÄCHS

Joachim Flick · Weingut in der Straßenmühle
D-65439 Flörsheim-Wicker · Telefon (0 61 45) 76 86

WEINGUT
ALEXANDER FREIMUTH

Owner: Alexander Freimuth
65366 Geisenheim-Marienthal,
Am Rosengärtchen 25
Tel. (0 67 22) 98 10 70, Fax 98 10 71
e-mail:
info@weingut-alexander-freimuth.de
Internet:
www.weingut-alexander-freimuth.de
*Directions: B 42, Geisenheim direction
of Marienthal suburb, at southern border of town in the vineyards*
Sales: Karin Freimuth
Opening hours: Mon.–Sat. by appointment
Restaurant/Wine bar: Open for 10 days
during Rheingau gourmet weeks in May

Vineyard area: 7.5 hectares
Annual production: 50,000 bottles
Top sites: Geisenheimer Kläuser-
weg, Rüdesheimer Bischofsberg
Soil types: Deep loess-clay
Grape varieties: 60% Riesling, 25%
Spätburgunder, 10% Weißbur-
gunder, 5% Rivaner
Average yield: 75 hl/ha
Best vintages: 2001, 2002, 2003
Member: VDP

This is one of those friendly, confidence-
inspiring family operations that quietly
delivers consistently reliable quality
every year. The main focus of production,
most of which is sold to restaurants and
private customers, continues to lie with
dry Riesling. It is in this field that Alexander Freimuth shows his strength in the
2003 vintage, presenting two very good
Erstes Gewächs (First Growth) wines.
Once again, his 2002 Spätburgunder (Pinot Noir) from the Rüdesheimer Magdalenenkreuz is a very attractive wine, with
aromas of blueberry and star anise, a
wine that spreads a feeling of warmth –
particularly with a view to its consumer-
friendly price!

2003 Geisenheimer Kläuserweg
Riesling Spätlese trocken "Zero"
13.5%, ♀ till 2006   83

2003 Geisenheimer
Riesling trocken
12.5%, ♀ till 2006   84

2003 Riesling Classic
12.5%, ♀ till 2006   84

2002 Riesling
trocken "Alte Reben"
13%, ♀ till 2006   87

2003 Rüdesheimer Bischofsberg
Riesling trocken Erstes Gewächs
13.5%, ♀ till 2010   88

2003 Geisenheimer Kläuserweg
Riesling trocken Erstes Gewächs
14%, ♀ till 2010   88

2002 Rüdesheimer Bischofsberg
Riesling Auslese
10.5%, ♀ till 2007   87

2003 Geisenheimer Mönchspfad
Riesling Trockenbeerenauslese
10.5%, ♀ till 2015   89

———— Red wines ————

2003 Rüdesheimer Magdalenenkreuz
Spätburgunder Rosé Kabinett
12%, ♀ till 2007   84

2002 "Pinot Noir"
Spätburgunder trocken
13%, ♀ till 2008   83

2001 Rüdesheimer Magdalenenkreuz
Spätburgunder trocken Barrique
12.5%, ♀ till 2009   85

2002 Rüdesheimer Magdalenenkreuz
Spätburgunder trocken Barrique
13%, ♀ till 2010   88

The wines: **100** Perfect · **95–99** Outstanding · **90–94** Excellent · **85–89** Very good · **80–84** Good · **75–79** Average

WEINGUT HAMM

Owner and manager: Karl-Heinz Hamm
65375 Oestrich-Winkel, Hauptstr. 60
Tel. (0 67 23) 24 32, Fax 8 76 66
e-mail: info@hamm-wine.de
Internet: www.hamm-wine.de
Directions: B 42; Winkel exit, turn left
immediately, right after 50 meters, right
again after 30 meters into Hauptstraße
Sales: Karl-Heinz and Christine Hamm
Opening hours: Mon.–Fri. 08:00 to
12:00 hours and by appointment
Wine bar: In winter from 18:00, Sun.
and public holidays from 12:00 hours,
closed Mon. and Tue., Jan. and Feb.
April–Oct. from 18:00, Sun. and public
holidays from 12:00 hours, closed Mon.
Worth seeing: Baroque Patrician building with Mediterranean-style courtyard

---

Vineyard area: 7 hectares
Annual production: 50,000 bottles
Top sites: Winkeler Jesuiten-
garten and Hasensprung
Soil types: Quartzite-slate, loess-clay
Grape varieties: 90% Riesling,
10% Spätburgunder
Average yield: 65 hl/ha
Best vintages: 2002, 2003
Member: VDP, Naturland

"Wein oder nicht sein" (Wine or not to
be) is the motto on the yellow label Karl-
Heinz Hamm puts on his summer wines,
collectively labelled with the HAMMlet
brand, with its obvious literary connota-
tions. In fact, this is a distinct style of
Riesling, most suited to quaffing. Hamm
is not only dedicated to organic wine
production, he is also quite open to self-
criticism, a feature not all that common among winemakers, freely admitting
that not everything went smoothly during
the 90's. The full-bodied wines of the
2002 vintage gave cause to accept him into
this guide, the 2003 vintage wines represent another significant improvement in
quality. In the words of Karl-Heinz
Hamm, it is "simply the best we have
ever harvested!"

2003 "HAMMlet" Riesling trocken
13%, ♀ till 2006   **83**

2002 Winkeler Hasensprung
Riesling Spätlese trocken
12%, ♀ till 2006   **84**

2003 Winkeler Dachsberg
Riesling Spätlese feinherb
13%, ♀ till 2008   **84**

2002 Winkeler Hasensprung
Riesling Spätlese feinherb – 4 –
12%, ♀ till 2007   **85**

2003 "HAMMlet" Riesling feinherb
11.5%, ♀ till 2007   **85**

2003 Winkeler Hasensprung
Riesling Spätlese feinherb
14%, ♀ till 2010   **85**

2003 Winkeler Hasensprung
Riesling Auslese
12%, ♀ till 2010   **85**

2003 Winkeler Hasensprung
Riesling Beerenauslese
8%, ♀ till 2012   **87**

2003 Winkeler Jesuitengarten
Riesling Beerenauslese
8.5%, ♀ till 2012   **89**

2003 Winkeler Hasensprung
Riesling Trockenbeerenauslese
6.5%, ♀ till 2015   **90**

2003 Winkeler Jesuitengarten
Riesling Trockenbeerenauslese
7.5%, ♀ till 2015   **91**

————— Red wine —————

2002 Spätburgunder trocken
14%, ♀ till 2009   **85**

WEINGUT
PRINZ VON HESSEN

**Owner: Hessische Hausstiftung,
Landgraf Moritz von Hessen**
Manager: Markus Sieben
Vineyard manager: Klaus Walter
Winemaker: Gerhard Kirsch
65366 Johannisberg, Grund 1
Tel. (0 67 22) 81 72, Fax 5 05 88
e-mail: weingut@prinz-von-hessen.com
Internet: www.prinz-von-hessen.com
*Directions: B 42 direction of Wiesbaden,
Industriegebiet Geisenheim exit, direc-
tion of Johannisberg, first building on left*
Opening hours: Mon.–Fri. 08:00 to
17:00, first and third Sat. of the month
11:00 to 15:00 hours, and by appointment
Worth seeing: Old barrel cellar

Vineyard area: 42 hectares
Annual production: 350,000 bottles
Top sites: Winkeler Hasensprung,
Jesuitengarten, Johannisberger Klaus
Soil types: Deep loess on gravel,
tertiary marl, decomposed quartzite
Grape varieties: 88% Riesling, 8%
Spätburgunder, 1% each of Weißbur-
gunder and Merlot, 2% other varieties
Average yield: 69 hl/ha
Best vintages: 1998, 1999, 2003
Member: VDP

Under the guidance of Markus Sieben
this large estate experienced a positive
development at the end of the 90's. Only
the best wines still bear a vineyard designation, all the others are marketed as
"Gutsriesling," estate varietal wine. Following on the progress seen in previous
years, the basic wines presented in 2001
and 2002 were rather mediocre. In the
2003 vintage, the basic wines are rather
poor, while the First Growths are on good
form, and the botrytis dessert wines are
simply outstanding: The Trockenbeerenauslese from the Klaus vineyard is one
of the best in the region, while the Beerenauslese, too, displays brilliant and rare
finesse. The 2002 vintage red wines are
also remarkably good.

2003 Winkeler Jesuitengarten
Riesling trocken Erstes Gewächs
12.5%, ♀ till 2007   **87**

2003 Johannisberger Klaus
Riesling trocken Erstes Gewächs
12.5%, ♀ till 2007   **87**

2003 Winkeler Hasensprung
Riesling trocken Erstes Gewächs
12.5%, ♀ till 2008   **88**

2003 Winkeler Hasensprung
Riesling Spätlese
10.5%, ♀ till 2010   **88**

2003 Johannisberger Klaus
Riesling Auslese Goldkapsel
8.5%, ♀ till 2014   **91**

2002 Winkeler Hasensprung
Riesling Eiswein
6.5%, ♀ till 2015   **92**

2003 Johannisberger Klaus
Riesling Beerenauslese
7%, ♀ till 2025   **94**

2003 Johannisberger Klaus
Riesling Trockenbeerenauslese
6%, ♀ till 2030   **95**

———— Red wines ————

2002 Frühburgunder
trocken Barrique
13%, ♀ till 2008   **85**

2002 Spätburgunder "S" Barrique
13.5%, ♀ till 2009   **87**

The wines: **100** Perfect · **95–99** Outstanding · **90–94** Excellent · **85–89** Very good · **80–84** Good · **75–79** Average

557

SCHLOSS JOHANNISBERG

Owner: Fürst von Metternich Winneburg'sche Domäne GbR
General manager: Wolfgang Schleicher
Technical manager: Hans Kessler
65366 Geisenheim-Johannisberg, Schloss
Tel. (0 67 22) 7 00 90, Fax 70 09 33
e-mail: info@schloss-johannisberg.de
Internet: www.schloss-johannisberg.de
Directions: B 42, Industriegebiet
Geisenheim exit, follow signs
Sales: Heribert Heyn, Frank Schuber
Opening hours: Mon.–Fri. 10:00 to 13:00 and 14:00 to 18:00, Sat., Sun. and public holidays 11:00 to 18:00 hours
Restaurant: With large terrace, daily from 11:30 to 23:00 hours, Tel. (0 67 22) 9 60 90
History: Founded as a Benedictine monastery around 1100
Worth seeing: Baroque château (18th cent.), basilica (12th cent.), cellar from 1721

Vineyard area: 35 hectares
Annual production: 250,000 bottles
Top site: Schloss Johannisberger
Soil types: Taunus quartzite, medium-deep loess soils
Grape varieties: 100% Riesling
Average yield: 70 hl/ha
Best vintages: 1999, 2001, 2003
Member: VDP

Schloss Johannisberg is a majestic sight, dominating the Rhine valley high above Geisenheim. Virtually throughout its history, fantastic wines have been produced here, and even today respectable quantities of these are stored in the "Bibliotheca subterranea," the underground cellar housing the treasures. The botrytis dessert wines of the 2003 vintage give eloquent evidence of the general standard: The classical Auslese has an elegant bouquet of blackcurrants, and is characterized by brilliant and persistent fruit, the Beerenauslese shows aromas of cinnamon and honey, while the outstanding Trockenbeerenauslese counts among the four best that have been bottled in this vintage in the whole country.

2003 Schloss Johannisberger
Riesling trocken "Gelblack"
13%, ♀ till 2006 — 82

2003 Schloss Johannisberger
Riesling Kabinett trocken "Rotlack"
13%, ♀ till 2006 — 82

2003 Schloss Johannisberger
Riesling Spätlese trocken "Grünlack"
13.5%, ♀ till 2007 — 85

2003 Schloss Johannisberger
Riesling halbtrocken "Gelblack"
12.5%, ♀ till 2006 — 82

2003 Schloss Johannisberger
Riesling Kabinett halbtrocken "Rotlack"
12%, ♀ till 2007 — 84

2003 Schloss Johannisberger
Riesling Spätlese "Grünlack"
11%, ♀ till 2009 — 86

2002 Schloss Johannisberger
Riesling Spätlese "Grünlack"
10%, ♀ till 2010 — 88

2003 Schloss Johannisberger
Riesling Beerenauslese "Rosa-Goldlack"
6.5%, ♀ till 2014 — 90

2002 Schloss Johannisberger
Riesling Auslese "Rosalack" – 9 –
10.5%, ♀ till 2014 — 91

2003 Schloss Johannisberger
Riesling Auslese "Rosalack"
9.5%, ♀ till 2014 — 91

2002 Schloss Johannisberger
Riesling Eiswein "Blaulack"
9%, ♀ till 2015 — 92

2003 Schloss Johannisberger
Riesling Trockenbeerenauslese "Goldlack"
6.5%, ♀ till 2035 — 99

WEINGUT JOHANNISHOF

Owner: Johannes Eser
Manager: Johannes Eser,
Hans Hermann Eser
Winemaker: Johannes Eser
65366 Johannisberg, Grund 63
Tel. (0 67 22) 82 16, Fax 63 87
e-mail: weingut.johannishof@t-online.de
Internet: www.weingut-johannishof.de
*Directions: B 42, Geisenheim exit,
in direction of Johannisberg, on the left
500 meters after the town entrance*
Sales: Elfriede Eser, Sabine Eser
Opening hours: Mon.–Fri. 08:00 to
12:00 and 13:00 to 18:00, Sat. 10:00 to
15:00 hours, and by appointment
History: First mentioned in documents
in 817, family-owned since 1685
Worth seeing: Vaulted cellar and rarities,
sculpture "Four Seasons," new vinotheque

Vineyard area: 17.7 hectares
Annual production: 120,000 bottles
Top sites: Geisenheimer
Kläuserweg, Johannisberger Hölle
and Klaus, Rüdesheimer Berg Rott-
land, Winkeler Jesuitengarten
Soil types: Loess, loess-clay, slate top
layer, decomposed quartzite
Grape varieties: 99% Riesling,
1% Weißburgunder
Average yield: 65 hl/ha
Best vintages: 2001, 2003
Member: VDP, Charta

In 2003, this consumer-friendly family
operation in Johannisberg produced the
best wine-range seen here since long:
From the outstanding Erstes Gewächs
(First Growth) through the elegantly fruity Spätlese to the Trockenbeerenauslese
wines, this is a range of consistently high
standard across the board – our compliments! Eser now indicates three of his Johannisberg vineyard sites on the label
with only an initial: "G" stands for Goldatzel, "V" for Vogelsang and "S" is for
the Schwarzenstein site. Only the Hölle
and Klaus vineyards still have the privi-
ege being mentioned fully on the label.

2003 Rüdesheimer Berg Roseneck
Riesling Kabinett trocken
13.5%, ♀ till 2006   83

2003 Johannisberger Hölle
Riesling trocken Erstes Gewächs
14%, ♀ till 2008   88

2003 Rüdesheimer Berg Rottland
Riesling trocken Erstes Gewächs
13%, ♀ till 2010   91

2003 Johannisberg "S"
Riesling Kabinett feinherb
13%, ♀ till 2008   85

2003 Johannisberg "V"
Riesling Kabinett
10.5%, ♀ till 2009   85

2003 Rüdesheimer Berg Rottland
Riesling Auslese
7.5%, ♀ till 2010   89

2003 Rüdesheimer Berg Rottland
Riesling Spätlese
7.5%, ♀ till 2011   90

2003 Rüdesheimer Berg Rottland
Riesling Beerenauslese
7.5%, ♀ till 2016   91

2003 Johannisberger Klaus
Riesling Trockenbeerenauslese
7.5%, ♀ till 2026   93

2003 Geisenheimer Kläuserweg
Riesling Trockenbeerenauslese
7%, ♀ till 2030   94

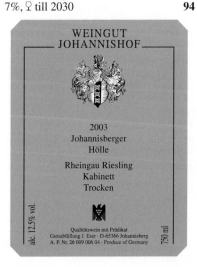

The wines: **100** Perfect · **95–99** Outstanding · **90–94** Excellent · **85–89** Very good · **80–84** Good · **75–79** Average

559

WEINGUT TONI JOST – HAHNENHOF

Owner: Peter Jost
55422 Bacharach, Oberstraße 14
Tel. (0 67 43) 12 16, Fax 10 76
e-mail: tonijost@debitel.net
Directions: A 61, Rheinböllen exit in direction of Bacharach, winery is in center of town
Sales: Linde and Peter Jost
by appointment only
Worth seeing: Old German tasting room in picturesque old part of town

---

Vineyard area: 3.2 hectares
Annual production: 30,000 bottles
Top site: Wallufer Walkenberg
Soil types: Loess-clay
Grape varieties: 80% Riesling, 15% Spätburgunder, 5% Weißburgunder
Average yield: 65 hl/ha
Best vintages: 1998, 1999, 2003
Member: VDP

Ever since 1953, the Jost winery, which is based in Bacharach, also owns some vineyards in the Rheingau region. Peter Jost's great-grandfather operated a mill in Walluf, and had two hectares of vineyard. This area has now been increased to 3.2 hectares, and is worked independently by an employee and his wife, who live in Walluf. The grapes are transported to Bacharach immediately after being picked, on the day of harvesting, and are usually pressed the same night. Apart from this, the young wines receive the same meticulous care and attention to detail that Jost lavishes on his Bacharach Rieslings. However, they only rarely reach the same level of quality as these. Bearing this in mind, the wines of the 2003 vintage – the 50th anniversary since the acquisition – represent an exception, as both an excellent Erstes Gewächs (First Growth) and several outstanding botrytis dessert wines were produced. Even the 2002 red wine from the Walkenberg vineyard, matured in barriques, was very well balanced. Our compliments!

2003 "Jodocus" Riesling trocken
12%, ♀ till 2006   **83**

2003 Weißer Burgunder trocken
13%, ♀ till 2007   **84**

2003 Wallufer Walkenberg
Riesling trocken Erstes Gewächs
13%, ♀ till 2008   **88**

2002 Wallufer Walkenberg
Riesling Spätlese
8%, ♀ till 2007   **87**

2003 Wallufer Walkenberg
Riesling Spätlese
8%, ♀ till 2010   **87**

2002 Wallufer Walkenberg
Riesling Beerenauslese Goldkapsel
🍷 auction wine, 9%, ♀ till 2015   **88**

2003 Wallufer Walkenberg
Riesling Beerenauslese
9%, ♀ till 2018   **92**

2003 Wallufer Walkenberg
Riesling Trockenbeerenauslese
🍷 auction wine, 7%, ♀ till 2030   **94**

——— Red wines ———

2001 Wallufer Walkenberg
Spätburgunder trocken
13%, ♀ till 2007   **84**

2002 Wallufer Walkenberg
Spätburgunder trocken Barrique
13%, ♀ till 2012   **85**

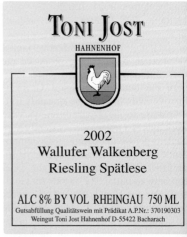

WEINGUT JAKOB JUNG

Owner: Ludwig Jung
65346 Erbach, Eberbacher Straße 22
Tel. (0 61 23) 90 06 20, Fax 90 06 21
e-mail: info@weingut-jakob-jung.de
Internet: www.weingut-jakob-jung.de
Directions: B 42, Erbach-Mitte exit
Sales: Brunhilde Jung
Opening hours: Mon.–Fri. 14:30 to
19:00 hours, Sat. 10:00 to 17:00 hours
Sun. by appointment
History: In family hands since 1799
Worth seeing: 200-year-old cellar
carved out of stone, eight meters
below the surface

Vineyard area: 10 hectares
Annual production: 80,000 bottles
Top sites: Erbacher Hohenrain,
Steinmorgen and Michelmark
Soil types: Deep loess-clay,
heavy tertiary marl
Grape varieties: 82% Riesling, 14%
Spätburgunder, 4% other varieties
Average yield: 67 hl/ha
Best vintages: 2001, 2002, 2003
Member: VDP

This is one of those rock-solid family-run
Rheingau wineries that first attracted attention with its wines in the early Nineties. Ludwig Jung is a prime example
of consistency – apart from the 2000 vintage, which is generally accepted as
having been very difficult, he has in recent years simply rolled out one good
vintage after another. The wines always
have their own individual style, are absolutely limpid, and always show a
piquant acidity. The 2003 vintage is no
exception – quite the contrary! From the
very attractive Erstes Gewächs (First
Growth) to the elegant Spätlese wines
from the Michelmark site and through to
the thoroughly impressive Trockenbeerenauslese from the Steinmorgen vineyard,
all the wines can be highly recommended.
The red wines, too, are remarkably good.

2003 Erbacher Hohenrain
Riesling trocken Erstes Gewächs
13.5%, ♀ till 2008   88

2003 Erbacher Michelmark
Riesling Spätlese Goldkapsel
⋎ auction wine, 10%, ♀ till 2010   88

2002 Erbacher Michelmark
Riesling Spätlese
9%, ♀ till 2009   89

2003 Erbacher Michelmark
Riesling Spätlese
9.5%, ♀ till 2010   89

2002 Erbacher Michelmark
Riesling Auslese
10%, ♀ till 2012   90

2003 Erbacher Michelmark
Riesling Auslese
10.5%, ♀ till 2012   90

2003 Erbacher Steinmorgen
Riesling Trockenbeerenauslese
6.5%, ♀ till 2025   91

2002 Erbacher Michelmark
Riesling Eiswein Goldkapsel
⋎ auction wine, 8%, ♀ till 2025   93

——————— Red wines ———————

2002 Erbacher Hohenrain
Spätburgunder trocken Barrique
13.5%, ♀ till 2010   88

2002 "Alexander Johannes"
Spätburgunder trocken Barrique
14%, ♀ till 2010   89

The wines: **100** Perfect · **95–99** Outstanding · **90–94** Excellent · **85–89** Very good · **80–84** Good · **75–79** Average

561

WEINGUT GRAF VON KANITZ

Owner: Sebastian Graf von Kanitz
Manager and winemaker:
Kurt Gabelmann
65391 Lorch, Rheinstraße 49
Tel. (0 67 26) 3 46, Fax 21 78
e-mail:
info@weingut-graf-von-kanitz.de
Internet:
www.weingut-graf-von-kanitz.de
*Directions: B 42, between Rüdesheim
and Loreley, follow signs from Lorch exit*
Sales: Kurt Gabelmann
Opening hours: Mon.–Fri. 09:00 to
18:00 hours, Sat. 10:00 to 13:00
and by appointment
History: Mentioned in 13th century,
later owned by Baron vom Stein, owned
by Graf von Kanitz family since 1926

Vineyard area: 13.5 hectares
Annual production: 70,000 bottles
Top sites: Lorcher Bodental-
Steinberg, Kapellenberg, Pfaffenwies
and Krone
Soil types: Quartzite, decomposed
slate and sandy clay
Grape varieties: 86% Riesling, 10%
Spätburgunder, 2% each of Müller-
Thurgau and Gewürztraminer
Average yield: 45 hl/ha
Best vintages: 1999, 2000, 2003
Member: VDP, EcoVin

The characterful wines made by Count
von Kanitz have for long been among our
most favored Rieslings of the Rheingau,
based on their characteristic terroir. They
require a few years of bottle maturation
to develop, and can be suprisingly long-
lived. A rumor spread in early 2004
that the estate was up for sale. As things
turned out, this has not come about.
Count von Kanitz was able to convince
Kurt Gabelmann, an ambitious winemaker
who was previously cellarmaster of the
state domain on the Nahe, to take over
here. It would seem that new aspirations
have been kindled here.

2002 Lorcher Kapellenberg
Riesling Spätlese trocken
12.5%, ♀ till 2006 — **84**

2003 Lorcher Pfaffenwies
Riesling Kabinett trocken
12%, ♀ till 2007 — **84**

2003 Lorcher Pfaffenwies
Riesling Spätlese trocken
12.5%, ♀ till 2007 — **84**

2001 Lorcher Krone
Riesling Erstes Gewächs
12%, ♀ till 2006 — **85**

2003 Lorcher Kapellenberg
Riesling Spätlese trocken
12.5%, ♀ till 2009 — **86**

2003 Lorcher Kapellenberg
Riesling Kabinett halbtrocken
11.5%, ♀ till 2006 — **83**

2002 Lorcher Kapellenberg
Riesling Kabinett halbtrocken
11.5%, ♀ till 2006 — **84**

2001 Lorcher Bodental-Steinberg
Riesling Auslese
10%, ♀ till 2007 — **86**

2001 Lorcher Bodental-Steinberg
Riesling Spätlese
9.5%, ♀ till 2006 — **86**

2002 Lorcher Bodental-Steinberg
Riesling Spätlese
10%, ♀ till 2006 — **86**

Snow-covered vineyards near Lorch in the Rheingau, with the Rhine in the background.
Photo: DWI/Hartmann

563

WEINGUT
AUGUST KESSELER

Owner: August Kesseler
Winemaker: Matthias Himstedt,
Thomas Muno
65385 Assmannshausen,
Lorcher Straße 16
Tel. (0 67 22) 25 13, Fax 4 74 77
e-mail: info@august-kesseler.de
Internet: www.august-kesseler.de
Directions: B 42, Assmannshausen exit, in
the center of town to the left of the church
Sales: Endre Kasa
by appointment
Worth seeing: Old double-storey wine
cellar in slate mountain, dating to 1793

Vineyard area: 20 hectares
Annual production: 115,000 bottles
Top sites: Assmannshäuser
Höllenberg, Rüdesheimer Berg
Schlossberg, Bischofsberg, Berg
Roseneck
Soil types: Slate-phyllite, slate,
quartzite soils, sandy clay
Grape varieties: 50% Riesling, 45%
Spätburgunder, 5% Silvaner
Average yield: 45 hl/ha
Best vintages: 1999, 2001, 2003
Member: VDP, Deutsches Barrique
Forum

August Kesseler is without doubt one of
the most talented winemakers in the
Rheingau, and he also stands out for his
exceptional talent to present both himself
and his winery in the most spectacular
way. He set out some fifteen years ago to
polish up the image of the traditional and
venerable Assmannshausen red wines by
using new oak. In the meantime, Kesseler
in true individualistic style demonstra-
tively turned away from this again, and
even cancelled his membership in the
German Barrique Forum. Today he is
back to using small, new oak barrels, and
has very recently taken up his membership in the Forum again. In between these
changes, there was a phase in which August Kesseler was primarily concerned

with running Schloss Reinhartshausen.
For the past few years, he has again been
concentrating fully on his own estate in
Assmannshausen, and the considerable
success of this is there for all to see. In the
1997, 1999 and 2001 vintages his red
wines from the Höllenberg and Berg
Schlossberg sites were among the best
and most elegant of their type in Germany, and now the 2002 vintage is out,
and makes no exception. Whereas the
Höllenberg wine impresses with its spicy
black cherry aromas, the wine from the
Schlossberg shows incredible complexity
and structure. As far as the white wines of
the 2003 vintage are concerned, the botrytis dessert wines can only be described
as magnificent. The Beerenauslese wines
produced by Kesseler are simply better
than anything he has done before. However, in some cases the quantities bottled
are so small that the greater part of these
wines will probably end up in the private
rarities cellar of the house. What's miss-
ing in the 2003 range were really good
dry white wines, it appears that another
vintage has gone by without an Erstes
Gewächs (First Growth) being produced.

2003 Riesling Kabinett trocken
12.5%, ♀ till 2007 **83**

2003 Rüdesheimer Berg Roseneck
Riesling Spätlese trocken
13%, ♀ till 2007 **84**

2002 Rüdesheimer Berg Roseneck
Riesling Spätlese trocken
12.5%, ♀ till 2006 **86**

2002 Lorcher Schlossberg
Riesling Spätlese trocken
12.5%, ♀ till 2006 **86**

2001 Rüdesheimer Berg Roseneck
Riesling Spätlese trocken
13%, ♀ till 2008 **87**

2000 Rüdesheimer Berg Schlossberg
Riesling Spätlese trocken
12%, ♀ till 2006 **8**

2002 Rüdesheimer Berg Schlossberg
Riesling Spätlese trocken
12.5%, ♀ till 2008 **8**

The estates: ♦♦♦♦♦ World's finest · ♦♦♦♦ Germany's best · ♦♦♦ Very good · ♦♦ Good · ♦ Reliabl

2001 Rüdesheimer Berg Roseneck
Riesling Erstes Gewächs
13%, ♀ till 2012 **91**

2003 Lorcher Schlossberg
Riesling Kabinett
11%, ♀ till 2007 **85**

2003 "Estate" Riesling
10.5%, ♀ till 2006 **85**

2002 Rüdesheimer Berg Schlossberg
Riesling Spätlese
10%, ♀ till 2010 **87**

2002 Rüdesheimer Berg Roseneck
Riesling Kabinett Goldkapsel
9.5%, ♀ till 2010 **87**

2003 Rüdesheimer Berg Schlossberg
Riesling Spätlese Goldkapsel
10%, ♀ till 2010 **88**

2001 Rüdesheimer Bischofsberg
Riesling Auslese Goldkapsel
↗ auction wine, 8.5%, ♀ till 2008 **89**

2002 Rüdesheimer Bischofsberg
Riesling Auslese Goldkapsel
↗ auction wine, 8.5%, ♀ till 2012 **89**

2000 Rüdesheimer Berg Roseneck
Riesling Spätlese Goldkapsel
8%, ♀ till 2010 **90**

2001 Rüdesheimer Berg Schlossberg
Riesling Spätlese Goldkapsel
8.5%, ♀ till 2015 **91**

2003 Rüdesheimer Bischofsberg
Riesling Auslese Goldkapsel
8%, ♀ till 2015 **91**

2003 Lorcher Schlossberg
Riesling Beerenauslese
8%, ♀ till 2018 **93**

2003 Rüdesheimer Berg Roseneck
Riesling Beerenauslese
7.5%, ♀ till 2020 **93**

2002 Rüdesheimer Bischofsberg
Riesling Beerenauslese Goldkapsel
↗ auction wine, 7.5%, ♀ till 2015 **94**

2003 Rüdesheimer Berg Roseneck
Riesling Beerenauslese Goldkapsel
↗ auction wine, 7.5%, ♀ till 2020 **94**

2001 Rüdesheimer Bischofsberg
Riesling Beerenauslese Goldkapsel
↗ auction wine, 6.5%, ♀ till 2022 **95**

2003 Rüdesheimer Bischofsberg
Riesling Trockenbeerenauslese Goldkapsel
↗ auction wine, 6%, ♀ till 2030 **96**

2003 Lorcher Schlossberg
Riesling Trockenbeerenauslese Goldkapsel
↗ auction wine, 7.5%, ♀ till 2030 **97**

——————— Red wines ———————

2001 Spätburgunder
trocken "Cuvée Max"
13.5%, ♀ till 2012 **87**

2002 Spätburgunder
trocken "Cuvée Max"
14%, ♀ till 2010 **88**

2001 Rüdesheimer Berg Schlossberg
Spätburgunder trocken
14.5%, ♀ till 2020 **89**

2001 Assmannshäuser Höllenberg
Spätburgunder trocken
13.5%, ♀ till 2018 **91**

2002 Assmannshäuser Höllenberg
Spätburgunder trocken
14%, ♀ till 2012 **91**

2002 Rüdesheimer Berg Schlossberg
Spätburgunder trocken
14.5%, ♀ till 2015 **91**

SPÄTBURGUNDER
RHEINGAU
ASSMANNSHÄUSER HÖLLENBERG
August **Kesseler**
2002
QUALITÄTSWEIN
TROCKEN
PRODUCE OF GERMANY
ALC. 14.0% VOL   NET CONT. 750 ML
ERZEUGERABFÜLLUNG: WEINGUT AUGUST KESSELER
D-65385 ASSMANNSHAUSEN A.P.NR. 22 016 004 04

he wines: **100** Perfect · **95–99** Outstanding · **90–94** Excellent · **85–89** Very good · **80–84** Good · **75–79** Average

WEINGUT BARON ZU KNYPHAUSEN

Owner: Gerko Freiherr zu Innhausen und Knyphausen
Winemaker: Rainer Rüttiger
65346 Erbach, Draiser Hof
Tel. (0 61 23) 6 21 77, Fax 43 15
e-mail: weingut@knyphausen.de
Internet: www.knyphausen.de
Directions: A 66, Eltville-West exit, in direction of Erbach, first estate on the left
Opening hours: Mon.–Fri. 08:00 to 12:00 hours and 14:00 to 18:00 hours
Sat. 10:00 to 16:00 hours
and by appointment
Guest house: Herrlichkeit Knyphausen
History: Monastery estate Drais founded by Cistercians 1141/42, purchased by Baron von Bodelschwingh 1818
Worth seeing: Manor buildings built 1727, carved wine totem

Vineyard area: 22 hectares
Annual production: 130,000 bottles
Top sites: Erbacher Marcobrunn, Steinmorgen, Hohenrain and Siegelsberg, Hattenheimer Wisselbrunnen
Soil types: Micaceous tertiary marl, some loess
Grape varieties: 96% Riesling, 4% Spätburgunder
Average yield: 65 hl/ha
Best vintages: 2000, 2002, 2003
Member: VDP

The Draiser Hof has a beautiful location on the outskirts of Erbach. Baron von Knyphausen has renovated the historical press house and one of the vaulted cellars so they can be used for all kinds of festivities, and has also built the guest house "Herrlichkeit." The 2001 vintage was just as reliably good as was the 2002 vintage. Of the 2003 wines we particularly liked the fruity Spätlese and Auslese wines. One of the points noted was that they had clearly been fermented further than in most other Rheingau wineries. The basic dry wines could still be improved.

2003 Riesling trocken
12%, ♀ till 2006 — **83**

2003 Hattenheimer Wisselbrunnen
Riesling trocken Erstes Gewächs
12.5%, ♀ till 2007 — **87**

2003 Kiedricher Sandgrub
Riesling Kabinett feinherb
11.5%, ♀ till 2006 — **84**

2003 Erbacher Steinmorgen
Riesling Kabinett
11%, ♀ till 2006 — **83**

2003 Kiedricher Sandgrub
Riesling Kabinett Charta
11.5%, ♀ till 2006 — **83**

2002 Erbacher Steinmorgen
Riesling Spätlese
8.5%, ♀ till 2007 — **87**

2003 Erbacher Steinmorgen
Riesling Spätlese
10%, ♀ till 2008 — **87**

2002 Erbacher Siegelsberg
Riesling Eiswein
11%, ♀ till 2008 — **88**

2003 Hattenheimer Wisselbrunnen
Riesling Auslese
10.5%, ♀ till 2009 — **88**

2003 Erbacher Steinmorgen
Riesling Auslese Goldkapsel
10.5%, ♀ till 2011 — **88**

2003 Hattenheimer Wisselbrunnen
Riesling Trockenbeerenauslese
7.5%, ♀ till 2015 — **90**

2003 Erbacher Michelmark
Riesling Beerenauslese
7.5%, ♀ till 2018 — **92**

WEINGUT ROBERT KÖNIG

Owner: Robert König jun.
Manager and winemaker:
Robert König jun.
65385 Assmannshausen,
Landhaus Kenner
Tel. (0 67 22) 10 64, Fax 4 86 56
Directions: Via Aulhausen suburb, signs
from Mühlberg parking lot
Sales: By appointment
Restaurant/Wine bar: During the
Rheingau culinary weeks and on all fol-
lowing weekends in May, as well as on
open-door days in the lower Rheingau –
always Sat. and Sun. from 11:00 hours
History: Winery established 1704

Vineyard area: 7.7 hectares
Annual production: 50,000 bottles
Top sites: Assmannshäuser
Höllenberg and Frankenthal,
Rüdesheimer Berg Schlossberg
Soil types: Decomposed Taunus
quartzite, decomposed phyllite slate
Grape varieties: 90% Spätburgunder,
5% Riesling, 2% Weißburgunder, 1,5%
Frühburgunder, 1,5% other varieties
Average yield: 64 hl/ha
Best vintages: 2001, 2002, 2003
Member: VDP

Although Josef König has been working
two hectares of vineyard since the Sixties, his attention was focussed mainly on
his flourishing construction business. It
was only his son Robert and grandson
Robert junior who have gone into wine
production full-time. The cellar was extended, and the vineyard area has grown.
In the past few years, König has presented very attractive red wines, this includes the 2002 vintage. The 2003 vintage
continues this high level of quality seamlessly. While the basic wines appear to go
overboard in their opulent style, there are
some really excellent Spätburgunder (Pinot Noir) wines at the higher quality levels. The dry Spätlese from the Frankenthal site is without doubt the best wine
König has presented in a long time.

——— Red wines ———

2003 Spätburgunder trocken
13%, ♀ till 2007   **82**

2003 Assmannshäuser Höllenberg
Spätburgunder trocken
13%, ♀ till 2008   **83**

2003 Assmannshäuser Frankenthal
Spätburgunder trocken
13%, ♀ till 2008   **84**

2003 Spätburgunder
Spätlese trocken
13.5%, ♀ till 2008   **85**

2003 Assmannshäuser Frankenthal
Spätburgunder Auslese trocken
15%, ♀ till 2010   **87**

2003 Assmannshäuser Höllenberg
Spätburgunder Auslese trocken
15%, ♀ till 2010   **87**

2002 Assmannshäuser
Frühburgunder Spätlese trocken
13.5%, ♀ till 2009   **88**

2003 Assmannshäuser Höllenberg
Frühburgunder Spätlese trocken
14%, ♀ till 2010   **88**

2001 Assmannshäuser Höllenberg
Frühburgunder Spätlese trocken
13.5%, ♀ till 2009   **89**

2003 Assmannshäuser Frankenthal
Spätburgunder Spätlese trocken
14%, ♀ till 2012   **90**

The wines: **100** Perfect · **95–99** Outstanding · **90–94** Excellent · **85–89** Very good · **80–84** Good · **75–79** Average

567

WEINGUT KÖNIGIN-VICTORIABERG

Owner: Henning Hupfeld
65375 Oestrich-Winkel,
Rheingaustraße 113 and Albansgasse 4
Tel. (0 67 23) 13 98, Fax 8 84 23
e-mail: koenigin.victoriaberg@t-online.de
Internet: www.koenigin-victoriaberg.de
Directions: B 42 in direction of Rüdesheim, Mittelheim exit, then turn left
Opening hours: Mon.–Sat. 09:30 to 19:00 hours by appointment
Worth a visit: Wine tastings and events in the vineyards and at Mittelheim
Worth seeing: Tudor style memorial in Königin-Victoria vineyard, vaulted cellar at Mittelheim

> Vineyard area: 5 hectares
> Annual production: 30,000 bottles
> Top site: Hochheimer Königin-Victoriaberg
> Soil types: Deep sandy loess-clay
> Grape varieties: 92% Riesling, 5% Chardonnay, 3% Spätburgunder
> Average yield: 65 hl/ha
> Best vintages: 1999, 2001, 2002
> Member: VDP

In 1845, Queen Victoria and her German husband Prince Albert visited Hochheim. In 1850 the entrepreneurial wine estate owner Papstmann was granted permission to name vineyards after the queen. Hochheim vineyards came to be owned by the Hupfeld family through marriage. Her sons Henning and Wolfram have been running the winery for many years, sharing the duties – Henning is in charge of the operation in Hochheim, and Wolfram runs the business in Mittelheim. The 2001 vintage wines produced by Henning Hupfeld followed on his excellent 1999 Riesling wines, and his 2002 vintage was just as good. Unfortunately, the same cannot be said of the 2003 vintage. Right across the board, these wines were rough and sour, and gave only little pleasure. We sincerely hope there will be a return to form next year.

2001 Hochheimer Königin-Victoriaberg
Riesling Spätlese trocken
12%, ♀ till 2005   83

2002 Hochheimer Königin-Victoriaberg
Riesling Kabinett trocken
11%, ♀ till 2006   84

2002 Hochheimer Königin-Victoriaberg
Riesling Kabinett halbtrocken
10%, ♀ till 2006   83

2001 Hochheimer Königin-Victoriaberg
Riesling Kabinett halbtrocken
10.5%, ♀ till 2005   84

2003 Hochheimer Königin-Victoriaberg
Riesling Kabinett
9.5%, ♀ till 2007   82

2003 Hochheimer Königin-Victoriaberg
Riesling Spätlese
9.5%, ♀ till 2007   82

2003 Hochheimer Königin-Victoriaberg
Riesling Auslese
9.5%, ♀ till 2008   85

2002 Hochheimer Königin-Victoriaberg
Riesling Kabinett
9%, ♀ till 2007   86

2001 Hochheimer Königin-Victoriaberg
Riesling Spätlese
8.5%, ♀ till 2006   87

2003 Hochheimer Königin-Victoriaberg
Riesling Beerenauslese
9%, ♀ till 2010   87

The estates: ✦✦✦✦✦ World's finest · ✦✦✦✦ Germany's best · ✦✦✦ Very good · ✦✦ Good · ✦ Reliabl

WEINGUT KRONE

Owner: Botho Jung
Manager and winemaker: Heinz Diehl
65385 Assmannshausen,
Niederwaldstraße 2
Tel. (0 67 22) 40 30, Fax 30 49
e-mail: info@hotel-krone.de
Directions: B 42 from Rüdesheim in direction of Koblenz, Assmannshausen exit, cross railroad track in direction of Aulhausen
Sales: By appointment
History: Estate founded 1860
Worth seeing: Historical hotel and restaurant Krone, natural cellar carved out of rock 60 meters below the Frankenthal vineyard

---

Vineyard area: 1.2 hectares
Annual production: 17,000 bottles
Top sites: Assmannshäuser Höllenberg and Frankenthal, Rüdesheimer Berg Schlossberg
Soil types: Slate
Grape varieties: 95% Spätburgunder, 5% Weißburgunder
Average yield: 35 hl/ha
Best vintages: 1999, 2001, 2002

Older inhabitants are in agreement that the Krone estate owns some of the best parcels of the famous Höllenberg vineyard with its high slate content. This potential has been more evident in the glass ever since Peter Perabo from Lorch has been responsible for the winemaking here. He has an excellent feeling for using just enough barrique without overwhelming the fruit. The 1997, 1999 and 2001 vintages all produced astonishingly good red wines, and even the wines of the 2000 vintage were very acceptable here. The red wines of the 2002 vintage provide a seamless transition to their predecessors, providing both elegance and an almost filigree structure with an unmistakably fruity cassis style. The fruity Weißherbst Spätlese (Rosé) from the Höllenberg site, matured in stainless steel, is also a very attractive wine.

2003 Weißer Burgunder trocken
12.5%, ♀ till 2007 **85**

2003 Spätburgunder Weißherbst
Blanc de Noirs
12%, ♀ till 2008 **87**

——— Red wines ———

2002 Spätburgunder Weißherbst
12%, ♀ till 2006 **86**

2003 Assmannshäuser Höllenberg
Spätburgunder Weißherbst Spätlese
9%, ♀ till 2010 **87**

2002 Rüdesheimer Berg Schlossberg
Spätburgunder Weißherbst Spätlese
11.5%, ♀ till 2007 **88**

2002 Assmannshäuser Höllenberg
Spätburgunder Weißherbst Eiswein
7%, ♀ till 2015 **90**

2002 Assmannshäuser
Spätburgunder trocken
13%, ♀ till 2010 **86**

2002 Assmannshäuser Höllenberg
Spätburgunder trocken
13%, ♀ till 2012 **88**

2001 Assmannshäuser Höllenberg
Spätburgunder trocken ***
13.5%, ♀ till 2015 **89**

2002 Assmannshäuser Höllenberg
Spätburgunder Spätlese trocken *
13.5%, ♀ till 2010 **89**

2002 Assmannshäuser Höllenberg
Spätburgunder Spätlese trocken **
13.5%, ♀ till 2012 **89**

2002 Assmannshäuser Höllenberg
Spätburgunder Spätlese trocken ***
13.5%, ♀ till 2010 **89**

The wines: **100** Perfect · **95–99** Outstanding · **90–94** Excellent · **85–89** Very good · **80–84** Good · **75–79** Average

569

WEINGUT
PETER JAKOB KÜHN

Owner: Peter Jakob Kühn
Winemaker: Peter Jakob Kühn
65375 Oestrich, Mühlstraße 70
Tel. (0 67 23) 22 99, Fax 8 77 88
e-mail: info@weingutpjkuehn.de
Internet: www.weingutpjkuehn.de
Directions: B 42, Oestrich exit, follow
the main road to the center of the village,
turn right after the pedestrian crossing,
last house on the right after 800 meters
Sales: Angela Kühn, Peter Kühn
Opening hours: Mon.–Sat. by appointment; from mid-May to mid-October
wine sales stall in courtyard, Sat. and
Sun. from 11:00 to 17:00 hours
Restaurant: From 1st May on three
weekends, 1st and 2nd weekend in Sept.
as well as 1st weekend in Dec.
Sat. 14:00 to 22:00 hours, Sun. from
13:00 hours
Specialties: Brawn with herbs and
cream, "Oestrich Onion,"
baked cheese medaillions

Vineyard area: 15 hectares
Annual production: 85,000 bottles
Top sites: Oestricher Lenchen
and Doosberg
Soil types: Clay with kaolin, gravelly
kaolin
Grape varieties: 85% Riesling,
15% Spätburgunder
Average yield: 59 hl/ha
Best vintages: 1999, 2002, 2003
Member: VDP

Hardly any other producer in the Rheingau experienced such a meteoric rise in
the Nineties. In no time at all, Peter Jakob
Kühn rose from being a nobody into the
small elite group of top producers in the
region. It seems that wind and weather
have no effect on the quality of wines
made by this friendly man from Oestrich,
his wines just keep on getting better each
year. Kühn has invested heavily in his
operation on the borders of the Oestricher
Lenchen vineyard, and has recently replaced the synthetic tanks with stainless
steel, as well as adding some oak barrels.
In the near future he plans to expand the
production area, and to establish a vinotheque. Peter Jakob Kühn continues to
produce the lion's share of his wines
in a dry style, which he distinguishes
from each other as different quality wines,
bearing up to three grapes on the label.
The highest category is reserved for the
Erste Gewächse (First Growths). We applaud his decision to state predicates only
on naturally sweet wines, this makes the
whole labelling system much easier and
consumer-friendly. Kühn also tries to
keep things simple, for instance, by
usually producing all the wines from the
Doosberg in a dry style, and makes fruity
sweet Rieslings only from the Lenchen
vineyard. Having said all that, we must
also state that we felt the wines of the
2000 and 2001 vintage were generally not
quite up to the usual standard, and that
specifically the more basic wines of the
2002 and 2003 vintages would benefit
from showing a little more character.
Apart from that, the 2003 vintage wines
are strongly reminiscent of the glorious
vintages of the Nineties. The dry wines
marked with grapes on the label are characterized by clear fruit, and the opulent
Erstes Gewächs (Frist Growth) has excellent structure. The botrytis dessert wines
surpass pretty much anything that Peter
Jakob Kühn has ever produced: from the
Beerenauslese from the Lenchen site
marked "E," which stands for the old site
designation Eiserberg, right through to the
fabulous Trockenbeerenauslese with its
gold capsule. Peter Jakob Kühn has been
searching for a long time to find the ideal
bottle closure as an alternative to natural
cork; he believes he has found it in stainless steel crown caps. Kühn reports that
an increasing number of his customers
accepts this decision, expresses gratitude
for the benefit of "definitely not having to
worry about cork taint any more."

2003 Oestricher Riesling trocken
12.5%, ♀ till 2006   8

2003 Oestricher Doosberg
Riesling trocken "1 Traube"
12.5%, ♀ till 2007   86

2003 Riesling Classic
12.5%, ♀ till 2007   86

2003 Oestricher Doosberg
Riesling trocken "2 Trauben"
13.5%, ♀ till 2008   87

2003 Mittelheimer St. Nikolaus
Riesling trocken "2 Trauben"
14%, ♀ till 2008   87

2003 Oestricher Doosberg
Riesling trocken Erstes Gewächs
14%, ♀ till 2010   89

2003 Oestricher Lenchen
Riesling Kabinett
9.5%, ♀ till 2008   85

2003 Oestricher Lenchen
Riesling Spätlese
11%, ♀ till 2010   85

2002 Riesling Classic
11.5%, ♀ till 2008   86

2002 Oestricher Lenchen
Riesling Auslese
7%, ♀ till 2012   89

2003 Oestricher Lenchen
Riesling Auslese
11.5%, ♀ till 2014   89

2003 Oestricher Lenchen
Riesling Beerenauslese "E"
13%, ♀ till 2015   89

2003 Oestricher Lenchen
Riesling Eiswein
7%, ♀ till 2015   91

2002 Oestricher Lenchen
Riesling Auslese Goldkapsel
⌐ auction wine, 7%, ♀ till 2014   91

2002 Oestricher Lenchen
Riesling Eiswein
7.5%, ♀ till 2014   92

2002 Oestricher Lenchen
Riesling Trockenbeerenauslese
⌐ auction wine, 6%, ♀ till 2018   92

2003 Oestricher Lenchen
Riesling Beerenauslese
9%, ♀ till 2018   92

2002 Oestricher Lenchen
Riesling Beerenauslese Goldkapsel
⌐ auction wine, 7.5%, ♀ till 2016   92

2002 Oestricher Lenchen
Riesling Beerenauslese
7.5%, ♀ till 2018   93

2003 Oestricher Lenchen
Riesling Trockenbeerenauslese
6.5%, ♀ till 2020   94

2003 Oestricher Lenchen
Riesling Beerenauslese Goldkapsel
⌐ auction wine, 7%, ♀ till 2020   94

2003 Oestricher Lenchen
Riesling Trockenbeerenauslese
Goldkapsel
⌐ auction wine, 6%, ♀ till 2020   97

——— Red wines ———

2002 "Purpur"
Cuvée trocken
14.5%, ♀ till 2008   86

2002 Spätburgunder
trocken Barrique
15%, ♀ till 2009   87

2001 Spätburgunder
trocken Barrique
14.5%, ♀ till 2010   88

Rheingau

Peter Jakob Kühn M

2003 Oestrich Doosberg
Riesling Trocken

Qualitätswein · Erzeugerabfüllung
A.P. Nr. 2924800304 · D-65375 Oestrich
Produce of Germany · White Wine

alc. 12.5% by vol.
750 ml

The wines: **100** Perfect · **95–99** Outstanding · **90–94** Excellent · **85–89** Very good · **80–84** Good · **75–79** Average

WEINGUT
FRANZ KÜNSTLER

Owner and manager:
Gunter Künstler
Vineyard manager: Rolf Schregel
Winemaker: Gunter Künstler
and Rolf Schregel
65239 Hochheim/Main, Kirchstr. 38
Tel. (0 61 46) 8 38 60, Fax 73 35
e-mail: info@weingut-kuenstler.de
Internet: www.weingut-kuenstler.de
Directions: A 671 Mainz–Wiesbaden,
Hochheim–Süd exit
Sales: Felix Bürklein and Monika Künstler
Opening hours: Mon.–Fri. 08:00. to
12:00 hours and 13:00 to 18:00 hours
Sat. 10:00 to 15:00 Hours
Worth seeing: Estate manor dating back
more than 500 years, with vaulted cellar
(1456)

Vineyard area: 25 hectares
Annual production: 150,000 bottles
Top sites: Hochheimer Hölle,
Kirchenstück and Domdechaney
Soil types: Clay and kaolin
Grape varieties: 85% Riesling, 14%
Spätburgunder, 1% Chardonnay
Average yield: 68 hl/ha
Best vintages: 1999, 2002, 2003
Member: VDP

There are not many German winemakers
who are as popular as Gunter Künstler.
This must be the main reason why so
many wine lovers have remained faithful
to this cult winemaker even though his
wines of the 2000 and 2001 vintages
were rather disappointing. The 2002 vintage saw a marked improvement, and the
range of 2003 vintage wines is almost
back to the old high standard. The dry
Riesling wines have a lot of body, and the
concentrated Spätlese from the Kirchenstück vineyard is again one of the highlights. With the botrytis dessert wines also adding to the overall luster of the
range, the day when we can proclaim
Künstler's return to the elite of the Rheingau producers cannot be far off.

2003 Hochheimer Hölle
Riesling Spätlese trocken
12.5%, ♀ till 2007 — 86

2003 Hochheimer Hölle
Riesling Auslese trocken
13.5%, ♀ till 2008 — 87

2003 Hochheimer Stielweg
Riesling trocken "Alte Reben"
12.5%, ♀ till 2008 — 87

2003 Hochheimer Reichestal
Riesling Kabinett
7%, ♀ till 2010 — 89

2003 Hochheimer Hölle
Riesling Auslese Goldkapsel
7.5%, ♀ till 2013 — 89

2002 Hochheimer Kirchenstück
Riesling Spätlese
7%, ♀ till 2010 — 90

2003 Hochheimer Kirchenstück
Riesling Spätlese
7%, ♀ till 2012 — 91

2003 Hochheimer Domdechaney
Riesling Trockenbeerenauslese
6%, ♀ till 2015 — 91

2003 Hochheimer Stielweg
Riesling Trockenbeerenauslese
6%, ♀ till 2015 — 91

WEINGUT LAMM-JUNG

Owner: Andreas and Gabriele Jung
Manager and winemaker:
Andreas Jung
65346 Eltville-Erbach,
Eberbacher Straße 50
Tel. (0 61 23) 6 21 48, Fax 6 18 92
e-mail: info@wein-rheingau.de
Internet: www.wein-rheingau.de
Directions: From the A 66 turn on to the
B 42, Eltville-Erbach exit
Sales: Jung family
Opening hours: Mon.–Fri. 10:00 to
18:00 hours, Sat.: 10:00 to 17:00 hours
and by appointment
Restaurant/Wine bar: Open in March,
Wed. to Sun., open from 17:00 hours
Specialties: Cheese matured in Riesling
History: Wines made by family for
seven generations

Vineyard area: 8 hectares
Annual production: 40,000 bottles
Top sites: Erbacher Hohenrain
and Steinmorgen
Soil types: Deep loess-clay
Grape varieties: 80% Riesling, 14%
Spätburgunder, 6% other varieties
Average yield: 65 hl/ha
Best vintage: 2003

The two wineries of the Lamm and Jung families were brought together by marriage in 1948. It was Josef Jung who took over the operation in 1979, and decided to concentrate on Riesling and Pinot Noir, and to invest in modern technology. This path has also been followed by Andreas Jung who has been running the winery in recent years. He benefited from his training at the leading Robert Weil winery in Kiedrich, and graduated as a cellar technician in Kreuznach. The focus of his work is to achieve particularly healthy grapes in the vineyard, and to harvest these as late as possible. The range of 2003 vintage wines shows a uniformly high standard, crowned by an outstanding Trockenbeerenauslese.

2003 Erbacher Michelmark
Riesling Kabinett trocken
12%, ♀ till 2007   83

2003 Riesling Classic
12.5%, ♀ till 2007   84

2003 Erbacher Michelmark
Riesling Spätlese trocken
13%, ♀ till 2007   85

2003 Erbacher Hohenrain
Riesling trocken "Bestes Fass"
13.5%, ♀ till 2007   85

2003 Erbacher Hohenrain
Riesling Kabinett halbtrocken
13%, ♀ till 2008   84

2003 Erbacher Hohenrain
Riesling Spätlese feinherb "S"
14%, ♀ till 2008   85

2003 Erbacher Honigberg
Riesling Spätlese
9.5%, ♀ till 2010   87

2003 Erbacher Michelmark
Riesling Trockenbeerenauslese
6.5%, ♀ till 2024   94

——— Red wine ———

2002 Spätburgunder
trocken Barrique "R"
13%, ♀ till 2009   87

---

he wines: **100** Perfect · **95–99** Outstanding · **90–94** Excellent · **85–89** Very good · **80–84** Good · **75–79** Average

573

WEINGUT HANS LANG

Owner and manager:
Johann Maximilian Lang
65347 Eltville-Hattenheim,
Rheinallee 6
Tel. (0 67 23) 24 75, Fax 79 63
e-mail: langwein@t-online.de
Internet: www.weingut-hans-lang.de
Directions: B 42, Hattenheim exit
Sales: Mr. Moos, Mr. and Mrs. Lang
Opening hours: Mon.–Fri. 08:00 to
12:00 and 13:00 to 17:00, Sat.: 09:00 to
13:00 hours, and by appointment

Vineyard area: 18 hectares
Annual production: 130,000 bottles
Top sites: Hattenheimer
Wisselbrunnen and Hassel
Soil types: Gravelly clay, slate, loess
Grape varieties: 70% Riesling, 15%
Spätburgunder, 10% Weißburgunder,
5% other varieties
Average yield: 68 hl/ha
Best vintages: 1997, 1999, 2002
Member: VDP,
Deutsches Barrique Forum

Each year Johann Maximilian Lang – Hans to his friends – scratches his head to see how he can further improve his level of quality. The specialties of this estate include bottle-fermented sparkling wines as well as full-bodied Pinot Noir and Pinot Blanc wines matured in barriques that can be among the best of their kind in the Rheingau. For instance, last year we were particularly enthusiastic about the 2001 Chardonnay. But the main focus continues to lie with classical Riesling wines, and this variety makes up three-quarters of the vineyard area. However, the basic wines of the 2003 vintage are much less attractive than their predecessors. Across the board they have a rather lemony nose and a boiled-sweets character on the palate. On the other hand, the Spätlese and Auslese wines are up to their usual high standard. The range is crowned by a Riesling Trockenbeerenauslese with an intense nose of apricot compote.

2002 Chardonnay trocken Barrique
13.5%, ♀ till 2008   **85**

2003 Weißer Burgunder
trocken "S"
13.5%, ♀ till 2007   **85**

2003 "Johann Maximilian"
Riesling trocken
12.5%, ♀ till 2006   **86**

2003 "Vom Bunten Schiefer"
Riesling trocken
12.5%, ♀ till 2007   **86**

2003 Hattenheimer Wisselbrunnen
Riesling trocken Erstes Gewächs
13.5%, ♀ till 2008   **88**

2003 Hattenheimer Hassel
Riesling Spätlese
9.5%, ♀ till 2007   **87**

2003 Hattenheimer Wisselbrunnen
Riesling Auslese
8.5%, ♀ till 2010   **88**

2003 Hattenheimer Hassel
Riesling Auslese
9%, ♀ till 2012   **89**

2002 Hattenheimer Wisselbrunnen
Riesling Auslese Goldkapsel
↗ auction wine, 7.5%, ♀ till 2012   **89**

2003 Hattenheimer Hassel
Riesling Beerenauslese
9.5%, ♀ till 2015   **90**

2002 Hattenheimer Wisselbrunnen
Riesling Trockenbeerenauslese
↗ auction wine, 6.5%, ♀ till 2015   **92**

2003 Hattenheimer Wisselbrunnen
Riesling Trockenbeerenauslese
7%, ♀ till 2020   **94**

HANS LANG

VOM BUNTEN SCHIEFER
RHEINGAU RIESLING

WEINGUT FREIHERR LANGWERTH VON SIMMERN

Owner: Georg-Reinhard Freiherr Langwerth von Simmern
Manager: Dirk Roth
Winemaker: Dirk Roth, Uwe Lex
65343 Eltville, Kirchgasse 6
Tel. (0 61 23) 9 21 10, Fax 92 11 33
e-mail: weingut-langwerth-von-simmern@t-online.de
Internet:
www.langwerth-von-simmern.de
Directions: From center of Eltville in direction of Wiesbaden, on right hand between Prince Elector's castle and church
Sales: Andrea Freifrau Langwerth von Simmern, Ascan von der Lancken
Opening hours: Mon.–Thur. 08:00 to 12:00 and 13:30 to 17:00, Fri. to 16:00 hrs.
Vinotheca: Fri. 16:00 to 19:00 hours, Sat. 10:00 to 17:00 hours
Wine bar: Gelbes Haus, Tue.–Sat. from 16:00, Sun. from 11:30 hours
Specialties: Regional Rheingau cuisine
History: Given by the Duke of Pfalz-Zweibrücken to his chancellor Johann Langwerth von Simmern, to hold in fee
Worth seeing: Langwerther Hof with park

Vineyard area: 26 hectares
Annual production: 160,000 bottles
Top sites: Erbacher Marcobrunn, Rauenthaler Baiken, Hattenheimer Nussbrunnen and Wisselbrunnen
Soil types: Tertiary marl, loess with limestone, sandy clay
Grape varieties: 96% Riesling, 2% Spätburgunder, 2% other varieties
Average yield: 55 hl/ha
Best vintages: 1998, 1999, 2003
Member: VDP

This renowned winery with its long tradition commands some of the best vineyard sites in Erbach, Hattenheim and Rauenthal, and for decades it belonged to the absolutely best producers in the Rheingau. While the standard of wines was a little patchy in the 80's and 90's, there were signs of a renaissance. Now we are pleased to report that the 2003 vintage has again produced a number of better wines, such as the well-structured First Growth, as well as the elegant Beerenauslese from the Marcobrunn site.

2003 Hattenheimer
Riesling Kabinett trocken
12.5%, ♀ till 2007   **83**

2003 Rauenthaler Baiken
Riesling Spätlese trocken
13.5%, ♀ till 2007   **84**

2003 Rauenthaler Baiken
Riesling Kabinett trocken
12.5%, ♀ till 2008   **85**

2003 Hattenheimer Mannberg
Riesling trocken Erstes Gewächs
13.5%, ♀ till 2008   **88**

2002 Erbacher Marcobrunn
Riesling Spätlese
10.5%, ♀ till 2008   **87**

2003 Hattenheimer Mannberg
Riesling Spätlese "Blaukapsel"
11%, ♀ till 2012   **87**

2003 Hattenheimer Mannberg
Riesling Auslese
9.5%, ♀ till 2015   **90**

2003 Erbacher Marcobrunn
Riesling Beerenauslese
10.5%, ♀ till 2016   **91**

2003 Rauenthaler Baiken
Riesling Trockenbeerenauslese
8%, ♀ till 2025   **93**

The wines: **100** Perfect · **95–99** Outstanding · **90–94** Excellent · **85–89** Very good · **80–84** Good · **75–79** Average

575

WEINGUT JOSEF LEITZ

Owner: Johannes Leitz
Manager and winemaker:
Johannes Leitz
65385 Rüdesheim, Th.-Heuss-Straße 5
Tel. (0 67 22) 4 87 11, Fax 4 76 58
e-mail: johannes.leitz@leitz-wein.de
Internet: www.leitz-wein.de
Directions: From Wiesbaden drive towards Rüdesheim in direction of Kloster Hildegard monastery
Sales: Johannes Leitz
by appointment only

Vineyard area: 15 hectares
Annual production: 120,000 bottles
Top sites: Rüdesheimer Berg
Schlossberg, Berg Roseneck
and Berg Rottland
Soil types: Decomposed slate
Grape varieties: 100% Riesling
Average yield: 68 hl/ha
Best vintages: 2001, 2002, 2003
Member: VDP

Johannes Leitz never fails to amaze us. Hardly any other Riesling producer in Germany managed to present such brilliant ranges of the 2000 to 2002 vintages as this young, outgoing man from Rüdesheim, who celebrated his 40th birthday last summer. His wines of the 2003 vintage, too, continue in the same vein, leaving no doubt as to their exceptional quality, and providing astonishing nuances in practically all categories, from the dry Spätlese wines to the elegantly juicy Spätleses from the Burg Roseneck site right up to the opulent Trockenbeerenauslese wines. However, above all the two previous vintages 2001 and 2002 really established his reputation as one of the leading producers. Johannes Leitz is not a man to ignore business opportunities, which can be seen in the fact that he increased his vineyard area by half last year, mainly in order to be able to meet international demand for his wines. The United States market alone absorbs more than three-quarters of his production, there the ele-

gantly fruity "Dragonstone," as well as the Spätlese from the Magdalenenkreuz vineyard are flying off the shelf. To go back in history – this success was not evident from the beginning. When his father died at the age of 33 in 1965, young Johannes was a mere 14 months old. The three hectares of vineyard were kept going as a side-line, while his mother's florist shop kept the family alive. Following on his apprenticeship and successful master's examination, Leitz took over the winery at the age of 22. In spite of all he has already achieved, Johannes Leitz still has a dream: At some stage he would like to see vines growing again on the well-preserved terraces between Rüdesheim and Assmannshausen, on land that is reputed to have produced some of the best Rheingau wines in the last century.

2003 Rüdesheimer Berg Rottland
Riesling Spätlese trocken – 22 –
14%, ♀ till 2008 **87**

2003 Rüdesheimer Berg Schlossberg
Riesling Spätlese trocken
13%, ♀ till 2008 **88**

2002 Rüdesheimer Berg Schlossberg
Riesling trocken
12.5%, ♀ till 2006 **88**

2003 Rüdesheimer Berg Schlossberg
Riesling Spätlese trocken "A.R."
13%, ♀ till 2008 **88**

2003 Rüdesheimer
Riesling trocken
13%, ♀ till 2008 **89**

2002 Rüdesheimer Berg Schlossberg
Riesling Spätlese trocken
12%, ♀ till 2010 **90**

2001 Rüdesheimer Berg Schlossberg
Riesling Spätlese trocken – 21 –
12.5%, ♀ till 2012 **92**

2003 Rüdesheimer Berg Rottland
Riesling Spätlese trocken – 20 –
13%, ♀ till 2010 **93**

2002 Rüdesheimer Berg Rottland
Riesling Spätlese trocken
13%, ♀ till 2012 **93**

The estates: World's finest · Germany's best · Very good · Good · Reliable

**2003 Rüdesheimer Berg
Kaisersteinfels**
Riesling Spätlese halbtrocken
Alte Reben
13.5%, ♀ till 2010　　　　**90**

2003 "Dragonstone" Riesling
8%, ♀ till 2008　　　　**85**

2003 Rüdesheimer Magdalenenkreuz
Riesling Spätlese
8%, ♀ till 2010　　　　**88**

2002 Rüdesheimer Magdalenenkreuz
Riesling Spätlese
9%, ♀ till 2010　　　　**89**

2002 Rüdesheimer Berg Schlossberg
Riesling Spätlese
8.5%, ♀ till 2010　　　　**89**

2002 Riesling Charta
12.5%, ♀ till 2007　　　　**89**

2003 Rüdesheimer Kirchenpfad
Riesling Auslese
7%, ♀ till 2012　　　　**90**

2002 Rüdesheimer Berg Roseneck
Riesling Spätlese
8.5%, ♀ till 2010　　　　**90**

2002 Rüdesheimer Berg Rottland
Riesling Auslese
8%, ♀ till 2015　　　　**90**

2001 Rüdesheimer Berg Schlossberg
Riesling Spätlese
8%, ♀ till 2010　　　　**90**

2003 Rüdesheimer Berg Roseneck
Riesling Spätlese "Botrytis"
8.5%, ♀ till 2012　　　　**90**

2002 Rüdesheimer Kirchenpfad
Riesling Beerenauslese
7%, ♀ till 2014　　　　**91**

2003 Rüdesheimer Berg Schlossberg
Riesling Spätlese
9%, ♀ till 2012　　　　**92**

**2003 Rüdesheimer Berg
Kaisersteinfels**
Riesling Trockenbeerenauslese
6%, ♀ till 2030　　　　**92**

2002 Rüdesheimer Kirchenpfad
Riesling Trockenbeerenauslese
↗ auction wine, 7%, ♀ till 2020　　　　**92**

**2002 Rüdesheimer Berg
Kaisersteinfels**
Riesling Beerenauslese
↗ auction wine, 6.5%, ♀ till 2015　　　　**93**

2003 Rüdesheimer Berg Rottland
Riesling Trockenbeerenauslese
6%, ♀ till 2030　　　　**94**

2001 Rüdesheimer Drachenstein
Riesling Beerenauslese
6.5%, ♀ till 2015　　　　**94**

2001 Rüdesheimer Berg Roseneck
Riesling Trockenbeerenauslese
↗ auction wine, 7%, ♀ till 2018　　　　**94**

2003 Rüdesheimer Berg Roseneck
Riesling Spätlese "Gesund"
8%, ♀ till 2012　　　　**94**

2003 Rüdesheimer Kirchenpfad
Riesling Trockenbeerenauslese
6%, ♀ till 2030　　　　**95**

2003 Rüdesheimer Magdalenenkreuz
Riesling Trockenbeerenauslese
6%, ♀ till 2030　　　　**95**

2002 Rüdesheimer Berg Schlossberg
Riesling Beerenauslese
↗ auction wine, 7%, ♀ till 2020　　　　**95**

LEITZ
WEINGUT

2002
Rüdesheimer
Berg Schlossberg

RHEINGAU | GERMANY

The wines: **100** Perfect · **95–99** Outstanding · **90–94** Excellent · **85–89** Very good · **80–84** Good · **75–79** Average

WEINGUT
FÜRST LÖWENSTEIN

Owner: Carl-Friedrich Erbprinz zu Löwenstein-Wertheim-Rosenberg
Manager and winemaker: Robert Haller
65375 Hallgarten, Niederwaldstraße 8
Tel. (0 67 23) 99 97 70, Fax 99 97 71
e-mail: hallgarten@loewenstein.de
Internet: www.loewenstein.de
Directions: B 42 Wiesbaden–Rüdesheim,
Hallgarten exit
Sales: Heide Hennecken
Opening hours: Tue.–Fri. 13:00 to
17:00, Sat. 10:00 to 14:00 hours, and by
appointment
History: The Dukes of Löwenstein have
been working vineyards at Hallgarten in
the Rheingau since 1875

Vineyard area: 22 hectares
Annual production: 60,000 bottles
Top sites: Hallgartener
Schönhell and Jungfer
Soil types: Clay, loess
Grape varieties: 95% Riesling, 3%
Spätburgunder, 2% Frühburgunder
Average yield: 54 hl/ha
Best vintages: 2001, 2002, 2003
Member: VDP

After the winery had been leased out for
20 years, manager Robert Haller took on
the management in 1997, initially operating from his base in Kreuzwertheim. In
the meantime the center of operations has
moved to the winery itself. The wines,
too, have found their style, and have improved with each vintage. The 2000 vintage was surprisingly good, and the two
successive vintages confirmed this positive trend. Now, the very attractive range
of 2003 vintage wines earns this producer
his third bunch of grapes – we were not
even put off by the white Bordeaux bottle
and the horrible label used to package
the "CF" Riesling. All the wines are of a
uniformly high standard, from the full-
bodied reds to the Spätlese with its apricot aromas right through to the opulent
Trockenbeerenauslese wines.

2003 Riesling trocken "CF"
12.5%, ♀ till 2006   **84**

2003 Hallgartener Jungfer
Riesling Spätlese trocken
13%, ♀ till 2008   **86**

2001 Hallgartener Schönhell
Riesling Erstes Gewächs
12%, ♀ till 2005   **87**

2002 Hallgartener Schönhell
Riesling trocken Erstes Gewächs
13%, ♀ till 2007   **87**

2002 Hallgartener Schönhell
Riesling Spätlese
8.5%, ♀ till 2007   **88**

2003 Hallgartener Schönhell
Riesling Spätlese
8.5%, ♀ till 2012   **89**

2002 Hallgartener Schönhell
Riesling Eiswein
7%, ♀ till 2014   **89**

2003 Hallgartener Schönhell
Riesling Trockenbeerenauslese
7%, ♀ till 2020   **93**

2002 Hallgartener Schönhell
Riesling Trockenbeerenauslese
7.5%, ♀ till 2015   **93**

——— Red wines ———

2002 Hallgartener Schönhell
Spätburgunder Spätlese trocken
14%, ♀ till 2010   **88**

2002 Hallgartener Schönhell
Frühburgunder Spätlese trocken "R"
13.5%, ♀ till 2010   **88**

2002 Hallgartener Schönhell
Pinot Noir Spätlese trocken "R"
13.5%, ♀ till 2010   **88**

WEINGUT WILHELM MOHR ERBEN

Owner and manager: Jochen Neher
65391 Lorch, Rheinstraße 21
Tel. (0 67 26) 94 84, Fax 16 94
e-mail: info@weingut-mohr.de
Internet: www.weingut-mohr.de
*Directions: Entrance is across the road
from the Rhine ferry pier, follow signs*
Sales: Saynur Sonkaya-Neher
Opening hours: Mon.–Sat. 10:00 to
12:00 hours and 14:00 to 17:00 hours
and by appointment
Restaurant/Wine bar: May and June,
Thu. and Fri. from 17:00 hours, Sat. and
Sun. from 15:00 hours
Specialties: Asparagus, game, trout
Worth seeing: Two deep vaulted cellars
carved out of the slate mountainside

Vineyard area: 4.5 hectares
Annual production: 35,000 bottles
Top sites: Lorcher Krone,
Bodental-Steinberg and Schlossberg,
Assmannshäuser Höllenberg
Soil types: Blue and red phyllite slate
Grape varieties: 62% Riesling, 24%
Spätburgunder, 10% Weißburgunder,
2% each of Silvaner and Scheurebe
Average yield: 70 hl/ha
Best vintages: 2001, 2002, 2003

Jochen Neher took over his parents' operation in 1992, after gaining experience in winemaking in other countries, including overseas regions. The good quality of wines produced in 2001 earned him a place in the Wine Guide, and the wines produced in the 2002 vintage confirmed that we were right to have confidence in his abilities. All of the dry Rieslings of the 2003 vintage are very good, while First Growth wines stand out head and shoulders. At this stage, only the rather mediocre red wines of the 2002 vintage have prevented us from awarding an even higher rating. But the winemaker assures us that his 2003 reds are the best that have been made here in the past decades.

2003 Riesling trocken
12%, ♀ till 2006 — 84

2003 Riesling Kabinett trocken
11.5%, ♀ till 2007 — 86

2003 Riesling Spätlese trocken
12.5%, ♀ till 2008 — 88

2002 Lorcher Krone
Weißer Burgunder trocken
13.5%, ♀ till 2008 — 88

2003 Lorcher Krone
Riesling trocken Erstes Gewächs
12.5%, ♀ till 2008 — 88

2003 Lorcher Bodental-Steinberg
Riesling trocken Erstes Gewächs
13%, ♀ till 2008 — 89

2003 Riesling
Spätlese halbtrocken
12%, ♀ till 2007 — 84

2003 Riesling Spätlese
11%, ♀ till 2008 — 85

2002 Lorcher Krone
Riesling Auslese
8.5%, ♀ till 2009 — 87

2002 Lorcher Kapellenberg
Riesling Auslese
8.5%, ♀ till 2009 — 87

2002 Lorcher Kapellenberg
Riesling Eiswein
6.5%, ♀ till 2010 — 88

The wines: **100** Perfect · **95–99** Outstanding · **90–94** Excellent · **85–89** Very good · **80–84** Good · **75–79** Average

579

WEINGUT HEINZ NIKOLAI

Owner: Heinz, Helga and Frank Nikolai
Manager: Heinz Nikolai
Winemaker: Frank Nikolai
65346 Erbach, Ringstraße 16
Tel. (0 61 23) 6 27 08, Fax 8 16 19
e-mail: weingut@heinz-nikolai.de
Internet: www.heinznikolai.de
Directions: A 66 in direction of Rüdesheim, B 42, Erbach-Mitte exit
Sales: Helga and Frank Nikolai
Opening hours: Mon.–Fri. 09:00 to 18:00, Sat. and Sun. 10:00 to 14:00 hours, by appointment
Restaurant/Wine bar: During the Rheingau culinary weeks in April/May from 16:00 to 24:00 hours
History: Winery in family hands since 1878, currently in the 5. and 6. generation
Worth seeing: Historical vaulted cellar

Vineyard area: 10 hectares
Annual production: 90,000 bottles
Top sites: Erbacher Steinmorgen and Michelmark, Hallgartener Jungfer
Soil types: Loess-clay
Grape varieties: 85% Riesling, 12% Spätburgunder, 2% Weißburgunder, 1% Müller-Thurgau
Average yield: 72 hl/ha
Best vintages: 2001, 2002, 2003

2003 "Primus Maximus"
Riesling Spätlese trocken
12.5%, ♀ till 2007 | 85

2003 Erbacher Steinmorgen
Riesling trocken Erstes Gewächs
12.5%, ♀ till 2007 | 85

2003 Riesling Classic
12%, ♀ till 2007 | 86

2003 Kiedricher Sandgrub
Riesling Kabinett
9.5%, ♀ till 2009 | 85

2003 Kiedricher Sandgrub
Riesling Eiswein
7.5%, ♀ till 2012 | 88

2002 Erbacher Honigberg
Riesling Auslese
9%, ♀ till 2009 | 89

2003 Erbacher Michelmark
Riesling Beerenauslese
8.5%, ♀ till 2014 | 89

2003 Erbacher Honigberg
Riesling Auslese
8.5%, ♀ till 2020 | 90

2002 Kiedricher Sandgrub
Riesling Eiswein
9%, ♀ till 2012 | 91

2003 Erbacher Steinmorgen
Riesling Trockenbeerenauslese
6.5%, ♀ till 2018 | 94

Although this winery is increasingly gaining a reputation for the good quality of its wines, it remains something of an insider's tip because of the extremely reasonable prices charged for good Riesling. We liked the 2002 wines here for their clearly structured fruit, and the wines of the 2003 vintage fit in seamlessly with this impression. In addition, this year Nikolai has managed to produce a number of tremendous botrytis dessert wines, which he compares to those of the great 1959 and 1971 vintages. The Auslese from the Honigberg site is simply oozing with clean, appetizing fruit, and the Trockenbeerenauslese, picked at a must weight of 246 Oechsle, is among the very best wines of the region.

WEINGUT DETLEV RITTER UND EDLER VON OETINGER

Owner: Detlev & Achim von Oetinger
Winemaker: Achim von Oetinger
65346 Erbach, Rheinallee 1–3
Tel. (0 61 23) 6 25 28, Fax 6 26 91
e-mail: von.oetinger@t-online.de
Directions: B 42 in direction of Rüdesheim, second Erbach exit, new building on right after 200 meters
Opening hours: Mon.–Fri. 14:30 to 22:00, Sat. and Sun. 11:00 to 22:00 hours
Wine bar: "Zum jungen Oetinger" directly on the Rhine, with shady garden terrace, Mon.–Fri. from 14:30, Sat. and Sun. from 11:00 hours, closed Tue.
Specialties: Traditional Rheingau cuisine

Vineyard area: 7.5 hectares
Annual production: 50,000 bottles
Top sites: Erbacher Marcobrunn and Siegelsberg
Soil types: Loess-clay
Grape varieties: 80% Riesling, 15% Spätburgunder, 5% Grauburgunder
Average yield: 68 hl/ha
Best vintages: 2001, 2002, 2003
Member: VDP

Ever since the original operation was split in 1958 there have been two Oetinger wineries in Erbach. In order to tell them apart, there is a consensus that Detlev von Oetinger, who took over the winery from his father Robert at the tender age of 21, is referred to as the "young" Oetinger, while Eberhard is the "old" Oetinger. We make no bones about the fact that we have found the wines made by Detlev von Oetinger increasingly attractive in recent years. This impression has been further confirmed by the wines his son Achim has presented in both 2001 and 2002 vintages. The 2003 vintage makes no exception. We particularly liked the elegant Auslese wine from the Marcobrunn vineyard, which we preferred to the very good Beerenauslese from the Hohenrain site in terms of its clarity of expression and refinement.

2003 Riesling trocken
13%, ♀ till 2006 — **83**

2003 Erbacher Siegelsberg
Riesling Spätlese trocken
13%, ♀ till 2007 — **84**

2002 Erbacher Marcobrunn
Riesling trocken Erstes Gewächs
13%, ♀ till 2007 — **88**

2003 Erbacher Steinmorgen
Riesling
12%, ♀ till 2008 — **83**

2003 Erbacher Hohenrain
Riesling Kabinett
10%, ♀ till 2010 — **85**

2002 Erbacher Siegelsberg
Riesling Spätlese
9.5%, ♀ till 2008 — **86**

2003 Erbacher Steinmorgen
Grauer Burgunder Auslese
8.5%, ♀ till 2012 — **88**

2003 Erbacher Hohenrain
Riesling Beerenauslese
➐ auction wine, 8%, ♀ till 2016 — **90**

2003 Erbacher Marcobrunn
Riesling Auslese
9%, ♀ till 2016 — **91**

The wines: **100** Perfect · **95–99** Outstanding · **90–94** Excellent · **85–89** Very good · **80–84** Good · **75–79** Average

WEINGUT
JOHANNES OHLIG

Owner and manager: Johannes Ohlig
65375 Oestrich-Winkel, Hauptstraße 68
Tel. (0 67 23) 20 12, Fax 8 78 72
e-mail: info@weingut-ohlig.de
Internet: www.weingut-ohlig.de
*Directions: B 42 Winkel exit, turn left
immediately into Rheinweg, 1st street on
right into Graugasse, gate after 100 meters*
Sales: Inga Ohlig
Opening hours: Mon.–Fri. 08:00 to
12:00 hours and 14:00 to 18:00 hours
Sat. by appointment
Wine bar: With attractive courtyard;
16:00 to 23:30 hours, Sun. and public
holidays from 15:00 hours, closed Wed.
Specialties: Cheese, wild boar brawn
Worth seeing: Historic buildings dating
back more than 400 years

Vineyard area: 9.5 hectares
Annual production: 70,000 bottles
Top sites: Winkeler Jesuitengarten
and Hasensprung, Geisenheimer
Kläuserweg, Johannisberger Klaus
Soil types: Deep stony loess-clay
Grape varieties: 83% Riesling, 14%
Spätburgunder 3% Müller-Thurgau
Average yield: 70 hl/ha
Best vintages: 2001, 2002, 2003

The Ohlig winery is housed in the historic
Zehntenhof (tithe farm), dating back 400
years, in the center of the town of Winkel.
Its attractive inner courtyard is home to a
restaurant and wine bar. Both the 2001
and 2002 vintages here were most attractive right across the board. The assessment of the 2003 vintage wines is equally positive, even though some of the dry
wines appear to be a little more alcoholic
than usual, and the botrytis wines do not
present an improvement on their counterparts of the 2002 vintage. While the
prices of most of the wines have been
set just a few Cents above those of the
previous vintage, the 2003 Spätlese from
the Kläuserweg vineyard has been increased by a whopping 25 percent!

2003 Winkeler Hasensprung
Riesling Spätlese trocken
13%, ♀ till 2006   **83**

2003 Winkeler Jesuitengarten
Riesling Spätlese trocken
13%, ♀ till 2006   **83**

2003 Riesling Classic
13%, ♀ till 2007   **84**

2003 Johannisberger Goldatzel
Riesling
11%, ♀ till 2007   **85**

2003 Geisenheimer Kläuserweg
Riesling Spätlese
9.5%, ♀ till 2008   **85**

2002 Geisenheimer Kläuserweg
Riesling Spätlese
10%, ♀ till 2008   **87**

2003 Winkeler Jesuitengarten
Riesling Auslese
10.5%, ♀ till 2010   **87**

2003 Winkeler Jesuitengarten
Riesling Beerenauslese
8%, ♀ till 2012   **88**

2002 Johannisberger Goldatzel
Riesling Eiswein
8.5%, ♀ till 2013   **90**

WEINGUT PRINZ

Manager: Fred Prinz
65375 Hallgarten, Im Flachsgarten 5
Tel. (0 67 23) 99 98 47, Fax 99 98 48
e-mail: prinzfred@gmx.de
Directions: B 42, Hattenheim exit, in direction of Hallgarten, at entrance to town follow road around town, 5th street left
Sales: Sabine Prinz
Opening hours: Mon.–Sat. by appointment only

Vineyard area: 4.5 hectares
Annual production: 20,000 bottles
Top sites: Hallgartener Jungfer
and Schönhell
Soil types: Loess-clay, multi-colored
slate, Taunus quartzite
Grape varieties: 92% Riesling,
8% Spätburgunder
Average yield: 60 hl/ha
Best vintages: 2000, 2001, 2003

For many years, this was the best part-time winery in the Rheingau. Now, that era has come to an end. Fred Prinz, who spent many years working for the Hessian State Domain, first in marketing, and later was also responsible for production, has said his farewells there, and has now almost trebled the vineyard area of what used to be his miniature operation. The wines of the 2000 vintage here were remarkably good against the general background of that extremely difficult vintage, and the Erstes Gewächs (First Growth) was even one of the very best dry wines of the region. Prinz was able to repeat this success with his 2001 wines, and those of 2002 were only marginally less impressive. The range of 2003 vintage wines is of most respectable quality, headed up – for the first time in the estate's history – by a Trockenbeerenauslese. However, we must admit that we found many of the dry wines to be somewhat on the baroque side in stature. We thus look forward with great interest to the 2004 vintage, to better assess the development of this much enlarged estate.

2003 Hallgartener Schönhell
Riesling Kabinett trocken
12.5%, ♀ till 2007 — **84**

2003 Hallgartener Jungfer
Riesling trocken Erstes Gewächs
13.5%, ♀ till 2007 — **85**

2002 Hallgartener Jungfer
Riesling trocken Erstes Gewächs
13%, ♀ till 2006 — **87**

2001 Hallgartener Jungfer
Riesling trocken Erstes Gewächs
12.5%, ♀ till 2009 — **89**

2003 Hallgartener Hendelberg
Riesling feinherb
12.5%, ♀ till 2007 — **85**

2002 Hallgartener Jungfer
Riesling Spätlese Goldkapsel
8%, ♀ till 2008 — **86**

2002 Hallgartener Jungfer
Riesling Spätlese
8.5%, ♀ till 2008 — **87**

2003 Hallgartener Jungfer
Riesling Spätlese
9%, ♀ till 2009 — **87**

2003 Hallgartener Jungfer
Riesling Auslese
8.5%, ♀ till 2010 — **87**

2003 Hallgartener Jungfer
Riesling Spätlese Goldkapsel
8%, ♀ till 2009 — **87**

2002 Hallgartener Jungfer
Riesling Auslese
9%, ♀ till 2010 — **88**

2003 Hallgartener Jungfer
Riesling Beerenauslese
7%, ♀ till 2015 — **92**

2003 Hallgartener Jungfer
Riesling Trockenbeerenauslese
7%, ♀ till 2030 — **94**

The wines: **100** Perfect · **95–99** Outstanding · **90–94** Excellent · **85–89** Very good · **80–84** Good · **75–79** Average

583

WEINGUT
WILFRIED QUERBACH

**Owner: Resi, Wilfried
and Peter Querbach
Manager and winemaker:
Wilfried and Peter Querbach**
65375 Oestrich, Lenchenstraße 19
Tel. (0 67 23) 38 87, Fax 8 74 05
e-mail: mail@querbach.com
Internet: www.querbach.com
*Directions: B 42, Oestrich exit, on main
road follow signs to Bürgerhaus, straight
on after railroad tracks, last building left*
Sales: Peter Querbach
Opening hours: Mon.–Fri. 08:00 to
12:00 hours and 13:00 to 18:00 hours
Sat. and Sun. by appointment
Wine bar: At winery on outskirts of town

Vineyard area: 10 hectares
Annual production: 80,000 bottles
Top sites: Oestricher Lenchen
and Doosberg, Winkeler Hasen-
sprung, Hallgartener Schönhell
Soil types: Deep clay and clay-loess
Grape varieties: 84% Riesling,
16% Spätburgunder
Average yield: 77 hl/ha
Best vintages: 2001, 2002, 2003
Member: VDP

Peter Querbachs hierarchy of wines is
based on "Schoppen" (quaffing wines),
Classic and Edition, all of them estate
blends that can be sourced from a number
of vineyards and communes. The next
step up is the commune blend, followed
by the classified vineyard sites and the
First Growth. In order to avoid cork taint
problems, Querbach now uses a stainless
steel crown closure for all his wines, and
has had even this procedure patented. The
dry wines of the 2003 vintage are quite
attractive. Botrytis dessert wines are not
really his specialty, but they, too, show
clear fruit character. A few years ago the
Querbachs built a modern cellar on the
border of the Oestricher Lenchen site,
and this complex includes a vinotheque
as well as ten guest rooms.

2003 Riesling trocken "Schoppen"
12.5%, ♀ till 2007 **84**

2003 Hallgartener
Riesling trocken
12%, ♀ till 2008 **87**

2003 Riesling Classic
12%, ♀ till 2008 **87**

2002 Oestricher Doosberg
Riesling trocken Erstes Gewächs
12%, ♀ till 2007 **89**

2003 Riesling halbtrocken
11.5%, ♀ till 2007 **84**

2003 "Edition" Riesling
12%, ♀ till 2007 **85**

2003 Riesling
11%, ♀ till 2009 **86**

2003 Oestricher Lenchen
Riesling
11%, ♀ till 2009 **86**

2003 Oestricher Doosberg
Riesling
12.5%, ♀ till 2008 **87**

2002 Oestricher Lenchen
Riesling "No. 1"
12%, ♀ till 2006 **87**

2003 Oestricher Lenchen
Riesling "No. 1"
12%, ♀ till 2007 **87**

2003 Oestricher Lenchen
Riesling Auslese
8%, ♀ till 2012 **89**

2003 Oestricher Lenchen
Riesling Trockenbeerenauslese
8.5%, ♀ till 2016 **90**

SCHLOSS REINHARTSHAUSEN

Owner: Freunde von Reinhartshausen GbR
Manager: Walter Bibo
Vineyard manager: Norbert Weiß
Winemaker: Günter Kanning
65346 Eltville-Erbach, Hauptstr. 41
Tel. (0 61 23) 67 63 33, Fax 42 22
e-mail:
service@schloss-reinhartshausen.de
Internet:
www.schloss-reinhartshausen.de
Directions: B 42, Erbach exit
Sales: Gerda Kruger
"Vinothek," Tel. (0 61 23) 67 63 99
Opening hours: Mon.–Fri. 09:00 to 18:00 hours, Sat., Sun., public holidays 11:00 to 17:00 hours
Restaurant: "Schloss-Schänke," Mon.–Fri. from 16:00, Sat. and Sun. from 11:00 hours
History: Founded 1337, palace with gala-hall built 1800, taken over by Princess Marianne of Prussia 1855
Worth seeing: Hotel Schloss Reinharts-hausen, Mariannenaue island

---

Vineyard area: 80 hectares
Annual production: 500,000 bottles
Top sites: Erbacher Marcobrunn and Schlossberg, Hattenheimer Nussbrunnen and Wisselbrunnen
Soil types: Deep marl and loess
Grape varieties: 85% Riesling, 5% Spätburgunder, 4% Weißburgunder, 3% Chardonnay, 3% other varieties
Average yield: 57 hl/ha
Best vintages: 1996, 1997, 2003
Member: VDP

We are pleased to report that the new manager Walter Bibo has right from the outset produced an outstanding range of wines. After years of decline, the wines of the 2003 vintage show exceptional quality, reminiscent of better times in the Nineties. We found not a single disappointing wine in the range. The company is provided by first class Spätlese and Auslese wines, serving as a background against which the magnificent Trocken-beerenauslese wines can really shine.

2003 Hattenheimer Nussbrunnen
Riesling Kabinett trocken
11.5%, ♀ till 2008 — **86**

2003 Riesling Classic
12.5%, ♀ till 2008 — **86**

2003 Hattenheimer Nussbrunnen
Riesling trocken Erstes Gewächs
13%, ♀ till 2009 — **88**

2003 Hattenheimer Wisselbrunnen
Riesling trocken Erstes Gewächs
13%, ♀ till 2010 — **88**

2003 Erbacher Marcobrunn
Riesling trocken Erstes Gewächs
13%, ♀ till 2010 — **88**

2003 Erbacher Schlossberg
Riesling trocken Erstes Gewächs
13%, ♀ till 2008 — **89**

2003 Hattenheimer Wisselbrunnen
Riesling Spätlese
9.5%, ♀ till 2012 — **89**

2003 Erbacher Marcobrunn
Riesling Auslese
9.5%, ♀ till 2014 — **89**

2003 Hattenheimer Wisselbrunnen
Riesling Auslese
9.5%, ♀ till 2012 — **89**

2003 Hattenheimer Nussbrunnen
Riesling Trockenbeerenauslese
Goldkapsel
⇗ auction wine, 7%, ♀ till 2025 — **94**

2003 Erbacher Marcobrunn
Riesling Trockenbeerenauslese
Goldkapsel
⇗ auction wine, 7%, ♀ till 2030 — **95**

The wines: **100** Perfect · **95–99** Outstanding · **90–94** Excellent · **85–89** Very good · **80–84** Good · **75–79** Average

585

WEINGUT
BALTHASAR RESS

Owner: Stefan and Christian Ress
Manager: Thomas Doll
Winemaker: Karl Klein, Thomas Doll
65347 Hattenheim, Rheinallee 7
Tel. (0 67 23) 9 19 50, Fax 91 95 91
e-mail: info@balthasar.ress.de
Internet: www.balthasar.ress.de
*Directions: Coming from Eltville on the
B 42, take the first Hattenheim exit after
the Shell filling station, then first right:
Rheinallee*
Sales: Vinotheque Rheinallee 50:
Mon.–Fri. 09:00 to 18:00 hours, Sat.
11:00 to 16:00 hours
Manor-house Rheinallee 7:
By appointment
Worth seeing: Estate cellar in historical
Heimes house, collection of modern art

Vineyard area: 33 hectares
Annual production: 250,000 bottles
Top sites: Hattenheimer Nuss-
brunnen, Rüdesheimer Berg
Schlossberg and Berg Rottland
Soil types: Loess, tertiary marl, quartzite
Grape varieties: 91% Riesling, 6%
Spätburgunder, 3% other varieties
Average yield: 65 hl/ha
Best vintages: 1999, 2001, 2003
Member: VDP

Let us start with a big compliment: We
cannot recall ever having tasted a better
"Von Unserm," an estate Riesling of
which no less than 45,000 bottles were
produced in the 2003 vintage. Apart from
this, it is particularly the Erste Gewächse
(First Growths) that show character, and
the botrytis dessert wines show a purity
of fruit and overall class as virtually
never before. This makes it all the more
difficult to understand the weaknesses
shown in other parts of the range, particularly the mediocre dry and off-dry Kabinett wines. All in all, though, the 2003
range here is by far the best of the past
ten years, and for that we congratulate
Stefan and Christian Ress.

2003 Riesling trocken
12%, ♀ till 2006   **81**

2003 "Von Unserm"
Riesling trocken
12%, ♀ till 2006   **84**

2003 Rüdesheimer Berg Schlossberg
Riesling trocken Erstes Gewächs
13%, ♀ till 2009   **88**

2003 Rüdesheimer Berg Rottland
Riesling trocken Erstes Gewächs
13%, ♀ till 2008   **88**

2003 Hattenheimer Schützenhaus
Riesling Kabinett
10.5%, ♀ till 2008   **86**

2003 Schloss Reichartshausener
Riesling Kabinett
11.5%, ♀ till 2008   **86**

2003 Schloss Reichartshausener
Riesling Spätlese
9%, ♀ till 2008   **86**

2003 Rüdesheimer Berg Rottland
Riesling Spätlese
10.5%, ♀ till 2009   **86**

2003 Hattenheimer Nussbrunnen
Riesling Auslese
8.5%, ♀ till 2010   **87**

2003 Rüdesheimer Berg Rottland
Riesling Beerenauslese
9.5%, ♀ till 2014   **89**

2003 Hattenheimer Nussbrunnen
Riesling Beerenauslese
8%, ♀ till 2018   **91**

2003 Hattenheimer Nussbrunnen
Riesling Trockenbeerenauslese
6.5%, ♀ till 2025   **95**

WEINGUT W. J. SCHÄFER

Owner: Josef Schäfer
65239 Hochheim, Elisabethenstraße 4
Tel. (0 61 46) 21 12 und 48 21, Fax 6 15 60
e-mail:
weingut-w.j.schaefer@t-online.de
Internet:
www.weingut-schaefer-hochheim.de
Directions: A 671, Hochheim exit,
on Ring as far as Delkenheimer Straße,
in direction of center, 6th street right
Sales: Jutta and Josef Schäfer,
Wilhelm J. Schäfer
Opening hours: Mon.–Fri. 10:00 to
20:00 hours, Sat. 09:00 to 18:00 hours
and by appointment

Vineyard area: 6.8 hectares
Annual production: 55,000 bottles
Top sites: Hochheimer Dom-
dechaney, Kirchenstück and Hölle
Soil types: Clay, sandy clay
Grape varieties: 85% Riesling, 10%
Spätburgunder, 5% Gewürztraminer
Average yield: 65 hl/ha
Best vintages: 1997, 1998, 1999

Wilhelm-Joseph Schäfer, the father, who
is also a passionate student of the region's
history, built up this business, which his
son Josef has now taken over, following
completion of his wine studies at Geisenheim. We saw a very successful range
produced here in 1999, and we have been
waiting for four years to experience a repeat. Unfortunately, the 2003 range of
wines makes no exception, and we are
still waiting. Most of the dry Rieslings are
characterized by excessively high alcohols, and the similarly alcoholic Gewürztraminer at 15.5 percent might please the
elder Schäfer, but not many others. Many
years ago he liked to give his Riesling
wines a bit more fruit by blending in a
small and permitted amount of Gewürztraminer. We have speculated whether
he did the same with the 2003 Auslese
from the Hölle vineyard. In any case, both
this rather floral Auslese and the Spätlese
were the wines we liked best.

2003 Hochheimer Stielweg
Riesling Kabinett trocken
11.5%, ♀ till 2006 **80**

2003 Hochheimer Stielweg
Gewürztraminer Auslese trocken
15.5%, ♀ till 2008 **81**

2003 Hochheimer Kirchenstück
Riesling Spätlese trocken
13.5%, ♀ till 2007 **82**

2003 Hochheimer Hölle
Riesling Kabinett trocken
13%, ♀ till 2006 **82**

2003 Hochheimer Reichestal
Riesling Kabinett halbtrocken
12%, ♀ till 2007 **82**

2003 Hochheimer Hölle
Riesling Spätlese halbtrocken
12.5%, ♀ till 2007 **83**

2003 Hochheimer Stein
Riesling Kabinett
9%, ♀ till 2008 **85**

2001 Hochheimer Hölle
Riesling Spätlese
8.5%, ♀ till 2007 **86**

2003 Hochheimer Hölle
Riesling Spätlese
8.5%, ♀ till 2010 **86**

2003 Hochheimer Hölle
Riesling Auslese
7%, ♀ till 2014 **88**

2001 Hochheimer Stielweg
Riesling Eiswein
8.5%, ♀ till 2010 **89**

2002 Hochheimer Stielweg
Riesling Beerenauslese
7.5%, ♀ till 2010 **90**

The wines: **100** Perfect · **95–99** Outstanding · **90–94** Excellent · **85–89** Very good · **80–84** Good · **75–79** Average

WEINGUT
SCHAMARI-MÜHLE

Owner and manager: Erik Andersson
65366 Johannisberg, Grund 65
Tel. (0 67 22) 6 45 37, Fax 74 21
e-mail: mail@schamari.de
Internet: www.schamari.de
Directions: B 42, Johannisberg exit,
Grund suburb, on main road
Sales: Erik Andersson
Opening hours: Mon.–Fri. 09:00 to
18:00 hours, and by appointment
Restaurant/Wine bar: Weinklause,
from April to Nov., open Fri. and Sat.
from 17:00 hours, Sun. from 15:00 hours
Specialties: Light regional dishes
History: Mill first mentioned 1593
Worth seeing: Mill building is a regis-
tered monument

Vineyard area: 5 hectares
Annual production: 30,000 bottles
Top sites: Geisenheimer Kläuser-
weg and Johannisberger Hölle
Soil types: Taunus quartzite, clay soils
Grape varieties: 60% Riesling, 25%
Spätburgunder, 15% other varieties
Average yield: 82 hl/ha
Best vintage: 2003

The history of Schamari mills is closely
linked to that of the Johannisberg monastery. Around the turn of the 20th century, it was the last operating mill in the
region, and was only shut down in 1929.
The restaurant and wine bar were built in
the 1930's. The complex was acquired by
the Swedish family Andersson in the Fifties, and their son Erik has been running
the estate since completion of his wine
studies in Geisenheim. We were pleasantly surprised last year to taste a range of
dry and off-dry wines that was clean and
lively across the board, while the botrytis
dessert wines were even remarkably
good. Most of the 2003 range is again of
such good quality that we are happy to
award a one-bunch rating. We particularly liked the fruity dessert specialties
from the Kläuserweg site.

2003 Johannisberger Erntebringer
Riesling trocken
11.5%, ♀ till 2006   82

2003 Geisenheimer Kilzberg
Riesling Kabinett trocken
12%, ♀ till 2006   82

2003 Johannisberger Erntebringer
Riesling halbtrocken
11.5%, ♀ till 2006   83

2003 Geisenheimer Kilzberg
Riesling Kabinett halbtrocken
11.5%, ♀ till 2007   83

2003 Geisenheimer Kläuserweg
Riesling Spätlese
9.5%, ♀ till 2010   87

2003 Geisenheimer Kläuserweg
Riesling Auslese
9%, ♀ till 2012   87

2003 Geisenheimer Kläuserweg
Riesling Beerenauslese
8%, ♀ till 2015   90

2003 Geisenheimer Kläuserweg
Riesling Trockenbeerenauslese
9.5%, ♀ till 2018   92

——— Red wine ———

2002 Johannisberger Erntebringer
Pinot Noir trocken Barrique
13%, ♀ till 2009   82

DOMÄNENWEINGUT SCHLOSS SCHÖNBORN

Owner: Paul Graf von Schönborn
Estate director: Günter Thies
Vineyard manager: Arnulf Kremer
Winemaker: Peter Barth
65347 Hattenheim, Hauptstraße 53
Tel. (0 67 23) 9 18 10, Fax 91 81 91
e-mail: schloss-schoenborn@t-online.de
Internet: www.schoenborn.de
Directions: B 42, Hattenheim exit
Sales: Günter Thies
Opening hours: Mon.–Fri. 08:00 to 16:30 hours, Sat. and Sun. by appointment
History: Documents trace winemaking by Schönborn family back to 1349
Worth seeing: 500-year-old barrel cellar

Vineyard area: 50 hectares
Annual production: 300,000 bottles
Top sites: Erbacher Marcobrunn, Hattenheimer Nussbrunnen and Pfaffenberg (monopole), Rüdesheimer Berg Schlossberg and Berg Rottland, Hochheimer Domdechaney
Soil types: Kaolin, loess, marl
Grape varieties: 91% Riesling, 6% Spätburgunder, 3% Weißburgunder
Average yield: 61 hl/ha
Best vintages: 1999, 2001, 2003
Member: VDP

There is hardly another winery in the Rheingau that enjoys ownership of such a range of top vineyard sites. Unfortunately, the quality of wines was rather spotty for some time, until signs of a renaissance became obvious in the mid-90's. Following on a very balanced range in 2001, the winery again presented quite an attractive collection in 2002. However, the 2003 vintage again shows up Schönborn as a temperamental diva. While the dry Kabinett wines reveal only moderate fruit, and there is little to praise of the First Growths, the top botrytis dessert wines are of tremendous quality, such as one rarely finds in the Rheingau. Nevertheless, we would prefer to see a little more homogeneity in this range.

2003 Erbacher Marcobrunn
Riesling Spätlese trocken
13.5%, ♀ till 2007 — **84**

2003 Hattenheimer Pfaffenberg
Riesling trocken Erstes Gewächs
13.5%, ♀ till 2008 — **87**

2003 Erbacher Marcobrunn
Riesling trocken Erstes Gewächs
13.5%, ♀ till 2007 — **88**

2003 Erbacher Marcobrunn
Riesling Spätlese
8.5%, ♀ till 2010 — **87**

2002 "Pfaffenberger"
Riesling Spätlese
8%, ♀ till 2010 — **89**

2003 Hattenheimer Pfaffenberg
Riesling Auslese ***
8.5%, ♀ till 2014 — **90**

2002 Erbacher Marcobrunn
Riesling Trockenbeerenauslese
↗ auction wine, 6.5%, ♀ till 2020 — **93**

2003 Erbacher Marcobrunn
Riesling Trockenbeerenauslese
↗ auction wine, 6%, ♀ till 2028 — **93**

2003 Hattenheimer Pfaffenberg
Riesling Beerenauslese
6%, ♀ till 2025 — **94**

2003 Hattenheimer Pfaffenberg
Riesling Trockenbeerenauslese
6%, ♀ till 2030 — **98**

SCHLOSS SCHÖNBORN

2001

RHEINGAU · RIESLING

HALBTROCKEN

The wines: **100** Perfect · **95–99** Outstanding · **90–94** Excellent · **85–89** Very good · **80–84** Good · **75–79** Average

WEIN- UND SEKTGUT F. B. SCHÖNLEBER

Owner: Franz & Katharina Schönleber
Manager: Bernd & Ralf Schönleber
Administrative manager:
Ralf Schönleber
Winemaker: Bernd Schönleber
65375 Oestrich-Winkel,
Obere Roppelsgasse 1
Tel. (0 67 23) 34 75, Fax 47 59
e-mail: info@fb-schoenleber.de
Internet: www.fb-schoenleber.de
Directions: B 42, Mittelheim exit
Sales: Schönleber family
Opening hours: Mon.–Sat. 07:30 to
11:30 hours and 13:00 to 19:00 hours
Wine bar: Wed.–Sat. 16:00 to 23:00, Sun.
15:00 to 23:00 hours, Tel. (0 67 23) 9 17 60
Hotel: Some rooms with view of Rhine

Vineyard area: 9.5 hectares
Annual production: 70,000 bottles,
incl. 15,000 bottles sparkling wine
Top sites: Oestricher Doosberg
and Lenchen, Mittelheimer
St. Nikolaus and Edelmann, Erbacher
Steinmorgen, Winkeler Hasensprung
Soil types: Clay, loess
Grape varieties: 92% Riesling, 6%
Spätburgunder, 2% Ehrenfelser
Average yield: 78 hl/ha
Best vintages: 2000, 2001, 2003

Bernd and Ralf Schönleber have invested heavily in modern cellar technology with the aim of producing top-quality wines. The winery was included in the guide four years ago, based on the excellent range of 1999 wines. In 2000 the Schönlebers proved they were capable of producing clean wines even in a difficult vintage. The 2001 vintage saw a second bunch of grapes, and this was confirmed by the following vintage. The range of 2003 makes no exception, providing a broad spectrum of good dry and elegantly fruity wines, crowned by excellent botrytis dessert wines. We were not quite as positive about the 2002 sparkling wines, which are normally very reliable.

2003 Oestricher Lenchen
Riesling Kabinett trocken
12.5%, ♀ till 2006 · · · · · · · · · · · · **84**

2003 Mittelheimer Edelmann
Riesling trocken Erstes Gewächs
13.5%, ♀ till 2007 · · · · · · · · · · · · **85**

2003 Oestricher Doosberg
Riesling trocken Erstes Gewächs
13.5%, ♀ till 2007 · · · · · · · · · · · · **85**

2003 Mittelheimer St. Nikolaus
Riesling trocken Erstes Gewächs
14%, ♀ till 2007 · · · · · · · · · · · · · · **86**

2003 Mittelheimer St. Nikolaus
Riesling halbtrocken
12%, ♀ till 2007 · · · · · · · · · · · · · · **85**

2003 Mittelheimer St. Nikolaus
Riesling Spätlese halbtrocken
12.5%, ♀ till 2008 · · · · · · · · · · · · **86**

2002 Mittelheimer Edelmann
Riesling Spätlese
9%, ♀ till 2007 · · · · · · · · · · · · · · · **87**

2003 Oestricher Doosberg
Riesling Auslese
7.5%, ♀ till 2010 · · · · · · · · · · · · · · **88**

2001 Mittelheimer St. Nikolaus
Riesling Auslese
8%, ♀ till 2012 · · · · · · · · · · · · · · · **89**

2003 Mittelheimer Edelmann
Riesling Trockenbeerenauslese
6.5%, ♀ till 2020 · · · · · · · · · · · · · · **92**

2003 Oestricher Lenchen
Riesling Trockenbeerenauslese
6%, ♀ till 2025 · · · · · · · · · · · · · · · **93**

RIESLING
QUALITÄTSWEIN MIT PRÄDIKAT
2002er Oestricher Doosberg
Spätlese halbtrocken
Gutsabfüllung
A.P.Nr. 28027 014 03
11,5 %vol   0,75l
RHEINGAU
WEIN- UND SEKTGUT FRANZ B. SCHÖNLEBER · D-65375 OESTRICH-WINKEL

WEINGUT SPEICHER-SCHUTH

Owner and manager: Ralf Schuth
65399 Kiedrich, Suttonstraße 23
Tel. (0 61 23) 8 14 21, Fax 6 16 15
e-mail:
info@weingut-speicher-schuth.de
Internet:
www.weingut-speicher-schuth.de
Directions: B 42, Eltville-Mitte exit, in
direction of Kiedrich
Sales: Ralf Schuth by appointment
Restaurant/Wine bar: Karl-Heinz and
Renate Schuth, Wed.–Sun. from 15:30
hours, closed in August
Specialties: Juicy vintner's steak

Vineyard area: 10 hectares
Annual production: 60,000 bottles
Top sites: Kiedricher Gräfenberg
and Sandgrub, Assmannshäuser
Hinterkirch and Höllenberg
Soil types: Stony, gravelly phyllites
with loess-clay, phyllite slate
Grape varieties: 80% Riesling,
20% Spätburgunder
Average yield: 55 hl/ha
Best vintages: 2000, 2002, 2003

Ralf Schuth is yet another of those producers who has in recent years discarded
natural cork closures in favor of stainless
steel crown closures. Following on a
good range produced in 2002, the 2003
vintage confirmed that Ralf Schuth now
appears to have found his own style.
Right across the board, the wines presented showed good quality, from the
crystal-clear estate Riesling through the
elegantly fruity single-vineyard wines
right up to the opulent Auslese from the
Kiedricher Wasseros site. Having said all
that, our favorite wine is the Riesling
Spätlese from the Kiedricher Gräfenberg
vineyard, picked at 115 degrees Oechsle,
which could easily have passed as an
Auslese predicate. More of the same,
please!

2003 Riesling trocken
11%, ♀ till 2006 — **84**

2003 Kiedricher Wasseros
Riesling trocken
11%, ♀ till 2007 — **86**

2003 Kiedricher Gräfenberg
Riesling trocken
11.5%, ♀ till 2007 — **86**

2003 Kiedricher Sandgrub
Riesling trocken "Erstes Gewächs"
12.5%, ♀ till 2008 — **88**

2003 Kiedricher Wasseros
Riesling Kabinett
10%, ♀ till 2009 — **87**

2002 Kiedricher Gräfenberg
Riesling Auslese
10%, ♀ till 2008 — **89**

2001 Kiedricher Gräfenberg
Riesling Eiswein
10%, ♀ till 2012 — **89**

2003 Kiedricher Gräfenberg
Riesling Spätlese
8.5%, ♀ till 2012 — **90**

2003 Kiedricher Wasseros
Riesling Auslese
8.5%, ♀ till 2012 — **91**

SPEICHER-SCHUTH
WEINGUT
RHEINGAU
2001
RIESLING SPÄTLESE
GRÄFENBERG

The wines: **100** Perfect · **95–99** Outstanding · **90–94** Excellent · **85–89** Very good · **80–84** Good · **75–79** Average

WEINGUT
JOSEF SPREITZER

Owner: Bernd and Andreas Spreitzer
Administrator: Bernhard Spreitzer
Winemaker: Andreas Spreitzer
65375 Oestrich, Rheingaustraße 86
Tel. (0 67 23) 26 25, Fax 46 44
e-mail: weingut-spreitzer@t-online.de
Internet: www.weingut-spreitzer.de
Directions: B 42, first Oestrich exit,
follow main road
Sales: Bernd and Mareike Spreitzer
Opening hours: Mon.–Fri. 09:00 to
12:00 and 13:30 to 18:30 hours,
Sat. 09:00 to 16:00 hours
Worth a visit: Culinary weeks for ten
days end April/early May
Specialties: Dishes related to Riesling
Worth seeing: Vaulted cellar (1745) with
oak barrels, villa in Belle Epoque style

Vineyard area: 14 hectares
Annual production: 105,000 bottles
Top sites: Oestricher Lenchen
and Doosberg, Winkeler Jesuiten-
garten, Hattenheimer Wisselbrunnen
Soil types: Deep clay and loess
Grape varieties: 97% Riesling,
3% Spätburgunder
Average yield: 68 hl/ha
Best vintages: 2001, 2002, 2003
Member: VDP

This is a typical family operation: Father
Bernhard Spreitzer keeps his watchful
eye on the operation as a whole, while his
sons Bernd and Andreas are responsible
for the vineyards and cellar respectively,
working hand in hand. They have been
producing a succession of good vintages
since the late Nineties. The highlight to
date in terms of quality has been the 2002
vintage, and the 2003 vintage now follows on seamlessly from that. We were
impressed yet again by a particularly homogeneous range, from the tremendous
First Growths up to the wonderfully clean
botrytis dessert wines. If they can keep
up this standard, they are certainly candidates for even higher ratings in future.

2003 Oestricher Lenchen
Riesling trocken Erstes Gewächs
12.5%, ♀ till 2010 — **90**

2003 Hattenheimer Wisselbrunnen
Riesling trocken Erstes Gewächs
12.5%, ♀ till 2010 — **92**

2003 Oestricher Lenchen
Riesling Spätlese
8.5%, ♀ till 2010 — **89**

2003 Oestricher Lenchen
Riesling Auslese
7.5%, ♀ till 2012 — **90**

2003 Oestricher Lenchen
Riesling Spätlese – 303 –
8%, ♀ till 2010 — **91**

2002 Oestricher Lenchen
Riesling Spätlese – 303 –
8.5%, ♀ till 2010 — **91**

2003 Oestricher Doosberg
Riesling Beerenauslese
8%, ♀ till 2018 — **92**

2003 Oestricher Lenchen
Riesling Trockenbeerenauslese
7%, ♀ till 2025 — **94**

2003 Oestricher Lenchen
Riesling Auslese Goldkapsel
↗ auction wine, 8%, ♀ till 2018 — **94**

2002 Oestricher Lenchen
Riesling Trockenbeerenauslese Goldkapsel
↗ auction wine, 6%, ♀ till 2030 — **95**

HESS. STAATSWEINGÜTER DOMAINE ASSMANNSHAUSEN

Owner: State of Hessen
Manager: Ralf Bengel
Administrator: Gregor Vollmer
Winemaker: Ralf Bengel, Frank Werle
65385 Assmannshausen,
Höllenbergstraße 10
Tel. (0 67 22) 22 73, **Fax** 4 81 21
e-mail: assmannshausen@weingut-kloster-eberbach.de
Internet:
www.weingut-kloster-eberbach.de
Directions: B 42, Assmannshausen exit, in direction of Aulhausen
Opening hours: April to Nov.:
Tue.–Sat. 12:00 to 18:00 hours; Dec. to March: Tue.–Fri. 12:00 to 18:00 hours
History: Assmannshäuser Höllenberg vineyard, mentioned as being owned by Cistercian nuns at Marienhausen in 1106

Vineyard area: 26 hectares
Annual production: 130,000 bottles
Top site: Assmannshäuser Höllenberg
Soil types: Taunus phyllite slate
Grape varieties: 98% Spätburgunder, 2% Frühburgunder
Average yield: 40 hl/ha
Best vintages: 1996, 1997, 2002
Member: VDP

The state domaine in Assmannshausen was one of the best producers of Pinot Noir in Germany long before red wine became fashionable in Germany. The wines are matured in traditional large oak vats, to date barrique maturation has played only a very small part. Tremendous red wines were produced here until the late 80's. In recent years, ever since Ralf Bengel, who used to be at the Graf Kanitz winery, took over the management, many things have improved here. The 2002 vintage presented was very good right across the board, and we look forward expectantly to the 2003 range, which has already received some enthusiastic preliminary reviews.

2003 Assmannshäuser Höllenberg
Spätburgunder "Blanc de Noir"
13.5%, ♀ till 2006 **82**

——— Red wines ———

2002 Assmannshäuser Höllenberg
Spätburgunder trocken
12%, ♀ till 2010 **86**

2002 Assmannshäuser Höllenberg
Frühburgunder trocken
13%, ♀ till 2009 **86**

2002 Assmannshäuser Höllenberg
Spätburgunder Spätlese trocken
13%, ♀ till 2009 **86**

2002 Spätburgunder
trocken Barrique
13.5%, ♀ till 2010 **86**

2002 Assmannshäuser Höllenberg
Spätburgunder Auslese trocken
13.5%, ♀ till 2012 **87**

2002 Assmannshäuser Höllenberg
Frühburgunder trocken Goldkapsel
13%, ♀ till 2012 **87**

2002 Assmannshäuser Höllenberg
Spätburgunder Spätlese trocken
Goldkapsel
13%, ♀ till 2012 **88**

2002 Assmannshäuser Höllenberg
Spätburgunder Auslese trocken
Goldkapsel
⤳ auction wine, 13.5%, ♀ till 2012 **88**

he wines: **100** Perfect · **95–99** Outstanding · **90–94** Excellent · **85–89** Very good · **80–84** Good · **75–79** Average

593

HESS. STAATSWEINGÜTER KLOSTER EBERBACH

Owner: State of Hessen
General manager: Dieter Greiner
Winemaker: Ralf Bengel
65343 Eltville,
Schwalbacher Straße 56–62
Tel. (0 61 23) 9 23 00, Fax 92 30 90
e-mail:
info@weingut-kloster-eberbach.de
Internet:
www.weingut-kloster-eberbach.de
Directions: A 66 Wiesbaden–Rüdesheim,
Martinsthal/Eltville-Nord exit
Sales: Jürgen Rödesheim, Anne Eppinger
Opening hours: Mon.–Fri. 09:00 to
18:00 hours, Sat. 10:00 to 16:00 hours
Restaurant/Wine bar: "Im Baiken,"
May to Oct., Tue.–Sat. from 17:00
hours, Sun. from 16:00 hours
"Klosterschänke Eberbach," daily from
10:00 to 22:00 hours
History: 850 years of winemaking tradi-
tion by Cistercian monks
Worth seeing: Kloster Eberbach with
Cistercian museum

Vineyard area: 131 hectares
Annual production: 1 mill. bottles
Top sites: Steinberger, Rauen-
thaler Baiken, Erbacher Marcobrunn,
Rüdesheimer Berg Schlossberg,
Hochheimer Domdechaney
Soil types: Decomposed slate,
quartzite-loess-clay- and marl soils
Grape varieties: 99% Riesling,
1% white Pinot varieties
Average yield: 70 hl/ha
Best vintages: 2000, 2001, 2003
Member: VDP

Dieter Greiner has brought some new life
to the historical surroundings of Kloster
Eberbach. The 2001 and 2002 ranges,
however, showed a rather split personality. We are pleased to report that the
range of 2003 wines is much more attractive. The very pleasant First Growths as
well as cleanly made Spätlese and Auslese
wines have given a lift to the whole range.

If they can produce more good results in
the basic wine range, the third bunch of
grapes will not be far off.

2003 Steinberger	
Riesling trocken	
12.5%, ♀ till 2006	**83**
2003 Rauenthaler Baiken	
Riesling trocken	
12.5%, ♀ till 2007	**84**
2003 Rauenthaler Baiken	
Riesling Kabinett trocken	
12.5%, ♀ till 2007	**85**
2003 Steinberger	
Riesling trocken Erstes Gewächs	
13%, ♀ till 2007	**87**
2003 Rauenthaler Baiken	
Riesling trocken Erstes Gewächs	
13%, ♀ till 2007	**87**
2003 Steinberger	
Riesling Kabinett	
9.5%, ♀ till 2010	**87**
2003 Steinberger	
Riesling Spätlese	
7.5%, ♀ till 2009	**87**
2003 Steinberger	
Riesling Auslese Goldkapsel	
↗ auction wine, 10.5%, ♀ till 2010	**88**
2003 Rauenthaler Baiken	
Riesling Auslese	
8.5%, ♀ till 2018	**90**

RHEINGAU

STAATSWEINGÜTER

KLOSTER EBERBACH

2003
RIESLING

CLASSIC

WEINGUT SCHLOSS VOLLRADS

Owner: Nassauische Sparkasse
Estate director: Dr. Rowald Hepp
Administrator: Gerd Wendling
Winemaker: Ralph Herke
65375 Oestrich-Winkel,
Schloss Vollrads
Tel. (0 67 23) 6 60, Fax 66 66
e-mail: info@schlossvollrads.com
Internet: www.schlossvollrads.com
Directions: B 42 in direction of Rüdesheim, 2nd Winkel exit, follow the signs
Sales: Mathias Ganswohl
Opening hours: Mon.–Fri. 08:00 to 12:00 hours and 13:00 to 17:00 hours Sat. 14:00 to 17:00 hours (Nov. and Dec.) April–Oct. Vinotheque and wine sales-stall in the courtyard, Sat., Sun. and public holidays 11:00 to 19:00 hours
Restaurant: Im Kavaliershaus, April–Oct. Mon.–Fri. 12:00 to 15:00 hours and 17:30 to 23:00 hours, closed Wed. Sat., Sun. and public holidays 12:00 to 23:00 hours Nov.–Mar. Fri.–Mon. 12:00 to 23:00 hours; closed Tue., Wed. and Thu.
History: First documented mention of wine sales here dates back to 1211

Vineyard area: 56 hectares
Annual production: 400,000 bottles
Top site: Schloss Vollrads
Soil types: Clay, loess
Grape varieties: 100% Riesling
Average yield: 54 hl/ha
Best vintages: 1998, 1999, 2003
Member: VDP

Dr. Rowald Hepp has had to face all kinds of challenges in his efforts to rebuild this flagship of German wine culture. After a number of vintages which were not quite convincing across the board, the 2003 vintage appears to present a big step forward. While one or the other basic wine can still be slightly improved upon, overall we tasted a most impressive range with two outstanding botrytis dessert wines as a crowning glory.

2003 Schloss Vollrads
Riesling trocken
12.5%, ♀ till 2007 — **84**

2003 Schloss Vollrads
Riesling Kabinett trocken
12%, ♀ till 2007 — **85**

2003 Schloss Vollrads
Riesling trocken Erstes Gewächs
13%, ♀ till 2010 — **86**

2003 Schloss Vollrads
Riesling Spätlese halbtrocken
12.5%, ♀ till 2010 — **88**

2003 Schloss Vollrads
Riesling "Edition"
12.5%, ♀ till 2008 — **87**

2002 Schloss Vollrads
Riesling "Edition"
12.5%, ♀ till 2007 — **87**

2003 Schloss Vollrads
Riesling Spätlese Goldkapsel
⤳ auction wine, 9.5%, ♀ till 2015 — **88**

2003 Schloss Vollrads
Riesling Auslese
8.5%, ♀ till 2016 — **89**

2003 Schloss Vollrads
Riesling Beerenauslese
8%, ♀ till 2020 — **91**

2003 Schloss Vollrads
Riesling Trockenbeerenauslese
6%, ♀ till 2035 — **93**

SCHLOSS VOLLRADS

2002
Trockenbeerenauslese
Rheingau · Riesling

Qualitätswein mit Prädikat

Gutsabfüllung
Weingutsverwaltung Schloss Vollrads KG
D-65375 Oestrich-Winkel
A.P.Nr. 2707402903

alc. 6.5% vol   375 ml

he wines: **100** Perfect · **95–99** Outstanding · **90–94** Excellent · **85–89** Very good · **80–84** Good · **75–79** Average

595

WEINGÜTER WEGELER – GUTSHAUS OESTRICH

Owner: Rolf Wegeler family
General manager: Dr. Tom Drieseberg
Manager: Michael Burgdorf
Winemaker: Andreas Holderrieth
65375 Oestrich-Winkel,
Friedensplatz 9–11
Tel. (0 67 23) 9 90 90, Fax 99 09 66
e-mail: info@wegeler.com
Directions: B 42, Oestrich exit,
continue to the center of town
Sales: Anja Wegeler-Drieseberg
by appointment

Vineyard area: 48 hectares
Annual production: 420,000 bottles
Top sites: Rüdesheimer Berg
Schlossberg and Berg Rottland,
Winkeler Jesuitengarten,
Geisenheimer Rothenberg
Soil types: Decomposed slate,
loess-clay
Grape varieties: 99% Riesling,
1% other varieties
Average yield: 58 hl/ha
Best vintages: 2000, 2002, 2003
Member: VDP

We are particularly pleased to report that this respected traditional winery appears to be back on form again, presenting first-class wines even in the dry category. Unfortunately Oliver Haag is destined to leave here, taking over his father's estate Fritz Haag in Brauneberg, his successor here is Michael Burgdorf, who comes from the Heyl zu Herrnsheim estate in Nierstein. Working closely with wine-maker Andreas Holderrieth, Haag in his finale has once again demonstrated the various terroir characteristics very well. Of the dry wines we particularly liked the Erstes Gewächs (First Growth) from the Jesuitengarten vineyard. We were especially impressed this year by the fruity sweet predicate wines, particularly those from the Geisenheimer Rothenberg site, crowned by a magnificent Trockenbee-renauslese.

2003 Riesling Spätlese trocken
12.5%, ♀ till 2007 — 85

2003 Winkeler Hasensprung
Riesling Spätlese trocken
12.5%, ♀ till 2007 — 86

2003 "Geheimrat J"
Riesling Spätlese trocken
12.5%, ♀ till 2008 — 87

2003 Rüdesheimer Berg Schlossberg
Riesling trocken Erstes Gewächs
12.5%, ♀ till 2007 — 87

2002 Winkeler Jesuitengarten
Riesling Erstes Gewächs
12.5%, ♀ till 2007 — 89

2003 Winkeler Jesuitengarten
Riesling trocken Erstes Gewächs
12.5%, ♀ till 2009 — 89

2003 Rüdesheimer Berg Rottland
Riesling Spätlese
8%, ♀ till 2012 — 90

2003 Geisenheimer Rothenberg
Riesling Auslese
7.5%, ♀ till 2012 — 90

2003 Rüdesheimer Berg Rottland
Riesling Spätlese Goldkapsel
𝅘 auction wine, 7.5%, ♀ till 2014 — 90

2003 Geisenheimer Rothenberg
Riesling Eiswein
7%, ♀ till 2014 — 91

2003 Geisenheimer Rothenberg
Riesling Auslese Goldkapsel
𝅘 auction wine, 7.5%, ♀ till 2016 — 93

2003 Geisenheimer Rothenberg
Riesling Trockenbeerenauslese
𝅘 auction wine, 6%, ♀ 2015 till 2030 — 95

WEINGÜTER
WEGELER

2002
Winkeler
Hasensprung

Riesling Spätlese
trocken

The majestic Schloss Vollrads castle is one of the symbols of the Rheingau region.
Photo: DWI/Hartmann

WEINGUT ROBERT WEIL

Owner: Suntory, Wilhelm Weil
Estate director: Wilhelm Weil
Vineyard manager: Clemens Schmitt
Winemakers: Christian Engel,
Michael Thrien, Stefan Bieber
65399 Kiedrich, Mühlberg 5
Tel. (0 61 23) 23 08 and 56 88, Fax 15 46
e-mail: info@weingut-robert-weil.com
Internet: www.weingut-robert-weil.com
Directions: A 66, then on to B 42, Eltville-Mitte exit, in the direction of Kiedrich, follow signs in Kiedrich
Sales: Martina Weil, Dirk Cannova, Jochen Becker-Köhn, Caroline Helmer
Opening hours: Mon.–Fri. 08:00 to 17:30 hours
Sat. 10:00 to 16:00 hours
Sun. 11:00 to 17:00 hours
History: Estate buildings constructed by an English nobleman, Baron Sutton, and acquired by Dr. Robert Weil in 1879
Worth seeing: Manor-house in the style of an English country manor, with park; the vinotheque has a special flair

Vineyard area: 65 hectares
Annual production: 450,000 bottles
Top sites: Kiedricher Gräfenberg and Wasseros
Soil types: Stony, gravelly soils with phyllite formation, partly with loess and clay added
Grape varieties: 98% Riesling, 2% Spätburgunder
Average yield: 55 hl/ha
Best vintages: 2001, 2002, 2003
Member: VDP

Only a handful of German wine estates has what one could call a château character, and the Robert Weil estate is probably the most characteristic one, since it also embraces the brand approach found in southwestern France. Whatever vintage variations may occur, the label is a guarantee for the quality of bottle contents. One must respect the way in which Wilhelm Weil has succeeded in turning this estate, which by now has grown to 65 hectares of vineyards, into a shining symbol of German Riesling culture, both domestically and in the most important export markets. For many years now, there has never been a doubt that this is one of the best producers in the world of botrytized dessert wines; only the 2000 vintage did not come quite up to standard, which at the time resulted in the loss of the fifth bunch of grapes in the ratings. However, the botrytis wines of the 2001 and 2002 vintages already showed a clear return to form, and the absolutely superb Trockenbeerenauslese wines of the 2003 vintage now definitely confirm the return of Weil to the small circle of top world-class producers. In fact, this year it was not only the fabulous botrytis wines that attracted our attention, rather it was the fact that Weil's Erstes Gewächs (First Growth) from the Gräfenberg vineyard is a truly monumental wine, and the achievement of no less than ten wines rated between 90 and 100 points. In our opinion, this is reason enough to award the winery the additional accolade of having produced the "Range of the year." Visitors to the cellar in Kiedrich will see not only rows of stainless steel tanks, but also a section filled with large oak vats, which have been installed in an area that used to house part of the older rarities. This section was first used in 2002 to mature the Erstes Gewächs (First Growth) wines. For most of the other wines, though, Wilhelm Weil has no intention of moving away from stainless steel tanks generally, as he sees these as the best guarantee for the clear fruit expression of his Riesling wines.

2003 Riesling trocken
11.5%, 1.0 liter, ♀ till 2006 — 80

2003 Riesling trocken
11.5%, ♀ till 2006 — 81

2003 Riesling Kabinett trocken
11.5%, ♀ till 2007 — 83

2003 Kiedricher Gräfenberg
Riesling Kabinett trocken
12%, ♀ till 2008 — 85

2003 Riesling Spätlese trocken
12.5%, ♀ till 2008 — 85

2002 Riesling Kabinett trocken
11%, ♀ till 2007   **86**

2002 Kiedricher Gräfenberg
Riesling Kabinett trocken
11.5%, ♀ till 2007   **86**

2002 Kiedricher Gräfenberg
Riesling Erstes Gewächs
13%, ♀ till 2008   **88**

2003 Kiedricher Gräfenberg
Riesling trocken Erstes Gewächs
13.5%, ♀ till 2012   **91**

2002 Riesling
Spätlese halbtrocken
11.5%, ♀ till 2008   **86**

2003 Riesling
Spätlese halbtrocken
12%, ♀ till 2008   **86**

2002 Riesling Kabinett
8%, ♀ till 2008   **86**

2003 Riesling Kabinett
8%, ♀ till 2010   **88**

2002 Kiedricher Gräfenberg
Riesling Spätlese
7.5%, ♀ till 2012   **90**

2003 Riesling Spätlese
8%, ♀ till 2012   **90**

2002 Kiedricher Gräfenberg
Riesling Auslese
7.5%, ♀ till 2014   **91**

2003 Kiedricher Gräfenberg
Riesling Spätlese
8%, ♀ till 2015   **92**

2002 Kiedricher Gräfenberg
Riesling Auslese Goldkapsel
⤳ auction wine, 7%, ♀ till 2018   **92**

2002 Kiedricher Gräfenberg
Riesling Eiswein
6.5%, ♀ till 2018   **93**

2003 Kiedricher Gräfenberg
Riesling Auslese
8%, ♀ till 2015   **93**

2002 Kiedricher Gräfenberg
Riesling Trockenbeerenauslese
5.5%, ♀ till 2020   **94**

2002 Kiedricher Gräfenberg
Riesling Beerenauslese
6.5%, ♀ till 2020   **95**

2003 Kiedricher Gräfenberg
Riesling Beerenauslese
7.5%, ♀ till 2020   **95**

2003 Kiedricher Gräfenberg
Riesling Trockenbeerenauslese
7%, ♀ till 2030   **97**

2003 Kiedricher Gräfenberg
Riesling Auslese Goldkapsel
⤳ auction wine, 8.5%, ♀ till 2020   **98**

2003 Kiedricher Gräfenberg
Riesling Beerenauslese Goldkapsel
⤳ auction wine, 6.5%, ♀ till 2025   **98**

2003 Kiedricher Gräfenberg
Riesling Trockenbeerenauslese
Goldkapsel
⤳ auction wine, 6%, ♀ till 2035   **100**

2003 Kiedricher Gräfenberg
Riesling Trockenbeerenauslese
Goldkapsel 316 Grad
⤳ auction wine, 6%, ♀ till 2035   **100**

the wines: **100** Perfect · **95–99** Outstanding · **90–94** Excellent · **85–89** Very good · **80–84** Good · **75–79** Average

Rheingau

Other recommended producers

Weingut Ferdinand Abel
65375 Oestrich-Winkel, Mühlstraße 32–34
Tel. (0 67 23) 28 53, Fax 8 74 54

We first noted the wines of this Oestrich producer with interest last year. From the 2003 vintage, we particularly liked both the off-dry and fruity Spätlese wines from the Lenchen vineyard (83 points). The Trockenbeerenauslese from the same site is exceptionally good (rated 91), and a veritable bargain. The restaurant with its interesting food is also to be recommended. Regular customers particularly appreciate the fact that glasses are always well filled here.

Weingut Fritz Allendorf
65375 Oestrich-Winkel, Kirchstraße 69
Tel. (0 67 23) 9 18 50, Fax 91 85 40
e-mail: Allendorf@allendorf.de
Internet: www.allendorf.de

In terms of vineyard area, this is one of the largest family-owned operations in the Rheingau area, and also a very active and dynamic one. In 2003 Uli Allendorf launched the so-called "Wine-Experience-World." Here, visitors can follow on the tracks of a wine's development in the vineyard, look behind the scenes in the cellar, and, of course, taste the wines produced here. However, the range of wines produced in 2003 achieves the overall good standard of the Rheingau in only a few cases. Therefore, we can only rate this estate as recommended at present.

Weingut August Eser
65375 Oestrich-Winkel, Friedensplatz 19
Tel. (0 67 23) 50 32, Fax 8 74 06
e-mail: mail@eser-wein.de
Internet: www.eser-wein.de

This old-established and family-owned operation in Oestrich was among the best wine producers in the middle Rheingau until the early Nineties. We have fond memories of the wonderful 1992 vintage, the wines of which are still in good condition to this day. We have no real explanation why Joachim Eser's wines since then

have not really been convincing. There is some sign, at least, in the 2003 Erstes Gewächs (First Growth) wines from the Rothenberg (86 points) and Lenchen (85) sites that indicates a slight renaissance may be underway.

**Georg-Müller-Stiftung –
Weingut der Stadt Eltville**
65347 Eltville-Hattenheim,
Eberbacher Straße 7–9
Tel. (0 67 23) 20 20, Fax 20 35

After purchasing the business in 2002, Peter Winter invested heavily in the operation, and this is beginning to bear its first fruits. While the dry Riesling wines are quite a mouthful, the elegantly fruity Spätlese wines from the Schützenhaus and Wisselbrunnen sites (both 84 points) are quite attractive. Easily our favorite is the Trockenbeerenauslese from the Wisselbrunnen site (91), which shows up clearly the ambitions that drive the new owner. The beautiful old cellar in Hattenheim is to be utilized in future for cultural and art events, Peter Winter is able to draw on the resources of his wife, who has an art gallery in Wiesbaden.

Major and minor vintages in the Rheingau region

Vintage	Rating
2003	🍇🍇🍇🍇🍇
2002	🍇🍇🍇
2001	🍇🍇🍇🍇🍇
2000	🍇🍇🍇
1999	🍇🍇🍇🍇
1998	🍇🍇🍇
1997	🍇🍇🍇
1996	🍇🍇🍇🍇
1995	🍇🍇🍇🍇
1994	🍇🍇🍇🍇

Vintage rating:

🍇🍇🍇🍇🍇 : Excellent vintage

🍇🍇🍇🍇 : Very good vintage

🍇🍇🍇 : Good vintage

🍇🍇 : Average vintage

🍇 : Poor vintage

Weinhof Gutsschänke Goldatzel

65366 Johannisberg, Hansenbergallee 1a
Tel. (0 67 22) 5 05 37, Fax 60 09
e-mail: wein@goldatzel.de
Internet: www.goldatzel.de

We first mentioned this winery last year, not only for its beautiful view of Schloss Johannisberg and the Rheingau region. On a fine day you literally have to fight for a space on the terrace. Of the 2003 vintage wines, we particularly liked the dry Spätlese from the Hölle site (83 points) and – even more so – the elegant Auslese from the Vogelsang vineyard (86). The other wines generally did not equal the good standard of the previous vintage.

Weingut Emmerich Himmel

65239 Hochheim,
Holger-Crafoord-Straße 4
Tel. (0 61 46) 65 90, Fax 60 15 70

Following on two difficult vintages, this winery showed a solid range of wines from the 2002 vintage, and was on its way back to a bunch of grapes standard. The wines of the 2003 vintage are also clean and have clear fruit, however they are once more too uniform, with too little character, and a little too much acidity. The wines we liked best were the dry Kirchenstück Auslese (83 points), the elegantly fruity Kabinett (83) as well as the botrytis dessert Auslese (88) from the Hölle site. Just consider: A winemaker by the name of Himmel (heaven), who has a vineyard in the Hölle (hell) site...

Weingut Hupfeld

65375 Oestrich-Winkel,
Rheingaustraße 113
Tel. (0 67 23) 99 92 59, Fax 99 92 59
Internet: weingut.hupfeld@t-online.de

While Wolfram Hupfeld is still some way from being awarded a bunch of grapes, we have in recent years noted slight improvements in quality here. The 2002 range of wines was already somewhat better than the two preceding rather mediocre vintages. Nevertheless, it is still true to say that the basic range of wines needs upgrading.

Klosterweingut Abtei St. Hildegard

65385 Rüdesheim, Klosterweg
Tel. (0 67 22) 49 91 30, Fax 49 91 85
e-mail: weingut @abtei-st-hildegard.de
Internet: www.abtei-st-hildegard.de

The Benedictine abbey of St. Hildegard houses 58 nuns, Sisters Andrea and Thekla are responsible for the wine production of a total of 6.5 hectares of vineyard. And they are doing this job successfully. Of the 2003 vintage, we particularly liked the hearty Classic Riesling (83), the invigorating Abtei-Sommer-Riesling (84) as well as the mouth-filling Weißherbst (Rosé 85 points). If all the other wines were of the same quality, the first bunch of grapes could be awarded. The nuns also produce liqueurs, wine jelly and German wheat (spelt) products.

Weingut Koegler – Hof Bechtermünz

65343 Eltville, Kirchgasse 5
Tel. (0 61 23) 24 37, Fax 8 11 18

This is a restaurant in the old heart of Eltville that is well worth a visit, with a most attractive hotel having been added recently. Following on significant variations in quality in recent years, the current range shows some really convincing red wines and botrytis dessert wines. If the winery remains on track, it will be one of the first candidates for a higher rating.

Weingut Dr. Nägler

65385 Rüdesheim, Friedrichstraße 22
Tel. (0 67 22) 28 35, Fax 4 73 63
e-mail: info@weingut-dr-naegler.de
Internet: www.t-online.de/home/h.naegler

The excellent potential of Nägler's vineyards in the Rüdesheimer Berg site should ensure the winery a place somewhere among the leading producers in this region. Since Tilbert Nägler has taken over the estate there have been small improvements noted each year, but these are still too small to say he has achieved his potential. Overall, we take a positive view of his 2003 wines, and we particularly liked the dry Spätlese from the Schlossberg vineyard (84 points) as well as the naturally sweet Auslese (85) from the same site.

Rheingau

Sektkellerei Solter

65385 Rüdesheim am Rhein,
Zum Niederwald-Denkmal 2
Tel. (0 67 22) 25 66, Fax 91 04 02

It is more than 20 years ago that Helmut Solter from Bischoffingen in Baden came to settle in the Rheingau. He set up his own business, a sparkling wine cellar, where he now produces around 250,000 bottles of sparkling wine each year, using traditional Champenoise methods. We found some of the older vintages such as 1993 and 1994, which Solter degorges as required, particularly interesting. We can also recommend the Roseneck wine bar/restaurant, which he runs in partnership with cellar master Schmoranz of the Breuer estate.

Weingut Trenz

65366 Johannisberg, Schulstraße 1
Tel. (0 67 22) 82 85, Fax 52 39
e-mail: info@weingut-trenz.de
Internet: www.weingut-trenz.de

This family operation was listed in the guide for the first time last year. The winery features both a vinotheque and a very cosy restaurant, both of which are very popular. Wines of particular interest this year were the dry Spätlese from the Johannisberger Vogelsang vineyard (84) as well as the elegantly fruity Weißherbst Auslese (Rosé, 85). The botrytis dessert wines have all been fermented too long, giving them an alcoholic character.

Other wineries tasted

- Weingut Crass, Erbach
- Weingut Carl Ehrhard, Rüdesheim
- Winzer von Erbach, Erbach
- Weingut Faust, Martinsthal
- Winzergenossenschaft Frauenstein, Wiesbaden
- Weingut Anthony Robert Hammond, Oestrich-Winkel
- Weingut der Landeshauptstadt Wiesbaden
- Weinwirtschaft Laquai, Lorch
- Weingut Heinz Lebert, Eltville-Erbach
- Weingut Karl-Joh. Molitor, Eltville-Hattenheim
- Weingut Schönleber-Blümlein, Oestrich-Winkel

Recommended by our wine producers

Hotels and inns

Assmannshausen: Krone
Eltville-Erbach: Tillmanns, Schloss Reinhartshausen
Eltville: Burg Crass, Gästehaus Kloster Eberbach
Geisenheim-Marienthal: Gietz
Hallgarten: Rebhang
Hattenheim: Kronenschlösschen, Zum Krug
Kaub: Deutsches Haus, Zum Turm
Oestrich-Winkel: Bellevue – Nägler, Kühns Mühle, Gästehaus Querbach, Schönleber, Schwan
Rüdesheim: Bären, Breuer's Schloss, Central, Felsenkeller, Lindenwirt, Jagdschloss Niederwald, Trapp
Schlangenbad: Parkhotel
Wiesbaden: Nassauer Hof

Gourmet restaurants

Hattenheim: Kronenschlösschen
Wiesbaden: Ente im Nassauer Hof

Restaurants, wine bars and winery facilities

Eltville-Erbach: Oetinger (2 x), Schlossschänke Reinhartshausen
Eltville-Rauenthal: Gutsausschank Im Baiken
Eltville: Weinpump, Vinothek Burg Crass
Flörsheim: Flörsheimer Warte
Hallgarten: Hallgartener Zange
Hattenheim: Adlerwirtschaft, Zum Krug
Hochheim: Rieslingstuben
Johannisberg: Gutsschänke im Schloss
Kaub: Zum Turm
Kiedrich: Schloss Groenesteyn
Martinsthal: Diefenhardt
Oestrich-Winkel: Grüner Baum, Corvers-Kauter, Zehntenhof
Rüdesheim-Eibingen: Fendel
Walluf: Beckers Weingarten, Zur Schlupp
Wiesbaden: Burg Sonnenberg, M, Tsva
Wiesbaden-Erbenheim: Domäne Mechtildshausen
Wiesbaden-Frauenstein: Sinz

Rheinhessen

"2003 wakes up the taste-buds"

There is no doubt that Germany's largest wine-growing region continues to post visible progress each year. This year is no exception, and we can report improved performance by some good wineries. And of the five wineries elevated to one-bunch status for the first time, only one is an older winery making a comeback, while the others appear in this category for the first time. It is not only the young wine-makers who are showing improvements, sometimes older producers can also convince us by presenting a particularly good range of wines.

The question is whether the 2003 vintage was helpful in achieving these improvements, and whether 2003 was indeed a great vintage in the Rheinhessen region – well, there is no clear-cut answer to this. Certainly the hot summer produced what the regional wine marketing office calls "phenomenal ripeness," which also resulted in opulent, often exotic aromas. There are quite a few wines with regard to which one can share the opinion of Bernd Kern of "Rheinhessenwein," or that of some producers ("powerful wines that wake up every single taste-bud," "exceptionally full body and quality"), but there were just as many cases of unselfcritical hype, in which producers wax lyrical over a "fantastic vintage," obviously with a view only to the must weights.

What good is it, if the sugar in the must allows you to make a wine with 14 percent alcohol or more, and the resulting wines are merely heavy and clumsy? Some producers are clearly able to handle the high must weights, and are still able to produce wines with both depth and finesse. Then there are wines that make you feel sated after the first sip, and all you notice is the unpleasantly high alcohol level, or unbalanced and excessive added acidity. As an exception, German wine producers in all regions were permitted to add acidity to their wines in 2003. It was noticeable that some producers in the Rheinhessen region did not have any experience with this phenomenon, or simply lacked the right touch, and either added the acidity at the wrong time, or sometimes overdosed. The resulting wines are green and grassy, often also showing noticeable bitterness. On the other hand, a few producers considered their options carefully, and used judicious acidification to achieve optimum results with their wines.

There is no doubt that the 2003 vintage will mature quickly. Many of the good wines we tasted were already remarkably accessible and mature, and ready to be enjoyed. It will be interesting to follow their further development. We believe that the really good Rheinhessen wines of the 2003 vintage have good staying power, and will not fade prematurely, simply because the underlying substance is so good. There are obvious parallels with the vintage of 1959. Here, too, the level of acidity was generally low, but anybody who has the privilege of tasting these wines today will generally be pleasantly surprised.

Once again, the decisive factor in determining the standard of the wine was the groundwork laid in the vineyard. It was important to reduce the stress on the vines at an early stage. On the other hand, premature pruning of the foliage could also be harmful, as this would increase the danger of sunburn for the grapes. In the words of Klaus-Peter Keller, "selective harvesting was more important than ever before." The Kellers, for instance, employed "vineyard grape tasters," who tasted grapes vine for vine, marking with a tag those vines whose grapes lacked aroma and racy fruit. The amount harvested was considerably reduced at a later stage. This is the sort of measure that underlines the fact that the Keller winery is a force to be reckoned with, not only in Rheinhessen. His philosophy is shared by other quality-conscious producers, for example Klaus Scherner from Flörsheim-Dalsheim: "Our older vineyards coped well with the conditions, while our young vines suffered in the extreme conditions. We had to reduce the grapes per vine radically simply to ensure the survival of the vines."

Rheinhessen

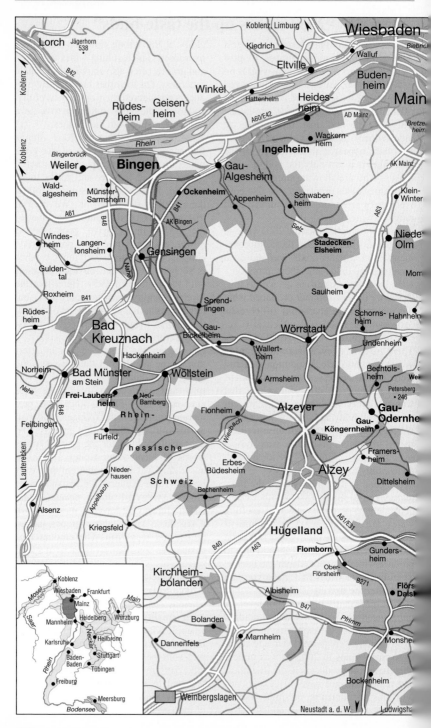

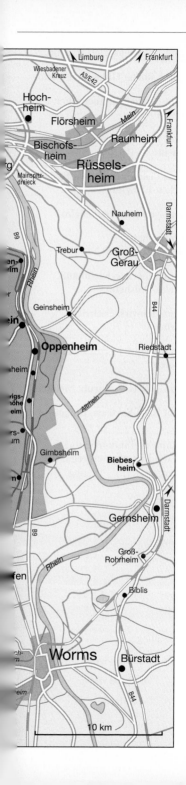

Meticulous care in the cellar was the order of the day. Since the heat-dried skins were thicker than hardly ever before, long standing times on the skins were called for, in order to extract piquant aromas and abundant mineral notes from the healthy grapes, many of which were considerably dried out. This leaded to remarkably good results particularly with the aromatic varieties (Rieslaner, Scheurebe, Gewürztraminer). Noble rot started developing at a reasonably early stage. The shrivelled berries, which often were particularly healthy, produced excellent wines with a long maturation potential.

The red wines of the 2003 vintage are a topic unto themselves. Great expectations here are not unreasonable. The regional marketing office promises "expressive fruit, juicy, powerful, with rich tannins." We can confirm this assessment, and noted that some of the wines were remarkably accessible at this early stage. The motto of the Rheinhessen Festival is: "Scandalously Good." This can also be applied to the Portugieser wines – quality-conscious producers have reduced yields to produce remarkably good red wines from this almost forgotten and little regarded variety. The red wines of the 2002 vintage also generally showed excellent form, and lots of power. Specialists such as Gerhard Gutzler were even still able to show an impressive 2001 wine.

The recently introduced "Classic" category plays a role for white wines. Many producers have still not understood what style is expected from a wine of this category. We were confronted with wines that had alcohol levels of 13.5 or even 14 percent. Another phenomenon we experienced: regional wine awards on bottles with very mediocre contents. It appears to be the motto of regional competitions that any wine that does not have obvious faults deserves at least a silver medal. The fatal attraction lies in the misconception created in the minds of producers, who believe they are on the right track if they do well in these competitions. There tends to be a rude awakening when customers realize they cannot rely on the number of medals awarded...

605

Rheinhessen

The leading producers in the Rheinhessen region

Weingut Keller,
Flörsheim-Dalsheim

Weingut Gunderloch, Nackenheim

Weingut Wittmann, Westhofen

Weingut Destillerie
Gerhard Gutzler, Gundheim

Weingut Freiherr
Heyl zu Herrnsheim, Nierstein

Weingut Manz, Weinolsheim

Weingut Sankt Antony, Nierstein

Weingut Georg Albrecht Schneider,
Nierstein

Weingut Wagner-Stempel,
Siefersheim

Wein- und Sektmanufaktur
Battenfeld-Spanier, Hohen-Sülzen

Weingut Brüder Dr. Becker,
Ludwigshöhe

Weingut Jean Buscher, Bechtheim

Fleischer und Weingut der Stadt
Mainz, Mainz-Hechtsheim

Weingut Gehring, Nierstein

Weingut Ökonomierat
Joh. Geil I. Erben, Bechtheim

Weingut K. F. Groebe, Biebesheim

Weingut Kissinger, Uelversheim

Weingut Kühling-Gillot, Bodenheim

Weingut Michel-Pfannebecker,
Flomborn

Weingut Karl-Hermann Milch,
Monsheim

Weingut Posthof Doll & Göth,
Stadecken-Elsheim

Weingut Sander, Mettenheim

Weingut Schales,
Flörsheim-Dalsheim

Weingut Scherner-Kleinhanß,
Flörsheim-Dalsheim

Weingut Heinrich Seebrich,
Nierstein

Weingut Seehof – Ernst Fauth,
Westhofen

Weingut J. & H. A. Strub, Nierstein

Weingut Villa Sachsen, Bingen

Major and minor vintages in the Rheinhessen region	
Vintage	Rating
2003	⚜⚜⚜
2002	⚜⚜⚜
2001	⚜⚜⚜
2000	⚜⚜
1999	⚜⚜⚜
1998	⚜⚜⚜⚜
1997	⚜⚜⚜
1996	⚜⚜⚜⚜
1995	⚜⚜⚜
1994	⚜⚜⚜

Vintage rating:

⚜⚜⚜⚜⚜ : Excellent vintage

⚜⚜⚜⚜ : Very good vintage

⚜⚜⚜ : Good vintage

⚜⚜ : Average vintage

⚜ : Poor vintage

Wein- und Sektgut
Ch. W. Bernhard,
Frei-Laubersheim

Weingut Fogt – Schönborner Hof,
Badenheim

Weingut Gallé, Flonheim

Geils Sekt- und Weingut,
Bermersheim

Weingut Göhring,
Flörsheim-Dalsheim

Weingut Hedesheimer Hof,
Stadecken-Elsheim

Weingut Georg Gustav Huff,
Nierstein-Schwabsburg

Weingut Huff-Doll, Horrweiler

Weingut Johanninger, Biebelsheim

Weingut Kreichgauer,
Dorn-Dürkheim

Weingut Axel Müller,
Flörsheim-Dalsheim

Weingut J. Neus, Ingelheim

Weingut Peth-Wetz,
Bermersheim

Weingut Riffel, Bingen-Büdesheim

Weingut Schätzel,
Nierstein

Weingut Adolf Schembs Erben,
Worms-Herrnsheim

Weingut Adolf Schick, Jugenheim

Weingut Spiess – Riederbacherhof,
Bechtheim

Staatliche Weinbaudomäne
Oppenheim, Oppenheim

Weingut Steitz, Stein-Bockenheim

Weingut Strohm, Offstein

Weingut Arndt F. Werner,
Ingelheim

Weingut Winter,
Dittelsheim-Hessloch

Weinkontor Dirk Würtz,
Gau-Odernheim

The best vineyard sites in the Rheinhessen region *

Bingen: Scharlachberg

Bodenheim: Burgweg

Dalsheim: Bürgel, Hubacker

Dienheim: Tafelstein

Nackenheim: Rothenberg

Nierstein: Brudersberg, Hipping,
Oelberg, Orbel, Pettenthal

Oppenheim: Kreuz, Sackträger

Westhofen: Aulerde, Kirchspiel,
Morstein

---

* Source: VDP Rheinhessen

Classification of producers

Highest rating,
for world-class wine producers

Excellent producers counted
as among the best in Germany

Very good producers
who have been making consistently
high quality wines for many years

Good producers who do better
than make just everyday wines

Reliable producers making
decent standard qualitiy wines

WEIN- UND SEKT- MANUFAKTUR BATTENFELD-SPANIER

Owner: H. O. Spanier and Heinrich Battenfeld
Manager: H. O. Spanier
67591 Hohen-Sülzen
Tel. (0 62 43) 90 65 15, Fax 90 65 29
e-mail: kontakt@battenfeld-spanier.de
Internet: www.battenfeld-spanier.de
Directions: A 61, Monsheim exit, on B 47 in direction of Hohen-Sülzen
Sales: Klaus Immes by appointment
History: Spanier winery founded 1990, merged with Heinrich Battenfeld 1996

Vineyard area: 16 hectares
Annual production: 70,000 bottles
Top sites: Flörsheimer Frauen-berg, Hohen-Sülzer Kirchenstück
Soil types: Limestone-rich marl, sandstone, sandy loess
Grape varieties: 50% Riesling, 20% Spätburgunder, 8% Weißburgunder, 5% each of Silvaner, Chardonnay and Portugieser, 7% other varieties
Average yield: 58 hl/ha
Best vintages: 2001, 2003
Member: EcoVin

This organically-run winery was founded in 1997, and is located in the southern Wonnegau area. Oliver Spanier's declared objective is to produce top wines based on low yields. In 2001, his best vintage to date, the yields were only 40 hl/ha. The 2002 vintage was not quite as good. However, in 2003 this talented winemaker has presented an outstanding collection, for which we are happy to award his second bunch of grapes. The highlights are two botrytis dessert wines, but even the dry wines are well-made. Spanier uses his own internal quality classification, the estate wine is the most basic level, and is remarkably good. The medium range is designated "S," while at the top of the pile are three vineyard-designated Rieslings with the designation "R." These are on a par with the First Growths.

2003 Silvaner trocken "S"
13.5%, ♀ till 2007   83

2003 Riesling trocken
12.5%, ♀ till 2006   84

2003 Weißer Burgunder
trocken "S"
13.5%, ♀ till 2007   85

2003 Chardonnay trocken "S"
13.5%, ♀ till 2007   85

2003 Riesling trocken "S"
13%, ♀ till 2008   86

2003 Hohen-Sülzer Sonnenberg
Riesling trocken "S" Alte Reben
13.5%, ♀ till 2009   87

2003 Kriegsheimer Rosengarten
Riesling trocken "R"
13.5%, ♀ till 2009   88

2003 Flörsheimer Frauenberg
Riesling trocken "R"
13%, ♀ till 2010   88

2003 Gewürztraminer trocken "S"
13%, ♀ till 2009   88

2003 Hohen-Sülzer Kirchenstück
Riesling trocken "R"
13%, ♀ till 2010   89

2001 Riesling Auslese "R"
8%, ♀ till 2006   87

2003 Riesling Auslese "R"
10%, ♀ till 2015   90

2003 Riesling
Trockenbeerenauslese
7.5%, ♀ till 2025   93

———— Red wine ————

2002 Spätburgunder trocken "S"
13%, ♀ till 2010   88

BATTENFELDSPANIER
WEIN-UND SEKTMANUFAKTUR
2001
RIESLING
ROSENGARTEN

WEINGUT
BRÜDER DR. BECKER

**Owner: Lotte Pfeffer-Müller,
Hans Müller
Manager: Hans Müller
Winemaker: Hans Müller
and Lotte Pfeffer-Müller
55278 Ludwigshöhe, Mainzer Str. 3–7
Tel. (0 62 49) 84 30, Fax 76 39
e-mail:
lotte.pfeffer@brueder-dr-becker.de
Internet: www.brueder-dr-becker.de**
*Directions: 25 kilometers south of
Mainz, via the B 9*
Sales: Lotte Pfeffer-Müller, Hans Mül-
ler, by appointment; open tasting every
1st Saturday of the month
Guest rooms: In old administrator's house
History: Winemaking since the late 19th
century
Worth seeing: Oak barrels in vaulted
cellar, organic viticulture

Vineyard area: 10.8 hectares
Annual production: 80,000 bottles
Top sites: Dienheimer Tafelstein
and Kreuz, Ludwigshöher Teufelskopf
Soil types: Loess, loess-clay
Grape varieties: 38% Riesling, 18%
each of Scheurebe and Silvaner,
10% Spätburgunder, 7% Grau- and
Weißburgunder, 6% Müller-Thurgau,
3% other varieties
Average yield: 67 hl/ha
Best vintages: 2001, 2002, 2003
Member: VDP, EcoVin

Organic methods were introduced in the
vineyards in the late Seventies. In the cellar, quaffing wines and aromatic varieties
are matured in stainless steel, while wines
intended for a longer maturation go into
oak. The wines need time to develop. In
recent years, the wines here have been
straightforward and clear, robust and
juicy. 2002 followed on seamlessly from
the good 2001 vintage. And in 2003 the
wines were even better. Under these circumstances we are happy to improve the
rating for the winery.

2003 Silvaner trocken
14%, ♀ till 2006   **82**

2003 Riesling trocken
14%, ♀ till 2006   **83**

2003 Ludwigshöher
Silvaner Spätlese trocken
13.5%, ♀ till 2006   **84**

2003 Weißer Burgunder trocken
13.5%, ♀ till 2006   **86**

2002 Dienheimer Tafelstein
Riesling trocken "Großes Gewächs"
12.5%, ♀ till 2007   **86**

2003 Dienheimer Tafelstein
Riesling trocken "Großes Gewächs"
13.5%, ♀ till 2009   **88**

2003 Ludwigshöher
Gewürztraminer Spätlese
14%, ♀ till 2008   **85**

2003 Dienheimer Tafelstein
Riesling Spätlese
10%, ♀ till 2009   **85**

2003 Dienheimer Tafelstein
Riesling Auslese
10%, ♀ till 2015   **89**

2003 Dienheimer Tafelstein
Ruländer Beerenauslese
14%, ♀ till 2015   **90**

Brüder Dr. Becker

2002
Grüner
Silvaner
trocken

Rheinhessen

The wines: **100** Perfect · **95–99** Outstanding · **90–94** Excellent · **85–89** Very good · **80–84** Good · **75–79** Average

WEIN- UND SEKTGUT CH. W. BERNHARD

Owner: Hartmut Bernhard
Winemaker: Hartmut Bernhard
55546 Frei-Laubersheim,
Philipp-Wehr-Straße 31–33
Tel. (0 67 09) 62 33, Fax 61 60
e-mail: info@chwbernhard.de
Internet: www.chwbernhard.de
Directions: A 61, Gau-Bickelheim exit,
8 kilometers on B 420 in direction of
Wöllstein/Frei-Laubersheim
Opening hours: Mon.–Sat. 08:00 to
20:00 hours and by appointment
History: 400 years of winemaking tradition
Worth seeing: Cellar with oak barrels,
scenically attractive loaction

Vineyard area: 10.2 hectares
Annual production: 75,000 bottles,
incl. 5,000 bottles sparkling wine
Top sites: Hackenheimer Kirch-
berg, Frei-Laubersheimer Fels,
Kirchberg and Rheingrafenberg
Soil types: Porphyry, sandy clay,
kaolin, loess and diluvial soils
Grape varieties: 22% Riesling, 21%
Spätburgunder, 8% Grauburgunder,
7% Müller-Thurgau, 6% each of Portu-
gieser and Kerner, 5% Silvaner, 4%
each of Weißburgunder and Auxer-
rois, 17% other varieties
Average yield: 78 hl/ha
Best vintages: 2001, 2002, 2003

The estate run by Hartmut and Petra
Bernhard is located close to Bad Kreuznach. The close proximity to the Nahe region is also evident in the mineral notes
and the lively acidity seen in some of the
wines. The vines are grown on six different soil types, which contributes to a
wide range of flavors. A special feature
here are the 60-year-old Auxerrois vines,
which yet again have produced one of the
best wines in the range. Apart from this,
the quality is solid, crowned by a Gewürztraminer Beerenauslese and a surprisingly elegant Ehrenfelser Trockenbeerenauslese.

**2003 Frei-Laubersheimer
Rheingrafenberg**
Grauer Burgunder trocken
14%, ♀ till 2006 **82**

2003 Hackenheimer Kirchberg
Weißer Burgunder Auslese trocken
15.5%, ♀ till 2007 **83**

2002 Hackenheimer Kirchberg
Riesling Spätlese trocken
12.5%, ♀ till 2006 **84**

2002 Frei-Laubersheimer Fels
Auxerrois Kabinett trocken
12%, ♀ till 2005 **84**

2003 Frei-Laubersheimer Fels
Auxerrois Auslese trocken
14.5%, ♀ till 2007 **86**

**2002 Frei-Laubersheimer
Rheingrafenberg**
Grauer Burgunder Spätlese trocken
12.5%, ♀ till 2006 **86**

2002 Hackenheimer Kirchberg
Riesling Spätlese halbtrocken
11.5%, ♀ till 2006 **84**

2001 Hackenheimer Kirchberg
Riesling Kabinett
10.5%, ♀ till 2006 **84**

2003 Frei-Laubersheimer Fels
Gewürztraminer Beerenauslese
10.5%, ♀ till 2015 **89**

**2003 Frei-Laubersheimer
Rheingrafenberg**
Ehrenfelser Trockenbeerenauslese
7.5%, ♀ till 2015 **90**

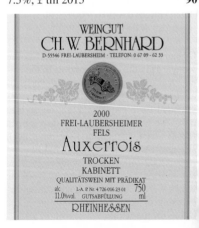

WEINGUT
CH. W. BERNHARD
D-55546 FREI-LAUBERSHEIM · TELEFON: 0 67 09 - 62 33

2000
FREI-LAUBERSHEIMER
FELS
Auxerrois
TROCKEN
KABINETT
QUALITÄTSWEIN MIT PRÄDIKAT
alc   I-A. P. Nr 4 726 016 23 01   750
11.0%vol. GUTSABFÜLLUNG   ml
RHEINHESSEN

WEINGUT JEAN BUSCHER

Owner: Jean Michael Buscher
Administrator and winemaker:
Jochen Drück
67595 Bechtheim, Wormser Straße 4
Tel. (0 62 42) 8 72, Fax 8 75
e-mail: weingut@jean-buscher.de
Internet: www.jean-buscher.de
Directions: B 9 Mainz–Worms, A 61,
Gundersheim exit
Sales: Jean Michael Buscher
Opening hours: Mon.–Fri. 08:00 to
17:00 hours and by appointment
History: Founded 1844
Worth seeing: Old vaulted cellar with
oak barrels, vintage rarities dating back
to 1911, cosy wine tasting room

Vineyard area: 16 hectares
Annual production: 170,000 bottles
Top sites: Bechtheimer Geyers-
berg, Stein and Rosengarten
Soil types: Loess-clay
Grape varieties: 25% Riesling, 16%
Spätburgunder, 15% Dornfelder,
10% each of Weiß- and Graubur-
gunder, 8% Portugieser, 6%
Schwarzriesling, 4% Silvaner,
6% other varieties
Average yield: 80 hl/ha
Best vintages: 2001, 2002, 2003

Michael Buscher is a marketing professional. Each year he commisions a label
to be designed by a well-known artist,
then has this embossed in metal, and presents it in the old barrel cellar, together
with paintings and sculptures. The quality of wines by now matches really the
slick presentations. The range has been en-
livened by the arrival of winemaker Jochen Drück. For some years now, the
wines have met even the expectations of demanding customers. This applies also to
the botrytis dessert wines, we particularly
liked a Riesling Trockenbeerauslese
that Buscher intends to sell on auction.
However, a few bottles of this will presum-
ably be added to the "treasure chest" of
rare wines.

2003 Riesling Kabinett trocken
12%, ♀ till 2006   **82**

2003 Silvaner
Spätlese trocken "Edition S"
13%, ♀ till 2006   **83**

2003 Weißer Burgunder
Spätlese trocken "Edition S"
13.5%, ♀ till 2007   **84**

2003 Riesling
Spätlese trocken "Edition S"
12.5%, ♀ till 2008   **85**

2003 Riesling
Spätlese halbtrocken
12%, ♀ till 2008   **84**

2003 Silvaner Auslese
9.5%, ♀ till 2010   **86**

2003 Riesling Spätlese
9.5%, ♀ till 2010   **87**

2003 Riesling Eiswein
9%, ♀ till 2015   **89**

2003 Riesling
Trockenbeerenauslese
ᚭ auction wine, 9%, ♀ till 2020   **91**

——————— Red wines ———————

2002 Cuvée Jean B. trocken
12.5%, ♀ till 2007   **83**

2003 Schwarzriesling
Auslese trocken "Edition S"
14%, ♀ till 2008   **87**

2002 Rosenmuskateller
10%, ♀ till 2010   **87**

The wines: **100** Perfect · **95–99** Outstanding · **90–94** Excellent · **85–89** Very good · **80–84** Good · **75–79** Average

611

FLEISCHER UND WEINGUT DER STADT MAINZ

Owner: Hans W. and Michael Fleischer
Winemaker: Michael Fleischer
55129 Mainz-Hechtsheim,
Rheinhessenstraße 103
Tel. (0 61 31) 5 97 97, Fax 59 26 85
e-mail: hansw.fleischer@gmx.de
Internet: www.weingut-fleischer.de
Directions: A 60, Mainz-Hechtsheim-West exit
Sales: Fleischer family
Opening hours: Mon.–Fri. 14:00 to 18:00 hours, Thur. to 20:00 hours
Sat. 10:00 to 17:00 hours
Restaurant: In winery of the City of Mainz, Harxheim, Obergasse 3, Tel. (0 61 38) 98 06 60, Mon.–Sat. from 17:00 hours, Sun. 11:30 to 14:00 hours, in the evenings from 18:00 hours as well as restaurant and wine bar "La Gallerie" in Mainz, Gaustraße
History: Winemaking here since 1742

Vineyard area: 20 hectares
Annual production: 170,000 bottles
Top sites: Mainz-Laubenheimer Edelmann, Bodenheimer Hoch
Soil types: Limestone formation with clay
Grape varieties: 22% Riesling, 10% Dornfelder, 9% Portugieser, 8% Silvaner, 7% Grauburgunder, 5% Kerner, 4% each of Weißburgunder, Spätburgunder and Müller-Thurgau, 27% other varieties
Average yield: 71 hl/ha
Best vintages: 2002, 2003

Michael and Hans Willi Fleischer cultivate around 20 hectares of best vineyard sites around Mainz, and this includes the vineyards of the City of Mainz wine estate, which they have leased since 1994. Michael Fleischer is a red wine specialist, but last year we particularly liked his white wines. This time around the whole range was of good quality. We were particularly impressed by the deft use of barrique in the red wines, which are still at the beginning of their maturation curve.

2003 Mainzer St. Alban
Grauer Burgunder trocken
15%, ♀ till 2006 — 83

2003 Mainzer St. Alban
Chardonnay trocken
13%, ♀ till 2006 — 84

2002 Mainzer St. Alban
Riesling Spätlese feinherb
11%, ♀ till 2007 — 86

2003 Mainzer St. Alban
Riesling Spätlese feinherb
12.5%, ♀ till 2008 — 87

2003 Riesling Classic
12.5%, ♀ till 2006 — 83

2003 Mainzer St. Alban
Riesling Spätlese
13.5%, ♀ till 2009 — 86

2002 Mainzer St. Alban
Riesling Eiswein
7.5%, ♀ till 2020 — 90

——— Red wines ———

2002 Mainzer St. Alban
Merlot trocken
14.5%, ♀ till 2009 — 83

2002 Spätburgunder trocken
14.5%, ♀ till 2008 — 85

2001 Mainzer St. Alban
Merlot trocken
14%, ♀ till 2006 — 85

2002 Mainzer St. Alban
trocken "Cuvée Moguntiacum"
15%, ♀ till 2009 — 85

2002 Cabernet Sauvignon trocken
14%, ♀ till 2009 — 86

2002 Merlot trocken "Fass Nr. 2"
15%, ♀ till 2010 — 86

2002 Mainzer St. Alban
Spätburgunder trocken "J.F."
14.5%, ♀ till 2010 — 86

WEINGUT FOGT – SCHÖNBORNER HOF

Owner: Karl-Heinz and Georg Fogt
Manager: Karl-Heinz Fogt
Winemaker: Georg Fogt
55576 Badenheim, Schönborner Hof
Tel. (0 67 01) 74 34, Fax 71 33
e-mail: weingutfogt@t-online.de
Directions: A 61 Gau-Bickelheim exit, in direction of Bingen, turn left to Badenheim, turn left twice once in village
Sales: Brunhilde and Dorothea Fogt
Opening hours: Sat. 10:00 to 16:00 hours and by appointment

Vineyard area: 23 hectares
Annual production: 60,000 bottles
Top sites: Wöllsteiner Äffchen, Hölle and Ölberg
Soil types: Kaolin-clay-gravel mixture
Grape varieties: 13% Müller-Thurgau, 12% Riesling, 11% Silvaner, 10% Dornfelder, 9% Kerner, 7% each of Portugieser, Weißburgunder and Spätburgunder, 6% Grauburgunder, 18% other varieties
Average yield: 80 hl/ha
Best vintages: 2000, 2001, 2003

This winery is located in close proximity to the Nahe region. The first bunch of grapes was awarded in 2002, and this status has been solidly confirmed for two years running, with good ranges being presented. A surprise this year was the fruity Morio Spätlese, which shows that this heavy-bearing variety holds potential when treated correctly. Last year, we criticized the red wines, and progress has clearly been made here. Positive development in future is also expected from some vineyards with old Riesling and Portugieser vines which have recently been taken over (first vintage 2004). In addition, improvements made in the cellar make working there easier for the Fogts (father and son). The relatively high average yield must be seen against the background that more than half of the wines produced here are still sold in bulk.

2003 Rivaner trocken
12.5%, ♀ till 2005 — **81**

2003 Wöllsteiner Hölle
Weißer Burgunder Spätlese trocken
14%, ♀ till 2006 — **82**

2003 Wöllsteiner Ölberg
Grauer Burgunder Spätlese trocken
14.5%, ♀ till 2006 — **82**

2003 Chardonnay Spätlese trocken
14.5%, ♀ till 2006 — **83**

2002 Weißer Burgunder
trocken "Holzfassausbau"
13.5%, ♀ till 2006 — **83**

2003 Badenheimer Galgenberg
Riesling Spätlese trocken
13%, ♀ till 2006 — **84**

2002 Badenheimer Römerberg
Weißer Burgunder trocken
13.5%, ♀ till 2006 — **84**

2002 Badenheimer Galgenberg
Riesling Spätlese halbtrocken
11.5%, ♀ till 2006 — **84**

2003 Riesling Classic
13%, ♀ till 2005 — **81**

2003 Morio-Muskat Spätlese
10%, ♀ till 2009 — **85**

2002 Badenheimer Römerberg
Riesling Spätlese
9.5%, ♀ till 2008 — **86**

2003 Huxelrebe Auslese
7%, ♀ till 2012 — **87**

——— Red wine ———

2002 Spätburgunder trocken
13.5%, ♀ till 2007 — **83**

2 0 0 3
CHARDONNAY
TROCKEN

The wines: **100** Perfect · **95–99** Outstanding · **90–94** Excellent · **85–89** Very good · **80–84** Good · **75–79** Average

WEINGUT GALLÉ

Owner: Klaus and Ortrud Gallé
Manager and winemaker: Klaus Gallé
55237 Flonheim, Langgasse 69
Tel. (0 67 34) 89 61, Fax 66 76
e-mail: o.galle@web.de
Directions: A 61/A 63, Flonheim exit
Sales: Ortrud Gallé
Opening hours: Mon.–Sat. by appointment

Vineyard area: 15 hectares
Annual production: 45,000 bottles
Top sites: No vineyard sites stated
Soil types: Decomposed sandstone, porphyry, loess, kaolin, marl
Grape varieties: 8% each of Riesling and Spätburgunder, 7% each of Grauburgunder and Chardonnay, 6% Müller-Thurgau, 5% each of Dunkelfelder and Dornfelder, 4% each of Weißburgunder and Portugieser, 3% each of Regent and St. Laurent, 40% other varieties
Average yield: 65 hl/ha
Best vintages: 2001, 2002, 2003

This winery was founded in 1995 by Klaus and Ortrud Gallé, and was soon attracting attention for its remarkably good Portugieser and Rivaner wines, a sign that low yields can benefit even these usually underrated varieties. Gradually, the vineyard area and the proportion of wine bottled have been expanded. Gallé (44) came to winemaking late in life, and had a secure income. In spite of this, the Gallés decided to opt out of their previous life, and found the winery offered in an advertisement. They have not regretted their decision, although currently they are still obliged to sell 60 percent of their production in bulk. Their promising entry to the Wine Guide last year was confirmed in the 2003 vintage by a hearty Rivaner, and a botrytized Riesling Auslese. The red wines of the 2002 vintage are also good. The highlight here is a selection wine made from the otherwise generally boring Portugieser grape.

2003 Rivaner trocken
12.5%, ♀ till 2006 — 83

2003 Riesling trocken
12.5%, ♀ till 2006 — 83

2003 Chardonnay trocken
12.5%, ♀ till 2007 — 84

2002 Riesling trocken Selection
12%, ♀ till 2006 — 85

2003 Riesling Auslese
12.5%, ♀ till 2010 — 87

———— Red wines ————

2002 Portugieser trocken
14%, ♀ till 2007 — 83

2002 Cabernet Sauvignon trocken
13.5%, ♀ till 2009 — 84

2001 Dunkelfelder trocken
13.5%, ♀ till 2007 — 86

2001 Cabernet Sauvignon trocken
13.5%, ♀ till 2007 — 86

2002 Portugieser
trocken Rheinhessen-Selection
13%, ♀ till 2008 — 86

WEINGUT GEHRING

Owner: Theo and Diana Gehring
Winemaker: Hans-Theo Gehring
55283 Nierstein, Außerhalb 17
Tel. (0 61 33) 54 70, Fax 92 74 89
e-mail: info@weingut-gehring.com
Internet: www.weingut-gehring.com
Directions: B 9, in Nierstein go on to the
B 420, between Nierstein and Dexheim
Sales: Diana Gehring
Opening hours: Mon.–Fri. 08:00 to
12:00 hours
Vinotheque: Mon.–Fri. 17:00 to 19:00
hours, and by appointment, closed Wed.
Restaurant and wine bar: "Vini Vita"

Vineyard area: 12.5 hectares
Annual production: 90,000 bottles
Top sites: Niersteiner Pettenthal,
Oelberg and Hipping
Soil types: Lower new red sandstone
with kaolin-slate
Grape varieties: 50% Riesling, 20%
Pinot varieties, 20% red varieties,
10% other varieties
Average yield: 65 hl/ha
Best vintages: 1998, 2001, 2003

This winery has been marketing wine in bottles since 1959, Theo Gehring took over the business from his parents in 1995. It did not take long for him and his wife Diana to implement their own ideas. A big change was due in mid-2001 when they moved from very cramped quarters in Nierstein to a farm complex in the middle of the vineyards. In terms of vineyards, they have some respectable parcels closer to the Rhine, in the famous Roter Hang. The potential of these sites was brought out very well in 2001. Last year we were more impressed by the basic wines. Theo Gehring has managed to master the challenges of the dry 2003 vintage very well, his range is not lacking in charm. The red wines as well as the Beerenauslese and Trockenbeerenauslese wines were not ready for tasting at time of going to press. Dry wines are designated with stars to indicate their quality.

2003 Niersteiner Hipping
Riesling trocken ***
13%, ♀ till 2007 — 85

2003 Niersteiner Pettenthal
Riesling trocken ***
12.5%, ♀ till 2007 — 85

2002 Niersteiner
Weißer Burgunder trocken
12%, ♀ till 2006 — 85

2003 Niersteiner Oelberg
Riesling trocken ***
12.5%, ♀ till 2007 — 86

2001 Niersteiner Pettenthal
Riesling trocken ****
12.5%, ♀ till 2006 — 86

2003 Chardonnay trocken ***
13.5%, ♀ till 2007 — 87

2003 Riesling halbtrocken *
12.5%, ♀ till 2008 — 85

2003 Niersteiner Pettenthal
Riesling Spätlese
9%, ♀ till 2009 — 86

2003 Niersteiner Hipping
Riesling Spätlese
9%, ♀ till 2010 — 88

2002 Niersteiner Oelberg
Scheurebe Eiswein
9%, ♀ till 2020 — 91

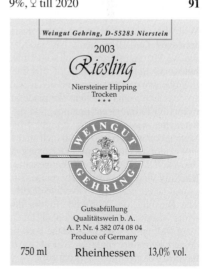

Weingut Gehring, D-55283 Nierstein
2003
Riesling
Niersteiner Hipping
Trocken
* * *

Gutsabfüllung
Qualitätswein b. A.
A. P. Nr. 4 382 074 08 04
Produce of Germany
750 ml   Rheinhessen   13,0% vol.

The wines: **100** Perfect · **95–99** Outstanding · **90–94** Excellent · **85–89** Very good · **80–84** Good · **75–79** Average

615

WEINGUT OEKONOMIERAT JOH. GEIL I. ERBEN

Owner: Karl and Johannes Geil-Bierschenk
Manager: Karl Geil-Bierschenk
Winemaker: Johannes Geil-Bierschenk
67595 Bechtheim, Kuhpfortenstraße 11
Tel. (0 62 42) 15 46, Fax 69 35
e-mail: info@weingut-geil.de
Internet: www.weingut-geil.de
Directions: Via B 9 or A 61, Gundersheim/Westhofen exit
Sales: Monika Geil-Bierschenk
Opening hours: Mon.–Sat. 08:00 to 12:00 hours and 13:00 to 17:00 hours or by appointment

---

Vineyard area: 28 hectares
Annual production: 200,000 bottles
Top sites: Bechtheimer Geyersberg, Rosengarten and Hasensprung
Soil types: Loess-clay, calcareous marl
Grape varieties: 30% Riesling, 9% each of Müller-Thurgau, Kerner and Spätburgunder, 8% Dornfelder, 7% Frühburgunder, 5% each of Silvaner and Weißburgunder, 18% other varieties
Average yield: 82 hl/ha
Best vintages: 2002, 2003

With the permission of his father Karl, Johannes Geil-Bierschenk has reduced the yields significantly, to sometimes below 50 hl/ha. The result of this meticulous work in vineyard and cellar was so convincing that last year we made an exception to our usual practice, and elevated the winery's rating straight from "also recommended" to two-bunch status, and celebrated this as our "Discovery of the year." The current range he presented has fully vindicated this early praise. Not a single wine was only of average quality. The Riesling was polished. In the dry white wines, the higher alcohol levels were well under control. And the botrytis dessert wines are nudging ever closer to the ranks of absolute top producers.

2003 Bechtheimer Rosengarten
Muskateller trocken
12.5%, ♀ till 2007 — **86**

2003 Bechtheimer Geyersberg
Silvaner trocken "S"
14%, ♀ till 2006 — **86**

2002 Bechtheimer Geyersberg
Riesling Spätlese trocken
12.5%, ♀ till 2006 — **87**

2002 Bechtheimer Geyersberg
Riesling Spätlese feinherb
12.5%, ♀ till 2007 — **88**

2003 Bechtheimer Geyersberg
Riesling Spätlese
9.5%, ♀ till 2010 — **87**

2003 Bechtheimer Geyersberg
Riesling Auslese
10%, ♀ till 2015 — **89**

2003 Bechtheimer Geyersberg
Riesling Beerenauslese
9%, ♀ till 2015 — **90**

2002 Bechtheimer Geyersberg
Rieslaner Auslese "S"
9.5%, ♀ till 2015 — **90**

2003 Bechtheimer Geyersberg
Rieslaner Trockenbeerenauslese
7.5%, ♀ till 2020 — **92**

2003 Bechtheimer Geyersberg
Riesling Trockenbeerenauslese
7%, ♀ till 2020 — **93**

GRÜNER SILVANER TROCKEN

SPÄTLESE -S-
2002

RHEINHESSEN

GEILS SEKT- UND WEINGUT

Owner and manager:
Rudolf and Birgit Geil
Winemaker: Rudolf Geil
67593 Bermersheim near Worms,
Zeller Straße 8
Tel. (0 62 44) 44 13, Fax 5 73 84
e-mail: mail@geils.de
Internet: www.geils.de
Directions: A 61, Gundersheim exit, continue through town to Bermersheim, at village square turn right into Zeller Straße
Sales: Rudolf and Birgit Geil
Opening hours: Mon.–Sat. by appointment
History: Family-owned since 300 years
Worth seeing: Historical barrel cellar

Vineyard area: 12.5 hectares
Annual production: 80,000 bottles
Top sites: Nieder-Flörsheimer
Frauenberg, Dalsheimer Bürgel
Soil types: Shell limestone, kaolin,
colored sandstone, loess
Grape varieties: 13% Riesling, 12%
Weißburgunder 11% Müller-Thurgau, 9% each of Spät- and Grauburgunder, 8% each of Silvaner
and Portugieser, 7% Huxelrebe,
23% other varieties
Average yield: 90 hl/ha
Best vintage: 2002

Rudolf Geil has had many ups and downs in his long winemaking life, and even as a teenager had to help his mother in the cellar, following his father's untimely early death. A few years ago the 43-year-old winemaker was motivated to change his priorities, and in this has been supported by his wife Birgit. Yields were brought down, and quality has gone up. Intense work in the vineyard, lots of patience during the harvest and slow fermentation in the cellar are ingredients that helped create an excellent range of white wines in the 2002 vintage. Things did not go quite as smoothly in 2003, but overall Geil proved he is worthy of the one-bunch status awarded last year.

2003 Chardonnay trocken
12.5%, ♀ till 2006 — 82

2002 "Ohne Namen"
Spätburgunder trocken weiß gekeltert
12%, ♀ till 2006 — 85

2003 Chardonnay & Weißer Burgunder
trocken "S"
14%, ♀ till 2008 — 86

2002 Chardonnay & Weißer Burgunder
trocken "S"
14%, ♀ till 2006 — 86

2002 Chardonnay trocken "S"
14%, ♀ till 2006 — 86

2003 Riesling trocken "S"
13%, ♀ till 2008 — 87

2002 Grauer Burgunder
trocken "S"
13.5%, ♀ till 2006 — 87

2002 Nieder-Flörsheimer Frauenberg
Riesling Auslese
12.5%, ♀ till 2008 — 86

——————— Red wine ———————

2000 "Nocturne" trocken
13%, ♀ till 2007 — 87

The wines: **100** Perfect · **95–99** Outstanding · **90–94** Excellent · **85–89** Very good · **80–84** Good · **75–79** Average

617

WEINGUT GÖHRING

Owner: Wilfried and Marianne Göhring
Manager: Wilfried Göhring
Winemaker: Gerd and Wilfried Göhring
67592 Flörsheim-Dalsheim,
Alzeyer Straße 60
Tel. (0 62 43) 4 08 and 90 82 17,
Fax 65 25
e-mail: info@weingut-goehring.de
Internet: www.weingut-goehring.de
Directions: A 61, Worms-Nord/
Mörstadt exit, Flörsheim-Dalsheim, in
suburb of Nieder-Flörsheim
Sales: Marianne and Wilfried Göhring
Opening hours: Mon.–Sat. 09:00 to
12:00 and 13:00 to 18:00, Sun. 10:00 to
12:00 hours, by appointment only
History: Winemaking here since 1819
Worth a visit: Wine festival at winery
on second-last weekend in August

Vineyard area: 16.5 hectares
Annual production: 110,000 bottles
Top sites: Nieder-Flörsheimer
Frauenberg and Goldberg,
Dalsheimer Bürgel and Sauloch
Soil types: Loess-clay, kaolin and
shell limestone
Grape varieties: 24% Pinot varieties,
18% Riesling, 11% Portugieser,
9% Dornfelder, 8% Müller-Thurgau,
4% Huxelrebe, 26% other varieties
Average yield: 84 hl/ha
Best vintages: 1997, 1998, 1999

The Göhrings have brought the cellar
up to date in recent years. However, converting the facilities to consistent quality
is apparently still a problem. It is true
that the standard overall was a little better
than last year, nevertheless the tasting
was a real roller-coaster ride. In a few
wines, one had obviously been a little
over-enthusiastic about adding acid. The
input of son Arno, who is already responsible for making individual wines, is a
real asset. A new addition to the range is
the powerful Rivaner, which is not over-
alcoholic in spite of a 15.5 percent alcohol
level, and shows stature.

2003 Dalsheimer Bürgel
Riesling trocken "S"
13.5%, ♀ till 2007   **83**

2003 "Adamah" Burgunder-Cuvée
trocken
14%, ♀ till 2006   **84**

2002 Dalsheimer Sauloch
Gewürztraminer trocken Selection
Rheinhessen
13%, ♀ till 2006   **84**

2002 Scheurebe trocken
13%, ♀ till 2006   **85**

2003 Nieder-Flörsheimer Goldberg
Rivaner trocken "S"
15.5%, ♀ till 2006   **85**

2003 Scheurebe trocken "S"
13.5%, ♀ till 2006   **85**

2001 Dalsheimer Bürgel
Weißer Burgunder trocken "S"
14%, ♀ till 2006   **85**

2003 Nieder-Flörsheimer Frauenberg
Huxelrebe Beerenauslese
10%, ♀ till 2010   **85**

2002 Nieder-Flörsheimer Frauenberg
Albalonga Auslese
8.5%, ♀ till 2008   **87**

2003 Nieder-Flörsheimer Frauenberg
Huxelrebe Trockenbeerenauslese
12%, ♀ till 2014   **89**

WEINGUT K. F. GROEBE

Owner: Friedrich Groebe
64584 Biebesheim, Bahnhofstr. 68–70
Tel. (0 62 58) 67 21, Fax 8 16 02
e-mail: weingut.k.f.Groebe@t-online.de
Internet: www.weingut-k-f-groebe.de
Directions: A 67, Biebesheim exit
Sales: Friedrich Groebe, by appointment
History: Founded around 1625, family
coat-of-arms since 1763 showing the old
Christian sign for wine
Worth seeing: 500-year-old vaulted
cellar in Westhofen, vineyard house
"Villa rustica" in Kirchspiel site

Vineyard area: 7.1 hectares
Annual production: 50,000 bottles
Top sites: Westhofener Aulerde,
Kirchspiel and Morstein
Soil types: Loess-clay, clay, limestone
and stone marl
Grape varieties: 62% Riesling, 12%
Silvaner, 10% each of Spät- and
Grauburgunder, 6% other varieties
Average yield: 72 hl/ha
Best vintages: 2000, 2001, 2003
Member: VDP

This winery is run from the offices in Biebesheim in Hessen, while the vineyards
are on the other side of the Rhine, in
the best sites of Westhofen, and the winery and barrel maturation cellar are here
too. The mix of varietals is also unusual.
More than 60 percent of the area is planted
to Riesling, and visitors can acquire rarities from this varietal dating back to
1911. Winemaker Friedrich Groebe who
occasionally feels misunderstood with regard to his characteristic oaked style, presented an excellent range of wines this
year, which instantly puts him back on a
two-bunch rating. In principle, the 2003
wines actually deserve an even higher
rating for the winery, which we will keep
in mind for the coming vintages, if this
high standard is maintained. Both the
First Growths as well as the botrytis dessert wines have certainly raised hopes.

2003 Westhofener
Grauer Burgunder trocken
14%, ♀ till 2006 — **85**

2003 Westhofener Aulerde
Riesling Kabinett trocken
11.5%, ♀ till 2007 — **87**

2003 Westhofener
Riesling Spätlese trocken
13.5%, ♀ till 2007 — **87**

2001 Westhofener Kirchspiel
Riesling trocken "Großes Gewächs"
12.5%, ♀ till 2006 — **87**

2003 Westhofener Aulerde
Riesling trocken "Großes Gewächs"
13.5%, ♀ till 2008 — **88**

2003 Westhofener Kirchspiel
Riesling trocken "Großes Gewächs"
13.5%, ♀ till 2008 — **89**

2003 Westhofener Aulerde
Riesling Kabinett
10%, ♀ till 2008 — **86**

2003 Westhofener Kirchspiel
Riesling Auslese Goldkapsel
9.5%, ♀ till 2012 — **87**

2003 Westhofener Kirchspiel
Riesling Spätlese
8%, ♀ till 2010 — **88**

2003 Westhofener Kirchspiel
Riesling Spätlese
7.5%, ♀ till 2010 — **89**

2003 Westhofener Kirchspiel
Riesling Beerenauslese
7%, ♀ till 2015 — **91**

2003 Westhofener Kirchspiel
Riesling Trockenbeerenauslese
10%, ♀ till 2020 — **94**

The wines: **100** Perfect · **95–99** Outstanding · **90–94** Excellent · **85–89** Very good · **80–84** Good · **75–79** Average

WEINGUT GUNDERLOCH

Owner: Fritz and Agnes Hasselbach
Winemaker: Fritz Hasselbach
55299 Nackenheim,
Carl-Gunderloch-Platz 1
Tel. (0 61 35) 23 41, Fax 24 31
e-mail: info@gunderloch.de
Internet: www.gunderloch.de
Directions: A 60, Nierstein exit, B 9,
Nackenheim exit, left as you enter town
Sales: Agnes Hasselbach-Usinger
Opening hours: Mon.–Fri. 09:00 to
17:00 hours, weekends by appointment
Wine tastings: By arrangement, can be
paired with suitable menu
Worth a visit: Literary menues
History: Winery founded 1890 by banker
Carl Gunderloch

Vineyard area: 14 hectares
Annual production: 95,000 bottles
Top sites: Nackenheimer
Rothenberg, Niersteiner Pettenthal
and Hipping
Soil types: Red kaolin-slate
Grape varieties: 80% Riesling,
5% Silvaner, 6% Pinot varieties,
9% other varieties
Average yield: 50 hl/ha
Best vintages: 2001, 2002, 2003
Member: VDP

The history of this estate dates back to 1890. That is when banker Carl Gunderloch from Mainz founded the winery, and from the outset pronounced himself in favor of "naturrein" wines, an old expression for "naturally pure" wines, i.e. wines that had not been chaptalized. In later years, the winery was even recognized in literature, a figure in the "Fröhliche Weinberg" (the happy vineyard) by renowned author Carl Zuckmayer, who himself hails from Nackenheim, was named Carl Gunderloch, whether by accident or by design. Because this fictitious person, as a number of other Nackenheim citizens in the play, was shown as a character with some weaknesses, outraged citizens protested in the 1920s, brandishing their pitch-forks at the premiere of the play in Mainz. However, a reconciliation with the famous author took place in 1971. In those days, the estate was still known as Gunderloch-Usinger, and had absolutely no reputation. Then, in the early Eighties, young Fritz Hasselbach, husband of Agnes Hasselbach-Usinger, took over the reins in the cellar. Gradually, he and his wife realized that less can sometimes be more. The change in style began in the late Eighties, when yields were drastically reduced. Selective picking led to better grape material. In cellars, the time factor became increasingly important. Fermentation times were increased, and maturation on the lees soon became the rule. The best estate wines are often released to the public only eighteen months after the harvest. Really outstanding Riesling Trockenbeerenauslese wines have been repeatedly successful in international competitions in recent years. The best of the fruity sweet wines have been firmly entrenched among the best of Germany wines for the past decade. The Auslese wines can be of world-class quality, and the Spätlese from the Rothenberg vineyard is easily on a par with the finest Mosel wines. The 2002 vintage produced an excellent range of wines: Apart from the fantastic botrytis dessert wines, the Rothenberg Spätlese was a highlight. It eventually took first place overall, and was named the "Riesling Spätlese of the year." The 2003 is a worthy successor in the long line of successes produced at this estate, as evidenced by the long list of wines scoring 90 points or better. For the future, the Hasselbachs are still determined to find the ideal wine style for their top vineyard Rothenberg and its terroir. In fact, an expert committee was convened in September 2004 to debate this question.

2003 Riesling trocken
12.5%, ♀ till 2006   82

2002 Riesling trocken
11.5%, ♀ till 2006   84

The estates: ♛♛♛♛♛ World's finest · ♛♛♛♛ Germany's best · ♛♛♛ Very good · ♛♛ Good · ♛ Reliable

2002 Niersteiner Pettenthal
Riesling trocken
12%, ♀ till 2006   **85**

2003 Niersteiner Pettenthal
Riesling trocken
13%, ♀ till 2008   **89**

2003 Nackenheimer Rothenberg
Riesling trocken "Großes Gewächs"
13%, ♀ till 2010   **90**

2002 "Red Stone" Riesling
11%, ♀ till 2007   **84**

2003 Jean Baptiste
Riesling Kabinett
11.5%, ♀ till 2008   **87**

2002 Jean Baptiste
Riesling Kabinett
10.5%, ♀ till 2007   **87**

2003 Nackenheimer Rothenberg
Riesling Kabinett
10%, ♀ till 2008   **88**

2002 Nackenheimer Rothenberg
Riesling Beerenauslese
7.5%, ♀ till 2012   **89**

2003 Riesling Spätlese
8%, ♀ till 2012   **90**

2003 Nackenheimer Rothenberg
Riesling Spätlese
8.5%, ♀ till 2012   **91**

2003 Nackenheimer Rothenberg
Riesling Auslese
7.5%, ♀ till 2015   **91**

2002 Nackenheimer Rothenberg
Riesling Auslese
8.5%, ♀ till 2012   **92**

2001 Nackenheimer Rothenberg
Riesling Spätlese
9%, ♀ till 2011   **92**

2003 Nackenheimer Rothenberg
Riesling Beerenauslese
7%, ♀ till 2020   **92**

2002 Nackenheimer Rothenberg
Riesling Spätlese
9%, ♀ till 2009   **93**

2001 Nackenheimer Rothenberg
Riesling Auslese
10%, ♀ till 2012   **93**

2003 Nackenheimer Rothenberg
Riesling Trockenbeerenauslese
8%, ♀ till 2026   **93**

2003 Nackenheimer Rothenberg
Riesling Auslese Goldkapsel
9.5%, ♀ till 2020   **93**

2002 Nackenheimer Rothenberg
Riesling Auslese Goldkapsel
8%, ♀ till 2020   **93**

2000 Nackenheimer Rothenberg
Riesling Auslese Goldkapsel
9%, ♀ till 2012   **93**

2002 Nackenheimer Rothenberg
Riesling Trockenbeerenauslese
7%, ♀ till 2024   **94**

2000 Nackenheimer Rothenberg
Riesling Beerenauslese
9%, ♀ till 2017   **94**

2001 Nackenheimer Rothenberg
Riesling Auslese Goldkapsel
10%, ♀ till 2014   **95**

2000 Nackenheimer Rothenberg
Riesling Trockenbeerenauslese
8.5%, ♀ till 2024   **96**

GUNDERLOCH

NACKENHEIM
ROTHENBERG
R I E S L I N G
Spätlese
2003

Qualitätswein mit Prädikat
WEINGUT GUNDERLOCH, Inh. F.Hasselbach,D-55299 Nackenheim
Gutsabfüllung A.P.Nr. 43790430304 Produce of Germany

750 ml   RHEINHESSEN   Alc.8.5 %/vol.

The wines: **100** Perfect · **95–99** Outstanding · **90–94** Excellent · **85–89** Very good · **80–84** Good · **75–79** Average

WEINGUT DESTILLERIE GERHARD GUTZLER

Owner: Gerhard Gutzler
Winemaker: Gerhard Gutzler
and Michael Gutzler
67599 Gundheim, Roßgasse 19
Tel. (0 62 44) 90 52 21, Fax 90 52 41
e-mail: weingut.gutzler@t-online.de
Internet: www.gutzler.de
Directions: A 61 Koblenz–Ludwigshafen, Gundersheim exit
Sales: Elke Gutzler, by appointment
Worth seeing: Barrel cellar, distillery

Vineyard area: 12 hectares
Annual production: 80,000 bottles
Top sites: Wormser Liebfrauenstift Kirchenstück, Westhofener Morstein and Steingrube, Niersteiner Ölberg
Soil types: Clay, kaolin und limestone, lower new red sandstone, sand, gravel
Grape varieties: 29% Spätburgunder, 26% Riesling, 16% white Pinot varieties, 9% Dornfelder, 6% Silvaner, 14% other varieties
Average yield: 70 hl/ha
Best vintages: 2001, 2002, 2003

Gerhard Gutzler began working in his parents' winery in 1985. He then initially gained a good reputation for his excellent distilled products. Then he realized the potential for reds in his vineyards. Since then he has collected a long string of awards at the annual Vinum Red Wine Competition, sometimes collecting several awards in a year. The foundation for these fine wines is created by dense planting in the vineyard more than 7,000 vines per hectare, which reduces the stress on each individual vine, and this is complemented in the cellar by a deft touch with correctly dosed maturation in barriques, which is often quite extended. The alcohol levels are occasionally quite high, but this is well balanced by good extract levels. The third bunch of grapes was awarded to Gutzler last year, and this year's range has easily vindicated that decision.

2003 Riesling trocken "GS"
13.5%, ♀ till 2007 — 87

2003 Chardonnay trocken "GS"
13.5%, ♀ till 2007 — 87

2002 Wormser Liebfrauenstift Kirchenstück
Riesling trocken
13%, ♀ till 2007 — 89

2003 Westhofener Kirchspiel
Riesling Trockenbeerenauslese
10%, ♀ till 2020 — 94

——————— Red wines ———————

2001 Cabernet Sauvignon trocken
14%, ♀ till 2008 — 87

2002 Spätburgunder trocken "GS"
14%, ♀ till 2009 — 87

2001 Westhofener Morstein
Spätburgunder trocken Barrique
13.5%, ♀ till 2008 — 88

2001 St. Laurent
trocken "GS" Barrique
13.5%, ♀ till 2008 — 88

2001 Spätburgunder
trocken "GS" Barrique
14%, ♀ till 2008 — 89

2002 Westhofener Morstein
Spätburgunder trocken
14%, ♀ till 2012 — 90

2002
GRAUER BURGUNDER
G S

Gutsabfüllung

WEINGUT
HEDESHEIMER HOF

Owner: Jürgen, Michael and Gerda Beck
Winemaker: Jürgen and Michael Beck
55271 Stadecken-Elsheim 1
Tel. (0 61 36) 24 87, Fax 92 44 13
e-mail: weingut@hedesheimer-hof.de
Internet: www.hedesheimer-hof.de
Directions: Via A 63, Nieder-Olm exit,
Stadecken-Elsheim, in suburb of
Stadecken
Opening hours: Mon.–Fri. 14:00 to
19:00 hours, Sat. 09:00 to 16:00 hours
and by appointment

Vineyard area: 22 hectares
Annual production: 180,000 bottles
Top sites: Stadecker Lenchen
and Spitzberg, Elsheimer Bockstein
and Blume, Jugenheimer Goldberg
Soil types: Heavy kaolin, clay with
loess deposits
Grape varieties: 19% Riesling, 17%
Spätburgunder, 13% Weißburgunder,
10% each of Portugieser and Grau-
burgunder, 7% each of Dornfelder
and Silvaner, 17% other varieties
Average yield: 70 hl/ha
Best vintages: 1997, 1998, 2002

Jürgen Beck and his son Michael have
opted for pruning the vines for low yields,
and have planted cover crops as a preferred alternative to fertilization. In recent
years there have been some changes in
cellar procedures (moving away again
from whole bunch pressing), and a restructuring of grape varieties. In the case
of the white wines, Riesling and Silvaner
are now accompanied by the white Pinot
varieties, while among the reds the classics are similarly dominant, including Pinot Noir, the early ripening clone Frühburgunder, St. Laurent and Portugieser.
Unfortunately, the reds are somewhat
overwooded (in barriques), and show no
finesse. The white wines presented also
had their ups and downs, and we felt
there was a lack of a definite style here.

2003 Stadecker Spitzberg
Riesling trocken "Rheinhessen Selection"
12.5%, ♀ till 2007 **84**

2002 Stadecker Lenchen
Weißer Burgunder Spätlese trocken
13%, ♀ till 2006 **85**

2002 Stadecker Lenchen
Grauer Burgunder Spätlese trocken
13%, ♀ till 2006 **85**

2003 Stadecker Spitzberg
Weißer Burgunder Beerenauslese
9%, ♀ till 2012 **85**

2003 Stadecker Lenchen
Riesling Trockenbeerenauslese
9%, ♀ till 2020 **89**

2002 Stadecker Spitzberg
Riesling Eiswein
9%, ♀ till 2020 **90**

———— Red wines ————

2003 Elsheimer Bockstein
Spätburgunder Weißherbst Beerenauslese
10.5%, ♀ till 2012 **88**

2002 Stadecker Lenchen
Portugieser trocken "Oporto"
14%, ♀ till 2006 **82**

2002 Elsheimer Bockstein
Spätburgunder trocken
14%, ♀ till 2007 **83**

The wines: **100** Perfect · **95–99** Outstanding · **90–94** Excellent · **85–89** Very good · **80–84** Good · **75–79** Average

623

WEINGUT FREIHERR HEYL ZU HERRNSHEIM

Owner: Ahr family Foundation
Commercial manager:
Carsten Klaus Ahr
Production manager: Bernhard Schmidt
55283 Nierstein, Langgasse 3
Tel. (0 61 33) 5 70 80, Fax 57 08 80
e-mail: info@heyl-zu-herrnsheim.de
Internet: www.heyl-zu-herrnsheim.de
Directions: B 9, between Mainz and
Worms, in Nierstein turn from market-
place into Langgasse
Sales: Andrea Gauer
Opening hours: Mon.–Fri. 08:00 to
12:00 hours and 13:00 to 17:00 hours
and by appointment
Worth seeing: Winery buildings in park
surroundings, some from 16th century,
historical halls for tastings
Worth a visit: Reconstruction of histori-
cal vineyard

Vineyard area: 17 hectares
Annual production: 150,000 bottles
Top sites: Niersteiner Bruders-
berg, Pettenthal and Oelberg,
Nackenheimer Rothenberg
Soil types: Red kaolin-slate
Grape varieties: 70% Riesling, 12%
Silvaner, 11% Weißburgunder, 4%
Spätburgunder, 3% other varieties
Average yield: 59 hl/ha
Best vintages: 1998, 1999, 2003
Member: VDP

This winery, which was formerly shaped
by Peter von Weymarn, is one of the
pioneers of organic viticulture. It has
been owned by the Ahr family Foundation since 1994, and since then it has experienced weaker phases as well as some
highlights (from 1997 to 1999), with wines
simply bursting with flavor and brilliance. However, 2000 to 2002 vintages
have been marked by uneven quality. In
the meantime the winery appears to be
finding its form. An excellent trio of First
Growth wines from the 2003 vintage
clearly demonstrates the potential of the

top vineyard sites. Also, Markus Ahr ha
withdrawn from the management of th
winery, and his brother Carsten Klaus ha
taken over at the helm.

2003 "Rotschiefer"
Silvaner trocken
12.5%, ♀ till 2006   8.

2003 Weißer Burgunder trocken
13%, ♀ till 2006   8

2003 "Rotschiefer"
Weißer Burgunder trocken
13%, ♀ till 2006   8

2002 Niersteiner Pettenthal
Riesling trocken "Großes Gewächs"
13%, ♀ till 2007   8

2001 Niersteiner Brudersberg
Riesling "Großes Gewächs"
13%, ♀ till 2007   8

2003 Niersteiner Pettenthal
Riesling trocken "Großes Gewächs"
13%, ♀ till 2009   8

2003 Niersteiner Oelberg
Riesling trocken "Großes Gewächs"
13%, ♀ till 2008   8

2003 Niersteiner Brudersberg
Riesling trocken "Großes Gewächs"
13%, ♀ till 2010   9

2002 Niersteiner Oelberg
Riesling Spätlese
9%, ♀ till 2008   8

2001 Niersteiner Pettenthal
Riesling Auslese
9.5%, ♀ till 2008   9

2001 Niersteiner Brudersberg
Riesling Auslese Goldkapsel
9.5%, ♀ till 2010   9

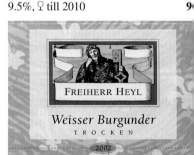

FREIHERR HEYL

Weisser Burgunder
T R O C K E N

2002

WEINGUT
GEORG GUSTAV HUFF

Owner: Dieter Huff
Winemaker: Dieter and Daniel Huff
55283 Nierstein-Schwabsburg,
Woogstraße 1
Tel. (0 61 33) 5 05 14, Fax 6 13 95
e-mail: info@weingut-huff.com
Internet: www.weingut-huff.com
Directions: B 9, in Nierstein go on to
B 420, turn right towards Schwabsburg
Sales: Helga Huff
Opening hours: Mon.–Fri. by appointment, Sat. 09:00 to 17:00 hours, Sun. 10:00 to 12:00 hours

---

Vineyard area: 15 hectares
Annual production: 150,000 bottles
Top sites: Niersteiner Hipping
and Schloss Schwabsburg
Soil types: Lower new red sandstone,
loess, kaolin
Grape varieties: 24% Riesling, 12%
each of Spätburgunder and Dornfelder, 10% Müller-Thurgau, 8%
Portugieser, 5% each of Chardonnay, Grauburgunder and Weißburgunder, 19% other varieties
Average yield: 81 hl/ha
Best vintages: 2001, 2002, 2003

This estate was founded around 1710 by Swiss immigrants, but it is only in recent years that it has attracted attention. There have been a number of good results in competitions, including a special state honors award, and a Pro Riesling award for the best Riesling range at the national wine awards. All that is encouraging for the elder Georg Gustav (81), Dieter and Helga Huff as well as their son Daniel, who is also already involved in the business. The motto "fully ripe grapes in the vineyard and minimal intervention in the cellar" is taken very seriously here. As in the previous year, we were presented with an attractive range of wines, the highlights of which were a Riesling as well as an exceptional Huxelrebe Trockenbeerenauslese.

2003 Chardonnay trocken
13%, ♀ till 2006 — **82**

2003 Niersteiner Ebersberg
Grauer Burgunder trocken
14%, ♀ till 2006 — **83**

2003 Niersteiner Hipping
Riesling Spätlese trocken
13%, ♀ till 2007 — **84**

2002 Riesling Auslese trocken
13%, ♀ till 2006 — **86**

2003 Niersteiner Rosenberg
Riesling trocken ***
13%, ♀ till 2007 — **87**

2002 Riesling Spätlese trocken
13%, ♀ till 2006 — **87**

2003 Niersteiner Schloss Schwabsburg
Riesling Auslese
10.5%, ♀ till 2012 — **84**

2002 Niersteiner Schloss Schwabsburg
Riesling Auslese
10.5%, ♀ till 2008 — **87**

2002 Niersteiner Schloss Schwabsburg
Riesling Eiswein
8.5%, ♀ till 2015 — **88**

2003 Niersteiner Bildstock
Huxelrebe Trockenbeerenauslese
9%, ♀ till 2020 — **89**

——— Red wines ———

2003 Spätburgunder trocken
14%, ♀ till 2007 — **83**

2003 Frühburgunder trocken
14%, ♀ till 2007 — **83**

2000 Dornfelder trocken
13%, ♀ till 2005 — **86**

The wines: **100** Perfect · **95–99** Outstanding · **90–94** Excellent · **85–89** Very good · **80–84** Good · **75–79** Average

WEINGUT HUFF-DOLL

Owner: Ernst, Ulrich and Gudrun Doll
55457 Horrweiler, Weedstraße 6
Tel. (0 67 27) 3 43, Fax 53 66
e-mail: weinguthuff-doll@arcormail.de
Directions: A 61, Bingen-Sponsheim
exit, in direction of Gensingen; A 60,
Gensingen exit
Sales: Mon.–Sun. by appointment
History: Winemaking since 1848

Vineyard area: 7 hectares
Annual production: 50,000 bottles
Top sites: Horrweiler Gewürzgärtchen and Goldberg
Soil types: Clay with kaolin
Grape varieties: 16% Grauburgunder,
13% each of Riesling and Weißburgunder, 9% each of Dornfelder, Müller-Thurgau and Spätburgunder, 5%
each of Chardonnay and St. Laurent,
21% other varieties
Average yield: 87 hl/ha
Best vintages: 2000, 2001, 2002

Things can sometimes move with great speed. Three years ago this winery, located in the small village of Horrweiler near Gensingen (which is between Bingen and Bad Kreuznach), was first mentioned in the Gault Millau wine guide. In the very next year it was already climbing in its ratings. Here nothing is left to chance, from pruning in the vineyard to the bottling line in the cellar. All the viticultural measures are aimed at producing ripe, healthy grapes in the vineyard, and then handling the grapes, must and wine as little as possible in the cellar to retain the quality. Last year, we tasted wines from the 2002 vintage that were strongly fruit-dominated, and very enjoyable to drink. The Doll family did not quite achieve the same high standard in the more difficult conditions of the 2003 vintage, but overall presented a very homogeneous range, which simply lacked real highlights. The winery on the Western border of the Rheinhessen region remains a good address for bargain-hunters.

2003 Horrweiler Gewürzgärtchen
Weißer Burgunder trocken
13.5%, ♀ till 2006 — 8

2003 Horrweiler Gewürzgärtchen
Grauer Burgunder trocken
14%, ♀ till 2006 — 8

2003 Horrweiler Gewürzgärtchen
Riesling trocken
13%, ♀ till 2007 — 8

2003 Silvaner
Spätlese trocken "Prestige"
14%, ♀ till 2006 — 8

2003 Riesling
Spätlese trocken "Prestige"
13.5%, ♀ till 2008 — 8

2002 "Prestige"
Grauer Burgunder Spätlese trocken
13.5%, ♀ till 2006 — 8

2002 "Prestige"
Riesling Spätlese trocken
13.5%, ♀ till 2006 — 8

2003 Horrweiler Goldberg
Riesling Spätlese
8%, ♀ till 2010 — 8

2002 Riesling Kabinett
12%, ♀ till 2006 — 8

2002 Riesling Spätlese
9%, ♀ till 2008 — 8

WEINGUT JOHANNINGER

Owner: Dieter Schufried, Markus Haas and Jens Heinemeyer
Viticulture: Dieter Schufried
Sparkling wine and distilling: Markus Haas
Winemaker: Jens Heinemeyer
55546 Biebelsheim, Hauptstraße 4–6
Tel. (0 67 01) 83 21, Fax 32 95
e-mail: johanninger@t-online.de
Internet: www.johanninger.de
Directions: A 61, Bad Kreuznach exit, in Gensingen turn south on to the B 50
Sales: Markus Haas, Jens Heinemeyer
Opening hours: Mon.–Sat. 08:00 to 18:00 hours or by appointment
Estate restaurant: "Remise," wine-culinary events by arrangement
Worth a visit: Culinary wine tastings

Vineyard area: 21 hectares
Annual production: 120,000 bottles
Top sites: Biebelsheimer Kieselberg, Kreuznacher Himmelgarten, Assmannshäuser Höllenberg, Lorcher Bodenthal-Steinberg
Soil types: Deep loess, limestone and red phyllite slate
Grape varieties: 65% Pinot varieties, 10% each of Silvaner and Riesling, 5% St. Laurent, 10% other varieties
Average yield: 70 hl/ha
Best vintages: 1999, 2001, 2003

In 1995 three wineries merged – one from Rheinhessen, one from the Rheingau and one from the Nahe. The headquarters is at Biebelsheim in Rheinhessen, where each of the partners has his duties. Dieter Schufried is responsible for the vineyards, Jens Heinemeyer handles the winemaking, and Markus Haas is responsible for the sparkling wines and distilled products. The trio endeavors to make the best of the resources in each region. They have not always succeeded in this. This time around, however, the range was homogeneous with good and very good wines. The attractive Pinot Noirs from the Rheingau deserve special mention.

2002 Weißer Burgunder & Chardonnay
trocken (Nahe)
13.5%, ♀ till 2006 — **82**

2003 Sauvignon Blanc
trocken (Rheinhessen)
14%, ♀ till 2006 — **82**

2002 Kreuznacher Himmelgarten
Grauer Burgunder trocken
"Alte Reben" (Nahe)
13%, ♀ till 2006 — **83**

2001 Weißer Burgunder & Chardonnay
trocken (Nahe)
12%, ♀ till 2005 — **83**

2003 "Berg"
Riesling trocken (Rheinhessen)
13.5%, ♀ till 2006 — **84**

2000 Chardonnay trocken (Nahe)
13%, ♀ till 2006 — **86**

2003 Biebelsheimer Kieselberg
Riesling Trockenbeerenauslese
(Rheinhessen)
12.5%, ♀ till 2020 — **89**

——— Red wines ———

2001 "Phyllit"
Spätburgunder trocken (Rheingau)
12.5%, ♀ till 2006 — **83**

2002 Biebelsheimer Kieselberg
St. Laurent trocken (Rheinhessen)
13%, ♀ till 2007 — **85**

2001 Lorcher Bodenthal-Steinberg
Spätburgunder trocken
"Alte Reben" (Rheingau)
13%, ♀ till 2008 — **86**

2002 Lorcher Bodenthal-Steinberg
Spätburgunder trocken
"Precoce" (Rheingau)
15%, ♀ till 2008 — **87**

The wines: **100** Perfect · **95–99** Outstanding · **90–94** Excellent · **85–89** Very good · **80–84** Good · **75–79** Average

627

Producer of the year 2000

Rheinhessen

WEINGUT KELLER

Owner: Klaus Keller
Winemaker: Klaus and
Klaus-Peter Keller
67592 Flörsheim-Dalsheim,
Bahnhofstraße 1
Tel. (0 62 43) 4 56, Fax 66 86
e-mail: Weingut_Keller@web.de
Internet: www.weingut-keller.de
Directions: A 61, Worms-Nord exit, via
Mörstadt to Flörsheim-Dalsheim, in sub-
urb of Dalsheim
Opening hours: Mon.–Fri. 08:00 to
11:30 and 13:00 to 18:00, Sat. 08:00 to
11:30 and 13:00 to 16:00 hours
Wine tastings by appointment only
History: The Keller family has been
making wine in Dalsheim since 1789 –
now in the eighth generation
Worth seeing: Natural stone tower in
the Dalsheimer Hubacker vineyard

Vineyard area: 12.5 hectares
Annual production: 100,000 bottles
Top sites: Dalsheimer Hubacker
and Bürgel, Westhofener Kirchspiel
and Morstein
Soil types: Decomposed limestone,
shell limestone, kaolin-marl, red
latosol, terra fusca
Grape varieties: 60% Riesling, 30%
Pinot varieties and Silvaner, 10%
Rieslaner and Scheurebe
Average yield: 59 hl/ha
Best vintages: 2001, 2002, 2003
Member: VDP

The Keller winery first attracted attention
in the late Eighties, busily collecting
medals at national wine awards. Since
then, a lot of gold been added to the
collection. In 2002 the winery was elevated, as it were, to Olympian heights,
receiving the Vinitaly Award in Verona.
Winners of this award in previous years
have included Château Margaux, Pen-
folds, Vega Sicilia and Mondavi. Behind
the success lie to like minds that got together in the Seventies, and implemented
their vision: Klaus Keller and his wife

Hedwig, who unfortunately passed away
much too soon – she has been given a memorial tower in the middle of the Hubacker vineyard. They realized that good
wine is made in the vineyard, and that
meticulous care of the vines, and highly selective hand-picking of perfectly
healthy grapes is more important than
just trying to keep the yields particularly
low. Son Klaus-Peter has completed his
studies in Geisenheim, and has in recent
years become an important factor in the
equation. His wife, Julia, who was trained
by Hans-Günther Schwarz, also has a
voice in the business. A positive factor
here is that for many years customers
have been able to buy every wine in the
range without thinking twice. Even the
more basic wines are exceptionally good.
The Kellers manage, as few others can, to
play at the top of the first league in three
separate divisions – red, white, and botrytis dessert wines. The current range
represents yet another improvement on
all that has gone before. Never yet have
they presented so many wines reaching or
exceeding 90 points, nor have they ever
scored so high at the top of the range. The
vintage conditions were completely different to those of other recent vintages,
and accordingly the Kellers reacted differ-
ently. They did not sit back patiently,
waiting until late in November to complete their harvest. They noted the early
ripening of the grapes, and were aware
of the danger of vine stress in the heat
and drouth, plus the fact that dry wines
would be much too alcoholic if the grapes
were just left to hang. Instead, they a-
stounded their neighbors by starting the
harvest much earlier than usual. If you
want to be a top winemaker, you must observe nature very closely, then you can
come to grips with it, and keep conditions
under control. Another thing kept under
control is the younger generation. There is
a passion here for passing on knowledge
and experience that has helped quite
a number of young winemakers who
trained here, to find their own place in the
pages of the Wine Guide.

The estates: ✦✦✦✦✦ World's finest · ✦✦✦✦ Germany's best · ✦✦✦ Very good · ✦✦ Good · ✦ Reliable

2002 Westhofener Kirchspiel
Riesling trocken "Großes Gewächs"
13%, ♀ till 2008   **90**

2003 Westhofener Morstein
Riesling trocken "Großes Gewächs"
13.5%, ♀ till 2010   **91**

2002 Dalsheimer Hubacker
Riesling trocken "Großes Gewächs"
13%, ♀ till 2008   **91**

2003 Dalsheimer Hubacker
Riesling trocken "Großes Gewächs"
13.5%, ♀ till 2010   **92**

2003 Westhofener Kirchspiel
Riesling trocken "Großes Gewächs"
13.5%, ♀ till 2010   **92**

2001 Dalsheimer Hubacker
Riesling trocken "Großes Gewächs"
13%, ♀ till 2007   **92**

2002 Westhofener Morstein
Riesling trocken "Großes Gewächs"
13%, ♀ till 2010   **93**

2003 "G-Max" Riesling trocken
13.5%, ♀ till 2012   **94**

2002 "G-Max" Riesling trocken
13%, ♀ till 2012   **94**

2001 Riesling trocken "G-Max"
13%, ♀ till 2009   **94**

2001 Dalsheimer Hubacker
Riesling Spätlese – 17 –
8%, ♀ till 2007   **90**

2003 Dalsheimer Hubacker
Riesling Spätlese Goldkapsel – 26 –
8.5%, ♀ till 2015   **91**

2002 Dalsheimer Hubacker
Riesling Spätlese Goldkapsel
7.5%, ♀ till 2015   **91**

2003 Westhofener Kirchspiel
Riesling Auslese *** Goldkapsel
7.5%, ♀ till 2020   **94**

2003 Dalsheimer Hubacker
Riesling Auslese *** Goldkapsel
7.5%, ♀ till 2020   **95**

2002 Dalsheimer Hubacker
Riesling Auslese *** Goldkapsel
7%, ♀ till 2020   **95**

2001 Monsheimer Silberberg
Rieslaner Trockenbeerenauslese
6.5%, ♀ till 2020   **96**

2002 Monsheimer Silberberg
Rieslaner Trockenbeerenauslese
Goldkapsel
6%, ♀ till 2025   **96**

2002 Dalsheimer Hubacker
Riesling Eiswein Goldkapsel
6%, ♀ till 2020   **96**

2001 Dalsheimer Hubacker
Riesling Auslese *** Goldkapsel
7.5%, ♀ till 2020   **96**

2003 Westhofener Morstein
Riesling Auslese *** Goldkapsel
7.5%, ♀ till 2020   **97**

2001 Dalsheimer Hubacker
Riesling Auslese *** Goldkapsel
7%, ♀ till 2020   **97**

2003 Scheurebe
Trockenbeerenauslese
6.5%, ♀ till 2030   **98**

2001 Dalsheimer Hubacker
Riesling Trockenbeerenauslese – 31 –
6.5%, ♀ till 2030   **98**

2003 Monsheimer Silberberg
Rieslaner Trockenbeerenauslese
Goldkapsel
6.5%, ♀ till 2030   **98**

2003 Dalsheimer Hubacker
Riesling Trockenbeerenauslese
Goldkapsel
6%, ♀ till 2040   **100**

KELLER

2003

Hubacker

Riesling

The wines: **100** Perfect · **95–99** Outstanding · **90–94** Excellent · **85–89** Very good · **80–84** Good · **75–79** Average

629

WEINGUT KISSINGER

Owner and winemaker:
Jürgen Kissinger
55278 Uelversheim, Außerhalb 13
Tel. (0 62 49) 79 69, Fax 79 89
e-mail: weingut.kissinger@t-online.de
Internet: www.WeingutKissinger.de
Directions: On the B 9 to Dienheim,
turn right in direction of Uelversheim
Sales: Jürgen Kissinger
Opening hours: Mon.–Sat. by appointment, each 1st Saturday of the month open tasting 10:00 to 16:00 hours
Worth seeing: Barrel cellar dating to 1722

Vineyard area: 11.7 hectares
Annual production: 70,000 bottles
Top sites: Dienheimer Tafelstein, Uelversheimer Tafelstein, Oppenheimer Herrenberg and Sackträger
Soil types: Loess and limestone-rich kaolin-clay
Grape varieties: 30% Riesling, 20% red varieties, 20% Pinot varieties, 10% Silvaner, 5% each of Müller-Thurgau and Chardonnay, 10% other varieties
Average yield: 74 hl/ha
Best vintages: 2001, 2002, 2003

The estate was founded in 1970, and marketing of bottled wines was started in the Seventies. However, development really only started when Jürgen Kissinger took over the winery in the Eighties. The move from cramped quarters to a new cellar improved the working environment. As this highly-motivated winemaker ferments most of his wines dry, it is particularly important to obtain fully ripe, healthy grapes from the vineyard. This has always been possible in recent vintages, and led to the production of thoroughly convincing ranges of wines. In 2003 Kissinger has again coped well with the conditions, although the high sugar-levels in the grapes resulted in high alcohol levels, particularly in the white Pinot varieties. Now we are just waiting for a really good Pinot Noir from here.

2003 Uelversheimer Tafelstein
Weißer Burgunder Spätlese trocken
15%, ♀ till 2006 **84**

2003 Grauer Burgunder
Spätlese trocken
14.5%, ♀ till 2006 **85**

2003 Uelversheimer Tafelstein
Chardonnay Auslese trocken
14%, ♀ till 2008 **86**

2003 Uelversheimer Tafelstein
Riesling Spätlese trocken
13.5%, ♀ till 2007 **87**

2002 Dienheimer Kreuz
Riesling Auslese trocken
12.5%, ♀ till 2006 **88**

2003 Dienheimer Kreuz
Riesling Auslese trocken
13.5%, ♀ till 2008 **89**

2003 Dienheimer Tafelstein
Riesling Spätlese halbtrocken
13%, ♀ till 2008 **85**

2002 Dienheimer Tafelstein
Riesling Spätlese halbtrocken
11.5%, ♀ till 2006 **86**

2002 Oppenheimer Sackträger
Riesling Spätlese
9.5%, ♀ till 2007 **86**

2003 Oppenheimer Sackträger
Riesling Auslese
11%, ♀ till 2012 **87**

WEINGUT KREICHGAUER

Owner: Axel and Anke Kreichgauer
Manager and winemaker:
Axel Kreichgauer
67585 Dorn-Dürkheim, Kirchgasse 2
Tel. (0 67 33) 70 05, Fax 96 08 06
e-mail: a.kreichgauer@t-online.de
Internet: www.weingut-kreichgauer.de
Directions: A 61, Alzey exit,
via Gau-Odernheim and Hillesheim
Sales: Anke Kreichgauer
Opening hours: Mon.–Fri. 09:00 to
20:00, weekends from 09:00 hours
by appointment

Vineyard area: 12.5 hectares
Annual production: 60,000 bottles
Top sites: Dorn-Dürkheimer
Hasensprung and Römerberg,
Wintersheimer Frauengarten
Soil types: Sandy loess and clay,
decomposed limestone
Grape varieties: 17% each of Riesling
and Spätburgunder, 12% Kerner,
11% Weißburgunder, 10% Graubur-
gunder, 6% Müller-Thurgau, 4% Char-
donnay, 23% other varieties
Average yield: 65 hl/ha
Best vintages: 2000, 2001, 2003

2003 Dorn-Dürkheimer Römerberg
Riesling trocken
12%, ♀ till 2006 **82**

2003 Dorn-Dürkheimer Hasensprung
Rivaner Classic
12%, ♀ till 2006 **82**

2003 Alsheimer Römerberg
Grauer Burgunder trocken
14.5%, ♀ till 2006 **83**

2003 Wintersheimer Frauengarten
Chardonnay trocken
13.5%, ♀ till 2006 **84**

2003 Dorn-Dürkheimer Römerberg
Riesling Spätlese trocken
13%, ♀ till 2006 **84**

2003 Dorn-Dürkheimer Römerberg
Riesling trocken "Alte Reben"
13.5%, ♀ till 2007 **85**

———— Red wines ————

2001 Alsheimer Römerberg
Dornfelder trocken
14%, ♀ till 2006 **83**

2001 "Anna-Maria Allessandra"
Cabernet Dorio trocken
13.5%, ♀ till 2007 **83**

2001 Dorn-Dürkheimer Römerberg
Cabernet Dorsa trocken
13.5%, ♀ till 2007 **85**

Just a few years ago, Axel Kreichgauer was one of the many bulk wine producers in Rheinhessen. But he has always tried to improve quality, even in his bulk wines, and by now he is selling 60,000 bottles of his own wine annually, producing more bottled than bulk wine now. A driving force in business is his wife Anke, a tax consultant, who is not shy to criticize her Axel if she thinks he has left a wine in barrique for too long. A good friend is winemaker Peter Jacob Kühn from the Rheingau, whose input and advice have also helped to improve quality here in recent years. Just as in the previous vintage, the current range makes a very good, solid impression. To date the Kreichgauers are selling their botrytis dessert wines in bulk, as they claim they do not have customers for these.

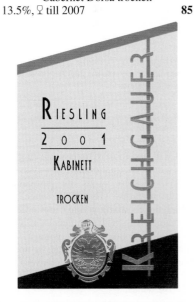

The wines: **100** Perfect · **95–99** Outstanding · **90–94** Excellent · **85–89** Very good · **80–84** Good · **75–79** Average

WEINGUT KÜHLING-GILLOT

Owner and manager:
Roland and Gabi Gillot-Kühling,
Carolin Gillot
Winemaker: Roland Gillot
and Carolin Gillot
55294 Bodenheim, Ölmühlstraße 25
Tel. (0 61 35) 23 33, Fax 64 63
e-mail: info@kuehling-gillot.de
Internet: www.kuehling-gillot.de
Directions: From Mainz on the B 9, in
old town center of Bodenheim
Opening hours: Mon.–Fri. 09:00 to
12:00 and 14:00 to 17:00, Sat. 10:00 to
12:00 hours, and by appointment
Restaurant: July and August, Fri.–Sun.
from 17:00 hours
Worth seeing: Park-sized garden with
Belle Epoque pavilion, collection of
Mediterranean and exotic trees

Vineyard area: 10 hectares
Annual production: 80,000 bottles
Top sites: Oppenheimer
Sackträger, Niersteiner Petten-
thal, Nackenheimer Rothenberg
Soil types: Loess with clay, red slate
Grape varieties: 44% Riesling, 10%
each of Portugieser, Spätburgunder
and Grauburgunder, 5% Chardon-
nay, 21% other varieties
Average yield: 70 hl/ha
Best vintages: 1999, 2002, 2003
Member: VDP

This winery was able to celebrate many
successes in recent years. If you go to the
open-air wine bar in the park in summer,
you will find most visitors preferring the
dry wines. Internationally, however, the
botrytis dessert wines are particularly
highly regarded. The 2003 range, for
which the charming young Carolin Gillot
is mainly responsible, reflects the problems of an extremely dry vintage. The
quality of the Qvinterra range is not as
homogeneous as usual. However, the
First Growth and the Eiswein are very attractive wines.

2003 "Qvinterra"
Silvaner trocken
13.5%, ♀ till 2006   **83**

2003 "Qvinterra"
Chardonnay trocken
13.5%, ♀ till 2006   **84**

2002 Oppenheimer Sackträger
Riesling trocken "Großes Gewächs"
12.5%, ♀ till 2007   **88**

2003 Niersteiner Pettenthal
Riesling trocken "Großes Gewächs"
12.5%, ♀ till 2010   **89**

2003 Oppenheimer Sackträger
Riesling Auslese
9%, ♀ till 2010   **86**

2002 Oppenheimer Sackträger
Riesling Spätlese
10%, ♀ till 2006   **86**

2003 Riesling Eiswein
7%, ♀ till 2020   **93**

——— Red wines ———

2002 "Giro IX" trocken
12.5%, ♀ till 2007   **84**

2001 Oppenheimer Kreuz
Spätburgunder trocken "Großes Gewächs"
14%, ♀ till 2008   **86**

WEINGUT MANZ

Owner: Erich and Eric Manz
Winemaker: Erich and Eric Manz
55278 Weinolsheim, Lettengasse 6
Tel. (0 62 49) 79 81 and 71 86,
Fax 8 00 22
e-mail: weingut@manz-weinolsheim.de
Internet: www.manz-weinolsheim.de
Directions: A 61 or A 63,
Gau-Bickelheim/Wörrstadt exit, B 420
Sales: Manz family, by appointment
History: First documented as farm in 1725
Worth seeing: Rustic wine tasting room in old barn, wine cellar

Vineyard area: 15 hectares
Annual production: 100,000 bottles
Top sites: Weinolsheimer Kehr,
Oppenheimer Herrenberg and
Sackträger, Niersteiner Hipping
Soil types: Calcareous marl with kaolin
and stone, decomposed limestone
Grape varieties: 30% Riesling, 40%
Pinot varieties, 30% other varieties
Average yield: 79 hl/ha
Best vintages: 2001, 2002, 2003

On his contract bottling line, Erich Manz (50) fills some three million bottles each year for other producers. But together with son Eric (27) he is showing some ambition with regard to his own winery, that has been expanded in recent years, has been given a new fermentation cellar, and is kept well-supplied with barriques. Recently, father and son took over another four hectares of excellent sites from the estate of the Protestant church. This was certainly of benefit to the overall image of the winery (the wines from these sites are labeled "EK" for Evangelische Kirche). The large range of 2002 wines presented was so convincingly good that we were happy to award the third bunch of grapes last year. Now, he successor vintage has brought some very opulent, but nevertheless well made wines from the Pinot varieties, as well as delicate, filigree Riesling wines in a number of variations. The red wines, too, have become quite good here.

2003 Grauer Burgunder
Spätlese trocken "Alte Reben"
15%, ♀ till 2007 — 85

2003 Niersteiner Hipping
Riesling Spätlese trocken
13.5%, ♀ till 2007 — 86

2003 Guntersblumer Steig-Terrasse
Gewürztraminer Spätlese trocken
13.5%, ♀ till 2007 — 86

2003 Guntersblumer Bornpfad
Weißer Burgunder Spätlese trocken (EK)
14.5%, ♀ till 2007 — 86

2003 Oppenheimer Herrenberg
Riesling Spätlese trocken (EK)
13.5%, ♀ till 2007 — 87

2003 Niersteiner Hipping
Riesling Spätlese
9.5%, ♀ till 2010 — 88

2003 Weinolsheimer Kehr
Riesling Auslese
8.5%, ♀ till 2012 — 89

2003 Oppenheimer Sackträger
Riesling Trockenbeerenauslese
7%, ♀ till 2020 — 92

2003 Niersteiner Hipping
Riesling Trockenbeerenauslese (EK)
7%, ♀ till 2020 — 92

2002 Weinolsheimer Kehr
Riesling Eiswein "2. Tag"
6%, ♀ till 2020 — 93

——— Red wines ———

2001 Oppenheimer Herrenberg
Spätburgunder trocken
14%, ♀ till 2008 — 87

2001 Cuvée "M" trocken
14%, ♀ till 2008 — 88

The wines: **100** Perfect · **95–99** Outstanding · **90–94** Excellent · **85–89** Very good · **80–84** Good · **75–79** Average

633

WEINGUT
MICHEL-PFANNEBECKER

**Owner: Heinfried and
Gerold Pfannebecker**
Winemaker: Gerold Pfannebecker
55234 Flomborn, Langgasse 18/19
Tel. (0 67 35) 3 55 and 13 63, Fax 83 65
e-mail: wgtmi.pfa@t-online.de
Internet: www.michel-pfannebecker.de
*Directions: A 61, Gundersheim exit, in
direction of Kirchheimbolanden,
on the main road*
Sales: Weekdays to 18:00 hours
by appointment

Vineyard area: 11.8 hectares
Annual production: 72,000 bottles
Top sites: Westhofener Stein-
grube, Flomborner Feuerberg and
Goldberg, Eppelsheimer Felsen,
Gundersheimer Höllenbrand
Soil types: Loess, clay, calcareous marl
Grape varieties: 30% Riesling, 13%
Silvaner, 12% Spätburgunder, 9%
Müller-Thurgau, 8% Portugieser, 7%
Grauburgunder, 6% Chardonnay, 5%
Weißburgunder, 10% other varieties
Average yield: 63 hl/ha
Best vintages: 1999, 2002, 2003

Heinfried and Gerold Pfannebecker, the
latter responsible for the cellar, have in
recent years invested considerably in the
cellar, while at the same time expanding
their Riesling plantings. They have also
increased the classic red varieties and Pinot varieties. Yields have been kept relatively low. It is true that the 2000 and
2001 vintages were not quite up to standard, but the 2002 vintage was back to
the good quality seen in the Nineties, followed by another rock-solid performance
in 2003. One noticeable fact: Virtually all
the bottles have stainless steel cap closures. One can assume that there were
considerable cork problems in the past.

2003 Flomborner Feuerberg
Riesling Spätlese trocken
13%, ♀ till 2006   **84**

2003 Flomborner Goldberg
Weißer Burgunder Spätlese trocken
13%, ♀ till 2006   **84**

2002 Westhofener Steingrube
Riesling Spätlese trocken – 13 –
12%, ♀ till 2006   **85**

2002 Westhofener Steingrube
Riesling Spätlese trocken – 6 –
12.5%, ♀ till 2006   **85**

2002 Flomborner Goldberg
Weißer Burgunder Spätlese trocken
12.5%, ♀ till 2006   **85**

2003 Westhofener Steingrube
Riesling "Rheinhessen Selection"
trocken
13%, ♀ till 2007   **86**

2003 Westhofener Steingrube
Riesling Spätlese feinherb
12.5%, ♀ till 2007   **86**

2003 Westhofener Steingrube
Riesling Auslese
9.5%, ♀ till 2010   **85**

2002 Flomborner Feuerberg
Riesling Eiswein
6.5%, ♀ till 2015   **90**

——— Red wines ———

2002 Gundersheimer Höllenbrand
Spätburgunder trocken
14%, ♀ till 2006   **82**

2001 Flomborner Goldberg
Spätburgunder trocken
13.5%, ♀ till 2006   **84**

WEINGUT
KARL-HERMANN MILCH

Owner: Karl-Hermann Milch
Winemaker: Karl-Hermann Milch
67590 Monsheim, Rüstermühle
Tel. (0 62 43) 3 37, Fax 67 07
e-mail: info@weingut-milch.de
Internet: www.weingut-milch.de
*Directions: A 61, Worms-Pfedders-
heim exit, B 47 in direction of Monsheim, in main road turn off to Mühlstraße, then 100 meters to winery*
Sales: Milch family
Opening hours: Mon.–Fri. by appointment, Sat. 09:00 to 12:00 hours and
13:00 to 17:00 hours
Worth seeing: Cross-vaulted cellar, barrel cellar, Belle Epoque paintings on
ceiling of tasting room

Vineyard area: 11.5 hectares
Annual production: 40,000 bottles
Top sites: Monsheimer
Rosengarten and Silberberg
Soil types: Loess-clay and sand
Grape varieties: 18% Spätburgunder,
15% each of Müller-Thurgau and
Dornfelder, 8% each of Riesling and
Scheurebe, 6% Chardonnay,
5% each of Frühburgunder and
Domina, 20% other varieties
Average yield: 77 hl/ha
Best vintages: 1999, 2002, 2003

Karl-Hermann Milch spent his training
years in top wineries: At Keller in Flörsheim-Dalsheim and at Knipser, who is in
Laumersheim in the Pfalz. He now has
his diploma as a viticultural technician,
and makes wines according to his own
vision, emphasizing the typical varietal
characteristics. His aim is to further reduce the share of wines sold in bulk. The
Pinot varieties are a hobby-horse of the
winemaker. We awarded him his second
bunch of grapes a year ago, and he has
confirmed this rating by presenting an extremely clean and clear 2003 range. The
only wine we were not happy with was a
barrique-matured Merlot.

2003 Monsheimer Silberberg
Chardonnay trocken "Blauarsch"
14.5%, ♀ till 2006   84

2002 Monsheimer Silberberg
Weißer Burgunder trocken
13%, ♀ till 2006   85

2002 Monsheimer Silberberg
Chardonnay trocken "S"
14%, ♀ till 2006   85

2003 Monsheimer Silberberg
Chardonnay und Grauburgunder trocken
14%, ♀ till 2007   86

2003 Monsheimer Silberberg
Weißer Burgunder Auslese trocken
13.5%, ♀ till 2008   87

2003 Monsheimer Rosengarten
Riesling feinherb
13%, ♀ till 2007   84

2003 Monsheimer Silberberg
Kerner Spätlese
11.5%, ♀ till 2008   84

———— Red wines ————

2002 Monsheimer Silberberg
Spätburgunder trocken "S"
13.5%, ♀ till 2007   83

2001 Monsheimer Rosengarten
Dornfelder trocken
13%, ♀ till 2005   84

2001 Monsheimer Rosengarten
St. Laurent trocken
13%, ♀ till 2006   85

2001 Monsheimer Silberberg
Spätburgunder trocken
14%, ♀ till 2006   86

2002 Monsheimer Silberberg
Frühburgunder trocken
13%, ♀ till 2008   87

The wines: **100** Perfect · **95–99** Outstanding · **90–94** Excellent · **85–89** Very good · **80–84** Good · **75–79** Average

WEINGUT AXEL MÜLLER

Owner and manager: Axel Müller
67592 Flörsheim-Dalsheim,
Ph.-Merkel-Straße 23
Tel. (0 62 43) 74 12, Fax 62 95
e-mail:
WeingutOttoMueller@t-online.de
Internet: www.weingut-otto-mueller.de
Directions: B 271, Alzey exit, in direc-
tion of Grünstadt, or Worms exit, B 47
Monsheim, B 271 Dalsheim
Sales: Birgit Müller
Opening hours: Mon.–Fri. 08:00 to
18:00, Sat. 09:00 to 18.00, Sun. 10:00 to
13:00 hours, by appointment
Worth seeing: Vaulted cellar, attractive
courtyard and gardens

Vineyard area: 12 hectares
Annual production: 100,000 bottles
Top sites: Dalsheimer Bürgel and
Sauloch
Soil types: Decomposed limestone,
kaolin and shell limestone
Grape varieties: 14% Müller-Thurgau,
13% Dornfelder, 12% Riesling, 10%
Portugieser, 8% Kerner, 7% Spät-
gunder, 6% each of Weiß- and Grau-
burgunder, 24% other varieties
Average yield: 85 hl/ha
Best vintage: 2002

This winery has been owned by the Müller family since 1625. The wines made by
Axel Müller show clear evidence of
modern cellar technology. They all have
very clear fruit, are typical of the varietal,
as well as clean and straightforward. This
style led to the winery being included in
the Guide two years ago. The second
range presented was significantly better,
and brought a better rating. In the 2003
vintage Müller obviously experienced
some problems getting to grips with the
extremely ripe grapes, and in some wines
the alcohol is too dominant. It seems to
us a little curious when a Silvaner with
14% alcohol is labeled as "Classic." The
prices here, nevertheless, continue to be
very consumer-friendly.

2003 Grauer Burgunder
Spätlese trocken
14%, ♀ till 2006 — **82**

2003 Riesling Auslese trocken
14%, ♀ till 2006 — **82**

2003 Weißer Burgunder
Spätlese trocken
13.5%, ♀ till 2006 — **82**

2003 Weißer Burgunder
Auslese trocken
14.5%, ♀ till 2006 — **82**

2002 Dalsheimer Burg Rodenstein
Riesling Kabinett trocken
11.5%, ♀ till 2006 — **84**

2002 Dalsheimer Steig
Gewürztraminer Kabinett trocken
12.5%, ♀ till 2006 — **84**

2003 Chardonnay
Spätlese halbtrocken
13.5%, ♀ till 2006 — **83**

2002 Riesling
Spätlese halbtrocken
12%, ♀ till 2006 — **84**

2003 Silvaner Classic
14%, ♀ till 2006 — **81**

——————— Red wines ———————

2003 Dalsheimer Burg Rodenstein
Spätburgunder Spätlese trocken
13%, ♀ till 2006 — **82**

2001 Dalsheimer Steig
Cabernet Sauvignon trocken
13%, ♀ till 2007 — **83**

2001 Dalsheimer Burg Rodenstein
Dornfelder trocken
13%, ♀ till 2006 — **85**

WEINGUT J. NEUS

Owner: Burchards family
Manager: Ulrich Burchards
55218 Ingelheim, Bahnhofstraße 96
Tel. (0 61 32) 7 30 03, Fax 26 90
e-mail: info@weingut-neus.de
Internet: www.weingut-neus.de
*Directions: A 60, Ingelheim-Ost
or -West exit, in direction of city center*
Sales: Ulrich Burchards
Opening hours: Mon.–Fri. 08:30 to
12:00 hours and 13:00 to 18:00 hours
Sat. 09:00 to 14:00 hours
Worth seeing: Vaulted cellar more than
100 years old, with oak barrels, historic
winery complex

Vineyard area: 13 hectares
Annual production: 80,000 bottles
Top sites: Ingelheimer Sonnen-
berg (monopole), Pares and Horn
Soil types: Loess, clay, shell limestone
Grape varieties: 65% Spätburgunder,
15% Portugieser, 8% each of Riesling
and Weißburgunder, 4% other varieties
Average yield: 60 hl/ha
Best vintages: 1999, 2002, 2003
Member: VDP

Ulrich Burchards, who is today in charge of the Neus winery, is the great-grandson of the founder. Selective hand-picking ensures only ripe, healthy grapes are brought into the cellar. In his red wines, the owner sticks totally to traditional mash fermentation, and oak maturation is designed to produce full-bodied Pinot Noirs with not much tannin. The winery has had its ups and downs in recent years. Following on two weaker vintages in 2000 and 2001, we downgraded the rating by one bunch of grapes. The two vintages presented since then have not yet been good enough to return to the former status. The red wines of the 2002 vintage either had some green notes, or were almost too commercially made and accessible. Just as in the previous vintage, we preferred the white wines, which make up only 20 percent of the range.

2003 Spätburgunder Weißherbst
weißgekeltert trocken
13%, ♀ till 2006 — 83

2003 Ingelheimer Horn
Riesling Spätlese trocken
12.5%, ♀ till 2007 — 84

2003 Ingelheimer Schlossberg
Weißer Burgunder Spätlese trocken
13.5%, ♀ till 2006 — 84

2002 Ingelheimer Schlossberg
Weißer Burgunder Kabinett trocken
12.5%, ♀ till 2005 — 84

2002 Ingelheimer Horn
Riesling Kabinett trocken
12%, ♀ till 2005 — 85

2002 Ingelheimer Schlossberg
Weißer Burgunder Auslese trocken
14%, ♀ till 2006 — 85

2002 Ingelheimer Schlossberg
Weißer Burgunder Spätlese trocken
13.5%, ♀ till 2006 — 86

——— Red wines ———

2002 Ingelheimer Pares
Spätburgunder Weißherbst Auslese trocken
14%, ♀ till 2006 — 87

2002 Ingelheimer Domina trocken
13%, ♀ till 2006 — 83

2002 Ingelheimer Pares
Spätburgunder Auslese trocken
13.5%, ♀ till 2007 — 83

2002 Ingelheimer Horn
Spätburgunder Spätlese trocken
13.5%, ♀ till 2007 — 83

2002 Ingelheimer Pares
Spätburgunder Spätlese trocken
13%, ♀ till 2007 — 84

2002
Ingelheimer Horn
SPÄTBURGUNDER
Spätlese · trocken
WEINGUT J.NEUS
RHEINHESSEN

The wines: **100** Perfect · **95–99** Outstanding · **90–94** Excellent · **85–89** Very good · **80–84** Good · **75–79** Average

WEINGUT PETH-WETZ

Owner: Johanna and Hartmut Peth
Manager: Hartmut Peth
Winemaker: Christian Peth
67593 Bermersheim, Alzeyer Straße 16
Tel. (0 62 44) 44 24, Fax 44 94
e-mail: info@weingut-peth-wetz.de
Internet: www.peth-wetz.com
Directions: A 61, Gundersheim exit, to
Bermersheim; A 61, Mörstadt exit, via
Gundheim to Bermersheim
Sales: Johanna Peth
Opening hours: Mon.–Sat. 09:00 to
18:00 hours, Sun. by appointment

Vineyard area: 15 hectares
Annual production: 30,000 bottles
Top sites: Dalsheimer Bürgel,
Bermersheimer Hasenlauf
Soil types: Limestone-rich loess-clay
Grape varieties: 16% Müller-Thurgau,
14% Riesling, 13% Spätburgunder,
8% each of Chardonnay and Bacchus,
7% each of Silvaner, Kerner and Por-
tugieser, 20% other varieties
Average yield: 76 hl/ha
Best vintages: 2002, 2003

Until 1998 Hartmut and Johanna Peth
sold the entire production in bulk. Then
their son Christian joined the business –
following on apprenticeships to Knipser
in Laumersheim and Keller in Flörsheim-
Dalsheim, and trips to the USA, Chile
and Australia to gain additional experience. Although he only completed his
studies in Geisenheim in January 2004,
he has already been working very hard
and has started experimenting in the cellar. The wines have become more juicy,
and more powerful. Of particular interest
is his ability to make interesting, sophisticated wines from the aromatic variety
Scheurebe, as well as from the Bacchus,
which elsewhere is a rather boring grape.
In recent times he has been marketing the
wines under the designation "Gravity," as
these wines are no longer pumped over.
So the share of bottled wines is increasing
from year to year. Continue on this path!

2002 "Gravity"
Chardonnay Auslese trocken *****
14%, ♀ till 2007 — **84**

2003 Dalsheimer Bürgel
Riesling Auslese trocken *****
13%, ♀ till 2007 — **86**

2003 Dalsheimer Bürgel
Riesling feinherb
12.5%, ♀ till 2007 — **82**

2003 Scheurebe Spätlese *
12%, ♀ till 2009 — **86**

2002 Westhofener Bergkloster
Scheurebe Spätlese ***
9%, ♀ till 2008 — **86**

2002 "Le mystère doux"
Bacchus Auslese
7.5%, ♀ till 2008 — **87**

2003 "Le mystère doux"
Bacchus Auslese
8%, ♀ till 2010 — **88**

2002 Westhofener Bergkloster
Scheurebe Beerenauslese
5.5%, ♀ till 2012 — **88**

———— Red wines ————

2002 Dornfelder trocken *
14.5%, ♀ till 2008 — **85**

2002 Spätburgunder
Auslese trocken ***
14.5%, ♀ till 2008 — **85**

2001 Dornfelder trocken *
13.5%, ♀ till 2007 — **86**

2001 Spätburgunder
Auslese trocken ***
14%, ♀ till 2007 — **87**

- 2002 -
Scheurebe
Beerenauslese

Weingut Peth-Wetz D · 67593 Bermersheim

WEINGUT POSTHOF DOLL & GÖTH

Owner: Karl Theo and Roland Doll
Winemaker: Karl Theo and
Roland Doll
55271 Stadecken-Elsheim,
Kreuznacher Straße 2
Tel. (0 61 36) 30 00, Fax 60 01
e-mail: weingut.posthof@doll-goeth.de
Internet: www.doll-goeth.de
*Directions: A 63 Mainz–Kaiserslautern,
Stadecken-Elsheim exit*
Sales: Christel Doll and Erika Doll
by appointment
History: The building was formerly an
Imperial post station, founded 1883
Worth seeing: Tasting room with panoramic view – tastings by appointment only,
collection of rare wines in vaulted cellar

Vineyard area: 15 hectares
Annual production: 150,000 bottles
Top sites: Stadecker Lenchen
and Spitzberg, Gau-Bischofsheimer Kellersberg
Soil types: Clay, kaolin
Grape varieties: 20% Riesling, 12%
each of Grauburgunder Silvaner
and Dornfelder, 10% each of Weißburgunder, Spätburgunder and St. Laurent, 14% other varieties
Average yield: 86 hl/ha
Best vintages: 2000, 2002, 2003

When two young winemakers, Erika Göth and Roland Doll, got married in 1993, one of the results was the merger of their two estates. The young wines are made and matured at the Doll winery in Stadecken-Elsheim. All grapes are hand-picked, then processed in the new, well-equipped cellar, resulting in clean, typical wines, which have, among others, received the State Honor Award in 2003. The botrytis dessert wines, in particular, again had an excellent standard. Apart from this, the range is not quite homogeneous. The two sparkling wines made from Riesling (Brut) and Scheurebe (dry) are quite good.

2003 Cuvée Gourmet
Spätlese trocken
13%, ♀ till 2006 · · · · · · · · · · · 83

2003 Weißer Burgunder
Spätlese trocken
13.5%, ♀ till 2007 · · · · · · · · · 84

2003 Stadecker Lenchen
Riesling Auslese trocken
13%, ♀ till 2008 · · · · · · · · · · 85

2002 Stadecker Lenchen
Riesling Kabinett trocken
11.5%, ♀ till 2005 · · · · · · · · · 85

2002 Stadecker Lenchen
Riesling Spätlese trocken
12%, ♀ till 2006 · · · · · · · · · · 85

2002 Riesling Classic
12%, ♀ till 2006 · · · · · · · · · · 85

2003 Stadecker Lenchen
Weißer Burgunder Trockenbeerenauslese
11%, ♀ till 2015 · · · · · · · · · · 88

2003 Stadecker Lenchen
Riesling Beerenauslese
11.5%, ♀ till 2015 · · · · · · · · · 89

2003 Gau-Bischofsheimer Kellersberg
Riesling Trockenbeerenauslese
11%, ♀ till 2020 · · · · · · · · · · 90

2002 Stadecker Spitzberg
Silvaner Eiswein
10.5%, ♀ till 2015 · · · · · · · · · 90

———— Red wines ————
2003 Spätburgunder Weißherbst
Auslese
14%, ♀ till 2009 · · · · · · · · · · 84

2003 Spätburgunder
Auslese trocken
15%, ♀ till 2008 · · · · · · · · · · 83

2002 Cuvée "R" trocken
12%, ♀ till 2006 · · · · · · · · · · 83

The wines: **100** Perfect · **95–99** Outstanding · **90–94** Excellent · **85–89** Very good · **80–84** Good · **75–79** Average

639

WEINGUT RIFFEL

Owner: Riffel family
Winemaker: Erik Riffel
55411 Bingen-Büdesheim, Mühlweg 9
Tel. (0 67 21) 99 46 90, Fax 99 46 91
e-mail: service@weingut-riffel.de
Internet: www.weingut-riffel.de
Directions: From Mainz A 60, Bingen-Ost exit, at lights in direction of Büdesheim; A 61, Bingen exit, keep left in direction of Büdesheim
Sales: Riffel family
Opening hours: Sat. from 10:00 to 16:00 hours and by appointment

---

Vineyard area: 11.5 hectares
Annual production: 90,000 bottles
Top site: Binger Scharlachberg
Soil types: Quartzite with clay, loess-clay, kaolin
Grape varieties: 28% Riesling, 13% Kerner, 11% Silvaner, 10% Müller-Thurgau, 8% Dornfelder, 5% each of Bacchus and Spätburgunder, 20% other varieties
Average yield: 92 hl/ha
Best vintage: 2003

Last year we forecast that the next higher rating was in reach. Erik Riffel did not disappoint us, and the positive development seen here in recent years has been rewarded with the first bunch of grapes. His father still ran the farm as a mixed operation, with fruit and other agricultural products, and a bit of wine. Today, Erik has no regrets that he has focused on the vines, concentrating particularly on white wines, which make up 85 percent of production. Around two-thirds of the wines are fermented dry. He owns around two hectares of the renowned Binger Scharlachberg site, which produces excellent Riesling. The winemaker implements cautious and minimal handling of grapes, and keeps the young wines on the lees for extended periods. The red wines have improved significantly. We are confident that the end of the path of improvement has not yet been reached.

2003 Silvaner trocken
13%, ♀ till 2005   **80**

2002 Weißer Burgunder
trocken "S"
13%, ♀ till 2006   **80**

2003 Riesling trocken
12%, ♀ till 2006   **84**

2003 Binger Scharlachberg
Silvaner Spätlese trocken
14%, ♀ till 2006   **84**

2003 Binger Scharlachberg
Riesling Spätlese trocken
13%, ♀ till 2007   **85**

2003 Binger Bubenstück
Weißer Burgunder Spätlese trocken
13.5%, ♀ till 2007   **85**

2003 Binger Scharlachberg
Riesling Spätlese trocken "Quarzit"
13%, ♀ till 2007   **86**

2003 Riesling halbtrocken
11.5%, ♀ till 2006   **82**

2003 Binger Scharlachberg
Riesling Spätlese
9.5%, ♀ till 2008   **84**

2003 Binger Scharlachberg
Riesling Auslese
9%, ♀ till 2012   **87**

——— Red wines ———

2002 Dornfelder trocken
13%, ♀ till 2007   **84**

2003 Binger Bubenstück
Spätburgunder trocken "Mariage"
13.5%, ♀ till 2008   **84**

WEINGUT SANDER

Owner: Gerhard and Stefan Sander
Manager: Gerhard Sander
Winemaker: Stefan Sander
67582 Mettenheim,
In den Weingärten 11
Tel. (0 62 42) 15 83, Fax 65 89
e-mail: info@weingut-sander.de
Internet: www.weingut-sander.de
*Directions: Via B 9 or A 61, at southern
end of Mettenheim*
Sales: Sander family
Opening hours: Mon.–Sat. 10:00 to
17:30 hours and by appointment
History: Grandfather Otto Heinrich
Sander was a pioneer of organic viticulture in the Fifties

Vineyard area: 24 hectares
Annual production: 200,000 bottles
Top sites: Mettenheimer Schlossberg and Michelsberg
Soil types: Loess and clay, sand and alluvial soil
Grape varieties: 18% Riesling, 13% Dornfelder, 10% Weißburgunder, 8% each of Spätburgunder and Kerner, 7% each of Müller-Thurgau and Portugieser, 29% other varieties
Average yield: 69 hl/ha
Best vintages: 2001, 2002, 2003
Member: Naturland

The pretty label with an image of the ladybug is not a marketing gimmick, but a symbol for the organic viticulture practiced here. Grandfather Otto was responsible for implementing the change to organic winemaking some 50 years ago. At the time he was considered a "Green weirdo," today he is respected as a pioneer. The following generations have felt themselves bound by his example. As the quality has been improving consistently, we awarded a second bunch of grapes last year. The 2003 vintage range has confirmed the appropriateness of this decision. We particularly liked the Sauvignon Blanc and Gewürztraminer, as well as the Huxelrebe Beerenauslese.

2003 Westhofener Aulerde
Grauer Burgunder trocken
13.5%, ♀ till 2006 — 83

2003 Mettenheimer Schlossberg
Riesling trocken "S"
13%, ♀ till 2006 — 83

2003 Sauvignon Blanc trocken
14%, ♀ till 2007 — 86

2002 Mettenheimer Schlossberg
Weißer Burgunder Spätlese trocken
13%, ♀ till 2006 — 86

2002 Sauvignon Blanc trocken
13%, ♀ till 2006 — 86

2003 Mettenheimer Schlossberg
Weißer Burgunder trocken "S"
13.5%, ♀ till 2007 — 86

2002 Mettenheimer Schlossberg
Gewürztraminer Spätlese trocken
12.5%, ♀ till 2007 — 87

2003 Riesling Spätlese
11%, ♀ till 2007 — 84

2003 Mettenheimer Schlossberg
Gewürztraminer Auslese
9%, ♀ till 2010 — 86

2002 Riesling "S"
12%, ♀ till 2007 — 87

2003 Mettenheimer Michelsberg
Huxelrebe Beerenauslese
9%, ♀ till 2012 — 88

——— Red wines ———

2003 Merlot trocken
14%, ♀ till 2007 — 84

2001 Dornfelder trocken
13%, ♀ till 2006 — 86

2001 Spätburgunder trocken
13%, ♀ till 2006 — 86

The wines: **100** Perfect · **95–99** Outstanding · **90–94** Excellent · **85–89** Very good · **80–84** Good · **75–79** Average

641

Rheinhessen

WEINGUT SANKT ANTONY

Owner: MAN AG, Munich
Manager: Dr. Alexander Michalsky
Administrator: Klaus Peter Leonhard
Winemaker: Günter Ewert
55283 Nierstein, Wörrstädter Str. 22
Tel. (0 61 33) 54 82, Fax 5 91 39
e-mail: St.Antony@t-online.de
Internet: www.st-antony.com
Directions: Via the B 9 or B 420
Sales: Traude Cersovsky, Regina Sauder
Opening hours: Mon.–Thur. 08:00 to
12:00 hours and 14:00 to 16:00 hours
Fri. 08:00 to 12:00 hours
and by appointment

Vineyard area: 22.5 hectares
Annual production: 170,000 bottles
Top sites: Niersteiner Oelberg,
Pettenthal, Orbel and Hipping
Soil types: Red slate
Grape varieties: 65% Riesling, 9%
each of Dornfelder and Spätbur-
gunder, 5% Silvaner, 3% Weißbur-
gunder, 9% other varieties
Average yield: 70 hl/ha
Best vintages: 1999, 2002, 2003
Member: VDP

The winery was established in 1920 to
manage a few vineyards that were part of
a former stone quarry owned by the Gute-
hoffnungshütte foundry (today part of
the MAN group). Later some parcels of
land in the best slate slopes around Nierstein were added. The winery was named
St. Antony in 1985, reflecting the name of
the first iron-works in the Ruhr region.
The wines are mostly fermented dry at
cool temperatures, then racked into traditional oak barrels and bottled late. Tremendous wines were produced here in the
early Nineties, but this was followed by a
rather difficult phase. The current general
manager Dr. Alex Michalsky is faced by
the prospect of the parent group wishing
to sell off the winery. In spite of this pressure, he has produced a respectable range
from the 2003 vintage, the only thing
lacking were the botrytis dessert wines.

2003 Niersteiner Orbel
Riesling trocken "Großes Gewächs"
13.5%, ♀ till 2008   **87**

2003 Niersteiner Orbel
Riesling Spätlese trocken
13%, ♀ till 2010   **88**

2003 Niersteiner Hipping
Riesling trocken "Großes Gewächs"
13.5%, ♀ till 2010   **88**

2003 Niersteiner Oelberg
Riesling trocken "Großes Gewächs"
12.5%, ♀ till 2010   **88**

2002 Niersteiner Oelberg
Riesling trocken "Großes Gewächs"
12.5%, ♀ till 2010   **88**

2003 Niersteiner Pettenthal
Riesling trocken "Großes Gewächs"
13.5%, ♀ till 2012   **89**

2002 Niersteiner Pettenthal
Riesling trocken "Großes Gewächs"
12%, ♀ till 2010   **89**

2003 Niersteiner Hipping
Riesling Spätlese
9.5%, ♀ till 2010   **88**

2003 Niersteiner Oelberg
Riesling Spätlese
9%, ♀ till 2012   **89**

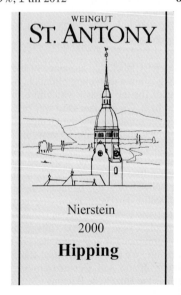

WEINGUT
ST. ANTONY
Nierstein
2000
Hipping

The estates: ⟂⟂⟂⟂⟂ World's finest · ⟂⟂⟂⟂ Germany's best · ⟂⟂⟂ Very good · ⟂⟂ Good · ⟂ Reliable

WEINGUT SCHAETZEL

Owner: Nanne Schätzel
Manager: Nanne Schätzel
Winemaker: Hans-Hermann in der
Beek and Kai Schätzel
55283 Nierstein, Oberdorfstraße 34
Tel. (0 61 33) 55 12, Fax 6 01 59
e-mail: weingut@schaetzel.de
Internet: www.schaetzel.de
Directions: B 9 Mainz–Worms, in Nierstein go on to B 420, follow Bildstockstraße to right until you reach Oberdorfstraße
Sales: Nanne Schätzel, by appointment
Worth seeing: 300-year-old manorhouse with tasting room, 700-year-old cross-vaulted cellar

---

Vineyard area: 5 hectares
Annual production: 35,000 bottles
Top sites: Niersteiner Pettenthal, Hipping, Oelberg and Heiligenbaum
Soil types: Red kaolin-slate, clay-loess with calcareous marl
Grape varieties: 50% Riesling, 15% Silvaner, 10% each of Spätburgunder and Müller-Thurgau, 8% Portugieser, 7% other varieties
Average yield: 60 hl/ha
Best vintages: 2001, 2002, 2003

Jakob Schlamp founded this estate in Nierstein around 1850. In 1874 his son Heinrich purchased the farm on which the winery is now located, formerly known as "General von Zastrow." The winery has always owned parcels of the famous Niersteiner Roter Hang site. Otto Schätzel, a descendant of the original owner, and his wife Nanne have been running the business for many years. Since 1996, son Kai has been making the wines. For the past few years, it appeared that this producer was treading water, but the latest vintage represents a real step forward, both in the quality of the wines themselves, and in their presentation and packaging. If Schätzel can improve the consistency of his basic wines, a higher rating cannot be far off.

2001 Niersteiner Hipping
Silvaner Spätlese trocken
12%, ♀ till 2005 — 83

2003 Niersteiner Hipping
Riesling Spätlese trocken
13.5%, ♀ till 2007 — 84

2003 Niersteiner Pettenthal
Riesling Spätlese trocken
13%, ♀ till 2007 — 85

2002 Niersteiner Pettenthal
Riesling Spätlese trocken
12%, ♀ till 2006 — 85

2002 Niersteiner Hipping
Silvaner Spätlese trocken "Selection II"
12%, ♀ till 2006 — 85

2002 Niersteiner Hipping
Riesling trocken
"Selection Heinrich Schlamp"
11.5%, ♀ till 2006 — 87

2003 Riesling
12%, ♀ till 2006 — 81

2003 Niersteiner Oelberg
Riesling Spätlese
12.5%, ♀ till 2008 — 85

2001 Niersteiner Oelberg
Riesling Spätlese
10.5%, ♀ till 2006 — 85

2003 "Heinrich Schlamp"
Riesling Auslese
12.5%, ♀ till 2010 — 86

2003 "Heinrich Schlamp"
Silvaner Auslese
13.5%, ♀ till 2010 — 87

2003 Niersteiner Oelberg
Riesling Trockenbeerenauslese
"Heinrich Schlamp"
10%, ♀ till 2020 — 90

The wines: **100** Perfect · **95–99** Outstanding · **90–94** Excellent · **85–89** Very good · **80–84** Good · **75–79** Average

643

WEINGUT SCHALES

Owner: Christel, Arno and Kurt Schales
General manager: Astrid Schales
Administrator: Burkhard Kirchner
Winemaker: Kurt and Christian Schales
67592 Flörsheim-Dalsheim,
Alzeyer Straße 160
Tel. (0 62 43) 70 03, Fax 52 30
e-mail: weingut.schales@t-online.de
Internet: www.schales.de
*Directions: A 61, Worms-Mörstadt exit,
Flörsheim-Dalsheim, in suburb of Dals-
heim, on the B 271*
Sales: Arno and Astrid Schales
Opening hours: Mon.–Fri. 08:00 to
12:00 and 13:30 to 18:00, Sat. 09:00 to
13:00 hours, Sun. by appointment
History: Family-owned since 1783
Worth seeing: Small wine museum,
barrel cellar, old tree press, large stock
of mature rarities (wines from 1780)

Vineyard area: 60 hectares
Annual production: 500,000 bottles
Top sites: Dalsheimer Hubacker,
Bürgel, Sauloch, Steig and Goldberg
Soil types: Decomposed shell lime-
stone, loess-clay and kaolin
Grape varieties: 30% Riesling, 25%
red varieties, 15% Weißburgunder,
10% Grauburgunder, 10% Müller-
Thurgau, 10% other varieties
Average yield: 73 hl/ha
Best vintages: 1998, 1999, 2003

This long-established wine estate has
grown to be one of the ten largest privately owned wineries in Germany. After
the death of brother Heinrich Schales,
shareholdings between Kurt, Arno and
his wife Christel have been re-allocated.
Christian Schales represents the younger
generation, and is also already active in
the business. Of the 2003 vintage we saw
an excellent range, on a par with the best
ever made here. Across the board, the
wines are delightfully crisp and refreshing, completely avoiding the dangers of
high alcohol or flabbiness. We can only
extend our compliments!

2003 Muskateller trocken
12%, ♀ till 2007 — 85

2003 Dalsheimer Hubacker
Weißer Burgunder trocken Selection
14%, ♀ till 2007 — 85

2003 Chardonnay Spätlese trocken
13.5%, ♀ till 2007 — 86

2003 Riesling Auslese trocken
12.5%, ♀ till 2009 — 88

2003 Dalsheimer Steig
Riesling trocken
12%, ♀ till 2008 — 88

2003 Weißer Burgunder
Auslese trocken
13.5%, ♀ till 2008 — 88

2003 Riesling Classic
12%, ♀ till 2006 — 84

2003 Huxelrebe Auslese
10%, ♀ till 2010 — 87

2003 Rieslaner Auslese
9%, ♀ till 2012 — 88

2003 Riesling Beerenauslese
8%, ♀ till 2015 — 90

2003 Huxelrebe
Trockenbeerenauslese
7%, ♀ till 2015 — 91

WEINGUT
ADOLF SCHEMBS ERBEN

Owner: Arno Schembs
Manager and winemaker: Arno Schembs
67550 Worms-Herrnsheim,
Schmiedgasse 23
Tel. (0 62 41) 5 20 56, Fax 59 17 20
e-mail: info@schembs-worms.de
Internet: www.schembs-worms.de
Directions: A 61, Worms-Nord exit
Sales: Arno Schembs
by appointment only
History: The winery developed from an
old-established cooperage
Worth seeing: Sales of wine in three ba-
roque manor-houses with Mediterranean
courtyards

Vineyard area: 8 hectares
Annual production: 45,000 bottles
Top sites: Wormser
Liebfrauenstift Kirchenstück,
Osthofener Goldberg
Soil types: Sandy clay with gravel
Grape varieties: 25% Riesling, 20%
Spätburgunder, 10% Dornfelder,
8% each of Schwarzriesling, Weiß-
burgunder and Portugieser,
21% other varieties
Average yield: 65 hl/ha
Best vintages: 2000, 2002, 2003

Arno Schembs is a creative man, and
each bottle here looks as though it were a
unique, hand-written original. But the
content of the bottles is also good. For
some years now Schembs has owned part
of the formerly world-famous Liebfrauenstift Kirchenstück vineyard site in
Worms, the original home of the once-
noble "Liebfrauenmilch." Here we were
only able to taste the previous vintage,
as the 2003 wines were only destined to
be bottled too late for our publishing deadline. By now, we see an upward trend. In
the past, it was mainly the reds that were
good here, but in the meantime the whites
are also pleasant and full-bodied. We will
only refrain from saying more about the
Riesling Trockenbeerenauslese.

2003 Grauer Burgunder trocken
13.5%, ♀ till 2007 **85**

2002 Wormser
Liebfrauenstift Kirchenstück
Riesling trocken
12.5%, ♀ till 2010 **88**

2003 Chardonnay halbtrocken
13%, ♀ till 2007 **85**

2003 Goldberg
Riesling Auslese "Variation No. 1"
11%, ♀ till 2010 **85**

———— Red wines ————

2002 "Cuvée 002" trocken ***
13%, ♀ till 2007 **85**

2002 Schwarzriesling trocken ***
13.5%, ♀ till 2008 **85**

2001 St. Laurent trocken
13%, ♀ till 2006 **85**

2001 Spätburgunder trocken
13.5%, ♀ till 2006 **86**

2001 Portugieser trocken
13%, ♀ till 2006 **86**

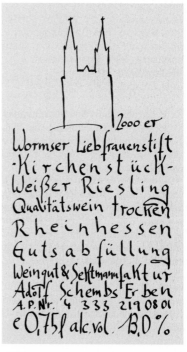

The wines: **100** Perfect · **95–99** Outstanding · **90–94** Excellent · **85–89** Very good · **80–84** Good · **75–79** Average

645

WEINGUT
SCHERNER-KLEINHANSS

Owner: Klaus R. Scherner
Winemaker: Klaus R. Scherner
67592 Flörsheim-Dalsheim,
Alzeyer Straße 10
Tel. (0 62 43) 4 35, Fax 56 65
e-mail:
scherner.kleinhanss@freenet.de
Internet: www.scherner-kleinhanss.de
Directions: A 61, Worms-Mörstadt exit
Sales: Monika Bank-Scherner
by appointment
Worth seeing: Half-timbered house
dating to 16th century, cross-vaulting in
tasting room and sales room

Vineyard area: 11 hectares
Annual production: 65,000 bottles
Top sites: Nieder-Flörsheimer
Frauenberg and Steig, Monsheimer
Rosengarten, Dalsheimer Bürgel
and Sauloch
Soil types: Clay, sand, gravel,
limestone-rich loess
Grape varieties: 22% Weißburgunder,
20% Riesling, 19% Spätburgunder,
5% each of Frühburgunder and Grau-
burgunder, 29% other varieties
Average yield: 60 hl/ha
Best vintages: 2001, 2002, 2003

The Petitjeans family fled from Burgundy
in the 16th century, crossing the Rhine
and translating the French name to Klein-
hanß. In 1726 Joseph Jodokus Scherner
established the winery in Dalsheim. In
1954 the two families were joined by
marriage. Today, Klaus R. Scherner is the
ninth generation to run this reliable family winery. Before starting his work here,
he spent some time gaining experience in
North America. The ranges he has presented in recent years have always been
very well made, with no evident weak
points. All told, a strong two-bunch producer that is frequently to be found
among the medal and trophy winners at
various competitions.

2003 Dalsheimer Sauloch
Weißer Burgunder Spätlese trocken
14%, ♀ till 2007   85

2003 Nieder-Flörsheimer Goldberg
Riesling Spätlese trocken "S"
13%, ♀ till 2007   85

2002 Nieder-Flörsheimer Goldberg
Riesling trocken "S"
12.5%, ♀ till 2006   88

2002 Dalsheimer Bürgel
Riesling Kabinett halbtrocken
11%, ♀ till 2007   87

2002 Dalsheimer Bürgel
Riesling Spätlese
8.5%, ♀ till 2008   88

2003 Nieder-Flörsheimer Frauenberg
Riesling Trockenbeerenauslese
13%, ♀ till 2020   89

2002 Nieder-Flörsheimer Frauenberg
Riesling Eiswein
12%, ♀ till 2015   90

————— Red wines —————
2002 Cuvée "J" trocken
14%, ♀ till 2006   84

2001 Spätburgunder
trocken "Turmalin"
13.5%, ♀ till 2007   85

2003 Nieder-Flörsheimer Frauenberg
Frühburgunder trocken
14%, ♀ till 2008   86

WEINGUT ADOLF SCHICK

Owner: Rainer Schick
Manager and winemaker:
Hermann Steitz
55270 Jugenheim, Kreinergasse 1
Tel. (0 61 30) 2 56, Fax 82 11
e-mail: weingut.schick@t-online.de
Internet:
www.weingutschickjugenheim.de
Directions: A 63, Nieder-Olm-Nord exit
Sales: Susanne Schick
Opening hours: Mon.–Fri. 09:00 to
12:00 hours and 13:00 to 18:00 hours
Sat. 09:00 to 16:00 hours
Hotel-Restaurant: Weedenhof
M. Knöll, Tel. (0 61 30) 94 13 37
History: First documented 1590
Worth seeing: Picturesque courtyard,
cellar with carved barrels

Vineyard area: 12 hectares
Annual production: 75,000 bottles
Top sites: Jugenheimer
Goldberg and Hasensprung
Soil types: Clay, partly with limestone
Grape varieties: 12% each of Riesling
and Spätburgunder, 10% Portugieser,
8% each of Weißburgunder and Dorn-
felder, 6% Müller-Thurgau, 5% each
of Kerner, Grauburgunder, Char-
donnay and Schwarzriesling,
24% other varieties
Average yield: 70 hl/ha
Best vintages: 2002, 2003

Rainer (66) and Edith Schick are passionate winemakers, and very pleased
that daughter Susanne has decided to join
the business. The young viticultural tech-
nologist has completed her studies in Bad
Kreuznach, and has brought some fresh
ideas to the operation. The homogeneous
range presented last year resulted in the
first bunch of grapes being awarded, and
this year's performance has confirmed
this rating. Following on a brief interlude
with Kurt Gabelmann as winemaker,
there is now a new motivated man in the
cellar – Hermann Steitz was previously
at Kruger-Rumpf on the Nahe.

2003 Jugenheimer Goldberg
Riesling Spätlese trocken – 31 –
13%, ♀ till 2006 — **83**

2002 Jugenheimer Goldberg
Gewürztraminer Spätlese trocken
13%, ♀ till 2006 — **83**

2002 Jugenheimer Goldberg
Grauer Burgunder Spätlese trocken
13%, ♀ till 2006 — **86**

2002 Jugenheimer Goldberg
Riesling Kabinett halbtrocken
11%, ♀ till 2006 — **84**

2002 Chardonnay
Spätlese halbtrocken
12%, ♀ till 2006 — **84**

2003 Jugenheimer Goldberg
Siegerrebe Auslese
10.5%, ♀ till 2008 — **84**

——— Red wines ———

2002 Jugenheimer Hasensprung
Spätburgunder Spätlese trocken
13%, ♀ till 2007 — **83**

2002 Schwarzriesling
Auslese trocken
13.5%, ♀ till 2008 — **84**

2001 Cabernet Mitos
trocken "Cuvée Lorenz"
13%, ♀ till 2006 — **84**

2002 Cabernet Mitos trocken
13%, ♀ till 2008 — **85**

2002er
Jugenheimer St. Georgenberg
Weißer Burgunder
Spätlese trocken
Qualitätswein mit Prädikat
ERZEUGERABFÜLLUNG
A. P. Nr. 4 367 119 17 03
0,75 L — alc. 12,0% vol
RHEINHESSEN

The wines: **100** Perfect · **95–99** Outstanding · **90–94** Excellent · **85–89** Very good · **80–84** Good · **75–79** Average

WEINGUT GEORG ALBRECHT SCHNEIDER

Owner: Albrecht Schneider
55283 Nierstein, Wilhelmstraße 6
Tel. (0 61 33) 56 55, Fax 54 15
e-mail:
Schneider-Nierstein@t-online.de
Internet: www.schneider-nierstein.de
Directions: Via the B 9 in direction of
Bad Kreuznach, 3rd street left
Sales: Ulrike and Albrecht Schneider
by appointment

Vineyard area: 14 hectares
Annual production: 90,000 bottles
Top sites: Niersteiner Hipping,
Oelberg, Orbel and Pettenthal
Soil types: Red kaolin-slate, loess-clay
Grape varieties: 50% Riesling,
25% Müller-Thurgau, 8% Kerner,
3% Dornfelder, 14% other varieties
Average yield: 80 hl/ha
Best vintages: 2001, 2002, 2003

Some winemakers are given responsibility only late in life, and manage to produce only 20 or 25 vintages. On the other hand, 2003 was the 36th vintage brought in by Albrecht Schneider, and he is nowhere near retirement age. However, his father passed away early, so that he was forced to take over responsibility at the age of 18. At the winery, the old Domherrenhof (cathedral master's estate) Harth, he implements whole bunch pressing, minimum intervention and leaves the Riesling to ferment over an extended period. The vineyards are spread over the best Nierstein sites. The winery's strength over many years has clearly been with the fruity Riesling wines, which also provide excellent value for money. This is also true of the 2003 vintage, which was largely successful. An interesting point on the dry wines: The Auslese actually has a lower alcohol level than does the Spätlese. The experiments with producing a Dornfelder red wine have so far not been particularly successful, and are not yet worth mentioning.

2003 Niersteiner Hipping
Riesling Spätlese trocken
14%, ♀ till 2006 — **84**

2003 Niersteiner Hipping
Riesling Auslese trocken
13.5%, ♀ till 2008 — **85**

2003 Niersteiner Oelberg
Riesling Spätlese halbtrocken
12%, ♀ till 2007 — **85**

2003 Niersteiner Orbel
Riesling Spätlese
10.5%, ♀ till 2010 — **86**

2003 Niersteiner Paterberg
Riesling Kabinett
11.5%, ♀ till 2008 — **87**

2002 Niersteiner Paterberg
Riesling Kabinett
9%, ♀ till 2007 — **87**

2003 Niersteiner Orbel
Riesling Auslese
9%, ♀ till 2012 — **88**

2002 Niersteiner Hipping
Riesling Spätlese
10%, ♀ till 2009 — **88**

2003 Niersteiner Hipping
Riesling Auslese
8.5%, ♀ till 2015 — **89**

2002 Niersteiner Hipping
Riesling Auslese
9%, ♀ till 2012 — **89**

2002
Niersteiner Rosenberg
Riesling Kabinett
Trocken
Qualitätswein mit Prädikat
Weingut Gg. A. Schneider, D55283 Nierstein
Gutsabfüllung A.P.Nr. 4 382 238 15 03
ALC.12.0 % **RHEINHESSEN** 750ml

WEINGUT
HEINRICH SEEBRICH

Owner and winemaker:
Heinrich Seebrich
Winemaker: Jochen Seebrich
55283 Nierstein, Schmiedgasse 3–5
Tel. (0 61 33) 6 01 50, Fax 6 01 65
e-mail: weingut.seebrich@t-online.de
Directions: Via B 9, in direction of Bad
Kreuznach, 5th street right
Opening hours: Mon.–Fri. 08:00 to
17:00 hours, by appointment
History: Winery was founded by current
family owners in 1783
Worth seeing: Old vaulted cellar, barrel
cellar

Vineyard area: 11.5 hectares
Annual production: 85,000 bottles
Top sites: Niersteiner Heiligen-
baum, Oelberg and Hipping
Soil types: Red kaolin-slate
Grape varieties: 40% Riesling, 11%
Dornfelder, 8% Müller-Thurgau, 7%
Weißburgunder, 6% Grauburgunder,
5% each of Silvaner and Spätburgun-
der, 18% other varieties
Average yield: 68 hl/ha
Best vintages: 2001, 2002, 2003

Heinrich Seebrich is primarily a specialist for delicately sweet Riesling. He is
particularly adept at producing wines
with juicy fruit and a piquant acidity from
grapes sourced from the famous Roter
Hang site. Son Jochen has been helping
actively since completing his studies as a
viticultural technician in Bad Kreuznach
four years ago. The old cellar with carved
oak barrels has witnessed the advent of an
increasing number of stainless steel
tanks, providing better conditions for the
fermentation of the musts. The quality of
the 2002 vintage was very solid, and was
followed by a 2003 vintage range that
was really enjoyable from Spätlese level
upward. The dry wines could do with a
bit more creativity.

2003 Niersteiner Oelberg
Riesling Auslese trocken
14%, ♀ till 2007 | 84

2002 Niersteiner Heiligenbaum
Riesling Spätlese halbtrocken
11.5%, ♀ till 2006 | 86

2003 Niersteiner Heiligenbaum
Riesling Spätlese feinherb
13.5%, ♀ till 2009 | 85

2003 Niersteiner Hipping
Riesling Spätlese
10.5%, ♀ till 2009 | 85

2003 Niersteiner Hipping
Riesling Auslese
10%, ♀ till 2012 | 86

2002 Niersteiner Hipping
Riesling Auslese
9.5%, ♀ till 2012 | 87

2001 Niersteiner Oelberg
Riesling Eiswein
8.5%, ♀ till 2010 | 88

2003 Niersteiner Oelberg
Riesling Beerenauslese
8%, ♀ till 2015 | 89

2002 Niersteiner Oelberg
Riesling Eiswein
8.5%, ♀ till 2020 | 92

SEEBRICH
WEINGUT

2002
Niersteiner Ölberg
Riesling
Spätlese

Qualitätswein mit Prädikat
A.P.Nr. 4 382 261 06 03
Gutsabfüllung - Produce of Germany
D-55283 Nierstein

Rheinhessen

750 ml   *alc. 9.5% vol.*

The wines: **100** Perfect · **95–99** Outstanding · **90–94** Excellent · **85–89** Very good · **80–84** Good · **75–79** Average

WEINGUT SEEHOF – ERNST FAUTH

Owner: Ernst, Ruth and Florian Fauth
Winemaker: Florian and Ernst Fauth
67593 Westhofen, Seegasse 20
Tel. (0 62 44) 49 35, Fax 90 74 65
e-mail: Weingut-Seehof@t-online.de
Directions: A 61, Gundersheim exit,
drive towards Westhofen
Sales: Fauth family
Opening hours: Mon.–Sat. by appointment
Guest rooms: With breakfast
History: Seehof is 1200 years old
Worth seeing: Seebach source behind the
house, its spring carrying most water in
Rheinhessen; 400-year-old vaulted cellar

Vineyard area: 14 hectares
Annual production: 38,000 bottles
Top sites: Westhofener Kirchspiel
and Morstein
Soil types: Limestone-marl, loess-clay
Grape varieties: 18% each of Riesling
and Müller-Thurgau, 10% Grau- and
Weißburgunder, 8% each of Kerner
and Silvaner, 5% each of Huxelrebe,
Portugieser and Scheurebe,
23% other varieties
Average yield: 82 hl/ha
Best vintages: 2001, 2002, 2003

Ernst and Ruth Fauth decided to give the
young generation a chance at independence early in life, and have not regretted
the decision. Florian Fauth served his apprenticeship at the top Pfalz wineries Dr.
Wehrheim and Mosbacher, and is adept
at implementing what he has learned.
This includes: Green harvesting to reduce
yields, careful pruning to optimize leaf
cover, late, selective harvesting to obtain
ripe, healthy grapes. Taken together, all
this effort produces very attractive wines.
The second bunch of grapes was awarded
in 2002, and this has since been twice
confirmed. Yet again the wines are lively
and juicy, with the dry wines showing restrained power. The racy Huxelrebe Spätlese is a bargain. The Scheurebe Trocken-
beerenausleses are brilliant.

2003 Westhofener Steingrube
Weißer Burgunder und Chardonnay
Spätlese trocken
14%, ♀ till 2006 — **84**

2003 Westhofener Steingrube
Chardonnay Spätlese trocken
13.5%, ♀ till 2007 — **85**

2003 Westhofener Morstein
Riesling trocken "S"
13.5%, ♀ till 2007 — **85**

2002 Westhofener Morstein
Riesling trocken Selection
12.5%, ♀ till 2006 — **87**

2003 Westhofener Rotenstein
Huxelrebe Spätlese
9%, ♀ till 2008 — **86**

2002 Westhofener Morstein
Riesling Spätlese
9.5%, ♀ till 2008 — **86**

2003 Westhofener Kirchspiel
Riesling Trockenbeerenauslese
6.5%, ♀ till 2015 — **88**

2003 Westhofener Morstein
Scheurebe Auslese
9.5%, ♀ till 2012 — **89**

2003 Westhofener Morstein
Scheurebe Trockenbeerenauslese
7%, ♀ till 2020 — **91**

2002 Westhofener Morstein
Scheurebe Trockenbeerenauslese
7%, ♀ till 2020 — **94**

WEINGUT SPIESS – RIEDERBACHERHOF

Owner: Jürgen Spiess
Manager: Jürgen and Burkhard Spiess
Winemaker: Burkhard Spiess
67595 Bechtheim, Gaustraße 2
Tel. (0 62 42) 76 33, Fax 64 12
e-mail: info@spiess-wein.de
Directions: B 9 or A 61,
Gundersheim/Westhofen exit
Sales: Spiess family
Opening hours: Mon.–Fri. 08:00 to
12:00 and 13:00 to 18:00, Sat. 08:00 to
18:00, Sun. 09:00 to 12:00 hours
History: Winemaking in family since 1509
Worth seeing: Barrique cellar with
columns, vaulted sparkling wine cellar,
tasting room panelled in cherry-wood

Vineyard area: 20 hectares
Annual production: 210,000 bottles
Top sites: Bechtheimer Hasensprung,
Heilig-Kreuz, Westhofener Kirchspiel
Soil types: Loess-clay, loess-marl
Grape varieties: 15% each of Riesling
and Spätburgunder, 13% Portugieser,
11% Dornfelder, 10% Weißburgunder,
5% Kerner, 4% each of Huxelrebe,
Silvaner and St. Laurent,
19% other varieties
Average yield: 78 hl/ha
Best vintages: 2001, 2002, 2003

Jürgen and Burkhard Spiess, 46 and 41
years young respectively, have achieved
a lot in recent years in this winery, which
previously was going nowhere. Two
years ago, the red wines produced by the
brothers were so good that we awarded
the first bunch of grapes. The standard
has been maintained in successive vintages. By now there are also larger quantities of Pinot Noir, Merlot and Cabernet available, which originally were produced only in miniscule quantities. We
have also noted that a number of the white
wines have improved. It is just a pity
that the highest classification, a Huxelrebe Trockenbeerenauslese, which is not
specificaly listed here, was disappointing.

2002 Bechtheimer Heilig-Kreuz
Weißer Burgunder Spätlese trocken
13%, ♀ till 2006   **84**

2002 Bechtheimer Rosengarten
Riesling trocken "S"
12.5%, ♀ till 2006   **85**

2003 Bechtheimer Stein
Gewürztraminer Spätlese halbtrocken
14%, ♀ till 2008   **85**

2003 Bechtheimer Hasensprung
Weißer Burgunder Auslese
10%, ♀ till 2009   **85**

2002 Bechtheimer Hasensprung
Kerner Auslese
9%, ♀ till 2008   **85**

2002 Bechtheimer Heilig-Kreuz
Riesling Spätlese
10.5%, ♀ till 2009   **87**

———— Red wines ————

2002 Westhofener Kirchspiel
Merlot trocken
15%, ♀ till 2007   **82**

2002 Bechtheimer Geyersberg
Cabernet Sauvignon trocken
14%, ♀ till 2008   **84**

2001 Westhofener Kirchspiel
Merlot trocken
15%, ♀ till 2006   **85**

2002 Bechtheimer Hasensprung
Spätburgunder Auslese trocken
14.5%, ♀ till 2009   **86**

2003 Bechtheimer Geyersberg
Cabernet Sauvignon trocken
14%, ♀ till 2009   **86**

2001 Cabernet Sauvignon trocken
15%, ♀ till 2008   **88**

The wines: **100** Perfect · **95–99** Outstanding · **90–94** Excellent · **85–89** Very good · **80–84** Good · **75–79** Average

STAATLICHE WEINBAU-DOMÄNE OPPENHEIM

Owner: State of Rheinland-Pfalz
Manager: Director Otto Schätzel
Administrator: Gunter Schenkel
Winemaker: Arndt Reichmann
55276 Oppenheim, Wormser Straße 162
Tel. (0 61 33) 93 03 05, Fax 93 03 23
e-mail: domaenenverkauf@dlr.rlp.de
Internet: www.domaene-oppenheim.de
Directions: Directly on the B 9, at town limits of Oppenheim in direction of Worms
Sales: Mrs. Preiß
Opening hours: Mon.–Thur. 09:00 to 12:00 hours and 13:00 to 16:00, Fri. to 18:00 hours, Sat. by appointment
History: Founded 1895 by Grand Duke Ludwig von Hessen as model operation
Worth seeing: Manor-house in Belle Epoque style, national heritage monument

---

Vineyard area: 22 hectares
Annual production: 140,000 bottles
Top sites: Niersteiner Oelberg, Pettenthal and Glöck (monopole), Oppenheimer Herrenberg
Soil types: Red kaolin-slate, limestone, marl, clay, loess
Grape varieties: 40% Riesling, 10% Silvaner, 9% Spätburgunder, 3% each of Weißburgunder, Grauburgunder, Chardonnay and St. Laurent, 29% other varieties
Average yield: 70 hl/ha
Best vintages: 1996, 1997, 1998
Member: VDP

The public servants may well be, as they themselves claim, "working within the framework of modern quality management standards." Our impression is that the opportunities provided by low yields and a minimal-handling approach have simply not been evident in the products. It can be conceded that the range of Rieslings tasted was quite respectable, but the other wines only serve to diminish the overall impression. In particular the red wines are nothing to crow about.

2003 Chardonnay trocken
14%, ♀ till 2005   8(

2003 Riesling Classic
12.5%, ♀ till 2006   8▮

2003 Niersteiner Oelberg
Riesling Spätlese
10.5%, ♀ till 2008   8▮

2003 Oppenheimer Herrenberg
Riesling Kabinett
11%, ♀ till 2008   8▮

2003 Riesling
10.5%, ♀ till 2008   84

2002 Oppenheimer Herrenberg
Riesling Spätlese
10%, ♀ till 2006   84

2001 Oppenheimer Herrenberg
Riesling Spätlese
9%, ♀ till 2006   85

2002 Oppenheimer Herrenberg
Riesling Auslese
8.5%, ♀ till 2007   86

2001 Niersteiner Oelberg
Riesling Spätlese
9.5%, ♀ till 2006   86

2003 Niersteiner Oelberg
Riesling Auslese
9.5%, ♀ till 2012   87

——— Red wine ———

2002 Spätburgunder trocken
14%, ♀ till 2006   80

Staatliche
Weinbaudomäne Oppenheim

2002

RIESLING

CLASSIC

RHEINHESSEN

WEINGUT STEITZ

Owner: Steitz family
Winemaker: Christian Steitz
55599 Stein-Bockenheim,
Mörsfelder Straße 3
Tel. (0 67 03) 9 30 80, Fax 93 08 90
e-mail: mail@weingut-steitz.de
Internet: www.weingut-steitz.de
Directions: A 61, Gau-Bickelheim exit,
via Wöllstein, Siefersheim and Wonsheim
Sales: Steitz family, by appointment
Guest house: In attractive garden with
swimming pool
Worth seeing: Mediterranean courtyard,
tasting room in barrel-vaulted cellar

Vineyard area: 13.5 hectares
Annual production: 100,000 bottles
Top sites: No vineyard sites stated
on labels
Soil types: Porphyry, loess-clay
Grape varieties: 30% white Pinot
varieties, 15% Spätburgunder,
12% Riesling, 10% each of Dornfel-
der, Müller-Thurgau and Portugieser,
5% Silvaner, 8% other varieties
Average yield: 80 hl/ha
Best vintages: 1999, 2000, 2003

Christian Steitz does not state vineyard
sites on his labels, and in most cases also
states no predicate classification (an exception is made for a few fruity wines).
On the other hand, he uses the designation "Classic" according to his own classification – causing some confusion with
his Riesling Auslese. This is a hospitable
family living in the "Switzerland of
Rheinhessen" close to the Nahe region,
and spares no effort in developing cus-
tomer loyalty. Groups of visitors can
participate in seminars, bicycle tours,
horse-carriage rides, enjoy gourmet events
or participate in working in the vineyard
or cellar. While quality last year was
somewhat uneven, this year we were presented with a better, more solid range of
wines, which is obviously the result of
some changes made in both the vineyard
and cellar procedures.

2003 Rivaner trocken
11%, ♀ till 2005   79

2003 Grauer Burgunder trocken
12.5%, ♀ till 2005   80

2002 Weißer Burgunder trocken
12.5%, ♀ till 2005   81

2003 Silvaner trocken "RS"
11%, ♀ till 2005   81

2003 Chardonnay trocken Classic
12.5%, ♀ till 2006   82

2003 Weißer Burgunder
trocken "S"
14.5%, ♀ till 2006   82

2003 Riesling Auslese Classic
9.5%, ♀ till 2009   83

2003 Weißer Burgunder Classic
13%, ♀ till 2006   83

2001 Riesling trocken Selection
12%, ♀ till 2006   83

2003 Riesling trocken "S"
13%, ♀ till 2008   86

2003 Riesling
11%, ♀ till 2007   82

2002 Riesling
11%, ♀ till 2006   83

——————— Red wines ———————

2002 St. Laurent trocken
12.5%, ♀ till 2006   82

2002 "No. 1"
Spätburgunder trocken
12.5%, ♀ till 2007   83

2001 Dornfelder trocken
13%, ♀ till 2006   83

2002 St. Laurent trocken Classic
12.5%, ♀ till 2006   83

The wines: **100** Perfect · **95–99** Outstanding · **90–94** Excellent · **85–89** Very good · **80–84** Good · **75–79** Average

WEINGUT STROHM

Owner: Rüdiger Strohm and
Lydia Bollig-Strohm
Manager and winemaker:
Rüdiger Strohm
67591 Offstein, Neu-Offsteiner Str. 44
Tel. (0 62 43) 90 51 17, Fax 90 51 18
e-mail: weingut-strohm@t-online.de
Internet: www.weingut-strohm.de
*Directions: A 61, Worms-Pfeddersheim
exit, B 47 in direction of Monsheim, at
Hohen-Sülzen turn left toward Offstein*
Sales: Lydia Bollig-Strohm
by appointment

Vineyard area: 15 hectares
Annual production: 35,000 bottles
Top sites: No vineyard sites stated
on labels
Soil types: Sandy clay
Grape varieties: 25% Riesling, 15%
Müller-Thurgau, 15% Dornfelder,
11% Silvaner, 10% Portugieser, 9%
Weißburgunder, 15% other varieties
Average yield: 85 hl/ha
Best vintages: 2002, 2003

Until 1998, the Strohm winery sold all its wine in bulk. Currently the share is still at around 75 percent, which puts a different perspective on the still relatively high average yields. By now, son Rüdiger, who took over not so long ago, is managing to bottle around 35,000 bottles annually. Lydia Bollig-Strohm (former Mosel and then German wine queen, who represented Germany's winemakers in 1991/2, and has been active in the business since 1998) says: "We have invested a lot of effort and enthusiasm, and by now are reasonably successful." The couple has developed a simple quality system. Predicate levels are not stated, customers can rely on a star rating system, which is defined by the expressivity of the wines. The good range presented last year, which led to the first bunch of grapes being awarded, was no flash in the pan. There is more potential for the future in this winery.

2003 Rivaner trocken *	
11.5%, ♀ till 2005	**81**
2002 Chardonnay trocken	
12%, ♀ till 2005	**83**
2003 Grauer Burgunder trocken **	
13.5%, ♀ till 2006	**84**
2003 Chardonnay trocken **	
13%, ♀ till 2006	**84**
2003 Silvaner trocken **	
13%, ♀ till 2007	**84**
2002 Riesling trocken **	
11.5%, ♀ till 2006	**84**
2003 Weißer Burgunder trocken **	
13%, ♀ till 2007	**85**
2003 "Cuvée Nobilis" trocken ***	
14%, ♀ till 2008	**86**
2003 Riesling trocken **	
12.5%, ♀ till 2007	**86**
2002 Riesling halbtrocken	
11%, ♀ till 2006	**82**
2003 Riesling halbtrocken *	
11.5%, ♀ till 2006	**83**
2003 Riesling halbtrocken **	
13.5%, ♀ till 2008	**86**
2002 Riesling ***	
8.5%, ♀ till 2008	**86**
2003 Riesling ***	
9.5%, ♀ till 2012	**89**

———— Red wines ————

2003 Dornfelder trocken *	
13.5%, ♀ till 2007	**82**
2001 Dornfelder trocken ***	
14%, ♀ till 2006	**85**

WEINGUT J. & H. A. STRUB

Owner: Walter Strub
Administrator: Georg Stiller
55283 Nierstein, Rheinstraße 42
Tel. (0 61 33) 56 49, Fax 55 01
e-mail: info@strub-nierstein.de
Internet: www.strub-nierstein.de
*Directions: From Mainz via the B 9,
from the West via A 61 and B 420;
in old town center, near marketplace*
Sales: Margit and Walter Strub
Opening hours: Mon.–Fri. 08:00 to
17:00 hours, by appointment
History: Winemaking in 11th generation
Worth seeing: Vaulted cellar and half-
timbered house from the 17th century,
generations barrel face from 1929

Vineyard area: 16.7 hectares
Annual production: 80,000 bottles
Top sites: Niersteiner Orbel,
Oelberg, Hipping and Pettenthal
Soil types: Red kaolin-slate, loess
and limestone
Grape varieties: 79% Riesling, 12%
Müller-Thurgau, 3% each of Spätbur-
gunder, Weißburgunder and
Grüner Veltliner
Average yield: 65 hl/ha
Best vintages: 2001, 2002, 2003

When it comes to Riesling, Walter Strub
relies on hand-picking, whole-bunch
pressing and temperature-controlled slow
fermentation to maintain the delicate fruit
of his young wines. 80 percent of production are either off-dry or fruity, and Strub
plans to increase the Riesling share in
years to come. This time, the range was
of good quality, as usual. The fruity
wines Strub makes are invigorating,
and show an excellent balance between
sweetness and acidity. It is a pity that we
were unable to taste more of the dry
wines, nor the Grüner Veltliner, which is
now bearing in the second year, because
the wines had not yet been bottled at the
time of going to press. Could they hold the
key to the awarding of a further bunch of
grapes?

2003 Niersteiner Paterberg
Riesling Kabinett
11%, ♀ till 2007 — 84

2003 Niersteiner Hipping
Riesling Kabinett
10.5%, ♀ till 2008 — 85

2003 Niersteiner Brückchen
Riesling Kabinett
12%, ♀ till 2008 — 85

2003 Niersteiner Paterberg
Riesling Spätlese
12%, ♀ till 2010 — 86

2002 Niersteiner Hipping
Riesling Kabinett
9.5%, ♀ till 2008 — 86

2003 Niersteiner Oelberg
Riesling Spätlese
11%, ♀ till 2010 — 87

2002 Niersteiner Oelberg
Riesling Spätlese
10%, ♀ till 2008 — 87

2001 Niersteiner Paterberg
Riesling Spätlese ***
8%, ♀ till 2007 — 87

2003 Niersteiner Paterberg
Riesling Spätlese ***
11%, ♀ till 2012 — 88

2001 Niersteiner Paterberg
Riesling Eiswein
8%, ♀ till 2010 — 89

The wines: **100** Perfect · **95–99** Outstanding · **90–94** Excellent · **85–89** Very good · **80–84** Good · **75–79** Average

655

WEINGUT VILLA SACHSEN

Owner: Michael Prinz zu Salm and partners
Manager and winemaker:
Markus Leyendecker
55411 Bingen, Mainzer Straße 184
Tel. (0 67 21) 99 05 75, Fax 1 73 86
e-mail: info@villa-sachsen.com
Internet: villa-sachsen.com
Directions: A 61, Bingen exit, in direction of car ferry, white villa on left between Bingen-Kempten and Bingen
Sales: By appointment
Restaurant: Summer terrace in July
History: Country villa in classic style built 1843; industrialist from Leipzig started winemaking in 1899
Worth seeing: Manor-house with park, cross-vaulted cellar

Vineyard area: 16.5 hectares
Annual production: 130,000 bottles
Top site: Binger Scharlachberg
Soil types: Slate, sandy clay
Grape varieties: 65% Riesling, 10% each of Weißburgunder and Grauburgunder, 6% each of Müller-Thurgau and Silvaner, 3% Spätburgunder
Average yield: 60 hl/ha
Best vintages: 1996, 1997, 1998
Member: VDP

This winery was for a long time unable to achieve its previous high standards. It has been privately owned again since 1994. Apart from the executive shareholder Michael Prinz zu Salm-Salm, the Klopfer, Diesler and Friedrichs families are involved in the business. Rolf Schregel who was the chief operating officer has left the estate. Looking at the 2003 vintage, for which Schregel was still responsible, only the wines from the renowned Scharlachberg site are in any way reminiscent of better times. However, the stage is set for an improvement: Markus Leyendecker who managed to make his mark at the Salm family estate in Wallhausen on the Nahe in just a few years, has taken over, and Felix zu Salm-Salm will join the old-established winery when he completes his studies in Geisenheim.

2003 Silvaner trocken
13%, ♀ till 2005 — **81**

2003 Riesling Spätlese trocken
13%, ♀ till 2006 — **82**

2003 Grauer Burgunder trocken
15%, ♀ till 2006 — **83**

2002 Riesling Spätlese trocken
12%, ♀ till 2005 — **83**

2001 Binger Scharlachberg
Riesling "Großes Gewächs"
12.5%, ♀ till 2006 — **86**

2003 Riesling Classic
12%, ♀ till 2005 — **80**

2003 Binger Scharlachberg
Riesling
9.5%, ♀ till 2007 — **84**

2003 Binger Scharlachberg
Riesling Auslese
9%, ♀ till 2008 — **84**

2001 Binger Scharlachberg
Riesling Spätlese
8.5%, ♀ till 2006 — **86**

VILLA SACHSEN

2002

Riesling
Auslese
Binger Scharlachberg

Weingut Villa Sachsen

WEINGUT WAGNER-STEMPEL

Owner: Wagner family
Manager: Lothar and Daniel Wagner
Winemaker: Daniel Wagner
55599 Siefersheim, Wöllsteiner Str. 10
Tel. (0 67 03) 96 03 30, Fax 96 03 31
e-mail: info@wagner-stempel.de
Internet: www.wagner-stempel.de
*Directions: A 61, Gau-Bickelheim exit,
via Wöllstein to Siefersheim*
Sales: Lore Wagner
Opening hours: Mon.–Sat. 09:00 to
12:00 hours and 13:00 to 17:00 hours
by appointment
Guest house: Above cross-vaulted cellar
Worth seeing: Picturesque courtyard
with old chestnut tree

Vineyard area: 13.5 hectares
Annual production: 80,000 bottles
Top sites: Siefersheimer
Höllberg and Heerkretz
Soil types: Porphyry and decomposed
porphyry, sandy clay, kaolin, loess
Grape varieties: 47% Riesling, 26%
white Pinot varieties, 8% Silvaner,
6% St. Laurent, 5% each of Spät-
and Frühburgunder, 3% other varieties
Average yield: 69 hl/ha
Best vintages: 2001, 2002, 2003
Member: VDP

Here, where the stony soils with their layers of porphyry are reminiscent of the neighboring Nahe region, father Lothar and son Daniel Wagner have dedicated their lives to produce quality wines. The winery complex not only gives them sufficient space to work, but also to present themselves to the public. Lothar Wagner and his wife Lore are frequently to be found in the kitchen, preparing food for visitors settled either in the beautifully restored cross-vaulted building, or outside under the open sky. Daniel is a young and ambitious winemaker, and his wines are polished, and show character. The excellent 2003 range is worth awarding the third bunch of grapes.

2003 Weißer Burgunder trocken
14%, ♀ till 2006   **86**

2003 "Vom Porphyr"
Riesling trocken
13%, ♀ till 2007   **86**

2003 Silvaner trocken "S"
14%, ♀ till 2007   **86**

2003 Chardonnay trocken "S"
14%, ♀ till 2008   **86**

2003 Siefersheimer Höllberg
Riesling trocken "Großes Gewächs"
13.5%, ♀ till 2009   **87**

2003 Siefersheimer Heerkretz
Riesling trocken "Großes Gewächs"
13.5%, ♀ till 2009   **88**

2002 Siefersheimer Höllberg
Riesling trocken "Großes Gewächs"
13%, ♀ till 2007   **88**

2002 Weißer Burgunder
trocken "S"
13.5%, ♀ till 2006   **88**

2002 Siefersheimer Heerkretz
Riesling trocken "Großes Gewächs"
13%, ♀ till 2007   **89**

2003 Siefersheimer Heerkretz
Riesling Spätlese
9%, ♀ till 2010   **89**

2003 Siefersheimer Heerkretz
Riesling Beerenauslese
8%, ♀ till 2015   **90**

2003 Siefersheimer Höllberg
Riesling Auslese
9.5%, ♀ till 2015   **91**

2003 Siefersheimer Heerkretz
Riesling Spätlese "S"
9%, ♀ till 2012   **91**

The wines: **100** Perfect · **95–99** Outstanding · **90–94** Excellent · **85–89** Very good · **80–84** Good · **75–79** Average

657

WEINGUT
ARNDT F. WERNER

Owner: Arndt and Birgit Werner
Manager and winemaker: Arndt Werner
55218 Ingelheim, Mainzer Straße 97
Tel. (0 61 32) 10 90, Fax 43 13 35
e-mail: weingut-a.werner@t-online.de
Internet: www.weingutwerner.de
Directions: A 60, Ingelheim-Ost exit, in
Ingelheim left at first traffic light, 2nd
street right, close to old town hall
Sales: Birgit Werner
Opening hours: Mon.–Fri. 09:00 to 13:30
and 14:00 to 19:00, Sat. 09:30 to 13:30
and 14:00 to 18:00 hours, by appointment
History: Founded 1819, located next to
the Imperial Palatinate of Charles the Great
Worth seeing: Large gardens in completely enclosed courtyard, tasting room
in cross-vaulted cellar

Vineyard area: 9 hectares
Annual production: 60,000 bottles
Top sites: Ingelheimer
Pares and Sonnenhang
Soil types: Loess with sand, clay
Grape varieties: 20% Spätburgunder,
15% Portugieser, 14% Silvaner,13%
Dornfelder, 8% Riesling, 7% Grau-
burgunder, 23% other varieties
Average yield: 56 hl/ha
Best vintage: 2003
Member: EcoVin, Bioland

Arndt Werner and his wife Birgit have
been running the winery in the 7th generation for the past 15 years. Even before
taking over, he had converted the vineyards to organic practices, indeed this is
one of the model estates for the Federal
Ministry of Agriculture, Nutrition and
Consumer Affairs. Almost two-thirds of
the vineyards are planted with red varieties, but the white wines too are not to be
sniffed at. For some years now the exemplary work in the vineyard has been evenly
matched by the meticulous care taken in
the cellar. The higher rating this year,
which was already on the cards last year,
is simply a logical result of these efforts.

2003 Ingelheimer Steinacker
Silvaner trocken
12.5%, ♀ till 2005   8

2003 Ingelheimer
Grauer Burgunder Spätlese trocken
13%, ♀ till 2006   8

2003 Ingelheimer
Chardonnay Spätlese trocken
13.5%, ♀ till 2007   8

2003 Ingelheimer
Weißer Burgunder Spätlese trocken
13.5%, ♀ till 2007   8

2003 Ingelheimer Steinacker
Riesling Spätlese halbtrocken
12%, ♀ till 2008   8

——— Red wines ———

2002 Ingelheimer
Cabernet Sauvignon trocken
14%, ♀ till 2006   8

2002 Spätburgunder
Selection Rheinhessen trocken
13%, ♀ till 2006   8

2003 Ingelheimer Regent trocken
13.5%, ♀ till 2007   8

2003 Ingelheimer Burgberg
Spätburgunder Selection Rheinhessen
trocken
14%, ♀ till 2008   8

2003 Frühburgunder trocken
14%, ♀ till 2008   8

WEINGUT WINTER

Owner and manager: Edmund Winter
Winemaker: Stefan Winter
67596 Dittelsheim-Hessloch,
Hauptstraße 17
Tel. (0 62 44) 74 46, Fax 5 70 46
e-mail: info@weingut-winter.de
Internet: www.weingut-winter.de
Directions: From North on A 61, Alzey
exit, in Gau-Odernheim turn right to-
ward Dittelsheim; from South on A 61,
Gundersheim exit, via Westhofen to
Hessloch and Dittelsheim
Sales: Winter family
Opening hours: Mon.–Fri. 08:00 to
19:00 hours, Sat. 09:00 to 17:00 hours,
Sun. by appointment
History: Werner Winter planted the first
Riesling and Silvaner around 1600

Vineyard area: 18 hectares
Annual production: 90,000 bottles
Top sites: Dittelsheimer
Leckerberg, Westhofener Aulerde
Soil types: Decomposed limestone,
deep kaolin-marl, loess-clay
Grape varieties: 23% Riesling, 11%
Grauburgunder, 10% Müller-Thurgau,
9% Kerner, 8% each of Dornfelder
and Portugieser, 31% other varieties
Average yield: 85hl/ha
Best vintage: 2003

Edmund and Hiltrud Winter laid a solid
foundation in this respectably sized 18-
hectares winery. Son Stefan has been involved full-time ever since he qualified as
a viticultural technician, but was able to
make his presence felt even before that –
no wonder when you have been trained
by Bassermann-Jordan and Klaus Keller.
In fact it was Klaus-Peter Keller who a
year ago suggested he should submit his
wines to the Guide. At the time we were
already very pleasantly surprised by the
high quality of the wines. In the succeeding vintage, father and son have
achieved an even better standard, being
capable of even greater things. We can
only congratulate this new talent.

2003 Bechtheimer Hasensprung
Riesling trocken "S"
13%, ♀ till 2007   83

2003 Dittelsheimer Leckerberg
Silvaner trocken "S"
14%, ♀ till 2006   85

2003 Dittelsheimer Geyersberg
Riesling trocken "S"
13.5%, ♀ till 2008   86

2003 Dittelsheimer Leckerberg
Riesling trocken "S"
13.5%, ♀ till 2008   87

2003 Silvaner Classic
12.5%, ♀ till 2005   79

2003 Riesling Classic
12.5%, ♀ till 2006   84

2003 Dittelsheimer Leckerberg
Riesling Spätlese
9%, ♀ till 2010   86

2003 Dittelsheimer Leckerberg
Huxelrebe Auslese
10%, ♀ till 2010   87

2003 Dittelsheimer Leckerberg
Riesling Auslese ***
9%, ♀ till 2012   90

2003 Dittelsheimer Leckerberg
Riesling Trockenbeerenauslese
6%, ♀ till 2020   92

The wines: **100** Perfect · **95–99** Outstanding · **90–94** Excellent · **85–89** Very good · **80–84** Good · **75–79** Average

659

WEINGUT WITTMANN

Owner: Günter and Philipp Wittmann
Winemaker: Philipp Wittmann
67593 Westhofen, Mainzer Straße 19
Tel. (0 62 44) 90 50 36, Fax 55 78
e-mail: info@wittmannweingut.com
Internet: www.wittmannweingut.com
Directions: A 61,
Gundersheim/Westhofen exit
Sales: Elisabeth Wittmann
Opening hours: Mon.–Fri. 08:00 to
12:00 hours and 13:00 to 17:00 hours
Sat. 11:00 to 15:00 hours
by appointment only
History: Ancestors first documented
1663 as hereditary leaseholders of the
Palatinate Elector's Seehof in Westhofen
Worth seeing: Large vaulted cellar,
Mediterranean-style garden

Vineyard area: 25 hectares
Annual production: 150,000 bottles
Top sites: Westhofener Morstein,
Kirchspiel and Aulerde
Soil types: Kaolin-marl, decomposed
limestone, loess, clay
Grape varieties: 47% Riesling, 30%
Pinot varieties, 10% Silvaner,
13% other varieties
Average yield: 60 hl/ha
Best vintages: 2001, 2002, 2003
Member: VDP, Naturland

If you enter the large complex on the outskirts of Westhofen you are automatically transported to the sunny South. The house is tastefully decorated, and lies in the midst of a Mediterranean-style garden. Below the broad stairs leading down into the ancient, cool vaulted cellar with its oak barrels you will find the rarities. Here you can see evidence that wine culture has a long tradition in the Wittmann family, only very few privately-owned estates have such a treasure chest of stocks from the past. The oldest bottles date back to the "Vintage of the century" 1921, and there are still stocks of the exceptional 1934 and 1937 vintages. This winery was already a tip 15 years ago, and in comparative tastings often outperformed many more famous wineries located on the Rhine front. A few years ago, Günter Wittmann remembered that he had been given responsibility early in life, and passed on responsibility for the cellar to son Philipp at an equally early stage. The son had already gained experience during his intensive training period in the Pfalz, and has enough drive and energy for two men. At the same time he shares with his father and his mother Elisabeth their enthusiasm for organic viticultural practices, which have been implemented here since 1990. All important decisions are taken by the family as a whole. His father spends most of his time tending the vineyards, which lie around Flörsheim-Dalsheim, Westhofen and Bechtheim in a fertile primordial section of the Rhine valley, with own specific mesoclimates. These advantages have been utilized for quite a few years. Since 1999 the Wittmanns have regularly presented one of the best ranges of not only Rheinhessen, but of Germany as a whole. From the dry Weißburgunder (Pinot Blanc) up to the botrytis dessert wines, it is practically impossible to discover any faults. One of the logical results was the designation "Rising star of the year 2001." As in so many other cases, the 2000 vintage showed up a few minor problems, but the 2001 vintage showed the estate back on form again. 2002 was a seamless continuation, if not even a shade better. The stressful, hot 2003 vintage was handled masterfully by the 30-year-old winemaker. In addition, the specialist for dry wines (90 percent share of the production) produced some outstanding botrytis dessert wines, and we would like to draw particular attention to the "S" Auslese wines from the top vineyard sites. The Trockenbeerenauslese wines are very good, and are again among the best produced in the region. Among organic wineries, Wittmann is clearly the undisputed number one.

2003 Westhofener
Riesling trocken "S"
13%, ♀ till 2008 **88**

2003 "Am Turm"
Riesling trocken Alte Reben
13%, ♀ till 2009   **90**

2003 Westhofener Morstein
Riesling trocken "Großes Gewächs"
13.5%, ♀ till 2010   **90**

2002 Westhofener Aulerde
Riesling trocken "Großes Gewächs"
13%, ♀ till 2007   **90**

2002 Westhofener Kirchspiel
Riesling trocken "Großes Gewächs"
13%, ♀ till 2007   **90**

2002 Weißer Burgunder
trocken "S"
13.5%, ♀ till 2007   **90**

2002 Chardonnay trocken "S"
13.5%, ♀ till 2007   **90**

2003 Weißer Burgunder
trocken "S"
14.5%, ♀ till 2008   **90**

2002 Westhofener Morstein
Riesling trocken "Großes Gewächs"
13%, ♀ till 2007   **91**

2003 Westhofener Kirchspiel
Riesling trocken "Großes Gewächs"
13.5%, ♀ till 2010   **91**

2003 Chardonnay trocken "S"
14.5%, ♀ till 2008   **91**

2001 Westhofener Aulerde
Riesling trocken "Großes Gewächs"
13%, ♀ till 2007   **92**

2001 Chardonnay trocken "S"
14%, ♀ till 2006   **92**

2001 Westhofener Morstein
Riesling trocken "Großes Gewächs"
13%, ♀ till 2007   **94**

2003 Westhofener Morstein
Riesling Spätlese
9.5%, ♀ till 2010   **89**

2003 Westhofener Aulerde
Riesling Auslese "S"
8%, ♀ till 2015   **91**

2002 Albalonga Beerenauslese
7%, ♀ till 2015   **92**

2003 Westhofener Kirchspiel
Riesling Auslese "S"
7.5%, ♀ till 2015   **92**

2003 Westhofener Morstein
Riesling Auslese "S"
8%, ♀ till 2020   **92**

2002 Westhofener Morstein
Riesling Auslese "S"
8.5%, ♀ till 2015   **92**

2003 Westhofener Aulerde
Riesling Trockenbeerenauslese
7%, ♀ till 2020   **93**

2002 Westhofener Aulerde
Riesling Trockenbeerenauslese
7%, ♀ till 2020   **93**

2001 Westhofener Morstein
Riesling Auslese "S"
8%, ♀ till 2010   **93**

2003 Westhofener Morstein
Riesling Trockenbeerenauslese
8%, ♀ till 2030   **94**

2003 Scheurebe
Trockenbeerenauslese
7.5%, ♀ till 2025   **94**

2001 Westhofener Aulerde
Riesling Trockenbeerenauslese
7.5%, ♀ till 2015   **94**

2003 Westhofener Aulerde
Riesling Trockenbeerenauslese "S"
6.5%, ♀ till 2030   **95**

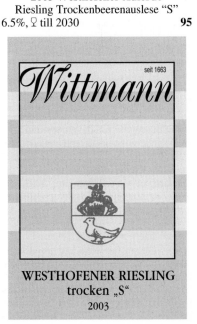

WESTHOFENER RIESLING
trocken „S"
2003

The wines: **100** Perfect · **95–99** Outstanding · **90–94** Excellent · **85–89** Very good · **80–84** Good · **75–79** Average

WEINKONTOR
DIRK WÜRTZ

Owner: Würtz family
Manager and winemaker: Dirk Würtz
55239 Gau-Odernheim, Königsmühle
Tel. (0 67 33) 94 86 01, Fax 94 86 02
e-mail: dasweinkontor@t-online.de
Directions: A 61, via Alzey interchange,
Gau-Odernheim exit, in town turn right
toward Westhofen, last street on right
Sales: Gabi Würtz, Benjamin Gillert
Opening hours: Mon.–Fri. 10:00 to
19:00 hours, Sat. 10:00 to 16:00 hours
Sun. by appointment
Worth seeing: Mill is 18th-century na-
tional heritage monument

Vineyard area: 6 hectares
Annual production: 26,000 bottles
Top site: Dienheimer Tafelstein
Soil types: Loess with limestone
Grape varieties: 80% Riesling, 10%
Spätburgunder, 5% each of Sil-
vaner and Chardonnay
Average yield: 32 hl/ha
Best vintages: 2001, 2003

Dirk Würtz (36) was at one stage the third
winemaker at the Robert Weil estate in
the Rheingau, but went off on his own
three years ago. His first vintage, in 2001,
produced two remarkably good Riesling
wines ("Würtz 1" and "Würtz 2"), but
these were followed by a weaker range in
2002. In the meantime, the boisterous,
ambitious Würtz has developed into a serious, good winemaker, and can now also
offer a wider range of wines at his picturesque Königsmühle complex on the
outskirts of Gau-Odernheim. 2003 saw
Würtz making his first fruity sweet wine,
a Spätlese made from grapes deemed not
good enough for a Trockenbeerenauslese
(which has not yet been released or tasted). Some of the wines are produced in
co-operation with Hubertus Weinmann
from the Neumer winery who implements organic practices. The wines are
produced from grapes sourced from both
estates.

2003 "Potate" Riesling trocken
12%, ♀ till 2006   **83**

2003 Silvaner trocken
12%, ♀ till 2006   **84**

2003 "Würtz 2" Riesling trocken
12.5%, ♀ till 2007   **84**

2003 "Würtz-Weinmann"
Riesling trocken
13%, ♀ till 2007   **87**

2002 Weißer Burgunder trocken
13%, ♀ till 2008   **88**

2003 Dienheimer Tafelstein
Riesling Spätlese "Würtz-Weinmann"
9%, ♀ till 2010   **88**

——— Red wine ———

2002 "Würtz-Weinmann"
Spätburgunder trocken
13%, ♀ till 2007   **85**

The estates: ❦❦❦❦❦ World's finest · ❦❦❦❦ Germany's best · ❦❦❦ Very good · ❦❦ Good · ❦ Reliable

Other recommended producers

Weingut Beiser

55578 Vendersheim, Außerhalb 1
Tel. (0 67 32) 87 32, Fax 50 61
e-mail: weingutbeiser@surfeu.de

Father Otto Beiser tends the 19 hectares of vineyard, while son Simon, qualified engineer for viticulture and enology, is responsible for the cellar. This year, only the Riesling and Gewürztraminer Spätlese wines (both 84 points) were convincing, while the reds were simply disappointing. No natural cork closures are used, only synthetic cork and screw caps.

Weingut Dautermann

55218 Ingelheim, Unterer Schenkgarten 6
Tel. (0 61 32) 12 79, Fax 43 11 91
e-mail: k.dautermann@t-online.de

Kurt Dautermann ist not yet able to implement all his ambitions in practice. There is considerable variation in the quality of the white wines, the one we liked best was the Silvaner Selection (84 points). Overall, the reds are clearly better, and here we particularly liked the 2002 vintage dry Spätburgunder (Pinot Noir) and Frühburgunder Auslese wines (both 85 points).

Weingut Werner Dettweiler

67587 Wintersheim, Karolinenhof
Tel. (0 67 33) 15 94, Fax 16 63
e-mail: weingut-dettweiler@freeenet.de

The wines are inexpensive, and the quality is very solid throughout. Werner Dettweiler is a winemaker who knows his job. There are some promising signs in the botrytis dessert department, the wines we liked best are an attractive Grauburgunder (Pinot Gris) Auslese (86 points) and a juicy Huxelrebe Auslese (85). Of the dry wines, we particularly liked the Spätburgunder (Pinot Noir) Rosé (82 points).

Weingut Frieder Dreißigacker

67595 Bechtheim, Untere Klinggasse 4-6
Tel. (0 62 42) 24 25, Fax 63 81
e-mail: info@dreissigacker-wein.de
Internet: www.dreissigacker-wein.de

Usually, Riesling is one of the strong suits of this relatively unknown winery, but in this vintage that expertise has only been realized in the attractive Trockenbeerenauslese (91 points). The balance of the range shows quite considerable variation, another wine we liked was an above-average Rieslaner Spätlese (84).

Weingut Eppelmann

55271 Stadecken-Elsheim 1, Kirchgasse 10
Tel. (0 61 36) 27 78, Fax 34 03
e-mail: info@weingut-eppelmann.de

A high tower points the way to the up-and-coming winery run by winemakers Udo and Timo Eppelmann. They make a promise in their price list ("honest and solid winemaking work"), and they keep it. The wines are grown on limestone-rich loess and heavy clay soils, and are all of decent quality. Most of the range features screw cap closures, right up to the Chardonnay Spätlese (82 points).

Weingut Kurt Erbeldinger und Sohn

67595 Bechtheim West 3, West 3
Tel. (0 62 44) 49 32, Fax 71 31
e-mail: erbeldinger-bechtheim@t-online.de
Internet: www.weingut-erbeldinger.de

In recent years, owner Stefan Erbeldinger has repeatedly produced attractive Riesling wines. In the meantime, the next generation has joined the business. The current range includes a good dry Gewürztraminer Auslese (83 points). The Riesling and Weißburgunder (Pinot Blanc) Trockenbeerenauslese wines were both not particularly convincing (both 85 points).

Weingut Gres

55437 Appenheim, Ingelheimer Straße 6
Tel. (0 67 25) 33 10, Fax 55 29
e-mail: weingut.gres@t-online.de

A year ago, Hans-Jürgen and Klaus Gres (who was inspired by visits to California and South Africa) got off to a good start. This year, the impression is rather mixed. The spectrum of the small range went from a bitter Frühburgunder Selection (75 points) via a respectable Riesling Selection (85 points) to an excellent Huxelrebe Auslese (88 points).

Rheinhessen

Weingut Hans-Ernst Gröhl

55278 Weinolsheim,
Uelversheimer Straße 4 + 6
Tel. (0 62 49) 9 39 88, Fax 9 39 98
e-mail: info@weingut-groehl.de

All of the wines produced by Eckehart Gröhl represent good value for money. The best wines in an extensive range, which has a solid homogeneous standard throughout, are the Riesling "G" as well as the Grauburgunder (Pinot Gris) "S" and a good dry Weißburgunder (Pinot Blanc, all rated 83 points).

Weingut Gysler

55232 Alzey-Weinheim,
Großer Spitzenberg 8
Tel. (0 67 31) 4 12 66, Fax 4 40 27
e-mail: alex.gysler@t-online.de

Young Alexander Gysler got off to a good start in winemaking, and has been in the category of grape-bunch-rated wineries. However, in the past two vintages he has not performed up to his abilities. This year, only a juicy Riesling Kabinett (83 points), a Huxelrebe Auslese (84) as well as a Spätburgunder Beerenauslese (85) give any indication of his potential.

Weingut Walter Hauck

55234 Bermersheim, Sonnenhof
Tel. (0 67 31) 12 72 and 31 95, Fax 4 56 52
e-mail: vinum@weingut-hauck.de

For the first time, young Heinz-Günter Hauck has presented a range of wines that is of solid quality across the board. The wines we liked best were a fruity Riesling Auslese, a dry Silvaner Auslese as well as a young Spätburgunder (Pinot Noir) – all rated 84 points. However, a little humility may be indicated. The use of the term "Unico" (referring to the world-class Spanish producer Vega Sicilia) appears somewhat optimistic.

Weingut Hemer

67550 Worms-Abenheim, Rathausstraße 1
Tel. (0 62 42) 22 22, Fax 90 46 49
e-mail: weingut.hemer@t-online.de

Last year we criticized the white wines here, and praised the reds. This year, too, we preferred the reds, headed up by a non-vintage "Anna Katharina" blend (87 points) as well as a serious Dornfelder (85). Slowly but surely, this winery is also gaining expertise with white wines, as shown by a Sauvignon Blanc as well as an elegantly dry Riesling (both 84)

Weingut Dr. Karl W. Heyden

55276 Oppenheim, Wormser Straße 95
Tel. (0 61 33) 92 63 01, Fax 92 63 02
e-mail: heydenwein@t-online.de

Dr. Karl W. Heyden and his son, a Geisenheim graduate, took over the vineyards of the Baumann family, who produced quite respectable wines here in the Eighties. Quite clearly, the strong suit here is Riesling. The wines we liked best were the dry Spätlese "Diamant" (86 points), a Beerenauslese (87) and the Trockenbeerenauslese (89 points).

Weingut Hildegardishof

55234 Bermersheim, Obergasse 5
Tel. (0 67 31) 4 29 99, Fax 4 65 18
e-mail: hildegardishof@t-online.de

Winemaker Hans Metzler, who has 16 hectares of vineyard, was formerly a top-class German bob-sled racer, and his winemaking ability is slowly also reaching higher levels. His initial appearance in the guide last year was promising, and this year he has increased the pace with good Riesling wines as well as a well-made Dornfelder (86 points), bringing him closer to being awarded his first bunch of grapes.

Weingut Hirschhof

67593 Westhofen, Seegasse 29
Tel. (0 62 44) 3 49, Fax 5 71 12
e-mail: hirschhof@t-online.de

Walter Zimmer, who practises organic wine production, showed slight signs of improved quality last year. This year he has again done a little better, which sets us thinking his first bunch of grapes might be awarded soon. We particularly liked the Riesling in liter bottles (82 points), the Sauvignon Blanc (87) as well as a remarkable Weißburgunder (Pinot Blanc) Trockenbeerenauslese (90).

Wein- und Sektgut Hofmann

55437 Appenheim, Obergasse 20
Tel. (0 67 25) 33 28, Fax 12 79
e-mail: weingut.hofmann@t-online.de

Parents Klaus and Irene as well as young Jürgen Hofmann are running this seven hectare winery. Their first appearance in the guide last year showed promising signs, and they have been able to continue in the same vein, presenting a respectable Grauburgunder (85 points), a very well-balanced Huxelrebe Beerenauslese (88) as well as the "Fusion" Riesling (86).

Wein- und Sektgut Georg Jakob Keth

67591 Offstein, Wormser Straße 35–37
Tel. (0 62 43) 75 22, Fax 77 51
e-mail: kontakt@weingut-keth.de

This winery has made a name for itself based on the red wines. However, one cannot help feeling that father Georg Jakob Keth and his son Matthias are not utilising their possibilities fully. The standard of the whites is variable (the best is a hearty Grauburgunder/Pinot Gris, 83 points). The reds are more interesting, and in some cases really good.

Weingut Klaus Knobloch

55234 Ober-Flörsheim, Saurechgässchen 7
Tel. (0 67 35) 3 44, Fax 82 44
e-mail: info@weingut-klausknobloch.de

Ralf Knobloch, a proponent of organic winemaking, names his top-wines after precious gems. However, as is the case with gems, the number of carats can be quite low, as with the Spätburgunder "Rubin." The best wines are the Riesling wines, consisting of a crisp estate wine, a fruity Auslese (both 83 points) as well as the juicy Höllenbrand No. 1 (85 points).

Weingut Krug'scher Hof

55239 Gau-Odernheim,
Am grünen Weg 15
Tel. (0 67 33) 13 37, Fax 17 00
e-mail: menger-krug@t-online.de

When he is working in the Menger-Krug sparkling wine cellar, Klaus Menger produces excellent sparkling wines, mostly sourced from the Pfalz region. This is not entirely the case when it comes to his wines. However, a dry Weißburgunder Spätlese (83 points) and an elegant Riesling Beerenauslese (89) show their potential. The range of wines of the Motzenbäcker estate in the Pfalz, which is owned by the same family, was a touch better.

Weingut Landgraf

55291 Saulheim, Außerhalb 9
Tel. (0 67 32) 51 26, Fax 6 26 46
e-mail: info@weingut-landgraf.de

Johannes Landgraf is an up-and-coming winemaker. However, of the Selection wines only the Silvaner (84 points) was in any way convincing, but provided less drinking pleasure than the regular Silvaner (85). The wines we liked best were a botrytized Riesling Auslese (87) as well as a formidable, mature barrique-aged 2001 Spätburgunder (86 points).

Weingut Klaus-Peter Leonhard

55283 Nierstein, Wörrstadter Straße 35
Tel. (0 61 33) 5 03 23, Fax 5 03 23
e-mail: klaus-peter.leonhard@epost.de

Klaus-Peter Leonhard did his practical training with Kurt Darting in Bad Dürkheim and at the Müller-Catoir estate, and works half-days at the St. Antony winery just down the road. In his own four hectares of vineyard he appears to have fared better in the 2003 vintage than he did in 2002. The wines are all made in a traditional, slightly fruity style as in the off-dry Riesling Spätlese halbtrocken (85 points) and the Scheurebe Spätlese (84).

Weingut Liebenauer Hof

67574 Ostofen,
Ludwig-Schwamb-Straße 22
Tel. (0 62 42) 23 56, Fax 36 90
e-mail: liebenauer-hof@t-online.de

The Liebenauer Hof estate was owned by the church from 1309 to 1815, at which time the May family took over control. Today Fritz and Karl May tend 12 hectares of vineyard, and their range of wines shows they have ambitions to improve. We liked the Riesling "S" (83 points), and particularly the well-balanced 2002 Spätburgunder (87 points).

Weingut G. & M. Machmer

67595 Bechtheim, Im Rosengarten
Tel. (0 62 42) 91 57 17, Fax 91 57 18
e-mail: mail@weingut-machmer.de

This family winery has 25 hectares of vineyard, and the average yield of 70 hl/ha indicates they are not just out to produce as much as possible. Father Georg is in charge of the vineyards, while son Markus works in the cellar. The range of white wines, which includes a full-bodied dry Riesling Spätlese (85 points) and a Riesling Trockenbeerenauslese (88) is already worthy of a bunch of grapes.

Weingut Mann & Fuchs

67591 Mölsheim, Hauptstraße 14
Tel. (0 62 43) 4 79, Fax 90 54 78
mann-fuchs@weingut-mann-fuchs.de

Markus Fuchs and his wife, both 27 years old, met while training to be viticultural technicians at Bad Kreuznach. His marriage brought Fuchs into contact with the winery of his in-laws. They are on the right track in terms of their white wines, the wines we liked best are the Riesling Auslese (85 points) and the Huxelrebe Beerenauslese (86), as well as the Spätburgunder Rosé Auslese (84 points).

Weingut Martinshof

55276 Dienheim, Rheinstraße 85
Tel. (0 61 33) 22 80, Fax 7 07 63
e-mail: info@wein-martinshof.de

This winery, which has 20 hectares of vineyard, has a winemaking tradition going back almost 300 years. Father Reinhard Martin and his son Achim (responsible for the cellar) have confirmed their good form with the 2003 vintage. The highlights are a Riesling Beerenauslese (86 points), a Huxelrebe Auslese (85) as well as a dry Riesling Spätlese trocken (84).

Weingut Meiser

55239 Gau-Köngernheim, Alzeyer Str. 131
Tel. (0 67 33) 5 08, Fax 83 26
e-mail: frank.meiser@weingut-meiser.de

Last year, the one-bunch status of this winery was already under threat, and this year's range of wines is yet again not de-signed to create a better impression. Some of the dry white wines have a far too high alcohol content, which comes across as a burn on the palate. As even the botrytis dessert wines are not convincing, the downgraded rating is inevitable.

Weingut J. Mett

55218 Ingelheim, Mainzer Straße 31
Tel. (0 61 32) 26 82, Fax 32 71
e-mail: info@weingut-mett.de

This winery has been family-owned since 1842. Jürgen Mett, the son of the current owner, has been responsible for the wines since 1990. Around 70 percent of production is red wine. The wines we liked best are a 2003 Spätburgunder Spätlese (86 points) as well as a 2002 dry Frühburgunder Auslese (84) and a Pinot Blanc de Noir (84). Mett has also been responsible for the vineyards of his parents-in-law Rainer and Gerti Weidenbach since early 2004.

Weingut Neef-Emmich

67593 Bermersheim, Alzeyer Straße 15
Tel. (0 62 44) 90 52 54, Fax 90 52 55
e-mail: info@neef-emmich.de

Dirk Emmich's talents are particularly evident in his Riesling wines. The wines we liked best are a dry Riesling Auslese (85 points) as well as a juicy sweet Auslese (84 points). He is even able to make quite an acceptable Beerenauslese from the Siegerrebe grape, a variety that has fallen almost totally out of favor.

Weingut Jakob Neumer

55278 Uelversheim,
Guntersblumer Straße 52–56
Tel. (0 62 49) 82 58, Fax 71 28
e-mail: kontakt@weingut-neumer.de

The owners of the winery, which was first established 300 years ago, are Lucia Weinmann, the granddaughter of the man who gave his name to the estate, and her husband Hubertus Weinmann. They work together with Dirk Würtz, a co-operation that has done their wines some good. The homogeneous range presented by this organic producer indicates that further improvements can be expected.

Weingut Nibelungenhof

67577 Alsheim, Mahlpfortstraße 27
Tel. (0 62 49) and 94 52 10, Fax 94 52 12
nibelungenhof.alsheim@t-online.de

Initially, Andrea Balz-Ries intended to become a biologist. In the end, though, she decided to take over the winery from her parents instead. This is the first time she has presented a range of wines, and the standard is promising, the highlights are a dry Riesling Spätlese as well as two fruity Spätlese wines, made from Riesling and Scheurebe (all rated 84 points).

Weingut Heinfried Peth

67593 Bermersheim, Wormser Straße 24
Tel. (0 62 44) 44 17, Fax 5 73 44
e-mail: info@wein-peth.de

The labels are still dominated by black, and are almost illegible. However the wines – allowing for some variability – made a better impression than in the previous vintage. This is particularly true of the two Rheinhessen Selection wines, a Grauburgunder (Pinot Gris) and a Riesling, both rated 85 points. An elegant dry Silvaner "A" is also good (84 points).

Weingut Wolfgang Peth

67592 Flörsheim-Dalsheim,
Alzeyer Straße 28
Tel. (0 62 43) 90 88 00, Fax 90 88 90
e-mail: wolfgang@peth.de

This winery is run by Wolfgang Peth, who has to try the best of the 20 different grape varieties grown on 15 hectares of vineyard. His wines are obviously improving a little from year to year. The range he presented was solid, with a good dry Scheurebe (83 points), and only Bacchus as well as a barrique-matured Spätburgunder are disappointing. An attractive guest house is part of the complex.

Weingut Raddeck

55283 Nierstein, Mühlgasse 33
Tel. (0 61 33) 5 81 15, Fax 5 83 31
e-mail: info@raddeckwein.de

Birgit and Hans Raddeck have gained a valuable assistant – son Stefan (25) will complete his studies at Geisenheim in

mid-2005, but was already the "best young winemaker" of the German agricultural youth association. As last year, we particularly liked the Riesling "S" (85 points) as well as a spicy Dornfelder barrique (85). In addition, there is a remarkable Huxelrebe Beerenauslese (88).

Weingut Gunther Rauh

55234 Dintesheim, Hauptstraße 2
Tel. (0 67 35) 3 29, Fax 6 37
e-mail: gunther@weingut-rauh.de

Together with his father, Gunther Rauh tends 12 hectares of vineyard, but is not yet able to show his talents in all his wines. Progress is evident in the good Spätburgunder (84 points) as well as an even better Dornfelder (86) and a Riesling Beerenauslese (87). On the other hand, the Rheinhessen Silvaner was not to our liking (81).

Sekthaus Raumland

67592 Flörsheim-Dalsheim,
Alzeyer Straße 134
Tel. (0 62 43) 90 80 70, Fax 90 80 77
e-mail: raumland@t-online.de

If we were to judge Volker Raumland's work purely based on his sparkling wines, this winery would easily be rated as worth two bunches of grapes. Some of his products, such as the Chardonnay, a Blanc de Noir, and a Rosé (all brut) are among the best one can find in Germany. In addition, the sparkling wine specialist is also pretty good at producing remarkably good red wines, such as a 2000 (87 points) and a 2003 Spätburgunder (84).

Weingut Russbach

55234 Eppelsheim, Alzeyer Straße 22
Tel. (0 67 35) 96 03 02, Fax 84 12
e-mail: info@weingut-russbach.de

In this estate dry wines make up 75 percent of production. Following on the critical comments voiced last year, some improvement is evident. Overall, the small range makes a good, serious impression. The wines we liked best were a Portugieser Rosé, a red blend matured in barrique called "Duett" (83 points) as well as the Huxelrebe Beerenauslese (84).

Weingut Scheffer

55576 Zotzenheim, Sprendlinger Straße 15
Tel. (0 67 01) 74 27, Fax 24 84
e-mail: weingutscheffer@t-online.de

This winery, located in Zotzenheim near Gau-Bickelheim, has grown to 11.5 hectares of vineyard area, and is showing some promising signs, such as a Silvaner Classic, two fruity wines made from Huxelrebe (Spätlese) and Riesling (Auslese), all of them rated at 83 points. The highlight was a Weißburgunder Spätlese (86).

Weingut Spohr

67550 Worms, Welchgasse 3
Tel. (0 62 42) 91 10 60, Fax 91 10 63
e-mail: weingut.spohr@t-online.de

In the past, this producer was noted more for the unusual bottle shapes and labels than for anything else. However, son Christian has been assisting his parents Rita and Heinz Spohr in recent years, and the current range shows definite signs of a positive trend in quality. We particularly liked the two Chardonnays (Spätlese and "S"), rated 85 and 86 points, as well as the juicy Riesling Spätlese (87).

Weingut Stallmann-Hiestand

55278 Uelversheim, Eisgasse 15
Tel. (0 62 49) 84 63, Fax 86 14
e-mail: info@hiestandwein.de

Werner Hiestand, formerly president of the Rheinhessen wine producers association, is back in action again, and is ably assisted by his son Christoph. What we would still like to see is a bit more consistency. Our favorites this year were a respectable Grauburgunder (Pinot Gris, 84 points), a full-bodied Weißburgunder "S" (86), as well as the 2002 Cabernet Dorsa "R" (86) and a surpisingly good Spätburgunder (Pinot Noir, 87 points).

Weingut P. J. Valckenberg

67547 Worms, Weckerlingplatz 1
Tel. (0 62 41) 9 11 10, Fax 91 11 61
e-mail: inland@valckenberg.com

Recently, owner Wilhelm Steifensand has given more prominence to the fact that the merchant house of Valckenberg also owns an estate with 14 hectares of vineyard. Enologist Tilman Queins focuses his attention on Riesling. The enormous potential here is indicated by two dry Spätlese wines (86 and 87 points) as well as by a fruity Spätlese (85) and an elegant Beerenauslese (88).

Weingut Villa Bäder

55599 Eckelsheim, An der Bellerkirche
Tel. (0 67 03) 15 74, Fax 41 18
e-mail: contact@villabaeder.de

This family-owned operation is located out of town, and includes a well-known vine nursery. Young Jens Bäder has studied enology, and has gained practical experience in Italy and Portugal. The wines he produces on 11 hectares of vineyard increasingly reflect his ambitions for improvement. In the small range submitted, we particularly liked the Grauburgunder (83 points) and a barrel sample of the 2002 Spätburgunder.

Weingut Wagner

55270 Essenheim, Hauptstraße 30
Tel. (0 61 36) 8 74 38, Fax 81 47 09
e-mail: info@wagner-wein.de

The young generation has been in charge here since 2002. Ulrich Wagner is responsible for quality, while his brother Dr. Andreas Wagner takes care of sales. They have presented an almost faultless range: The best wines are the dry Spätlese wines of the "Jean" range, a Riesling (85 points) and a Weißburgunder (Pinot Blanc, 84), while the highlight is an Ortega Trockenbeerenauslese (89 points).

Weingut Weedenbornhof

55234 Monzernheim, Am Römer 4–6
Tel. (0 62 44) 3 87, Fax 5 73 31
weingut-weedenbornhof@t-online.de

Owners Heidrun and Udo Mattern tend 12 hectares of vineyard. We tasted a thoroughly solid range, including a good Grauburgunder (Pinot Gris), Riesling as well as a juicy Scheurebe and a red blend named "MM" (all 83 points). An attractive and original idea: Visitors have the opportunity of lunching with the winemaking family every Thursday.

Weingut E. Weidenbach

55218 Ingelheim, Bahnhofstraße 86
Tel. (0 61 32) 21 73, Fax 4 14 18

Rainer and Gerti Weidenbach have handed over their vineyards to son-in-law Jürgen Mett (see that entry). The Weidenbachs intend marketing their wines separately for a while, but the goal is to merge the two wineries into a single unit.

Weingut Dirk Wendel

67551 Worms-Pfeddersheim,
Zellertalstraße 48
Tel. (0 62 47) 57 20 and 15 40, Fax 57 18
e-mail: weingut.wendel@t-online.de

A pleasant surprise. We tasted a good range, including elegant Gewürztraminer and Silvaner wines (each 86 points) as well as the very promising red wines of the 2003 vintage. Winemaker Dirk Wendel took over the winery with its six hectares of vineyard five years ago.

Weingut Schloss Westerhaus

55218 Ingelheim
Tel. (0 61 30) 66 74, Fax 66 08
e-mail: info@schloss-westerhaus.de

Dr. Heinz von Opel is chairman of the regional VDP. Slowly, the changes introduced by enologist Paul Shefford appear to be showing effect. The wines we liked include a dry Riesling Spätlese, a fruity Riesling Kabinett, a Spätburgunder Rosé Spätlese (all 83 points) as well as a 2002 Spätburgunder (84 points).

Other wineries tasted

- Brenner, Bechtheim
- Brühler Hof, Volxheim
- Dätwyl, Wintersheim
- Espenhof, Flonheim-Uffhofen
- Fischborn-Schenk, Biebelsheim
- Geil, Eimsheim
- Hemmes, Bingen-Kempten
- Julius, Gundheim
- Oberstleutnant Liebrecht, Bodenheim
- Rappenhof, Alsheim
- Schlossmühlenhof, Kettenheim
- Axel Schmitt, Ober-Hilbersheim
- Singer-Fischer, Groß-Winternheim
- Wernersbach, Dittelsheim-Heßloch

Recommended by our wine producers

Hotels and inns

Alzey: Am Schloss
Flörsheim-Dalsheim: Jost
Flonheim-Uffhofen: Espenhof
Jugenheim: Weedenhof
Mainz: Dorint, Favorite, Hilton, Hyatt
Mainz-Weisenau: Quartier 65
Mainz-Finthen: Atrium
Nierstein: Rheinhotel, Wein- & Parkhotel
Osthofen: Zum Schwanen
St. Johann: Golfhotel
Schwabenheim: Pfaffenhofen
Siefersheim: Wagner-Stempel
Sörgenloch: Schloss Sörgenloch
Sprendlingen: Blessing
Stadecken: Christian
Steinbockenheim: Steitz
Worms: Prinz Carl

Restaurants, wine bars, winery facilities

Alzey: Am Schloss, Wein-Zinken
Alzey-Weinheim: Poppenschenke
Bermersheim: Weingewölbe
Eckelsheim: Kulturscheune
Essenheim: Domherrenhof
Flörsheim-Dalsheim: Krause
Flonheim: Dohlmühle
Flonheim-Uffhofen: Espenhof
Hackenheim: Metzlers Weinstube
Ingelheim: Millennium
Jugenheim: Weedenhof
Mainz: Alte Patrone, Bassenheimer Hof, Brasserie im Hilton, Geberts Weinstuben, Haus des Deutschen Weines, Beichtstuhl
Mainz-Finthen: Gänsthaler, Steins Traube
Mainz-Kastel: Der Halbe Mond
Nackenheim: Altes Zollhaus, Jordan's St. Gereon
Nierstein: Alter Vater Rhein
Ober-Hilbersheim: Altes Pfarrhaus
Oppenheim: Fässje, Gutsausschank Diez
Osthofen: Hotel Zum Schwanen,
Schwabenheim: Engel, Immerheiser, Pfaffenhofen
Selzen: Kapellenhof
Sörgenloch: Schloss Sörgenloch
Wackernheim: Kirschgarten
Wahlheim: Sandmühle
Wöllstein: Wöllsteiner Weinstube
Worms-Rheindürkheim: Zum Schiffchen
Zornheim: Zornheimer Weinstube

Solid basic wines plus top quality

In the Saale-Unstrut region, too, the 2003 vintage is one of the most unusual experienced in the past 40 years. Following on a very warm spring with below-average rainfall, the vegetation remained almost five weeks ahead of normal development. Temperatures of almost 40° C were no exception in July and August, presenting a challenge to wine producers' ability. Particularly soils rich in shell limestone suffered from the lack of water. The first rains only fell early in September, at a time when many producers had already started harvesting. The overall result is a total harvest volume that is down by almost 20 percent on average, paired with very high quality and a very solid standard for everyday quaffing wines. In addition, the wines produced here in 2003 exhibit a wide range of taste and character such as has never before been achieved in this region.

Most wine producers have had to adapt their normal production philosophy to some extent in order to maintain balance in their wines, avoiding excessively high alcohol levels. In the botrytis dessert wine category, the Auslese wines show particularly high extract and full body, coupled with pleasantly refreshing acidity, while highly concentrated Beerenauslese wines round off the picture of this vintage. Although only few producers in this region are engaged in the laborious business of producing high-quality red wine, there are a number of Portugieser, Spätburgunder (Pinot Noir) and even a few Zweigelt wines worth looking for.

The Pawis winery has used this vintage to further establish its leading position in this region, and coped best with the extreme conditions of the vintage. All the wines here show real class. The Bad

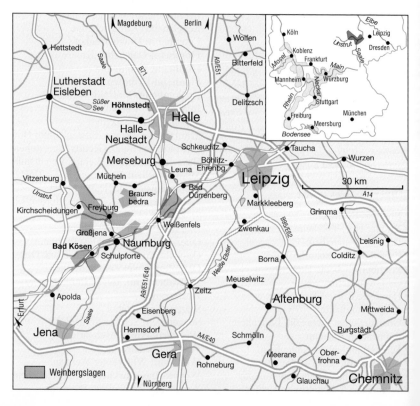

Sulza winery in Thüringen (which has been awarded a bunch of grapes for the first time) and the Herzer winery also showed a strongly positive development. Moderate improvement was seen at the Böhme and Gussek wineries, as well as at the Lützkendorf estate. Also worth a try are the wines from the wineries in the extreme north, the Kirmann winery on the outskirts of the Harz mountains, and the Dr. Manfred Lindicke winery in Werder near Potsdam. Unfortunately, the difficult vintage also showed that the larger wineries were apparently less well-equipped to handle the challenge. Renewed restructuring at the state domain Kloster Pforta also led to rather mediocre results.

The Saale-Unstrut growing region is in the federal state of Sachsen-Anhalt, stretching south of the city of Halle, and is the most northerly wine-growing region in Europe. The harsh continental climate and regular spring frosts mean the growing of vines is limited to a few selected locations. Viticulture is only possible here by planting early-ripening varieties on south-facing slopes above the rivers, to fully utilize what microclimatic benefits there are. Most of the vines are planted on shell limestone in the vallies close to the Burgendreieck (triangle of castles). Here, close to the towns of Freyburg, Naumburg and Bad Kösen, the small rivers Saale and Unstrut flow together. A further very small pocket of vines can be found some 50 kilometers to the north, on the Süßer See (Sweet Lake) near Eisleben.

Wine has been grown along the middle Saale and the lower Unstrut rivers since medieval times. The first official document in this regard records the donation of some vineyard land by Emperor Otto II. to the Memleben monastery in 998. Slightly later, the Cistercian abbey of Kloster Pforta, founded in 1137, was also dedicated to growing vines on the Saale and Unstrut. Having shrunk at one stage to a mere 75 hectares of vineyard, the area had grown again to 506 hectares. 1990 saw a new low point at only 340 hectares; in the meantime, the total vineyard area has again grown to its current level of 650 hectares. In the same time, the number of producers has climbed to more than 50. The new or re-establishment of many vineyards has given producers the opportunity to concentrate on the grape varieties preferred by consumers. The leading varieties planted now are Müller-Thurgau, which covers 23 percent of vineyard area, as well as Pinot Blanc (12 percent) and Silvaner (9 percent).

The leading producers in the Saale-Unstrut region

Weingut Lützkendorf, Bad Kösen

Weingut Pawis, Freyburg/Unstrut

Weingut Klaus Böhme, Kirchscheidungen

Winzerhof Gussek, Naumburg

Thüringer Weingut Bad Sulza

Major and minor vintages in the Saale-Unstrut region	
Vintage	Rating
2003	❦❦
2002	❦❦
2001	❦❦
2000	❦❦❦
1999	❦❦
1998	❦❦
1997	❦❦
1996	❦
1995	❦❦
1994	❦❦❦

Vintage rating:

❦❦❦❦❦ : Excellent vintage

❦❦❦❦ : Very good vintage

❦❦❦ : Good vintage

❦❦ : Average vintage

❦ : Poor vintage

WEINGUT KLAUS BÖHME

Owner: Klaus Böhme
06636 Kirchscheidungen, Lindenstr. 42
Tel. (03 44 62) 2 03 95, Fax 2 27 94
e-mail: weingut.boehme@t-online.de
Internet: www.weingut-klaus-boehme.de
*Directions: A 9 from Leipzig, Naumburg
exit, on the country road running along
the Unstrut to Kirchscheidungen*
Sales: Ina Paris, by appointment
History: Farming and winemaking in
the family for 300 years
Worth seeing: Picturesque estate complex with old cobble-stone paving

---

Vineyard area: 8 hectares
Annual production: 55,000 bottles
Top sites: Burgscheidunger
Veitsgrube, Dorndorfer Rappental
Soil types: Decomposed shell limestone
Grape varieties: 20% each of Müller-
Thurgau and Weißburgunder, 15%
Silvaner, 10% Kerner, 10% Riesling,
5% each of Traminer and Gutedel,
15% red varieties
Average yield: 66 hl/ha
Best vintages: 2000, 2001, 2003

This winery was established by one of
Böhmes ancestors in the late 19th century. At that time, the grapes were transported in baskets by ferry across the Unstrut river, then crushed and the must
transported by horse-drawn carriage to
the cellar in the lower village. All this is
history. Klaus Böhme and his wife Ina
Paris were among the first private wine
producers to invest in a modern cellar.
Ever since, the wines here have been
clean and typical of their varieties each
year. The quality of 2002 wines was not
quite as homogeneous as those of the previous vintage, but the winemaker's signature is clearly evident. In the 2003 vintage, Klaus Böhme produced a larger part
of his range with some residual sugar, in
order to maintain the balance. Although
the vineyard character of some of these
wines may be a little restrained, they are
enjoyable and pleasant to drink.

2003 Burgscheidunger Veitsgrube
Silvaner trocken
12%, ♀ till 2005   **81**

2003 Burgscheidunger Veitsgrube
Weißer Burgunder trocken
12.5%, ♀ till 2006   **83**

2002 Dorndorfer Rappental
Traminer Spätlese trocken
11%, ♀ till 2006   **84**

2003 Dorndorfer Rappental
Weißer Burgunder Spätlese trocken
13%, ♀ till 2007   **85**

2002 Dorndorfer Rappental
Riesling Spätlese halbtrocken
11%, ♀ till 2006   **84**

2003 Dorndorfer Rappental
Riesling feinherb
11.5%, ♀ till 2006   **83**

2003 Burgscheidunger Veitsgrube
Kerner Spätlese feinherb
12%, ♀ till 2006   **84**

2003 Dorndorfer Rappental
Riesling Spätlese feinherb
12%, ♀ till 2006   **84**

2003 Dorndorfer Rappental
Riesling Auslese
10.5%, ♀ till 2007   **86**

WINZERHOF GUSSEK

Owner: André Gussek
06618 Naumburg, Kösener Straße 66
Tel. (0 34 45) 7 81 03 66, Fax 7 81 03 60
e-mail: winzerhofgussek@t-online.de
Directions: A 9 from Leipzig, Naumburg exit; A 4 from Eisenach, Apolda exit
Sales: André and Alexandra Gussek by appointment
Worth seeing: Memorial for rootstock grower Dr. Carl Börner, regularly changing art exhibitions

---

Vineyard area: 5.8 hectares
Annual production: 35,000 bottles
Top sites: Naumburger Steinmeister, Kaatschener Dachsberg
Soil types: Loess, clay and decomposed shell limestone
Grape varieties: 30% Müller-Thurgau, 17% Zweigelt, 16% Riesling, 9% Silvaner, 7% each of Spätburgunder, Weißburgunder and Portugieser, 7% other varieties
Average yield: 47 hl/ha
Best vintages: 2000, 2001, 2003

André Gussek was winemaker at the Kloster Pforta state winery. In 2002 this ambitious winemaker gave up his position there to concentrate fully on his own winery, which he had already founded ten years earlier. Here he cultivates the only steep terraced vineyard in Thüringen, the Kaatschener Dachsberg, as well as part of the Steinmeister site in Naumburg. His 2001 wines were among the best produced in the Eastern states of Germany, the 2002 wines were not quite as good, which was determined by the vintage characteristic. Gussek has shown with his range of 2003 wines that his meticulous quality management in the vineyard pays off particularly in exceptional vintages. The wines are full of character. We liked best the Weißburgunder and the full-bodied Müller-Thurgau Eiswein. The red wines are well-made, but do not achieve the concentration shown by their predecessors in the 1999 and 2000 vintages.

2003 Kaatschener Dachsberg
Riesling Kabinett trocken
12.5%, ♀ till 2006 — **83**

2003 Kaatschener Dachsberg
Silvaner Spätlese trocken
13%, ♀ till 2006 — **85**

2002 Kaatschener Dachsberg
Grauer Burgunder Spätlese trocken Barrique
14%, ♀ till 2007 — **85**

2003 Kaatschener Dachsberg
Riesling Spätlese feinherb
12.5%, ♀ till 2007 — **84**

2003 Kaatschener Dachsberg
Weißer Burgunder Spätlese feinherb
13.5%, ♀ till 2006 — **86**

2003 Naumburger Steinmeister
Müller-Thurgau Eiswein
10.5%, ♀ till 2012 — **89**

——————— Red wines ———————

2003 Kaatschener Dachsberg
Spätburgunder trocken
13.5%, ♀ till 2007 — **84**

2002 Kaatschener Dachsberg
Zweigelt trocken Barrique
13.5%, ♀ till 2008 — **84**

WEINGUT LÜTZKENDORF

Owner: Uwe Lützkendorf
06628 Bad Kösen, Saalberge 31
Tel. (03 44 63) 6 10 00, Fax 6 10 01
e-mail:
weingut.luetzkendorf@t-online.de
Internet: www.weingut-luetzkendorf.de
Directions: A 9 from Leipzig,
Naumburg exit, via the B 180 and B 87
Sales: Udo Lützkendorf
Opening hours: Mon.–Sun. 10:00 to
20:00 hours by appointment
Restaurant: Open daily from 10:00 to
20:00 hours, reservations essential
Specialties: Thüringen sausage from
own butchery

Vineyard area: 9.6 hectares
Annual production: 60,000 bottles
Top sites: Karsdorfer Hohe Gräte,
Pfortenser Köppelberg
Soil types: Red marl, decomposed
shell limestone, kaolin and limestone
Grape varieties: 38% Silvaner,
13% Weißburgunder, 11% Riesling,
5% Traminer, 33% other varieties
Average yield: 40 hl/ha
Best vintages: 2001, 2002, 2003
Member: VDP

Since the reunification of Germany, Udo
Lützkendorf, who was formerly in charge
of the collective wine estate in Naumburg, and his son Uwe have expanded the
vineyard area considerably. In particular
the 1999 and 2000 vintages showed what
can be produced along the Saale and Unstrut rivers in a good vintage. The wines
they have produced since have also been
good, and are developing very well. On
occasion this has meant downgrading an
Auslese to a standard quality wine, in order to find the right balance in the Silva-
ners and Pinot Blancs. The highlights of
the 2003 vintage are the Traminers from
the exceptional Karsdorfer Hohe Gräte
site. The Weißburgunder Auslese "S" is
particularly good. The Traminer Auslese
shows more class and finesse than the "S"
version of the same varietal.

2003 Karsdorfer Hohe Gräte
Weißer Burgunder trocken
13%, ♀ till 2006   **85**

2003 Karsdorfer Hohe Gräte
Weißer Burgunder Auslese trocken
13%, ♀ till 2007   **87**

2003 Karsdorfer Hohe Gräte
Riesling trocken "S"
13%, ♀ till 2007   **87**

2003 Karsdorfer Hohe Gräte
Weißer Burgunder Auslese trocken "S"
13%, ♀ till 2008   **88**

2002 Karsdorfer Hohe Gräte
Traminer Spätlese trocken
13%, ♀ till 2007   **89**

2003 Karsdorfer Hohe Gräte
Traminer Auslese "S"
13.5%, ♀ till 2007   **86**

2003 Karsdorfer Hohe Gräte
Traminer Auslese
13.5%, ♀ till 2006   **87**

2002 Karsdorfer Hohe Gräte
Silvaner Auslese
13%, ♀ till 2007   **88**

2002 Karsdorfer Hohe Gräte
Riesling Spätlese
12%, ♀ till 2008   **88**

2002 Karsdorfer Hohe Gräte
Traminer Eiswein
7.5%, ♀ till 2015   **90**

KARSDORFER
HOHE GRÄTE
WEISSBURGUNDER
AUSLESE 2000
SAALE UNSTRUT
Qualitätswein mit Prädikat
A.P.Nr. 006-004-01 Gutsabfüllung
14,0%vol · 0,5l
WEINGUT LÜTZKENDORF · D-06628 BAD KÖSEN
SAALBERGE 31 · TELEFON (03 44 63) 610 00

WEINGUT PAWIS

Owner: Bernard and Kerstin Pawis
Manager and winemaker: Bernard Pawis
06632 Freyburg/Unstrut,
Lauchaer Straße 31c
Tel. (03 44 64) 2 83 15, Fax 6 67 27
e-mail: info@weingut-pawis.de
Internet: www.weingut-pawis.de
Directions: A 9 Berlin–Nürnberg, Weißen-
fels or Naumburg exit, direction of Freyburg
Sales: Pawis family
Opening hours: Mon.–Sat. 10:00 to
19:00 hours, Sun. 10:00 to 12:00 hours
at the cellar Lauchaer Straße 31c
Restaurant: Ehrauberge 12
Wed.–Mon. 14:00 to 24:00 hours
Specialties: Hearty home cooking
Worth seeing: Underground cellar,
tasting room with a view of Neuenburg
castle and the Edelacker vineyard

Vineyard area: 8.5 hectares
Annual production: 75,000 bottles
Top sites: Freyburger Edelacker
and Mühlberg
Soil types: Limestone, loess
Grape varieties: 30% Riesling,
12% Müller-Thurgau, 10% Silvaner,
9% each of Grau- and Weißburgun-
der, 30% red varieties
Average yield: 58 hl/ha
Best vintages: 2001, 2002, 2003
Member: VDP

Ever since Herbert and Irene Pawis established this winery in 1990, the wine
bar at the vineyard has been a popular
meeting place. The estate has been developing rapidly since son Bernard took over
the helm in 1998. We were surprised to
see the remarkable quality of the 2000
vintage, and even more so of the 2001
wines. Then in 2002, the young winemaker surpassed himself. Now, the 2003
wines reflect the meticulous work done by
Bernard Pawis in the vineyard. All his
wines have class, from the most basic quaffing wine right up to the First Growths.
This range puts Bernard Pawis right at the
top of the pack in this region.

2003 Großjenaer Blütengrund
Riesling Kabinett trocken
12.5%, ♀ till 2006 — **85**

2003 Freyburger Edelacker
Weißer Burgunder Spätlese trocken
13.5%, ♀ till 2007 — **86**

2003 Freyburger Edelacker
Grauer Burgunder Spätlese trocken
13.5%, ♀ till 2007 — **87**

2003 Freyburger Edelacker
Weißer Burgunder Spätlese trocken
"Holzfassausbau"
13.5%, ♀ till 2007 — **87**

2003 Großjenaer Blütengrund
Riesling Spätlese trocken
12.5%, ♀ till 2006 — **88**

2003 Freyburger Edelacker
Riesling Spätlese trocken
"Großes Gewächs"
13%, ♀ till 2008 — **88**

2003 Freyburger Edelacker
Weißer Burgunder Spätlese trocken
"Großes Gewächs"
13.5%, ♀ till 2008 — **88**

2003 Freyburger Edelacker
Riesling Eiswein
8%, ♀ till 2015 — **89**

The wines: **100** Perfect · **95–99** Outstanding · **90–94** Excellent · **85–89** Very good · **80–84** Good · **75–79** Average

675

THÜRINGER WEINGUT BAD SULZA

Owner: Burkhardt family, City of Bad Sulza, Andreas Clauß
Manager and winemaker: Andreas Clauß
99518 Bad Sulza, Ortsteil Sonnendorf 17
Tel. (03 64 61) 2 06 00, Fax 2 08 61
e-mail: info@thueringer-wein.de
Internet: www.thueringer-wein.de
Directions: Drive out of Bad Sulza in direction of Naumburg, turn left up to Sonnendorf after two kilometers
Sales: Clauß family
Opening hours: Mon.–Sat. 09:00 to 18:00 hours, Sun. 10:00 to 13:00 hours
Worth a visit: Wine tastings in vaulted cellar for 15 or more persons

> Vineyard area: 23 hectares
> Annual production: 120,000 bottles
> Top sites: Bad Sulzaer Sonnenberg, Auerstedter Tamsel
> Soil types: Decomposed shell limestone
> Grape varieties: 19% Müller-Thurgau, 18% Regent, 9% each of Gutedel and Kerner, 7% each of Riesling, Grauburgunder and Cabernet Dorsa, 24% other varieties
> Average yield: 35 hl/ha
> Best vintages: 2002, 2003

This winery was the first to be founded in Thüringen in 1992, and moved to a former farm complex in Sonnendorf in 1998, which gave new impetus to the development. Extensive replanting was only completed in 1999, expanding the range of varieties, which was previously primarily focused on Müller-Thurgau. Its 30 hectares of vineyard, of which 23 hectares are currently in production, make this the biggest privately-owned winery in the Saale-Unstrut region. The 2002 vintage range was again very solid, and in 2003 Andreas Clauß was able to improve even further. Virtually all wines are fermented dry. The white wines are fresh and spicy, some of them have exotic fruit aromas. Our favorites are the Traminer as well as the Kerner wines.

2003 Gutedel trocken
12%, ♀ till 2005   82

2003 Müller-Thurgau trocken
12%, ♀ till 2005   82

2003 Müller-Thurgau
Spätlese trocken
12%, ♀ till 2006   83

2003 Riesling Kabinett trocken
11.5%, ♀ till 2006   83

2003 "Justinus K."
Kerner trocken
12.5%, ♀ till 2006   84

2003 Weißer Burgunder
Spätlese trocken
13%, ♀ till 2006   84

2003 Traminer Spätlese trocken
13.5%, ♀ till 2006   84

2002 Weißer Burgunder
trocken Barrique
13%, ♀ till 2007   85

2003 Traminer Auslese trocken
13.5%, ♀ till 2007   86

2003 Kerner Spätlese
11.5%, ♀ till 2006   85

THÜRINGER WEINGUT BAD SULZA

2003
Müller-Thurgau
Spätlese trocken

"im Holzfass gereift"

SAALE-UNSTRUT

Other recommended producers

Weingut Günter Born

06179 Höhnstedt, Wanslebener Straße 3
Tel. (03 46 01) 2 29 30, Fax 2 00 39
e-mail: weingut-born@t-online.de
Internet: www.weingut-born.de

Günter Born and his father established the first privately-owned winery of the region on the slopes of the town of Höhnstedt on the Süßer See (Sweet Lake) in 1993. Wines with a certain charm are grown on seven hectares of vineyard. Maturation in stainless steel tanks ensures fresh, zesty wines with a slightly piquant finish. The 2003 vintage wines show that Günter Born is able to cope with the demands of an extreme vintage. The wines are characterized by pleasant fruit, and an easy-drinking, quaffing style. There is hope that we may yet see Günter Born's wines among the top products of the region.

Winzervereinigung Freyburg

06632 Freyburg, Querfurter Straße 10
Tel. (03 44 64) 3 06 23, Fax 3 06 30
e-mail:
info@winzervereinigung-freyburg.de
Internet:
www.winzervereinigung-freyburg.de

This co-operative is by far the largest wine producer in East Germany (365 hectares, 521 members), and has, following on considerable investment in the cellar and the introduction of a vineyard control system, improved considerably in quality. The 2003 vintage is the best ever in the 70-year history of the co-operative. In particular, the white Pinot varieties deserve a closer look.

Weingut Frölich-Hake

06618 Naumburg-Roßbach,
Am Leihdenberg 11
Tel. (0 34 45) 26 68 00, Fax 26 68 01
e-mail: weingut-froelich-hake@t-online.de
Internet: www.weingut-froelich-hake.de

The small winery run by Volker Frölich and Sandra Hake first attracted attention when it was awarded an honors award medal. Following on a decent range of wine from the 2002 vintage, we tasted 2003 wines that were fairly lean, and had some bite to them, but also showed a bit of character and finesse. A dry Silvaner Spätlese and a nicely mature 2000 Riesling Sekt (both 83 points) show the way for what is possible here. The modern label design seems a bit contrived, and a trifle garish.

Weingut Herzer

06618 Naumburg-Roßbach,
Am Leihdenberg 7
Tel. (0 34 45) 20 21 98, Fax 20 22 09
e-mail: weingutherzer@gmx.de

Last year, the winery of Stephan Herzer, which has a respectable vineyard area of 17 hectares, was a minor discovery, brought to our attention by a reader of the Wine Guide. The winery, which first produced wines from its grapes in the 2000 vintage, has been improving ever since. The most harmonious range so far has been that of the 2002 vintage, while the 2003 range was less homogeneous. The wines we liked best were a dry Kerner Spätlese (84 points) and a fruity Grauburgunder (Pinot Gris) Auslese (85). These wines make us optimistic as to the future potential of this producer.

Harzer Weingut Kirmann

06484 Westerhausen, Gartenstraße 532
Tel. (0 39 46) 70 14 66, Fax 68 98 13
e-mail: harzer-weingut@t-online.de
Internet: www.harzer-weingut.de

The Kirmann family decided in 1989 to revive winemaking in the Harz mountains. The Westerhäuser Königstein vineyard is one of the most northerly of the region. The Kirmanns made their first wine in 1995. Our attention was first drawn to the winery by the 2002 Traminer Eiswein, which is fresh, with bracing acidity. A 2001 barrique-matured Weißburgunder shows that the owners knew their business even before this. Further highlights followed in 2003: The Traminer Spätlese (83 points) as well as a Traminer Auslese (84) show that this winery is definitely headed in the right direction.

Saale-Unstrut

Landesweingut Kloster Pforta

06628 Bad Kösen, Saalhäuser
Tel. (03 44 63) 30 00, Fax 3 00 25
e-mail: lwg-kloster-pforta@t-online.de

The state winery of the state of Sachsen-Anhalt has been operating since 1993 from the old Cistercian abbey Pforta, where Fichte and Nietzsche went to school. The barrel cellars are located in the medieval vaults, hewn from shell limestone. The winery has 19 vineyards with steep south-facing slopes on the Saale river. Now the whole operation is to be sold. The wines of the 2002 vintage were not of the same quality as those of 2001. Winemaker Hubert Zöllin was replaced after only a short time by Giso Rösch, who did not cope well with the extreme conditions of the 2003 vintage. We can but hope that there will be a considerable improvement next year.

Weingut Rollsdorfer Mühle

06317 Seeburg,
Ortsteil Rollsdorf, Raststätte 1
Tel. (03 45) 29 05 60 79, Fax 29 05 60 79
e-mail:
winzer@weingut-rollsdorfer-muehle.de
Internet:
www.weingut-rollsdorfer-muehle.de

René Schwalbe took over this historic water-driven mill in 1996, and produced his first wine the following year. Since then, quality has improved continuously. Following on a reliable range in the 2000 vintage, the 2001 range presented by Schwalbe was his best yet. The 2002 vintage is not of the same high quality. In the 2003 vintage, too, we fail to see any clear direction. The wine we liked best was a dry Kerner Auslese (84 points). We look forward with interest to next year – perhaps the winery can assume the title as best producer in the Süßer See area.

Weingut Rudolf Thürkind

06632 Gröst, Neue Dorfstraße 9
Tel. (03 46 33) 2 28 78, Fax 9 07 62
e-mail: info@weingut-thuerkind.de
Internet: www.weingut-thuerkind.de

Rudolf Thürkind has a day job as winemaker for the Freyburg co-operative, and in his spare time he runs, together with his wife Birgit, his own winery with just on six hectares of vineyard. The doors of the wine bar are wide open from April to September. Visitors, enjoying a glass of wine from the Gröster Steinberg together with some fresh homemade sausage, can sit back and enjoy the quiet of the old farm complex. Following on the awarding of the First State Honor Award in 2001, you can be sure that you will not be sitting there on your own. We tasted only a few wines from the 2002 vintage, all of which left a good impression. The 2003 range, too, leaves us optimistic. The wines show some character, headed up by a Weißburgunder (Pinot Blanc) Auslese (85 points). We suggest Thürkind continues in the same vein.

Other wineries tasted

- Weingut Deckert, Freyburg
- Weingut Böhme, Gleina
- Thüringer Weingut Zahn, Großheringen
- Naumburger Wein- und Sektmanufaktur
- Dr. Manfred Lindicke, Werder/Havel

Recommended by our wine producers

Hotels and inns
Freyburg: Edelacker, Rebschule, Zur Sonnenuhr, Unstruttal
Bad Kösen: Rittergut Kreipisch, Villa Ilske, Schöne Aussicht,
Naumburg: Zum alten Krug, Zur alten Schmiede
Tröbsdorf: Zum grünen Tal

Restaurants and wine bars
Freyburg: Alte Remise – Schloss Neuenburg, Unstruttal
Bad Kösen: Saalhäuser Weinstuben
Naumburg: Weindepot bei Bock's, Domschänke, Gasthaus zum alten Krug, Ottonenkeller im Hotel Stadt Aachen

Happy times for small producers

The wine producers of Saxony, too, faced hitherto unknown challenges in the extreme weather conditions of the 2003 vintage. The exposed vineyard sites of Meißen and Radebeul suffered in the heat and drouth. Nevertheless, good quality wines were produced here, with overall an attractive level of acidity. The level of ripeness of grapes was perfect, and a few rain showers in September posed no threat to the harvest, which yielded a small crop.

The vintage can be regarded as a happy occurrence for those small wineries that had correctly anticipated the extreme conditions, and had done the preparatory work in their vineyards. It is here that the continuous improvements in quality can best be seen, producing wines that have their own character, with both power and a deep structure. The Traminer grape, in particular, produced some real highlights.

Great things have already been achieved at Schloss Proschwitz, yet these are early days, and not all the facettes possible here have yet been revealed in the wines. The basic wines, in particular, show above-average quality. Klaus Zimmerling has shown further improvements in 2003, and has presented the best vintage of his career. Martin Schwarz can without doubt be described as the great new discovery in the east, he has shown his mettle for many years as cellarmaster at Schloss Proschwitz, and has now created great excitement with his own range of wines. The ever-lively, friendly Friedrich Aust is also well on his way to joining the top producers in this region, a compliment that cannot be made this year with regard to the state winery. The potential in terms of top-class vineyards is there, but the restructuring programme still needs some time to take effect.

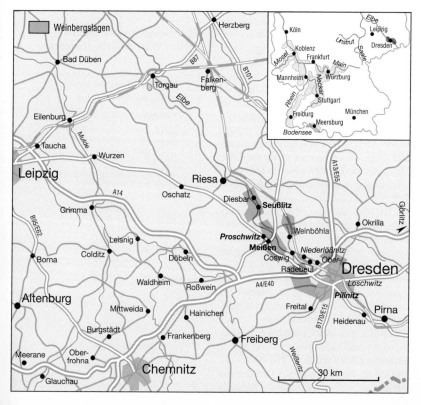

Sachsen

Sachsen (Saxony) is the most easterly wine-growing region in Germany, stretching along the steep slopes above the Elbe river. It reaches from Pirna, to the south of Dresden, to Seußlitz, to the north of Meißen. The region is characterized by a harsh continental climate with hot summers and cold winters; spring frost threatens the flowering stage, and often lead to reduced yields. Viticulture is thus restricted to a few, carefully selected locations with south-facing slopes and favorable microclimatic conditions. The soils composition, steepness of slope and direction of exposure all play a tremendously important role. Near Meißen the soils are charaterized by decomposed granite, while between Radebeul and Dresden it consists mainly of decomposed gneiss. Porphyry is found in some spots.

Records of wine-growing in Saxony dated back to medieval times. During Napoleonic times, when the vineyard area along the Elbe had grown to more than 1,500 hectares, the first viticultural school in Europe was founded in Meißen. Wars and deseases reduced the vineyard area to 70 hectares in the Seventies. Now the vineyards have grown again to 445 hectares. The wine industry in Saxony is in good shape, and is looking to a bright future, in spite of low yields and climatic risks.

Müller-Thurgau, which covers 22 percent of the vineyard area, is still the most important grape variety grown along the Elbe. However, more noble varieties are beginning to play a more important part: Riesling now accounts for 16 percent of the total. The potential stars of the future are probably the Pinot varieties, which are well suited to the conditions found here. Varieties such as Elbling and Goldriesling are also of some importance as easy-drinking quaffing wines for summer. However, we have our reservations as to whether the increasing plantings of red varieties make much sense in this climatic zone.

The wines are usually available only locally, so you will have to travel if you wish to experience these products. The villas looking out on the Elbe between Dresden and Meißen as well as the ruggedly romantic Sächsische Schweiz (Saxonian Switzerland) rock formations have their attractions for visitors. Although some wine producers from the area are starting to make headlines, most Germany still associate the region with famous author Karl May, the most famous son of the area.

The leading producers in the Sachsen region

Weingut Schloss Proschwitz, Meißen

Weingut Klaus Zimmerling, Dresden-Pillnitz

Weingut Martin Schwarz, Radebeul

Sächsisches Staatsweingut – Schloss Wackerbarth, Radebeul

Major and minor vintages in the Sachsen region

Vintage	Rating
2003	⚜⚜
2002	⚜⚜
2001	⚜⚜
2000	⚜⚜
1999	⚜⚜⚜
1998	⚜⚜⚜
1997	⚜⚜
1996	⚜
1995	⚜⚜
1994	⚜⚜⚜

Vintage rating:

⚜⚜⚜⚜⚜ : Excellent vintage

⚜⚜⚜⚜ : Very good vintage

⚜⚜⚜ : Good vintage

⚜⚜ : Average vintage

⚜ : Poor vintage

WEINGUT
SCHLOSS PROSCHWITZ

Owner: Dr. Georg Prinz zur Lippe
Marketing/sales manager: Peter Bohn
Administrator: Steffen Seiler
Winemaker: Martin Schwarz
01665 Zadel über Meißen, Dorfanger 19
Tel. (0 35 21) 7 67 60, Fax 76 76 76
e-mail: schloss-proschwitz@t-online.de
Internet: www.schloss-proschwitz.de
Directions: A 4 Dresden–Chemnitz, Wilsdruff exit, via Meißen to Zadel; A 13 Berlin–Dresden, Radeburg exit, via Meißen
Sales: Vinotheque at winery
Opening hours: Mon.–Sun. 10:00 to 18:00 hours
History: Oldest wine estate in Saxony
Worth seeing: Beautifully restored baroque château Schloss Proschwitz

---

Vineyard area: 55 hectares
Annual production: 300,000 bottles
Top sites: Schloss Proschwitz, Seußlitzer Heinrichsburg
Soil types: Granite rock with loess
Grape varieties: 20% Grauburgunder, 11% Elbling, 10% each of Weiß- and Spätburgunder, 8% each of Müller-Thurgau and Riesling, 7% Traminer, 26% other varieties
Average yield: 45 hl/ha
Best vintages: 1999, 2000, 2002
Member: VDP

After 1989, Prince zur Lippe was able to repurchase the wine estate located opposite the Burgberg hill in Meißen, as well as the old family property Schloss Proschwitz. However, the new winery is located in a quadrangular complex in Zadel, and is more than 300 years old. Following on the excellent range of wines produced in 1999, the 2000 and 2001 vintages were difficult here. The winemaker comments: "Our wines need time to develop." This is true, the Scheurebe and Pinot Gris wines are particularly enjoyable after two or three years. In future, the top quality wines are to be defined more clearly against the basic wines.

2003 Goldriesling trocken
12%, ♀ till 2006   **82**

2003 Scheurebe Spätlese trocken
13%, ♀ till 2007   **85**

2002 "Drei Musketiere"
Weißer Burgunder trocken Barrique
13%, ♀ till 2007   **87**

2002 Seußlitzer Heinrichsburg
Traminer Auslese ***
12%, ♀ till 2009   **88**

2002 Riesling Eiswein
9%, ♀ till 2016   **89**

2002 Traminer Eiswein
10%, ♀ till 2014   **90**

——————— Red wines ———————

2002 Dornfelder trocken Barrique
13.5%, ♀ till 2008   **84**

2002 "Edition Meißen"
Spätburgunder trocken Barrique
14%, ♀ till 2006   **85**

The wines: **100** Perfect · **95–99** Outstanding · **90–94** Excellent · **85–89** Very good · **80–84** Good · **75–79** Average

681

WEINGUT
MARTIN SCHWARZ

Owner: Martin Schwarz
01445 Radebeul, Weinbergstraße 34
Tel. (03 51) 8 95 60 72, Fax 8 95 60 79
e-mail: barriquewein@aol.com
Directions: A 14/A 4 from Leipzig,
Dresden-Neustadt exit; A 13 from Berlin,
Wilder Mann exit
Sales: By appointment

Vineyard area: 1.1 hectares
Annual production: 3,500 bottles
Top site: Radebeuler
Goldener Wagen
Soil types: Decomposed granite
and syenite
Grape varieties: 25% each of Trami-
ner and Müller-Thurgau, 20% Spät-
burgunder, 15% Weißburgunder,
10% Grauburgunder, 5% Portugieser
Average yield: 32 hl/ha
Best vintage: 2003

The likeable winemaker of the Schloss Proschwitz winery started last year working the steep slopes of the Radebeul vineyards, and to make wines from them. The results of his efforts are simply phenomenal, which has inspired us to award Martin Schwarz his first bunch of grapes straight away. Practically each one of his wines is the best of its type in the region, his use of oak in practically all wines is very well balanced and integrated. The two Traminer wines are complex, and virtually explode on your taste-buds. The off-dry version carries the winemaker's initial "M," whereas the fruity sweet Auslese bears the initial of his life partner Grit Geißler ("G"). The red wine, which was only bottled this fall, shows the potential of old vines. There are two disappointments: Because of the size of the operation, only small quantities of the wines are available, and some of the vineyards not owned by the estate will only be partly available as suppliers for the next vintage. We must look forward with interest and pleasurable anticipation

to the next vintage. Our congratulations on a job well done!

2003 Müller-Thurgau trocken
12%, ♀ till 2006   86
2003
Weißburgunder & Grauburgunder
trocken Barrique
13%, ♀ till 2007   88
2003 Traminer
Spätlese halbtrocken "M"
13.5%, ♀ till 2008   88
2003 Traminer Auslese "G"
11%, ♀ till 2009   90

———— Red wine ————

2003 Spätburgunder & Portugieser
trocken Barrique
14%, ♀ till 2007   87

Sachsen

SÄCHSISCHES STAATSWEINGUT – SCHLOSS WACKERBARTH

Owner: Sächsische Aufbaubank (State development bank for Saxony)
Chief executive: Sonja Schilg
Winemaker: Jürgen Aumüller
01445 Radebeul, Wackerbarthstraße 1
Tel. (03 51) 8 95 50, Fax 8 95 51 50
e-mail:
kontakt@schloss-wackerbarth.de
Internet: www.schloss-wackerbarth.de
Directions: A 14/A 4 from Leipzig, Dresden-Neustadt exit; A 13 from Berlin, Wilder Mann exit
Sales: Jörg Hahn
At market: 09:30 to 20:00 hours
Restaurant: 12:00 to 22:00 hours
History: Built 1728/29 by Count August von Wackerbarth, restored 1999 to 2002, oldest sparkling wine cellar in Saxony
Worth seeing: Baroque palace in extensive park, terraced vineyards
Guided tours: 10:00 to 19:00 Uhr, Oct.–April to 16:30 Uhr

Vineyard area: 93 hectares
Annual production: 430,000 bottles
Top sites: Radebeuler Goldener Wagen, Seußlitzer Heinrichsburg
Soil types: Decomposed stone, porphyry, clay and sand
Grape varieties: 28% Riesling, 13% Elbling, 11% Müller-Thurgau, 10% Kerner, 9% Weißburgunder, 7% Grauburgunder, 5% Traminer, 17% other varieties
Average yield: 40 hl/ha
Best vintages: 2000, 2001, 2002

The state winery of the federal state of Saxony, located at the baroque Schloss Wackerbarth palace was taken over by the state of Saxony in 1991. Now that extensive construction and restoration work has been completed, the unique ensemble of buildings shines again in all its glory. This is a unique location, and there is a point to be made in the contrast between a modern Napa Valley-style "experience"

winery and the baroque palace dating to 1727. Following on from the very good wines in the 2000 vintage, and quite decent wines in 2002, we are somewhat disappointed by the current 2003 vintage. The wines are correctly made, but we would like to see more of a difference between the basic everyday wines and the top-level specialties. The Traminer Auslese is an exciting example of what can be produced here. We are confident that Jürgen Aumüller will succeed in impressing his style on the wines increasingly in the years to come.

2003 Scheurebe trocken
12.5%, ♀ till 2006 **84**

2003 Radebeuler Lößnitz
Riesling Spätlese trocken
13.5%, ♀ till 2006 **85**

2003 Riesling halbtrocken
12.5%, ♀ till 2006 **84**

2001 Radebeuler Lößnitz
Traminer Spätlese
12%, ♀ till 2005 **85**

2003 Radebeuler Lößnitz
Traminer Spätlese
12.5%, ♀ till 2006 **85**

2003 Radebeuler Lößnitz
Traminer Auslese
13%, ♀ till 2008 **86**

2000 Radebeuler Steinrücken
Riesling Trockenbeerenauslese
10.5%, ♀ till 2012 **90**

———— Red wine ————
2002 Radebeuler Lößnitz
Spätburgunder Spätlese trocken
13.5%, ♀ till 2008 **84**

The wines: **100** Perfect · **95–99** Outstanding · **90–94** Excellent · **85–89** Very good · **80–84** Good · **75–79** Average

WEINGUT
KLAUS ZIMMERLING

Owner: Klaus Zimmerling
01326 Dresden-Pillnitz, Bergweg 27
Tel. (03 51) 2 61 87 52
Directions: Via Dresden to Pillnitz
Sales: Klaus Zimmerling
by appointment
Worth seeing: Wine cellar in
Pillnitzer Schloss

Vineyard area: 4 hectares
Annual production: 15,000 bottles
Top site: Pillnitzer Königlicher
Weinberg
Soil types: Sand and clay on
decomposed stone
Grape varieties: 22% Riesling,
18% each of Grauburgunder and Ker-
ner, 12% each of Gewürztraminer and
Müller-Thurgau, 7% Weißburgunder,
6% Traminer, 5% Bacchus
Average yield: 21 hl/ha
Best vintages: 2001, 2002, 2003

2003 Weißer Burgunder
Sächsischer Landwein trocken "R"
12.5%, ♀ till 2007   **85**

2002 Weißer Burgunder trocken
12%, ♀ till 2006   **86**

2001 Riesling trocken
12%, ♀ till 2005   **86**

2003 Riesling
Sächsischer Landwein trocken
11.5%, ♀ till 2007   **87**

2002 Grauer Burgunder
trocken "R"
13%, ♀ till 2007   **87**

2003 Riesling
Sächsischer Landwein trocken "R"
13%, ♀ till 2007   **89**

2003 Gewürztraminer
Sächsischer Landwein
14%, ♀ till 2008   **87**

2003 Grauer Burgunder
Deutscher Tafelwein
12%, ♀ till 2008   **88**

2003 Traminer Eiswein
12%, ♀ till 2012   **92**

Even in the days of the German Democratic Republic, Klaus Zimmerling
wanted to be a winemaker. He spent a
year as an apprentice in the Wachau in
Austria, and has consistently improved
his skills since then. His four hectares of
vineyard are now all in production. Nevertheless, Zimmerling who implements
organic viticultural practices, rarely ob-
tains yields of more than 20 hectoliters
per hectare. This means that the wines also strongly reflect the structure of the soil,
which incidentally is quite similar to that
in the Wachau. Following on from the
2001 wines, which were clean and not too
opulent, 2002 brought wines that were
better than ever before. The wines of the
2003 vintage are full-bodied with a good
acid structure and the potential for long
maturation. The Traminer Eiswein is one
of the best sweet wines ever produced in
the region. The labels, which show various sculptures produced by his wife, the
Polish artist Malgorzata Chodakowska,
are fast becoming collector's items.

The estates: ⚭⚭⚭⚭⚭ World's finest · ⚭⚭⚭⚭ Germany's best · ⚭⚭⚭ Very good · ⚭⚭ Good · ⚭ Reliable

Other recommended producers

Weingut Friedrich Aust
01445 Radebeul, Weinbergstraße
Tel. (03 51) 89 39 01 00, Fax 89 39 00 98
e-mail: friederick.aust@gmx.de

Friedrich Aust is a stonemason, and tends three hectares of vineyard in his spare time. The 2001 and 2002 vintages already held out some promise. The wines of the 2003 vintage are developing slowly. New vines are going into production next year, so perhaps wines will not be sold out at quite such an early stage.

Weingut Hanke
06917 Jessen, Alte Schweinitzer Straße 80
Tel. (0 35 37) 21 27 70, Fax 20 05 61
e-mail: ingo.hanke@t-online.de

This winery, with its vineyard site Jessener Gorrenberg, is the Northern star of viticulture in Saxony. Frank and Ingo Hanke showed a deft hand in their wines of the 2002 vintage. The dry 2003 Riesling Spätlese (85 points) this year showed what can be produced on the sandy soils.

Weingut Hoflössnitz
01445 Radebeul, Knollweg 37
Tel. (0 35 1) 8 30 13 22, Fax 8 30 83 56
e-mail: weingut@hofloessnitz.de

For 50 years no own wines were produced on this estate, which was founded in 1401. Today, Steffen Rößler produces organic wines that show some class. One should look out for the Weißburgunder wines sourced from the steep slopes behind the winery. Authentic vintner's fare can be enjoyed in the wine bar.

Weinstube Joachim Lehmann
01162 Seußlitz, An der Weinstraße 26
Tel. (03 42 67) 5 02 36

The fresh wines produced by Joachim Lehmann are best enjoyed in summer, on the terrace of his wine bar in Seußlitz, in the shade of the chestnut trees. The floods in the summer of 2002 caused extensive damage here. Of the 2003 vintage, we particularly liked the fruity Heinrichsburg Riesling Spätlese (84 points).

Weingut Vincenz Richter
01662 Meißen, Dresdener Straße 147
Tel. (0 35 21) 73 16 06, Fax 73 19 23
e-mail: weingut@vincenz-richter.de

Thomas Herrlich has expanded the vineyard holdings to eight hectares, has installed new technology in the cellar, and recently acquired the old city-owned winery located below the Meißner Kapitelberg site. The 2002 wines had a distinct character, while the 2003 wines are lacking the minerality usually so typical here, a result of this very hot vintage.

Weinhaus Walter Schuh – Elbtalkellerei Meißen
01640 Sörnewitz, Dresdner Straße 314
Tel. (0 35 23) 8 48 10, Fax 8 48 20

Walter Schuh has restored the Elbtal (Elbe valley) winery. The 2002 vintage saw the quality of the wines, produced from five hectares of vineyard, make a big step forward. However, the 2003 wines appear somewhat artificial, we liked best the Grauburgunder Auslese (84 points).

Other wineries tasted

- Steffen Loose, Niederau
- Winzerhaus Matyas, Coswig
- Lutz Müller, Dresden
- Klaus Seifert, Radebeul
- Sächs. Winzergenossenschaft Meißen
- Jan Ulrich, Diesbar-Seußlitz

Recommended by our wine producers

Hotels and inns

Dresden: Hilton, Bülow-Residenz, Pattis
Meißen: Burgkeller, Kämpfes Weinterrassen, Mercure
Pillnitz: Schlosshotel
Radebeul: Steigenberger Parkhotel
Zadel: Schloss Proschwitz

Restaurants and wine bars

Meißen: Bauernhäusel, Kämpfes Weinterrassen, Vincenz Richter
Radebeul: Goldener Anker, Goldener Wagen, Hoflössnitz
Seußlitz: Merkers Weinstuben Diesbar

Success has to be earned

producers in the Württem-
 by and large been quite
 past two or three years.
However, the 2003 vintage represents an interruption, a temporary pause in what has been a very positive trend in the development of this growing region. Once again it has been shown that, while most of the vineyard area in this region is planted to red varieties, the real challenge remains Riesling. In spite of all the different red varieties planted, Riesling ranks second overall in importance behind Trollinger, and is the most widely planted white grape variety (20 percent). And it is this variety that poses particular problems in an extreme vintage like 2003.

The soils are mainly rich and fertile, heavy with humus top-soil, these make the vine lazy, tapping only water and nutrient resources close to the surface in the good years experienced recently. When conditions are not so ideal, as was the case in 2003, the vines rapidly become stressed, which one can readily taste in the wines later on. Right across the region, many of the Riesling wines show powerful, dense structure – which is no surprise considering the alcohol levels – but the significant lack of fruit as well as the often-found hard phenolic finish show up the problems of this vintage.

Looking at the red wines, the vintage at first sight appears to be more successful. Generally high must weights made it unnecessary to chaptalise the must. Quite the contrary – the addition of acidity was permitted for the first time, and this was widely implemented. Interestingly this was done mainly to establish a more stable biological condition for the musts, rather than to actually improve the balance or backbone of the wines.

Despite the deep, juicy character that is increasingly becoming evident in many of the 2003 red wines, one cannot ignore the fact that a lot of the wines have simply gone overboard, and at 14.5 percent alcohol – and more – lack anything resembling balance. Thus, it is a vintage that is good in parts, perhaps it will serve to shake some winemakers wide awake, reminding them that even in this otherwise so successful region success does not simply rain down from heaven, but can require a lot of hard and dedicated work in a difficult vintage.

Happily, there are quite a few positive developments to be reported. Thus the concept of "Justinus K.," launched by the research institute at Weinsberg, has seen the development of the erstwhile stepchild grape Kerner into an interesting and moreover marketable wine.

In addition, the young generation of winemakers continues to present a highly motivated front. This can be said particularly of the winemakers united under the banner of "Junges Schwaben" (Young Swabia), who present a happy and slightly irreverent image, but also, and in particular, of Rainer Schnaitmann in Fellbach. His success story is impressive, and has few parallels in Germany: Having established his winery only in 1997, the ambitious shooting star is already firmly ensconced among the top producers of the region.

Another remarkable rise has been witnessed in Untertürkheim, a suburb of Stuttgart lying on the Neckar river. The cooperative there has progressed within a few short years from being a traditional, average winery to being today by far the best co-operative cellar in Württemberg. On the other hand, we noticed a certain degree of stagnation in the case of Gert Aldinger, who has dominated the region in recent years. His current range continues to provide some outstanding wines, but overall does not quite achieve the level seen last year. This may be a temporary lull, but the general impression is that the president of the Württemberg VDP is no longer so singularly dominant in all categories as he was in recent years. We are certainly interested to see how Aldinger will react to the veritable explosion in quality shown by his colleague and neighbour Schnaitmann.

It is also interesting to observe how the "old masters" of the region face up to the challenge of the new rising stars. One of the developments we note with pleasure is seeing how one of the quiet men of the region, the classical producer Hans Haidle from Remstal, continues to move ever closer to the top echelon of producers – a slow but constant improvement that we have been observing with approval for a number of years. Another of the old masters appears to have missed the train in keeping up with the dynamic developments in the region. Michael Graf Adelmann, for long the most prominent ambassador of Württemberg wine culture, continues to produce a few superb wines, but overall one cannot help feeling that a fresh viticultural breeze would do a lot of good at the picturesque castle of Burg Schaubeck.

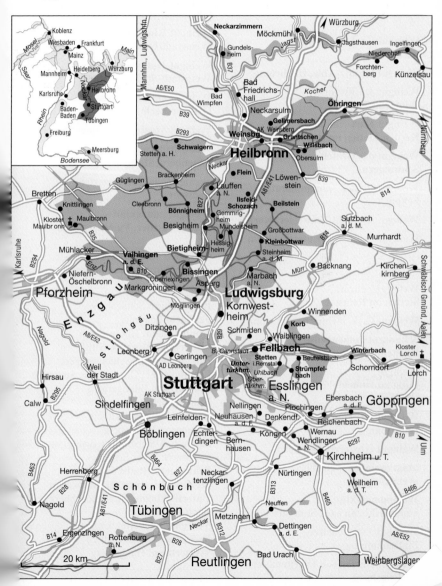

Württemberg

The leading producers in the Württemberg region

Weingut Gerhard Aldinger,
Fellbach

Weingut Ernst Dautel, Bönnigheim

Weingut Graf Adelmann,
Kleinbottwar

Weingut Drautz-Able, Heilbronn

Weingut J. Ellwanger,
Winterbach

Weingut Karl Haidle,
Kernen-Stetten im Remstal

Weingut des Grafen Neipperg,
Schwaigern

Weingut Rainer Schnaitmann,
Fellbach

Weingut Albrecht Schwegler, Korb

Weingut Wöhrwag, Untertürkheim

Weingut Beurer,
Stetten im Remstal

Weingut G. A. Heinrich, Heilbronn

Schlossgut Hohenbeilstein,
Beilstein

Weingut
Fürst zu Hohenlohe-Oehringen,
Öhringen

Weingut Kistenmacher-Hengerer,
Heilbronn

Weingut Kusterer, Esslingen

Staatsweingut Weinsberg,
Weinsberg

Weinmanufaktur
Untertürkheim e.G., Stuttgart

Weingut Wachtstetter,
Pfaffenhofen

Weingut Herzog von Württemberg,
Ludwigsburg

Weingut Amalienhof, Heilbronn

Weingut H. Bader, Kernen-Stetten

Weingärtnergenossenschaft
Grantschen,
Weinsberg-Grantschen

Weingut Erich Hirth,
Obersulm-Willsbach

Weingut Klopfer,
Weinstadt-Großheppach

Weingut Kuhnle,
Weinstadt-Strümpfelbach

Weingut Gerhard Leiss,
Gellmersbach

Weingut Medinger, Kernen-Stetten

Weingärtnergenossenschaft
Rotenberg, Stuttgart

Weingut Sankt Annagarten,
Beilstein

Weingut Sonnenhof –
Bezner-Fischer, Vaihingen-Enz

The best vineyard sites in the Württemberg region *

Besigheim: Wurmberg
Bönnigheim: Sonnenberg
Fellbach: Lämmler
Gundelsheim: Himmelreich
Heilbronn: Wartberg, Stiftsberg
Hohenbeilstein: Schloßwengert
Kleinbottwar: Oberer Berg, Süßmund
Maulbronn: Eilfingerberg
Mundelsheim: Käsberg
Neckarsulm: Scheuerberg
Neipperg: Schlossberg
Schnait: Altenberg, Burghalde
Schozach: Roter Berg
Schwaigern: Ruthe
Stetten: Pulvermächer, Brotwasser
Untertürkheim: Gips, Mönchberg, Herzogenberg
Verrenberg: Verrenberg
Weinsberg: Schemelsberg
Winterbach: Hungerberg

* Source: VDP Württemberg

WEINGUT GRAF ADELMANN

Owner: Michael Graf Adelmann
Administrator: Peter Albrecht
71711 Kleinbottwar, Burg Schaubeck
Tel. (0 71 48) 92 12 20, Fax 9 21 22 25
e-mail: weingut@graf-adelmann.com
Internet: www.graf-adelmann.com
Directions: A 81 Stuttgart–Heilbronn,
Großbottwar exit
Opening hours: Mon.–Fri. 09:00 to
12:00 hours and 14:00 to 18:00 hours
Sat. 09:00 to 13:00 hours
History: Winemaking since 1297, di-
rectly subject to the emperor until 1803
Worth seeing: Burg Schaubeck castle,
13th century, with half-timbered court-
yard, located in an old English-style park

Vineyard area: 18 hectares
Annual production: 120,000 bottles
Top sites: Kleinbottwarer
Süßmund and Oberer Berg
Soil types: Red marl, shell limestone
Grape varieties: 26% Riesling, 15%
Lemberger, 13% Trollinger, 9% Grau-
burgunder, 7% each of Samtrot,
Clevner and Spätburgunder, 4%
Muskattrollinger, 12% other varieties
Average yield: 65 hl/ha
Best vintages: 1997, 1999, 2001
Member: VDP, Deutsches
Barrique Forum, Hades

Time seems to be standing still when you
look at the idyllic gardens of the Burg
Schaubeck castle. And we cannot help
thinking that the same applies to the cellars of this wine estate. In fact, the classics such as Muskattrollinger, Lemberger, Muskateller and Riesling from the
"Brüssele'r Spitze" are good wines, but
just "good" should not really be good
enough for this centuries-old homestead
of Württemberg wine. We can recommend the 2002 Samtrot "Spitze," and the
2001 blend "Vignette" is outstanding.
Perhaps the planned investment in cellar
technology will bring some fresh drive
into this winery.

2003 Kleinbottwarer Oberer Berg
Muskateller Spätlese trocken
13%, ♀ till 2006   85

2003 Kleinbottwarer Süßmund
Riesling Spätlese trocken
"Brüssele'r Spitze"
12.5%, ♀ till 2007   86

2001 Grauer Burgunder
trocken "Hades"
12.5%, ♀ till 2007   87

2001 Kleinbottwarer Süßmund
Riesling Spätlese
13%, ♀ till 2006   86

——— Red wines ———

2002 Lemberger trocken
13%, ♀ till 2006   86

2002 "Der Loewe von Schaubeck"
Lemberger trocken
12.5%, ♀ till 2007   86

2002 Kleinbottwarer
Samtrot trocken "Brüssele'r Spitze"
13%, ♀ till 2008   87

2000 "Vignette" trocken "Hades"
13%, ♀ till 2008   88

2001 "Vignette" trocken "Hades"
13%, ♀ till 2010   91

The wines: **100** Perfect · **95–99** Outstanding · **90–94** Excellent · **85–89** Very good · **80–84** Good · **75–79** Average

689

WEINGUT
GERHARD ALDINGER

Owner: Gert Aldinger
Manager: Gert and Hansjörg Aldinger
Viticulture: Rainer Bubeck
Winemaker: Marc Jäger
70734 Fellbach, Schmerstraße 25
Tel. (07 11) 58 14 17, Fax 58 14 88
e-mail: Gert.Aldinger@t-online.de
Internet: www.weingut-aldinger.de
Directions: From Stuttgart via the B 14,
Fellbach-Süd exit, follow signs
Sales: Sonja Aldinger
Opening hours: Mon.–Fri. 09:00 to
12:00 hours and 15:00 to 18:00 hours
Sat. 09:00 to 12:00 hours
and by appointment
History: Winemaking in the family
since 1492

Vineyard area: 20 hectares
Annual production: 160,000 bottles
Top sites: Untertürkheimer Gips,
Fellbacher Lämmler, Stettener
Pulvermächer and Mönchberg
Soil types: Gypsum-red marl, red marl,
decomposed sandstone
Grape varieties: 30% Riesling, 30%
Trollinger, 15% Spätburgunder,
5% each of Lemberger, Cabernet
Sauvignon, Merlot, Sauvignon
Blanc and Weißburgunder
Average yield: 70 hl/ha
Best vintages: 1999, 2001, 2002
Member: VDP

Last year, we used the development of the Gert Aldinger family winery in Fellbach as an example of the positive and pleasing developments in Württemberg as a whole. It is thus only right that we should do the same to show up the problems experienced in the region with the most recent vintage. Just as most of his colleagues in the region, the "Dominator" of recent years has not managed the challenges of the 2002 vintage with regard to red wines (rain just before the harvest) and of the 2003 vintage with regard to white wines (heat stress). Certainly, Aldinger has again produced a large number of outstanding wines, but looking at the range overall we detect a certain stagnation, and possibly even a step backward, compared to the previous vintage. However, we are confident in hoping that this is only a temporary interlude, and that the ambitious regional VDP president will soon be back at work defending his regional dominance – which was evident last year – again. The fascinating development of this estate is an important model for the whole region. It is only 15 years ago that most producers were content to leave the production of top wines to the established estates, often run by the former nobility, in the lowlands, and to concentrate on basic, well-made quaffing wines in liter bottles (60 percent of total production at the time) to quench the thirst in the many wine bars of the Remstal valley and in the nearby state capital. However, Aldinger chose to deviate from this path, and the path he took has taken him, with a lot of ambition and hard work, right to the top of the pile in Württemberg. An important factor in this was almost certainly also the (always fair) competition and exchange of ideas with his friend and vineyard neighbor Hans-Peter Wöhrwag. However, it would be an incomplete picture if one were to hang the entire success story on the person of Gert Aldinger. He himself always stresses that the strength of his business lies in the structures of his team, which has been developed over many years, a team in which the owner and his family as well as the leading employees are always pulling in the same direction. It was only because of these strong, organic structures that setbacks such as the devastating hails of June 2000 could be mastered. And the indication is there that this structure will be maintained in future, as evidenced by the fact that son Hansjörg has joined his father's business, having first gained experience as second winemaker at the W. Bründlmayer top-estate in Austria.

The estates: ❦❦❦❦❦ World's finest · ❦❦❦❦ Germany's best · ❦❦❦ Very good · ❦❦ Good · ❦ Reliable

2002 Untertürkheimer Gips
Weißer Burgunder trocken **
13.5%, ♀ till 2005   **86**

2003 "Cuvée S"
Sauvignon Blanc trocken
12%, ♀ till 2006   **87**

2003 Fellbacher Lämmler
Riesling trocken "Großes Gewächs"
13%, ♀ till 2008   **87**

2001 Cuvée "S"
Sauvignon Blanc trocken
12.5%, ♀ till 2006   **88**

2002 Cuvée "S"
Sauvignon Blanc trocken
12.5%, ♀ till 2006   **88**

2001 Fellbacher Lämmler
Riesling Spätlese trocken
"Großes Gewächs"
13%, ♀ till 2006   **89**

2002 Fellbacher Lämmler
Riesling Spätlese trocken
"Großes Gewächs"
13%, ♀ till 2007   **90**

2003 Stettener Pulvermächer
Riesling **
12.5%, ♀ till 2006   **87**

2003 Stettener Pulvermächer
Gewürztraminer Trockenbeerenauslese
7%, ♀ till 2011   **88**

2001 Fellbacher Lämmler
Riesling Auslese
10%, ♀ till 2007   **89**

2002 Fellbacher Lämmler
Riesling Auslese
8%, ♀ till 2010   **91**

2002 Riesling Eiswein
8%, ♀ till 2012   **92**

2001 Riesling Eiswein Nr. 27
7.5%, ♀ till 2013   **94**

——— Red wines ———

2002 Stettener Mönchberg
Lemberger trocken **
13%, ♀ till 2006   **86**

2001 Fellbacher Lämmler
Spätburgunder trocken **
13.5%, ♀ till 2006   **87**

2003 Untertürkheimer Gips
Samtrot trocken **
14%, ♀ till 2008   **87**

2000 Untertürkheimer Gips
Spätburgunder trocken ***
13.5%, ♀ till 2006   **88**

2002 "Cuvée C" trocken
13.5%, ♀ till 2009   **88**

2002 "Cuvée M" trocken
13.5%, ♀ till 2010   **88**

2002 Untertürkheimer Gips
Spätburgunder trocken ***
13.5%, ♀ till 2009   **88**

2002 Fellbacher Lämmler
Lemberger trocken ***
13.5%, ♀ till 2009   **88**

2001 Cuvée "C" trocken
13.5%, ♀ till 2010   **89**

2001 Cuvée "M" trocken
13.5%, ♀ till 2009   **89**

2001 Untertürkheimer Gips
Spätburgunder trocken ***
13.5%, ♀ till 2009   **89**

2001 Fellbacher Lämmler
Lemberger trocken ***
13.5%, ♀ till 2009   **90**

WÜRTTEMBERG

CUVÉE S

2003 SAUVIGNON BLANC

TROCKEN

GA

13%VOL   GUTSABFÜLLUNG WEINGUT ALDINGER   0,75L

QUALITÄTSWEIN • D-70734 FELLBACH • A.P.NR. 403 030 04

The wines: **100** Perfect · **95–99** Outstanding · **90–94** Excellent · **85–89** Very good · **80–84** Good · **75–79** Average

WEINGUT AMALIENHOF

Owner: Martin Strecker and
Regine Böhringer
Winemaker: Gerhard and
Martin Strecker
74074 Heilbronn, Lukas-Cranach-Weg 5
Tel. (0 71 31) 25 17 35, Fax 57 20 10
e-mail: Amalienhof@t-online.de
Internet: www.weingut-amalienhof.de
*Directions: On the B 27, at city exit of
Heilbronn, in direction of Sontheim*
Sales: Strecker family, Stephan Meier
Opening hours: Mon.–Sat. 08:00 to
12:00 and 13:00 to 18:00, Tue. 13:00 to
20:00, Sat. 13:00 to 16:00 hours
Sun. by appointment
Worth seeing: Beilsteiner Steinberg estate
Worth a visit: Wine festival on 4th weekend in September, with more than
100 wines available for tasting, thematic
wine tastings Tuesdays from 19:00 hours

Vineyard area: 29 hectares
Annual production: 250,000 bottles
Top sites: Beilsteiner Steinberg
(monopole), Heilbronner Stiftsberg
Soil types: Multi-colored marl,
gypsum-red marl
Grape varieties: 31% Riesling,
22% Trollinger, 14% Samtrot,
10% Lemberger, 4% Wildmuskat,
19% other varieties
Average yield: 70 hl/ha
Best vintages: 1997, 2001, 2002

Gerhard Strecker re-established the monopole vineyard Beilsteiner Steinberg in
the Seventies. The winery itself is located
in Heilbronn. A specialty of the estate is
the Wildmuskat grape, which is made in
dry as well as in Auslese style, and most
recently also as a sparkling wine, and represents a real asset to the usual range of
aromas. A similar comment can be made
about the "Bariton," a new variety developed here on this estate. However, the
main focus is on Riesling, which in the
2003 vintage produced correctly made
wines, but with very restrained fruit.

2003 Riesling Classic
12%, ♀ till 2005   **82**

2002 Beilsteiner Steinberg
Riesling Kabinett trocken
11%, ♀ till 2006   **83**

2003 Beilsteiner Steinberg
Riesling Spätlese trocken
12.5%, ♀ till 2006   **83**

———— Red wines ————

2002 Beilsteiner Steinberg
Dornfelder trocken "Holzfassausbau"
12.5%, ♀ till 2006   **83**

2002 Beilsteiner Steinberg
Samtrot Spätlese trocken
12.5%, ♀ till 2006   **84**

2002 Beilsteiner Steinberg
Lemberger Spätlese trocken
12%, ♀ till 2006   **84**

2003 Beilsteiner Steinberg
Wildmuskat trocken
13%, ♀ till 2006   **85**

2000 Beilsteiner Steinberg
Wildmuskat Auslese trocken Barrique
13%, ♀ till 2006   **85**

2002 Wildmuskat Spätlese
12%, ♀ till 2006   **84**

WEINGUT H. BADER

Owner and manager: Hans Bader
71394 Kernen-Stetten,
Albert-Moser-Straße 100
Tel. (0 71 51) 4 28 28, Fax 4 54 97
e-mail: info@weingut-bader.de
Internet: www.weingut-bader.de
Directions: B 10/B 14 via Fellbach or
Waiblingen, to Kernen-Rommelshau-
sen, then Kernen-Stetten, follow signs
Sales: Iris Bader
Opening hours: Mon.–Fri. 16:00 to
18:00 hours, closed Wed.
Sat. 09:00 to 13:00 hours
and by appointment

Vineyard area: 5 hectares
Annual production: 35,000 bottles
Top sites: Stettener Pulver-
mächer and Häder
Soil types: Decomposed sandstone,
colored marl, gypsum-red marl
Grape varieties: 44% Riesling, 12%
each of Trollinger and Spätburgun-
der, 6% Dornfelder, 5% each of
Weißburgunder and Heroldrebe, 4%
each of Lemberger and Portugieser,
8% other varieties
Average yield: 63 hl/ha
Best vintages: 2001, 2002, 2003

Reliability and continuity are the catch-
phrases for this family winery in Stetten.
The highlights here are always the steely-
racy dry Riesling wines from the Pulvermächer site, which this year were presented in their usual high quality – which
sets them apart from most of their competitors, as generally this variety in 2003
was a little weaker than usual. A highlight
is the very good Riesling Selection. A
new addition is the wine named "Vis à
Vis," a blend of Riesling and Sauvignon
Blanc: From our point of view, a better
option than the straight varietal Sauvignon. In the red wines, too, we detect signs
of improvement: They may not be particularly spectacular, but they do provide
good value for money.

2003 Riesling trocken
13%, ♀ till 2005 — **83**

2002 Stettener Pulvermächer
Riesling Spätlese trocken
12.5%, ♀ till 2005 — **84**

2003 Weißer Burgunder trocken
13.5%, ♀ till 2006 — **84**

2003 "Vis à Vis" trocken
13.5%, ♀ till 2005 — **84**

2003 Riesling trocken Selection
13%, ♀ till 2006 — **85**

2003 Stettener Pulvermächer
Riesling Kabinett
12%, ♀ till 2006 — **83**

———— Red wines ————

2002 Dornfelder trocken
12.5%, ♀ till 2006 — **82**

2001 Lemberger trocken
13%, ♀ till 2005 — **83**

2000 Cuvée "Iris" trocken
13%, ♀ till 2005 — **84**

2002 Spätburgunder trocken
13%, ♀ till 2006 — **84**

2002 Lemberger trocken
13%, ♀ till 2006 — **84**

2001 Spätburgunder
trocken Barrique
13.5%, ♀ till 2005 — **84**

WEINGUT H. BADER

VISAVIS

2003
WEISSWEIN TROCKEN
WÜRTTEMBERG

13,5 % VOL 0,75 L

QUALITÄTSWEIN · A.P.NR. 59900304
GUTSABFÜLLUNG · WWW.WEINGUT-BADER.DE
WEINGUT H. BADER · D-71394 KERNEN-STETTEN

The wines: **100** Perfect · **95–99** Outstanding · **90–94** Excellent · **85–89** Very good · **80–84** Good · **75–79** Average

WEINGUT BEURER

Owner: Siegfried and Jochen Beurer
Winemaker: Jochen Beurer
71394 Stetten im Remstal,
Lange Stráße 67
Tel. (0 71 51) 4 21 90, Fax 4 18 78
e-mail: info@weingut-beurer.de
Internet: www.weingut-beurer.de
Directions: From Stuttgart via B 14 into
the Remstal valley, Kernen exit, direc-
tion of Stetten, main road direction of
Esslingen, Lange Straße/Weinstraße
Sales: Beurer family
Opening hours: Fri. 14:00 to 19:00
hours, Sat. 09:00 to 14:00 hours
and by appointment

Vineyard area: 6 hectares
Annual production: 50,000 bottles
Top sites: Stettener
Pulvermächer and Häder
Soil types: Red marl
Grape varieties: 50% Riesling,
25% other white varieties,
25% red varieties
Average yield: 60 hl/ha
Best vintages: 2000, 2001, 2002
Member: Junges Schwaben

We admire the courage that Jochen Beurer shows, allowing all his wines to ferment spontaneously, using only natural yeasts. In this he has managed to achieve an unmistakable style of his own. This is particularly evident in the Riesling wines, which in their style are unique in Württemberg, their yeasty mineral character presents quite a challenge to the inexperienced palate, particularly when they are young. Beurer has also not been able to quite make up for the lack of fruit that is chracteristic of this variety in Württemberg in the 2003 vintage, but the marked personality of the wines provides at least some compensation. Only in the botrytis dessert wines we have to say that Beurer could have done better. The elegant Riesling Spätlese from the previous vintage shows that his wines are quite capable of maturing.

2003 Sauvignon Blanc trocken	
14.5%, ♀ till 2006	86

2002 Stettener Pulvermächer
Riesling Spätlese trocken
12.5%, ♀ till 2007   87

2002 Grauer Burgunder trocken
13%, ♀ till 2006   87

2003 Riesling Auslese
11%, ♀ till 2009   88

2003 Riesling Eiswein
8.5%, ♀ till 2010   88

2003 Riesling Beerenauslese
6.5%, ♀ till 2010   88

2002 Riesling Eiswein
9.5%, ♀ till 2011   90

———— Red wines ————

2002 "Secundus" trocken
14.5%, ♀ till 2006   86

2002 Spätburgunder trocken
13%, ♀ till 2006   86

Vineyards as far as the eye can see – here in Württemberg, close to Schwaigern.
Photo: DWI/Dieth

WEINGUT ERNST DAUTEL

Owner: Ernst Dautel
74357 Bönnigheim, Lauerweg 55
Tel. (0 71 43) 87 03 26, Fax 87 03 27
e-mail: weingut.dautel@t-online.de
Internet: www.weingut-dautel.de
Directions: A 81 Heilbronn–Stuttgart,
Mundelsheim exit, via Kirchheim
to Bönnigheim
Sales: By appointment
History: Winemaking in the family
since 1510

Vineyard area: 10.5 hectares
Annual production: 75,000 bottles
Top sites: Besigheimer Wurmberg,
Bönnigheimer Sonnenberg
Soil types: Shell limestone, red marl
Grape varieties: 23% Riesling, 18%
Lemberger, 12% each of Trollinger
and Spätburgunder, 8% each of
Weißburgunder and Schwarz-
riesling, 5% Müller-Thurgau, 4%
each of Chardonnay and Kerner,
6% other varieties
Average yield: 72 hl/ha
Best vintages: 1999, 2001, 2002
Member: VDP,
Deutsches Barrique Forum

The 2003 vintage was something of an anniversary for Ernst Dautel. It was the 25th vintage this exceptional winemaker has brought into the cellar since he decided to go into business on his own. But the vintage had no gifts to bear for Dautel. When tasting the wines it becomes evident how hard he has had to work to maintain the high standard of the previous vintage, or at least not to remain much below that level. We can only express our respect for this effort, but of course we must also hope that he will return next year to the form that one would expect of a top producer rated four bunches of grapes. Considering that Ernst Dautel today stands at the pinnacle of winemaking in Württemberg, on a level shared only by his colleague Aldinger, then this is surprising, considering the humble beginnings of this estate. After leaving the co-operative, the 1978 vintage was the first to be brought in as an independent winemaker, sourced from two hectares of vineyards that at the time belonged to his parents, and was bottled at their facility in Meimsheim. But Dautel's ambitions grew rapidly, once he had completed building a new facility at Bönnigheim (from the 1984 vintage on), the foundation was laid for both a quantitative, but primarily a qualitative growth. It did not take long for the busy winemaker to establish himself among the avantgarde of the region. In the late Eighties, he campaigned for permission to be allowed to plant Chardonnay on an experimental basis. That, and the creation of this "Kreation" blend show his enological foresight, a characteristic not widely spread at the time. The fruits of these efforts became evident at the latest with the 1993 vintage. At the time, this guide rated his Spätburgunder (Pinot Noir) "S" as the best red wine in Germany. Ever since, Dautel has always successfully defended his position near the top of the regional rankings, and has always been considered a safe, reliable option in Württemberg. And if one sees the energy with which he is pursuing additional plans – the new barrique cellar is but one example – then we live in hope that this will be the case again in future. Last year, when we awarded Ernst Dautel and his extremely supportive wife Hannelore the fourth bunch of grapes this came in recognition of their efforts over the past quarter century, and we look forward with pleasant anticipation to see Dautel accepting this as an inspiration for even better performances in future.

2003 Besigheimer Wurmberg
Riesling trocken ***
12.5%, ♀ till 2007   **85**

2002 Besigheimer Wurmberg
Riesling trocken ***
12.5%, ♀ till 2006   **86**

2002 "Kreation" trocken *
12.5%, ♀ till 2006   **86**

The estates: ✦✦✦✦✦ World's finest · ✦✦✦✦ Germany's best · ✦✦✦ Very good · ✦✦ Good · ✦ Reliable

2003 Bönnigheimer Sonnenberg
Weißer Burgunder trocken ✳✳✳
13%, ♀ till 2006   **86**

2003 "Kreation" trocken ✳✳✳
12.5%, ♀ till 2006   **86**

2003 Bönnigheimer Sonnenberg
Riesling trocken "Großes Gewächs"
12.5%, ♀ till 2008   **86**

2001 Bönnigheimer Sonnenberg
Riesling trocken ✳✳✳
13%, ♀ till 2006   **87**

2002 Bönnigheimer Sonnenberg
Weißer Burgunder trocken ✳✳✳
12.5%, ♀ till 2005   **87**

2003 Weißer Burgunder
trocken ✳✳✳✳
13.5%, ♀ till 2008   **87**

2002 Chardonnay trocken ✳✳✳✳
13%, ♀ till 2007   **88**

2002 Bönnigheimer Sonnenberg
Riesling Spätlese trocken
"Großes Gewächs"
12.5%, ♀ till 2007   **88**

2001 Chardonnay trocken ✳✳✳✳
13%, ♀ till 2007   **89**

2003 Chardonnay trocken ✳✳✳✳
13.5%, ♀ till 2008   **89**

2001 Bönnigheimer Sonnenberg
Riesling Auslese
10%, ♀ till 2007   **88**

2002 Bönnigheimer Sonnenberg
Riesling Auslese
10%, ♀ till 2008   **88**

2003 Bönnigheimer Sonnenberg
Riesling Beerenauslese
8.5%, ♀ till 2009   **90**

2002 Bönnigheimer Sonnenberg
Weißer Burgunder Beerenauslese
10%, ♀ till 2009   **91**

2002 Bönnigheimer Sonnenberg
Riesling Eiswein
10.5%, ♀ till 2011   **91**

2003 Bönnigheimer Sonnenberg
Riesling Trockenbeerenauslese
7%, ♀ till 2012   **91**

——— Red wines ———

2001 Bönnigheimer Sonnenberg
Samtrot trocken ✳✳✳
12.5%, ♀ till 2007   **86**

2002 Bönnigheimer Sonnenberg
Spätburgunder trocken ✳✳✳
12.5%, ♀ till 2007   **86**

2003 Bönnigheimer Sonnenberg
Lemberger trocken ✳✳✳
13%, ♀ till 2008   **86**

2001 Bönnigheimer Sonnenberg
Lemberger trocken ✳✳✳
13%, ♀ till 2006   **87**

2000 Spätburgunder trocken ✳✳✳✳
13%, ♀ till 2007   **88**

2000 "Kreation" trocken ✳✳✳✳
13%, ♀ till 2008   **88**

2001 Spätburgunder "S" trocken ✳✳✳✳
13%, ♀ till 2008   **88**

2002 Spätburgunder "S" trocken ✳✳✳✳
13%, ♀ till 2009   **88**

2002 Lemberger "S" trocken ✳✳✳✳
13%, ♀ till 2009   **88**

2001 Lemberger "S" trocken ✳✳✳✳
13%, ♀ till 2009   **89**

2002 "Kreation" trocken ✳✳✳✳
13%, ♀ till 2009   **89**

2001 "Kreation" trocken ✳✳✳
13.5%, ♀ till 2009   **90**

DAUTEL

Kreation
weiss
trocken
★ ★ ★
2000

WÜRTTEMBERG

The wines: **100** Perfect · **95–99** Outstanding · **90–94** Excellent · **85–89** Very good · **80–84** Good · **75–79** Average

WEINGUT DRAUTZ-ABLE

**Owner: Christel Able,
Richard Drautz
Manager: Richard Drautz
Adminsitrator: Thomas Gramm
Winemaker: Richard Drautz,
Thomas Gramm
74076 Heilbronn, Faißtstraße 23
Tel. (0 71 31) 17 79 08, Fax 94 12 39
e-mail: wgda@wein.com
Internet: www.wein.com**
Directions: On outskirts of Heilbronn
Sales: Monika Drautz
Opening hours: Mon.–Fri. 08:00 to
12:00 hours and 13:30 to 18:00 hours
Sat. 09:00 to 16:00 hours
History: Family coat-of-arms awarded
in 1496
Worth seeing: Wein-Villa of the Heil-
bronn estates

Vineyard area: 17.2 hectares
Annual production: 140,000 bottles
Top sites: Heilbronner Stiftsberg and
Wartberg, Neckarsulmer Scheuerberg
Soil types: Multi-colored marl,
red marl, decomposed sandstone
Grape varieties: 20% Trollinger, 19%
Riesling, 13% Lemberger, 10% Spät-
burgunder, 9% Schwarzriesling, 5%
Weißburgunder, 24% other varieties
Average yield: 81 hl/ha
Best vintages: 1998, 1999, 2002
Member: VDP, Hades,
Deutsches Barrique Forum

This, the leading wine estate in Heilbronn, had an evident weak phase at the
beginning of the decade, but this has in
the meantime been completely overcome.
Apart from the excellent red "Jodokus"
from the 2001 vintage, we very much
liked the basic 2003 Lemberger estate
wine. It proves yet again that well-made
wines can be found here even at moderate
prices. The tasting of the 2002 white
"Jodokus" was also interesting: a powerful
wine with the aroma of a Sauternes, but
on the palate it is full-bodied rather than
sweet and botrytized.

2003 Heilbronner Stiftsberg
Riesling Spätlese trocken
"Großes Gewächs"
14%, ♀ till 2007   86

2003 Sauvignon Blanc
trocken "Hades"
13%, ♀ till 2007   86

2001 Weißer Burgunder
trocken "Hades"
15%, ♀ till 2007   89

2002 "Jodokus" "Hades"
15%, ♀ till 2008   88

———— Red wines ————

2003 Lemberger trocken
13%, ♀ till 2006   85

2001 Spätburgunder
trocken ***** "Hades"
14%, ♀ till 2007   86

2002 Lemberger trocken "Hades"
13%, ♀ till 2007   87

2001 Samtrot
trocken ***** "Hades"
13.5%, ♀ till 2007   87

2001 Lemberger trocken "Hades"
13%, ♀ till 2007   88

2001 "Jodokus" trocken "Hades"
13.5%, ♀ till 2008   89

WEINGUT J. ELLWANGER

Owner and manager: Jürgen Ellwanger
Viticulture: Jörg Ellwanger
Winemaker: Andreas Ellwanger
73650 Winterbach, Bachstraße 21
Tel. (0 71 81) 4 45 25, Fax 4 61 28
e-mail: info@weingut-ellwanger.de
Internet: www.weingut-ellwanger.de
Directions: From Stuttgart B 14, Waiblingen exit, B 29 in direction of Schorndorf
Sales: Sieglinde Ellwanger
Opening hours: Tue.–Fri. 09:00 to 12:00 and 15:00 to 19:00, Sat. 08:00 to 15:00 hours, and by appointment

Vineyard area: 19 hectares
Annual production: 120,000 bottles
Top sites: Winterbacher Hungerberg, Grunbacher Berghalde and Klingle, Schnaiter Altenberg
Soil types: Heavy red marl and gravel
Grape varieties: 20% Riesling, 15% each of Trollinger and Lemberger, 10% each of Spätburgunder and Zweigelt, 10% Weiß- and Grauburgunder, 7% Kerner, 5% Merlot, 8% other varieties
Average yield: 70 hl/ha
Best vintages: 1999, 2001, 2002
Member: VDP, Hades, Deutsches Barrique Forum

The "Hades" wines produced by Jürgen Ellwanger in the 2002 vintage were by and large of the same good quality as those of the previous vintage. Only the Pinot Noirs and "Nikodemus" – for many years now one of the best red wines in Württemberg – fall a little short of the mark. On the other hand, we were again really enthusiastic about the barrique-matured Zweigelt. The 2003 Riesling wines are full-bodied and well-made, but follow the general trend in the region, the vintage character precludes them from showing charm and fruit of the previous vintage. The Riesling and Spätburgunder (Pinot Noir) Eisweins presented by Ellwanger this year head the list of the best botrytis dessert wines in Württemberg.

2003 Winterbacher Hungerberg
Weißer Burgunder Spätlese trocken
14.5%, ♀ till 2006   **86**

2003 Schnaiter Altenberg
Riesling Spätlese trocken
"Großes Gewächs"
13%, ♀ till 2008   **86**

2002 Winterbacher Hungerberg
Riesling Auslese
10.5%, ♀ till 2008   **90**

2003 Schnaiter Altenberg
Riesling Eiswein
9.5%, ♀ till 2012   **92**

——— Red wines ———

2002 Spätburgunder
trocken "Hades"
13%, ♀ till 2009   **87**

2002 Lemberger trocken "Hades"
13%, ♀ till 2010   **88**

2003 Merlot trocken "Hades"
14.5%, ♀ till 2011   **88**

2002 Zweigelt trocken "Hades"
14%, ♀ till 2009   **89**

2002 "Nikodemus" trocken "Hades"
13.5%, ♀ till 2010   **89**

2001 "Nikodemus" trocken "Hades"
13.5%, ♀ till 2010   **91**

2003 Schnaiter Altenberg
Spätburgunder Eiswein
10%, ♀ till 2010   **91**

Weingut J. Ellwanger
Nikodemus
2000
trocken

Württemberg
13% Vol. · 0,751 · Qualitätswein · AP-Nr. 270 048 02
Gutsabfüllung Jürgen Ellwanger · D-73650 Winterbach

The wines: **100** Perfect · **95–99** Outstanding · **90–94** Excellent · **85–89** Very good · **80–84** Good · **75–79** Average

WEINGÄRTNER-GENOSSENSCHAFT GRANTSCHEN

Chairman: Friedrich Wirth
General manager: Bruno Bolsinger
Winemaker: Fritz Herold
**74189 Weinsberg-Grantschen,
Wimmentaler Straße 36**
Tel. (0 71 34) 9 80 20, **Fax** 98 02 22
e-mail: info@grantschen.de
Internet: www.grantschen.de
*Directions: A 81 Heilbronn–Stuttgart,
Weinsberg-Ellhofen exit*
Sales: Wolfgang Dämon
Opening hours: Mon.–Fri. 09:00 to
17:00 hours, Sat. 09:00 to 12:30 hours
History: Founded 1947

Vineyard area: 147 hectares
Number of members: 195
Annual production: 1.6 mill. bottles
Top site: Grantschener
Wildenberg
Soil types: Decomposed red marl
Grape varieties: 28% Riesling, 25%
Trollinger, 22% Lemberger, 15%
Schwarzriesling, 5% Kerner,
5% other varieties
Average yield: 100 hl/ha
Best vintages: 1997, 1999, 2003
Member: Deutsches Barrique Forum

General manager Bolsinger and winemaker Herold were the first in Württemberg to realize that top wines can be produced in co-operatives if you know how to motivate the members. When the legendary "Grandor" was first created 15 years ago, this opened the door for co-operatives to produce top-class wines. We had been looking forward to the release of the 2000 version with great interest: It is an elegant, sublime wine with silky finesse. But that is not the only reason why the current range can be described as a successful one. The barrique-matured white Pinot blend is well-balanced, and the 2003 Lemberger Spätlese is attractively juicy. And Trollinger fans will just love the Spätlese.

2002 Grantschener Wildenberg
Chardonnay trocken Barrique
13.5%, ♀ till 2006 — **84**

2003 Riesling
Auslese trocken Barrique
13%, ♀ till 2007 — **84**

2003 Chardonnay mit Weißburgunder
Auslese trocken Barrique
13.5%, ♀ till 2007 — **86**

——— Red wines ———

2003 Trollinger Spätlese trocken
12.5%, ♀ till 2005 — **83**

2003 Lemberger Spätlese trocken
12.5%, ♀ till 2007 — **86**

2001 "SM" trocken
12.5%, ♀ till 2007 — **86**

2000 Lemberger Spätlese trocken
12%, ♀ till 2005 — **86**

2000 Cuvée "SM" trocken Barrique
12.5%, ♀ till 2006 — **86**

2000 Grantschener Wildenberg
Lemberger Spätlese trocken Barrique
12%, ♀ till 2005 — **86**

2000 "Grandor" trocken
13%, ♀ till 2007 — **88**

The estates: ♦♦♦♦♦ World's finest · ♦♦♦♦ Germany's best · ♦♦♦ Very good · ♦♦ Good · ♦ Reliable

WEINGUT KARL HAIDLE

Owner and manager: Hans Haidle
Viticulture: Werner Kuhnle
Winemaker: Hans Haidle
and Frank Haller
71394 Kernen-Stetten im Remstal,
Hindenburgstraße 21
Tel. (0 71 51) 94 91 10, Fax 4 63 13
e-mail: info@weingut-karl-haidle.de
Internet: www.weingut-karl-haidle.de
Directions: A 8, Köngen exit, via Esslin-gen; from Stuttgart: B 14, B 29, Kernen exit
Sales: Bärbel and Susanne Haidle
Opening hours: Mon.–Fri. 08:00 to
12:00 hours and 13:00 to 18:00 hours
Sat. 09:00 to 13:00 hours
Worth seeing: Castle ruins above the estate, museum underneath the Yburg castle

---

Vineyard area: 19 hectares
Producers community: 3.8 hectares
Number of members: 12
Annual production: 140,000 bottles
Top sites: Stettener Pulvermächer
and Häder, Schnaiter Burghalde
Soil types: Red marl
Grape varieties: 40% Riesling, 15%
Trollinger, 8% Spätburgunder, 7%
each of Kerner and Lemberger,
23% other varieties
Average yield: 62 hl/ha
Best vintages: 2001, 2002, 2003
Member: VDP

As in the previous vintage, Hans Haidle was able to surprise us with a very homogeneous range at a high level. 2003 saw him again shining with his racy Rieslings from the Pulvermächer site, the highlight of these is the "Großes Gewächs" (First Growth), the best dry Riesling of the vintage in Württemberg. And the "Justinus K." is a powerful, spicy wine that is probably the best dry Kerner ever made in Germany. In addition, the barrique-matured wines were also very good, in particular the juicy Lemberger as well as the delicate blend "Ypsilon," so all that remains for us to do is to extend our congratulations on this fine range.

2003 Stettener Pulvermächer
Riesling Spätlese trocken
13%, ♀ till 2007   **87**

2003 "Justinus K."
Kerner trocken
16%, ♀ till 2006   **88**

2003 Stettener Pulvermächer
Riesling Spätlese trocken
"Großes Gewächs"
13.5%, ♀ till 2008   **88**

2002 Stettener Pulvermächer
Riesling Spätlese
13%, ♀ till 2006   **87**

2002 Stettener Pulvermächer
Riesling Trockenbeerenauslese
8.5%, ♀ till 2014   **92**

——————— Red wines ———————

2002 Zweigelt trocken Barrique
13.5%, ♀ till 2009   **88**

2002 Spätburgunder
trocken Barrique
13.5%, ♀ till 2009   **88**

2002 Lemberger trocken Barrique
13.5%, ♀ till 2010   **89**

2002 "Ypsilon" trocken Barrique
13.5%, ♀ till 2010   **90**

KARL HAIDLE
WEINGUT

2003
Stettener Pulvermächer
Riesling Kabinett
Trocken

The wines: **100** Perfect · **95–99** Outstanding · **90–94** Excellent · **85–89** Very good · **80–84** Good · **75–79** Average

Württemberg

WEINGUT G. A. HEINRICH

Owner: Martin Heinrich
Winemaker: Martin Heinrich and Martin Streicher
74076 Heilbronn, Riedstraße 29
Tel. (0 71 31) 17 59 48, Fax 16 63 06
e-mail: heinrich_ga.weingut@t-online.de
Internet: www.weingut-heinrich.de
Directions: Winery situated on the outskirts of Heilbronn at the foot of the Wartberg hill
Sales: Christel Heinrich
Opening hours: Mon.–Fri. 09:00 to 12:00 and 13:30 to 18:00, Sat. 09:00 to 14:00 hours, and by appointment
Restaurant: 14 days each in Nov. and Feb., from 11:00 to 24:00 hours
Specialties: Swabian-style ravioli (Maultaschen), boiled meat
Worth seeing: Viticultural vineyard path directly at the winery, historical tree press

> Vineyard area: 12 hectares
> Annual production: 85,000 bottles
> Top sites: Heilbronner Wartberg and Stiftsberg
> Soil types: Red marl, decomposed reed sandstone, loess-clay
> Grape varieties: 26% Trollinger, 21% Riesling, 20% Lemberger, 5% each of Schwarzriesling and Spätburgunder, 3% each of Weißburgunder and Gewürztraminer, 17% other varieties
> Average yield: 85 hl/ha
> Best vintages: 1997, 1999, 2001

Martin Heinrich always takes his time about getting his red flagships, the "Wollendieb" and "G.A.1" blends, ready for the bottle, and so it is that the 2001 vintages of these wines have only recently been released for sale. It has been worth the wait: Two very good wines that show further improvements. In addition, the basic range of wines from the 2003 vintage was of consistent quality, including the Pinot Noir, Pinot Blanc and the Riesling of the "Edition S" range. By the way: Customers can keep their wines here to mature under optimum conditions.

2003 Weißer Burgunder trocken
12%, ♀ till 2006 — 84

2003 Weißer Burgunder
trocken "Edition S"
13.5%, ♀ till 2006 — 85

2003 Riesling
trocken "Edition S"
13.5%, ♀ till 2006 — 85

2003 Riesling Spätlese
12.5%, ♀ till 2006 — 84

——— Red wines ———

2002 "Fass IV" trocken
13%, ♀ till 2006 — 84

2001 Heilbronner Stiftsberg
Lemberger trocken
13%, ♀ till 2005 — 85

2002 Lemberger trocken
13.5%, ♀ till 2006 — 85

2003 Spätburgunder
trocken "Edition S"
13.5%, ♀ till 2007 — 85

2000 Heilbronner Stiftsberg
Cuvée "G.A.1" trocken
13%, ♀ till 2006 — 86

2000 Heilbronner Stiftsberg
Cuvée "Wollendieb" trocken
14%, ♀ till 2007 — 87

2001 Cuvée "G.A.1" trocken
13.5%, ♀ till 2007 — 87

2001 Cuvée "Wollendieb" trocken
13.5%, ♀ till 2009 — 88

WEINGUT G.A. HEINRICH ®
2000ER
TROLLINGER · TROCKEN
QUALITÄTSWEIN
HEILBRONNER WARTBERG
GUTSABFÜLLUNG
WEINGUT G.A.HEINRICH
D-74076 HEILBRONN
RIEDSTRASSE 29
A.P.NUMMER 21202101
0,75L WÜRTTEMBERG 12,5%VOL

The estates: ✦✦✦✦✦ World's finest · ✦✦✦✦ Germany's best · ✦✦✦ Very good · ✦✦ Good · ✦ Reliable

WEINGUT ERICH HIRTH

Owner: Erich Hirth
74182 Obersulm-Willsbach,
Löwensteiner Straße 76
Tel. (0 71 34) 36 33, Fax 86 22
e-mail: erich.hirth@t-online.de
Directions: A 81 Heilbronn–Stuttgart,
Kreuz Weinsberg interchange, Ellhofen
exit, in direction of Obersulm
Sales: Gudrun Hirth
Opening hours: Mon.–Fri. 16:00 to
18:00 hours, except Wed., Sat. 09:00 to
12:00 hours and by appointment

Vineyard area: 8.6 hectares
Annual production: 45,000 bottles
Top sites: Willsbacher Diebles-
berg, Lehrensteinfelder Steinacker
Soil types: Red marl, decomposed
sandstone
Grape varieties: 30% Schwarzriesling,
22% Riesling, 16% Lemberger, 9%
Trollinger, 5% each of Samtrot and
Spätburgunder, 13% other varieties
Average yield: 68 hl/ha
Best vintages: 2001, 2002, 2003

Erich Hirth was winemaker at the co-operative in Flein, before setting up his own winery in 1986. Initially we praised him for the fact that his basic red wines were real bargains for the thrifty Swabian winelovers; in the meantime we are happy to admit that Hirth is becoming increasingly interesting even for the discerning palate. 2003 was successful for him. In spite of the hot vintage, the red wines are not overly heavy, and show an elegant balance – obviously the time of picking was carefully judged. This is particularly evident in the two top wines of the estate, the Lemberger Spätlese and the "Optimus" blend. They are beautifully balanced, and the fine tannins are perfectly integrated. Both wines were rated a point higher than in the previous vintage. Only the Riesling Spätlese, which is correctly made, has suffered from the vintage character, and remains a little below its predecessor in quality.

2003 Willsbacher Dieblesberg
Riesling Spätlese trocken
14%, ♀ till 2006 — **83**

2002 Willsbacher Dieblesberg
Riesling Spätlese trocken
13%, ♀ till 2006 — **84**

——— Red wines ———

2003 Willsbacher Dieblesberg
Lemberger trocken
13.5%, ♀ till 2006 — **83**

2003 Willsbacher Dieblesberg
Dornfelder trocken
13%, ♀ till 2006 — **83**

2002 Willsbacher Dieblesberg
Samtrot Kabinett trocken
13%, ♀ till 2005 — **84**

2002 Willsbacher Dieblesberg
Lemberger Spätlese trocken
13%, ♀ till 2006 — **85**

2001 Willsbacher Dieblesberg
Cuvée "Optimus" trocken
12.5%, ♀ till 2006 — **85**

2003 Willsbacher Dieblesberg
Spätburgunder Spätlese trocken
13.5%, ♀ till 2006 — **85**

2003 Willsbacher Dieblesberg
"Optimus" trocken
13.5%, ♀ till 2007 — **86**

2003 Willsbacher Dieblesberg
Lemberger Spätlese trocken Barrique
13.5%, ♀ till 2007 — **86**

The wines: **100** Perfect · **95–99** Outstanding · **90–94** Excellent · **85–89** Very good · **80–84** Good · **75–79** Average

SCHLOSSGUT HOHENBEILSTEIN

Owner: Hartmann Dippon
Manager and winemaker:
Hartmann Dippon
71717 Beilstein, lm Schloss
Tel. (0 70 62) 93 71 10, Fax 9 37 11 22
e-mail:
info@schlossgut-hohenbeilstein.de
Internet:
www.schlossgut-hohenbeilstein.de
Directions: A 81 Heilbronn–Stuttgart
Opening hours: Mon.–Fri. 09:00 to
12:00 hours and 14:00 to 18:00 hours
Sat. 09:00 to 14:00 hours
Worth seeing: "Langhans" ruins and
falconry at castle

Vineyard area: 14 hectares
Annual production: 100,000 bottles
Top site: Hohenbeilsteiner
Schloßwengert (monopole)
Soil types: Red marl
Grape varieties: 25% Riesling, 20%
Trollinger, 12% Lemberger, 9% Spät-
burgunder, 8% Samtrot, 6% Schwarz-
riesling (Pinot Meunier), 5% Kerner,
15% other varieties
Average yield: 68 hl/ha
Best vintages: 2000, 2001, 2002
Member: VDP, Naturland,
Deutsches Barrique Forum

Hartmann Dippon is really an enthusiastic
and untiring proponent of organic winemaking practices. His current range shows
that the good wines produced here are by
no means a flash in the pan. Of the Riesling wines, we particularly liked the Kabinett. The 2003 "Großes Gewächs" has a
marked botrytis character, and is exceptional. Just to be fair, however, we must
mention there are a number of weak
wines in the range: the Weißburgunder
Auslese, the Trollinger Kabinett, and the
very basic Muskattrollinger. As we walk
back down from the château we comfort
ourselves with a view of the beautiful,
meticulously restored dry-stone walls.

2003 Weißer Burgunder
Auslese trocken
13.5%, ♀ till 2006   **82**

2003 Riesling Kabinett trocken
12.5%, ♀ till 2005   **83**

2003 Weißwein Cuvée trocken
12.5%, ♀ till 2005   **83**

2002 Hohenbeilsteiner Schloßwengert
Riesling Spätlese trocken
"Großes Gewächs"
12%, ♀ till 2006   **86**

2003 Hohenbeilsteiner Schloßwengert
Riesling Spätlese trocken
"Großes Gewächs"
13.5%, ♀ till 2007   **86**

2003 Riesling Auslese
13%, ♀ till 2008   **87**

——— Red wines ———

2002 Cuvée "Robert Vollmöller"
trocken
13%, ♀ till 2006   **84**

2002 Lemberger
trocken "Holzfassausbau"
13%, ♀ till 2006   **84**

2001 Spätburgunder
trocken Barrique
13%, ♀ till 2006   **87**

2002 Lemberger trocken Barrique
13.5%, ♀ till 2007   **87**

Württemberg

WEINGUT FÜRST ZU HOHENLOHE-OEHRINGEN

Owner: Fürst (Prince) Kraft zu Hohenlohe-Oehringen
Manager: Siegfried Röll
Winemaker: Siegfried Röll and Justus Kircher
74613 Öhringen, Im Schloss
Tel. (0 79 41) 9 49 10, Fax 3 73 49
e-mail: schlosskellerei@gmx.de
Internet: www.verrenberg.de
Directions: A 6 Heilbronn–Nürnberg, Öhringen exit
Sales: Siegfried Röll
Opening hours: Mon.–Fri. 08:00 to 17:00 hours, Sat. 09:00 to 12:00 hours
Restaurant: Schlosshotel Friedrichsruhe
Specialties: Top-class regional cuisine
History: Winemaking since 1360

Vineyard area: 17 hectares
Annual production: 140,000 bottles
Top site: Verrenberger Verrenberg (monopole)
Soil types: Red marl, shell limestone
Grape varieties: 40% Riesling, 20% Lemberger, 15% Spätburgunder, 8% Trollinger, 6% Weißburgunder, 11% other varieties
Average yield: 60 hl/ha
Best vintages: 2001, 2002, 2003
Member: VDP, Hades, Deutsches Barrique Forum

The château's cellar dating to the 17th century, located on the picturesque market place of Öhringen is worth seeing, and provides the appropriate backdrop for the wines of the Verrenberger Verrenberg. Manager Siegfried Röll has a reputation as one of the leading red wine specialists in the region, and he underlines this with his four 2003 Auslese wines made from Lemberger, Samtrot, Schwarzriesling and Spätburgunder, all of them big wines with lots of tannin. Yet again, the red wines of the "Hades" series were most convincing. For many years now they have been among the best of their style in Württemberg.

2003 Verrenberger Verrenberg
Riesling Spätlese trocken "Butzen"
12%, ♀ till 2006 — 85

2003 Verrenberger Verrenberg
Riesling Spätlese trocken "Großes Gewächs"
12%, ♀ till 2006 — 86

2003 Verrenberger Verrenberg
Riesling Spätlese
12%, ♀ till 2006 — 85

2003 Verrenberger Verrenberg
Riesling Eiswein
6.5%, ♀ till 2010 — 88

——— Red wines ———

2003 Verrenberger Verrenberg
Lemberger Auslese trocken
14%, ♀ till 2009 — 86

2003 Verrenberger Verrenberg
Schwarzriesling Auslese trocken
13.5%, ♀ till 2007 — 86

2003 Verrenberger Verrenberg
Samtrot Auslese trocken
14%, ♀ till 2007 — 86

2003 Verrenberger Verrenberg
Spätburgunder Auslese trocken
14%, ♀ till 2008 — 87

2001 Lemberger trocken "Hades"
14%, ♀ till 2010 — 89

2001 "Ex flammis orior"
trocken "Hades"
13%, ♀ till 2010 — 89

2001 "In senio" trocken "Hades"
14%, ♀ till 2011 — 90

The wines: **100** Perfect · **95–99** Outstanding · **90–94** Excellent · **85–89** Very good · **80–84** Good · **75–79** Average

1705

WEINGUT KISTENMACHER-HENGERER

Owner: Hans Hengerer
74074 Heilbronn,
Eugen-Nägele-Straße 23–25
Tel. (0 71 31) 17 23 54, Fax 17 23 50
e-mail: kistenmacher-hengerer-
wein@t-online.de
Directions: Outskirts of Heilbronn-Ost,
near youth hostel
Sales: Sabine Hengerer
Opening hours: Mon.–Fri. 16:00 to
18:30, Sat. 09:00 to 11:00 and 13:00 to
16:00 hours, and by appointment
History: Winemaking here since 1504

Vineyard area: 8.2 hectares
Annual production: 80,000 bottles
Top sites: Heilbronner Wartberg
and Stiftsberg
Soil types: Red marl and decomposed
sandstone
Grape varieties: 30% Trollinger, 20%
Riesling, 8% each of Kerner and Lem-
berger, 5% each of Schwarzriesling,
Spätburgunder, Samtrot, Muskattrol-
linger and Merlot, 9% other varieties
Average yield: 80 hl/ha
Best vintages: 1997, 1999, 2001
Member: Junges Schwaben

Hans Hengerer may be a member of the winemaking group "Junges Schwaben" (Young Swabia), but his youthful stage is truly a thing of the past. The quality of his wines is by now too reliable to refer to him as youthful. This estate produces good, sometimes even very good wines at surprisingly attractive prices. The white wines of the 2003 vintage are all correctly made, and we can blame the dry vintage for the fact that they do not posess the fruit and balance of the 2002 vintage. Looking to the top-ranking reds, here, too, the 2002 wines are not quite as good as the successful wines from the 2000 vintage. However, there are again some outstanding bargains: The Muskateller Auslese is a delicious aperitif!

2003 Riesling trocken
13%, ♀ till 2005   **82**

2003 "Theresa" Riesling trocken
13.5%, ♀ till 2005   **83**

2003 Cuvée "Josephine"
Spätlese trocken
13.5%, ♀ till 2005   **83**

2003 Riesling Spätlese trocken
14%, ♀ till 2006   **84**

2002 Heilbronner Wartberg
Riesling Spätlese
12%, ♀ till 2006   **85**

2003 Muskateller Auslese
13.5%, ♀ till 2007   **87**

———— Red wines ————

2003 Pinot Meunier
"Blanc de Noir" trocken
14.5%, ♀ till 2005   **83**

2003 Lemberger Spätlese trocken
14%, ♀ till 2006   **84**

2003 Samtrot Auslese trocken
14.5%, ♀ till 2007   **85**

2001 Heilbronner Stiftsberg
"Jubiläums-Cuvée" trocken
13%, ♀ till 2007   **86**

2002 Cuvée "Max"
trocken Barrique
13.5%, ♀ till 2007   **86**

2002 Lemberger
trocken "Edition S" Barrique
14%, ♀ till 2007   **86**

2002 Spätburgunder
trocken "Edition S" Barrique
13.5%, ♀ till 2007   **86**

The estates: ✛✛✛✛✛ World's finest · ✛✛✛✛ Germany's best · ✛✛✛ Very good · ✛✛ Good · ✛ Reliable

WEINGUT KLOPFER

Owner and manager: Wolfgang Klopfer
71384 Weinstadt-Großheppach,
Gundelsbacher Straße 1
Tel. (0 71 51) 60 38 48, Fax 60 09 56
e-mail: weingut-klopfer@freenet.de
Internet: www.klopfer-weingut.de
Directions: From Stuttgart via the B 14
in direction of Waiblingen, then B 29,
Weinstadt-Großheppach exit
Sales: Dagmar Klopfer
Opening hours: Tue. and Fri. 16:00 to
19:00 hours, Sat. 09:00 to 13:00 hours
and by appointment
Worth seeing: Attractive modern win-
ery buildings at foot of vineyard slopes

Vineyard area: 9 hectares
Annual production: 65,000 bottles
Top sites: Großheppacher
Wanne and Steingrüble
Soil types: Gypsum-red marl, shell
limestone, decomposed sandstone
Grape varieties: 23% Riesling, 20%
Trollinger, 10% each of Spätburgun-
der, Lemberger and Schwarzriesling,
7% Portugieser, 4% each of Weißbur-
gunder and Merlot, 12% other varieties
Average yield: 80 hl/ha
Best vintages: 2001, 2002

The rise of this likable family winery
continues apace, although just currently a
few setbacks are evident. The fact that the
white wines of the 2003 vintage were not
as good as their predecessors can be for-
given, and explained in terms of the dry
vintage character. But a Sauvignon Blanc
absolutely devoid of expression and an
unbalanced, over-alcoholic Gewürztraminer did come as a surprise to us. Overall, we still believe that the development
from being an occasional hot tip to being
a reliable, continuous producer of fine
wines is there, in principle. For instance,
the 2002 vintage of the top red blend
"Modus K" has now reached and even
surpassed the reliably good quality of the
Merlots, giving Wolfgang Klopfer two
thoroughbred red wines in his stable.

2003 Cannstatter Zuckerle
Riesling Spätlese trocken
13.5%, ♀ till 2006 — **83**

2002 Großheppacher Steingrüble
Riesling Spätlese trocken
12.5%, ♀ till 2005 — **84**

2002 Cuvée "Modus K" trocken
14%, ♀ till 2006 — **85**

2003 Geradstettener Lichtenberg
Riesling Eiswein
9%, ♀ till 2010 — **87**

——————— Red wines ———————

2003 Endersbacher Wetzstein
Dornfelder trocken
13.5%, ♀ till 2005 — **82**

2003 Kleinheppacher Greiner
Trollinger trocken
12%, ♀ till 2005 — **82**

2003 Großheppacher Wanne
Trollinger Spätlese trocken
12.5%, ♀ till 2005 — **83**

2002 Kleinheppacher Greiner
Lemberger trocken
12%, ♀ till 2006 — **84**

2002 Kleinheppacher Greiner
Spätburgunder trocken "Holzfassausbau"
13.5%, ♀ till 2006 — **84**

2002 Merlot trocken
13.5%, ♀ till 2007 — **86**

2001 Merlot trocken
13%, ♀ till 2006 — **87**

2002 Cuvée "Modus K" trocken
13%, ♀ till 2008 — **87**

The wines: **100** Perfect · **95–99** Outstanding · **90–94** Excellent · **85–89** Very good · **80–84** Good · **75–79** Average

707

WEINGUT KUHNLE

Owner: Werner and Margret Kuhnle
Manager and winemaker:
Werner Kuhnle
71384 Weinstadt-Strümpfelbach,
Hauptstraße 49
Tel. (0 71 51) 6 12 93, Fax 61 07 47
e-mail: info@weingut-kuhnle.de
Internet: www.weingut-kuhnle.de
Directions: B 14 from Stuttgart to
Remstal valley
Sales: Margret Kuhnle
Opening hours: Fri. 16:00 to 19:00
hours, and by appointment
Worth a visit: Culinary wine-tastings
with local food specialties
History: Winery housed in old forester's
building dating to 18th century
Worth seeing: Path in vineyard lined by
20 bronze sculptures

Vineyard area: 19 hectares
Annual production: 130,000 bottles
Top sites: Stettener Pulvermächer,
Strümpfelbacher Altenberg and
Nonnenberg, Schnaiter Burghalde
Soil types: Multi-colored marl, reed
sandstone
Grape varieties: 25% Trollinger, 20%
Riesling, 10% Spätburgunder, 8%
each of Chardonnay and Kerner, 5%
Muskattrollinger, 24% other varieties
Average yield: 70 hl/ha
Best vintages: 1999, 2001, 2003

Right in the center of the village of
Strümpfelbach, an historic heritage site,
lies the Kuhnle winery, which also pays
great attention to the maintenance of its
own attractive half-timbered buildings. In
the current range, the red wines of the
2003 vintage are miles better than the
white wines. The Rieslings were rather
unspectacular, but the reds, with no fewer
than five wines scoring 86 points or better, are a strong suit. If they can raise the
quality level of the white wines to this
standard next year, a higher rating would
be the consequence for the winery of
Werner and Margret Kuhnle.

2003 Strümpfelbacher
Riesling trocken
12.5%, ♀ till 2005   **80**

2003 Strümpfelbacher Nonnenberg
Riesling Auslese trocken
13.5%, ♀ till 2007   **84**

2003 Chardonnay Auslese trocken
14%, ♀ till 2007   **85**

———— Red wines ————

2003 Schnaiter Sonnenberg
Spätburgunder Auslese trocken
14.5%, ♀ till 2008   **86**

2003 Regent Auslese trocken
13.5%, ♀ till 2007   **86**

2001 "Cuvée Auslese" trocken
13.5%, ♀ till 2007   **86**

2002 Lemberger trocken Barrique
14%, ♀ till 2008   **86**

2002 Merlot trocken Barrique
14.5%, ♀ till 2008   **87**

2003 Strümpfelbacher Nonnenberg
Schwarzriesling Auslese
13%, ♀ till 2007   **86**

2003 Spätburgunder Weißherbst
Trockenbeerenauslese
7%, ♀ till 2013   **89**

WEINGUT KUSTERER

Owner: Hans and Monika Kusterer
Manager: Hans Kusterer
73728 Esslingen, Untere Beutau 44
Tel. (07 11) 35 79 09, Fax 3 50 81 05
e-mail: info@weingut-kusterer.de
Internet: www.weingut-kusterer.de
Directions: A 8 Stuttgart–München,
Esslingen exit
Sales: Kusterer family
Opening hours: Tue. 16:00 to 19:00
hours, Sat. 09:00 to 13:00 hours
and by appointment
Worth seeing: Medieval press
Worth a visit: Guided tours through ter-
raced vineyards dating to Staufen times,
and historical town center of Esslingen

Vineyard area: 5 hectares
Annual production: 40,000 bottles
Top sites: Esslinger Schenken-
berg and Neckarhalde
Soil types: Colored and bulbous marl
Grape varieties: 34% Trollinger, 20%
Riesling, 12% each of Spätburgunder
and Lemberger, 8% each of Graubur-
gunder and Zweigelt, 3% Merlot,
3% other varieties
Average yield: 62 hl/ha
Best vintages: 1997, 1999, 2001

The Kusterer winery has established itself as one of the most reliable producers
in the region. However, one cannot ignore the fact that the current range is not
quite as homogeneous as that of the previous vintage. Mainly it is the somewhat
tart and harsh Rieslings that we noted,
which stand in contrast to the harmonious
style seen here usually. The red wines are
significantly better, although the Spätburgunder (Pinot Noir) and Zweigelt both
show a hefty dose of wood. The highlight
of the range is the top blend "Mélac." The
winery itself is located in the heart of the
old part of Esslingen, just five minutes
away from the Frauenkirche church and
the vineyards. In a medieval cellar building Hans Kusterer uses to present his
wines.

2003 Esslinger Schenkenberg
Riesling Kabinett trocken
13%, ♀ till 2006   83

2003 Esslinger Schenkenberg
Riesling Auslese trocken
13.5%, ♀ till 2007   84

2002 Esslinger Schenkenberg
Grauer Burgunder Spätlese trocken
12.5%, ♀ till 2005   86

———— Red wines ————

2002 Esslinger Schenkenberg
Lemberger trocken
13%, ♀ till 2006   85

2002 Esslinger Neckarhalde
Spätburgunder trocken
13%, ♀ till 2006   85

2002 Esslinger Schenkenberg
Zweigelt trocken
13%, ♀ till 2007   86

2001 Esslinger Schenkenberg
Spätburgunder Spätlese trocken
13%, ♀ till 2006   87

2001 Esslinger Schenkenberg
Cuvée "Mélac" trocken
13.5%, ♀ till 2008   87

2000 Esslinger Schenkenberg
Cuvée "Mélac" trocken
13%, ♀ till 2008   88

WEINGUT GERHARD LEISS

Owner and manager: Wolf-Peter Leiss
74189 Gellmersbach,
Lennacher Straße 7
Tel. (0 71 34) 1 43 89, Fax 2 06 21
e-mail: info@weingut-leiss.de
Internet: www.weingut-leiss.de
*Directions: A 81 Heilbronn–Stuttgart,
Weinsberg exit*
Sales: Christa Leiss
Opening hours: Mon.–Fri. 17:30 to
19:00 hours, Sat. 09:00 to 18:00 hours
Restaurant: Wine bar with
home-made regional specialties

Vineyard area: 10 hectares
Annual production: 95,000 bottles
Top sites: Gellmersbacher
Dezberg, Erlenbacher Kayberg
Soil types: Red marl
Grape varieties: 26% Riesling, 22%
Trollinger, 19% Lemberger, 10%
Schwarzriesling, 6% Kerner, 4%
each of Müller-Thurgau and Ge-
würztraminer, 9% other varieties
Average yield: 94 hl/ha
Best vintages: 2001, 2002, 2003

Ever since Gerhard Leiss took over the winery (founded in 1959) from his parents, the vineyard area has been increased more than ten-fold, and the quality of the wines has been continuously improved. The main attraction of the winery today is the attractive vaulted sandstone cellar used as a barrel maturation cellar. We were presented with good red wines from here, including the blend "Nobilis." The current range bears testimony to the reliability of this producer. Whereas in many other wineries the 2003 white wines are distinctly inferior to previous vintages, Leiss has been able to maintain his standard, as evidenced by a charming Riesling Classic and an elegantly balanced Riesling Spätlese. In addition, his idea of presenting the Muskattrollinger as an aromatic but lightweight Rosé shows that one can make a delightful summer wine out of this variety.

2003 Riesling Classic
12.5%, ♀ till 2005 — 83

2003 Gellmersbacher Dezberg
Grauer Burgunder Spätlese trocken
13.5%, ♀ till 2006 — 84

2002 Gellmersbacher Dezberg
Grauer Burgunder trocken
13.5%, ♀ till 2006 — 85

2003 Gellmersbacher Dezberg
Riesling Spätlese "feinherb"
12.5%, ♀ till 2007 — 85

——— Red wines ———

2003 Gellmersbacher Dezberg
Muskattrollinger Weißherbst
11%, ♀ till 2005 — 82

2002 Erlenbacher Kayberg
Spätburgunder trocken
14%, ♀ till 2006 — 84

2002 Erlenbacher Kayberg
Lemberger trocken
13%, ♀ till 2006 — 85

2002 Cuvée "Nobilis" trocken
13.5%, ♀ till 2007 — 86

WEINGUT MEDINGER

Owner and manager:
Barbara Medinger-Schmid
and Markus Schmid
Winemaker: Barbara Medinger-
Schmid
71394 Kernen-Stetten, Brühlstraße 6
Tel. (0 71 51) 4 45 13, Fax 4 17 37
e-mail: weingut.medinger@t-online.de
Internet: www.weingut-medinger.de
Directions: From Stuttgart B 14/B 29,
Kernen exit, in direction of Kernen-Stetten
Sales: Markus Schmid
Opening hours: Mon.–Fri. 18:00 to
19:30 hours, Sat. 15:30 to 18:00 hours
Worth seeing: Bell-shaped press from
16th century, newly laid-out vineyard trail

Vineyard area: 5.2 hectares
Annual production: 40,000 bottles
Top sites: Stettener Pulver-
mächer, Mönchberg and Häder,
Strümpfelbacher Altenberg
Soil types: Red marl, marl
Grape varieties: 28% Riesling, 20%
Trollinger, 11% each of Regent
and Lemberger, 10% Dornfelder,
8% Spätburgunder, 4% each of
Cabernet Cubin and Schwarz-
riesling, 4% other varieties
Average yield: 65 hl/ha
Best vintages: 2001, 2002, 2003

Barbara Medinger-Schmid and her husband were able to maintain their standard
in this vintage. In spite of the dry, hot
conditions experienced in 2003, their
Riesling wines from the top Pulvermächer site were as fresh and racy as
ever. An interesting addition to the range
is a barrique-matured blend of Chardonnay and Kerner ("CK"), which has some
New World touches. Of the red wines, we
particularly liked a Cabernet Cubin that is
full of character, while the 2001 Lemberger, which was also matured in barrique,
has not managed to integrate its rather
green tannins. The highlight of the range
is a clean but rather full-bodied Eiswein.

2003 Stettener Pulvermächer
Riesling Kabinett trocken
12%, ♀ till 2006 **84**

2003 Stettener Pulvermächer
Riesling Kabinett trocken "S"
13.5%, ♀ till 2006 **84**

2003 Stettener Pulvermächer
Riesling Spätlese trocken
14%, ♀ till 2007 **85**

2003 Cuvée "CK" trocken Barrique
14.5%, ♀ till 2007 **85**

2003 Stettener Pulvermächer
Riesling Eiswein
11.5%, ♀ till 2010 **88**

———— Red wines ————

2001 Lemberger trocken Barrique
13%, ♀ till 2006 **83**

2001 Stettener
Spätburgunder trocken
13%, ♀ till 2005 **84**

2002 Strümpfelbacher Altenberg
Lemberger trocken
13%, ♀ till 2006 **84**

2002 Spätburgunder trocken
13%, ♀ till 2006 **84**

2002 Cabernet Cubin
trocken Barrique
14%, ♀ till 2007 **86**

STETTENER
HÄDER

2002er
Riesling
Qualitätswein
Württemberg

WEINGUT 🍇 MEDINGER

Gutsabfüllung: Brühlstraße 6 · D-71394 Kernen-Stetten
Tel. 07151/4 45 13 · A.P.Nr. 903 005 03 · 1 l · 12% Vol.

The wines: **100** Perfect · **95–99** Outstanding · **90–94** Excellent · **85–89** Very good · **80–84** Good · **75–79** Average

711

WEINGUT
DES GRAFEN NEIPPERG

Owner: Karl Eugen Erbgraf zu Neipperg
Winemaker: Bernd Supp
74193 Schwaigern, Schlossstraße 12
Tel. (0 71 38) 94 14 00, Fax 40 07
e-mail: neipperg@t-online.de
Directions: A 6, Bad Rappenau exit
Sales: Mrs. Binkele
Opening hours: Mon.–Fri. 08:00 to 11:30 and 13:00 to 16:00, Sat. 10:00 to 12:30 hours
Restaurant: Zum Alten Rentamt
History: Winemaking documented 1248
Worth seeing: Castle complex from Staufen times in Neipperg, château in Schwaigern

---

Vineyard area: 29.6 hectares
Annual production: 180,000 bottles
Top sites: Schwaigerner Ruthe, Neipperger Schlossberg
Soil types: Red marl, reed sandstone
Grape varieties: 21% Lemberger, 16% Riesling, 9% each of Trollinger and Schwarzriesling, 7% Müller-Thurgau, 6% Spätburgunder, 4% Dornfelder, 3% each of Samtrot, Muskateller and Weißburgunder, 19% other varieties
Average yield: 54 hl/ha
Best vintages: 1997, 1999, 2001
Member: VDP

There is never any doubt that this estate in Schwaigern is one of the big traditional names in the region. However, we must say that the red wines of the 2002 vintage did not quite fulfil our expectations. The Schwarzriesling, Samtrot and particularly the Lemberger are very well made wines with character, but considering the tremendous potential of this property they could be much better. Looking at the 2003 white wines, the special position taken here by the Muskateller is evident. There is a lovely series of wines from this varietal, and these impressed us much more than did the somewhat rustic Rieslings.

2003 Neipperger Schlossberg
Riesling Spätlese trocken
13%, ♀ till 2006 — **86**

2003 Schwaigerner Ruthe
Riesling trocken "Großes Gewächs"
13%, ♀ till 2007 — **86**

2003 Neipperger Schlossberg
Muskateller Spätlese
12%, ♀ till 2006 — **87**

2003 Neipperger Schlossberg
Muskateller Auslese
12.5%, ♀ till 2008 — **87**

2003 Neipperger Schlossberg
Muskateller Beerenauslese
11.5%, ♀ till 2009 — **89**

——— Red wines ———

2003 Neipperger Schlossberg
Schwarzriesling Auslese trocken
14%, ♀ till 2008 — **86**

2003 Schwaigerner Ruthe
Lemberger Spätlese trocken
13%, ♀ till 2008 — **86**

2002 Neipperger Schlossberg
Samtrot trocken Barrique
13%, ♀ till 2008 — **86**

2003 Neipperger Schlossberg
Lemberger Auslese trocken
14%, ♀ till 2008 — **87**

2002 Schwaigerner Ruthe
Lemberger trocken Barrique
14%, ♀ till 2008 — **87**

2001 Cuvée "S.E." trocken
13%, ♀ till 2008 — **89**

WEINGÄRTNER-GENOSSENSCHAFT ROTENBERG

Manager: Martin Kurrle
70327 Stuttgart, Württembergstr. 230
Tel. (07 11) 33 76 10, Fax 33 10 15
e-mail: info@wg-rotenberg.de
Internet: www.wg-rotenberg.de
Directions: B 10, Untertürkheim exit, in direction of Stuttgart-Rotenberg, on the right just before entering town
Sales: Thomas Jud
Opening hours: Mon.–Fri. 09:00 to 12:00 and 13:00 to 18:00, Sat. 09:00 to 12:00 and 13:00 to 16:00 hours
History: Founded 1936
Worth seeing: Grave chapel on the Württemberg hill, Rotenberg press in the middle of vineyards, with beautiful view

Vineyard area: 49.5 hectares
Number of members: 76
Annual production: 450,000 bottles
Top site: Rotenberger Schlossberg
Soil types: Shell limestone, red marl
Grape varieties: 50% Trollinger, 10% Riesling, 7% each of Heroldrebe and Kerner, 5% each of Lemberger, Dornfelder and Müller-Thurgau, 11% other varieties
Average yield: 94 hl/ha
Best vintages: 2001, 2002

This mini co-operative is located in a most attractive site in the vineyards of the suburb of Rotenberg, on the outskirts of Stuttgart, and is a hot tip among leading restaurants in the area. There is great demand for the barrique-matured red wines produced here, as well as for the top Riesling, named "Katharina." But even the more basic wines can be attractive here. Other wines worthy of some consideration are a well-made clean Silvaner, a Kerner that is slightly reminiscent of a Sauvignon, and the red made from the Heroldrebe, which has an aroma of raspberries, and is a lovely everyday quaffing wine.

2003 Silvaner "sur lie" trocken	
13%, ♀ till 2005	**83**
2003 "Justinus K."	
Kerner trocken	
14%, ♀ till 2005	**84**
2001 Cuvée "Cantica" trocken	
14.5%, ♀ till 2005	**86**
2003 Riesling "Katharina"	
trocken	
13.5%, ♀ till 2007	**86**
2002 Riesling "Katharina"	
trocken	
13%, ♀ till 2006	**87**
2000 Kerner	
Beerenauslese Barrique	
12.5%, ♀ till 2007	**86**

———— Red wines ————

2002 Lemberger trocken	
13%, ♀ till 2005	**83**
2003 Heroldrebe trocken	
13%, ♀ till 2005	**83**
2001 Lemberger trocken Barrique	
13%, ♀ till 2006	**86**
2001 Spätburgunder	
trocken Barrique	
13%, ♀ till 2007	**86**
2002 Lemberger trocken Barrique	
13.5%, ♀ till 2007	**86**
2002 Spätburgunder	
trocken Barrique	
13%, ♀ till 2007	**86**
2002 Cuvée "Cantus"	
trocken Barrique	
14%, ♀ till 2008	**86**

The wines: **100** Perfect · **95–99** Outstanding · **90–94** Excellent · **85–89** Very good · **80–84** Good · **75–79** Average

WEINGUT
SANKT ANNAGARTEN

Owner: H. + R. Wiedenmann GbR
Manager and winemaker:
Hans Wiedenmann
71717 Beilstein, St.-Anna-Gärten 1
Tel. (0 70 62) 31 66, Fax 2 28 51
e-mail: info@sankt-annagarten.de
Internet: www.sankt-annagarten.de
Directions: A 81 Heilbronn–Stuttgart,
Ilsfeld-Auenstein exit, two kilometers in
direction of Beilstein
Sales: Renate and Hans Wiedenmann
Opening hours: Mon.–Fri. 09:00 to
12:00 hours and 13:30 to 19:00 hours
Sat. 09:00 to 15:00 hours
Worth seeing: Beautifully located Sankt
Annasee lake, winery is at foot of Lang-
hans castle ruins

Vineyard area: 8.5 hectares
Annual production: 70,000 bottles
Top site: Beilsteiner Wartberg
Soil types: Decomposed red marl
Grape varieties: 21% Trollinger, 20%
Riesling, 15% Schwarzriesling, 12%
Lemberger, 8% Samtrot, 7% Grau-
burgunder, 4% Spätburgunder,
3% Kerner, 10% other varieties
Average yield: 90 hl/ha
Best vintages: 1999, 2000, 2002

We always enjoy traveling to Beilstein to
see the Wiedenmann family, who run a
typically Swabian family winery: likable,
firmly established, incredibly hard-
working, with solid quality, loyal private
customers, and a long-term approach to
investments that takes full cognizance of
the next generation. In the current range,
there was a certain degree of stagnation
among the white wines, due to the vintage character, while the reds were significantly improved. The Cabernet blend
as well as the Samtrot Auslese show that
the red wines now have more depth and
character. The only wine to slightly upset
the overall positive impression was the
Schwarzriesling Spätlese that had too
much volatile acidity.

2003 Beilsteiner Wartberg
Riesling Kabinett trocken
12.5%, ♀ till 2005   83

2002 Beilsteiner Wartberg
Grauer Burgunder Kabinett trocken
12%, ♀ till 2005   84

2003 Beilsteiner Wartberg
Grauer Burgunder Spätlese trocken
13%, ♀ till 2006   84

2003 Beilsteiner Wartberg
Riesling Spätlese trocken
13%, ♀ till 2006   84

2003 Beilsteiner Wartberg
Riesling Auslese trocken
13%, ♀ till 2007   84

——————— Red wines ———————

2002 Beilsteiner Wartberg
Lemberger trocken
13%, ♀ till 2006   84

2001 Beilsteiner Wartberg
Lemberger trocken "Holzfassausbau"
13%, ♀ till 2005   84

2003 Beilsteiner Wartberg
Lemberger Spätlese trocken
13%, ♀ till 2006   85

2003 Beilsteiner Wartberg
Samtrot Auslese trocken
14%, ♀ till 2007   86

2002 Beilsteiner Wartberg
Cuvée Cabernet trocken "Holzfassausbau"
13%, ♀ till 2007   86

WEINGUT RAINER SCHNAITMANN

Owner: Rainer Schnaitmann
70734 Fellbach,
Untertürkheimer Straße 4
Tel. (07 11) 57 46 16, Fax 5 78 08 03
e-mail:
weingut.schnaitmann@t-online.de
Internet: weingut-schnaitmann.de
Directions: From Stuttgart via the B 14,
Fellbach-Süd exit, follow signs
Opening hours: Tue. and Fri. 16:30 to
18:30 hours, Sat. 09:00 to 13:00 hours

Vineyard area: 9.8 hectares
Annual production: 70,000 bottles
Top site: Fellbacher Lämmler
Soil types: Red marl, gypsum-red marl,
decomposed sandstone
Grape varieties: 20% Trollinger, 17%
Riesling, 16% Spätburgunder, 14%
Lemberger, 12% Schwarzriesling, 6%
each of Merlot and Sauvignon Blanc,
9% other varieties
Average yield: 59 hl/ha
Best vintages: 2001, 2002, 2003

It seems like a fairy tale: The Schnait-mann winery was founded only seven years ago, and is already among the absolute top producers in the region. We were openly enthusiastic about the current range. Last year, Schnaitmann already produced by far the best Pinot in Württemberg. This year he has repeated this performance, adding yet another very fine Pinot Noir as well as a Frühburgunder so that he can fill all three top Pinot placings himself – what a success! Add to this the enchanting Samtrot, the Lemberger, the Cabernet blend and the botrytis dessert wines: The ambitious Rainer Schnaitmann has presented himself as a master of all categories in this vintage. And if you consider that a new cellar complex is almost completed, and that many of the vineyards are still young and will improve in the years to come, then one can anticipate that his exceptional run of successes is to be continued in future.

2003 Fellbacher Lämmler
Riesling trocken **
13.5%, ♀ till 2006   **86**

2003 Fellbacher Lämmler
Riesling Auslese
11%, ♀ till 2009   **89**

2003 Fellbacher Lämmler
Riesling Beerenauslese
10%, ♀ till 2011   **90**

——— Red wines ———

2003 Lemberger trocken **
13.5%, ♀ till 2007   **86**

2003 Samtrot trocken **
14.5%, ♀ till 2007   **87**

2002 "Simonroth"
Lemberger trocken
13.5%, ♀ till 2009   **89**

2002 "Simonroth"
Cuvée "C" trocken
13.5%, ♀ till 2009   **89**

2002 "Simonroth"
Spätburgunder "S" trocken
13.5%, ♀ till 2009   **90**

2002 "Simonroth"
Spätburgunder "R" trocken
13.5%, ♀ till 2010   **91**

2003 Frühburgunder trocken ***
15%, ♀ till 2009   **91**

The wines: **100** Perfect · **95–99** Outstanding · **90–94** Excellent · **85–89** Very good · **80–84** Good · **75–79** Average

WEINGUT
ALBRECHT SCHWEGLER

Owner: Albrecht Schwegler
71404 Korb, Steinstraße 35
Tel. (0 71 51) 3 48 95, Fax 3 49 78
e-mail: weingut.a.schwegler@web.de
Internet: www.albrecht-schwegler.de
Directions: B 14 Stuttgart–Nürnberg,
Korb exit
Sales: Andrea Schwegler
by appointment

Vineyard area: 1.2 hectares
Annual production: 7,000 bottles
Top sites: Korber Hörnle and
Sommerhalde
Soil types: Red marl
Grape varieties: 40% Blauer Zweigelt,
16% each of Lemberger and Regent,
9% Cabernet Franc, 7% Syrah,
6% each of Merlot and Trollinger
Average yield: 45 hl/ha
Best vintages: 1997, 1998, 2000

The Schwegler winery is something of the "boutique winery" of Württemberg. That involves miniscule production from only 1.2 hectares, but outstanding quality at high prices. In general, the winery concentrates on the production of two blends, the "Saphir" (made of Zweigelt and Lemberger) and the slightly lighter "Beryll." In particularly good vintages they also produce the exceptionally rare red wine "Granat" (garnet), which also includes Merlot in the blend. This is a wine that can benefit more from maturation than any other wine produced in the region, and should therefore not be drunk too young. The 1997 vintage is only starting to enter its optimum drinking stage, and the 1993 vintage is currently in outstanding condition. The 2000 vintage was not so good, so no "Granat" was produced, but this has in effect benefited the other blends. We had been waiting in anticipation of the 2001 "Granat," and it exceeded our expectations. It is one of the very best wines in Württemberg, and the highest-scoring "Granat" ever – but you should leave it in the cellar for another five years if you really want to enjoy the experience.

——————— Red wines ———————

"d'r Oifache"
trocken
12.5%, ♀ till 2006 — **83**

2000 "Beryll"
trocken
13%, ♀ till 2006 — **87**

2000 "Saphir"
trocken
13.5%, ♀ till 2008 — **89**

2001 "Granat"
trocken
13.5%, ♀ 2008 till 2014 — **92**

AS

ALBRECHT SCHWEGLER

SAPHIR

2000

ABFÜLLER: ALBRECHT SCHWEGLER
STEINSTRASSE 35 · 71404 KORB
QUALITÄTSWEIN WÜRTTEMBERG
AP 418 001 03

0,75 l   13,5 Vol. %

WEINGUT SONNENHOF – BEZNER-FISCHER

**Owner: Albrecht W. and
Charlotte Fischer
Winemaker: Kilian Klein
71665 Vaihingen-Enz,
Ortsteil Gündelbach, Sonnenhof
Tel. (0 70 42) 81 88 80, Fax 81 88 86
e-mail: info@weingutsonnenhof.de
Internet: www.weingutsonnenhof.de**
*Directions: A 81 Heilbronn–Stuttgart,
Vaihingen-Enz exit, follow the B 10*
Opening hours: Mon.–Fri. 08:00 to
12:00 hours and 13:00 to 18:00 hours
Sat. 09:00 to 12:00 hours
and 13:00 to 17:00 hours
History: Winemaking since 1522

Vineyard area: 35 hectares
Annual production: 240,000 bottles
Top sites: Gündelbacher Wacht-
kopf, Hohenhaslacher Kirchberg
Soil types: Red marl formations,
primarily colored marl
Grape varieties: 28% Trollinger, 20%
Lemberger, 13% Riesling, 9% Spät-
burgunder, 6% Schwarzriesling,
5% Dornfelder, 19% other varieties
Average yield: 83 hl/ha
Best vintages: 1999, 2002, 2003
Member: Hades, Deutsches
Barrique Forum

It has been another successful year for the Sonnenhof in Gündelbach. The Fischers have produced several remarkably good white wines from the 2003 vintage, the Grauburgunder (Pinot Gris) Spätlese, as well as the Chardonnay Auslese and the Muskateller Auslese. The barrique-matured Chardonnay, too, was able to maintain the standard of the previous vintage. Of the reds, we liked a Spätburgunder (Pinot Noir) Auslese that has enough structure to balance the slight residual sugar. However, we were a little disappointed by the rather light-bodied blend "Julius," which was nowhere close to the outstanding quality of its predecessor from the 1999 vintage.

2003 Gündelbacher Wachtkopf
Grauer Burgunder Spätlese trocken
13.5%, ♀ till 2006   **85**

2003 Gündelbacher Wachtkopf
Chardonnay Auslese trocken
14%, ♀ till 2007   **86**

2003 Gündelbacher Wachtkopf
Muskateller Auslese trocken
13.5%, ♀ till 2006   **86**

2002 Chardonnay trocken "Hades"
13%, ♀ till 2007   **86**

2002 Gündelbacher Wachtkopf
Riesling Auslese
10.5%, ♀ till 2007   **86**

——— Red wines ———

2003 Hohenhaslacher Kirchberg
Trollinger Auslese trocken
13%, ♀ till 2006   **83**

2003 Gündelbacher Wachtkopf
Muskattrollinger Spätlese trocken
13%, ♀ till 2006   **83**

2001 Cuvée "Julius"
trocken "Hades"
13.5%, ♀ till 2006   **85**

2001 Lemberger trocken "Hades"
13.5%, ♀ till 2007   **87**

2003 Gündelbacher Stromberg
Spätburgunder Auslese
13%, ♀ till 2008   **85**

The wines: **100** Perfect · **95–99** Outstanding · **90–94** Excellent · **85–89** Very good · **80–84** Good · **75–79** Average

STAATSWEINGUT WEINSBERG

Owner: State of Baden-Württemberg
Director: Dr. Günter Bäder
Enologist: Dr. Dieter Blankenhorn
Winemaker: Gerhard Wächter
74189 Weinsberg, Traubenplatz 5
Tel. (0 71 34) 50 41 67, Fax 50 41 68
e-mail: staatsweingut@lvwo.bwl.de
Internet: www.lvwo.de
Directions: A 81 Heilbronn–Stuttgart, Weinsberg exit
Sales: Ilona Liepelt, Martin Schwegler
Opening hours: Mon.–Fri. 09:00 to 17:00 hours and by appointment
History: Oldest viticultural college in Germany, founded 1868
Worth seeing: Modern cellar complex, archtiectural award for new sales facility

---

Vineyard area: 40 hectares
Annual production: 300,000 bottles
Top sites: Burg Wildeck, Weinsberger Schemelsberg (both monopole)
Soil types: Gypsum-red marl, colored marl, shell limestone, Neckar rubble
Grape varieties: 20% Riesling, 14% Lemberger, 10% Trollinger, 8% Spätburgunder, 6% Samtrot, 42% other varieties
Average yield: 70 hl/ha
Best vintages: 1999, 2000, 2001
Member: VDP, Hades, Deutsches Barrique Forum

Weinsberg is regarded as the heart of wine-growing in Württemberg, and it is beating as youthfully as ever! The state winery is attached to the oldest viticultural and enological college in Germany, and serves as a source of innovation for the whole region. Thus the successful concept "Justinus K." for the problematical variety Kerner was born here, other successful ideas include the popular Muskateller perlé wine and the fortified wine "XP." The basic wines produced here are also appealing. We look forward with anticipation to the 2001 version of the red flagship "Traum" (Dream).

2003 "Justinus K."
Kerner trocken
15%, ♀ till 2006 — 84

2003 Riesling trocken "S"
13%, ♀ till 2006 — 85

2002 Riesling trocken "S"
12.5%, ♀ till 2006 — 86

2002 Grauer Burgunder
trocken "Hades"
13%, ♀ till 2006 — 87

2001 Grauer Burgunder
trocken "Hades"
13.5%, ♀ till 2005 — 88

——— Red wines ———

2001 Lemberger trocken "Hades"
13%, ♀ till 2007 — 86

2000 Spätburgunder
trocken "Hades"
13%, ♀ till 2006 — 86

2002 Lemberger trocken "S"
13%, ♀ till 2006 — 86

2001 Spätburgunder trocken "S"
13%, ♀ till 2006 — 86

2001 Cuvée "Traumzeit" trocken
13%, ♀ till 2007 — 87

2002 Lemberger Eiswein
8%, ♀ till 2010 — 89

The estates: ✝✝✝✝✝ World's finest · ✝✝✝✝ Germany's best · ✝✝✝ Very good · ✝✝ Good · ✝ Reliable

WEINMANUFAKTUR UNTERTÜRKHEIM E.G.

Manager: Günter Hübner
Winemaker: Jürgen Off
70327 Stuttgart,
Strümpfelbacher Str. 47
Tel. (07 11) 3 36 38 10, Fax 33 63 81 24
e-mail: info@weinmanufaktur.de
Internet: www.weinmanufaktur.de
*Directions: Via the B 10,
Untertürkheim exit*
Opening hours: Mon.–Fri. 08:00 to
18:00 hours, Sat. 09:00 to 13:00 hours
History: Founded 1887
Worth seeing: Barrel cellar, sparkling
wine cellar in former air-raid shelter

Vineyard area: 75 hectares
Number of members: 73
Annual production: 750,000 bottles
Top sites: Untertürkheimer
Mönchberg and Altenberg
Soil types: Decomposed red marl
Grape varieties: 42% Trollinger,
25% Riesling, 7% Müller-Thurgau,
6% Kerner, 5% Spätburgunder,
15% other varieties
Average yield: 110 hl/ha
Best vintages: 2001, 2002, 2003

A crown appears in the coat-of-arms of the Untertürkheim Weinmanufaktur – and this co-operative, which is by far the best in Württemberg, certainly deserves it. What a success story this is! When the name was changed to "Weinmanufaktur," this was followed up with a comprehensive change in philosophy. The various ranges of wines are marked by stars, and the difference is also there in the taste. We must show our respect not only for the top wines, the basic wines are well-made, too. An almost spectacular series of top red wines all rated 86 to 88 points has ensured the well-earned higher rating for the team. We can extend our sincere compliments to the folks at Untertürkheim, and are happy to award them the title of "Estate manager of the year 2005." Congratulations!

2003 Riesling trocken *
12%, ♀ till 2005   83

2002 Grauer Burgunder
trocken ***
13.5%, ♀ till 2006   83

2001 Grauer Burgunder
trocken ***
13%, ♀ till 2006   86

2003 Riesling trocken
13.5%, ♀ till 2007   86

2003 Riesling Beerenauslese
9.5%, ♀ till 2009   89

——————— Red wines ———————

2003 Trollinger trocken *
12.5%, ♀ till 2005   82

2003 Cuvée "Mönch Berthold"
trocken **
13.5%, ♀ till 2006   85

2003 Spätburgunder trocken *
14%, ♀ till 2006   85

2002 Merlot trocken *
14%, ♀ till 2007   86

2001 Spätburgunder trocken *
14%, ♀ till 2007   87

2001 Cuvée "Mönch Berthold"
trocken ***
14%, ♀ till 2008   87

2002 Cuvée "Mönch Berthold"
trocken ***
14%, ♀ till 2008   87

2002 Dornfelder trocken *
14%, ♀ till 2007   87

2002 Spätburgunder trocken *
14%, ♀ till 2008   87

2002 Lemberger trocken *
13.5%, ♀ till 2009   88

WEINGUT
WACHTSTETTER

Owner and winemaker:
Rainer Wachtstetter
74397 Pfaffenhofen,
Michelbacher Straße 8
Tel. (0 70 46) 3 29, Fax 93 10 00
e-mail: info@wachtstetter.de
Internet: www.wachtstetter.de
Directions: A 6 Steinsfurt exit, A 81 Ilsfeld or Ludwigsburg-Nord exit
Sales: Rainer Wachtstetter
Opening hours: Mon.–Thur. by appointment, Fri. u. Sat. 09:00 to 18:00 hours
Restaurant: Gasthaus Adler
Fri.–Sun. 11:30 to 24:00 hours
Specialty: Suckling pig from own butchery

Vineyard area: 11 hectares
Annual production: 100,000 bottles
Top sites: Pfaffenhofener
Hohenberg and Heuchelberg
Soil types: Red marl and reed sandstone
Grape varieties: 20% Lemberger, 17%
each of Trollinger and Riesling, 12%
Spätburgunder, 8% Schwarzriesling,
7% Samtrot, 5% Dornfelder,
14% other varieties
Average yield: 80 hl/ha
Best vintages: 1999, 2001, 2003
Member: Junges Schwaben

Rainer Wachstetter has impressivley underlined his position as a red wine specialist. His barrique-matured range "Ernst Combé" (named after his grandfather, and founder of the winery) is of a high standard across the board. On the other hand, the "normal" wines, matured in traditional large oak vats, prove the point that high quality red wines need not always be barrique-matured: The "Cuvée Louis" and the Lemberger are very good. Indeed, even the 2003 white wines have improved a little. The sparkling wines are also well above average. There is no doubt that Rainer Wachtstetter is currently the best all-rounder of the winemakers that is untied under the title of "Junges Schwaben" (Young Swabia).

2003 Riesling Spätlese trocken
13.5%, ♀ till 2006 **85**

2001 Pfaffenhofener Hohenberg
Riesling Spätlese trocken
13%, ♀ till 2005 **86**

2003 Gewürztraminer
Auslese trocken
14.5%, ♀ till 2006 **86**

2003 Riesling Spätlese
13%, ♀ till 2006 **84**

——— Red wines ———

2002 Cuvée "Louis" trocken
13%, ♀ till 2006 **85**

2003 Lemberger Spätlese trocken
13.5%, ♀ till 2007 **86**

2002 "Ernst Combé"
Spätburgunder trocken Barrique
13.5%, ♀ till 2007 **86**

2002 Lemberger "Felix"
trocken "Holzfassausbau"
13.5%, ♀ till 2006 **86**

2001 "Ernst Combé"
Lemberger trocken
13%, ♀ till 2007 **87**

2002 "Ernst Combé"
Dornfelder trocken Barrique
13.5%, ♀ till 2007 **87**

2001 "Ernst Combé" Cuvée trocken
13.5%, ♀ till 2007 **88**

2002 "Ernst Combé"
Lemberger trocken
13.5%, ♀ till 2008 **88**

2002 "Ernst Combé"
Cuvée trocken Barrique
14%, ♀ till 2008 **88**

WEINGUT WÖHRWAG

Owner: Hans-Peter Wöhrwag
Winemaker: Carsten Kämpf
70327 Untertürkheim,
Grunbacher Straße 5
Tel. (07 11) 33 16 62, Fax 33 24 31
e-mail: info@woehrwag.de
Internet: www.woehrwag.de
Directions: Via the B 10,
Untertürkheim exit
Sales: Christin Wöhrwag
Opening hours: Mon.–Fri. 08:00 to
12:00 hours and 15:00 to 18:30 hours
Sat. 09:00 to 13:00 hours

Vineyard area: 20 hectares
Annual production: 150,000 bottles
Top site: Untertürkheimer
Herzogenberg (monopole)
Soil types: Red marl, marl
Grape varieties: 40% Riesling, 8%
Trollinger, 13% Lemberger, 7%
Spätburgunder, 5% Grauburgun-
der, 3% each of Weißburgunder,
Müller-Thurgau and Dornfelder,
8% other red varieties
Average yield: 60 hl/ha
Best vintages: 1999, 2001, 2002
Member: VDP

There is no doubt that Hans-Peter Wöhrwag and his wife Christin, who hails from
the Rheingau, are considered to be Riesling specialists in the overall picture of
the Swabian wine industry. It is therefore
particularly surprising to record that this
likable winemaking family from Untertürkheim has allowed others in recent
years to forge ahead and increasingly to
hand over their erstwhile leading position
to them. This is particularly evident in the
botrytis dessert wines of this variety. Just
a few years ago, Wöhrwag was the recognized leader in this category. The 2003
range, too, remains well below the potential here. On the other hand, the elegant
Lemberger and the outstanding Cabernet-
Lemberger blend "X" are very good, and
we were also impressed by the Pinot Gris,
which is almost in a New World style.

2003 Untertürkheimer Herzogenberg
Riesling trocken "Großes Gewächs"
14%, ♀ till 2007   **86**

2003 Pinot Gris trocken
14.5%, ♀ till 2007   **87**

2003 Untertürkheimer Herzogenberg
Riesling Auslese Goldkapsel
7%, ♀ till 2009   **88**

2003 Untertürkheimer Herzogenberg
Riesling Eiswein
7%, ♀ till 2011   **89**

2002 Untertürkheimer Herzogenberg
Riesling Beerenauslese
8.5%, ♀ till 2011   **91**

——————— Red wines ———————

2002 Untertürkheimer Herzogenberg
Spätburgunder trocken ***
13.5%, ♀ till 2008   **86**

2002 Cuvée "Philipp" trocken
13%, ♀ till 2007   **86**

2002 Untertürkheimer Herzogenberg
Lemberger trocken ***
13.5%, ♀ till 2008   **87**

2002 Cuvée "X" trocken
13.5%, ♀ till 2010   **89**

The wines: **100** Perfect · **95–99** Outstanding · **90–94** Excellent · **85–89** Very good · **80–84** Good · **75–79** Average

Württemberg

WEINGUT HERZOG VON WÜRTTEMBERG

Owner: Carl Herzog v. Württemberg
Commercial manager: Hartmut Otter
Technical manager: Bernhard Idler
Administrator: Michael Herzog von Württemberg
Winemaker: Bernhard Idler
71634 Ludwigsburg, Schloss Monrepos
Tel. (0 71 41) 22 10 60, Fax 22 10 62 60
e-mail: weingut@hofkammer.de
Internet:
www.weingut-wuerttemberg.de
Directions: A 81 Heilbronn–Stuttgart, LB-Nord exit, in direction of LB-Monrepos
Sales: Hilde Meyer-Trump, Jan Steingaß
Opening hours: Mon.–Fri. 09:00 to 18:00 hours, Sat. 10:00 to 14:00 hours
Wine bar: Open every day
History: Private wine estate of the House of Württemberg since 1677
Worth seeing: Palace grounds Monrepos with Schlosshotel

Vineyard area: 40.6 hectares
Annual production: 300,000 bottles
Top sites: Stettener Brotwasser, Maulbronner Eilfingerberg, Untertürkheimer Mönchberg, Asperger Berg, Mundelsheimer Käsberg
Soil types: Reed sandstone, shell limestone, gypsum-red and colored marl
Grape varieties: 41% Riesling, 22% Trollinger, 17% Lemberger, 5% Spätburgunder, 3% Weißburgunder, 12% other varieties
Average yield: 68 hl/ha
Best vintages: 1999, 2001, 2002
Member: VDP

Thanks to the dedicated work of the team surrounding Duke Michael, this largest privately owned wine estate in the region is on its way back to its former reputation. However, the First Growths of the 2003 vintage are not on a par with their predecessors. We were pleasantly impressed by the Lemberger from the vineyards in Maulbronn, and the Riesling and Traminer Auslese wines were also quite good.

2003 Stettener Brotwasser
Riesling Kabinett trocken
12%, ♀ till 2005 — 83

2003 Stettener Brotwasser
Riesling Spätlese trocken
"Großes Gewächs"
13%, ♀ till 2006 — 85

2003 Maulbronner Eilfingerberg
Riesling Spätlese trocken
"Großes Gewächs"
13.5%, ♀ till 2006 — 85

2003 Maulbronner Eilfingerberg
Riesling Auslese
13.5%, ♀ till 2008 — 86

2003 Maulbronner Eilfingerberg
Traminer Auslese
13%, ♀ till 2007 — 86

——— Red wines ———

2003 Hohenhaslacher Kirchberg
Trollinger Spätlese trocken
12.5%, ♀ till 2006 — 83

2002 Untertürkheimer Mönchberg
Spätburgunder Auslese trocken
13%, ♀ till 2007 — 85

2003 Maulbronner Eilfingerberg
Lemberger trocken
13%, ♀ till 2007 — 85

2002 Maulbronner Eilfingerberg
Lemberger "Herzog Eberhard Ludwig" trocken Barrique
13%, ♀ till 2007 — 85

The estates: �♥ World's finest · ♥♥♥♥ Germany's best · ♥♥♥ Very good · ♥♥ Good · ♥ Reliable

HERZOG VON WÜRTTEMBERG

Seit 1677

2002
MAULBRONNER
EILFINGERBERG
LEMBERGER
TROCKEN

722

Weingut Robert Bauer

74223 Flein, Heilbronner Str. 56
Tel. (0 71 31) 25 16 62, Fax 57 32 88

Robert Bauer, an individualistic winemaker highly respected by his fans, has sold his winery in Flein to the Albrecht family, already based in the same town. Martin Albrecht junior is now working together with Robert Bauer, and is learning the ropes of the place. We will follow the future developments here with interest.

Weingut Dr. Baumann – Schloss Affaltrach

74182 Obersulm, Am Ordenschloss 15-21
Tel. (0 71 30) 4 74 40, Fax 47 44 44

Unfortunately, the current range presented at the Affaltrach palace ranks far below that of the previous vintage. None of the Classic red wines, made from Lemberger, Trollinger and Pinot Meunier, justifies a recommendation. Even the charming Rieslings of the previous vintage are absent in the 2003 vintage. On the other hand, the elegant Frühburgunder Spätlese is well-made this year. As usual, the range includes some botrytis dessert wines, this year comprising a Riesling Trockenbeerenauslese and two Eisweins, a Riesling and a Trollinger.

Weingut Graf von Bentzel-Sturmfeder

74360 Ilsfeld-Schozach, Sturmfederstr. 4
Tel. (0 71 33) 96 08 94, Fax 96 08 95
e-mail: weingut@sturmfeder.de
Internet: www.sturmfeder.de

The trend here continues to develop positively. It is gratifying to see how this traditional winery, a VDP member, is slowly but surely working its way back into the top league of Württemberg producers. This development is shown clearly by the aromatic fresh 2003 Rieslings (Kabinett and "Großes Gewächs"/First Growth): They are tasty and well-made, but with potential to develop and improve. If this potential can be developed further, this winery will soon be back in the ranks of wineries rated with a bunch of grapes.

Weingut Manfred Birkert

74626 Adolzfurt, Unterheimbacher Str. 28
Tel. (0 79 46) 4 84, Fax 33 78

It was clearly not an easy year for Manfred Birkert at his winery in Adolzfurt. The aromatics and freshness of his wines, which we have applauded in recent vintages, was somewhat lacking in the current range of wines. The rather rustic dry Riesling Auslese, the Muskateller and particularly the Sauvignon Blanc all show marked signs of overripe grapes. The wine we liked best was the 2003 Samtrot Auslese (84 points) We are looking forward with interest to the barrique-matured wines of the 2002 vintage, which are only scheduled for release next year.

Weingut Bruker

71723 Großbottwar, Kleinaspacher Str. 18
Tel. (0 71 48) 92 10 50, Fax 61 90
e-mail: Herbert-Bruker@Hotel-Bruker.de

While the current range presented by the family winery of Herbert Bruker and his son Markus is not homogeneous, this in itself is a good sign. Wines of the 2003 vintage that we liked include the elegant Lemberger Auslese (85 points), as well as the Pinot Meunier Auslese, the Trollinger Auslese and the Lemberger Spätlese – all good wines; however the Spätburgunder (Pinot Noir) Auslese is unbalanced and too alcoholic. We would also like to see more than an 81-point rating for a Riesling "Alte Reben" (old vines). The wines produced here can perhaps best be enjoyed in the restaurant attached to the winery, there is also an attractive hotel, which makes a perfect base for excursion into the Swabian wine-growing areas.

Weingut Bernhard Ellwanger

71384 Weinstadt-Großheppach,
Rebenstraße 9
Tel. (0 71 51) 6 21 31, Fax 60 32 09

Assisted by his family, Sven Ellwanger has made the best of the challenges of the 2003 vintage, as evidenced in the attractive aromatic, fruity Riesling Spätlese (85 points). However, the best wine produced here is yet again the barrique-matured

Spätburgunder (Pinot Noir) (86). At the same time, you should not ignore the 2003 Dornfelder as an attractive quaffing wine with a bit of class. We were disappointed only by the Sauvignon Blanc, which has very little varietal character this year, and is rather rustic in style (82). Also, the white blend "Kreation Ellwanger" is no feather in the cap of this winery, which on the whole is showing a positive development. The highlight this year of the Ellwanger estate was the Kerner Trockenbeerenauslese (87 points), which is very moderately priced.

Fellbacher Weingärtner eG

70734 Fellbach, Kappelbergstraße 48
Tel. (07 11) 5 78 80 30, Fax 57 88 03 40
Internet: info@fellbacher-weine.de

The co-operative in Fellbach has in recent times been influenced by its dynamic neighbors Aldinger and Schnaitmann, improving in quality and image, so their inclusion in the recommended list in this year's edition of the Guide is well-earned. The range is solid across the board, and we really did not find any failures. We thus look forward to observing, and reporting on, the future development at this co-operative.

Weingärtner Flein-Talheim

74223 Flein, Römerstraße 14
Tel. (0 71 31) 5 95 20, Fax 59 52 50
e-mail: flein.talheim@t-online.de
Internet: www.WG-Flein-Talheim.de

The current range produced by the "past masters" at Flein is unfortunately not quite as homogeneous as that of the previous vintage, when we specifically praised the Riesling wines. In 2003, the wines produced from this variety are regrettably lacking in the fruit and acidity shown by their predecessors. The only praiseworthy exception is the dry Auslese, rated a respectable 86 points – it shows what great Rieslings can be produced here. Another wine we liked was the 2003 Muskateller (84), which makes a pleasant aperitif. Looking to the red wines of 2003, we particularly liked the elegant Samtrot Spätlese, with sublet sweetness nicely bal-

anced by silky tannins (84). However, the dry Auslese of this variety is out of balance, and strongly characterized by volatile acidity.

Weingut Heid

70734 Fellbach, Cannstatter Straße 13/2
Tel. (07 11) 58 41 12, Fax 58 37 61

We have high hopes for this small winery in the pretty historic section of Fellbach. Heid was able to fulfil these expectations, specifically with his dry 2003 Riesling Auslese (86 points) as well as with the Riesling Eiswein of the previous vintage (89). On the other hand, the 2003 red wine "Melchior" was a major disappointment, unbalanced and strongly characterized by volatile acidity. The 2002 "Melchisedec" as well as the Lemberger are much better wines. Overall one notices that some of the current red wines are quite strongly defined by a hard, acidic structure. We know Marcus Heid has both ambition and ability, and hope he will be able to find more balance and finesse in future.

Major and minor vintages in the Württemberg region	
Vintage	Rating
2003	⚜⚜⚜
2002	⚜⚜⚜
2001	⚜⚜⚜⚜
2000	⚜⚜⚜
1999	⚜⚜⚜
1998	⚜⚜⚜
1997	⚜⚜⚜⚜
1996	⚜⚜⚜
1995	⚜⚜⚜
1994	⚜⚜⚜

Vintage rating:

⚜⚜⚜⚜⚜ : Excellent vintage

⚜⚜⚜⚜ : Very good vintage

⚜⚜⚜ : Good vintage

⚜⚜ : Average vintage

⚜ : Poor vintage

Weingut F. & I. Heinrich

74182 Obersulm-Sülzbach, Kümmelstr. 2
Tel. (0 71 34) 1 74 69, Fax 90 10 78
e-mail: info@weingut-heinrich.com

Things appear to be moving here ever since Alexander Heinrich joined his parents' winery in Obersulm-Sülzbach. The tasty 2003 red wines, the Lemberger Auslese and the Spätburgunder (Pinot Noir) Spätlese (both 84 points) show that the winemaker has some ambition. The 2003 Riesling Kabinett wines are also well made. However, the 2002 Trollinger in liter bottles (77) was a negative example, as was the exorbitant price for the mediocre blend "L'CaZa." We will certainly continue to track this interesting newcomer.

Rebhof Helmut Hirth

74182 Obersulm-Willsbach
Tel. (0 71 34) 2 09 71, Fax 2 09 72
Internet: rebhof@t-online.de

A possibly interesting new producer, our attention was attracted by a good 2002 Dornfelder as well as a decent 2003 Riesling (both 83 points). However, the best wine currently is the 2002 Lemberger (84). In our opinion the Auxerrois, which has a strong aroma of bitter almonds, is a complete flop. However, we will continue to observe the development of Helmut Hirth with interest.

Weingut Keck

74676 Niedernhall, Weinsteige 1
Tel. (0 79 40) 5 58 84, Fax 22 85
e-mail: info@weingut-keck.de

We cannot really figure out this producer. On the one hand he is capable of producing some very attractive 2002 wines, such as the Dornfelder and the Dornfelder-Lemberger blend, while at the same time presenting a wine from the Bacchus grape variety showing definite mature characteristics, as well as Rieslings that are also no longer particularly fresh. The red blend "Sirona" has a bouquet dominated to the extreme by oak (vanilla and caramel), reminiscent of Caribbean rum.

Schloss Lehrensteinsfeld

74251 Lehrensteinsfeld, Im Schloss
Tel. (0 71 34) 1 79 32, Fax 1 30 59

The biggest surprise of our tastings in Württemberg was the range presented by this winery! This Riesling specialist is at last again producing remarkable wines from this variety. It would appear that the new winemaker Christoph Ruck and his youthful style have managed to inject new life into the old castle cellar in a very short time. Rieslings rated 85 to 86 points – it is a long time since that was last seen here. We await the further developments with great interest.

Weingut Schäfer-Heinrich

74074 Heilbronn, Im Letten 3
Tel. (0 71 31) 16 24 54, Fax 16 56 59

Andreas and Elke Hieber have implemented organic practises in their winery (member of EcoVin), and appear to have mastered the difficult 2003 white wine vintage quite well, as evidenced by the tasty Riesling and Grauburgunder (Pinot Gris) Spätlese wines. However, the 2002 red wines are much weaker, even the barrel-matured Lemberger, usually considered to be the hot tip of this producer, was disappointing this year.

Weingut Schmalzried

71404 Korb, Kirchstraße 61/3
Tel. (0 71 51) 3 26 52, Fax 30 27 50
Internet: www.weingutschmalzried.de

It is always a special pleasure to visit Hermann Schmalzried, who is as friendly as he is chaotic. He is the pioneer of organic wine farming in Württemberg, and is a good source for many informative anecdotes on the production of organic wines, as well as being a constant source of interesting surprises in terms of the quality of his wines.

Weingut der Stadt Stuttgart

70173 Stuttgart, Dorotheenstraße 2
Tel. (07 11) 2 16 71 40, Fax 2 16 76 83

Overall, 2003 was a successful vintage for the city's wine estate. This is shown by two very decent Riesling Auslese wines (dry and sweet, each 84 points) as well as by the elegant, well-balanced red St. Laurent (85). The Spätburgunder (Pinot Noir) Auslese might have been rated even higher if it would have less alcohol. The 2002 barrique-matured version, just like its predecessor, suffers from an overdose of oak.

Weingut Zimmerle

71404 Korb, Kirchstraße 14
Tel. (0 71 51) 3 38 93, Fax 3 74 22
e-mail: info@zimmerle-weingut.de

The Zimmerle winery in Korb has been absent from this guide for three years, and returns with a flourish, presenting a very attractive range of wines. It appears they have worked hard at their quality profile in the interim, and it gives us pleasure to welcome Friedrich Zimmerle back in the circle of recommended wineries. He has certainly earned this, particularly with respect to the 2003 vintage wines of the "Astrum***" series.

Weingut Zipf

74245 Löwenstein, Vorhofer Straße 4
Tel. (0 71 30) 61 65, Fax 97 25

Jürgen Zipf is a member of the "Junges Schwaben" (Young Swabia) group, and thus one of the up-and-coming young producers in Württemberg. His current range shows a significant improvement. We were happy to taste several racy Rieslings, headed up by the Selection (85 points), as well as some red wines full of character, such as the 2002 blend "Junges Schwaben" (86) as well as a charming and well-balanced 2002 Spätburgunder (Pinot Noir, 85). We hope he continues in this vein.

Other wineries tasted

- Dolde, Frickenhausen-Linsenhofen
- Kurz-Wagner, Talheim
- Steinbachhof, Vaihingen-Gündelbach
- Rolf Willy, Nordheim
- Konrad Zaiss, Stuttgart

Recommended by our wine producers

Hotels and inns

Asperg: Adler
Abstatt: Sperber
Bönnigheim: Adler
Güglingen: Herzogskelter
Hebsack: Lamm
Ilsfeld: Ochsen
Ludwigsburg: Schlosshotel Monrepos
Oberstenfeld: Ochsen
Öhringen: Schlosshotel Friedrichsruhe
Remshalden: Lamm
Weinsberg: Rappenhof
Weinstadt-Strümpfelbach: Lamm

Gourmet restaurants

Öhringen: Schlosshotel Friedrichsruhe,
Stuttgart: Speisemeisterei, Wielandshöhe

Restaurants, wine bars and swabian inns

Abstatt: Sperber
Bietigheim: Schiller
Bönnigheim: Adler, Ratsstüble
Endersbach: Weinstube Muz
Esslingen: Träuble
Fellbach: Hirschen
Flein-Thalheim: Landgasthof Haigern
Gellmersbach: Kelterstube
Hebsack: Lamm
Heilbronn: Ratskeller, Rauers Weinstube, Weinstube Braun
Kernen/Stetten: Ochsen
Öhringen: Weinstube Reiss
Remshalden: Lamm
Steinreinach: Gasthaus Lamm
Stuttgart-Uhlbach: Weinstube Ochsen
Stuttgart: Délice, Weinstube zur Kiste, Weinstube Klink, Weinstube Schellenturm, Weinstube Stetter
Sülzbach: Alter Klosterhof
Waiblingen: Bachofer
Weinstadt-Strümpfelbach: Hirsch
Weinstadt: Adler in Baach

Index of the Estates

The full presentation of the best estates is to be found on the pages printed in boldface type.

Index of the Estates

Index of the Estates

Index of the Estates

Index of the Estates

Index of the Vineyard Sites

Index of the Vineyard Sites

Index of the Vineyard Sites

Index of the Vineyard Sites

Index of the Vineyard Sites

Index of the Vineyard Sites

Index of the Vineyard Sites

www.gaultmillau.de

Index of Individuals

Index of Individuals

Index of Individuals

Edling, Lisa 242
Ehlen, Stephan 293
Eifel, Alexandra 294
Eifel, Anne 296
Eifel, Brigitte 296
Eifel, Franz-Josef 295
Eifel, Gerhard 291
Eifel, Heinz 296
Eifel, Marietta 294
Eifel, Waltraud 291
Eisenlohr 532
Eller, Martin 464
Ellwanger, Andreas 699
Ellwanger, Jörg 699
Ellwanger, Jürgen 699
Ellwanger, Sieglinde 699
Ellwanger, Sven 723
Elten, Bernd van 226
Emmerich, Alfred 80
Emmerich, Gotthard 251, 252
Emmerich, Rita 251
Emmich, Dirk 666
Emrich-Montigny, Ursula 409
Ende, Dieter 424
Engel, Christian 598
Engel, Erwin 280
Engist, Herbert Daniel 110
Engist, Simone 110
Enk, Steffen 440
Eppelmann, Timo 663
Eppelmann, Udo 663
Eppinger, Anne 594
Erbeldinger, Stefan 663
Erbes, Stefan 297
Erdmann, Tanja 244
Erhard, Sabine 198
Erhard, Walter 198
Eser, Elfriede 559
Eser, Hans Hermann 559
Eser, Joachim 600
Eser, Johannes 559
Eser, Sabine 559
Espe, Hans-Bert 175
Ewert, Günter 642
Eymael, Doris 509
Eymael, Jan 509
Eymael, Robert 286, 343
Eymann, Rainer 469

F
Faber, Gerd 357
Fader family 470
Fader, Karl-Heinz 470
Fader, Knut 470

Faller, Norbert 109
Faubel, Christa 522
Faubel family 522
Faubel, Gerd 522
Faubel, Silke 522
Faust, Volker 145
Fauth, Ernst 650
Fauth family 650
Fauth, Florian 650
Fauth, Ruth 650
Fendel, Ferdinand 270
Fendel, Jens 270
Fendel-Hetzert family 553
Fendt, Jürgen 19
Ferdinand, Erzherzog in Innsbruck 485
Feser, Elke 136
Fetz, Andrea 266
Fetz, Heinz-Uwe 266
Fichte 678
Finkenauer, Anton 412
Finkenauer, Carl 412, 422
Finkenauer family 412
Finkenauer, Hans-Anton 412
Firnbach, Reinhard 195
Fischer, Albrecht W. 717
Fischer, Charlotte 717
Fischer, Christina 10
Fischer, Thomas 483
Fitz, Konrad M. 471
Fleischer family 612
Fleischer, Hans Willi 612
Fleischer, Michael 612
Flemming, Alison 44
Flick, Reiner 554
Fobian, Stefan 348
Fogt, Brunhilde 613
Fogt, Dorothea 613
Fogt, Georg 613
Fogt, Karl-Heinz 613
Forster, Georg 440
Franckenstein, Freiherren 112
Frank, Horst 348
Franke, Annetrud 517
Franz, Werner 365
Franzen, Iris 298
Franzen, Martin 503
Franzen, Ulrich 298
Freimuth, Alexander 555
Freimuth, Karin 555
Frey, Achim 104
Frey, Jürgen 472
Frey, Peter 472
Frey, Ursula 472

Frey, Winfried 472
Friedrich, Christoph J. 404
Friedrich family 299
Friedrich, Franz-Josef 299
Friedrich, Mechtilde 299
Friedrichs family 656
Fries, Anke 300
Fries, Reiner 300
Frieß, Christian 195
Frieß, Rudolf 20
Fröhlich, Clemens 235
Fröhlich, Eva 199
Fröhlich, Hans 430
Fröhlich, Ingrid 235
Fröhlich, Karin 430
Fröhlich, Meike 430
Fröhlich, Michael 199
Fröhlich, Tim 17, 398, 430
Frölich, Volker 677
Fuchs, Brunhilde 301
Fuchs, Bruno 301
Fuchs, Markus 666
Fuchs, Ranke 666
Fuhrmann, Karl 509
Full, Reinhold 231
Fürst, Monika 200
Fürst, Paul 18, 31, 58, 200, 205
Fürst, Sebastian 200

G
Gabel, Rainer 509
Gabelmann, Kurt 424, 562, 647
Gallé, Klaus 614
Gallé, Ortrud 614
Galli, Andrea 324
Gälweiler, Albert 440
Gälweiler, Andreas 440
Gälweiler, Dr. Leo 440
Gamber, Klaus 487
Ganswohl, Mathias 595
Gartner, Gerhard 324
Gass, Stéphane 10
Gatzmaga, Andreas 76
Gatzmaga family 76
Gatzmaga, Günter 76
Gauer, Andrea 624
Gaul, Karl-Heinz 473
Gaul, Rosemarie 473
Gehring, Diana 615
Gehring, Hans-Theo 615
Geiben, Peter 318
Geier, Kordula 206
Geil, Birgit 617
Geil, Rudolf 617

Index of Individuals

Index of Individuals

Index of Individuals

Index of Individuals

Index of Individuals

Piedmont, Claus 354
Piedmont, Monika 354
Pieroth, Andreas 46
Pieroth, Elmar 46
Pieroth, Dr. Johannes 46
Pix, Helga 154
Pix, Reinhold 154
Plunien, Helmut 194
Podzun, Hans-Jürgen 5
Praß, Bernhard 271
Preiß, Mrs. 652
Preißinger, Eugen 224
Preußen, Marianne Prinzessin von 585
Prinz, Fred 583
Prinz, Sabine 583
Probst, Marion 155
Probst, Reiner 155
Probst, Werner 233
Prüm, Dr. Manfred 14, 31, 58, 274, 355
Prüm, Peter 380
Prüm, Raimund 357
Prüm, Wolfgang 355

Q

Queins, Tilman 668
Querbach, Peter 584
Querbach, Resi 584
Querbach, Wilfried 584

R

Raddeck, Hans 667
Raddeck, Stefan 667
Rapp, Walter 425
Rasenberger, Dr. Herbert 46
Rathgeber, Kurt 467
Ratzenberger family 263
Ratzenberger, Jochen jun. 246, 263
Rau, Johannes 241
Rauen, Harald 358
Rauen, Irmtrud 359
Rauen, Maria 358
Rauen, Stefan 359
Rauen, Walter 359
Rauh, Gunter 667
Raumland, Volker 667
Ravensburg, Freiherren Göler von 156
Ravensburg, Ritter Berthold Göler von 156
Rebholz, Birgit 512
Rebholz family 512

Rebholz, Hansjörg 18, 31, 58, 492, 512
Rebitzer, Karl-Heinz 195
Regnery, Franz-Josef 360
Regnery, Peter 360
Reh, Andrea 44
Reh, Carl 44
Reh, Günther family 324
Reh, Sigrid 361
Reh, Winfried 361
Reh-Gartner, Annegret 324
Rehbein, Werner 101
Reichmann, Arndt 652
Reimann, Martin 420
Reinert, Annetrud 362
Reinert, Johann Peter 362
Resch, Anna Lioba 363
Resch, Franz-Andreas 363
Resch, Monika 363
Ress, Christian 586
Ress, Stefan 586
Reuther, Thomas 521
Richter, Claus-Martin 366
Richter, Dr. Dirk 365
Richter family 366
Richter, Ökonomierat Horst 365
Richter, Thomas 366
Richter, Wolfgang 280
Riedel, Dr. Martin 417
Rieflin, Hans-Peter 152
Riffel, Erik 640
Riffel family 640
Rinker family 134
Rinker, Regina 134
Rinker, Thomas 134
Riske, Bernd 87
Riske, Mechthild 81
Riske, Volker 81
Ritzau, Dr. Michael 417
Rödesheim, Jürgen 594
Rohr, Michael 426
Rohr, Monika 426
Rohrer, Josef 180
Röll, Siegfried 705
Rombach, Christoph 95
Rößler, Steffen 685
Rösch, Giso 678
Rosch, Werner 368
Roßwog, Rainer 136
Roth, Christa 530
Roth, Dirk 575
Roth, Herbert family 530
Roth, Gerhard 213
Roth, Herbert 530
Rothweiler, H. 238, 241

Rotthaus, Thorsten 514
Rotzinek family 418
Ruck, Birgit 214
Ruck, Christoph 725
Ruck, Johann 214
Ruck, Johannes 214
Rudloff, Dorothea 215
Rudloff family 215
Rudloff, Peter 215
Rumpf, Cornelia 419
Rumpf, Stefan 419
Rundquist, Erik 47
Rundquist-Müller, Barbara 382
Rüttiger, Rainer 566

S

Salm-Salm, Felix zu 656
Salm-Salm, Michael Prinz zu 427, 656
Salwey, Benno 157
Salwey, Konrad 157
Salwey, Wolf-Dietrich 157
Sander family 641
Sander, Gerhard 641
Sander, Otto Heinrich 641
Sander, Stefan 641
Sauder, Regina 642
Sauer, Albrecht 208
Sauer, Anne 208
Sauer, Edgar 226
Sauer family 208
Sauer, Heiner 537
Sauer, Helga 218
Sauer, Horst 184, 216, 236
Sauer, Magdalena 216
Sauer, Margarete 208
Sauer, Michael 208
Sauer, Monika 208
Sauer, Paul 208
Sauer, Rainer 218
Schächtele, Marlene 95
Schaefer, Christoph 372
Schaefer family 372
Schaefer, Willi 17, 372
Schäfer, Gitta 69
Schäfer, Josef 587
Schäfer, Jutta 587
Schäfer, Klaus-Rainer 377
Schäfer, Marion 168
Schäfer, Paul-Josef 69
Schäfer, Paul-Michael 69
Schäfer, Dr. Ralf 96
Schäfer, Sebastian 398, 428
Schäfer, Wilhelm Josef 587
Schäffer, Egon 219

Index of Individuals

Index of Individuals

Notes

Copyright

English-Language Edition

Christian Verlag, Amalienstraße 62, 80799 München

Publishers: Johannes Heyne, Martin Dort

www.gaultmillau.de

Senior editors: Armin Diel, Joel Payne
Editor: Gerhard Benz
Corrector: Dr. Christian Topp
Translator: Peter Gebler

Copyright © 2005 by Christian Verlag, Munich
© Gault Millau by DAMEFA S.A., Paris
Johannes Heyne Verlag, Munich

Typeset: Typomaß, Am Kalkofen 11, 67824 Feilbingert
Maps: Wittmann, Kaufbeuren
Photographer: Armin Faber & Partner, Düsseldorf

Printed and bound in Germany by Kösel, Krugzell

ISBN 3-88472-675-7